A Concise Anglo-Saxon dictionary

J.R. Clark-Hall

© Copyright – J.R. Clark-Hall

© Copyright 2008 – BN Publishing

Cover Design: J. Neuman

www.bnpublishing.net

info@bnpublishing.net

ALL RIGHTS RESERVED

For information regarding special discounts for bulk purchases, please contact BN Publishing

sales@bnpublishing.net

PREFACE TO THE SECOND EDITION

The first edition of this dictionary having been exhausted, it has been extensively revised, and certain new features and alterations have been introduced into it.

1. The principle of arranging all words according to their actual spelling has been to a considerable extent abandoned. It was admittedly an unscientific one, and opened the door to a good many errors and inconsistencies. The head form in this edition may be either a normalised form or one which actually occurs.

2. Words beginning with *ge-* have been distributed among the letters of the alphabet which follow that prefix, and the sign + has been employed instead of *ge-* in order to make the break in alphabetical continuity as little apparent to the eye as possible. The sign ± has been used where a word occurs both with and without the prefix.

3. References to Cook's translation of Sievers' *Anglo-Saxon Grammar*, and to the Grammatical Introduction to Sweet's *Reader* have been taken out, as Wright's or Wyatt's *Old English Grammar* will have taken their place with most English students.

4. A new feature which, it is hoped, will prove widely useful, is the introduction of references to all, or nearly all, the headings in the *New English Dictionary* under which quotations from Anglo-Saxon texts are to be found. A vast mass of valuable information as to the etymology, meaning and occurrence of Old English words is contained in that Dictionary, but is to a very large extent overlooked because it is to be found under the head of words which are now obsolete, so that unless one happens to know what was the last form which they had in Middle English, one does not know how to get at it. This information will be made readily available by the references in the present work, which will form a practically complete index to the Anglo-Saxon material in the larger dictionary and will at the same time put the student on the track of interesting Middle English examples of the use of Old English words. Besides directing the reader (by means of quotation marks) to the heading in the *New English Dictionary* where the relevant matter may be found, an indication has been given of the texts from which quotations are made therein, when these do not exceed four or five.

5. There have been many valuable contributions to Anglo-Saxon lexicography (by Napier, Swaen, Schlutter, Förster, Wülfing and

others) since the first edition of this Dictionary appeared, and these have been made use of, but (as before) unglossaried matter has not been systematically searched for words not hitherto recorded in Anglo-Saxon Dictionaries.

6. The number of references to passages has been very largely increased. All words occurring only in poetical texts have been marked. If they occur more than once they bear the sign †, if only once, a reference to the passage is generally given. If not they are marked ‡. As regards prose texts, the rule has been only to give references to particular passages in the case of rare words,—more especially ἅπαξ λεγόμενα. The references to AO, CP and Æ which were given in the earlier edition have been retained, as a useful indication that the word occurs in Early West Saxon or Late West Saxon prose, as the case may be.

7. By various devices it has been found possible, while much increasing the amount of matter in the book, to add very slightly to the number of pages, and at the same time to reduce the number of columns on a page from three to two. Most of these devices are more or less mechanical, but one method of saving space may be mentioned. Certain compound words, descriptive of places, which, as far as I know, occur only in charters and which may often be more correctly regarded as proper nouns, have not been separately inserted. Their meaning can however always be ascertained by referring to their components, and where the abbreviation Mdf is inserted the reader will understand that examples of words so compounded, or of the components, or of both, will be found in Birch's *Cartularium Saxonicum,* or in Earle's *Land Charters,* and that references to those examples are given in Middendorff's *Altenglisches Flurnamenbuch.*

8. In the List of Abbreviations, etc. at the commencement of the book, editions of texts which are furnished with a glossary have been specially indicated.

J. R. C. H.

January 1916

PREFACE TO THE THIRD EDITION

In this new edition account has been taken of the important publications concerned with Anglo-Saxon lexicography which have appeared within the last sixteen years, and notably of the final instalments of '*Bosworth-Toller*' (BT) and the *New English Dictionary* (NED). A considerable number of words from twelfth-century texts, which have not been recorded in BT, has been inserted in the Dictionary, as there seemed to the writer that there was no sufficient ground for their exclusion.

Generally speaking, the preface to the Second Edition still holds good, except that a few words now marked † do not occur exclusively in poetical texts but appear very rarely elsewhere, e.g. in glosses. References to lines have been given in the case of all poetical words which occur only once, the sign ‡ being thus rendered unnecessary; and as regards prose words, references to page and line have usually been limited to those occurring once, or very rarely, or to passages which are not noted in other dictionaries.

In the same preface it was stated that references to the texts from which quotations have been made in the NED have only been given as a rule when the numbers did not exceed four or five. As regards the cases in which the quotations contained in the NED are more numerous, this has been indicated in the present edition by the NED word being printed in small capitals, an asterisk being added where inflectional or other forms are specially illustrated in that Dictionary by examples.

For the rest, the number of references has again been materially increased, an indication having often been given of one or two texts in which the more common words are to be found. It may be added that a few words have been given on the authority of BT, NED or Sweet alone when I have not been able to trace their source, or to verify the references given in those dictionaries.

J. R. C. H.

EASTBOURNE

April 1931

LIST OF SIGNS AND ABBREVIATIONS
WITH THEIR EXPLANATION

Note 1. Where references are in *italic type*, quotations from the texts indicated will be found in the *New English Dictionary*, under the head of the English word which is distinguished in the article by quotation marks (see Preface). When the quotations in the NED have been too numerous to allow of reference to them in this Dictionary, the Modern English word has been put in SMALL CAPITALS; and an asterisk is affixed to it when examples of inflectional or other forms ·of an Anglo-Saxon word are given in the NED. In references to special passages volumes have been marked off from pages by an inverted full stop, and lines or verses have been shown, *where they follow other numerals,* by small superior figures. Occasionally where lines have not been numbered in a quoted text, the mark ' has been inserted to show that the quotation is in the lower part of a page. References to page and line have, as a rule, been restricted to words only occurring once.

Note 2. In the following list the number (1) after an edition of a text indicates that the edition is supplied with a complete referenced glossary or word-index, (2) that it has a complete glossary, but without references, and (3) that it has a partial glossary or word-index.

Note 3. Some of the abbreviations given below are used in combination, *e.g.* MtLR = the Lindisfarne and Rushworth MSS of St Matthew; BJPs = the Bosworth and the Junius Psalters; asf. = accusative singular feminine; EK = Early Kentish.

Note 4. If any meanings of adverbs are given, they are *additional* to those which may be inferred from the corresponding adjective.

Note 5. In settling the spelling and alphabetical order of words preference has been given to EWS forms in ie or īe whenever they occur. Where other spellings (i, y; ī, ȳ) have been adopted ' = ie' or ' = īe' has been added in the case of the more important forms.

' ' Quotation marks are used to enclose the English words which should be looked up in the NED in order to find etymological information as to, and examples of the use of, the Anglo-Saxon words to which the articles in this Dictionary relate, see Note 1 above. If they enclose Latin words, they indicate the lemmata of Anglo-Saxon words in glosses or glossaries etc., or the Latin equivalent of such words in the Latin texts from which they are translated. The Latin is especially so given when ·the Ags. word seems to be a blindly mechanical and literal equivalent.

* is prefixed to hypothetical forms. Normalised forms of Ags. words which actually exist are not usually so marked. See also Note 1.

' See Note 1 above.

+ = ge-.

± indicates that the Ags. word to which it is prefixed is found both with and without the prefix ge-.

† = occurs only or mainly in poetical texts. (For references to those texts v. GK.)

a. = accusative.

A = Anglian, or, if followed by numerals, Anglia, Zeitschrift für Englische Philologie, Halle, 1877 etc.

AB = Anglia Beiblatt.

AA = Alexander's Letter, in Three English Prose Texts, ed. S. Rypins (EETS), 1924 (1).

Æ = Ælfric. (References followed by numerals in parentheses relate to certain Homilies attributed to Ælfric in HL.) References to books in Ælfric's version of the Heptateuch, in Grein's *Ælfric de vetere et novo Testamento* (Bibl. der Ags. Prosa, vol. 1), or in S. J. Crawford's Heptateuch (EETS), 1929, are given under the abbreviations of their titles (GEN etc.). Words peculiar to Crawford's text are marked C. See also ÆT.

ÆGR = Ælfric's Grammatik und Glossar, ed. J. Zupitza, Berlin, 1880.

ÆH = Ælfric's Homilies, ed. B.Thorpe, London, 1844–6. (Quoted by vol., page and line.)

ÆL = Ælfric's Metrical Lives of Saints, ed. W. W. Skeat (EETS), 1881–1900 (3).

ÆP = Ælfric's Hirtenbriefe (Pastoral Letters), ed. B. Fehr, Hamburg, 1914 (Bibl. der Ags. Prosa, vol. 9).

ÆT = the prefatory matter in Ælfric's Heptateuch (see Æ). Quoted from Crawford by line only up to p. 75, and after that by page and line.

AF = Anglistische Forschungen, ed. J. Hoops, Heidelberg.

ALM = the poem on Alms, in GR.

AN = the poem of Andreas, in GR; or ed. G. P. Krapp, Boston, U.S.A., 1905 (1).

ANDR = the prose legend of St Andrew, in BR.

ANS = Herrig's Archiv für das Studium der neueren Sprachen, Brunswick, 1846 etc.

ANT = Analecta Anglo-saxonica by B. Thorpe, London, 1846 (2).

anv. = anomalous verb.

AO = Alfred's translation of Orosius, ed. H. Sweet (EETS), 1883. (v. also Wfg.)

AP = the poem of the Fate of the Apostles, in GR; or included with Andreas in Krapp's edition (v. AN).

APs = the Arundel Psalter, ed. G. Oess (AF vol. 30), Heidelberg, 1910.

APT = Anglo-Saxon version of Apollonius of Tyre, ed. B. Thorpe, London, 1834.

AS = King Alfred's version of Augustine's Soliloquies, ed. Endter, Hamburg, 1922, or H. L. Hargrove (Yale Studies in Old English), Boston, U.S.A., 1912 (1). References are to Endter. See also SHR.

Az = the poem of Azarias, in GR.

B = the poem of Beowulf, in GR; also ed. A. J. Wyatt and R. W. Chambers, Cambridge, 1914 (1); or ed. W. J. Sedgefield, Manchester, 1912 (1); or F. Klaeber (Klb.), Boston, U.S.A., 1922 (1).

BAS = The Admonition of St Basil, ed. H. W. Norman, London, 1849.

BB = Bonner Beiträge zur Anglistik, ed. M. Trautmann.

BC = Cartularium Saxonicum, ed. W. de Gray Birch, London, 1883 etc., 3 vols.

Bd = Bede.

BDS = Beiträge zur Geschichte der deutschen Sprache, ed. E. Sievers, Leipzig, 1874 etc.

BF = Byrhtferth's Manual, ed. S. J. Crawford (EETS), 1929. Also in A vol. 8, from which the quotations in NED are made.

BH = the Anglo-Saxon version of Bede's Ecclesiastical History, 2 vols., ed. T. Miller (EETS), 1891–6. (Reference is usually made to the pages in vol. 1 as regards the various readings recorded in vol. 2—not to the pages in the latter vol.) Sch = ed. J. Schipper, Hamburg, 1899.

BK = Texte und Untersuchungen zur AE Literatur, etc., by R. Brotanek, Halle, 1913.

BL = The Blickling Homilies, ed. R. Morris (EETS), 1874–80 (1).

BLPs = Blickling Glosses to the Psalms, at the end of BL.

Bo = King Alfred's translation of Boethius, with the Metres of Boethius, ed. W. J. Sedgefield, Oxford, 1899 (1).

BPs = die AE Glossen im Bosworth-Psalter, ed. U. Lindelöf (Mémoires de la Soc. néo-philologique à Helsingfors, tom. 5), 1909 (3).

BR = An Anglo-Saxon Reader, ed. J. W. Bright, New York, or London, 1923 (1).

Br = the poem of Brunanburh, in GR or †CHR.

BT = An Anglo-Saxon Dictionary, by J. Bosworth and T. N. Toller, Oxford, 1882–98; BTs = the Supplement, 1908–21; BTac = Additions and Corrections at the end of the Supplement.

BTK = C. G. Bouterwek, de officiis horarum, in pref. to Caedmon's Biblische Dichtungen, Gütersloh, 1854 (pp. 194–222).

ByH = 12th Century Homilies in MS Bodley 343, ed. A. O. Belfour (EETS vol. 137), 1909.

CAS = Legends of St Andrew and St Veronica, in Cambridge Antiq. Society's Publications, 1851.

CC = The Crawford Charters, ed. A. S. Napier and W. H. Stevenson (Anecdota Oxoniensia), Oxford, 1895.

CHR = Two of the Saxon Chronicles Parallel, ed. J. Earle and C. Plummer, Oxford, 1892 (1). The poetical passages are marked †CHR.

CHRD = the Rule of Chrodegang, ed. A. S. Napier (EETS), 1916.

CM = the tract 'de Consuetudine Mona-
chorum,' in Anglia, vol. 13, pp. 365–
454.

Coll. Monast., v. WW.

Cos = Altwestsächsische Grammatik,
by P. J. Cosijn, Haag, 1888.

cp. = compare.

CP = King Alfred's trans. of Gregory's
Pastoral Care, ed. H. Sweet (EETS),
London, 1871.

Cp = the Corpus Glossary, in OET, or in
WW (cols. 1–54) or (if the numbers
are followed by a letter) in A Latin-
Anglo-Saxon Glossary, ed. J. H.
Hessels, Cambridge, 1890 (1).

CPs = Der Cambridge-Psalter, ed. K.
Wildhagen, Bibl. der Ags. Prosa, vol.
7, Hamburg, 1910. (CHy = Cambridge Hymns in the same vol.) (3).

Cr = the poem of Crist, in Gr.

Cra = the poem of Men's Crafts, in Gr.

Creat = the poem of the Creation, in
Gr.

Ct = Charters, wills and other like documents, as contained in BC, CC, EC,
KC, TC and WC.

d. = dative. dp. = dat. pl. ds. = dat.
singular; etc.

Da = the poem of Daniel, in Gr; or ed.
T. W. Hunt (Exodus and Daniel),
Boston, 1885.

DD = the poem 'Be Dōmes Dæge' ('de
die judicii'), ed. J. R. Lumby
(EETS), London, 1876 (1); or in Gr
(vol. 2, pp. 250–272).

Deor = the poem of Deor's Complaint,
in Gr and Kl.

Deut = Deuteronomy (see Æ).

DHy = the Durham Hymnarium, ed.
J. Stevenson (Surtees Society, vol.
23), London, 1851. (Gl by H. W.
Chapman, Yale Studies, No. 24,
Boston, 1905.)

Dom = the poem 'Be Dōmes Dæge'
from the Exeter Book, in Gr (vol.
3, pp. 171–4).

DR = the Durham Ritual, ed. J.
Stevenson (Surtees Society), London,
1840, as re-edited by Uno Lindelöf,
1927. Lines of Anglo-Saxon only
counted. [Gl by Lindelöf, Bonn,
1901 (BB vol. 9).]

E = Early.

EC = Land Charters and other Saxonic
Documents, ed. John Earle, Oxford,
1888 (3).

EETS = Early English Text Society's
Publications.

EHR = English Historical Review.

EK = Early Kentish.

El = the poem of Elene, in Gr; or ed.
Kent, Boston, 1889.

Ep = the Epinal Gloss., in OET.

EPs = Eadwine's Canterbury Psalter,
ed. F. Harsley (EETS), London, 1889.
Late text. (EHy = Hymns in the
same vol.)

Erf = the Erfurt Gloss., in OET.

ES = Englische Studien, Heilbronn and
Leipzig, 1876 etc.

Ettm. = L. Ettmüller, Lexicon Anglo-
saxonicum, 1851.

EWS = Early West Saxon.

Ex = the poem of Exodus, in Gr or in
Hunt's edition (v. Da). If followed
by two kinds of numerals = Exodus
in Ælfric de vetere et novo Testamento
in the Bibl. der Ags. Prosa, vol. 1,
Cassel, 1872, or in Crawford's
Heptateuch (ExC).

exc. = except.

f. = feminine. fp. = fem. plural.

FAp = the poem 'Fata Apostolorum,'
in Gr.

FBO = Das Benediktiner Offizium, ed.
E. Feiler (AF vol. 4), Heidelberg,
1901.

Fin = the poem of Finnsburg, in Gr,
and most editions of Beowulf.

FM = The Furnivall Miscellany, Oxford, 1901.

FT = the poem 'A Father's Teachings,'
in Gr.

FTp = Falk-Torp, Wortschatz der
Germ. Spracheinheit, Göttingen,
1909.

g. = genitive. gs. = gen. singular. gp. =
gen. pl.; etc.

G = the Anglo-Saxon Gospels, ed. W. W.
Skeat, Cambridge, 1871–87, or by
Bosworth (B) or Kemble (K). See
also LG, NG, RG, WG. (Gl to WG
by M. A. Harris, Yale Studies, vol. 6,
Boston, 1899.)

GBG = The meaning of certain terms in
Ags. Charters, by G. B. Grundy,
English Association Essays and
Studies, vol. 8, 1922.

GD = Die Dialoge Gregors den Grossen,
ed. Hans Hecht (Bibl. der Ags. Prosa,
vol. 5), Cassel, 1900–7.

Gen = the poem of Genesis, in Gr. If
followed by two kinds of numerals =
Genesis in Ælfric de vetere et novo
Testamento, in the Bibl. der Ags.
Prosa, vol. 1, Cassel, 1872, or in
Crawford's Heptateuch (GenC).

Ger. = German.

GF = Legends of St Swithhun etc., ed. J. Earle, London, 1861 (Gloucester Fragments).

GK = Grein's Sprachschatz der Ags. Dichter, revised by Köhler and Holthausen, Heidelberg, 1912. (A complete referenced glossary to GR.)

GL = Glossary. Used also as a comprehensive sign for all or any of the extant Anglo-Saxon glosses or glossaries: Cp, Ep, Erf, GPH, HGL, KGL, Ln, OEG, WW etc.

GN = The Gnomic Verses, in GR. GNE = those in the Exeter Book and GNC those in the Cotton MS. Separate edition also by B. C. Williams, New York, 1914 (1).

GPH = Prudentius Glosses, in Germania, Vierteljahrsschrift für deutsche Altertumskunde, vol. 11 (ns).

GR = Bibliothek der Angelsächs. Poesie, ed. C. W. M. Grein and revised by R. P. Wülker, Cassel, 1883–98.

GU = the poem of St Guthlac, in GR.

GUTH = the (prose) Life of St Guthlac, ed. C. W. Goodwin, London, 1848 (pp. 8–98), or (pp. 100–176) ed. P. Gonser (AF vol. 27), Heidelberg, 1909.

HELL = the poem of Hell, in GR.

HEPT = Heptateuchus, etc., Anglo-Saxonice, ed. E. Thwaites, Oxford, 1698. See also Æ.

HEX = The Hexameron of St Basil, ed. H. W. Norman, London, 1849, or ed. S. J. Crawford (HEXC), Bibl. der Ags. Prosa, vol. 10, 1921.

HGL = Glosses in (Haupt's) Zeitschrift für deutsches Altertum, vol. 9 (1853).

HL = Homilien und Heiligendleben, ed. B. Assmann, Bibl. der Ags. Prosa, vol. 3, Cassel, 1889. v. also Æ and SHR (3).

HR = Legends of the Holy Rood, ed. R. Morris (EETS), 1871.

HU = the poem 'The Husband's Message,' in GR.

HY = the collection of 'Hymns' at the end of most of the Ags. versions of the Psalms. v. the various Psalters (PS). [The numbering of verses etc. usually follows that in Wildhagen's Cambridge Psalter (CPS).] †HY = the 'Hymnen und Gebete,' in GR.

i. = instrumental (case).

IF = Indogermanische Sprachforschungen, 1891 etc.

IM = 'Indicia Monasterialia,' ed. F. Kluge, in Techmer's Internationale Zeitschrift für allgemeine Sprachwissenschaft, vol. 2, Leipzig, 1885, pp. 118–129.

intr. = intransitive.

JAW = Eigentümlichkeiten des Anglischen Wortschatzes, by R. Jordan (AF vol. 17), Heidelberg, 1906.

JGPh = Journal of (English and) Germanic Philology, Urbana, 1897 etc.

Jn = the Gospel of St John. v. G and NG (JnL = Lindisfarne MS; JnR = Rushworth MS, v. LG, RG).

Jos = Joshua (see Æ).

JPs = der Junius-Psalter, ed. E. Brenner (AF vol. 23), Heidelberg, 1909 (JHy = the Hymns in the same vol.).

JUD = the poem of Judith, in GR, or ed. A. S. Cook, Boston, 1889 (1); or if followed by two kinds of numerals = Judges, in Crawford's Heptateuch.

JUL = the poem of Juliana, in GR.

K = Kentish.

KC = Codex Diplomaticus Aevi Saxonici, ed. J. M. Kemble, 6 vols., London, 1839–48. (3) at end of vol. 3.

KGL = Kentish Glosses to the Proverbs of Solomon (= WW 55–88, or, if quoted by number, in KL).

KL = Angelsächsisches Lesebuch, by F. Kluge, 3rd edition, Halle, 1902 (2).

KLED = F. Kluge's Etymologisches Wörterbuch, or J. F. Davis' translation, London, 1891.

KPs = Psalm 50 (Kentish), in GR, KL or SwtR.

L. = Latin.

LCD = Leechdoms, Wortcunning and Starcraft of the Anglo-Saxons, ed. O. Cockayne, London, 3 vols., Rolls Series, 1864–6 (vol. 2, and pp. 1–80 of vol. 3 are referred to by the folio of the MS, so that the references may also be available for G. Leonhardi's edition of that part of the LCD, in the Bibl. der Ags. Prosa, vol. 6) (3).

LEAS = the poem 'Be manna lease,' in GR.

LEV = Leviticus, in Æ.

LF = An OE Ritual text, ed. B. Fehr, and Keltisches Wortgut im Eng. by M. Förster, in F. Liebermann's Festgabe, Halle, 1921.

LG = the Lindisfarne Gospels, in Skeat's ed. of the Anglo-Saxon Gospels (v. G). (Glossary by A. S. Cook, Halle, 1894.) LRG = Lindisfarne and Rushworth Gospels. v. RG.

Lieb. = F. Liebermann (v. LL).

Lk = the Gospel of St Luke. v. G and

NG (LkL = Lindisfarne MS; LkR = Rushworth MS; v. LG, RG).

LL = the Anglo-Saxon Laws, as contained in Liebermann, Schmid, Thorpe or Wilkins. If followed by numerals not in parentheses, or only partially in parentheses, the reference is to 'Die Gesetze der Angelsachsen,' by F. Liebermann, 3 vols., Halle, 1903–16 (1); if by numerals *entirely* in parentheses, to vol. 2 of 'Ancient Laws and Institutes,' by B. Thorpe, 2 vols., London, 1840 (3).

Ln = the Leiden Glossary, ed. J. H. Hessels, Cambridge, 1906 (1).

Lor = the Lorica Hymn, in Kleinere angelsächsische Denkmäler, by G. Leonhardi (Bibl. der Ags. Prosa, vol. 6), Hamburg, 1905.

LPs = Der Lambeth-Psalter, ed. U. Lindelöf, Acta Soc. Sc. Fennicae, vol. 35, Helsingfors, 1909 (1). (LHy = the Hymns in the same vol.)

LV = Leofric's Vision, ed. A. S. Napier, in the Transactions of the Philological Society for 1907–10, pp. 180–188.

LWS = Late West Saxon.

M = Mercian.

m. = masculine. ms., mp., etc. = masc. sing., masc. plur., etc.

MA = the poem of the Battle of Maldon, in Gr, also in Br, Kl or Sweet's Anglo-Saxon Reader, Oxford.

Mdf = Altenglisches Flurnamenbuch, by H. Middendorff, Halle, 1902. [See Preface.]

Men = the Menologium, at the end of Chr, or in Hickes' Thesaurus, vol. 1

Met = the Metres of Boethius; v. Bo.

MFB = Max Förster's contribution to A. Brandl's Festschrift (Anglica II, pp. 8–69 in Palaestra 148), Leipzig, 1925. (Quoted by line; v. also RWH.)

MFH = Vercelli-Homilies, ed. in the Festschrift für L. Morsbach (Studien zur Eng. Philologie, vol. 50), Halle, 1913, ed. Max Förster, pp. 20–179; v. also VH.

MH = An Old English Martyrology, ed. G. Herzfeld (EETS), London, 1900. See also Shr.

Mk = the Gospel of St Mark; v. G and NG. (MkL = Lindisfarne MS; MkR = Rushworth MS of St Mark; v. LG, RG.)

MLA = Publications of the Modern Language Association of America, Baltimore.

MLN = Modern Language Notes, Baltimore, 1886 etc.

MLR = Modern Language Review, Cambridge, 1905 etc.

Mod = the poem 'Bi Manna Mōd,' in Gr.

MP = Modern Philology, Chicago.

Mt = the Gospel of St Matthew; v. G and NG. (MtL = Lindisfarne MS; MtR = Rushworth MS of St Matthew; v. LG, RG.)

n. = nominative, *or* neuter, *or* note. (np., nap., etc. = nom. plural, nom. and acc. plur., etc.)

N = Northumbrian.

Nar = Narratiunculae, ed. O. Cockayne, London, 1861.

NC = Contributions to Old English Lexicography by A. Napier, in the Philological Society's Transactions for 1903–1906, London (mostly late texts).

NED = the New English Dictionary, ed. Sir J. A. H. Murray and others, Oxford, 1888–1915. (See Prefaces, and Note 1.)

neg. = negative.

NG = the Northumbrian Gospels, contained in Skeat's edition (v. G, LG, RG).

Nic = the Gospel of Nicodemus, in MLA 13·456–541, MP 1·579–604 and RWH 77–88 (referred to by pages in those texts).

NP = Neophilologus, Groningen, 1915 etc.

NR = The Legend of the Cross (Roodtree), ed. A. S. Napier (EETS), London, 1894.

Num = Numbers (see Æ).

obl. = oblique.

occly. = occasionally.

OEG = Old English Glosses, ed. A. Napier (Anecdota Oxoniensia), Oxford, 1900 (1).

OEH = vol. 1 of Morris, Old English Homilies (pp. 296–304 only) (EETS), 1867.

OET = The Oldest English Texts, ed. H. Sweet (EETS), 1885 (1).

OF. = Old French.

OHG. = Old High German.

ON. = Old Norse.

OP = Oratio Poetica, in DD (Lumby).

OS. = Old Saxon.

p. = page, *or* plural.

Pa = the poem of the Panther, in Gr.

Part = the poem of the Partridge, in Gr.

PH = the poem of the Phoenix, in GR or BR.

pl. = plural.

PPs = the Paris Psalter, ed. B. Thorpe, London, 1835. The prose portion (Psalms 1–50) also ed. Bright and Ramsay, Belles Lettres Series, Boston, 1907, and the remainder (verse portion) in GR.

PR = Proverbs, at end of SOL (Kemble), pp. 258–268.

Ps = any one or more of the Anglo-Saxon Psalters. [NB. In the numbering of the Psalms, the Authorised Version is usually one ahead of the MSS.] v. A, B, C, E, J, L, R, S and VPs; also Hy. PsC = Psalm 100 in GR.

PST = Philological Society's Transactions (v. also LV and NC).

QF = Mone, Quellen u. Forschungen zur Geschichte der teutschen Lit. u. Sprache, Aachen und Leipzig, 1830.

RB = der Benedictinregel, ed. A. Schröer, Bibl. der Ags. Prosa, vol. 2, Cassel, 1885–8 (3).

RBL = the Anglo-Saxon and Latin Rule of St Benet (Interlinear Glosses), ed. H. Logeman (EETS), London, 1888.

RD = The Riddles of the Exeter Book, in GR, or ed. F. Tupper Junr., Boston, 1910 (1).

RG = the Rushworth Gospels, in Skeat's ed. of the Anglo-Saxon Gospels (v. G). Mt (all), Mk 1–2^{15} and Jn 18$^{1-3}$ are in a Mercian dialect, and are usually known as R^1; the rest (R^2) is in a Northumbrian dialect (v. also LG). Glossary to R^1 by Ernst Schulte, Bonn, 1904; to R^2 by U. Lindelöf, Helsingfors, 1897.

RIM = The Rhyming Poem, in GR.

ROOD = the poem 'Dream of the Rood,' in GR.

RPs = der Regius-Psalter, ed. F. Roeder (Studien in Eng. Philologie, vol. 18), Halle, 1904. (RHy = the Hymns in the same vol.)

RSL = Transactions of the Royal Society of Literature, London.

RUIN = the poem of the Ruin, in GR.

RUN = the Rune-poem, in GR.

RWH = Homilies in MS Vesp. D. XIV (12th cent.), ed. R. D. N. Warner (EETS vol. 152), 1917. (pp. 77–88 = NIC, and pp. 134–139=MFB.)

s. = strong; also = singular. sv. = strong verb. swv. = strong-weak verb.

SAT = the poem 'Christ and Satan,' in GR.

sb. = substantive.

Sc = Defensor's Liber Scintillarum, ed. E. Rhodes (EETS), London, 1889 (3). Lines of Ags. only counted.

SCR = Screadunga, by C. G. Bouterwek, Elberfeld, 1858.

SEAF = the poem of the Seafarer, in GR.

SF = Streitberg Festgabe, Leipzig, 1924.

SHR = the Shrine by O. Cockayne, London, 1864–70 [pp. 29–33 and 46–156 = MH; pp. 35–44 = HL pp. 199–207; pp. 163–204 = AS].

SHy = Surtees Hymnarium = DHy.

SkED = An Etymological English Dictionary by W.W. Skeat, Oxford, 1910.

SOL = the poem Solomon and Saturn, in GR (if followed by page and line, or marked SOLK, the reference is to the prose version, ed. J. M. Kemble). Ags. proverbs (PR) are included at pp. 258–268.

SOUL = the poem of the Soul, in GR.

SPs = Psalterium Davidis Latino-Saxonicum, ed. J. Spelman, London, 1640. No Hymns. (Stowe MS, but includes marginal readings from APs, CPs and EPs.)

S^{2}Ps = Psalter Glosses in Salisbury Cathedral Library MS 150 (noted in CPs).

STC = Life of St Christopher, in 3 OE Prose Texts (v. AA).

Swt. = The Student's Dictionary of Anglo-Saxon by H. Sweet, Oxford, 1897.

SwtR = Sweet's Anglo-Saxon Reader, Oxford, 1922.

TC = Diplomatarium Ævi Saxonici, ed. B. Thorpe, London, 1865 (3).

tr. = transitive.

TF = The Capitula of Theodulf, at the end of CHRD.

usu. = usual, usually.

v. = vide, or very.

VH = an art. in A vol. 54 pp. 9–24 on the Homilies in the Vercelli Book; v. also MFH.

v.l. = varia lectio.

VPs = the Vespasian Psalter, in OET (1). [VHy = Hymns at the end of the Psalter.] Glossary also by Conrad Grimm (AF vol. 18), Heidelberg, 1906.

V^{2}Ps = Psalter-Glosses in Cotton Vitellius E 18 (noted in CPs).

W = (I) Wulfstan's Homilies, ed. A. Napier, Berlin, 1883. Glossary by

L. H. Dodd, New York, 1908. (II) West Saxon.

WA = the poem of the Wanderer, in GR.

WAL = the poem of Waldhere, in GR.

WC = D. Whitelock, Anglo-Saxon Wills, Cambridge, 1930.

WE = Wonders of the East, in 3 OE Prose Texts (v. AA).

Wfg = die Syntax in den Werken Alfreds, by J. E. Wülfing, Bonn, 1894–1901 (copious material, and indexes to words in AO, BH, Bo, CP, AS, PPs, etc.).

WG = West Saxon Gospels (v. G).

WH = the poem of the Whale, in GR.

WID = the poem of Widsith, in GR, or ed. R. W. Chambers, Cambridge, 1912.

WIF = the poem of 'the Wife's Complaint,' in GR.

WNL = Wanley's Catalogue, in vol. 2 of G. Hickes' Thesaurus Antiquae Literaturae Septentrionalis, Oxford, 1705.

WS = West Saxon.

Wt = An Old English Grammar by J. and E. M. Wright, 2nd edition, Oxford, 1914.

WW = Old English Vocabularies, ed. by T. Wright and R. P. Wülker, London, 1884. Cols. 1–54 = Cp; 55–88 = KGL; pp. 89–103 = *Colloq. Monast.* in NED.

Wy = the poem 'Be manna wyrdum,' in GR.

WYN = Wynfrith's Letter, in MLR vol. 18.

ZDA = Zeitschrift für deutsches Altertum, Leipzig and Berlin, 1853 etc.

ZDPh = Zeitschrift für deutsche Philologie, Halle, 1869 **etc.**

A CONCISE
ANGLO-SAXON DICTIONARY

A

ā I. (āwa, ō) adv. *always, ever, at all, continuously, for ever*, Æ,AO,CP. ā on ēcnisse; ā butan ende *world without end: at any time : in any degree*. [*ON.* ei, ey] II. f. = ǣ

ā- (unemphatic verbal prefix); I. orig. = *forth, away*, but as a rule only intensive in meaning. II. = on- III. ym(b)- IV. = ā(I.) in pronouns and participles, and gives a sense of indefiniteness. V. = ǣ-

āǣ (Bf) = ā

āǣlan = onǣlan; **āǣðan** = āīeðan; **āb** = ōweb

ābacan⁶ *to bake*, ÆH 2·268⁹

ābǣdan *to compel, restrain, ward off : exact, take toll : force out, extract.*

ābǣligan = ābylgan

ābǣran *to disclose, bring to light*, DD 41.

ābǣre (W 274²⁴) = ǣbǣre

ābǣrnan = onbǣrnan; **abal** (Gen 500) = afol

ābannan⁷ *to summon, convoke, command : announce, proclaim.* ā. ūt *call out, assemble*, Chr. ['abanne']

ābarian *to lay bare, disclose*, Jos,RBL : *strip*, CM.

abbad = abbod

abbod (a, u) m. '*abbot*,' BH,Chr; Æ. [*L.* abbatem]

abboddōm m. *abbatial jurisdiction*, BH.

abboðesse f. *abbess*, Chr.

abbodhād m. *abbatial rank, dignity*, LL.

abbodlēast f. *lack of an abbot*, BC 1·155'.

abbodrīce n. *abbey, abbacy, office or jurisdiction of an abbot* (used even of a convent of nuns).

abbot, abbud = abbod

ābēatan⁷ *to beat, strike, break to pieces, make to fall*, Cr. ['abeat']

ābēcēdē f. *ABC, alphabet*, Bf 180, 194.

ābedecian (eðe-) *to get by asking*, Bo,Chrd.

abedisse = abbodesse; **ābēgan** = ābȳgan

ābelgan³ *to make angry, irritate, offend, Sol*; Æ,AO,CP : *hurt, distress : be angry with*. ['abelgen']

ābeligan = ābylgan

ābēodan² *to order, proclaim, bid, command, direct : summon, call out : announce, relate, declare, present, offer, AO*; Æ. hǣl ā. *to wish one good luck, greet, bid farewell to.* ['abede']

ābeofian = ābifian; **ābēogan** = ābūgan

ābeornan³ *to take fire*, PPs 105¹⁶.

ābēowan (WW 217⁴⁶) = ābȳwan

āberan⁴ *to bear, carry, Mt : endure, suffer, Bo*; Æ,CP : *bear (a child), Æ : take away, remove : reveal :* (refl.) *restrain oneself : do without*, NC 268. ['abear']

ā-berd, -bered *crafty, cunning*, Lcd,Sc.

āberendlic *bearable*, LL.

ābernan (N) = ābeornan

āberstan³ *to burst out, break out*, Æ,CP : *break away, escape.* ūt ā. *break out.*

ābeðecian = ābedecian; **ābicgan** = ābycgan

ābīdan¹ *to 'abide,' wait, remain, delay, remain behind, Chr*; AO : *survive : wait for, await*, Æ : *expect*, Mt 11⁸.

ābiddan⁵ *to ask for, request, require, demand, pray, pray to, pray for, Æ : get by asking, obtain, Æ,AO,CP : call out (an army).*

ābies f. *silver fir-tree*, AA 12⁶. [*L.*]

ābifian (eo) *to tremble, quake, shake.*

ābilgð, ābilhð = ǣbylgð; **ābiran** = āberan

ābir(g)ing f. *taste* (BTs)

ābisgian (y, -seg-) *to busy, occupy, employ, CP : be busy with, engage in, undertake : take up, fill*, GD.

ābisgung (y) f. *occupation : trouble*, CP.

ābītan¹ *to bite in pieces, tear to pieces, devour, gnaw, Æ,AO : taste, partake of, consume.* [= on-b.]

ābit(e)rian *to turn bitter*, CP 341²⁴ : *embitter.*

āblācian *to become pale, grow faint : become tarnished*, CP 135².

āblǣcan *to bleach, whiten*, BJPs 50⁹.

āblǣcnes f. *pallor, gloom*, Lcd 1·294 n 6.

āblǣcung f. *pallor*, HGl 518.

āblǣst *inspired, furious : blowing fiercely* (of flame), StC 69⁵.

āblāwan⁷ *to blow, blow away, breathe upon, Æ : puff up, swell*, Lcd 93b. ['ablow']

āblāw-nes, -ung f. *inflation*, Lcd.

āblegned *ulcerated*, Lcd.

āblendan *to blind, put out the eyes of, Æ, CP : dazzle, deceive, delude, Æ.* ['ablend']

āblered *bare, uncovered, bald*, ES 8·62. [blere]

āblīcan¹ *to shine, glitter*, Ps.

āblicgan = āblycgan; **āblignes** = ǣbylgnes

āblindan *to make blind*, Bl 151⁴.

āblindian *to become blind*, Lcd,MH.

āblinnan³ *to cease, leave off, desist*, Æ,AO, CP

āblinnednes (A5·465) = āblinnendnes
āblinnendlīce indefatigably, HGL429³².
āblinnendnes f. cessation, ÆL23b⁹⁸.
āblisian (Æ) = āblysian
āblissian to make glad, please, GD335n.
āblongen = ābolgen, pp. of ābelgan.
āblycgan (i) to grow pale, Æ : make afraid.
āblynnan = āblinnan
āblysian to blush, Ps.
āblysung f. blushing, shame, RB133¹¹.
ābodian to announce, proclaim, LkR12³.
ābolgennes f. irritation, WW230¹⁹. [ābel-gan]
āborgian to be surety for, LL : (w. æt) borrow.
āborian = ābarian
ābracian to engrave, emboss, GL.
ābrǣdan I. to spread out, dilate : stretch out, Æ. II. bake, LCD44a.
ābraslian to crash, crackle, GD236¹². [brastlian]
ābrēac pret. 3 sg. of ābrūcan.
ābrēat pret. 3 sg. of ābrēotan.
ābrecan⁴ (tr.) to break, break to pieces, break down, conquer, capture, violate, destroy, Æ,AO,CP : (intr.) break out, away, forth, Æ,AO,CP.
ābrēdan = ābregdan
ābredwian to lay low, kill, B2619.
ābrēgan to alarm, terrify, BH,GD.
ābregdan³ to move quickly, draw, unsheath, wrench, pull out, Mt : withdraw, take away, draw back, free from, Æ,AO. ūp ā. to draw up, raise, lift up, Æ. : start up, awake. ['abraid']
ābrēotan² to destroy, kill : fail, deteriorate.
ābrēotnes f. extermination, OET182.
ābrēoðan² (intr.) to fail, decay, deteriorate, perish, be destroyed, Ma; Æ. ābroðen (pp.) degenerate, reprobate, ÆGr. (tr. and wk.) destroy. [v. 'brethe']
ābrerd- = onbryrd-
ābroðennes f. baseness, cowardice, W.
ābrūcan³ to eat, A11·1¹⁷.
ābryrd- = onbryrd-
ābrȳtan to destroy, CPs36⁹.
ābūfan (= on-) adv. above, CHR1090E.
ābūgan² (= on-) to bow, incline, bend, submit, do reverence, B,Chr; Æ : swerve, turn (to or from), deviate, CP : withdraw, retire : be bent or turned, turn oneself. ['abow']
ābunden unimpeded, WW.
ābūrod not inhabited, TC162'.
ābūtan (e³, o³) I. prep. acc. on, 'about,' around, on the outside, round about, Chr. II. adv. 'about,' nearly, Chr. [= onbūtan]
ābycgan to buy, pay for, requite : redeem : perform, execute.

ābyffan to mutter, WW447²⁴.
ābȳgan (ē, ē²; = īe²) to bend, deflect : subdue, bring low : convert.
ābȳgendlic v. un-ā
ābyl(i)gan (æ², e²) to irritate, provoke, MtR,W.
ābyrg- = ābirg-; **ābysg-** = ābisg-
ābȳwan (ēo) to rub off, polish, cleanse, purify.
ac I. conj. but : but also, moreover, nevertheless, however : because, for (?). ac gif unless, except, BL151'. [Goth. ak] II. interrog. particle why, wherefore, whether : in direct questions = L. nonne, numquid.
āc f. gds. and np. ǣc 'oak,' Æ,Ct,Lcd;Mdf : ship of oak, RUN77 : (w. nap. ācas) name of the rune for a. [OHG. eih]
ācǣgan = aciegan
ācǣglod studded with pegs? (BTs), AA31².
ācǣnn- = ācenn-; **ācǣrran** = ācirran
ācalan⁶ to become frost-bitten, LCD2b.
acan⁶ to 'ache,' suffer pain, Æ.
acas, acase f. (NG) = æcs
ācbēam m. oak-tree. **accent** m. accent. [L.]
ācbearo m. oak-grove, KC5·232'.
accutian? = ācunnian
āccynn n. a kind of oak, WW430⁶.
ācdrenc m. oak drink, drink made from acorns? WW.
ace = ece
ācealdian to become cold, CP. ['acold']
ācēapian to buy off, buy out, Ct,LL.
ācēlan to cool off, still, quiet, Met. ['akele']
ācelma = æcelma; **ācen** = æcen
ācennan to bring forth, produce, renew, Æ,Bo,RG : attribute to. ['akenne(d)']
ācennedlic 'genuinus,' native, CHRD,RPs.
ācennednes (WG; Æ), -cennes (NG; AO,CP) f. birth. ['akenn(ed)nes']
ācennend m. parent, DR197¹¹.
ācennicge f. mother, DR.
ācenning f. birth, BK16.
ācēocian (tr.) to choke : (intr.) burn out.
ācēocung f. rumination, WW179².
āceorfan³ to cut off, hew down, AO,CP. onweg ā. to cut away. of ā. to cut off, AO.
ācēosan² to choose, AO,CP.
acer = æcer; **ācerr-** = ācirr-
ācīgan (= īe) to call, summon.
ācirran (æ, e, y; = ie) (tr.) to turn, turn away or aside : (intr.) turn oneself, go, return.
-ācirrednes v. onweg-ā.
ācl = ācol; **āclǣc** = āglǣc
āclǣnsian to cleanse, purify, Æ.
āclēaf n. oak leaf, LCD.
āclēofan² to cleave, EC351¹⁰.
ācleopian to call out, WW378⁵.
+āclian† to frighten, excite. [ācol]

āclungen *contracted*, WW 239³⁷. [clingan]
ācmelu n. *acorn meal*, LCD.
ācmistel f. *mistletoe*, LCD. ācn- = ēacn-
ācnāwan¹ *to know, recognise, understand*.
ācnyssan *to drive out, expel*, SPs 35¹³.
ācofrian *to recover*, Lcd. ['acover']
ācol† *affrighted, dismayed*.
ācōlian *to grow cold*, CP.
ācolitus m. *acolyte*, LL. [*L.*]
ācolmōd† *fearful minded, timid*
+ācolmōdian *to alarm, sadden*, WW 209¹⁶.
ācordian *to make terms, reconcile*, CHR 1120.
ācorenlic *eligible, worthy of choice*, CP 409³⁶.
ācostnian *to try, test, prove*, CM,WW.
ācræftan *to think out, devise*, AO 46²⁹.
ācrammian *to cram*, WW 236¹⁰.
ācrēopian *to creep, crawl*, ExC 16²⁰.
ācrimman³ (y) *to cram, stuff*, WW.
ācrind f. *oak-bark*, LCD.
ācrummen pp. of ācrimman.
acs = æx; ācs-= āsc-; acse = asce
ācstybb m. *oak-stump*, KC (v. MLR 17).
āctān m. *oak-twig*, LCD.
āctrēo n. *oak-tree*, WIF 28, 36.
ācucian (Æ) = ācwician
ācul = ācol; ācum, ācuma (Æ) = ācumba
ācuman⁴ *to come, come forth (from)*, Æ :
bear, bring : endure, withstand, Æ : *get to
or from, reach*, Gen. ['acome']
ācum-ba m., -be fn. 'oakum,' *hards, tow*,
Lcd,OEG,WW : *ashes of oakum : parings,
clippings*. [cemban]
ācumendlic *tolerable*, Æ : *possible*.
ācumendlicnes f. *possibility*, OEG 3393.
ācunnan (NG) = oncunnan
ācunnian *to try, test, prove : experience*, CP.
ācunnung f. *experience, trial*, GD.
ācusan *to accuse*, MtL 12¹⁰. [*L.*]
ācwacian *to tremble*, GD,PPs.
ācwæncan = ācwencan
ācweccan (tr.) *to move, swing, shake, vibrate*,
Ma; Æ : (intr.) *quiver*, Æ. ['aquetch']
ācwelan⁴ *to die, perish*, Æ,AO,CP.
ācwellan *to kill, destroy*, JnL; Æ,AO,CP.
['aquell']
ācwellednes (eæ²) f. *slaughter*, EPs 43²².
ācwencan (æ²) *to quench, extinguish*, Mt;
AO. ['aquench']
ācweorna m. *squirrel*, Gl. ['aquerne']
ācweorran³ *to guzzle, gorge*, EPs 77⁶⁵.
ācwern = ācweorna
ācwerren = ācworren pp. of ācweorran.
ācweðan⁵ *to say, speak out, declare, utter,
express, answer, banish*, Gen : *reject, banish*, GEN
304. ['aqueath']
ācwician (tr.) *to quicken, vivify*, Ps : (intr.)
revive, BH. ['aquick']
acwīnan¹ *to dwindle away, disappear, go
out (of fire)*, BH,LPs.

ācwincan³ *to vanish, be extinguished or
eclipsed*, Æ.
ācworren pp. of ācweorran.
ā-cwucian, -cwycian = ācwician
ācwudu m. *an oak wood*, KC 6·218'.
ācwylman (= ie) *to kill, slay*.
ācwylmian (= ie) *to be tormented*, W 220⁵.
ācwyncan = ācwincan
ācynned = ācenned pp. of ācennan.
ācyrr- = ācirr-
ācȳðan *to show, proclaim, reveal, announce,
confirm, prove*.
ād mn. *heap, funeral pile, pyre*, AO : *fire,
flame*. [OHG. eit]
ādǣlan *to divide, separate*, BL,BO.
ādēadian *to fail, decay, mortify, become
torpid or callous*, Æ.
ādēafian *to become deaf*, WW 179²⁵.
ādēafung f. *deafening, making deaf*, Lcd.
[v. 'adeave']
ādel I. = ādl. II. = ādela
ādela m. *mud, dirt, filthy place*, Æ. ['addle']
ādelfan³ *to delve, dig, excavate*, Æ,AO,CP.
ādeliht *filthy*, WW.
ādelsēað m. *sewer, sink*, Æ.
ādēman *to judge, try, deprive of or exclude
from by a legal decision : try; afflict*.
ādeorcian *to become dull, obscure, tarnished*,
CP : *grow dark*, W.
āderian *to hurt*, GD 219¹⁹.
adesa m., adese f. 'adze,' *hatchet*, BH,W.
ādexe = āðexe
ād-faru f. ds. -fære *way or path to the funeral
pile*, B 3010.
ādfīni n. *limit? ash-heap of a beacon?*
EC 354⁵.
ādfȳr n. *sacrificial fire*, Ex 398.
+ ādgian = +ēadgian
ādīdan (GENC 7²², 9¹¹) = ādȳdan
-ādihtian v. fore-ā.
ā-dīlegian, -dīl(i)gian (ȳ) *to destroy, blot out,
annihilate, devastate*, CP.
ādimmian *to become dim or dull, to darken,
obscure*, BO; CP. [v. 'dim']
ādl fn., ādle f. *disease, infirmity, sickness*,
AO,CP.
ādlēg m. *flame of the funeral pile*, PH 222.
± ādlian *to be diseased or ill, languish*, Æ :
cause disease, DR : *become ill*, ANS
120·297.
ādlig *sick, diseased*, Æ.
ādliga m. *sick person*. ādliht = ādeliht
ādloma m. *one crippled by fire*, GU 884.
[lama?]
ādlsēoc *in bad health : sick of a contagious
disease?* ES 39·322.
ādl-ðracu f. gs. -ðræce *force of disease*,
GU 935.
ādlung f. *illness*, ÆH 1·122³¹.

ādlwērig *weary from illness*, Gu 981.
ādōn (for conj. v. dōn) *to take away, send away : cast out, expel, destroy* : (w. preps. tō, on, fram, etc.) *put, place, take, remove, set free*, AO,CP.
adosa = adesa; **ādrǣdan** = ondrǣdan
ādrǣfan (ē) *to drive away, shut out, expel*, NED; AO,CP. ['*adrefe*']
ādrǣnct = ādrenced pp. of ādrencan.
ādragan⁶ *to draw (sword)*, HL 15³⁵⁶.
ādrēfan = ādrǣfan
adreminte f. *feverfew* (BT).
ādrencan *to submerge, immerse, drown*, Ps; AO. ['*adrench*']
ādrēogan² *to act, do, practise, Æ : bear, suffer, endure*, An; CP : *pass time, live, Æ.* ['*adree*']
ādrēogendlic '*agendus*,' '*gerendus*,' DHy, RBL.
ādrēohan = ādrēogan
ādrēopan² *to drip, drop*, An.
ādrēosan² *to fall to pieces, decline, vanish, fail.*
ādrīfan¹ (īe) *to drive, drive away, drive out, pursue, follow up*, LL; Æ,AO,CP : *stake out (a ford) : chase (metal), Æ.* ['*adrive*']
ādrīgan = ādrȳgan
ādrincan³ *be drowned, extinguished*, BH; AO. ['*adrink*']
ādrūgian, ādrūwian (Æ,Mt) *to dry up.* ['*adroughe*']
ādrȳgan (ī) *to dry up : dry, wipe dry*, CP.
ādrysnan *to extinguish, repress*, NG.
adsa = adesa; **adulsēað** = adelsēað
ādumbian *to become dumb, keep silence*, Mk; Æ. [v. '*dumb*' vb.]
a-dūn, -dūna, -dūne adv. *down, downward*, Æ. [= ofdūne]
adūne(ā)stīgan *to descend*, CPs.
adūnfeallan *to fall down*, EPs 144¹⁴.
adūnweard adv. *downwards*, ChrL. ['*a-downward*']
ādūstrigan = andūstrian
ādwǣscan (ē) *to put out, quench, extinguish, blot out, destroy*, AO : *suppress*, Æ,CP.
ā-dwelian *to wander, stray*, Æ,LL.
ādwellan, pret. 3 sg. -dwealde *to seduce, lead astray : hinder*, Æ.
ādwēscan = ādwǣscan
ādwīnan¹ *to dwindle or waste away*, Bf 74¹¹
ādȳdan (ī; = īe) *to destroy, mortify, kill*, Æ. ['*adeaden*']
ādȳfan (= īe) *to overpower with sound*, Sol 152¹³.
ādylf = ādealf pret. of ādelfan.
ādȳlgian, ādȳlegian = ādīlegian
ādymman = ādimmian
ādysgian *to make foolish*, W 185¹².
ǣ- accented verbal prefix, = (1) *without*; (2) ā-.

ǣ I. f. also ǣw f. (and m. or n.? in *NG*) *law (divine or human), custom, covenant*, AO, CP; *WG,NG.* butan ǣ *outlaw* : (esp. in pl.) *rite, ceremony : faith, religion*, unrihte ǣ *false religion.* Crīstes ǣ *gospel : scriptures, revelation : marriage, Æ : (lawful) wife.* For some comps. v. ǣw-. ['*æ*']
II. = ēa I. III. interj. *oh! alas!*
ǣa I. = ēa I. II. gp. of ǣ; **ǣal-** = eal-
ǣalā interj. = ēalā; **ǣar** = ēar-
āeargian *to become remiss*, AO 212²⁰.
ǣbǣre (ā¹, ē¹) *manifest, notorious, public, open, evident, clear*, LL. ['*eber*']
āebbian *to ebb away, recede*, Chr.
ǣbbung (= ebb-) f. '*ebbing*.' sǣ æ. *gulf, bay*, WW 154.
ǣbebod n. *injunction of the law, command*, PPs 118¹⁰².
ǣbēc fp. *books of the law*, WW 439¹⁵.
ǣbēre = ǣbǣre; **ǣbesn** = ǣfesn
ǣbilg-, -bili(g)- = ǣbylg-; **ǣblǣc-** = āblǣc-
ǣblǣce *lustreless, pale, pallid*, Æ.
ǣbod m. *business*, WW 114³⁶ : *statute*, WW 114³⁵.
ǣboda m. *messenger, preacher*, Gu 909
ǣbrǣce -breca = ǣwbrǣce, -breca
ǣbrecð f. *sacrilege*, LPs.
ǣbrucol *sacrilegious*, GPH 402.
æbs f? *fir-tree*, Æ. [L. abies]
ǣbylg n. = ǣbylgð
ǣbylga m. *anger*, LPs 77⁴⁹.
±ǣbyl-gan, -i(g)an *to exasperate, offend*, Æ.
ǣbylgnes (ā¹) f. *anger, offence*, Æ.
ǣbylgð, -bylgðu (ā¹) f. *anger*, AO.
ǣbylig- = ǣbylg-; **ǣ-bylð, -bylygð** = ǣbylgð
ǣc I. f. = āc; II. (N) = ēac
ǣcambe f. = ācumbe
ǣcan = īecan; **ǣccyrn** = æcern
æce, ǣce = ece, ēce; **ǣced** = eced
ǣcēlan = ācēlan
ǣcelma m. *chilblain*, OEG,WW.
ǣcelmehte (ēcil-) *having chilblains*, OEG 1523.
ǣcen I. *a wood of oaks.* II. *oaken*, WW 270¹⁴. III. = ēacen pp. of ēacan.
æcer nap. æcras m. *field, cultivated land*, Mt; AO,CP; Mdf : *a certain quantity of land, strip of plough-land* (GBG), '*acre*,' Æ; v. LL 2·267 : *crop.*
æcerceorl m. *rustic, ploughman, armer*, Chrd,WW.
æceren = æcern
æcerhege m. *hedge of a field*, KC 3·33².
æcermǣlum *by acres*, KC 6·98⁵.
æcermann m. *farmer*, WW. ['*acreman*']
æcern (i²) n. *nut, mast of trees, Æ : 'acorn*,' WW.
æcernspranca m. *oak sapling?* ÆGr 69¹⁵.

æcersǣd n. *seed enough for an acre?* CHR 1124.

æcerteoðung f. *tithe of the produce of the soil*, W310²⁴.

æcertȳning f. *fencing*, EC377⁹.

æcerweorc n. *field-work*, GPH391.

æces = æx

æcest, æceð pres. 2 and 3 sg. of acan.

ǣcilma = ǣcelma; **æcirn** = æcern

ǣclǣca = āglǣca; **ǣclēaw** = ǣglēaw

ǣcnōsle *degenerate, not noble*, WW.

+**ǣcnōsliende** *degenerating*, WW218¹².

ǣcræft† m. *knowledge of law or ordinances, religion.*

ǣcræftig *learned in the law*, DA; as sb. = *lawyer, scribe, Pharisee*, MtL.

æcras v. æcer; **æcren** = æcern

æcs f. *'axe', pickaxe, hatchet*, CP; *Mt* (æx).

æcst, æcð pres. 2 and 3 sg. of acan.

ǣcumba = ācumba; **æcur** = æcer

ǣcyrf m. *(wood-)choppings*, BH224¹⁵.

æd (NG) = æt; **æd-** = ed-

ǣdderseax (WW) = ǣdreseax

ǣddre, ǣdr = ǣdre

ǣdre I. f. *artery, vein, pulse, nerve, sinew*, AO : pl. *veins*, B : *kidneys*, Ps73²¹ : *runlet of water, fountain, spring, stream*. ['eddre'] II. adv. *at once, directly, instantly, quickly* : (†) *fully, entirely*. [OS. ādro]

ǣdreseax (daer) n. *lancet*, WW410¹⁰.

ǣdrīfan = ādrīfan; **ædwist** = edwist

æfæst = æfest; **ǣfæst** = ǣwfæst

æfdǣll -dell (NG) = ofdǣle

æfdȳne m. *declivity*, GL.

ǣfelle *without skin, peeled*, WW190³¹.

æfen = efen

ǣfen (ē) nm. *'even,' evening, eventide*, B, MkL,Gu (ēfn), RB : *eve*, CHR. tō ǣfenes *till evening.*

ǣfencollatio *the 'collatio' read before compline*, CHRD60³⁵.

ǣfendrēam m. *even-song*, RB.

ǣfengebed n. *evening service*, WW129³⁴.

ǣfengereord n. *evening meal, supper* (often used in pl. of one meal).

ǣfengereordian *to sup, give supper to*, CM1030.

ǣfengereordung f. *supper*, NC269.

ǣfengeweorc n. *evening work*, LCD70b.

ǣfengi(e)fl n. *evening repast, supper*, AO,CP.

ǣfen-glōm (Gu), -glōma (BF) m., -glōmung (omm-, BH) f. *gloaming, twilight*. [v. 'even']

ǣfengrom *fierce at eve*, B2074.

æfenian = ǣfnian

ǣfenlāc n. *evening sacrifice, evening prayer*, PPs140³.

ǣfenlǣcan *to grow towards evening*, Lk24²⁹.

ǣfenlēoht n. *evening light*, B403. [v. 'even']

ǣfenlēoð† n. *evening song.*

ǣfenlic *of the evening*; adv. -līce.

ǣfenlof n. *lauds (service)*, CM1035.

ǣfenmete m. *supper*, MtR; WW. [v. 'even']

ǣfenoffrung f. *evening sacrifice*, CHRD30²².

ǣfenrǣding f. *reading (during the evening meal at a monastery), 'collatio,'* CM.

ǣfenrepsung f. *nightfall*, Æ.

ǣfen-rest, -ræst† f. *evening rest*, B.

ǣfensang m. *'evensong,'* Æ,RB.

ǣfensceop m. *evening singer, bard*, RD9⁵. [scop]

ǣfenscīma m. *evening splendour*, GEN2448.

ǣfensprǣc f. *evening talk*, B759.

ǣfensteorra m. *the evening star, Hesperus*, Bo; Æ. ['evenstar']

ǣfen-tīd (Mk) f., -tima (GD) m. *eventide*, Æ. [v. 'even']

ǣfenðēnung f. *evening service*, TF : *evening repast, supper*, RBL.

ǣfenðēowdōm m. *evening service or office*, WW129³⁴.

ǣfenung = ǣfnung; **ǣfer** = ǣfre

æferðe f. *name of a plant*, LCD.

æfes- = efes-

æfesa? m., æfese (m.) f. = æfesn

āefesian *to shear*, ÆGR157¹⁶.

æfesn, æfesen f. *relish, dainty, special pasturage, pannage; the charge for special pasturage*, LL.

æfesne? = æpsen?

æfest mf. *envy, hatred, malice, spite*, CP; El,Ps : *zeal, rivalry*, CHRD. ['evest']

ǣfest = ǣwfæst

æfestful *full of envy*, APT.

±**æfest-ian**, -igian *to be or become envious.*

æfestig *envious*, CP : *zealous*, CP.

æfestlīce = ofostlīce

æfgælð f. *superstition*, OEG.

æfgerēfa (-groefa) *'exactor,'* LkL12⁵⁸.

æfgrynde n. *abyss*, PPs35⁶.

æfhynde = ofhende

æfian (-an?) *to be in a miserable condition*, CR1357 (or æfnan? Gollancz).

æfisc (EC291) = efesc

æflāst m. *a wandering from the way?* Ex473.

±**æfnan** (e) *to carry out, do, perform, fulfil* : *cause* : *endure, suffer* : (+) *hold, sustain.*

æfne = efne

±**ǣfnian** *to grow towards evening*, Æ.

ǣfnung f. *'evening,' sunset*, Æ.

ǣfre adv. *'ever,' at any time*, Sat,Mt : *always, constantly, perpetually*, Æ,Cr,RB, Sat; CP : *henceforth* : ne ǣ. ; ǣ. ne (=nǣfre) *never*; ǣ. tō aldre *for ever*. ǣ. ǣlc, W,Chr. ǣ. ǣnig *any at all*, KC.

æfreda m. *what is taken or separated from,* OEG (Napier). [æf; *hreda (hreddan)] : *tow, oakum* (BTs).

æfremmende *pious, religious,* JUL648.

æfse I. = efes; II. = æbs

æfsecgan *to confute,* ES42¹⁶³.

æfst = æfest

æfsweorc n. *pasturage,* WW410¹⁹ (= *æfesweorc).

æft = eft

æftan adv. *from behind, behind, in the rear,* Br. ['aft']

æftanweard adj. *behind, in the rear, following,* RD63⁵.

æftemest adj. *last, hindmost,* Æ,AO.

æfter I. prep. (w. d., i. and—chiefly N.—a.) (local and temporal) 'after', along, behind, B,Chr,G : through, throughout, during : (causal) following, in consequence of, according to, for the purpose of, Æ : (object) after, about, in pursuit of, for, B. II. adv. after, then, afterwards, thereafter : thereupon, later, back (= in return). æ. ðon, ðæm, ðisum; æ. ðæm (ðon, ðan) ðe; afterwards, thereafter.

æftera = æfterra

æfterǣ f. *the book Deuteronomy,* ÆT333 (æftre-).

æfterboren adj. 'afterborn,' posthumous, ÆGr.

æftercnēoreso posterity, DR61⁹.

æftercweðan⁵ to speak after, repeat: renounce, abjure, CHR1094. æftercweðendra lof praise from posterity.

æftercyning m. later king, BH140B²⁴.

æfterealu n. small beer, WW129⁴.

æfterfili-, æfterfilig- = æfterfylg-

æfterfolgere m. follower, AO142²³.

æfter-folgian, -fylgan (AO) to follow after, succeed, pursue.

æfterfylgednes f. sequel, ÆL23b³⁶⁵.

æfterfylgend m. follower, successor, AO. adv. -līce in succession.

æfterfylgendnes f. succession, DHy11⁴.

æfterfylgung (eft-, e³) f. pursuit, KGL371.

æfterfylig- = æfterfylg-

æfter-genga, -gengea m. follower, successor : descendant, Æ.

æftergengel m. successor, KC5·30.

æftergengnes f. succession, Æ : posterity : inferiority.

æftergyld n. further payment, LL.

æfterhǣ̄ða m. autumn drought, AO102⁷.

æfterhyrigan to imitate, BH.

æfterlēan n. reward, recompense, restitution, retribution, GEN76.

æfterlic second, WW505¹⁹.

æfterra (comp.) second, following, next, latter, lower, CP.

æfter-rāp (Æ) -rǣpe m. crupper.

æfterrōwan⁷ to row after, ES41³²⁵.

æfterryne m. 'occursus,' CPs18⁷.

æftersang m. (after-song), matins, CM.

æftersingallic (= -sanglic) of matins, CM 476.

æftersingend m. succentor, WW129²³.

æftersōna soon, afterwards, again, NG.

æftersprǣc f. after-claim, LL398,7.

æftersprecan⁵ to claim, LL226,9⁴.

æfterspyrian to track out, search, inquire into, examine, CP.

æfterweard adj. after, following, further, behind, in the rear, later, Æ. on æfterweard-an, -um at the end.

æfterweardnes f. posterity, WW464¹⁸.

æfterwriten written afterwards, LCD69b.

æfter-yld, -yldo f. †advanced age, old age : after age, later time, BH. [ield(o)]

æfteweard = æfterweard

æftewearde adv. behind, Æ(Ex33²³).

æftra = æfterra

æftresta superl. last.

æftum adv. after, MtR24²¹.

æftyr = æfter

æfðanc, æfðanca (o, u) m. insult, offence : grudge, displeasure, anger.

æf-weard (CP), -ward (BH) absent.

æfweardnes f. absence, Bo,GD.

æfwela f. decrease of wealth, LCD3·170¹³.

æfwendla (WW223¹) = æfwyrdla

æfwyrdelsa (e²) m. injury, damage, loss.

æfwyrdla, m. injury, damage, loss : fine for injury or loss.

æfwyrð(u)? f. degradation, disgrace, RBL.

æfyllende fulfilling the law, pious, CR 704.

æfyn = æfen

æfyrmða fp. sweepings, rubbish, ÆGR. [feorman]

æg n. (nap. ægru) 'egg,' Ct,G,Lcd,Lk,Met.

æg = ieg; **ægan** = āgan

æge = ege; **ægen** = āgen

ægera (K) dp. of æg.

ægerfelma f. egg-skin, LCD20b.

ægergelu n. yolk of egg, GL. [æg, geolu]

ægesetnes f. law-giving, the (Old) Testament, BF136⁵.

ægflota m. seafarer, sailor, AN258. [ieg]

æggemang n. egg-mixture, WW.

æg-hwā mf., -hwæt n. pron. each one, every one, everything, who or whatever. æghwæt neut. anything.

æghwǣr everywhere, in every direction, Mk; Æ : in every case, in every respect : anywhere. ['aywhere']

æghwæs (gs. of æghwā) altogether, in every way, entirely, wholly, throughout, in general.

æghwæt v. æghwā.

æghwæðer (ǣgðer, āðer). I. pron. adv. *every one, 'either,' both, AO,KC,Mt* (gð) : *each, An.* II. conj. æghwæðer (ge)...ge; ǣgðer...and *both*...and; *as well*...as.

æg-hwanan, -hwanon(e), -hwannon, -hwanum *from all parts, everywhere, on every side, in every way.*

æg-hwǣr, -hwēr = æghwǣr

æghwelc = æghwilc

æghweðer = æghwæðer

æghwider *on every side, in all directions : in any direction, anywhere.*

æghwilc adj. *each, every, whosoever, whatsoever, all, every one, Bo,Met* : *any.* ǣ. ānra *each.* ǣ. ōðer *each other, Ma.* æghwilces *in every way.* [v. '*each*']

æg-hwonan, -hwonon (CP), -hwonene = æghwanan

æghwyder = æghwider; æghwylc = æghwilc

ǣgift f. (m? n?) *restitution, repayment.*

ǣgilde (y²) adv. *receiving no 'wergild' as compensation, LL.*

ǣgilt = ǣgylt; ǣglǣc = āglǣc

ǣglēaw *learned in the law, An,Lk.*

ǣglēca = āglǣca

ǣglīm m. *white of egg, WW 164¹². [līm]*

ǣgmang (WW 4²⁹) = ǣggemang

ǣgmore f. *root of the eye, socket? LCD 3·985. [ēage]*

ǣgnan sb. pl. *awns, sweepings, chaff, GL.* [v. egenu]

ǣgnes = āgnes, v. āgen; ǣgnian = āgnian

ǣgru v. ǣg; ǣgsa = egesa

ǣgscill (y) f. *eggshell, LCD.*

ǣgðer = æghwæðer

ǣgweard f. *watch on the shore, B 241.* [īeg]

ǣgwern = æghwǣr

ǣgwyrt f *dandelion, LCD 158b.*

ǣgylde = ǣgilde

ǣgylt (i²) m. *sin, offence, WW.* [ǣw, gylt]

ǣgype (= ie²?) *without skill or cunning* (BTs),PPs 106¹⁰. [gēap]

æhher (MkR 4²⁸) = ēar

ǣhīw n. *pallor, OEG 4897.*

ǣhīwe *pallid : deformed, OEG 2⁴⁹⁸.*

ǣhīwnes f. *pallor, LCD 1·294³.*

ǣhlȳp m. *breach of the peace, assault, LL.* [cp. æthlȳp]

æht = eaht

æht I. f. (rare in sg.) *possessions, goods, lands, wealth, cattle, Mk; AO : serf : ownership, control.* [āgan : '*aught*' sb.] II. = ōht

ǣhtan *to persecute, LkL 21¹².*

ǣhtboren *born in bondage, RB 138²⁰.*

ǣhte = āhte pret. sg. of āgan.

ǣhteland n. *territory, BH 358¹⁴.*

ǣhtemann m. *farmer, Æ : serf, LL.*

ǣhteswān m. *swineherd who was a chattel on an estate, LL 449,7.*

ǣhtgesteald n. *possession, JUL 115.*

ǣhtgestrēon n. *possessions, PH 506.*

ǣhtgeweald† mn. *power, control.*

æhtian = eahtian

+ǣhtle f. *esteem, B 369.*

æhtowe (LkR 2²¹) = eahta

ǣhtspēd f. *wealth, riches, LPs 103²⁴.*

ǣhtspēdig *rich, BL,JUL.*

ǣhtwela† m. *wealth, riches.*

ǣhtwelig *wealthy, rich, JUL 18.*

ǣ-hwænne, -hwǣr, -hwār = āhwænne, āhwǣr

ǣhwyrfan = āhwierfan

æhx = æcs; ǣlg = ǣg

æl- prefix = I. eal(l)- ; II. el(e)-

æl m. *piercer, 'awl,' Æ.*

ǣl m. '*eel,' Lcd,WW*; Mdf.

ǣlā = ēalā

ǣlǣdend m. *legislator, SPs 9²¹.*

ǣlǣrend m. *teacher of (God's) law, EL 506.*

ǣlǣte I. n. *desert place.* II. *desert, W 47²¹* : *empty, ERHy 9⁵³.* III. f. *divorced woman, LL.*

ǣlǣten I. = ālǣten pp. of ālǣtan. II. = ælǣte II.

ǣlagol *law-giving, GPH 397³⁶³.*

±ǣlan *to kindle, light, set on fire, burn, Æ,CP.*

ǣlārēow (-lārua) m. *teacher of the law, Pharisee, NG.*

ǣlātēow m. *legislator, CJPs 9²¹.*

ǣlað = ealað; ǣlbeorht = eallbeorht

ælbitu (GL) = ilfetu

ǣlc, elc, ealc, ylc (VPs); v. '*EACH*.' I. (pron. subst.) *any, all, every, each (one), Æ,AO,CP.* ǣlc...ōðrum *the one...the other.* II. (adj. pron.) *each, Lcd : any, CP.*

ælceald *altogether cold, very cold, MET 24¹⁹.*

ælcor, ælcra = elcor, elcra

ælcræftig *almighty, all-powerful, MET 20³⁸.*

ǣlcuht (AO) = ælcwuht n. *everything.*

æld = æled; ǣld- = ield-

ældewuta (NG) = ealdwita

ǣlecung = ōleccung

ǣled† m. gs. ǣldes *fire, firebrand.* ǣ. weccan *to kindle a fire, WH 21. [ON. eldr]*

ǣledfȳr n. *flame of fire, PH 366?*

ǣledlēoma m. *fire-brand, B 3125.*

ǣlednes = ālǣtnes

ælegrǣdig *greedy, ÆL 18²¹³. [eall-]*

ælegrēne = eallgrēne

ælelendisc = elelendisc

ælemidde f. *exact middle, Æ.*

ǣlenge I. *lengthy, tedious, vexatious, C.P.* ['*elenge*'] II. (i²) *weariness, MET 151⁴.*

ǣlengnes f. *tediousness, Sc,WW.*

ælepe? 'origanum,' wild marjoram, WW 299¹⁹. [ælene? BTs]
ælepūte f. 'eel-pout,' burbot, WW.
æleð pres. 3 sg. of alan; æleð, ælð = æled
ælewealdend = eallwealdend
ælf mf. (pl. ielfe, ylfe) 'elf,' sprite, fairy, goblin, incubus, B,Lcd.
ælfādl f. nightmare, LCD 123b.
ælfæle = ealfelo
æl-faru, -fær f. whole army, host, Ex66.
ælfcynn n. elfin race, LCD 123a.
ælfen (e¹) f. nymph, spirit, WW 352¹⁰.
ælfer = ælfaru
æl-fisc, -fix m. eel, TC 242¹¹.
ælfitu = ilfetu
æl-fremed, -fremd, (el-) strange, foreign, Æ : (+) estranged, LPs57⁴ : (w. fram) free, separated from, Æ.
ælfremedung f. 'alienatio,' RHy5¹⁴.
ælf-scīene (ī²ȳ²)† bright as an elf or fairy, beautiful, radiant.
ælfsiden f. elvish influence, nightmare, LCD 120b.
ælfsogoða m. hiccough (thought to have been caused by elves), LCD 124b.
ælfðēodlīce = elðēodiglīce
ælfðone f. nightshade, LCD 123b.
ælfylce (= el-) n. strange land, EL36 : oreign band, enemy, B 2371
ǣlhyd f. eel receptacle? eel-skin? (BTs), LL455,17
ǣlic of the law, legal, lawful, Æ. adv. -līce.
ǣlīf (ā) n. eternal life, MFH 150.
ælifn f. sustenance, GL? (v. ES42·166)
ǣling f. burning, Æ : ardour, MET.
ǣling- = æleng-; æll- = æl-, eal(l)-, el(l)-
ælmes = ælmesse
ælmesæcer m. ground of which the yield was given as alms, first-fruits, A 11·3⁶⁹.
ælmesbæð n. gratuitous bath, W 171².
ælmesdǣd f. almsdeed, Æ.
ælmesdönd alms-giver, CHRD 93²⁸.
ælmesfeoh n. alms : Peter's pence, Rome-scot, LL. ['almsfee']
ælmesfull charitable, CHR,LL.
ælmesgedāl n. distribution of alms, LL,W.
ælmesgeorn charitable, Æ.
ælmesgifa (y³) m. giver of alms, W 72⁴.
ælmesgifu f. alms, charity, W 159²⁰.
ælmeshand almsgiving, charitableness, CHRD 12¹⁹.
ælmeshlāf (e¹) m. dole of bread, TC474'.
ælmeslāc giving of alms, NC269.
ælmeslēoht n. a light in church provided at the expense of a pious layman, LL (288¹).
ælmeslic charitable : depending on alms, poor. -līce; adv. charitably, OET (Ct).
ælmeslond (a¹) m. land granted in frankal-moigne, (BT)

ælmesmann m. 'almsman,' bedesman, beggar, Lcd; Æ.
ælmespening m. alms-penny, KC (v. MLR17).
ælmesriht n. right of receiving alms, W.
ælmesse f. 'alms,' almsgiving, Da,Mt; Æ, CP. [L. eleēmosyna]
ælmessylen (e³) f. almsgiving, GD,LL.
ælmestlīce = ælmeslīce
ælmesweorc n. almsdeed, BL25¹⁷.
ælmidde = ælemidde; ælmiehtig = ælmihtig
ælmihtig (ea², e²) adj. 'almighty,' Ps,TC; AO,CP : m. the Almighty, B.
ælmihtignes f. omnipotence, AS59¹⁹.
ælmyrca m. one entirely black, Ethiopian, AN432.
ælmysse = ælmesse
ǣlnet n. eel net, BH304¹¹.
ǣlpig (CHR 1085) = ānlīpig
ælren adj. of an alder tree, KC3·316'. ['al-dern']
ælreord = elreord
ælsyndrig separately, LkR2³.
æltǣwe (ēo, ō) complete, entire, perfect, healthy, sound, true, Æ,AO,CP : noted, Æ. [Goth. tēwa] -līce adv.
ælðēod, (ælðīed) = elðēod
æl-walda, -wealda = ealwealda
ælwiht† m. strange creature, monster [=*elwiht] : (in pl.) = eallwihta.
æmbern = embren
ǣmelle insipid, WW 429³⁰.
ǣmelnes f. slackness, sloth, Æ : weariness, disgust, WW.
ǣmen, ǣmenne (AO) uninhabited, desolate, desert.
ǣmend = ǣmynd
ǣmenne solitude, AS4¹ (v. Wfg3).
ǣmerge f. embers, ashes dust, Lcd; Æ. ['ember']
ǣmet- = ǣmett-
ǣmetbed n. ant-hill, LCD 121b.
ǣmethwīl (ā¹) f. leisure, Æ.
ǣmethyll m. ant-hill, CP191²⁵.
ǣmetian = ǣmtian
ǣmetta m. leisure, rest, CP. [mōt]
ǣmette f. 'emmet,' ant, WW; Æ.
ǣmettig (CP), -m(e)tig (Æ) 'empty,' vacant, Æ,Bl : unoccupied, without employment, Æ : unmarried, CP.
ǣmettigian = ǣmtian
æmn- = eimn-, efen-
ǣmōd (ā) dismayed, disheartened, Æ,AO.
ǣmt- = ǣmett-
±ǣmtian to 'empty,' Æ : to be at leisure, have time for, Æ,CP.
ǣmtignes f. emptiness, GD 35¹⁷.
ǣmuða m. 'cæcum intestinum,' WW 160¹¹.
ǣmynd (e²) f. jealousy, LCD 1·384'.

æmyrce *excellent*, WW 393³⁸.

æmyrie = æmerge; æmytte = æmette

æn = ān; +æn- = +en- +ænan (ē)? *to unite oneself to, join with,* AS 39⁶.

ænbrece = unbrece; ænd- = end-

æne (āne) *once, at some time,* Æ,B : *at any time : at once.* ['*ene*']

æned = ened

ænes adv. *once,* GD,LL

ænetre = ānwintre

ænett, ænetnes = ānet; ænga = ānga

ængancundes *in a unique way?* (BTs), LCD 162b.

ænge, ængel = enge, engel

Ænglisc = Englisc; ænid = ened

ænig adj. pron. and sb. '*any,*' *any one,* Mk,Jn. ænige ðinga *somehow, anyhow.* adv. *only,* Ps,RD (v. BTac). [ān]

ænigge = ānēage

ænigmon *any one, some one,* NG.

æniht = āwuht; æninga = ānunga

ænlænan = onlænan; ænlefan = endlufon

ænlep- = ānlep-

ænlic *one, 'only,' singular, solitary,* Ps : *unique, glorious, noble, splendid, excellent,* Bo; Æ,AO. adv. -līce, WW.

ænlīpig (Æ) = ānlīpig

ænne (AO,CP) v. ān.

ænote *useless,* LL 254,3⁸⁴.

ænrædnis = ānrædnes; ænyge = ānēage

ænytte = ānet; æpl = æppel

æpled = æppled

æppel m. (nap. æpplas, rarely ap(p)la, æppla) *any kind of fruit, fruit in general :* '*apple,*' CP,Gen : *apple of the eye, ball, anything round,* Bo,CP,Sol.

æppelbære *fruit-bearing,* GEN 1¹¹,HEXC 198.

æppelbearu m. *orchard,* PPs 78².

æppelberende *apple-bearing,* DR 98¹⁶.

æppelcynn n. *kind of apple,* LCD 67a.

æppelcyrnel n. *apple-pip,* WW 440²³.

æppelfæt n. *apple-vessel,* ZDA 31·15⁴⁰¹.

æppelfealu *apple-yellow, bay,* B 2165.

æppelhūs n. *fruit storehouse,* WW.

æppelscealu f. *apple-core,* WW 371¹.

æppelscrēada np. *apple-parings,* WW 118¹.

æppeltrēow n. '*apple-tree,*' WW.

æppeltūn m. *fruit garden, orchard,* Æ,CP.

æppelðorn m. *crab-apple tree,* BC 3·93'.

æppelwīn n. *cider,* WW 430⁹.

æppled† *shaped like an apple, round, embossed,* El,Jul. ['*appled*']

æppul- = apul-; æps = æsp, æbs.

æpsen *shameless?* OEG 7³⁰¹ and n.

æpsenes f. *shame, disgrace,* Sc 174⁹.

ær I. adv. comp. æror; sup. ærost, ær(e)st '*ERE,*' *before that, soon, formerly, beforehand, previously, already, lately, till;* (comp.) *sooner, earlier;* (sup.) *just now, first of all : early, prematurely.* on ær; ær ðissum *previously, formerly, beforehand,* CP. tō ær *too soon.* ær oððe æfter *sooner or later.* hwonne ær *how soon? when?* hwēne ær *just before.* on ealne ærne mergen *very early in the morning.* ne ær ne siððan *neither sooner nor later.* ær and sið *at all times.* II. conj. '*ere,*' *before that, until,* Æ,AO,CP. ær ðam (ðe) *before.* III. prep. (w.d.) *before.* IV. adj. *only in comp. and sup.* (ærra, ærest) q.v. V. f. = ār f. VI. n. = ār n. VII. = ēar II.

ær- = *early, former* (v MP 28·157)

æra I. m. *scraper, strigil,* GL. II. = ærra

æræt m. *too early eating,* W.

ærbe- = yrfe-, ierfe-

ærbeðoht *premeditated,* LL 428¹².

ærboren *earlier born, first-born* (or ? *two words*), GEN 973.

ærc = earc; ærce = arce

ærcwide m. *prophecy?* MOD 4.

ærdæd f. *former deed,* Lk,W.

ærdæg m. (nap. ærdagas) *early morn, dawn :* in pl. *former days, past times,* AO.

ærdēað m. *premature death,* EX 539.

ærdian = eardian

ærdon = ærndon? from ærnan (GR),MA 191.

ærdung = eardung

ære I. = ȳre. II. *in comp.* = -*oared.*

ærēafe (= æ²) *detected,* TC 230¹⁶.

æreldo '*anteritus,*' WW 347¹².

æren I. *made of brass, brazen,* Æ,AO,CP : *tinkling?* [ār; cp. Ger. ehern] II. *oar-propelled,* GD 347.

ærendbōc f. *message, letter,* DA,WW 511²⁵.

ærenddraca (AO,CP) = ærendraca

ærende n. '*errand,*' *message,* BH,Gu; AO : *mission,* An,Chr : *answer, news, tidings,* Æ.

ærendfæst *bound on an errand,* ÆL 26²²¹.

ærendgāst m. *angel,* GEN 2296.

ærendgewrit n. *written message, letter,* Æ, CP.

±ærendian *to go on an errand, carry a message, send word to,* CP : *intercede,* Æ : *seek for, obtain,* BH 2·132⁵ : (+) *speed, succeed,* W 238⁹. ['*ernde*']

ærendraca m. *messenger, apostle, ambassador, angel,* Æ,AO : *representative, substitute, proxy,* BH 276¹⁹.

ærendscip n. *skiff, small boat,* WW 287²⁸.

ærendsecg m. *messenger,* GEN 658.

ærendsprǣc f. *message,* RD 61¹⁵.

ærendung f. *errand : errand-going : intercession,* RB. ['*ernding*']

ærend-wraca (AO), -wreca (CP) = ærendraca

ærendwrit = ærendgewrit

ærenscip = ærendscip; ærer = æror

ǣrest I. adv. and superl. adj. *first, at first, before all*, Æ,CP. ðā, ðonne, siððan ǣ. *as soon as.* ǣ. ðinga *first of all.* **II.** = ǣrist

ǣrfæder m. *forefather*, B2622.

ǣrfæst = ārfæst; **ǣrfe** = ierfe, yrfe

ǣrgedōn *done before*, CP.

ǣrgefremed *before committed*, LL(434^14).

ǣrgelēred *previously instructed*, MtL14^8.

ǣrgenemned, -gesæd = ǣrnemned

ǣrgestrēon† n. *ancient treasure.*

ǣrgeweorc† n. *work of olden times.*

ǣrgewinn n. *former strife or trouble, old warfare*, ÇROSS19.

ǣrgewyrht† n. *former work, deed of old.*

ǣrglæd *bright in armour*, Ex293.

ǣrgōd† *good from old times*, B.

ǣrhwīlum† *erewhile, formerly.*

ærian = erian; **ǣrig** (OET) = earh

ǣriht† n. *code of law or faith*, EL.

ǣring f. *day-break, early morn*, JUL„MkL.

ǣrisc = ēarisc

ǣrist I. (ē) mfn. *rising*, VPs : *resurrection, awakening*, CP,Jn. [*'arist'*] **II.** = ǣrest

ǣrlēof? 'gratus' OEG56^296.

ǣrlēst = ārlēast

ǣrlic (ā) adj.; -līce adv. *'early,'* Jn.

ǣrlyft f. *early morning air*, WW415^13.

ærm = earm

ǣrmorgen (a^1, a^2, e^2) m. *dawn, day-break.*

ǣrmorgenlic *of early morning*, DR.

ærn (ea) n. *dwelling, house, building, store, closet* (v. GBG).

ǣrn = ǣren

ærnan (strictly causative) *to 'run,' ride, gallop*, BH : (+) *to ride, run to, reach, gain by running or riding*, AO.

ǣrndian = ǣrendian

ǣrne-mergen, -merigen (Æ) = ǣrmorgen

ǣrnemergenlic *matutinal*, CM277.

ǣrnemned (æ^2) *aforementioned*, LL.

ǣrneweg m. *road for riding on, race-course*, BH398^30; Bo112^23. [iernan]

ærnian = earnian

ærning f. *'running,' riding, racing*, Bo,GD : *flow of blood*, MtL9^20 (iorn-).

ærnð = ernð

ærnðegen (rend-) m. *house-officer*, GL.

ærnung = earnung; **ǣron** = ǣrran

ǣror I. adv. *earlier, before, beforehand, formerly*, B,Rood; Æ,AO : *rather.* **II.** prep. (w. d.) *before.* [*'ever'*]

ǣrost = ǣrest

ǣrra m. ǣrre fn. adj. *earlier, former, preceding*, Bo,El; CP. on ǣrran dæg *the day before yesterday.* [*'ere,' 'ever'*]

ǣrror = ǣror; **ǣrs** = ears

ǣrsceaft f. *ancient building*, RUIN16.

ǣrschen, ǣrshen = erschen; **ǣrst** = ǣrest

ǣrstæf = ārstæf

ǣr-ðam, -ðon, -ðamðe v. ǣr; **ǣrð-** = yrð-

ǣrwacol *early awake*, Æ.

+ǣrwe *depraved, wicked*, EPs100^4.

ǣrwela m. *ancient wealth*, B2747.

ǣrworuld f. *ancient world*, CR937.

ǣrynd = ǣrend; **ǣryr** = ǣror

ǣryst I. = ǣrist. **II.** = ǣrest

ǣs n. *food, meat, carrion* : *bait.* [*OHG.* ās]

æsc I. m. nap. ascas '*ash'-tree*, Gl,KC; Mdf : name of the rune for æ : (†) *spear, lance*, B : *ship*, Æ. **II.** = æcs

æscǣre *unshorn, untrimmed*, LL. [scieran]

æscan *to demand (legally)*, LL177'.

æscapo (WW273^35) = æsceapa

æscbedd n. *an ash-plot*, KC5·126'.

æscberend† m. *spear-bearer, soldier.*

æsce = asce

æsce f. *asking, inquiry, search*, LL : *claim (to insurance money for theft of cattle)*, LL175^2. [*'ask'* sb.]

æsceap (ē^1) n. *remnant, patch*, LkL,WW.

æsceda fp. *refuse*, WW148^33.

æscegeswǣp n. *cinders, ashes*, TC318'.

æscen I. fm. *vessel of ash-wood, bucket, pail, bottle, cup.* **II.** adj. *made of ash-wood, ashen*, LCD.

æscfealu *ashy-hued*, WW204^23.

æscgrǣg *ashy gray*, WW204^24.

æschere m. *naval force*, MA69.

æscholt† n. *spear of ash-wood, spear-shaft, lance* (v. also Mdf).

æscian = āscian

æscmann m. *ship-man, sailor, pirate*, CHR, WW. [æsc]

æscplega m. *play of spears, battle*, JUD217.

æscrind f. *bark of the ash-tree*, LCD.

æscrōf† *brave in battle.*

æscsteall? (æts-) m. *place of battle*, WALD1^21.

æscstede m. *place of battle*, MOD17; Mdf.

æscstederōd f. *cross marking a battlefield?* (BTs), KC3·135'.

æscstybb m. *stump of an ash-tree*, BC.

æsctīr m. *glory in war*, GEN2069.

æscðracu f. *battle*, GEN2153.

æscðrot-e, -u f. *a plant, ferula? vervain?* LCD.

æscwert = æscwyrt

æscwiga† m. *(spear-)warrior.*

æscwyrt f. *verbena, vervain.*

ǣsellend (y^2) m. *lawgiver*, Ps.

æsil = hæsel

ǣslītend m. *law-breaker*, LPs.

ǣsmæl *smallness of the eye*, LCD.

ǣsmogu np. *slough (of snake)* LCD88a. [āsmūgan]

æsne- = esne-; **æsp** = æspe I.

æspe I. f. *aspen-tree, white poplar*, GL; Mdf. [*'asp^1'*] **II.** = æbs

æsphangra m. *aspen wood*, KC.

æspreng, æspring(e) = æspryng
æsprind (ps) f. *aspen bark*, Lcd. ['*asp*']
æspringnes = āsprungenes
æspryng nf. *spring, fountain*, CP. [ēa] : *departure*, CREAT 77.
æst I. = ǣrest. **II.** = ēst
æstǣnan = āstænan; **æstan** = ēastan
æstel m. *some thin kind of board?* CP 9, ÆGR 31⁹, WW 327¹ (v. BTac and NED s.v. '*astel*')
æsul = esol
æswǣpa sbpl. *sweepings, rubbish*, OEG.
æswic I. m. *offence, stumbling-block, infamy, seduction, deceit*. **II.** adj. *apostate*, GD 304²⁸.
æswica m. *offender, deceiver, hypocrite, traitor*, GD.
æswice m. *violation of God's laws* (or? *adultery*), W 164³.
±**æswician** to *offend, deceive*, Æ : *apostatize*, WW 342¹² : *desert*, Æ.
æswicnes f. *stumbling-block*, LPs 105³⁶ : *reproach*, 122⁴.
æswicung f. *offence, stumbling-block*, Æ : *deceit*, Æ : *sedition*, WW 116²⁶.
æswind *idle, slothful*, WW 422¹³. [swīð]
æsyllend = ǣsellend
æt I. prep. (w. d. and, more rarely, a) (local) 'AT,' *near, by, in, on, upon, with, before, next to, as far as, up to, into, toward, Chr* : (temporal) *at, at the time of, near, in, on, to, until* : (causal) *at, to, through* : (source) *from* : (instrumental) *by*. æt fēawum wordum *in few words*, BH : *in respect to, as to*. **II.** adv. *at, to, near*. æt nehstan, æt siðestan *finally*. æt- in composition = *at, to, from*.
ǣt I. (ē) mfn. *eatables, food, meat, flesh*, Æ, Gu; AO. ǣt and wǣt *food and drink*, Æ : *the act of feeding, eating*, PPs; MkL. ['*eat*' sb.] **II.** pret. 3 sg. of etan.
æt- = oð-; **ǣt-** = āte-; **-ǣta** v. self-ǣta.
ǣtǣwian = ǣtīewan
ǣetan⁵ to *eat, devour*, AS 18², 38².
ætbēon anv. to *be present*, DHy.
ætberan⁴ to *carry to, bring, produce, show*, Da : *carry off*, B. ['*atbear*']
ætberstan³ to *break out, or away, escape from*, Æ. ['*atburst*']
ætbrēdan = ætbregdan
ætbrēdendlic *ablative*, ÆGR 23⁷.
æt-bregdan, -brēdan³ to *take away, carry off, deprive of, snatch away, draw off, withdraw*, Mt; Æ : *release, rescue, enlarge* : *prevent*, ÆL 31¹²⁶. ['*atbraid*']
ætclifian to *adhere*, BJPs 101⁶.
ætclīðan to *adhere*, OET 181.
ætdēman to *refuse, give judgment against*, EC 202¹⁹.

ætdōn anv. to *take away, deprive*, LL (246¹⁰).
ǣte = āte
ætēaca (eth-) m. *addition*, OEG 53¹⁸.
ætēacnes (BH) = ætȳcnes
ætealdod *too old*, Æ (2¹⁵⁹).
ætēaw- = ætīew-, ætȳw-
ætēcan = ætȳcan; **ætegār** = ætgār
æteglan to *harm*, PPs 88¹⁹.
ætēode pret. 3 sg. of *ætgān.
ǣteorian = āteorian
ætēow- = ætīew-, ætȳw-, oðīew-
ǣtercyn = ātorcyn
ǣtere (ē¹) m. '*eater*,' *glutton*, KGl; NG.
ǣtern I. (NG) *viper*. **II.** = ǣtren
ætēw- = ætīew-, ætȳw-
ætfæstan (= oð-) to *inflict on, afflict with* : *fasten to, drive into, impart to*, CP 115¹⁹ : *commit, entrust* : *marry to*.
ætfæstnian to *fasten? entrust?* AS 22¹⁰.
ætfaran⁶ to *escape*, SHR 14²³.
ætfeallan⁷ to *fall, fall out* : *fall away, fail, be reduced*, LL; Æ : *happen*. ['*atfall*']
ætfele m. *adhesion*, PPs 72²³.
ætfeng m. *attaching, distraint* v. LL 2·279.
ætfeohtan² to *grope about*, WY 18
ætfēolan³ (T²) to *stick to* : *adhere, apply oneself to, continue in*, CP.
ætfeorrian to *take from*, Sc 160⁷ : *remove oneself from*, CHRD 93³.
ætferian to *carry away, bear off*, CHRD, LL.
ætfilan = ætfēolan
ætflēon² to *flee away, escape by flight*, Æ. ['*atflee*']
ætflōwan⁷ to *flow together, accumulate*, SPs 61¹⁰.
ætfōn⁷ to *seize upon, lay claim to*, LL. ['*atfong*']
ætforan I. prep. w. d. *before, in the presence of, in front of, close by*, JnL; Æ. ['*atfore*'] **II.** adv. *beforehand* (time).
ætfyligan, -fylgan to *adhere, cling to*, GD.
æt-gædere (AO), -gæddre (CP) -gædre, -gæderum adv. *together, united, at the same time*. [gadrian]
æt-gǣre n., -gār m. *spear, dart, javelin*, GL.
ætgangan⁷ to *go to, approach*, Az 183. ['*atgo*']
ætgeddre, -gedre = ætgædere
ætgenumen *taken away*, WW 529³⁹.
ætgiefa† (eo, i) m. *food-giver, feeder*.
ætgifan⁵ to *render, give*, B 2878.
ætglīdan¹ to *slip away, disappear*, OEG 7¹³².
ætgrǣpe *seizing*. æ. weorðan *seize*, B 1268.
æthabban to *retain*, Æ.
æthealdan⁷ to *keep back*, Sc 109¹⁸.
æthebban⁶ to *take away, take out, hold back*, Æ : *exalt oneself*, CP 113¹³.

æthindan prep. w. d. *behind, after, Chr*; Æ.
['*athinden*']

æthléapan[7] *to run away, flee, escape,* W162[5].

æthlýp m. *assault,* LL. [cp. ǣhlýp]

æthrīnan[1] *to touch, move, Mt*; Æ. ['*atrine*']

æthrine m. *touch,* LCD.

æthwā *each, every one,* LL,PA.

æthwāre *somewhat,* HGL421[37].

æt-hwega, -hwæga, -hweg(u) adv. *somewhat, tolerably, a little : how.*

æthweorfan[3] *to return, go back,* B2299.

æthwōn adv. *almost, nearly.*

æthȳd '*eviscerata,' deprived of its sinews,* MtL, WW392' (v. A47·34).

ætīernan[3] *to run away,* Æ. ['*atrin*']

ætīewan (oð-; ē, ēa, ēo, ī, ȳ) pret. sg. -īe(w)de, (tr.) *to show, reveal, display, disclose, manifest, Mt*; CP : (intr.) *show oneself, become visible, appear, Mt.* ['*atew*'] For compounds see ætȳw-.

ǣting (ē) f. *eating,* Sc170[5] : *pasture?* Mdf.

ǣtinge (=y[2]) *speechless,* OEG46[45].

ætis pres. 3 sg. of ætwesan, ætbēon.

ætīw-=ætīew-, ætȳw-

ætlǣdan (=oð-) *to drive away,* Æ. ['*atlead*']

ǣtlic (ē) adj. *eatable,* WW,LkL.

ætlicgan[5] *to lie idle,* ÆGr2[22]. ['*atlie*']

ætlimpan[3] *to fall away, escape, be lost,* Æ.

ætlūtian *to lurk, hide,* Æ. ['*atlutien*']

ætnēhstan (ȳ) adv. *at last.*

ætnes f. *edibility,* WW226[11].

ætnīman[4] *to take away, deprive of,* Ex414.

ætol=etol

ǣton pret. pl. of etan.

ǣtor, ǣtorcynn=ātor, ātorcynn

ǣtran=ǣtrian

ætreccan w. d. and a. *to declare forfeit, deprive of,* LCD.

ǣtren *poisoned, poisonous, MtL* (-ern). ['*attern*']

ǣtrenmōd *of venomous spirit, malignant* (or? two words), GNE163.

ǣtrennes f. *poisonous nature,* LCD55a.

±ǣtrian *to poison,* AO : *become poisonous.* ['*atter*']

ǣtrig *poisonous, Lcd*; Æ. ['*attery*']

ætrihte (y) I. adj. *right at, near, present, close at hand.* II. adv. *almost, nearly, immediately.*

ætsacan[6] *to deny, Lk*; Æ : *renounce, Mk.* ['*atsake*']

ætsamne (æ, e, o) adv. *united, together, at once,* AO.

ætscēotan[2] *to escape, disappear,* MFH150.

ætsittan[5] *to sit by, remain, stay, Chr.* ['*atsit*']

ætslāpan[7] *to sleep beside,* LCD83a.

ætslīdan[1] *to slip, glide, fall,* Æ.

ætsomne (Æ)=ætsamne

ætspornan[3] (u) *to strike against, stumble, go wrong,* CP : *rebel* (æt).

ætspornung f. *offence, stumbling-block, misfortune,* CM230.

ætspringan[3] *to rush forth, spurt out,* B1121. ['*atspring*']

ætspringnes, -sprung(en)nes f. *failing,* Ps118[58].

ætspurnan=ætspornan

ætspyrning=ætspornung

ætst=itst pres. 2 sg. of etan.

ætst-=oðst-

ætstæl m. *aid, assistance* (GK);=ætsteall (BT), GU150.

ætstæppan[6] *to step up to,* B745.

ætstandan[6] *to stand still, stand at, near, in or by,* Æ : *remain, stand up : check, resist,* Æ : *cease, Lk*; Æ. ['*atstand*']

ætstandend m. *bystander, attendant,* Æ.

ætstandende *standing by,* GD284[21].

ætsteall m. *assistance, meeting with hostile intent* (GK) : *station, camp station* (BT), or ? æscsteall (Sedgef.), WALD1[21].

ætstentan=ætstyntan

ætstillan *to still,* LCD25b.

ætstrengan *to withhold wrongfully,* LL206'.

ætstyntan *to blunt, dull, weaken,* GL,Hy.

ætswerian[6] *to deny on oath,* LL.

ætswīgan *to keep silence,* GD217[18].

ætswimman[3] *to escape by swimming, swim out,* CHR918.

āettan (āyttan) *to eat up,* LPs79[14].

ǣtter, ǣttor=ātor; **ǣttr-**=ǣtr-

ætōringan[3] *to take away from, deprive of,* AN,GD.

ætwegan[5] *to bear away, carry off,* B1198.

ætwela *abundance of food, feast,* SOUL123.

ætwenian *to wean from,* LL368'.

ætwesan anv. *to be present,* BF,BH276[20].

ætwesende *at hand, imminent,* WW.

ætwindan[3] *to escape,* Æ. ['*atwind*']

ætwist I.† f. *presence.* II.=edwist

ætwītan[6] *to reproach (with), censure, taunt,* B,Met,Ps; CP. ['*atwite*']

ætwrencan *to seize by fraud,* PR34.

ætȳcan *to add to, increase,* BH. [īecan]

ætȳcnes f. *increase,* BH.

ǣtȳnan=ontȳnan; **ǣtynge**=ǣtinge

ætys=ætis pres. 3 sg. of ætwesan.

æt-ȳwan, -ȳwian=ætīewan

ætȳwednes f. *showing, appearance, manifestation, revelation,* GD.

ætȳwigendlic *demonstrative,* ÆGR.

ætȳwnes f. *showing, manifestation, revelation : apparition,* Æ : *Epiphany.*

ætȳwung f. *manifestation, Epiphany,* CM531.

ǣðan I. (±) *to make oath, swear.* +ǣðed *under oath,* LL210,6. [āð] II.=īeðan

æðel=æðele; ǣðel=ēðel
æðelboren of noble birth, distinguished, Æ : free-born, Æ : inborn, natural.
æðelborennes f. nobility of birth or nature, Æ : inborn nature, OEG 4518.
æðelcund of noble birth, GD.
æðelcundnes f. nobleness, Bo 46¹³.
æðelcyning m. noble king (Christ), Æ.
æðelduguð f. noble retinue, CR 1012.
æðele noble, aristocratic, excellent, famous, glorious, Ex,Gen; Æ,AO,CP:splendid,fine, costly, valuable : lusty, young : pleasant, sweet-smelling, Gen : (+) natural, congenial, suitable. ['athel']
æðel-ferðingwyrt, -fyrdingwyrt f. stitchwort (plant), LCD.
+æðeliant† to make noble or renowned, Hy. ['i-athele']
æðelic=æðellic; ǣðelic=ēaðelic
æðeling m. man of royal blood, nobleman, chief, prince, Chr; AO (v. LL 2·274) : †king, Christ, God, Cr : †man, hero, saint; in pl. men, people, Gen. ['atheling']
æðelinghād n. princely state, LCD 3·438⁵.
æðellic noble, excellent. adv. -lice.
æðelnes f. nobility, excellence, BL,MH.
æðelo=æðelu
æðelstenc m. sweet smell, PH 195.
æðeltungol† n. noble star.
æðelu fn. nobility, family, descent, origin, B; CP : nature : noble qualities, genius, talents, pre-eminence, Bo : produce, growth. ['athel']
ǣð-=ēð-
ǣðm (ē) m. air, breath, breathing, B; CP : vapour, Sat. : blast, Æ. ['ethem']
ǣðmian to fume, exhale, emit a smell, GL, MH.
ǣðre=ǣdre
ǣðreclic terrible, RPs 95⁴.
ǣðret-=ǣðryt-
ǣðrot n. disgust, weariness, GL,RB. [āðrēotan]
ǣðryt I. troublesome, wearisome, disgusting. II. n. weariness, disgust, tediousness, Æ.
ǣðryte=ǣðryt I.
ǣðrytnes f. tedium, v. OEG 4582.
±ǣðryttan to weary. Æ,RWH 123⁸
æðða (Bd, Death-song)=oððe
ǣw I.=ǣ. II.=ǣwe
ǣwǣde without clothes, WW 230³⁸.
ǣwan to despise, scorn, KPs 129.
ǣwbrǣce despising the law, Æ : adulterous, LL.
ǣwbreca (i, y) m. adulterer, LL. ['eaubruche²']
ǣwbryce m. adultery, Æ; LL. ['eaubruche¹']

ǣw-da, -damann m. witness, compurgator, LL.
ǣwe I. fn. married woman, Æ : married people. II. lawful : married : born of the same marriage.
ǣwelm=ǣwielm
ǣwenbröðor m. brother by the same marriage, WW 413²⁹.
ǣwene doubtful, uncertain, DEUT 28⁶⁶.
ǣwerd adj.? religious, or sb.? regular priest, ANS 128·298. [cp. ǣweweard]
ǣwerd-=ǣfwyrd-, ǣwierd-
ǣweweard m. priest, BL 161'.
ǣwfæst upright, pious, devout, religious, Æ,CP : married, Æ.
ǣwfæsten n. legal or public fast, A 11·102.
ǣwfæstlic lawful : religious, CP (ǣf-). adv. -lice.
ǣwfæstnes f. religion, piety, Æ,BH.
ǣwicnes f. eternity, RPs 102¹⁷ (v. p.303).
ǣwielm (e, i, y), -wielme m. source, fount, spring, beginning, AO,CP. [=ēawielm]
+ǣwierdlian (e²) to injure, BH 202b³⁰.
ǣwintre=ānwintre; ǣwis-=ǣwisc-
ǣwisc I. nf. offence, shame, disgrace, dishonour, AO. [Goth. aiwisks] II. disgraced, shameless, indecent.
ǣwisc-=ēawisc-
ǣwiscberende shameful, WW 264⁴².
ǣwisce=ǣwisc I.
ǣwisc-ferinend (GL), -firina (NG) m. shameless sinner, publican.
ǣwisclic disgraceful, infamous, OEG.
ǣwiscmōd† ashamed, abashed, cowed.
ǣwiscnes (ēa-) f. shameless conduct : openness, WW : reverence, CP 34³⁶.
ǣwita m. counsellor, EL 455.
ǣwlic legal, lawful. adv. -lice.
±ǣwnian to marry, Æ.
ǣwnung f. wedlock, OEG.
ǣwul basket with a narrow neck for catching fish, WW 181¹¹. [?=cawl, BTs]
ǣwumboren lawfully born, LL 76'.
ǣwunge=ǣwnung; ǣwunge=ēawunge
ǣwyll m. stream, BC 1·542.
ǣ-wylm, -wylme=ǣwielm
ǣwyrdla=ǣfwyrdla
ǣwyrp m. what is cast away, RB : an abortion, LL. [āweorpan]
ǣwysc-=ǣwisc-; æx=æcs, eax; æxe= asce
æxfaru f. 'apparatus,' naval expedition? (=æsc-? v. ES 37·184), GL.
æxian=ascian; æxl=eaxl; æxs=æcs
áfædan=áfēdan
áfægan to depict, figure, BH 58²⁵. [fāg]
áfægrian (æ) to ornament, adorn, BH 38b²⁷.
á-fælan, -fællan=áfyllan II.
áfæman to foam out, PPs 118¹³¹.

āfǣran *to frighten,* *PPs,Mk,Chr*; AO,CP. ['*afear,*' '*afeared*']

āfǣst=æwfæst

āfǣstan I. *to fast,* LL,W. **II.** *to let out on hire,* MkR 12[1].

āfǣstlā interj. *certainly! assuredly! Æ.*

āfǣstnian (e) *to fix upon, fasten, make firm, confirm,* AO : *enter, inscribe, Æ : build.*

āfǣttian *to fatten, anoint,* APs 22[5]; LPs 140[5].

āfandelic=āfandodlic

āfandian *to try, test, prove, tempt,* Lk,Lcd; Æ,CP : *find out, experience, Æ.* āfandod (and āfanden?) *approved, excellent, Æ.* ['*afond*']

āfand-igendlic, -odlic *proved, approved, laudable.* adv. -odlīce.

āfandung f. *trial, experience,* Æ,GD,WW.

āfangennes f. *reception, assumption,* EHy 15[35].

afara=eafora

āfaran *to go out, depart, march, travel,* Da; Æ,AO. ['*afare*']

āfeallan[7] *to fall down, fall in battle,* Lk; CP : *fall off, decay.* ['*afalle*']

āfeallan=āfyllan

āfēdan *to feed, nourish, bring up, maintain, support, Æ;* AO : *bring forth, produce.* ['*afede*']

āfēgan *to join,* DR (oe).

āfehtan (DR)=āfeohtan

āfellan=āfyllan; **āfelle**=ǣfelle

āfeohtan[3] *to fight, fight against, attack,* AO : *tear out, destroy.*

āfeormian *to cleanse, purge, purify,* Æ,Lcd.

āfeormung f. *scouring, cleansing, purging,* CM,Lcd,Sc.

ā-feorran, -feorrian (CP)=āfierran

āfeorsian *to remove, do away, expel, dispel, Æ : go away.*

afer=eafor; **āfer**=āfor; **āfǣran**=āfǣran

āfercian *to support,* CHRD 90[11].

aferian *to provide horses for team work* (as *service for a lord*), v. LL 445, 446 and 3·247.

ā-ferian (GL), -ferran=āfierran

āferscan *to become fresh,* Bo 86[20].

āfersian=āfeorsian

āfestnian (WW 49[8])=āfæstnian

afetigan=hafetian

āfierran (eo, i, y) *to remove, withdraw, depart : estrange from, take away, expel, drive away,* CP. [feorr]

āfierrednes (y) f. *removal,* NC 270.

āfigen *fried,* GL.

āfilgan=āfylgan

āfindan[3] (=on-) *to find, find out, discover, detect,* Jn; Æ : *experience, feel, Æ.* ['*afind*']

āfir-=āfierr-, āfeor-, āfyr-

āflǣgen pp. of āflēan.

āflǣman=āflīeman

āflēan[6] *to strip off, flay,* GD.

āflēgan (DR)=āflīegan; **āflēman**=āflīeman

āflēon[2], -flēogan *to fly, flee away, Gu : fly from, escape.* ['*aflee*']

āflēotan[2] *to skim,* Lcd.

āflīan=āflīegan

+**aflīan**? *to get, obtain?* OEG 7[118] (v. BTac).

āflīegan (ī, ē, ȳ) *to put to flight, expel, Æ.* ['*afley*']

āflīegung (ī) f. *driving away,* Lcd 1·338[12].

āflīeman (ȳ) *to put to flight, expel, scatter, disperse, rout, Chr;* CP : *banish.* ['*afleme*']

āflīg-=āflīeg-

-**āflīung** v. mete-ā.

āflote '*afloat,*' KC 4·24[1]. [=on flote]

āflōwan[7] *to flow, flow away or from, pass away,* AO,CP.

āflȳg-, āflȳh-=āflīeg-

āflygennes f. *attack* (BTs),Lcd 1·336[7].

āflȳman=āflīeman; **āfōgian**=āwōgian

afol n. *power, might,* LL (304 n 1).

āfōn (=on-) *to receive, take in, take, Mk, Ps : lay hold of, seize, MtR,Jul : hold up, support.* ['*afong*']

āfondian=āfandian

āfor *bitter, acid, sour, sharp : dire, fierce, severe, harsh, impetuous.* [OHG. eipar]

afora=eafora

āforhtian *to be frightened, take fright, wonder at, Æ.*

ā-frēfran, -frēfrian *to comfort, console, make glad,* CP. [frōfor]

āfrem-dan, -dian *to alienate, Æ : become alienated.*

āfremðan (VPs)=āfremdan

āfremðung f. *alienation,* VHy 6[28].

āfrēon *to deliver, free,* DR,LkR.

āfrēoðan[2] *to froth,* Lcd 45 b.

afslōg=ofslōg; **after**=æfter

āfūlian *to become foul, putrefy, rot, be corrupt, defiled.*

afulic *perverse,* MtL. ['*awkly*']

āfulliend m. *fuller,* MkR 9[3].

āfunde rare wk. pret. 3 sg. of āfindan.

āfundennes f. *invention, device, discovery, Æ.*

āfȳlan *to foul, stain, defile, corrupt,* CP; Æ. ['*afile*']

āfylgan (i[2]) *to pursue,* GEN 14[16].

āfyllan I. (w. g. or d.) *to fill, fill up, replenish, satisfy, Æ;* AO : *complete, fulfil.* ['*afill*'] **II.** (y;=ie) *to cause to fall, fell, beat down, overturn, subvert, demolish, abolish,* Lk; Æ : *slay, kill.* ['*afelle*']

āfyndan=āfindan; **āfyr-**=āfierr-, āfeor-

āfȳran *to emasculate.* āfȳred (CP), āfȳrd pp. as sb. *eunuch.*

āfyrhtan *to frighten, terrify,* Æ,AO.

āfȳrida=āfȳred; āfyrran=āfierran

āfyrsian=āfeorsian

āfyrðan (i) to remove, LCD 1·294².

āfȳsan (intr.) to hasten : inspire with longing, BL : (tr.) urge, impel, excite : drive, drive away. [fūs]

āga m. proprietor, owner, GD 230¹¹.

āgǣlan to hinder, keep back, preoccupy, detain, hold back, retard, delay, AO : neglect, CP : profane.

āgǣlwan (e) to terrify, astonish, AO.

āgalan⁶ to sound forth, sing, chant, B,W.

āgald=āgeald pret. 3 sg. of āgieldan.

āgāllan to become slack, CP 65¹⁸.

āgan I. (conj. Wt 546) to own, possess, have, obtain, An,Bo,Mt; AO,CP : have control over, take charge of : give, give up, deliver, restore : have to pay, 'owe*,' Mt,Lk : have to do, ANS 123·417. ā. ūt find out, discover. II. pret. 3 sg. of āginnan (onginnan).

āgān (conj. v. gān) to go, go by, pass (of time), Mk: pass into possession (of inherited property), TC 486' : occur, befall, Æ : come forth, grow, Ps : approach : lose strength. of ā. go away. ['ago']

āgangan=āgān

āge f. possessions, property, SAT,BH 196¹⁸. [ON. eiga]

āgēan=ongēan; āgehwǣr=æghwǣr

āgeldan I. †to punish. II.=āgieldan

āgelwan=āgǣlwan; āgēman=āgȳman

±āgen I. 'own,' proper, peculiar, Æ,BH,G, Met,Sat; AO,CP,CHR; proper (gram.), ÆGR. ā. cyre freewill. āgnes ðonces voluntarily, spontaneously. II. n. property, LL : own country. III. pp. of āgan.

āgēn=ongēan

āgēnbewendan to return, G.

āgēncuman⁴ to return, Lk 8⁴⁰.

āgend m. owner, possessor, master, lord, LL. se ā. the Lord, B,Ex.

āgendfrēa I. m. lord, owner. II. f. mistress? GEN 2237.

āgendfrēo=āgendfrēa

āgendlīce properly, as one's own : imperiously, CP 145⁵ : correctly, v. MLR 17·165.

āgen-friga, -frige=āgendfrēa

āgēngehweorfan³ to return, Lk 2⁴³.

āgēnhwyrfan (y;=ie) to return, Mk 6³¹.

āgēniernan³ to run against, meet, Mk.

āgēnlǣdan to lead back, WW 91⁹.

āgenlīc own : owed, due, DR.

āgennama m. proper name, ÆGR 25¹⁶.

āgennes f. property, Æ.

āgēnsendan to send back, Lk.

āgenslaga m. slayer of oneself, suicide, Æ.

āgēnstandan⁶ to press, urge, Lk.

āgenung=āgnung

āgēode=āēode pret. 3 sg. of āgān.

āgeolwian to become yellow, LCD,W.

āgēomrian to mourn, grieve, GD.

āgeornan (=ie) to desire, be eager for, GD 205¹⁹.

āgēotan² to pour out, pour forth, shed, An, MtL; CP : melt, found (of images) : destroy : deprive (of), JUD 32. ['ageten']

āgētan=āgītan

āgiefan⁵ (eo, i, y) to give, impart, deliver, give up, yield, relinquish, Mt : restore, return, repay, pay, AO. eft ā. give back, return. ['agive']

āgieldan³ (e, i, y) to pay, repay, compensate, yield, restore, reward, AO : offer oneself, offer up (as a sacrifice) : perform (an office), Æ : allow : to punish? PH 408.

āgīemelēasian (i, y) to neglect, despise, CP.

āgīemelēasod neglectful, careless, NC 337.

āgieta=āgīta; āgifan (AO,CP)=āgiefan

āgifian to bestow, grant, DR 124¹⁹

āgift=ægift; āgildan (CP)=āgieldan

āgilde=ægilde

āgiltan=āgyltan

āgīmelēasian (C)=āgīemelēasian

āgimmed set with precious stones, Æ.

āginnan=onginnan

āgīta m. prodigal, spendthrift, CP.

āgītan (y²) to find, find out, RB,W.

āgītan (ē,=ie) to waste, destroy, Chr. ['aget']

āglāchād m. state of misery, RD 54⁵.

āg-lǣc, -lāc† n. trouble, distress, oppression, misery, grief.

āglǣca† (ē) m. wretch, monster, demon, fierce enemy.

āglǣccræft (āc-) m. evil art, AN 1364.

āglǣcwīf n. female monster, B 1259.

āglǣdan? to cause to slip. v. AB 19·163.

āglēca=āglǣca

āglīdan¹ to glide, slip, stumble, LCD,WW.

agn-=angn-

āgnere m. owner, ÆGR 110¹⁹.

āgnes=āgenes gmn. of āgen adj.

āgnett n. interest, usury, LkL 19²³ (or ? āgnettung). v. ES 42·163).

āgnettan to appropriate, GL.

±āgnian to 'own,' MtL,Rd : claim : appropriate, usurp, Bo; CP : make over (to), Æ : dedicate, adopt, CP : enslave, Ex.

āgnidan¹ to rub off, WW 386¹⁶.

āgniden I. f. rubbing, GL? (v. A 31·533). II. used, threadbare, WW 220²⁴.

āgniend (āh) m. owner, possessor, GEN 14²².

±āgniendlīc possessive, genitive (case), ÆGR.

+āgnod own, CP 262²³.

āgnung f. owning, ownership, possession : claim, declaration or proof of ownership : (+) acquisition, KC 2·304⁵.

āgotenes f. effusion, shedding, Æ,LCD.

āgrafan[6] *to carve, hew, sculpture,* Æ : *engrave, inscribe,* Æ.
āgrafenlic *sculptured,* ARSPs 105[19].
āgrāpian *to grasp tightly,* ÆL 8[121].
āgrētan (oe) *to attack,* LkLR 9[42].
agrimonia '*agrimony,*' Lcd.
āgrīsan[1] (ȳ) *to quake, fear,* LL. ['*agrise*']
āgrōwen *overgrown,* HExC 196.
āgrymetian *to rage,* GD.
āgrȳndan *to descend,* Men 111.
āgrȳsan=āgrīsan
agu f. *magpie,* WW 132[11].
Agus-tus, -tes (AA 8[11]) m. *August.*
āgyf-, āgyld-=āgief-, āgield-, ǣgild-
āgylpan[3] (=ie) *to exult in* (w.d.), Soul 165.
āgyltan *to offend, sin, do wrong,* Æ; CP. ['*aguilt*']
āgyltend m. *debtor,* EHy 13[6].
āgylting f. *guilt, offence,* DR.
āgyltnes f. *guilt,* NC 270.
āgȳman (ē; =īe) *to regard,* AS : *heal, cure.*
āgȳmelēasian=āgīemelēasian
āgymmed=āgimmed; agynnan=onginnan
āgytan=āgitan
ah (AO,CP)=ac (conj. and adv.)
āh pres. 3 sg. of āgan; āh-=āg-
āhabban *to restrain,* Æ : (refl.) *abstain* (fram), BH : *support,* Cp 1947.
āhaccian *to pick out,* ÆL 23[78].
āhæbban=āhebban
āhældan=āhildan
āhafennes f. *rising, lifting up, elevation,* Ps.
āhalsian *to implore,* RBL 15[3].
āhangian *to hang,* LkL 23[39].
āhātan *to name,* MtL 27[16].
āhātian *to become hot,* WW 214[81].
āhealdan[7] (=on-) *to hold, keep,* DR, JnL.
āhealtian *to limp, crawl,* LPs 17[46].
āheardian *to be or become hard, grow hard or inured,* CP : *endure.*
āheardung f. *hardening,* Lcd.
āhēawan[7] *to cut off, out or down,* Æ,CP : *cut wood into planks.*
āhebban[6] (occl. wk. pret. āhefde and pp. āhefed) (often w. ūp) *to lift up, stir up, raise, exalt, erect,* Lk; CP : *take away, remove : support, uphold : leaven.* ['*aheave*']
āhebbian=āebbian; āhefednes=āhafennes
āhefegian (CP), -hef(i)gian (æ) *to make heavy, oppress : become heavy.*
āheld (VPs)=āhild pp. of āhildan.
āhellian? *to cover over, conceal, hide,* OEG 5410.
āhelpan[3] *to help, support,* DR.
āhēnan *to humble,* LkL : *accuse,* NG. [hīenan; hēan]
āheolorian *to weigh, consider,* GL.
āhēran=āhȳran
āherian *to praise,* DR.

āhērian=āhȳrian
āherstan (BPs 101[4])=āhyrstan
āheten pp. of āhatan.
āhicgan=āhycgan; āhienan v. āhēnan.
āhierdan (i, y) *to make hard, harden,* CP : *encourage, animate.* [heard]
āhierding (y) *hardening,* Sc 232[19].
āhīeðan=āhȳðan
āhildan (æ, e, y;=ie) *to bend, incline,* Æ : *rest, lay down* (tr. and intr.) : *turn away, avert : cast down, destroy.*
āhildnes '*declinatio,*' RPs 72[4].
āhirdan (CP)=āhierdan; āhīðan=āhȳðan
āhladan[6] *to draw out, lead out, draw forth,* Æ : *exclude,* Bk 18.
āhlǣca=āglǣca
āhlǣnan *to set oneself up,* Mod 53.
āhlǣnsian *to become lean,* Æ.
āhlēapan[7] *to leap, spring up,* AO.
āhlēfan (oe) *to pull out,* DR 55[10].
āhlēoðrian *to sound, resound,* GD.
āhliehhan[6]† *to laugh at, deride : exult.*
āhlin-ian, -nan=ālynnan
āhlocian *to dig out,* Gl, MtR 5[29]. [?=*ālocian, cp. lucan (BTs) and v. ES 42·165]
āhlōwan *to roar again,* WW 492[11].
āhlūttrian *to cleanse, purify,* Gl, Lcd.
āhlyhhan=āhliehhan
āhlȳt(t)rian=āhlūttrian
āhn-=āgn-
āhnēapan[2] *to pluck off,* Gu 819.
āhnescian *to become soft or effeminate,* AO : *weaken.* [hnesce]
āhnīgan[1] *to fall down : bow down : empty oneself,* DR.
āhogian *to think out, be anxious about,* GD.
āholan=āholian
āholian *to hollow, scoop out,* CP. ūt ā. *to root out, pluck out : engrave, emboss.*
āhōn[7] *to hang, suspend, crucify,* MkLR; AO,CP. ['*ahang*']
āhopian *to hope for* (tō), Bl 17[23].
āhrǣcan *to spit out,* Lcd 9a.
āhrǣscian *to shake off?* (BTs),LPs 108[13].
āhreddan *to set free, save, rescue, re-capture,* AO; Æ. ['*aredde*']
āhredding f. *salvation, deliverance,* EC, HL 9[281].
āhrēofian *to become leprous,* MH 174[12].
āhrēosan[2] *to rush : fall, fall down,* Æ : *be destroyed.*
āhrepian *to treat,* FBO 80[5].
āhrēran (=on-) *to move, shake, make to tremble,* CP.
āhrīnan[1] (=on-) *to touch, handle,* Lk. ['*arine*']
āhrisian (y) *to shake, stir up,* CP, Ps : *shake off.* ['*arese*']
āhrȳnan=āhrīnan

āhrȳran (=īe) *to cause to fall, destroy,* GL.
āhrȳsian=āhrisian
ahse=asce; āhsian=āscian
aht, āht=eaht, āwiht; ahta=eahta
āhte, āhton pret. 3 sg. and pl. of āgan.
āhtes (=g. of āht) *of any account or value.*
āhtlīce *stoutly, manfully,* CHR 1071E.
āhwā pron. *any one,* LL.
āhwǣnan *to vex, grieve, afflict,* Lcd; Æ. [' *awhene* ']
āhwænne adv. *when, whenever :* at some *time, any time,* RB : *at all times.*
āhwǣr (ā, ē) *anywhere,* Bo,LL,Ps : *at any time, ever, in any way.* [' *owhere* ']
āhwǣrgen=āhwergen
āhwǣt n. *anything,* CM 371.
āhwǣðer (āwðer, āðer, āðor) I. pron. *some one, something; any one : anything.* II. adv. and conj. *either,* AO,CP. āðer...oððe= *either...or,* AO. [' OUTHER ']
āhwanon=āhwonan; āhwǣr=āhwǣr
āhwelfan=āhwylfan
āhwēnan=āwēnan
āhweorfan³ (tr.) *to turn, turn away, convert :* (intr.) *turn aside, turn away,* Gen : *avert.* [' *awherf* ']
āhwēr=āhwǣr; āhwerfan=āhwierfan
āhwergen (æ²) *anywhere :* in any case.
āhwettan *to whet, excite, kindle,* AO : *hold out to, provide : reject.*
āhwider *in any direction, from any source,* Æ.
āhwierfan *to turn away, turn from, avert,* CP.
āhwilc=ǣghwilc; āhwistlian v. āwistlian.
āhwītian *to whiten,* BJPs 50⁹.
āhwonan *from any source, anywhere,* BH, Bo.
āhwonne=āhwænne; āhwyder=āhwider
āhwylfan (e;=ie) *to cover over, submerge, subvert,* Æ : *roll to,* RWH 78¹⁹. up ā. *pull up, loosen.*
āhwyrfan=āhwierfan
āhycgan† *to think out, devise.*
āhȳdan *to hide, conceal,* GD,W.
āhyldan=āhildan
āhyldendlic *enclitic,* ÆGR 265¹. [āhildan]
āhyltan *to trip up,* PPs 139⁵.
āhȳran (ē) *to hire,* G.
āhȳrd-=āhierd-
āhȳrsian=āhrisian
āhyrstan (e²;=ie) *to roast, fry,* LCD 33b; BPs 101⁴.
āhyspan *to reproach,* LPs 101⁹.
āhȳðan (īe, ī) *to plunder, destroy, devour,* EL,VPs. [hūð]
āīdan (ȳ)? ' *eliminare* ' (v. OEG 7¹⁰⁹n; BTs)
ā-īdlian, -īdlan, -īdelian *to be or make useless, frustrate, empty, annul,* Æ,CP : *profane :* be free from : *deprive (of).* [īdel]

ālernan³ *to run away, run out, go over :* pass *by, go,* CHR.
āleðan (ǣ, ī, ȳ) *to lay low, demolish, destroy, cast out,* GEN,WW.
al=eall, æl
āl n. *fire, burning,* OEG 4389; 4470. [cp. ǣlan]
ālādian *to excuse,* Bo 144⁵. ālādiendra ' *excussorum* '(=*excussatorum,*) BJPs 126⁴.
ālæccan *to catch, take,* CHR 1123.
ālǣdan (tr.) *to lead, lead away, carry off, withdraw, conduct, bring,* Æ : (intr.) *be produced, grow, come forth.*
ālǣnan *to lend,* WW : *grant, lease,* Æ. [' *alene* ']
ālǣr=alor
ālǣran *to teach,* PPs 118¹⁰⁸.
ālǣson pret. pl. of ālesan.
ālǣtan⁷ *to let go, give up, leave, lose, resign, lay aside,* Jn; AO,CP : *let, allow : release, pardon, forgive : deliver,* Æ. [' *alet* ']
ālǣtnes (ǣ¹, ē²) f. *desolation : loss : remission* (of sins).
alan⁶ *to nourish, produce,* RIM 23. [Goth. alan]
ālangian (impers.) *to affect with longing,* Soul 154. [' *along* ']
ālatian *to grow sluggish or dull,* GL.
alað=ealað (v. ealu)
ālāðian¹ (GL) *to be or become hateful : hate : threaten.*
alb f. *white garment, ' alb,'* LL. [L.]
ald (EWS,EK,A)=eald; āld=ādl
aldaht=ealdoð
ālecgan *to put, place, lay down, lay aside, give up, cease from, abandon,* LL; Æ,AO, CP : *put down, allay, suppress, abolish, conquer, destroy, overcome, refute,* Æ,LL : *lay upon, inflict : diminish, lessen, withhold,* Æ. ālecgende word, ālecgendlic word *deponent verb.* [' *allay* ']
āled pp. of (1) ālecgan; (2) ālǣdan (=ālǣd).
ālēfan=ālīefan
ālēfednes f. *infirmity,* ÆL 21⁹⁹.
ālēfian *to injure, maim; enfeeble,* Æ. pp. *ill,* Æ. [lef]
ālenian (K)=ālynnan
ālēodan²† *to spring up, grow.*
āleofian=ālifian, ālibban
ālēogan² *to lie, deny, deceive, be false to, leave unfulfilled,* Æ,AO.
ālēon¹ (=on-) *to lend, give up,* DR.
āleonian=ālynnan
ālēoran *to depart, flee away,* RPs 10³ : pass *away,* ARPs 56².
āleoðian=āliðian; aler=alor
ālēs-=ālīes-
ālesan⁶ *to pick out, choose,* AS,BH.
ālet (DA 254)=ǣled

ālētan=ālǣtan; ālēōran=ālȳōran
alewe, al(u)we f. 'aloe,' Jn,Lcd.
ālēwed ptc. feeble, weak, ill, RB51¹⁶. [lēf]
alexandre f. horse-parsley, Lcd. ['alexanders']
alfæle (AN770)=ealfelo
ālfæt n. cooking vessel, cauldron, LL. [ǣlan]
ālgeweorc n. fire-making, tinder, GL.
algian=ealgian; alh=ealh
ālibban to live, pass one's life, AO.
ālicgan⁵ to be subdued, fail, cease, yield, perish, AO.
āliefan (ē, ī, ȳ) to allow, give leave to, grant, AO,CP : hand over, yield up.
āliefedlic lawful, permissible. adv. -līce (Æ,CP).
āliesan (ē, ī, ȳ) to loosen, let loose, free, redeem, release, absolve, Mt; AO,CP. ['alese']
ālies-ednes (Mt), -(e)nes (Cr,MtLR) (ē, ȳ) f. redemption, ransom : remission (of sins), ERHy9⁷⁷. ['alese(d)ness']
āliesend (ē, ī, ȳ) m. liberator, deliverer, Redeemer, CP.
āliesendlic (ȳ) loosing, liberating, BH.
āliesendnes=āliesednes
āliesing, -liesnes=āliesednes
ālif=ǣlif
ālifan=āliefan; āliflan=ālibban
ālih (DR) imperat. sg. of ālēon.
ālihtan I. to lighten, relieve, alleviate, take off, take away, CP,LL : 'alight,' ÆGr. II. to light up, Æ,Met (=onlihtan).
ālimpan³† to occur, happen.
ālinnan=ālynnan; āliesend=āliesend
ālīōian (eo) to detach, separate, Gen : set free. ['alithe']
all (strictly Anglian, but found in AO,CP) =eal, eall
almes-=ǣlmes-; aln-=ealn-
alo-=ealu-
āloccian to entice, AO.
alor, al(e)r m. 'alder,' Gl,KC,Lcd; Mdf.
alorbedd (ælr-) alder bed, KC5·153'.
alordrenc m. drink made of alder sap? Lcd 40a.
alorholt nm. alder-wood, WW.
alorrind m. alder-bark, Lcd 12b.
aloð=ealu; alr=alor; alswā=ealswā
alter, altar(e), altre m. 'altar,' G; CP. [L.]
ālūcan² to pluck up, pull out, separate, take away, GD.
ālūtan² (=onl-) to bend, incline, bend or bow down, Æ. āloten pp. submissive.
aluwe, alwe=alewe; alwald-=eal(l)weald-
ālybban=ālibban; ālȳfan (Æ)=āliefan
ālȳfed I.=āliefed pp. of āliefan. II.=ālēfed pp. of ālēfian; ālȳfed-=aliefed-
ālȳht-=onliht-; ālyhtan=ālihtan

ālȳman to come forth, GL : show forth.
ālynnan, -lynian (e, eo, i) to deliver, let go, release, loosen, Æ.
ālȳs-=ālies-
ālȳōran (ē;=īe) to lather, LCD. [lēaðor]
am (NG)=eom; am-=an-
ām m. reed or slay of a loom? RD36⁸ (v. LL3·524 and BTs)
āmǣllian=āmeallian
āmǣnsumian=āmānsumian
āmǣran I. to extol, GD206²⁴. II. (usu. ūtāmǣr(i)an) to exterminate, BH.
āmæstan to feed with mast, fatten, feed up, CP.
āmagian? (hamacgian) to revive, be restored to health, LCD3·184'. (or ? +magian, v. BTac)
āman=onman
āmang prep. w. d. among, amongst : while, whilst, during. ā. ðām, ðissum meanwhile. [=gemang]
āmanian to exact, require, LL202,1.
āmāns-ian, -ung=āmānsum-ian, -ung
āmānsumian to excommunicate, curse, proscribe, outlaw, BH; Æ,AO. ['amanse']
āmān-sumung, -sumnung f. excommunication, curse, Æ. ['amansing']
āmarian to disturb, trouble, confound. [cp. āmierran]
āmasian to amaze, confound, W137²³.
āmāwan⁷ to cut down, PPs101⁴.
āmb (LL455,15)=ām; ambeht=ambiht
amber (e¹, o¹, æ², o², u²) mfn. vessel, pail, cask, pitcher, tankard, Gl,MkL : dry or liquid measure (? four bushels), AO,Ct, WW. ['amber']
ambiht (e¹, o¹, y¹, e²) I. n. office, service : commission, command, message. II. m. attendant, messenger, officer.
+ambiht-an, -ian (embe-) to minister, serve, NG.
ambihtere (embe-) m. servant, LkL22²⁶.
ambihtþēra (o¹) obedient servant, Gu571.
ambihtþūs n. workshop, 'officina,' CM1087.
ambihtmann m. manservant, LL.
ambihtmecg† (o¹, e², y²) m. servant, Ps.
ambiht-nes, -sumnes (emb-) f. service, NG.
ambihtscealc† m. functionary, retainer.
ambihtsecg sm. minister, GEN582.
ambihtsmið m. court smith or carpenter, LL3, 7.
ambihtðegn (omb-)† m. attendant, servant.
ambrōsie ambrosia, GUTH90⁸.
ambyht=ambiht
ambyre unfavourable? (BTac), AO19¹³.
ambyrian (OEG11¹⁴²)=onbyrgan II.
āmeallian (æ) to become insipid, v. OEG61⁴.
āmearcian to mark out, delineate, define, describe : destine, assign, appoint.

amel m. *sacred vessel*, WW 348. [*L.*]
āmelcan² *to milk*, LCD.
āmeldian *to let out, make known, betray*, Æ,AO.
āmeltan³ v. āmolten.
ameos *bishop-weed*, LCD 71b. [*Gk.*]
amerian=hamorian
āmerian *to test, examine* : *purify, refine*, LCD.
āmerran=āmierran
āmetan⁵ *to measure, estimate* : *mete out, assign, grant, bestow*, Æ.
āmētan *to paint, depict*, CP : *adorn*, Æ.
āmetendlic *compendious, measurable, limited*, LPs 38⁶. adv. -līce.
āmethwīl=ǣmethwīl
āmetsian *to provision*, CHR 1006 E.
āmiddan=onmiddan
āmidian *to be foolish*, RHy 6⁶.
āmidlian *to bridle*, BYH 56²⁷,WW 226³⁸.
āmierran (e, i, y) *to hinder, obstruct, prevent, delay*, CP : *mar, injure, disturb, scatter, consume, waste, spoil, destroy, Lk, Bo* ; AO,CP : *lose*. ['*amar*']
āmigdal m. *almond*, LCD. [*Gk.*]
āmōd=ǣmōd
āmolcen pp. of āmelcan.
āmolsnian *to decay, weaken*, W 147²⁹.
āmolten *molten*, ÆL 5²³⁴.
amore=omer
am-pelle (o², u²) f. *flask, vessel*, Æ. [*L.*]
ampre I. '*varix*,' *tumour, swelling*, Gl. ['*amper*'] II. f. *dock, sorrel*, LCD.
āmundian *to protect, defend*, Æ.
āmyltan (tr.) *to melt*, Æ.
āmyrdrian (LL 348,56A)=āmyrðrian
āmyrgan *to delight, cheer*, SOL 240.
āmyrian=āmerian
āmyrran=(1) āmierran ; (2) (LL 348,56G,B) āmyrðran
ā-myrðran, -myrðrian *to murder, kill, LL* ; CHR 1049 C. ['*amurder*']
an I. adv. and prep.=on. II. pres. 1 sg. of unnan.
an- in composition represents (1) and- ; (2) un- ; (3) in- ; (4) on-.
ān I. adj. strong mfn. (asm. ānne, ǣnne) '*ONE*,' *Æ,Chr.* in plur. *each, every one, all.* ān and (æfter) ān *one by one.* ānes hwæt *some single thing, a part* : *a, an* : *alone, sole, only* ; in this sense it is used also in the weak form (sē āna ; hē āna, AO,CP) and with a pl. : *lonely?* AN 258 : *singular, unique* : *single, each, every one, all* (gp. ānra) : *any.* II. adv. (also wk. āna) *alone, only.* on ān *continually, continuously, ever, in one, once for all, immediately.* ðæt ān *only that.* ān and ān *one by one*, Æ.
ana=heonu ; āna v. ān.

ānad, ānædt n. *waste, desert, solitude*. [*Ger.* einöde]
ānægled *nailed down*, AA 6⁶.
anǣl-=onǣl-
anǣðelian=unǣðelian
ananbeam m. *spindle-tree*, LCD 29b.
anawyrm m. *intestinal worm*, LCD 43b.
anbærnes=onbærnes
anbestingan³ *to thrust in, insert*, CP.
anbid (=on-) n. *waiting, expectation, hope*, AO,CP : *interval*, AO.
±an-bidian (on-) (intr.) *to wait, stay* : (tr.) w. g. *wait for, expect.*
anbidstōw (on-) f. *place of meeting*, LL.
±anbidung m. *waiting for, expectation* : *delay*, OEG 3396.
anbiht=ambiht ; anbindan=onbindan
anbiscopod=unbiscopod
ānborent ptc. *only-begotten.*
anbringelle=onbringelle
anbrōce (EL 1029)=unbrǣce?
anbrucol (=on-) *rugged*, GPH 402.
anbryrd-=onbryrd-
ānbūend m. *hermit, anchorite*, GU 59.
anbūgan (AO,CP)=onbūgan
anbyhtscealc=ambihtscealc
ānbȳme *made of one trunk, dug-out (ship)*, WW 181³³.
+anbyrdan (and-) *to strive against, resist, oppose*, LL.
anbyrdnes f. *resistance*, LL 214,14.
anbyrignes (=on-) f. *tasting, taste*, WW.
ān-cenned (æ²), -cend, *only-begotten*, Æ.
ancer=ancor
an-clēow n., -clēowe f. '*ankle*,' *Lcd,WW.*
ancnāwan=oncnāwan
ancor m. '*anchor*,' *B,Bo* ; CP. [*L. from Gk.*]
ān-cor, -cora m. *anchorite,hermit*, WW ; Æ. ['*anchor*']
ancorbend (oncer-) m. *cable*, B 1918.
ancorlic *like a hermit*, WW 463⁷.
ancorlif n. *solitary life*, BH.
ancorman m. *man in charge of the anchor*, WW 166⁷.
ancorrāp (o¹, y²) m. *anchor-rope, cable*, WH 14.
ancorsetl (e²) n. *prow of a ship*, WW.
ancorsetl n. *hermitage*, Æ.
ancorsetla m. *hermit*, Æ.
ancorstōw f. *solitary place*, BH 424¹².
ancorstreng (ancer-) m. *cable*, AS 22¹⁹.
ancra=ancor
ancra (a¹?) m. *anchorite, hermit, monk*, WW ; Æ. ['*anchor*']
ancsum=angsum
ancuman⁴ *to arrive*, GEN 1884.
āncummum *one by one, singly*, NG.
āncyn adj. *only*, A 2·358 ; LPs 21²¹.

and (e) conj. 'AND' : *but* : *or*, LL 2·13.
gelice and...*like as if*...AO.
and-=an-, on-, ond- (*opposition, negation*;
Ger. ent-); *and occasionally* a-.
anda m. *grudge, enmity, envy, anger,
vexation, Mt*; Æ : *zeal*, Æ,CP : *injury,
mischief* : *fear, horror*, NG. ['*ande*,'*onde*']
ándæge† *for one day, lasting a day.*
andæt-=andet-
ándaga m. *appointed day*, Æ.
±ándagian *to fix a day for appearance* :
adjourn, EC 163'.
andb-=anb-, onb-
andbicnian *to make signs to*, WW 378³
(andbēt-).
andbita m. *feast (of unleavened bread)*, WW.
andclēow=anclēow
andcweðan '*contradicere, frustrari*,' HGL
491.
andcwiss f. *answer*, GU 992.
andcȳðnes f. *evidence*, BH 158⁵.
andd-=and-, ond-; ande=ende
andēages (ǣ) *eye to eye, openly?* B 1935.
andēaw *arrogant, ostentatious*, Sc.
andefn, -efen f. *measure, quantity, amount*,
AO : *capacity, nature*, CP.
andel-bær, -bære *reversed*, OEG.
andergilde *in repayment, in compensation*,
PR 41.
andet-=andett-
andetla m. *declaration, confession*, LL 18,22.
±andetnes (ond- CP) f. *confession*, Æ :
thanksgiving, praise.
andetta (o¹, æ²) m. *one who confesses*, BL,
LL. a. bēon *to acknowledge.*
±andettan *to confess, acknowledge*, Æ,CP :
give thanks or praise : *promise, vow.* [and,
hātan]
andettere m. *one who confesses*, Æ,CHRD.
andettian=andettan
andettung m. *confession, profession*, CP.
andfang n. *acceptance*, WW.
andfangol '*susceptor*,' LPs 45¹².
ándfealdlīce=ānfealdlīce
andfeax *bald*, W 46¹.
andfeng (on-) m. *seizing, receiving, taking*,
Æ,RB : *defence* : *defender* : *attack, assault* :
revenue, means, Lk 14²⁸,BK 10 : *illegal occupation (of land).*
andfenga m. *receiver, defender, undertaker*,
Ps.
andfenge I. (anf-, onf-) *acceptable, agreeable, approved, fit, suitable*, Æ,CP : *that can
receive* : *taken.* II. m. *undertaker, helper*,
PPs.
andfengend m. *helper, defender*, PPs : *receiver.* gafoles a. *tax collector.*
andfengnes f. *acceptance, receiving* : *receptacle* : *acceptableness*, W 253²¹.

andfengstōw f. *receptacle*, CHRD 109³.
andfex=andfeax; andgelōman=andlōman
andget=andgit
andgete *plain, manifest*, CR 1243. [andgiete]
andgiet (ond-; e, i, y) n., andgiete f. *understanding, intellect, Mt*; Æ,CP : *knowledge,
perception*, CP : *sense, meaning*, Æ,CP : *one
of the five senses* : *plan, purpose.* ['*angit*']
andgietful (e,i,y) *intelligent, sensible*, RB,W.
andgietfullic (i,y) *intelligible, clear*, ÆGR 4¹¹.
adv. -līce, CP.
andgietlēas (i) *foolish, senseless*, Æ.
andgietlēast (i,y) f. *want of understanding*,
Æ.
andgietlic (i) *intelligible, clear*, AS 5¹⁶. adv.
-līce, WW.
andgiettācen n. *sensible token, sign*, GEN
1539.
andgit=andgiet
andgitol *intelligent, sensible*, RB,WW.
andhēafod n. *heading, unploughed headland
of a field*, EC.
andhetan, andhettan=andettan
andhweorfan³ *to move against, blow against*,
B 548. [or ? onhweorfan]
andian *to be envious or jealous*, Æ.
andiendlīce *enviously*, TF 108¹⁸.
andig *envious, jealous*, OEG.
andlāman=andlōman
andlang (o¹, o²) I. adj. *entire, continuous,
extended.* andlangne dæg, niht *all day
(night) long*, An,Gu. ['*along*'] II. prep.
w. g. '*along*,' *by the side of*, Æ,Chr,KC ;
AO.
andlangcempa (anl-) *soldier fighting in line*,
WW 450¹⁸.
andlanges adv. prep. *along*, Ct.
andlata (CR 1436)=andwlita
andlēan† n. *retribution, retaliation.*
and-leofen (ie, i, y) f., -leofa m. *nourishment, food* : *money, wages.* [libban]
andlīcnes=onlīcnes
andliefen (AO,CP), andlifen=andleofen
andlōman (ā², u²) m. pl. *utensils, implements, vessels*, GL.
andlong=andlang; andlyfen=andleofen
andmitta=anmitta; andrǣdlīce=undrǣd-
līce
Andrēasmæsse f. *St Andrew's day* (30 Nov.),
ÆGr 43¹¹. [v. '*mass*']
andrecefæt? n. *wine or oil press*, WW
123³⁷.
andribb n. '*pectusculum*,' *breast*, ExC 29²⁶,²⁷
andriesne=ondrysne
an-drysen-, -drysn-=ondrys(e)n-
andsaca† m. *adversary* : *denier, apostate.*
andsacian *to dispute, deny*, CP.
andsæc m. *denial, oath of purgation*, El,LL :
refusal : *strife, resistance.* ['*andsech*']

andsǣte adj. *hateful, odious, repugnant*, ÆGr : *hostile*. ['*andsete*']
andslyht† (=ie) m. *blow*, B (hond-).
andspurnan³ (y) *to stumble against*, NG.
andspurnes (y) f. *offence*, MtR.
āndstreces=ānstreces
and-sumnes, -sundnes (=on-) f. *purity, chastity, virginity*. v. OEG 1696.
±andswarian *to* '*answer*,' *Lk*; Æ,CP.
andswaru f. '*answer*,' *reply, B,Jn*; CP.
and-swerian (VPs), -sworian=andswarian
andsȳn=ansīen
andtimber (y²)=ontimber
andǒr-=onǒr-
andung f. *jealousy*, LPs 77⁵⁸.
andūstrian *to deny* (*with oaths*), MtR 26⁷⁴.
andūstrung f. '*abominatio*,' MtR 24¹⁵.
andwǣscan=ādwǣscan
andward-=andweard-
andweal-=onweal-
±andweard *present, actual, existing*, Æ,CP : *opposite to*.
±andweardian *to present, bring before one*. (+andweardian also=andwyrdian.)
andweardlic *present, actual*. adv. -līce.
andweardnes f. *presence*, CP : *present time*, BH : *dispensation*, W 243³⁵.
andwendednes=onwendednes
andweorc n. *matter, substance, material*, CP : *cause*.
andwerd=and-weard, -wyrd
andwīg m. *resistance*, Gu 147.
andwille=ānwille
andwirdan=andwyrdan
andwīs *expert, skilful*, Jul 244.
andwīsnes f. *experience*, WW 20⁵.
andwist f. *support*, An 1542.
andwlata=andwlita
+andwlatod *shameless*, OEG 8³⁶⁵.
andwlita (a, eo) m. *face, forehead, countenance, form, B,MtR*; AO,CP. ['*anleth*']
andwlite n.=andwlita
andwliteful '*vultuosus*,' GPH 393.
andwrāǒ *hostile, enraged*, Pa 17.
andwreðian (?=āwr-) *to support*, Chrd 62²⁹.
and-wurd, -wyrd=andweard
±and-wyrdan, -wyrdian (e, i) *to answer*, Æ,AO,Mt; CP. ['*andwurde*']
andwyrde n. *answer*, AO.
andwyrding f. *conspiracy*, WW 373¹¹.
andyde pret. of andōn (ondōn).
andytt-=andett-
āne=(1) āne, (2) heonu
ān-ēage, -ē(a)gede (ÆL) '*one-eyed*,' *blind of one eye*.
ānecge adj. *having one edge*, WW 142³⁷.
+āned v.+ānian.
ānēge, ānēgede=ānēage
ānēhst=anīhst

ānemnan *to announce, declare, Gu*. ['*aname*']
ānerian *to deliver, rescue*, LPs 24¹⁵; EPs 49²².
ānes=ānes; ānesclan=āhnescian
ānett mn., ānetnes f. *solitude, seclusion*, CP.
anf-=onf-
ān-feald, -fald, -fealdlic *single, unmixed, unique, superior*, CP : *simple, modest, honest, sincere, Mt*; CP : *fixed, invariable: singular* (gram.), ÆGr. ā. gerecednes *or* sprǣc prose. ['*afald*'] adv. -līce.
ānfealdnes f. *unity, concord*, AO : *simplicity*, CP.
anfealt f. *anvil*, OEG 11⁶⁷ and n. [cp. anfilte]
anfeng=andfeng
ānfēte *one-footed*, RD 59¹.
an-filt (*Æ*), -filte (*Gl*), n. '*anvil*.'
anfindan=onfindan
ānfloga m. *lonely flier*, Seaf 62.
anfōn (AO)=onfōn
anforht *fearful*, Cross 117.
ānforlǣtan⁷ *to let go, lose, relinquish, abandon, surrender*, CP : *omit, neglect*.
ānforlǣtnes f. *loss, desertion*, Bl 85' : *intermission*.
anforngean *in front of*, RWH 45¹².
anga (o) m. *stimulus, sting, goad*, CP.
āngat (ā, ē) *sole, only* : *solitary*.
angbrēost n. *tightness of the chest, asthma*, Lcd.
ange=enge
angeald pret. 3 sg. of angildan.
angēan=ongēan
angel I. m. '*angle*,' *hook, fish-hook, Bo, MtL* (ongul). II. m.=engel
Angel n. *Anglen, a district in Schleswig, from which the Angles came*, AO.
Angelcynn n. *the English people : England*, AO.
āngeld=āngilde
Angelfolc n. *the English people*, BH 472¹⁷.
angelic *like, similar*, Bo 44¹⁸.
angeltwicce fm. *a certain worm used as bait, earthworm?* Lcd,WW. ['*angletwitch*']
Angelðēod f. *the English people : England*.
Angelwitan (o²) mp. *English councillors*, LL 236 G 2.
āngenga I. *solitary, isolated*, Æ. II. m. *solitary goer, isolated one*, B.
angerǣd=ungerād
āngetrum n. *illustrious company*, Ex 334.
angeweald=onweald
±anglan *to be in anguish*, RPs 60³; 142⁴.
anglen=anginn; angil=angel I.
angildan=ongieldan
āngilde (e, y) I. n. *single payment or rate of compensation for damage, LL : the fixed price at which cattle and other goods were received as currency*, LL. ['*angild*'] II. adj. *to be compensated for*. III. adv. *simply, only*, LL.

ångildes=ångilde III.

anginn n. *beginning, Æ; AO,CP : intention, design, enterprise, undertaking, CP : action, onset, attack : rising (of sun) : tip (of finger),* BF154⁶. ['*angin*']

anginnan (AO)=onginnan

angitan=ongietan; **angitful**=andgietful

Angle mp. *the Angles or English* (v. Angel).

angmōd *sad, sorrowful, Æ,*RB.

angmōdnes f. *sadness, sorrow,* W188⁶.

angnægl m. *corn, 'agnail,'* Lcd30b.

angnere (on-) m. *corner of the eye,* WW 423³⁴.

angnes f. *anxiety, trouble, pain, fear,* Lcd, Ps.

angol-=angel-

angrisla (y) m. *terror,* Bl203⁷.

angrislic (y²) *grisly, terrible.* adv. -(en)līce.

ang-set, -seta m. *eruption, pustule, carbuncle,* WW.

angsum *narrow, hard, difficult.* adv. -sume.

±**angsumian** *to vex, afflict, Æ.*

angsumlic *troublesome, painful,* RB5¹⁹. adv. -līce, Æ.

angsumnes f. *pain, Æ : sorrow, trouble : difficulty, perplexity.*

āngum=ǣnigum dat. of ǣnig.

ångyld, āngylde=ångilde

angyn, angytan=anginn, ongietan

anh-=onh-

ānhaga (o²)† m. *solitary being, recluse.*

anhende (=on-) *on hand, requiring attention,* AO88²⁴.

ānhende *one-handed, lame, weak, Æ.*

ānhīwe '*uniformis,*' OEG1046.

anhoga m. *care, anxiety,* Gu970.

ānhoga=ānhaga

ānhorn, ānhorna m. *unicorn,* Ps.

ānhrǣdlīce=ānrǣdlīce

ānhundwintre *a hundred years old,* Gen 47⁹.

ānhȳdig† *resolute, firm, constant, stubborn, brave.*

ānhyrne I. m. *unicorn.* II.=ānhyrned

ānhyrn-ed, -e(n)de *having one horn,* Ps.

+**ānian** *to unite,* BH214⁹. ['*one*' vb.]

ānīdan (ē, ȳ;=īe) *to restrain, repel : force.* ūt a. *expel, drive out.* [nīed]

ānig=ǣnig; **ān-īge**, -igge=ānēage

anīhst (=īe) *last, in the last place,* Wid 126.

āniman⁴ (y) *to take,* GD : *take away or from, deprive of, Mt;* CP. ['*anim*']

āninga=ānunga

āniðrian *to cast down,* Chr675e.

anl-=andl-, onl-; **anlēc**=anlēc

±**ānlǣcan** *to unite,* ÆL : *collect,* ÆL.

ānlaga *acting alone,* WW491²³.

anlang-=andlang-; **ānlāp-** (NG)=ānlīp-

anlēc (on-) m. *respect, regard, Æ.*

ānlegere *consorting with one man,* WW 171¹⁵.

ān-lēp-=ānlī(e)p-

ānlic '*only,*' *unique, Lk : solitary, Ps : catholic : beautiful.* [cp. ǣnlic]

+**anlīcian**=+onl-

ān-līepig, -līpig (Chr), līpe (CP), -līpie (æn-; ē, ȳ) I. adj. *single, separate, solitary, private, individual, special, PPs,BH, MtR.* ['*anlepi,*' '*onlepy*'] II. adv. *alone, only, severally.*

ānlīpnes (on-, ē², ȳ²) f. *loneliness,* BH128²³.

ānlīpum (ē²) *singly,* MtR26²².

ānlȳp-=ānlī(e)p-

+**anmēdan** *to encourage,* AO. [mōd]

ānmēde n. *unanimity, concord,* PPs54¹³.

anmēdla m. *pomp, glory : pride, presumption, arrogance : courage.* [mōd]

anmitta m. *weight, balance, scales,* Gl. [and, mitta]

ānmōd *of one mind, unanimous, El; Æ: steadfast, resolute, eager, bold, brave, fierce, proud,* CP. ['*anmod*'] adv. -līce.

ānmōdnes f. *unity, unanimity,* CP: *steadfastness, resolution,* Lcd3·170²².

ann pres. 3 sg. of unnan.

anna=heonu; **ānne** (AO,CP) v. ān.

ānnes f. *oneness, unity, BH; Æ : agreement, covenant, Chr : solitude, Gu.* ['*annesse*']

ānnihte adv. *one day old,* Lcd.

anoða=anda

ānpæð† m. *narrow path.*

anpolle f. (Æ)=ampella; **anr-**=onr-

ānrǣd *of one mind, unanimous : constant, firm, persevering, resolute, Æ.* ['*anred*']

ānrǣdlic *constant, resolute : undoubting,* Bl13¹³. adv. -līce *unanimously : resolutely, persistently, constantly, earnestly, Æ : definitely, decidedly.*

ānrǣdnes f. *unanimity, agreement : constancy, firmness, diligence, AO; Æ.* ['*anrednesse*']

ānreces (Chr1010cde)=ānstreces

ānrēd-=ānrǣd-; **anribb**=andribb; **ans-**=ands-, ons-, uns-

an-scēatan (Cp) -scēotan (Erf)=onscēotan

ānseld n. *lonely dwelling, hermitage,* Gu 1214.

ānsetl n. *hermitage,* RB135⁹.

ānsetla m. *anchorite, hermit,* GD,RB.

ansīen I. (on-; ē, ī, ȳ) fn. *countenance, face, CP,G : form, figure, presence : view, aspect, sight, thing seen, AO : surface.* ['*onsene*'] II.† f. *lack, want.*

ansīene (on-, ȳ²)† *visible.*

anspel n. *conjecture,* WW382⁵.

anspilde *salutary,* Lcd11b.

ānsprǣce *speaking as one,* PPs40⁷.

ānstandende ptc. *standing alone*, RB9⁷. as sb. *hermit*, Æ.

ānstapa m. *lonely wanderer*, PA 15.

ānstelede *one-stalked, having one stem*, LCD.

ānstīg f. *narrow path? path up a hill?* (GBG) KC.

ānstonde=ānstandende

ānstræc (ǣ?) *resolute, determined*, CP.

ānstreces (ē?) *at one stretch, continuously, continually*, CHR 894A.

ansund *sound, whole, entire, perfect, healthy*, Æ (on-) : *solid*, BF80²⁶.

an-sundnes, -sumnes f. *soundness, wholeness, integrity*.

ānswēge *harmonious, accordant*, WW 129⁴⁴.

ansȳn=ansīen; **ant-**=and-, ont-, unt-

Antecrist m. *Antichrist*. [L.]

antefn m. *antiphon, 'anthem,' BH*; Æ.

antefnere (CM), antemnere (ÆP 154⁶) m. *book of antiphons*.

āntīd (and-?) f. *similar time?* (*i.e.* the corresponding time of a following day) *appropriate time?* (Klb.) B 219.

antifon=antefn

antre f. *radish*, LCD.

ānum *alone, solely*, Æ.

anunder=onunder

anung f. *zeal*, NG.

ānunga (i²) *at once, forthwith* : *quickly, shortly* : *entirely, altogether, throughout, by all means, uninterruptedly*, B : *necessarily, certainly*.

anw-=andw-, onw-, unw-

anwedd n. *security, pledge*, TC 201¹⁶.

ānwīg n. *single combat, duel*, Æ,AO.

ānwīglīce *in single combat*, WW 512²¹.

ānwiht=āwiht

ānwille I. adj. *wilful, obstinate, CP, WW*; Æ. ['onwill'] II. adv. *wilfully, obstinately*.

ānwillīce *obstinately*, CP.

ānwilnes f. *self-will, obstinacy, persistence*, CP. mid ānwilnesse *wantonly, wilfully*.

ānwintre adj. *one year old, yearling*, Ex 12⁵.

ānwīte n. *single fine*, LL 64,31¹.

anwlōh (DAN 585)=onwealg?

ānwuht=āwiht

ānwunung f. *solitary abode*, RB 134¹².

ānwylnes=ānwilnes

+**anwyrdan** *to conspire*, WW 209⁴².

+**anwyrde** *known, acknowledged, confessed*.

anxsum-=angsum-

ānȳdan=ānīdan; **anȳhst**=anīhst

ānyman=āniman; **anȳwan**=onȳwan

apa m. *'ape,' Gl,Lcd*.

āpǣcan *to seduce, lead astray*, LL.

āparian *to discover, apprehend*, G,EC 164¹⁷.

apelder-=apuldor-

āpinsian *to weigh, estimate, ponder, recount*, CP. [L. pensare]

āpinsung f. *weighing*, OEG 1757.

apl=appel

āplantian *to plant*, ÆH.

āplatod *beaten into (metal) plates*, OEG. [v. 'plate']

āpluccian *to pluck, gather*, ÆGR 170¹⁴,BF 198²¹.

apostata m. *apostate*, LL (322¹⁴).

apostol (CHR), apostel m. *messenger, JnL* : *'apostle,' MtR* : *disciple*, ÆH 1⁵²⁰. [L. from Gk.]

apostolhād† m. *apostleship*.

apostolic *apostolic, BH*; Æ. ['apostly']

appel, apple=æppel

Aprelis m. *April*, BF,MEN 56.

āpriccan *to prick*, W 146²¹.

Aprilis (BF 84)=Aprelis

aprotane f. *southernwood, wormwood*, LCD 22a. [L. abrotonum; from Gk.]

apulder, apuldor fm. *apple-tree*, LCD,WW.

apuldorrind f. *bark of apple-tree*, LCD.

apuldortūn (e³) m. *apple-orchard*, WW.

apuldre, apuldur=apulder

āpullian *to pull*, LCD 1·362¹⁰.

āpundrian? *to measure out, requite?* (GK) : *estimate?* (BTac), EL 580.

āpyffan *to exhale, breathe out*, GL.

āpyndrian *to weigh*, HGL 512⁷⁸ (āwynd-?).

āpȳtan *to put out (eyes)*, NC 338.

ār m. I.† *messenger, servant, herald, apostle, angel*. [Got. airus] II. f. *'oar,' Chr,Gn*. III. f. *honour, worth, dignity, glory, respect, reverence, BH,Gen,JnLR,Ph*; AO, CP : *grace, favour, prosperity, benefit, help*, B : *mercy, pity, An* : *landed property, possessions, revenue*, Æ,AO : *ecclesiastical living, benefice* : *ownership*, LL : *privilege*, LL, 76,42². ['are,' 'ore'] IV. n. *'ore,' brass, copper*, Æ,BH,CP,G,Ps; AO. V. (NG)=ǣr

āracsian=ārasian

ārǣcan wv. *to reach, get at, Chr* : *hold forth, reach out*, Æ : *get (a thing for a person)*, ÆGr. ['areach']

ārǣd I. (ē) m. *welfare*, LL 184n. II. *prepared, resolute, determined*, WA 5; GNE 192?

arǣda (Bo 46²²)=aroda? v. arod.

ārǣdan¹ (but usu. wk.) *to appoint, prepare* : *arrange, settle, decide, BH* : *guess, prophesy, interpret, utter, Lk,Bo,Da,CP* : *read, read out, read to (any one)*, CP. ['aread']

ārǣdnes (ē²) f. *condition, stipulation*, BH.

ārǣfan *to set free, unwrap*, WW.

ārǣfn-an, -ian *to carry out, accomplish* : *endure, suffer*, Æ,AO : *keep in mind, ponder*, Æ. [æfnan]

ārǣfniendlīc *endurable, possible*, WW.

ārǣman *to raise, elevate (oneself)*, Æ : (†) *rise, stand up*.

āræpsan (*-ræf-) *to intercept*, GL.

ārǣran *to lift up, raise, set up, create, establish, An,Chr,Jn* : *build, erect, Jn* : *rear (swine)*, LL449 : *spread, disseminate* : *disturb, upset.* ūp ā. *bring up, raise up, exalt, CP.* ['*arear*']

ārǣrend m. *one who arouses*, DHy18¹⁵.

ārǣrnes f. *raising, elevation*, AO.

ārǣsan *to rush*, ÆH140¹³.

āræflan *to unravel, disentangle*, CP.

āräslan *to lay open, search out, test, detect, discover* : *reprove, correct, CP* : *suspect*, BHo256²⁹. ārāsod *skilled*, BF94¹.

ārblǣd n. *oar-blade*, Æ.

arblast m. *cross-bow*, CHR1079D. [*O.Fr.* arbaleste]

arc mf. (also earc, earce) *ark, coffer, chest, box*, Æ. [*L.* arca]

arce I. (æ, e) m. *archiepiscopal pallium*, CHR. II. f. (BF192³³)=arc

arcebiscop (æ¹,e¹,y³,e⁴,eo⁴) m. '*archbishop,*' CP,Chr,KC.

arcebiscopdōm m. *post of archbishop*, CHR 616.

arcebiscophād (eo) m. *post of archbishop*, BH49²³.

arcebiscoprīce n. '*archbishopric,*' *post of archbishop, Chr.*

arcebiscopstōl m. *archiepiscopal see*, CHR.

arcedīacon m. '*archdeacon,*' WW.

arcehād (e) m. *post of archbishop*, ÆH.

arcerīce n. *archbishopric*, CHR1051.

arcestōl (æ¹) m. *archiepiscopal see*, CHR.

ārcræftig *respected, honourable*, DA551.

ārdǣde *merciful*, BL131².

ārdagas mp. *festival days*, WW206³¹.

ardlic=arodlic; āre f.=ār III.

āréaflan *to separate, divide*, Ex290.

āreccan *to spread out, put forth, stretch out: lift up, erect, build up* : *say, relate, declare, speak out, explain, expound, translate, CP,G* : *astonish* : *adorn? deck?* RIM10. ['*arecche*']

ārécelēasian *to be negligent, neglect*, A9·102⁶⁸, VH,WYN66.

ared=arod

ārēd=ārǣd

āreddan=āhreddan

āredian *to make ready, devise, provide, arrange, carry out, CP: find, find one's way, reach : find out, understand.* [rǣde]

ārēfnan=ārǣfnan

ārendan *to tear off*, LCD101a.

ārengan *to make proud, exalt*, A11·117³²? (? ʾarencan, BTs).

āréodian *to redden, blush: put to shame*, RPs69⁴.

ārēosan=āhrēosan; ārēran=ārǣran

ārētan *to cheer, gladden*, Æ. [rot]

arewe=arwe

ārfæst *respected, honest, pious, virtuous*, Æ, CP : *merciful, gracious, compassionate*, Æ : *respectful.*

ārfæstlic *pious*, DR,RWH94¹⁴. adv. -līce.

ārfæstnes f. *virtue, honour, grace, goodness, piety : pity, mercy*, Æ.

ārfæt nap. -fatu, n. *brazen vessel*, Æ.

ārfest=ārfæst

ārful *respected, venerable : favourable, kind, merciful : respectful.* adv. -līce *graciously*, Æ.

arg (NG)=earg; argang=earsgang

ārgeblond=ēargebland

argentille f. *argentilla (plant)*, GL. [*L.*]

ārgeotere m. *brass-founder*, AO54²⁰.

ārgesweorf n. *brass filings*, LCD30b.

ārgeweorc n. *brass-work*, WW398³⁴.

ārgifa m. *giver of benefits*, CRAFT11.

arhlīce=earglīce

ārhwæt *eager for glory*, †CHR937A.

±ārian *to honour, respect*, Æ,CP : *endow : regard, care for, favour, be merciful to, spare, pardon*, Æ; CP. ['*are*']

ārīdan¹ *to ride*, AO118³³.

āriddan=āhreddan

ārl(g)end mf. *benefactor, benefactress*, LCD, W257⁴.

āriht '*aright,*' *properly*, LL.

āriman *to number, count, enumerate*, CP; AO : *relate.* ['*arime*']

ārinnan³ *to run out, pass away*, SOL479.

ārīsan I. (sv¹) *to* '*ARISE,*' *get up*, Æ,CP : *rise: spring from, originate : spring up, ascend.* II.= āræsan I.

ārist=ǣrist

ārlēas *dishonourable, base, impious, wicked*, Æ,CP : *cruel*, JUL4. [*Ger.* ehrlos] adv. -līce Æ.

ārlēasnes f. *wickedness*, BH,Bo.

ārlēast f. *disgraceful deed*, MET.

ārlic I. *honourable : fitting, agreeable, proper*, AO : *delicious.* II.=ǣrlic

ārlīce adv. I. *honourably, becomingly, graciously, kindly, pleasantly, mercifully*, CP. II. (RG)=ǣrlīce

ārloc n. '*oarlock,*' *rowlock*, WW288⁶.

arm=earm

armelu '*harmala,*' *wild rue*, Lcd.

ārmorgen=ǣrmorgen

arn pret. 3 sg. of iernan. arn-=earn-

arod (wk. aroda) *quick, bold, ready*, CP.

ārod pp. of ārian.

arodlic *quick.* adv. -līce *quickly : vigorously*, Æ,CP.

arodnes f. *spirit, boldness*, CP41¹⁷.

arodscipe m. *energy, dexterity*, CP.

ārōm? *copperas*, LCD (v. MLR17·165).

aron (NG) used as pres. pl. of wesan.

ārsāpe f. *verdigris*, Lcd 3·14³¹. [sāpe]
ārscamu f. *shame, modesty*, PPs 68¹⁹.
ārsmiŏ m. *coppersmith*, WW 99³.
ārstæft m. (often in pl.) *support, assistance, kindness, benefit, grace*.
art, arŏ (NG)=eart, pres. 2 sg. of wesan.
ārŏegn m. *servant*, BH 378¹¹.
ārŏing n. *a thing of value*, LkR 21¹.
arud=arod
ārung f. *honour, respect, reverence*, AO : *pardon*.
ārunnen=āurnen, pp. of ārinnan.
arwe (rew-, ruw-) f. '*arrow*,' *An,Chr*.
ārwela v. ēarwela
ār-weorŏ, -weorŏe *honourable, venerable, revering, pious*, CP. adv. -weorŏe.
ārweorŏful (u²) *honourable*, Æ.
±ārweorŏlan (u², y²) *to honour, reverence, worship, extol*.
ārweorŏlic *venerable, honourable*. adv. -līce *reverentially, solemnly, kindly*, Æ. ['*arworthly*']
ārweorŏnes f. *reverence, honour*, CP.
ārweorŏung (y²) f. *honour*, Ps.
ārwesa *respected*, RB 115²⁰.
+ārwierŏan? (y²) *to honour*, LkL 6³⁴ (BTs).
ārwierŏe=ārweorŏ
ārwlŏŏe f. *oar-thong, rowlock*, Æ.
arwunga, arwunge (A)=earwunga
ārwurŏ, -wyrŏ=ārweorŏ
āryd-dan, -dran, -tran *to strip, plunder*, GL.
āryderian *to blush, be ashamed*, BRPs 69⁴.
ārȳpan *to tear off, strip*, RD 76⁷.
ārȳŏ v. ēarȳŏ.
āsadlan *to satiate, surfeit*, MFH 150.
āsæcgan=āsecgan; āsægdnes=onsægednes
āsǣlant *to bind, fetter, ensnare*.
āsǣndan=āsendan
asal, asald (NG)=esol
āsānian *to droop, flag*, Gu 1148, LV 57.
āsāwan⁷ *to sow, sow with*, Æ.
asca (NG) m.=asce; āscacan=āsceacan
āscādan=āscēadan
āscæcan=āsceacan
āscæfen pp. of āsceafan.
āscǣre=æscǣre; āscafan=āsceafan
āscamelic *shameful*, HGl 500.
āscamian (ea) *to feel shame*, Ps,Cr. ['*ashame(d)*']
ascas nap. of æsc.
asobacen (ax-) *baked on ashes*, GD 86³⁰.
asce (æ, cs, x) f. (*burnt*) '*ash*,' Lcd : *dust (of the ground)*, MtL.
āsceacan⁶ (a) *to shake off, remove*, Mt : *depart, flee, desert, forsake*, Æ : *shake, brandish*, Ph. ['*ashake*']
āscēadan⁷ (ā) *to separate, hold aloof or asunder, exclude*, CP : *make clear, cleanse, purify*.
āsceafan (a) *to shave off*, Lcd.

āscealian *to peel off*, WW 398¹⁰.
āsceaman *to be ashamed*, WW 229²⁰.
āscearpan=āscirpan
āscellan=āscillan, āscilian
āscēofan=āscūfan; āsceon-=onscun-
āsceortian=ascortian
āscēotan² *to shoot, shoot out*, Æ,AO : *drop out, fall*, Æ : *lance (surgery)*, ÆL 20⁶³ : *eviscerate*, OEG 46⁴⁷.
āsceppan=āscieppan; āscer-=āscir-
āscian (ācs-, āhs-, āx-) *to* '*ASK*,' *inquire, seek for, demand*, CP : *call, summon* : *examine, observe* : (+) *learn by inquiry, discover, hear of*, CHR : (†) *announce*.
āsciendlic (āx-) *interrogative*, ÆGR 260¹⁴.
āscieppan⁶ *to make, create*, Ex : *appoint, determine, assign*, AO. ['*ashape*']
āscihtan (=y²) *to drive away*, RPs 87¹⁹.
āscildan (=ie) *to protect*, DR.
āscilian *to separate, divide*, v. OEG 1367n.; FM 100.
āscimian *to shine*, Lcd 86b.
āscinan¹ *to flash or shine forth, beam, radiate, be clear*, GD.
āsciran (e, y;=ie) *to cut off, cut away*, Æ.
āscirian (y;=ie) *to cut off, separate, divide, remove*, Æ : *set free, deprive of* : *arrange, destine*.
āscirigendlic (y²) *disjunctive*, ÆGR 259¹⁴.
āscirpan (e, ea, y;=ie) *to sharpen, make acute*, CP.
āscortian (eo) *to become short, fail*, Æ : *pass away, elapse*.
āscrēadian *to prune, lop*, ÆH 2·74¹².
āscrencan *to displace, trip up, cause to stumble*, CP. ['*aschrench*']
āscrepan⁵ *to scrape, clear away*, GL,Lcd.
āscrūtnian (ūdn) *to investigate, examine*, BF.
āscūfan² *to drive out, remove, expel, banish*, Æ : *push (away), give up (to)*.
ascun-=onscun-
±āscung f. '*asking*,' *questioning, inquiring, question*, Bo,Met; Æ,CP.
āscyhhan *to scare away, reject*, RPs 50¹³.
āscylfan *to destroy*, GPH 393⁴⁹.
āscylian, āscyllan=āscilian
āscyndan *to separate, part (from)* : *drive away (from)*, Æ : *take away*, RHy 12¹².
āscyr-=āscir-
āscȳran *to make clear*, Æ. [scīr]
āsealcan (GEN 2167)=āseolcan
āsēarian *to wither, dry up*, Lcd; CP. ['*asear*']
āsēcan *to seek out, select* : *search out, examine, explore* : *seek for, require, ask*, PPs : *search through, penetrate*. ['*aseek*']
āsecgan I. *to say out, express, tell, narrate, explain, announce*, AO. II.=onsecgan
āsecgendlic *utterable*, Æ.
āsēdan (oe) *to satiate*, WW 45⁸. [sǣd]

āsegendnes f. *an offering*, AA 36¹⁷.
āsellan *to give up, hand over, deliver* : *expel, banish.*
āsencan *to sink, immerse*, OEG 829.
āsendan *to send away, send forth, send, give up, Mt*; Æ. ['*asend*']
āsengan (JUL 313)=āsecgan
āseolcan³ *to become slack, remiss, relaxed, weak*, Æ,CP.
āsēon I. sv⁵ *to look upon, behold*, HL 16²⁵⁵.
II. sv¹ *to strain*, LCD.
āseonod *relaxed*, WW 228²⁵. [seonu]
āsēoðan² *to seethe, boil*, CP : *refine, purify* : *examine.*
āsēowan *to sew*, Cp 421 P (io).
āsetnes f. *institute, law*, LL.
asettan=onsettan
āsettan *to set, put, place* : *store up*, Lk 12¹⁹ (MLR 17) : *fix, establish, appoint, set up or in, erect, build, plant, AO,Mt*; Æ : *apply,* PPs 68²⁸ : *transport oneself over, cross (the sea, etc.)* : *take away*, LL 11,12. sīð *or* sīðas ā. *to perform a journey, travel.* ['*aset*']
āsēðan *to affirm, confirm*, Æ. [sōð]
āsīcan I. sv¹ *to sigh*, Sc. II. (=ȳ) *to wean*, CPs 130².
āsiftan *to sift*, LCD 13b.
āsīgan¹ *to sink, sink down, decline, fall down, Chr*; CP. ['*asye*']
āsincan³ *to sink down, fall to pieces*, Æ.
āsingan³ *to sing out, sing, deliver (a speech), compose (verse)*, BH.
āsittan⁵ *to dwell together, settle*, El : *apprehend, fear* : *run aground.* ūt a. *starve out.* ['*asit*']
āslacian *to become slack, decline, diminish*, Æ,CP : *grow tired* : *make slack, loosen, relax, dissolve.*
āslacigendlic *remissive*, ÆGR 228⁵.
āslæccan *to slacken, loosen*, WW.
āslǣcian=āslacian
āslǣpan⁷ (ā) *to slumber, dream* : *be paralysed*, LCD : *be benumbed*, MFH 91⁶.
āslǣwan *to blunt, make dull*, OEG 18b⁶⁵.
āslāpan=āslǣpan
āslāwian *to become sluggish, be torpid*, CP. [slāw]
āslēan⁶ *to strike, beat, cut*, Æ : *erect* : *make way* : *paralyse.* of ā. *strike off, behead, Mt*; AO. ['*aslay*']
āslēpen=āslēopen pret. opt. 3 pl. of āslūpan.
āslīdan¹ *to slide, slip, fall, Ps*; Æ,CP. ['*aslide*']
āslīding f. *slipping*, GPH 388⁶².
āslītan¹ (ȳ) *to slit, cleave, cut off, destroy*, CP.
āslūpan² *to slip off, escape, disappear* (of), Gen. ['*aslip*']
āslȳtan=āslītan

āsmēagan *to consider, examine, investigate, devise, elicit, treat of, think*, Æ : *look for, demand.*
āsmēagung f. *scrutiny, consideration*, APT 3¹⁶.
āsmēan=āsmēagan
±āsmir-ian, -wan *to smear, anoint*, LEV 2⁴.
āsmīðian *to do smith's work, fashion, forge, fabricate*, Æ,WW.
āsmorian *to smother, strangle*, AO,CP.
āsmorung f. *choking, suffocation*, LCD 18a.
āsmūgan=āsmēagan
āsnǣsan (ā²) *to spit, impale, stab*, LL 68,36. ['*asnese*']
asnīðan¹ *to cut off*, LCD.
āsoden (WW 20⁴⁴) pp. of āsēoðan.
āsogen pp. of āsūgan.
āsolcen (pp. of āseolcan) *sluggish, idle, indifferent, dissolute*, Æ.
āsolcennes f. *sleepiness, sloth, laziness, W*; Æ. ['*aswolkeness*']
āsolian *to become dirty*, A 2·374.
āspanan⁶ *to allure, seduce, persuade, urge, insinuate*, AO.
āspannan⁷ *to unbind, unclasp*, GD 214²⁴.
āsparian *to preserve*, GD 159²⁴.
āspeaft (JnL 9⁶)=āspeoft
āspēdan *to survive, escape*, AN 1628.
āspelian *to be substitute for, represent, take the place of*, LL,RB. ā. of *be exempt from*, CHRD.
āspendan *to spend, expend, distribute, squander, consume, AO*; Æ. ['*aspend*']
āspeoft pret. 3 sg. *spit out*, JnR 9⁶. [v. speoft]
āsperian=āspyrian
aspide m. *asp, adder, serpent, Ps*; Æ. ['*aspide*']
āspillan *to destroy*, JnL 12¹⁰.
āspinnan³ *to spin*, WW.
āspirian=āspyrian
āspīwan¹ (ȳ) *to spew up, vomit*, Æ,CP.
āsplǣtan? *to split.* v. ES 49·156.
āspornan *to cast down*, EPs 145⁷. [spurnan]
āsprēadan *to stretch out, extend*, EPs 35¹¹.
āsprecan *to speak out, speak*, PPs.
āsprengan *to cause to spring, fling out*, ÆL 8²¹³.
āsprettan=āspryttan
āsprindlad *ripped up*, LCD 80b.
āspringan³ (y) *to spring up or forth, break forth, spread*, Æ; AO : *arise, originate, be born*, Æ : *dwindle, diminish, fail, cease.* āsprungen *dead.* ['*aspring*']
āspringung f. *failing*, VPs 141⁴.
āspritan=āspryttan
āsproten pp. of āsprūtan.
ā-sprungennes, -sprungnes f. *failing, exhaustion, death* : *eclipse.*

āsprūtan² (=ēo) *to sprout forth,* PPs 140⁹.
āspryngan=āspringan
āspryttan¹ (e, i) *to sprout out, bring forth,* Æ.
āspylian *to wash oneself,* Bo 115⁷.
āspyrgend m. *investigator,* VHy 13²⁵.
āspyrging f. *'adinventio,'* WW 513¹⁵.
āspyrian (e, i) *to track, trace out, investigate, study, explore, discover,* BF,SOLK.
āspȳwan=āspīwan
assa m. *he-ass,* Æ,Mt,Jn; CP. ['ass']
assen f. *she-ass,* WW 108²⁶.
assmyre f. *she-ass,* GEN 32¹⁵.
āst f. *kiln,* WW 185³⁰; A 9·265. ['oast']
āstǣgan *to go up, embark,* MkR 6³².
āstǣlan *to lay to one's charge,* LL (264¹⁵).
āstǣnan¹ *to adorn with precious stones,* W.
āstæppan *to imprint (a footstep),* NC 344¹ (v. MLR 17).
āstærfan (*MtR*)=āstyrfan
āstandan⁶ *to stand up, stand forth, rise up, arise,* B; Æ : *continue, endure,* Lk; CP. ['astand']
āstandennes f. *perseverance,* ÆL 23b²⁷² : *existence, subsistence.*
āstēapan=āstȳpan
āstellan I. *to set forth, set, put, afford, supply, display, appoint,* AO,CP : *set up, establish, confirm, institute, ordain, undertake, start,* AO; Æ : *undergo,* Æ. II. *to fly off, rush.*
āstemnian *to found, build,* BH 4¹⁷.
āstemped *engraved, stamped,* WW 203²⁷.
āstencan *to scatter,* GD 42³³.
āstēop-=āstȳp-
āsteorfan³ *to die,* MH 62²⁷.
āstēp-=āstȳp-; **āster-**=āstyr-
asterion *'asterion,' pellitory,* Lcd 1·164.
āstīflan *to become stiff,* Æ.
āstīfician=āstȳfecian
āstīgan¹ *to proceed, go,* Æ : (usu. w. ūp, niðer, *etc.*) *rise, mount, ascend, descend,* Jn; Æ,CP : *be puffed up,* AO 264⁸. ['astye']
āstīgend m. *rider,* ARHy 4¹.
āstigian *to ascend, mount,* MkL,WW 93²¹.
āstīgnes (æ¹) f. *ascent,* EPs 103⁴.
āstihtan *to determine on, decree,* CHR 998.
āstihting (OEG)=ātyhting
āstillian *to still, quiet,* RWH 75³⁰.
āstingan³ *to bore out, pierce out,* CHR : *stab.*
āstintan=āstyntan; **āstirian**=āstyrian
āstīðian *to become hard, dry up, wither* : *grow up? become powerful?* TC 203²⁰.
āstondnes=āstandennes
āstrǣlian *to cast forth, hurl,* RPs 75⁹.
āstreccan *to stretch out, stretch forth, extend, lay low,* Æ : *prostrate oneself, bow down,* CP. ['astretch']
āstregdan *to sprinkle,* GD,LL.
āstregdnes? f. *sprinkling,* DR.
āstrenged (*made strong*), *malleable,* WW.

āstrīenan† (ēo, ȳ) *to beget.*
āstrogden pp. of āstregdan.
āstrowenes f. *length,* HGL 443.
āstrȳnan=āstrīenan
āstundian *to take upon oneself,* Æ.
āstȳfecian *to suppress, eradicate,* CP.
āstyllan=āstellan
āstyltan *to be astonished,* LkLR.
āstyntan (i) *to blunt, repress, restrain, stop, overcome,* Gl. ['astint']
āstȳpan (ē, ēa, ēo) *to deprive, bereave,* GD.
āstȳpte *orphans.* [stēop]
āstȳp(ed)nes (ē², ēo²) f. *privation, bereavement,* GD,WW.
āstȳran *to guide, control,* AS 9¹³.
āstyrfan (æ, e;=ie) *to kill, destroy,* Cr,Mt. ['asterve']
āstyrian *to stir up, excite, move, move forward, raise,* JnMk; Æ : *be roused, become angry,* Æ. āstyred weorðan *be or become anxious,* Æ. ['astir']
-āstyriendlic v. un-ā.
āstyrigend m. *a stirrer-up,* GPH 393⁷⁸.
āstyrred *starry,* Sc.
āstyrung f. *motion,* LCD.
ā-sūcan², -sūgan *to suck, suck out, drain: consume,* WW 501³³ (ōsogen).
ā-sundran, -sundron=onsundran
āsundrian=āsyndrian
āsūrian *to be or become sour,* LCD,WW.
āswǣman *to roam, wander about* : *pine, grieve,* Æ : *be ashamed,* LPs 24²⁰.
āswǣrn-=āswarn-
āswǣtan *to burst out in perspiration,* MH 20¹³.
āswāmian *to die away,* GEN 376 : *cease.*
āswāpan⁷ (but pp. āswōpen) *to sweep away, remove, clean,* CP.
āswārcan *to languish,* LPs 38¹².
āswārcnian *to confound,* BSPs 70²⁴.
āswārnian *to be confounded,* Ps.
āswārnung f. *shame, confusion,* LPs 43¹⁶.
āswaðian *to investigate,* OEG 5¹¹.
āsweartian *to turn livid, become ashy or black,* CP.
āswebban† *to lull, soothe, set at rest* : *put to death, destroy,* Jud. ['asweve']
āswefecian *to extirpate,* WW.
āswellan³ *to swell,* CP.
āsweltan³ *to die,* CHR.
āswencan *to afflict,* DR.
āswengan *to swing off, shake off, cast forth.* ā. on *cast upon,* RPs 21¹¹.
āsweorcan³ *to droop,* Jos 2¹¹.
āsweorfan³ *to file off, polish,* GPH.
āswēpa=æswǣpa
āswerian⁶ *to swear,* PPs 131¹¹.
āswic-=æswic-
āswīcan¹ *to desert, abandon, betray, deceive,* Mt : *offend, irritate, provoke.* ['aswike']

āswīfan[1] *to wander, stray*, WW.
āswind=āeswind
āswindan[3] *to become weak, shrink, fade away, perish, decay, dissolve*, Bo; Æ,CP. ['*aswind*']
āswingan[3] *to scourge*, DR42[6].
āswōgan[7] *to cover over, choke*, CP411[17].
āsworettan *to sigh, grieve*, GD.
āswornian (NC271)=āswarnian
āswundennes f. *idleness*, BH160[25].
āsynderlīc *remote*, OEG2514.
±āsynd-ran, -rian (u[2]) *to separate, divide, disjoin, sever*, Soul; Æ,CP : *distinguish, except*. ['*asunder*']
āsyndrung f. *division*, WW.
at=æt; ātǣfran (CP467[19])=ātīefran
ātǣsan *to wear out, injure, strike, smite*, Æ : *wound*, CP296[18].
atāwian=ætīewan
āte (ǣ) f. '*oats*,' Lcd : *wild oats, tares*, Gl,WW.
āteallan=ātellan; ātēfran=ātīefran
ategār=ætgār; atel=atol
ātellan *to reckon up, count*, Bo; AO. ā. wið *balance against* : *tell, enumerate*, CP : *explain, interpret*. ['*atell*']
ātemian *to tame, subdue, render quiet*, CP.
ātendan *to set on fire, kindle, inflame*, Chr : *trouble, perplex*, BF94[9]. ['*atend*']
ātending f. *incentive*, Sc221[17].
ātēon[2] *to draw up, out, off or from, remove, pull out, lead out, draw*, B,BH; AO,CP. ūp ā. *draw up, move away* : *protract*, Æ : *move, journey, roam* : *deal with, dispose of, apply, use*, Mt; Æ,CP. ['*atee*']
ātēorian *to fail, become exhausted, weary, cease*, Ps; Æ : *be defective*, ÆGr. ['*atire*']
ātēori(g)endlīc *transitory, perishable*, Æ : *failing* : *defective*, ÆGr.
ātēorodnes f. *cessation, exhaustion*, Æ(3[495]); BPs118[53].
ātēorung f. *failing, weariness*, Æ.
ātēowan=ōðīewan; āter=ātor
āteran[4] *to tear away*, CP359[20].
āteriendlīc=āteoriendlīc
āterima (ētr-) *oat-bran*, Lcd 3·292'.
ātertānum dp. *with poisoned twigs or poison-stripes?* (or ? -tēarum *with poison-drops*) B1460.
āteshwōn adv. *at all*, CM987. [āwiht]
athēd (Gl)=æthȳd
ātīdrian *to grow weak*, GD59[26] (ydd).
ātīefran (ǣ, ē, ī, ȳ) *to draw, depict*, CP.
ātīewan=ōðīewan; ātiht-=ātyht-
ātillan *to touch, reach*, GenC11[4].
ātimbr-an, -ian *to erect, build*, AO,CP.
ātimplian *to provide with spikes*, NC271.
ātīwan=ōðīewan
ātland *oat-land*, EC208'.

ātlēag m. *oat-field*, EC448[9].
atol I. (e[2], u[3]) *dire, terrible, ugly, deformed, repulsive, unchaste*, B. ['*atel*'] II.† n. *horror, evil*.
+atolhīwian *to disfigure, make hideous*, WW220[31].
atolian *to disfigure*, WW220[26].
atolic, atollic *dire, terrible, deformed, repulsive*, Æ. adv. -līce.
ātor, āt(to)r, (ǣ) n. *poison, venom*, Lcd; AO, CP : *gall*, Gl. ['*atter*']
ātorbǣre *poisonous*, ÆH1·72[22].
ātorberende *poisonous, venomous*, Lcd,W.
ātorcoppe (ǣ) f. *spider*, Lcd; LPs38[12] (-loppe). ['*attercop*']
ātorcrǣft (āttor-) m. *art of poisoning*, W.
ātorcyn (ǣ) n. *poison*, Sol219.
ātordrinca m. *poisonous draught*, MH.
ātorgeblǣd n. *swelling caused by poison*, Lcd162b.
ātorlāðe f. *plant used as antidote to poison, betonica?* Lcd,WW. ['*atterlothe*']
ātorlīc *poison-like, bitter*, WW. ['*atterlich*']
ātorsceaða† m. *poisonous enemy*.
ātorspere n. *poisoned spear*, RD18[9].
ātorðīgen (ātt-) f. *taking of poison*, Lcd1·4[5].
ātr=ātor; ātr-=ādr-
ātrahtnian *to treat, discuss*, BF72,142.
ātredan[5] *to extract, extort*, LL.
ātreddan *to search out, examine*, PPs.
ātrendlian *to roll*, Met5[17]. [v. '*trendle*']
ātres gs. of ātor.
atrum n. *ink*, A13·28[15]. [L. atramentum]
ātter, āttor=ātor
attrum=atrum
atul=atol; ātur=ātor
ātwēonian *to cause doubt*, BF182[8].
ātyddrian=ātīdrian
ātȳdran *to beget, create*, El1279. [tūdor]
ātȳfran=ātīefran
ātyhtan (i) *to entice, allure, incite* : *be attentive* : *produce*, RD51[3] : *stretch, extend, turn*.
ātyhting (i) f. *intention, aim* : *instigation*, OEG2[304].
ātymbran=ātimbran
ātȳnan I. *to shut off, exclude*, PPs,WW. [tūn] II.=ontȳnan
ātyndan=ātendan; ātȳrian=ātēorian
atȳwan=ōðīewan
āð m. '*oath*,' (*judicial*) *swearing*, B,Chr,Mt; AO : *fine for an unsuccessful oath*, KC (v. BTac).
āð-=ōð-
aðamans m. *adamant*, CP271[2]. [L.]
āðbryce m. *perjury*, W164[7].
āðecgan *to take food, consume?* Lcd57a : *oppress?* RD1[3,7] (Tupper).
āðegehāt=āðgehāt
āðegen *distended (with food)*, WW.

āðencan *to think out, devise, contrive, invent,* AO : *intend,* B.
āðenenes f. *extension,* VHy 7⁴⁸.
ā-ðennan, -ðenian *to stretch out, extend, draw out, expand,* AO : *apply (the mind),* CP : *prostrate.*
āðenung f. *stretching out, distension,* LCD 71b : '*stratum,*' ALRPs 131⁸.
āðēodan=āðīedan
āðēostrian (ē, īe, ī) *to become dark, obscured, eclipsed, Bo;* CP,VPs. ['*athester*']
āðer=āhwæðer
āðerscan *to thresh out,* ÆL 31¹²¹⁷.
āðēstrian=aðēostrian; āðēwan=āðȳwan
āðexe f. *lizard,* Cp 1182.
āðfultum m. *confirmation (confirmers) of an oath,* LL.
āðgehāt (āðe-) n. *promise on oath, oath,* WW.
āðiddan (=y) *to thrust, push,* OEG 50⁸.
āðīedan (ēo, ȳ) *to separate,* CP.
āðierran *to clean,* CP.
āðiestrian (CP)=āðēostrian
āðindan⁸ *to swell, puff up, inflate, increase,* CP : *melt, pass away.* (cp. ðindan)
āðindung f. *swelling,* LCD 93a.
ā-ðīstrian, -ðīsðrigan (CP)=āðēostrian
āðl (BH,VPs)=ādl
āðloga m. *perjurer,* CR 165.
āðol=ādl
āðolian *to hold out, endure, suffer,* Æ.
āðolware mp. *citizens,* GnE 201.
āðor=āhwæðer
āðracian *to dread : frighten.* [=onðracian]
āðrǣstan *to twist out, wrest out,* GL.
āðrāwan⁷ *to curl, twist, twine,* Æ.
āðrēatian *to dissuade from,* CP 293¹⁰ : *chide, rebuke,* GenC 37¹⁰.
āðrēotan² (pers. and impers.) *to tire of, weary, be tiresome to, displease, disgust,* Æ,AO,CP.
āðrescan=aðerscan
āðrīetan (ȳ) *to weary,* Æ,AO.
āðringan⁸ *to crowd or press out : rush forth, break out.* ūt ā. *emboss.*
āðriostrian (MtR 24²⁹)=āðēostrian
āðristlan *to be bold, presume,* GD 70³⁰.
āðrotennes f. *wearisomeness,* WW 409²².
āðrotsum *irksome,* WW 510¹².
āðrōwian *to suffer,* LCD 68b.
āðroxen pp. of āðerscan.
āðrunten (pp. of *āðrintan) *swollen,* RD 38².
(or? āðrūten)
āðrūten? (pp. of *āðrūtan) *swollen,* LCD.
āðryccan *to press, oppress,* DR.
āðrȳn *to rob? drive out?* GL (ES 43·331)
ā-ðrysemian, -ðrysman (AO) *to suffocate, smother.* ['*athrysm*']
āðrytnes (ǣ¹,e²) f. *weariness,* DHy. [ðrēotan]
āðstæf m. *oath,* CPs 104⁹.

āðswara m?=āðswaru
āðswaring=āðswerung
āðswaru f. *oath-swearing, oath,* Æ.
āðswerian? *to vow with an oath,* WW 387⁹.
āðswerung f. *oath-swearing,* CHR,RSPs 104⁹.
āðswyrd (ǣ¹, eo²) n. *oath-swearing,* EJVPs 104⁹; B 2064.
āðum m. *son-in-law,* Æ; AO : *brother-in-law.* ['*odam*']
āðumswerian mp. *son-in-law and father-in-law,* B 84.
āðundennes f. *swelling, tumour,* LCD : *contumacy,* WW 87¹⁷.
āðwǣnan *to diminish, soften,* LCD.
āðwēan⁶ *to wash, wash off, cleanse, baptize, anoint,* Æ,CP.
āðwedd n. *promise on oath,* WW 115¹⁶.
āðweran⁴ *to stir up, churn,* LCD.
āðwīnan *to vanish,* NC 338.
āðwītan¹ *to disappoint,* SPs 131¹¹.
āðwyrðe *worthy of credit.* v. LL 2·376.
āðȳan=āðȳwan
āðȳdan=āðīedan
āðȳlgian *to bear up,* ARSPs.
āðȳn=āðȳwan
āðȳnnian (i) *to make thin, reduce,* DHy 8¹⁰.
āðȳstrian (Æ)=āðēostrian
āðȳtan I. *to sound, blow (a horn),* DD 109. II. *to expel,* WW 19¹².
āðȳwan (ē) *to drive away,* AO : *press out or into, squeeze out.*
āuht=āwiht; āuðer=āhwæðer
āw=ǣ; āwa=ā
āwacan⁶ (on-) *to awake,* Æ : *arise, originate, spring forth, be born.* ['*awake(n)*']
āwacian *to awake,* Æ.
āwācian *to grow weak, decline, fall, belittle,* Æ,CP : *fall away, lapse, desist from, abstain,* Æ : *mollify, appease,* MFH 142⁶.
āwacnian=āwæcnian; āwæc-āwǣcan *to weaken,* BHB 250⁴.
āwæc-nian, -nan (on-; a, e) *to awaken, revive,* Æ : *arise, originate, spring from,* AO. ['*awake(n)*']
āwǣgan *to deceive : destroy, annul, make nugatory,* Æ.
āwǣlan *to harass, afflict,* NG.
āwǣled pp. of āwilwan.
āwæltan=āwyltan
āwæmmian=āwemman
āwænd-=āwend-, onwend-
āwænian=āwenian
āwærd pp. of āwierdan.
āwærged=āwierged
āwærlan *to avoid,* DR 39¹³.
āwǣscan=āwascan; āwǣstan=āwēstan
āwandian *to fear, hesitate,* ÆGr 162².
āwanian *to diminish, lessen,* DR,KC.

āwannian *to become livid or black and blue,* GD 20³² (v. NC 332).

āwansian *to diminish,* KC 4·243⁶.

āwǣr=āhwǣr

āwǣrnian *to be confounded,* APs. (=āswarnian)

āwascan⁶ (æ) *to wash, bathe, immerse,* LCD.

āweallan⁷ *to well up, flow out, break forth, issue, swarm,* CP : *be hot, burn.*

āweardian *to guard, defend,* AO 202²⁴ (v.l.).

āweaxan⁶ *to grow, grow up, arise, come forth,* CP.

āweb=ōweb; **āwec-**=āwæc-

āweccan *to awake, rouse, incite, excite,* Mk, Lk; Æ,CP : *raise up, beget.* ['awecche']

āwecenes (æ) f. *incitement,* GD 199⁷.

āwecgan *to undermine, shake, move,* Æ.

āwēdan *to be or become mad, rage,* AO; Æ. ['awede'; wōd]

āwefan⁵ *to weave, weave together,* Æ.

āweg (=on-) '*away,*' *forth, out,* Chr,Mt; CP.

āwegan⁵ *to lift up, carry away,* Ex : *weigh, weigh out,* Æ : *estimate, consider : distinguish.* ['aweigh']

āwegāworpnes f. *abortion,* LL (154').

āwegcuman⁴ *to escape,* AO 102¹⁰.

āwegēade *went away,* JnL 4⁵⁰ [v. '*away*'; ēode]

āwegflēon² *to fly or flee away,* OEG 2169.

āweggān *to go away,* BH 326¹⁰.

āweggewītan¹ *to depart,* AO 74²⁶.

āweggewītenes f. *departure,* Æ : *aberration (of mind),* JPs 115¹¹.

āwegweard *coming to a close,* RWH 133³⁷.

āwehtnes f. *arousing,* BH 422²⁰.

awel (o², u²) m. *hook, fork,* GL.

āwellan=āwillan

āwemman (æ²) *to disfigure, corrupt,* BF,HL.

āwemmendnes f. *corruption,* LPs 15¹⁰.

āwēnan *to consider,* RBL 4¹² (āhw-).

āwendan (=on-) *to avert, turn aside, remove, upset,* Ps : *change, exchange, alter, pervert,* Æ; CP : *translate,* Æ,CP : *turn from, go, depart,* Ps; AO : *return : subdue.* ['awend']

āwended-=āwendend-

āwendendlic *that can be changed, changeable,* Æ.

āwendendlicnes f. *mutability,* Æ.

āwende(n)dnes f. *change, alteration,* Æ.

āwendennes f. *change,* OEG 191.

āwending f. *subversion, change,* ES 39·322, Sc 188⁴.

āwenian *to disaccustom, wean,* BH,Ps.

āwēodian *to root out, extirpate,* LL,W.

āweorpan³ *to throw, throw away, cast down, cast out, cast aside, degrade, depose,* Mt; Æ, AO,CP. āworpen *divorced, rejected, destroyed, apostate.* of, ūt ā. *to throw out.* ['awarp']

āweorpnes=āworpennes

āweorðan³ *to pass away, vanish, become worthless,* Mt : (NG)=+weorðan. ['aworth']

āweosung f. '*subsistentia,*' WW 516⁴.

āwer=āhwǣr

āwerdan=āwierdan

āwerde (æ²) m. *worthless fellow,* WW 111²⁹.

āwerg-=āwierg-, āweri-, āwyrig-

āwerian I. *to defend,* AO : *hinder, restrain,* CHR : *protect, cover, surround, enclose : ward off from oneself, spurn from oneself.* II. *to wear, wear out (clothes),* RB.

āwerpan=āweorpan

āwescnes (VPs)=āewiscnes

āwēstan *to lay waste, destroy,* AO; Æ. ['awest']

āwēst(ed)nes f. *desolation, destruction,* LCD.

āwēstend m. *devastator,* W 200¹⁹.

āwexen=āweaxen pp. of āweaxan.

+āwian=+īewan

āwīdlian *to profane, defile,* LL,OEG.

āwierdan (e, y) *to spoil, injure, hurt, corrupt, seduce, destroy, kill,* CP.

āwierding (y) f. *corruption, blemish,* HGL 421⁵⁷.

āwierdnes (y) f. *hurt, harm, destruction,* Æ : *defilement.*

āwierg-an, -ian (æ, e, i, y) I. *to curse, damn, denounce, outlaw,* Æ,Mt,CP,VPs. sē āwier(ge)da *fiend, devil.* ['awarie'] II. (i, y) *to strangle, suffocate,* AO; Æ. ['aworry']. For compounds see āwyrg-.

āwiht I. n. '*aught,*' *anything, something,* Ps. II. adv. *at all, by any means.* tō āhte *at all.* III. *good, of value,* Æ.

āwildian *to become wild,* Æ,LL.

āwillan (e, y;=ie) *to bring into commotion, boil,* Æ.

āwille (WW)=ānwille II.

awil-wan, -wian (æ;=ie) *to roll* (tr.).

āwindan³ *to wind, bend, plait : slip from, withdraw, escape,* CP : *become relaxed? cramped?* (BTac), W 148³.

āwindwian (y) *to winnow, blow away, disperse,* Ps.

āwinnan³ *to labour, strive,* JnL : *gain, overcome, endure,* Da. ['awin']

āwirgan=āwiergan

āwirgnes=āwyrgednes; **āwisc-**=æwisc-

āwisnian *to become dry, wither,* LkL.

āwistlian *to hiss,* W 147³¹. [hwistlian]

āwītegian *to prophesy,* VH 9.

āwlacian *to be or become lukewarm,* LCD,RB.

āwlǣtan *to befoul, make loathsome, defile,* Æ.

āwlancian *to exult, to be proud,* OEG 1159.

āwlencan *to make proud, enrich,* DR 59¹.

āwlyspian *to '*lisp,*'* MLN 4·279 (NC 338).

āwo=ā (āwa)

āwoffian *to become proud, insolent : rave, be delirious, insane*, Æ.
āwōgian *to woo*, Æ.
āwōh (*crookedly*), *wrongfully, unjustly*, LL. [=on wōh]
āwol=āwel; **āwolfigan**=āwoffian
āwonian (DR)=āwanian; **āwor**=āfor
āwordennes f. *degeneration*, WW 87²¹.
āworpednes (EPs 21⁷)=āworpennes
āworpenlic *worthy of condemnation*, CP. adv. -lice *vilely*.
āworp(en)nes f. *rejection, what is cast away : exposure* (*of children*) : *a casting out*, BH 482¹¹.
āwrǣnan *to make wanton*, LCD 54b.
āwrǣnsian, *to wax wanton*, A 30·128.
āwrǣstan *to wrest from, extort*, WW 397³⁷.
āwrecan⁵ *to thrust out, drive away : strike, pierce : utter, sing, relate, recite : punish, avenge*, Chr,LL. ['*awreak*']
āwreccan *to arouse, awake*, Æ.
āwregennes=onwrigenes
āwrēon¹,² (=on-) *to disclose, discover, reveal : cover*, NG.
āwreðian *to support, uphold*, CP.
āwrīdian *to originate, spring from*, A 11·2.
āwrigenes=onwrigennes
āwringan³ *to wring, squeeze out*, Æ : *express*, Bf 100¹⁰.
āwrit n. *a writing*, DR (io²).
āwrītan *to write, write down, describe, compose*, CP; Æ,AO,CHR : *mark, inscribe, draw, carve, copy*, Æ. ['*awrite*']
āwrīðan¹ I. *to turn, wind, bind up, bind, wreathe.* II.=onwrīðan
āwrygenes=onwrigenes
āwðer, āwðor=āhwæðer
āwuht=āwiht; **āwul**=āwel
āwuldrian *to glorify*, DR,JnL.
āwundrian *to wonder, wonder at, admire*, G,GD.
āwunian *to remain, continue*, BH.
āwunigende ptc. *continual*, BL 109².
āwurt-walian, -warian=āwyrtwalian
āwurðan=āweorðan; **āwyht**=āwiht
āwylian (Æ)=āwilwian
āwyllan=āwillan; **āwylm**=æwielm
āwyltan (æ;=ie) *to roll, roll away*, Æ : *harass*, DR.
āwyndwian=āwindwian
āwyrcan *to do*, Bo 149¹⁶,LL.
āwyrd- (Æ)=āwierd-; **āwyrdla**=æfwyrdla
āwyrg-=āwierg-, āwyrig-
āwyrgedlic (NIC 490²⁰) *detestable, shameful, abominable.*
āwyrgednes (o³) f. *wickedness*, Æ : *curse, cursing.* [wearg]
āwyrgendlic (CAS 34²²)=āwyrgedlic
āwyrigende *accursed*, ÆL 18³²⁴.

āwyrigung f. *a curse*, ÆL 15¹¹⁵.
āwyrn (MEN 101)=āhwergen
āwyrpan (=ie) *to recover* (*from illness*), ÆL 20⁶⁵ (v.l.), A 41·109⁸⁵.
āwyrtlian=āwyrtwalian
āwyrttruman *to root out*, MFH 161
āwyrtwalian *to root out*, CP.
āwyrðung f. *stain, aspersion*, HGL 421.
ax-=asc-, ox-; **āx-**=āsc-; **axe**=æcs
āȳdan (OEG 8¹⁰⁶)=āīdan; **āȳdlian**=āīdlian
āyldan *to delay*, GD 21²². [ieldan]
āyppan '*experiri*' (*aperire ?*) DR 70⁵.
āyrnan=āiernan
āȳtan *to drive out*, OEG 4080. [ūt]
āyttan=āettan

B

bā nafn. and am. of bēgen *both*.
bac- v. bæc.
bacan⁶ *to '*bake*,'* Æ.
bacas nap. of bæc II.
bacca m. *ridge*, BC (bacce f. Mdf).
bacu nap. of bæc I.
bād I. f. *forced contribution, impost, pledge*, LL : *expectation.* [bīdan] II. (±) pret. 3 sg. of bīdan.
-bādere v. nied-b.
bādian *to take a pledge or fine*, LL.
bæ-=ba-, be-, bea-
bæc I. n. '*back*,' Bo,MtL,Ps; CP. on b. *backwards, behind, '*aback*.*' on b. settan, lǣtan *to neglect*. ofer b. *backwards, back*. under b. *behind, backwards, back*. ofer b. būgan *to turn back, flee.* clǣne b. habban *to be straightforward, honest*, LL 128,5. II. mfn. *beck, brook*, KC. [v. ES 29·411,GBG and '*bache*']
+bæc n. *bakemeats*, GEN 40¹⁷ : *baking*, ÆGR 176.
bæcbord n. *left side of a ship, larboard*, AO.
bæce I. *back parts*, WW 160¹⁰. II.=bæc II.
bǣce=bēce
bǣcen=bēacen-
bæcere I. m. '*baker*,' WW. II.=bæzere
bæcering m. *gridiron*, WW.
bæcern n. *bakery, bakehouse*, Æ.
bæcestre fm. *baker*, Æ. ['*baxter*']
bæceð, bæcð, pres. 3 sg. of bacan.
bæcistre=bæcestre
bæcling(e), bæclinga (on) adv. *backwards, behind*, JnR: *back to back*, RWH 86²⁷. on b. gewend *having one's back turned*, Æ. ['*backlings*']
bæcslitol adj. *backbiting*, W 72¹⁶.
bæcðearm m. *rectum*; pl. *bowels, entrails*, Æ.
+bæcu np. *back parts*, LPs.
bæd I. pret. 3 sg. of biddan. II.=bed

bædan *to defile*, EPs 78[1].
bǣdan *to urge on, impel*, CP : *solicit, require : afflict, oppress.*
bædd=bedd
bæddæg=bæðdæg
bǣddel m. *effeminate person, hermaphrodite,* WW. [v. '*bad*']
bæddryda=bedrida
bǣdend m. *inciter*, WW.
bǣdewēg n. *drinking vessel*, GU,BH 370[30]. [wǣge]
bǣdling m. *effeminate person, WW.* ['*badling*']
bǣdon pret. pl. of biddan.
bædryda=bedrida; bædzere=bæzere
bæfta, bæftan (*Mt*; Æ)=beæftan
bæftansittende *idle*, ÆGR 52[2].
-bæftian (ea[1], a[2]) v. hand-b.
bǣg=bēag; bǣgen=bēgen; bǣh=bēag
bǣl n. *fire, flame, B : funeral pyre, bonfire, B.* ['*bale*']
bǣlblys, -blyse, -blæse† f. '*blaze*' *of a fire, funeral blaze, Gu.*
bǣlc I.† m. *pride, arrogance.* II. m. *covering, cloud?* Ex 73.
bǣlcan *to cry out*, MOD 28.
+bǣlcan *to root up*, CPs 79[14].
bǣldan=bieldan
bǣldo (CP), bǣldu=bieldo
bǣlegsa m. *terror of fire*, Ex 121.
bǣlfȳr n. '*bale-fire*,' *funeral or sacrificial fire, B.*
bǣlg, bǣlig (NG)=belg
bǣlstede m. *place of a funeral pile*, B 3097.
bǣl-ōracu f. (ds. -ōræce) *violence of fire*, PH 270.
bǣlwudu m. *wood for a funeral pile*, B 3112.
bǣlwylm m. *flames of a funeral fire*, JUL 336.
bǣm=bām (v. bēgen); bænd=bend
+bǣne n. *bones*, GD 86[11]n.
bǣnen *made of bone*, Æ,LCD.
bær I. gsmn. bares '*bare*,' *uncovered, Bo : naked, unclothed, Gen.* II. pret. 3 sg. of beran.
bǣr I. f. '*bier*,' *El*; Æ : *handbarrow, litter, bed, BH, JnR.* [beran] II. *a pasture*, KC. III.=bār (AB 14·233).
+bǣran *to behave, conduct oneself, CP : fare,* B 2824 : '*exultare*,' PPs. ['*i-bere*']
bǣrbǣre *barbarous*, EPs 113[1].
bǣrdisc m. *tray*, WW. [beran]
bǣre=bere pres. 1 sing. of beran.
bǣre-=bere-
-bǣre suffix (from beran); forms derivatives from substantives, as in cwealmbǣre. [*Ger.* -bar]
bǣre=bǣr
+bǣre n. *manner, behaviour, El* : *gesture, cry : action.* ['*i-bere*'; beran]

bærfōt *barefoot*, LL,W.
bærhtm (A)=bearhtm
bærlic I. adj. *of barley*, KC 6·79[10]. II. *open, clear, public.* adv. -līce.
bǣrmann m. *bearer, porter*, Æ. ['*berman*']
bǣrn=bereærn
±bǣrnan (e) *to cause to burn, kindle, burn, consume, Sol*; AO,VPs. [v. '*burn*']
bǣrnelāc (e) n. *burnt-offering*, PPs.
bǣrnes=bǣrnnes
+bǣrnes f. *bearing, manner*, WW 529[13].
bǣrnett (y[2]) n. *burning, burn, cautery*, Æ : *arson*, LL.
bǣrning f. *burning : burnt offering*, BPs 50[18].
bǣrnīsen n. *branding-iron*, OEG 7[113].
bǣrnnes, bǣrnes f. *burning*, BH.
bǣro=bearu; bǣron pret. pl. of beran.
bǣrs m. *a fish, perch*, GL. [*Ger.* barsch]
+bǣrscipe (LkL)=+bēorscipe
bǣrst pret. 3 sg. of berstan.
bǣrstl-=brastl-
bǣrsynnig (eo[2]) m. *notorious sinner, publican*, NG.
+bǣru v. +bǣre and BTs; bǣrwe=bearwe
bæst m? n? *inner bark of trees*, '*bast*,' Æ, OET.
bæsten *made of bast*, JUD 15[18].
bæstere=bæzere
bǣtan I. *to bait, hunt, worry*, Æ. [v. '*bait*'] II. *to beat against the wind?* (BT) : *make fast?* (Sedgef.=III), Bo 144[81]. III.(±) *to furnish with a bit or bridle, saddle, curb.*
+bǣte(l) n. *bit, bridle*, pl. *trappings*, BH.
bǣtera, bǣttra=betera
bǣting (ē) f. *beating (against the wind?)* (BTs), *cable* (Sedgef.), Bo 144[81].
bæð n. nap. baðu '*bath*,' *action of bathing, Lcd* : *laver, AO,Bl* : *liquid in which one bathes, medicinal spring, BH,Jul,KC.* ganotes b. *gannet's bath (i.e. the sea)*, B.
bæð(c)ere=bæzere
Bǣðdæg m. *Epiphany (day of Christ's baptism)* DR 2[1].
bǣðern n. *bath-house*, NC 272.
bæðfæt n. *bathing-tub*, LL 455,17.
bæðhūs n. *bathing-place*, Æ.
bæðian=baðian
bæðsealf f. *bathing-salve*, LCD.
bæðstede m., bæðstōw f. *bathing-place*, WW.
bæðweg† m. *sea*, AN,EX.
bæzere m. *baptizer, baptist*, G. [*L.* baptista]
bal-=beal-
balc, balca m. *bank, ridge, Bo,WW.* ['*balk*']
ballīce (NG)=bealdlīce
bal-sam, -samum n. '*balsam*,' *balm, Lcd, WW.*
balsmēðe f. *bergamot*, LCD 3·90'.

balsminte f. *spear-mint, water-mint,* WW 136⁶.

bal-zam n., **-zame** f., **-zamum** (AA) n.= balsam

bām dmfn. of bēgen.

+ban=+bann

bān n. *'bone,' tusk,* Æ,Gl,Jn; AO,CP : *the bone of a limb.*

+bān *bones,* GD86¹¹.

bana (o) m. *killer, slayer, murderer,* B,Chr : *the devil* : f. *murderess,* A10·155. ['bane']

bānbeorge f. *leg-armour, greaves,* WW.

bānbryce m. *fracture of a bone,* LCD.

bāncofa† m. *the bodily frame.*

ban-coða m., **-coðu** f. *baneful disease.*

band pret. 3 sg. of bindan.

bānece *in pain in the thigh,* LCD.

bān-fæt† n. nap. **-fatu** *body, corpse.*

bānfāg *adorned with bonework* (deer antlers?), B781.

bangār (o) m. *murdering spear,* B2031.

bāngeberg n.=bānbeorge

bāngebrec n. *fracture of a bone,* AN1439.

bānhelm m. *helmet, shield?* FIN30 (v. also bārhelm).

bānhring† m. *vertebra, joint.*

bānhūs† n. *body, chest, breast.* bānhūses weard *the mind,* Ex523.

bānlēas *boneless,* RD46³.

bānloca† m. *joint, limb.*

+bann n. *proclamation, summons, command,* Æ,CP : *indiction* (*cycle of* 15 *years*).

±bannan⁷ *to summon, command, proclaim.* b. ūt *call out,* CHR.

bannend m. *summoner,* GL.

+banngēar (o¹, -ē²) n. *indiction, year of the indiction,* Ct.

bannuc m. *a bit, small piece,* ZDA; OEG. [v. LF123 and 'bannock']

bānrift (y) n. *leggings, leg-armour, greaves,* GL,WW (-rist).

bānsealf f. *salve for pain in the bones,* LCD 138b.

bānsele m. (*bone-house*), *body,* DOM102.

bānwærc m. *pain in the bones,* WW200¹².

banweorc n. *homicide, manslaughter,* LL 244'.

bānwyrt f. *violet? small knapweed?* LCD.

bār (ǣ) m. *'boar,'* ÆGr.

bara, bare wk. forms of bær adj.

barda m. *beaked ship,* WW289¹².

bārhelm m. *helmet with the image of a boar?* FIN30 (v. also bānhelm).

barian *to lay bare, uncover* : *depopulate,* W310⁵. [bær I.]

barice=barricge; **barm**=bearm

barn I. pret. 3 sg. of biernan. II.=bearn

barricge '*braugina,*' '*baruina,*' WW.

bārspere n. *boar-spear,* BF,GL.

bārsprēot m. *boar-spear* (Swt).

barstlung=brastlung

barð m. *barque,* '*dromo,*' WW181²⁹.

barða=barda

baru napn. of bær adj.

basilisca (ea¹) m. *basilisk,* EPPs90¹².

basing m. *cloak,* Æ.

±bāsnian *to await, expect,* AN,GEN.

bāsnung f. *expectation,* DR.

bastard m. *bastard,* CHR1066D. [OFr.]

basu (e, ea, eo) gsmn. baswes *purple, scarlet, crimson.* baswa stān *topaz.*

basuhǣwen *purple,* WW430⁷.

+baswian *to stain red,* ES33·177.

bāt I. fm. *'boat,' ship, vessel,* CHR. II. pret. 3 sg. of bītan.

batian *to heal* : *grow better* : *improve in health,* CP173²⁰.

bātswegen m. *boatman,* EC254⁵.

batt *bat, cudgel, club,* OEG18b18.

bātwā=būtū

bātweard m. *ship's watchman,* B1900.

bað=bæð

±baðian *to wash, lave, 'bathe'* (tr. and intr.), *give baths* (*to others*), LCD; Æ,AO.

baðu v. bæð.

be- prefix. 1. specializes the meaning of a tr. vb. (as in behōn, besettan). 2. makes an intr. vb. transitive (beswīcan, beðencan). 3. is privative (bedǣlan, belīðan). 4. does not alter the meaning (becuman).

be prep. w. d. and instr. (of place) 'BY,' *near, in, on, upon, with, along, at, to* : (of time) *in, about, by, before, while, during* : *for, because of, in consideration of, by, by means of, through, in conformity with or imitation of, in comparison with,* Æ,AO : *about, concerning, in reference to* : *on penalty of.* be āwihte *in any respect.* be sumum dǣle *partly.* be ānfealdum *single.* be twifealdum *twofold.* be eallum *altogether.* be fullan *in full, fully, perfectly* : *in excess.* be ðām mǣstan *at the most.* be ðām (ðān) ðe *because, as, according as, how.* be norðan, sūðan *to the north, south of...,* AO. be æftan=beæftan

±bēacen (ē) n. *'beacon,' sign, token, phenomenon, portent, apparition,* JNL : *standard, banner,* B : *audible signal,* CHRD32²⁶.

bēacenfȳr n. *beacon fire, lighthouse,* OET 180⁷ (ē).

bēacenstān m. *stone on which to light a beacon fire,* WW.

bēacn- v. also bīcn-.

+bēacnian *to make signs, indicate,* B,BO.

+bēacnung f. '*categoria,*' WW382³².

bead=bed

bēad I. pret. 3 sg. of bēodan. II. (NG)=bēod

beado=beadu; beadowig=bǣdewēg
beadu† f. gds. beaduwe, beadowe *war, battle, fighting, strife*.
beaducāf *bold in battle*, RD 1¹¹.
beaducræft m. *skill in war*, AN 219.
beaducræftig† *warlike*.
beaducwealm m. *violent death*, AN 1704.
beadufolm f. *battle-hand*, B 990.
beadugrīma m. *war-mask, helmet*, B 2257.
beaduhrægl n. *coat of mail*, B 552.
beadulāc† n. *war-play, battle*.
beadulēoma m. *(battle-light), sword*, B 1523.
beadumægen n. *battle-strength, force*, Ex 329.
beadumēce m. *battle-sword*, B 1454.
beadurǣs m. *rush of battle*, MA 111.
beadurinc† m. *warrior, soldier*.
beadurōf† *strong in battle, renowned in war*.
beadurūn f. *secret of a quarrel*, B 501.
beaduscearp *keen in battle (sword)*, B 2704.
beaduscrūd n. *coat of mail*, B 453; 2660?
beadusearo n. *war equipment*, Ex 572.
beaduserce f. *coat of mail*, B 2755.
beaduðrēat m. *war-band, army*, EL 31.
beaduwǣpen† n. *weapon of war*, RD.
beaduwang† m. *battlefield*, AN 413.
beaduweorc† n. *warlike operation*.
beaduwrǣd (o²) m. *fighting troop*, LCD 125b.
beæftan I. adv. *after, hereafter, afterwards, behind*, AO; CP (bi-). ['*baft*'] II. prep. w. d. *after, behind*, Chr,Mt. ['*baft*']
beǣwnian *to join in marriage, marry*, CHR 1052 D. [ǣw]
beaftan *to strike (the hands) together? lament?* MtL 11¹⁷. ['*beft*']
bēag I. (ǣ, ē) m. *ring (as ornament or as money), coil, bracelet, collar, crown, garland*, Æ,WW; CP. ['*bee*'; būgan] II. pret. 3 sg. of būgan.
bēag-gifa, -gyfa† m. *ring-giver, lord, king, generous chief*.
bēaggifu (bēah-)† f. *ring-giving*.
bēaghord (h)† n. *ring-hoard*, B.
bēaghroden† *diademed, adorned with rings or armlets*.
bēaghyrne (h) f. *corner of the eye*, WW 156⁴¹.
±bēagian (ē) *to crown*, Ps.
bēag-sel n., -sele† m. *hall in which rings are distributed*.
bēagðegu (h) f. *receiving of rings*, B 2176.
bēagwīse n. *round shape*, GD 343¹⁵.
bēagwriða (h) m. *armlet*, B 2018.
bēah I.=bēag. II. pret. 3 sg. of būgan.
beāh-=bēag-
beāhsian *to ask advice*, BL 199'; 205'.
bealanīð=bealunīð
bealcan, bealcettan *to 'belch,' utter, bring up, splutter out, give forth, emit*, Mod,Ps; Æ : *come forth*.

beald (a) '*bold,*' *brave, confident, strong*, Ps; AO,CP : *presumptuous, impudent*, CP.
bealde adv. *boldly, courageously, confidently* : *without hesitation, immediately*.
bealdian *to be bold*, B 2177. ['*bold*']
bealdlīce (a¹) '*boldly,*' Jul.
bealdnes (a) f. *boldness*, MH 6²⁵.
bealdor† m. *lord, master, hero*.
bealdwyrde *bold of speech*, Æ.
beale-=bealu-
bealg, bealh pret. 3 sg. of belgan.
beallucas mp. '*testiculi,*' WW. ['*ballock*']
bealo, bealo-=bealu, bealu-
bealu I.† gs. b(e)al(u)wes n. '*bale,*' *harm, injury, destruction, ruin, evil, mischief*, Chr,Ps,Sat : *wickedness, malice* : *a noxious thing*, Æ. II. adj. *baleful, deadly, dangerous, wicked, evil*.
bealubend m. *pernicious bond*, W 178².
bealubenn f. *mortal wound*, Ex 238.
bealublonden *pernicious*, GN E 198.
bealuclomm mf. *oppressive bond*, HELL 65.
bealucræft m. *magic art*, MET 26⁷⁵.
bealucwealm m. *violent death*, B 2265.
bealudǣd† f. *evil deed, sin*.
bealuful '*baleful,*' *dire, wicked, cruel*, Cr.
bealufūs *prone to sin*, RIM 50.
bealu-hycgende, -hȳdig *meditating mischief*, B.
bealuinwit n. *deceit, treachery*, PPs 54²⁴.
bealulēas† *harmless, innocent*, Chr,Gn. ['*baleless*']
bealunīð† m. *malice, wickedness*.
bealurāp m. *oppressive fetter*, CR 365.
bealusearu n. *wicked machination*, JUL 473.
bealusīð† m. *hurt, adversity* : *death*.
bealusorg f. *dire sorrow*, PH 409.
bealuspell n. *baleful message*, Ex 510.
bealuðonc m. *evil thought*, JUL 469.
bealuwes, bealwes v. bealu.
bēam I. m. *tree*, KC,Rd : '*beam,*' *rafter, piece of wood*, Chr,Mt; CP,Mdf : *cross, gallows*, Cr : (†) *ship*, Rd : *column, pillar* : *sunbeam*, Chr,Ps : *metal girder*, AO. II. (NG)=bȳme
bēamere (Mt)=bȳmere
bēamsceadu† f. *shade of a tree*.
bēamtelg m. *ink or dye from wood*, RD 27⁹.
bēamweg m. *road made with logs*, BC 1·417'.
bēamwer m. *wooden weir?* BC 2·242'.
bēan (īe) f. '*bean,*' *pea, legume*, Lcd; Mdf.
bēan-belgas (LkL), -coddas (Lk) mp. *bean-pods, husks or cods*. [v. '*belly,*' '*cod*']
bēanbroð v. bēonbroð.
bēancynn n. *a kind of bean*, WW 205³.
bēanen adj. *of beans*, LCD 1·282⁹.
bēanlēag f. *land where beans grow*, KC 5·265. [v. '*bean*']

bēanmelu n. _bean-meal_, Lcd 31b.
bēansǣd n. _bean-seed._
bēansc(e)alu f. _bean-pod_, OEG 608.
bēanset n. _bean-plot_, KC 1·315′.
bēar (NG)=bēor
bearce (æ) f. _barking_, Gl.
beard m. '_beard_,' VPs; Æ.
+bearded _having a beard_, GD 279[14].
beardlēas _beardless, youthful_, ÆGR,Gl.
bearg I. (e) m. '_barrow_' _pig, hog_, Mt,Rd.
II. pret. 3 sg. of beorgan.
bearh=bearg I and II; bearht=beorht
bearhtm I. (br-, e, eo, y) m. _brightness,
flash_ : _twinkling (of an eye), instant._ adv.
bearhtme _instantly._ II.=breahtm
bearhtmhwæt _swift as the twinkling of an
eye, momentary_, Az 107 (br-).
bearhtmhwīl f. _moment, twinkling of an eye,
point of time_, GD.
bearm I. (a) m. _lap, bosom, breast, Lk_ :
middle, inside : (†) _possession._ II. _emotion,
excitement?_ PPs 118. III.=beorma
bearm-clāð, -hrægl n. _apron_, WW 127[2]. [v.
'_cloth_']
bearmtēag _yeast-box_, LL 455,17.
bearn I. (a, eo) n. _child, son, descendant, offspring, issue_, B,Mt,TC; AO,CP. lēoda b.
children of men. mid bearne _pregnant_, LL.
['_bairn_'] II.=barn pret. 3 sg. of biernan.
III. pret. 3 sg. of beiernan. IV.=bereærn
bearnan (N)=biernan
bearncennicge _mother_, DR.
bearn-ēaca (Æ,CP), -ēacen (CP), -ēacnod,
-ēacnigende (Æ) _pregnant._
bearnende (NG)=biernende ptc. of biernan.
bearngebyrda fp. _child-bearing_, B 946.
bearngestrēon n. _procreation of children_,
Rd 21[37].
bearnlēas _childless_, Æ.
bearnlēast (ē[2]) f. _childlessness_, Bo 24[10].
bearnlufe _affection (for a child), adoption_,
BH 454[11].
bearn-myrðra m., -myrðre f. _murderer or
murderess of a child_, W.
bearntēam m. _offspring, posterity, AO_ : _pro-
creation of children_, HL. ['_bairnteam_']
bearo=bearu
bears=bærs; bēarscipe=bēorscipe
±bearu gs. bearwes m. _grove, wood, BH_;
CP; Mdf. [berwe]
bearug=bearg
bearunæs m. _woody shore_, Rd 58[5].
bearwe (æ) f. _basket, wheelbarrow_, LL 455,15.
bearwes v. bearu; beasu=basu I.
+bēat n. _scourging_, Æ,H 1·406[8].
±bēatan[7] pret. bēot and (rarely) beoft (ES
38·28) _to_ '_beat_,' _pound, strike, thrust, dash_,
Bo,Bl,Ps : _hurt, injure_, Da 265 : _tramp,
tread, B._

bēatere m. _beater, boxer_, Æ.
bēaw m. _gad-fly_, WW.
bebaðian _to bathe, wash_ (tr. intr. and refl.),
Ph. ['_bebathe_']
bebēodan[2] _to offer, commit, entrust_, CP :
bid, enjoin, instruct, command, require,
Æ,Lk; AO,CP : _announce, proclaim._
['_bibede_']
bebēodend m. _commander, master_, CP.
bebēodendlic _imperative_, ÆGR.
bebeorgan[3] _to be on one's guard, defend,
protect, B._ ['_bibergh_']
beber (WW 11[14])=befer
beberan[4] _to carry to, supply with_, LL 4,18.
bebindan[3] _to bind about, bind fast_, Æ.
be-birgan, -birigan=bebyrgan
bebītan (bi-) _to bite_, Cp 251M.
beblāwan _to blow upon_, Lcd,LPs.
bebod n. _command, injunction, order, decree_,
Mt; Æ,AO,CP. ðā bebodu _the (ten) com-
mandments._
beboddæg m. _appointed day_, A 11·102[67].
bebodian wv.=bebēodan
bebodrǣden f. _command, authority_, LPs
118[110].
bebrǣdan _to spread, cover_, MH 44[19].
bebrecan[4] _to break to pieces_, Sol 295.
bebregdan[3] _to pretend_, LkL 20[20].
bebrūcan[2] _to practise_, Æ : _consume (food)_,
GD.
bebūgan[2] _to flow round, surround, enclose_ :
turn from, shun, avoid, El : _reach, extend._
['_bibugh_']
bebycgan _to sell_, LRG,MH.
bebycgung f. _selling_, WW.
bebyrdan _to fringe, border_, WW 375[41].
be-byrgan (AO) -byrian I. _to raise a mound
to, bury, inter_, Æ. ['_bebury_'] II.=be-
beorgan
be-byrgednes, -byrig(ed)nes f. _burial, bury-
ing._
bebyrgung f. _burial_, ÆL,GD.
bebyrig-=bebyrg-
bebyrwan (?=-bȳwan, BTs) _to rub over_,
GD 318[8].
bec=bæc; bēc v. bōc.
becæflan _to ornament_, WW 137[22].
+bēcan _to make over in writing, grant by
charter_, EC 202′.
becarcian _to be anxious (about)_, MFB 99.
becc=bæc II.
becca m. _pick, mattock_, WW; Æ. ['_beck_';
v. also IF 24 and LF 140]
beccen m. _buyer_, WW (KGL) 75[36]. [=byc-
gend]
bece m.=bæc II.
bēce (oe) f. '_beech_' _(tree)_, Gl. (v. also
bōc.)
becēapian[1] _to sell_, Æ : _buy_, Æ.

becefed=becæfed, pp. of becæfian.
becen I. '*beechen,*' *made of beechwood*, Lcd, WW. **II.** (NG)=bēacen
beceorfan³ *to cut, cut off, separate*, Æ. hēafde b. *to behead.*
beceorian *to murmur at, complain of*, CHR, RB.
becēowan² *to gnaw in pieces*, SOUL 111.
becēpan I. *to take notice of*, LPs. **II.**= becȳpan
beceð pres. 3 sg. of bacan.
becidan *to complain of*, ÆH 2·470⁶.
becierran (e, y) *to turn, turn round, pass by, avoid*, Met; CP : *wind, twist : pervert*, Chr : *give up, betray*. ['*bicharre*']
beclǣman *to plaster over, poultice*, LCD.
beclǣnsian *to cleanse*, SPs 18¹⁴.
beclemman *to bind, enclose*, SOL 71.
beclencan *to hold fast*, LPs 104¹⁸.
beclēsung=beclȳsung
beclingan³ *enclose, bind*, EL 696.
beclippan (CP)=beclyppan
beclisung=beclȳsung
beclypian (eo;=i) *to accuse, challenge, sue at law*, LL. ['*beclepe*']
beclyppan *to clasp, embrace*, Mk : *encompass, hold*, Ps; Æ. ['*beclip*']
beclypping f. *embrace*, OEG.
beclȳsan *to close, shut up, enclose, confine, imprison*, Lk; Æ. [clūse; '*beclose*']
beclȳsung f. *enclosure, cell*, OEG 1522 : *period, syllogism*, OEG.
bēcn=bēac(e)n; **bēcn-**=bi(e)cn-
becnāwan⁷ *to know*, RB 38¹⁷.
becnedan⁵ *to knead up*, LCD 93a.
bēcnydlic=bīcnendlic
becnyttan *to knit, tie, bind*, Æ,CP.
becol-a? m., -e? f. *spectre*, WW 530²³.
bōc-rǣde, -rǣding, -trēow=bōc-rǣding, -trēow
becrēopan² *to creep into, crawl*, AO : *be hidden*, Æ.
becst pres. 2 sg. of bacan.
becuman⁴ *to come, approach, arrive, enter, meet with, fall in with*, AO,B; Æ,CP : *happen, befall, fall in* with, Æ,Bo : (impers.) *befit*, MkL 14³¹. ['*become*']
bēcun (NG)=bēacen
becwelan⁴ *to die*, LL 400,1.
becweðan⁵ *to say : speak to, address, exhort*, A,Ps : *admonish, blame : 'bequeath,' leave by will*, KC; Æ.
becweðere m. *interpreter, translator*, EHy 16 (proem.).
becwyddod *bespoken, deposited*, WW 115³⁹.
becwylman? *to torment* (BTs).
becyme m. *event, result*, BH 372¹⁹.
becȳpan (ē;=ie) *to sell*, G,RB.
becyrran=becierran

±**bed I.** n. *prayer, supplication*, Æ,CP : *religious ordinance, service*, Æ. **II.**=bedd. **III.**=bæd pret. 3 sg. of biddan.
bedǣlan *to deprive, strip, bereave of, rob*, Æ : *release, free from*. ['*bedeal*']
bēdan=bēodan; +**bēdan**=+bǣdan
bedbǣr (ē) f. *portable bed*, NG.
+**bedbigen** f. *payment for prayers*, LL 258,51. [bycgan]
bedbolster m. *bolster, pillow*, WW 124²⁰. ['*bedbolster*']
bedbūr n. *bed-chamber*, HGL 481.
±**bedcleofa** (e, i, y) m. *bed-chamber*, Ps : *lair*.
bed-cofa m., -cofe f. *bed-chamber*, GL,HL.
bedd n. '*bed*,' *couch, resting-place*, Jn,KC; CP : *garden-bed, plot*, LCD; Mdf.
+**bedda** mf. *bedfellow, consort, wife, husband*, B; Æ. ['*i-bedde*']
±**beddagas** mpl. *Rogation days*, ÆH.
beddclāð m. *bed-covering*; pl. *bed-clothes*, HL.
beddolyfa=bedcleofa
+**bedde** (KC 3·50³)=+bedda
beddgemāna m. *cohabitation*, CP 99²⁵.
beddian *to make a 'bed,'* WW : *provide one with a bed*, LL.
bedding f. '*bedding,' bed-covering*, LPs, WW; Æ : *bed.*
bedd-rēaf, -reda=bed-rēaf, -reda
beddrest† f. *bed*, WW 154¹.
beddstōw f. *bed*, BH 410¹².
-**bede** v. ēað-b.
be-dēaglian (-dēahl) *to conceal*, GU,KGL.
bedecian *to beg*, Æ,CP.
bedēglian=bediglian; **bedēlan**=bedǣlan
bedelfan³ *to dig round*, Lk : *bury*, Rood; AO. ['*bedelve*']
bedelfung f. *digging round*, WW 149¹¹.
beden pp. of biddan.
be-dēpan (VPs), -deppan=bedipan, -dyppan
bedfelt mn. *bed-covering*, RB 91¹⁶.
bedgerid n. *food in an ant's nest*, LCD 118a.
+**bedgiht** f. *evening*, WW 117⁸.
±**bedhūs** n. *chapel, oratory*, Æ.
+**bedian** *to pray, worship*, BH 408²⁹.
bedician *to surround with a dyke, embank, fortify*, CHR 1016 E.
bedidrian=bedydrian
be-diglian (-dihl-; ē, ēo, īo;=īe) *to conceal, hide, obscure, keep secret*, Æ : *be concealed, lie hid.*
bedigling f. *secret place*, RPs 80⁸.
beding=bedding
bediolan (K)=bedīglian
bedipan (ē, ȳ) *to dip, immerse : anoint*, CPs 140⁵.
+**bedmann** m. *worshipper, priest*, Bo,LL.
bedol=bedul
bedōn *to shut*, PPs 147². ['*bedo*']

±**bedrǣden** f. *prayer, intercession*, Æ.
bedragan v. pp. bedrōg.
bedrēaf n. *bed-clothes, bedding*, Ct,RB.
bedreda (i, y) m. (and adj.) *bedridden (man)*, Æ. ['*bedrid*']
bedrōf=bedrēaf
bedrēosan² *to overcome, deceive?* GEN 528, 823 : *deprive of, bereave, despoil.*
bedrest=beddrest; **bedrida**=bedreda
bedrīfan¹ *to drive, beat, strike, assail*, AO : *follow up, pursue : surround, cover.*
bedrincan³ *to drink up, absorb*, LCD.
bedrīp n. *compulsory service rendered to a landowner at harvest time*, LL. [v. '*bedrip*']
bedrōg *beguiled*, GEN 602.
bedrūgian *to dry up*, LCD 1·336⁴.
bedryda=bedreda
bedrȳpan *to moisten*, GPH 391¹⁸.
+**bedscipe**† m. *cohabitation, wedlock*, GEN.
+**bedsealm** m. *precatory psalm*, LCD 51a, 138a.
+**bedstōw** f. *place of prayer, oratory*, BH, BL.
bedstrēaw n. *straw for bedding*, ÆL 31⁵⁷².
bedtīd f. *bed-time*, WW 176².
+**bedtīd** *time of prayer*, MH 126¹⁸.
bed-ōegn, -ōēn m. *chamber-servant, chamberlain*, WW.
bedu f. *asking, prayer*, CP. [*Goth.* bida]
bedūfan² *immerse, submerge, drown*, Æ. ['*bedove*']
bedul *suppliant*, WW 180¹².
bedwāhrift n. *bed-curtain*, Ct.
bedydrian *to conceal from*, Æ : *deceive*, Æ. ['*bedidder*']
bedȳfan *to immerse*, GD 73²⁴; CPs 68¹⁶.
bedȳglan=bedīglian; **bedȳpan**=bedīpan
be-dyppan (e), *to dip, immerse*, Æ,Mt. ['*bedip*']
bedyrnan *to conceal*, Æ. [dierne]
beēastan *to the east of*, Chr; AO. ['*beeast*']
beēastannorōan *to the north-east of*, AO.
beebbian *to leave aground by the ebb tide, strand*, CHR 897A.
beefesian *to cut off the hair*, ÆL 33⁸⁴.
beegōan *to harrow*, BYH 74¹¹.
beerf-=beyrf-; **befǣdman**=befǣōman
befǣlon pret. 3 pl. of befēolan.
befǣstan *to fasten, fix, ground, establish, make safe, put in safe keeping*, Æ,CP : *apply, utilize : commend, entrust to*, Æ, CP.
befǣstnian (ea) *to fix*, Æ : *pledge, betroth.*
befǣttian *to fatten, anoint*, LPs 140⁵.
befǣō-man, -mian *to encircle*, Æ.
befaran⁶ *to go, go round or among, traverse, encompass, surround*, AO : *come upon, surprise, catch*, LL 230,13¹.

befealdan⁷ *to fold, roll up, envelop, clasp, surround, involve, cover*, Æ; CP : *attach.* ['*befold*']
befealdian (intr.) *to roll up*, MFH 117¹¹.
befealh pret. of befēolan
befeallan I. (sv⁷) *to fall*, CP,Mt; Æ : *deprive of, bereave of : fall to, be assigned to* : '*befall*,' ÆGR. II.=befyllan
befeastnian (NG)=befæstan
befēgan *to join*, ÆL 23⁴⁸⁵.
befelgan=befylgan; **befellan**=befyllan
befelōrǣd (HGL 489)=hefeldōrǣd
befeohtan³ *to take by fighting*, Rd 4³². ['*befight*']
befēolan³ *to put away, bury : deliver, grant, consign, entrust to*, Ps : *betake oneself to, apply oneself, devote oneself to, persist, persevere*, CP : *importune : put up with, be pleased with*. ['*bifele*']
befēon *to deprive of property*, OEG 3157.
befer (eo¹, y¹, o²) m. '*beaver*,' ÆGr; Mdf.
beferan *to surround*, Æ : *come upon, overtake, pass by : go about : fall among*, NG.
beficlan *to deceive*, LL (320').
befīlan, befilgan=befylan, befylgan
beflod (HGL 480) pp. of befēon.
beflēan⁶ *to peel, skin, flay*, WW. beflagen flǣsc *entrails*. ['*beflay*']
beflēogan³ *to fly upon*, BH. ['*befly*']
beflēon³ (w. a.) *to flee from, flee, escape, avoid*, Ps; CP. ['*beflee*']
beflōwan⁷ *to flow round, over*, Wif. ['*beflow*']
befōn⁷ *to surround, clasp, include, envelop, encase, clothe*, Bl; Æ,AO,CP : *comprehend, seize, attach (at law), lay hold of, catch, ensnare*, Gen : *contain, receive, conceive : explain*, CP. wordum b. *tell, relate.* on b. *have to do with, engage in.* ['*befong*']
befor=befer
beforan I. prep. a. (w. d.) (local) '*before*,' *in front of, in the presence of*, Æ,Bl,G; CP : (temporal) *before, prior to, sooner than*, G. β. (w. a.) (local) *before, in front*, B : (temporal) *before, formerly, in former times, earlier, sooner : at hand, openly*, An.
beforhtian *to dread*, Æ 23b⁸²⁵.
befōtian *to cut off one's feet*, Æ 25¹¹⁷.
befrēogan *to free, liberate*, Ps.
be-frīnan, -frignan³ *to question, ask, learn*, Æ.
befrīnung f. *inquiry*, OEG 2309.
befrȳnan=befrīnan; **beftan**=beæftan
befullan *entirely, completely, perfectly*, CP 5³⁰.
befȳlan (ī) *to befoul, defile*, Lcd; Æ. ['*befile*']
befylgan *to follow after, pursue, persevere with*, LCD.

befyllan I. *to fell, lay low, strike down,* GEN : *take by killing, bereave,* GEN. [feallan] **II.** *to fill up,* BH 64⁵n (Schipper). [full]

bēg=bēag

bēga gmfn. of bēgen.

begalan⁶ *to sing incantations over, enchant,* Lcd; Æ. ['*bigale*']

begān *to go over, traverse,* Æ : *get to, come by, fall into* : *go to, visit, care for, cultivate, Lcd;* AO : *inhabit, occupy, Æ,BH,Lcd : surround, beset, overrun, Chr,Job: practise, do, engage in, perform, attend to, be diligent about,* Æ,CP : *honour, serve, worship : profess.* on borh b. *pledge oneself,* CP. ūtan b. *besiege, Chr.* ['*bego*']

bēgan=bīegan, bēagian

begang (i¹, o²) mn. *way, course, circuit, extent : district, region : business, undertaking, practice, exercise, service, reverence, worship : cultivation,* GD. [=bīgeng]

beganga=bīgenga; **begangan**=begān

be-gangnes, -geongnes (DR), -gannes (WW), f. '*calendæ,*' *celebration.*

begangol (bigeong-) m.? *cultivator,* LkR : *worship,* DR.

begbēam m. *bramble, thorn-bush,* G,WW.

bēge=bēgen; **bēgea**=bēga

bēgean=bīegan

begēat I. m. *attainment,* Æ : *acquisitions, property,* Æ. **II.** pret. 3 sg. of begēotan.

begeg-=begeng-; **begēm-**=begīm-

begēmen (KGL)=begīmen

bēgen nm. (but where one thing is m. and the other f. or n., the nom. is bā, bū), nf. bā, nn. bū; gmfn. bēg(e)a, bēgra; dmfn. bæm, bām; am. bū; af. bā; an. bū *both, El,G,Lcd.* v. also būtū. ['*bo*']

begenga m. *cultivator,* MtR.

bege(n)gnes (i¹) f. *application, study,* GD, WW.

begēomerian *to lament,* W 75¹⁵.

begeondan (AO,CP), begeonde, -geonan prep. w. a. d.; and adv. '*beyond,*' *on the other side,* Æ,*Chr,J*n.

begeong-=begang-; **begēotan**=begietan

begēotan² *to pour over or upon, anoint, infuse, flood (with), sprinkle, cover with fluid, Chr;* Æ. ['*bigeten*']

beger n. *berry,* GL.

beget=begeat pret. 3 sg. of begietan.

begeten pp. of (1) begēotan, (2) begietan.

bēgian=bēagian

begiellan³ (i¹, e²) *to scream, screech, Seaf* 24. [v. '*yell*']

begietan⁵ (e, i, y) *to get, find, acquire, attain, receive, take, seize,* AO,CP : *happen : beget.*

begietend (e) m. *one who gets,* WW 214²⁵.

begīman (ȳ;=īe) *to look after, take care of : do service, attend : take heed, observe.*

begīmen f. *attention, observation,* GL,LCD.

begīmend (ȳ) m. *guide, ruler,* Sc.

begīming (ȳ) f. *invention, device : observance : care, regard,* OEG.

begīnan¹ *to open the mouth wide, swallow,* GD,RD.

beginnan³ *to* '*begin,*' Æ; AO,CP : *attempt, undertake,* Æ : *attack,* AO.

begīr=beger; **begīrdan**=begyrdan

begitan (AO,CP)=begietan

begleddian *to befoul, pollute,* Æ : *stain, dye,* Æ.

beglīdan¹ *to leave, desert,* PPs 56¹.

begnagan⁶ *to gnaw,* MH 118¹⁰.

begneorð? *attentive,* BH 370² (?=*becneord, BT).

begnīdan¹ *to rub thoroughly,* LCD 50a.

begnornian *to mourn for,* B 3179.

begong=begang

bēgra gmfn. of bēgen.

begrǣtan⁶=begrētan

begrafan⁶ *to bury, El* 835. ['*begrave*']

begrētan *to lament,* PPs 77⁶³.

begrindan³† *to grind, polish, sharpen,* RD 27⁶ : *deprive of, rob,* GEN 1521.

begrīpan¹ *to grip, seize : chide, Ps.* ['*begripe*']

begriwen ptc. *steeped in,* Æ.

begroren *overwhelmed,* SAT 52.

begrornian=begnornian

begrynian *to ensnare, entrap,* WW 92¹⁰. [grin]

begyldan *to adorn with gold,* CVPs 44¹⁰.

begylpan (=ie) *to boast, exult,* B 2007?

begȳm-=begīm-

begyrdan *to gird, clothe, Ps;* Æ : *surround, fortify,* BH; CP. ['*begird*']

begytan=begietan; **bēh**=bēag, bēah

behabban *to include, hold, surround, comprehend, contain,* AO,CP : *detain, withhold.*

behādian *to unfrock (a priest),* LL.

behæfednes f. *restraint, temperance,* WW 504¹⁰.

behæpsian *to fasten a door,* ÆL 31²¹⁴.

behǣs f. *vow,* CHR 1093. [v. '*behest*']

behǣttian *to scalp,* Æ : *make bald,* OEG.

behaldan=behealdan

behamelian *to mutilate,* ÆL 25¹²⁷, MH 216²⁴.

behammen '*clavatus,*' (of shoe) *patched* (BT), *studded with nails* (Napier), GD 37¹³.

behāt n. *promise, vow, Lk;* Æ : *threat,* LCD. ['*behote*']

behātan⁷ (often w. d. pers.) *to promise, vow, pledge oneself,* Æ; CP : *threaten.* ['*behight**']

behātland n. *promised land,* GD 204¹².

behāwian *to see clearly, take care, consider, Mt.* ['*bihowe*']

behēafdian *to 'behead,' Mt*; Æ,AO.
behēafdung f. *beheading,* Æ.
behēafodlic *capital (punishment),* OEG 4042.
behealdan⁷ *to hold, have, occupy, possess,* Gen : *guard, preserve,* CP : *contain, belong,* KC : *keep, observe, consider, Bl,Ps*; AO, CP : '*behold,' look at, gaze on, observe, see,* Æ,CP : *signify,* Æ : *avail, effect : take care, beware, be cautious,* CP : *restrain : act, behave.*
behealdend m. *beholder, spectator,* BH 26²³.
behealdennes f. *observance,* DR : *continence,* DR.
behealdnes f. *regard, observation,* Æ.
behēawan⁷ *to cut, chip, chop, beat,* CP : *cut off from, deprive of.*
behēdan (KGL)=behȳdan
be-hēfe, -hēf(e)lic *suitable, proper, necessary,* G; Æ. ['*biheve*']
behēfnes f. *convenience, utility,* GL.
behēfð(u) f. *want, need,* RWH 134,136
behegian *to hedge round,* MLR 17·166.
behelan⁴ *to cover over, hide,* AA,BH,BL.
beheldan=behealdan
behelian *to cover over, conceal, bury,* CP.
behelmian *to cover over,* SOL 104.
behēofian *to lament,* LPs,Sc.
be-heonan, -heonon prep. (w. d.) and adv. *on this side of, close by.*
be-hēot, -hēt pret. 3 sg. of behātan.
behicgan=behycgan; **behīdan**=behȳdan
behīdiglīce=behȳdiglīce
behīenan (CHR)=beheonan
behildan *to depart,* EPs 138¹⁹.
behindan I. prep. (w. d., a.), adv. '*behind,' after, Chr,Leas,LG,Met*; CP.
be-hinon, -hionan=beheonan
behīring=behȳrung
behīwian *to dissimulate,* RBL 16⁷.
behlæmman=behlemman
behlænan† *to surround.*
behlēapan⁷ *to leap upon, settle on, fix upon, devote oneself to,* CP.
behlehhan=behlyhhan
behlemman† *to dash together.*
behlēotan *to assign by lot,* MLR 17·166.
behlīdan¹ *to close, cover over,* Æ,AO.
behliden=beliden pp. of belīðan.
behligan¹ *to accuse,* RWH 4¹.
behlyhhan⁶ (e;=ie)† *to deride, exult over,* Gu. ['*bilaugh*']
behlȳðan *to rob, deprive of,* RD 15¹⁰.
behōf n. *behoof, profit : need,* OEG 27⁸⁴.
behōfian (abs. and w. g.) *to have need of, require, want, BH,Lcd*; Æ,CP : (impers.) *it behoves, concerns, belongs, is needful or necessary, MtL,Jn.* ['*behove*']
behōflic *necessary, MkL.* ['*behovely*']

behogadnes f. *practice,* WW 427⁸⁷.
behogian *to care for,* RB. ['*bihogien*']
behogod *careful, prudent,* DR. adv. -līce.
behōn⁷ *to hang round,* CP. ['*behung*']
behorsian *to deprive of horses,* CHR.
behrēosan² *to fall : cover, shelter.* pp. behroren *divested of.*
behrēowsian *to rue, repent of, make amends,* Æ : *compassionate,* Æ. ['*bireusy*']
behrēowsung f. *repentance, penitence,* Æ. ['*bireusing*']
behrēowsungtīd f. *time of repentance, Septuagesima,* Æ.
behrīman *to cover with hoar-frost,* WIF 48.
behringan *to surround,* CP.
behrōpan⁷ *to plague, importune,* Lk 18⁵.
behrūmian *to besmirch,* WW.
behrūmig *sooty,* MH 52²⁷.
bēhð f. *witness, sign,* JUD 174.
behwearf I. (eo) pret. 3 sg. of behweorfan.
II. (EPs)=behwearft
behwearft m. *exchange,* LPs 43¹³.
behweolfan (A)=behwylfan
behweorfan³ *to turn, change, spread about : see to, arrange, prepare, treat,* Æ : *bury,* Æ.
behwerfan=behwirfan
behwirfan (e, y;=ie) *to turn, change, convert,* CP : *exchange : prepare, instruct, exercise.*
behwon *whence,* BH.
behwylfan (eo;=ie) *to cover, vault over,* Ex,MFH.
behwyrfan (Æ)=behwirfan
behycgan *to consider, bear in mind : confide, trust* (on).
behȳdan (ī) *to conceal, shelter, Mt*; Æ. ['*behide*']
behȳd(ed)nes f. *concealment,* LL : *secret place,* LPs.
behȳdig *careful, watchful, anxious,* Æ. adv. -hȳdiglīce, -hȳdelīce.
behȳdignes f. *solicitude, care, anxiety.* v. MP 1·393. [hygdig]
behygd-=behȳd-
behyhtan *to trust,* W 48⁸.
behyldan *to flay, skin,* AO.
behylian *to cover, veil,* ÆL 33²³⁷.
behȳpan (ē;=īe) *to surround,* BH 188¹⁴. [hȳpe]
behȳpian *to heap up,* OEG 3322.
behȳran *to let on hire,* WW.
behȳrung f. *letting, loan,* WW.
behȳðelīce *sumptuously,* WW 513⁶.
beiernan³ (i, y) *to run up to, over, or into : incur : occur to.*
beigbēam=begbēam; **beinnan**=binnan
beinsiglian *to seal up,* RHy 6³⁴.
beirnan=beiernan
beiundane=begeondan; **bel-**=behl-

belācan[7] *to enclose*, RD 61[7].
belādian *to excuse, clear*, Æ,AO,CP.
belādiendlic *apologetic, that can be excused*, OEG.
belādigend m. *apologist*, WW 332[2].
belādung f. *apology, excuse*, WW.
belǣdan *to lead astray*, RB. ['belead']
belǣfan *to leave, spare* : *be left, remain, survive*, Ps; Æ. ['beleave']
belǣndan=belandian
belǣðan *to make hateful, pervert*, W 47[7].
be-lǣwa (Æ), -lǣwend m. *betrayer*.
belǣwan *to betray*, Æ.
belǣwung f. *betrayal, treachery*, Æ.
belāf pret. of belīfan.
belandian *to deprive of lands*, CHR 1091.
belcedswēora adj. *having an inflated neck*, RD 79[1]. [bælc]
belcentan, belcettan=bealcettan
beld, beldo=bieldo
+beldan I. *to cover, bind (a book)?* JnL p 188[3]. II.=+bieldan
belē- (NG)=belǣ-
belēan[6] *to censure, reprove* : *charge with* : *dissuade, forbid, prevent*, CP.
belecgan *to cover, invest, surround, afflict*, An; AO : *attribute to, charge with, accuse*. ['belay']
belēfan=belȳfan; belendan (CHR 1096)=belandian
belene (eo[1], o[2]) f. *henbane*, GL,LCD.
belēogan[2] *to deceive by lying*, GD : (impers.) *be mistaken*. ['belie']
belēoran *to pass by, pass over*, MkL,VPs.
beleorendlic *past*. DR.
belēosan[2]† *to be deprived of, lose*.
belēweda (LL 438[5])=belǣwend
belewit=bilewit
belflȳs n. *bell-wether's fleece*, LL 451,14.
belg (æ, i, y) m. *bag*, Mt,WW : *purse, leathern bottle, pair of bellows, pod, husk*. ['belly']
+belg m. *anger : arrogance*, RB 69[20].
±belgan[3] (intr., refl.) *to be or become angry*, Æ,AO,CP : *offend, provoke*.
belgnes f. *injustice*, MtL 20[13] (bælig-).
+belh=+belg
belhring m. *bell-ringing*, RB 67[20].
belhūs=bellhūs
belibban=belīfian
belicgan[5] *to lie round, surround*, Gen : *hedge in, encompass*, Æ; AO. ['belie']
belīfan[1] (ȳ) *to remain over, be left*, Æ. pp. belifen *dead*, AO. ['belive']
belīfend m. *survivor*, OEG.
belīfian *to deprive of life*, Æ; belig=belg
belīman *to glue together*, Sc 96[19].
belimp n. *event, occurrence, affair*. of belimpe *by chance*.

±belimpan[3] *to concern, regard, belong to, conduce to, Bo*; CP : *happen, befall, B*; Æ : *become* : (impers.) *befit*. ['belimp']
belis(t)nian *to castrate*, Æ. belis(t)nod pp. as sbm. *eunuch*. wæs b. 'stupratur,' HGL 507.
bellōan[1]† *to deprive of*. pp. beliden *departed, dead*, AN 1087.
bell=belle
bellan[3] *to bellow, bark, grunt, roar*, Rd. ['bell']
belle f. *'bell,'* KC; Æ,CP.
bellhūs n. *'bell-house,' belfry*, LL,WW.
belltācen n. *indication (sounding of the hour) by a bell*, HL 11[65].
belltīd f. *a canonical hour marked by the ringing of a bell*. (cp. belltācen)
belōcian *to behold*, RPs 44[5].
belone=belene
belt m. *'belt,' girdle*, WW.
belūcan[2] *to lock, shut up, close, Bl,CP,Mt*; AO : *surround, enclose, embody, VPs* : *stop, impede, block up, choke*, Æ : *preserve, protect* : *shut out, exclude*, Æ: *sum up, define*, RWH 137[4]. ['belouke']
belune=belene
belūtian *to lie hid*, GD 293[15].
belȳfan (ē;=īe) *to believe*, Æ. pp. belȳfed *having belief*.
belympan=belimpan
belyrtan (N) *to deceive*, MtL 2[16]. ['belirt']
belytegian *to allure, seduce*, AO 112[26]. [lytig]
bemǣnan *to 'bemoan,' bewail, lament*, Æ.
bemancian *to maim*, LCD 3·214[20].
bēmare=bȳmere; bēme=bīeme
bemeldian *to disclose, reveal, denounce* (BTs).
bēmere=bȳmere
bemetan[5] *to account, consider*, AO. ['bemete']
bemīðan[1] *to hide, conceal*, CP : *lie hid*.
bemurc(n)ian, *to murmur at*, AO 48[17].
bemurnan[3] (also wk.) *to mourn, bewail, deplore, be sorry for* : *care for, take heed for*.
bemūtian *to exchange for*, GU 42. [L. mutare]
bemyldan *to bury*, WW. [molde]
ben-=benn
bēn I. f. (±) *prayer, request, Lk*; AO, CP : *compulsory service*, LL 447 (v. 2·418, Fron.). ['bene'] II. pret. 3 sg. of bannan.
bēna m., bēne f. *suitor, petitioner*, AO.
benacian *to lay bare*, Hy. [nacod]
benǣman (ē) *to take away, deprive of, rob of*, Æ,AO. [niman]

benc f. 'bench,' B.
bencian to make benches, LL455,13.
bencsittend† m. one who sits on a bench.
bencswēg m. bench-rejoicing, sound of revelry, B1161.
bencðel† n. bench-board, wainscotted space where benches stand, B. [v. 'theal']
bend mfn. (+b. MtL) bond, chain, fetter, BH,Bl,Mt,Ps; CP : band, ribbon, ornament, chaplet, crown, WW. ['bend']
bēndagas mpl. days of prayer, Rogation days, Bf166¹⁴.
±bendan to bend (a bow), Ps : bind, fetter, Chr. ['bend']
bendfeorm=bēnfeorm
-bene v. ēað-b.
beneah (pret. pres. vb.) pl. benugon, pret. benohte to have at one's disposal, possess, enjoy : require.
beneced=benacod pp. of benacian.
benēman=benǣman
benemnan to name : stipulate, settle, declare, asseverate.
benēotan²† to deprive of, rob.
beneoðan (i, y) prep. w. d. 'beneath,' under, below, Æ,Bo,KC,LL.
bēnfeorm f. food during (or after) compulsory labour for the lord? LL452' and 3·252.
bengeat n. wound-gash, B1121.
benīdan (ē) to compel, A11·110.
beniman⁴ to take, assume, obtain, AO : take away from, deprive of, bereave, rob, BH, Gen,Met; AO,CP : contain : catch, apprehend. ['benim']
benīming f. deprival, WW (bi-).
benīðan=beneoðan
bēnlic (oe) that may be entreated, DR. adv. -līce beseechingly, DR.
benn† f. wound, mortal injury. [bana]
+benn n. edict, WW398⁸⁷. [=+bann]
bēnn pret. 3 sg. of bannan.
benne f. reed-grass, BC (Mdf).
±bennian† to wound, Rd.
benohte v. beneah.
benorðan in the north, northwards (of), Chr1087; AO. ['benorth']
benoten pp. of benēotan.
benotian to use, consume, Chr. ['benote']
bēnrīp n. compulsory service rendered to a landowner at harvest time, LL448. [cp. bedrīp]
±bēnsian to pray, supplicate, BH.
benst pres. 2 sg. of bannan.
bēntīd f. prayer time, Rogation days, Men 75.
bēntigðe, bēntīð(ig)e granting requests, gracious, LPs : obtaining requests, successful, Chr.
benð pres. 3 sg. of bannan.

benugon v. beneah.
bēnyrð f. ploughing required from a tenant LL448,5².
benyðan=beneoðan
bēo I. f. nap. bēon; dp. bēo(u)m 'bee,' Lcd Ps,WW; Æ. II. pres. 1 sg. of bēon.
bēobrēad n. honey with the comb, Lk,Met VPs; Æ. ['bee-bread']
bēoce=bēce
bēoceorl m. bee-master, bee-keeper, Ll 448,5.
bēocere m. bee-keeper, LL. [MHG. bīkar]
+beod=+bed
bēod m. table, Mt : bowl, dish. ['beod']
bēodærn n. refectory, dining-room, Æ (-ern). on bēoderne at table.
beodan=bidon pret. pl. of bīdan.
±bēodan² to command, decree, summon, Chr; Æ,AO,CP. b. ūt call out (an army), banish : declare, inform, announce, proclaim, Gu,LL : threaten : offer, proffer, give, grant, surrender, Æ,Gen; AO : (refl.) show oneself, behave : exact, collect. ['bid,' 'i-bede']
bēodbolle f. table-bowl, Gl.
bēodclāð m. table-cloth, carpet, ÆGr 34⁸.
bēoddern=bēodærn
bēoddian to do joiner's work, LL455, 13.
bēodend m. preceptor, CM967.
bēodendlic=bebēodendlic
bēodern (Æ)=bēodærn
bēodfæt n. table-vessel, cup, WW204²⁵.
bēodfers n. grace at meal-time, GD,RB.
bēodgæst m. table-companion, An1090.
bēodgenēat† m. table-companion, B.
bēodgereord n. feast, NC,Gen1518.
bēod(h)rægl n. table-cloth, WW126³³.
bēodlāfa fp. table-leavings, Bl53¹³,VH9.
bēodland n. land from which the table of monasteries, etc., was supplied, glebe-land, Ct.
bēodrēaf n. table-cloth, TC530'.
bēod-scēat n., -scȳte m. table-napkin, towel, WW449²².
bēodwyst f. a table with food on it, LPs22⁵. [wist]
beofer (o²)=befer; beofian=bifian
beoft redupl. pret. of bēatan; beoftadon is from a later wk. *beoftian (ANS141·176).
beofung=bifung
bēogang m. swarm of bees, WW.
+bēogol (ū, ȳ) submissive, obedient : forgiving, Æ. [būgan]
bēohāta m. chief? prince? Ex253. [bēot-?]
beolone=belene
bēom I. dp. of bēo I. II.=bēam. III.= bēo pres. 1 sg. of bēon.

bēomōder f. *queen-bee*, OEG.

bēon I. anv. [conj. in full (WS and A) Wt 548] *to* 'BE*,' *exist, become, happen.* b. ymbe *to have to do with.* b. *of to be gone.* (v. also eom, wesan.) **II.** nap. of bēo I.

bēona gp. of bēo I.

bēonbrēad=bēobrēad

bēonbrōð n. *mead?* (or? bēanbrōð, ES 38·302).

bēonnon pret. pl. of bannan.

bēor n. *strong drink,* ' *beer*,' *mead, Lk,WW* (v. A 27·495 and FTP 276).

+**bēor** m. *pot-companion, guest,* Æ.

beora=bearu; ±**beoran**=beran

bēorbyden f. *beer-barrel,* LL 455,17.

beorc I. (e, i, y) f. ' *birch*,' *Gl,Lcd*; Mdf : *name of the rune for* b. **II.** (±) n. *barking,* ÆGR,LCD.

beorcan³ (tr.) *to* ' *bark*,' *ÆGr,CP* : (intr.) *bark at,* Lcd.

beorce=beorc

beorcholt (y) *birch wood,* WW 138,361.

beorcragu (e¹) f. *lichen from a birch-tree,* LCD 99b.

beorcrind (e¹) f. *birch-bark,* LCD 119b.

beord (BH 392²⁷)=bord

bēordrǣst(e) f. *dregs of beer,* LCD.

beorg m. *mountain, hill, AO,Lk*; Mdf : *mound,* ' *barrow*,' *burial place,* Æ,Lcd.

+**beorg** n. *protection, defence, refuge, W.* [' *bergh*']

beorgælfen f. *oread* (Swt).

±**beorgan I.** sv³ (w. d.) *to save, deliver, preserve, guard, defend, fortify, spare, An, Ps*; AO,CP : (w. refl. d.) *beware of, avoid, guard against.* [' *bergh*'] **II.**=birgan

beorg-hlīð† (u) n. nap. -hleoðu *mountain-height, mountain-slope.*

+**beorglic** *fitting, profitable,* LL,W : *safe, prudent,* Æ.

beorgseðel n. *mountain dwelling,* GU 73. [setl]

beorgstede m. *mound,* PH 284 (rh).

±**beorh** (1)=beorg; (2) imperat. of beorgan.

beorhlēode (WW 178⁴¹)=burglēode

+**beorhnes** f. *refuge,* CPs 30³.

+**beorhstōw** f. *place of refuge,* PPs 31⁸.

beorht (e, y) **I.** 'BRIGHT,' *shining, brilliant, light, clear* : *clear-sounding, loud* : *excellent, distinguished, remarkable, beautiful, magnificent, noble, glorious* : *pure, sublime, holy, divine.* **II.** n. *brightness, gleam, light* : *sight.* ēagan b. *twinkling of an eye.*

beorhtan=bierhtan

beorhtblōwende *bright-blooming,* LCD 1·404⁹.

beorhte *brightly, brilliantly, splendidly, B, Met* : *clearly, lucidly, distinctly,* CP.

beorhthwīl (RWH 41¹⁸)=bearhtmhwīl

beorhtian (e) *to glisten, shine, BH,Ps* : *to sound clearly, B* : *to make bright, VPs.* [' *bright*']

+**beorhtian**=+beorhtnian

beorhtlic *brilliant, clear, shining, splendid.* adv. -līce, *Mk*; Æ. [' *brightly*']

beorhtm=bearhtm

beorhtnan *to grow bright,* OEG 534.

±**beorhtnes** (æ) f. ' *brightness*,' *clearness, splendour, beauty, JnL,Lk*; CP : *lightning,* LPs 109³.

±**beorhtnian** (e) *to glorify,* NG.

beorhtrodor m. *shining heavens,* Ex 94.

beorhtte (=*beorgihte) pl. *mountainous,* AO 10²⁵.

beorhtu=bierhtu

beorhtword (y¹) *clear-voiced,* SAT 238.

bēorhyrde m. *cellarer, butler,* CRA 75.

beorm-=bearm-

beorma m. ' *barm*,' *yeast, leaven, Mt.*

+**beormad** *leavened,* MtR 13³³. [' *barm*']

beorn I.† m. *man* : *noble, hero, chief, prince, warrior, B,Ma* : *rich man,* RUN 12. [' *berne*'] **II.**=barn pret. 3 sg. of biernan. **III.**= bearn

beornan (VPs)=biernan

beorncyning m. *lord of heroes,* B 2148.

beorne=byrne

Beornice mp. *Bernicians, inhabitants of part of Northumbria,* BH.

beorning (=ie) f. *incense,* LkL 1¹¹.

beornðrēat m. *troop of men,* PA 50.

beornwiga m. †*warrior, hero.*

bēorscealc *reveller, feaster,* B 1240. [v. A 46·233]

±**bēorscipe** m. *feast, banquet, revel,* Æ,CP.

bēorsele† m. *beer-hall, banqueting hall.*

bēorsetl n. *ale-bench,* JUL 687.

beorswinig (NG)=bærsynnig

bēorðegu† f. *beer-drinking.*

-beorðling (ie) v. hyse-b.

±**beorðor** (e, o, u, y) n. *child-bearing, childbirth* : *what is born, foetus, offspring.*

beorðorcwelm m. *abortion,* WW 348²³.

beorðor-ðīnen, -ðīnenu (broðor-) f. *midwife,* GEN 38²⁸.

beoruh=beorg; **beosmrian**=bismerian

bēost m. *beestings, the first milk of a cow after calving, WW* : *swelling* (*of the ground*)? v. Mdf. [' *beest*']

beosu=basu

±**bēot I.** n. *boastful speech, boast, threat,* Æ, Gen. on b. *boastfully* : *promise, vow,* AO : *command* : *peril, danger,* DA 265. [=behāt; ' *beot*,' ' *i-beot*'] **II.** pret. 3 sg. of bēatan.

±**bēotian I.** *to threaten, JUL* : *boast, vow, promise,* AO. [' *beoten*'] **II.**=bōtian

±**bēotlic** *arrogant, exulting, boastful, threatening,* Æ. adv. -līce.

bĕotmæcg m. *leader*, DA 265.
bĕoton pret. pl. of bĕatan.
bĕotung f. *threatening*, BH,LCD.
bĕotword† n. *boast*, B : *threat*, JUL.
bĕoðĕof m. *bee-thief*, LL 54,9².
bĕoum dp. of bĕo.
bĕow n. *barley*, GL.
bĕowan=bȳwan
bĕowyrt f. *bee-wort, sweet flag*, LCD.
bepǣcan *to deceive, seduce, Mt*; Æ. ['*bi-peche*']
bepǣcend m. *deceiver*, Æ.
bepǣcestre f. *whore*, ÆGR 175⁹.
bepǣcung f. *deception*, OEG.
beprīwan (ē) *to wink*, BO,W.
bĕr (NG)=bǣr
bera m. '*bear*,' Æ.
beræccan=bereccan
berǣdàn *to deprive, take by treachery, rob* : *betray*, Æ : *deliberate on* : *get the better of.*
berǣsan *to rush upon or into*, Æ,CP.
±beran⁴ (eo) *to* '*bear,*' *carry, bring, take away, carry out, extend, AO,B*; Æ,CP : *bring forth, produce, Bl,Mt,Gen*; Æ : *be situated by birth, LL* : *wear, AO* : *endure, support, sustain, LL,Mt*; CP. (with ūp) *set forth, open* (*a case*), CHR 1052E. berende *fruitful.* +boren *born.* [v. also '*i-bere*']
berascin n. *bear-skin*, EC 250¹⁷.
+berbed '*vermiculatus,*' *barbed*, DR 4³.
ber-bēne, -bīne f. *verbena*, LCD.
berc=beorc, berec-
+berd-, +bēre=+byrd-, +bǣre
bere m. *barley*, Æ,JnLR. ['*bear*']
bereærn n. '*barn,*' Lk. [bere, ærn]
berĕafere m. *despoiler*, OEG 46³⁶.
berĕafian *to* '*bereave,*' *deprive of, take away, seize, rob, despoil, Bo*; Æ,AO.
berĕafigend m. *despoiler, robber*, APT,GL.
berebrytta m. *barn-keeper*, LL 451,17.
berĕcan *to cause to smoke, smoke* (tr.), LCD 1·106¹⁶.
bereccan *to relate* : *excuse or justify oneself*, CP.
berecorn n. *barley-corn*, GL,LL.
berecroft m. *barley-field*, KC 3·260¹ (berc-).
+bered *crushed, kneaded*, WW : *harassed, oppressed*, NG.
berĕfian (KGL)=berĕafian
bereflōr m. *barn-floor, threshing-floor*, LkL. [v. '*bear*']
beregafol n. *rent paid in barley*, LL 116,59¹. [cp. gafolbære]
beregræs n. *barley-grass, fodder*, WW 148²⁶.
berehalm n. *barley-haulm, straw*, LCD 157a.
bereland (ber-) *barley-land*, KC 3·367⁹.
beren I. *of barley*, Æ. II.=biren. III.=bereærn
berend m. *bearer, carrier*, GL.

berendan *to peel, take off husk*, LCD.
berende *fruitful*, BH. [beran]
berendlīce *with fecundity*, DR 32⁸.
berendnes f. *fertility*, DR 108¹¹.
berenhulu f. *barley-husk*, SC 95¹⁹.
berĕnian *to bring about*, EX 147 : *ornament, mount* (*with silver*), KC 6·101'.
berĕocan² *to fumigate*, LL (164⁵).
berĕofan²† *to bereave, deprive, rob of.*
berĕotan² *to bewail*, HELL 6.
berĕowsian=behrĕowsian
-berere v. wæter-b.
berern (NG)=bereærn
beresǣd n. *barley*, BH 366²⁷.
beretūn m. *barley-enclosure, threshing-floor, barn, MtL*; Æ. ['*barton*']
berewæstm m. *barley-crop*, LCD 1·402⁸.
berewíc f. *barley-yard, demesne farm*, TC. ['*berewick*']
berg=(1) bearg, (2) beorg
berg-=beri-, birg-, byrg-
berh=bearh pret. 3 sg. of beorgan.
berht, berht-=beorht, beorht-, bierht-
berhtm-=breahtm-
berian I. *to make* '*bare,*' *clear*, B 1239. [bær] II.=byrgan II.
+berian=+byrian
bericge=barricge
berídan¹ *to ride round, surround, besiege, LL* : *overtake, seize, occupy*, CHR. ['*beride*']
berie f. '*berry,*' Lcd : *grape*, Æ : *vine*, WE 63²⁰.
berig I. n. *berry*, RPs 77⁴⁷. II.=byrig, ds. of burg.
berigdrenc m. *drink made of mulberries*, WW 114²².
berige=berie; berigea=byrga
berind(r)an *to strip off bark, peel*, LCD.
beringan=behringan
berinnan² *to run upon, run over, wet, bedew*, Cr 1176. ['*berun*']
berísan¹ *to be fitting*, ByH 78¹³.
berland, bern=bereland, bereærn
bern-=bærn-, biern-
bernan (VPs); v. AB 40·343)=bærnan
bernhus n. *barn*, GD 68²². [=beren-]
berōfon (pret. pl. of *berafan or *berebban) *despoiled*, GEN 2078.
berŏwan⁷ *to row round*, CHR 897A.
berst=byrst
+berst n. *bursting*, LCD,W 186⁷.
±berstan³ (intr.; tr. at RD 2⁸) *to break,* '*burst,*' *fail, fall, B,Lcd,LL,Ma*; Æ,AO : *break away from, escape* : *break to pieces, crash, resound.*
berthwíl=bearhtmhwíl; bertūn=beretūn
berð-=beorð-, byrð-
+bĕru=+bǣru, +bǣre
berŭmod=behrŭmod pp. of behrŭmian.

berunnen pp. of berinnan.

berwe ds. of bearu.

berwinde f. '*bearbind*,' *navel-wort*, WW 300[19].

berȳfan *to deprive*, MOD 63. [rēaf]

berȳpan (=ie) *despoil of, strip, spoil, rob*, Æ.

besǣgan *to sink*, GPH 388[85].

besǣncan=besencan

besǣtian *to lay wait for*, AO 146[11].

besārgian *to lament, bewail, be sorry for, pity*, Æ. [sārig]

besārgung f. *compassion*, Æ.

besāwan[7] *to sow*, Æ.

bescēad (bi-) n. *distinction*, G.

bescēadan[7] *to separate, discriminate : scatter, sprinkle over*, LCD 20b.

bescēad(uw)ian, *to overshadow*, Sol; RWH 138[5], RPs 139[8]. ['*beshade*']

besceafan[6] *to scrape thoroughly*, LCD 143b.

bescēan pret. 3 sg. of bescīnan.

besceatwyrpan '*despondi*,' v. OEG 4555; 2[346]; ES 42·170.

bescēawere m. *observer*, DHy 24[15].

bescēawian *to look round upon, survey, contemplate, consider, watch*, Æ,AO : *look to, care for*. bescēawod *thoughtful, prudent*, LCD 3·436[11].

bescēawiendlic *contemplative*, OEG 991.

bescēawodnes f. *vision, sight*, EPs 9[12].

bescēawung f. *contemplation*, GD,GL.

besceddan=besceadan

bescencan *to give to drink*, GU 596.

bescēofan=bescūfan

besceoren (WW 217[24])=bescoren pp. of bescieran.

bescēotan[2] *to shoot into, plunge into, implant : happen, occur*, AO.

be-sceran, -scerwan=bescieran

bescerian=bescierian

bescieran[4] *to shear, shave, cut hair, give the tonsure*, Æ,AO. ['*beshear*']

bescierednes (y[2]) f. *deprivation*, WW 351[13].

bescierian *to separate from, deprive of*, CHR : *defraud*.

bescīnan[1] *to shine upon, light up, illuminate*, Rd; Æ. ['*beshine*']

bescir-an, -ian=bescier-an, -ian

bescītan[1] *to befoul*, WW 507[28].

bescrēadian *to scrape off, clean off*, ES 42·171.

bescrepan[5] *to scrape*, LCD 101a.

bescrȳdan *to clothe*, RWH 136[32].

bescūfan[2] *to shove, impel, thrust down, hurl, throw*, Æ,AO : *force*, Æ.

bescȳlan (=ie) *to look askance*, BO 121[30]. [sceol]

bescyldian *to shield, defend*, WYN.

bescyr-=bescier-

besēcan *to beseech, beg urgently*, MFH 151.

besecgan *to announce, introduce : defend, excuse oneself* : (w. on) *accuse*, Æ.

beselian=besylian

besellan *to surround, cover (over) : hand over*, RPs 105[41].

besema=besma

besencan *to cause to sink, submerge, immerse, drown*, Bl,Mt; AO,CP : *plunge into (fire)*, GD 317. ['*besench*']

besendan *to send*, Æ.

besengan *to singe, burn*, AO.

besēon I. sv[5] (tr., intr. and refl.) *to see, look, look round, behold*, Æ,Mk,Ps; AO : *observe : look after, go to see, visit : provide for.* b. tō *look upon, have regard to*, CP. ['*besee*'] II. sv[1] *to suffuse*, CR 1088.

besēoðan *to boil down*, LCD.

besēowian (ī, ȳ) *to sew together, sew up*, Ep, WW. ['*besew*']

be-serian, -serwan=besierwan

besettan *to put, place, set near, appoint*, Æ : *own, keep, occupy* : '*beset*,' *cover, surround with, adorn*, B ; Æ,CP : *besiege, invest*, AN : *institute, set going.*

besibb *related*, RWH 139[4]. (as sb.).

besīdian *to regulate the size of anything*, RB 89[18]. [sīd]

besierwan *to ensnare, surprise, deceive, defraud, oppress*, AO. [searu]

besīgan (on) *to rush*, v. OEG 4126.

besilfran *to silver*, VPs 67[14].

besincan[3] (intr.) *to sink*, AO. ['*besink*']

besingan[3] *to sing of, bewail : sing charms, enchant*, Æ.

besirwan (AO,CP)=besierwan

besittan[5] *to sit round, surround, beset, besiege*, Chr; AO : *hold council : occupy, possess.* ['*besit*']

besīwian=besēowian

beslǣpan[7] *to sleep*, LL (284[2]).

beslēan[6] *to strike, beat, cut off, take away, deprive by violence*, Æ.

beslēpan *to slip· on, cover, put on, clothe*, BO,Ps.

beslītan[1]† *to slit, tear*, SOUL.

besma m. '*besom*,' *broom, rod*, AO,Mt.

besmēagan *to consider about*, ÆL 23b[633].

+**bēsmed** *bellied* (of sails), WW 515[9]. [bōsm]

bēsming f. *curve, curvature*, WW. [bōsm]

besmirwan (y[2]; =ie[2]) *to* '*besmear*,' WW.

besmītan[1] *to soil, defile, pollute, dishonour*, Bl; Æ,CP. ['*besmit*']

besmitenes f. *soil, stain, defilement, degradation, dirtiness*, Æ.

besmittian *to defile*, RB,MP 1·613.

besmiðian *to work (in metal), forge, surround with forged work*, B,EETS 46·17.

besmocian *to smoke, envelop with incense*, ANS 84·3.

besmyred=besmirwed pp. of besmirwan.
besnǣdan† to cut, mutilate, DA.
besnīwian to cover with snow, WW. ['be-snow']
be-snyðian, -snyððan† to rob, deprive of.
besolcen stupefied, dull, inactive, slow, CP.
besorg dear, beloved, Æ.
besorgian to regret : be anxious about, dread, shrink from, Æ.
besorh=besorg
bespǣtan to spit upon, ÆH 2·248′,RWH 137²⁴.
bespanan⁶ to lead astray, entice, incite, urge, persuade, AO.
besparrian to bar, shut, GL.
bespirian=bespyrigan
besprecan⁵ to speak about : speak against, accuse of, Ps : claim at law, LL : complain, AO. ['bespeak']
besprengan to besprinkle, Lcd : bespatter, CHRD 64³⁶. ['bespreng']
bespyrigan to track, trace, LL.
besta, beste wk. forms of superl. adj. betst.
bestǣlan (ē) to lay a charge against, convict.
bestæppan⁶ to tread upon, step, go, enter, Æ.
bestandan⁶ to stand round or about, beset, surround, Æ : attend to, Æ : beset, harass, Jn. ['bestand']
bestealcian to move stealthily, steal, 'stalk,' ÆL 32⁴⁰. [stealc]
bestefnod ptc. having a fringe, WW 375⁴¹.
bestelan⁴ to move stealthily, steal away, steal upon, AO,LL; Æ,CP : (†) deprive. ['besteal']
bestēlan=bestǣlan; **bestēman**=bestȳman
bestēpan (=īe) to deprive of (children), GD 76¹⁸.
bestingan³ to thrust in, push, Æ.
bestrēdan to bestrew, cover, BHB 154²⁷.
bestrēowian to 'bestrew,' besprinkle, Job.
bestreðian (y²) to bestrew, cover over, RD.
bestrican¹ to make a stroke, LCD 186b. [strīca]
bestrīdan¹ to 'bestride,' mount, Æ.
bestrīpan to strip, plunder, Chr. ['bestrip']
bestrūdan⁷ to spoil, plunder, rob, GEN, WW 424²³.
bestrȳpan=bestrīpan
bestryððan=bestreððan
bestuddian to be careful for, trouble about, RWH 134¹⁰.
bestȳman† (ē;=īe) to bedew, wet, flood. [stēam]
bestyrian to heap up, BH. ['bestir']
bestyrman to agitate, Bo 9¹¹.
besu=basu
besūpan² to sup up, swallow, LCD 113b.
besūtian to besmirch, GPH 403²⁶.
besūðan in the south, southwards (of).

beswǣlan to burn, singe, scorch, B; Æ. [v. 'sweal']
beswǣpan=beswāpan
beswǣtan to sweat, toil, Sc 111¹⁴.
beswāpan⁷ to clothe, cover over, veil, protect, BH; CP : persuade, BH. ['beswape']
beswelgan to swallow up, EPs 106²⁷; 123³.
beswemman to make to bathe, Bo 115³.
beswencan to afflict, CPs 68¹³.
besweðian (bi-) to swathe, wrap up, wind round, CR, JnL.
beswic n. treachery, deceit, AO,CP : snare.
beswica (bi-) m. deceiver, BL.
beswican¹ to deceive, seduce, betray, circumvent, frustrate, Bl,Mt; AO,CP : to overcome, supplant, AO. ['beswike']
beswicend m. deceiver, seducer, GL.
beswicenes f. deception, MH : surrender, GL.
beswicfalle f. trap, WW 17¹.
beswician to escape, be free from, BH.
beswicol deceitful, CP 238¹⁶. (bi-)
beswicung f. deception, WW.
beswincan³ to toil, exert oneself, make with toil, Jn : till, plough, Æ. beswuncen exhausted, tired out. ['beswink']
beswingan³ to flog, scourge, beat, strike, Æ; CP. ['beswinge']
beswylian to drench, flood, ROOD 23. [swilian]
besyftan to sprinkle, ÆL 23¹⁵⁵. [siftan]
besylfran=besilfran
besylian to sully, defile, stain, Æ.
besyr-ewian, -i(a)n=besierwan
bet adv. better, Bo. ['bet']
-bēta v. dǣd-b.
betācnian to betoken, designate, RWH 136²⁰.
betǣcan (w. d.) to make over, give up to impart, deliver, entrust, commend to, Lk, Mt,WW; AO,CP : betroth : appoint (for), set apart as, dedicate : show, point out, Lk : give orders, RB 130⁴ : pursue, hunt, WW 92²³. ['beteach']
±bētan to amend, repair, restore, cure, CP : make good, make amends, reform, remedy, compensate, atone, pay 'bōt' for an offence, Æ,CP,Lcd,Mt; AO : attend to (fire or light), AO. ðurst b. quench thirst. [bōt; 'beet' vb.]
betast=betst
betboren of higher birth, LL.
bēte f. 'beet,' beetroot, Lcd. [L. beta]
-bēte v. twi-b.; **bētel**=(1) bīetl; (2) bītol
beteldan³† to cover, hem in, surround : overload, oppress.
betellan to speak about, answer, defend oneself (against a charge), exculpate oneself, Chr; Æ. ['betell']
bētend m. restorer, RUIN 28.
+bētendnes f. amendment, OEG 58⁶.

betēon[1,2] *to cover, surround, enclose*, AO; Æ, CP : *dispose of, bestow, bequeath* : *impeach, accuse*. ['*betee*']

betera '*better*,' AO,Bl,Bo,Mk. w. g. *better in respect of*....

-bētere v. dǣd-b.

±beterian *to 'better,' improve*, CP : *trim (lamp)*, GD.

±beterung f. *improvement*, Æ.

betest=betst; betienan (WW 383[17])=betȳnan

betīhtlian *to accuse*, LL.

betillan=betyllan

betimbran *to construct, build*, B. ['*betimber*']

betīnan=betȳnan; bēting=bǣting

bētl=bīetl

betlic† *grand, excellent*.

bētnes f. *reparation, atonement*, LL (264[16]).

betoce=betonice

betogenes f. *accusation*, LL.

betolden pp. of beteldan.

betonice f. '*betony*,' Lcd.

betost=betst; betr-=beter-

betræppan=betreppan

betredan[5] *to tread upon, cover*, CPs 138[10].

betrendan *to roll*, ES 37·180.

betreppan *to entrap, catch*, Chr. ['*betrap*']

be-trymman, -trymian *to enclose, surround, besiege*.

betst I. superl. adj. '*best*,' *first*, AO,B,Chr, Cr; CP. as sb. *people of position*, Chr,WW. II. adv. *in the best manner, most*, Bo.

betstboren *best-born, eldest*, Æ.

bett=bet

be-tuh, -tuoxn (CP), -tux=betwux

betuldon pret. pl. of beteldan.

+bētung f. *repair, maintenance*, LL.

betwēnan=betwēonan

betweoh, betweohs (Æ)=betwux

betwēonan, betwēonum I. prep. w. g. d. a. *between, among, amid, in the midst*, B,Bl, G,Ps. II. adv. '*between*,' BH : *in the meantime, meanwhile* : *in turn, by turns*, CM (-twȳn-).

betweox (LL), betweoxn, betwih(s) (RG)= betwux

betwīn-=betwēon-

betwīnforlētnes f. *intermission*, DR.

betwux (Æ,AO,CP), betwuht, betwix, betwux(t), betwisc prep. w. d. a. *between, among, amongst, amidst* : *during*. b. ðisum *meanwhile*. b. ðǣm ðe *whilst*. ['BETWIXT']

betwuxālegednes f. *interjection*, ÆGR 278[3].

betwuxāworpennes f. *interjection*, ÆGR 10[20].

betwuxblinnes (twih) f. *intermission*, DR 12[3].

betwuxfæc (yx) *internal*, OEG 3861.

betwuxgangende (twih) *separating*, VPs 28[7].

betwuxgesett (eoh, ih, yh) *interposed*, BF 66[32], BH 288[23].

betwuxlicgan[6] (twih) *to lie between*, BH 72[10].

betwuxsendan *to send between*, CM 104.

betwuxt, -twyh, -twyx(t)=betwux

betȳhtlian=betīhtlian

betyllan *to allure, decoy*, BH 358[4].

betȳnan (ī, īe) *to hedge in, enclose, shut, bury*, AO,CP : *shut out* : *end*, BH. [tūn]

betȳnung f. *conclusion*, OEG 3210.

betyran *to pitch, stain a dark colour*, LCD. [teoru]

betyrnan *to turn round* : *prostrate oneself*, RB.

beð I.=bið pres. 3 sg. of bēon. II.=bæð

beðæncan=beðencan

beðan=beðian

beðearfan *to need*, RWH 6[36].

beðearfende *needy, indigent*, KGL 708.

beðearflic *profitable*, ÆL 23b[242].

beðearfod *needy*, ES 8·474[50].

beðeccan *to cover, protect, cover over, conceal*.

beðen=beðung

beðencan *to consider, remember, take thought for, take care of, care for*, Gu : (refl.) *reflect, 'bethink' oneself*, Lk; Æ : *trust, confide in, entrust to*, AO.

be-ðenian, -ðennan *to cover, stretch on or upon, spread over*, RD.

beðēodan *to be joined (to)*, RB 134[20].

beðerscan *to winnow, thresh*, PPs 43[7].

beðettan *to bathe, foment*, LCD 3·90[15] (A 30·397).

±beðian *to heat, warm, foment*, Lcd; Æ : *cherish*. ['*beath*']

beðrāwan[7] *to twist*, GPH 391[16].

beðridian (y) *to circumvent, overcome, force*, AO.

beðringan[8]† *to encircle, encompass* : *beset, oppress, burden*.

beðryccan *to press down*, CR 1446.

beðrydian, beðryððan=beðridian

beðrȳn *to press*, NC 273.

beððan=beðian

beðuncan (RD 49[7])=beðencan

beðung f. *bathing, bath, fomentation, cataplasm*, Lcd; Æ,CP. ['*beathing*'; bæð]

be-ðurfan swv. pres., 3 sg. -ðearf, pl. -ðurfon, pret. -ðorfte. (w. g. or a.) *to need, have need of, want*, Æ,CP.

beðwēan[6] *to moisten, wet*, LPs 6[7].

beðwyrian *to deprave*, WW 386[7]. [ðweorh]

beðȳn *to thrust*, AO 158[6].

beufan=bufan; beūtan=būtan

bewacian *to watch, guard*, Æ.

bewadan[6] *to emerge*, RD 88[34].

bewǣfan *to enfold, wrap round, cover over, clothe*, Æ,CP.

bewǣgan *to deceive, frustrate*, BVPs.

bewægnan *to offer, proffer*, B1193.
bewǣlan *to oppress, afflict*, AN 1363.
bewǣpnian *to disarm*, Æ.
bewǣrlan *to pass by* : *be free from*, DR.
bewarenian *to guard against, be on one's guard*, CP.
bewarian *to keep watch, guard, preserve, ward off*, CP.
bewarnian=bewarenian
bewāwan[7] *to blow upon*, WA 76. (biwāune= biwāwene)
bewealcan *to involve*, CHRD 74³³.
beweallan[7] *to boil away*, LCD.
bewealwian *to wallow*, Bo 115⁹.
beweardian *to guard, protect* : *observe closely*.
beweaxan[7] *to grow over, cover over, surround*, Æ.
beweddendlic *relating to marriage*, OEG 1122.
beweddian *to betroth, marry*, Æ : *give security*. ['*bewed*']
beweddung f. *betrothal*, LL442Ha.
bewefan[5] *to cover over*, LCD 3·146⁴.
bewegan[5] *to cover*, Bo,WY.
bewēled (oe², ȳ²) *poisoned, polluted*, GD, JPs,WW; ES38·344. [wōl]
bewellan (=ie) *to knead, mix together*, GD, WW.
bewendan *to turn, turn round, Mk*; (refl.) *Mt*9²² : *turn one's attention, convert*, Æ. ['*bewend*']
bewenian† *to entertain, take care of, attend upon*, B.
beweorcan=bewyrcan
beweorpan³ *to cast, cast down, plunge, throw*, Æ,AO : *beat*, Æ : *surround*.
beweorðian *to adorn*, DD 118.
beweotian=bewitian
bewēpan[7] *to weep over, mourn, bewail*, Æ. pp. bewōpen *tearful, weeping*, AO 92³⁰. ['*beweep*']
bewōpendlic *lamentable*, GL,HL 12⁶⁶.
bewēpnian=bewǣpnian
bewerenes f. *prohibition*, BH 86¹³.
bewerian *to guard, protect, defend*, Æ,AO : *check, prevent, forbid*, Æ.
bewerigend m. *protector, keeper*, Æ.
bewerung f. *defence, fortification*, CM,SC.
bewestan prep. w. d. or adv. *to the west of, Chr*; AO. ['*bewest*']
bewīcian *to encamp*, CHR 894w.
bewindan³ *to wind round, clasp, entwine, envelop, encircle, surround, B,Mt*; AO,CP : *brandish (a sword)* : *turn, wind, revolve*. hēafe b. *bewail*. ['*bewind*']
bewindla (bi-) m. *hedge, border*, BC(Mdf).
bewitan swv., pres. 3 sg. -wāt, pret. 3 sg. -wiste *to keep, care for, watch over, superintend, administer, lead, guide*, Æ,AO.

bewitian (eo) *to observe, attend to, care for· administer* : *perform*.
bewlātian *to look at, behold*, LPs 32¹⁴.
bewlītan¹ *to look round*, GEN 2925.
bewōpen pp. of bewēpan.
bewrecan⁵† *to drive* : *drive away, banish drive round, beat round*.
bewrencan *to deceive*, PR 34.
bewrēon¹·² *to cover, hide, cover over, enwrap protect, clothe, Sol,Met*; CP. ['*bewry*']
bewreðian *to sustain, support*, RD 81²¹.
bewrigennes f. *a covering*, WYN 10¹³.
bewrītan¹ *to record?* CREAT 19 : *score round*, LCD 1·244.
bewrīðan¹† *to bind, wind about, surround*, CR.
bewrixl(i)an *to change* : *exchange, sell*, PPs.
bewuna adj. indecl. *accustomed, wont*, AO.
bewyddian=beweddian; **bewȳled**=bewēled
bewyllan (=ie) *to boil away*, LCD.
bewylwian (=ie) *to roll down, roll together*, SC,WW.
bewȳpð=bewēpð pres. 3 sg. of bewēpan.
bewyrcan *to work, construct, surround with, enclose, cover, B*; Æ,AO : *work in, insert, adorn, Lcd*. ['*bework*']
bewyrpan=beweorpan
beyrfeweardian *to disinherit*, A 13·321.
beyrnan=beiernan; **bezera**=bæzere
bi, **bī** (1)=be (prep.); (2) f.=bēo
bi- v. also be-; **bīad**=bēod
biblioðēce f. biblioðeoco (AO), bibliðēca m. *library* : *bible*, Æ. ['*bibliotheca*' (*L*.)]
bībrēad=bēobrēad
bicce, bice f. '*bitch,*' *Lcd,WW*.
biccen=byccen
bicgan (Æ)=bycgan; **bicge**=bicce
±bīcn-an, -ian=bīecnan
+bīcnend (ē), ±bīcni(g)end m. '*index,*' *indicator, discloser*, SC : *forefinger*, GL.
bīcnendlic, +bīcni(g)endlic *allegorical* : (gram.) *indicative*, ÆGR 124¹⁴.
bīcnol *indicating, indicative*, GPH 398¹⁹³.
±bīcnung (ēa, ē) f. *beckoning, nodding* : *token, symbol, figure*, Æ : *figurative speech*.
bīcwide m. *byword, proverb, fable, tale*, Æ. ['*bequeath*']
bīd n. *lingering, hesitation, delay, halt*, Rd. ['*bide*']
±bīdan¹ (intr.) *to stay, continue, live, remain, delay, AO,G,Ps* : (tr. usu. w. g.) *wait for, await, expect, B,Bl,Mt*; AO,CP : *endure, experience, find* : *attain, obtain* : *own*. ['*bide*']
biddan⁵ *to ask, entreat, pray, beseech, A,AO, Bl,G* : *order, command, require*, AO,CP. b. and bēodan, hālsian *to beg and pray*. ['*bid*']

+**biddan**⁵ (often refl.) *to beg, ask, pray, Bl, Mt*; Æ,CP : *worship*, Æ,AO. [' *i-bid* ']
biddend *petitioner*, Sc 32³.
biddere m. *petitioner*, GD,WW.
bidenfæt=bydenfæt
biderīp=bedrīp
bideð (CP) pres. 3 sg. of biddan.
bīdfæst† *firm, forced to stand out*.
bīding f. *abiding place, abode*, Gu 180.
bīdsteall† m. *halt, stand*.
bīe=bēo pres. 1 sg. of bēon.
bīecn=bēacen
bīecn-an, -ian (ē, ī, ȳ) *to make a sign, 'beckon,' wink, nod, Lk*; CP : *signify* : *summon*. [bēacen] For comps. see bīcn-.
bīegan (ē, ī, ȳ) *to bend, turn, turn back, incline, Bo,Mk* : *depress, abase, humiliate* : *subject* : *persuade, convert*. [' bey,' būgan]
±**bīeldan** (æ, e, i, y) *to encourage, excite, impel, exhort, confirm, CP,Ma*; Æ,AO. [' bield '; beald]
bīeld-o, -u (y) f. *boldness, courage, arrogance, confidence, BH*; CP. [' bield ']
bīelg=belg; **bielw-**=bilew-
bīeme (ē, ī, ȳ) f. *trumpet, CP,Mt,WW* : *tablet, billet*. [' beme ']
bīen=bēan; **bīencoddas**=bēancoddas
+**bīerde**=+byrde
+**bīerhtan** (e, y) *to brighten, be or make bright, illuminate, enlighten, CP* : *make clear* : *celebrate*. [beorht]
bīerhtu (e, eo, i, y) f. *brightness, effulgence, brilliance, CP*. [beorht]
bīerm=bearm
bīernan³ (ea, eo, i, y) tr. and intr. *to 'burn,' be on fire, give light, Æ,Lk,Ex,Sol,VPs*.
bīersteð, bierst pres. 3 sg. of berstan.
bīerð pres. 3 sg. of beran.
bīesen=bisen; **bīesgian**=bisgian
bīeter-=biter-
bīetl (ē, ī, ȳ) m. *'beetle,' mallet, hammer, CP,Jud*.
bīetr-=biter-
bīeð=bēoð pres. pl. of bēon.
bīfēran *to feed*, Guth 126⁸⁸.
bifian *to tremble, be moved, shake, quake, Bo,Ps*; Æ. [' bive ']
bifigendlic (byfg-) *terrible*, Chrd 93²⁷.
bifung (y) f. *trembling, shaking*, ÆH.
-bifung (eo¹) v. eorð-b.
bīfylce n. *neighbouring people*, BH 196¹. [folc]
big=be; **big-**=be-, bī-, bycg-; **bīg**=bēag
bīgan=bīegan; **bīge**=byge
+**bīgednes** f. *inflection, declension, case*, ÆGr.
bigegnes=begengnes
bīgels m. *arch, vault*, Æ : *curvature*, OEG 2228.

+**bīgendlic** *inflectional*, ÆGr 91⁸.
+**bīgendnes**=+bīgednes
bīgeng f. *practice, exercise, observance, worship, ÆGr* : *cultivation*, Æ. [' bigeng ']
bīgenga m. *inhabitant* : *cultivator*, Æ : *worshipper*, Æ : *benefactor*.
bīgenge n. *practice, worship*, Sc,SPs.
bīgengere m. *worker*, WW : *worshipper*, KC.
bīgengestre f. *handmaiden, attendant, worshipper*, GL.
bīgengnes=begengnes
+**bīgeð**=+bygeð pres. 3 sg. of +bycgan.
bīging (=īe) f. *bending*, WW 216³⁸.
bīgleaf- (eo, i)=bīleof-
bīgnes f. *power of bending, bending, winding*, BH,GD. [bīegan]
+**bīgnes** f. *'confrequentatio,'* EPs 117²⁷.
+**bīgð**=+bīgeð
bīgyrdel m. *girdle, belt, purse, Æ,Mt* : *treasury*. [' bygirdle ']
bīgytan=begietan
bihianda (MtL 5²⁷)=behindan
bīhst=bȳhst pres. 2 sg. of būgan.
+**bīhð** (Gu 346)=+byht
bīl=bill; **bīlcettan**=bealcettan
bīldan=bieldan
bīle m. *'bill,' beak, trunk (of an elephant), WW* : *prow*.
bīle=bȳle; **bīlefa**=bīleofa
bīlehwīt=bilewit
bīleofa (i²) m., bīleofen f. *support, sustenance, food, nourishment, Æ,WW* : *money, pay*. [' bylive '; libban]
bīlēofian *to support, feed upon*, Guth 34⁷.
bilewet=bilewit
bilewit *innocent, pure, simple, sincere, honest, BH,Mt*; Æ,CP : *calm, gentle, merciful, gracious* : *plausible*. [' bilewhit ']. adv. -lice.
bilewitnes f. *mildness, simplicity, innocence, purity*, Æ,CP.
bilgesieht=billgesliht
bilgst, bilhst pres. 2 sg. of belgan.
bilgð pres. 3 sg. of belgan.
bilherge=billere
bīlibb-, bīlif-=bīleof-; **billg**=belg
billw-=bilew-
bill n. *'bill,' chopper, battle-axe, falchion, sword, B,WW*.
billere m. *'bibulta' (plant)*, WW.
billgesliht n. *sword-clash, battle*, †Chr 937.
billhete m. *murderous hate, strife*, An 78.
+**bilod** *having a bill or beak*, HexC 256. [bile]
bil-swæð n. (nap. -swaðu) *sword track, wound*, Ex 329.
bilw-=bilew-; **bīlyht**=bȳliht
bīma (m.?), bīme=bīeme; **bin**=binn
bīnama m. *pronoun*, Bf 94¹⁵.

+**bind** n. *binding, fetter : costiveness : a bind* (measure), TC328' (v. BTs).

±**bindan** sv³ *to tie, 'bind,' fetter, fasten, restrain, Æ,Bl,G,WW*; AO,CP : *adorn*.

binde f. *head-band?* KC6·133. ['*bind*']

bind-ele, -elle f. *binding,* LL : *bandage,* LCD.

bindere m. '*binder,*' Rd28⁶.

binding f. *binding,* OEG324b.

binn f. '*bin,' basket, crib, manger, Bl, LkL,WW (Keltic,* LF124).

binna (*LG*)=binnan

binnan I. prep. (w. d. a.) *within, in, inside of, into, Jn.* II. adv. *inside, within, less than, during, whilst, LG.* ['*bin*']

binne=(1) binn; (2) binnan (RG)

bint pres. 3 sg. of bindan.

bio-=beo-, bi-; **biosmrung**=bismerung

birce=beorc, beorce; **bird** (*LkLR*)=bridd

+**bird**=+byrd; **birele**=byrele

biren f. *she-bear,* OET(Ct).

birg=byrg

+**birg** n. *taste,* DR116².

+**birgan** (e, eo, y) *to taste, eat,* BH,NG.

birging (y) f. *taste,* LCD.

birgnes (eo, y) f. *taste,* BH,WW.

birgð, birhð pres. 3 sg. of beorgan.

birht-=bierht-

birig, birig-=byrig, byrg-

birihte (y) prep. w. d. *near, beside,* AN 850.

birihto=bierhtu; **birle**=byrele

+**birman** (y;=ie) *to ferment, leaven,* LCD 37a. [beorma]

birnan (*Æ*)=biernan

birst, birsteð pres. 3 sg. of berstan.

birst pres. 2 sg., bir(e)ð pres. 3 sg. of beran.

biryhte=birihte

bisæc n? m? *wallet,* MtR10¹⁰. [*LL.* bi-saccium]

bisæc *contested, disputed,* LL.

bisæc f. *visit,* Gu188.

bisceop (e², o², u²) m. '*bishop,' CP : high-priest, chief priest (Jewish), heathen priest, AO,MkL.*

bisceopcynn (o²) n. *episcopal (high-priestly) stock,* ÆP116¹².

bisceopdōm m. *episcopate, bishopric, Chr :* excommunication. ['*bishopdom*']

bisceopealder m. *high-priest,* HL.

bisceopfolgoð m. *episcopate,* GD65²¹.

bisceopgegyrelan mpl. *episcopal robes,* BH90².

bisceophād m. '*bishophood,' office of bishop, ordination as bishop, episcopate, bishopric, Ps*; CP.

bisceophādung f. *episcopal ordination,* ÆL 31²⁸⁶.

bisceophām m. *bishop's estate,* EC365¹⁷.

bisceophēafodlīn (o²) n. *head ornament worn by bishops,* WW152²³.

bisceophīred (o) m. *clergy subject to a bishop,* MH,WW.

bisceopian *to confirm,* LL. ['*bishop*']

bisceopland (o) n. *episcopal or diocesan land,* LL173¹⁰.

bisceoplic '*bishoply,' episcopal,* BH.

bisceoprīce n. '*bishopric,' diocese, province of a bishop, BH : episcopal demesne or property,* WC16².

bisceoprocc (o²) m. *bishop's rochet, dalmatic,* LCD3·202'.

bisceoprōd f. *bishop's cross,* KC4·275¹¹.

bisceopscīr, -scӯr f. *diocese : episcopate,* BH.

bisceop-seld, -setl, -seðl n. *bishop's seat or see, bishopric,* BH,CHR.

bisceopseonoð m. *synod of bishops,* A11·8¹.

bisceopstōl m. *episcopal see, bishopric, KC : CP : bishop's palace,* GD. ['*bishopstool*']

bisceopsunu m. *godson at a 'bishoping' or confirmation,* CHR,LL.

bisceopðēnung f. *office of a bishop,* BH.

bisceopung f. *confirmation, Æ,*CHRD.

bisceopweorod (o²) n. *bishop's company,* BH309¹¹ (Schipper).

bisceopwīte n. *fine payable to a bishop?* (BTs), *forced entertaining of a bishop?* (Lieb : v. LL2·667).

bisceopwyrt f. *bishop's-wort, betony, vervain, marshmallow,* LCD,WW.

bisceopwyrtil (o²) *vervain,* WW134⁴¹.

bisceop=bisceop

bi-sceran, -scerian (i², y²)=be-scieran, -scierian

biscop, bisc(u)p=bisceop

bisegu=bisgu

bīsen, bisene (ie, y) fn. *example, pattern, model, JnLR; Æ,*AO,CP : *similitude, parable, parallel : rule, command, precept.* ['*bysen*']

bisene (y) *blind, MtL;* NC274; JAW22. ['*bisson'?*]

±**bīsenian** (ie, y) *to give, set an example, instruct by example, Bo; Æ : follow an example or pattern, CP : express figuratively.* ['*bysen*' vb.]

bīsenung f. *example, pattern,* Æ.

bises m. *the extra day intercalated in leap year,* MEN32. [*L.* bissextus]

±**bisgian** *to occupy, employ, Æ,Bo;* CP : *trouble, afflict,* Lcd,Met. ['*busy*']

bisgu, bisigu f. *occupation, labour, Bo; Æ,* CP : *affliction, trouble.* ['*busy*']

bisgung f. *business, occupation, care,* CP.

bisig (y) '*busy,' occupied, diligent,* Ma,Sol.

bisignes f. '*business,' MtL* (Cont. p. xx).

bismær-=bismer-; **bisme**=besma

bismer (y) nmf. *disgrace, scandal, shame, mockery, insult, reproach, scorn, AO,Bl*; CP : *filthiness, defilement, Æ.* tō bismere *ignominiously, shamefully* : *blasphemy* : *infamous deed,* AO. [*'bismer'*]

bismerful (y) *infamous, shameful, ignominious, Æ.*

bismergléow (y) n. *shameful lust,* Æ 236²⁴¹.

±**bismerian** (y) *to mock, revile, illtreat, blaspheme, Mk*; Æ,AO. [*'bismer'* vb.]

bismeriend m. *mocker,* KGL 298.

bismerléas (y) *blameless,* CR 1326.

bismerléoð n. *scurrilous song,* GL.

bismerlic *shameful, ignominious, contemptuous,* AO : *ridiculous, frivolous.* adv. -lice.

bismernes f. *pollution* : *insult* : *contemptibleness.*

bismer-sprǣc, -spǣc f. *blasphemy,* G.

±**bismerung** (y) *mockery, scorn* : *blasphemy* : *infamy, disrepute,* AO.

bismerword (æ²) n. *reproach, insult,* LL 10¹¹.

bismor, bism(o)r-=bismer, bismer-

bisn-=bisen-

+**bisnere** f. *imitator,* DR 45⁷.

bispell (big-) n. *example, proverb, Æ* : *parable, fable, allegory, story, MtL*; CP. [*'byspel'*]

bispellbōc (big-) f. *book of Proverbs,* ÆT 496.

bissextus, gen. -te *the intercalary day of leap year* : *leap year.* [L.]

bist pres. 2 sg. of bēon.

bist=bīdst pres. 2 sg. of bīdan.

biswǣc (e²) *tripping up, treachery,* RPs 40¹⁰.

biswic=beswic

bit pres. 3 sg. of biddan.

bit pres. 3 sg. of (1) bīdan; (2) bītan.

bita m. **I.** *'bit,' morsel, piece, Jn*; Æ. **II.** *biter, wild beast.*

±**bītan¹** *to 'bite,' tear, B,Rd*; Æ : *cut, wound* : (+) *dash down,* MkL 9¹⁸.

bite m. *'bite,' sting, AO,Lcd* : *sword-cut, Ap,B* : *cancer.*

bitela m. *'beetle,' Gl.*

biter *'bitter,' sharp, cutting, Gu*; Æ : *stinging, PPs* 117¹² : *exasperated, angry, embittered* : *painful, disastrous, virulent, cruel, B,Bl.* adv. -lice, Mt.

bitere=bitre

±**biterian** *to be or become bitter, CP* : *make bitter.* [*'bitter'* vb.]

biternes f. *'bitterness,' grief, Æ,Bl*; CP.

biterwyrde *bitter in speech, Æ.*

biterwyrtdrenc m. *drink of bitter herbs,* WW 114¹⁸.

bītl=bīetl

bitmǣlum *piecemeal, bit by bit,* ÆGR 239¹⁰.

bitol n. *bridle,* SPs 31⁹.

bitor=biter

bitre *bitterly, sharply, painfully, severely* : *very.*

bitres, bittres gsmn. of biter.

bitst pres. 2 sg. of biddan.

bītst pres. 2 sg. of bīdan and bītan.

bitt I. pres. 3 sg. of (1) biddan; (2) beodan. **II.**=bytt

bītt pres. 3 sg. of bītan.

+**bitt** n. *biting, gnashing,* ÆH.

bitter=biter

bittor, bittre=biter, bitre; **bitula**=bitela

bið pres. 3 sg. of bēon.

biwāune v. bewāwan.

biwist fm. *sustenance, food, provision, necessaries, Æ,Bo.* [*'bewiste'*]

biword (u) n. *proverb, household word* : *adverb,* BF 94²⁰.

biwyrde n. *'byword,' proverb, WW.*

bixen=byxen

blāc I. (ǣ) *bright, shining, glittering, flashing, Rd* : *pale, pallid, wan, AO,CP.* [*'bleak,'* but v. FTP 286] **II.** pret. 3 sg. of blīcan.

blac=blæc

blāchlēor† *with pale cheeks.*

blācian *to turn pale, Æ.*

blācung f. *a turning pale, pallor, Æ.*

bladesian *to flame, blaze, be hot* : *emit an odour,* OEG 554.

bladesnung (at-) f. *odour,* WW 405¹.

bladesung (æ¹) f. *shining, lightning,* EPs 76¹⁹

blæc (a) **I.** *'black,' dark, Æ,B,BH,KC.* **II.** n. *ink, LL,WW.* [*'bleck'*]

blǣc=blāc

blǣcan *to bleach, whiten* : (+) *disfigure,* CPs 79¹⁴. [blāc]

blæcce f. *black matter,* OEG 652.

blǣce n.? *irritation of the skin, leprosy,* LCD.

blǣcern n. *lamp, candle, light,* CP.

blǣcernleoht (ā) n. *lantern-light,* LV 59.

blæcfexede *black-haired,* ÆH 1·456¹⁶. [feax]

blæcgymm m. *jet,* BH 26¹⁶.

blæchorn (e) n. *ink-horn,* ANS 119·125,IM 128¹⁸.

blǣco f. *pallor, WW*; LCD. [*'bleach'*]

blǣcpytt m. *bleaching-pit?* EC 383'.

blǣcða *leprosy,* WW 53²⁸.

blǣcðrustfel n. *leprosy,* Cp 103B (? two words).

blæd n. (nap. bladu) *'blade,' WW* : *leaf, Gen.*

blǣd (ē) **I.** m. *blowing, blast, BH* : *inspiration, Ph* : *breath, spirit, Æ* : *life, mind* : *glory, dignity, splendour* : *prosperity, riches, success.* [*'blead'*; blāwan] **II.**=blēd I.

blǣdāgende *renowned,* B 1013.

+**blǣdan** *to puff up, inflate,* APs 34²¹

blǣdbylig m. *bellows,* WW 241³³.

blǣddæg† m. *day of prosperity.*

blædderwǣrc m. *pain in the bladder*, LCD.
blǣddre=blǣdre
±**blǣdfæst†** *glorious, prosperous.*
+**blǣdfæstnes** f. *success*, ÆL23b[492].
blǣdgifa† m. *giver of prosperity*, AN.
blǣdhorn m. *trumpet*, Æ.
blǣdnes f. *blossom, fruit*, BF86[2]. [blēd]
blǣdre (ē) f. *blister, pimple*, Æ,Lcd; AO : *'bladder,'* Gl,Lcd. [blāwan]
blǣdwela m. *abundant riches*, CR1392.
blǣge f. *gudgeon, bleak*, WW. ['blay']
blǣgettan (a) *to cry*, GD278[12].
blǣhǣwen *light blue*, LEV8[7].
blæs=blæst
blæsbelg (OET28)=blæstbelg
blǣse (a) f. *firebrand, torch, lamp*, Æ,Jn. ['blaze']
blǣsere m. *incendiary*, LL.
blǣshorn m. *trumpet*, LL194,8.
blæst m. *blowing*, *'blast'* (*of wind*), *breeze*, Ex : *flame.*
blǣstan *to blow, belch forth.*
blǣstbelg m. *bellows*, GL.
blæstm m? *flame, blaze*, MFH90[7].
blǣtan *to 'bleat,'* ÆGr,Rd.
blǣtesung=bladesung; **blǣts-**=blēts-
blǣwen (WW163[29])=blǣhǣwen
blǣwest, blǣwst pres. 2 sg., blǣw(e)ð pres. 3 sg. of blāwan.
blagettan=blǣgettan
blan pret. 3 sg. of blinnan.
blanca† m. (*white?*) *horse*, B. ['blonk']
±**bland†** n. *blending, mixture, confusion.*
±**blandan**[7] *to blend, mix, mingle*, Rd : *trouble, disturb, corrupt.* ['bland']
blandenfeax† *grizzly-haired, grey-haired, old.* [blandan]
blann pret. 3 sg. of blinnan.
blase, blasere=blǣse, blǣsere
blāstbelg=blǣstbelg; **blaster**=plaster
blāt† *livid, pale, wan, ghastly* : *low, hoarse* (*sound*)? or *pale?* (BTs), AN1279. [cp. blēat] adv. blāte *lividly, pallidly*, MET.
blates(n)ung=blades(n)ung
blātian *to be livid, pale*, GEN981 (GK).
±**blāwan**[7] (ō) (tr. or intr.) *to 'blow,' breathe*, Mt,Lk,Jn; Æ : *be blown, sound* : *inflate* : (+) *kindle, inflame*, WW208[14] : (+) *spit*, MkLR7[33].
blāwend m. *inspirer*, ÆH2·478[8].
blāwende *blowing hard* (wind), ANS120[298].
blāwere m. *'blower,'* CP.
blāwung f. *'blowing,' blast*, Æ : *inflation.*
bleac=blæc
blēat *miserable?* Gu963. ['blete']. adv. blēate, B2824.
blēað *gentle, shy, cowardly, timid*, Rd : *slothful, inactive, effeminate*, AO. ['blethe']
blec=blæc; **blēc-**=blǣc-

bled. blēd-=blæd, blēt-
blēd I. (ǣ) f. *shoot, branch, flower, blossom, leaf, foliage, fruit*, Mt,Lcd; CP : *harvest, crops.* ['blede'; blōwan] II.=blǣd I.
blēdan *to 'bleed,' let blood*, Sol.
blēdhwǣt *growing quickly? profusely?* RD2[9].
blēdre=blǣdre
bledu f. *dish, bowl, goblet*, ÆL.
blegen, blegne f. *'blain,' boil, blister, ulcer*, Lcd.
+**blegenod** *blistered*, Lcd1b, 18b. [v. 'blain']
blencan *to deceive, cheat*, Mod. ['blench']
blēnd (e) pret. 3 sg. of blandan.
blendan I. *to blind, deprive of sight*, Bo,Chr : *deceive.* ['blend'] II. *to mix*, WW425[38].
blendian (CHR1086)=blendan I.
blendnes f. *blindness*, DR38[5].
blent pres. 3 sg. of (1) blendan, (2) blandan.
±**blēo** n. gs. blēos, ds. blēo, gp. blēo(na), dip. blēom, blēo(w)um *colour*, Æ,Bo,Met; CP : *appearance, form*, Sol. ['blee']
blēobord n. *coloured board, chess-board*, WY 71.
blēobrygd n? *combination of colours, scintillation*, PH292. [bregdan]
blēocræft m. *art of embroidery*, WW354[9].
+**blēod** *beautiful*, CR909 : *variegated*, KGL (īo).
bleodu=bledu
blēofæstnes f. *delight*, RPs138[11].
blēofāg *variegated*, GL.
bleoh=blēo
blēomete m. *dainty food*, GD99[18].
blēona gp. of blēo.
blēorēad *purple*, WW.
blēostǣning f. *tesselated pavement*, WW 444[10].
blēot pret. 3 sg. of blōtan.
blēoum dip. of blēo.
blēow pret. 3 sg. of (1) blāwan, (2) blōwan.
blēowum dip. of blēo.
blere, blerig *bald*, WW.
blese=blǣse
blētan=blǣtan
±**blē**(later e)**tsian** *to consecrate, ordain*, Mt, JnL(oe) : *'bless,' give thanks, adore, extol*, Da,Lk,Ps: *sign with the cross*, Æ: *pronounce or make happy*, Æ,G,Gen. [blōd; v. NED]
blētsingbōc f. *blessing-book, benedictional*, EC250'.
blētsingealm m. *the Benedicite*, RB36[18].
blētst pres. 2 sg. of blōtan.
blētsung f. *consecration*, Chr : *'blessing,' benediction*, Chr; Æ : *favour* (*of God*), Bl,VPs.
blēw=blēow pret. 3 sg. of blāwan.
blēwð pres. 3 sg. of blōwan.
blīcan[1] *to glitter, shine, gleam, sparkle, dazzle*, Sol235 : *appear*, SOL144. ['blik']

bliccettan *to glitter, quiver,* GL.
bliccettung f. *glittering, shining,* VPs.
blice m. *exposure,* LL 5,34.
-blicgan=-blycgan
blician *to shine,* A 2·357,OEG 1499.
blicð pres. 3 sg. of blican.
blids=bliss
blin imperat. of blinnan.
blind '*blind,*' Mk,Mt; Æ,CP : *dark, obscure, opaque, DD*; Æ : *internal, not showing outwardly* : *unintelligent, Mt* : *not stinging,* WW 322²⁹. adv. -līce *blindly, rashly,* AO.
blindboren *born blind,* JnL 9³².
blindenetele *archangelica (plant),* WW 136, 544.
+**blindfellian** *to blind, blindfold,* HL 8²⁷⁶.
-blindian v. of-b.
blindnes f. *blindness,* Æ.
blinn n? *cessation,* BH,EL.
±**blinnan**⁸ *to cease, leave off, rest from, Mt;* CP : *lose, forfeit, An*: *be vacant* (bishopric). ['*blin*'; be, linnan]
blinnes f. *cessation, intermission,* LL (156⁵).
blis (CP)=bliss; **blisa**=blysa
bliscan=blyscan
blisgere m. *incendiary,* LL. [blysige]
bliss f. '*bliss,' merriment, happiness, Bl,Ps;* CP : *kindness, friendship, grace, favour, Met* : *cause of happiness, Ps.* [bliðe]
±**blissian** (intr.) *to be glad, rejoice, exult, CP,Lk;* Æ : (tr.) *make happy, gladden, endow,* †Hy : *applaud,* ANS 109·306. ['*bliss*']
blissig *joyful,* RPs 112⁹.
blissgendlic *exulting,* ÆH 1·354¹¹.
blissung f. *exultation,* EPs 64¹⁸.
blið=bliðe
±**bliðe** I. '*blithe,' joyous, cheerful, pleasant, Bl,Cr;* Æ,AO,CP : *gracious, well-disposed, friendly, kind, El* : *agreeable, willing* : *quiet, peaceful, gentle, Ps.* II. adv. *Ps.*
bliðelic *gentle, pleasant, glad, well-wishing.* adv. -līce *Lk;* AO. ['*blithely*']
bliðemōd *glad, cheerful* : *well-wishing, friendly,* BH.
bliðheort *happy, joyful,* An : *kind, merciful,* Gen.
+**bliðian** *to make glad,* RPs 91⁴.
bliðnes f. *joy, gladness, pleasure, Lcd;* AO. ['*blitheness*']
bliðs=bliss
bliwum=blēo(w)um, dp. of blēo.
blod=bold
blōd n. '*blood,'* Æ,Chr,G,Lcd; AO,CP : *vein.*
blōd-=blōt-
blōd-dolg, -dolh n. *bleeding wound,* LCD.
blōddrync m. *bloodshed,* AO 162³.
blōdegesa m. *bloody horror,* Ex 477.

+**blōdegian**=blōdgian
blōden *bloody,* WW 217⁸⁵?
blōdfāg† *blood-stained, bloody.*
blōdgemang n. *a blood-mixture,* WW 220⁷.
blōdgemenged *blood-stained,* W 182¹¹.
blōdgēot=blōdgȳte
blōdgēotend m. *shedder of blood,* LPs 50¹⁶.
blōdgēotende *bloody,* LPs 5⁸.
±**blōdgian** *to be bloodthirsty,* WW 215⁴³ : *make 'bloody,'* B.
blōdgyte m. *bloodshed,* AO.
blōdhrǣcung f. *spitting of blood,* WW 113⁶.
blōdhrēow *sanguinary, cruel,* Ps.
blōdig '*bloody,' WW*; AO.
blōdigtōð *bloody-toothed,* B 2083.
blōd-lǣs, -lǣswu f. *blood-letting, bleeding, Lcd.* ['*bloodles*']
blōdlǣstīd f. *time for blood-letting,* LCD 55a.
blōdlǣte f. *blood-letting, bleeding,* LCD 6a.
blōdlǣtere m. '*blood-letter,' WW.*
blōdlēas *bloodless,* ÆGR 56¹⁴.
blōdrēad *blood-red,* LCD.
blōdrēow=blōdhrēow
blōdryne m. *issue of blood, bloody flux* : *bursting of a blood-vessel,* AO 288²⁷.
blōdscēawung f. *supply of blood?* LCD 83a.
blōdseax (æ, e) n. *lancet,* GL.
blōdseten *something to stop bleeding,* LCD.
blōdsihte f. *flowing of blood,* LCD 64a.
blōdðigen f. *tasting of blood,* LL.
blōdwīte n. *blood-offering,* LPs 15⁴ (*i.e. penalty for bloodshed?* v. LL 2·25 and 318): *right to exact such a penalty,* KC 4·216⁵. ['*bloodwite*']
blōdyrnende *having an issue of blood,* BH 78¹⁶ B.
bloedsung (DR 123³)=bletsung
blōma m. *lump of metal, mass, WW.* ['*bloom*']
blon pret. 3 sg. of blinnan.
blonca=blanca; **blond-**=bland-
blonn pret. 3 sg. of blinnan.
blōsa, blōsma=blōstma
blōstbǣre=blōstmbǣre
blōstm (Æ), blōstma mf. '*blossom,' flower, fruit, Bl,Lcd.*
blōstmbǣre (Æ), -bǣrende *flower-bearing.*
blōstmfrēols m. *floral festival,* OEG 4720.
blōstmian *to 'blossom,' bloom,* BH.
blōstmig (sm-) *flowery,* WW 256⁸.
±**blōt** n. *sacrifice,* AO. [blōd]
blōt-=blōd-
blōtan⁷ (and ? wv) *to sacrifice, kill for sacrifice,* AO,CP.
blōtere m. *sacrificer,* GPH 398⁹⁹.
blōtmōnað m. *month of sacrifice* (8 Oct.– 8 Nov.), *November.*
blōtorc m. *sacrificial vessel,* GPH 397.

+blōtsian *to bless*, Percy Soc. vol. 88 p. iii.
blōtspiung f. *spitting of blood*, WW 113⁷.
blōtung f. *sacrifice*, AO 102¹⁶.
±blōwan I. sv⁷ *to 'blow,' flower, flourish, blossom*, Lcd. II.=blāwan
blōwendlic *blooming*, WW 240²⁸.
blunnen pp., blunnon pret. pl. of blinnan.
-blycgan v. ā-b.; blys, blyss=bliss
blysa m. *firebrand, torch*, Æ.
blyscan '*rutilare*,' HGL434⁷⁵ (v. OEG 1196 and '*blush*').
blyse f.=blysa; blysere=blæsere
blysian *to burn, blaze*, PPs 17⁸.
blysige=blyse; blyssian (Æ)=blissian
blȳðe, blȳðelīce=blīðe, blīðelīce
bō=bā, nafn. of bēgen.
bōc I. fn. ds. and nap. bēc '*beech'-tree*, WW; Mdf: *beech-nut*, CHRD 15¹⁰: '*book,' writing, Bible, Bl,CP,Jn*; Æ,AO : *deed, charter, conveyance, Mk,TC*. Crīstes b. *gospel*. II. pret. 3 sg. of bacan.
bōcæceras mpl. *freehold lands*, KC.
bōcblæc (e) n. *ink*, W 225¹.
bōcce=bēce
bōc-cest, -cist(e) f. *book-chest*, APT,RBL.
bōccræft m. *learning, science*, Bo. ['*book-craft*']
bōccræftig *book-learned*, BF 192⁸, JUL 16.
bōcere m. *scholar, scribe, writer*, Æ.
bōcfell n. *parchment, vellum*, LL. ['*book-fell*']
bōcfōdder n. *bookcase*, WW 194¹³.
bōcgesamnung f. *library*, WW 203¹⁵.
bōcgestrēon n. *library*, BH.
bōchaga n. *beech-hedge*, BC 1·515.
bōchord n. *library*, WW. ['*bookhoard*']
bōchūs n. *library*, WW 185³⁵.
±bōcian *to grant by charter : supply with books*.
bōclæden (e²) n. *literary Latin, learned language, Chr*. ['*bocleden*']
bōcland n. *land held by written title*, LL; Æ,AO. v. LL 2·323. ['*bookland*']
bōclār f. '*book-lore,' learning*, LL.
bōcleden=bōclæden
bōclic *of or belonging to a book*, Æ : *scientific*, BF 60⁸ : *biblical, scriptural*. b. stæf '*ars liberalis*,' HGL 503.
bōcon pret. pl. of bacan.
bōcrǣdere m. *reader of books*, WW 439²⁵.
bōcrǣding f. *reading of books*, WW.
bōcrēad *red colour used in illuminating manuscripts, vermilion*, WW.
bōcrēde f. *reading of books*, A 10·143¹⁰¹.
bōcriht n. *right given by will or charter*, LL 444(1).
bōcstæf m. nap. -stafas *letter, character*, El. ['*bocstaff*'; Ger. buchstabe]
bōcstigel f. *beech-wood stile*, BC 1·515.

bōc-tǣcung, -talu f. *teaching or narrative, written in books*, LL.
bōctrēow n. *beech-tree*, ÆGR,WW.
bōcung f. *conveyance by charter or deed*, KC 5·257¹².
bōcweorc n. *study of books*, LL (314¹⁸).
bōcwudu m. *beech-wood*, RD 41¹⁰⁶.
±bod (+exc. N) n. *command, message, precept, Bo,Hy*; Æ : *preaching*. ['*bode,' 'i-bod*']
boda m. *messenger, herald, apostle, angel*, Æ,CP : *prophet*. ['*bode*']
bodan=botm
bode pret. of bōgan.
bodeg=bodig
boden pp. of bēodan.
bodere m. *teacher*, NG.
±bodian *to tell, proclaim, announce*, †Hy; AO,CP : *preach, Mt*; Æ,CP : *foretell, El : boast*. ['*bode*']
bodiend m. *proclaimer, teacher, preacher*, GL,HL.
bodig n. '*body,' trunk, frame, bodily presence*, Æ,BH,Gl,Lcd; CP : *main part*, LCD.
bodigendlic *to be celebrated*, ÆL 7²³³.
bodlāc n. *decree, ordinance*, CHR 1129.
±bodscipe† m. *command, message*, GEN.
bodung f. *message, recital, preaching*, Æ : *interpretation : assertiveness*, RB 136²².
bodungdæg m. *Annunciation Day*, ÆH 1·200²⁵.
bōg m. *arm, shoulder*, Æ; CP : '*bough,' twig, branch, Mt*; CP : *offspring*. [būgan]
boga m. '*bow*' (weapon), *Gn*; Æ : *arch, arched place, vault*, B : *rainbow*, Æ,Lcd : *folded parchment*. [cp. Ger. bogen]
bōga=bōg
bōgan *to boast*, RB.
boganet=bogenett
bogefōdder m. *quiver*, WW 143¹⁹.
bogen I. *name of a plant*, LCD. II. pp. of būgan.
bogenett n. *wicker basket with a narrow neck for catching fish*, WW.
bogetung f. *curve*, WW 355¹⁵.
bōgh=bōg
bōgian I. ±(intr.) *to dwell*, Æ : (tr.) *to inhabit*. II.=bōgan
bogiht *full of bends*, MtL 7¹⁴.
bōgincel n. *small bough*, OEG.
bōgung (bōung) f. *boastfulness, arrogance, display*, Æ.
bōh=bōg
bohscyld m. *curved shield?* (WC 172n), EC 226'.
bohte pret. 3 sg. of bycgan.
bōhtimber n. *building-wood*. [v. AS 1³ and ES 42·172]
bōian=bōgan

bol? m. *bole, trunk,* Lcd 143a.
bolca m. *gangway of a ship,* An,B,Gl.
bold (=botl) n. *house, dwelling-place, mansion, hall, castle,* B : *temple.* ['*bold*']
boldāgend† m. *homestead-owner.*
boldgestrēon (botl)† *household goods,* Gen.
boldgetæl *collection of houses* : (*political*) *district, county, province,* GD.
boldgetimbru npl. *houses,* Sol 412.
boldweard (botl-) m. *housekeeper, steward,* Ægr,WW.
boldwela† (botl-) m. *wealth* : *splendid dwelling, paradise, heaven: village,* Gen 1799.
bolgen pp. of belgan.
bolgenmōd† *enraged.*
bolla m., bolle f. '*bowl,*' *cup, pot, beaker, measure,* Æl,Jn,Lcd.
bolster mn. '*bolster,*' *cushion,* B; CP.
+bolstrian *to support with pillows, prop up,* Bf 74¹⁶.
bolt m. '*bolt*' : *cross-bow for throwing bolts or arrows,* WW.
bolttimber n. *building timber, beams.* [v. AS 1³ and ES 42·172]
bōn I. f. *ornament,* Chr 1063 D. **II.**=bōgan
bon-, bond-=ban-, band-
bōnda m. *householder,* LL : *freeman, plebeian* : *husband.* ['*bond*']
bōndeland n. *land held by a* bōnda, Chr 777 E. [*ON.* bōndi]
bōne=bēn
+bōnian *to ornament,* TC. [bōn]
bonn=bann
bor *borer, gimlet,* Gl : *lancet, scalpel, graving tool,* Gl. [borian]
bora m. *ruler,* Sat 500. [? rǣdbora]
borcen pret. 3 sg. of beorcan.
borcian *to bark,* Rd 84⁶.
bord n. '*board,*' *plank,* Æ : *table,* Ps : *side of a ship,* Gen : *ship,* El,Gn : *shield,* El. innan, ūtan bordes *at home, abroad,* CP.
borda m. *embroidery, ornament,* Gl.
bordclāð m. *table-cloth,* OEG 56²².
bordgelāc n. *weapon, dart,* Cr 769.
bordhæbbende *shield-bearing,* B 2895.
bordhaga m. *cover of shields,* El 652.
bordhrēoða (ē)† m. *shield-ornament* : *phalanx.*
bordrand m. *shield,* B 2559.
bordrima (e²) m. *rim, edge,* Ln.
bordrīolg *a stream running in a channel made of planks?* (BTs),EC 450¹¹.
bordstæð n. *sea-shore,* An 442.
bordðaca m. *shield-covering, testudo,* Gl : *board for roofing,* WW.
bordweall m. *wall of shields, phalanx* : *buckler, shield* : *side of ship,* Rd 34⁶.
bordwudu m. *shield,* B 1243
boren (B,Chr,Cp) pp. of beran. ['*y-born*']

borettan *to brandish,* Gl.
borg m. *pledge, security, bail, debt, obligation,* LL (v. 2·331; 641); CP : *bondsman : debtor.* ['*borrow*' sb.]
borgbryce m. *breach of surety,* LL. ['*borrow-breach*']
borgen pp. of beorgan.
borggelda m. *borrower* : *lender,* CPs 108¹¹.
borgian *to* '*borrow,*' Mt,Ps : *lend : be surety for,* OEG 3812.
borgiend m. *lender, usurer,* SPs 108¹⁰.
borg-sorg (burg-) f. *trouble on account of lending or security,* Rim 63.
borgsteall *a steep path up a hill?* BC,KC (v. BTac and Mdf).
borgwedd n. *pledge,* WW 279¹⁶.
borh=borg
borhfæst *fast bound,* HL 203²⁵⁴.
±borhfæstan *to bind by pledge or surety,* Chr.
borhhand fm. *security, surety* (person), Æ.
borhlēas *without a pledge, without security,* LL 230,5.
borian *to bore, perforate,* Gl.
borlīce *very, extremely, fitly, excellently,* Bf.
born=barn pret. 3 sg. of biernan.
+borsnung=+brosnung
borsten pp. of berstan.
borðor=beorðor
bōsig m? n? *stall, crib,* LkLR. ['*boosy*']
bōsm (CP), bōsum m. '*bosom,*' *breast, womb,* Æ : *surface,* An : *ship's hold,* Gen.
bōsmig *sinuous,* OEG 8².
bōt f. *help, relief, advantage, remedy,* An,Da, Lcd; AO : *compensation for an injury or wrong,* LL (v. 2·336) : (*peace*) *offering, recompense, amends, atonement, reformation, penance, repentance,* B,Bl; CP. tō bōte *to* '*boot,*' *besides, moreover.*
bōtan=bētan
bōtettan *to improve, repair,* W.
bōtian *to get better,* BH,Lcd.
±botl (Æ,CP)=bold
bōtlēas *unpardonable, not to be atoned for by* bōt, LL,W.
botm m. '*bottom,*' *ground, foundation,* B, Sat,WW : *abyss,* Gen.
bōtwyrðe *pardonable, that can be atoned for by* bōt, LL,W. [cp. bōtlēas]
bōð=bōgeð pres. 3 sg. of bōgan.
bōðen mn? *rosemary* : *darnel,* Æ : *thyme,* GPH 390.
bōung=bōgung
box mn. *box-tree,* KC,WW : '*box,*' *case,* M., WW. [L.]
boxtrēow n. *box-tree,* ÆGr 20¹⁹.
braccas mp. *breeches,* Lcd 3·198'. [L.]
bracce (Mdf)=brǣc I.
brachwīl f. *moment,* Bf 118²⁴.
-bracian v. ā-b.

brād I. comp. brādra, brǣdra '*broad*,' *flat, open, extended, spacious, wide,* Bl,Gen, Chr,Ps; Æ,AO,CP : *ample, copious,* B,El. **II.** n. *breadth,* LV,Rim.

brādæx f. *broad axe,* Gl.

brādbrim† n. *wide sea.*

brāde† *far and wide, broadly, widely,* W.

brādelēac n. *leek,* Gl.

brādhand f. *palm of the hand,* WW 264³⁴.

brādian *to extend, reach,* AO 234¹⁰ : (+) VPs 47³.

brādlāstæx f. *broad axe,* Gl.

brādlinga *flatly, with the hand open,* IM.

brādnes sf. *breadth, greatness, extent, surface,* Æ : *liberality.*

brādpanne = brǣdepanne

bræc I. *a strip of untilled land?* (BT),KC. **II.** = pret. 3 sg. of brecan. **III.** (+) (e) n. *noise, sound,* CP.

bræc I. (±) n. *catarrh, cough.* **II.** f. *breaking, destruction,* ÆL 5²⁹². **III.** = brēc nap. of brōc I.

bræcce *breeches,* Cp 1788. [L.]

bræccoōu f. *falling sickness, epilepsy,* WW 112²⁷.

bræcdrenc (ē) *cough medicine,* WW 351⁸⁸.

+**bræceo** = bræc I.

bræclian *to crackle, make a noise,* GD 236¹².

bræcon pret. pl. of brecan.

±**bræcsēoc** *epileptic, lunatic,* BH,Lcd.

brǣd I. f. *breadth, width,* AO. [brād] **II.** f. *flesh,* Ph 240. [OHG. brāt] **III.** m. *trick, fraud, deceit, craft,* LL,MtL. [=*brægd; '*braid*'] **IV.** pret. 3 sg. of brēdan, bregdan. **V.** pres. 3 sg. and pp. of brǣdan.

brǣd- = brægd- (bregd-)

±**brǣdan** (e) **I.** *to make broad, extend, spread, stretch out,* BH; AO : *be extended, rise, grow.* ['*brede*'; brād] **II.** *to roast, toast, bake, broil, cook,* WW. ['*brede*']

brǣde m. *roast meat,* WW. ['*brede*']

-brǣdels v. ofer-b.

brǣdepanne f. *frying-pan* (v. WW 363n3).

brǣding I. f. *extension,* Bo 46⁶ : *bedding, bed?* DR. **II.** f. *roast meat,* OEG 3760.

brǣdingpanne = brǣdepanne

brǣdīsen (ē) n. *chisel,* Gl,WW.

brǣdra v. brād.

brǣd-u, -o f. *breadth, width, extent,* Ps. ['*brede*']

+**brægd** = brǣd III; **brægdan** = bregdan

brægdboga m. *deceitful bow,* Cr 765.

brægden (e) **I.** (±) *deceitful, crafty,* AO. adv. -līce. [bregdan] **II.** *fraud,* LL.

brægdwīs *crafty,* Gu 58. [bregd]

brægen (a, e) n. '*brain*,' Lcd,Ps; Æ,CP.

brægenpanne f. *brain-pan, skull,* OEG 2815.

brægensēoc *brain-sick, mad,* OEG.

brægn = brægen

brægnloca (hrægn-) m. *brain-house, head,* Rd 72⁸¹.

brægpanne = brægenpanne

bræhtm (A) = breahtm

brǣmbel, brǣmel = brēmel

brǣme (NG) = brēme; **brǣr** = brēr

bræs n. '*brass*,' *bronze,* WW.

bræsen '*brazen*,' *of brass,* LPs; Æ.

bræsian *to do work in brass, make of brass,* ÆGr 215¹⁷. ['*braze*']

bræsne = bresne

brǣð m. *odour, scent, stink, exhalation, vapour,* AO,WW. ['*breath*']

brǣw (ēa) m. *eye-brow, eye-lid,* BH,Lcd,Ps, WW; CP. ['*bree*']

bragen = brægen

brahton = brohton pret. pl. of bringan.

brand (ō) m. *fire, flame,* B; Æ : '*brand*,' *torch,* JnL,Da; Æ : *sword, weapon,* B,TC.

brandhāt† *burning hot, ardent.*

brandhord (o¹) n? *treasure exciting ardent desires* (BT); *care, anxiety* (GK), Rim 46.

brand-īren, -īsen o. *fire-dog, trivet, grate,* WW. ['*brandise*']

brandōm (o¹) m. '*rubigo*,' WW 44¹⁴.

brandrād (o², e²) f. *fire-dog, trivet,* WW. ['*brandreth*']

brandrida m. *fire-grate,* WW 266²⁶.

brandstæfn (o¹) *high-prowed?* An 504. [= brant-?]

brang pret. 3 sg. of bringan.

brant† (o) *deep, steep, high,* An,El. ['*brant*']

braslan = bræsian

+**brastl** (-sl) n. *crackling* (*of flames*), DD,W.

brastlian (-sl) *to roar, rustle, crackle,* Æ. ['*brastle*']

brastlung f. *crackling, rustling, crashing,* Æ.

bratt m. *cloak,* MtL 5⁴⁰. ['*bratt*'; v. LF 125]

brēac pret. 3 sg. of brūcan.

brēad n. *bit, crumb, morsel* : '*bread*,' JnL.

+**breadian** (e) *to regenerate, restore,* Ph 372, 592.

brēag = brǣw

breahtm I. (bearhtm; æ, e, eo, y) m. *cry, noise, revelry.* **II.** = bearhtm

breahtmian (earht) *to creak, resound,* Gl.

breahtmung f. '*convolatus*,' WW 376³.

breahtumhwæt = bearhtmhwæt

breard = brerd; **brēat-** = brēot-

brēað *brittle,* Lcd 1·260⁷.

brēaw = brǣw

brēawern n. *brew-house,* WW 145²⁹.

+**brec** = + bræc III.

brēc v. brōc; ±**brēc** = ±bræc

±**brecan I.** sv⁴ *to 'break,' shatter, burst, tear,* B,Bl,G,Ps : *curtail, injure, violate, destroy, oppress,* B,Chr,Da,KC ; AO,CP : *break into, rush into, storm, capture* (*city*), Ma, Chr ; CP : *press, force : break or crash through, burst forth, spring out,* An,Ph : *subdue, tame,* CP. **II.** *to roar?* CR 951.

brēchrægl n. *breeches,* PPs 108⁸⁸.

brecmǣlum=brytmǣlum

±**brecnes** f. *breach,* EPs.

-brecð v. ǣ-, eodor-b.

brecða m. *broken condition.* mōdes b. *sorrow of heart,* B171.

brecung f. *'breaking,'* LkR.

bred n. *surface : board, plank,* CP : *tablet,* Æ. ['*bred*']

brēd=(1) brȳd, (2) brād, (3) brǣd III.

brēdan I. *to produce, or cherish, a brood,* Æ. ['*breed*'] **II.** (±)=bregdan. **III.** (±)= brǣdan I. and II.

breden (i, y) *of boards, wooden,* Æ,Chr.

brēdende *deceitful, cunning,* AO. [bregdan]

brēdettan=brogdettan

+**bredian**=breadian

brēdi(ng)panne=brǣdepanne

brēdīsern=brǣdīsen

bredweall m. *wall of boards, palisade,* ES 20·148.

+**brēfan** *to write down shortly,* BF 72²⁰. [cp. *Ger.* brief]

brēg (VPs)=brēaw ; **brega** (Æ)=brego

brēgan *to alarm, frighten, terrify,* Lk ; Æ, CP. ['*bree*' ; brōga]

bregd=brǣd III.

+**bregd I.** n. *quick movement, change,* Ph 57. [v. '*braid*'] **II.**=brǣd III.

bregdan³ (brēd-) *to move quickly, pull, shake, swing, throw* (*wrestling*), *draw* (*sword*), *drag,* B,Ma : *bend, weave, 'braid,' knit, join together,* ÆGr : *change colour, vary, be transformed,* Ex,Sol,Gu : *bind, knot :* (intr.) *move, be pulled : flash,* Æ. up b. *bring up* (*a charge*) : (+) *scheme, feign, pretend :* (+) *draw breath, breathe.*

bregden=brægden

+**bregdnes** (ē?) f. *quick movement? sudden terror?* MFH 133¹⁷ (v. BTac).

+**bregdstafas** mp. *learned arts,* Sol 2.

bregen=brægen

brēgendlic *terrible,* RPs 46³.

brēgh=brēaw

brēgnes f. *fear, terror,* EPs 87¹⁷.

brego† (eo) m. *ruler, chief, king, lord.* b. engla, mancynnes *God.*

bregorīce n. *kingdom,* Gen 1633.

bregorōf *majestic, mighty,* B 1925.

bregostōl† m. *ruler's seat, throne : rule, dominion.*

bregoweard† m. *ruler, prince, lord,* Gen.

bregu=brego

breht-=breaht-, beorht-, bierht-

brehtnian=bearhtmian

brēman I. (±) *to honour, extol : respect, fulfil,* Chrd 18³⁵ : *celebrate,* Chrd 114¹⁷. [brēme] **II.** (oe) *to rage,* NG.

brēmbel (Æ), brēmber=brēmel

brēme (oe, ȳ) **I.** adj. *famous, glorious, noble,* PPs ; AO. ['*breme*'] **II.** adv. *An.*

brēmel (ǣ) m. *brier, 'bramble,' blackberry bush,* Æ,Lcd ; Mdf. [brōm]

brēmelæppel m. *blackberry,* Lcd. [v. '*apple*']

brēmelberie f. *blackberry,* Lcd. ['*brambleberry*']

brēmelbrǣr (ǣ¹) m. *bramble-brier,* WW 269³⁸.

brēmellēaf n. *bramble-leaf,* Lcd.

brēmelrind f. *bramble-bark,* Lcd.

brēmelðyrne f. *bramble-bush,* Æ.

brēmen=brēme I.

brēmendlic *noted,* OEG.

brēmer=brēmel

brēmlas nap. of brēmel.

bremman *to rage, roar,* JnL, WW. [*Ger.* brummen]

bremung f. *roaring,* WW 242³⁹.

brencð pres. 3 sg. of brengan.

brene=bryne

breneð=berneð (pres. 3 sg. of bernan) (Run 43)

±**brengan** *to bring,* AO,CP : *produce,* NG.

brengnes f. *oblation :* (+) *food, support,* MkL 12⁴⁴.

brenting m. *ship,* B 2807. [brant]

breo-, brēo-=bre-, brē-

brēod (NG)=brēad

breodian *to cry out,* Mod 28.

breodwian *to strike down, trample?* Gu 258, Lcd 32¹¹.

breoht-=bearht-, beorht-

brēosa (īo) m. *gadfly,* WW. ['*breeze*']

brēost nmf. (usu. in pl.) '*breast,' bosom,* B, G,Lcd ; AO,CP : *stomach, womb : mind, thought, disposition,* Gen ; CP : '*ubertas,*' CPs 35⁹.

brēostbān n. *'breast-bone,'* WW 158.

brēostbeorg=brēostgebeorh

brēostbyden (e²) f. *breast,* Gl.

brēostcearu† f. *heart-care, anxiety.*

brēostcofa† m. *heart, affections.*

breostgebeorh m. *bulwark,* WW 466¹⁴.

brēostgehygd†, -hȳd† fn. *thought.*

brēostgeðanc† m. *mind, thought.*

brēostgewǣdu† np. *corslet,* B.

brēostgyrd f. *sceptre?* OEG 3303 ; 2¹⁸⁸.

brēosthord† n. *thought, mind.*

brēostlīn n. *stomacher,* WW 407².

brēostloca† m. *mind, soul.*

brēostnet† n. *coat of mail.*
brēostnyrwet n. *tightness of chest,* LCD 189b.
brēostrocc m. *chest-clothing,* WW 151³⁹.
brēostsefa† m. *mind, heart.*
brēosttoga m. *chieftain,* SOL 184.
brēostðing n. *region of the heart,* LCD 3·146¹⁸.
brēostwære m. *pain in the chest,* LCD.
brēostweall m. *breastwork, rampart,* WW 490¹³.
brēostweorðung f. *breast-ornament,* B 2504.
brēostwylm (e²) m. *breast-fountain, teat,* SPs 21⁸ : *emotion, sorrow,* B.
Breot-=Bryt-
brēotan²† *to break in pieces, hew down, demolish, destroy, kill.*
Breotas=Brittas
Breoten, Breoton=Bryten
breoton=bryten; brēoton pret. pl. of brēatan.
brēoðan² *to decay, waste away,* LCD 63a, RPs 4¹⁶.
±brēowan² *to 'brew,'* AO.
brēowlāc n. *brewing,* ÆL 17¹⁰³.
brēr (ǣ) f. *'brier,' bramble,* Lcd,WW.
brerd (ea, eo, y) m. *brim, margin, border, surface,* Jn,WW : *shore, bank,* Æ. ['*brerd*']
brerdful *brim-full,* ÆL 6²⁸². ['*brerdful*']
brērhlǣw m. *brier-hillock,* EC 450⁹.
brērðyrne f. *brier-bush,* KC 6·221¹³.
brēsan=brȳsan; bresen=bræsen
bresne (æ)† *mighty, strong.*
Bret=Bryt; bret-, brēt-=bryt-, brȳt-
brēt pret. 3 sg. of brēdan, bregdan.
brēð=brǣð; brēðel=brīðel
brēðer ds. of brōðor.
brēw (KGL)=brǣw
bric-, brīc-=bryc-, brȳc-
briceð pres. 3 sg.; bricst pres. 2 sg. of brecan.
brid=bridd; brīd=brȳd
bridd m. *young 'bird,' chicken,* Gl,Lk; Æ, CP,Mdf.
bridel, bridels (ȳ) m. *'bridle,' rein, curb, restraint, Run;* Æ,CP.
bridelshring m. *bridle-ring,* EL 1194.
bridelōwangas mp. *reins,* WW 97¹⁰.
briden=breden
brid-gift, -gifu=brȳd-gift, -gifu
±brīdlian *to 'bridle,' curb, Bo;* CP.
briengan=bringan
brig=brycg; brīg=brīw
brigd n. *change or play of colours,* PA 26. [bregdan]
brigdils (GL)=brīdels
briht-=beorht-, bierht-
brim† n. *surf, flood, wave, sea, ocean, water, B :* *sea-edge, shore.* ['*brim*']

brimcealdt† *ocean-cold,* PH.
brimclif n. *cliff by the sea,* B 222.
brimfaroð n. *sea-shore* (BT), DA 322 (or ? 2 words).
brimflōd m. *flood, sea,* Az,WW.
brimfugol m. *sea-bird, gull,* WA 47.
brimgiest m. *sailor,* RD 4²⁵.
brimhengest† m. *(sea-horse), ship.*
brimhlæst f. *sea-produce, (fish),* GEN 200.
brimlād† f. *flood-way, sea-way.*
brimlīðend† m. *seafarer, B : pirate,* MA.
brimmann† m. *sailor, pirate,* MA.
brimrād† f. *(sea-road), sea,* AN.
brimsa? *gadfly?* (v. Ln 49⁸² and NC 354).
brimstæð n. *sea-shore,* AN 496.
brimstrēam† m. *current, sea : rapid, river.*
brimðyssa† m. *ship.*
brimwīsa m. *sea-king, captain,* B 2930.
brimwudu† m. *(sea-wood), ship.*
brimwylf f. *(she-)wolf of the sea or lake,* B 1507.
brimwylm m. *ocean surge, sea-wave,* B 1494.
bring m. *offering,* CPs 50²⁰.
bringād† f. *epilepsy?* (or? hringādl v. MLR 19·201).
±bringan³ (e, ie, y) (and wv) *to 'bring,' lead, bring forth, carry, adduce, produce, present, offer, B,Gen,Jn,Met ;* AO,CP.
-bringelle v. on-b.; brīosa=brēosa
brīst, brītst pres. 2 sg., brīt pres. 3 sg. of bregdan.
Brit-, brit-=Bryt-, bryt-
brīðel (e) *fragile, weak,* LCD 1·384¹⁴ (BTac).
brīw m. *pottage, porridge,* ÆGr,Lcd. ['*bree*']
±brīwan *to prepare food, cook, make pottage : make a poultice,* LCD 25a.
brīwðicce *as thick as pottage,* LCD 190a.
broc I. (±) n. *affliction, misery, care, toil, adversity, Bl,Bo,TC;* Æ,AO,CP : *disease, sickness, Æ : fragment, G : breach.* ['*broke*'; brecan] II. n. *use, benefit.* III. *a kind of locust?* WW 460. ['*brock*'] IV.=brocc
brōc I. f. pl. brēc *breeches, RB,WW :* *the breech? Lcd* (ES 38·345). II. m. *'brook,' torrent, Bo,WW ;* Mdf.
brocc m. *badger, Lcd.* ['*brock*']
broccen *of badger's skin,* WW 152¹.
brocchol n. *badger's hole,* EC 239¹².
broccian *to tremble,* GD 156.
brocen pp. of (1) brecan, (2) brūcan.
brocenlic *fragile,* BYH 130²⁹.
±brocian *to crush, hurt, afflict, molest,* Æ, AO,CP : *blame.* [broc]
broclic *full of hardship,* W 248¹.
brōcminte f. *brookmint, horsemint,* LCD, WW.
brōcriō *a tributary stream,* KC 5·194'.
brōcsēoc=brǣcsēoc

brocung f. *affliction, sickness,* ÆH 1·472[7].
brod *shoot, sprout,* LHy 6[3].
brōd f. '*brood,*' Æ : *foetus* : *breeding, hatching,* WW 380[44].
broddetan=brogdettan
broddian=brōdian
brōden pp. of brēdan.
brōdenmǣl† n. *damascened sword.*
brōder=brōðor; **brōdet-**=brogdet-
brōdian *to glitter, shine,* OEG.
brōdig adj. *broody,* BF 78[16].
brōga m. *terror, dread, danger,* CP : *prodigy.*
brogden (*El*) pp. of bregdan. ['*browden*']
brogdenmǣl=brōdenmǣl
brogdettan *to shake, brandish* : *tremble, quake* : *glitter,* HGL 435?
brogdettung f. *trembling, shaking* : *figment, pretence,* CPs 102[14].
±**brogne** *bough, bush, branch,* DR (v. ES 38·340 and JAW).
broht '*viscellum,*' WW 54[1]. (?=broð '*juscellum,*' MLR 19·201)
brōht pp., **brōhton** pret. pl. of bringan.
brōhðrēa m. *dire calamity,* GEN 1813. [brōga]
brōm m. '*broom,*' *brushwood,* Lcd; Mdf.
brōmfæsten n. *enclosure of broom,* WW 414[7].
brōmig *broomy,* BL 207[27]? (BTs and ac).
bron-=bran-; **brond**=brand, brant
brord m. *prick, point* : *blade* (*e.g., of grass or corn*) : *herbage,* BH 366[26].
±**brosnian** *to crumble, decay, fall to pieces, rot, wither, be corrupted,* AO,CP.
brosniendlic (Æ), +**brosnodlic** (BL,W) *corruptible, perishable, transitory.*
±**brosnung** f. *decay, corruption, ruin,* Æ.
+**brot** n. *fragment,* G. [breotan]
Broten=Bryten
broten pp. of brēotan.
brotettan *to burst forth, shoot, sprout?* HGL 435, OEG 1218n (or?=brogdettan, BTs)
brōtetung=brogdettung
broð n. '*broth,*' WW. [brēowan]
brōðar, brōðer=brōðor
brōðhund (WW 329[38]; 548[19])=roðhund?
brōðor m. ds. brēðer '*brother**,*' *Chr,Mt,Lk.* nap. (±) brōðor, brōðru, *Gen,Jn* : *fellowman, Ps* : *co-religionist, Mt* : *monk.*
brōðorbana m. *fratricide* (*person*), GEN 1526.
brōðorcwealm m. *fratricide* (*act*), GEN 1030.
brōðordohter f. *niece,* WW 173[30].
brōðorgyld n. *vengeance for brothers?* Ex 199.
brōðorlēas *brotherless,* RD 85[16].
brōðorlic '*brotherly,*' ÆGr.
brōðorlīcnes f. *brotherliness,* BH.
brōðorlufu (-e[2]) *love,* DR.
brōðorrǣden f. *fellowship, brotherhood,* Æ : *membership of a brotherhood.* ['*brotherred*']

brōðorscipe m. *brotherliness, love, MtL* : (+) *brotherhood, fraternity,* AO. ['*brothership*']
brōðorsibb f. *kinship of brothers* : *brotherly love.*
brōðorslaga m. *brother-slayer,* Æ.
brōðorslege m. *fratricide* (*act*), CP.
brōðorsunu m. *brother's son, nephew,* CHR.
brōðorsybb=brōðorsibb
broðor-ōīnen, -ōīnenu=beorðorðīnen
brōðorwīf n. *brother's wife, sister-in-law,* BH.
brōðorwyrt (e[2]) f. '*pulegium,*' *penny-royal,* WW 300[24].
+**brōð-ru,** -ra mp. *brothers, brethren, Mt.* ['*i-brotheren*']
brōður=brōðor
+**browen** pp. of brēowan.
brū f. nap. brū(w)a, gp. brūna '*brow,*' *eyebrow, eye-lid, eye-lash, Rd,WW.*
±**brūcan**[2] *to* '*brook,*' *use, enjoy, possess, partake of, spend, B,Wa.* brocen cyrtel *a coat which has been worn,* Æ : *eat, Æ,JnL* : *execute an office,* CP : *cohabit with.*
brūcendlice *serviceably,* OEG 53[1].
brūcung f. *function, occupation,* BC 1·154[13].
brūdon, brugdon pret. pl. of brēdan, bregdan.
brūn '*brown,*' *dark, dusky, Ex,Met* : *having metallic lustre, shining* (v. NED).
brūna gp. of brū.
brūn-basu, -be(o)su *brownish-purple,* OEG.
brūnecg† *with gleaming blade.*
brūneða m. *itch, erysipelas,* LCD 18a.
brūnewyrt=brūnwyrt
brūnfāg *burnished? brown-hued?* B 2615.
brungen pp., **brungon** pret. pl. of bringan.
brūnian *to become brown,* LCD 106b.
brunna=burna
brūnwann *dusky,* AN 1308.
brūnwyrt f. '*brownwort,*' *water-betony, wood-betony,* Lcd.
bruðon pret. pl. of brēoðan.
brūwa nap. of brū.
±**bryce** (i) I. m. '*breach*' ('*bruche*'), *fracture, breaking, infringement, Gu,LL;* Æ : *fragment,* OEG. [brecan] II. *fragile, brittle, worthless, fleeting, Bl.* ['*bryce*'] III. n. *use, enjoyment, service, exercise, advantage, gain, profit, fruit,* Æ,CP.
brȳce *useful, profitable,* PPs. ['*briche*']
-brycel v. hūs-b.
bryceð pres. 3 sg. of brecan.
brycg f. '*bridge,*' Æ; AO,Mdf.
brycgbōt (i) f. *repairing of bridges,* LL.
brycggeweorc (i[1]) n. *work of building or repairing bridges,* Ct,LL.
brycgian *to* '*bridge,*' *make a causeway, pave, An.*
brycgweard (i[1]) m. *keeper or defender of a bridge, Ma* 85. ['*bridgeward*']

brycgwyrcende '*pontifex*'! DR 194'.

±brȳc-ian, -sian *to use, enjoy*, DR : *profit, benefit.*

brycŏ pres. 3 sg. of brecan.

brȳcŏ pres. 3 sg. of brūcan.

brȳd I. (ē, i) f. '*bride*,' *betrothed or newly-married woman, wife, consort*, G,WW ; Æ, CP. brȳdes wǣde *wedding garment* : (†) (*young*) *woman*. II.=brygd

bryd-, brȳd-=bred-, brīd-

brȳdbedd n. *bridal bed*, Æ.

brȳdblētsung (ī) f. *marriage blessing*, LL 72,38¹.

brȳdboda m. *paranymph, bridesman*, OEG 18b⁷¹.

brȳdbūr (BL) n., brȳdcofa (HGL) m. *bride-chamber, bed-chamber.*

+bryddan *to frighten, terrify*, SOL 16.

-brȳde v. un-b.

brȳdeala, brȳdealo(ŏ) n. *bride-ale, marriage-feast*, Chr. ['*bridal*']

brȳdelic=brȳdlic

brȳdgifta fpl. *betrothal, espousals*, APT.

brȳdgifu (ī) f. *dowry*, ÆGR 57¹⁴ : (pl.) *espousals*, WW 171⁵.

brȳdguma (Æ,CP), brȳdiguma (Æ) m. '*bridegroom*,' Jn : *suitor.*

brȳdhlōp n. *ceremony on conducting a bride to her new home, bridal, wedding*, Chr,MtL. ['*bridelope*']

brȳdhūs n. *bride-chamber*, APs 18⁶.

+brȳdian *to marry*, MH.

brȳdlāc n. *bridal, wedded condition*, Æ : (pl.) *marriage ceremony*, LL ; Æ. ['*bridelock*']

brȳdlēoŏ n. *epithalamium*, OEG.

brȳdlic *bridal.* b. gewrit *Song of Solomon*, WW 388²⁰. ['*bridely*']

brȳdloca m. *bride-chamber*, BL.

brȳdlōp=brȳdhlōp

brȳdlufe f. *love of a bride*, JUL 114.

brȳdniht f. *wedding-night*, MH 14²⁶.

brȳdrǣst f. *bridal bed*, GD.

brȳdrēaf n. *wedding garment*, MtL 22¹¹.

brȳdsang m. *epithalamium*, WW.

brȳdsceamol? *bridal bed*, DR 110¹ (BTs).

brȳdŏing np. *nuptials*, Bl. ['*brydthing*']

brygc=brycg

brygd I. (bryd) m. *drawing out, unsheathing, brandishing*, LL 356,2. II.=brǣd III.

bryht=beorht; bryhtan=bierhtan

±brygdan *to seize property improperly held by another*, LL. [=*brigdan? BTs]

brym, brymm m. *surf, sea*, AB 35·240.

brȳm-=brēm-

bryne m. *burning, conflagration*, BH : *fire, flame, heat*, MtL ; AO : *inflammation, burn, scald*, Lcd : *torch* : *fervour, passion.* ['*brune*'; beornan]

brȳne f. '*brine*,' WW ; Æ.

bryneādl f. *fever*, WW 238²⁶.

brynebrōga m. *fire-terror*, Az 161.

brynegieldt (i³) m. *burnt-offering*, GEN.

brynehāt *burning hot*, DOM 51.

brynelēoma m. *fire-gleam, flame*, B 2313.

brynenes f. *hard, fiery trial*, HGL 469.

brynetēar m. *hot tear*, CR 152.

bryne-wylm, -welmt m. *wave of fire, flame, burning heat.*

bryngan=bringan

brynig *fiery, burning*, DD 211.

brynstān m. *brimstone*, RWH 143³¹.

bryrd=brerd

bryrdan *to urge on, incite, encourage*, MET 13⁸. [brord]

bryrdnes f. *incitement, instigation*, BH.

±brȳs-an, -ian (ē; =īe) *to* '*bruise*,' *crush, pound*, BH,DD : *season*, Sc 20²⁰.

+brȳsednes f. *bruising, crushing*, WW 211²².

brȳsewyrt f .*daisy, soap-wort*, Lcd 1·374. ['*bruisewort*']

brystmian=brytsnian

brȳt pres. 3 sg. of brēotan.

Bryt (e, i) m. *Briton* : *Breton.*

bryta=brytta

±brȳtan *to crush, pound* : (+) *break up, destroy.*

-brytednes v. for-b.

Bryten (e, eo, i, o) f. *Britain.*

bryten (eo) *spacious, roomy*, SAT 687.

brytencyning m. *powerful king*, WY 75.

brytengrūnd m. *broad earth*, CR 357.

Brytenlond n. *Britain* : *Wales.*

brytenrīce (eo) n. I. *spacious kingdom*, Az 107. II. *kingdom of Britain.*

Brytenw(e)alda m. *wielder of Britain, Bretwalda, chief king*, CHR,KC.

brytenwongas mp. *spacious plains, the world*, CR 380.

brȳtest pres. 2 sg. of brēotan.

brytian=bryttian

brȳting (ē) f. *breaking (of bread)*, LkL 24³⁵.

Bryt-land, -lond=Brytenlond

brytmǣlum *piecemeal*, OEG 1553n.

brytnere m. *steward*, CP 459¹¹.

±brytnian (i) *to divide, distribute, dispense, administer*, B ; CP. ['*britten*']

brytnung f. *distribution*, WW 222⁴³.

brȳtofta pl. *espousals*, WW 171⁵. [brȳd, ŏoft]

Bryton=Bryten

±brytsen f. *fragment*, FM,G.

brytsnian *to parcel out, distribute*, OEG 2195 : (+) *enjoy, possess*, ES 8·473³³.

brȳtst pres. 2 sg. of brēotan.

Brytt- v. also Bryt-.

bryttat (e) m. *dispenser, giver, author, governor, prince, lord.* sinces b. *treasure-giver, lord.* [brēotan]

+bryttan=+brȳtan

Bryttas mp. *Britons*, BH : *Bretons*, CHR.

±**bryttian** (i) *to divide, dispense, distribute,* CP : *rule over, possess, enjoy the use of.*
Bryttisc (e) '*British,*' *Chr.*
Bryttwealas, Brytwalas mp. *Britons of Wales,* CHR.
Brytwyllsc *British, Welsh,* CHR.
bryðen f. *brewing, drink, Gu,Lcd.* ['*bruthen*'; broð]
brywlāc (Æ)=brēowlāc
bū I. n. nap. bȳ *dwelling.* [*Ger.* bau] II. v. bā, bēgen.
±**būan** anv. (intr.) *to stay, dwell, live,* AO : *lie* (*of land*), WE66¹⁶ : (tr.) *inhabit, occupy : cultivate.* [*Ger.* bauen]
būc, bucc m. *belly, stomach,* Æ : *pitcher,* Æ : *beaver* (*of helmet*)? ['*bouk*']
bucca m. '*buck*,' *he-goat, male deer,* Æ,Lcd, WW; CP.
budda m. *beetle,* WW543¹⁰.
būde 3 sg., būdon pl. pret. of būan.
budon pret. pl. of bēodan.
būend m. *dweller, inhabitant,* G,LPs.
bufan I. prep. (w. d.) *over, 'above,'* Æ,Chr; AO : (w. a.) *on, upon, above,* AO. II. adv. *above, overhead, before,* Æ.
bufan-cweden, -nemd, -sprecen *above-mentioned,* GD.
bufon=bufan; **būg-**=bū-
±**būgan** I. (sv³) *to 'bow,' bow down, turn, bend, stoop, sink,* Æ,AO,Rood : *submit, give way,* Æ,B,Chr : *depart, flee, retire,* Æ,AO : *join, go over to,* Æ : *convert,* Æ. II.=būan
būgol v. bēogol
būh imperative of būgan.
būian=būan; **būl**=būla I.
bula m. *bull, steer,* EC449²².
būl(a) m. *bracelet, necklace, brooch* [bȳl]
bulberende *wearing an ornament,* WW 195³⁷; OEG8³¹⁹.
bulentse f. *a plant,* LCD44b.
bulgon pret. pl. of belgan.
bulluc m. *male calf, 'bullock,'* Sc.
bulot, bulut *ragged robin, cuckoo-flower,* LCD.
būn=būan
bund f? *bundle,* MtL13³⁰.
būnda=bōnda
bunden (B) pp., bundon pret. pl. of bindan. ['*y-bound*']
bundenheord *with bounden tresses,* B3151.
+**bundennes** f. *obligation,* LPs.
bundenstefna adj. (*ship*) *with an ornamented prow,* B1911.
bune I.† f. *cup, beaker, drinking vessel.* II. *reed, cane?* WW198¹³. ['*bun*']
+**būnes** f. *dwelling,* NC292.
būr n. '*bower,' apartment, chamber, Gen, WW : storehouse, cottage, dwelling,* B,KC; Æ. [būan]

±**būr** (usu.+; but būr at LL92,6³) m. *freeholder of the lowest class, peasant, farmer.* ['*gebur*']
būrbyrde (æ²) *of peasant birth,* Ct.
būrcniht n. *chamberlain, eunuch,* HL.
būrcot n. *bed-chamber,* CP.
burg (burh) f. (gds. and nap. byrig) *a dwelling or dwellings within a fortified enclosure, fort, castle,* Chr,WW; CP : '*borough,' walled town,* AO,Mt; Æ. [v. GBG and Mdf]
burg- v. also burh- and beorg-.
burgāgend m. *city-owner,* EL1175.
burgat=burggeat
burgbryce m. *breaking into a (fortified) dwelling,* LL : *penalty for that offence,* LL.
burgen=byrgen
būrgerihta np. *peasant's rights or dues,* LL446,4.
būrgeteld† n. *pavilion, tent,* JUD.
burgfæsten n. *fortress,* GEN1680.
burgfolc n. *townspeople,* B2220.
burggeat n. *castle gate, city gate.*
burghege m. *fence of a 'burg,'* Ct.
burg-hlið† n. nap. -hleoðu *fortress-height* (or?=beorg-hlið).
burglagu f. *civil law,* GPH388.
burg-lēod, -lēoda m. *citizen,* AO.
burgloca† m. *fortified enclosure, walled town.*
burglond n. *native city,* CR51.
burgon pret. pl. of beorgan.
burgræced n. *fortress,* RUIN22.
burgrūn f. *sorceress*; pl. *fates, furies,* GL.
burg-sæl† n. nap. -salu *city-hall, house.*
burgsǣta (ē²) m. *town-dweller, citizen,* WW.
burgscipe m. *borough,* WW497¹⁹.
burgsele m. *castle-hall, house,* RIM30.
burgsittende† mpl. *city-dwellers.*
burgsorg=borgsorg
burgsteall m. *citadel? city?* WW205³⁶. (or? borg-)
burgstede† m. *city, castle.*
burgstrǣt *town road,* BC3·15¹¹.
burgtūn m. *city,* Wif31. ['*borough-town*']
burgðelu f. *castle floor,* Fin30 (burh-). [v. '*theal*']
burg-waran, -waru fp., -ware (AO,CP), -waras mp. *inhabitants of a 'burg,' burghers, citizens.*
burgweall m. *city-wall,* Æ.
burgweg m. *road, street,* Æ.
burgwīgend m. *warrior,* EL34.
burh=burg
burhbiscop m. *bishop of a city,* HR15¹⁶.
burhbōt f. *liability for repair of the walls of a town or fortress,* LL.
burhealdor m. *burgomaster, mayor,* Æ.
burhgeard m. *castle yard,* EC328'.

burhgemet n. *measure used in a town*, LL 477,6.

burhgemōt n. *town's meeting*, LL.

burhgerēfa m. *chief magistrate of a town, provost, mayor*, WW. ['*borough-reeve*']

burhgerihta np. *town due*, TC 432, 433.

burhgeŏingŏ f. *town council (as judicial body)*, LL 228,1².

burhmann m. *citizen*, WW. ['*borough-man*']

burhrǣdden f. *citizenship*, WW 441¹⁰.

burhrest f. *chamber-couch*, IM 125⁸⁶. [? = *bûrrest, ES 38·347]

burhriht n. *town right, town law*, LL 477,6.

burh-rûn, -rûne f. *fury, sorceress*, WW 245¹⁶.

±**burhscipe** m. *township, civil district*, Gl, LL. ['*boroughship*']

burhscir f. *city limits, city, township*, Æ.

burhsprǣc f. *courtly speech*, GL.

burhstaŏol m. *foundation of the wall of a* '*burg*,' LCD 1·328'.

burhŏegn m. *living in a* '*burg*'; or? = bûrŏegn

burhwarumann m. *burgess*, BH 40³¹.

burhwealda m. *burgess*, BH 40³¹ᴮ.

burhweard† m. *city defender*.

burhwela m. *treasure of a city*, B 3100.

burhwelle f. *spring in a* '*burg*'? KC 3·394'.

burhwerod n. *townsfolk*, KC, WW.

burhwita m. *town councillor*, CC.

bûrland n. *land occupied by peasants*, EC 384', (+) BC 201¹⁴.

burn f., burna (CP) m., burne f. *brook, stream*, Jn (v. GBG and Mdf) : *spring or well water*, Cp, WW. ['*burn*']

burnon pret. pl. of biernan.

burnsele m. *bath-house*, RUIN 22.

burnstŏw f? *bathing-place*, KC.

bûrrēaf n. *tapestry (for a bûr)*, TC 530'.

bûrscipe = burhscipe

burse f. *bag, pouch*, LCD.

burston pret. pl. of berstan.

bûr-ŏegn, -ŏēn m. *page, chamberlain*, CC, MA.

burŏre f. *birth, issue*, BL 105²⁰.

buruh = burg

bûst pres. 2 sg. of bûan.

bût m. *a vessel*, LL 455' (? = bûc; BTs).

bûta = (1) bûtan, (2) bûtū

bûtan (o²) I. prep. w. d. and (rarely) a. *out of, outside of, off, round about*, Æ : *except, without, all but, but only*, Chr : *besides, in addition to* : *in spite of*. II. conj. (w. ind.) *except, except that, but, only*. b. ŏæt *except* : (w. subj.) *unless, save that* : (w. subst.) *except, but, besides, if only, provided that*, AO. III. adv. *without, outside*, Chr. ['*BOUT*,' '*BUT*']

bûte = (1) bûtan, (2) bûtū

butere f. '*butter*,' Lcd; Æ : *milk for butter-making*, LCD (v. A 52·186). [*L.*]

buter-flēoge, -flēge f. '*butterfly*,' WW.

butergeŏwēor n. *butter-curd, butter*, WW 98³.

+**buterian** *to butter*, LCD 121a.

buter-ic, -uc = butruc

buterstoppa m. *butter-vessel*, WW 280²⁵.

bûton = bûtan; **butre** = butere

butruc m. *(leather) bottle*, Æ.

butsecarl m. *boatman, mariner*, Chr. ['*buscarl*']

buttorflēoge = buterflēoge

buttuc m. *end, small piece of land*, KC 4·19'.

bûtū (bûtwu, bûta, bûte) *both* (neuter). v. also bēgen.

butueoh (CHR) v. betwux.

bûtun = bûtan; **buturuc** = butruc

bûtwû = bûtū; **bûwan** = bûan

bŷ = bû; **bŷan** (N) = bûan

byccen (i) *of a goat, goat's*, CHRD 48²⁶.

bŷcera m. = bēocere

±**bycgan** (i) *to* '*buy*,' *pay for, acquire*, Mt, Jn : *redeem, ransom* : *procure, get done* : *sell*, LL.

bycgend v. beccen; **bŷcn-** = bēacn-, biecn-

byd-, byd' = bed-, bid-, bid-

bydel m. '*beadle*,' *apparitor, warrant officer*, Lk; Æ : *herald, forerunner*, Æ : *preacher*, Æ. [bēodan]

bydelæcer m. *land of a* '*bydel*,' KC 6·152'.

byden f. *measure, bushel* : *bucket, barrel, vat, tub*. [*Low L.* butina; *Ger.* bütte]

bydenbotm m. *bottom of a vessel*, WW 123⁴.

bydenfæt n. *bushel, barrel*, BL.

bŷdla m. *worshipper*, NG.

bŷencg (DR) = bŷing; **bŷend** = bûend

byf- = bif-, beof-

-byffan v. ā-b.

byg-, bŷg- = big-, bē-, bî, bîg-

bŷgan = bîegan

byge (ŷ? ; i) m. *curve, bend, corner, angle, cone (of a helmet)*, AO, CP : *traffic, commerce*, LL 128,5.

bŷgel, bŷgle = bēogol

bygen f. *purchase*, LL (328¹¹).

bygendlic *easily bent, flexible*, BH.

bygeŏ pres. 3 sg. of bycgan.

bŷgeŏ pres. 3 sg. of bûan.

+**bygu** f. *a bend*, KC. [= byge]

byht m. I. (±) *bend, angle, corner*, Ct : *bay*, '*bight*.' [bûgan] II.† n? *dwelling*. [bûan]

+**byhte** = byht I. + **byhŏ** = byht II.

bŷhŏ pres. 3 sg. of bûgan.

bŷing = bû I.

bŷl m? bŷle f? '*boil*,' *carbuncle*, WW.

bylcettan = bealcettan

±**byld** = bieldo

bylda m. *builder? householder?* CRA 75. [bold]

byldan I. *to build, construct*, KC. II. = bieldan

byldu, byldo=bieldo; **bӯle**=bӯl
byledbrēost (=bylged-?) *puff-breasted*, RD
81[1].
bylewit=bilewit; **bylg**=belg
bylgan *to* '*bellow*,' *MH*.
+**bylgan** *to anger, provoke*, GD.
bylgð pres. 3 sg. of belgan.
bylig=belg, bylg
bӯlIht (īly-) *ulcerous*, LCD 63b.
bylwet, byl(y)wit=bilewit
bӯme (Æ)=bīeme
bӯmere (*WW*), bӯmesangere (ē, ēa; =īe) m.
trumpeter, Æ. ['*bemer*']
bӯmian (=īe) *to blow the trumpet*, *Ps,WW* :
trumpet forth, BF 172[28]. ['*beme*']
bynd=bind
byndele, byndelle=bindele
bӯne *cultivated, inhabited, occupied*, AO.
[būan]
+**bӯran** *to colonize*, WW 210[14].
byrc, byrce=beorc, beorce
byrcð pres. 3 sg. of beorcan.
byrd I. (i) f. *birth* (pl. w. sg. meaning),
APT 11[20]. **II.** f. *burden*, GD 215[1].
+**byrd I.** fn.; +byrdo, -u f. *birth, Cr* : *descent, parentage, race, BH* : *offspring*, BL :
nature, quality, rank, Æ,AO : *fate*.
['*birde*'; beran] **II.** *burdened*, MtR 11[45].
III.=+byrded
+**byrdan** *to beard, fringe, embroider*, GL.
-**byrdan** v. an-b-, +ed-b.
+**byrdboda** m. *herald of a birth*, OP 17.
+**byrddæg** m. *birthday*, Mt 14[6].
byrde *of high rank, well-born, noble, rich*,
AO.
+**byrde I.** *innate, natural*, BO,EL. **II.**=
+byrd I.
+**byrdelīce** *energetically, zealously*, CP 160[19].
byrden=byrðen
byrdicge f. *embroideress*, WW 262[18].
byrdinenu=byrððinenu
byrding f. *embroidering*, WW 294[10].
-**byrding** v. hyse-b.
byrdistre *embroiderer* (v. ANS 123·418).
+**byrdlic** *harmonious*, AS 5[13].
byrdling *tortoise*, OEG 23[21].
-**byrdling** v. in-, frum-b.
byrdscype m. *child-bearing*, CR 182.
+**byrd-tīd** (G) f., -tīma (W) m. *time of birth*.
+**byrdu**=+byrd I.
+**byrdwiglere** m. *birth-diviner, astrologer*,
WW 108[14].
+**byrdwītega** m. *astrologer*, WW 189[1].
byre I.† m. (nap. byras, byre) *child, son,
descendant* : *young man, youth*. [beran]
II. m. *mound*. **III.** (±) m. *time, opportunity*, Æ : *occurrence*, AS 62? **IV.** m.
strong wind, storm, GPH 400.
bӯre n. *stall, shed, hut*, Gl. ['*byre*']

+**byredlic** *suitable, fitting, convenient, congenial*, DR. adv. -līce.
byrele (i) mf. *cup-bearer, butler, steward, B*,
Gen. ['*birle*']
byrelian *to give to drink, serve with drink*,
Gu. ['*birle*' vb.]
+**byrelic**=+byredlic
byren I. (and byrene) f. *she-bear*, MH,WW.
[bera] **II.**=beren
-**bӯren** v. nēahge-b.
byres f. *borer, graving tool, awl, chisel*, GL.
[borian]
byreð I.=bierð pres. 3 sg. of beran. **II.**=
pres. 3 sg. of byrian I.
byrg gds. and nap. of burg.
byrg- v. also byrig-, birg-.
+**byrg**, bēon on gebyrge (w. d.) *to help,
protect*. [beorgan]
byrga m. *security, surety, bail, one who gives
bail*, GL. [Ger. bürge]
±**byrgan I.** (i) *to raise a mound, hide, 'bury,'
inter, Hy*; AO. **II.**=birgan. **III.**=beorgan
+**byrgednes** f. *burial*, BH (Sch.) 546[3].
byrgels (e, i) m. *tomb*, Æ,Ct. ['*buriels*']
byrgelslēoð (e[1]) n. *epitaph*, HGL 427.
byrgelssang m. *dirge*, OEG : *epitaph*, HGL
427.
byrgen (i, u) f. *burying-place, grave, sepulchre, El,Mt*; Æ,AO,CP : *burial*. ['*burian*';
beorgan]
+**byrgen I.** f. *caul? grave?* (BTs), LCD 185a.
II. '*tinipa*,' WW 277[2].
byrgend m. *grave-digger*, PPs 78[3].
byrgenlēoð n. *epitaph*, BH 94[12].
byrgensang m. *dirge*, OEG.
byrgenstōw f. *burying-place*, W.
byrgere m. *corpse-bearer*, WW. ['*burier*']
byrgian=byrgan
byrging I. f. *burial*, A 11·173. **II.**=birging
byrglēoð n. *dirge, epitaph*, GL.
byrht, byrht-=beorht, beorht-, bierht-
byrhtm=breahtm
±**byrian I.** (impers.) *to happen, pertain to,
belong to, befit*, Æ,Chr,Mk,MtR; AO,CP.
['*bir*'; '*i-bure*'] **II.**=byrgan
byric=beorc
byrig=burg, and gds. of burg.
byrig-=byrg-, burh-
byrigberge f. *mulberry*, LCD 86a.
byrignes I. f. *burial*, BH : *grave*, BYH
124. ['*buriness*'] **II.**=birgnes
-**bӯrild** v. nēah-geb.; **byris**=byres
byrisang (i) m. *dirge*, HGL 488[67].
byrl-=byrel-
byrla m. *trunk (of body)*, LCD 58b.
+**byrman** (i; =ie) *to ferment, leaven* : *swell
up, be proud*. [beorma]
+**byrmed** n. *leavened bread*, Ex 12[15],[19].
byrnan (Æ)=biernan

byrne I. f. *corslet, WW*; CP. [*'burne'*] **II.**=burne, burn. **III.**=bryne
byrnete f. *barnacle,* NC275.
byrn-ham, -hama† m. *corslet.*
+**byrnod** *corsleted, ÆGr*256¹⁶. [*'i-burned'*]
byrnsweord n. *flaming sword,* Bl109³⁴.
byrnwiga† m. *corsleted warrior,* AA.
byrn-wīgend, -wīggend† m. *corsleted warrior.*
byrs, byrse=byres
byrst I. (e) m. *loss, calamity, injury, damage, defect,* Æ. [berstan] **II.** n. *(land-)slip,* KC3·52⁹ (v. also KC5·112¹⁹ and Mdf). **III.** f. *'bristle,' Ep,Lcd,WW*; Æ. [*'birse,' 'brust'*] **IV.** pres. 3 sg. of berstan. **V.** pres. 2 sg. of beran.
+**byrst** *furnished with bristles,* OEG23³.
byrstende *'rugiens'?* DR122⁷.
byrstful *disastrous,* Chr1116.
byrstig *broken, rugged,* OEG,RWH141³⁸. [berstan]
+**byrtīd**=+byrdtīd
byrð pres. 3 sg. of beran.
byrðen f. *'burden,' load, weight, Bl,G,WW*; Æ,CP : *charge, duty.*
+**byrðen** f. *what is born, a child,* W251ᴅ¹⁴.
byrðenmǣlum *a heap at a time,* ÆH 1·526'.
byrðenmǣte (ē³) *burdensome,* KGl1011
byrðenstān m. *millstone,* MtL18⁶.
byrðenstrang *strong at carrying burdens,* ÆH1·208¹³.
byrðere=byrðre
byrðestre (e) f. *female carrier,* HGl498¹⁸.
byrðling (e) m. *carrier,* OEG4922.
byrðor=beorðor
byrðre I. m. *bearer, supporter,* ÆH. [beran] **II.** f. *child-bearer, mother,* W251¹³.
+**byrðtid**=+byrdtīd
byrðōīnenu f. *midwife,* GPH392.
bysceop=bisceop; **byseg-**=bysg-
bysen=bisen; **bysig-,** bysg-=bisg-
bysmer, bysmor=bismer; bysmr-=bismr-
bysn=bisen
byst=bist pres. 2 sg. of bēon.
bȳsting (=īe) f. *'beestings,'* WW129². [bēost]
byt I.=bit pres. 3 sg. of biddan. **II.**=bytt
bȳt pres. 3 sg. of (1) bēodan, (2) bēatan.
bȳtel, bȳtl=bīetl; **byter**=biter
bytla†=bylda
bytlan, ±bytlian *to build, erect,* Æ,CP. [botl]
+**bytlu** np. *building, dwelling,* Æ.
±**bytlung** f. *building,* Æ.
bytme f? *keel : head of a dale,* Ct.
bytming f. *hold, keel of ship,* ÆH1·536.
bytne=bytme
bȳtst pres. 2 sg. of bēatan and bēodan.

bytt I. f. *bottle, flagon, Mt,WW*; Æ : *cask.* [*'bit'*] **II.** *small piece of land,* KC3·85¹¹. **III.** pres. 3 sg. of biddan.
bytte=bytt I.
byttehlid n. *butt-lid,* WW213²³.
byttfylling f. *filling of casks,* LL178,8¹.
byð=bið pres. 3 sg. of bēon.
bȳð pres. 3 sg. of būan.
byðme=bytme
bȳwan (ēo; =īe) *to rub, brighten, furbish up, adorn,* B,WW.
byxen (i) *made of boxwood,* WW. [box]

C

cæb-, cǣc-=cæf-, cēac-
cæcepol *taxgatherer,* WW111⁹. (hæce-)
cæderbēam=cederbēam; **cæf** = ceaf
cæfertūn=cafortūn
cæfester (cæb-) n. *halter,* Gl. [L. capistrum]
-**cæflan** v. be-, ofer-, ymb-c.
cæfing f. *hair-ornament,* Gl.
cæfl m. *halter, muzzle,* WW.
cǣg, cǣge f., cǣga m. *'key'* (lit. and fig.), Ex,G,LL,MH,Rd : *solution, explanation,* CP.
cǣgbora m. *key-bearer, jailor,* Gl,MH.
cǣghiorde m. *keeper of keys, steward,* WW.
cǣgloca m. *locked depository,* LL362,76¹.
-**cǣglod** v. ā-c.
cæh-=ceah-; **cæl-**=cel-, ceal-, ciel
cælð pres. 3 sg. of calan.
cæm-; cæn-=cem-; cen-, cyn-
cǣpehūs=cīepehūs
cæppe f. *'cap,' WW* : *cope, hood.* [Lat.]
cæpse f. *box,* NC276. [L. capsa]
cær-=car-, cear-, cer-, cier-
cærse (e) f. *'cress,' water-cress,* Lcd; Mdf.
cærsiht *full of cress,* KC3·121¹⁸.
cærte=carte
cǣs=cēas pret. 3 sg. of cēosan.
cǣse=cȳse; **cæstel**=castel
cæster (NG)=ceaster
cāf *quick, active, prompt,* Æ : *strenuous, strong : bold, brave.* adv. cāfe, El. [*'cofe'*]
cāflic *bold.* adv. -līce *promptly, vigorously : boldly,* ÆL. [*'cofly'*]
cāflwyrt=cawlwyrt
cāfnes f. *energy,* ÆH2·282⁴.
cafortūn (æ, ea¹, e²) m. *vestibule, court, courtyard,* Æ : *hall, residence,* Æ.
cāfscipe m. *alacrity, boldness,* RB,W.
+**cafstrian** *to bridle, curb,* CP218²³. [cæfester]
cahhetan=ceahhetan; **cāl**=cawl, cawel
calan⁶ *to grow cool or cold,* BH,Bo.

calc I. m. *shoe, sandal,* Mk6⁹. [*L.*] **II.**= cealc
calcatrippe=coltetræppe
calcrond *shod (of horses),* GNE 143.
cald (A)=ceald
cälend m. *the beginning of a month,* AO : *month, Men* : (†) *span of life.* ['*calends*']
cälendcwide m. *tale of days,* SOL479.
calf (A)=cealf
calfur (VPs) nap. of cealf.
calic m. '*chalice,*' *Lcd,Lk,Mt,Ps.* [*L.*]
-calla (ZDA 10·345) v. hilde-c.
calu (cal(e)w- in obl. cases) '*callow,*' *bare, bald, Rd,Pr.*
calwer (*Gl*)=cealer
calwer-clīm, -clympe *curds?* WW.
cäma m. *muzzle, collar, bit,* PPs31¹¹. [*L.*]
camb (o) m. '*comb,*' *crest, Ep,WW* : *honey-comb,* LPs.
cambiht *combed, crested,* WW.
cambol=cumbol
camel m. '*camel,*' *Mt,Mk.*
cammoc (u²) nm? '*cammock,*' *rest-harrow, Lcd,WW.*
±camp (o) I. mn. *combat, battle, struggle, warfare, B,Rd.* ['*camp*'] II. *field, plain?* EC 183². [*L.* campus]
campdōm m. *military service, warfare,* Æ.
campealdor m. *commander,* OEG4433.
campgeféra m. *fellow-soldier,* GL.
camphād m. *warfare,* BH.
±campian (o) *to strive, fight, Gu;* Æ. ['*camp*']
camplic *military,* Æ,CHRD.
campræden f. *war, warfare,* AN 4.
campstede† m. *battlefield.*
campung f. *fighting, warfare,* BL,GL.
campwæpen (o¹) n. *weapon,* RD 21⁹.
campweorod (e², ea², e³) n. *army, host,* BH.
campwīg (o¹) n. *battle, combat.* JUD 333
campwīsa m. *director of public games,* HGL 405.
campwudu m. *shield?* EL51.
can pres. 1 and 3 sg. of cunnan.
cän m. *germ, sprout?* PPs79¹⁰. [*OS.* cīnan]
±canc n. *jeering, scorn, derision,* GL.
canceler m. *chancellor,* CHR 1093. [*Low L.* cancellarium]
cancer m. *cancer,* Æ. [*L.*]
canceradl f. *cancer,* LCD 41a.
cancerwund f. *cancerous wound,* LCD.
cancet(t)an, *to cry out, mock, deride,* GL, LL.
cancetung f. *boisterous laughter,* WW 382³⁶.
cancor=cancer
candel (o¹, o²) fn. *lamp, lantern,* '*candle,*' *Gl;* Æ. [*L.* candela]
candelbora m. *acolyte* (Swt).
candelbryd (?=bred; BTs) *flat candlestick,* IM 120.

candellēoht n. '*candle-light,*' RB.
Candelmæsse f. '*Candlemas,*' *the feast of the Purification, Chr.*
Candelmæsseæfen n. *Candlemas eve,* LL.
Candelmæssedæg m. *Candlemas day,* NC 276.
candelsnȳtels m. *candle-snuffers,* WW 126²⁸. [v. '*snitels*']
candelstæf m. *candlestick, Mt,WW.* ['*candlestaff*']
candelsticca m. '*candlestick,*' EC 250'.
candeltrēow n. *candelabrum,* MtR 5¹⁵.
candeltwist m. *pair of snuffers,* GL.
candelwēoce f. '*candle-wick,*' *torch, WW.*
candelwyrt f. *candlewort,* WW 137⁹.
cann I. f. *cognizance, averment, asseveration, clearance,* LL. II. (±) pres. 3sg. of cunnan.
canne f. '*can,*' *cup, WW.*
cannon sbp. *reed, cane,* AA30¹⁹. [*L.* canna]
canon m. *canon, rule.* canones bēc *canonical books.* [*L.* canon]
canonbōc *a book of canons,* LL (316¹⁴).
canonic I. m. *canon,* LL. II. *canonical,* Æ.
canoniclic (e³) *canonical* (BT).
cans=canst pres. 2 sg. of cunnan.
cantel m? n? *buttress, support,* BF 142²³.
cantelcāp m. *cope,* CHR 1070 E.
cantercæppe f. *cope (vestment),* Ct.
cantere m. *singer,* CM 904.
canterstæf m. *chanter's staff,* EC 250¹⁵.
cantic (Æ), canticsang (CPs), m. *canticle, song.* [*L.*]
-cāp v. cantel-c.
capellan m. *chaplain,* EC,CHR (late). [*L.*]
capian *to look.* ūp c. *to look up, lie on its back (of the moon),* LCD 3·266²³. capiende '*supinus,*' GPH 393a.
capitel=capitol
capitelhūs n. *chapter-house,* IM 122⁴.
capit-ol, -ul, -ula m. *chapter (cathedral or monastic)* : *chapter (division of a book), lesson,* LL : *anthem.* ['*chapitle*']
capitolmæsse f. *early mass, first mass,* WW 101¹⁶.
+capitulod *divided into chapters,* LL (204²).
cappa=cæppe
capun m. '*capon,*' WW. [*L.* capōnem]
carbunculus m. *carbuncle,* CP. [*L.*]
carc-ern (AO,CP), -ærn n. *prison, jail.* [*L.* carcer]
carcernðȳstru f. *prison darkness,* LL.
carcernweard m. *jailor,* MH 24¹⁵,¹⁹.
-carcian v. be-c.
cārclife=gārclife; **care-**=car-
carful (ea) *anxious, sad, Gu,Soul* : '*careful,*' *attentive, painstaking, Ps,WW* : *troublesome.* adv. -līce, LL.
carfulnes f. *care, anxiety* : '*carefulness,*' Æ, Lcd.

cargealdor (ea¹) n. *sorrowful song*, JUL618.
cargēst (ea¹) m. *sad spirit, devil*, GU365.
carian *to ' care' for, be anxious, grieve*, B,Cr; ÆE.
caricum dp. of sb. *with dried figs*, ÆL23b⁶⁸¹. [*L.* carica]
carig (ea, e)† *sorrowful, anxious*, Cr,Soul : *grievous*, DD. ['*chary*']
carl m. *man*, LCD. [*ON.* karl]
carlēas '*careless*,' *free from care*, Ex,RB.
carlēasnes, carlēast f. *freedom from care, security*, WW. ['*carelessness*']
carlfugol (ea¹, e³) m. *male bird, cock*, RWH 148⁴.
carlīce (ea) *wretchedly*, PPs85⁶.
carlmann m. *male, man*, CHR1086.
carr m. *stone, rock*, NG. [*Keltic*]
carseld (ea) n. *home of care*, SEAF5.
carsīð (ea) *painful journey*, B2396.
carsorg f. *sad anxiety*, GEN1114.
carte (æ) f. *paper for writing on*, Æ : *document, deed* : *letter*, RWH87³⁴. [*L.* charta]
caru (ea) f. '*care,' concern, anxiety, sorrow*, B,Lk,Ps; AO.
carwylm (æ², e²)† m. *welling sorrow*.
casebill n. *club*, GPH394 (v. A31·66).
cāserdom m. *imperial sway*, DR,LL.
Cāsere (Cāser, JnL) m. *Cæsar, emperor*, Bo; Æ,AO. ['*Kaser*']
cāsering f. *coin with Cæsar's head on it, drachma, didrachma*, NG.
cāserlic *imperial*, WW427⁴⁰.
cāsern f. *empress*, AO266¹⁴.
cassuc m. *hassock, sedge*, LCD.
cassuclēaf np. *hassock or sedge leaves*, LCD 170a.
castel I. m. '*castle,' fort*, Chr : *walled enclosure?* Ct (v. GBG). II. n. *town, village*, Mt,Mk,Lk.
castelmann m. *townsman*, CHR.
castelweall (æ¹) m. *city wall, rampart*, RWH134²⁷.
castelweorc n. *castle-building*, CHR1137.
castenere m. *cabinet, chest*, TC531⁷.
casul m. *over-garment, ' birrus,' cloak*, WW 196³⁹. ['*casule*']
cāsus m. (*grammatical*) *case*, ÆGR.
catt m., catte f. '*cat,*' Gl; Mdf.
caul [S6N1]=cawl I. and II.
caulic *a medicine*, LCD102b.
cawellēaf n. *cabbage-leaf*, LCD166b.
cawelsǣd n. *cabbage-seed*, LCD187a.
cawelstela m. *cabbage-stalk*, LCD3·102⁷.
cawelstoc (cāl-) m. *cabbage-stalk*, LCD1·378⁸.
cawelwurm m. *caterpillar*, WW121²⁹. [v. '*cawel*']
cawl I. (e, ea, eo) m. *basket*, AO,Gl. ['*cawl*'] II. (ā?) m. '*cole*' ('*caul,' ' cawel*'), *kale, cabbage*, Lcd.

cēac sm. *basin, pitcher, jug*, Æ,CP : *kettle, cauldron* (*for hot-water ordeal*), LL24; 104; 116.
cēacādl (ēo) f. *jaw-ache*, LCD109a,113a.
cēacbān n. '*cheek-bone,' jaw*, WW.
cēacbora m. *yoke for buckets*, GL.
cēace (ē, ei, ēo) f. '*cheek,' jaw, jawbone*, G, Lcd,VPs,WW.
ceacga m. *broom, furze*, BC,KC.
ceacl=ceafl
ceaf (e) n., nap. ceafu '*chaff,*' Æ,Mt,Lk, WW; CP.
ceaf-=caf-, ceaf-, cief-
ceaffinc m. *chaffinch*, ANS76·206.
ceafl m. *jaw, cheek, jaw-bone, cheek-bone*, Æ,Whale. ['*jowl*']
ceaflādl (cealf-) f. *disease of the jaws*, LCD90b.
ceafor (e) m. *cock-' chafer,' beetle*, Ps,WW; Æ.
ceahhe f. *daw*, KC3·48'.
ceahhetan *to laugh loudly*, BH428¹.
ceahhetung f. *laughter, jesting*, Æ.
cealc (a) m. '*chalk,' lime, plaster*, AO; Mdf : *chalkstone, pebble*, Ep,WW.
+cealcian (æ) *to whiten*, MtL23²⁷.
cealcpyt m. *chalk-pit*, KC5·346. [v.'*chalk*']
cealcsēað m. *chalk-pit*, KC.
cealcstān m. *limestone, chalk*, GL,LCD.
ceald (a) I. adj. '*cold*' ('*cheald*'), *cool*, A, Mt,Jn; AO,CP. adv. cealde. II. n. *coldness, cold*.
cealdheort (a) *cruel*, AN138.
cealdian *to become cold*, Rim. ['*cold*']
cealdnes f. *coldness, cold*, ÆL23b¹⁷⁵.
cealer m. '*galmaria,' pressed curds, jelly of curds or whey*, GL. ['*calver*']
cealerbrīw m. *pottage of curds*, LCD.
cealf I. (æ, e) nm. (nap. cealfru) '*calf,*' Æ, G,Gl. II.=ceafl
+cealfe *great with calf*, GENC33¹³.
cealfādl=ceaflādl
cealfian *to calve*, Æ.
cealfloca m. *calf-pen*, KC1·312⁶.
cealfre=cealre, cealer
cealfwyrt (a) '*eruca,*' WW136¹⁷.
ceallian *to ' call,' shout*, Ma91. [*ON.* kalla]
cealre=cealer and das. of cealer.
cēap (ē, ȳ) m. *cattle*, CP : *purchase, sale, traffic, bargain, gain*, B; CP : *payment, value, price*, LL : *goods, possessions, property*, Chr; AO : *market*, Æ. dēop c. *high price.* būtan cēape *gratis.* ['*cheap*']
cēapcniht m. *bought servant, slave*, GL.
cēapdæg m. *market-day*, WW.
cēapēadig? *rich, wealthy*, GNE108.
cēapealeðel n. *alehouse*, LL(410¹⁸)? (v. BTs).
cēapgyld n. *purchase money, market price* : *compensation*, v. LL2·338.

±cēapian *to bargain, trade, Mt* : *buy, Jn,Cr*;
AO : *endeavour to bribe,* DA 739. ['*cheap*']
cēapland *purchased land,* TC 580¹³.
cēapman m. '*chapman,*' *trader, BH,LL.*
cēapsceamul m. *seat of custom or toll,*
treasury, G.
cēapscip n. *trading vessel,* AO 116⁴.
cēapsetl (ē¹) n. *toll-booth,* G.
cēapstōw f. *market-place, market,* CP.
cēapstrǣt (ē, ȳ) f. *market-place,* ÆGr.
cēapung f. *traffic, trade, LL.* ['*cheaping*']
cēapunggemōt n. *market,* WW 450¹.
cear = car
cearcetung f. *gnashing, grinding,* W 200¹⁸.
cearcian *to creak, gnash,* Æ. ['*chark*']
cearde = cierde pret. 3 sg. of cierran.
+cearfan (NG) = +ceorfan
cearm m. *noise,* W 186¹⁸.
cear-rige, -ruce *a vehicle?* Gl.
ceart I. *wild common land,* KC. II. = crǣt
cearwund *badly wounded?* LL 6,63 and 3·12
(or ? scearw- BTs).
cēas I. = cēast. II. pret. 3 sg. of cēosan.
-cēasega v. wæl-c.
cēaslunger *contentious,* CHRD 19¹².
cēast (ǣ, ē) f. *strife, quarrelling, contention,*
WW : *reproof.*
ceastel = castel
ceaster (æ, e) f. *castle, fort, town,* CP :
†*heaven, hell.*
ceasteræsc m. *black hellebore,* LCD.
ceasterbūend m. *citizen,* B 768.
ceastergewar- = ceasterwar-
ceasterherpað *high road?* (BTs),KC 5·217¹.
ceasterhlid n. *city gate,* CR 314.
ceasterhof n. *house in a city,* AN 1239.
ceaster-lēod f. np. -lēode *citizens,* NC 276.
ceasternisc (æ) *urban, municipal,* TC 244¹³.
ceaster-sǣtan, -sǣte mp. *citizens,* TC.
±ceaster-waran mp., -ware, -waru f.
burghers, citizens.
ceasterweall (e¹) m. *city wall,* MH 150⁹.
ceasterwīc f. *village,* BL 69³⁵.
ceasterwyrt f. *black hellebore,* LCD.
cēastful *contentious,* Sc 105⁵.
ceastre = ceaster
cēaw pret. 3 sg. of cēowan.
ceawl (*MtL*) = cawl I.
cēce (*VPs*) = cēace
cēcel (coecil) *a little cake, Ep.* ['*kechel*']
cecil '*suffocacium,*' WW 49²⁸.
cecin '*tabetum,*' *a board,* WW 279¹.
cēde (VPs) = cīegde pret. 3 sg. of cīegan.
cedelc f. *the herb mercury,* Lcd,WW. ['*ked-*
lock']
ceder nmf. *cedar,* BLPs. [*L.* cedrus]
ceder-bēam mn., -trēow (ȳ) n. *cedar-tree,*
Ps.
cedor- = ceder-

cēdrisc *of cedar,* DR 65¹⁵.
cef (Æ) = ceaf; cef- = ceaf-, cif-
cēgan (VHy), cēgian = cīegan
cehhettung = ceahhetung
ceíce (MtLR); ceig- (N) = cēace; cīg-
ceir *cry, clamour,* DR.
cel = cawl
cēlan (ǣ) *to cool, become cold, be cold, MH,*
VPs (oe) : (+) *quench* (*thirst*), *refresh.*
['*keel*']
celc (1) (VPs) = calic. (2) = cealc
celde f. *copious spring?* KC 3·429¹³.
celdre = ceoldre; cele = (1) ceole; (2) ciele
celen-dre f., -der n. '*coliander,*' *coriander,*
Lcd.
cele-ðonie, -ðenie, cileðonie f. *celandine,*
swallow-wort, LCD.
celf (A) = cealf; celic = calic
+celfe (GEN 33¹³) = +cealfe
cēling f. *cooling,* Æ : *cool place,* Æ.
celis '*peditis,*' *foot-covering,* A 37·45.
celiwearte = cielewearte
cell m. (*monastic*) *cell,* CHR 1129.
cellender n., cellendre f. = celendre
cellod (ē?)† part. *round? hollow? embossed?*
beaked? FIN 29 (or ? celced = cealced); MA
283.
celmertmonn m. *hireling,* NG (v. ES
42·172).
±cēlnes f. *coolness, cool air, breeze,* CP.
[cōl]
celod v. cellod.
celras = ceallras, nap. of cealer.
±cemban (æ) *to comb,* Æ. ['*kemb*']
cemes f. *shirt,* GD. [*L.* camisia]
cempa (æ) m. *warrior, champion, Gl,Ma*;
Æ,AO,CP. [camp; '*kemp*']
cempestre f. *female warrior,* OEG.
cēn† m. *pine-torch, pine* : *name of the rune*
for c. [*Ger.* kien]
cendlic = cynlic
cēne *bold, brave, fierce, CP,Ex,Lcd,Ma,Ps*;
Æ,AO : *powerful, Ps* : *learned, clever, Met*
10⁵¹. ['*keen*'] *also adv.*
cenep m. *moustache,* CHR : *bit* (*of a bridle*),
WW 486¹⁶. [*ON.* kanpr]
cenlic = cynlic
cēnlīce *boldly,* Æ. ['*keenly*']
±cennan *to conceive, bring forth,* Æ : *beget,*
create, produce, Mt,VPs; CP : *nominate,*
choose out, Æ : *assign, attribute, give* :
declare, show oneself, clear oneself, make
a declaration in court (v. LL 2·32; 279,
'cennan,' 'Anefang'), *B,LL,Ps.* ['*ken*']
cennend m. *parent,* BL.
cennendlic *genital,* GD.
cennes f. *produce, what is produced,* EHy
6²² : *childbirth* : *birthday.*
+cennes f. *summons,* BH 436¹⁵ (cæne-).

cennestre f. *mother*, Æ.
cenning f. *procreation*, CP : *parturition, birth*, Æ : *declaration in court* (v. cennan).
cenningstān (y¹) m. *testing-stone*, LL192,4.
cenningstow f. *birthplace*, Æ.
cenningtīd f. *time of bringing forth*, Æ.
cennystre=cennestre
Cent, Centescīr f. *Kent*. [*L.* Cantia]
centaur m. *centaur*, WW.
centaurie f. *centaury* (plant), LCD.
Centingas mp. *Kentish men*, CHR.
Centisc *Kentish*, CHR.
Cent-land, -lond (AO) n. *Kent*.
Centrīce n. *kingdom of Kent*.
centur m. *centurion*, G.
Centware mp. *inhabitants of Kent*, CHR.
cēnðu f. *boldness*, B2696.
cēo f. *chough, jay, jackdaw*, ÆGR.
cēoce (WW)=cēace; -cēocian v. ā-c.
ceod? ceode? *bag, pouch*, CP,LL.
ceodor-=ceder-; ceofl, ceol (NG)=cawl I.
cēol m. *ship*, AN,B,CHR.
ceolas mp. *cold winds, cold*, Az103. [ciele?]
ceolbor-=cilfor-
ceoldre I. f. *milk-pail*, WW33¹⁷. II.=cealre
ceole (e) f. *throat : gorge, chasm : beak of ship*, GL. [*Ger.* kehle]
ceolor m. *throat*, GL : *channel*, Ct.
cēol-ðel n., -ðelu? f. *deck of a ship*, HU8.
ceolwærc m. *pain in the throat*, LCD113a.
ceorcing f. *complaining*, GPH398.
±ceorfan³ *to cut, cut down, slay*, Mk,Æ; LkL : '*carve*,' *cut out, engrave : tear*.
ceorfæx f. *axe*, AO160¹⁶.
ceorfingīsen n. *branding iron*, Sc43².
ceorfsæx n. *surgeon's knife, scalpel*, Æ.
±ceorian *to murmur, complain*, Æ,AO.
ceorig *querulous, complaining*, OEG.
ceorl m. '*churl*,' *layman, peasant, husband-man*, CP : *freeman of the lowest class*, LL; AO,CP : *man : husband*, Jn,WW; CP : †*hero, noble man*.
ceorlǣs (=ceorllēas) *unmarried* (of women), LL360,73B.
ceorlboren *low-born, not noble*, LL.
ceorlfolc n. *common people*, ÆGR.
±ceorlian *to marry* (of the woman), LL,Mt; Æ. ['*churl*']
ceorlic=ceorllic
ceorlisc (ie) *of a* '*ceorl*,' '*churlish*,' *common, rustic*, LL,WW. adv. -lisce.
ceorllic *common, belonging to the people generally*. adv. -līce *commonly, vulgarly, popularly*.
ceorlman m. *freeman*, LL73; 463.
ceorlstrang *strong as a man*, WW108¹⁸.
ceorm=cirm
ceorran I. (sv³) *to creak*, LCD160a. II. (+) =cierran

ceorung f. *murmuring*, Æ.
±cēosan² *to* '*choose*·' ('*i-cheose*,' '*y-core*'), *seek out, select*, AO; Æ : *decide, test : accept, approve*, B,Gen.
ceosel (i, y) m. *gravel, sand, shingle*, Ep,Mt; Æ. ['*chesil*']
ceoselbǣre *gravelly, shingly*, A13·32.
ceoselstān m. *sand-stone, gravel*, WW.
ceoslen (OEG7¹⁶¹), ceoslig (4⁴⁰) *gravelly*.
ceosol I. m? n? *gullet, maw*, GL. II.=ceosel
±cēowan² *to* '*chew*,' *gnaw*, Æ,Soul : *eat, consume*, Æ.
ceowl (NG)=cawl
cēowung (ī, ȳ) f. '*chewing*,' WW.
cēp=cēap; cēp-, cēpe-=cēap-, cȳp-
cēpan I. *to seize*, Æ : *seek after, desire*, Æ : *await*, Æ : *receive*, RBL : '*keep*,' *guard, observe, attend, watch, look out for, take heed*, Æ,Chr,Lcd,Ps : *take*, Æ : *avail oneself of, betake oneself to, take to, bear* : *meditate : regulate by*. II.=cȳpan
cēpnian *to await eagerly*, NC276.
cer=cierr
ceren I. (æ, y) n? *new wine, sweet wine*, GL, LCD. [*L.* carenum] II.=cyrn
cer-felle, -fille f. '*chervil*,' Lcd,WW. [*L.* cerefolium]
cerge=carig; cerlic=cirlic
cerm=cirm; cerr=cierr
cers-=cærs-; cert-=cyrt-
certare *charioteer*, ÆL18²⁹⁵.
ceruphin *cherubim*, EL750.
ces-=ceos-; cēs-=cīs-, cȳs-
cēs-=cēas pret. 3 sg. of cēosan.
Cēsar (AO)=Cāsere
cester=ceaster; cestian=cystian
cēte=cȳte; cetel, cetil=citel
cēðan=cȳðan; cewl (NG)=cawl
chor, chora m. *dance, choir* (*singers*), CP : *church-choir* (*place*). [*L.* chorus]
chorglēo n. *dance*, LPs.
cian sbpl. *gills*, GL. [*Ger.* kieme]
cicel=cycel
cicen (y) n. '*chicken*,' Mt,WW.
cicene (Æ)=cycene
cicropisc *cyclopean?* WW217¹³.
+cīd n. *strife, altercation*, CP,DR,GD : *reproof*, RB.
±cīdan (w. d. or wið) *contend, quarrel*, Æ, WW : *complain*, Æ : '*chide*,' *blame*, Mk; Æ,CP.
cīdde (1) pret. 3 sg. of cīdan. (2)=cȳðde pret. 3 sg. of cȳðan.
cīdere m. *a chider*, CHRD41³⁰.
cīdung (ȳ) f. *chiding, rebuke*, AO,EPs.
ciefes=cifes
±cīegan (ē, ī, ȳ) (tr.) *to call, name*, Æ : *call upon, invoke, summon, convene*, CP : (intr.) *call out*. For comps. v. cīg-.

ciele (e, i, y) m. *coolness, cold, 'chill,' frost,* *Bl,CP,VPs*; AO. [ceald]

cielegicel† (y¹) m. *icicle.*

cielewearte (e¹, y¹) f. *goose-skin,* WW.

cielf=cealf

cielle (i, y) f. *fire-pan, lamp,* BH,GD. [*OHG.* kella]

cīepa (e, i, y) m. *merchant, trader,* Æ,CHRD.

cīepe=cīpe

cīepehūs (æ¹) n. *storehouse,* WW 186¹¹.

cīepemann (CP), cīepmann (LL) m. *merchant.*

cīepeðing (ē, ȳ) np. *merchandise,* BH,GL.

cīeping (ē, ī, ȳ) f. *marketing, trading,* CP : *market-place, market : merchandise : market dues,* WW 145²⁸.

cīeplic (ȳ) *for sale, vendible,* Sc 98¹⁷.

cierice=cirice; **cierlisc**=ceorlisc

cierm=cirm

cierr (e, i, y) m. *turn, change, time, occasion,* Æ,CP,Lk,Lcd : *affair, business.* æt sumum cierre *at some time, once.* ['*chare*']

±**cierran** (eo, i, y) (tr. and intr.) *turn, change,* Ps,Sat : (intr.) *turn oneself, go, come, proceed, turn back, return,* Mt; Æ : *regard : translate : persuade, convert, be converted, agree to,* CP : *submit,* CHR,W : *make to submit, reduce.* ['*chare*,' '*i-cherre*']

+**cierrednes** (y) *conversion,* Æ : *entrance, admission,* RB.

±**cierring** (e, y) f. *turning,* LPs 9⁴ : *conversion,* NC 341.

cīest, cīesð pres. 3 sg. of cēosan.

cīfes (ie, e, y) f. *concubine, harlot,* AO. [*Ger.* kebse]

cīfesboren adj. *bastard,* OEG 5042.

cīfesdōm m. *fornication,* OEG 5042.

cīfesgemāna m. *fornication,* LL (Wilk.) 84¹.

cīfeshād (y) m. *fornication,* WW.

cīgan=cīegan

+**cīgednes** f. *calling, summons : name* (cīed-), OEG 1503.

+**cīgendlic** *calling, vocative,* ÆGR 23².

cīgere (ei) *one who calls,* DR 194¹.

+**cīgnes** f. *calling, invocation, entreaty : name,* A 10·143⁷⁹.

±**cīgung** f. *calling, invocation,* GD 289, NC 292.

cild (y) (nap. cild, cild-ra, -ru; gp. -ra) n. '*child*,*' *infant,* Ct,G,Lcd,WW; Æ,AO, CP : *a youth of gentle birth,* KC.

Cildamæssedæg m. *Childermas, Innocents' Day* (Dec. 28).

cildatrog=cildtrog

cildclāðas mp. *swaddling-clothes,* Gl. [v. '*cloth*']

cildcradol m. *cradle,* Æ.

cildfaru f. *carrying of children,* GEN 45¹⁹.

cildfēdende *nursing,* MtR 24¹⁹.

cild-fōstre, -fēstre f. *nurse, LL.* [v. '*foster*']

cildgeogoð f. *childhood,* ÆL 30³²⁰.

cildgeong *youthful, infant,* LCD,RB.

cildhād m. '*childhood,' MkL.*

cildhama m. *womb,* GL : *after-birth,* WW.

cildisc '*childish,*' Gen.

cildiugoð=cildgeogoð

cildlic *childish, young, BH;* Æ. ['*childly*']

cildru v. cild.

cildsung f. *childishness,* LL (314').

cildtrog (cilt-, cilda-) m. *cradle,* GL.

cile (AO)=ciele

cilforlamb (eo¹) n. *ewe-lamb,* Æ,WW. ['*chilverlamb*']

cilic m. *sack-cloth of hair,* NG. [*L.* cilicium]

cille=cielle, cyll; **cim-**=cym-

cimbal(a) m. '*cymbal,' Lcd,VPs.* [*L.*]

cimbalglīwere m. *cymbal-player,* GD 61²⁰.

cimbing f. *commissure, joining,* WW 15⁵; 206¹². [v. '*chime*']

cimbīren n. *edge-iron? (joining-iron, clamp?* BTs), LL 455,15.

cimbstān m. *base, pedestal,* Sc 226². [v. '*chimb*']

cin=(1) cinn; (2) cynn, n.; **cin-**=cyn

cīnan¹ *to gape, yawn, crack,* GL,LCD. ['*chine*']

cinbān n. *chin-bone, jaw-bone,* Æ.

cinberg f. *defence of the chin or cheek, cheek-guard,* Ex 175. [beorg]

cincung f. *boisterous laughter,* WW 171³⁹.

cind=cynd

cine I. f. *sheet of parchment (folded),* '*diploma,*' Æ. II. f. *chink, fissure, depth, cavern,* Æ,Bo,WW. ['*chine*']

cine-=cyn(e)-

cineht (io) *chinky, cracked,* WW 43³⁷.

cing, cining=cyning

cinn (1) n. '*chin,' WW.* (2)=cynn n.

cinnan *to gape, yawn?* RIM 52.

cintōð m. *front tooth, grinder,* GL.

cinu=cine II.

cio-=ceo-; **cīo**=cēo

cip=cipp; **cīp-**=cēap-, cīep, cȳp-

cīpe (īe) f. *onion,* GL,LCD. [*L.* cepa]

cīpelēac n. *leek,* WW 380²⁹.

cipersealf (y) f. *henna-ointment,* WW 205¹¹. [*L.* cypros]

cipp (y) m. *log, trunk,* WW : *coulter, plough-share,* WW : *weaver's beam,* LL 455,15¹.

cir=cierr; **circ-**=ciric-

circian *to roar,* LCD 1·390¹¹ (v. A 31·56).

circolwyrde m. *computer, mathematician,* BF 66⁹.

circul m. *circle : cycle, zodiac,* LCD. [*L.* circulum]

circulādl f. *the shingles,* LCD.

cirebald (AN 171)=cynebeald?

ciricǣw nf. *marriage to the church* (as when one takes orders), LL.

ciricbelle f. '*church-bell*,' *Lcd.*

ciricbōc f. '*church-book*,' *manual of the church services, W.*

ciricbōt f. *repair of churches*, LL.

ciric-brǣc f., -bryce m. *sacrilege*, Æ.

ciric-dor n., -duru *church-door*, LL.

cirice (ie, y) f. '*church*,' *religious community*, Æ,BH,CP,G,LL,OET : *church (building), temple, AO,Bl,Chr,Ct*; CP : *congregation (non-Christian), Ps.*

ciricend m. *an ecclesiastic*, MtLp 8[10].

ciricfriŏ mn. *right of sanctuary* : *penalty for breach of the right.* v. LL 2·537.

ciricfultum m. *support from the church*, LL.

ciricgang (y) m. *going to church*, LL 473,7 : *churching, purification (of the B.V.M.),* CM 484.

ciricgemāna (y) m. *church-membership*, W 103[23].

ciricgeorn *zealous in church-going*, LL,W.

ciricgeriht (y) n. *church-due*, LL (328[1]).

ciricgriŏ (y) n. *church-peace, right of sanctuary*, LL : *penalty for breach of the right*, LL 263,3; v. 2·537. ['*church-grith*']

cirichād m. *an order of the church*, LL.

cirichālgung f. *consecration of a church*, CHR.

cirichata m. *church-tormentor, persecutor*, W.

ciricland (y) n. *land of the church*, GD.

ciriclic (circ-) *ecclesiastical*, BH,Chr,Wnl. ['*churchly*']

ciricmǣrsung (y) f. *dedication of a church*, W 277[10].

ciricmangung f. *simony*, LL.

ciricmitta m. *church measure (of ale)*, TC 144'.

ciricnēod f. *requirements of the church*, LL.

ciricnytt f. *church service*, CRA 91.

ciricragu f. *church-lichen or moss*, LCD 51b.

ciricrēn (y[1]) n. *sacrilege*, LL 254 K. [rān]

ciricsang m. *hymn* : *church-singing*, BH.

ciricsangere m. *church-singer*, BH 466[17].

ciricsceat m. '*church-scot*,' *church-due at Martinmas*, BH,W.

ciricsceatweorc n. *work connected with the grain given as church-scot*, KC.

ciricsōcn (y[1]) f. *church-privilege, sanctuary*, LL : *territory of a church* : *attendance at church.* ['*churchsoken*']

cirictīd (y[1]) f. *service-time*, LL (314[20]).

cirictūn m. *churchyard*, LL (250[7]).

ciricŏēn m. *minister of a church*, LL.

ciricŏēnung (y) f. *church-duty or service*, LL.

ciricŏīng n. *object belonging to a church*, LL 381,27.

ciricŏīngere m. *priest*, WW 155[29] (yrc).

ciricwæcce f. *vigil*, LL.

ciricwǣd f. *vestment*, LL 258,51.

ciricwāg m. *wall of a church*, LL.

ciricwaru f. *congregation*, LL 400'; 2·539.

ciricweard (e[2], y[2]) m. *church-keeper, warden, sexton*, Æ. ['*churchward*']

cirisbēam m. *cherry-tree*, GL. [*L.* cerasum]

cirlic I. (e, y) *charlock*, LCD. II.=ciriclic

cirlisc=ceorlisc

cirm (e, eo, y;=ie) m. *cry, shout, outcry, uproar*, Gl,MtR. ['*chirm*']

cirman (e, y;=ie) *to cry, cry out, call, shriek*, Gu,Jud. ['*chirm*']

cirnel (GL)=cyrnel

cirps (y) *curly*, Æ. ['*crisp*']

±cirpsian (y) *to crisp, curl*, CHRD,GL.

cirr=cierr

cīs (=īe) *fastidious*, LCD,CHRD 23[9]. [cēosan]

cīse=cȳse

cisel, cisil=ceosel

ciseræppel m. *dried fig*, WW 367[2]. [=ciris-?, *cherry* (BTs)]

ciser-bēam, cisir-=cirisbēam

cīsnes f. *fastidiousness*, LCD 65a,RB 63[12].

cist (e, y) I. f. '*chest*,' *casket*, Gl,JnR : *coffin*, BH,Lk : *rush basket*, WW : *horn (as receptacle?)*, WW. II.=cyst I.

cīst pres. 3 sg. of cēosan.

ciste=cist I.

cistel I. '*cistella*'? Ct (v. GBG). II.=cystel

cistenbēam m. *chestnut-tree*, GL. [*L.* castanea]

cīstmēlum *earnestly*, OEG 4[32]. [cēast]

citel (e, y) m. '*kettle*,' *cauldron*, Ep,Lcd.

citelflōde (y[1]) f. *bubbling spring*, BC 2·371[9].

citelhrūm (e) m. *kettle-soot*, LCD 50a.

citelian *to tickle* (Ettm., Leo).

citelung f. *tickling*, WW 278[6]. ['*kittling*']

citelwylle (y[1]) *bubbling spring*, BC 2·270[4].

citere, citre (y) f. *cithara*, CJVPs.

cīŏ m. *seed, germ, shoot*, Æ : *mote, CP.* ['*chithe*']

cīŏfæst *well-rooted*, ÆH 1·304'.

cīwung=cēowung; clā=clēa, clāwu

clābre (GL)=clǣfre; clac-=clæc-, cleac-

clacu f. *injury*, W 86[10] (v. FTP 55).

+clǣded (MkL 5[15]) pp. of +clāŏian.

cladersticca m. *rattle-stick*, GL.

clǣclēas *harmless*, WW 419[1] : *uninjured.* [clacu]

clǣdur (ea) *rattle*, GL. [clader]

clǣferwyrt f. *clover*, LCD.

clǣfre f. '*clover*,' *trefoil*, Lcd,WW; Mdf.

clǣg m. '*clay*,' WW.

clǣig '*clayey*,' Ct.

±clǣman *to smear, caulk, plaster, anoint*, Æ,Lcd. ['*cleam*']

clǣming f. *blotting, smearing*, ÆGR 256[4].

clǣmman (e) *to press*, GD.

clǣmnes f. *torture*, BH 290[2].

clǣne (ā, ē) **I.** '*clean*,' *CP,Ct,LL* : *pure, chaste, innocent, Æ,Bl* : *unencumbered, unfettered* : *hallowed* : *clear, open, El,Lcd,Ps.* on clǣnum felda *in the open field* (*of battle*), CP227²⁵ : *honourable, true* : *acute, sagacious, intellectual.* **II.** adv. *clean, clearly, fully, purely, entirely, Æ,Ct*; AO, CP.

clǣngeorn *yearning after purity, celibate* : *cleanly*, CHRD 19¹⁹,²⁰.

clǣnheort *pure in heart, Æ.*

clǣnlic ('*cleanly*'), *pure, Bo,Met* : *excellent.* adv. -līce (*Bf*)=clǣne II.

clǣnnes f. (*moral*) '*cleanness*,' *purity, chastity, BH*; Æ,CP.

clǣnsere (e) m. *priest*, CP139¹⁵ ; W72⁶.

±**clǣnsian** (āsn-) *to* '*cleanse*' ('*yclense*'), *purify, chasten, Æ,CP* : *clear out, purge, Lcd* : (w. a. and g.) *justify, clear oneself, LL.*

clǣnsnian=clǣnsian

±**clǣnsung** f. '*cleansing*,' *purifying, chastening, castigation, expiation, Mk*; Æ : *purity, chastity.*

clǣnsungdæg m. *day for purging*, LCD 1·330⁸.

clǣnsungdrenc (sn) m. *purgative*, MH72²⁷.

clæppan (a¹) *to clap, beat, throb*, LCD 3·88⁵.

clæppettan *to palpitate*, LCD,WW.

clæppetung f. *clapping* : *pulsation, pulse, Æ.*

clǣsn-=clǣns-; **clǣð**=clāð

clæweða=cleweða

clāf pret. 3 sg. of clīfan.

clāfre (GL)=clæfre

clām I. m. *paste, mortar, mud, clay, Æ,Lcd* : *poultice.* ['*cloam*'] **II.**=clēam dp. of clēa.

clamb pret. 3 sg. of climban.

clamm m. *band, bond, fetter, chain, An,Bl, Rd* : *grip, grasp.* ['*clam*']

clān-=clǣn-

clang pret. 3 sg. of clingan.

clap-=clæp-

+**clāsnian** (JVPs)=clǣnsian

clātacrop=clāte

clāte f. *bur, burdock, clivers, Gl,Lcd.* ['*clote*']

clatrung f. *clattering, noise*, WW377²⁷.

clāð m. '*cloth*,' *Mt* : '*clothes*,' *covering, sail, Bo,Cp,Ps,Chr,Jn,Lcd*; AO,CP. under Crīstes clāðum *in baptismal garments*, CHR688E.

clāðflyhte m. *patch*, MtR9¹⁶.

+**clāðian** (clēðan) *to* '*clothe*,' LG.

clāðwēoce f. *wick of cloth*, GPH391.

clauster=clūstor

clāwan⁷ *to claw, Æ*GR,WW.

clāwian *to scratch,* '*claw*,' *Æ*GR170¹¹n.

clawu (ā?) f. nap. clawe '*claw*,' *Æ,Gl,Ph* : *hoof, Æ* : *hook* : (pl.) *pincers? Æ.*

clāwung f. *griping pain*, LCD.

clea-=clǣ-, cleo-

clēa=clawu

cleac f. *stepping-stone*, KC4·36. [*Keltic*]

cleacian *to hurry, Æ*L23⁴⁹³.

clēaf pret. 3 sg. of clēofan.

clēm-, clēn-=clǣm-, clǣn-

-clencan v. be-c.

clengan *to adhere*, RD29⁸.

cleo-; clēo-=cli-; clīe-, clū-

clēo=clēa, clawu

cleofa (ea, i, y) m. *cave, den, BH* : *cell, chamber, cellar, Æ,Ps.* ['*cleve*']

clēofan² *to* '*cleave*,' *split, separate, A,Bo,Ct.*

cleofian=clifian; **cleofu**=nap. of clif

clēofung f. '*cleaving*,' WW.

clēone=clēowene, ds. of clēowen, clīewen

cleop-=clip-

clep-=clæp-, clip-; **clerc**=cleric

cler-ic (-ec, -oc; clerus, PPs67¹³) m. '*clerk*' *in holy orders, WW* : *clerk in minor orders, LL* : *educated person, Chr.* [*L. clericus*]

clerichād m. *condition of a* (*secular*) *clerk, clerical order, priesthood*, CHR,RB.

cleweða (æ¹) m. *itch*, CP71¹⁹. [*clāwan*]

clib-=clif-

clibbor *clinging*, MEN245. [clifian]

+**clibs** (e; cleps; clæsp, y) *clamour*, CP.

clid-ren, -rin f. *clatter*, Ep,Erf928.

cliepian=clipian

clīewen, cliewen? (ēo, īo, ī, ȳ) n. *sphere, ball, skein, Æ,CP,Ph,WW* : *ball of thread or yarn, KC* : *mass, group.* ['*clew*']

clif n. (nap. cleofu, clifu) '*cliff*,' *rock, promontory, steep slope, An,B,Ct*; Æ,CP.

clifa=cleofa; **clifæhtig**=clifihtig

clīfan¹ *to* '*cleave**,' *adhere, Æ,CP.*

clīfe f. '*clivers*' ('*cleavers*'), *burdock, Lcd, WW.*

clifeht=clifiht

clifer m. nap. clifras *claw*, GPH; Æ. ['*cliver*']

cliferfōte *cloven-footed, Æ*L25⁷⁹.

clif-hlēp, -hlȳp m. *a cliff-leap, plunge to ruin?* (BTs),GL.

+**clifian** (eo, y) *to adhere, Æ,CP.*

clifig, clif-iht, -ihtig *steep*, GL.

clifr- v. clifer.

clifrian *to scarify, scratch, Æ*,CHRD.

clifrung f. *clawing, talon*, GPH398.

clifstān m. *rock*, WW371³³.

clifwyrt f. *cliff-wort, water-wort, foxglove*, WW134³ and N.

+**cliht** pp. of +*cliccan, clyccan.

-clīm v. calwer-c.

climban³ (y) *to* '*climb*,' *Sol.*

climpre=clympre

clincig *rough*, DHy104¹⁸.

clingan³ *to stick together, An* : *shrink, wither, pine, Æ,Sol.* ['*cling*']

clipian (e, eo, y) (tr. and intr.) *to speak, cry out, call, DR,Chr,Mt,Jn,Ps;* CP : (±) *summon, invoke, Æ* : (w. d.) *cry to, implore.* ['*clepe,*' '*yclept*']

clipigendlic (y) *vocalic,* ÆGR5 : *vocative* (gram.), ÆGR23.

clipol *sounding, vocal,* BF94[29] : *vocalic, vowel,* BF100[16].

clipung (e, eo, y) f. *cry, crying, clamour, MtR* : (±) *prayer,* Ps : *call, claim,* CHR 1129. ðā clypunga *kalends.* ['*cleping*']

clipur m. *bell-clapper,* WNL109b[16, 20].

cliroc=cleric; +**clistre**=+clystre

clite f. *coltsfoot,* LCD146a.

cliða (eo, y) m. *poultice, Æ,*LCD.

-cliðan v. æt-c.

cliðe f. *burdock,* GL. [v. '*clithe,*' '*clithers*']

cliðwyrt f. '*rubea minor,*' '*clivers,*' *Lcd* 173b.

cliwe, clīwen=clīewen

cloccettan *to palpitate,* LCD82b.

cloccian to cluck, make a noise, BF78[17].

clodhamer m. *fieldfare,* WW287[17].

clof-=cluf-

+clofa m. *counterpart (of a document),* CC 80. [clēofan]

clofe f. *buckle,* GL.

clofen pp. of clēofan.

clomm I. m.=clamm. II. pret. 3 sg. of climban.

clop m? *rock?* v. Mdf.

clott *lump, mass,* HGl488. ['*clot*']

clucge f. *bell,* BH340[6].

clūd m. *mass of stone, rock, Æ,AO* : *hill,* ES38·13. ['*cloud*']

clūdig *rocky, hilly, AO.* ['*cloudy*']

clufeht(e) (i²) *bulbous, Lcd.* [v. '*cloved*']

clufon pret. pl. of clēofan.

clufðung, clufðunge f. *crowfoot : a vegetable poison.* v. OEG896.

clufu f. *clove (of garlic, etc.), bulb, tuber,* LCD. [clēofan]

clufwyrt f. '*batrachion,*' *buttercup, Lcd.* ['*clovewort*']

clugge=clucge

clumben pp. of climban.

clum(m)ian *to murmur, mumble, mutter,* W.

clungen pp. of clingan.

clūs, clūse f. *bar, bolt : enclosure : cell, prison.* [L. clausum]

cluster=clyster; **clūster**=clūstor

clūstor n. *lock, bar, barrier : enclosure, cloister, cell, prison.* [L. claustrum]

clūstorcleofa m. *prison-cell,* AN1023.

clūstorloc n. *prison,* GL.

clūt m. '*clout,*' *patch, cloth, Ep* : *piece of metal, plate, Æ.*

+clūtod '*clouted,*' *patched, Æ.*

±clyccan *to clutch, clench, IM,Sc.* ['*clitch*']

clyf=clif; **clyf-**=clif-, cleof-

+clyft adj. *cleft,* GPH393. [clēofan]

clymmian *to climb, ascend,* SOL414.

-clympe v. calwer-c.

clympre m. *lump of metal,* LCD,RD,WW. ['*clumper*']

clyne n. *lump of metal,* GL.

clynian I. *to roll up, enfold,* GPH. II.= clynnan

clynnan (intr.) *to resound, ring,* EL51 : (tr.) *knock,* NG.

clyp-=clip-

clypnes f. *embrace,* BH238[3].

clypp m., **clypping** f. *embracing,* GD.

±clyppan *to embrace, clasp, Æ,LG* : *surround, enclose, VPs* : *grip, Gen* : *prize, honour, cherish, CP.* ['*clip*']

-clȳsan v. be-c. [clūse]; +**clysp**=+clibs

clyster, +clystre n. '*cluster,*' *bunch, branch, Æ,Cp,WW.*

clȳsung f. *enclosure, apartment, Æ* : *closing, period, conclusion of a sentence, clause.*

clyða=cliða; **clȳwen**=clīewen

cnæht (NG)=cniht

cnæpling m. *youth, Æ.* [cnapa]

cnæpp (e) m. *top, summit, Æ,Lk* : *fibula, button,* WW. ['*knap*']

+cnǣwe (w. g.) *conscious of, acknowledging, Æ* : *known, notorious, manifest, Æ.*

cnǣwð pres. 3 sg. of cnāwan.

cnafa, cnapa m. *child, youth, Æ,Sc* : *servant, Æ,Mt,Ps.* ['*knape,*' '*knave*']

±cnāwan[7] (usu. +) *to* '*know*' ('*y-know*'), *perceive, Æ,B,Bl,Jul,OEG* : *acknowledge : declare* : (+) *ascertain.*

+cnāwe=+cnǣwe

cnāwelǣcing f. *acknowledgement,* KC 4·193[12].

cnāwlǣc (ē²) *acknowledgement,* CHR963 (ES42·176).

+cnāwnes f. *acknowledgement,* EC265[2].

cnēa gp. of cnēo(w).

cnearr m. *small ship, galley (of the ships of the Northmen),* †CHR. [ON. knorr]

±cnēatian *to argue, dispute,* GL.

cnēatung f. *inquisition, investigation,* OEG : *dispute, debate,* Sc.

cnedan[5] *to* '*knead*,*' *Lcd,LkL.*

cneht (VPs)=cniht; **cnēo**=cnēow

cnēodan, cneoht=cnōdan, cniht

+cneord *eager, zealous, diligent, Æ,*BH.

±cneordlǣcan *to be diligent, study, Æ.*

cneordlic *diligent, earnest, zealous, Æ.* adv. -lice.

±cneordnes f. *zeal, diligence, study,* GL.

cnēordnes (Æ)=+cnēorenes

+cnēor-(e)nes, -ednes f. *generation, race,* GL.

cnēores=cnēoriss

cnēorift n? *napkin* (BTs), *kneehose?* (Kluge), GL.

cnēorisbōc f. *Genesis*, WW 414²⁹.

cnēorisn (Bl), cneor(n)is(s) f. *generation, posterity, family, tribe, nation, race*.

cneorōlǣcan=cneordlǣcan

cnēow I. (cnēo) n. '*knee*,' *AO* : *step in a pedigree, generation, LL*; Æ. II. pret. 3 sg. of cnāwan.

cnēowbīgung f. *kneeling, genuflection*, CM.

cnēow-ede, -ade *having big knees*, WW.

cnēowgebed n. *prayer on one's knees*, Æ.

cnēowholen m. '*knee-holly*,' *butcher's broom*, Lcd.

cnēowlan I. (±) *to kneel*, Æ 2¹⁵⁴. ['*knee*'] II. *to know carnally*, ÆL 12⁷.

cnēowlian *to* '*kneel*,' LL.

cnēowmǣg m. (nap. -mǣgas, -māgas) *kinsman, relation, ancestor*.

cnēowrīm† n. *progeny, family*, GEN.

cnēowslbb f. *generation, race* (BDS 8·527).

cnēowung f. *kneeling, genuflection*, CM.

cnēowwærc m. *pain in the knees*, LCD.

cnēowwyrst f. *knee-joint*, WW.

cnepp=cnæpp; cnēw=cnēow

cnīdan¹ *to beat*, MtR 21³⁵.

cnleht=cniht

cnīf m. '*knife*,' *WW*.

cniht (e, eo, ie, y) m. *boy, youth, AO,Bl,LL* : *servant, attendant, retainer, disciple, warrior, Chr,Mt,Met* : *boyhood, ÆGr* : *junior member of a guild* (BTac),Ct. ['*knight*']

cnlhtcild (eo¹) n. *male child, boy*, BH 284³⁰, MH 12⁹.

cnlhtgebeorðor n. *child-birth, child-bearing*, BL 3¹².

cnlhtgeong *youthful*, EL 640.

cnihthād m. *puberty, youth, boyhood, Æ, Bo*; AO : *(male) virginity*. ['*knighthood*']

cnlhtlugoð f. *youth*, BF 12³.

cnlhtlēas *without an attendant*, ÆL 23³⁹⁵.

cnlhtlic *boyish, childish, Guth*. ['*knightly*']

cnlhtðēawas mp. *boyish ways*, GD 111⁹.

cnlhtwesende† *when a boy, as a youth*, B.

cnlhtwīse f. *boyishness*, GUTH 12¹³.

cnlssan=cnyssan

cnītian *to dispute*, Sc 51¹².

cnlttan=cnyttan; cnocian=cnucian

±cnōdan (ēo) *to attribute to, assign to, load with*, CP.

cnoll m. '*knoll*,' *Ps*; Mdf : *summit, Æ, Bo*.

cnop '*ballationes*,' *knob*, WW 8²⁸; 357³².

-cnoppa v. wull-c.

+cnos n. *collision*, WW 376². [cnyssan]

cnōsl n. *stock, progeny, kin, family* : *native country*.

cnosslan *to strike, hit upon*, SEAF 8.

cnotmǣlum '*strictim*,' A 13·35²⁰¹.

cnotta m. '*knot*,' *fastening, Æ* : *knotty point, puzzle, Æ*.

±cnucian (o) *to* '*knock*' *(door)*, *Æ,G* : *beat, pound, IM,Lcd*.

cnūlan, cnūwian *to pound*, LCD.

+cnycc n. *bond*, DR 59,66.

±cnyccan pret. 3 sg. cnycte, cnyhte *to tie*.

+cnycled *bent, crooked*, WW 458³³.

cnyht=cniht; cnyhte v. cnyccan.

cnyll m. *sound or signal of a bell*, RB,WW. ['*knell*']

±cnyllan *to toll a bell*, RB : *strike, knock, LkR,MtL*; LV 28. ['*knell*']

cnyllslan (LkL)=cnyllan; cnyrd-=cneord-

±cnyssan *to press, toss, strike, hew to pieces, dash, crash (together), beat, Æ,AO,CP* : *overcome, overwhelm, oppress*, CP.

cnyssung f. *striking, stroke*, ÆGR.

±cnyttan *to fasten, tie, bind, '*knit*' ('*i-knit*,' Mt,WW), Æ,Lcd*; CP : *add, append*, BF 32³⁰. [cnotta]

cnyttels m. *string, sinew*, OEG 2935.

coc=cocc

cōc m. '*cook*,' *Æ,Ps*; CP. [*L. coquus*]

cocc m. *cock, male bird, Æ,CP,Lcd,Mt*; Mdf.

coccel m. '*cockle*,' *darnel, tares, Bf,Mt*.

cocer (o², u²) m. *quiver, case, sheath, Æ* : *spear*, Ps.

cōcerpanne f. *cooking-pan, frying-pan*, PRPs.

+cōcnlan (cōca-) *to season food*, WW 504¹².

cōcnung f. *seasoning*, LCD,WW.

cocor=cocer

cōcormete m. *seasoned food*, WW 281⁶.

+cōcslan *to cook, roast*, RPs 101⁴.

cōcunung=cōcnung; cocur (Æ)=cocer

codd m. '*cod*,' *husk, Lcd* : *bag, Mt* : *scrotum*.

coddæppel m. *quince*, WW 411¹⁵.

codlc (coydic) '*lapsana*,' *charlock?* A 37·47.

cofa m. *closet, chamber* : *ark* : *cave, den*. ['*cove*']

cofgodas mp. *household gods*, GL.

cofincel n. *little chamber*, WW.

-cofrian v. ā-c.

cohhetan *to make a noise, cough?* JUD 270.

col n. (nap. colu, cola) '*coal*,' *live coal*, *Æ,CP,Lcd,VPs*.

cōl I. '*cool*,' *cold, B,Bo,Lcd* : *tranquil, calm*. II. pret. 3 sg. of calan.

cōlcwyld f. '*frigida pestis*,' *ague?* WW 243¹¹.

-cole v. ōden-, wīn-c.

cōlian *to* '*cool*,' *grow cold, be cold, An,Gu,Lcd*.

collandre f. *coriander*, LCD.

coll-, cōll-=col-, cōl-; -colla v. morgen-c.

collecta f. *collect, ÆP,CM*.

+collenferhtan *to make empty*, LPs 136⁷.

collen-ferhð, -fyrhð, -ferð† *proud, elated, bold*. [*cwellan (to swell)?*]

collon-croh, -crog m. *water-lily, nymphæa*, LCD,WW.

colmāse f. '*coal-mouse*,' *tit-mouse*, *WW*.
cōlnes f. '*coolness*,' *Ps*.
colpytt m. (*char*-)*coal pit*, Ct.
colsweart *coal-black*, NC277.
colt m. '*colt*,' Æ.
coltetræppe f. *a plant*, '*caltrop*,' *WW*.
coltgræg f? *colt's-foot*, WW136[18].
coltræppe=coltetræppe
col-ðrǣd, -ðrēd m. *plumb-line*, GL.
columne f. *column*, AA6.
cōm pret. 3 sg. of cuman.
coman (AO70[24])=cuman
comb, combol=camb, cumbol
comēta m. *comet*, †CHR975. [*L*.]
commuc=cammoc
communia *psalm sung at Eucharist*, ÆP 168[16].
cōmon pret. pl. of cuman.
comp=camp
con (v. '*con**')=can pres. 1, 3 sg. of cunnan.
condel=candel
conn=cann pres. 1, 3 sg. of cunnan.
consolde f. *comfrey*, LCD125b. [*L*.]
const=canst pres. 2 sg. of cunnan.
consul m. *consul*, AO. [*L*.]
coorte f. *cohort*, AO240, 242. [*L*.]
cop=copp
cōp m? '*ependytes*,' *cope, vestment*, GL.
+cōp *proper, fitting*, CP.
copel *unsteady, rocking?* (BTs),BC3·624.
cōpenere m. *lover*, CP405[14].
coper, copor n. '*copper*,' *Lcd,WW*. [*L*. cuprum]
coplan *to plunder, steal*, WW379[17].
+cōplic *proper, fitting*, GD. adv. -līce, Bo.
copp I. m. *top, summit*, HGl. ['*cop*'] II. m. *cup*, NG. ['*cop*']
-coppe v. ātor-c.
copped *polled, lopped, pollard*, Ct. ['*copped*']
cops (*WW*)=cosp
+cor n. *decision*, OET436[15,16]. [cēosan]
corclō m. *increase? choice growth?* LCD 3·212[9] (v. A31·56).
+corded *having a cord?* WW187.
cordewānere m. '*cordwainer*,' *shoemaker*, EC257'. [*OFr*.]
±coren (pp. of cēosan) *chosen, elect, choic?, fit*, Æ : *precious, dear*.
corenbēg m. *crown*, A11·172. [*L*. corona]
+corenlic *elegant*, WW393[37]. adv. -līce, WW396[26].
±corennes f. *choice, election* : (+) *goodness*.
±corenscipe m. *election, excellence*, DR.
corfen pp. of ceorfan.
corflian *to mince*, IM,LCD. [ceorfan]
corn n. '*CORN*,' *grain*, *Chr,CP*; Æ,AO : *seed, berry*, *CP,Jn,Lcd*; Æ : *a corn-like pimple, corn*, LCD.
cornæsceda fp. *chaff*, WW118[1].

cornappla np. *pomegranates*, OEG.
corn-bǣre (Æ), -berende *corn-bearing*.
corngebrot n. *corn dropped in carrying t barn*, LL451,17.
corngesǣllg *rich in corn*, LCD3·188[11].
corngesceot n. *payment in corn*, Ct.
cornhūs n. *granary*, WW185[28].
cornhwicce (æ², y³) f. *corn-bin*, Æ.
cornlād f. *leading of corn*, LL453,21[4].
cornsǣd n. *a grain of corn*, GD253[1].
corntēoðung f. *tithe of corn*, W.
corntrēow n. *cornel-tree*, WW.
corntrog m. *corn-bin*, WW107[1].
cornuc, cornuch (WW25)=cranoc
cornwurma m. *scarlet dye*, GL.
corōna m. *crown*, NC277. [*L*.]
+corōnian *to crown*, PPs5[13].
corsnǣd f. *piece of consecrated bread which an accused person swallowed as a test of innocence*, LL.
corðor†, corðer† fn. *troop, band, multitude, throng, retinue* : *pomp*.
corwurma=cornwurma; **cos**=coss
cosp m. *fetter, bond*, Bo. ['*cops*']
+cospende, +cosped *fettered*, LPs.
coss m. '*kiss*,' *embrace*, Æ,Lk,WW.
cossetung f. *kissing*, NG.
cossian *to* '*kiss*,' ÆGr,BH,G.
cost I. m. *option, choice, possibility* : *manner, way*, DR : *condition*. ðæs costes ðe *on condition that*. ['*cost*'; v. NC341] II. (±) †*tried, chosen, excellent*. [cēosan] III. m? *costmary, tansy*, Lcd. ['*cost*']
costere I. m? *spade, shovel*, WW106[18]. II. m. *tempter*, Æ.
±costian (w. g. or a., also intr.) *to tempt, try, prove, examine*, AO,CP. [Ger. kosten]
costigend m. *tempter*, BL.
costn-=cost-
+costnes f. *proving, temptation, trial*, BH 218[10].
costnungstōw f. *place of temptation*, DEUT 6[16].
±costung, costnung f. *temptation, testing, trial, tribulation*, Mt; Æ,CP. ['*costnung*']
cot (AO) n. (nap. cotu) ; cote (*LL?*) f. '*cot*,' *cottage, bed-chamber, den*, AO,Lk,Mt; Mdf. [v. also '*cote*']
cotlīf n. *hamlet, village, manor*, Chr : *dwelling*. ['*cotlif*']
cotsetla (cote-) m. *cottager*, LL. ['*cotsetla*']
cotstōw f. *site of cottages*, KC.
cott=cot
cottuc, cotuc m. *mallow*, GL.
coða m., coðe f.=coðu
coðig *diseased*, CHRD62[9].
coðlīce *ill, miserably*, MET25[36].
cōðon (AO)=cūðon pret. pl. of cunnan.

coðu f. *disease, sickness,* Æ,*Chr,Lcd.*
['*cothe*']
+cow n. *thing to be chewed, food,* NC292.
cowen pp. of cēowan.
crā n.? *croaking,* WW208¹⁰.
crabba m. '*crab,*' WW : *Cancer* (*sign of the zodiac*), *Lcd.*
cracelung? '*crepacula,*' OEG56²⁴⁹.
crācettan (ǣ) *to croak,* GD119²⁵. [crā]
crācetung (ǣ) f. *croaking,* GUTH48⁴.
cracian *to resound,* '*crack,*' Ps.
cradol, cradel m. '*cradle,*' *cot, WW.*
cradolcild n. *child in the cradle, infant,* W158¹⁴.
crǣ=crāwe
crǣcet-=crācet-
crǣf-=craf-
crǣft m. *physical strength, might, courage,* A,*AO,Sol* : *science, skill, art, ability, talent, virtue, excellence, Bo*; Æ,*CP* : *trade, handicraft, calling, BH,CP,RB*; Æ : *work or product of art, Hex* : *trick, fraud, deceit,* BL : *machine, instrument.* in pl. *great numbers, hosts?* DA393 (v. MP26·434). ['*craft*']
crǣfta=crǣftiga
±crǣftan *to exercise a craft, build* : *bring about, contrive,* Æ.
crǣftelīce=crǣftlīce
+crǣftgian *to strengthen, render powerful,* AO.
crǣftglēaw *skilful, wise,* †CHR975.
crǣf-t(i)ca, -t(e)ga=crǣftiga
crǣftig *strong, powerful, AO* : *skilful, cunning, ingenious, Bl* : *learned, instructive,* BF132⁸ : *knowing a craft, scientific,* RB. ['*crafty*']
crǣftiga m. *craftsman, artificer, workman,* Æ,*CP* : *architect,* BH.
crǣftiglīce *skilfully,* WW.
crǣftlēas *artless, unskilful,* RBL52¹.
crǣftlic *artificial,* BF112²⁵ : *skilful.* adv. -līce
crǣftsprǣc f. *scientific language,* ÆGR18¹⁵.
crǣftwyrc n. *skilled workmanship,* Sc109⁵.
crǣt n. nap. cr(e)atu *cart,waggon,chariot,* Æ.
crǣtehors n. *cart-horse,* WW108²⁴.
crǣtwǣn m. *chariot,* AO.
crǣtwīsa m. *charioteer,* ÆL18²⁹⁵.
crǣwð pres. 3 sg. of crāwan.
craflan (æ) *to* '*crave,*' *ask, implore, demand, Chr,LL* : *summon, Lcd.*
crafing (æ) f. *claim, demand,* TC645⁴.
±crammian *to* '*cram,*' *stuff,* ÆGr.
crammingpohha m. '*viscarium,*' CHRD68⁹.
crampul m. *crane-pool,* Ct(Swt). [=cran, pōl]
cran m. '*crane,*' WW.
crancstæf m. *weaving implement, crank,* LL455,15 and 3·254.

crang pret. 3 sg. of cringan.
cranic m. *record, chronicle,* Æ. [L.]
cranicwrītere m. *chronicler,* OEG7²⁴.
cranoc m. '*crane,*' WW (corn-).
crat (WW140⁸¹)=crǣt; cratu v. crǣt.
crāwa m., crāwe f. '*crow,*' *raven, Gl,Ps.*
±crāwan⁷ *to* '*crow,*' *Mt*; CP.
crāwan-lēac (crāw-) n. *crow-garlic,* WW.
crēac-=crēc-
crēad pret. 3 sg. of crūdan.
creaft-=crǣft-
crēap pret. 3 sg. of crēopan.
crēas *fine, elegant,* NC277 : *dainty,* BDS 48·460.
crēaslic *dainty, rich.* v. NC277.
crēasnes f. *elegance* : *presumption, elation,* OEG1108.
creat=crǣt
Crēcas (ēa, v. AB40·342) mp. *the* '*Greeks,*' AO,BH.
Crēce=Crēcas
Crēcisc *Grecian, Greek,* AO.
crēda m. *creed, belief, confession of faith,* Æ. [L. credo]
credic? *a bowl,* OEG29³.
creft (AS)=crǣft
crencestre f. *female weaver, spinster,* KC 6·131'. [cranc]
±crēopan (occly. refl.) *to creep, crawl,* Æ, *Bo*; AO,CP.
creopel=crypel
crēopere m. *cripple,* ÆL,GF. ['*creeper*']
crēopung f. '*creeping,*' *Gl.*
crēow pret. 3 sg. of crāwan.
crepel=crypel
cressa m. (GL), cresse f.=cærse
cribb (y) f. '*crib,*' *stall,* Cr1426 : *couch,* CHRD31³.
cricc=crycc
crīde pret. 3 sg. of crīgan.
crīgan? *to bubble up.* v. OEG7¹⁰¹.
±crimman³ *to cram, put in, insert,* LCD, WW.
crinc '*cothurnus,*' ZDA33·250³.
crincan=cringan
cring (gr-) *downfall, slaughter,* EL115.
±cringan³† *to yield, fall* (*in battle*), *die.*
cringwracu (gr-) f. *torment,* JUL265.
cripel=crypel; crippan=cryppan
crīpð pres. 3 sg. of crēopan.
crisma m. *chrism, holy oil,* LL : *chrisome-cloth,* BH : *anointing,* CHR.
crismal m? n? *chrismale,* W36¹⁷.
crismhālgung f. *consecration of the chrism,* WNL121b'.
crismlīsing (ȳ²) f. *chrism-loosing, loosing of the chrismale, confirmation,* CHR.
crisp (BH)=cirps ['*crisp*']
Crīst m. *Anointed One, Christ,* Æ,CP.

cristalla m. *crystal*, Æ.
cristallisc *of crystal*, AA 7⁶.
cristelmǣl=cristesmǣl
cristelmǣlbēam m. *tree surmounted by a cross? upright shaft of a cross?* EC 385'.
cristen '*Christian*,' *AO,BH*; Æ. ðā crist-nan=*the English as opposed to the Danes*, CHR 894.
cristen m., crīst(e)na m. '*Christian*,' *Ao*.
cristendōm m. '*Christendom*,' *the church, Christianity*, *AO,Jud*; Æ.
cristenlic *Christian*, DR 91'.
cristenmann m. *a Christian*, MH 170²⁵.
cristennes f. *Christianity* : *Christian baptism*, LL 412,1; 413,13a.
Cristes-mǣl (CHR), -mēl mn. (*Christ's mark*), *the cross*. wyrcan C. *to make the sign of the cross*.
Cristesmæsse f. *Christmas*, CHR 1021 D.
cristlic *Christian*, LL (Thorpe) 1·318¹¹n4.
cristna=cristen
cristnere m. *one who performs the rite of* cristnung, MH 92¹.
cristnes=cristennes
±cristnian *to anoint with chrism (as a catechumen)*, '*christen*,' *baptize*, *BH*.
cristnung f. *christening, anointing with chrism or holy oil*, W 33¹⁶.
crið=crīgeð (v. crīgan)?
crocc f., crocca m. '*crock*,' *pot, vessel, Lcd*.
crocchwer? m. *earthen pot*, OEG 4672.
croced=croged
+crōcod *crooked, bent*, NC 292.
crocsceard n. *potsherd*, Æ.
crocwyrhta m. *potter*, ÆGR.
+crod v. hlōð-gec.; lind-gec.
croden pp. of crūdan.
croft m. '*croft*,' *small field*, *KC*; GL.
crog, croh m. *saffron*, *Lcd*. [v. '*crocus*']
crōg m. *crock, pitcher, vessel*, *Gl*. ['*croh*']
crōgcynn n. *kind of vessel, wine-jar*, WW 210³⁹.
+crōged (ōc) *saffron-hued*, OEG 5204n.
crōh I. m. *shoot, twig, tendril*. II. (*WW* 431') =crōg ['*croh*']
crohha=crocca; croma=cruma
crompeht '*placenta*,' *a flat cake, crumpet*, WW 241³⁴(A 40·352); A 37·48.
crong=crang pret. 3 sg. of cringan.
crop=cropp
cropen pp. of crēopan.
crop-lēac, -lēc n. *garlic* LCD,WW.
cropp, croppa m. *cluster, bunch* : *sprout, flower, berry, ear of corn*, *Ep,LkL,WW* : '*crop*' (*of a bird*), Æ : *kidney* : *pebble*.
croppiht *clustered*, LCD 38b.
crūc m. *cross*, *Lcd*; LV 74. ['*crouch*']
crūce f. *pot, pitcher*, *Gl*. ['*crouke*']
crucethūs n. *torture-chamber*, CHR 1137.

crūdan²† *to press, hasten, drive*.
cruft m? crufte f. *crypt*, GL. [*L.*]
cruma (o) m. '*crumb*,' *fragment*, *Mt,WW*.
crumb, crump *crooked, bent, stooping*, *Gl*. ['*crump*']
crumen (crumm-) pp. of crimman.
cruncon pret. pl. of crincan.
crundel mn. *ravine, chalk-pit, quarry*, Ct (v. GBG and Mdf).
crungen pp. of cringan.
crupon pret. pl. of crēopan.
crūse f? *cruse*, A 37·50.
crūs(e)ne f. *fur coat*, GL. [cp. *Ger.* kürschner]
crybb=cribb
crycc (i) f. '*crutch*,' *staff*, *BH*; Æ.
cryccen *made of clay*, GPH 398.
crȳdeð pres. 3 sg. of crūdan.
crymbing f. *curvature, bend, inclination*, WW 382². [crumb]
+crymian, +crymman (tr.) *to crumble*, LCD 3·290²⁸.
+crympan *to curl*, WW 378²⁶.
crypel I. (eo) m. '*cripple*,' *LkL*. II. (o²) *crippled*, HL 179³²². III. (e, i) m. *narrow passage, burrow, drain*, OEG; v. Mdf.
crypelgeat n. *small opening in a wall or fence?* BC 2·399¹.
crypelnes f. *paralysis*, Lk.
crȳpeð, crȳpð pres. 3 sg. of crēopan.
±cryppan *to crook (finger), close (hand), bend*, IM.
cryps=cirps; crysm-=crism-
crȳt=crȳdeð pres. 3 sg. of crūdan.
cū f. gs. cū(e), cȳ, cūs; ds. cȳ; nap. cȳ, cȳe; gp. cū(n)a, cȳna; dp. cūm; '*cow*,' *Æ,G, VPs*; Mdf.
cūbutere f. *butter*, LCD. [cū]
cūbȳre m. *cow-byre, cow-shed*, Ct.
cuc=cwic
cūcealf (æ) n. *calf*, *Erf*, LL. ['*cowcalf*']
cuceler, cuce(le)re=cucler(e)
cucelere '*capo*,' WW 380²⁵.
cucler, cuculer, cuclere m. *spoon, spoonful*, LCD. [cp. *L.* cochlear]
cuclermǣl n. *spoonful*, LCD.
cucu (Æ,AO,CP) v. cwic.
cucurbite f. *gourd*, LCD 92a. [*L.*]
cudele f. *cuttlefish*, WW 181⁷.
cudu (Æ)=cwudu
cūēage f. *eye of a cow*, LL 116Bn.
cueðan=cweðan
cufel f. '*cowl*,' *hood*, BC (at NED 2 p. ix).
cūfel=cȳfl
cufle, cuffie=cufel
cugle, cug(e)le, cuhle f. *cap*, '*cowl*,' *hood, head-covering*, RB, WW (v. '*cowl*').
cūhorn m. *cow's horn*, LL 116.
cūhyrde m. '*cowherd*,' LL.

cūle=cugle

culfer, cul(e)fre f. '*culver*,' *pigeon, dove, Gen,VPs,WW*.

culmille f. *small centaury*, LCD 22a.

culpan as. of *culpa? m. or *culpe? f. *fault, sin*, CR 177.

culpian *to humble oneself, cringe*, Bo 71²⁴.

culter m. '*coulter*,' *WW* : *dagger, knife*, *WW*. [*L.* culter]

culufre=culfre; **cūm** v. cū.

cuma mf. *stranger, guest*, Æ,AO,CP. cumena hūs, inn, wīcung *inn, guest-chamber*.

cuman⁴ *to* 'COME*,' *approach, get to, attain*, Æ,AO,CP. c. ūp *land, be born* : (±) *go, depart*, Æ,AO : *come to oneself, recover* : *become* : *happen* (also c. forð) : *put* : (+) *come together, arrive, assemble*, Æ : (†) w. inf. of verbs of motion, forming a sort of periphrastic conjugation for such verbs. cōm gangan *he came*. cōm swimman *he swam, etc.*

cumb I. m. *valley*, BC; Mdf. ['*coomb*'] **II.** m. *liquid measure*, BC. ['*coomb*']

cumbelgehnād (BR 49)=cumbolgehnāst

cumbl=(1) cumbol; (2) cumul

cumbol† n. *sign, standard, banner*.

cumbolgebrec (KPs 11), -gehnāst, BR 49 (*v.l.*), n. *crash of banners, battle*.

cumbolhaga m. *compact rank, phalanx*, JUL 395.

cumbolhete m. *warlike hate*, JUL 637.

cumbolwīga† m. *warrior*, JUD.

cumbor, cumbul=cumbol

cumen pp. of cuman.

cumendre f. *godmother, sponsor*. [=cumedre, *cumædre. v. A37·52]

cūmeoluc f. *cow's milk*, LCD 15a.

Cumere? -eras? np. *Cumbrians*, ÆL 21⁴⁵¹.

cumfeorm f. *entertainment for travellers*, Ct. [cuma, feorm]

cū-micge (LCD 137a) f. -migoða (LCD 37a) m. *cow's urine*.

cuml=cumbl

cumlīðe *hospitable*, Æ,W. [cuma]

cumlīðian *to be a guest*, RBL 11¹.

cumlīðnes f. *hospitality*, Æ : *sojourn as guest*, RB.

cummāse f. *a kind of bird*, '*parra*,' WW 260¹⁹.

cumpæder m. *godfather*, CHR 894A. [*L.* compater]

cumul, cuml n. *swelling*, LCD.

cūna v. cū; **cund**=cynd

-cund adjectival suffix denoting derivation, origin or likeness. (-kind) as in deofolcund, god-cund.

cuneglæsse f. *hound's-tongue*, LCD 41b. [*L.* cynoglossum]

cunel(l)e, cunille f. *wild thyme*. [*Ger.* quendel]

cuning=cyning

±**cunnan** pres. 1 and 3 sg. can(n), pl. cunnon; pret. cūðe, pp. cūð swv. *to be or become acquainted with, be thoroughly conversant with, know*, AO,B,Lcd,Mt; CP : *know how to, have power to, be able to, can*, Æ,CP : *express* (*thanks*), CHR 1092 : *have carnal knowledge*, CR 198. ['*can**,' '*con**']

cunnere m. *tempter*, NG.

±**cunnian** (w. g. or a.) *to search into, try, test, seek for, explore, investigate*, B,Bo,Cr, Sol; Æ,CP : *experience* : *have experience of, to make trial of* : *know*. ['*cun*']

cunnung f. *knowledge* : *trial, probation, experience* : *contact, carnal knowledge*, DR 110¹ (A45·187).

cuopel f? *small boat*, MtL. ['*coble*']

cuppe f. '*cup*,' *Lcd,WW*; Æ.

curfon pret. pl. of ceorfan.

curmealle (e, i) f. *centaury*, LCD.

curnstān=cweornstān

curon pret. pl. of cēosan.

curs m. *imprecatory prayer, malediction*, '*curse*,' *Ct,LL,Sc*. [v. MP 24·215]

cursian I. *to '*curse*,'* Ps. **II.** *to plait?* MkR 15¹⁷.

cursumbor *incense*, MtL 2¹¹.

cursung f. '*cursing*,' *damnation*, LkL : *place of torment*, MtL.

cūs v. cū.

cūsc *chaste, modest, virtuous*, GEN 618. [*Ger.* keusch]

cūscote (eo, u) f. '*cushat*' *dove, wood-pigeon*, Gl.

cūself f. *cow's fat, suet*, GPH 392. [sealf]

cū-sloppe, -slyppe f. '*cowslip*,' *Lcd,WW*.

cūsnes=cīsnes

cūtægl m. *tail of a cow*, LL 169,59B.

±**cūð** *known, plain, manifest, certain*, Rd; Æ,AO,CP : *well known, usual*, Da,Ps : *noted, excellent, famous*, Ex : *intimate, familiar, friendly, related*. ['*couth*']

cūða m. *acquaintance, relative*, CP.

cūðe I. *clearly, plainly*, Ps. ['*couth*'] **II.** pret. 3 sg. of cunnan.

cūðelic=cūðlic

±**cūðian** *to become known, take knowledge of, regard*, JVPs 143³.

cūðlce=cūðlice

±**cūðlǣcan** *to make known* : *make friends with*, ÆL.

cūðlic *known, certain, evident*. adv. -līce *clearly, evidently, certainly, openly*, BH, Jul; Æ,CP : *familiarly, kindly, affably*, An,BH; Æ : *therefore, to be sure, hence*. ['*couthly*']

cūðnes f. *acquaintance, knowledge*, HL.

cūðnoma m. *surname*, NG.

cūðon pret. pl. of cunnan.

cūwearm *warm from the cow (milk)*, LCD 126a.

cuwon pret. pl. of cēowan.

cwacian *to 'quake,' tremble, chatter (of teeth)*, Æ,AO,Cr,LkL,VPs.

cwacung f. *'quaking,' trembling*, Æ,VPs; AO.

cwæc-=cwac-

cwǣdon pret. pl. of cweðan.

cwæl pret. 3 sg., **cwǣlon** pret. pl., of cwelan.

cwæl-=cwal-, cwiel-, cwil-

cwǣman=cwēman; **cwǣn**=cwēn

cwærtern=cweartern

cwǣð pret. 3 sg. of cweðan.

cwal-=cweal-

cwalstōw (LL556,10²)=cwealmstōw

cwalu f. *killing, murder, violent death, destruction*, Æ,CP. [cwelan]

cwānian† (tr. and intr.) *to lament, bewail, deplore, mourn*. [Goth. kwainon]

cwānig *sad, sorrowful*, EL377.

cwānung f. *lamentation*, NC279.

cwartern=cweartern

cwatern *the number four at dice*, GL. [L.]

cwēad n. *dung, dirt, filth*, LCD. [Ger. kot]

cweaht pp. of cweccan.

cweald pp. of cwellan.

cwealm (e) mn. *death, murder, slaughter : torment, pain : plague, pestilence*, ÆH; AO. ['qualm'; cwelan]

+cwealmbǣran (e, y) *to torture*, LPs.

cwealmbǣre *deadly, murderous, bloodthirsty*, Æ.

cwealmbǣrnes (e) f. *mortality, destruction, ruin*, Æ.

cwealmbealu n. *death*, B1940.

cwealmberendlic (y¹) *pestilent, deadly*, NC279.

cwealmcuma m. *death-bringer*, B792.

cwealmdrēor m. *blood shed in death*, GEN 985.

+cwealmful (y¹) *pernicious*, HGL428.

cwealmlic *deadly*, WYN 281b (MLR 17·166).

cwealmnes f. *pain, torment*, BH40³³.

cwealmstede m. *death-place*, GL.

cwealmstōw f. *place of execution*, Æ,Cp. [v. 'qualm']

cwealmðrēa m. *deadly terror*, GEN 2507.

cwearn=cweornstān

cweartern (a, æ, e) n. *prison*, Æ.

cwearternlic *of a prison*, GPH400.

cwearte(r)nweard? *jailor*, GPH399.

±**cweccan** *to shake, swing, move, vibrate*, Mt,VPs; Æ : *shake off, give up*, CHRD 99³⁴. ['quetch'; cwacian]

cweccung f. *moving, shaking, wagging*, LPs 43¹⁵.

cwecesand m. *quicksand*, WW357⁶.

+**cwed** n. *declaration*, WW423²².

cweddian=cwiddian; **cwedel**=cwedol

cweden pp. of cweðan.

+**cwedfæsten** f. *appointed fast*, A11·99; ES 43·162.

cwedol *talkative, eloquent*, LCD.

+**cwedrǣden** (i, y) f. *agreement*, AO : *conspiracy*.

+**cwedrǣdnes** (y) f. *agreement, covenant*, NC292.

+**cwedstōw** f. *appointed place, place of meeting*, GD183⁷.

cwehte pret. sg. of cweccan.

cwelan⁴ *to die*, Lcd; Æ,CP. ['quele']

cweldeht *corrupted, mortified*, LCD47b. [=*cwildeht]

cwelderǣde (æ¹)? *evening rider? bat*, SHR 29⁸. [ON. kveld]

±**cwellan** *to kill, murder, execute*, Æ, CP; AO. ['quell']

cwellend m. *killer, slayer*, GPH400.

cwellere m. *murderer, executioner*, BH,Mk; Æ. ['queller']

cwelm=cwealm (but v. MFH106), cwielm

cwelmere ꝩelre=cwellere

±**cwēmə** d.) *to gratify, please, satisfy*, propit. E,AO,CP,Sol : *comply with, be obedient to, serve*. ['queme,' 'i-queme']

±**cwēme** *pleasant, agreeable, acceptable*, NG, WG. ['i-queme']

cwēme-, cwēmed=cwēm

±**cwēming** f. *pleasing, satisfaction, complaisance*, CP.

±**cwēmlic** *pleasing, satisfying, suitable*. adv. -lice *graciously, kindly, humbly, satisfactorily*.

±**cwēmnes** f. *pleasure, satisfaction, mitigation*.

+**cwēmsum** *pleasing*, OEG5000.

cwēn (ǣ) f. *woman*, Sc; Æ : *wife, consort*, AO,Gen : *'queen,' empress, royal princess*, Æ,AO,Chr,VPs : *Virgin Mary*, Bl,Cr. [Goth. kwēns]

-cwencan v. ā-c.

cwene f. *woman*, Rd,W : *female serf*, *'quean,' prostitute*, AO. [Goth. kwinō]

cwenfugol *hen-bird*, RWH148⁵.

cwēnhirde m. *eunuch*, MtL19¹².

cwēnlic *queenly*, B1940.

cweodu=cwudu

cweorn f. *'quern,' hand-mill, mill*, Æ,MtL; CP.

cweornbill *'lapidaria,' a stone chisel for dressing querns* (BT),WW438¹⁸.

cweornburna m. *mill-stream*, Ct.

cweorne=cweorn

cweornstān m. *mill-stone*, MtL. ['quern-stone']

cweorntĕð mp. *molars, grinders*, GL.

-cweorra v. mete-c.; -cweorran v. ā-c.

cweorð *name of the rune for* cw(q).

cwern (NG)=cweorn; cwertern=cweartern

±cweðan[5] *to say, speak, name, call, proclaim, summon, declare, BH,Bl,VPs; Æ, AO,CP :* (+) *order, give orders : propose,* AO 68[16] : ±c. (tō) *agree, settle, resolve, Chr :* (+) *consider, regard,* ÆL 1[117]. c. on hwone *assign to one.* cwyst ðū lā *sayest thou?* '*numquid.*' cweðe gē *think you?* ['*quethe*']

cwic [cuc, cucu (this last form is archaic, and has an occasional asm. cucone, cucune)] 'QUICK,' *living, alive, CP; AO :* as sb. *living thing,* PPs 103[24].

cwicæ̆ht f. *live-stock,* LL 60,18[1].

cwicbēam m. *aspen, juniper, Gl,Lcd.* ['*quick-beam*']

cwicbēamen *of aspen,* LCD 3·14[25].

cwicbēamrind f. *aspen bark,* LCD.

cwicclīende *moving rapidly? tottering?* OEG 2234.

cwice fm. '*couch*' ('*quitch*')-*grass, Gl,Lcd.*

cwicfȳr n. *sulphur,* LkR 17[29].

cwichege *a quick hedge,* KC 3·380[11].

cwichrērende *living and moving,* CREAT 5.

±cwician *to quicken, create, JnL : come to life, come to one's self, Æ,Lcd.* ['*quick*']

cwiclāc n. *a living sacrifice,* NG.

cwiclīc *living, vital,* DR. adv. -līce *vigorously, keenly, Ps.* ['*quickly*']

cwiclīfigende† *living.*

cwicrind=cwicbēamrind

cwicseolfor n. '*quicksilver,*' Lcd; WW.

cwicsūsl nf. *hell-torment, punishment, torture, Æ.*

cwicsūslen *purgatorial,* APT 26.

cwictrēow n. *aspen,* WW.

cwicu=cwic

+cwicung f. *restoration to life,* GD 218[17].

cwicwelle *living (of water),* JnR.

cwid-=cwed-, cwud-

cwidbōc f. *Book of Proverbs, CP : book of homilies,* MFH 136,152.

cwiddian (e, y) *to talk, speak, say, discuss, report : make a claim against,* LL 400,3[1].

cwiddung (y) f. *speech, saying, report, Æ.*

cwide (y) m. +cwide n. *speech, saying, word, sentence, phrase, proverb, argument, proposal, discourse, homily, Bo; Æ,CP : opinion : testament, will, enactment, agreement, decree, decision, judgment, TC; Æ.* ['*quide*'; cweðan]

cwidegiedd (i) n. *speech, song,* WA 55.

cwidelēas (y) *speechless, Æ : intestate,* EC 212[17].

±cwielman (æ, e, i, y) *to torment, afflict, mortify, destroy, kill, Bl,VPs; AO,CP.* ['*quelm*'] For compounds v. cwylm-.

cwiferlīce *zealously,* RB 122[2]. ['*quiverly*']

cwild (y;=ie) mfn. *destruction, death, pestilence, murrain.* [cwelan] For compounds v. also cwyld-.

cwildbǣre (æ, y) *deadly, dangerous, pestiferous,* Sc : *stormy.* adv. -bǣrlīce.

cwildberendlīc (y) *deadly,* NC 279.

cwild(e)flōd nm. *deluge,* CJVPs 28[10], 31[6].

±cwildful (y) *deadly,* OEG.

cwildrōf *deadly, savage,* Ex 166.

cwildseten (u, y) f. *first hours of night,* GL.

cwildtīd (u) m. *evening,* WW 211[42]. [*ON.* kveld]

cwilman=cwielman

cwilð pres. 3 sg. of cwelan.

-cwīnan v. ā-c.; -cwincan v. ā-c.

cwine=cwene

+cwis *conspiracy,* OEG 4955.

-cwisse v. un-c.

cwist pres. 2 sg. of cweðan.

cwið I. (also cwiða) m. *belly, womb,* LCD. [*Goth.* kwiðus] II. pres. 3 sg. of cweðan.

cwīðan *to bewail : accuse,* LL.

cwīðe=cwide

cwīðenlīc *natural,* WW 412[30].

cwīðnes f. *complaint, lament,* GD.

cwīðst pres. 2 sg. of cweðan.

cwīðung (qu-) f. *complaint,* WW 488[37].

cwolen pp. of cwelan.

-cwolstan v. for-c.

cwōm pret. 3 sg. of cuman.

cwuc, cwucu=cwic

cwudu (eo, i) n. *what is chewed, cud, Æ : resin of trees.* hwīt c. *chewing gum, mastic.*

cwyc=cwic; cwyd-=cwed-, cwid-, cwidd-

cwydele f. *pustule, tumour, boil,* WW 112, 161.

cwyl-=cwild-; cwyld=cwild

cwylla m. *well, spring,* KC 2·265[30]. [*Ger.* quelle]

cwylm=cwealm; cwylman=cwielman

cwylmend m. *tormentor, destroyer,* GD.

+cwylmful *pernicious,* HGL 428.

cwylmian (intr.) *to suffer :* (tr.) *torment, kill, crucify, Æ.* [cwealm]

cwylming f. *suffering, tribulation, Æ :* (metaph.) *cross : death.*

cwylttīd (WW 117[8])=cwildtīd

cwylð pres. 3 sg. of cwelan.

cwyne=cwene; cwyrn=cweorn

±cwȳsan *to squeeze, dash against, bruise, Æ.*

cwyst pres. 2 sg. of cweðan.

cwyð pres. 3 sg. of cweðan.

cwȳðan, cwyðe=cwīðan, cwide

cȳ v. cū.

cycel (i) m. *small cake,* Lcd 159b. ['*kichel*']

cycen=cicen, cycene

cycene f. '*kitchen,*' Æ,WW. [*L.* coquina]

cycenðēnung f. *service in the kitchen*, NC 279.

cycgel m. '*cudgel*,' BDS,CP.

+cȳd(d) (*Chr,HR*)=+cȳðed pp. of +cȳðan. ['*ykid*']

cȳdung=cīdung

cȳe I. v. cū. II.=cēo

cȳt f. *tub, vat, cask, bushel*, Æ. ['*keeve*']

cyfes=cifes

cȳfl m. *tub, bucket*, BC.

cȳgan, cȳgling=cīegan, cȳðling +cygd=+cīd; +cȳgednes=+cigednes

cylcan '*ructare*,' OEG 20².

cyld=(1) cild; (2) ceald

cyle=ciele

cylen f. '*kiln*,' *oven*, Cp,WW. [*L.* culina]

cyleðenie=celeðonie; cylew=cylu

cylin=cylen

cyll f. *skin, leather bottle, flagon, vessel, censer*, Æ,AO,CP. [*L.* culeus]

cylle I. m.=cyll. II.=cielle

cyllfylling f. *act of filling a bottle*, GD 250²⁷.

cyln=cylen

cylu *spotted, speckled*, WW 163²⁹.

cym imperat. of cuman.

cymbala=cimbala

cyme (i) m. *coming, arrival, advent, approach*, Bo,MtR; AO,CP : *event : result*, BH 372B¹⁹. ['*come*']

cȳme (ī) *comely, lovely, glorious*, PPs.

cymed n. *germander*, LCD.

cymen I. mn. '*cumin*,' CP,Mt. [*L.*] II. pp. of cuman. III. (and cymin)=cinimin

cȳmlīc† '*comely*,' *lovely, splendid*, Ps. adv. -līce, B.

cȳmnes f. *fastidiousness, daintiness*, GL.

cymst pres. 2 sg., cym(e)ð 3 sg. of cuman.

cyn=(1) cynn; (2) cinn

cȳna gp. of cū.

cyncan aş. of sb. *small bundle, bunch?* (BTs),LCD 2·58²².

±cynd (usu.+) nf. *origin, generation, birth : race, species*, Bl,Bo,El : *place by nature : nature*,'*kind*' ('*i-cunde*'), *property, quality : character*, Bo : *offspring : gender*, Ph : '*genitalia*,' Æ.

+cyndbōc f. *Book of Genesis*, ÆT 77⁴⁶.

+cynde *natural, native, innate*, B,Bo,Gen, WW; Æ,AO,CP : *proper, fitting*, Met : *lawful, rightful*, Chr,Met. ['*kind*,' '*i-cunde*']

±cyndelic '*kindly*,' *natural, innate*, Bl,Bo, Lcd : *generative, of generation*, LL 7,64 : *proper, suitable*, Bo : *lawful*, BH. adv. -līce, Bo.

+cyndlim n. *womb*, Lk : pl. '*genitalia*.'

+cyndnes f. *nation : produce, increase*, RHy 6²².

+cynd-o, -u f.=cynd

cyne=cine II. ; cȳne=cēne

cynebǣnd m. *diadem*, NC 279.

cynebeald† *royally bold, very brave*, B.

cynebearn (a³) n. *royal child, Christ*, CHR, LCD.

cyneboren *royally born*, Æ.

cynebōt f. *king's compensation*, LL 462',463'.

cynebotl n. *palace*, Æ,WW.

cynecynn n. *royal race, pedigree or family*, Æ,AO.

cynedōm (cyning-, *Da*) m. *royal dignity, kingly rule, government*, Chr,Gl; AO : *royal ordinance or law* : '*kingdom*' ('*kindom*'), *royal possessions*.

cyneg=cyning

cyne-geard, -gerd=cynegyrd

cynegewǣdu np. *royal robes*, BH 32²⁵.

cynegierela (e³) m. *royal robe*, MET 25³³.

cynegild n. *king's compensation*, LL 462.

cynegōd† *noble, well-born, excellent*.

cynegold† n. *regal gold, crown*.

cyne-gyrd, -ge(a)rd f. *sceptre*, Æ,GL.

cynehād m. *kingly state or dignity*, CP.

cynehām m. *royal manor*, EC.

cyne-helm, -healm m. *diadem, royal crown*, Æ : *royal power*.

±cynehelmian *to crown*, MFB,Sc.

cynehlāford m. *liege lord, king*, Æ.

cynehof n. *king's palace*, GPH 391.

cynelic I. *kingly, royal*, CP : *public*. adv. -līce. II.=cynlic

cynelicnes f. *kingliness*, BH 194³⁴.

cynemann m. *royal personage*, NG.

cynerēaf n. *royal robe*, VH 10.

cyneren=cynren

cynerīce (cyning-) n. *rule, sovereignty*, Chr, Ct; CP : *region, nation*, AO. ['*kinrick*,' '*kingrick*']

cyneriht n. *royal prerogative*, EC 202¹⁸.

cynerōf† *noble, renowned*.

cynescipe m. *royalty, majesty, kingly power*, Æ.

cynesetl (æ³) n. *throne, capital city*, Æ,AO.

cynestōl m. *throne, royal dwelling, city*, Æ, AO,CP.

cynestrǣt f. *public road*, WW 71⁶.

cyneðrymlic *very glorious*, NC 279.

cyneðrymm† m. *royal glory, majesty, power : kingly born*, DA 706.

cynewāðen *of royal purple*, TC 538¹⁰. [?=cynewǣden]

cynewīse f. *state, commonwealth*, BH.

cynewīðe f. *royal diadem*, GL.

cyneword n. *fitting word*, RD 44¹⁶. [cynn]

cynewyrðe (u) *noble, kingly*, BF 74¹³, MFH 157.

cyng, cynig=cyning

cyning m. '*king*,' *ruler*, Bo,Bl,Chr,Ct; Æ, AO,CP : *God, Christ*, Bl,Ct : (†) *Satan*.

cyning-=cyne-

cyningǣðe *man entitled to take oath as a king's thane,* LL112,54BH.

cyningeswyrt f. *marjoram,* WW301[17].

cyningfeorm f. *king's sustenance, provision for the king's household,* KC2·111'.

cyninggeníola m. *great feud,* EL610.

cyninggereordu np. *royal banquet,* WW 411[28].

cynlic I. *fitting, proper, convenient, becoming, sufficient.* adv. -līce. **II.**=cynelic

cynn I. (i) n. *kind, sort, rank, quality : family, generation,. offspring, pedigree, 'kin,' race, people,* Æ,CP,Chr : *gender, sex,* Æ : *propriety, etiquette.* **II.** adj. *becoming, proper, suitable,* CP.

+**cynn**=+cynd; **cynn-**=cenn-, cyn-

cynnig *noble, of good family,* OEG.

cynnreccenes f. *genealogy,* NG.

cynren (y²), cynrēd (EPs) n. *kindred, family, generation, posterity, stock,* CP : *kind, species.*

cynresu *a generation,* Mt (pref.).

cȳo, cyp=cēo, cipp; **cȳp-**=cīep-

cȳpa m. I. (also cȳpe) f. *vessel, basket,* Lk, OEG. ['*kipe*'] **II.** (ē, ī) m. *chapman, trader, merchant,* Æ.

±**cȳpan** (ī;=īe) *to traffic, buy, sell, barter.* [*Ger.* kaufen]

+**cȳpe** adj. *for sale,* ÆH.

cȳpe-=cēap-, cīepe-

cȳpedæg m. *market day,* OEG.

cȳpend m. *one who sells, merchant,* Mt.

cypera m. *spawning salmon,* MET19[12] : '*esox,*' *pike?* A38·516.

cyperen (Æ)=cypren; **cypp**=cipp

cypersealf (i) f. *henna-ointment,* WW205[11] [*L.* cyperos]

cypren *made of copper, copper,* AO. [copor]

cypresse f. *cypress,* LCD3·118'. [*L.*]

cypsan=cyspan; **cyr-**=cer-, cier-, cir-

cyre m. *choice, free-will,* Æ. ['*cure*']

cyreāð m. *oath sworn by an accused man and by other chosen persons.* v. LL2·293.

cyrelīf n. *state of dependence on a lord whom a person has chosen? : person in such a state* (v. BTs and NC279).

cyren=(1) ceren, (2) cyrn

cyrf m. *cutting, cutting off,* Æ : *what is cut off.* ['*kerf*']

cyrfæt=cyrfet

cyrfel m. *little stake, peg,* WW126[18].

cyrfet m. *gourd,* LCD. [*Ger.* kürbis]

cyrfþ pres. 3 sg. of ceorfan.

ðyric-=ciric-

cyrige v. wæl-c.

cyrin, cyrn (e) f. '*churn,*' WW.

cyrnel (i) mn. (nap. cyrnlu) *seed,* '*kernel,*' *pip,* Æ,Lcd : *(enlarged) gland, swelling,* Lcd. [corn]

+**cyrnod,** +cyrnlod *granulated, rough,* OEG.

cyrps=cirps

cyrriol *the Kyrie Eleison,* BF126³.

cyrs-=cærs-, cris-

cyrstrēow n. *cherry-tree,* WW 138. [ciris; *L.*]

+**cyrtan** *to shorten,* GPH400.

cyrtel m. (*man's*) *tunic, coat,* Æ,AO : (*woman's*) *gown,* Ct. ['*kirtle*']

cyrten I. *fair, comely,* Æ : *intelligent.* adv. -līce (and cyrtelīce) *elegantly, neatly, fairly, well, exactly.* **II.** *ornament?* WW216[7].

cyrtenes (e¹) f. *elegance, beauty,* OEG.

±**cyrtenlǣcan** (e¹) *to beautify, make elegant,* Æ : (+) *make sweet,* OEG.

cyrð pres. 3 sg. of cyrran.

cys-=cyse-, ceos-

cȳse (æ, ē;=īe) m. '*cheese,*' WW.

cȳsefæt n. *cheese vat,* WW379[27] (v. LL 3·255).

cȳsehwǣg n. *whey,* LCD119b.

cȳsfæt (LL455,17)=cȳsefæt

cȳsgerunn n. *curd-like mass,* WW98³ (v. A51·158).

cysirbēam=cirisbēam

cȳslybb n. *rennet,* Cp,Lcd. ['*cheeselip*']

±**cyspan** *to fetter, bind,* Æ. [cosp]

±**cyssan** *to* '*kiss,*' Æ,BH,Mt. [coss]

cȳssticce n. *piece of cheese,* CHRD15.

cyst I. fm. *free-will, choice, election :* (w. gp.) *the best of anything, the choicest,* Æ : *picked host : moral excellence, virtue, goodness,* CP, Æ : *generosity, munificence,* CP. [cēosan] **II.**=cist I.

cȳst pres. 3 sg. of cēosan.

cystan *to spend, lay out, get the value of,* CHR1124.

cystbēam=cistenbēam

cystel, cysten (=cist-) f. *chestnut-tree,* LCD, WW.

cystelīce=cystiglīce

cystian (e) *to put in a coffin,* W. [cist]

cystig *charitable, liberal, generous,* CP; Æ : *virtuous, good.* ['*custi*'] adv. -līce.

cystignes, cystines f. *liberality, bounty, goodness,* Æ : *abundance.*

cystlēas *worthless, bad,* GEN1004.

cystlic=cystig; **cystnes**=cystignes

cȳsð=cīesð pres. 3 sg. of cēosan.

cȳswucu f. *the last week in which cheese was allowed to be eaten before Lent,* Mt(B)5[48]n.

cȳswyrhte f. (*female*) *cheese-maker,* LL 451,16.

cȳta m. '*kite,*' *bittern,* Cp.

cȳte (ē) f. *cottage, hut, cabin,* Æ : *cell, cubicle,* Æ.

cytel=citel; **cytere**=citere

cytwer m. *weir for catching fish,* KC3·450.

cȳð=(1) cȳðð, (2) cīð

±**cȳðan** *to proclaim, utter, make known, show forth, tell, relate, Cp,Cr,HR,Jn*; CP : *prove, show, testify, confess, Mt,VPs* : *become known : exercise, perform, practise,* B : (+) *confirm,* LL : (+) *make celebrated.* wundor c. *perform a miracle.* ['*kithe*'; '*y-kid*']

+**cȳðednes** f. *testimony,* LPs 121⁴.

cȳðere m. *witness, martyr,* Æ.

cȳðig *known* : (+) *knowing, aware of,* DR.

cȳðing f. *statement, narration,* GD 86¹⁴.

±**cȳðlǽcan** *to become known,* GL.

cȳðling=cȳðing

±**cȳðnes** f. *testimony : testament* (often of Old and New Test.), Æ : *knowledge, acquaintance.*

cȳðð, cȳððu f. *kinship, relationship :* '*kith,*' *kinsfolk, fellow-countrymen, neighbours,* Lk : *acquaintance, friendship* : (±) *native land, home, Bo;* AO,CP : *knowledge, familiarity, Æ,BH.*

cywes-=cyfes-

cȳwð pres. 3 sg. of cēowan.

cȳwung=cēowung

D

dā f. '*doe*' (*female deer*), ÆGr; WW 320³⁵.

dǣd I. (ē) f. (nap. dǣda, dǣde) '*deed,*' *action, transaction, event, Æ,B,Bl,VPs.* **II.**=dēad

dǣdbana m. *murderer,* LL 266,23.

dǣdbēta m. *a penitent,* Æ.

dǣdbētan *to atone for, make amends, be penitent, repent,* Æ. [dǣdbōt]

dǣdbētere m. *a penitent,* CHRD 80²⁴.

dǣdbōt f. *amends, atonement, repentance, penitence, Mt;* AO. ['*deedbote*']

dædbōtlihting f. *mitigation of penance,* LL (288').

dǣdbōtnes f. *penitence,* Sc 41⁴.

dǣdcēne *bold in deed,* B 1645.

dǣdfrom *energetic,* PPs 109⁸.

dǣdfruma† m. *doer of deeds (good or bad), worker.*

dǣdhata m. *ravager,* B 275.

dǣdhwæt† *energetic, bold.*

dǣdlata m. *sluggard,* OET 152⁸.

dǣdlēan n. *recompense,* Ex 263.

dǣdlic *active,* ÆGR.

dǣdon=dydon pret. pl. of dōn.

dǣdrōf† *bold in deeds, valiant.*

dǣdscūa (CR 257)=dēaðscūa?

dǣdweorc n. *mighty work,* Ex 575.

dæf-=daf-

±**dæftan** *to put in order, arrange,* Æ,CP.

+**dæfte** *mild, gentle, meek, Mt.* ['*daft*']

+**dæftelīce,** +dæftlīce *fitly, in season, in moderation, gently,* CP.

+**dæftu** f. *gentleness,* GD 202¹².

dæg m. gs. dæges; nap. dagas '*day*,' *lifetime, Æ,Mt,Mk;* AO,CP : *Last Day, Bl* : *name of the rune for* **d.** andlangne d. *all day long.* dæges, *or* on d. *by day.* tō d., tō dæge *to-day.* d. ǣr *the day before.* sume dæge *one day.* ofer midne d. *afternoon.* on his dæge *in his time.* dæges and nihtes *by day and by night.* lange on d. *far on, late in the day.* emnihtes d. *equinox.* ealle dagas *always, Mt.*

dægcandel (o²)† f. *sun.*

dægcūð *open, clear as the day,* DD 40.

dǣge f. (*female*) *bread maker,* WW 277². ['*dey*']

dǣge-=dæg-

dægehwelc *daily,* DR 90'.

dægenlic *of this day,* A 17·121.

dæges adv. v. dæg.

dæges-ēage, -ēge n. '*daisy,*' *Lcd,WW.*

+**dægeð** pres. 3 sg. *dares? braves?* W 220²⁸.

dægfæsten n. *a day's fast,* LCD,LL.

dægfeorm f. *day's provision,* EC 226².

dæghlūttre adv. *clearly, as day,* Gu 665.

dæghryne=dægryne

dæghwǣm (ǣ²) adv. *daily,* Gu,Lcd.

dæghwāmlic (ǣ²) *of day, daily,* Æ. adv. -līce, Æ,AO.

dæghwīl f. (pl.) *days, lifetime,* B 2726.

dæghwonlic=dæghwāmlīce

dæglang (o²) *lasting a day,* SOL 501.

dæglanges adv. *during a day,* Æ.

dæglic=dæghwāmlic

dægmǣl nm. *horologe, dial,* BF,LCD.

dægmǣlspilu f. *gnomon of a dial,* WW 126³¹.

dægmēlscēawere m. *astrologer,* WW.

dægmete m. *breakfast, dinner,* WW 267¹³.

dægol=dīegol

dæg-rēd (or ? dægred) (Æ,CP), -rǣd n. *day-break, dawn, Lk.* ['*dayred*']

dægrēdlēoma m. *light of dawn,* NC 280.

dægrēdlic *belonging to morning, early,* WW.

dægrēdoffrung f. *morning sacrifice,* ExC 29⁴¹.

dægrēdsang m. *matins,* RB,CM.

dægrēdwōma† m. *dawn.*

dægrīm† n. *number of days.*

dægrima m. *dawn, daybreak, morning,* Æ. ['*dayrim*']

dægryne *daily, of a day,* WW 224²⁹.

dægsang m. *daily service,* W 290²².

dægsceald m? (*shield by day?*) *sun,* Ex 79.

dægsteorra m. '*daystar,*' *morning star,* Æ, Lcd.

dægswǣsendo np. *a day's food,* LL (220 n3).

dægtīd f. *day-time, time, period.* on dægtīdum *at times,* RD.

dægtīma m. *day-time, day*, LPs 120⁶.
dægðerlic *of the day, of to-day, daily, present*, Æ.
dægðern f. *interval of a day*, LCD.
dægðerne adj. *for use by day, every-day*, CM.
dægwæccan fp. *day-watches*, WW 110²⁴.
dægweard m. *day-watchman*, WW 110²⁵.
dægweorc n. *work of a day, fixed or stated service, Ex* : *day-time*. ['*daywork*']
dægweorðung f. *feast-day*, EL 1234.
dægwilla *wished for day*, GEN 2776.
dægwine n? *day's pay*, GL.
dægwist f. *food, meal*, Æ,RB.
dægwōma (Ex,Gu)=dægrēdwōma
dæl I. nap. dalu n. '*dale,' valley, gorge, abyss, AO* : *hole pit, Gl* (v.GBG). II. pret. 3 sg. of delan.
dæl (ā) m. (p. dæl-as, -e) *portion, part, share, lot, Cp,Bl,Bo,G,VPs*; AO,CP : *division, separation, Æ* : *quantity, amount, Lcd* : *region, district, AO* : *part of speech, word, ÆGR.* d. wintra *a good number of years.* be dæle *in part, partly.* be healfum dæle *by half.* be ænigum dæle *at all, to any extent.* be ðæm dæle *to that extent.* cýðan be dæle *to make a partial or 'ex parte' statement.* sume dæle, be sumum dæle *partly.* ['*deal*']
±dælan *to divide, part, separate, share, Da*; Æ,CP : *bestow, distribute, dispense, spend, hand over to, An,Mk* : *take part in, share with, Gen* : *be divided* : *diffuse* : *utter.* †hilde, earfoðe dælan *to fight, contend, Ma.* ['*deal*']
+dæledlīce *separately*, WW 487¹⁹.
dælend m. *divider*, Lk 12⁴.
dælere m. *divider, distributor, WW* : *agent, negotiator, Æ* : *almsgiver, Æ.* ['*dealer*']
dæling f. *dividing, sharing*, HGL 423.
+dælland=+dālland
dællēas *deficient, unskilled, WW* : *destitute of, without*, W.
dælmælum adv. *by parts or pieces*, ÆGR, LCD.
dæl-neom-, -nym-=dælnim-
dælnes f. *breaking (of bread)*, LkL p11¹¹.
dælnimend m. *sharer, participator, VPs*; Æ : *participle*, ÆGR. [v. '*deal*']
dælnimendnes f. *participation*, BJPs 121³.
dælnimung f. *participation, portion, share*, Ps,RBL.
dælnumelnes=dælnimendnes
dæm-, dæn-=dēm-, den-; dæp=dēop
dære v. daru; dærēd (S²Ps 62⁷)=dægrēd; dærne=dierne
dærst, dærste, dræst (e¹) f. *leaven*, NG,DR : (pl.) *dregs, refuse, Lcd,Ps.* ['*drast*']
+dærsted *leavened, fermented*, NG.

dæð, dæwig=dēað, dēawig
+dafen I. n. *what is fitting*, GD 84⁶. II. *becoming, suitable, fit, proper.*
+dafenian (often impers.) *to beseem, befit, be right*, Æ.
+dafenlic *fit, becoming, proper, suitable, right.* adv. -līce.
±dafenlicnes f. *fit time, opportunity*, Æ.
+daflic=+dafenlic; dafn-=dafen-
+dafnlendlic=+dafenlic
dāg m? (dāh) '*dough,' Lcd* : *mass of metal.*
dagas, dages v. dæg.
dagian *to dawn, be day*, BH; Æ. ['*daw*']
dagung f. *daybreak, dawn*, BH. on dagunge *at daybreak.* ['*dawing*']
dāh, dāl=dāg, dæl
+dāl n. *division, separation, sharing, giving out, CP* : *distinction, difference* : *destruction* : *share, lot*, GD 311¹¹.
+dālan (VH 10)=+dǣlan
dalc m. *bracelet, brooch*, GL.
dalf (NG)=dealf pret. 3 sg. of delfan.
dalisc (? for *dedalisc) '*dedaleus,'* WW 221³.
+dālland n. *land under joint ownership, common land divided into strips.* v. LL 2·443.
dālmǣd f. *meadow-land held in common and apportioned between the holders*, KC 3·260³.
dalmatice? f. *dalmatic* (vestment), GD 329²⁴.
dalu v. dæl; darað, dareð=daroð
darian *to lurk, be hidden*, ÆL 23³²².
daroð† m. *dart, spear, javelin.* daroða lāf *those left by spears, survivors of a battle.*
daroðhæbbende *spear-bearing*, JUL 68.
daroðlācende† (eð) mp. *spear-warriors.*
daroðsceaft (deoreð-) m. *javelin-shaft*, GEN 1984.
daru f. gds. dære *injury, hurt, damage, calamity*, Æ.
datārum m. (indecl.) *date*, BF 46.
dað '*bloma,' mass of metal*, WW 141³⁶.
Davīdlic (DHy).
Davītic adj. *of David*, LCD 3·428¹⁷.
dēacon=dīacon
dēad (±) '*dead,' Æ,B,Mt* ; AO,CP : *torpid, dull* : *still, standing (of water).* d. blōd *congealed blood.*
dēad-=dēað-
dēadboren *still-born*, LCD 1·206⁶.
±dēadian *to die*, JnL. ['*dead*']
dēadlic *subject to death, mortal, perishable, Æ* : *causing death, 'deadly,' fatal, AO* : *about to die.* adv. -līce.
dēadrægel n. *shroud*, WW 37⁶. [hrægl]
dēadspring m. *ulcer*, LCD.
dēadwylle *barren*, AO 26¹⁶.
dēaf I. '*deaf,' Mt,Jul*; VPs : *empty, barren*, CP 411²⁰. II. pret. 3 sg. of dūfan.

-dēaflan v. ā-d.; **dēaflic**=dēfelic
dēafu f. *deafness*, LCD.
deag=dæg
dēag I. *hue, tinge*, Æ,WW : '*dye*,' WW.
II. pres. 3 sg. of dugan.
dēagel=dī(e)gol
dēaggede *gouty*, WW161³¹. [dēaw]
±**dēagian** *to* '*dye*,' OEG.
dēagol=dīegol
dēagung f. '*dyeing*,' *colouring*, Æ.
dēagwyrmede *gouty*, WW161³¹. [dēaw]
dēah=dēag I. and II.
dēahl, deal=dīegol, deall
dealf pret. 3 sg. of delfan.
deall† *proud, exulting, bold, renowned.*
dēap-=dēop-
dear pres. 3 sg. of *durran.
dearc, deareð=deorc, daroð
dearf I. pret. 3 sg. of deorfan. II. *bold*,
NG.
dearflic *bold; presumptuous*, NG.
dearfscipe m. *boldness, presumption*, NG.
dearn-unga, -unge (e², i²) *secretly, privately,
insidiously*, Æ,AO,CP.
dearoð=daroð
dearr pres. 3 sg. of *durran.
dearste (VPs)=dærste
dēað (ēo) m. '*death*,' *dying*, An,Bo,G; CP :
cause of death, Bl : in pl. '*manes*,' *ghosts*.
dēað-=dēad- (v. ES39·324).
dēaðbǣre *deadly*, CP.
dēaðbǣrlic (dēad-) *deadly*, Mk16¹⁸.
dēaðbǣrnes (ē²) f. *deadliness, destructive-
ness*, LkL,OEG.
dēaðbēacnigende *boding death*, DD,W.
dēaðbēam m. *death-bringing tree*, GEN638.
dēaðbedd† n. *bed of death, grave*, B.
['*death-bed*']
dēaðberende *fatal, deadly*, CP.
dēaðcwalu† f. *deadly throe, agony*, EL: *death
by violence*, B.
dēaðcwealm m. *death by violence*, B1670.
dēaðcwylmende *killed*, LPs78¹¹.
dēaðdæg† m. '*death-day*,' OET; VH.
dēaðdenu† f. *valley of death*.
dēaðdrepe m. *death-blow*, Ex495.
dēaðfǣge *doomed to death*, B850.
dēaðfiren f. *deadly sin*, CR1207.
dēaðgedāl n. *separation of body and soul by
death*, GU936.
dēaðgodas mp. *infernal deities*, WW447¹⁹.
+**dēaðian** *to kill*, DR48⁷.
dēaðlēg m. *deadly flame*, GR983.
dēaðlic '*deathly*,' *mortal*, Bl : *deadly* : *dead*.
dēaðlicnes f. *mortal state* : *deadliness,
liability to death*, BL.
dēaðmægen n. *deadly band*, GU867.
dēaðrǣced (=e²) n. *sepulchre*, PH48.
dēaðrǣs m. *sudden death*, AN997.

dēaðrēaf n. *clothing taken from the dead,
spoils*, WW397³².
dēaðrēow *murderous, fierce*, AN1316.
dēað-scūa, -scufa m. *death-shadow, spirit of
death, devil.*
dēaðscyld f. *crime worthy of death*, LL130'.
dēaðscyldig (LL), dēadsynnig (NG) *condemned to death.*
dēaðsele† m. *death-hall, hell.*
dēaðslege m. *death-stroke*, RD6¹⁴.
dēaðspere n. *deadly spear*, RD4⁶³.
dēaðstede m. *place of death*, EX589.
dēaðsynnignes f. *guiltiness of death*, DR
42'.
dēaððēnung f. *exequies, last offices to the
dead, funeral*, NC,WW.
dēaðwang m. *plain of death*, AN1005.
dēaðwēge n. *deadly cup*, GU964. [wǣge]
dēaðwērig *dead*, B2125.
dēaðwīc n. *dwelling of death*, B1275.
dēaðwyrd f. *fate, death*, WW408²³.
dēaw mn. '*dew*,' Æ,Cp,VPs.
+**dēaw** *dewy, bedewed*, LCD10a, 35a.
dēawdrīas m. *fall of dew?* DA277. [drēosan]
dēawig (ǣ, ē) '*dewy*,' *Ex* : *moist*, Lcd.
dēawigendlic? *dewy*, HGL408.
dēawigfeðera† *dewy-feathered.*
dēawung f. *dew*, EHy7⁶⁴.
dēawwyrm m. '*dew-worm*,' *ring-worm,
tetter*, Lcd.
decan m. *one who has charge of ten monks*,
RB125n.
±**dēcan** *to smear, plaster*, Æ, Lcd. ['*deche*']
decanhād m. *office of a* '*decan*,' RBL54³.
decanon=decan
December m. g. -bris *December*, MEN.
declīnian *to decline*, ÆGR88,100.
declīnigendlic *subject to inflection*, ÆGR88.
declīnung f. *declension*, BF94¹⁶.
dēd I. (A)=dǣd. II.=dēad
dēde (KGL)=dyde pret. 3 sg. of dōn.
+**dēfe** (doefe once, in NG) *befitting, suitable,
proper* : *meek, gentle, kindly, good*. also
adv.
+**dēf-elic, -edlic** *fit, becoming, proper*. adv.
-līce, BH.
defen-=dafen-; **dēflic**=dēfelic
+**dēfnes** f. *mildness, gentleness*, LPs89¹⁰.
+**deftlīce**=+dæftlīce; **deg**=dæg
dēg (NG)=dēag pres. 3 sg. of dugan.
dēg-=dēag-, dīeg-, dīg-; **degn**=ðegn
dehter ds. of dohtor.
dehtnung (KGL)=dihtnung; **del**=dæl
dela nap. of delu.
dēlan=dǣlan
+**delf** n. *digging, excavation*, Æ,AO : *what is
dug, trench, quarry, canal*, Mdf.
delfan³ *to* '*delve*,' *dig, dig out, burrow*, Æ,
Bo,G,VPs; AO : *bury*.

delfere m. *digger*, Bo 140¹³.
delfīn *dolphin*, WW 293¹³. [*L.*]
delfīsen n. *spade*, WW.
delfung f. *digging*, WW 149¹⁰.
+delgian=+telgian
dell nm. *dell, hollow, dale*, BH; Mdf.
delu f. *teat, nipple*, CP 405¹. [*OHG.* tili]
dem=demm
dēma m. *judge, ruler*, Æ,CP.
±dēman *to judge, determine, decide, decree, sentence, condemn*, BH,Cra,El,G,VPs; CP : *assign* : '*deem*' ('*i-deme*'), *consider, think, estimate, compute*, Æ,BH,Cp : (†) *praise, glorify* : (†) *tell, declare*, FAp.
dēmedlic *that may be judged*, GD 336²⁰.
dēmend† m. *judge, arbiter*.
dēmere m. *judge*, MtL (oe). ['*deemer*']
demm m. *damage, injury, loss, misfortune*, AO,CP.
-demman v. for-d.
dēmon *demon, devil*, DR.
den=denn, denu; **dēn**=dōn pp. of dōn.
Denalagu, f. *the 'Dane law,' law for the part of England occupied by the Danes*, LL.
den-bǣr f., **-berende** n. *swine-pasture*, Mdf.
dene=denu
Dene mp. *the 'Danes,'* Chr; AO.
deneland (æ) *valley*, LPs 59⁸.
Denemearc (æ¹, a³, e³), **Denmearce** f. *Denmark*.
dengan (ncg) *to beat, strike*, CHRD 60³⁰.
denge=dyncge
Denisc '*Danish*,' Chr. wk. nap. ðā Deniscan *the Danes*.
denn n. '*den,' lair, cave*, B,WW; Æ : *swine-pasture*. v. Mdf.
dennian *to stream?* BR 12 (v. ANS 118·385).
denstōw f. *place of pasture*, BC 3·144²¹
denu f. **I.** *valley, dale*, Æ,Lk,VPs; Mdf. ['*dean*'] **II.** (MFH 108)=denn
dēof=dēaf pret. 3 sg. of dūfan.
dēofel-, dēofl-=dēofol-
deofenian=dafenian
dēofol mn. gs. dēofles, nap. dēoflu, dēofol *a 'devil,' demon, false god*, B,Cr,G,VPs; AO : *the devil*, Cp,G,Jul,Sol,VHy; Æ: *diabolical person*, JnLR. [*L.* diabolus]
dēofolcræft m. *witchcraft*, AO,BH.
dēofolcund *fiendish*, JUD 61.
dēofolcynn n. *species of devil*, RWH 105²¹.
dēofoldǣd f. *fiendish deed*, DA 18.
dēofol-gield (AO,CP), **-gild, -geld** (AO,VHy), **-gyld** (Æ) n. *devil-worship, idolatry : idol, image of the devil*, Æ.
dēofolgielda (y³) m. *devil-worshipper, idolater*, ÆH 1·70′.
dēofolgieldhūs n. *idol-temple*, AO 284⁹.
dēofolgītsung (dīwl-) f. *unrighteous mammon*, LkL 16¹¹.

dēofollic *devilish, diabolical, of the devil*, Æ. ['*devilly*'] adv. -līce.
dēofolscīn n. *evil spirit, demon*, Sc. ['*devilshine*']
dēofolscīpe m. *idolatry*, NC 286.
dēofolsēoc *possessed by devils, lunatic*, Æ.
dēofolsēocnes f. *demoniacal possession*, G.
dēofolwītga m. *wizard, magician*, DA 128.
dēoful=dēofol
dēog pret. 3 sg. of dēagan (MLR 24·62).
dēohl, dēogol=dīegol
±dēon *to suck*, LG (JAW 19).
dēop **I.** '*DEEP,' profound* : *awful, mysterious*, CP : (†) *heinous* : *serious, solemn, earnest*. d. cēap *high price, great price.* **II.** n. *deepness, depth, abyss*, Ex,Mt : *the 'deep,' sea*, Lk.
dēope adv. *deeply, thoroughly, entirely, earnestly, solemnly*, Ps. ['*deep*']
dēophycgende† dēophȳdig† *deeply meditating, pensive*.
±dēopian (ēa) *to get deep*, DR 81²⁴,LCD 125b.
dēoplic *deep, profound, thorough, fundamental*, Æ,CP : *grievous.* adv. -līce '*deeply*,' Bo,WW : *ingeniously*, BF 64, 70.
dēopnes f. *depth, abyss*, LPs,Nic : *profundity, mystery*, Hy; Æ : *subtlety, cunning*, W. ['*deepness*']
dēopðancol *contemplative, very thoughtful*, BF 164²⁸; W 248⁷. adv. -līce.
dēor **I.** n. *animal, beast* (usu. *wild*), Lk,Met, WW; Æ,CP : '*deer,' reindeer*, AO. **II.** *brave, bold*, An,Sal,Seaf,Sol : *ferocious*, B : *grievous, severe, violent*, Da,Sol. ['*dear*'] **III.**=dēore
±dēoran (ȳ)† *to hold dear, glorify, endear.*
dēorboren *of noble birth*, LL 104,34¹.
deorc '*dark,' obscure, gloomy*, B,Ps : *sad, cheerless*, Wa : *sinister, wicked*, Lk,Sat. adv. deorce.
deorcegrǣg *dark grey*, WW.
deorcful *dark, gloomy*, Sc. ['*darkful*']
deorcian *to grow dim*, LPs.
deorclīce '*darkly,' horribly, foully*, GPH 391²².
deorcnes f. '*darkness,'* Sc 228³.
deorcung f. *gloaming, twilight*, WW; Æ. [v. '*dark*' vb.]
dēorcynn n. *race of animals*, Bo.
dēore **I.** '*dear,' beloved*, G,Jul : *precious, costly, valuable*, AO,Bo : *noble, excellent*, Ps,Rd. **II.** adv. *dearly, at great cost*, Met, WW. **III.** adv. *fiercely, cruelly.* [dēor II.]
dēoren *of a wild animal*, GL.
deoreðsceaft=daroðsceaft
±deorf n. *labour*, WW 91 : *difficulty, hardship, trouble, danger*, Æ. ['*derf*']

dēorfald m. *enclosure for wild beasts*, WW 201²⁴.

±**deorfan**³ *to exert oneself, labour*, Æ : *be in peril, perish, be wrecked*, AO. ['*derve*']

dēorfellen *made of hides*, WW 328¹⁸.

+**deorflēas** *free from trouble*, GL.

+**deorfnes** f. *trouble, tribulation*, LPs 45².

dēorfriŏ n. *preservation of game*, *Chr* 1086. [v. '*frith*']

+**deorfsum** (y¹) *troublesome, grievous*, CHR 1103; 1005.

dēorgēat n. *gate for animals*, Ct.

dēorhege m. *deer-fence*, LL.

deorian (CHR)=derian

dēorlic *brave, renowned*, B 585.

dēorlīce '*dearly*,' *preciously, richly*, El : *sincerely, acceptably*, AS 4¹⁹ (or ? dēoplīce).

dēorling (ī, ȳ) m. '*darling*,' *favourite, minion*, Æ,Bo,CP : *household god*.

dēormōd† *courageous, bold*.

dēornett n. *hunting-net*, WW 183¹².

deornunga=dearnunga

deorsterlīce=dyrstiglīce

dēortūn m. *park*, GL.

dēor-wierŏe (CP), -wurŏe (Æ), -wyrŏe *precious, dear, costly*, Bl,Bo. ['*dearworth*']

dēorwyrŏlic (eo², u²) *precious, valuable*. adv. -līce *splendidly*, Æ : *as a thing of value*, Æ.

dēorwyrŏnes (u²) f. *treasure*, Bo : *honour, veneration*, RWH 139¹⁸ ['*dearworthness*']

dēoŏ (NG)=dēaŏ; **dēpan**=dȳpan

dēpe=dēop; **deppan**=dyppan; **dēr**=dēor

Dēra, Dēre mp. *Deirans, inhabitants of Deira*.

+**derednes** f. *injury*, LCD 1·322¹.

derian (w. d.) *to damage, injure, hurt*, Bo, Chr; Æ,AO,CP. ['*dere*']

deriendlic *mischievous, noxious, hurtful*, Æ.

dērling (NG)=dēorling

derne=dierne

dernunga (NG)=dearnunga

derodine m. *scarlet dye*, CP 83²⁵.

derste (VPs)=dærste

derung f. *injury*, GD.

desig=dysig; **dēst** v. dōn.

dēŏ I. 3 p. sg. pres. of dōn. **II.** '*manipulus*,' *sheaf?* EPs 125⁶.

+**dēŏan** (=īe) *to kill*, NG : *mortify*, DR.

dēŏing f. *putting to death*, DR 72¹³.

deŏŏan? *to suck*, LkR 11²⁷.

dēwig=dēawig

dīacon (ā) m. '*deacon*,' *minister, Levite*, Æ,BH,*Jn*. [L. diaconus]

dīacongegyrela m. *deacon's robe*, BH 90².

dīaconhād m. *office of a deacon*, ÆH.

dīaconrocc m. *dalmatic*, CM 723.

dīaconŏēnung f. *office of a deacon*, BH 272¹⁷.

dīan (A)=dēon

dīc mf. '*dike*,' *trench, ditch, moat*, AO,BH, Chr,Ct; Æ; Mdf : *an earthwork with a trench*.

+**dīcan**=+dīcian

dīcere m. *digger*, WW 149¹⁶. ['*diker*']

±**dīcian** *to make a dike or bank*, BH. ['*dike*']

dīcsceard n. *breach of a dike*, LL 455,13. [v. '*shard*']

dīcung f. *construction of a dike*, WW. ['*diking*']

dīcwalu f. *bank of a ditch?* KC 5·334'.

dīde, didon=dyde, dydon (v. dōn).

dīegan *to die*, NR 38.

dīegel=dīegol

±**dīeglan**, -lian *to hide, cover, conceal, hide oneself*, CP.

dīegle=dīegol

dīegol (ǣ, ē, ēa, ēo, ī, ȳ) **I.** adj. *secret, hidden, obscure, unknown, deep*, B,DD. ['*dighel*'] **II.** n. *concealment, obscurity, secrecy, mystery* : *hidden place, grave*.

dīegolful (ē¹) *mysterious*, RD 80¹⁴.

±**dīegollīce** (ē, ēa, ēo, ī, ȳ) *secretly*, AO,CP : *softly* (*of the voice*), ÆP 28.

dīegolnes f. (ē, ī, īo, ȳ) *privacy, secrecy, solitude*, CP : *secret, secret thought, mystery*, Æ,AO,CP : *hiding-place, recess*, Æ.

dīelf=dealf pret. 3 sg. of delfan.

dīelgian=dīlegian

dīend m. *suckling*, NG. [dēon]

dīere (ȳ) '*dear*,' *beloved*, Lk : *precious, costly*, AO : *noble, excellent*.

±**dīernan** (e, y) *to keep secret, hide, restrain, repress*, Æ,AO : *hide oneself*. ['*dern*']

dīerne (æ, e, y) **I.** *hidden, secret, obscure, remote*, B,El,Lk,Ps; CP : *deceitful, evil, magical*, B,CP,Gen. ['*dern*'] For comps. v. dyrne-. **II.** (y) n. *secret*, GnE. ['*dern*']

dīerra comp. of dīere, dēore.

dīgan=dēagian

+**dīgan** (ē, ȳ; =īe) *to endure, survive, overcome* : *escape* : *profit*, LCD.

dīgel=dīegol (wk. dīgla, dīgle).

dīgl-, dīhl-=dīegl-, dīegol-

dīgner=dīnor

dīgol, dīgul=dīegol

dīhnian=dihtian

diht n. *arrangement, disposal, deliberation, purpose*, Æ : *administration, office* : *direction, command, prescription*, Æ : *conduct*, Æ : (+) *piece of writing, composition, literary work*.

±**dihtan**, dihtian *to arrange, dispose, appoint, direct, dictate, impose*, Æ,G : *compose, write*, Æ : *make, do*. ['*dight*']

dihtere m. *informant, expositor*, WW : *steward*, Æ (=dihtnere) : *one who dictates*, Guth. ['*dighter*']

dihtfæstendæg m. *appointed fast*, Swt (? for riht-).

dihtig=dyhtig

dihtnere m. *manager, steward*, ÆH 2·344[5].

dihtnian=dihtian

±**diht-nung**, -ung f. *ordering, disposition*.

dile m. '*dill*,' *anise*, Gl,Mt,Lcd; CP.

±**dilegian** *to destroy, blot out*, CP : *perish*, LL. ['*dilghe*']

dilemengan v. for-d.

dilfö pres. 3 sg. of delfan.

diligan (CP)=dilegian

dilignes f. *annihilation, destruction*, GL.

dill, dim=dile, dimm

dimhīw *of dark colour*, DD 106.

dim-hof n., -hofe f. *place of concealment*, Æ.

dimhūs n. *prison*, OEG.

dimlic (y) *dim, obscure, secret, hidden*, Æ.

dimm '*dim*,' *dark, gloomy, obscure*, Bo,Gen, Sat : *blurred, faint*, MH : *wicked* : *wretched, grievous*.

dimmian *to be or become dim*, Lcd.

dimnes (y) f. '*dimness*,' *darkness, obscurity, gloom*, Lcd,VPs; Æ : *evil* : *obscuration, moral obliquity*, LL 476,14 : *a dark place*.

dimscūa m. *darkness, sin?* An 141.

dincge=dyncge; **dīner**=dīnor

ding I. v. dung I. **II.**=dung II.

dinglung f. *manuring*, WW 104[8]. [v. '*dung*']

dinig? (A 8·450)=dung

dīnor m. *a piece of money*, ÆGR. [L. denarius]

dīo-=dēo-; **dīowl-** (NG)=dēofol-

dippan=dyppan

dirige *dirge*, '*vigilia*,' CM 433,444.

dīrling (CP)=dēorling

dirn-=diern-, dyrn-; **dis-**=dys-

disc m. '*dish*,' *plate, bowl*, Gl,Mt.

discberend m. *dish-bearer, seneschal*, WW.

discipul m. '*disciple*,' *scholar*, BH,MtL.

discipula *female disciple*, BH 236[34].

discipulhād m. '*disciplehood*,' BH 362.

disc-ðegn, -ðēn m. *dish-servant, waiter, seneschal, steward*, Æ.

disg, disig=dysig

dism (ðism) m. '*vapor*,' '*fumus*,' ES 41·324.

disma m., disme f. *musk*, OEG 46[4] (A 30·123) : '*cassia*,' Ps 44[9] (y).

distæf m. '*distaff*,' WW; Æ.

dīō-=dēð-

dīwl-=dēofol; **dob-**=dof-, dop-

dix (LL 455)=disc

dōc m. *bastard son*, WW.

docce f. '*dock*,' *sorrel*, Lcd.

docga m. '*dog*,' GPH.

dōcincel n. *bastard*, GL.

dōefe v. +dēfe.

doeg, doema (NG)=dæg, dēma

dōere m. *doer, worker*, DR 198[6].

doeð-=dēað-

dofen pp. of dūfan.

dofian (dobian) *to be doting*, GL.

dofung f. *stupidity, frenzy, madness*, GL (?+at OEG 418).

döger=dōgor; **dogga**=docga

dogian *to endure?* RD 1[9].

dōgor mn. (ds. dōgor(e)) *day*, AO,CP.

dōgor-gerīm, -rīm† n. *series of days, time, allotted time of life*.

dōh=dāg; **dohtar**, dohter=dohtor

dohte pret. 3 sg. of dugan.

dohtig *competent, good, valiant*, '*doughty*,' Chr. [dugan]

dohtor f. gs. dohtor, ds. dohtor, dehter, nap. ±doh-tor, -tra, -tru '*daughter*,' Mt; Æ,AO,CP : *female descendant*, Jn.

dohtorsunu m. *daughter's son, grandson*, Chr 982 c.

dohx=dox

dol I. adj. *foolish, silly*, Seaf; CP : *presumptuous*. [v. '*dull*'] **II.** n. *folly*, CP.

dolc=dalc; **dolcswaðu**=dolgswaðu

dolfen pp. of delfan.

dolg (dolh) nm. *wound, scar, cut, sore* : *boil, tumour*, Æ.

dolgbenn f. *wound*, An 1399.

dolgbōt f. *fine or compensation for wounding*, LL 62,23[2].

±**dolgian** *to wound*, Rd.

dolgilp m. *idle boasting*, B 509.

dolgrūne f. *pellitory*, Lcd 25a.

dolgsealf f. *poultice for a wound*, Lcd.

dolgslege† m. *wounding blow*, An.

dolgswæð n., dolgswaðu f. *scar*, Æ.

dolh=dolg

dolhdrenc m. *drink for a wound, antidote*, Lcd.

dolhsmeltas mp. *linen bandages*, WW 107[33].

dolhwund *wounded*, Jud 107.

dol-lic *audacious, rash, foolhardy, foolish*. adv. -līce, CP : *bewildered*, Bf 144[1].

dolmanus=dulmunus

dolsceaða m. *fell destroyer*, B 479.

dolscipe m. *folly, error*, CP 387[34].

dolsmeltas=dolhsmeltas

dolsprǣc f. *silly talk*, CP 385[6].

dolwillen I. *rash, bold*, Jul 451. **II.** n. *rashness, madness*, Jul 202.

dolwīte n. *pain of a wound?* (BTs), *punishment of the wicked, pains of hell?* (Tupper), Rd 27[17].

dōm m. '*doom*,' *judgment, ordeal, sentence*, BH,JnL; Æ,CP : *decree, law, ordinance, custom*, Æ,VPs : *justice, equity*, Mt,VPs : *opinion, advice* : *choice, option, free-will* : *condition* : *authority, supremacy, majesty, power, might*, Jn; AO : *reputation, dignity, glory, honour, splendour*, AO : *court, tribunal, assembly* : *meaning, interpretation*.

-dōm masc. abstract suffix=*state, condition, power, etc.*, as in frēodōm.

dōmærn n. *judgment-hall, tribunal*, Æ.

dōmbōc f. *code of laws, statute-book, manual of justice*, Æ,LL. ['*doombook*']

dōmdæg m. '*doomsday,*' *judgment-day, Mt.*

dōmēadig† *mighty, renowned.*

dōmere m. *judge, Bo,LL*; CP. ['*doomer*']

dōmern (Æ)=dōmærn

dōmfæst† *just, renowned, mighty.*

dōmfæstnes f. *righteous judgment*, LPs 100¹.

dōmgeorn† *ambitious : righteous.*

dōmhūs n. *law-court, tribunal*, GL.

dōmhwæt adj. *eager for renown? strenuous in judgment?* CR 428.

dōmian† *to glorify, magnify*, DA.

dōmlsc adj. *of the day of judgment*, SOL 148'.

dōmlēas† *inglorious, powerless.*

dōmlic *famous, glorious, praiseworthy : judicial*, Æ : *canonical*, CM 268. adv. -līce.

domne mf. *lord*, CHR : *nun, abbess.* [*L.*]

dōmsetl n. *judgment-seat, tribunal*, Æ.

dōmsettend m. *jurisconsult*, WW 429⁶.

dōmstōw f. *tribunal*, W 148³¹.

dōmweorðung† f. *honour, glory.*

±dōn anv. pres. ptc. dō(e)nde, pres. 2 sing. dēst, 3 dēð, pret. sg. dyde, pl. dydon (æ,i), pp. dōn to '*DO**' ('*i-do*'), *make, act, perform : cause* (often followed by the inf. with a passive sense—as in hig dydon rīcu settan *they caused kingdoms to be founded*, i.e. *they founded kingdoms*—or by ðæt) : *add* (*to*) : *put, place, take* (*from, to or away*) : *give, bestow, confer : consider, esteem : observe, keep* : to avoid repetition of another verb, Æ : (+) *arrive at*, CHR : (+) *halt, encamp, cast anchor*, CHR : (+) *reduce*, CHR. d. tō hīerran hāde *promote, advance to a higher position.* d. tō nāhte *annul, make of none effect.* d. tō witanne *cause to know.* betre, furðor, d. *prefer.* +d. forð *manifest, show forth.* d. ūp *put ashore.* +d. ūp *exhume.*

dōnlic *active*, RBL.

dop-ened, -ænid f. *diver, water-fowl, moorhen, coot*, GL.

dopfugel m. *water-fowl, moorhen*, GL.

-doppa v. dūfe-d.; **-doppe** v. fugol-d.

doppettan *to plunge in, immerse*, Æ.

dor n. (nap. doru, dor) *door, gate : pass, Lcd, Ps.* [v. '*door*']

dora m. *humble-bee, Ep,Lcd,WW*; Æ. ['*dor*']

dorfen pp. of deorfan.

dorste (Æ,AO,CP) pret. 3 sg. of *durran.

dorweard m. *doorkeeper*, DR,MkRL.

dott m. *head of a boil, Lcd.* ['*dot*']

-dōung v. on-d.

dox *dark-haired, dusky, A,WW.* ['*dusk*']

doxian *to turn dark, VH* (v. ES 43·330). ['*dusk*']

draca m. *dragon, sea-monster, B,MH,Ps : serpent, Pa,Ps : the devil : standard representing a dragon or serpent*, GPH 392. ['*drake*']

drā-centse, -cente, -conze f. *dragon-wort*, LCD. [*L.* dracontea]

dræce (N)=draca

drǣdan⁷ *to dread, fear*, Sc 67¹.

drǣf=drāf; **drǣf-=**drēf-

±drǣfan *to drive, drive out*, CHR.

drǣfend I. m. *hunter*, CRA 38. **II.=**drēfend

+drǣg† n. *concourse, assembly : tumult.*

drǣge f. *drag-net*, WW. [drāgan]

drǣgeð pres. 3 sg. of dragan.

drǣgnett n. *drag-net*, WW. ['*draynet*']

drǣhð, drǣgð pres. 3 sg. of dragan.

drǣn, drænc=drān, drinc

drǣp pret. 3 sg. of drepan.

drǣst=dǣrst

drǣstig *full of dregs, rubbishy, WW.* [dǣrste; '*drasty*']

drǣt pres. 3 sg. of drǣdan.

drāf I. f. *action of driving, Bl : expulsion, LL : '*drove,*' herd, Chr;* Æ : *company, band, W;* Æ : *road along which cattle are driven, KC* 5·217⁶. [drīfan] **II.** pret. 3 sg. of drīfan.

dragan⁶ *to drag, '*draw*,*' JnL,CP : go : protract*, CHRD 57⁷.

drāgense=drācentse

drān (ǣ) f. '*drone,*' WW; Æ.

dranc pret. 3 sg. of drincan.

drapa=dropa; **drēa=**drȳ

drēag, drēah pret. 3 sg. of drēogan.

+dreag=+drǣg

drēahnian (ē) *to '*drain,*' strain out, Lcd,Mt.*

dreaht pp. of dreccan.

drēam m. *joy, gladness, delight, ecstasy, mirth, rejoicing, Ct,Chr,Sat; AO : melody, music, song, singing,* Æ. ['*dream*']

drēamcræft m. *art of music*, Bo 38⁷,MH 212³⁰.

drēamere m. *musician*, Bo 38⁷.

drēam-hæbbende (GEN 81), -healdende (B 1227) *happy, joyful.*

drēamlēas† *joyless, sad.*

drēamlic *joyous, musical*, GL.

drēamnes f. *singing*, LPs 136³.

drēap pret. 3 sg. of drēopan.

drēap- (VPs)=drēop-

drēariend *inrushing tide?* WW 225¹².

drēarung=drēorung

drēas pret. 3 sg. of drēosan.

±dreccan *to vex, irritate, trouble, torment, oppress, afflict,* Æ,Gen,OET. ['*dretch*']

±drec(c)ednes (Æ), dreccung (Sc) f. *tribulation, affliction.* ['*dretching*']

drēd=drǣd pret. 3 sg. of drǣdan.

±**drēfan** to stir up, excite, disturb, trouble, vex, afflict, B,Jn; Æ,CP. [drōf; 'dreve']

+**drēfedlīc** oppressive, AO 38¹⁴.

±**drēfednes** (ǣ) f. tribulation, trouble, distress, scandal, disorder.

±**drēfend** (ǣ) m. disturber, LPs,RB.

drefllan to 'drivel,' WW.

+**drēfnes** f. confusion : tempest, OEG.

drēfre m. disturber, RB 121¹². [drōf]

drēfung f. disturbance, WW 109².

drēge, drēgan=drȳge, drȳgan

drēhnian (Mt)=drēahnian

dreht pp. of dreccan.

+**drehtnes** f. contrition, BH 424¹³.

drēm-=drȳm-

drenc m. 'drink,' drinking, draught, Æ,Lcd, WW; CP : drowning. ['drench,' 'drunk']

drencan to give to drink, to ply with drink, make drunk, Ps; CP : soak, saturate : submerge, drown, Æ. ['drench']

drenccuppe f. drinking-cup, WW 329¹⁹.

drence-=drenc-, drinc-, drync-

drencflōd† m. flood, deluge.

drenchorn m. drinking-horn, Ct. ['drench']

drenchūs n. drinking-house, WW 186²⁵.

dreng m. youth, warrior, Ma 149. ['dreng'; ON.]

drēocræft (BL)=drȳcræft

dreofon=drifon pret. pl. of drīfan.

+**drēog** I. n. a dressing for keeping (shoes) in good condition, Æ : usefulness? gravity? RB 123⁶. tō +d. gān to ease oneself, RB 32²². II. fit, sober, serious : tame, gentle (horse), GD 78¹².

±**drēogan²** to lead a (certain) life, do, work, perform, fulfil, take part in, conduct, Gu,Ps; AO. wide d. wander : be busy, employed : experience, suffer, endure, sustain, tolerate, Ex; CP : to enjoy. ['dree,' 'i-dree']

+**drēoglǣcan** to put in order, regulate, arrange, attend to, Æ.

+**drēoglīce** (h) discreetly, carefully : meekly, modestly, humbly.

drēoh=drēog

±**drēopan²** to drop, drip, PPs. ['dreep']

drēopian (ēa) to drop, drip, trickle, Ps.

drēopung (ēa) f. dropping, VV²Ps.

drēor† m. blood. [drēosan]

dreord pret. 3 sg. of drǣdan.

drēorfāh bespattered with gore, B 485.

drēorgian=drēorigian

drēorig adj. †bloody, blood-stained, B : cruel, grievous, Gu : sad, sorrowful, Æ : headlong? ['dreary'] adv. -līce sorrowfully, Æ. ['drearily']

drēorigferð sorrowful, Cr 1109.

drēorighlēor sad of countenance, WA 83.

drēorigian to be 'dreary,' sad, Ruin; Æ.

drēorigmōd sad in mind, Gen 2804. ['drearymood']

drēorignes f. sadness, sorrow, GD; Æ. ['dreariness']

drēorlīc, drēorlic=drēorig

drēorsele m. dreary hall, WIF 50.

drēorung† (ēa) f. falling, distilling, dropping. [drēosan]

±**drēosan²** to fall, perish : become weak, fail.

drēosendlīc perishable, ByH 130⁸.

drep=ðrep?

+**drep** m. stroke, blow, An 1446.

±**drepan⁵** to strike, kill, overcome, B. ['drepe']

drepe† (y) m. stroke, blow, violent death.

+**drettan** to consume, PPs 70¹².

drī-=drȳ-

±**drīf** f. fever, MkR 1³¹; ANS 84·324.

+**drīf** I. n. a drive, a tract through which something moves rapidly (BTs), SoLK 186. II. what is driven, stubble, EPs 82¹⁴.

±**drīfan¹** to 'drive*,' force, hunt, follow up, pursue, Æ,AO,CP : drive away, expel, BH, Gen,Met,Mk,Ps : practise, carry on, RB ; Æ : rush against, impel, drive forwards or backwards, Cr,KC : undergo.

drīg(l)ð, **drīhð** pres. 3 sg. of drēogan.

+**drīhð** f. sobriety, gravity, LL (314,318).

drīm=drēam

±**drinc** (y) 'drink,' beverage, Bo,Chr,G : draught, Cp,Mt : drinking, carousal. [v. also 'drunk']

drinc- v. also drync-, drenc-.

drinca (m.), **drince** (f.)=drinc

+**drinca** m. cup-bearer, RWH 39².

±**drincan¹** to drink, Æ,Lk; AO,CP : be entertained, LL 3,3 : to swallow up, engulf, Æ. pp. druncen refreshed, elate (with drink), drunk.

drincere m. 'drinker,' drunkard, MtL.

drīorig=drēorig

drisne (y) f. 'capillamenta'? v. A 41·108.

+**drītan¹** 'cacare,' Lcd 1·364⁹. ['drite']

drīting f. 'egestio' (sc. ventris), WW ; A 8·449. [v. 'drite']

±**drōf** dirty, muddy, swampy, turbid, troubled, Lcd. ['drof'; drēfan]

drōfe grievously, severely, Lcd 3·286¹¹.

+**drōfednes**=+drēfednes

drōfig troubled, Bas 44¹⁶.

drōflic troublesome, tormenting, Dom 19.

drōg pret. 3 sg. of dragan.

droge f? excrement, Lcd 118b.

drogen pp. of drēogan.

drōgon pret. pl. of dragan.

drōh pret. 3 sg. of dragan.

drohnian=drohtnian

droht I. m? n? condition of life. II. (ō?) pull, draught, WW 486²⁷.

drohtaŏ m. *mode of living, conduct : environment, society : condition, employment.*
drohtian (CP), drohtnian (Æ) *to conduct oneself, behave, associate with, lead a life, live, continue.* [drēogan]
droht-(n)oŏ, -nung=droht-aŏ, -ung
±**drohtnung** f. *condition, way of life, reputation, conduct,* Æ,CP.
dronc=dranc pret. 3 sg. of drincan.
dropa m. *a 'drop,'* Az,Lcd,Lk,VPs; AO, CP : *gout? Lcd : humour, choler.*
+**dropa** m. *a kind of date,* OEG 474.
dropen I. pp. of drēopan. II. (B 2891)= drepen pp. of drepan.
drop-fāg, -fāh I. *spotted, speckled,* Lcd. II. *starling,* Gl.
dropian *to 'drop,' drip, trickle,* Ps.
dropmǣlum *drop by drop, Æ.* ['dropmeal']
droppetan, -ian *to drop, drip, distil,* Ps.
droppetung, drop(p)ung (Ps) f. *'dropping,' dripping, falling, Æ.*
droren pp. of drēosan.
+**drorenlic** *perishable,* NC 293.
drōs, drōsna (Æ) m., drōsne (VPs) f. *sediment, lees, dregs, dirt, ear-wax,* WW. [drēosan; 'dros,' 'drosen']
drūgaŏ=drūgoŏ
±**drūgian** *to dry up, wither,* LRG,Ps. [drȳge]
drugon pret. pl. of drēogan.
drūgoŏ f., drūgoŏa m. *'drought,' dryness,* WW : *dry ground, desert, LPs.* [drȳge]
drūgung=drūgoŏ
druh m. *dust?* Soul 17.
druncen I. n. *drunkenness, LG,LL.* ['drunken'] II. pp. of drincan. III. adj. '*drunken,' drunk, Sc*; AO.
druncenes=druncennes
druncengeorn *drunken,* HL,RB.
druncenhād m. *drunkenness,* Chr 1070.
druncenig *drunken,* LkL 12⁴⁵.
druncenlǣwe 'inebrians,' CPs 22⁵.
druncennes f. *'drunkenness,' AO,Lk;* Æ.
druncenscipe m. *drunkenness,* HL 12n³⁴.
druncenwillen *drunken,* CP 401²⁹.
druncmennen n. *drunken maidservant?* Rd 13¹.
±**druncnian** *to be drunk, Æ : get drunk : furnish with drink,* EPs 22⁵ : *sink, drown, MtL.* ['drunken']
druncning f. *drinking,* LPs 22⁵.
druncon pret. pl. of drincan.
drupian=dropian
drupon pret. pl. of drēopan.
drūpung f. *drooping, torpor, dejection,* Wyn 59.
druron pret. pl. of drēosan.
drūsian† *to droop, become sluggish, stagnant, turbid.* [drēosan]

drūt f. *beloved one,* DD 291.
drūw-=drūg-
drȳ (ē, ī) m. *magician, sorcerer,* Æ,AO : *sorcery.* [Kelt. drūi]
+**drycned** *dried up, emaciated,* AO 102¹⁰.
drȳcræft (ēo) m. *witchcraft, magic, sorcery,* Æ,AO : *magician's apparatus,* ÆH 2·418⁸.
drȳcræftig *skilled in magic,* Bo 116³,Ex 7¹¹.
drȳcræftiga m. *sorcerer,* GD 27¹⁵.
drȳecge=drȳicge
drȳfan=(1) drīfan; (2) drēfan
±**drȳgan** (ī) *to 'dry,' dry up, rub dry, Bo,Jn*; CP.
drȳge (ī) *'dry,' A,Bo,Mt : parched, wiᵗhered, Lk.* on drȳgum *on dry land.* tō drȳgum *to the dregs.*
drȳgnes (ī) f. *dryness,* Ps.
drȳgscēod *dry-shod,* W 293¹⁷.
drȳhst pres. 2 sg. of drēogan.
dryht (i) I.† f. (±) *multitude, army, company, body of retainers, nation, people, Ex :* pl. *men.* ['dright'; drēogan] II. (+) f. *fortune, fate,* OEG.
+**dryhta** m. *fellow-soldier* (BT).
dryhtbealo=dryhtenbealu
dryhtbearn n. *princely youth,* B 2035.
dryhtcwēn f. *noble queen,* Wid 98.
dryhtdōm m. *noble judgment,* VPs 9¹⁷.
dryht-ealdorman (Chrd), -ealdor (WW) m. '*paranymphus,' bridesman.*
dryhten (i) m. *ruler, king, lord, prince, Æ,B : the Lord, God, Christ,* CP. ['drightin']
dryhtenbēag (drihtin-) m. *payment* (to a lord) *for killing a freeman,* LL 3,6.
dryhtenbealu† n. *great misfortune.*
dryhtendōm m. *lordship, majesty,* An 1001.
dryhtenhold (i) *loyal,* Gen 2282.
dryhtenlic *lordly : divine, of the Lord, Æ.* adv. -līce.
dryhtenweard m. *lord, king,* Da 535.
dryhtfolc† n. *people, troop, Ex.* ['drightfolk']
dryhtgesīŏ m. *retainer, warrior,* Fin 44.
dryhtgestrēon n. *princely treasure,* Rd 18³.
dryhtguma m. †*warrior, retainer, follower, man : bridesman.*
dryhtin-=dryhten-
dryhtlēoŏ n. *national song, hymn,* El 342.
dryhtlic (i) *lordly, noble, B,Gen.* d. gebed *the Lord's Prayer.* ['drightlike'] adv. -līce.
dryhtmann m. *bridesman,* Gl.
dryhtmāŏm m. *princely treasure,* B 2483.
dryhtnē m. *warrior's corpse,* Ex 163.
dryhtscipe† m. *lordship, rulership, dignity : virtue, valour, heroic deeds.*
dryhtsele† m. *princely hall,* B.
dryhtsibb† f. *peace, high alliance,* B.
dryhtwēmend, -wēmere (i) m. *bridesman,* OEG 1774.

dryhtwerast mp. *men, chieftains*, GEN.

dryhtwuniende *living among the people*, CRA 7.

dryhtwurð (i) *divine*, ÆL.

dryhtwurða (i) m. *theologian*, ÆL.

drȳhð pres. 3 sg. of drēogan.

drȳicge f. *witch*, MH 28³ (-egge), NC 282.

drȳlic *magic, magical*, NAR 50¹³.

drȳman (ē;=īe) *to sing aloud, rejoice*, LPs. ['*dream*']

drȳmann m. *sorcerer, magician*, Æ.

±drȳme (ē), +drȳmed *melodious, harmonious, cheerful*, Æ,GL.

drync m. *drink, potion, draught, drinking*, Cp; AO,CP. ['*drunk*'] (v. also drinc.)

drync- v. also drenc-, drinc-.

dryncehorn (i) *drinking-horn*, TC 555⁶.

dryncelēan (i) n. *scot-ale, the ale given by a seller to a buyer on concluding a bargain* (BT). v. LL 2·56.

dryncfæt n. *drinking vessel*, AA 7⁶.

dryncgemett (i) n. *a measure of drink*, CHRD 15²⁴.

+dryncnes f. *immersion, baptism*, ÆL 23b, 723.

dryncwīrig *drunk*, WW 437²¹. [wērig]

±drȳpan (=īe) *to let drop, cause to fall in drops*, Æ,AO : *moisten*, Æ. ['*dripe*']

drype=drepe

dryppan? *to drip* (v. NED '*drip*,' BTs and FTP 214).

dryret m. *ceasing, decline* : *fall, deposit*. [drēosan]

dryslic *terrible*, WW 191²⁸.

drysmiant *to become obscure, gloomy*.

±drysnan *to extinguish*, NG. [drosn]

+drysnian *to vanish, disappear*, LkL 24³¹.

dubbian *to* '*dub*,' *strike, knight (by striking with a sword)*, Chr 1085 E.

dūce f. '*duck*,' Ct.

±dūfan² *to duck*, '*dive*,' Rd; Æ : (+) *sink, be drowned*, AO,CP.

dūfedoppa m. *pelican*, LPs. ['*divedap*']

dugan pres. 1, 3 dēag, dēah, pl. dugon, pret. dohte swv. (usu. impers.) *to avail, be worth, be capable of, competent, or good for anything*, Chr,MtL : *thrive, be strong* : *be good, virtuous, kind*, B,Fa,Sat. ['*dow*']

dug-að, -eð, -oð=duguð

duguð fm. *body of noble retainers, people, men, nobles, the nobility*, An,Ex; AO : *host, multitude, army* : *the heavenly host* : *strength, power* : *excellence, worth*, Hy; Æ, AO : *magnificence, valour, glory, majesty* : *assistance, gift* : *benefit, profit, wealth, prosperity, salvation*, Cr : *what is fit or seemly, decorum*. ['*douth*']

duguðgifu (a², e²) f. *munificence*, GL.

duguðlic *authoritative, chief, noble*, OEG. adv. -līce.

duguðmiht f. *supreme power*, LCD.

duguðnǣmere m. '*municeps*,' OEG 7¹².

duhte=dohte (v. dugan).

dulfon pret. pl. of delfan.

dulhrune=dolgrune

dulmunus? m. *a kind of warship*, AO 46,80.

dumb '*dumb*,' *silent*, An,Mt; Æ,CP.

-dumbian v. ā-d.

dumbnes f. *dumbness*, NC 282.

dun=dunn

dūn fm. nap. dūna, dūne '*down*,' *moor, height, hill, mountain*, Bl,Chr,Mt; Æ; Mdf. of dūne *down, downwards*.

dūn-ælf, -elf, -ylf f. *mountain elf*, BF,GL.

dūne *down, downwards*, LkL 4³¹. [dūn]

dūnelfen f. *mountain elf*, WW 189⁹.

dūnestīgende *descending*, VPs 87⁵.

dunfealu *dun-coloured*, WW.

dung I. f. ds. dyng, ding *prison*, AN 1272. II. f. '*dung*,' WW.

dungrǣg *dark, dusky*, WW 246⁴. [dunn]

dunh-=dimh-

dūnhunig n. *downland honey*, LCD 132a.

duniendlic (dunond-) *falling down, tottering*, LPs 108¹⁰ (BTs).

dūnland n. *downland, open country*, ÆT, LCD.

dūnlendisc *mountainous*, ÆGR 11¹⁵.

dūnlic *of a mountain, mountain-dwelling*, WW 376⁶.

dunn '*dun*,' *dingy brown, dark-coloured*, Ct,WW.

dunnian *to obscure, darken*, Bo. ['*dun*']

dunondlic v. duniendlic.

Dūnsǣte mp. *inhabitants of the mountains of Wales*, LL.

dūn-scræft n. nap. -scrafu *hill-cave*.

dure=duru

durfon pret. pl. of deorfan.

durhere (durere) m. *folding door*, GL.

durran* (+in NG) swv. pres. I, 3 sg. dear(r), 2 dearst, pl. durron, subj. durre, dyrre, pret. sg. dorste (u, y), pl. dorston *to* '*dare*,' *venture, presume*, Æ,AO,BH,Bo,Met.

durstodl n. *door-post*, WW.

duru (dure) f. gs. dura, ds. and nap. dura, duru '*door*,' *gate, wicket*, B,Bl,G,VPs; CP, CHR.

duruhaldend (e²) *doorkeeper*, JnL 18¹⁷.

durustod (WW)=durstodl

duruðegn m. *doorkeeper*, AN 1092.

duruðīnen f. *female doorkeeper*, Jn 18¹⁶,¹⁷.

duruweard m. *doorkeeper*, Æ,JnL (durweard). ['*doorward*']

dūst (u) n. '*dust*,' Æ,Lcd,MH,Mt; AO,CP.

dūstdrenc m. *drink made from the pulverized seeds of herbs*, LCD 114a.

dūstig *dusty*, OEG 15; 3⁹.

dūstscēawung f. *(viewing of dust), visit to a grave*, BL113²⁹.

dūstswerm m. *dust-like swarm*, OEG 23⁵².

dūsŏ=dūst

dūŏhamor (ȳ¹, o², e³) m. *papyrus, sedge*, WW 135⁸⁵, 492⁴⁰.

dwæl-=dwel-; +**dwǣrian**=+ŏwǣrian

±**dwǣs** I. *dull, foolish, stupid.* II. m. *clumsy impostor*, ÆL 23⁶⁹⁶.

±**dwǣscan** *to put out, extinguish, destroy*, GD,LCD.

dwǣsian *to become stupid*, Æ (6¹⁴⁶).

dwǣslic *foolish*, W. adv. -līce, LL.

+**dwǣsmann** m. *fool*, ÆL 17¹⁰¹.

dwǣsnes f. *stupidity, foolishness*, Æ.

dwal-=dwol-

dwǎn pret. 3 sg. of dwīnan.

dwealde pret. 3 sg. of dwellan.

dwel-=dwol-

±**dwellan** *to go astray : lead astray, deceive*, Æ.

dwellan pret. sg. dwealde, pp. dweald *to lead astray, hinder, prevent, deceive*, Æ,Bo, Rd : *to be led astray, wander, err*, Æ,Mt. ['*dwele*,' '*dwell*']

dwelsian *to wander*, LPs 118¹¹⁰.

+**dweola** (BH), +dweolsa=+dwola

dweoligan=dwellan

dweorg (e, i) m. '*dwarf*,' Gl. [Ger. zwerg]

dweorge-dwosle, -d(w)os(t)le f. *pennyroyal, flea-bane*, GL,LCD.

dweorh=dweorg

±**dwild** (y;=ie) n. *wandering*, BF 172⁸ : *error, heresy*, Chr. ['*dwild*']

+**dwildæfterfolgung** (dwel-) f. *heresy*, A 8·450; 13·318.

+**dwildlic** (y) *deceptive?* W 196²⁰.

+**dwildman** m. *heretic*, CHRD,NC.

-**dwilman** v. for-d.

±**dwimor** (e²) n. *phantom, ghost, illusion, error*, Æ.

+**dwimorlic** *illusory, unreal.* adv. -līce, Æ.

dwīnan¹ *to waste away, languish, disappear*, Lcd,WW. ['*dwine*']

+**dwol** *heretical*, GD.

±**dwola** m. *error, heresy*, BH,MtLR : *madman, deceiver, heretic*, Æ,Bl : '*nenia*,' MtL p 8⁹. ['*dwale*,' '*dwele*']

+**dwolbiscop** m. *heretical bishop*, GD.

±**dwolcræft** m. *occult art, magic*, AN,BL.

dwolema=dwolma

+**dwolen†** *perverse, wrong, erroneous*, GL.

+**dwolenlic** *foolish*, CHRD 115⁵.

+**dwolfær** n. *a going astray*, RHy 6³⁶.

+**dwolgod** m. *false god, idol, image*, W 106³⁰.

+**dwolhring** m. *erroneous cycle*, BH 470²¹.

±**dwolian** *to be led astray, err, wander*, BH; CP. ['*dwele*']

dwollic *foolish : erroneous, heretical*, Æ. adv. (±) -līce.

±**dwolma** m. *chaos*, WW 378¹⁶.

±**dwolman** m. *one who is in error, heretic*, Æ,AO,CP.

+**dwolmist** m. *mist of error*, Bo,MET.

dwolscipe m. *error*, BF 130¹⁸.

+**dwolsprǣc** f. *heretical talk*, ÆL 23³⁶⁹.

+**dwolsum** *misleading, erroneous*, ÆT 80¹.

dwolŏing n. *imposture, idol : sorcery*, LCD.

dwolung f. *foolishness, insanity*, WW 390³¹.

dwomer=dwimor

+**dwol-**=dwol-

dworgedwostle=dweorgedwosle

dwyld=dwild

dwy-mer, -mor=dwimor

dwyrgedwysle=dweorgedwosle

dybbian *to pay attention to*, OEG 645.

dȳdan (=īe) *to kill*, LL 132,1. [dēad]

dyde pret. 3 sg., dydon pret. pl. of dōn.

dyder-=dydr-

dydrian *to deceive, delude*, Bo 100⁵.

dydrin m? *yolk*, LCD. [Ger. dotter]

dydrung f. *delusion, illusion*, Æ.

±**dȳfan** (=ī) *to dip, immerse*, BH,RD. ['*dive*']

dȳfing f. *immersion*, W 36⁹.

dȳfst pres. 2 sg. of dūfan.

dȳgel-, dȳgl-, dȳhl-=dīegol-, dīeg(o)l-

dyht, dyhtan=diht, dihtan

dyhtig (o) '*doughty*,' *strong*, B,Chr,Gen. [dugan]

dyl-=dil-; +**dȳlegian**=+dīlegian

dylmengon (=dilemengum? dat. of sb.) *dissimulation*, CHRD 45¹⁰.[cp. fordilemengan]

dylsta m. *festering matter, filth, mucus* LCD.

dylstiht *mucous*, LCD 26a.

dym-, dyn-=dim-, din-; ±**dyn**=dyne

dyncge f. *dung, manure, litter : manured land, fallow land*, OEG. [dung]

±**dyne** m. '*din*,' *noise*, Sat,Sol.

+**dyngan** (AO), dyngian (WW) *to* '*dung*.'

dynian *to make a* '*din*,' *sound, resound*, B; Æ.

dȳnige f. *a plant*, LCD 113b. [dūn]

dynn, dynnan=dyne, dynian

dynt m. '*dint*,' *blow, stroke, bruise, stripe*, CP,JnL : *thud*, Bo 117³⁰.

dȳp=dēop

dȳpan (ē;=īe) I. (±) *to dip : baptize*, MtR : (+) *anoint*, EPs 140⁵. ['*depe*'] II. *to make greater*, LL 388¹. ['*deep*']

dȳpe=dēope

dyple *double*, BF 186¹⁵.

dyppan (e, i) *to* '*dip*,' *immerse*, Lcd,Mk : *baptize*, MtR.

dȳr=dēor; **dyre** ds. of duru.

dȳre adj.=dīere

+**dyre** n. *door-post, door*, Æ.

±**dyrfan** (=ie) *to afflict, injure : imperil, endanger.* v. ES 39·342. [deorfan]
dyrfing (=ie) f. *affliction,* GPH 395.
dyrfð pres. 3 sg. of deorfan.
dyrn-=diern-, dern-
dyrneforlegen *adulterous,* LL (144').
dyrneforlegernes f. *fornication,* BH 280³.
dyrne(ge)legerscipe (e¹) m. *adultery, fornication,* JnLR 8³.
dyrnegeligre I. (ie, e) n. *adultery,* AO,CP.
II. m. *fornicator,* DR 107¹.
dyrneleger (e¹) *adulterous,* NG.
dyrnelegere (e¹) **I.** *licentiously,* NG. **II.** (RWH 78⁴)=dyrnegeligre I.
dyrngewrit n. *apocryphal book,* WW 347³⁸.
dyrnhæmende (i) *fornicating, adulterous,* WW 383⁴⁰.
dyrnlic *secret,* LL. adv. -lice, LCD 3·424'.
dyrnlicgan⁵ *to fornicate,* CPs 108³⁹.
dyrnmaga m. *president at mysteries,* GPH 397.
dyrnunga=dearnunga; **dyrodine**=derodine
dȳrra=dierra; **dyrre** v. *durran.
+**dȳrsian** *to praise, glorify, hold dear, prize,* JUD 300. [diēre]
+**dyrst** f. *tribulation,* HELL 108.
dyrste=dorste pret. 3 sg. of *durran.
+**dyrstelice**=dyrstiglice
±**dyrstig** *venturesome, presumptuous, daring, bold,* CP. adv. -lice. [*durran]
+**dyrstiglan** *to dare, presume,* BH 468¹⁹.
±**dyrstignes** f. *boldness, insolence, daring, presumption, arrogance, rashness,* Æ,CP.
dyrstingpanne=hyrstingpanne
±**dyrstlǣcan** *to presume, dare,* Æ.
dyrstlǣcung f. *courage, boldness,* GD 71¹⁹.
+**dyrstlic**=+dyrstig
±**dyrstnes**=dyrstignes
dyru ds., dyrum dp. of duru.
dȳr-wurðe, -wyrðe=dēorwierðe
dys-=dis-; **dyseg**=dysig, dysg-
dyselic (Æ)=dyslic
±**dysgian** *to act foolishly, make mistakes,* Bo; Æ : *blaspheme,* G. ['dizzy']
dysgung f. *folly, madness,* LCD 53b.
dysian=dysgian
dysig (e, i) **I.** *foolish, ignorant, stupid,* Bl, Mt,VHy; Æ,CP. ['dizzy'] **II.** n. *foolishness, error,* AO,CP. **III.** m. *fool,* VPs 91⁶.
dysigan=dysgian
dysigcræftig? (i¹, ea³) *skilled in foolish arts,* ANS 128·300 (BTac).
dysigdōm m. *folly, ignorance,* CM,Sc.
dysiglic *foolish,* VH 10. adv. -lice, VH 10.
dysignes f. *folly, madness, blasphemy,* BH, Mk; Æ,AO : *foolish practice,* NC 300²⁵. ['dizziness']
dysigu=dysig II.
dyslic *foolish, stupid,* Æ,CP. adv. -lice.

dȳstig *dusty,* WW 517²³. [dūst]
dyttan *to shut to, close, stop,* Lk,PPs. ['dit']
dȳð f. *fuel, tinder,* OEG 2⁴³; cp. 1655n.
dȳð-homar, -homer=dūðhamor

E

ð ds. of ēa.
ēa I. f. (usu. indecl. in sg., but with occl. gs. ēas; ds. īe, ē, ǣ, ēæ; nap. ēa, ēan; gp. ēa; dp. ēa(u)m, ēan) *water, stream, river,* Æ, Chr,Ps; AO. ['ea'; 'æ'] **II.** interj. v. ēalā.
ēac I. adv. *also, and, likewise, moreover,* B, Ep,Mt; AO,CP. ge...ge ēac *both...and also.* nē...nē ēac...*neither...nor even....* ēac swā, ēac swilce *also, likewise, moreover, as if.* ēac gelīce *likewise.* ēac hwæðre *however, nevertheless.* ēac ðon *besides.* ['eke'] **II.** prep. w. d. *together with, in addition to, besides.*
ēaca m. *addition, increase, reinforcement, advantage, profit, usury, excess,* Chr,Sol; Æ,AO,CP. tō ēacan (w. d.) *in addition to, besides, moreover,* Bo. ['eke']
ēacan *to increase,* Bo,LL.
ēacen *increased, augmented : richly endowed, strong, great, vast, vigorous : pregnant.*
ēacencræftig *huge,* B 2280.
ēacerse f. *water-cress,* Lcd 35b. [ēa; v. 'cress']
ēacian *to increase,* CP 163,231.
±**ēacnian** *to add, increase, be enlarged : become pregnant, conceive, bring forth,* Æ,CP.
ēacnlendlic adj. *to be increased,* OEG 1078.
±**ēacnung** f. *increase,* GL : *conception, bringing forth,* Æ.
ēad† n. *riches, prosperity, good fortune, happiness.*
ead-=ed-; **ēad-**=eað-
ēaden† (pp. of *ēadan) *granted (by Fate,* [ēad]
eadesa=adesa
ēadfruma† m. *giver of prosperity.*
ēadga wk. form of ēadig.
ēadgian=ēadigan
ēadgiefa† m. *giver of prosperity.*
ēadgiefu† f. *gift of prosperity.*
ēadhrēðig† *happy, blessed, triumphant.*
ēadig *wealthy, prosperous,* Cr : *fortunate, happy, blessed, perfect,* Gu,VPs; Æ,CP. ['eadi']
±**ēadigan** *to count fortunate, call blessed,* HL : *enrich, make happy.*
ēadiglic *prosperous, rich, happy, blessed.* adv. -lice, B. ['eadily']
ēadignes f. *happiness, prosperity,* Æ.

eadlēan=edlēan

ēadlufu f. *blessed love*, JUL 104.

ēadmōd, ēadmōd=ēaðmōd

ēadmētto=ēaðmēttu

ēadnes f. *inner peace, ease, joy, prosperity, Run : gentleness.* ['*eadness*'; ēað]

ēadocce f. *water-lily*, WW 116[16]. ['*edocke*']

eador=(1) geador, (2) eodor

ēadorgeard m. *enclosure of veins, body ?* (GK), AN 1183 (or ? ealdor-).

eaduse (A 10·143[90])=adesa

ēadwela† m. *prosperity, riches, happiness.*

ēæ v. ēa, **eæ-**=ea-; **eafera**=eafora

ēafisc† m. *river-fish.*

eafor I. mn? *the obligation due from a tenant to the king to convey goods and messengers?* KC (v. IF 48·262). **II.** (afer) *draught-horse*, v. LL 498f and 2·57. **III.**=eofor

eafora† m. *posterity, son, child; successor, heir.* [cp. Goth. afar]

eafoð† n. *power, strength, might*, B.

eafra=eafora; **eaftra**=æfterra

ēagbræw m. *eyelid*, Lcd 1·352. ['*eyebree*']

ēagduru f. *window*, MH.

ēage (ē) n. '*eye*,' G,Lcd,RB,VPs; AO,CP : *aperture, hole*, Lk.

ēagece m. *eye-ache*, LCD.

ēagflēah m. *albugo, a white spot in the eye*, WW.

ēaggebyrd f. *nature of the eye*, PH 301.

ēaggemearc (ēah-) n. *limit of view, horizon*, DD 148.

ēaghring (ēah-, ēh-) m. *eye-socket, pupil*, Æ.

ēaghōyrl=ēagðyrel

ēaghyll m. *eyebrow?* WW 415[22].

ēaghyrne (hēah-) m. *corner of the eye*, WW 156[41].

ēagmist (ēah-) m. *dimness of the eyes*, LCD 11a.

ēagor=ēgor; **eagospind**=hagospind

ēagsealf f. '*eye-salve*,' WW.

ēagsēoung f. *eye-disease, cataract*, WW 414[12].

ēagsȳne *visible to the eye*, AN. adv. -sȳnes, Æ.

ēagðyrel n. *eye-hole, window*, BH. ['*eye-thurl*']

ēag-wærc (y[2]), -wræc m. *pain of the eyes*, LCD.

ēagwund f. *wound in the eye*, LL 20,47.

ēagwyrt f. *eye-wort, eye-bright*, LCD 117a.

ēah-=ēag-, ēa-

eaht (a, æ, e) f. *assembly, council.* e. besittan *to hold a council : esteem, estimation, estimated value.*

ēaht=æht

eahta (a, æ, e) '*eight*,' B,Chr,Men; CP.

eahtafeald *eightfold*, Æ.

eahtahyrnede *eight-cornered*, ÆH 2·496'.

eahtan† I. *to persecute, pursue.* II. *to estimate, appreciate.*

eahtanihte *eight days' old (moon)*, LCD 3·178[14].

eahtatēoða '*eighteenth*,' AO.

eahta-tīene, -tȳne '*eighteen*,' Lk (eht-).

eahtatig *eighty*, AO.

eahtatȳnewintre *eighteen years old*, ÆL 33[86]

eahtawintre *of eight years old*, Æ.

eahtend m. *persecutor*, PPs 118[150].

-eahtendlic v. unge-e.

eahtēoða=(1) eahtatēoða, (2) eahtoða

eahtere (e[1], æ[1]) m. *appraiser, censor*, LCD.

eahteða (AO)=eahtoða

±eahtian (æ, e) *to estimate, esteem*, CP : *consult about, consider, deliberate : watch over*, Æ : *speak of with praise.* [Ger. achten]

ēahtnes=ēhtnes

eahtoða '*eighth*,' Men; CHR.

eahtung f. *estimation, valuation*, CP : (+) *deliberation, counsel*, PPs.

eal=eall, æl (LL); **eala**=ealu

ēalā interj. *alas! oh! lo!* Æ,AO,CP. [ēa II.]

ēalād f. *watery way*, AN 441.

ēaland n. *island*, CHR : *maritime land, seaboard*, B 2334.

ealað v. ealu.

ealbeorht=eallbeorht; **ēalc**=ǣlc

eald (a) comp. ieldra, yldra; sup. ieldest, yldest '*OLD*,' *aged, ancient, antique, primeval*, Æ,CP; AO : '*elder*,' *experienced, tried : honoured, eminent, great.* ðā ieldstan men *the chief men.*

ealda m. *old man*, RHy 6[25] : *chief, elder : the Devil*, Leas. ['*old*']

ealdbacen *stale*, ÆP 31[7].

eald-cȳðð (AO), -cȳððu f. *old home, former dwelling-place : old acquaintance*, Æ.

ealddagas (æa[1]) mp. *former times*, AO.

ealddōm m. *age*, AO 76[2].

ealde=ielde

ealdefæder m. *grandfather*, CHR.

ealdemōdor f. *grandmother*; Ct.

ealder=ealdor

ealdfæder m. *forefather*, Æ,B. ['*eldfather*']

ealdfēond (ī)† m. *old foe, hereditary foe, the devil.*

ealdgecynd† n. *original nature*, MET.

ealdgefā m. *ancient foe*, AO 118[84].

ealdgefēra m. *old comrade*, AO 152[24].

ealdgemǣre *ancient boundary*, BC 3·546'.

ealdgenēat m. *old comrade*, MA 310.

ealdgenīðla† m. *old foe, Satan.*

ealdgeriht (a[1]) n. *ancient right*, TC 70[22].

ealdgesegen f. *ancient tradition*, B 869.

ealdgesīð† m. *old comrade.*

ealdgestrēon n. *ancient treasure*, AO.

ealdgeweorc† n. *old-standing work, the world*, MET.

ealdgewinn n. *old-time conflict*, B 1781.

ealdgewinna m. *old enemy*, B 1776.

ealdgewyrht† n. *former deeds : deserts of former deeds?* B 2657.

ealdhettende mp. *old foes*, JUD 321.

ealdhláford m. *hereditary lord*, AO,CP.

ealdhríðer? n. *an old ox*, LL.

±**ealdian** (a) *to grow old*, *Jn,VPs*; Æ. ['*eld,*' '*old*']

ealdland n. *land which has been long untilled?* (BTs), *ancestral property?* (Earle), EC 327¹⁴.

ealdlandræden f. *established law of landed property*, LL 448,4⁶ (or ? two words, BT).

ealdlic *old, venerable*, Æ.

ealdnes f. *old age*, Æ. ['*eldness,*' '*oldness*']

ealdor (a¹, e²) I. m. *elder, parent*, BH,Gen. pl. *ancestors : civil or religious authority, chief, leader, master, lord, prince, king*, G; Æ : *source : primitive*, ÆGR. [eald; '*alder*'] II. n.(f?) (†) *life, vital part :* (†) *age, old age : eternity*. on ealdre tō ealdre *for ever, always*. āwa tō ealdre, tō wīdan ealdre *for ever and ever*. [*Ger.* alter]

ealdorapostol (a) m. *chief apostle*, NC,BH 314⁷.

ealdorbana (a¹) m. *life-destroyer*, GEN 1033.

ealdorbealu† n. *life-bale, death*.

ealdorbiscop m. *archbishop*, Æ : *high-priest*, Æ.

ealdor-bold, -botl n. *palace, mansion*, BH.

ealdorburg f. *metropolis*, BH,GL.

ealdorcearu (a¹) f. *great sorrow*, B 906.

ealdordæg† m. *day of life*, B.

ealdordēma† (a¹) m. *chief judge, prince*, GEN.

ealdordēofol m. *chief of the devils*, NC 282.

ealdordōm (a¹) m. *power, lordship, rule, dominion, authority, magistracy, PPs*; Æ, AO,CP : *superiority, preeminence : beginning?* JUL 190. ['*alderdom*']

ealdordōmlic *preeminent*, EPs 50¹⁴ (cp. ealdorlic).

ealdordōmlicnes f. *authority, control*, RBL 68¹².

ealdordōmscipe? m. *office of alderman*, CHR 983 C.

ealdorduguð† f. *nobility, flower of the chiefs*.

ealdorfrēa (a¹) m. *lord, chief*, DA 46.

ealdorgeard m. *enclosure of life, body*, AN 1183? (or? ēador-).

ealdorgedāl† n. *death*.

ealdorgesceaft f. *state of life*, RD 40²³.

ealdorgewinna† m. *deadly enemy*.

ealdorlang *life-long, eternal*, †CHR 937A.

ealdorlēas I. *lifeless, dead*, B 15. II. *deprived of parents, orphaned : without a chief*.

ealdorlegu† f. *destiny : death*, GU.

ealdorlic '*principalis,*' *chief, princely, excellent : authentic*. adv. -līce.

ealdorlicnes f. *authority*, CP.

ealdormann (o³) [v. LL 2·359] m. '*alderman,*' *ruler, prince, chief, nobleman of the highest rank, high civil or religious officer, chief officer of a shire*, Chr; Æ,AO,CP : as trans. of foreign titles, JnL,Mt.

ealdorneru† f. *life's preservation, safety, refuge*, GEN.

ealdorsācerd m. *high-priest*, AN,G.

ealdorscipe m. *seniority, headship, supremacy, sovereignty*, Æ.

ealdorstōl m. *throne*, RIM 23.

ealdorðegn m. *chief attendant, retainer, distinguished courtier, chieftain : chief apostle*, MFH,VH.

ealdorwisa (a¹) m. *chief*, GEN 1237.

ealdoð (ald-aht, -ot) *vessel*, GL.

ealdriht n. *old right*, LL 11,12.

Eald-Seaxe, -Seaxan mp. *Old-Saxons, Continental Saxons*, AO.

ealdspell n. *old saying, old story*, Bo.

ealdspræc f. *proverb, by-word*, PPs 43¹⁵.

ealdung f. *process of growing old, age*, Æ,AO.

ealdur=ealdor

ealdwerig (=-wearg) *accursed from old times*, EX 50.

ealdwīf n. *old woman*, GEN 18¹³.

ealdwita m. *venerable man, priest, sage* : BH,LL.

ealdwrītere m. *writer on ancient history*, OEG 5449.

ēales v. ealh.

ealfara m. *pack-horse*, AA 13⁷ and n.

ealfela† *very much*.

ealfelo *baleful, dire*, AN 771 (ælfæle), RD 24⁹.

ealgearo† *all ready, prepared*.

±**ealgian** *to protect, defend*, Æ.

ealgodwebb n. '*holosericus,*' *all-silk cloth*, WW 395¹⁵.

ealgodwebben *all-silk*, WW 501².

ealh† (a) m., gs. ēales *temple*.

ealhstede† m. *temple*, DA.

ēalifer f. *liver-wort?* Lcd. ['*eileber*'?]

ēalīðend m. *seafaring man*, AN 251.

eall I. adj. (has no weak form) '*ALL**,' *every, entire, whole, universal*, Æ,Chr. pl. all men, Æ. II. adv. *fully, wholly, entirely, quite*, Cr,GD,Gen. e. swā *quite as, just as*. e. swā micle swā *as much as*. mid ealle, mid eallum *altogether, entirely*, CP. ealra swīðost *especially, most of all*. ealne weg (also contr. ealneg) *always*. ofer e. (neut.) *everywhere, into all parts*. III. n. *all, everything*, Æ.

ealla=gealla

eallbeorht† (æl-) *all-bright, resplendent,* Sat. [v. '*all*']

eallcræftig† (æl-) *all-powerful.*

eallencten m. *season of Lent,* RB66⁵.

eallenga=eallunga

ealles, ealle adv. (g. of eall) *entirely, wholly, fully, quite.* e. for swīðe *altogether, utterly.*

eallgelēaflic *universally believed, catholic,* BH (Sch) 648⁸.

eallgōd *all-good,* ÆT 65.

eallgrēne *all-green, green, An : young, fresh,* RV²Ps 127³. [v. '*all*']

eallgylden (æl-) *all-golden,* B,CP 169²¹.

eallhālgung f. *consecration,* A 41·106.

eallhālig '*all-holy,*' Met; PPs 131⁸.

eallhwīt *entirely of white,* Ct.

eallic *universal, catholic,* GD.

eallinga=eallunga

ealliren *entirely of iron,* B 2338.

eallīsig *all-icy, very cold,* Bo,MET.

eallmægen† n. *utmost effort,* MET.

eallmǣst (al-, æl-) adv. *nearly all,* '*almost,*' *for the most part,* Æ,Chr.

eallmiht f. *omnipotence,* PPs 135¹².

eallmihtig=ælmihtig

eallnacod *entirely naked,* GEN 871.

eallneg=ealneg

eallnīwe *quite new,* Æ. [v. '*all*']

eallnunge=eallunga

eallofrung f. *holocaust,* WW 130¹² (eal-).

eallreord=elreord

eallrihte adv. *just, exactly,* RB 131¹³.

eallseolcen *entirely made of silk,* GL.

eallswā *just as, even as,* '*as,*' *as if, so as, likewise,* Æ,Mt.

eallswilc *just such,* Æ,CHR.

ealltela adv. *quite well,* GEN 1905.

eallunga adv. *altogether, entirely, utterly, quite, indeed,* Æ,Bo,Mt; CP. ['*allinge*']

eallwealda† I. *all-ruling, almighty.* II. m. *God, the Almighty.*

eallwealdend (alw-) m. *ruler of all,* Hu; ÆL. ['*all-wielding*']

eallwealdende (alw-) '*all-wielding,*' *all-ruling,* Æ.

eallwihta† (æl-) fp. *all creatures,* W.

eallwriten adj. *holograph,* WW 463²⁸.

eallwundor n. *marvel,* Ex 578.

ealm-=eallm-; **ealmihtig**=ælmihtig

ealneg (AO,CP), ealneweg, ealnuweg, ealnig, ealning(a) *always, quite, perpetually.*

ealnunga=eallunga; **ealo**=ealu

ealofrung f. *holocaust,* WW 130¹².

ēalond=ēaland; **ealoð** (AO) v. ealu.

ealsealf f.' *ambrosia,' an aromatic plant* (BT).

ealswā=eallswā; **ealtēawe**=æltēawe

ealu (ealo) m? n? gds. ealoð (AO), ealað; gp. ealeða '*ale,' beer,* Æ,Lcd. [v. A 27·495]

ealubenc† f. '*ale-bench,*' B.

ealuclyfa m. *beer-cellar,* OEG 4⁴².

ealufæt n. *ale-vat,* LCD 53b.

ealugafol n. *tax or tribute paid in ale,* LL 448.

ealugāl *drunk with ale,* GEN 2408.

ealugālnes f. *drunkenness,* MFH 94¹.

ealugeweorc (o²) n. *brewing,* AO 222⁷.

ealuhūs (a²) n. *alehouse,* LL 228,1².

ealumalt (alo-) n. *malt for brewing,* LCD 157a.

ealuscerwen f. (*ale-deprival*), *deprival of joy, distress, mortal panic?* B 770.

ealuscop m. *singer in alehouses,* LL.

ealusele m. *alehouse,* AB 34·10.

ealuwǣge† n. *ale-flagon, ale-can,* B. [v. '*ale*']

ealuwosa (o²) m. *ale-tippler,* WY 49.

ealw-=eallw-; **eam** (VPs)=eom (v. wesan).

ēam I. m. *uncle* (usu. maternal; paternal uncle=fædera), Æ,B; AO. ['*eme*'] II. dp. of ēa.

+ēane *yeaning,* GEN 33¹³.

±ēanian *to bring forth young* (usu. lambs), LPs 77⁷¹. ['*ean*']

ēaōfer m. *river-bank,* MET 19²².

eapel, eapl=æppel; **eappul-**=æppel- ear' *occa,' harrow?* OEG 2359 (v. A 36·72).

ēar I. n. '*ear*' (*of corn*), Cp,Mt; AO. II. (ǣ)† m. *wave, sea, ocean.* III.† m. *earth : name of the rune for* ēa. IV.=ǣr. V.=ēare

ēar- v. ār-

ēaracu f. *river bed,* KC 5·122¹⁵.

earan-=earon; **earb-**=earf-

ēarblǣd (ē¹) n. *stalk, blade (of corn), straw.*

earc, earce (a, æ, e) f. *chest, coffer, Rd : ' ark,' Mt,Ps;* CP. [*L.*]

ēarclǣnsend m. *little finger,* WW 265¹.

earcnanstān=eorcnanstān

ēarcoðu f. '*parotis,' a tumour near the ears,* WW 113³¹.

eard m. *native place, country, region, dwelling-place, estate, cultivated ground, B,Ps,* Æ,AO,CP : *earth, land : condition, fate,* †Hy. ['*erd*']

eardbegenga m. *inhabitant,* LPs.

eardbegengnes f. *habitation,* RLPs.

eardeswrǣcca (LPs 118¹⁹)=eardwrecca

eardfæst *settled, abiding,* AO.

eardgeard† m. *place of habitation, world.*

eardgyfu f. *gift from one's homeland,* PPs 71¹⁰.

±eardian tr. and intr. *to inhabit, dwell, abide, live,* AO,B,G; Æ,CP. ['*erde*']

eardiend m. *dweller,* GD.

eardiendlic *habitable,* BH 366¹⁰.

eardland n. *native land,* PPs 134¹².

eardlufe f. *dear home?* B 693.

eardrīce n. *habitation,* GU 825.

eardstapa m. *wanderer*, WA6.
eardstede m. *habitation*, PH 195.
±eardung f. *living* : *abode, tabernacle*, Ps.
['erding']
eardungburg f. *city of habitation*, Ex 1[11].
eardunghūs n. *tabernacle, habitation*, GD.
eardungstōw f. *tabernacle, habitation*, Mt;
CP. ['erdingstow']
eardweall m. *land-rampart, bulwark*, B
1224?
eardwīc† n. *dwelling*.
eardwrecca m. *exile*, LL51n5.
eardwunung f. *dwelling in one's own
country*, W120[13].
ēare n. '*ear*,' Mt,Rd,VPs; Æ,CP.
ēarede *having a handle*, WW122[89].
ēarefinger m. *little finger*, ÆGr; WW.
['earfinger']
ēarelipprica=ēarliprica
earendel (eo) m. *dayspring, dawn, ray of
light*, BL,CR.
earfað-=earfoð-
earfe, earbe f? *tare*, LCD. [L. ervum]
earfed-=(1) earfoð-; (2) yrfe-
earfeð=earfoð
ēarfinger=ēarefinger; earfod-=earfoð-
earfoðcierre (að-) *hard to convert*, MH112[20].
earfoðcynn n. *depraved race*, PPs77[10].
earfoðdæde *difficult*, CP147[12].
earfoðdæg m. *day of tribulation*, PPs76[2].
earfoðe I. n. *hardship, labour, trouble, difficulty, suffering, torment, torture*, AO,CP.
[Ger. arbeit] II. adj. *hard, difficult,
troublesome*, Æ,Bo. ['arveth'] III. adv.
with difficulty.
earfoðfēre *difficult to pass through*, AS44[25].
earfoðfynde *hard to find*, ÆL23[82]. [cp.
ēaðfynde]
earfoðhāwe *difficult to be seen*, MET.
earfoðhwīl f. *hard time*, SEAF3.
earfoðhylde *dissatisfied*, ÆH1·400[1].
±earfoðian *to trouble*, Ps.
earfoðlǣre *hard to teach*, GD110[19] : *un-
disciplined*, CHRD18[6].
earfoðlǣte *hard to discharge*, WW113[20].
earfoðlic *difficult, full of hardship*, Æ.
['arvethlich'] adv. -līce *with difficulty,
painfully, reluctantly, hardly, scarcely*, Mt.
['arvethliche']
earfoðlicnes (Æ)=earfoðnes
earfoðmæcg† m. *sufferer*.
earfoðnes f. *difficulty, hardship, trouble,
affliction, pain, misfortune*, Æ. ['arveth-
ness']
earfoðrecce *hard to relate*, W22[14].
earfoðrihte *hard to correct, incorrigible*,
CHRD42[1].
earfoðrīme *hard to enumerate*, Bo1[7].
earfoðsǣlig *unhappy, unfortunate*, CRA8.

earfoðsīð† m. *troublesome journey* : *misfortune*.
earfoðtǣcne *difficult to be shown*, MET20[147].
earfoððrāg f. *sorrowful time*, B283.
earfoðwylde *hard to subdue*, LCD3·436[12].
earg (earh) *slothful, sluggish*, Gn : *cowardly*,
BH; AO : *craven, vile, wretched, useless*,
MtL. ['argh'] adv. earge.
eargēat=earngēat
ēargeblandt (ār-) n. *wave-blend, surge*.
ēargespeca m. *whisperer, privy councillor*,
WW351[2]. [=-spreca]
±eargian (i, y) *to shun, fear, turn coward*,
Æ : *terrify*.
earglic *slothful, shameful, bad*, Æ. adv.
-līce, *timidly, fearfully?* Gen20[4] : *basely*,
Chr1086. ['arghly']
eargnes (arog-) f. *licentiousness*, MkR8[38].
ēargrund m. *bottom of the sea*, Az40.
eargscipe m. *idleness, cowardice* : *profligacy*.
earh I. f. '*arrow*,' An,LL. II.=earg
earhfaru f.† *flight, or shooting, of arrows*.
ēarhring m. '*ear-ring*,' Æ; WW.
ēarisc (ǣ, ēo) f. *rush, reed, flag*, GL,LCD. [ēa]
ēarīð m. *water-stream*, GUTH20[5].
ēarlæppa m. *external ear*, WW157. ['earlap']
ēarliprica m. *flap of the ear, external ear*, NG.
ēarlocc m. *lock of hair over the ear*, WW
152[30].
earm (a) I. m. '*arm*' (of the body, sea, etc.),
AO,LkL : *foreleg*, Æ : *power*, Jn. II. *poor,
wretched, pitiful, destitute, miserable*, Chr,
Mk; Æ,CP. ['arm']
earm-bēag, -bēah m. *bracelet*, B,GL.
earmcearig† *full of sorrows*.
earme adv. *miserably, badly*, GEN.
earmella m. *sleeve*, RB136[23].
earmful *wretched, miserable*, LCD3·440' :
poor in spirit, humble, VH10.
earmgegirela m. *bracelet*, WW386[13].
earmheort *humble, poor in spirit*, CP209[2] :
tender-hearted, merciful.
earmhrēad f. *arm-ornament*, B1194.
earmian *to pity, commiserate*, CHR,HL.
earming m. *poor wretch*, Æ. ['arming']
earmlic *miserable, pitiable, mean*, Met. adv.
-līce, BH. ['armlich(e)']
earmscanca m. *arm-bone*, LL82,55.
earmsceapen *unfortunate, miserable*.
earmslīfe f. *sleeve*, RBL93[9].
earmstoc n. *sleeve*, IM128[110].
earmstrang *strong of arm, muscular*, WW
158[7].
earmswīð *strong of arm, muscular*, WW
435[33].
earmðu f. *misery, poverty*, Bo. ['armthe']
earn I. m. *eagle*, El,Mt; Æ. ['erne'] II.=
ærn. III.=arn (v. iernan).

earnan (VPs)=ǣrnan

earncynn n. *eagle tribe*, Lev 11[13].

earn-gēap (v. AB 19·164), -gēat, -gēot f. *vulture*, Gl.

±earnian (a) (w. g. a.) *to ' earn,' merit, win*, Ct : *labour for*, Bo,Gu.

earningland n. *land earned or made freehold* (=bōcland; BT), Ct.

earnung f. *merit, reward, consideration, pay*, Æ : *labour*, Bo 52[20].

earo=gearo

earon (VPs)=sindon pres. 3 pl. of eom (v. wesan).

ēaron=gēarum dp. of gēar.

earp *dark, dusky*, RD 4[42]. [ON. jarpr]

earpa=hearpa

ēarplætt m. *box or blow on the ear*, ÆH 2·248'.

±ēarplætt(ig)an *to box the ears, buffet*, ÆH, RWH 137[25].

ēar-prēon, -ring m. *ear-ring*, Æ.

earre (N)=ierre

ears (æ) m. *fundament, buttocks*, WW. ['*arse*']

ēarscripel (ēo[1], y[2]) m. *little finger*, Gl.

ēarsealf f. *ear-salve*, Lcd.

earsendu np. *buttocks*, WW.

earsgang (ars-) m. *privy*, Lcd,OEG : *excrement*, Lcd : '*anus*' (BT).

ēarslege m. *a blow that strikes off an ear*, LL 20,46.

earsling *backwards*, Ps. ['*arselings*']

earslȳra? m? *buttocks, breech*, Æ. [līra]

earsode '*tergosus*,' WW. ['*arsed*']

ēarspinl f. *ear-ring*, KGl 960.

earsðerl n. '*anus*,' WW 160[1].

eart 2 sg. of eom pres. of wesan.

earð I.=eorð, yrð. II.=eart

ēarðan=ǣr ðam (v. ǣr II.).

earðe (N)=eorðe

ēarðyrel n. '*fistula, arteria*,' *ear-passage?* (BT),WW 238[29]. [or=ears-ðyrel, -ðerl?]

earu=gearu; earun (VPs)=earon

ēarwǣrc n. *ear-ache*, Lcd 14b.

ēarwela (ā[1]) m. *watery realm*, An 855.

earwian (APs 22[5])=gearwian

ēarwicga (ēo) m. '*earwig*,' Lcd,WW.

earwunga *gratuitously* : *without a cause*, PPs.

ēarȳð (ā[1]) f. *wave of the sea*, An 535.

ēas v. ēa.

ēase '*caucale*' (*caucalia?*), *lipped vessel, beaker*, WW 202[1] (v. IF 48·266).

ēaspring=ǣspryng

ēast I. adj. comp. ēast(er)ra, sup. ēastmest, ēastemest *east, easterly*. II. adv. *eastwards, in an easterly direction, in or from the east*, BH,Gen,Met. ['*east*']

ēastæð (e[2]) n. *river-bank, sea-shore*, Ma 63.

ēastan, ēastane *from the east, easterly*, AO. ['*east*']

ēastannorðan *from the north-east*, WW.

ēastannorðanwind m. *north-east wind*, WW 364[5].

ēastansūðan *from the south-east*, WW 3[4].

ēastansūðanwind m. *south-east wind*, WW 144[3].

ēastanwind (e[2]) m. '*east wind*,' WW 143[36].

ēastcyning m. *eastern king*, AO 148[35].

ēastdǣl m. *eastern quarter, the East*, Æ,AO.

ēaste f. *the East*, OEG 1894.

ēastemest (AO) v. ēast.

ēastende m. '*east-end*,' *east quarter*, Chr; AO,LV.

ēastene=ēastane

Eastengle mpl. *the East-Anglians* : *East Anglia*.

Ēasterǣfen m. *Easter-eve*, BH,Chr.

Ēasterdæg m. *Easter-day, Easter Sunday, day of the Passover*, Æ. on ōðran Easterdæge *on Easter Monday*, Chr 1053c.

Ēasterfæsten n. *Easter-fast, Lent*, BH,Chr.

Ēasterfeorm f. *feast of Easter*, LL 450,452'.

Ēasterfrēolsdæg m: *the feast day of the Passover*, Jn 13[1].

Ēastergewuna m. *Easter custom*, ÆL 23b[643].

Ēasterlic *belonging to Easter, Paschal, Lk*. ['*Easterly*']

Ēastermōnað m. *Easter-month, April*, Men, MH.

Ēasterne *east, ' eastern,' oriental*, Æ,Gen, WW.

Ēasterniht f. *Easter-eve*, Hell 15; MP 1·611'.

ēasterra v. ēast.

Ēastersunnandæg (tor) m. *Easter Sunday*, W 222[21].

Ēastersymbel (tro) n. *Passover*, Jn 19[42] (mg).

Ēastertīd f. *Easter-tide, Paschal season*, Æ.

Ēasterðēnung f. *Passover*, Mt 26[19]. [v. '*theine*']

Ēasterwucu f. *Easter-week, Guth*. [v. '*week*']

ēasteð=ēastæð

ēasteweard (e[2]) *east, eastward*, Mt.

ēastfolc n. *eastern nation*, WW 396[30].

ēastgārsecg m. *eastern ocean*, AO 132[29].

ēastgemǣre n. *eastern confines*, AO 132[29].

ēasthealf f. *east side*, Chr 894A.

ēastland n. *eastern land, the East*, Æ : *Esthonia*, AO. ['*Eastland*']

ēastlang *to the east, eastwards, extending east*, Chr 893A.

ēastlēode mp. *Orientals*, BH 254[33].

ēastmest v. ēast.

ēastnorð *north-easterly*, AO 16.

ēastnorðerne *north-east*, ApT 11[2].

ēastnorðwind m. *north-east wind*, GL.
ēastor-=ēaster-
ēastportic n. *eastern porch*, ÆH 2·578[12].
ēastra v. ēast.
Ēastre (usu. in pl. Ēastron, -an; gs. -es in N) f. '*Easter,*' BH,WW : *Passover*, Bl, Mk : *spring*.
ēastrēam m. *stream, river*, DA 385.
+ēastrian *to elapse (during Easter)*, W 208[24].
ēastrīce n. *eastern kingdom, eastern country, empire : the East*, Æ,AO : *East Anglia*.
ēastrihte (y[2]) *due east, eastwards*, AO 17[14].
ēastrihtes (ēst-) *due east*, KC 3·449'.
Ēastro, Ēastru, np.=Ēastre; Ēastro-=Ēaster-
ēastrodor m. *eastern sky*, PPs 102[12].
Ēastron dp. of Ēaster.
ēastsǣ f. *east sea*, BH.
Ēast-Seaxan, -Seaxe mpl. *East-Saxons, people of Essex : Essex*.
ēaststæð n. *east bank of a stream*, Ct.
ēastsūð *south-eastwards*, AO. be ēastsūðan *to the south-east*.
ēastsūðdǣl m. *south-east part*, BH 264[22].
ēastsūðlang *from east to south*, AO 22[17].
ēastðēod f. *an eastern people*, AA 4[17].
ēast-weard, -werd *east, 'eastward,'* Ct,Mt.
ēastweardes *eastwards*, ÆL.
ēastweg† m. *path in or from the east*.
eata (N)=eta imperat. of etan.
eatan=etan; eatol=atol
ēað (ē, ȳ)=(1) ēaðe, (2) īeð
ēað-bede, -bēne *easy to be entreated*, Ps.
ēaðbe-gēate, -gēte *easy to get*, LCD.
ēaðbylgnes f. *irritability*, NC 288.
ēaðbylige (y[1], e[2]) *easily irritated*, VH 10, W 253[11].
ēaðcnāwe *easy to recognise*, ÆGR 147[8].
ēaððǣde (ȳ) *easy to do*, LCD,W.
ēaðe (ē, ēo) I. *easy, B : smooth, agreeable, kindly : easily moved*. II. adv. *easily, lightly, soon*, Met; AO,CP : *willingly, readily*, An. ē. mæg *perhaps, lest*. ['*eath*']
III. n. *an easy thing*, W 185[1].
ēaðelic (ǣ) *easy, possible*, Mt : *insignificant, scanty, slight*, BH; Æ. ['*eathly*'] adv. -līce (Lk).
ēaðelicnes (ēð-) f. *easiness*, WW 400[39].
ēaðfēre *easy for travelling over*, WW 146[29].
ēaðfynde (ē, ȳ)† *easy to find*.
ēaðgeorn (ēð-) *easily pleased*, WW 218[16].
ēaðgesȳne (e[1], y[1], ē[3])† *easily seen, visible*, Cr. [v. '*eathe*']
ēað-gēte, -gēate *easy to obtain, prepared, ready*, Æ. [v. '*eathe*']
ēaðhrēðig=ēadhrēðig
ēaðhylde *contented, satisfied*, RB.
ēað-lǣce (ā[2]), -lǣcne *easy to cure*, LCD.

ēaðlǣre (ēad-) *capable of being taught, instructed*, Jn 6[45] : *easily taught*, CHRD 96[13].
±ēað-mēdan, -mēttan, -mēdian *to humble, humble oneself, prostrate oneself, adore : lower*.
ēaðmēde=(1) ēaðmōd, (2) ēaðmēdu
ēaðmēdlīce (ēad-) *humbly*, CHR 1070.
ēaðmēdu, -mēdo (CHR) f. *gentleness, humility*, Ps : *obedience, submission, reverence : good-will, kindness, affability*. ['*edmede*']
ēaðmēdum *humbly, kindly*, AN.
ēaðmelte=ēaðmylte
ēað-mēttu, -mētto np. *humility, weakness, impotency*, AO.
ēað-mōd (CP), -mēde *humble-minded, gentle, obedient*, Mt,Ps : *benevolent, friendly, affectionate, gracious*. ['*edmede*']
ēaðmōdheort *humble-minded*, Az 152.
±ēaðmōdian *to humble or submit oneself, obey :* (+) *condescend :* (+) *adore, worship*.
ēaðmōdig=ēaðmōd
ēaðmōdlic *humble, respectful*, CP. adv. *humbly, meekly*, CP : *kindly*.
ēaðmōdnes (ēad-) f. *humility, meekness*, Bo; AO : *kindness, condescension*. ['*edmodness*']
ēaðmylte *easily digested*, LCD.
ēaðnes f. *easiness, lightness, facility, ease : gentleness*.
ēaðrǣde (ēð-) *easy to guess*, ES 36·326.
ēaðwylte (ēð-) *easily turned*, OEG 1151.
ēaum dp. of ēa.
ēaw=(1) ēa; (2) ēow V.; (3) ǣ(w)
ēawan=īewan
ēawdnes f. '*ostensio,*' *disclosure*, LL 412,3.
ēawenga (AO)=ēawunga
ēawesc-=ēawisc-; ēawfæst=ǣwfæst
ēawian=īewan
ēawisc- v. also ǣwisc- (but see SF 395).
ēawisclic *manifest, open*, DR. adv. -līce, BH.
ēawlā=ēalā; ēawu=ēowu
ēawunga (CP,Æ), ēawunge (LG) adv. *openly, plainly, publicly*. [īewan]
ēawyrt f. *river-wort, burdock*, LCD.
eax (æ) I. f. *axis, axle, axle-tree*, Bo,Gl. ['*ax*'] II.=æcs
eaxelgespann n. *place where the two beams of a cross intersect*, ROOD 9.
eaxl, eaxel (æ) f. *shoulder*, Æ.
eaxlclāð m. *scapular*, LEV 8[7].
eaxle=eaxl
eaxlgestealla† m. *shoulder-companion, comrade, counsellor : competitor?* HGL(BTs).
eb-=ef-, eof-; ēb-=ǣb-
ebba (æ) m. '*ebb,*' *low tide*, MA.
±ebbian *to '*ebb,*'* GEN.
ebind (Ln 33[6])=+bind

ebol- (N)=yfel-

Ebrēisc (e, i) *Hebrew, Bf,Jn.* ['*Hebreish*']

ēc=ēac

ēca wk. m. form of ēce adj.

ēcambe=ācumbe; **ēcan**=īecan

ēccelic=ēcelic

ece (æ) m. '*ache,' pain, BH,Lcd;* Æ. [acan]

ēce *perpetual, eternal, everlasting, Ct,VPs;* Æ,CP : *durable,* ÆP 126²⁶. adv. *eternally, ever, evermore.* ['*eche*']

eced (æ) mn. *acid, vinegar,* Æ. [*L.* acētum]

eced-drenc (LCD), -drinca (VH) m. *acid drink, vinegar.*

ecedfæt n. *vinegar-vessel,* GL.

ecedwīn (æ) n. *wine mingled with myrrh,* MkL 15²³.

ēcelic *eternal, everlasting.* adv. -līce, *VPs.* ['*echliche*']

ēcen=ēacen; **ecer**=æcer

ēcere gfs. of ēce adj.

ecg f. '*edge,' point, B,Lk;* Æ,CP; Mdf : (†) *weapon, sword, battle-axe, B.*

±**ecgan** *to sharpen : harrow, Cp.* ['*edge*']

ecgbana† (o²) m. *slayer with the sword,* B.

ecgheard *hard of edge,* AN 1183.

ecghete† m. *sword-hatred, war.*

ecghwæs? *keen-edged,* B 1459,2778 (Trautmann).

ecglāst mf. *sword's edge,* SOL 150¹⁹,²¹.

ecgplega m. *battle,* JUD 246.

ecgōracu f. *hot contest,* B 596.

ecgung f. *harrowing,* WW 104¹².

ecgwæl n. *sword-slaughter,* GEN 2089.

ēcilm- (M)=æcelm-

eclinga (=ecgl-) *on the edge,* IM.

eclypsis n. *eclipse,* AA 42¹³. [*L.*]

ēcnes f. *eternity, VPs.* ā on ēcnesse *for ever and ever.* ['*echeness*']

ēcre dfs. of ēce.

ēcsōð, ēcsōðlīce (NG) *verily.*

ed- prefix, denotes *repetition, turning.*

ēd-=ēað-

+**edbyrdan** *to regenerate,* SOUL 100.

+**edcēlnes** f. *refreshment,* VPs 65¹¹ (oe).

+**edcennan** *to regenerate, create,* ÆH.

edcenning f. *regeneration,* ÆH.

+**edcīegan** (ē²) *to recall,* LPs 101²⁵.

edcierr (e, i, y) m. *return,* CP.

+**edcucoda** (ea¹) m. *man restored to life,* Æ.

edcwic *regenerate, restored to life,* CM 499.

±**edcwician** (cwyc-, cuc-) *to re-quicken, revive,* Æ.

edcwide (eð-) m. *relation, narrative,* WW 43.

edcynn-=edcenn-; **edcyrr**=edcierr

ēde=ēowde; **eder**=eodor; **edesc**=edisc

+**edfrēolsian** *to re-grant by charter,* EC 197n.

edgeong† *becoming or being young again.*

edgift f. *restitution,* TC 202'.

edgrōwung f. *growing again,* WW 149²¹.'

edgung=edgeong

edgyldan² (=ie) *to remunerate,* Sc 162¹¹.

edgyldend m. *remunerator,* Sc 127¹⁷.

+**edhīwian** *to re-shape, conform, reform,* Sc 58.

edhwierfan (æ) *to return, retrace one's steps,* RHy,RPs.

edhwyrft† m. *change, going back (to a former state of things), reverse.*

+**edhyrtan** *to refresh, recruit,* GPH 390.

edisc (e²) m. *enclosed pasture, park, Ct,Gl, Ps;* Mdf. [v. '*eddish*']

edischenn (e²) f. *quail, VPs;* ExC 16¹³. [v. '*eddish*']

ediscweard m. *park-keeper, gardener,* GL.

ediung=edgeong

±**edlæcan** *to repeat, renew,* ÆL.

edlæcung f. *repetition,* LL (416').

edlæht pp. of edlæcan.

edlæs-=edles-

+**edlæstan** *to repeat,* ANS 84·6.

edlēan n. *reward, retribution, recompense, requital, Bo;* Æ,CP. ['*edlen*']

+**edlēanend** m. *rewarder,* OET 420²⁸.

±**edlēanian** (ēa) *to reward, recompense,* Ps.

edlēaniend m. *rewarder,* GD.

±**edlēanung** f. *recompense, remuneration, retribution,* GL.

edlēc-=edlæc-

±**edlesende** *relative, reciprocal,* ÆGR.

edlesendlic *relative, reciprocal.* adv. -līce, Æ.

edlesung (æ², y²) f. *relation, relating,* ÆGR.

edmæle (ē) n. *religious festival,* WW 45⁹.

edmēltid f. *festival time,* TC 158²⁰.

ēdmōd=ēaðmōd; **ednēow-**=edniw-

edniwan adv. *anew, again,* OEG.

ednīwe I. *renewed, new,* Æ. II. adv. *anew, again,* Æ.

±**ednīwian** (ēo) *to renew, restore, reform,* Æ.

ednīwigend m. *restorer,* A 11·115⁹.

ednīwinga (ēo², u³) *anew, again,* AA 26³.

±**ednīwung** f. *renewal, reparation, renovation,* Æ,CP.

ēdo (NG)=ēowde; **edor**=eodor

ēdr-=ædr-; **edrec**=edroc

edreccan *to chew, ruminate,* WW 533³⁸. [=eodorcan]

edric=edroc; **edrine**=edryne

edring f. *refuge?* (GK),SOUL 107. [or? īeðr-]

edroc m. *gullet,* GL : *rumination,* GL.

edryne m. *return, meeting,* ERPs 18⁷.

edsceaft f. *new creation, regeneration : new creature,* Bo.

edslhð (etsith) f. *looking again, respect,* WW 43³³.

+**edstalian** *to restore,* CM 366¹⁵.

±**edstaðelian** *to re-establish, restore,* Æ.

±**edstaðeligend** m. *restorer,* Æ.

±**edstaðelung** f. *re-establishment, renewal,* Æ.

edstaðol-=edstaðel-

edðingung f. *reconciliation,* WW 172⁴⁰.

+**edðräwen** *twisted back,* OEG 1062.

ēdulfstæf=ēðelstæf

ed-walle, -welle=edwielle

edwendan *to return,* RPs 77³⁹.

ed-wend(en)† f. *change, reversal, end,* B.

edwīd=edwīt

edwielle (a, e, i) f. *eddy, vortex, whirlpool,* GL.

edwihte? *something, anything,* GEN 1954.

edwille=edwielle

ed-winde, -wind f. *'vortex,' whirlpool,* GL.

edwist f. *being, substance,* Æ : *sustenance, food.*

+**edwistian** *to feed, support,* LPs 22² : *make to share?* 140⁴.

edwistlic *existing, substantive,* ÆGR 201⁸.

edwīt n. *reproach, shame, disgrace, scorn, abuse,* Ps; AO,CP. ['edwit']

edwītan¹ *to reproach,* VPs. ['edwite']

edwītful *disgraceful,* GL. adv. -līce.

edwītian=edwītan

edwītlīf n. *life of dishonour,* B 2891.

edwītscipe m. *disgrace, shame,* WALD 1¹⁴.

edwītsprǣc† f. *scorn,* AN,PPs.

edwītspreca m. *scoffer,* Gu 418.

edwītstæf† m. *reproach, disgrace,* PPs.

edwylm m. *whirlpool of fire,* WHALE 73.

±**edwyrpan** (=ie) *to amend, recover, revive.*

edwyrping f. *recovery,* ÆH 2·26²⁹.

+**edyppol** adj. *that is to be reviewed,* GPH 396.

efe-=efen-

efen (æfen, efn, emn) I. adj. *'even,' equal, like, level,* AO : *just, true,* Æ : *calm, harmonious, equable,* CP. on efen v. onemn.

II. adv. *evenly,* Æ,Ps : *equally,* Bo : *exactly, just as,* B,Cr : *quite, fully,* CP,Gen : *namely,* Gu,Met.

efen- often=L. con-

ōfen n.=æfen

efenæðele (emn-) *equally noble,* Bo.

efenāmetan=efenmetan

efenapostol (efn(e)-) m. *fellow-apostle,* DR.

efenbehēfe (efn-) *equally useful or needful,* MET 12⁷.

efenbeorht† *equally bright,* MET.

efenbisceop (-cop) m. *co-bishop,* BH 112²⁷.

efenblissian *to rejoice equally,* BH,GD.

efenblīðe *rejoicing with another,* MH 28⁸.

efenboren *of equal birth,* LL (256 n 5).

efenbrād *as broad as long,* ES 8·477.

efenbyrde *of equal birth,* ÆL 33³.

efenceasterwaran mp. *fellow-citizens,* BH 62²⁰; GD 205¹.

efencempa m. *fellow-soldier,* Æ.

efencrīsten (em-) *fellow-Christian,* LL. ['even-Christian']

efencuman⁴ *to come together, agree,* BH.

efendȳre *equally dear,* LL.

efenēadig *equally blessed,* †Hy 8²¹.

efeneald *contemporary, coeval,* Æ,Wid. ['evenold']

efeneardigende *dwelling together,* CR 237.

efenēce† (efn-) *co-eternal,* CR. adv. B.

efenedwistlic *consubstantial,* ÆH.

efenēhð f. *neighbourhood? neighbouring district?* CHR 894A (v. BTs).

efenesne (efne-) m. *fellow-servant,* DR,MtL.

efenetan *to eat as much as,* RD 41⁶³.

efenēðe *just as easy,* MET 20¹⁶⁷ (efn-).

efenfela (eo³) num. adj. *just so many, as many,* AO (em-).

efenfrē-fran, -frian '*consolari,*' EPs 125¹.

efengedǣlan (efn-) *to share alike,* Ex 95.

efengefēon⁵ *to rejoice together, sympathise,* BH.

efengelic *like, co-equal,* G.

efengelīca m. *equal, fellow,* W.

efengemæcca (efn-) m. *companion, fellow, consort,* CP.

efengemyndig *commemorative,* BL 101¹.

efengespittan '*conspuere,*' MkL 14⁶⁵.

efengōd (emn-) *equally good,* Bo.

efenhāda m. *an equal in rank, co-bishop,* GD 43²².

ēfenhālig *equally holy,* BL 45¹⁸.

efenhēafda m. *fellow, comrade,* NC 283.

efenheafodling m. *mate, fellow,* GUTH 14³.

efenhēah *equally high,* SOL 85´.

efenhēap m. *band of comrades,* WW 375²⁰.

efenhemman? *to fetter,* EPs 145⁷.

efenheort(e)? -nes? *harmony,* DR (æfne-).

efenherenes f. *praising together,* CPs 32¹.

efenherian *to praise together,* VPs 116¹.

efen-hlēoðor (PH 621) n., -hlēoðrung (WW 213³⁷) f. *harmony, union of sounds or voices.*

efenhlēoðrian *to sing together,* NC 283.

efenhlȳte (ē³) *equal in rank,* BH.

efen-hlytta, -hlēta m. *sharer, partner,* ÆH.

efenlēoðe (ē) *just as easy,* MET 20¹⁶⁷.

±**efenlǣcan** *to be like* : *make like, match, imitate,* Æ. ['evenleche']

efenlǣcend m. *imitator,* ÆH.

efenlǣcere m. *imitator,* OEG 1957.

+**efenlǣcestre** f. *female imitator,* Sc 71¹¹.

±**efenlǣcung** f. *copying, imitation,* Æ.

efenlang (em-) *equally long* : prep. (w. d.) -lange *along.*

efenlāste f. *the herb mercury,* Lcd. ['evenlesten']

efenlēof (em-) *equally dear,* AO.

efenleornere m. *fellow-disciple,* OEG 56²⁶⁴.

±**efenlic** *even, equal, comparable to, of like age*, Cr. [*'evenly'*] adv.-**līce** *equally, evenly, alike : patiently.*

efenlīca (efn-) m. *equal*, MET 20[19].

+**efenlīcian** *to make equal, liken*, BH 372[31] : *adjust :* (±) *conform to*, AV²Ps 25³.

efenlīcnes f. *evenness, equality*, CP,Ps. (ēm-). [*'evenliness'*]

efenling (efn-) m. *consort, fellow*, EPs 44⁸. [*'evenling'*]

efenmǣre (efn-) *equally famous*, MET 10³².

efenmæsseprēost m. *fellow-priest*, GD 283³.

efenmedome (efn-) *equally worthy*, MH 134⁹.

efenmetan⁵ *to assemble together*, EPs 61⁹ : *compare*, VPs 48²¹.

efenmicel *equally great : just as much as*, LCD.

efenmid adj. *middle*, PPs 73¹².

efenmihtig *equally mighty*, W 16⁷.

efenmōdlīce *with equanimity*, OEG 2978.

efennēah adv. *equally near*, Bo,MET.

efenneahtlic *equinoctial*, A 52·190.

efennēhð=efenēhð

efennes f. *equity, justice*, Ps : *comparison.* [v. *'even'*]

efen-niht f., -nihte? n. *equinox* (23 Sep.).

efenrēðe (emn-) *equally fierce*, AO 68⁶.

efenrīce *equally powerful*, BH 416⁹.

efensācerd m. *fellow-priest*, A 11·7⁴.

efensāre (emn-) *equally bitterly*, CP 413²⁹.

efensārgian *to sorrow with, commiserate*, Æ.

efensārgung f. *sympathy*, GD 180⁸.

efensārig adj. (w. d.) *equally sorry (with)*, AO : *compassionate*, GD.

efenscearp *equally sharp*, PPs 63³.

efenscolere (emn-) m. *fellow-pupil*, AO 132¹.

efenscyldig *equally guilty*, LL 364,76².

efensorgian (efn-) *to be sorry for*, GD 345¹⁸.

efenspēdiglic *consubstantial*, BH 312.

efensprǣc (efne-) *confabulation*, LkL p11¹¹.

efenstǎllian *to prepare, make ready, execute*, WW 208²⁶. [=*efenstaðelian]

efensung=efesung

efenswīðe (efn-) *just as much*, CP.

efentēam (efne-) m. *conspiracy*, JnL 9²².

efenðegn (efne-) m. *fellow-servant*, NG.

ēfenðēnung f. *supper* (BT).

efen-ðēow, -ðēowa m. *fellow-servant*, Æ,CP. -ðēowen f. *fellow-servant (female)*, HL 18²⁵⁶.

efenðrōwian *to compassionate, sympathise*, CP (efn-), Æ (em-).

efenðrōwung f. *compassion*, Sc 147,148.

efenðwǣre *agreeing*, CM 32.

efenunwemme *equally inviolate*, LL 250,14.

efenwǣge f. *counterpoise*, GL.

efenweaxan *to grow together*, LCD.

efenwel *as well*, LL (324¹). e. and *equally as well as*, AS 61¹¹ (æmn-).

efenweorð *of equal rank : very worthy equivalent.*

efenwerod n. *band of comrades*, WW 381¹⁶.

efenwesende *contemporaneous, co-existent*, CR 350.

efenwiht n. *equal, fellow, associate*, CHR,W.

efenwrītan (emn-) *'conscribere,'* EPs 149⁹.

efenwyrcend (æ) m. *cooperator*, BH 464²⁵.

efenwyrhta (em-) m. *fellow-worker*, Æ.

efenwyrðe=efenweorð

efenyrfeweard m. *co-heir*, WW; BH. [v *'even'*]

efeostlīce (CHR 1114 E)=ofostlīce

efer, eferfearn=eofor, eoforfearn ; **ēfer** v. ȳfre.

ēfern (N)=ǣfen

efes, efesc f. *'eaves' (of a house)*, LPs *brim, brink, edge, border (of a forest), side*, Chr.

efesdrypa=yfesdrype

±**efesian** *to clip, shear, cut*, ÆGr. [*'evese'*]

efest (VPs)=æfest, ofost

±**efestan** *to hasten, hurry*, Æ. [=ofestan]

efestlīce *hurriedly*, NG.

efestung f. *hastening*, GD,VPs.

efesung f. *shearing, shaving, tonsure*, Cp, WW. [*'eavesing'*]

efeta (WW) m., efete (Æ) f. *'eft,' newt, lizard*, Æ.

efgǣlð (OEG 8¹⁶⁸)=æfgælð ; **efn**=efen

±**efnan** I. *to make even, level*, Rd 28⁸ : *liken, compare*, MtL. [*'even'*] II.=æfnan

efne I. adv. *'even,' evenly*, Bo,Ps : *quite, fully*, CP,Gen : *equally, exactly, indeed, precisely, just, only, simply, merely*, B,Cr : *alike, likewise : just now : namely*, Gu,Met. e. swā *even so, even as, just as if, when.* e. swā ðēah *even though*. e. tō *next to.* II. (æ,eo) interj. *behold! truly! indeed!* Æ. [efen] III. f? *alum*, WW. IV.? (æ) n. *material*, DR 116'.

efne-=efen-

efnenū interj. *behold now*, CLPs 7¹⁸.

efnes *quite, exactly*, DD,W.

±**efnettan** (emn-) *to equal, emulate : make even, adjust :* (+) *compare.*

efnian=efnan I.

efning m. *partner*, BHCA 194⁴.

ēfod (RPs 49⁹)=ēowd

efol-=eoful-; **efor**=eofor; **ēfre**=ǣfre

efsian=efesian

efst-=efest-

eft adv. *again, anew, a second time*, Æ,VPs; CP : *then, thereupon, afterwards, hereafter, thereafter*, Chr; Æ : *back*, CHR : *likewise, moreover*, Mt. [*'eft'*]

eftācenned *born again*, DR.

eftācenn(edn)es f. *regeneration*, DR,MtR.

eftǣrist (ē) *resurrection*, NG.

eftārīsan[1] *to rise again*, VPs.

eftbētung f. *making whole*, NG.

eftboren *born again*, JnLR 3[5].

eftbōt f. *restoration to health*, NG.

eftcerran=eftcyrran

eftcneoreso *regeneration*, DR 108'.

eftcuman[4] *to come back*, BH,Bo.

eftcyme† m. *return*.

eftcymeð pres. 3 sg. of eftcuman.

eftcynnes (=cen-) f. *regeneration*, NG.

eftcyrran (=ie) *to turn back, return*, Æ.

eftdrægend (? -ðræcend) 'recalcitrans' LkLp 3[6].

eftedwītan[6] *to reprove*, MtL 21[42].

efter=æfter

eftern? *evening*, LkL 24[29].

eftflōwan[7] *to flow back*, HGL 418; 462.

eftflōwung f. *redundance*, HGL 418[45].

eftforgifnes f. 'remissio,' 'reconciliatio,' NG,DR.

+eftgadrian *to repeat*, GD 277[1].

eftgeafung f. *remuneration*, DR 59[1].

eftgecīgan *to recall*, BH 250[21].

eftgecyrran=eftcyrran

eftgemyndgian *to remember*, DR.

eftgemyndig *remembering*, NG,DR.

eftgian *to repeat*, CP 421[10,11] : (+) *restore, strengthen*.

efthweorfan[3] *to turn back, return*, BH.

efthwyrfan (i[2]) *to return*, EPs 108[14], V[2]Hy 6[15] : *recur*, ÆL 23B[613].

eftlēan n. *recompense*, CR 1100.

eftlēaniend m. *rewarder*, DR 89'.

eftlīsing (ē) f. *redemption*, NG.

eftlōcung f. 'respectus,' *regard*, DR 86'.

eftmyndig *remembering*, NG.

eftnīwung f. *restoration*, DR.

eftonfōnd? *receiver*, MtL p16[8].

eftryne m. 'occursus,' *return*, VPs 18[7].

eftscēogian *to put one's shoes on again*, CM 687.

eftsel(e)nes f. *requital*, NG,DR.

eftsittan[5] 'residere,' ÆGR 157[5].

eftslō* m. *journey back, return*, B.

eftslōgende *turning back, retreating*, WW 491[19].

eftsōna *a second time*, Mk : *repeatedly : soon after, again, likewise*, Mt. ['eftsoon']

eftspellung f. *recapitulation*, WW 491[24].

efttōselenes=eftselenes

eftðingung f. *reconciliation*, DR 88[5].

eftwyrd f. *judgment day, resurrection day?* (or ? adj. *future*, GK),Ex 539.

eftyrn=eftryne

efulsung=yfelsung; ēg=īeg

ēg-=æg-, ēag-, īeg-; eg v. eg-lā-eg.

-ēgan v. on-ē.

egcgung (WW 104[12])=ecgung

egde (OET,Ep)=egðe

ege (æ) m. 'awe,' *fear, terror, dread*, Chr,Ps, MtL; Æ,AO,CP : *overawing influence, Æ : cause of fear*, VPs.

egean (WW 459[15])=ecgan

egeful 'awful,' *inspiring or feeling awe*, Æ,Bo. adv. -līce.

egelāf? f. *survivors of a battle*, Ex 370 (or ? ēgorlāf, GK).

egelēas *fearless*, CP. ['aweless'] adv. -līce, CP.

egelēasnes f. *boldness*, BL 85'.

egelic *terrible*, SPs 75[7].

egenu f. *chaff, husk*, WW 412[9].

egesa m. *awe, fear, horror, peril : monstrous thing, monster : horrible deed*, W 281[4]. [ege]

egesful=egeful

egesfullic *terrible*, BH. adv. -līce.

egesfulnes f. *fearfulness, fear*, JPs,LL.

egesgrīma m. *terror-mask, ghost*, GL,MH 54[1].

±egesian[1] *to frighten*, AO,CP : *threaten*, OEG 2481.

egesig (eisig) *terrible*, SAT 36.

egeslic *awful, dreadful, terrible, threatening*, CP. adv. -līce *sternly*, GD 59[20].

egesung f. *threatening, terror*, CHRD,RBL.

egeswīn n. *a kind of fish*. v. NC 284.

egeðe=egðe

egeðgetigu npl. *harrowing implements*, LL 455,17.

egewylm m. *terrible wave*, PPs 106[24].

+eggian *to egg on, incite*, MkL 15[11].

ēghw-=æghw-

egide I.=ecgede pret. 3 sg. of ecgan.
II.=egðe

egile=egle

Egipte (y) mp. *Egyptians*, ÆT.

Egiptisc (y) *Egyptian*, ÆT.

egis-=eges-; egiðe=egðe

egl fn? *mote, beard, awn, ear (of barley)*, Lk : *claw, talon*. ['ail']

eg-lā-eg 'euge!' BRPs 69[4].

±eglan tr. (Jud,Lcd) and impers. (Chr,LL) *to trouble, plague, molest, afflict*, Æ,CP. ['ail']

egle I. *hideous, loathsome, troublesome, grievous, painful*, RD. ['ail'] II.=egl

eglian=eglan

-ēgnan v. on-ē.

ēgnes f. *fear*, EPs 88[41].

egnwirht 'merx,' EPs 126[3] (=gēnwyrht? BT; āgenwyrht? ES 38·1).

ēgo (NG)=ēage

ēgor n? *flood, high tide*, WW 386[29]; 474[4].

ēgorhere† m. *flood, deluge*, GEN.

ēgorstrēam† (ēa), m. *sea, ocean*.

egs-=eges-; ēgs-=ēges-, īegs-

+egðan *to harrow*, BF 30[17].

egðe f. *harrow, rake*, GL.

egðere m. *harrower*, GL.
egðwirf n. *a young ass used for harrowing?*
(BTac),BC 3·367'.
Egypt-=Egipt-
eh=eoh; ōh-=ēag-, īeg-, īg-
eher (NG)=ēar; ehhēoloðe=hēahhēoloðe
ehsl=eaxl; eht=æht, eaht
ōht? (æ) f. *pursuit*, B 2957? [=ōht]
ehta=eahta
±ēhtan *to attack, persecute, pursue, harass,*
Æ,AO,CP : (+) *acquire, purchase*, Æ.
[ōht]
ehtefeald=eahtafeald
ēhtend m. *pursuer, persecutor*, AO.
ēhtere m. *persecutor*, Æ,CP.
ēhtian=ēhtan
ēhtnes f. *persecution*, Æ,AO,CP.
ēhtre=ēhtere
ēhtung f. *persecution*, AO 274¹⁰.
ehtuwe (RD 37⁴)=eahta
ēig=īeg; eige=ege; eis-=eges-
el-, ele- (prefix) *foreign, strange.*
ōl=(1) īl, (2) ǣl; elan=eglan
elboga (Æ)=elnboga
ēlc (NG)=ǣlc; elch=eolh
elcian *to put off, delay*, Æ.
elciend m. *procrastinator*, ÆL 12¹⁶⁶.
elcor adv. *else, elsewhere, otherwise, except,*
besides, BH. ['elchur']
elcora,˙elcra, elcran (æ¹) adv. *else, otherwise.*
elcung f. *delay*, Æ.
elcur=elcor; eld=ield; eldor=ealdor
ele m. *oil*, Lcd,Mt; Æ,AO,CP. ['ele'; L.]
ele-=el-
elebacen *cooked in oil*, ÆT.
elebēam m. *olive-tree*, Æ : *elder? privet?*
elm-tree? (GBG),EC 379'.
elebēamen *of the olive-tree*, WW 128⁷.
elebēamstybb m. *stump of an elder*, EC 190'.
elebearu m. *olive-grove*, NG.
eleberge f. *olive*, GD,Ps.
eleboga (WW)=elnboga
elebytt f. *oil-vessel, chrismatory*, WW 432²⁵.
electre=elehtre
eledrōsna pl. *dregs of oil*, Lcd 1·310'.
elefæt n. *oil-vessel, ampulla*, WW. ['elvat']
elegrēofa m. *oil-vessel?* OEG (v. BTs).
elehorn m. *oil-flask*, WW 434⁷.
elehtre f. *lupine*, Lcd. [L. electrum]
elelēaf n. *olive-leaf?* Lcd 102b.
elelēast f. *lack of oil*, GD 44²¹.
elelendisc *strange, foreign*, GL,Ps. as sb.
stranger, exile. [ellende]
elene=eolone; elesdrōsna=eledrōsna
elesealf f. *oil-salve, nard*, HGl 405.
eleseocche f. *oil-strainer*, WW 154¹².
elestybb=ellenstybb
eletredde f. *oil-press*, GD.
eletrēow n. *olive*, GD, Ps.

eletrēowen *of olive-trees*, Swt.
eletwig n. *oleaster*, WW 460²⁸.
ēleð m. *allodium, freehold*, Gu 38. [=ēðel]
elewana m. *lack of oil*, GD 44⁹.
elfen=ælfen
elfetu=ilfetu; elfremed=ælfremed
elh=eolh
elhygd f. *distraction, ecstasy*, GD,Lcd.
ell m. *the letter l*, ÆGr 200.
ell-=el-
ellærn (Cp), ellarn=ellen II. and III.
elland† n. *foreign country*, B. ['eilland']
elle I. (pl. of *el) *the others*, MtR 26⁶. [v
elra] II.=ealle. III.=ellen II.
ellefne (An)=endleofan
ellen I. nm. (always n. in †) *zeal, strength,*
courage, B,Bo,Gu : *strife, contention*, WW
424¹². on e. *boldly.* ['elne'] II. n. '*elder*'-
tree, Gl,Lcd; Mdf. III. adj. *of elder-wood*,
Lcd.
ellenahse f. *elder ash*, Lcd 121b. [=asce]
ellencræft m. *might, power*, PPs 98⁶.
ellendǣd† f. *heroic deed.*
ellende I. adj. *foreign, strange, exiled.* II. n.
foreign parts.
ellenga=eallunga
ellengǣst m. *powerful demon*, B 86.
ellengrāfa m. *elder-grove*, BC 2·469²⁷.
ellenheard† *mighty, brave, bold.*
ellenhete m. *jealousy*, A 11·98²⁶.
ellenlǣca m. *champion, combatant*, WW.
ellenlēaf n. *elder-leaf*, Lcd 122a.
ellenlēas *wanting in courage*, Jul. ['ellen-
laes']
ellenlic *brave*, Æ. adv. -līce.
ellenmǣrðu† f. *fame of courage*, B.
ellenrind f. *elder-bark*, Lcd.
ellenrōf† *courageous, powerful*, Æ.
ellensēoc *mortally wounded*, B 2787.
ellensprǣc f. *strong speech*, Gu 1128.
ellen-stubb, -stybb m. *elder-stump*, Ct.
ellentān m. *elder-twig*, Lcd 116b.
ellentrēow n. *elder-tree*, KC 3·379¹⁵.
ellenðrīste *heroically bold*, Jud 133.
ellenweorc† n. *heroic deed: good work*, VH
11.
ellenwōd I. f. *zeal*, PPs 68⁹. II. *furious,*
Jul 140: *zealous, earnest*, OEG 364.
ellenwōdian *to emulate*, CPs,WW.
ellenwōdnes f. *zeal*, BH,EPs.
ellenwyrt f. *elderwort, dwarf-elder*, Lcd,WW.
ellenwyrttruma m. *root of elder*, Lcd 101a.
elleoht n. *elision of the letter l*, OEG 5471.
ellern=ellen II.
elles adv. *in another manner, otherwise*, Mt;
Æ,CP : '*else*,' *besides*, Bl,Seaf; Æ,CP :
elsewhere, OEG 2²⁵². e. hwǣr, hwergen,
hwider *elsewhere*. e. hwæt *anything else,*
otherwise.

ellicor (CHRD 80²²)=elcor

ellnung=elnung

ellor† *elsewhere, elsewhither, to some other place. e. londes in another land.*

ellorfūs† *ready to depart.*

ellorgāst† (ǣ) m. *alien spirit,* B.

ellorsīð m. *death,* B 2451.

ellreord, ellreordig=elreord

ellðēod=elðēod

elm m. *'elm,' elm-tree,* Lcd. [L. ulmus]

elm-=ælm-; **elmboga**=elnboga

elmrind f. *elm-bark,* Lcd.

eln f. *fore-arm, 'ell'* (a foot and a half to two feet), *Mt,WW;* Æ,AO,CP.

elnboga m. *'elbow,' WW*(ele-); CP.

elne, elnes ds. and gs. of ellen.

elngemet n. *ell-measure,* GEN 1309.

±elnian *to emulate, be zealous : strengthen, comfort oneself : gain strength,* Lcd.

elnung f. *comfort, consolation,* ÆL 23⁵²⁵ : *emulation, zeal,* Æ.

elone=eolone; **elotr, eloðr** (GL)=elehtre

elpan- (VPs), **elpen-**=elpend-

elpend (y¹) m. *elephant,* AO.

elpendbǣnen (elpan-, ylpen-) *of ivory,* Ps 40⁹.

elpendbān n. *ivory,* AA 6¹⁸,GL.

elpendtōð m. *ivory,* WW 397²⁷.

elpent=elpend

elra comp. adj. *other,* B 753. [*el; Goth. aljis]

el-reord (BH), **-reordig** (AA) *of strange speech, barbarous.*

elreordignes f. *barbarism,* GL(Swt).

-els masc. suffix for inanimate things, as in rēcels, wǣfels.

eltst (Æ)=ieldest superl. of eald.

elðēod f. *strange people, foreign nation,* (in pl.) *foreigners, enemies :* (pl.) *all people, all nations,* CR 1084, 1337 : *exile,* AO.

elðēod(g)ian *to live abroad, wander as a pilgrim :* (+) *make strange, disturb,* Sc 106¹⁹.

elðēodgung=elðēodung

elðēodig (æ¹) *foreign, strange, barbarous, hostile, Bo,Met* (æl-); AO,CP : *exiled.* wk. form mp. el-ðēodian, -ðēodigan *strangers, foreigners, pilgrims, proselytes.* ['altheodi']

elðēodige (īo) *abroad,* LkR 15¹³.

elðēodiglic (æ¹) *foreign, strange, born abroad.* adv. -līce.

elðēodignes (æ¹) f. *foreign travel or residence, pilgrimage, exile,* AO,CP,CHR.

elðēodisc *foreign, strange,* Mt 27⁷.

elðēodung f. *residence or travel abroad,* BH 332¹⁸.

elðīd-, elðīed-, elðīod-=elðēod-

eluhtre=elehtre; **elwiht**=ælwiht

em m? *the letter* m.

em-=ef(e)n-, emn-, ym-, ymb-, ymbe-

ēm-=ǣm-

emb, embe=ymb, ymbe

embeht (NG)=ambiht

embehtian=ambihtan; **embiht**=ambiht

embren (æ¹, i²) n. *bucket, pail,* GL. [Ger. eimer]

emdenes, emdemes=endemes

emel=ymel; **emer**=omer

emleoht n. *elision of m before vowels in scanning verse,* OEG 5473.

emn, emne=ef(e)n, efne

emnet n. *plain,* AO 186²². [efen]

emtwā (on) *into two equal parts, in half,* Æ.

-en suffix I. *diminutive* (neut.) as in mægden (from mægð). II. *to form feminines* (a) *with mutation* (gyden, *from* god). (b) *without mutation* (ðēowen *from* ðēow). III. *adjectival, with mutation, denoting material.*

ēn-=ān-, ǣn-; **end** conj.=and

+endadung f. *finishing,* DR 105¹⁴.

ende m. *'end,' conclusion, Ct,Met,Mt,Ps : boundary, border, limit, Ps;* Æ,AO,CP : *quarter, direction : part, portion, division, Chr;* AO : *district, region, AO : species, kind, class : death.* æt (ðǣm) e. *finally.*

ende-berd-, -bird-, -bred-=endebyrd-

endebyrd f. *order,* MET 13⁴.

±endebyrdan *to arrange, ordain, dispose,* Æ.

endebyrdend m. *one who orders or arranges,* OEG.

endebyrdes† *in an orderly manner, regularly, properly,* MET.

endebyrdian=endebyrdan

endebyrdlic *ordinal,* ÆGR 282¹⁴. adv. (±) -līce *in an orderly manner, in order, in succession,* Æ,CP.

endebyrdnes f. *order, succession, series, arrangement, method, rule,* Æ,CP : *grade, degree, rank, condition,* Æ,CP.

endedæg† m. *last day, day of death.*

endedēað m. *death as the end of life,* CR 1653?

endedōgor† mn. *last day, death-day.*

endefæstend m. *finisher,* DR 27¹⁵.

endefurh f. *end-furrow,* KC 3·384¹⁶.

endelāf f. *last remnant, last,* B 2813.

endelēan† n. *final retribution.*

ende-lēas, -lēaslic (Æ) *'endless,' boundless, eternal, Bo.* adv. -līce, Æ.

endelēasnes f. *infinity, eternity,* ÆGR 116¹⁰.

endelīf n. *life's end, death,* EL 585.

endeman m. *man of the world's (supposed) final age,* Æ.

endemes (Æ,CP), **endemest** adv. *equally, likewise, at the same time, together, unanimously : fully, entirely : in procession.*

endemest (ænde-) *last,* MFH 157.

endemestnes? f. *extremity*, RBL33¹⁵ (?= endenēhstnes, BTs).

ende-nēhst, -nēxt (ī, ȳ) *extreme, final, last*, Æ.

enderīm m. *number*, Sat 12.

endesǣta m. *border-watchman*, B 241.

endespǣc f. *epilogue*, CM 1166.

endestæf† m. *end, conclusion*.

endetīma m. *end of life, last hour*, LL.

endeðrǣst (ænde-) f. *end, destruction*, GD 337⁹.

±**endian** to '*end*,' *finish*, G; Æ : *abolish, destroy*, Ps; AO,CP : *to come to an end, die*, Gu; AO. [v. also '*yend*']

end-lefte (AA 16',31'), -lifta=endlyfta

endleofan (e², i², u², y²; o³) num. '*eleven*,' Æ,BH.

endlifangilde *entitled to eleven-fold compensation*, LL 3,1; 470,7.

endlyfenfeald *eleven-fold*, ByH 36¹⁴.

end-lyfta, -leofta, -leofeða '*eleventh*,' Bl,Mt.

endlyfte *in the eleventh place, eleventhly*, LL 182,11.

+**endodlic** *finite*, Bo 44²¹.

±**endung** f. '*ending*,' *end*, Mt; CP : (+) *death*. ['*yend*']

endwerc n. *pain in the buttocks*, Lcd 174a. [wærc]

ened (æ¹, i²) mf. *drake, duck*, Gl. ['*ende*']

enelēac=ynnelēac

ēnetere=ānwintre; **ēnga**=ānga

enge I. (a, æ) *narrow, close, straitened, constrained* : *vexed, troubled, anxious* : *oppressive, severe, painful, cruel*. II. (a, o) adv. *sadly, anxiously*.

+**enged** *troubled, anxious*, WW 357⁷.

engel (æ) m. '*angel*,' *messenger*, Mt; Æ,CP. [L. angelus]

Engel=Angel

engelcund *angelic*, Gu 72.

engelcynn† n. *race or order of angels*.

engellic *angelic, of angels*, ÆH.

engetrēow=hengetrēow

Englaland n. *country of the Angles*, '*England*,' BH.

Englan, Engle mp. *the Angles* (as opposed to the Saxons) : *the English generally*. [Angel]

engelic=engellic

Englisc '*English*,' Ct,LL; CP. on E. *in (the) English (language)*, ÆGr,BH,Mt.

Engliscman m. '*Englishman*,' LL.

engu† f. *narrowness, confinement*.

enid=ened; **ēnig**=ǣnig; **ēnitre**=ānwintre

enlefan=endlufon; **ēnlīpig**=ānlīpig

enne-lēac, -lēc=ynnelēac; **eno**=heonu

ent m. *giant*, Æ,AO (v. AB 40·21ff).

entcynn n. *race of giants*, Num 13³⁴.

entisc *of a giant*, B 2979.

entse=yndse

enu=heonu

ēnwintre=ānwintre

eobor, eobot=eofor, eofot; **ēoc**=gēoc

ēode (B,G,Gl) I. pret. 3 sg. of gān. ['*yode*'] II.=ēowde

eodor† m. *hedge, boundary* : *limit, region, zone* : *enclosure, fold, dwelling, house* : *prince, lord*.

eodor-brecð f., -brice m. *breach of an enclosure, house-breaking*, LL.

eodorcan *to chew, ruminate*, BH 346². [=edrocian]

eodorgong (eder-) m. *begging*? (GK) : *robbery*? (Liebermann), Cr 1676. (v. also BTac.)

eodorwīr m. *wire fence*, RD 18².

eodur=eodor; **eofel**=yfel

eofer=eofor; **eofera**=eafora

eofermodig=ofermodig

eofet=eofot; **eofne**=efne

eofole f? *danewort, endive*? Lcd.

eofon=heofon

eofor (e¹, ea¹, e²) m. *boar, wild boar*, Lcd,Ps : *boar-image on a helmet*. ['*ever*']

eofora=eafora

eoforcumbol n. *boar-image on a helmet? boar-shaped ensign?* EL 76; 259.

eoforfearn (e¹) n. *a kind of fern, polypody*, Lcd,WW. ['*everfern*']

eoforhēafodsegn (ea¹) n. *banner with a boar's head design?* B 2152 (? two words, Klb. p. 196).

eoforlīc m. *boar-image (on a helmet)*, B 303.

eoforspere (u²) n. *boar-spear*, OEG 7⁵⁶.

eoforsprēot n. *boar-spear*, Gl.

eoforswīn n. *boar*, Lcd 98b.

eoforðring m. (*boar-throng*), *the constellation Orion*, Cp 1464 (ebur-).

eoforðrote f. *carline thistle*, Lcd.

±**eofot** n. *crime, sin, guilt*, LL.

eofoð=eafoð; **eoful-** (A)=yfel-

eofur (VPs)=eofor; **eofut** (NG)=eofot

ēogor=ēgor; **eogoð**=geoguð

eoh† nm., gs. ēos *war-horse, charger* : *name of the rune for* e. [Goth. aihwa]

ēoh† [=īw] m. '*yew*'-*tree*, WW : *name of the rune for* ēo.

eola, eolc=eolh; **eoldran**=ieldran

eolene=eolone

ēoles gs. of eolh.

eolet n. *voyage?* (Cosijn), B 224.

eolh m. [g. ēoles] *elk*, Gl : *name of a rune*, Run 15. [OHG. elho]

eolh-sand (-sang, HGl 431) n. *amber*, Gl.

eolhsecg (eolhx-, eolx-, ilug-) m. '*papyrus*,' *reed, sedge*, Gl.

eolhstede (An)=ealhstede

eolone f. *elecampane*, Gl,Lcd.

eoloð=ealað (v. ealu).

eolxsecg=eolhsecg

eom I. v. wesan. II.=heom, him dp. of hē, hēo, hit.

eond=geond

eonde?=ende (but v. JAW31).

eonu=heonu

eor-; ēor-=ear-, ier-; ēar-

eorcnanstān (AA), eorc(l)anstān† m. *precious stone*. [*Goth.* -airkns]

ēored (o²) nf. *troop, band, legion, company*: *chariot?* AA13⁵. [eoh, rād]

ēoredcist (o², ie³, e³, y³)† f. *troop, company*.

ēoredgeatwe fpl. *military apparel*, B2866.

ēoredgerīd n. *troop of horsemen*, WW229¹.

ēoredhēap m. *troop, host*, DD113.

ēoredmæcg m. *horseman*, RD23³.

ēoredmann m. *trooper, horseman*, BH,WW.

ēoredmenīgu f. *legion*, GD73,74.

ēoredōrēat m. *troop, host*, RD4⁴⁹.

ēored-weorod, -wered n. *band, company*, GD71⁶.

eorl m. *brave man, warrior, leader, chief*, B, Cr,Gen,Rd: *man*: '*earl*,' *nobleman* (origly. a Danish title=the native 'ealdorman'), Ct,LL,Ma.

eoricund *noble*, LL.

eorldōm m. *earldom, rank of an earl*, CHR.

eorlgebyrd† f. *noble birth*, MET.

eorlgestrēon† n. *treasure, wealth*.

eorlgewǣde n. *armour*, B1442.

eorlic (1)=ierlic; (2) eorllic

eorlisc *of noble rank*, LL173.

eorllic *chivalrous, manly*, B,WW4¹6³³.

eorlmægen† n. *band of noble warriors*.

eorlriht n. *earl's right*, LL458,5.

eorlscipe† m. *manliness, courage*.

eorlweorod n. *host of noble warriors*, B2893.

eormencynn (y¹)† n. *mankind*.

eormengrund n. *wide world*, B859.

eormenlāf f. *huge legacy*, B2234.

eormenstrȳnd f. *race, generation*, SOL329.

eormenðēod (y¹) f. *mighty people*, MEN139.

eorn-=georn-

eornes f. *anger*, BL123⁸; HL.

eornest=eornost

eornost f. *earnestness, zeal*, Æ,CP: *seriousness*, W: *battle*. on eornost(e) *in earnest, earnestly, truly*. ['*earnest*']

eornoste (e²) I. '*earnest*,' *zealous, serious*, Æ. II. adv. *courageously*: *fiercely*.

eornostlīce I. adv. '*earnestly*,' *strictly, truly, in truth, indeed*, Mt,LL. II. conj. *therefore, but*.

eornust=eornost; ēorod=ēored

eorp=earp; eorre (AA37¹⁶)=ierre

eorð=eorðe, heorð

eorð-æppel m. nap. -æppla '*earth-apple*,' *cucumber*, Æ: '*mandragora*,' WW.

eorðærn† (e²) n. *earth-house, grave*, WW.

eorðbeofung (i²) f. *earthquake*, AO.

eorðberge f. *strawberry*, WW242⁶. [berie]

eorðbīgenga m. *earth-dweller*, BH268³¹.

eorðbīgennes f. *agriculture*, WW144²¹.

eorðbrycg f. *bridge of poles covered with earth*, BC3·223²¹.

eorð-būend†, -būg(ig)end m. *earth-dweller, man*, Æ.

eorðburh=eorðbyrig

eorðbyfung=eorðbeofung

eorðbyrgen f. *grave*, NC284.

eorðbyrig f. *earthwork, mound, embankment, road*, Ct,GL.

eorðcafer m. *cockchafer*, WW122¹⁶. [ceafor]

eorð-cenned, -cend *earth-born*, PS.

eorðcræft m. *geometry*, OEG3119.

eorðcry(p)pel m. *paralytic, palsied man*, NG.

eorðcund, eorðcundlic (CP) *earthly, mortal*.

eorðcyning m. *earthly king, king of the country*.

eorðcynn n. *human race*, EX370.

eorðdenu n. *valley*, NC284.

eorðdraca m. *dragon that lives in the earth*, B. [v. '*earth*']

eorðdyne m. *earthquake*, Chr1060. ['*earthdin*']

eorðe f. *ground, soil*, Æ,B,LkL; AO,CP: '*earth*,' *mould*, Gu: *world*, Æ,B,Mt: *country, land, district*, Jn.

eorðen adj. *of or in the earth*, OEG3312?

eorðern=eorðærn

eorðfæst '*earthfast*,' *firm in the earth*, Æ.

eorðfæt n. *earthly vessel, body*, SOUL8.

eorðg(e)alla, m. *earth-gall, lesser centaury*, Lcd; GL. [v. '*earth*']

eorðge-byrst, -berst n. *landslip*, Ct.

eorðgemǣre n. *boundary of the earth*, PPs21²⁵.

eorðgemet n. *geometry*, GL.

eorðgesceaft f. *earthly creature*, MET20¹⁹⁴.

eorðgræf n. *hole in the earth*, RD59⁹.

eorðgrǣp f. *earth's embrace*, RUIN6.

eorðhele m. *a covering of the ground*, EX16¹⁴.

eorðhrērnes f. *earthquake*, BL,NG.

eorðhūs n. *cave-dwelling, den*, ÆL.

eorðīfig (ea¹, ȳ²) n. *ground-ivy*, Lcd, WW: '*terebinthus*,' DR68'. [v. '*earth*']

eorðlic '*earthly*,' *worldly*, Bl,Mt; Æ. adv. -līce.

eorðling=yrðling

eorðmægen n. *earthly power*, RIM69.

eorð-mata [-maða?] m. '*vermis*,' *worm*, GL.

eorðmistel m. *basil (plant)*, LCD33a.

eorðnafela (a³, o³) m. *asparagus*, LCD.

eorðnutu f. '*earth-nut*,' *pig-nut*, Ct. [hnutu]

eorðreced n. *cave-dwelling*, B2719.

eorðrest f. *bed laid on the ground*, WW 362¹¹.
eorðrīce n. *earthly kingdom*, CP : *earth*, LCD.
eorðrima m. *a plant*, LCD 120a.
eorðscræf n. ds. -scrafe *cave-dwelling, cavern*, CP : *sepulchre*.
eorðsele† m. *cave-dwelling*.
eorðslihtes *close to the ground*, NUM 22⁴.
eorðstede m. *earth*, PPs 73⁷.
eorðstirung=eorðstyrung
eorð-styren (GD), -styrennes (NG), -styrung (Æ) f. *earthquake*.
eorðtilia m. '*earth-tiller,*' *husbandman, farmer*, Æ(Gen); W 305³¹. [=yrðtilia]
eorðtilð f. '*earth-tilth,*' *agriculture*, WW.
eorðtūdor n. *human race*, PPs 117²².
eorðtyrewe f. *earth-tar, bitumen*, AO 74¹⁷.
eorðu (N)=eorðe
eorðwæstm f. *fruit of the earth*, BH,LL.
eorð-waran (CP), -ware mpl., -waru fpl. *earth-dwellers*, AO. ['*earthware*']
eorðweall m. *earth-wall, mound*, B,BH.
eorðweard m. *region of earth*, B 2334.
eorðweg† m. *earth*, EL,Ps.
eorðwela m. *wealth : fertility*, AO.
eorðweorc n. *work on the land*, Ex 1¹⁴.
eorðwerod n. *inhabitants of earth*, W 25²¹; 203⁵.
eorð-westm, -ȳfig=eorð-wæstm, -ifig
ēorwicga=ēarwicga
ēos gs. of eoh.
eosel, eosol=esol
eosen=iesen
ēost-=ēast-; **eosul**=esol
eotan (VPs)=etan; **Eotas**=Eotenas
eoten† m. *giant, monster, enemy*. [v. '*eten*']
Eotenas mpl. *Jutes*, B.
eotend=etend
eotenisc *gigantic*, B. ['*etenish*']
Eotolware mp. *Italians*, BH 108¹¹.
ēoton=æton pret. pl. of etan.
eotonisc=eotenisc
eotonweard f. *watch against monsters?* B 668.
ēoðe (N)=ēaðe
ēow I. dat. of gē pers. pron. *to you*, 'YOU.' II. interj. *wo! alas!* III.=gīw. IV.=īw. V. m. *sheep*.
ēowā=ēow II.; **ēowan**=īewan
ēowberge=īwberge; **ēowcig**=ēowocig
ēowd f. *sheepfold*, Æ : *flock, herd*, Æ. ['*eowde*']
ēowde fn. *flock (of sheep), herd*, An,Ps. ['*eowde*']
ēowdescēap n. *sheep of the flock*, PPs 64¹⁴.
ēowe I. gs. of ēowu. II.=ēowu
ēowed, ēowede=ēowd, ēowde
ēowende (dat.) '*testiculis,*' LL 64,25¹.
ēower I. gp. of gē pers. pron. (2nd pers.). II. possess. pron. YOUR, *yours*.

ēowerlendisc *of your land*, '*vestras,*' ÆGR 94¹.
ēowestre (ē¹, ēa¹, i²) mf. *sheepfold*, GD.
ēowian=īewan
ēowic acc. pl. of ðū (v. gē).
ēowistre=ēowestre
ēowocig '*yolky,*' *greasy with yolk, as unwashed wool*, Lcd 16a (v. NED).
ēowod, ēowode=ēowd, ēowde
ēowohumele f. *female hop-plant*, LCD.
ēowomeoluc f. *ewe's milk*, LCD 70a.
ēowu f. '*ewe,*' Æ,KC,LL.
ēowunga=ēawunga
epactas sbp. *epacts*, LCD.
epistol, epistola m. *letter*, AA.
epl, eppel=æppel; **eppan**=yppan
er-=ær-, ear-, ier-, yr-
ēr=(1) ær, (2) ȳr, (3) ēar I.
erce=arce; **ercna(n)stān** (NG)=eorcnanstān
eretic *heretic*, BH 312¹⁹. [L.]
erian, erigean *to plough*, Æ,Bo,Lk; CP. ['*ear*']
erinaces pl. *hedgehogs*, PPs 103¹⁷.
eringland n. *arable land*, KC 6·200⁷.
erinung f. *ploughing*, WW 104⁶.
ernð (æ) f. *crop of corn*, BHc 44²³.
ersc m? *stubble-field*, EC 282'; 290'.
erscgrāfa *a copse near a stubble-field?* KC 374'.
erschen f. *quail*, Æ,WW.
ēsa v. ōs.
ēsceap=æsceap; **esl**=eaxl
esne m. *labourer, slave, servant, retainer : youth, man*, CP. [Goth. asneis]
esnecund *of a labourer*, WW 212⁴⁴.
esnemon (æ¹) m. *hireling*, JnR 10¹³.
esnewyrhta m. *mercenary, hireling*, GD,LL.
esnlīce *like a man, manfully*, Æ,CP.
esol mf. *ass*, CP. [L. asellus]
esole f. *she-ass*, BL.
ess m. *name of the letter* s, ÆGR.
essian *to waste away*, RPs 118¹³⁹.
ēst mf. *favour, grace, bounty, kindness, love*, An,B : *pleasure*, Lk : *harmony, consent* : (usu. in pl.) *delicacies*, WW; Æ. ['*este*']
ēstan (w. d.) *to live luxuriously*, W 190¹⁷.
ēstan=ēastan
ēste *gracious, liberal*, B,Gen. ['*este*']
ēstelic *kind, gracious*, EPs 68¹⁷ : *devout*, DR : *delicate, dainty (of food)*, MFH 157. adv. -līce, CP : *courteously*, An 292 : *luxuriously*, WW. [v. '*este*']
ēstful *gracious, devoted, devout*, Æ : *fond of luxuries*, WW 218¹⁸,¹⁹. ['*estful*'] adv. -līce.
ēstfulnes f. *devotion, zeal*, CP : *daintiness*, WW : *luxury, lechery*. [v. '*este*']
ēstgeorn *delicate, fond of luxuries*, WW 218¹⁸.

éstig *gracious, liberal*, PA 16.
éstines f. *benignity*, EPs 64¹².
éstlic=éstelic
éstmete m. *dainty (food), delicacy, luxury*, ÆGr. [v. 'este']
-estre=f. *agent, as in* wítegestre, *prophetess*.
éstum† *freely, willingly, gladly*.
esul=esol
esulcweorn f. *mill-stone turned by an ass*, CP 31¹⁷.
éswic=æswic
et I.=æt prep. II. pres. 3 sg. of etan.
et-=æt-, ed-; **ét** (NG)=æt
±**etan**⁵ (ea, eo) *to 'eat,'* Æ,AO,Jn : *devour, consume*, Jn; CP : (tr.) *feed* : (reflex.) *provision oneself* : (+) *eat together.* [v. also 'yeten']
etelond n. *pasture land*, KC 2·95¹⁴.
etemest=ytemest; **eten**=eoten
etend I. m. *eater, glutton.* II. *voracious, gluttonous*, WW 396,523 (eot-).
etenlǽs f. *pasture*, LL 452,20.
eting f. *eating*, Sc 170⁵.
etol (ettul) *voracious*, ÆGr 69⁷,WW 226¹.
etolnes (ettul-) f. *greediness, gluttony*, Sc 55⁶.
etonisc (B)=eotenisc; **etsomne**=ætsamne
etst=itst pres. 2 sg. of etan.
ettan *to graze, pasture land*, AO 18²⁵.
ettul=etol
éð I. comp. adv. *more easily.* II.=ýð
eð-=æð-, ed-
éð-=ǽð-, éað-, íeð-
eðcwide (GL)=edcwide
éðel (oe, N) mn. gs. éðles *country, native land, ancestral home*, Lk,Met; CP : *name of the rune for œ.* †hwǽles é. *the sea*, CHR 975A. ['ethel']
éðelboda m. *land's apostle, native preacher*, GU 976.
éðelcyning m. *king of the land*, CR 997.
éðeldréam m. *domestic joy*, GEN 1607.
éðeleard m. *native dwelling*, GEN 1945.
éðelfæsten n. *fortress*, RD 72²².
éðelland† n. *fatherland, country.*
éðelléas† *homeless, exiled.*
éðelmearc† f. *boundary of one's country, territory*, GEN.
éðelríce† n. *native country.*
éðelriht† n. *hereditary right.*
éðel-seld†, -setl† n. *settlement*, GEN.
éðelstæf (ul, yl) m. *heir, successor*, GEN 2223.
éðelstaðol m. *settlement*, GEN 94.
éðelstól† m. *hereditary seat, habitation : royal city, chief city.*
éðelstów† f. *dwelling-place*, GEN.
éðelturf† f. (ds. -tyrf) *fatherland.*
éðelðrymm m. *glory of one's own land*, GEN 1634.

éðelweard† m. *lord of the realm, man.*
éðelwynn† f. *joy of ownership*, B.
éðgung f. *breath, breathing, inspiration : hard breathing*, RB 68³.
±**éðian** *to breathe*, GD : *smell.* ['ethe']
éðmian=æðmian
éðr (N)=ǽðr, ǽdre; **éðr-**=íeðr-
eðða (MtR)=oððe
éðung I. f. *laying waste, destroying*, GL. [éðe, íðan] II.=éðgung
éðwíte *easily turned*, OEG 1151.
éuwá interj. *woe!* GL.
evangelista m. *evangelist*, VH 11.
éw-=ǽw-, éaw-, éow-, íew-; **éwe**=éowu
ex, exe f. *brain*, LCD (v. A 30·129).
ex=eax; **exen** v. oxa.
exlistealla (HGL 405)=eaxlgesteallA
exorcista m. *exorcist*, ÆL 31¹⁴¹.

fá v. fáh I.
faca gp. of fæc.
fácen n. nap. fácnu *deceit, fraud, treachery, sin, evil, crime*, Mt,LL; Æ,AO : *blemish, fault (in an object)*, LL 114,56; 398,9. ['faken']
fácendǽd f. *sin, crime*, PPs 118⁵³.
fácen-ful, -fullic *deceitful, crafty.* adv. -líce.
fácengecwis f. *conspiracy*, WW.
fácenléas *guileless*, VH 11 : *pure*, NG.
fácenlic *deceitful*, RB 95¹²,¹⁵. adv. -líce, Æ. ['fakenliche']
fácensearu† n. *treachery.*
fácenstafas mp. *treachery, deceit*, B 1018.
fácentácen n. *deceitful token*, CR 1566.
facg m. *plaice? loach?* WW 180³².
fácian *to try to obtain, get*, AO 152⁷ : *get to, reach*, BC 2·305'.
fácn=fácen; **fácne**=fǽcne
fácnesful=fácenful
facum dp. of fæc.
±**fadian** *to arrange, dispose, guide*, LL; Æ. ['fade' v. IF 48·257]
fadiend m. *manager*, OEG 56³⁰⁸.
±**fadung** f. *arrangement, order, disposition, dispensation, rule*, Æ : *interpretation, version*, BF 238¹⁶.
fadur (A)=fæder
fæc (e) n. *space of time, while, division, interval*, Lk; Æ,CP : *period of five years, lustrum*, WW 431¹⁶. ['fec']
fǽcan *to wish to go*, LL 128B².
fæccan=feccan
fæcele (e¹) f. *torch*, WW. [*Ger.* fackel]
fǽcenlíce=fácenlíce
fǽcful *broad, spacious*, Sc 185¹⁵.
fæcile (GL)=fæcele

fǣcne I. *deceitful, treacherous*, Ps : *vile, worthless.* II. adv. *deceitfully, maliciously, disgracefully* : (†) *exceedingly.* ['*faken*']
fǣcnig *crafty*, RPs 72¹⁸.
+fǣd I. *orderly, well-conducted*, LL : *calm, composed*, W 51²⁴. II. n? *discretion*, LL (244¹⁵). [fadian]
fǣd-=fēd-
fæder (e¹) m. usu. indecl. in sg. '*father*,' Æ, VPs; AO,CP : *male ancestor*, LkL,Mt : *the Father, God, Jn,Mt,VPs* : (in pl.) *parents*, Æ. eald f. *grandfather.* ðridda, fēowerða f. etc. *great-grandfather, great-great-grandfather*, etc.
fædera (e¹) m. *paternal uncle*, AO. [cp. *Ger.* vetter]
+fædera m. *male sponsor, godfather*, Æ. [*Ger.* gevatter]
fæderæðelo† npl. *patrimony* : *paternal kinship.*
+fædere f. *female sponsor, godmother*, LL.
fæderen *paternal*, ÆT,Sc.
+fæderen *born of the same father*, AO 114¹⁴.
fæderenbrōðor m. *brother* (*from the same father*), PPs 68⁸.
fæd(e)rencnōsl n. *father's kin*, LL 54,9.
fæderencynn n. *father's kin*, CHR.
fæderenfeoh=fæderfeoh
fæderenhealf f. *father's side*, CHR 887A.
fæderenmǣg m. *paternal kinsman*, CHR 887 E.
fæderenmǣgð f. *paternal kindred*, LL 392,3.
fæderēðel m. *fatherland*, AO.
fæderfeoh n. *dowry paid by the father of the bride*, LL.
fædergeard m. *father's dwelling*, GEN 1053.
fædergestrēon n. *patrimony*, GL.
fæderhīwisc n? '*paterfamilias*,' NG.
fæderingmǣg=fæderenmǣg
fæderland n. *paternal land, inheritance*, CHR 1101.
fæderlēas *fatherless*, W.
fæderlic '*fatherly*,' *paternal, ancestral*, El. adv. -līce.
fædern-=fæderen-
fæderslaga m. *parricide*, WW.
fæderswica m. *traitor to one's father*, ÆL 19²²⁴.
+fædlic *fit, suitable, proper.* adv. -līce *orderly, quietly* : *craftily?* CPs 82⁴. [fadian]
fædm=fæðm; **fædr-**=fæder-
+fædred (AO)=+fæderen
fæðne (LkR 1²⁹)=fæmne
+fæge *popular with, acceptable to*, B 915. [*OHG.* gifag]
fægan *to paint*, GL.
fæge '*fey*,' *doomed* (*to death*), *fated, destined*, An,B,Ma : *dead* : *unhappy, accursed*, Cr : *feeble, cowardly*, Gu.

±fægen (w. g.) '*fain*,' *glad, joyful, rejoicing*, B,Bo ; AO,CP.
fægenian=fægnian
fægennes f. *joy*, NC 285.
fæger I. '*fair*,' *lovely, beautiful*, B,Bo,Gen; AO,CP : *pleasant, agreeable*, Ex : *attractive*, Gen; Æ. II. n. *beauty*, Bo : *beautiful object.*
fæger-=fægr-
fægerlīce *splendidly*, LkL 16¹⁹.
fægernes f. '*fairness*,' *beauty*, LPs,Sc; Æ.
fægerwyrde *smooth-speaking*, FT 12.
fægn=fægen
fægnes (LPs 44¹⁵)=fāgnes
+fægnian (a) (w. g. etc.) *to rejoice, be glad, exult*, Bo,Met : *fawn*, Æ : *applaud.* ['*fain*']
±fægnung f. *rejoicing*, Æ, ELSPs.
+fægon pret. pl. of +fēon.
fægre (e) *fairly, elegantly, beautifully*, Æ, Gen : *pleasantly, softly, gently, kindly*, Gen,Men : *well, justly* : *early*, LkR 24¹. ['*fair*']
±fægrian *to become beautiful*, Seaf : *adorn, decorate.* ['*fair*']
fǣgð? f. *imminent death*, AN 284(GK).
fǣhan=fǣgan; **fǣht**=feoht
fǣhð f. *hostility, enmity, violence, revenge, vendetta*, AO. [fāh; cp. *Ger.* fehde]
fǣhðbōt f. *payment for engaging in a feud*, LL 266,25; 286,5²ᵈ.
fǣhðe, fǣhðo, fǣhðu=fǣhð
fæl-=feal-, fel-, fiel-, fyl-
fǣlǣcan=fālǣcan
fǣle† I. *faithful, trusty, good*, Ps : *dear, beloved.* ['*fele*'] II. adv. *truly, well, pleasantly.*
±fǣlsian *to cleanse, purify* : *expiate*, WW : (+) *pass through.*
fǣman *to foam*,' MkL. [fām]
fǣmhādlic=fǣmnhādlic; **fǣmig**=fāmig
fǣmnanhād=fǣmnhād
fǣmne (ē) f. *maid, virgin, bride*, Æ : (+) *woman* : *virago.*
fǣmne(n)dlic=fǣmnhādlic
fǣmnhād m. *virginity, maidenhood*, AO.
fǣmnhādesmon m. *virgin*, RB 136²⁴.
fǣmnhādlic (OEG), fæmn(en)lic *maidenly, virginal.*
fǣn=fen
fær n. nap. faru (±) *way, journey, passage, expedition*, Bf,Ex,Lk. mannes f. *highway*, ÆL 25⁴⁴¹ : *movement*, MET 31⁴ : *proceedings, life*, Æ : *movable possessions, means of subsistence*, HL : *ark, ship.* ['*fare*']
fǣr (ē) I. m. *calamity, sudden danger, peril*, B,Ex : *sudden attack* : *terrible sight*, BL 199²⁴. ['*fear*'] II.=fēfer. III.=fæger.
fǣr-=fer-, fear-, feor-, fier-, for-
fǣr- prefix=(1) *sudden, fearful*; (2) fēr-
fǣrærning f. *quick riding*, GD 14²⁴.

fǣran (ē) *to frighten*, Æ; CP: *raven*, MtL 7¹⁵. ['*fear*']

fǣrbēn-a, -u m. *peasant, small-holder?* (Lieb.), LL 383,50 : '*epibata*,' Erf 1112.

fǣrbifongen *beset by dangers*, B 2009.

fǣrblǣd (ē¹) m. *sudden blast (of wind)*, JUL 649.

fǣrbryne m. *scorching heat*, EX 72.

fǣrclamm (ē) m. *sudden seizure*, EX 119.

fǣrcoðu f. *apoplexy*, LCD.

fǣrcwealm m. *sudden pestilence*, LL,W.

fǣrcyle m. *intense cold*, GEN 43.

fǣrdēað m. *sudden death*, MH,WW 351¹⁹.

fǣrdryre m. *sudden fall*, CRA 48.

fǣredlīc (Æ)=fǣrlic; **fǣreht**=fǣrriht

fǣreld (a¹) nm. *way, journey, track, passage, expedition*, Æ,AO,CP : *retinue, company*, AO : *course of life, conduct*, Æ : *movement, progress, power of locomotion*, Æ : *vehicle*, OEG : *the Passover*, Æ.

fǣreldfrēols m. *Passover-feast*, JOS 5¹⁰.

fǣrelt (AO,CP)=fǣreld

fǣrennes=fǣrnes

fǣreð pres. 3 sg. of faran.

fǣrfyll (on) *headlong*, WW 426⁸.

fǣrgripe† m. *sudden grip*, B.

fǣrgryre† m. *awful horror*.

fǣrhaga m. *hedge of terrors*, GU 933.

fǣring (ē) f. I.† *journey, wandering*. II. *accusation*, WW 27⁸. III. *ecstasy*, WW 398¹⁶.

fǣringa (ē) *suddenly, unexpectedly, quickly, forthwith, by chance*, Lk; Æ,CP. ['*feringe*']

fǣrlīc *sudden, unexpected*, AO,WW; Æ,CP, *rapid*. adv. -līce, Lk. ['*ferly*']

fǣrnes f. *passage, traffic*, BH,MtR.

fǣrnīð m. *hostile attack*, B 476.

fǣrrǣs m. *sudden rush*, LkL 8³³.

fǣrrǣsende (ē¹) *rushing headlong*, DR 125¹⁶.

fǣrriht n. *passage-money*, ÆL 23b³⁵².

fǣrsceatt m. *passage-money, fare*, ANDR.

fǣrsceaða m. *enemy*, MA 142.

fǣrscyte m. *sudden shot*, CR 766.

fǣrsearo n. *sudden artifice*, CR 770.

fǣrsēað m. *deep pit*, WW 193⁶.

fǣrslide m. *sudden fall*, PPs 114⁸.

fǣrspell† n. *dreadful tidings*.

fǣrspryng m. *sudden eruption*, LCD 134a.

fǣrst pres. 2 sg. of faran.

fǣrsteorfa m. *murrain*, LCD 177a.

fǣrstice m. *sudden stitch (pain)*, LCD 3·52¹¹.

fǣrstylt m? *amazement*, LkL 5²⁶.

fǣrswīge (ē) f. *amazement*, MkL 5⁴².

fǣrswile m. *sudden swelling*, LCD 27b.

fǣrð I.=ferð. II.=pres. 3 sg. of faran.

fǣrunga, fǣrunge (Æ)=fǣringa

fǣruntrymnes f. *sudden sickness*, LCD 107b.

fǣrweg m. *cart road*, Ct.

fǣrwundor n. *terrible wonder*, EX 279.

fǣs (a, ea) n. *fringe, border*, MtL. ['*fas*']

fǣsceaftnes=fēasceaftnes

fǣsl† n? *seed, offspring, progeny*, GEN.

fǣsnian=fǣstnian

fǣst I. '*fast*,' *fixed, firm, secure*, Bo,Lcd; CP : *constant, steadfast*, BH : *stiff, heavy, dense*, Lcd : *obstinate, bound, costive*, Lcd; Æ : *enclosed, closed, watertight*, CP : *strong, fortified*, BH; Æ,AO: *reputable? standard?* (BTs), AO 286⁴. II. (GU 192)=fǣsten

±fǣstan I. *to fasten, make firm, ratify, establish*, LkL : *entrust, commit*. ['*fast*'] II. *to* '*fast*' ('*i-fast*'), *abstain from food*, Bf, Bl,Lcd; CP : *atone for (by fasting)*, DA 592.

fǣste (e) '*fast*,' *firmly, securely*, BH,Bo; Æ : *straitly, strictly* : *heavily (sleep)* : *speedily*.

fǣsten n. I. *fastness, stronghold, fortress*, AO,CP : *cloister*, Æ : *enclosure, prison* : *fastener*. II. (±) *fast (abstinence from food)* Bl,LL,Mt,VPs; CP : *firmament, sky*. ['*fasten*']

fǣstenbryce m. *breach of fast*, LL,W.

fǣstendæg m. *fast-day*, Ct; RB,W. [v. '*fasten*']

fǣstendīc m. *fort-ditch, moat*, KC 1·257'.

fǣstengangol=fǣstgangol

fǣstengeat n. *castle-gate*, JUD 162.

fǣstengeweorc n. *liability for repair of the defences of a town*, KC.

fǣstenlic (ern) *quadragesimal, Lenten*, DR.

fǣstentīd f. *fast*, LL. [v. '*fasten*']

fǣstenwuce f. *week of fasting*, ÆL 23b¹¹¹.

fǣstermōdor=fōstormōdor

fǣstern n. *fast* : *Quadragesima*, LG. [=fǣsten II.]

fǣstern-=fǣsten-

fǣstgangol (o², e³) *steady, faithful*, CRA 80.

fǣsthafol *retentive, tenacious*, Æ : *sparing, miserly*, CP.

fǣsthafolnes f. *economy*, CP 453²⁸ : *stinginess*, DD.

fǣstheald *firmly fixed*, ÆL 23⁴²³.

fǣsthȳdig† *constant, steadfast*.

±fǣstlan (ea) *to commend, entrust, commit*, LkL.

fǣsting f. *commendation, trust, guardianship*, GD 239¹⁵,LL 58,7 : *quartering (of the king's servants)*, KC 2·60'.

fǣstingan=fǣstnian

fǣstingmann m. *a kind of retainer*, EC.

fǣstland (o²) n. *land easily defended*, AA 25⁸.

fǣstlīc *firm, fixed, steadfast, resolute*. adv. -līce *certainly*, AS 32²¹ : (+) *fixedly, steadily, constantly*, Bo : *unceasingly*, Æ,Bl : *verily, but*, NG : *strictly*, CHRD. ['*fastly*']

fǣstmōd *constant in mind*, AO 288¹⁷.

fæstnes f. *firmness, massiveness, stability,* Bo : '*fastness,*' *stronghold, Æ : firmament,* Æ.

fæstnian *to* '*fasten,*' *fix, secure, bind,* An, Ps : *confirm, ratify, conclude* (*peace*), Ct, Ma : *betroth* : *bestow upon, secure for,* VH 11.

±**fæstnung** f. *fastening, bond : strengthening, stability* : *security, safety* : *protection, shelter* : *confirmation, ratification, pledge, engagement* : *exhortation,* MkL p 25.

fæstrǽd *firm, constant, steadfast,* B,Bo ; Æ, CP. ['*fastrede*']

fæstrǽdlic *constant, steadfast,* Bo 20²¹. adv. -lice.

fæstrǽdnes f. *constancy, fortitude,* Bo.

fæststeall *standing firmly,* PPs 121².

fæsð=fæst

fæt n. nap. *fatu vat, vessel, jar, cup,* Æ,B, JnL,WW ; AO,CP : *casket,* El 1026 : *division,* Bf 4²⁶. ['*fat*']

fǽt I.† n. *plate, beaten out metal* (*especially gold*), *gold ornament.* II.=fǽtt I.

±**fǽtan** *to cram, put* (*in*), *load,* CP : *adorn.*

fǽted I.† *ornamented with gold.* [pp. of fǽtan] II.=fǽtt

fǽtedhlēor *with cheek ornaments,* B 1026.

fǽtedsinc n. *beaten gold,* An 478.

fǽtels, fǽtel m. *vessel,* AO,Lcd ; Æ : *pouch, bag, sack,* Æ,CP. ['*fetles*']

fǽtelsian *to put into a vessel,* Lcd 1·328¹⁷.

fǽtelsod=fætelsod

fǽtfyllere (a¹, e²) m. *cupbearer,* GD,TC,WW.

fǽtgold n. *beaten gold,* B 1921.

fǽthengest m. *riding-horse,* Rd 23¹⁴.

fætian=fetian

fǽtnes f. '*fatness,*' Ps ; Æ,CP : *the richest part of anything,* Ps.

+**fǽtnian**=+fǽttian

fǽtt I. (ē) '*fat,*' *fatted,* Æ,AO,Lk,Ps,Rd. II. =fǽted

fǽttian (+) *to become fat,* Ps : (+) *anoint,* Ps : *fatten.* ['*fat*']

+**fǽttig** *fat, rich,* CPs 19⁴.

fǽðe=fēðe

fǽðel *play-actor?* v. OEG 39².

fǽðer=feðer

fæðm (e) m. fæðme f. *outstretched or encircling arms, embrace, grasp,* An,Rd : *protection : interior, bosom, lap, breast, womb* : '*fathom,*' *cubit,* Æ,Cp,WW ; Æ : *power,* B,Cr : *expanse, surface.*

fæðman, fæðmian *to surround, envelop, clasp, embrace,* An,B. ['*fathom*']

fæðmlic *embracing, enclosing, sinuous,* WW 486⁴.

-**fæðmnes** v. on-f.

fæðmrim n. *fathom, cubit,* Ph 29.

fæx=feax

fāg I. *variegated, spotted, dappled, stained, dyed,* B,Gl,Lcd : *shining, gleaming,* Ps. ['*faw*'] II.=fāh I.

fāg-=fāh-; **fāge** f. (WW 94)=facg

fagen, fagen-=fægen, fægn-

fāgettan *to change colour,* Lcd 3·240²³. mid wordum f. *speak evasively.*

fāgetung f. *change* (*of colour*), ÆH 2·538'.

±**fāgian** *to change in colour, vary, be variegated,* RB 137⁸.

fāgnes f. *scab, ulcer, eruption, Æ : variety of colour, brilliancy,* HL,OEG.

fagnian=fægnian

fāgung f. *variety* (*esp. of colour*), DR,GD.

fāgwyrm m. *basilisk,* VPs 90¹³.

fāh I. nap. fā *hostile, B :* (±) *proscribed, outlawed, guilty, criminal,* B. ['*foe*'; fēogan] II. (±) m. '*foe,*' *enemy, party to a bloodfeud,* LL ; Æ,AO. III.=fāg I.

fahame '*polentum,*' WW 40²⁸.

fāhmann m. '*foeman,*' *object of a bloodfeud,* LL 50,5.

fahnian=fægnian

fala I. (WW 52¹¹) ? đ. of *fealh *tube? pipe? plank?* (BTs) (ES 38·337). II.=fela

fālǽcan *to be at enmity with, show hostility to,* LL 160,20⁷.

fal-d, -æd, -od, -ud m. '*fold,*' *stall, stable, cattle-pen,* Gl,Jn,LL.

fald- (N)=feald-

faldgang m. *going to the* (*sheep-*)*fold,* W 170²⁰ᴇ.

faldhrīðer n. *stalled ox,* MFH 158.

faldian *to make a fold, hurdle off sheep,* LL 454,9. ['*fold*']

falew-=feal(e)w-

fall- (VPs; NG)=feall-; **falod**=fald

fals I. '*false,*' WW ; LL,W 272⁴. II. n. *falsehood, fraud, counterfeit.* [L.]

falðing *mass, load,* WW 33⁸.

falu=fealu ; **falud**=fald

fām n. '*foam,*' BH,Ep ; Æ : *sea,* Rd.

fāmbig=fāmig · **-fāmblāwende** v. līg-f.

fāmgian *to foam, boil,* Ex 481.

fāmig (ǣ) '*foamy,*' Rd.

fāmigbord *with foaming banks* (*of a stream*), Met 26²⁶.

fāmigbōsm *with foamy bosom,* Ex 493.

fāmigheals† *foamy-necked.*

fana m. *banner, standard,* Met ; OEG : *plant, iris?* Lcd. ['*fane*']

+**fāna** gp. of +fā.

fanbyrde *standard-bearing,* v. OEG 1744.

fand pret. 3 sg. of findan.

fandere m. *trier, tester,* Sc 206⁴.

±**fandian** (*often w. g., but also d. and a*), *to try, attempt, tempt, test, examine, explore, search out, experience, visit,* AO,B,Gen, Mk,Run ; CP. ['*fand,*' '*fond*'; findan]

fandung f. *investigation, trial, temptation, test, proof, A,Gen*; Æ,CP. ['*fanding*']
fane (1) (NG, o¹)=fann. (2)=fanu
fang m. *plunder, booty, Chr* 1016. ['*fang*']
fangen pp. of fōn.
+fangian *to join, fasten,* Bo 96¹⁴.
fann f. ' *winnowing,* '*fan,*' *Cp,Lk,LL.* [L. vannus]
fannian *to* '*fan,*' *winnow, Sc* 186¹⁷.
fant (o) m. *fount,* '*font,*' *LL* : *baptismal water,* HL 15²⁹³.
fantbæð n. *baptismal water, laver of baptism,* ÆL,W.
fantblētsung f. *consecration of a font,* ÆP 188¹².
fantfæt n. *baptismal font,* ÆH 2·268′.
fanthālgung (o¹) f. *consecration of a font,* W 36².
fanthālig *holy from connection with the font,* LCD 140b.
fantwæter (o¹) n. '*font-water,*' *water used at baptism, laver of baptism,* Lcd; Æ.
fanu=fana
fāra gp. of fāh I.
+fara m. *travelling companion, comrade,* BH,RD.
±faran⁶ *to set forth, go, travel, wander, proceed, Bl,Chr,Gen,JnL;* AO,CP : *be, happen, exist, act, Bo* : '*fare*' ('*i-fare*'), *get on, undergo, suffer,* Æ : (+) *die,* AO,CP : (+) *attack, overcome, capture, obtain,* AO.
farað-=faroð-; **fareld**=færeld
fareð-=faroð-
Fariseisc *of or belonging to the Pharisees,* OEG,WG.
farm=feorm
farnian *to prosper,* DR 176¹³.
faroð† m. *shore : stream.*
faroðhengest (ea¹) m. *sea-horse, ship,* EL 226.
faroðlācende† *swimming, sailing.* as sb. *sailors.*
faroðrīdende *sailing,* AN 440.
faroðstrēt f. *path of the sea,* AN 311,900.
faru f. *way, going, journey, course,* Æ : *expedition, march* : *procession, retinue, companions : life, proceedings, adventures,* Æ : *movable possessions.*
fas-=fæs-; **fatian** (NG)=fetian
fatu v. fæt.
faðe, faðu f. *father's sister, paternal aunt,* Æ.
faðusunu m. *father's sister's son,* CHR 1119.
faul m? *evil spirit,* LCD 43a.
fēa I. (±) m. *joy,* AO,CP. **II.** n.=feoh. **III.** (fēawa) adj. nap. fēawe, superl. fēawost, fēast '*few,*' *B,BH,Chr,Mt,VPs.* fēawum sīðum *seldom.* adv. *even a little, at all.*
feadur (A)=fæder;±**fēagan**(NG,Ps)=±fēon
feah=feoh

±**feaht I.** pret. 3 sg. of feohtan. **II.**=feoht
feal-=fel-
+feald n. *region, abode?* WALD 2¹⁰.
±**fealdan⁷** *to* '*fold,*' *wrap up, furl, entangle,* Æ,Bo,Rd : *roll about,* MkR 9²⁰.
fealdestōl=fyldstōl
feale, fealewes v. fealu.
fealewian=fealwian; **fealfor**=felofor
fealg pret. 3 sg. of fēolan.
fealga v. fealh.
fealgian *to fallow,* LL 454,9 (v. A 36·71).
fealh I. f. nap. fealga, *fallow land.* **II.** (e) f. '*felloe,*' *felly (of a wheel), Bo,WW.* **III.** pret. 3 sg. of fēolan. **IV.** v. fala.
+fēalic *joyous, pleasant.* adv. -līce, W 284¹⁶.
feall=fiell
feallan⁷ (±) *to* '*fall*' ('*i-falle,*' '*y-falle*'), *Bl, Ps* : *fall headlong, fail, decay, die, B,Ps;* AO,CP : *inflict (on), attack : flow,* AO 19¹⁸ : (+) *overthrow,* DR 115⁶ (æ).
fealle f. *snare, trap,* OEG 4979. ['*fall*']
feallen(d)lic *unstable, perishable, transient,* BL,W.
fealletan (a¹) *to fall down,* '*concidere,*' (mistaken for *concidere*), MkLR 5⁵.
-feallung v. feax-f.
+fealnis (æ) f. *ruin,* LkL 2³⁴.
fealo=(1) fealu; (2) fela
fēalōg w. g. *destitute,* Gu 217.
fealohilte *yellow-hilted,* MA 166.
fealu I. (feale) adj. gsm. feal(e)wes, fealuwes '*fallow,*' *yellow, tawny, dun-coloured, grey, dusky, dark, B,Rd;* Æ. **II.** n. *fallow ground,* EC 179′.
fealu-=felo-
fealuwian=fealwian; **fealwes** v. fealu.
fealwian *to become* '*fallow,*' *fade, wither, Sol : grow yellow, ripen.*
fēanes f. '*fewness,*' *paucity, BH,Ps.* [= fēawnes]
+fēanes f. *joy,* GUTH 134,VH 12.
fear=fearr; **fēar**=fearh
fēara gen. of fēa.
fearh m. gs. fēares *little pig, hog, Ep, WW.* ['*farrow*']
fearhhama m. *hide of pig,* WW 161⁵ (IF 48·254).
fearhryðer (e¹) n. *bull,* BL. [fearr]
+fearhsugu f. *sow in farrow,* WW.
fearlic *of a bull,* OEG 11¹⁸⁷
fēarlic=fǣrlic
fearm m. *freight, cargo,* GEN 1394.
fearn n. '*fern,*' *Bo,Cp*; Æ; Mdf.
fearnbed n. *fern-bed,* BC,WW.
fearnbracu f. *fern-brake,* KC 5·173¹⁸.
fearnedisc n. *fern-pasture,* BC 1·519².
fearnhege m. *hedge with ferns,* KC 3·54′.
fearnig *fern-covered,* Ct.
fearnlæs n. *fern-pasture,* KC 2·59¹⁹.

fearoð-=faroð-
fearr I. m. *beast of burden, ox, bull,* Æ,AO.
II. =feorr
feas (VPs)=fæs
fēasceaft† *destitute, miserable, helpless, poor.*
fēasceaftig *destitute, poor,* SEAF 26.
fēasceaftnes (ǣ[1]) f. *poverty,* OEG 1171.
feast-=fæst-
featu (VPs)=fatu nap. of fæt.
fēaw-=fēa-; **fēawa**=fēa
fēawlic *few,* EPs 104[12].
fēawnes f. *fewness, paucity,* LPs 101[24].
feax (æ, e) n. *hair, head of hair,* B,BH,Lcd;
Æ,CP. ['*fax*']
feaxclāð n. *cap,* WW 411[17].
+feaxe *furnished with hair,* BH 96[11].
feaxēacan m. pl. *forelocks,* WW 343[33].
feaxede *hairy, bushy : long-haired (of a
comet),* Chr 892. ['*faxed*']
+feaxen (WE 61[14]?)=+feaxe
feaxfang n. *seizing or dragging by the hair,*
LL 5,33.
feaxfeallung f. *shedding of hair, mange,*
WW 113[30].
feaxhār *hoary, grey-haired,* RD 73[1].
feaxnǣdel f. *crisping-pin,* WW 108[2].
feaxnes (æ, e) f. *head of hair,* WW.
feaxnett n. *hair-net,* WW.
+feaxod=+feaxe
feaxprēon m. *hair-pin,* WW 107[38].
feaxscēara (e[1]) fp. *scissors for hair-cutting?
curling-tongs?* WW 241[41].
feaxwund f. *wound under the hair,* LL 20,45.
feb-=fef-; **fec**=fæc
±feccan (æ) to '*fetch*,' *bring, bring to, draw,*
Æ,Mt : *seek : gain, take.* [=fetian]
fecele=fæcele; **fecgan**=feccan
±fēdan to '*feed*,' *nourish, sustain, foster,
bring up, Bl,Mt,Ps;* Æ,CP : *bear, bring
forth, produce.* pp. +fēd, OEG. [fōda]
fēdednes=fēdnes
fēdelfugol (oe[1]) m. *fatted bird,* MtR 22[4].
fēd-els, -esl m. *feeding, keep : fatted animal
(bird?),* WW; Cp. ['*feddle*']
fēdelsswīn *fattened pig,* NC 343.
feder, federa=fæder, fædera
fēding f. '*feeding*,' CP.
fēdnes (æ) f. *nourishment,* BH 88[6].
fedra=fædera
fēfer mn. gs. fēfres '*fever*,' Lk,G; CP.
fēferādl f. '*fever*,' AO.
fēfercyn n. *a kind of fever,* Lcd 5b.
fēferfūge f. *feverfew,* Lcd,GL. [L. febrifugia]
fēferian *to be feverish, suffer from fever,*
Lcd.
fēferig (o[2]) *feverish,* Lcd 1·334'.
fēfersēoc *feverish,* WW 405[34].
fēfor, fēfur=fēfer
fēfr-=fēfer-

+fēg n. *joining, joint,* Æ : *composition :
diagram,* BF 10[2]. [*Ger.* gefüge]
fēgan I. (±) *to join, unite, fix, adapt,* Lcd,
Rd; Æ,CP : *compose, confine.* ['*fay*'] **II.**
(WW 469[8])=fǣgan?
+fēgednes f. *conjunction, connection : bond,
fetter,* DHy 5[6] : *figure,* ÆGR 105[20].
feger, fegere=fæger, fægre
±fēging f. *conjunction, composition,* ÆGR
10[8].
+fēgnes f. *association, companionship : conjunction,* BF 94[23].
feh=feoh
+feh=+feah pret. 3 sg. of +fēon.
feht *sheepskin with the fleece on it?* TC 119[21];
v. ES 37·177.
+feht=+feoht; **fehtan** (N)=feohtan
fēhð pres. 3 sg. of fōn.
fel=fell; **fēl**=fēol
fela (ea, eo) **I.** sbn. and adj. (w. g., or in
agmt. : rarely inflected) *many, much,* Chr.
II. adv. *very much, many.* ['*FELE*']
felaǣte '*mordax*,' QEG 23[15].
felafǣcne *very treacherous,* GnE 148.
felafeald *manifold, many times over,* Ps.
['*felefold*']
felafealdnes (fele-) f. *multitude,* EPs 5[11].
felafrēcne *very fierce, bold,* RUN 2.
felagēomor *very sad, sorrowful,* B 2950.
felageong *very young,* FT 53.
felageonge *much-travelled,* CREAT 3. [gan-
gan]
felahrōr *full of exploits,* B 27.
felaïdelspræce *emptily chattering,* CP 174[25].
felalēof *very dear,* WIF 26.
felameahtig† *most mighty.*
felamōdig† *very bold,* B.
±fēlan I. (w. g.) *to touch, 'feel'* ('*y-fele*'),
AO : *perceive,* Rd. **II.** (VPs)=fēolan
felaspecol *talkative,* Lcd,Ps.
fela-specolnes, -sprecolnes f. *talkativeness,*
BH,Sc.
felasprǣc (eo) f. *much speaking, loquacity,*
MtR 6[7].
felasprǣce *talkative,* CP 281[14].
felasynnig *very guilty,* B 1379.
felawlonc *very stately,* RD 13[7].
felawyrde *talkative,* W 40[18].
felawyrdnes f. *talkativeness,* GD 208[4].
felcyrf m. *foreskin* (BT).
feld m. ds. felda, felde *open or cultivated
land, plain, Bf,Met,RBL;* AO,CP; Mdf :
battlefield. on clǣnum felda *in the open
field (of battle),* CP 227[25]. ['*field*']
feldælbin (WW 352[10])=feldelfen
feldbēo f. *humble-bee,* WW.
feldbisceopwyrt f. *field-bishopwort,* ANS
84·325.
feldcirice f. *country church,* LL 264,5[1]; 282,3[2].

felde=fylde pret. 3 sg. of fyllan.
feldefare? f. *fieldfare?* WW 287¹⁷ (-ware).
feldelfen f. *wood-nymph*, *WW* 189⁶. [v. *'elven'*]
feldgangende† *roaming over the land*, Sol.
feldhrīðer n. *field-ox*, NC 285 (cp. feldoxa).
feldhūs† n. *tent*, Ex.
feldlǣs (ē²) n. *pasture in open country*, KC.
feldland n. *'field-land,' meadow-land, plain*, Æ.
feldlic *rural*, ÆGR : *growing wild*, ÆH.
feldmǣdere f. *field-madder, rosemary*, Lcd; WW 300¹⁰. [v. *'field'*]
feldminte f. *field-mint, wild mint*, WW.
feld-more, -meru f. *parsnip*, Lcd.
feldoxa f. *field-ox* (i.e. an ox out to grass, not a stalled ox), ÆH 2·576'.
feldrude f. *wild rue*, Lcd 3·325.
feldsǣten f. *field*, LPs 77¹². [seten]
feldswamm m. *fungus, toadstool*, WW 404²⁶.
feldwēsten n. *desert*, Deut 1¹.
feldwōp m. *plantain*, Gl (?=*feldhoppe, ANS 119·435; FM 200) : *peewit?* (BTs).
feldwyrt f. *gentian*, Lcd.
+fēle *sensitive*, Lcd.
fele-=felo-
felefeald=felafeald
fēlelēas *insensible, dead*, Wy 40.
felg(e) f. *'felloe,' rim of a wheel*, Bo. [fēolan]
felge-role, -roðe *'polipodium,'* A 24·432 (v. MLN 23·186).
felh=fealh pret. 3 sg. of fēolan.
felhð (KGL)=fylgð pres. 3 sg. of fylgan.
feligean=fylgan
fell I. n. *'fell,' skin, hide*, B,Jul,Lcd; Æ,AO, CP : *garment of skin*, Chrd 64³³. [L. pellis] II. m.=fiell
fell-=fyll-
fellen (i¹) *made of skins*, Æ.
fellerēad (ēo³ ; =*pællerēad? ES 43·31) *purple*, NG.
fellstycce n. *piece of skin*, Lcd 1·330⁵.
fēllun=fēollon pret. pl. of feallan.
-felma v. æger-f.; **felmen-**=fylmen-
±fēlnes f. *sensation, feeling*, Æ.
felo-=fela-
felofe(o)rð (eo¹, e², u², ea³) *stomach, maw* (*of an animal*), Lcd,Gl.
felofor (ea¹, eo¹, u², e³) m. *bittern*, Gl.
fēlon (A)=fulgon pret. pl. of fēolan.
+fēlsian=+fælsian
felst pres. 2 sg. of feallan.
felt m? n? *'felt,' WW*.
felt-ere, -erre *a plant*, Lcd.
feltūn m. *privy, dunghill*, CP. [=feld-]
feltūngrēp f. *dunghill*, NC 285.
feltwurma m. *wild marjoram*, Lcd.
feltwyrt f. *mullein (plant)*, ÆGR, Lcd.

felð=fielð pres. 3 sg. of feallan; **fēlð**=fyʒlð
felða (Cp 128 s) rare gp. of feld.
felu-=felo-; **fēm-**, fēmn- (VPs)=fǣmn-
fen=fenn
fenampre (o²) f. *a marsh plant*, Lcd 38b.
fencerse f. *water-cress*, Lcd. [v. *'fen'*]
fenester n? m? *window*, GD 220. [L.]
fenfearn n. *marsh-fern, 'salvia,' water-fern*, WW 135⁴.
fenfisc m. *fen-fish*, Lcd 95b (n.).
fenfreoðo f. *fen-refuge*, B 851.
fenfugol m. *moor-fowl*, Lcd 95b?
±feng m. *grip, grasp, embrace : capture : prey, booty*. [fōn]
fēng pret. 3 sg. of fōn.
fengel† m. *lord, prince, king*, B.
fengelād n. *marsh-path, fen*, B 1359.
fengnes f. *'susceptio,'* CPs 82² (? for and-f.).
fengnett n. *(catching-)net*, PPs 140¹².
fengon pret. pl. of fōn.
fengtōð (æ) m. *canine tooth*, LL 81 n16.
fenhleoðu np. *fen-coverts*, B 820. [hlið]
fenhop n. *fen-hollow*, B 764.
fenix m. *the bird 'phœnix,'* ÆGr,Ph : *date-palm*.
fenland n. *fen-land, marsh*, Æ,AO.
fenlic *marshy*, Æ,Guth. [*'fenlich'*]
fenminte f. *water-mint*, Lcd 14b.
fenn nm. *mud, mire, dirt*, CP,WW : *'fen,' marsh, moor*, B,Bo; AO : *the fen country*, Chr 905.
fenn-=fen-
fennig I. *marshy*, WW : *muddy, dirty*, CP. [*'fenny'*] II.=fynig
fennðæc n. *covering of thatch from a fen*, OET (Bd²).
fenol=finul; **fenompre**=fenampre
fenȳce f. *snail?* OET,WW : *tortoise?* RD 41⁷¹.
fēo=feoh; also ds. of feoh.
fēode pret. 3 sg. of fēogan.
+fēogan (fīa, N; fēon) *to hate, persecute*, LG. [*'ivee'*]
feogað *hatred*, MtR.
fēogȳtsung (BH 130³⁴)=feohgītsung
feoh n. gs. fēos, ds. fēo *cattle, herd*, LL,Sol; AO : *movable goods, property*, Bo,Ps; AO : *money, riches, treasure*, B,BH,Mt,OET; Æ,CP. *wið licgendum fēo for ready money*, ÆL 9⁶⁴ : *name of the rune for f*. [*'fee'*]
feohbehāt n. *promise of money*, Chr 865 E.
feohbīgenga m. *cattle-keeper*, AA 28².
feohbōt f. *money compensation*, LL 46 n5; 258,51.
feohfang n. *offence of taking a bribe*, LL 318,15¹.
feohgafol n. *usury*, Chrd 76³².
feohgehāt n. *promise of money*, Chr 865 A.
feohgeorn *covetous, greedy*, LL,RWH.

feohgerêfa m. *steward*, LkLR 12⁴².
feohgesceot n. *payment of money*, BK 28, 29.
feohgesteald n. *possession of riches*, JUL 685.
feohgestrēon n. *treasure, possessions, riches*, CHRD,W.
feoh-gīdsere, -gīetsere (CP)=feohgītsere
feohgīfre *avaricious*, WA 68.
feohgift† f. *bounty-giving, largess*.
feohgītsere m. *miser*, Bo,MET.
feohgītsung f. *avarice*, CP 1496.
feohgōd n. *property (in cattle)*, LL 60 n 1.
feohgyrnes (=eo²) f. *greed*, LL 396,4.
feohhūs n. *treasure-house*, WW.
feohlǣnung f. *lending of money*, WW 115⁴⁵.
feohland n. *pasture*, PPs.
feohlēas *without money* : *not to be bought off, past compensation*, B 2441.
feohlēasnes f. *want of money*, Swt.
feohsceatt n. *money-payment*, DA 744.
feohspēda fp. *riches*, GD 273².
feohspilling f. *waste of money*, CHR 1096.
feohstrang *well off*, GL.
±feoht (i, o, y) n. *action of fighting*, B,Ps : 'fight,' battle, AO : strife, Mod.
±feohtan³ (e) *to fight, combat, strive*, Chr, Lk,Rd,LL; Æ,AO,CP. : (+)*gain by fighting, win*. on f. *attack, fight against*.
+feohtdæg m. *day of battle*, PPs 139⁷.
feohte f.=feoht
feohtehorn (y¹) m. *battle-horn*, PPs 74⁹.
feohtend m. *fighter*, OEG 3805.
feohtere m. *fighter*, ES 39³²⁶.
feohtgegyrela m. 'falarica,' WW 399³⁰.
feohtlāc n. *fighting*, LL. ['fightlac']
feohtling (y¹) m. *fighter*, GD 110¹³; MP 1·610.
+feohtsumnes f. *joyfulness*, NC 292. [+fēon]
feohtwīte (i¹, y¹, ȳ²) n. *penalty for fighting*, LL.
feohwīte n. *fine for coining false money*, LL 319 col. 2.
fēol pret. 3 sg. of feallan.
fēol (ē, ī) f. 'file,' Cp,Rd; ÆL.
feola=fela
fēolaga m. *partner*, 'fellow,' Chr 1016 D. [ON. fēlagi]
fēolagscipe m. *fellowship*, TC.
±fēolan³ (ē) *to cleave, be joined to, adhere* : *enter, penetrate, pass into, through or over, betake oneself to*, CHR : *undergo* : *persevere in*. [Goth. filhan]
fēold pret. 3 sg. of fealdan.
feolde=folde
fēoldon pret. pl. of fealdan.
fēolheard *hard as a file? hard enough to resist the file? file-hardened?* MA 108 (or ?=*felaheard).
fēolian *to file*, ÆL 32²⁰³.

fēoll pret. 3 sg., fēollon pret. pl. of feallan.
feologan *to become discoloured?* LCD 125b.
feolu=fela; **feolu-fer**, -ferð, -for=felofor
feon=fenn
fēon I. (±, usu. +) sv⁵ w. in or g. *to be glad, rejoice, exult*, CP. II. (ēa) *to gain*, MtL 16²⁶. III.=fēogan
fēond (īe, ȳ) m. ds. fīend, fēonde, nap. fiend, fēond *adversary, foe, enemy*, B,Bf,Mt; AO,CP [f.=female enemy] : 'fiend,' devil, Gu; CP : the Devil, Lcd,Hy. [pres. ptc. of fēogan]
fēondǣt m. *eating things sacrificed to idols*, PPs 105²⁴.
fēondgrāp f. *grip of a foe*, B 636.
fēondgyld n. *idolatry, idol*, GD,PPs : *demoniacal possession?* MtL 4²⁴.
fēondlic *hateful, hostile, fiendish*, WW; Æ. adv. -līce, Jul. ['fiendly']
fēondrǣden f. *enmity*, Æ.
fēondrǣs m. *hostile attack*, GEN 900.
fēondsceaða† m. *enemy, robber*.
fēondscipe m. *hostility, hatred*, AO,CP.
fēondsēoc *devil-possessed, demoniac*, BH 184⁵.
fēondulf m. *public enemy, criminal, malefactor*, GPH 396. [fēond, wulf]
fēong=fēoung; **feonn**=fenn
feor=feorr; **fēor**=feorh, fēower
fēora gp. of feorh.
+fēora=+fēra
feorbūend *dwelling far off*, B 254.
feor-cumen, -cund=feorran-cumen, -cund
feorcȳðð f. *distant land*, B 1838.
feord, feord-=fierd, fierd-, fyrd-
fēores gs. of feorh; **feorg**=feorh
feorh (e) mn. gs. fēores, nap. feorh *life, principle of life, soul, spirit*, AO,CP. tō wīdan fēore *for eternity, for ever*. f. gesellan, āgiefan *to die* : *living being, person*.
feorhādl f. *fatal disease*, Æ.
feorhbana† m. *man-slayer*, GL.
feorhbealu† n. *deadly evil, violent death*, B.
feorhbenn f. *deadly wound*, B 2740.
feorhberend† m. *living being*.
feorhbold n. *body*, ROOD 73.
feorhbona=feorhbana
feorhbora m. *life-bearer*, RD 92².
feorhcwalu† (e) f. *slaughter, death*, GL.
feorhcwealm† m. *slaughter, death*, GEN.
feorhcynn† n. *race of mortals*, B.
feorhdagas mp. *days of life*, GEN 2358.
feorhdolg n. *deadly wound*, CR 1455.
feorhēacen *living*, GEN 204.
feorhfægen *fain of life, glad to preserve one's life*, ÆL 23³⁰⁹.
feorhgebeorh n. *refuge*, EX 369.
feorhgedāl† n. *death*.

feorhgener n. *preservation of life*, LL 204,7³.

feorhgenīðla† m. *mortal foe*, B.

feorhgiefa† m. *giver of life*.

feorhgiefu f. *gift of life*, RIM 6?

feorh-gōme? f. *means of subsistence*, or -gōma? m. *jaw*. CR 1547.

feorhhord† n. *breast, soul, spirit*.

feorhhūs n. *soul-house, body*, MA 297.

feorhhyrde m. *life's guardian, protector*, BH.

feorhlāst m. *step taken to preserve life, flight? step stained by one's life-blood?* (BTs), *track of vanishing life?* (Klb), B 846.

feorhlēan n. *revenge for bloodshed? gift for life saved?* (BTs), EX 150.

feorhlegu† f. *death*, B, EL.

feorhlic (fera-, ferh-) *vital*, HGL 453.

feorhlīf n. *life*, PPs 142².

feorhloca m. *breast*, GU 625.

feorhlyre m. *loss of life*, LL 466,3.

feorhneru f. *preservation of life, refuge, salvation : nourishment of life, food*.

feorhrǣd m. *salvation*, AN 1656.

feorhscyldig *guilty of death*, LL.

feorhsēoc *mortally wounded*, B 820.

feorhsweng m. *fatal blow*, B 2489.

feorhðearf f. *urgent need*, PPs 69¹.

feorhwund f. *deadly wound*, B 2385.

feorland (o²) n. *distant land*, PA 10.

feorlen=fyrlen

feorlic *far off, alien, strange*, RWH 137'.

feorm (a, æ, o, y) f. *food, provision, sustenance : entertainment, meal, feast, supper*, Æ, AO, CP : *goods, possessions : stores : rent in kind*, EC : *profit, benefit*, CP : *tilling*, LL 454,8.

feorma=forma

feormehām m. *farm*, CHR 1087.

feormend I. m. *entertainer*, WY 30. II. *cleanser, polisher, furbisher*, B 2256.

feormendlēas *wanting a burnisher*, B 2761.

feormere m. *purveyor*, KC 4·278²¹.

feormfultum m. *help in food*, LL 356,69¹.

±**feormian** I. *to entertain, receive as guest : cherish, support, sustain, feed : consume : benefit, profit :* (+) *harbour (stolen goods)*, LL 108,4⁶. II. *to scour, cleanse, furbish*, Lk. ['farm']

feormung f. I. *harbouring*, LL. II. *furbishing, cleansing*, LL.

feornes f. *distance*, BH 72¹⁰.

feorr I. comp. fi(e)rra, fyrra; sup. fierresta 'far,' *remote, distant*, Wif ; CP. II. adv. comp. fierr, firr, fyr(r); sup. fi(e)rrest, fyrrest 'far,' *far away, distant, remote*, BH, Cr, RBL, VPs ; CP : *far back (in time) : further, besides, moreover*.

feorran I. adv. *from afar, from a remote time or place*, B, El, Gen : *far off, at a distance*, Bo ; Æ, CP. ['ferren'] II. (æ, y) *to remove, avert, turn aside, withdraw*, B : *proscribe*. ['far']

feorrancumen *come from afar, strange*, LL.

feorrancund (B), feorrcund (LL) *come from afar, foreign born*.

feorrane, feorren(e)=feorran I.

feorrian (ea) *to keep apart*, Æ : (±) *depart*, NG.

feorrung f. *removal, departure*, GD 49¹⁶.

feorsian (y) *to go beyond : put far from, expel : depart, remove, separate*, Ps. ['ferse']

feorsibb *distantly related*, LL 346,51.

feorsn=fiersn

feor-stuðu, -studu (e¹) f. *support*, WW.

feorting f. '*pedatio*,' WW 162⁴².

feorð=ferhð

fēorða (ēa, N) '*fourth*,' Lk, MkL ; AO, CP. fēorðe healf *three and a half*.

feorðandǣl *fourth part*, Æ.

feorðe *fourthly*, LL 158,15.

feorðēod *a far country*, WYN 186.

fēorð-ling, -ung m. *fourth part :* '*farthing*,' MkL, LkL ; Æ. ['ferling']

fēorum dp. of feorh.

feorweg† m. *remote part*.

feorwit=fyrwit

fēos gs. of feoh.

feostnode (CHR 963 E)=fæstnode pret. 3 sg. of fæstnian.

feot-=fet-

fēoð pres. 3 sg. of fēogan.

fēoðer-, fēoðor-=fēower-, fiðer-

fēoung f. *hatred*, CP. [fēogan]

feow-, fēower- v. also fiðer-.

fēower, fēowere [indecl. before a sb. but when alone, usu. g. fēow(e)ra, d. fēowerum] '*four*,' Cr ; Æ, AO, CP : *four times*.

fēowerdōgor mn. and adj. *four days*, JnR 11³⁹.

fēowerecg(ed)e *four-cornered, square*, LCD.

fēowerfeald *four-fold*, Lk 19⁸.

fēowerfealdlīce *quadruply*, BL.

fēowerfēte *four-footed*, AO ; Æ. ['four-foot']

fēower-fōte (BH), -fōtede (HL) *four-footed*.

fēowergild n. *four-fold compensation*, LL 228'.

fēowerhwēolod (fȳr-) *four-wheeled*, RHy 4¹⁹ (v. ES 38·15).

fēowernihte *four days old*, BH 392¹².

fēowerscȳte *four-cornered, square*, AO. [scēat]

fēowertēme (fēoður-) *four-teamed*, VHy 6³⁴.

fēower-tēoða, -tēogða '*fourteenth*,' BH, MH ; AO.

fēowertīene (ē³, ȳ³) '*fourteen*,' MtL ; AO.

fēowertīeneniht (ȳ) *fortnight, LL.* [v. '*fourteen*']

fēowertīenewintre (ȳ) *fourteen years old, LL.*

fēowertig '*forty,*' *MtL*; AO.

fēowertigfeald *forty-fold,* Æ,WW.

fēowertiggēare adj. *of forty years,* ÆL3⁴⁶⁹.

fēowertiglic *quadragesimal,* BH.

fēowertigoða '*fortieth,*' Æ (-tēoða; in error).

fēowertȳne=fēowertīene

fēowerða (*Mt*)=fēorða

fēowerwintre *four years old,* ÆGR287¹⁹.

fēowr-=fēower-, fēor-

fēowra v. fēower.

±**fēowung** f. *rejoicing, joy,* OEG1118. [+fēon]

fēowur-=fēower-; **fer**=fær

fer-=fær-, fear-, fier-, feor-, for-, fyr-

fēr=(1) fær I.; (2) fēfer; **fēr-**=fǣr-, fȳr-

+**fēra** (fera in A only) m. *associate, comrade, fellow-disciple,* Æ,G,OET; AO,CP : *wife : man, servant,* v. LL2·427f. ['*fere,*' '*y-fere*']

fēran *to go, come, depart, set out, march, travel,* B,*JnL* (oe); CP : *behave, act* : (+) *accomplish, attain, obtain* : (+) *fare, speed, undergo, suffer : bring,* MkR1³². ['*fere*']

fērbedd n. *portable bed, litter,* WW154⁴.

fērblǣd=færblǣd

fercian (ē?) *to convey, bring, Chr : support,* ÆL23⁵⁹⁷ : *stuff up (with lies),* ÆL23⁷¹³ : *proceed,* BF68²⁹. ['*ferk, firk*']

fercung f. *sustenance, provision, food,* Æ (9¹⁷²), CHRD.

ferdwyrt ? *a plant* (or ?=feld-), LCD57b.

fēre *able to go, fit for (military) service,* CHR.

+**fēre** I. n. *company, community.* II. m. *companion.* III. *accessible,* PH4. [faran]

+**fēred** *associated,* WW216¹³.

ferele f. *rod,* GD. [*L.* ferula]

fērend† m. *sailor,* WH : *messenger,* JUL.

fērende *mobile,* GD.

feresceat m. *passage-money,* WW34³.

feresōca? '*sibba,*' WW277²³.

fereð pres. 3 sg. of (1) faran, (2) ferian.

fēreð pres. 3 sg. of fēran.

fergan=ferian

fergenberig (N)=firgenbeorg

ferht I. (=eo) *honest,* GL. II.=ferhð

ferhtlic (=eo) *just, honest,* PPs95¹⁰.

ferhð I.† (ferð) mn. *mind, intellect, soul, spirit : life : person,* SEAF26. **wīdan** f. *eternally, for ever.* II.=fyrhð

ferhðbana m. *murderer,* EX399.

ferhðcearig *of anxious mind,* GEN2217.

ferhð-cleofa, -cofa† m. *breast.*

ferhðfrec *bold, brave,* B1146.

ferhðfriðende (rð) *sustaining life,* RD39³.

ferhðgenīðla m. *mortal enemy,* B2881.

ferhðgewit (rð) n. *understanding,* CR1184.

ferhðglēaw† *wise, prudent.*

ferhðgrim (rð)† *savage,* JUL,WA.

ferhðloca† m. *breast, body.*

ferhðlufu (y) f. *heartfelt love,* AN83.

ferhðsefa† (i, y) m. *mind, thought,* EL.

ferhðwērig† *soul-weary, sad.*

±**ferian** *to carry, convey, bring,* An,B,El; Æ : (with refl. a.) *betake oneself to, be versed in : depart, go,* MA. ['*ferry*']

feri(g)end m. *leader, bringer,* SOL80.

fering f. *vehicle,* GD.

+**fērlǣcan** (ē²) *to associate, unite,* Æ.

+**fērlic** *associated.* adv. -līce *sociably, together;* -līðlīce GD313²⁴.

±**fērnes** f. *passage, transition, passing away,* BL163¹² (v. BTs).

+**fērrǣden** (usu. +) f. *companionship, fellowship,* Æ,AO,CP : *friendship : society, fraternity, congregation,* Æ.

fers nm. *verse,* Æ : *sentence,* Æ. [*L.*]

fersc '*fresh*' (*not salt*), AO : *not salted,* KC.

-ferscan v. ā-f.

fersceta m. *freshet,* A20·382.

±**fērscipe** m. *fraternity, community, retinue : order, clan : society, fellowship, companionship,* CP : *wedlock,* OEG2544.

+**fērscipian** *to accompany,* DR.

fersian *to versify,* ÆGR218³.

ferð=ferhð

ferðan=furðum

ferðe m. *skin, hide?* LCD8b.

ferwett-=fyrwit-

fēsan, fēsian=fȳsan, fȳsian

fest=fæst; **fēst**=fȳst; **fēster-**=fōstor-

fēstermenn mp. *bondsmen,* BC,LL.

fēstrian=fōstrian

fet pres. 3 sg. of fetian.

fēt I. pres. 3 sg. of fēdan. II. ds. and nap. of fōt.

+**fetan⁴** *to fall,* MtR13⁷,⁸. (v. FTP225).

fetel, fetels m. *belt,* Bo,Met. ['*fettle*']

fetelhilt n. *belted or ringed sword-hilt,* B1563.

fētels=fǣtels

±**fetelsod** *provided with a sheath?* BC3·215².

feter=fetor

+**feterian†** *to fetter, bind.*

±**fetian** (æ) *to bring near, fetch, obtain,* AO, B,Gen,Sol : *bring on, induce,* Pr : *marry.* ['*fet,*' '*y-fet*']

fetor (eo¹, e²) f. '*fetter,*' *shackle,* Cp,MkL, Ps : *check, restrain,* WA.

fetorwrāsen f. *fetter, chain,* AN1109.

+**fetran,** +fetrian=+feterian

fētt I. pres. 3 sg. of fēdan. II.=fǣtt

fettan=fetian

fette pret. 3 sg. of fetian.

fēð=fēhð pres. 3 sg. of fōn.

fēða m. *foot-man, foot-soldier,* AO : *band of foot-soldiers, troop,* Æ.

fēðan *to go on foot?* Æ (116⁴⁴⁹).
fēðe n. *power of locomotion, walking, gait, pace,* Æ,AO.
fēðecampa† m. *foot-soldier,* B.
fēðegang m. *journey on foot,* GEN 2513.
fēðegeorn *anxious to go,* RD 32⁹.
fēðegest† m. *guest coming on foot, traveller.*
fēðehere m. *infantry,* AO.
fēðehwearf m. *band of footmen,* GU 162.
fēðelāst† m. *step, track, course.*
fēðelēas† *footless, crippled.*
fēðemann m. *pedestrian,* LRG,WW 481³ : *foot-soldier,* WW 399²⁷.
fēðemund f. *fore-paw,* RD 16¹⁷.
feðer (æ) f. nap. feð(e)ra, feð(e)re '*feather,*' *Lcd,Ph;* pl. *wings, Bo,Mt,OET;* CP : *pen, Lk;* CP.
feðer-=fēower-, fiðer-; feðeran=fiðerian
feðerbǣre *having feathers, winged,* GPH 390.
feðerbedd n. '*feather-bed,*' WW 124¹⁹.
feðerberend m. *feathered creature,* WW 465²⁰. [v. '*feather*']
feðercræft m. *embroidery,* WW 491³.
feðergearwe fp. *feathers of the arrow,* B 3119.
feðergeweorc n. *feather-embroidery,* WW 459²⁷.
feðerhama m. *wings, plumage, Cp,Gen.* ['*featherham*']
fēðespēdig *speedy of foot,* CRA 53.
fēðewīg† m. *battle on foot, affray.*
feðm=fæðm
feðorbyrste *split into four,* LCD 148a.
feðra, feðre v. feðer.
fēðre *loaded,* A2·373.
feðrian *to become fledged,* OEG 26²⁷.
+fēðrian *to load,* AS 1¹⁰. [fōðor]
feðriht *feathered,* MtL p 7¹⁷.
fēðu (WW 110²⁹)=fēða
fēðung f. *walking, motion,* ÆH 2·134.
fex=feax
fiag- (N)=fēog-; fibulae (GL)=fīfele
+fic n. *deceit,* EL,RB [v. '*fickle*']
fīc m. *fig, fig-tree, MtR : (fig-disease), venereal ulcer, hemorrhoids,* LCD. ['*fike*'; *L.* ficus]
fīcādl f. *fig-disease* (v. fīc), LCD.
fīcæppel m. *fig,* Æ,GL.
fīcbēam m. *fig-tree,* Æ,CP.
fician *to flatter,* AB 34·10.
fīclēaf n. *fig-leaf,* GEN 3⁷.
fīcol '*fickle,' cunning, tricky,* KGl; W.
fīctrēow n. *fig-tree,* G.
ficung f. *fraud, trickery,* LL 242,24; 254, 28³.
fīcwyrm m. *intestinal worm,* LCD 122a.
fīcwyrt f. *fig-wort,* WW 134³².
fieftiene=fīftiene
fieht pres. 3 sg. of feohtan.

±fiell (æ, e, ea, y) mn. *fall, destruction,* AO, CP : *death, slaughter : precipice : case, inflection,* ÆGR 91¹⁴. [feallan] For comps. v. fyll-.
fielt pres. 3 sg. of fealdan.
fielð pres. 3 sg. of feallan.
fiend=fēond, also ds. of fēond.
+fīend (ȳ) mp. *foes, enemies, Lk;* AO. ['*i-feond*']
fiendwīc n. *enemy's camp,* LPs 77²⁸.
fier v. feorr II.; fier-=fēower-
fierd (æ, e, eo, y) f. *national levy or army, Chr : military expedition, campaign, Ma, PPs;* AO : *camp.* ['*ferd*'] For comps. v. fyrd-.
fieren-=firen-; fierfēte=fēowerfēte
-fierme (eo) v. or-f.
fierra, fierrest, fierresta v. feorr II.
fiersn (e, eo, y) f. *heel,* GEN,WW. [*Ger.* ferse]
fierst=first
fīf usu. indecl. before sb.; but when alone, has na. fife, g. fīfa, d. fīfum '*five,*' *Bf,G, Gen.*
fīfalde f. *butterfly,* GL. [*Ger.* falter]
fīfbēc fp. *Pentateuch,* WW 470⁸.
fīfe v. fīf.
fīfecgede *having five angles,* ÆGR 289¹⁵.
fīfel n. *(huge) sea-monster, giant,* WALD 2¹⁰.
fīfelcynn n. *race of sea-monsters,* B 104.
fīfeldōr n. *door of sea-monsters, river Eider,* WID 43.
fīfele f. *buckle,* WW 403⁷. [*L.* '*fibula*']
fīfelstrēam m. *ocean, sea,* MET 26²⁶.
fīfelwǣg m. *ocean, sea,* EL 237.
fīffalde=fīfalde
fīffeald '*five-fold,*' *ÆGr : five each,* CM 840.
fīffētede *five-footed (verse),* OEG 130.
fīffingre f. '*potentilla,' 'primula,' cinquefoil, oxlip?* Lcd. ['*fivefinger*']
fīfflēre *five-storied,* Æ. [flōr]
fīfgēar n. *period of five years, lustrum,* WW 431¹⁶.
fīfhund(red) num. *five hundred,* EL,GL.
fīflæppede *having five lobes,* LCD 59b.
fīf-lēaf n., -lēafe f. '*potentilla,' cinquefoil,* Lcd. ['*fiveleaf*']
fīfmægen n. *magic power,* SOL 136. [fifel]
fīfnihte *five days old,* ANS 129·22.
fīfta '*fifth,' Æ,Chr,Lcd;* AO,CP.
fīftafæder v. fæder.
fīfte *fifthly,* LL 158,16.
fīfteg=fīftig; fīftegōða=fīftēoða
fīftēne=fīftiene
fīfteogoða (i²) '*fiftieth,*' *ÆGr;* CP.
fīf-tēoða (ȳ¹), tēða, -tegða '*fifteenth,*' BH, Lcd.

fīftīene (ȳ[1], ē[2], ȳ[2]) (often w. g.) *'fifteen,'* B,Bf,Gu; AO.
fīftīenenihte *fifteen days old,* LCD 3·180.
fīftīenewintre (e[2]) *fifteen years old,* BL 213[1].
fīftig num. *'fifty,'* ÆB : sb. *a set of fifty,* Mk.
Fīftigdæg m. *Pentecost,* MkL p 5[10].
fīfti(g)esman m. *captain of fifty,* Ex 18[21], DEUT 1[15].
fīftigeōa, fīftigoōa=fīfteogoōa
fīftigfeald *'fifty-fold,' containing fifty,* Æ.
fīftigwintre *fifty years old,* Jn 8[57].
fīftȳne (Æ)=fīftīene
fīfwintre *five years old,* ÆGR 287[14].
-fīgen v. ā-f.
+fīgo ? np. *a disease, 'cimosis'* (? +fligo, v. BTac), LCD 1a, 14a.
fīhl, fihle m? *cloth, rag,* NG. [?=fliht]
fiht I. pres. 3 sg. of feohtan. **II.**=feht
fiht-=fyht-; **fihtan**=fȳhtan
+fīhō pres. 3 sg. of +fēon.
fil (GL)=fēol
+fīlan=+fȳlan; **+fīlce**=+fylce
fild sb. *curdled milk,* LCD 53b (LF130).
fildcumb m. *milk-pail,* LCD 122b.
filde *field-like, of the nature of a plain,* AO 74[12].
+filde n. *field, plain,* AO 12[10]. [feld]
fileōe n. *hay,* PPs 36[2].
filgō, filhō pres. 3 sg. of fēolan.
fili-=fylg-
filiende ptc. *rubbing,* WW 407[36].
filiōe=fileōe
filiōlēag m. *meadow,* Ct.
fill=fyll
fille f. *thyme,* LCD,OEG 56[38]. [=cerfille?]
fillen I.=fellen **II.** (?) f. *a dropping,* LCD 18a (fyln).
filmen (y) n. *'film,' membrane, thin skin,* Lcd; Æ : *foreskin,* Æ.
filst-=fylst-
filō pres. 3 sg. of feallan.
fin f. *heap, pile.* v. OEG 2456.
fin-=fyn-
fina m. *woodpecker,* WW 49[2].
finc m. *'finch,'* Ep,WW.
find=fiend
findan[3] (but occl. wk. pret. funde) (±) *to 'find' ('y-find,' 'y-found'), meet with,* B, BH,Gen,Jul,LG,Met : *discover, obtain by search or study, recover,* Cr,MtL,Ps : *provide : consider, devise, arrange, dispose, decide,* AO,CP : *show, inform.* f. *æt obtain from.*
findend m. *finder,* GPH 391.
+findig (y) *capable,* ÆGR 69[4].
finding f. *invention, initiative,* CM 1082.
finel=finol
finger m. *'finger,'* Bf,MtL,VPs; Æ,CP.

finger-æppla, -appla npl. *finger-shaped fruits, dates,* ÆL,OEG.
fingerdocca? m? *finger-muscle,* GL.
fingerlic *belonging to a finger or ring,* WW 291[26].
fingerliō n. *finger-joint,* NC 343.
fingermæl n. *finger's length,* NR 22[8].
finn m. *'fin,'* Æ.
finol (e[1], u[2], y[2]) m. *'fennel,'* Ep,WW. [L. foenuculum]
finolsæd n. *fennel-seed,* LCD 157a.
finst=findest pres. 2 sg. of findan.
fint pres. 3 sg. of findan.
finta† m. *tail : consequence, result.*
finu(g)l m., finu(g)le f.=finol
fīo=fēo; **fīr**=fȳr
fīras† mp. *men, human beings.*
fird=fierd; **fird-**=fierd-, fyrd-
firen f. *transgression, sin, crime : outrage, violence : torment, suffering.*
firenbealu n. *transgression,* CR 1276.
firencræft m. *wickedness,* JUL 14.
firendæd† f. *wicked deed, crime.*
firenearfeōe n. *sinful woe,* GEN 709.
firenfremmende *sinful,* CR 1118.
firenful (y) *sinful, wicked,* Æ.
firengeorn *sinful,* CR 1606.
firenhicga (y[1], y[2]) m. *adulterer,* GPH 389.
firenhicge (fyrn-) f. *adulteress,* OEG.
firenhicgend (fyrn-) *adulteress, harlot,* OEG.
±firenian (y) *to sin : commit adultery : revile.*
firenleahter (y[1]) m. *great sin,* ÆH 2·420[16].
firenlic (y) *wicked.* adv. -līce *vehemently, rashly,* WALD 1[20] : *sinfully.*
firenligerian *to commit fornication,* RSPs 105[39].
firenlust m. *lust, sinful desire, luxury, wantonness,* AO,CP.
firenlustful *wanton, luxurious,* A 12·502[10].
firenlustgeorn *wanton,* W 253[5].
firensynn f. *great sin,* JUL 347.
firensynnig *sinful,* CR 1379.
firentācnian (y) *to commit misdeeds,* RHy 6[21].
firenōearf (y) f. *dire distress,* B 14.
firenōēof (i[2], ēa[2]) m. *robber,* DR.
firenum *excessively, very, intensely : malignantly.* [dp. of firen]
firenweorc† n. *evil deed, sin,* CR.
firenwyrcende† *sinning, sinful,* PPs.
firenwyrhta (y)† m. *evil-doer,* PPs.
firfoda=fȳrfoda
firgenbēam (y) m. *mountain tree,* B 1414. [Goth. fairguni]
firgenbeorg (fergenberig) *mountain,* RUNE-CASKET (v. FM 368).
firgenbucca m. *ibex,* LCD.

firgendstrēam=firgenstrēam

firgen-gāt f. nap. -gǣt *ibex*, GL.

firgenholt n. *mountain-wood*, B 1393.

firgenstrēam† m. *mountain-stream, woodland-stream*.

firgin-=firgen-; **fīrh**=fyrh

fīrht=friht; **fīrhð**=ferhð

firigendstrēam=firgenstrēam

firinggāt=firgengāt; **firmdig**=frymdig

firmettan *to ask, beg*, AO 186⁶.

fīrn-=firen-, fyrn-

fīrr, firra, firre, firrest v. feorr.

first I. (e, ie, y) mn. *period, space of time, time, respite, truce*, B,Chr; CP. ['*frist*']
II. (ie) f. *ceiling, (inner) roof*, WW : *ridgepole*. ['*first*'] III.=fyrst

firsthrōf n. *ceiling, ridge-pole*, OEG 2812.

first-mearc, -gemearc fm. *period of time, appointed time, interval, respite*.

fīrð-=fyrð-; **firwet**=fyrwit

fisc m. '*fish*,' VPs; Æ,AO,CP; Mdf.

fisc-að, -(n)oð m. *fishing*, AO : *fishpond* : *a catch of fish* : *fishing rights*. [v. NC 286]

fiscbrȳne m. *fish-brine*, WW 128³⁹. [v.'*fish*']

fisccynn n. *fish tribe*, ÆT.

fiscdēah f. *fish-dye, purple*, OEG 5193.

fiscere m. '*fisher*,' *fisherman*, AO,Mt : *kingfisher (bird)*.

fiscfell (NG)=fiscpōl

fiscflōdu? m. *fish-flood, sea*, OET 127⁴.

fischūs n. *place where fish is sold*, WW 184⁴⁰.

fiscian *to '*fish*,'* Bo.

fisclacu f. *fishpond or stream*, BC 2·374¹⁶.

fiscmere m. *fishpond*, WW 484¹¹.

fiscnað=fiscað

fiscnett n. *fishing-net*, MET 176¹¹.

fiscnoð, fiscoð=fiscað

fiscpōl m. *fishpond*, JnL,WW. ['*fishpool*']

fiscrūt m. *small fish*, MtL 15³⁴.

fiscwelle m. *fishpond*, A 13·321.

fiscwer m. '*fish-weir*,' *fish-trap*, LL 454,9 : *fishing-ground*, Lk.

fiscwylle *full of fish*, BH. [weallan]

fisting f. '*fesiculatio*,' WW. ['*fisting*']

fitelfōta *white-footed* (BTs),WW 161²⁰.

fitersticca m. *tent-nail*, WW 187⁵.

fitt I. f? *struggle, contest, fight*, Gen 2072. ['*fit*'] II. f. '*fit*,' *song, poem*, Bo; GL (FTP 226).

fiðele f. *fiddle* (BT).

fiðelere m. '*fiddler*,' WW 311²³.

fiðelestre f. *female fiddler*, WW 311²⁴.

fiðer-=fēower-, feðer-

fiðerbǣre *feathered*, OEG.

fiðercian *to flutter*, GD 100¹⁹. [fiðere]

fiðerdǣled *quadripartite, quartered*, OEG.

fiðere (y) n. nap. fið(e)ru, fiðera(s) *wing*, Æ,CP.

fiðerfeald *four-fold*, EHy 4¹⁹.

fiðerflēdende (y¹) *flowing in four streams*, GPH 390.

fiðerflōwende *flowing in four streams*, OEG 48².

fiðerfōtnieten (e¹) m. *four-footed animal*, AA 23²⁰.

fiðerhama (y¹) m. *wing-covering*, ÆL 34⁷⁴.

+**fiðerhamod** *covered with feathers*, ÆH 1·466²⁷.

fiðerhiwe '*quadriformis*,' OEG 177.

+**fið(e)rian** *to provide with feathers or wings*, Bo; PPs. ['*feather*']

fiðerlēas *without wings*, Wy 22.

fiðerrica (y¹) m. *tetrarch*, ÆH.

fiðerrice (y²) n. *tetrarchy*, CHR 12 c.

fiðerscēatas mp. *four quarters?* SOL 32.

fiðersleht m. *flapping of wings, joy?* OEG 4892.

fiðertēme (eo¹, u²) *with four horses abreast*, VHy 5³⁴. [v. '*team*']

fiðertōdǣled=fiðerdǣled; **fiðru** v. fiðere.

fixa, fixas, fixum=fisca, fiscas, fiscum, gp., nap. and dp. of fisc.

fixen=fyxen

fixian, fixoð, fixnoð=fiscian, fiscað

flā f. *arrow*, AO. ['*flo*';=flān]

flacg *cataplasm, plaster*, WW 380²⁸.

flacort† *flying (of arrows)*. [cp. Ger. flackern]

flæ-=flea-, fleo-

flǣ-=flēa-, flēo-, flīe-

flǣre f. *earlap*, WW 157¹².

flǣsc (DD 51)=fleax

flǣsc (ē) n. '*flesh*,' Æ,Cp,Lk,VP; CP : *body (as opposed to soul)*, B,Jn : *carnal nature*, Mt : *living creatures*, Lk,Ps.

flǣscǣt m. *animal food*, RB.

flǣscbana m. *murderer, executioner*, GD.

flǣscbesmitennes f. *defilement of the flesh*, Sc 69¹¹.

flǣsccofa m. *body*, LPs 118¹²⁰.

flǣsc(c)wellere m. *executioner*, WW 382²⁹.

flǣsccȳping f. *meat-market*, WW 145²⁶.

flǣsceht *fleshy*, LCD 83a.

flǣscen *of flesh, like flesh*, GPH; Æ. ['*fleshen*']

flǣscennes (BF 142¹²)=flǣscnes

flǣscgebyrd f. *incarnation*, OEG 429.

flǣschama (o²)† m. *body, carcase*.

+**flǣschamod** *incarnate*, Æ.

flǣschord n. *body*, SOUL 103.

flǣschūs n. '*flesh-house*,' *place where meat is sold*, WW.

flǣsclic '*fleshly*,' *corporeal, carnal*, Æ,BH, Bl,Bo.

flǣsclicnes f. *incarnate condition*, Æ. ['*fleshliness*']

flǣscmangere m. *butcher*, WW. ['*fleshmonger*']

flǣscmaðu f. *maggot*, WW 122¹³.

flǣsc-mete m. nap. -mettas *flesh, animal food, LL*; Æ,CP. ['*fleshmeat*']

±**flǣscnes** f. *incarnation*, CHR.

+**flǣscod** *incarnate*, Æ.

flǣscsand *portion of meat*, CHRD 14'.

flǣscstrǣt f. *meat-market*, Æ.

flǣsctǎwere m. *torturer of the flesh, executioner*, WW 189¹⁹.

flǣsctōð m. *one of the teeth*, WW 415²⁴.

flǣscōēnung f. *allowance of food*, CHRD 15¹¹.

flǣscwyrm m. *maggot*, Lcd. ['*fleshworm*']

flǣslic=flǣsclic

flæðecomb m. *weaver's comb*, WW.

flæx (MtR)=fleax

flagen pp. of flēan.

flǎh I. n. *wickedness, treachery*, RIM 47.
II.† adj. *wily, deceitful, hostile*. [*ON*. flār]

flǎn mf. *barb, arrow, javelin, dart*, B,Ma; Æ,AO,CP. ['*flane*']

flǎnboga† m. *bow*, B.

flanc m. *flank*, OEG 50³⁵.

flǎngeweorc† n. *shooting-gear, arrows*.

flǎnhred? *arrow-swift? arrow-equipped? (of death)*, RIM 72.

flǎniht (e) *relating to darts*, WW 425³⁴.

flǎnōracu† f. *onset, attack*.

flasce (x) f. '*flask,*' *bottle*, GD,WW.

flǎt pres. 3 sg. of flītan.

flaxe=flasce

flaxfōte *web-footed*, HEXC 251. [=flox-]

flēa I. mf. '*flea,*' Ep,Lcd. II. (LCD)=flēah n.

flēag pret. 3 sg. of flēogan.

flēah I. n. *albugo, a white spot in the eye*, CP 69. II. m.=flēa I. III. pret. 3 sg. of flēogan. IV. pret. 3 sg. of flēon.

flēam m. *flight*, B; Æ,AO. on f. gebrengan *to put to flight*. on f. weorðan *to flee*. ['*fleme*']

flēamdōm m. *flight*, NC 287.

flēamlǎst m. *apostasy*, WW 500³.

flēan⁶ *to* '*flay,*' Cp.

±**fleard** n. *nonsense, vanity, folly, deception, fraud, superstition, LL*; OEG. ['*flerd*']

fleardere m. *trifler*, CHRD 20¹².

fleardian *to be foolish, err, go astray*, CHRD, LL.

flēat I. pret. 3 sg. of flēotan. II.=flēot

fleaðe, fleaðorwyrt f. *water-lily*, LCD.

flēawyrt f. *fleabane*, WW. ['*fleawort*']

fleax (æ, e) n. '*flax,*' *linen*, CP; Æ.

fleax- v. flex-.

flecta=fleohta; **fled**=flett

-flēdan v. ofer-f.

flēde adj. *in flood, full, overflowing*, AO. [flōd]

flēding f. *flowing*, ÆH 2·180².

flēg- (N)=flēog-

flēge *little ship*, JnL 6²²(oe).

flehta, flehtra=fleohta; **flēm-**=flīem-

flene=flyne; **flēo**=flēa

+**flenod** *describes some attribute of a cloak*, WW 187¹⁴.

±**flēogan²** (intr., cp. flēon) *to* '*fly,*' B,El, Jud,Jul; Æ,CP : *flee, take to flight*, Ma.

flēoge (ē, ȳ) f. *any winged insect*, '*fly,*' Æ, MtL; CP.

flēogenda m. *bird*, CPs.

flēogende '*flying,*' *winged*, ÆGr 44⁹.

flēogendlic *flying, winged*, ÆGR 55².·

flēogryft n. *fly-curtain*, WW 373²¹.

flēohcynn m. *a kind of flies*, PPs 104²⁷.

flēohnet n. '*fly-net,*' *curtain*, Jud.

fleohta (flecta) m. *hurdle*, Cp 600. [*Ger*. flechte]

±**flēon³** *to fly from*, '*flee*,' *avoid, escape*, An, B,G,Met,VPs; AO,CP : *put to flight*, Æ : *fly* (intr.), Æ.

flēos (VPs)=flīes; **fleos-**=fles-

flēot (ēa) m. I. *water, sea, estuary, river*, AO. II. *raft, ship*, Hy. ['*fleet*']

flēotan² *to float, drift, flow, swim, sail*, Æ,B, CP : (tr.) *skim*, LCD. ['*fleet*']

flēote=flīete

flēotende *floating*, Gen 1447. ['*fleeting*']

flēotig *fleet, swift*, RD 52⁴.

flēotwyrt f. *seaweed*, LCD 101a.

fleoðe (ea) f. *water-lily*, LCD.

flēow pret. 3 sg. of flōwan.

flēowð=flēwð pres. 3 sg. of flōwan.

-flēre v. ðri-, fīf-.

flēring f. *story (of a building)*, Æ. [flōr]

flēs=flīes; **flēsc**=flǣsc

fleswian (eo) *to whisper? pull a wry face?* BH 122¹⁷ (JAW 30). [or ? flēswian *dissemble*, ES 44·470]

flet=flett; **flēt**, flēte=flīete

fletrǣst f. *couch*, B 1241.

fletsittend† m. *sitter in hall, courtier, guest*.

flett n. *floor, ground*, B,LL : *dwelling, hall, mansion*, B,LL. ['*flet*']

flettgefeoht n. *fighting in a house*, LL 18,39.

flettgesteald† n. *household goods*, GEN.

flettpǣð m. *floor of a house*, GEN 2729.

fletwerod n. *hall-troop, body-guard*, B 476.

fleðecamb=flæðecomb

flēwsa m. *flowing, flux, issue (bodily disorder)*, LCD. [flōwan]

flēwð pres. 3 sg. of flōwan.

flex=fleax

flexæcer (y³) m. *flax land*, KC 5·389¹⁶.

flexgescot n. *contribution of flax*, W 171²⁷.

flexhamm m. *flax field*, KC 5·374'.

flexlīne f. *flax-winder, reel? flax line? thread?* LL 455,15.

flicce n. '*flitch*' *of bacon, ham*, Gl,KC.

flicorian (e²) *to move the wings, flutter*, Æ. ['*flicker*']

FLÏE

122

FLYGEPÏL

flïe=flēah I.

flïehð pres. 3 sg. of flēon.

flïema (ē, ī, ȳ) m. *fugitive, exile, outlaw, Æ, Gen*; AO. Godes f. *excommunicate person*, LL352,66. ['*fleme*']

±flïeman (ǣ, ē, ȳ) *to put to flight, .drive away, banish, Gen*; CP. ['*fleme*'; flēam]

flïeman-feorm, -feorming f. *offence of, or penalty for, sheltering fugitives from justice*, LL102,30; 2·302.

+flïeme (ē) adj. *fugitive*, DR147[8].

flïeming (flȳmig) sb. *fugitive*, OEG2965.

flïes (ē, ēo, ī, ȳ) n. '*fleece,*' *wool, fur, sealskin, LL,Ps.*

flïet (WW489[3])=flēot; flïetan=flītan

flïete (ē, ēo, ȳ) f. I. *cream, curds.* II. *punt, boat, raft*, WW.

flïg=flēah I.; flïg-=flēog-, flȳg-

flïgel m? n? '*flail,*' *A* 9·264.

fliht=flyht; fliht-, flihte-=flyhte-

flïhð pres. 3 sg. of flēon.

flïma=flïema

flint m. '*flint,*' *rock, Æ,Cr,Ep,WW.*

flinten *of flint*, W252[1].

flintgrǣg *grey like flint*, RD4[19].

flïo=flēah I.; flïs=flïes

±flit (usu. +) n. *strife, Ps : dispute, contention : 'scandalum'*; tō+flītes *emulously.* ['*flite*']

±flïtan[1] *to strive, quarrel, dispute, contend, B,BH*; Æ,CP. ['*flite*']

flïtcræft m. *dialectics, logic*, OEG.

flïtcræftlïc *logical*, HGL481.

flïtere m. *disputer, chider, brawler, schismatic, Gl.* ['*fliter*']

±flit-ful (OEG), -fullic (CHR) *contentious.*

+flïtfulnes f. *litigiousness*, A11·102[84].

±flïtgeorn I. (±) m. *contentious person*, BF, LCD. II. (+) *contentious*, RB130[20].

+flïtgliw n. *mockery*, WW.

+flïtlïce *emulously*, BH406[17].

±flïtmǣlum *contentiously, emulously*, OEG, RBL.

-flïtme? v. un-f.

flïusum (OET)=flēosum dp. of flēos.

flōc n. *flat fish, flounder*, WW.

flōcan *to clap, applaud*, RD21[34].

flocc m. '*flock,*' *company, troop, Æ,Chr.*

floccmǣlum *in troops*, AO. ['*flockmeal*']

flocgian *to spring forth*, GPH399.

flocrād f. *invading band, troop*, CHR.

flōd mn. *mass of water, 'flood,' wave, Æ,Gen, Chr,Mt,VPs*; AO,CP : *flow (of tide as opposed to ebb), tide, flux, current, stream*, AO : *the Flood, Deluge, B,Lk*; Æ.

flōdblāc *pale as water? pale through fear of drowning*, Ex497.

flōde f. *channel, gutter, Gl : flood?* (Earle) EC120[31].

flōdegsa m. *flood-terror*, Ex446.

flōden *of a river*, WW240.

flōdhamm m. *piece of land surrounded by water?* KC1·289[16].

flōdlic *of or belonging to a stream*, ÆGR54[9].

flōdweard f. *sea-wall*, Ex493.

flōdweg† m. *watery way, sea.*

flōdwudu m. *ship*, CR854.

flōdwylm† m. *flowing stream, raging billows.* [weallan]

flōdȳð f. *wave of the sea*, B542.

+flog n. *infectious disease*, LCD3·34[9].

flogen I. pp. of flēon. II. pp. of flēogan.

flogettan *to fluctuate : flutter*, Sc,GD100[19].

flogoða m. *liquor*, GPH402.

flōh f. *chip*, WW416[4].

flohtenfōte *web-footed*, LCD33b.

flōr fm. ds. flōra, flōre '*floor,*' *pavement, ground, B,Bo,Lk*; Æ : *bottom (of a lake, etc.), Sat.*

flōrisc *flowery*, CM44.

flōrstān m. *paving-stone, tessella*, WW150[27].

flot n. *deep water, sea.* on flot(e) '*afloat,*' *Chr,Ma.*

flota m. (*floater*), *boat, ship, vessel : fleet, Chr : crew : sailor :* (†) *pirate.* ['*flote*']

+flota m. *floater (whale)*, WH7.

floten pp. of flēotan.

floterian *to flutter, fly, flicker, Æ : float, be carried or tossed by waves*, Æ.

flothere m. *piratical fleet*, B2915.

flotian *to 'float,' Chr.* [flēotan]

flotlic *nautical, naval*, WW205[27].

flotmann m. *sailor, pirate*, ÆL,W.

flotorian=floterian

flotscip n. *ship, bark*, WW.

flotsmeru n. *floating grease, fat*, LL453,4.

flotweg m. *ocean*, HU41.

flōwan[7] *to 'flow,' stream, issue, Bf,Sol,VPs*; AO,CP : *become liquid, melt, VPs : abound, PPs :* (+) *overflow*, AO.

flōw(ed)nes f. *flow, flux, overflow, torrent*, CP.

flōwende '*flowing,*' *Ma* 65.

flōwendlïc *flowing*, LPs147[18].

flōwing f. '*flowing,*' *flux, MtL.*

fugl- (OET26)=fugl-

flugol *fleet, swift : fleeting*, Sc.

flugon I. pret. pl. of flēogan. II. pret. pl. of flēon. III.=fulgon pret. pl. of fēolan.

flustrian *to plait, weave*, WW485[1] (IF 48·254).

fluton pret. pl. of flēotan.

flycerian=flicorian

-flÿcge v. unfl-.

flyctīclāð (GL)=flyhteclāð

flyge† (i) m. *flight.*

flȳge=flēoge

flygepïl n. *flying dart*, Mod27. [v. '*pile*']

flygerēow *wild in flight*, Gu 321.
flȳgul=flugol
flȳhst pres. 2 sg. of flēon.
flyht (i) m. *flying, 'flight,'* Æ,OET. on flyhte *on the wing*.
flyhte m. *patch*, MkLR 2²¹.
flyhteclāð (i) m. *patch, Cp.* [v. '*cloth*']
flyhthwæt† *swift of flight*, Ph.
flȳhð pres. 3 sg. of flēon.
flȳm-=flīem-
flyne (e) f. *batter*, Lcd.
flȳs (Æ)=flīes; **flyt**, flȳt-=flit, flīt-
flȳt pres. 3 sg. of flēotan.
flȳte=flēot(e), flīete
flȳtme f. *fleam (blood-letting instrument)*, Gl. [*L.* phlebotomum]
flyð=flyht
±**fnæd** n. nap. fnadu *fringe, border, hem*, Æ.
fnǣran, fnǣrettan *to breathe heavily, snort, fume.* v. NC 356.
fnæs I. n. dp. fnasum *fringe*, WW 425²⁷.
    II. pret. 3 sg. of fnesan.
fnǣst m. *blowing, blast, breath*, Lcd: *voice*, LF 56³. ['*fnast*']
fnǣstian *to breathe hard*, Lcd. [v. '*fnast*']
fnēosung f. *sneezing*, WW. [v. '*fnese*']
fnēsan⁵ *to pant, gasp*, GD : (+) *sneeze*, Lcd.
fnora m. *sneezing*, Æ,Gl.
fō pres. 1 sg. of fōn.
foca m. *cake (baked on the hearth)*, ÆL 18¹⁶⁴.
fōd-=fōdd-
fōda m. '*food,' nourishment*, Æ,CD : *fuel, Sc.*
fōdder (o², u²) I. n. gs. fōd(d)res '*fodder,' food*, Æ,LL : *darnel, tares*, MtL 13 (fōter). II. n. *case, sheath*, Gl,MH. III. *hatchet?* WW.
fōdderbrytta m. *distributor of food, herdsman*, WW 111³⁹.
fōddergifu (u²) *food*, PPs.
fōdderhec *rack for food or fodder*, LL 455,17.
fōddornoð m. *sustenance*, GD 193¹⁷.
fōddorðegu† f. *feeding, repast, food.*
fōddurwela m. *wealth of food, provisions*, Rd 33¹⁰.
fōdnoð m. *substance, food*, TC.
fōdrað (OET 180²⁰)?=fōdnoð
fōdrere m. *forager*, AO 156³⁵.
foe- (N)=fe-, fē-
+**fōg** I. n. *joining, joint.* II. n. *suitability*, Lcd 10b. III. *suitable*, Lcd 89b.
+**fōgstān** (fōh) m. *hewn stone*, CP 253¹⁹.
fōh imperat. of fōn.
foht=feoht
fohten pp. of feohtan.
fol (wk. adj.)=full
+**fol** adj. *with foal*, Gen 32¹⁵.
fol-=ful-
fola m. '*foal,' colt*, Bl,MkL ; Æ.

folc n. '*folk,' people, nation, tribe,* Æ,B, Chr ; AO,CP : *a collection or class of persons, laity*, Bl,Bo : *troop, army.*
folcāgende† *ruling.*
folcbealo n. *great tribulation*, Men 125.
folcbearn† n. *man*, Gen.
folccū (folcū) f. *people's cow*, PPs 67²⁷.
folccūð *noted : public*, BH.
folccwēn f. *queen of a nation*, B 641.
folccwide n. *popular saying*, NC 287.
folccyning† m. *king of a nation.*
folcdryht† f. *multitude of people.*
folcegetrum=folcgetrum
folcegsa m. *general terror*, PPs 88³³.
folcfrēa m. *lord of the people*, Gen 1852.
folcfrig *having full rights of citizenship*, LL 13,8 ; 344,45. [v. '*folk*']
folcgedrēfnes f. *tribulation*, NC 287.
folcgefeoht n. *pitched battle*, AO.
folcgemōt n. *meeting of the people of a town or district*, LL. ['*folkmoot*']
folcgerēfa m. *public officer*, WW.
folcgeriht=folcriht
folcgeslō† m. *prince, noble, chief, officer.*
folcgestealla† m. *companion in war*, Gen.
folcgestrēon n. *public treasure*, Gen 1981.
folcgetæl n. *number of fighting men*, Ex 229.
folcgetrum† n. *army, host*, Gen.
folcgewinn n. *fighting, war*, Met 1¹⁰.
folcherepað m. *highway*, KC.
folcisc *of the people, popular, secular, common*, LL.
folclǣsung=folclēasung
folclagu f. *law of the people, public law*, LL.
folcland n. *land held by freemen according to tribal rules of family inheritance*, LL (v. 2·403 and NED). ['*folkland*']
folclār f. *homily*, GD.
folclēasung f. *slander*, LL. [v. '*folk*']
folclic *public, Æ : common, popular : secular : populous*, OEG.
folcmægen† n. *public force, army, tribe.*
folcmǣgð† f. *tribe, nation*, Gen.
folcmǣlum=floccmǣlum
folcmǣre *celebrated*, Gen 1801.
folcmōt=folcgemōt
folcnēd f. *people's need*, PPs 77¹⁶.
folcrǣd† m. *public benefit.*
folcrǣden† f. *decree of the people*, Cra 42.
folcriht I. n. *right of the people, common law*, LL. ['*folkright*'] II. adj. *according to common law*, LL 30¹³.
folcsæl n. *house*, Rd 2⁵.
folcscearu† f. *people, nation, province : people's land*, B 73 (Earle).
folcsceaða m. *villain*, An 1595.
folcscipe m. *nation, people*, Rd 33¹⁰.
folcslite n. *sedition*, WW 116²⁶.
folcsōð n. *simple truth?* ÆL 23⁶⁶.

folcstede† m. *dwelling-place, B : battlefield.* [v. '*folk*']

folcstōw f. *country place,* BH 160¹⁶.

folcswēot m.? *troop, multitude,* Ex 577.

folctalu f. *genealogy,* Ex 379.

folctoga† m. *chieftain, commander.*

folctruma m. *host,* LPs.

folcū=folccū

folcweleg *populous,* WW 476¹⁶.

folcwer† m. *man,* GEN.

folcwiga m. *warrior,* RD 15²³.

folcwita m. *public councillor, senator,* CRA 77.

folcwōh n. *deception of the public,* ÆL 23²⁶¹.

foldærn† n. *earth-house, grave.*

foldāgend m. *earth-possessor, earth-dweller,* PH 5. (MS folcāgend)

foldbold n. *house, castle,* B 773.

foldbūend m. *earth-dweller, man, inhabitant of a country,* CP.

folde (eo) f. *earth, ground, soil, terra firma, B,Jud : land, country, region, Gen : world.* ['*fold*']

foldgræf† n. *earth-grave.*

foldgrǣg *grey as the earth?* GNC 31.

foldhrērende *walking on the earth,* PA 5.

foldrǣst f. *rest in the earth,* CR 1029.

foldwæstm m. *fruits of the earth,* PH 654.

foldweg† m. *way, path, road : earth.*

foldwela m. *earthly riches,* RIM 68.

foldwong† m. *plain, earth.*

folen, folgen pp. of fēolan.

folgað (AO)=folgoð

folgere m. '*follower,' attendant, disciple, Bo, WW ; Æ,CP : successor,* AO 150²⁷ : *freeman who is not a householder.*

±folgian (often w. d.) *to '*follow,*' Jn,Lk : accompany, Chr,Ps : follow after, B :* (+) *attain,* CP 383²⁷ : *obey, serve, observe, El.* (v. also fylgan.)

folgoð m. *body of retainers, following, retinue : pursuit, employment, service, dignity, office, rule,* Æ,AO,CP : *jurisdiction, district : condition of life, destiny.*

folm†, folme f. folma m. *palm, hand.* [fēlan]

fon=fann; **fon-**=fan-

fōn⁷ (±) *to take, grasp, seize, catch, B, BH,Gen,Ma ;* AO,CP : *capture, make prisoner, Chr : receive, accept, assume, undertake, B,Sol ;* CP : *meet with, encounter.* f. on *take up, begin, resume, take to,* Æ,Bo,Chr : *attack,* CHR 1085E. f. tō rīce *ascend the throne, Chr ;* AO. f. tōgædre *join together, join issue, engage in battle.* him tōgēanes feng *clutched at him, B.* him on fultum feng *helped them,* JUD 300. hlyst +f. *listen.* ['*fang,' 'i-fang*']

fond=fand pret. 3 sg. of findan.

fong-=fang-; **fonn**=fann; **font**=fant

fonu=fanu

for I. prep. (with d., inst. and a.) (local) *before, in the sight of, in or into the presence of, as far as,* IM 119¹³ : (temporal) *during, before,* Æ : (causal) '*FOR,' on account of, for the sake of, through, because of, owing to, from, by reason of,* Æ : *as to : in order to : in place of, instead of, equivalent to, at the price of,* Æ : *in preference to, Rood : in spite of, Chr.* for worulde *as regards this world,* Æ. for Dryhtne *by God.* II. conj. *for, because.* for hwȳ, for hwām, for hwon *wherefore?* for ðām, for ðon, for ðȳ ('*forthen*') *therefore,BH : because, since.* for ðām ðe (ðȳ), for ðȳ ðe *because,* AO. for ðȳ ðæt, for ðām ðæt *in order that.* III. adv. *too, very,* Æ. for ān *only.*

for- I. denotes loss or destruction (as in fordōn, forgiefan), or is intensitive or pejorative, as in forbærnan, forrotian. It is not connected with the preposition '*for.*' [*Ger.* ver-] II. occly.=fore-

fōr I. f. *going, course, journey, expedition, BH ;* AO : *way, manner of life.* ['*fore*'] II. m. *pig, hog,* OEG. III. pret. 3 sg. of faran.

fora (N)=foran; **fora-**=fore-; **forad**=forod

foran I. prep. (w. d.) *before, opposite.* II. adv. *before, in front, forward, Rd ;* Æ, AO,CP : *to the front, Da.* foran ongean *opposite.* fōran tō *opposite : beforehand.* ['*forne*']

foranbodig n. *thorax, chest,* WW 158⁴¹.

forandæg *early part of the day,* Æ(NC).

forane *opposite : beforehand.*

foranhēafod n. *forehead,* Æ.

foranlencten m. *early spring,* LCD 96a.

foranniht f. *early part of the night, dusk, evening,* Æ.

forannihtsang m. *compline,* BTK 194,218.

forāð=foreāð

forbærnan *to cause to burn, burn up, consume by fire, be consumed,* Æ,Chr ; AO. ['*forburn*']

forbærnednes f. *burning,* LCD.

forbearan=forberan

forbearnan=forbærnan

forbed n. *portable bed, litter,* ZDA 31.

forbēgan=forbīgan

forbelgan³ *to be enraged,* BL.

forbēn f. *prayer,* DHy 138¹³.

forbēodan *to '*forbid,' prohibit, Chr,G ;* Æ : *restrain, Ps : refuse, Lk : repeal, annul,* LL 42,49.

forbēodendlic *dehortative, dissuasive,* ÆGR 225¹¹.

forbeornan³ (e, y) *to burn, be consumed by fire,* AO,B. ['*forburn*']

forberan I. (sv⁴) *to 'forbear,' abstain from, refrain,* CP : *suffer, endure, tolerate, humour,* CP,B,BH,Mt : *restrain.* II.=foreberan

forberendlīce *tolerably,* Sc 137⁶.

forbernan=forbærnan

forberstan³ *to break, burst asunder, vanish, fail,* LL : *let go by default,* EC 201'. ['*forburst*']

forbētan=forebētan

forbīgan (ē, ȳ) *to bend down, bow down, depreciate, abase, humiliate, degrade.*

forbīgels m. *arch, arched roof,* WW 126³.

forbindan³ *to bind* (*up*), *muzzle,* CP 105⁷. ['*forbind*']

forbīsen=forebysen

forbītan¹ *to bite through,* HL 18³⁹¹.

forblāwan⁷ *to blow,* AO : *blow out, inflate,* Lcd. ['*forblow*']

forblindian *to blind,* MkR 6⁵².

fōrbōc f. *itinerary,* OEG 2023.

forbod n. *prohibition,* LL ; CP. ['*forbode*']

forboda=foreboda

forbrecan⁵ (æ²) *to break in pieces, bruise, violate, crush, destroy,* Jn ; AO,CP. *forbrocen broken down, decrepit.* ['*forbreak*']

for-brēdan³, -bregdan *to tear, pull, snatch away : draw over, cover : change, transform,* Bo. ['*forbraid*']

forbrītan *to break in pieces, crush, bruise.*

forbrȳt-ednes (ESPs), -ennes (V²Ps) f. *contrition.*

forbrytian, forbryttan=forbrītan

forbūgan² *to bend from, refrain from, avoid, decline,* Æ,Ma ; CP : *flee from, escape,* CP : *hold down.* ['*forbow*']

forbȳgan=forbīgan

for-byrd, fore- f. *abstention,* AO 30³⁵ : *long-suffering,* CP 41¹⁷.

forbyrdian *to wait for,* EPs 32²⁰.

forbyrdig *forbearing,* NC 287.

forbyrnan (Æ)=forbeornan

force f. forca m. '*fork,*' Æ,WW.

forcēap *forestalling* (*in trade*), LL 234,2¹⁰. [=*forecēap]

forcel m. *pitchfork,* NC 287.

forceorfan³ *to carve out, cut down, cut off, cut through, divide,* Æ,Chr ; AO,CP. ['*forcarve*']

forcēowan² *to bite off,* Bo 36²³.

forcierran (e², y²) *to turn aside, prevent, avert, avoid,* CP : *turn oneself away, escape : pervert.*

forcierrednes (e², y²) f. *perversity,* GD 119¹⁵ : *turning aside,* BPs 125¹.

forcierring (e, y) f. *turning aside,* CVPs 125¹.

forcilled *chilled,* LCD.

forcippian (y) *to cut off,* RHy 2¹². [v. '*chip*']

forclǣman *to stop up,* GL.

forclas pl. of forcel.

forclingan³ *to wither, shrink up,* CAS 36¹⁹, Cp. ['*forcling*']

forclyccan *to stop, close* (*ears*), RPs 57⁵.

forclȳsan *to close up,* LCD 3·92'.

forcnīdan=forgnīdan

forcostian *to tempt,* ByH 98³².

forcrafian *to require,* RBL 82⁵.

forcuman⁴ *to come before, prevent, surprise : harass, wear out, destroy : reject,* LG : *overcome, conquer, obtain : surpass.*

forcunnian *to tempt, try,* G.

for-cūð (Æ) *bad, wicked, infamous, foul, despicable, despised,* Æ,Bo ; AO,CP. adv. -cūðe. ['*forcouth*']

forcūð-līc, -līce=for-cūð, -cūðe

forcweðan⁵ *to speak ill of, abuse, revile,* CP : *reprove : refuse, reject,* CP : *boast, promise great things,* GnE 49.

forcwolstan³? *to swallow,* LCD 18a.

forcwȳsan *to shake violently,* SPs 109⁷.

forcyppian=forcippian

forcyrran (Æ)=forcierran

forcȳðan *to reprove, rebuke : refute?* SOL.

ford m. ds. forda '*ford,*' Æ,AO ; Mdf.

fordǣlan *to spend,* Lk(B) 8⁴³.

fordēad *dead,* MtL 28⁴.

fordelfan³ *to delve, dig up,* EC 120²⁸.

fordēman *to condemn, sentence, doom,* Mt ; Æ : *prejudice,* EC 145' : *decide,* Sc 125⁶. ['*fordeem*']

fordēmedlic *to be condemned,* GD 208⁹.

fordēmednes f. *condemnation, proscription,* BH 34⁵.

fordēmend m. *accuser,* JnL p5⁹.

fordēming f. *plunder, spoliation,* OEG 3149.

fordemman *to dam up, block up,* EPs 57⁵.

fordettan (KGl)=fordyttan

fordīcigan *to shut out by a ditch, block up,* CP.

fordīlemengan *to gloss over,* CHrd 18⁹.

for-dīlgian, -dīlegian, -dīligian *to blot out, destroy, abolish,* BH. ['*fordilghe*']

fordimmian *to obscure, darken,* Sc. ['*fordim*']

fordittan=fordyttan

fordōn anv. *to undo, bring to nought, ruin, destroy,* BH,MtL ; Æ,AO : *abolish,* Chr : *kill,* LL : *corrupt, seduce, defile.* pp. fordōn *corrupt, wicked, abandoned.* ['*fordo*']

fordrǣfan *to drive, compel,* LL 24,62.

fordrencan (æ) *to make drunk, intoxicate,* Æ. ['*fordrench*']

fordrīfan¹ *to drive, sweep away : drive on, impel, compel,* AO : *drive away, expel,* Chr ; Æ : *overtax.* ['*fordrive*']

fordrifnes f. *objection, opposition,* MkL Pref 2¹⁵.

fordrincan³ *to make drunk, be drunk,* CP.

fordrūgian *to become dry, wither,* Met ; ÆL ['*fordry*']

fordruncen pp. *drunk, CP.* ['*fordrunken*']
fordruncnian (fore-) *to be made drunk*, LL.
fordrūwian=fordrūgian
forduttan (VPs)=fordyttan
fordwer m. *weir at a ford*, KC.
fordwilman *to confound*, Bo 14⁵.
fordwīnan *to vanish*, ÆL. ['*fordwine*']
fordyslic *very foolish*, Bo 42¹⁰.
fordyttan (e, i, u) *to obstruct, block up, close, Cp,VPs*; Æ. ['*fordit*']
fore I. prep. w. d. a. (local) *before, in the sight of, in presence of, B* : (causal) *because of, for the sake of, through, on account of, by reason of, from, BH* : (temporal) *before, Cr* : *for, instead of.* II. adv. *before, beforehand, formerly, once, Ps.* ['*fore*']
fore-=for-
foreādihtian *to arrange, order beforehand*, CP 9⁹.
forealdian *to grow old, decay, BH*; Æ,CP. ['*forold*'] .
foreāstreccan *to lay low, overthrow*, EPs 105²⁶.
foreāð m. *preliminary oath, LL* (v. 2·546). ['*foreoath*']
for-ēaðe (Æ), -ēaðelīce *very easily.*
forebē(a)cen n. *sign, portent, prodigy, Æ.*
forebegān *to intercept*, CHR 1009 E.
foreberan *to prefer*, BH 294⁷.
forebētan *to make legal amends (vicariously)*, LL.
forebirig=forebyrig ds. of foreburh.
forebiscop m. *high-priest*, MtL 1¹⁸ (mg).
forebisegian *to preoccupy*, OEG 1236.
foreblǣsting (ē) f. *shoot, branch*, EPs 79¹².
fōrebōc (HGL 454)=fōrbōc
forebod n. *prophecy, preaching*, NG.
foreboda m. *forerunner, messenger, crier*, ANS 84¹⁴.
forebodere m. *herald, crier*, DR 48,194.
forebodian *to announce, declare*, ASPs.
forebodung f. *prophecy*, NG.
forebrǣdan *to prolong*, EPs 119⁵ : *overshadow*, MkL 9⁷.
forebrēost n. *chest*, WW.
foreburh f. *outwork* : *outer court, vestibule*, Æ.
forebyrd=forbyrd
forebysen f. *example*, CHR(Thorpe) 67'.
foreceorfan³ '*praecidere*,' ÆGR 172⁴.
foreceorfend m. *front tooth*, WW 264¹¹.
forecēosan *to choose in preference*, BCJRPs 131¹³,¹⁴.
foreclipian (y) '*proclamare*,' BHy 3⁴; ANS 122·265.
forecnēo(w)ris(n) f. *progeny*, ERPs.
forecnyll m. *first ringing (of a bell)*, RBL 82¹¹.

forecostigan *to profane*, EPs 88³².
forecostung f. *profanation*, EPs 88³⁵.
forecuman⁴ *to come before, prevent, BH* : *overcome? Ps* : *come out, come upon*, NG. ['*forecome*']
forecweden *aforesaid*, GD 12,344.
forecweðan⁵ *to preach, predict*, G,DR.
forecwide m. *prophecy* : *introduction, heading (of chapter)*, NG.
forecyme m. *proceeding forth*, MtL p4³.
fore-cynren, -cynrēd n. *progeny*, RPs, WW.
forecȳðan *to make known (beforehand), tell forth*, EPs,TC : *prophesy*, GD 339³¹.
fored=forod
foreduru f. -dyre, -dere n. *vestibule*, GL.
foredyrstig? *presumptuous*, LL 409,22.
forefæger *very fair*, ES 8·479⁸⁹.
fore-feng, -fong=forfang
forefēran *to go before*, BL,LkLR.
forefex (=ea²) n. *forelock*, OEG 5326; 2⁴⁵³.
foreflēon *to flee*, MkL 14⁵².
forefōn⁷ *to prevent, anticipate*, CPs,DR.
foregān anv., foregangan⁷ *to go before, precede, BH,VPs*: *go in front of, project*: *excel.* ['*forego*']
forege-=for(e)-
foregearwung f. *preparation, parasceve*, G.
foregebiddan⁵ *to intercede*, RB 62⁸.
foregeblind *blinded*, MkL 6⁵³.
foregecēosan *to choose beforehand*, Æ.
foregegān=forgangan
foregehāt n. *vow*, ÆL 23b⁵⁴³.
foregehātan *to promise* : *invite*, NG.
foregelēoran *to pass away*, LkL.
foregenga m. *forerunner* : *predecessor, ancestor, CP* : *attendant*, JUD 127.
foregengel (for-) m. *predecessor*, CHR 963 E.
foregescēaw-=foresceaw-
foregeseocgan *to predestine*, MtL p 1⁹.
foregesettan=foresettan
foregeswuteliende '*indagande*,' OEG 1504.
foregetēon² *to point out*, HGL 411.
foregeðingian=foreðingian
foregeðistrod *darkened*, MkL 6⁵².
foregidd n. *proverb*, JnR 16²⁹.
foregielpan³ *to boast greatly*, AO 4¹⁸,BF 188¹³.
foregīmnes (ē³) f. *observation*, LkL 17²⁰.
foregīsl m. *preliminary hostage*, CHR 878.
foreglēaw *foreseeing, provident, wise, prudent, Æ.* adv. -līce.
foregyrnan *to show before*, Sc 203¹⁷.
forehālig *very holy*, ANS 84·3.
forehrādian *to hasten before*, CHRD 26¹⁸.
forehūs n. *porch*, LV 33.
foreiernan (for-) *to run before, outrun, JnL 20⁴.* ['*forerun*']
fore-iernend, -iernere m. *forerunner*, WW.

forelád-téow, -twa m. *chief, leader*, LkLR 22²⁶.

foreléédan *to lead forth*, MtL 15¹⁴.

foreléérend m. *teacher*, BL 149¹³.

forelár f. *preaching*, MtL p 16⁵.

forelcian *to delay*, RWH 142²⁴.

foreldan=forieldan

forelegnis=forlegis

foreléoran *to go before, pass by*, NG.

foreléornes (EPs 100³)=forléornes

forelocc m. '*forelock*,' OEG.

forelócian '*prospicere*,' EPs 101²⁰ : '*respicere*,' EPs 101¹⁸.

foreméére *illustrious, renowned, famous*, Æ.

foreméérlic *eminent*, Bo 75²⁴.

foreméérnes f. *eminence, fame*, Bo.

foremanian *to forewarn*, BH 412³⁰.

foremanig *very many*, MtL p 18¹².

foremeahtig=foremihtig

foremearcod *before-mentioned*, CM 378.

foremearcung (e²) f. *title, chapter*, NG.

foremihtig (ea) *most mighty*. adv. -líce.

foremunt m. *promontory*, WW 464¹⁷.

forenama m. '*pronomen*,' RBL 11¹³.

forene=forane

forenemnan *to mention beforehand*, VH 12.

forenyme m. *taking before*, WW 42⁷.

forerím m. *prologue*, Mt(K) pref. 1¹.

forerynel m. *forerunner, herald, morning star*, Æ,CP.

foresacan⁶ *to forbid*, MtL 3¹⁴.

foreséd *aforesaid*, Æ. ['*foresaid*']

fore-séégdnes, -saga f. *preface*, NG.

foreséndan=foresendan

forescéawere (for-) m. '*provisor*,' ES 39·327.

forescéawian *to* '*foreshow*,' *foresee*, Æ : *preordain, decree, appoint*, Æ : *provide, furnish with*, Æ.

foresceáwodlíce *with forethought, thoughtfully*, CM 76.

foresceáwung f. *contemplation, foresight, providence*, Sc; Æ. ['*foreshowing*']

forescéotan (Bo 124¹¹)=forscéotan

forescieldnes f. *protection*, EPs 120⁵.

forescynian *to shun*, NG.

forescyttels m. *bolt, bar*, CR 312.

forescýwa m. *shadow*, DR 13¹⁴.

forescýwung f. *overshadowing*, DR 28⁶.

foreséécan *to appeal* (*for justice*), LL 152,3 and nn.

foresecgan *to mention before*, Æ : *proclaim, preach* : *foretell*, BH. ['*foresay*']

foreseld n. *first seat*, MtL 23⁶.

foresellan *to spend, advance* (*money*), LL (or ? 2 words).

foresendan *to send before*, ÆGr; CM 448. [v. '*fore*']

foreséon⁵ *to* '*foresee*,' Ps : *provide*, BH : *provide for*, BH.

foreséond m. *provider*, BH 338¹⁰.

foreséones f. *care, foresight, providence*, BH.

fore-setnes, -sete(d)nes f. *proposition, purpose*, BF 2⁶ : *preposition*, ÆGr 267¹⁵.

foresettan *to place before, shut in*, VPs : *propose* : *prefer* : *precede*. ['*foreset*']

foresingend m. *precentor*, WW 129²¹.

foresittan⁵ *to preside over*, BH.

fore-sméagan, -sméan *to think beforehand*, G,GL.

foresnotor *very wise*, B 3163.

fore-spÆéc, -speca=fore-sprÆéc, -spreca.

fore-sprÆéc (CP), -sprec, -spÆéc (WW) f. *advocacy, defence, excuse* : *agreement, arrangement* : *preamble, preface, prologue*, Æ,CP : *promise*. ['*forespeech*']

forespreca m. *intercessor, advocate, mediator* : *sponsor*, LL 442,1.

foresprecan⁵ I. *to speak or answer for, be surety for, intercede for*, CP : *say before*. **foresprecen** *above-mentioned, aforesaid*, Bo. ['*forespoken*'] **II.**=forsprecan

forestÆéppan⁶ (e³) *to precede, go before, anticipate*, Æ : *excel* : *forestall, prevent*.

forestÆéppend m. *precursor*, Lk 22²⁶.

forestÆéppung f. *anticipation*, BF 172¹⁷.

forestandan⁶ *to preside, lead* : *excel*, WW 464¹⁵ : *prevail against*, MtL 16¹⁸.

forestapul *going before*, GPH 396.

foresteall (for-) m. *intervention, hindrance* (*of justice*) : *ambush, assault, offence of waylaying on the highway*, Æ,LL : *fine for such an offence* : *resistance, opposition*. ['*forestall*']

forestemman *to prevent, hinder*, NG.

forestéora m. *look-out man, pilot*, WW 464⁸.

foresteppan⁶=forestÆéppan

forestigan¹ *to excel*, ÆGr 154¹¹n.

forestige m. *vestibule*, OEG 4688 and n.

forestihtian *to fore-ordain*, Æ.

forestihtung f. *predestination*, Æ.

foreswerian⁶ *to swear before*, NUM 11,14.

foretÆécn n. '*fore-token*,' *prognostic, prodigy, sign, wonder*, Bo; CP.

foretÆécnian *to foreshow*, BH 216¹⁷.

foreteohhian *to fore-ordain*, WW 219³¹.

foreteohhung f. *predestination*, Bo.

foretéon *to fore-ordain, frame beforehand, arrange*, BH,PPs.

foretéð mp. *front teeth*, WW. ['*foretooth*']

foretíge m. *forecourt, porch*, Mt 11¹⁶.

foretrymman *to testify*, JnL 13²¹.

foretýned *shut in*, BH 386².

foreðanc m. *forethought, providence, consideration, deliberation*, CP.

foreðancful *prudent*, AS 14⁵.

foreðanclic *thoughtful, careful, prudent*, CP. adv. -líce.

foreðancol (u³) *prudent*, CP305².
foreðancolnes f. *prudence*, PPs48³.
foreðencan *to premeditate, consider, be mindful*, *CP*. [*'forethink'*]
foreðēon *to surpass, excel*, RB131¹⁹.
foreðīngere m. *intercessor, mediator*, Æ.
foreðīngian *to plead for, intercede, defend*, Bo,LL.
foreðīngiend m. *intercessor*, WNL294³⁰,³².
fore-ðīngrǣden (WNL), -ðingung (Æ) f. *intercession*.
foreðonc=foreðanc; **forewall**=foreweall
foreward=foreweard
forewarnian *to take warning beforehand : forewarn*, NC288.
foreweall m. *rampart, bulwark, Ex.* [*'forewall'*]
foreweard (a², e²) I. fn. *condition, bargain, agreement, treaty, assurance, Chr.* [*'foreward'*] II. m. *outpost, scout.* III. adj. *'forward,' inclined to the front, Æ : fore, early, former, BH*; Æ. f. gēar *new year.* IV. adv. (-wearde at AS55¹⁴) *in front, CP : towards the future, Gen.* on f. *at the beginning*, BF174 : *above all*, BYH40⁶. fram foreweardum *once more*, RB.
foreweardnes (e³) f. *beginning*, BF198².
foreweorðan³ *to predestinate*, MkLp1¹⁶
fore-wesan anv. pret. 3 sg. -wæs *to be over, rule over*, BH.
forewīs *foreknowing*, HL18³⁶³.
forewitan swv. *to foreknow*, Bo. [*'forewit'*]
forewītegian *to prophesy*, ÆH.
forewītegung f. *prophecy*, ÆL,OEG.
forewitig *knowing*, LCD3·436 : *foreknowing*, Æ : *prophetic*, OEG.
forewitol *foreknowing*, CHR1067D.
forewittlendlic *prescient*, ŒEG1502.
foreword n. *stipulation, condition*, KC, LL.
forewost=forwost.
forewrēgan=forwrēgan
forewriten *above or before-written*, CM.
forewrītennes f. *proscription, exile*, WW466⁵.
forewyrcend m. *servant*, ÆL2¹⁵⁶.
forewyrd f. *agreement, condition*, GL.
±**forewyrdan** (æ³) *to agree*, KC3·274¹².
forfang (forefeng) n. *capture, (legal) seizure, recovery of cattle or other property*, LL : *reward for rescuing property*, LL (v. 388–391 and 2·279). [*'forfang'*]
forfangfeoh n. *reward for rescuing cattle or other property*, LL390,3².
forfaran⁶ *to pass away, perish, Chr : lose : destroy, ruin, cause to perish, LL : intercept, obstruct.*
forfeallan *to overwhelm*, AA35⁴.
forfeng I. pret. 3 sg. of forfōn. II.=forfang

forfēran *to depart, die, Chr*; Æ. [*'forfere'*]
forferian *to let die*, LL58,17.
forflēon² *to flee from, escape, avoid, evade*, Æ.
forflȳgan *to put to flight*, ZDA31·16⁴¹⁸.
forfōn⁷ *to seize : anticipate, forestall : surprise : prevent : forfeit.*
forfyllan *to stop up, obstruct*, WW463¹⁰.
forg-=foreg-
forgǣgan *to transgress, trespass, prevaricate*, Æ : *pass by, omit, neglect*, OEG,W.
forgǣgednes f. *transgression, trespass*, Æ.
forgǣgend m. *transgressor*, CHRD41³¹.
forgǣgung f. *fault, excess*, Sc115⁹.
forgǣlan *to avoid*, LkL.
for-gān, -gangan I. *to go or pass over, by or away, Æ,MtL : 'forgo,' abstain from, neglect, lose, Æ*; CP,Æ. II.=foregān
forgeare *very certainly*, ÆL23⁵⁵⁶.
forgedōn=fordōn
forgeearnung f. *merit*, DHy132¹.
forgefenes=forgiefnes
forgēgan=forgǣgan
forgeldan=forgieldan
forgēm-=forgiem-
forgenge *hard to carry out?* (BTs), TC159².
forgeorne *very earnestly, very attentively*, BL.
forgeot-=forgit-, ofergit-
forget=forgiet pres. 3 sg. of forgietan.
forgief- v. also forgif-
forgiefan⁵ (i, y) *to give, grant, allow, BH,Bl; CP : 'forgive,' overlook, Gen,Lk,Mt; AO, CP : give up, leave off, CP : give in marriage.*
forgiefen (e², ea², i²) *indulgent, AO : mild, tolerable*, NG.
for-giefnes (e, i, y) f. *pardon, 'forgiveness,' remission, Bl; CP : indulgence, permission, BH : gift?* CR425.
forgieldan⁸ (e, i, y) *to pay for, CP : requite, reward, Bl; AO,CP : indemnify, make good : pay double (as penalty), LL : give : give up, forfeit*, VH12. [*'foryield'*]
forgielpan³ *to boast in public, trumpet forth*, W234¹⁶.
forgieman (ē, i, ȳ) *to neglect, pass by, transgress*, B. [*'foryeme'*]
forgiemelēasian (ī, ȳ) *to neglect, abandon, give up, omit*, CP.
forgietan⁵ (i, y) w. a. or g. *to 'forget,' Bf, Bo,G,Ps; AO,CP. For comps. v. forgit-.*
forgif- v. also forgief-.
forgifendlic (y²) *dative*, ÆGR22¹⁶.
forgifenlic *excusable, tolerable, Mt.* [*'forgivelich'*]
forgifestre f. *female giver*, DHy49⁶.
forgifu f. *'gratia,' DHy78⁷ (? 2 words).*
forgifung f. *gift*, WW115¹².
forgildan=forgieldan
forgīm-=forgiem-

forgit-=forgiet-, ofergi(e)t-

forgitel (eo², y², o³, u³) *forgetful, Æ.* ['*forgetel*']

forgitelnes (y²) f. *forgetfulness, oblivion, LPs.* ['*forgetelness*']

forgiten pp. *forgetting, forgetful, Æ,Bl.*

forgiting f. *forgetfulness,* CM 1065.

forglendrian *to devour, swallow up,* W.

forgnagan⁶ *to eat up, Æ.* ['*forgnaw*']

forgnīdan¹ *to grind together, dash down, crush, break, LPs.* ['*forgnide*']

forgniden *contrite,* SPs 50¹⁸.

forgnidennes f. *tribulation,* APs 146³,LPs 13³.

forgnȳdan=forgnīdan

forgrindan³ I. *to grind down, ruin, destroy, consume.* II. (=y²) *to send to the bottom, destroy,* A 11·2⁴⁰. [grund]

forgrindet n. *grinding, pounding,* Cp. 776c.

forgrīpan¹ *to seize, assail, attack, overwhelm.*

forgrīwan *to sink (in vice),* NC (BTs).

forgrōwen *grown up? overgrown? Rim* 46. [v. '*forgrow*']

forgumian (LL 474,2)=forgīman

forgyf-=forgief-, forgif-

forgyldan=forgieldan

forgyltan *to sin, be or become guilty,* W. forgylt *condemned, guilty.*

forgȳm-=forgīem-

forgyrd=forðgyrd

forgyrdan *to enclose, encircle,* CHR 189 n 4.

forgyt-=forgiet-, forgit-

for-habban, pret. 3 sg. -hæfde *to hold in, restrain, retain, keep back : draw back, refrain from, avoid, Æ.* forhæfed *continent, abstemious, celibate,* CP.

forhæbbend m. *abstinent, continent person.* OEG 1254.

forhæfd=forhēafod

forhæf(e)(d)nes f. *temperance, continence, self-restraint, abstinence, BH; Æ,CP : parsimony,* OEG 3748. ['*forhevedness*']

forhæfendlīce *continently,* CHRD 42²⁹.

forhēlan *to injure?* WW 464⁴.

forhǣtan *to overheat,* LCD 91b.

forhǣōed *burnt up,* WW 234¹.

forhātan⁷ *to renounce, forswear, Æ.* se forhātena *the devil,* GEN 609. ['*forhight*']

forheafdnes (AS 23⁷)=forhæfednes

forhēafod n. '*forehead,*' *brow, skull,* WW; Æ. [=fore-]

forhealdan⁷ *to forsake, fall away from, rebel against, B : let go,* LL 360,11 : *defile, pollute,* BL : *withhold,* LL 130,6¹ : *misuse, abuse,* Bo. ['*forhold*']

forhealdnes f. *unchastity,* NC 288.

forheard *very hard,* MA 156.

forheardian *to grow hard,* LVPs 89⁶.

forhēawan⁷ *to hew in pieces, cut down, kill, Ma.* ['*forhew*']

forhefednes=forhæfednes

forhegan (KGL)=forhogian

forhelan⁴ *to cover over, conceal, hide, protect, Æ,Bo;* CP. sacne f. *conceal a guilty man.* ['*forhele*']

forhelian *to hide,* OEG 5410n : *cover, clothe,* CHRD 108¹³.

forhergend m. *ravager,* GL.

for-hergian, -herigean, -heregian *to plunder, harry, ravage, devastate, destroy,* AO,CP. [*Ger.* verheeren]

for-hergung, -her(g)iung f. *harassing, devastation,* AO 74³⁶.

forhicgan=forhycgan

forhīenan *to cast down, defeat, humiliate, outrage, oppress, waste,* AO. [*Ger.* verhöhnen]

forhigan=forhycgan

for-hoged-, -hogd-=forhogod-

forhogian *to neglect, disregard, despise, BH; Æ,CP.* ['*forhow*']

forhogiend m. *despiser,* CHRD,GD.

forhogi(g)endlic *contemptible,* Sc.

forhogod pp. of forhycgan.

forhogodlic *contemptuous,* BL 77²³. adv. -līce.

forhogodnes f. *contempt,* BHB 342¹⁰.

forhogung f. *contempt,* BPs,CM.

forhohnes=forhogodnes

forhradian *to hasten,* CP : *prevent, anticipate, frustrate, Æ,CP.*

forhraðe *very speedily, quickly, soon, Æ.*

forhrēred *annulled,* WW.

forht *afraid, timid, cowardly,* AO,CP: *frightful, terrible.* adv. forhte *despairingly.*

forhtful *fainthearted, timorous,* WW 93⁹.

±**forhtian** (tr. and intr.) *to be afraid, surprised, fear, dread, Æ.*

forhtiendlic *timorous,* WW 442⁵ : *dreadful,* GD.

forhtige *humbly, submissively,* RB 70⁵.

forhtigend *timid,* W : *dreadful,* W.

forhtlic *fearful, afraid : dreadful.* adv. -līce.

forhtmōd *timorous, timid, Æ.*

forhtnes f. *fear, terror, Æ.*

forhtung f. *fear, ÆH.*

forhugian=forhogian

forhwæn, forhwan=forhwon

forhwega (æ²) *somewhere, somewhere about, Æ,AO.*

forhweorfan³ *to come to an end, be destroyed,* W 183⁴.

forhwerf-=forhwierf-

for-hwī, -hwig=forhwȳ

forhwierfan (e, i, y) *to change, transform : remove, transfer : pervert,* CP.

forhwierfedlic (y²) *perverse*, BL 31⁴.
forhwierfednes (y²) f. *perversity*, NC 288.
forhwon *wherefore, why, for what reason*, BH:
forhwȳ (ī²) *why, wherefore*, Ps. ['*forwhy*']
forhwyrf-=forhwierf-
forhycgan *to disdain, despise, reject*, CP.
forhȳdan *to hide*, Ps; CP. ['*forhide*']
forhygdelic *despised*, LPs 118¹⁴¹.
forhylman *to refuse obedience to*, AN 735.
forhȳnan=forhīenan
forhyrdan (i) *to harden*, EPPs 94⁸. [heard]
forieldan *to put off, delay*, CP.
foriernan=foreiernan
forierð (y) *a head-land* (v. heafodlond) *in the case of land with furrows at right angles to those of the adjacent land* (BTs), KC 5·153²¹.
forinlīce *thoroughly, exceedingly*, Bo 94⁶.
forinweardlīce *thoroughly, genuinely*, Bo 137¹⁵.
forlācan⁷† *to mislead, seduce, deceive, betray*.
forlǣdan *to mislead, seduce*, Æ,AO,CP : *bring out* (=forð-), Æ. [*Ger.* verleiten]
forlǣran *to teach wrongly, lead astray, seduce, pervert*, An,CP; Æ. ['*forlere*']
forlǣtan⁷ *to let go, relinquish, surrender, lose, leave, abandon, neglect*, An,Bl; Æ,CP : *remit, pardon, excuse* : *loose, release* : *let, permit, allow*, BH : *grant, give*. ūp, in f. *to direct upwards, within*. ān(n)e f.=ānforlǣtan. ['*forlet*']
for-lǣtennes (Æ), -lǣt(ed)nes f. *leaving, departure, absence* : *loss, perdition* : *intermission, cessation, end* : *remission* : *divorce*.
forlǣting f. *leaving, intermission*.
forlǣtu sbpl. *losses, sufferings*, VH 12.
forlǣðan *to loathe*, W 165³.
forlēan *to blame much*, A 12·517.
forlecgan *to cover up*, LCD 25a.
forlegen pp. of forlicgan.
forlegenes=forlegnes
forlegenlic *mean-looking, ugly* (Swt).
for-legis, -leges f. *prostitute, adulteress*, CP.
for-legis-, -legor-=forliger-
forlegnes f. *fornication*, BH,CP.
forlegnis f. *prostitute*, CP.
forlēogan² *to lie, perjure oneself, slander*, Æ.
forlēoran (EPs 143¹⁴)=forelēoran
forlēornes f. *transgression*, EPs 100⁸ (cp. ofer-l.).
forleornung f. *deception*, BL 183³⁴.
forleorte redupl. pret. sg. of forlǣtan.
forlēosan² *to lose, abandon, let go*, B ; Æ,AO, CP : *destroy, ruin*, Gen. ['*forlese*']
forlēt-=forlǣt-
forlettan (fore-) *to prevent*, MkL 10¹⁴.

forlicgan⁵ *to commit adultery or fornication*, AO,LL;Æ,CP:*fail,lapse, be neglected*, LL 178,7:*screen* (*a thief*), LL 274,12. ['*forlie*'] pp. forlegen used as sb. *adulterer, fornicator*.
forlicgend m. *fornicator*, Sc,WW.
forliden I. *much-travelled*, CAS 9·11. **II.** pp. of forlīðan.
forlidennes=forliðennes
forligan=forlicgan
for-ligenes, -lignes=forlegnes
forliger I. n. *adultery, fornication, wantonness, immorality*, Æ. **II.** m. *whoremonger, adulterer*, Æ : f. *fornicatress, adulteress*. **III.** adj. *adulterous*.
forligerbed n. *bed of fornication*, ÆH.
forligere=forliger I.
forligeren adj. *fornicating*, OEG 8²³².
forligerhūs n. *house of ill fame*, OEG.
forligerlic *unchaste, impure*, OEG. adv. -līce.
forligerwīf (e², o³) n. *prostitute*, MH 140¹⁹.
forliges=forlegis
forliggang m. *adultery, fornication*, WW 499¹².
forligrian *to commit fornication*, ERSPs 72²⁶.
forlīr=forliger II.
forlīsgleng *harlot's dress*, OEG 8³⁶¹ (= forlegis-).
forlīðan¹ *to suffer shipwreck*, OEG.
forliðennes f. *shipwreck*, OEG.
for-long, -longe adv. *long ago*, NG.
forlor m. *loss, destruction*, AO,CP. tō forlore gedōn *to destroy*, CP.
forlorenes f. *state of being forlorn, perdition, destruction*, VPs. ['*forlornness*']
for-lorian, -losian *to lose*, NG.
forlustlīce *very willingly*, Bo 51¹⁸.
forlytel *very little*, Bo.
form=feorm; **form-** (NG)=frum-
forma (eo) *first, earliest*, B,Bo,Mt; CP. ['*forme*'] on forman *at first*.
for-mǣl, -māl fn. *negotiation, agreement, treaty*, LL. [mǣl II.]
formǣr-=foremǣr-
formanig (æ², o², e³) *very many*, MA,RB.
formelle f. *bench*, ANS 84·9. [*L.* formella]
formeltan³ (y) *to melt away, dissolve, liquefy, burn up*, AO; Æ. ['*formelt*']
formengan *to associate*, CP 395⁴.
formesta=fyrmesta wk. superl. of forma.
formete m. *food for a journey*, Æ.
formicel (y²) *very great*, CP,LL.
formogod *corrupted*, ÆL 23³⁷⁵.
formolsnian *to rot away, crumble, decay*, Æ.
formolsnung f. *corruption*, OEG 1251.
formycel=formicel; **formyltan**=formeltan

formyrðrian *to murder*, LL,W.
forn I. f? m? *trout*, WW 180³⁹. **II.**=foran
fornǣman *to be worn out, afflicted (with grief)*, GD 245³.
forne=foran adv.; **forne** f.=forn
forneah *very nearly, almost, about*, Æ,AO, CP.
for-nēan (Æ), -nēh, -nēon=fornēah
fornerwian (=ie²) *to check the growth or fecundity of*, LCD 3·164'.
Fornētes folm *a plant*, LCD (v. BTs).
fornēðan *to expose to danger, sacrifice*, AO 222¹.
forniman⁴ *to take away, deprive of, plunder waste, devastate, destroy, consume*, B,Lcd; Æ,AO : *annul* : *disfigure* : *overcome*. ['*fornim*']
fornȳdan (=īe) *to coerce, compel*, W 158¹⁰.
fornyman=forniman
fornytlice *very usefully*, GD 174²⁰.
forod (a², e²) *broken down, worn out, useless, void, abortive*, Æ,AO,CP.
foroft *very often*, Æ.
forpǣran *to turn away, lose, spoil, pervert, destroy*, Æ,CP.
forpyndan *to do away, remove*, CR 97.
forracu f. *itinerary*, OEG 7¹²¹.
forradian=forhradian
forrǣda? m. *traitor, plotter*, MP 1·592.
forrǣdan *to plot against, betray*, W : *condemn : injure*. ['*forrede*']
forraðe (Æ)=forhraðe
forrepen *taken*, JnL p5⁸. [hrepian]
forrīdan¹ *to intercept by riding before*, CHR 894 A.
forridel m. *fore-rider, forerunner, messenger*, Æ. ['*forridel*']
forrotednes (a³, o³) f. *corrupt matter, rottenness*, Æ.
forrotian *to rot away, decay*, CP, WW : *putrefy*, Æ. ['*forrot*']
forrynel=forerynel
forsacan⁶ *to object to, reject, oppose, deny, refuse*, AO,Cp,LL : *give up, renounce*, AO, CP. ['*forsake*']
forsacennes f. *denial*, RWH 102¹⁰.
forsacung f. *denial*, RWH 144²⁵.
forsǣcan=forsēcan
forsǣtian *to lay wait for, beset, surround*, AO 146¹⁰.
forsǣtnian=forsetnian
forsǣwestre=forsewestre
forsawen=forsewen
forsc=frosc
forscǣd-=forscēad-
forscǣncednes (LPs 40¹⁰)=forscrencednes
forscamian *to make ashamed* (impers. w. a.), CP,Sc : *be ashamed*. ['*forshame*']
forscamung f. *modesty*, GPH 390.

forscapung f. *mishap, mischance*, AO 40, 50.
forscēadan⁷ *to scatter, disperse*, CP : *damn, condemn?* GU 449 (GK).
forsceamian=forscamian
forsceap n. *evil deed?* GEN 898.
forscēaw-=forescēaw-
forscending f. *confusion*, LkR 21²⁵.
forsceorfan³ *to gnaw off, bite, eat up*, AO 226⁹.
forscēotan *to anticipate, forestall, prevent*, BO.
forsceppan=forscieppan
forsceta *flood-gate*, BLPs 41⁸. [=forsscēta]
forscieppan⁶ *to change, transform*, Æ. ['*forshape*']
forscip n. '*foreship*,' *prow*, WW. [=fore-]
forscired *the dead?* VH 12.
forscrencan (æ²) *to supplant, overcome, vanquish, cast down*, Æ : *dry up*, OEG 4926.
forscrencednes (scænc-) f. *supplanting, deceit*, LPs 40¹⁰.
forscrencend m. *supplanter*, ÆH 1·198'.
forscrīfan¹ *to decree*, GL : *proscribe, condemn, doom*, Æ : (†) *bewitch*.
forscrincan³ (intr.) *to shrink, dry up, wither away*, Æ,Mt. ['*forshrink*']
forscūfan² *to cast down (pride)*, EX 204.
forscyldig *wicked*, Æ (58¹⁷⁰).
forscyldigian *to condemn*. pp. *guilty*, Æ.
forscyppan=forscieppan
forscyrian *to separate*, MFH 159.
forscyttan *to exclude, prevent, obviate*, Æ. ['*forshut*']
forsēarian *to sear, dry up, wither*, Æ,CP.
forseawennes=forsewennes
forsēcan I. *to afflict, attack*. **II.**=foresēcan
forsecgan *to accuse falsely, slander, accuse*, Æ : *to speak about, discourse on*.
forsegen-=forsewen-
forsēgon=forsāwon pret. pl. of forsēon.
forsellan *to sell*, ÆP 202⁷ : *give up, lose*, LL.
forsencan *to reject*, CP 345¹³.
forsendan *to send away, banish, send to destruction*, AO.
forsēon⁵ *to overlook, neglect, scorn, despise, reject, renounce*, Bl; Æ,AO,CP : *refrain from*. ['*forsee*']
forsēones=foresēones.
forsēoðan² *to wither, consume*, ÆH 1·84¹⁵.
forsērian (AS 10³?)=forsēarian
forsetnian (æ) *to beset*, ERPs 21¹⁷.
forsettan I. *to hedge in, obstruct*, BH : *oppress*. ['*forset*'] **II.**=foresettan
forsettednes=foresetnes
forsewen I. f. *contempt*, LPs 122⁴. **II.** pp. of forsēon.
forsewenlic *despicable, ignominious, wretched, of poor appearance*. adv. -līce, Æ.

forsewennes f. *contempt*, Æ,AO.
forsewestre (æ²) f. *female despiser*, OEG 4430.
forsingian=forsyngian
forsittan⁵ *to neglect, delay*, LL : *block, obstruct, besiege*, AO : *injure : absent oneself (from)*. ['*forsit*']
forsīð=forðsīð
forsīðian *to perish*, B1550.
for-slǣwan, -slāwian *to be slow, unwilling, delay, put off*, Bo; CP. ['*forslow*']
forslēan⁶ *to cut through, strike, break, kill, destroy*, AO.
forslegenlic *mean, ignominious*, MH156²⁰.
forsliet m. *slaughter*, WW28¹⁶. [slieht]
forslītan *to consume, devour*, PPs77⁴⁶.
forsmorian *to smother, choke, stifle*, Æ.
forsorgian *to despond*, W69¹⁶.
forsōð *indeed, verily*, Bo. ['*forsooth*']
forspǣc=foresprǣc
forspanan⁶ *to mislead, lead astray, seduce, entice*, Æ; CP. ['*forspan*']
forspaning f. *allurement*, OEG.
forspeca=forespreca
forspecan=forsprecan
forspēdian *to speed, prosper*, SPs (? forswefian).
forspendan *to spend, give out, squander, consume*, AO. ['*forspend*']
forspennen (OEG612)=forspenning
forspennend m. *procurer*, ÆGR36¹¹.
forspenn-ende, -endlic *seductive, voluptuous, defiling*, OEG.
forspennestre f. *procuress*, ÆGR36¹².
forspenning f. *enticement, seduction, evil attraction*, ÆL.
forspild m. *destruction*, CP294¹⁹.
forspildan *to waste, lose, disperse, bring to nothing, destroy, ruin, kill*, CP. ['*forspill*']
forspillan (AO)=forspildan
forspil(le)dnes f. *waste, destruction, perdition*, Æ.
forspillian *to wanton*, OEG.
forsprec-=foresprec-; **forspyll-**=forspill-
for-sprecan, -specan⁵ *to speak in vain : state amiss : deny : denounce : lose (a case)*.
forspyrcan (=ie) *to dry up*, PPs101³.
forst (frost) m. '*frost*,' Gl,Ph,Rd. [frēosan]
forstæppan=forestæppan
forstal (LL)=foresteall
forstalian (refl.) *to steal away*, LL.
forstandan⁶ *to defend, help, protect*, LL : *withstand, prevent, hinder, resist, oppose*, Met : *benefit, avail*, CP : *understand*, Bo; CP : *signify, be equal to*, EC,LL. ['*forstand*']
forsteall=foresteall
forstelan⁴ *to steal away, steal, rob, deprive*, MtR,LL; Æ. ['*forsteal*']

forstig *frosty*, ÆL23b⁵⁷⁵. [v. fyrstig]
forstlic *glacial, frozen*, WW175¹⁶.
forstoppian *to stop up, close*, LCD15b.
forstrang *very strong*, RD51⁴.
forstregdan³ *to destroy*, JPs105²³.
forstrogdnes f. '*precipitatio*,' NC289 (v. BTs).
forstyltan *to be amazed*, MkLR.
forstyntan *to blunt, break, crush*, WW375⁶ : *check, impair*, WYN132.
forsūcan² *to suck up*, OEG3343.
forsūgan² *to suck in*, LCD.
for-sugian (Æ,AO), -suwian (Æ)=forswigian
forsuwung f. *silence*, OEG2085.
forswǣlan *to burn, burn up, inflame, consume*, Æ. ['*forsweal*']
forswǣð (DHy38¹⁶)=fōtswæð
forswāpan⁷† *to sweep away, drive off*.
forswarung f. *perjury*, CHRD40³⁴.
forswefian (-sweb-) *to prosper*, EPs88²³ (forð-), 117²⁵.
forswelan⁴ *to burn, burn up*, PH532.
forswelgan³ *to swallow up, devour, consume, absorb*, B; Æ,CP. ['*forswallow*']
forsweltan³ *to die, disappear*, Bo; WW. ['*forswelt*']
forsweogian=forswigian
forsweolgan=forswelgan
forsweorcan³ *to grow dark, obscure*, B,W.
forsweorfan³ *to polish, cleanse*, WW227¹⁷ : *grind away, demolish*, WW218²⁸.
forsweotole *very clearly*, AS2¹⁷.
forswerian⁶ (refl. and intr.) *to swear falsely*, Æ,LL : *make useless by a spell*, B. ['*forswear*']
forswigian *to conceal by silence, suppress, pass over*, Æ,CP : *be silent*.
forswīð *very great*, CREAT26.
forswīðan, forswīðian *to crush, press upon, overcome, repress*, CP.
forswīðe adv. *very much, utterly*, Bo.
forsworcenlic *dark, obscure*, DHy24¹⁰.
forsworcennes f. *darkening, darkness*, Æ, W.
forsworen (pp. of forswerian) '*forsworn*,' *perjured*, Æ,Chr,WW.
forsworennes f. *perjury*, Æ. ['*forswornness*']
for-swugian (CP), -sygian=forswigian
forsyngian (i) *to sin greatly*, LL. ['*forsin*'] pp. as sb. forsyngod m. *sinner*.
fortācen=foretācn
fortendan *to burn away, sear*, AO46¹⁴.
fortēon² *to mislead, seduce*, Cr : *draw over, cover, obscure*. ['*fortee*']
fortiht-=fortyht-
for-timbran, -timbrian *to close up, obstruct*, CVPs62¹².

fortog n. *gripes*, LCD 109⁶.
fortogen *pulled together*, WW 106¹⁴.
fortogenes f. *griping, spasm*, LCD 89a.
fortogian *to contract*, LCD 3·120⁸.
fortredan⁵ *to tread down, trample on*, Æ; CP. ['*fortread*']
fortreddan *to tread down*, BH 44²³.
fortreding f. *treading down, crushing*, SC 95¹⁰.
fortrendan *to block (by rolling a stone)*, v. OEG 114.
fortrūgadnes, fortrūwednes=fortrūwodnes
fortrūwian *to be presumptuous, over-confident, rash*, CP.
fortrūwodnes f. *presumption*, CP.
fortrūwung f. *presumption*, Bo,CP.
fortrymman *to testify, confirm*, NG.
fortyhtan *to seduce*, EL 208.
fortyhtigend m. *polluter, defiler*, OEG 3337.
fortyllan *to seduce*, CR 270.
fortymbrian=fortimbrian
fortȳnan *to shut in, enclose, block up*, CP.
forð I. adv. '*FORTH*,' *forwards, onwards, further*, Æ : *hence, thence : away*, Æ : *continually, still, continuously, henceforth, thenceforward, simultaneously.* f. mid ealle *forthwith*. and swā f. *and so forth*, ÆGr. swā f. swā *so far as*, LL. f. on *continually*. fram orde oð ende f. *from the beginning to the end*. f. ðæt *until*. **II.** prep. *during*, Bo.
forð- (N)=furð-
forðācigan *to call forth*, BH 444²⁴.
forðādilgian *to bring to nothing, blot out*, MFH 160.
forðǣm, forðām, forðan (CP), forðon (AO, CP) **I.** conj. *for (the reason) that, owing to (the fact) that, for, because, on that account, therefore, seeing that*. for ðǣm ðe, etc. with same signification. **II.** adv. *for that cause, consequently, therefore*.
forðāgoten *poured forth*, ÆL 23b⁷⁹⁶.
forðahting (=eaht-) f. *exhortation*, CM 447.
forðancful *very thankful*, ES 18·336; 43·162.
forðātēon² *to bring forth, produce*, Æ. pp. forðātogen.
forðāurnen ptc. *elapsed*, BH 280²¹.
forðbǣre *productive*, GEN 132.
forðbecuman⁴ *to come forth*, BH,PPs.
forðberan⁴ *to bring forth, produce*, BH; Æ. ['*forthbear*']
forðbesēon⁵ *to look forth*, LPs 101²⁰.
forðbi, forðbie prep. *by, past*, CP 197¹³.
forðbigferende *passing by*, NC 343.
forðblǣstan *to blow forth, burst out*, WW 393³³,WYN 24.
forðblāwan *to blow or belch forth*, WW 397¹⁰.
forðboren *of noble birth*, LL.

forð-brengan, -bringan *to bring forth, produce*, Bl,Lk : *bring to pass, accomplish* : *bring forward : adduce, quote*, Æ. ['*forthbring*']
forðbylding f. *emboldening, encouragement*, CHR 999 E.
forðclypian *to call forth*, Gal (Lye). ['*forthclepe*']
forðcuman⁴ *to come forth, proceed, arrive at, succeed : come to pass, come true : be born*.
forðcyme m. *coming forth, birth*, Æ. ['*forthcome*']
forðcȳðan *to announce, declare*, CVPs 118²⁶.
forðdǣd f. *advantage*, Æ.
forðdōn *to put forth*, BH. ['*forthdo*']
forðeahtung (a²) f. *exhortation*, A 13·447.
forðearle *very much, greatly, strictly*, Æ.
forðearlice *absolutely, entirely*, RB 11¹⁹.
forðeccan *to shield, protect*, APs 18⁶.
forðelgian (KGL)=forðyld(g)ian
forðencan I. (æ) *to mistrust, despise, despair*, Ps. pp. forðōht *despaired of*; as sb. *poor wretch*, Æ. ['*forthink*'] **II.**=foreðencan
forðēoflan (īo) *to steal*, MkL 10¹⁹.
forðēon I. *to crush, oppress*, ROOD 54. **II.**=foreðēon
forðēostrian (īe) *to darken*, LPs 104²⁸.
forðerscan³ *to beat down*, GD 57⁴.
forðfǣder m. *forefather, ancestor*, Æ. ['*forthfather*']
forðfæderen *paternal*, CHRD 96⁶.
forðfaran⁶ *to depart, die*, Bo,Chr; Æ. ['*forthfare*']
±**forðfēran** *to depart, die*, Æ.
forðfērednes f. *death*, BHcs 290²⁹.
forðfēring f. *death*, SC 65⁸.
forðflōwan *to flow*, BH 418²¹.
forðfolgian *to follow*, CM 1052.
forðfōr I. f. *departure, death*, BH. ['*forthfore*'] **II.** pret. 3 sg. of forðfaran.
forðforlǣtenes f. *licence*, Bo 12².
forðframian *to grow to maturity*, WW 465¹⁰.
forðfromung f. *departure*, CVPs 104³⁸.
forðfyligan *to follow, fall out, happen*, CM 1109.
forðgān anv., pret. 3 sg. -ēode *to go forth, advance, proceed, pass by, go away, go on, precede, succeed*, Chr,Mk. ['*forthgo*']
forðgang m. *going forth, progress, advance, success : privy, drain : purging, evacuation*, ÆL 16²⁰⁷.
forðgangan⁷ *to go forth*, Ma. ['*forthgang*']
forðgecigan *to call forth*, REPs 67⁷ : *exhort*, BH 54¹⁵.
forðgeclipian (y) *to call forth, provoke*, SC, EPs.

forðgefaran=forðfaran
forðgefēran=forðfēran
forðgegyrdu *ornaments of a* forðgyrd, WW 195²⁹.
forðgelǣstan=forðlǣstan
forðgelang *dependent*, LL (280¹²).
forðgelēoran *to pass away, die*, BH.
forðgelēorednes f. *departure, death*, GD 282¹¹.
forðgelōcian (BPs 101²⁰)=forðlōcian
forðgenge *increasing, thriving, effective, successful*, Æ,CP.
forðgeong=forðgang
forðgeorn *eager to advance*, MA 281.
forðgēotan² *to pour forth*, BH. ['*forthyete*']
forðgerīmed *in unbroken succession*, B 59.
forðgesceaft† f. *creature, created being or thing, world : future destiny.*
forðgestrangian '*confortare*,' LPs 68⁵.
forðgesȳne *visible, conspicuous*, CRA 1.
forðgewītan¹ *to go forth, pass, proceed, go by : depart, die.* forðgewiten tīd, tīma *past tense*, ÆGR.
forðgewitenes f. *departure*, LPs 104³⁸.
forðgyrd m. *fore-girdle, martingale*, WW.
forðheald *bent forward, stooping : inclined, steep*, RB 5²⁰.
forðhealdan⁷ *to hold to, follow out, keep up, observe*, Æ.
forðheold I.=forðheald. II. pret. 3 sg. of forðhealdan.
forðherge m. *van (of an army)*, Ex 225.
forðhlīfian *to be prominent*, BH 322²⁴.
forðhnigan¹ *to fall down, fall forward*, VH 13.
forðhrēosan *to rush forth*, Sc 101¹³.
forðī=forðȳ
±forðlan *to put forth, contribute : further, advance : carry out, accomplish*, Chr. ['*forth*']
forðīg=forðȳ
forðindan³ *to swell up*, LCD 127a.
forðingian *to arrange for a man's wergild*, LL (Wilk.) 39³⁴.
forðlǣdan *to lead forth, bring forth*, Sat; Æ. ['*forthlead*']
forðlǣdnes f. *bringing forth*, BH 76¹⁵.
forðlǣstan *to persevere in, accomplish*, BH 352¹⁴.
forðlǣtan⁷ *to send forth, emit*, BL.
forðlēoran *to proceed*, BH 312²⁷.
forðlīc *forward, advanced*, CHR 1066 D: *thoroughly*, RWH 138¹⁶. adv. -līce.
forðlīfian=forðhlīfian
forðlōcian *to look forth*, BL.
forðlūtan *to lean forward, fall down*, VPs : *be prone (to)*, CHRD 54³¹.

forðmǣre *very glorious*, CREAT 69.
forðman m. *man of rank*, NC 289.
forðmest *foremost*, MtL. ['*forthmost*']
forðolian *to go without, lack*, WA 38.
forðon I. *forthwith*, MH. ['*forthon*'] II.= forðæm
forðoncol=foreðancol; **forðor**=furðor
forðrǣcan (tr.) *to protrude*, ÆL 25¹³⁵.
forðrǣsan *to rush forth, rise up : jut out, protrude*, RPs 72⁷. [rǣsan]
forðrǣstan (ē) *to crush, afflict, oppress*, VPs : *suppress, stifle : destroy*, CPs 104¹⁶. ['*forthrast*']
forðrǣst(ed)nes (ē) f. *tribulation*, VPs.
forðres-=forðrys-
forðriccednes=forðryccednes
forðriht adj. *direct, plain*, WW. ['*forthright*' adj.]
forðrihte adv. *straightway, at once : unmistakeably, plainly : straight on*, ZDA 9·406. ['*forthright*' adv.] -rihtes *without a break*, RBL 48⁶.
forðringan *to rescue from, defend against*, B 1084 : *elbow out, displace*, RB 115⁷.
forðroccetan *to belch forth*, APs 18³.
forðryccan *to press, squeeze, crush, oppress, suppress.*
forðryccednes (i) f. *pressure, oppression*, G, Ps.
forðrycnes f. *extortion, oppression, tribulation*, LL; MFH 159 (fore-).
forðryne m. *onward course*, GEN 215.
for-ðrysman, -ðrysmian *to choke, suffocate, strangle : becloud*, WW 246⁶. [ðrosm]
forðscacan⁶ *to pass away*, RPs 143⁴.
forðscencan *to pour forth, give to drink*, WW 464⁹.
forðscype m. *progress*, BHc 92¹⁴.
forðsetennes f. '*propositio*,' MtR 12⁴.
forðslō m. *going forth, decease*, Chr; Æ,CP. ['*forthsithe*']
forðsnoter (tt)† *very wise*, EL.
forðspell n. *declaration*, MOD 47.
forðspōwnes f. *prosperity*, BH 106²⁵.
forð-stæppan, -steppan⁶ *to issue forth, proceed, pass by*, ÆL,BF 184,198.
forðstæpping f. *advance*, DHy 80¹⁴.
forðstefn m. *prow*, LCD 3·180⁴.
forðswefian=forswefian
forðsyllan *to give out, pay out*, LL 175,3.
forðtēge (KGL)=forðtīge
forðtēon² *to draw forth, bring forth*, GEN 1¹².
forðtīge (e², y²) m. *vestibule*, OEG 3828.
forððegn m. *chief noble*, ÆL 6¹²⁵.
forððēon *to profit*, GD 200¹¹.
forðum=furðum
forðung f. *furtherance*, LCD 3·198' (v. ANS 125·49).

forðweard (e²) I. *inclined forwards or towards* : *advanced, progressing, growing, ready* : *enduring, everlasting, continual* : *future.* adv. *continually,* PPs : *prospectively,* ÆGr : *from now on* : *forwards, onwards,* W 17⁸. ['*forthward*'] II. m. *lookout man, pilot,* GEN 1436.
forðweardes (e²) *forwards,* HL 16²⁰³.
forðweardnes f. *progress,* GD 117¹⁹.
forðweaxan *to break forth, burst forth,* GD. ['*forthwax*']
forðwegt m. *journey, departure.* in (on) forðwege *away.*
forðwerd=forðweard
forðwīf n. *matron,* WW 309⁴⁴.
forðwyrft *tortured, mutilated,* v. OEG 5028.
forðȳ I. conj. *for that, because, therefore,* Jn. ['*forthy*'] II. adv. *for that, therefore, consequently.*
for-ðyldian, -ðyld(i)gian, -ðyl(de)gian *to bear, support, endure, wait patiently,* Æ.
forðylm-an, -ian *to shut in, enclose, envelop, obscure, cover over, overwhelm* : *choke, suffocate, consume.*
forðyppan *to make manifest,* CVPs.
forðyrnan³ *to run before, precede* : *continue,* Æ.
forðyrrian *to dry up,* LCD 82b.
forðysmed *obscured,* WW 246⁶.
forðȳðe=forðȳ; **forud**=forod
for-ūtan, -ūton adv.; prep. w. d. *except, without,* Chr 1122. ['*forout*']
forwærnan=forwiernan
forwærnian (WW 442¹⁸)=forweornian
forwana m. *abundance?* CP 465¹⁶.
forwandian *to hesitate, be reluctant,* CP : *be ashamed* : *reverence.*
forwandung f. *shame,* VPs 68²⁸.
forwarð=forwearð pret. 3 sg. of forweorðan.
forweallan *to boil away,* LCD 95a.
forweard I. (NG) *beginning, front* : *heading, title, chapter.* II. adv. *continually, always,* GEN 788. [?=forðweard; ·or foreweard, JGPh 12·257]
forweardmercung f. *heading,* JnL p 3¹.
forweaxan⁷ *to progress, grow too much, become overgrown,* CP; AO. ['*forwax*']
forweddod *pledged,* WW 115⁴⁴. [wedd]
forwegan⁵ *to kill,* MA 228.
forwel adv. *very, very well,* Æ.
forwened '*insolens,*' GL. [wenian]
forwēned '*suspectus,*' BDS 30·12¹⁰⁶. [wēnan]
forwenednes f. '*insolentia,*' ANS 79·89.
forweoren=forworen
forweornan=forwiernan
forweornian *to dry up, wither, fade, grow old, rot, decay,* Æ.

forweorpan *to throw, cast out, cast down, drive off, reject, throw away, squander,* B. ['*forwerpe*']
forweorpnes f. *migration,* MtL 1¹⁷.
forweorðan³ (y) *to perish, pass away, vanish,* Mt; AO,CP,Æ : *deteriorate, sicken.* f. on mōde *be grieved.* ['*forworth*']
forweorðenes=forwordenes
forweorðfullic *excellent,* Bo 65¹⁵.
forwercan=forwyrcan; **forwerd**=foreweard
forwered=forwerod
forweren (WW 217¹⁵)=forworen
forwerennes (RPs 70¹⁸)=forwerodnes
forwerod *worn out, very old,* Æ. [werian]
forwerodnes (e³) f. *old age,* SPs 70¹⁹.
forwest=forewost
forwiernan (e, eo, i, y) *to hinder, prohibit, prevent, repel, refuse, repudiate, deny, withhold, oppose,* AO,B; CP. ['*forwarn*']
forwiernedlice (e²) *continently,* W 284⁸.
forwiernednes (y²) f. *restraint, self-denial, continence,* BH 160¹⁰,MFH 118.
for-wird, -wirn-=for-wyrd, -wiern-
forwisnian (eo) *to dry up, decay, rot.*
forwitan=forewitan
forwitolnes f. *intelligence, diligence,* RBL 58¹⁰. [=fore-]
forwlencan *to fill with pride, puff up,* CP. ['*forwlench*']
forword I. n. *iota,* MtL 5¹⁸. II.=foreword
forwordenes f. *destruction, failure,* CHR 1105.
forwordenlic *perishable,* W 263¹³ : *perishing,* ByH 130²⁹.
forworen (pp. of *forweosan) *decrepit, decayed,* OEG 2109.
forwost (e²) m. *chief, captain,* NG.
forwracned *banished,* RB 82².
forwrecan⁵ *to drive forth, carry away* : *expel, banish.*
forwrēgan *to accuse, calumniate,* Chr. ['*forwray*']
forwrēon¹ *to cover over,* LkR 23⁴⁵.
forwrītan¹ *to cut in two,* B 2705.
forwrīðan¹ *to bind up,* LCD 122a.
forwundian *to wound,* Chr. ['*forwound*']
forwundorlic *very wonderful,* GD. adv. -līce.
forwurðan=forweorðan
forwynsumian *to enjoy thoroughly,* VH 13.
forwyrcan I. (e) *to do wrong, sin,* Æ,CP. forworht mann *criminal,* CP : *ruin, undo, destroy,* Cr ; Æ,AO,CP : *condemn, convict, curse* : *forfeit.* ['*forwork*'] II. *to barricade, obstruct, close up.*
forwyrd fn. *destruction, ruin, fall, death,* Æ,CP. [forweorðan]
forwyrdan *to destroy,* GD 201¹⁵.
forwyrdendlic *perishable,* Sc 43¹¹ (wyrð-).

forwyrht f. *misdeed*, LL : *ruin*, MFH 160.
forwyrhta m. *agent, deputy : evil-doer, malefactor, ruined person.* [fore-]
forwyrn- (Æ)=forwiern-
forwyrpnes f. *casting out*, LPs 21[7].
foryld=foreald; foryldan=forieldan
foryldu f. *extreme old age*, RB 114[11].
foryrman *to reduce to poverty, bring low*, BH,W. [earm]
foryrð=forierð
fōster=fōstor
fōstor m. *sustenance, maintenance, food, nourishment*, Lcd; Æ. ['*foster*']
fōstorbearn n. *foster-child*, GL.
fōstorbrōðor m. '*foster-brother*,' WW.
fōstorcild (e²) n. *foster-child*, ÆL.
fōstorfæder m. '*foster-father*,' Cp,MH.
fōstorland (e²) n. *land granted for the support of the recipients*, TC. [v. '*fosterland*']
fōstorlēan n. *payment for maintenance*, LL 442,2; MEN 152.
fōstorling m. *foster-child, nursling, pupil*, WW. ['*fosterling*']
fōstormann (ē) m. *bondsman, security*, LL 668,18.
fōstormōdor f. '*foster-mother*,' MH.
fōstornōð m. *pasture, sustenance*, EPs 22².
fōstorsweostor f. *foster-sister* (BT).
fōstrað (e²) m. *food : manna*, JnL 6[49].
-fōstre v. cild-f.
fōstrian (ē) *to '*foster*,' nourish, Sc;* MFB 205.
fōstring m. *foster-child, disciple*, NG.
fōstur=fōstor
fōt m. ds. fēt, fōte, nap. fēt, fōtas 'FOOT' (as *limb and as measure*), B,LL,NG: Æ,AO,CP.
fōtādl fn. *gout in the feet :* '*morbus regius*,' OEG (v. BTs).
fōtādlig *having gout in the feet*, ÆH 2·26[19].
fōtbred n. *foot-board, stirrup*, WW 107[6].
fōtclāð m. *joining, patch*, MtL 9[16].
±fōtcopsian, +fōtcypsan *to fetter*, Pss.
fōt-cosp, -cops m. *foot-fetter*, VPs,WW; Æ. [v. '*cops*']
fōtcoðu f. *gout in the feet*, OEG : '*morbus regius*' (v. fōtādl).
fōtece m. *gout in the feet*, LCD.
fōter=fōdder I.
fōtfeter f. *fetter of the feet*, WW 116[8].
fōtgangende *going on foot*, OEG 5254.
fōtgemearc n. *space of a foot*, B 3043.
fōtgemet n. *foot-fetter*, EPs 104[18].
fōtgewæde fn? *covering for the feet*, RB 88[14].
+fōtian *to hasten up*, MkL 15[44].
fōt-lāst (Æ), -læst mf. *footprint, spoor : foot.*
fōtlic *on foot*, ÆH 2·468[21] : *pedestrian*, GPH 403.
fōtmæl n. *foot-measure, foot*, WE 55[1].
fōtmælum adv. *step by step, by degrees*, CM 883.

fōtrāp m. *the loose part of the sheet by which a sail is trimmed to the wind*, '*propes*,' WW 167[11].
fōtsceamol (e², e³, u³) m. *footstool*, Æ.
fōtsceanca m. *foreleg*, Lcd 1·362'. [v. '*shank*']
fōtsetl n. *footstool*, CHR 1053 C.
fōtsid *reaching to the feet*, NC 289.
fōtspor n. *footprints, spoor*, LCD.
fōtspure n. *foot-rest, foot-support*, CHR 1070 E.
fōtstän m. *base, pedestal*, WW 191[85].
fōtstapol m. *footstep*, LPs 17[37].
fōtswæð n. (nap. -swaðu), fōtswaðu f. *footprint, footstep : foot*, Æ.
fōtswyle (i) m. *swelling of the foot*, LCD.
fōtðwēal n. *washing of the feet*, W,WW.
fōtwærc n. *pain in the foot, gout*, LCD 1·342[10].
fōt-welm, -wylm, -wolma m. *instep*, Æ (v. I F 48·254).
fōð ind. pres. pl. of fōn.
fōð-or I. (-er, -ur) n. *load, cartload, Chr : food, fodder.* ['*fother*'] II. *covering, case, basket*, GL.
fōðorn m. *lancet?* LCD 19b (v. BTac).
fōwer=fēower
fox m. '*fox*,' Lk,VPs.
foxesclāte f. *burdock*, LCD 54a.
foxesclife f. *foxglove? greater burdock?* WW 135n1.
foxesfōt m. *fox-foot, xiphion*, LCD.
foxesglōfa m. *foxglove*, WW 296[25].
foxhol n. *fox-hole*, KC.
foxhyll m. *fox-hill*, SR 57'.
foxung f. *foxlike wile, craftiness*, ÆL 16[162].
fra=fram; fraced, fraceð, fracod=fracoð
fracoð I. adj. *vile, bad, wicked, criminal, impious, filthy, abominable*, BH : *useless, worthless*. ['*fraked*'] II. n. *insult, contumely, disgrace : wickedness.*
fracoðdæd (-od) f. *misdeed*, W 188[15].
fracoðe adv. *shamefully*, PPs.
fracoðlic *base, ignominious, shameful, lewd*, Æ,CP. adv. -līce, CP.
fracoð(lic)nes f. *vileness, coarseness, obscenity*, Æ.
fracoðscipe (-od) *scandalous conduct*, RB 141[5].
fracoðword n. *insulting word*, GD 152[7].
fracud, fracuð=fracoð; fræ-=frēa-
fræc=frec; fræc-=frēc- (v. ES 39·327 ff. as to these four forms).
fræcuð (GL)=fracoð
fræfel n? *and adj. cunning*, GL.
fræfelian *to be cunning*, GL.
fræfellice (e¹) *shamelessly*, AO : *carefully : astutely.*
fræfelnes f. *sharpness, shrewdness*, OEG.

+**fræge** (ē) I.† n. _hearsay, report, knowledge._
mine +f. _as I have heard say._ II. adj. _well-known, celebrated, reputable,_ CP : _notorious, disreputable._ [fricgan]

frægn I. pret. 3 sg. of frignan. II. fregen II.

frægning f. _questioning,_ GD 323²³.

fræm-=frem-

fræng=frægn

±**fræpgian** (NG) _to accuse,_ MtL : _reverence,_ LG.

fræt I.† _perverse, proud, obstinate_ : _shameful._
II. pret. 3 sg. of fretan.

frætegung (Æ)=frætwung

frætenes f. _ornament,_ WW 524⁵.

frætew-=frætw-

frætgenga (ē¹) m. _apostasy,_ GL.

frætig _perverse, proud,_ JUL 284.

frætlæppa m. _dew-lap,_ WW 179³.

fræton pres. pl. of fretan.

frætwa, frætwe fp. _treasures, ornaments, trappings, armour_ : m. _adorner,_ CR 556.
[+tāwe]

frætwædnes=frætwednes

±**frætwan,** fræt(te)wian _to ornament, adorn,_ AO : _clothe, cover over,_ CP 83¹⁰.

frætwednes (æ², o²) f. _adorning, decoration, ornament,_ BH.

frætwian v. frætwan.

±**frætwung** f. _adorning, ornament,_ Æ.

fragendlic=framigendlic

+**frāgian** _to learn by inquiry,_ MtL 2¹⁶.

fram (o) I. prep. w. d. (instr.) (local) 'FROM,'
_by,_ Æ,Chr : (temporal) _from, since_ :
(agent) _by_ : _as a result of_ : (with verbs of saying and hearing) _of, about, concerning._
f. gān _to depart._ comps. v. fram-, from-.
II. adv. _from, forth, out, away._ III. adj.
(eo) _strenuous, active, bold, strong._ [_Ger._
fromm]

framācyrran=framcyrran (In this and the following words fram- may often be taken as a separate preposition).

framādōn anv. _to take from, do away, cut off, cut out,_ LCD,LPs.

framādrȳfan¹ _to drive away, expel,_ WW 98¹⁹.

framāhyldan _to turn from,_ LCD 1·328¹⁰.

framānȳdan _to drive away,_ LCD 1·226¹³.

framāscæcan⁶ _to shake off,_ GD,Sc.

framāstyrian _to remove,_ RPs 65²⁰.

framātēon² _to draw away from,_ Ps.

framāteran⁴ '_diripere_,' ÆGR 168¹⁰.

framāwendan _to turn from or away,_ Sc 169².

framāweorpan³ _to cast away,_ ÆGR.

frambige m. _backsliding, apostasy, default,_ KC,W.

frambringan³ _to take away,_ LCD.

framcyme (o) m. _issue, posterity,_ GEN 1765.

framcynn† (o) n. _issue, posterity_ : _origin._

framcyrran (e) _to turn from, avert_ : _take from._

framdōn anv. _to put off, stop, interrupt,_ Sc 131⁸.

frameald _very old,_ KC 3·60¹⁷.

fram-fær, -færeld mn. _departure,_ Æ.

framfaru (o) f. _excess,_ DR 17⁸.

framfundung f. _departure,_ BH.

framgewītan¹ _to apostatize,_ Sc 83².

framian _to avail, benefit,_ RB.

framierning (o¹, e²) f. _outflowing,_ DR 8¹.

framigendlic _effective, beneficial,_ LCD.

framlād (o) f. _departure,_ GEN 2098.

framlēce _turned from,_ GPH 401.

framlic _strong, daring,_ BH 30²⁸. adv. -lice
boldly, strongly, strenuously, quickly.

framlōcian (o) _to look back,_ CP 403⁶.

framnes (o) f. _vigour, excellence,_ AA 10¹⁷.

framrinc (o) _chief, prince,_ RHy 4¹.

framscipe (o) I. m. _exercise, action_ : _progress, success,_ BH 92¹⁴. II. m. _fraternity,_ BH 160⁶.

framsīð (o) m. _departure,_ GD.

framslitnes (o) f. _desolation,_ NG.

framswengan _to swing away, shake off,_ WW 524³⁰.

framung=fremung

framweard (o) _about to depart, departing, doomed to die,_ Bo,Seaf; CP : _with his back turned,_ LCD 126a. ['_fromward_']

framweardes (o) adv. _away from,_ Lcd.
['_fromwards_']

framwesende _absent,_ DR 178'.

frān pret. 3 sg. of frīnan.

franca m. _lance, javelin,_ ÆL.

±**frāsian** _to ask, inquire, find out by inquiry_ :
tempt, try.

frāsung f. _questioning, temptation,_ GU 160,
Mt p 19.

fratwian=frætwian

frēa† I. m. gs. frēan _ruler, lord, king, master_ :
the Lord, Christ, God : _husband._ [_Goth._
frauja] II. (VPs)=frēo·I.

frēa- intensive prefix (=_L._ prae-).

frēabeorht _glorious,_ BL.

frēabeorhtian (æ) _to proclaim,_ CPs 41⁹.

frēabodian _to proclaim, declare,_ LPs 118¹⁷².

frēabregd? _mighty device,_ MLR 22·3.

frēadrēman _to exult,_ LPs.

frēadrihten† m. _lord and master._

frēafætt (ǣ¹) _very fat,_ WW 532²⁴.

frēaglēaw _very wise,_ DAN 88.

frēahrǣd (ǣ¹, -hrǣð) _very quick,_ GL.

frēamǣre (ǣ¹) _very celebrated,_ PA,WW.

frēamicel (ǣ¹) _preeminent,_ WW 530¹³.

frēamiht _great strength,_ RPs 42².

freamsum=fremsum

frēan=frēon

frēaofestlice (ǣ¹) _very quickly,_ WW 530¹³.

frēareccere m. _prince,_ LRPs 118¹⁶¹.

frēas pret. 3 sg. of frēosan.

frēasian=frāsian

frēatorht *very bright, radiant,* GL.
frēaðanclan *to exult,* RPs 52⁷.
frēawine† m. *lord and friend,* B.
frēawlitig *very beautiful,* NC 290.
frēawrāsn f. *splendid chain,* B 1451.
frēbran=frēfran
frec (æ, i) *greedy,* MtL; Æ : *eager, bold, daring,* Met : *dangerous* (v. ES 39·327 ff.). ['*freck*']
freca† m. *warrior, hero.*
frēced-=frēcen-; **frēcelnes**=frēcennes
frēcelsod *exposed to danger,* WW 465²⁵.
frēcendlic, frēcenlic (CP) *dangerous, mischievous, perilous, terrible.* adv. -līce, AO.
frēcennes f. *harm, danger,* CP.
frecful (æ) *greedy,* OEG 2445.
frecian *to be greedy,* WW (BTs).
freclīce *greedily,* GD 31¹.
frecmāse f. *titmouse,* WW.
frēcn-=frēcen-
frēcne (æ) I. *dangerous, perilous,* CP : *terrible : savage, wicked : daring, bold.* [v. ES 39·328 f.] II. n. *peril.* III. adv. *dangerously : fiercely, severely : boldly, audaciously.*
frecnes f. *greediness,* GL.
±frecnian *to make bold,* DA 184 : *endanger, imperil,* ÆL 30·436.
frecwāsend m. *gluttony,* A 6·100.
+frēdan *to feel, perceive,* Æ,Bo; CP. ['*frede*'; frōd]
+frēdendlic *perceptible,* ÆGR 4⁶.
+frēdmǣlum *little by little,* OEG 3245.
+frēdnes f. *feeling, perception,* Bo.
+frēdra *more acute,* CP 123¹⁹.
frefellīce=fræfellīce
frōfer (CHRD), frēfernes (LkL) f. *consolation.*
frefīlce=fræfellīce
±frēfran *to cheer, console,* BH; CP. ['*frover*']
frēfrend (ie²) mf. *comforter, consoler : the Comforter* (*Holy Ghost*), BL.
frēfrian (*Jn*; Æ)=frēfran
frēfriend=frēfrend
frēfrung f. *consolation,* GEN 37³⁵, LPs 93¹⁹.
+frēge, +frǣge
fregen, fregn I.=frægn pret. 3 sg. of frignan. II. n. *question,* AN 255.
fregensyllic *very strange,* WNL 223a²⁴.
fregnan=frignan
fregnðearle *inquiringly,* ÆL 23⁵⁶⁶.
fregnung f. *questioning,* MkL p4¹⁹.
freht=friht
frem=fram adj.
fremde *foreign, alien, strange,* JnL,LL; AO,CP : *unfriendly,* Sol (-ede) : *estranged from, devoid of, remote from.* ['*fremd*']
±fremdian *to estrange,* RB : *curse, anathematize, excommunicate.*

freme I.† *vigorous, flourishing,* B,Gen. ['*frim*'; fram] II.=fremu
fremede=fremde
fremedlǣcan *to alienate,* RPs 57⁴.
fremedlīce *perfectly,* Sc 129³.
±fremednes f. *fulfilment, effect,* Æ.
fremful *useful, profitable, beneficial,* Lcd : *well-disposed,* WE 67³. ['*fremeful*'] adv. -līce *efficaciously.*
fremfullic=fremful
fremfulnes f. *utility, profit,* RB 83¹⁶.
±fremian *to avail, benefit, do good,* Æ,Mt. ['*freme*']
fremigendlic *profitable,* LCD,OEG.
fremlic (eo, o) *profitable,* BH 30²⁸.
fremman *to further, advance, support,* An, B : *frame, make, do, accomplish, perfect, perpetrate, commit, afford,* B,Gen; CP. ['*freme*']
±fremming f. *purpose, effect, performance, progress,* Æ.
fremnes=fremednes
fremsum *beneficent, benign, kind, gracious,* Æ,CP. adv. -sume.
fremsumlic *benignant, kind,* GD 280. adv. -līce, CP.
fremsumnes f. *benefit, benignity, kindness, liberality.*
fremð- (NG)=fremd-
+fremðian (MkL 14⁷¹)=fremdian
fremðlic=frymðlic
fremu f. *advantage, gain, benefit,* Bo,Ep, Lcd; CP. ['*freme*']
fremung (eo, o) f. *advantage, profit, good,* LL.
frence f. *a coarse cloak,* WW 212²⁶.
Frencisc '*French*,' Chr.
frēnd=frēond
frendian (WW 484³¹)=fremdian
freng=fræng pret. 3 sg. of frignan.
frēo I. nap. often frīge '*free*,' Bo,Ex,G; Æ, CP : (†) *glad, joyful* : (†) *noble, illustrious,* Gen. [frēo- v. also frīg-, frið-] II.† f. *woman, lady.* III. m.=frēa. IV. imperat. of frēogan. V. f? *freedom, immunity* (Swt).
frēobearn† n. *child of gentle birth,* WW.
frēoborh=friðborh
frēobrōðor m. *own brother,* Ex 338.
frēoburh f. *city,* B 694.
frēod I.† f. *peace, friendship : good-will, affection.* II. pp. of frēogan. III.=frēot
frēode pret. 3 sg. of frēogan.
frēodohtor f. *freeborn daughter,* W 193⁶.
frēodōm m. '*freedom*,' *state of free-will, charter, emancipation, deliverance,* Bf,Bo; AO,CP.
frēodryhten†=frēadrihten
frēodscipe (ES 39·340)=frēondscipe?

±**frēogan** to 'free' ('y-free'), liberate, manumit, Æ,Chr; AO : love, embrace, caress, think of lovingly, honour.
+**frēoge**=+fræge; **frēoh**=frēo
+**frēogend** (ī) m. liberator, CPs.
frēolāc n. free-will offering, oblation, LPs 50²¹.
frēolǣta m. freedman, WW.
±**frēolic** free, freeborn : glorious, stately, magnificent, noble, B,Rd : beautiful, charming. ['freely'] adv. -līce 'freely,' readily, Bo,VPs : as a festival, ÆP196¹².
frēols I. mn. freedom, immunity, privilege : feast-day, festival. [origl. frīheals] II. adj. free, festive.
frēolsǣfen m. eve of a feast, LL383,56.
frēolsbōc f. charter of freedom, Ct.
frēolsbryce (i) m. breach of festival, LL,W.
frēolsdæg m. feast-day, festival-day, Æ.
frēolsdōm=frēodōm
frēols-end, -iend m. liberator, EPs.
frēolsgefa m. emancipator, LL13,8.
frēolsgēr (=ēa²) n. year of jubilee, WW420³¹.
±**frēolsian** (ī, ȳ) to deliver, liberate, BL, EPs : to keep a feast or holy day, celebrate, Æ. ['frels']
frēolslic festive, festival, CM350. adv. freely : solemnly.
frēolsmann m. freedman, KC3·295⁶.
frēolsniht f. eve of a festival, NC290.
frēolsstōw f. festival-place, LL338,38.
frēolstīd f. festival, feast-day, Æ.
frēolsung f. celebration of a feast, LL.
freom=fram III.; **freom-**=fram-, frem-
frēomǣgt m. free kinsman, GEN.
frēomann m. 'free-man,' freeborn man, Gen, LL.
frēonama m. surname, BH.
frēond m. ds. friend, nap. friend, frēond, frēondas 'friend,' relative, B,Chr,El,Gen; AO,CP : lover.
frēondheald amiable, LCD3·192¹⁵.
frēondhealdlic related, akin, WW217²⁹.
frēondlār f. friendly counsel, B2377.
frēondlaðu f. friendly invitation, B1192.
frēondlēas 'friendless,' JnL : orphan. f. mann outlaw, LL.
frēondlēast f. want of friends, LL336,35.
frēondlic 'friendly,' well-disposed, kindly, BH; W. adv. -līce, CP.
frēondlīðe kind to one's friends, ES39·340.
frēondlufu f. friendship, love, GEN1834.
frēondmyne f. amorous intention, GEN1831.
frēondrǣden f. friendship, Bo; Æ : conjugal love. ['friendrede']
frēondscipe m. 'friendship,' B,Lcd; AO, CP : conjugal love.
frēondspēd f. abundance of friends, GEN 2330.

frēondspēdig rich in friends, LL(286¹³).
frēone asm. of frēo adj.
frēonoma=frēonama
frēorig† freezing, frozen, cold, chilly : blanched with fear, sad, mournful. [frēosan]
frēorig-ferð, -mōd† sad, GU.
frēoriht n. rights of freemen, LL,W.
±**frēosan²** to 'freeze,' Æ,Bl,Gn.
frēosceat m. freehold property, RB138²¹.
frēot m. freedom, LL. frēotes ðolian to be reduced to slavery.
frēotgifa m. liberator, WW.
frēot-gifu, -gift f. emancipation, WW.
frēotmann m. freedman, BK,TC,W.
freoð-=frið-; **-frēoðan** v. ā-f.
freoðo-, freoðu-=friðo-, friðu-
frēowif (ī¹) n. free-woman, LL7,73.
frēowine=frēawine; **Fresan**=Frisan
Freslic (y) in the Frisian manner, Frisian, CHR. [Frisan]
±**fretan⁵** to devour, eat, consume, Æ,B. Chr,LG; CP : break, Ex147. ['fret,' 'y-fret']
fretgenga=frætgenga
frettan to feed upon, consume, CHR,PPs. [fretan]
frettol greedy, gluttonous, WW171³⁴.
fretw-=frætw-
freðo=frið
frī=frēo I.; **frīa**=frēa
frīand (A)=frēond
frīborh (v. LL2·81)=friðborh
fric (NG)=frec
fricca, friccea m. herald, crier, CP (? v. ES 39·336).
fricgan⁵† to ask, inquire into, investigate : (+) learn, find out by inquiry.
frician to dance, Mt. ['frike']
frician† w. g. to seek, desire.
friclo f. appetite, LCD73a.
frico f. 'usura,' MtL25²⁷ (v. ES39·328f.).
fricolo (OP21)=friclo
frictrung (OET26)=frihtrung
frīdhengest v. friðhengest.
frīnan=frīnan, frignan
frīend v. frēond.
+**frīend** (ȳ) pl. friends, AO,Lk. ['i-freond']
frīg=frēo; **Frīgdæg**=Frīgedæg
frīge I.† fp. love. II. v. frēo.
frīgea m. lord, master, LL (=frēa).
Frīgeǣfen m. Thursday evening, Æ.
Frīgedæg m. 'Friday,' LL,Ma; Æ.
frigenes=frignes
Frīgeniht f. Thursday night, LL,W305²⁴.
frigest, frigeð pres. 2, 3 sg. of fricgan.
±**frignan³**, frīnan² ask, inquire, B,BH,Cp, Ps; AO,CP : †learn by inquiry. ['frayne']
±**frignes** f. interrogation, question, BH.

frīgnes f. *freedom*, CHR 796.
frignung f. *question*, GD 137²⁹.
frigst, frihst pres. 2 sg. of fricgan.
friht (e, y) n. *divination*, DR,LL.
frihtere m. *diviner, soothsayer*, NAR 37².
frihtrian *to divine*, KL.
frihtrung f. *soothsaying, divination*, WW.
frimdig=frymdig; **frīnan**=frignan
frīnd=friend; **frīo**=frēo
frīs (ȳ) *crisped, curled*, GNE 96.
Frisan (e) mp. *Frisians*, AO.
frisca=frysca
fristmearc (GL)=firstmearc
frit, friteð, fritt pres. 3 sg. of fretan.
frið (y) mn. *peace, tranquillity, security, refuge*, AO,Chr,MtL; CP, Æ. f. niman *to make peace* : *privilege of special protection, and penalty for the breach of it*, LL 10,5 : *restoration of rights* (*to an outlaw*), LL 316,13. ['*frith*']
frīð *stately, beautiful*, RD 10⁹.
frīða (eo) m. *protector*, PPs 70³.
frīðāð m. *oath of peace*, CHR 1012 E.
frīðbēna m. *suppliant, refugee*, LL.
frīðborh m. *surety for peace*, LL.
frīðbræc f. *breach of the peace*, LL.
frīðburg f. *town with which there is peace, city of refuge*, LL 222,2¹.
frīðcandel f. *the sun*, GEN 2539.
frīðelēas=friðlēas
frīðgeard m. *enclosed space, asylum, sanctuary*, LL : *court of peace* (*heaven*), CR.
frīðgedāl n. *death*, GEN 1142. [ferhð?]
frīðgegilda m. *member of a peace-guild*, LL 173 Pro.
frīðgeorn *peaceable*, MtL 5⁹.
frīðgewrit m. *peace agreement*, LL 144.
frīðgild n. *peace-guild*, LL 181. [v. '*frith*']
frīðgīsl m. *peace-hostage*, LL 378,9¹.
frīðhengest (frīd-) m. *stately horse?* (*ON.* friðr), *or horse of peace?* (frið-h.), RD 23⁴.
frīðherpað m. *king's highway*, KC 5·214′.
frīðhūs n. *sanctuary*, WW 186²³.
frīðian (eo) *to give '*frið*' to, make peace with, be at peace with* : (±) *cherish, protect, guard, defend, keep*, AO,Chr; CP : *observe*. ['*frith*']
frīðlend m. *helper, defender*, PPs,W 239⁷.
frīðland n. *friendly territory*, CHR.
frīðlēas *peaceless, outlawed*, LL 318.
frīðlic *mild, lenient*, LL.
frīðmāl n. *article of peace*, LL 220 Pro.
frīðmann m. *man under special peace-protection*, LL 222.
frīðo=friðu
frīðobēacen (eo¹) n. *sign of peace*, GEN 1045.
frīðoscealc (eo¹)† m. *angel*, GEN.
frīðosibb f. *peace-bringer*, B 2017.
frīðospēd (eo¹)† f. *abundant peace*.
frīðotācn n. *sign of peace*, GEN 2369.

frīðoðēawas (eo¹) mp. *peaceful state*, GEN 79.
frīðowær (eo¹)† f. *treaty of peace*.
frīðowang (eo¹) m. *peaceful plain*, B 2959.
frīðowaru (eo¹)† f. *protection*.
frīðo-webba (eo¹) m., -webbe† f. *peacemaker*.
frīðscip n. *ship for defence*, LL 441 (? read fyrdscip).
frīðsōcn f. *sanctuary, asylum*, LL.
frīðsplott m. *peace-spot, asylum*, LL (248⁵).
frīðstōl m. *sanctuary, asylum,refuge*, LL,Ps. ['*frithstool*']
frīðstōw f. *refuge, sanctuary*, CP.
frīðsum *pacific, peaceful* : (+) *safe, fortified*.
frīðsumian *to make peaceful, reconcile*, NC 290.
frīðu (eo) fm. *peace, safety, protection*, AO, Chr,MtL : *refuge, asylum*. [v. '*frith*']
frīðu-=friðo-; **frocga**=frogga
frōd† *wise* : *old*. [ON. frōðr]
frōdian *to be wise*, RIM 32.
frōfer=frōfor; **frōferian**=frēfran
±frōfor fmn. (e², u²) gs. frōfre *consolation, joy, refuge*, Æ; CP : *compensation, help, benefit*. ['*frover*']
frōforbōc (e²) f. *book of consolation*, Bo 50⁶.
frōforgāst (frōfre-) m. *consoling spirit, Holy Ghost, Comforter*, BH,Jn; Æ. [v. '*frover*']
frōforlīc (e²) *kind, helpful*, W. adv. -līce, W 295³.
frōfornes f. *consolation*, LkL 6²⁴ (oe).
frōforword n. *word of consolation*, GD 344²⁸.
frōfrian=frēfran
frogga m. '*frog*,' Æ,WW.
froht (NG)=forht
from=fram; **from-** also=frem-, frum-
froren pp. of frēosan.
frosc m. *frog*, Æ (frox); GL. ['*frosh*']
frost=forst
frōwe f. *woman*, DD 291. [Ger. frau]
frox (Æ)=frosc
frugnen pp., frugnon pret. pl. of frignan.
frum I. *primal, original, first*. II.=fram
fruma m. *beginning, origin, cause*, B,Mt; AO,CP : *creation*, CHR 33 : *originator, inventor, founder, creator* : *first-born*, CPs 135¹⁰ : (†) *prince, king, chief, ruler*. on fruman *at first*. wæstma fruman *first-fruits*. ['*frume*']
frumācennes f. *nativity*, JnL p 5¹⁹.
frumbearn† n. *first-born child*.
frumbyrd f. *birth*, TC 369⁹.
frumbyrdling n. *youth*, WW 171²³. ['*frumberdling*']
frumcenned *first-begotten, first-born*, Æ,AO : *original, primitive*, ÆGR.
frumcennende *primitive*, OEG 1775.
frumcnēow n. *primal generation*, Ex 371.

frumcyn† n. *ancestry, origin, descent, lineage : race, tribe.*
frumcynnend=frumcenned
frumcyrr m. *first time,* LL 164,25².
frumdysig n. *first offence, beginning of sin,* CHRD 18¹⁶.
frum-gār†, -gāra† m. *leader, patriarch, chieftain, noble.* [cp. L. primi-pilus]
frumgesceap n. *creation of the world,* CR 840.
frumgeweorc n. *original construction,* A 11·174⁶.
frumgewrit n. *deed, document,* W 252¹².
frumgifu f. *prerogative, privilege,* GL.
frumgripa m. *firstling,* W 113⁶.
frumgyld n. *first instalment,* LL 190.
frumhēowung (=ī²) f. *original formation,* WW 467²⁷.
frumhrægl n. *first garment* (sc. *of fig-leaves*), GEN 943.
frumildo f. *early age,* WW 341²². [ieldo]
frumlēoht n. *dawn,* AF 4·56.
frumlic *original, primitive,* GL. adv. -līce, GL.
frumlīda m. *chief sailor.* v. OEG 32.
frumlȳhtan *to dawn,* BL 207³⁵.
frummeoluc f. *'nectar' (new milk?* BTs), WW 456¹⁸.
frummynetslæge m. *first coinage,* ÆL 23⁴⁷⁹.
frumræd m. *primary ordinance,* LL 246.
frumrǣden f. *space of time,* AN 147.
frumrinc=framrinc
frumrīpa m. *first-fruits,* LL 40,38.
frumsceaft m. *first creation, origin, primeval condition,* B,BH : *creature : home.* ['*frumschaft*']
frumsceapen *first created, first,* Æ.
frumsceatt m. *first-fruits,* ELPs.
frumscepend m. *creator,* DR 16¹⁰.
frumscyld f. *original sin,* SOL 445.
frumsetnes f. *authority,* DR 123⁸.
frumsetnung f. *foundation, creation,* JnR 17²⁴.
frumslǣp m. *first sleep,* Æ,AO.
frumspellung f. *first relation, original story,* OEG 1153; 2³¹.
frumsprǣc f. *opening words,* ÆL 23¹²⁰ : †promise.
frumstaðol m. *first state,* RD 61³.
frumstemn m. *prow,* WW 288²¹.
frumstōl m. *first or principal seat, paternal home,* LL.
frumtalu f. *first statement in an action?* (Lieb), *of a witness?* (BT), LL 385 and 3·226.
frumtīd f. *beginning,* GD 212⁵.
frumtyhtle f. *first accusation, first charge,* LL 336,35. [tēon II.]
frumð=frymð
frumwæstm mf. *first-fruits,* Æ.

frumweorc n. *primeval work, creation,* AN 805.
frumwīfung f. *first marriage,* W 304²⁷.
frumwylm (e²) m. *new-born zeal,* RB 135⁵ : *first inflammation,* LCD 30b.
frumwyrhta m. *creator,* DR 37⁴.
frunen pp., frun(n)on pret. pl. of frīnan.
frungon=frugnon pret. pl. of frignan.
fruron pret. pl. of frēosan.
frȳ=frēo; fryccea=fricca
fryht=friht
fryht- (N)=forht-, fyrht-
frylsian (Bo)=freolsian
frym-=frum-, fyrm-
frymdig (i) *curious, inquisitive,* Æ : *desirous.* f. bēon *to entreat.*
frymetling f. *young cow,* LL 451,13.
frymð I. mf. *origin, beginning, foundation,* Bo; Æ,AO : *creature,* (in pl.) *created things,* El. ['*frumth*'] II.=fyrmð
frymð-lic, -elic *primeval, primitive, first : chief.* adv. -līce, OEG 5211.
frymðu, frymðo (MtL)=frymð
frymðylde *of early age?* v. OEG 2381.
frȳnd (Æ) nap. of frēond.
+frȳnd=+frīend
frȳs=frīs
Frysan=Frisan
frysca I. (i) m. *kite, bittern,* GL. II. '*pusio*'? GL (v. A 19·495).
frȳsð pres. 3 sg. of frēosan.
fryt pres. 3 sg. of fretan.
fryð=frið; fryð- also=fyrð-
fugel m. gs. fugles '*fowl,*' *bird,* B,Mt; CP.
fugelbona m. *fowler,* CRA 80.
fugelcynn n. *bird-tribe,* Æ. ['*fowlkin*']
fugeldæg (u²) m. *day on which poultry might be eaten,* TC 460²⁰.
fugeldoppe f? *water-fowl,* WW 131²⁰.
fugelere (AO)=fuglere
fugeleswȳse f. *larkspur,* WW 298²⁴.
fugelhwata m. *augur,* WW 140⁵.
fugellīm m. *bird-lime,* OEG 3105.
fugelnett n. *bird-net,* WW 277¹⁵.
fugelnoð, fugeloð *bird-catching, fowling,* Æ.
fugeltimber n. *young bird,* PH 236.
fugeltrēo n. *prop (of a snare for birds),* WW 349¹⁹.
fugelweohlere m. *augur,* WW 108¹². [wiglere]
fugelwylle (o²) *swarming with birds,* BH 30¹⁰ [weallan]
fuglere m. '*fowler,*' AO.
fuglesbēan f. *vetch,* GL.
fuglian *to catch birds,* ÆGr. ['*fowl*']
fuglung f. *bird-catching,* WW 268,352.
fugol-, fugul-=fugel-; fuhl-=fugl-
fūht *damp, moist,* LCD,CHRD 64³⁶. [Ger. feucht]

fūhtian *to be moist*, NC 290.

fuhton pret. pl. of feohtan.

ful I. n. *beaker, cup*, Æ. **II.**=full

fūl I. '*foul,' unclean, impure, vile, corrupt, rotten*, Æ,Bl,Cp,Cr,Gl; CP : *guilty*, LL. f. bēam *black alder*, LCD 29b. **II.** n. *filth, foulness, impurity, crime, offence*, El,OET. ['*foul*']

fulbeorht *very bright, resplendent*, CP 87²³.

fulbrecan⁴ *to violate*, LL 280,2².

fulðon anv. *to complete, perform*, RB 70²¹ : *arrange*, ÆL 33¹⁴²⁵.

fūle adv. *foully*, Æ.

fulēode pret. 3 sg. of fullgān.

fūletrēo n. *black alder*, Cp 430 A.

fulfæstnian *to ratify fully*, CHR 675 E.

fulfaran⁶ *to travel*, LL 383,56.

fulfealdan⁷ '*explicare*,' ÆGR 138⁹.

fulgeare *quite well*, ÆL 3⁴⁵⁶. [gearwe]

fulgōd *very good*, ÆL 6¹²⁴.

fulgon pret. pl. of fēolan.

fulhār *entirely grey, very hoary*, WW 380¹³.

fulhealden *contented*, WW 211³⁰.

fulht- =fulwiht-

fūlian *to be or become* '*foul*,' *decay, rot*, AO, Ps,Sc.

full I. adj. (w. g.) 'FULL,' *filled, complete, perfect, entire, utter*, Æ,AO,CP : *swelling, plump*, LCD. be fullan *fully, perfectly, completely*. **II.** adv. *very, fully, entirely, completely, thoroughly*, Bo,Chr,Met,Ps. f. nēah *almost, very nearly*. ['*full*' adv.] **III.**=ful

full- v. also ful-.

fulla I. m. *fulness*, ÆL 13¹⁰⁴. **II.** m. *assembly?* Ct (Swt).

fullǣst (ā, ē; fylst) m. *help, support*, Ex, Met. ['*filst*']

±**fullǣstan** (ē) w. d. *to help, support*, AO, Lk. ['*filst*']

fullǣðele *very noble*, Bo 24⁷.

+**fullan**=+fyllan

fullberstan³ *to burst completely*, W 267¹⁸.

fullbētan *to make full amends*, ÆGR,RB.

fullblīðe *very glad*, JUD 16²³.

fullboren *fully born*, CP 367¹⁸ : *of noble birth*.

fullbryce m. *complete breach of the peace*, LL : *violation of the rights of a clerical offender*, LL.

fullclǣne *very pure*, AS 30².

fullcuman⁴ *to attain*, RWH 136¹.

fullcūð *well-known, notorious, famous*, HL 201²¹¹.

-fulle v. sin-f.

fullendian *to complete*, BH. ['*fullend*']

fullere m. '*fuller,' bleacher*, Mk.

fullest=fullǣst

fullflēon² *to take to flight, escape completely*, ÆGR 179¹⁶.

fullforðian *to fulfil*, NC 291, RWH 138²⁵.

fullfrem-ed, -edlic *perfect*, CP. adv. -līce *fully, perfectly, completely*, Bl. ['*fullfremed*(ly)']

fullfremednes f. *perfection*, BH; CP. ['*fullfremedness*']

±**full-fremman**, -fremian *to fulfil, perfect, practise, complete*, Bo; CP. ['*fullfreme*']

fullfyligan *to follow, obey*, W 95¹⁹ : *pursue*, EPs 7⁶.

fullfyllan *to* '*fulfil*,' ÆGr 153¹.

full-gān pret. 3 sg. -ēode anv., -gangan⁷ *to accomplish, fulfil, perform, carry out*, Æ : *follow, imitate, obey* : *help*, AO.

fullgearwian *to finish, complete*, GD 126² : *prepare fully*, CP.

fullgedrifen (w. g.) *full* (*of wild beasts*), SOL 150²³.

fullgeorne *very eagerly*, CP 255²².

fullgewēpned *fully armed*, CHR 1083.

fullgrōwan⁷ *to grow to perfection*, CP 67²³.

fullhāl *thoroughly well*, GD 248¹.

fullhealden *contented*, WW 211³⁰.

±**fullian I.** *to complete, fill up, perfect*. **II.** (*Jn*)=fulwian

fullic *full : universal, catholic*, CHy 15. adv. -līce *entirely*, '*fully,' perfectly, completely*, Bf,BH; Æ.

fūllic *foul, unclean, objectionable, shameful, base*, LCD,W. adv. -līce.

fulligan=fulwian

fullmægen n. *great power*, W 186¹⁴.

fullmannod *fully peopled*, Bo 40¹⁷.

full-medeme *excellent, perfect*, GD. adv. -medomlīce, GD 320²¹, 331¹³.

fullnes f. *fulness*, DR 11¹³.

fūllnes=fūlnes

fulloc *final or definite agreement?* LL 385.

fulloft adv. *very often*, CP.

fullraðe adv. *very quickly*, AO.

fullricene *very quickly, immediately*, PPs 140².

fullrīpod *mature*, RB 139⁹.

fullslēan *to kill outright*, ÆP 138⁴.

fullsumnes f. *abundance*, EPs 48⁷.

fullðungen (ful-) *full-grown*, RB 133¹.

fullðungennes f. *full development*, MFH 160.

fulluht=fulwiht

fullunga adv. *fully*, N

fullwearm *fully warm*, CP 447⁵.

fullweaxan *to grow to maturity*, CP 383³⁰, ByH 6¹¹.

fullwelig *very rich*, Bo 24⁷.

fullwēpnod *fully armed*, CHR 1070 E.

fullwer m. *complete* '*wer,' full atonement*, RD 24¹⁴?

fullwērig *very tired*, MFH 160.

fullwyrcan *to complete, fulfil*, ÆL.

fulnēah I. adj. *very near.* II. adv. *very nearly, almost,* CP.

fūlnes f. *foulness, filthy smell,* BH,GL.

fūlon rare pret. pl. of fēolan.

fūlstincende *foul-stinking,* GD,LCD.

fultēam (Erf.)=fultum

fultem- (CP), fultom-=fultum-

fultrūwian *to confide in,* Bo 60²³.

fultum (ēa) m. *help, support, protection, B, Gl;* Æ,AO,CP:*forces, army,* AO. [' *fultum* ']

+**fultuma** m. *helper,* SPs 18¹⁶.

±**fultum-an,** -ian *to help, support, assist,* Æ,CP : (†) *be propitious to, overlook.*

±**fultum(i)end** m. *helper, fellow-worker,* Æ, CP.

fultumlēas *without help,* AO 56²¹.

fulwa m. *fuller,* MH 26²⁶.

fulwere m. *baptizer, baptist,* MH 14,102.

±**fulwian** *to baptize,* BH,Jn,MH; AO,CP. ['*full*']

fulwiht, fulluht (Mt) mfn. *baptism, Christianity, Mt;* AO,CP. ['*fullought*']

±**fulwiht-an,** -ian *to baptize,* CHR,NG.

fulwihtbæð n. *baptismal bath, font,* Æ (fulluht-).

fulwihtbēna m. *applicant for baptism,* WW 207¹⁶.

fulwihtele m. *baptismal oil,* LL (258¹⁵).

fulwihtere m. *baptizer : the Baptist,* Æ,G.

fulwihtfæder m. *baptismal father, godfather, baptizer,* BL 205¹⁷.

fulwihthād m. *baptismal order or vow,* BL 109²⁶.

fulwihtnama m. *baptismal name, Christian name.*

+**fulwihtnian** (fulhtn-) *to baptize,* NC 291.

fulwihtstōw f. *baptistry,* BL 140²⁰.

fulwihttīd f. *time of baptism,* MEN 11.

fulwihtðēaw m. *rite of baptism,* MET 1³³.

fulwihtðēnung (-uht) f. *baptismal service,* W 38⁹.

fulwihtwæter n. *laver of baptism,* NC 291.

fulwihtwere m. *baptist,* BL 161⁶.

fulwuht=fulwiht

funde wk. pret. 3 sg., funden pp. of findan.

-fundelnes, -fundennes v. on-f.

fundian I. (w. of, tō) *to tend to, wish for, strive after, go, set out, go forward, hasten,* Æ,B,Cr,Gen,Gu; CP : *spread?* LCD 125b. ['*found*'] II.=fandian

fundon pret. pl. of findan.

fundung f. *departure,* Chr 1106; ByH 12²⁰. ['*founding*']

funta? funte? *spring? brook?* KC (v. ES 54·102) or ?=finta (IF 48·255).

fūra v. furh.

furh f. gs. fūre, ds. fyrh, furh, gp. fūra '*furrow,*' *trench,* BC,Bo; Æ.

furhwudu m. *pine,* Cp 420 P.

±**fūrian** *to furrow,* OEG.

furlang n. *length of furrow,* '*furlong,*' BH, Lk : *land the breadth of a furrow,* KC.

furðan, furðon=furðum

furðor adv. (of place and time) '*further,*' *more distant, forwards, later,* Æ,Bf,Chr; CP : *more : superior,* CP 117². f. dōn *to promote,* CP.

furðorlucor (e²) cp. adv. *more perfectly,* MFB 133 and n 30.

furðra cp. adj. '*further,*' *greater, superior, Jn.*

furðum (-an, -on) adv. *even, exactly, quite, already, just as, at first, Bl,Mt;* AO,CP : *further, previously.* syððan f. *just as soon as.* ['*forthen*']

furðumlic *luxurious, indulging,* AO 50³⁰.

furður=furðor; **furuh**=furh

fūs *striving forward, eager for, ready for, inclined to, willing, prompt, B;* Æ : *expectant, brave, noble : ready to depart, dying.* ['*fous*']

fūslēoð† n. *death-song, dirge.*

fūslic *ready to start : excellent.* adv. -līce *readily, gladly.*

fūsnes f. *quickness,* EHy 6²⁵.

fustra (OEG 1428). ?=fyrstān (BTs).

fȳf-=fīf-; **fyhfang**=feohfang

fyht-=feoht-

fȳhtan (ī) *to moisten,* OEG. [fūht]

fyl=fiell, fyll

±**fȳlan** *to befoul, defile, pollute,* Æ.

+**fylce** n. *band of men, army, host,* CP. [folc]

±**fylcian** *to marshal troops,* CHR 1066,C,D. [folc]

fyld m. *fold, crease,* OEG.

fyld(e)stōl m. *folding-stool,* ZDA 31·10. ['*faldstool*']

fylen=fellen?

±**fylgan** w. d. or a. *to* '*follow,*' *pursue,* LG; Æ,CP : *persecute : follow out, observe, obey : obtain : attend to : practise, Bl.*

fylgend m. *follower, observer,* BH 472⁷.

fylgestre f. *female follower,* OEG 1228.

fylgian=fylgan

fylging f. I. *following,* DR. II. (æ) *fallow-land.* [fealh]

fylian, fyligan=fylgan

fyligendlic *that can or ought to be imitated,* CM 803.

fylignes f. *following, practice,* BH 160²³.

fyll=(1) fyllu; (2) fiell

±**fyllan** I. *to* '*fill,*' *fill up, replenish, satisfy, An,Gen;* Æ : *complete, fulfil, Az.* [full] II.± (æ, e;=ie) wv. *to cause to fall, strike down,* '*fell*' ('*y-fell*'), *cut down,* AO,Bl,Ps, Rd : *throw down, defeat, destroy, kill, BH, Cr,Ps : tumble : cause to stumble, MtR.*

+**fylled** (wdg.) *bereft.*

fyllað m. *filling, filling up,* GEN 1513.

+**fyllednes** (i) f. *fulness, completion, fulfilment*, Æ.

fyllen (=i) f. *a dropping*, LCD 18a.

-**fyllen** (fylen) v. mōnað-f.

fyllend=fylgend

+**fyllendlic** *filling, expletive*, ÆGR 261[5] : *capable of completion*, WW 209[38].

fyllesēoc (=ie) *epileptic*, LCD,WW 112[27].

fyllesēocnes f. *epilepsy*, LCD 1·164[9].

fylleðflōd m. *high tide*, GL.

fyllewærc (e[1];=ie) n. *epilepsy*, LCD 65a.

±**fylling** f. *filling*, GD : *completion*, LRSPs.

+**fyllingtīd** f. *compline*, WW 207[44]n.

±**fyllnes** f. *fulness, plenitude, satiety* : *supplement* : *completion, fulfilment*.

fyllo, fyllu f. *fulness (of food),* '*fill*,' *feast, satiety*, AO,B ; CP : *impregnation*.

fylmen=filmen

fylnes I. (±) f. *fall, stumbling-block, offence, ruin*, NG. II.=fyllnes

fȳlnes=fūlnes

fylst I. m. *help, aid*, Mt ; Æ,AO. II. pres. 2 sg. of feallan. III. pres. 2 sg. of fyllan.

+**fylsta** m. *helper*, Æ.

±**fylstan** (w. d.) *to aid, support, help, protect*, Æ,AO. [=fullæstan]

±**fylstend** m. *helper*, Æ,BRPs.

fylt pres. 3 sg. of fealdan.

fylð I. pres. 3 sg. of fyllan. II. pres. 3 sg. of feallan.

fȳlð f. '*filth*,' *uncleanness, impurity*, Mt,Sc, W. [fūl]

fylwērig *faint to death*, B 963. [fiell]

fyn-=fin- ; **fȳnd**=fēond ; +**fȳnd**=+fiend

fyndele m. *invention, devising*, Sc. ['findal']

fyne m? n? *moisture, mould*, WW 183[19].

fynegian *to become mouldy*, LL. ['finew']

fynig (i) *mouldy, musty*, Jos. ['fenny']

fyniht *fenny, marshy*, LCD 92a.

fyr v. feorr.

fȳr (ī) n. '*fire*,' Ex,G,VPs ; Æ,AO,CP : *a fire*, Gen.

fȳran I.=fēran. II. (±) *to cut a furrow*, OEG 2492n : *castrate*, LCD 3·184[19].

fȳras=firas

fȳrbǣre *fire-bearing, fiery*, OEG.

fȳrbæð† n. *fire-bath, hell-fire*, CR.

fȳrbend m. *bar forged in the fire*, B 722.

fȳrbēta m. *fireman, stoker*, WW.

fȳrbryne m. *conflagration*, AO 252[20].

fyrclian (ȳ?) *to flash, flicker*, CHR 1106.

fȳrclomm m. *band forged in the fire*, SAT 39.

fȳrcrūce f. *crucible, kettle*, GL.

fȳrcynn n. *fire*, AO 252[20]c.

fyrd=fierd

fyrdcræft (i) m. *warring host*, NUM 22[4].

fyrdend *enrolled for military service*, ÆL 25[363].

fyrdesne m. *warrior*, BH 148[6].

fyrdfæreld n. fyrdfaru f. *going to war, military service*, LL. [v. 'ferd']

fyrdfōr f. *military service*, KC.

fyrdgeatewe fp. *war-gear*, RUN 27.

fyrdgemaca m. *fellow-soldier*, Æ.

fyrdgesteallat m. *comrade in arms*.

fyrdgetrum† n. *band of warriors*, Ex.

fyrdhama (o²) m. *corslet*, B 1504.

fyrdhrægl n. *corslet*, B 1527.

fyrdhwæt† *warlike, brave*.

fyrdian (ie) *to go on an expedition*, CHR.

fyrding (e) f. *soldiering* : *army, expedition, militia*, LL ; Æ : *camp* : *fine for evading military service*, LL : *march, progression*, BF 46[28]. ['ferding']

fyrdlāf f. *remnant of an army*, ÆL 25[377].

fyrdlēas (ie) *without an army*, CHR 894 A.

fyrdlēoð† n. *war-song*, B.

fyrdlic *martial*, Æ.

fyrdmann m. *warrior*, BO 40[18].

fyrdnoð (e) m. *liability to military service*, BC 3·71[7].

fȳrdraca m. *fire-spewing dragon*, B 2689. ['firedrake']

fyrdrian *to serve in the army*, ÆL 28[11].

fyrdrinc† (e) m. *warrior, soldier*.

fyrdsceorp n. *armour*, RD 15[13].

fyrdscip n. *battle-ship*, LL.

fyrdsearu† n. *accoutrements*, B.

fyrdsōcn f. *military service*, Ct.

fyrdstemn m. *body of soldiers who serve for a fixed term, army-corps*, CHR 921.

fyrdstrǣt f. *military road*, KC.

fyrdtīber n. *military sacrifice?* (Swt), WW 418[22] ; A 15·187.

fyrdtruma m. *martial band, army*, ÆH 1·442'.

fyrdung=fyrding

fyrdwǣn (i) m. *military carriage?* EC 250'.

fyrdweard f. *military watch*, LL 444,1.

fyrdwerod n. *host, army*, WW 399[30].

fyrdwīc n. *camp*, Æ.

fyrdwīsa m. *chieftain*, CRA 77.

fyrdwīse f. *military style*, AA 14[5].

fyrdwīte n. *fine for evading military service*, LL.

fyrdwyrðe *distinguished in war*, B 1316.

-**fȳrede** v. twi-, ðri-f.

fyren=firen

fȳren *of fire, fiery*, Bl,MH ; AO,CP : *on fire, burning, flaming*. ['firen']

fȳrenful *fiery*, LPs,W.

fyrengāt (WW 423[11])=firgengāt

fȳrentācen n. *fiery sign*, MFH 131[12].

fyrentācnian *to pollute with sin*. RHy 6[21].

fȳrenðecele f. *firebrand*, BH 476[15].

fyres=fyrs

fyrest=fyrst, fyrmest superl. adj.

fyrewyt=fyrwit

fýrfeaxen *fiery-haired,* WW 425,519.

fýrfōda (ī) m. *fuel, twigs for burning,* OEG 7⁸⁸.

fýrgearwung f. *cooking,* WW 401⁹.

fýrgebeorh *fire-screen,* LL 455,17.

fýrgebræc n. *crackling of fire,* GEN 2560.

fyrgen=firgen

fýrgnāst m. *spark of fire,* AN 1548. [*ON.* gneisti]

fyrh I. f. *fir,* KC 6·102'. **II.** v. furh.

fýrhāt *hot as fire, burning, ardent,* El. ['*firehot*']

fýrheard *hardened by fire,* B 305.

±**fyrht I.** *afraid, timid.* [forht] **II.**=friht

±**fyrht-an,** -ian (fryht-, N) *to fear, tremble,* DR : *frighten, terrify,* BH. ['*fright,*' vb.]

fyrhtnes f. *fear,* AO,MtL.

±**fyrhto,** fyrhtu (fryht-, N) f. '*fright,*' *fear, dread, trembling,* Ps,VHy; Æ,AO,CP : *horrible sight,* NR 26⁶,⁹. [forht]

fyrhð=ferhð

±**fyr(h)ð,** fyrhðe nf. *wooded country,* Ct. ['*frith*']

fýrhūs n. '*caminatum,*' *house or room with a fireplace in it?* WW; CHRD 45⁶. ['*firehouse*']

fýrhwēolod v. fēowerhwēolod.

fyrian (B 378)=ferian

fýrian I. *to supply with firing,* LL. ['*fire*' vb.] **II.** (±) *to cut a furrow.* [furh]

fyrlen I. (eo, e) *far off, distant, remote,* Æ. **II.** n. *distance,* Æ.

fýrlēoht n. *gleam of fire,* B 1516. ['*firelight*']

fýrlēoma m. *gleam of fire,* SAT 128.

fýrlīce=færlīce

fýrloca m. *fiery prison,* SAT 58.

fyrm I. (=ie) *cleansing,* LL 454⁸. **II.**=feorm

fyrm-=frym-

fýrmǣl m. *mark burnt in by fire,* AN 1136.

fyrmest (o) superl. of forma **I.** '*foremost,*' *first,* LCD; Æ,CP : *most prominent, chief, best,* El,Mt. **II.** adv. *first of all, in the first place, at first, most, especially, very well, best.*

fyrmð (=ie) f. **I.** *harbouring, entertainment,* LL. **II.** *cleansing, washing.*

fyrn I. (i) adj. *former, ancient,* Rd. **II.** adv. (±) *formerly, of old, long ago, once,* Gu; ÆL. ['*fern*']

fyrn-=firen-

±**fyrndagas** mp. *days of yore,* An; ÆL. [v. '*fern*'] frōd fyrndagum *old, aged.*

fyrngēar n. *former year(s),* Gn,Ps : *preceding year,* LCD 3·228. ['*fernyear*']

fyrn-geflit† n. nap. -geflitu *former quarrel, old strife.*

fyrngeflita m. *old-standing enemy,* PA 34.

fyrngemynd n. *ancient history,* EL 327.

fyrngesceap n. *ancient decree,* PH 360.

fyrngesetu np. *former seat, habitation,* PH 263.

fyrngestrēon n. *ancient treasure,* SOL 32.

fyrngeweorc† n. *former, ancient work,* PH.

fyrngewinn n. *primeval struggle,* B 1689.

fyrngewrit† n. *old writings, scripture,* EL.

fyrngewyrht n. *former work, fate,* GU 944.

fyrngidd n. *ancient prophecy,* EL 542.

fyrnmann m. *man of old times,* B 2761.

+**fyrnnes** f. *antiquity,* CHRD 25,26.

fyrnsægen f. *old saying, ancient tradition,* AN 1491.

fyrnsceaða m. *old fiend, devil,* AN 1348.

fyrnstrēamas mp. *ocean,* WH 7.

fyrnsynn (JUL 347)=firensynn

fyrnweorc† n. *work of old, creation.*

fyrnwita (eo²)† m. *sage, counsellor.*

fýr-panne, -ponne f. '*fire-pan,*' *brazier,* WW.

fyrr v. feorr.

fýrrace (fērrece) f. *fire-rake,* WW 273⁶.

fyrran=feorran

fyrs I. m. '*furze,*' *gorse, bramble,* Bo,WW. **II.** n.=fers

fýrscofl f. '*fire-shovel,*' WW 358¹⁶.

fyrsgāra m. *furzy corner,* KC 4·8'.

fyrsian=feorsian

fyrsīg (=īeg) f. *furzy island,* KC 5·300¹⁷.

fyrslēah m. *furzy lea,* KC 5·232'.

fyrsmeortende v. smeortan; **fyrsn**=fiersn

fyrspearca m. *fire-spark,* WW 100².

fyrspenn m. *a pen of furze,* EC 266'.

fyrst I. '*first,*' Chr,Ex : *foremost, principal, chief,* LL. **II.** adv. *in the first place, firstly, at first, originally,* Ct. **III.** (Æ)=first I. and II.

+**fyrst** n. *frost,* LL 454,11.

fyrst-=first-

fýrstān m. '*firestone,*' *stone used for striking fire, flint,* WW.

fyrstig '*frosty,*' BH 216²⁷. [v. forstig]

fýrsweart *black with smoke,* CR 984.

fýrtang f. '(*fire-*)*tongs,*' LL 453,15. [v. '*fire*']

fýrtorr m. *beacon, lighthouse,* WW.

fýrð=fyrhð; **fýrð-**=fēorð-

fýrðolle f. *furnace,* EPS 20⁹ : *stage on which martyrs were burned,* OEG

±**fyrðran** (GL,AO), fyrðian (Bo; Æ) *to further, urge on, advance, promote, benefit.*

fyrðriend m. *promoter,* BC.

+**fyrðring** f. *removal,* CHRD 79¹⁵.

fyrðringnes f., fyrðrung (Lcd; W) f. *furtherance, promotion.* ['*furthering*']

fyrwit (e²) **I.** n. *curiosity, yearning,* Æ. **II.** adj. *curious, inquisitive.*

fyrwitful (æ¹, e²) *curious, anxious,* LkL 12²⁶.

fyrwitgeorn *curious, anxious, inquisitive.*

fyrwitgeornes (e², e³, y³) f. *curiosity,* BL 69²² : *fornication?* MFH 146¹¹.

fyrwitgeornlīce (e²) *studiously*, GD 174²⁸.

fyrwitnes f. *curiosity*, Æ.

fȳrwylm m. *wave of fire*, B 2672.

±fȳsan *to send forth, impel, stimulate* : *drive away, put to flight, banish* : (usu. reflex.) *hasten, prepare oneself*, An,Gen. ['*fuse*']

fȳsian (ē) *to drive away*, LL,W. ['*feeze*']

fȳst (ē) f. '*fist*,' Æ,Gl; CP.

fȳstgebēat n. *blow with the fist*, CP 315.

+fȳstlian *to strike with the fist*, Sc 7¹⁴.

fȳstslægen *struck with the fist*, WW 396³³.

fyðer-=fiðer-, fēower-

fyðera, fyðeras, fyð(e)ru, nap. of fiðere.

fyðerling=fēorðling

fyx=fisc

fyxe f. *she-fox, vixen*, KC 2·29'.

fyxen (i) adj. *of a fox*, LCD.

fyxenhȳd (i) f. *she-fox's skin*, LCD 1·342¹¹.

G

gā imperat. and pres. ı sg. ind. of gān.

gab- (GL)=gaf-

gabote (u²) f. *side-dish*, EGL. [*L.* gabata]

gād I.† n. *lack, want, need, desire*. [*Goth.* gaidw] II. f. '*goad*,' *point, arrow-head, spear-head*, Cp,Sol.

±gada m. *comrade, companion*, ÆL. [*Ger.* gatte]

+gadere *together*, ÆL 30³⁸⁵.

+gaderednes f. *gathering, abscess*, LCD.

gaderian (Æ)=gadrian

±gaderscipe (æ) m. *matrimony*, OEG.

gadertang (æ, ea) *continuous, united*, KC.

gadertangnes (æ) f. *continuation*, Sc 52¹.

±gaderung (æ) f. *gathering together* : '*gathering*,' Bf,Lcd : *union, connection*, BH : *assembly*, Jn : *text*, Mtp 8¹⁷.

±gaderwist (o²) f. *companionship*, WW 174⁴⁵.

+gaderwyrhtan np. *assembled workmen*, ÆL 6·186.

gadinca m. *wether sheep*, WW.

gād-īren (LL 455,15), -īsen n. *goad*.

gador=geador; gador-=gader-, gadr-

±gadrian (æ) *to* 'GATHER,' *unite* : *agree*, (refl.) *assemble*, Chr : *collect, store up*, Æ, CP : *pluck (flowers, etc.)* : *compile* : *associate (with)* : *concentrate (thoughts)*, Bo. [geador]

gadrigendlic *collective*, ÆGR 229⁴.

gǣ=geā; gǣc=gēac

gǣd n. *society, fellowship*, SOL 449.

gǣd=gād I.

gǣdeling† m. *kinsman, fellow, companion in arms, comrade*, B,Da. ['*gadling*']

gǣder-, gǣdr-=gader-, gadr-

gǣf=geaf pret. 3 sg. of giefan.

gǣfe=giefu

gǣfel (MtL)=gafol

gǣfon=gēafon pret. pl. of giefan.

-gǣgan v. for-, ofer-g.

gǣgl-=gagol-

gǣl-=geal-

gǣlan *to hinder, impede, keep in suspense*, CP : (intr.) *linger, delay* : *dupe*, KGL. [gāl]

gǣleð pres. 3 sg. of galan.

gǣling f. *delay*, CP 39¹.

gǣlnes=gālnes

gǣlsa (ē) m., gǣls (OEG 611) f. *pride, wantonness, luxury*, Æ,W : *(worldly) care*, MtL 13²² : *a greedy person*, LCD. [gāl]

gǣlslic '*luxuriosus*,' NC 291.

gǣlð pres. 3 sg. of galan.

-gǣlwan v. ā-g.

gǣmnian=gamenian; gǣn-=gēan-

-gǣnan v. tō-g.; +gǣnge=+genge

gǣp=gēap; gǣr-=gear-, grǣ-

gǣr=gēar

gǣred *wedge-shaped*, BC 3·251'. [gār]

-gǣrede v. twi-, ðri-g.

gǣrs (grǣs) n. '*grass*,' *blade (of grass), herb, young corn, hay, plant*, An,Cp,CP,G; Æ : *pasture*, Ct. v. also grǣs, grǣs-

gǣrsama=gǣrsuma

gǣrsbedd n. *(grass-bed), grave*, PPs 102¹⁵.

gǣrscīð m. *blade of grass*, AO 38¹¹.

gǣrsgrēne *grass-green*, WW 199²⁴.

gǣrs-hoppa m., -hoppe (e¹) f. '*grasshopper*,' *locust*, MtR (grǣs-), Ps,VPs.

gǣrsstapa=gǣrstapa

gǣrsswȳn n. *pasturage-swine*, LL 445,2.

gǣrstapa m. *grasshopper, locust*, Æ,AO.

gǣrstūn m. *grass-enclosure, meadow*, LL. ['*garston*']

gǣrstūndīc m. *meadow-dike*, Ct.

gǣrsum mn., gǣrsuma f. *jewel, costly gift, treasure, riches*, Chr. ['*gersum*']

gǣrswyrt f. '*herba*,' *grass*, APs 36².

gǣrsyrð f. *pasturage in return for ploughing-labour*, LL 447,4,1c. ['*grassearth*']

gǣsne (ē, ēa) w. g. or on. *deprived of, wanting, destitute, barren, sterile*, An,Cr,Jul : *dead*. ['*geason*']

gǣst=giest

gǣst I. m.=gāst. II. pres. 2 sg. of gān.

gǣstan *to frighten*, Jul 17. ['*gast*']

gǣsð=gāst

gǣt=geat; gǣt nap. of gāt.

gǣtan=gēatan

gǣten *of or belonging to a goat*, LCD,WW 152¹.

gǣð pres. 3 sg. of gān.

gaf=geaf pret. 3 sg. of giefan.

gafel=gafol

gafeluc m. *spear, javelin, OEG,WW*; ÆL. ['*gavelock*']
gaffetung f. *scoffing, mocking*, Æ.
gafol (æ, ea¹; e, u²) I. n. gs. gafles *tribute, tax, duty, due, debt, AO,Gl,MtL : interest, usury, profit, rent, Gl,Mt*; Æ (v. A36·60, 377 and LF168). ['*gavel*'] II. f. *fork*, Æ, *LL,WW*; OET463 (v. A36·60). ['*yelve*']
gafolbere m. *barley paid as rent*, TC145².
gafolfisc m. *fish paid as rent*, TC307'.
gafolfrēo (e²) *tax-free*, KC4·191,215.
gafolgerēfa (æ¹, e²) m. *taxgatherer*, MtR.
gafolgielda (i³, y³) m. *tributary, tenant, debtor*, AO.
gafolgyld n. '*fiscus,*' *revenue?* GPH395.
gafolgyldere m. *tributary, debtor*, Æ.
gafolheord f. *taxable swarm (of bees)*, LL 448,5.
gafolhwītel m. *tribute-blanket, a legal tender instead of coin for the rent of a hide of land*, LL 108,44¹.
±**gafolian** (e²) *to rent (land), Ct : confiscate, seize as tribute*, WW. ['*gavel*']
gafolland n. *leased land, land let for rent or services*, LL126,2.
gafollic *fiscal*, OEG6²⁰.
gafolmǣd f. *meadow which was mown as part of the rent*, TC145³.
gafolmanung (ea¹, o³) f. *place of tribute or custom*, MkR2¹⁴.
gafolpenig m. *tribute-penny*, LL446.
gafolrǣden f. *tribute, rent*, LL.
gafolrand (e²) m. *compasses*, WW.
gafolswān m. *swine-herd who paid rent in kind for permission to depasture his stock*, LL448,6.
gafoltīning f. *fencing-wood given as part of the rent*, TC145⁸.
gafolwydu (y³=u) m. *firewood supplied as part of the rent*, TC145⁶.
gafolyrð f. *ploughing, etc. done by a gebūr as part of his rent*, LL447; 3·249.
±**gafsprǣc** f. *foolish speech, scurrility*, ÆL.
gaful=gafol
gagātes, gagātstān (WW148⁵) m. *agate, jet, BH.* ['*gagate*']
gagel m? '*gale,*' *bog-myrtle, Lcd*; Mdf.
gagelcroppan mpl. *tufts of gale*, LCD33a.
gagelle, gagolle f.=gagel
gagol=(1) gāl; (2) gagel
gagolbǣrnes (gægl-) f. *wantonness*, CP,WW.
gagolisc (æ, e, ea) *light, wanton*, BH400¹³, MHc156¹⁸.
gāl I. n. *lust, luxury, wantonness, folly, levity.* II. adj. *gay, light, wanton, Bo,BH : proud, wicked.* ['*gole*']
±**galan⁶** *to sing, call, cry, scream, B,Met : sing charms, practise incantation.* ['*gale*']
galder-=galdor-

galdor (ea) n. *sound, song, incantation, spell, enchantment*, Æ.
galdorcræft m. *occult art, incantation, magic*, BL,LL.
galdorcræftiga m. *wizard*, LL38,30,VH14.
galdorcwide m. *incantation*, RD49⁷.
galdorgalend (e²) m. *enchanter*, WW448²².
galdorgalere m. *wizard*, WW346¹⁵.
galdorlēoð n. *incantation*, WW509¹⁷.
galdorsang n. *incantation*, W253¹⁰.
galdorword n. *magic word*, RIM24.
galdre m. *wizard, magician*, Æ.
galdricge f. *enchantress*, GL.
galdru nap. of galdor.
galere m. *wizard, snake-charmer*, WW.
gālferhð *wanton, licentious*, JUD62.
gālfrēols m. *revel, 'lupercalia,'* OEG.
gālful *wanton, lustful, luxurious.* adv. -līce.
galg-=gealg-
gālian *to be wanton*, Sc87¹⁰.
Galilēisc *Galilean*, G.
galla (VPs; DR)=gealla
gallac=galloc
Galleas, Gallias mp. *Gauls, Franks, French.*
galled'=gealled
gāllic *wanton, lustful, BH,Bo*; Æ. ['*golelich*'] adv. -līce, CHRD108¹⁸.
Gallie=Galleas
Gallisc *Gaulish, French*, AO.
galloc (u²) m. *comfrey, gall-apple, GL, LCD.*
gālmōd *wanton, licentious*, JUD256.
gālnes f. *frivolity, wantonness, lust, Sc*; Æ. ['*goleness*']
gālscipe m. *excess, luxury, lasciviousness, wantonness, Æ : pride.* ['*goleship*']
gālsere m. *licentious person*, W72⁶.
gālsmǣre *frivolous, facetious, jocose*, RB 30⁸. [v. '*smere*']
galung f. *incantation*, OEG4940. [galan]
Galwalas mp. *Gauls, Frenchmen : France*, CHR.
gambe=gombe
gamel=gamol; **gamelic**=gamenlic
gamen (o) n. *sport, joy, mirth, pastime, 'game,' amusement, B,Met*; Æ,CP.
gamenian *to pun, play, joke, Æ,Sc.* ['*game*']
gamenlic *belonging to games, theatrical, Gl : ridiculous.* adv. -līce *artfully*, Æ. ['*gamely*']
gamenung f. *jesting, pastime*, BAS,LPs.
gamenwāð (o¹) f. *merry journey*, B854.
gamenwudu (o¹)† m. *harp*, B.
gamnian=gamenian
gamol† *old, aged, hoary, ancient.* [ge-, mǣl]
gamolfeax† *grey-haired.*
gamolferhð *old, aged*, GEN2867.
gamolian (o¹, e²) *to grow old*, GNE11.
gān pret. 3 sg. of gīnan.

±**gān** pret. 3 sg. ēode, anv. *to* 'GO*' ('*i-go*'), *come, move, proceed, advance, traverse, walk,* Æ; CP : *depart, go away* : *happen, turn out, take place* : (+) *get, gain, conquer, occupy, overrun,* AO : (+) *observe, practise, exercise, effect.*

gandra m. '*gander*,' ÆGr; Ct.

ganet=ganot

gang I. (eo, o, iong) m. *going, journey, progress, track, footprint,* B,Lcd,LG,RB; Æ : *flow, stream, way, passage, course, path, bed,* AO,Bl,LG : *drain, privy,* Æ : (in pl.) *steps, platform, stage,* GPH394 : *legal process,* LL396,2. ['*gang*,' '*gong*,' '*yong*'] II. imperat. and pret. sg. of gangan.

+**gang** n. *hap, occurrence,* WW394[9] : *passage (lapse) of time,* GD179[10].

±**gangan**[7] (*B,Bl*) pret. geng (eo, a)=gān

gangdæg m. *one of the three processional days before Ascension day, Rogation day, Chr.* ['*gangdays*']

gangehere=ganghere

gangelwæfre=gangewifre

gangende *alive,* W : *going on foot,* Æ,AO.

gangern n. *privy,* WW184[15]. [ærn]

gangewifre (eo[1], o[1]; æ[2]; æ[3]) f. (*a weaver as he goes*), *spider,* Lcd,Ps.

ganggeteld n. *portable tent,* WW187[3].

ganghere m. *army of foot-soldiers,* AO154[24].

gang-pytt (*Scr*21[7]) m., -setl n., -stōl m., -tūn m. (Æ) *privy.* [v. '*gong*']

gangweg m. *thoroughfare, WW.* ['*gangway*']

Gangwuce f. *Rogation week, the week of Holy Thursday, Mk.* ['*gangweek*']

gānian *to yawn, gape, open,* Gl,Ps. ['*gane*']

ganot m. '*gannet*,' *sea-bird, water-fowl,* B, *Chr.* ganotes bæð *the sea.*

ganra=gandra

gānung f. *yawning,* WW162[37] : *gaping (in scorn),* WW476[9]. ['*ganing*']

-**gapian** v. ofer-g.

gār† I. m. '*spear*,' *dart, javelin,* B,PPs. ['*gare*'] II. *tempest? piercing cold? sharp pain?* Gen316. III.=gāra (Mdf).

gāra m. *corner, point of land, cape, promontory,* AO. [gār; '*gore*']

gāræcer n. *a pointed strip of land,* KC5·153'.

gārbēam m. *spear-shaft,* Ex246.

gārberend† m. *warrior.*

gārcēne *bold in fight,* B1958.

gārclife f. *agrimony,* Lcd.

gārcwealm m. *death by the spear,* B2043.

gare=gearo; **gāre**=gār

gārfaru† f. *warlike expedition.*

gārgetrum *armed company,* Cr673.

gārgewinn† n. *fight with spears, battle.*

gārhēap m. *band of warriors,* Ex321.

gārholt n. *shafted spear,* B1835.

gārlēac n. '*garlic*,' Lcd; Æ.

gārmitting f. *battle,* †Chr937.

gārnīð m. *conflict, war,* GnE128.

gārrǣs m. *battle,* Ma32.

gārsecg m. *ocean, sea,* AO.

gārtorn m. *fighting rage,* Sol145.

gār-ðracu f. ds. -ðræce *battle,* El1186.

gārðrīst *bold, daring,* El204.

garuwe=gearwe

gār-wiga, -wīgend m. *spearman, warrior,* B.

gārwudu m. *spear-shaft, lance,* Ex325.

gāsrīc m. *savage animal,* OET127.

gast=giest

gāst (ǣ) m. *breath,* Ps,VPs : *soul, spirit, life,* Gen,Ex,Mt; CP : *good or bad spirit, angel, demon,* BH,Mt; Æ : *Holy Ghost,* A,Jn, VPs : *man, human being, Gu.* ['*ghost*']

gāstan *to meditate?* AS2[20] (or ? geāscian).

gāstberend (æ)† m. *living soul, man.*

gāstbona m. *soul-slayer, the Devil,* B177.

gāstbrūcende *practising in the spirit,* Æ.

gāstcofa m. *breast,* Leas13.

gāstcund (ǣ) *spiritual,* Gu743.

gāstcwalu (ǣ) f. *torment, pains of hell,* Gu651.

gāstcyning m. *soul's king, God,* Gen2883.

gāstedom (ǣ) n. *spirituality,* MFH112[8].

gāstgedāl† n. *death.*

gāstgehygd† n. *thought.*

gāstgemynd (ǣ) n. *thought,* Gu574.

gāstgenīðla (ǣ) m. *devil,* Jul245.

gāstgerȳne† n. *spiritual mystery* : *thought, consideration.*

gāstgewinn (ǣ) n. *pains of hell,* Gu561.

gāstgifu f. *special gift of the Holy Spirit* (e.g. *gift of tongues*), WW200[8].

gāsthālig† *holy in spirit, holy.*

gāstlēas *lifeless, dead,* El. ['*ghostless*']

gāstlic *spiritual, holy,* Æ,Bf; CP : *clerical (not lay),* BH; Æ,CP : *ghastly, spectral, Nic.* adv. -līce *spiritually,* Æ. ['*ghostly*']

gāstlufu (ǣ)† f. *spiritual love,* Az.

gāstsunu† m. *spiritual son.* Godes g. *Christ.*

gat=geat

gāt f. gs. gǣte, gāte, nap. gǣt, gēt *she-*'*goat*,' Cr,Ep,Lcd,Rd.

gātahierde=gāthyrde

gātahūs n. *goat-house,* WW185[8].

gātbucca m. *he-goat, WW.* ['*goat-buck*']

gātehǣr n. *goat's hair,* ÆT79[82,87].

gātetrēow n. *cornel tree?* Lcd32b.

gāthyrde (io) m. '*goat-herd*,' LL,WW.

gatu v. geat.

gāð pres. pl. of gān.

ge conj. *and, also,* Cr,Lcd. ge...ge *both... and,* B,Chr : *not only...but also; whether... or.* ǣg(hwæ)ðer ge...ge *both...and; either ...or.* ['*ye*']

ge- prefix (indicated by the sign + in this Dict.), original meaning *together*; but it has usually lost all collective or intensive force.

gē I. (īe) pron. 2 pers. pl., dp. ēow, ap. ēow (ic) '*ye*,' *you*, B,G,Mt. **II.**=gēa

gēa adv. '*yea*,' *yes*, Æ,B,BH,G,WW.

geabul=gafol

gēac m. *cuckoo*, Cp, Gu. [v. '*gowk*,' '*yeke*']

gēacessūre f. *wood-sorrel*, GL.

geador† *unitedly, together*.

geadrung=gaderung

geaduling=gædeling

geaf pret. 3 sg. of giefan.

geaf-=gif-; **geafl**=gafol

geaflas† *jaws*, WW.

geafol=gafol

gēafon pret. pl. of giefan.

geafu=giefu

gēagl I. mn. *jaws, throat, gullet*, LCD. **II.**=gāl

geaglisc=gagolisc

gēaglswile m. *swelling of the jaws*, LCD.

geagn-=gegn-; **gēahl**=gēagl

gēahð=gēað

geal pret. 3 sg. of giellan.

gealādl f. *gall-disease, jaundice*, LCD 40b.

gēalāgē (gēa lā gēa, AS) *yea, amen*, RHy.

geald pret. 3 sg. of gieldan.

geald-=gald-

gealg (-lh) *sad*, Æ,WW.

gealga I. (a) m. '*gallows*,' *cross*, B,Jul,WW; CP. **II.** m. *melancholy*, WW 445,499.

gealgian=geealgian

gealgmōd† *sad, gloomy, angry*.

gealgtrēow (a) n. '*gallows-tree*,' *gallows, cross*, B,DR.

gealh=gealg; **gēalhswile**=gēaglswile

gealla (a, e) m. **I.** '*gall*,' *bile*, Mt,VPs,WW; Æ,CP. **II.** *a galled place on the skin*, LCD. ['*gall*'] (I. and II. possibly the same word, v. NED.)

geallādl f. '*melancholia*,' v. OEG 7²²³.

geallede '*galled*' (*of horses*), LCD.

gealp pret. 3 sg. of gielpan.

gealpettan (a) *to boast, live gluttonously?* NC 291,MFH 144.

gealpettung (æ) f. *boastfulness*, NC 291.

gēamrung (VPs)=gēomrung

gēamung=gēmung

gēan, gēana=gēn, gēna

gēan-, see also gegn-

geanbōc? f. *duplicate charter, counterpart*, Ct.

gēancyme (ē) m. *meeting*, EPs 63³,ARSHy.

gēancyrr m. (-cyrnes? f. RPs 18⁷) *meeting*, SPs 18⁷ : *return*. ['*gainchare*']

gēandele? (ē) *steep*, HGL 416.

gēandȳne *arduous*, LL (134⁶).

gēanfær n. *going again, return*, CHR 1119.

gēangang (ǣ) *return?* LL 8,84.

gēangewrit (ē) '*rescriptio*,' OEG 862.

gēanhweorfan³ *to return*, HGL.

gēanhworfennes f. *return*, HGL 470.

gēanhwurf m. *return*, OEG 559.

gēanhwyrft (ǣ) m. *turning again*, LPs 125¹.

gēannes f. *meeting*, OEG 4610.

gēanoð? *complaint*, OEG xiv. [*Goth.* gaunōðus]

gēanryne m. *meeting*, ERLPs 58⁶.

geantalu f. *rejoinder, contradiction*, Ct (v. talu, LL 3·226).

gēanðingian *to reply*, GEN 1009.

geanul '*obvius*,' GPH 399.

gēap I. (ǣ, ē) *open, wide, extensive, broad, spacious, lofty, steep, deep* : *bent, crooked* : *deceitful, cunning*, Æ,Shr : *intelligent, shrewd*, LCD. ['*yepe*'] **II.** pret. 3 sg. of gēopan.

gēaplic *deceitful, cunning*, Æ. adv. -līce, Æ, Bf,KGl. ['*yeply*']

gēapneb adj. (*epithet of corslet*) *meshed*, WALD 2¹⁹ (?=*gēapweb wide-meshed*).

gēapnes f. *astuteness*, WW 192¹.

gēapscipe m. *cleverness, cunning, craft, deceit, trickery, artifice*, Æ. ['*yepship*']

gēapweb v. gēapneb.

gear pret. 3 sg. of georran.

gēar (ē, ǣ) nm. '*YEAR*,' Æ,AO,CP (as to epacts v. Bf 60). tō gēare *in this year* : *yearly tribute* : *name of the rune for* g.

geara=gearwe; **geara-**=gearo-

gēara *of '*yore*,' formerly, in former times, once, long since*, B,BH,Met,RG,WW; AO, CP. gēara gēo=gēogēara (gp. of gēar).

gearbōt f. *penance lasting a year*, LL (278¹¹).

±gearcian *to prepare, procure, supply*, Æ (Gen). ['*yark*']

gearcung f. *preparation*, Æ.

±gearcungdæg m. *preparation-day, day before the Sabbath*, G.

gēarcyning m. *consul*, WW 375².

geard I. m. '*yard*,' *fence, enclosure, court, residence, dwelling, land*, B,Gen,Gu; Mdf. in geardum *at home, in the world* : *hedge*, GD,MtR. **II.**=gierd

gēardagas† mp. *days of yore*, W : *lifetime*.

geardsteall m. *cattle-yard*, KC 3·391⁸ (v. BTs).

geardung f. *habitation*, APs 77⁶⁰.

gēare=gearwe I. and II.

geare-=gear-, gearo-; **gēare**=gēara

gēarfæc n. *space of a year*, W 72¹.

gearfoð=earfoð

gēargemearc n. *space of a year*, Gu 1215.

gēargemynd n. *yearly commemoration*, NC 292. ['*year's mind*']

gēargeriht n. *yearly due*, W 113⁹.

gēargerím (ǣ) n. *numbering by years*, v. ES 39·342.

gēargetæl (æ[1], a[3], e[3]) n. *number of years*, LCD,LL.
gēarhwamlīce *yearly*, EC226[6].
gēarlanges *for a year*, Æ.
gēarlēac=gārlēac
gēarllc '*yearly,' of the year, annual, Bas,Cp, LL*; Æ. adv. -līce, WW; CP.
gearllīce=gearolīce
gēarmǣlum *year by year*, MET 1[5].
gēarmarcet n. *annual fair*, TC372[15].
gearn (e) n. '*yarn,' spun wool*, Gl.
gearnful (NG)=geornful
gearnung=geornung
gearnwinde f. *yarn-winder, reel*, Cp,WW; LL455,15. ['*yarn-wind*']
gearo (gearu) I. (wk gearwa) gsmn. -(o)wes; asm. gearone; napn. gearu *prepared, ready, equipped, finished*, An,B,Bl,Bo,Cr; CHR. ['*yare*'] II. (e[1], a[2], e[2])=gearwe adv. (B, Cr,G,Met.).
gēaro=gēara
gearobrygd m. *quick movement, deft playing (of an instrument)*, CRA 50.
gearofolm *with ready hand*, B2085.
gearolīce *readily, fully, clearly*, El. ['*yarely*']
gearor comp. of gearo adj. and gearwe adv.
gearo-snotor, -snottor† *very skilful*.
gearoðoncol *ready-witted*, JUD 342.
gearowes gsmn. of gearo.
gearowita m. *intellect, understanding*, Bo.
gearowitol (rw-) *sagacious*, OEG 56[108] : *austere*, LkL 19[21].
gearowitolnes (a[2]) f. *sagacity*, W53[16].
gearowyrde *fluent of speech*, BH. [v. '*yare*']
gearowyrdig *ready of speech*, MOD 51.
gēarrīm n. *number of years*, AO.
gēartorht *perennially bright*, GEN 1561.
gēarðēnung f. *annual service*, LL382,38.
gearu=gearo
gearugangende *going swiftly*, RD41[17].
gēarwǣstm *yearly fruit*, EC168'.
gearwan=gierwan
gearwanlēaf=geormanlēaf
gearwe I. (gearo) adv. comp. gear(w)or; sup. gear(w)ost *well, effectually, sufficiently, thoroughly, entirely*, Æ,AO,CP : *quickly : near*. ['*yare*'] II.† f. (usu. pl.) *clothing, equipment, ornament, trappings, harness, armour*. III. (a, æ) f. '*yarrow,*' Cp,Lcd,WW.
±gearwian (æ, e, i, ie, y) *to equip, prepare, facilitate, do, make ready*, Bo,G; Æ,CP : *construct, erect, make : procure, supply : clothe, adorn : grant*, DR 18[11]. ['*yare*']
±gearwung f. *preparation : working : parasceve*.
gearwungdæg (eo[1]) m. *parasceve*, JnR.
+gearwungnes f. *preparation*, LPs (but v. BTs).
gēasceaft v. gēosceaft.

gēasne (Jul)=gǣsne
geaspis *jasper*, ZDA 34·239.
geat n. (æ, e) nap. gatu (geatu VPs) '*gate,' door, opening*, Æ,BH,Bl,Ct,G,Ps; AO,CP; Mdf.
gēat pret. 3 sg. of gēotan.
gēatan (ǣ, ē, ēo) *to say 'yea,' consent, grant confirm*, Chr. ['*yate*']
geatolic† *adorned, magnificent, stately*.
geatwa=geatwe
geatwan *to equip*, RD 29[6].
geatwe fp. *arms, equipments, trappings, ornaments*, Bl,CHR. [=getāwa]
geatweard m. *gate-keeper, door-keeper, porter*, Jn. ['*gateward*']
gēað† f. *foolishness, mockery*. [gēac]
gebellic (OET,Cp 881)=gafollic
gēc (OET)=gēoc; gecel, gecile (GL)=gicel
gecs-=geocs-
ged=gǣd, gidd; gedd=gidd
gederian=(1) gaderian; (2) derian
gee=gēa
gef=(1) geaf pret. 3 sg. of giefan; (2) (N) gif
gef-=gief-
gēgan *to cry out*, BHT 88, WW355[13] (v. JAW 17).
geglisc=gagolisc
gegn=gēn; gegn- see also gēan-.
gegncwide† m. *reply, answer, retort* : (in pl.) *conversation*.
+gegnian *to meet*, DR45[11]. ['*yain*']
gegninga=gegnunga
gegnpæð m. *opposing path*, RD 16[26].
gegnslege m. *battle*, AN 1358.
gegnum† adv. *away, forwards, straight on, thither*.
gegnunga adv. *immediately, directly : certainly, plainly, precisely : completely, fully*.
gegoð=geoguð; geher (NG)=ēar
Gehhol=Geohol, Gēol
gehðu† (eo, i) f. *care, anxiety, grief*.
-gelan v. tō-g.
geld=gield; geld-=gild-, gyld-
-gelan v. ā-g.
gelde *sterile*, WW 226[22]; 394[26]. ['*yeld*']
gell-=geall-, giell-
gellet n? *bowl*, LCD 122a.
gelm=gilm; gelo=geolu
gelostr=geolster; gelp=gielp
gēlsa=gǣlsa; gelt (KGL)=gylt
gēm-=gīem-; gēmer-=gēomr-
gemstān (ES 7·134)=gimmstān
gēmung (ēa, ī, ȳ;=īe) f. *marriage*, MtR,DR.
gēmungian *to marry*, DR 109[17].
gēmunglic *nuptial*, MtR,DR.
gēn I. (ie) (A, rare in prose) adv. *yet, now, still, again : further, besides, also, moreover : hitherto*. II. adj. *direct*, AA 8[10]. III.=gēgan, gōian

gēn-=gēan-, gegn-; gĕna=gēn I.
gend=geond
gende=gengde pret. 3 sg. of gengan.
gĕnde=v. gēn III.
geng I.=geong. II.=gang. III. pret. 3 sg. of gangan.
+genga m. *fellow-traveller, companion*, W.
gengan, pret. gengde *to go*, Æ. [gong]
±genge I. *prevailing, effectual, appropriate*, BH,Gu : *seasonable : agreeable*. ['genge'] II. n. *troop*, Chr; FBO,W. ['ging'] III. f. *privy*, Æ,WW. ['gong']
-gengel v. æfter-, for(e)-g.
genigend=giniend pres. ptc. of ginian.
gĕnlād *estuary*, KC 1·238⁶.
gĕno, gēnu=gēn
gēo (īu) adv. *once, formerly, of old, before, already, earlier,* CP (gīo).
geoc (iu) n. '*yoke*,' Bo,CP,Gl,Mt; Æ, AO : *yoke of oxen, etc.*, LL,WW : *a measure of land*, Ct,WW : *consort*, NG.
gĕoc† (ēoc) f. *help, support, rescue : safety : consolation.*
geocboga (iuc-) m. *yoke-bow, yoke*, WW.
gĕocend† m. *preserver, Saviour.*
±geoclan (iuc-) *to '*yoke,' *join together*, Æ, WW.
gĕoclan (w. g. or d.) *to preserve, rescue, save*, Æ.
geocled n. geocleta (ioc-) m. *a measure of land*, Ct, OET (v. LL 2·527). ['yoklet']
gĕocor† *harsh, terrible : bitter, sad.* adv. gĕocre DA 211.
geocsa (i) m. *sob*, Met : *hiccough*, G,Lcd. [=gesca; 'yex']
geocslan (i) *to sob*, Bo. ['yex']
geocstecca m. *yoke-stick* (BTs), WW 35,459. [sticca]
geocsung f. *sobbing*, WW 179,423. ['yexing']
geoctĕma (ioc-) m. *animal yoked with another*, WW 106³⁶.
geocða=gicða
gĕodǣd (iū-)† f. *deed of old, former deed.*
gĕodæg (īu) m. *day of old*, BF,Bo.
geof=gif; geof-=gief-, gif-
geofen=geofon
geofena gp. of geofu=giefu
geofola m. *morsel, bit of food*, WW. [=giefla]
geofon (i, y)† n. *ocean, sea, flood.*
geofonflōd m. *ocean flood*, Az 125.
geofonhūs n. *ship*, GEN 1321.
geogað=geoguð
gĕo-gĕara, -gĕare adv. *of old*, BH.
gĕog(e)lere m. *magician*, W 98⁹; HGL. [*Ger.* gaukler]
geoguð (o²) f. '*youth*,' Bl,Cp,G; Æ, AO : *young people*, B,CP : *junior warriors (as opposed to duguð)* : *young of cattle.*

geoguðcnōsl n. *young offspring*, RD 16¹⁰.
geoguðfeorh† n. *time of youth.*
geoguð-hǣd (Bl,Sc) m., -hādnes f. *state of youth : adolescence.* ['youthhood']
geoguðlic *youthful*, BH. ['youthly']
geoguðlust m. *youthful lust*, BL 59⁹.
geoguðmyrð f. *joy of youth* (GK), *tenderness of youth?* (BTs),RD 39².
Geohol, Geohhol=Gēol; Geoh(h)el-=Gēol-
geohsa=geocsa
geoht (iuht) n. *yoke, pair*, v. OEG 7¹³⁵.
gȝohwīlum *of old*, Bo 8⁷.
geohðu=gehðu
Gĕol n., Gēola m. '*Yule*'-*tide, Christmas*, BH,KC,LL,MH. ǣrra Gēola *December.* æftera Gēola *January.*
geolca=geoloca; geold=gield
Gĕoldæg (Geoh(h)el-) m. *Yule-day, day at Yuletide*, MA.
geole=geolwe
gĕolēan (iū-) n. *reward for past deed*, WAL 2⁷.
geolca=geoloca; geolerēad=geolurēad
geolhstor=geolster
Gĕolmōnað (Iūl-) m. *December*, MEN (CHR p 280).
geolo=geolu
geoloca, geol(e)ca m. '*yolk*,' Æ,Lcd,Met. [geolu]
geolorand† m. *buckler covered with yellow linden-bark.*
geol-ster, -stor mn. *matter, pus, poison, poisonous humour, disease*, OEG.
geolstrig *secreting poison, purulent*, OEG.
geolu gmn. geolwes '*yellow*,' B,Gl,Lcd. geolwe ādl *jaundice.*
geoluhwīt *pale yellow*, WW. [v. 'yellow']
geolurēad *reddish yellow*, WW 375¹⁸. [v. 'yellow']
geolwe *yellowish*, LCD.
±geolwian *to become yellow*, OEG, Sc. [v. 'yellowed']
gĕomann (īu)† m. *man of past times.*
gĕomēowle (io)† f. *aged wife?* B.
gĕomer-=gēomor-, gĕomr-
gĕomor (īo¹, u²) *troubled, sad, miserable*, B, Hu. ['yomer'] adv. -more.
gĕomorfrōd *very old*, GEN 2224.
gĕomorgidd† n. *dirge, elegy.*
gĕomorlic *sad, painful, miserable*, B; AO. adv. -līce, Sol. ['yomerly']
gĕomormōd *sorrowful*, Æ.
gĕomornes f. *tribulation*, LPs 118¹⁴³.
gĕomorung=gēomrung
gĕomrian *to be sad, complain, lament, bewail, mourn*, B,Bl,DHy; Æ,AO,CP. ['yomer']
gĕomrung (e, ea) f. *groaning, moaning, grief*, Æ.
geon adj. pron. '*yon*,' CP.

geon-=geond-; **gĕona** (NG)=gēna, gēn

geonað pres. 3 sg. of geonian.

geond (e, i, ie, y) **I.** prep. (w. a. and, rarely, d.) *throughout, through, over, Bo,G : up to, as far as, during.* geond...innan *throughout.* ['*yond*'] **II.** adv. *yonder, thither, BH, RG.*

geondan prep. (w. a.) *beyond,* CHR 1052.

geondblāwan[7] (i[1]) *to inspire, illuminate,* GL.

geondbrǣdan *to cover entirely,* B 1239 : *enlarge, extend,* VH 14.

geonddrencan (i) *to drink excessively, get drunk,* CHRD,KGL 58[40].

geondeardian *to inhabit,* RPs 32[8].

geondfaran[7] *to traverse, pervade,* BF,GD.

geondfēolan[3] (only in pp. geondfolen) *to fill completely,* GEN 43.

geondfēran *to traverse : surpass,* ÆL 23b[333].

geondflōwan[7] *to flow over or through,* HELL 105.

geondflōwende *ebbing and flowing,* OEG 2363.

geondfolen v. geondfēolan.

geondgangan[7] *to traverse, go round,* RB, VPs.

geondgēotan[2] (tr. and intr.) *to pour, pour upon, suffuse, spread, soak,* Æ.

geondhweorfan[3]† *to pass over, pass through.*

geondhyrdan *to harden thoroughly,* SOL 150[28].

geondlācan[7] *to traverse, flow over,* PH 70.

geondleccan *to water, irrigate,* LPs 103[13], CHRD 108.

geond-leccung (gynd-) f. *moistening, watering,* Sc 27[7].

geondlīhtan (ȳ[2]) *to illuminate, enlighten,* CP.

geondlīhtend (ēo) m. *illuminator,* DHy 128[5].

geondmengan *to confuse, bewilder,* SOL 59.

geondrēcan *to fill with smoke,* LCD 124a.

geondsāwan[7] *to strew, scatter,* DA 278.

geondscēawian *to look upon,* GUTH,WA : *consider, have regard to,* LPs 118[6].

geondscīnan[1] *to shine upon, illuminate,* CP.

geondscrīðan[1] *to pass through, traverse, stride to and fro,* BF,W 250[3] : *ramble (of the mind),* MFH 147.

geondscrīðing f. *course, passage,* OEG 263.

geond-sēcan pret. 3 sg. -sōhte *to search thoroughly,* CP : *pervade.*

geondsendan *to overspread,* GEN.

geondsēon[5] *to examine,* B 3087.

geondsmēagan *to investigate, discuss,* BH, GL.

geondspǣtan *to squirt through,* LCD 78a.

geondsprengan *to besprinkle,* GUTH,RBL.

geondspringan[3] *to penetrate, be diffused,* OEG 2840.

geondsprūtan[2] *to pervade,* CR 42.

gĕond-strēdan, -stregdan *to scatter, suffuse, besprinkle,* Æ.

geondstrēdnes f. *dispersion,* APs 146[2].

geondstyrian *to stir up, agitate,* MET 6[15].

geondðencan† *to reflect upon, consider.*

geondwadan[6] (i[1]) *to know thoroughly, be versed in,* CP 9[10].

geondwlītan[1]† *to look over, contemplate, examine, scan.*

geondyrnan[3] (=ie[2]) *to run over,* ÆGR 277[3].

geong I. (e, i, u) '*young,*' *youthful,* Æ,AO, CP : *recent, new, fresh* : comp. gingra '*younger,*' LL,Ps : superl. gingest '*youngest,*' AO : *last,* B,CP. **II.** (LG)=gang. ['*yong*'] **III.**=geng pret. 3 sg. of gangan.

gēong=gōung

geonga (iu-) m. *young man,* Lk,WW.

geongan (LG)=gangan. ['*yong*']

geongerdōm=geongordōm

geongewifre=gangewifre

geonglǣcan (gyng-, iung-) *to pass one's youth, grow up,* HGL 508; OEG 4361.

geonglic *young, youthful,* Æ. ['*youngly*']

geonglicnes f. *youth,* Sc 124[3].

geongling (iu-) m. *a youth,* GD; ÆGR 3[1]. ['*youngling*']

geongordōm, geongorscipe m. *discipleship, allegiance,* GEN. [OS. jungardōm; jungarskepi]

geongra (i) m. *youth : disciple, follower, dependant, servant, vassal,* BH,Gen; AO, CP : *assistant, deputy,* Æ. ['*younger*']

geongre (i) f. *female attendant, assistant,* JUD 132 : *deputy,* BH 340[17].

geonian=ginian

geonlic (MFH 103[20])=geonglic

geonofer adv. *thither.*

geonsīð m. *departure hence, death,* MFH 163.

geonung=ginung

gēopan[2] *to take in,* RD 24[9].

geormanlēaf n. *mallow,* LCD.

geormenletic *mallow,* WW 135[27]. [?=-lēaf]

georn I. (usu. w. g.) *desirous, eager, earnest, diligent, studious,* AO,Bl,Gu; CP. ['*yern*'] **II.**=gearn pret. 3 sg. of +iernan.

geornan (M)=giernan

georne adv. *eagerly, zealously, earnestly, gladly,* B,Bo,Chr; Æ,AO,CP : *well, carefully, completely, exactly,* Æ : *quickly,* W. ['*yerne*']

geornes=geornnes

georneste (WW 499[1])=eornoste

georn-ful, -fullic *desirous, eager, zealous, diligent,* Bo,G; AO,CP. ['*yearnfull*'] adv. -lice, Æ.

geornfulnes f. *eagerness, zeal, diligence, Bo, RB;* Æ,AO,CP : *desire.* ['*yearnfulness*']

geornian=giernan

geornlic adj. *desirable,* AO. adv. -lice *zealously, earnestly, diligently, carefully, Cp BH,G;* Æ,CP. ['*yernly*']

geornnes (i, ie, y) *desire, endeavour : zeal, industry : importunity*, NG.

geornung (i, ie, y) f. *'yearning,' desire*, CP, Sc : *diligence*.

geornust-=eornost-

georowyrde (BH)=gearowyrdig

georran=gyrran; **georst**=gorst

georst-=gierst-

georstu interj. *O!* VPs. [hīeran]

gēosceaft m. *destiny, fate*, B 1234.

gēosceaftgǣst m. *doomed spirit*, B 1266.

geostra, geostran (ie, ei, y) *'yester'(-day, -night)*, Æ,B,G,Ps.

gēot=gīet.

gēotan I. (sv²) *to pour, pour forth, shed*, Æ, BH,CP,Cr,Lcd; AO,CP : *gush, flow, flood, overwhelm, El,Gu* : (±) *found, cast*, Æ,Ps. ['*yet*'] **II.**=gēatan

gēotend m. *artery*, WW 352²⁵.

geotendǣder f. *artery*, Lcd.

gēotenlic *molten, fluid*, GPH 394.

gēotere m. *founder (of metal)*, AO 54. ['*yeter*']

-gēoting v. in-, on-g.

gēotton pret. pl. of gēotan II.

geoðu=geohðu=gehðu; **gēow**=gīw

gēower (GPH 395)=ēower

gēowian=+ēowan=+īewan

gēowine (īu) m. *departed friend*, Seaf 92.

geox=geocs-; **gēp**=gēap

ger-=gær-, gearw-, gier-; **gēr**=gēar

gerd(A)=gierd; **gerd-**=gyrd-

gerew-, gerw-=gearw-, gierw-

gernwinde=gearnwinde

gērscipe m. *jest?* Rim 11.

gēs v. gōs.

gesca, gescea (eo, i) m. *hiccough, sobbing*, Gl,Lcd.

gēse (ī, ȳ) adv. *'yes,'* Æ,Bo,CP,G.

gesen *entrails, intestines*, WW 231³⁹.

gēsine, gēsne=gǣsne

gest, gēst=giest, gāst; **gest-**=giest-

gēstende (OEG 2499)=ȳstende; **get**=geat

gēt I.=gǣt, nap. of gāt. **II.**=gēat pret. 3 sg. of gēotan. **III.** (VPs), gēta=gīet(a)

gētan I. *to destroy, kill*, B 2940 (? for gītan or grētan). **II.**=gēatan

gētenwyrde *consenting, agreeing*, Ct (Swt). [gēatan]

gi- (NG, etc.)=ge-; **gib**=gif

giccan *to 'itch,'* Lcd.

gicce (y) *'itch,'* Ln 33³.

giccig *purulent, itchy*, HGl 453.

gicel(a) (y) m. *icicle, ice, DD,WW.* ['*ickle*']

gicelgebland n. *frost*, RHy 7⁷⁰.

gicelig *glacial, icy*, OEG.

gicelstān (y¹) m. *hailstone*, Bl 261,LRPs 147¹⁷.

gicenes (y) f. *itching, itch*, Gl.

gicer (y) n. *acre*, OET 114⁹².

gicða (ie, io, y) m. *scab, itch, itching,* Æ,CP : *hiccough?* Lcd (v. BTs). ['*yekth*']

gid-=gyd-; **gīd-**=gīt-; **gidd-**=giedd-

gīe=gē; **giecða** (CP)=gicða?

giedd (e, i, y) n. *song, poem*, B : *saying, proverb, riddle : speech, story, tale, narrative : account, reckoning, reason*, VH 14. ['*yed*']

±gieddian (i, y) *to speak formally, discuss : speak with alliteration, recite, sing*, Bo; AO. ['*yed*']

gieddung (e, i, y) f. *utterance, saying, prophecy, song, poetry, poetical recitation, metre*, LG; Æ. ['*yedding*']

gief (rare EWS)=gif; **gief-**=gif-, geof-

giefa (eo, i, y) m. *donor*, CP.

giefan⁵ (e, ea, eo, i, ia, io, y) w. d. and a. *to 'give*,'* bestow, allot, grant*, Æ; AO,CP : *commit, devote, entrust*, Da : *give in marriage*, Chr.

giefend (e) m. *giver*, DR.

giefernes (CP)=gīfernes

giefl (i, y)† n. *morsel, food* (v. also geofola).

giefnes (e) f. *grace, pardon*, DR,†Hy.

giefu (e, eo, i, y) f. *giving, gift*, B,Bo,Mt; AO,CP. *tō giefe, giefes gratis, freely : favour, grace*, Bl,Lk : *liberality : sacrifice : name of the rune for* **g.** ['*give*']

gield (eo, i) n. *service, offering, worship, sacrifice, Jul : money-payment, tax, tribute, compensation, substitute*, LG,LL : (±) *guild, brotherhood*, Ct : *idol, god.* ['*yield*']

gield- v. also gild-.

±gieldan³ (e, i, y) *to 'yield*,'* pay*, AO,LG : CP : *pay for*, Æ,LL : *reward, requite, render*, B,Bl,CP,Gen,Ps : *worship, serve, sacrifice to*, CP : *punish*.

-gieldere (y) v. gafol-g.

gieldra=ieldra comp. of eald.

-giella (e, i) v. stān-g.

giellan³ (e, i, y) *to 'yell,' sound, shout*, An, Fin,Rd.

giellende *'yelling,'* Ex,Lcd,Wid.

gielp (e, i, y) mn. *boasting, pride, arrogance : fame, glory*, Æ,B,BH,Bo; AO,CP. ['*yelp*']

gielpan³ (i, y) *to boast, exult*, B,Bo,Da,W; AO,CP : *praise*, CP. ['*yelp*']

gielpcwide† m. *boastful speech.*

gielpgeorn (i, y) *eager for glory*, BH 92⁴ : *arrogant*, W.

gielpgeornes (i) f. *desire for glory, pride, arrogance*, W.

gielphlǣden (i) *boastful*, B 868.

gielping (y) f. *glory, boasting*, Sc 144¹¹. ['*yelping*']

gielplic (i) *vainglorious, boastful : ostentatious, showy.* adv. -līce.

gielpna (i) m. *boaster*, CP.

gielpnes (e) f. *boastfulness*, LPs.

gielpplega (y) m. *war*, Ex 240.

gielpsceaða† (e¹, a²) m. *boastful enemy*.

gielpspr̄c f. *boastful speech*, B 981.

gielpword (y) n. *boast*, AO.

gielt=gylt; **giem**=gimm

gíeman (ē, ī, ȳ) (w. g. or a.) *to care for, heal,* CP : *correct, reprove* : *take notice of, take heed to, regard, observe*, Æ,Bl,Bo,Cr; AO, CP : *take charge of, control*, Æ(Gen). ['*yeme*']

gíeme f. *care*, AO,CP. ['*yeme*']

gíemelēas (ē, ȳ) *careless, negligent*, CP : *neglected, uncared for, stray* : *incurable*, MtLp20¹¹. ['*yemeles*']

gíemelēasian *to neglect, despise*, BH 362¹³.

gíemelēaslic *careless*, CP. adv. -līce, *Lcd*. ['*yemelesliche*']

gíemelēasnes (ē, ȳ) f. *negligence*, BH 242²⁸.

gíeme-lēast, -līest f. *carelessness, neglect*, CP : *presumption*, RB 77⁵. ['*yemelest*']

gíemen (ē, ī, ȳ) f. *care, oversight, heed, diligence, rule*, AO,CP.

gíemend (ȳ) m. *governor*, Sc 117⁷ : *keeper* : *observer*.

gíem(e)nes (ē) f. *care, anxiety*, DR,NG.

gíeming f. *care, anxiety*, CP : *custody* : *rule*.

gíen, gíena=gēn, gēna; **giend**=geond

gieng=geong

gierd (ea, i, y) f. '*yard*,' *rod, staff, twig*, Æ, G,Lcd; CP : *measure of length*, LL : g. landes *an area of land about one-fourth of a hide*, EC,KC,LL.

gierdweg (y) m. *road fenced on either side? road made with faggots?* (BTs),KC.

gierdwíte (y) n. *affliction caused by* (*Moses'*) *rod*, Ex 15.

gierede pret. 3 sg. of gierwan.

±gierela (e, i, y) m. *dress, apparel, adornment*, AO,CP : *banner*, WW 435¹⁵. [gearwian]

±gier(e)lian (e) *to clothe*, G,Ps.

+gierelic (e) adj. *of clothes*, WW 503¹⁸.

gierian=gearwian

+giering f. *direction*, RPs 138³.

gierman (y) *to cry, mourn*, LPs 37⁹. ['*yarm*']

±giernan (eo, y) (w. g.) *to* '*YEARN*' *for, strive, be eager, desire, entreat, seek for, beg, demand*, AO,CP. [georn]

giernendlic (y) *desirable*, Sc 111¹³, (+) EPs 18¹¹.

giernes=geornnes

gierning (CP)=geornung; **gierran**=gyrran

gierst-=giestr-

±gierwan (e, ea, y) *to prepare*, AO : *cook*, CP : *deck, dress, clothe, adorn* : *direct*, CP.

giest (æ, e, i, y) m. '*guest*,' B,Gen,RB : *stranger*, MtL,Rd.

giestærn (e, y) n. *guest-chamber* : *inn* : *shelter*.

giesterdæg (e, io) '*yesterday*,' JnRL 4⁵².

giesternlic (eo, y) *of yesterday*.

giesthof (æ) n. *guest-house*, Cr 821.

giesthūs (a, æ, e, y) n. '*guest-house*,' ApT, Mk ; CP.

giestian (y) *to lodge, be a guest*, Sc 153'.

giestig (e) adj. *being a stranger*, MtL 25³⁸.

giesting (e) f. *exile*, GL.

giestlíc (a¹) *hospitable*, GEN 209.

giestlíðe (i¹) *hospitable*, MH 168²⁴,WW 97¹⁵.

giestlíðian (æ¹) *to be hospitable*, NAR 38¹⁸n.

giestlíðnes (æ, e, i, y) f. *hospitality, shelter*, BH.

giestmǽgen (i) n. *band of guests*, GEN 2494.

giestning (e) f. *hospitality, lodging*, NC 296.

giestran (e¹,o²)adv.*yesterday*,Rd. ['*yestern*']

giestranǽfen m. *yesterday evening*, DD. adv. -ǽfene, Æ,GD. ['*yesterneve*']

giestrandæg (eo, y) m. '*yesterday*,' Æ,G, PPs.

giestranniht (y) f. '*vesternight*,' B 1334.

giestsele (e, y) †m. *guest-hall*.

gíet I. (ē, ī, ȳ) adv. '*YET*' : *still* : *besides* : *hitherto* : *hereafter* : *even* : *even now*. ðā g. *yet, still, further, also*. nū g. *until now* : *hitherto, formerly* : *any longer* II. pres. 3 sg. of gēotan.

gíeta=gíet

gíetan (i) *to get*, RBL 56¹⁵.

gíetsere, gíetsian=gítsere, gítsian

gif I. (e, ie) conj. (w. ind. or subj.) '*IF*,' Chr; CP : *whether, though*, B. II. n. *gift, grace*, AN 575,BH 34¹⁷.

gifa, gifan=giefa, giefan

gifect (GL)=gefeoht; **gifel**=giefl

gifen I. pp. of giefan. II.=geofon

gifer m. *glutton*, SOUL 118.

gifere=gífre

gíferlíce *greedily*, BH,OEG. ['*yeverly*']

gífernes f. *greediness, gluttony, avarice*, Bo, Bl; Æ,CP. ['*yeverness*']

gifeðe I. *granted by fate, given*. II. n. *fate, lot*, B 3085.

gifǽst *endowed, talented* : (w. g.) *capable of*.

gifheall f. *hall in which gifts were made*, B 838.

gifian (ea, eo) *to present, endow* : *glorify*, DR 78¹⁴ : (+) '*prestolari*,' DR 20⁸.

gifig *rich*, A 11·171.

gifl=giefl

gifnes† f. *grace, favour*.

gifol (e) *liberal, generous, bountiful*, CP : *gracious*, WW 66¹.

gifola m. *giver*, AS 2⁸.

gifolnes (io) f. *liberality*, CP 321²².

gífre *useful*, RD 27²⁸; 50³.

gífre *greedy, rapacious, ravenous*, B,Bo; CP : *desirous of*. ['*yever*']

gifsceatt m. *present*, B378.

gifstōl† m. *gift-seat, throne.*

gift (y) nf. *'gift,' portion, marriage gift (by the bridegroom), dowry* : (pl.) *nuptials, marriage,* Æ. [giefan]

giftbūr m. *bride-chamber*, BF6²⁰,EPs18⁵.

giftelic=giftlic

giftfeorm f. *marriage-feast*, NC297.

gifthūs (y) n. *house at which a wedding is being celebrated*, Mt22¹⁰.

giftian (y) *to give in marriage (of the woman)*, G.

giftlēoð n. *epithalamium*, WW165³³.

giftlic *nuptial, belonging to a wedding,* Æ.

gifu (Æ)=giefu; **giful**=gifol

gifung (y) f. *consent*, BH86²⁵.

gīg (Cp142G)=gīw

gīgant m. *giant*, B,BL. [*L.* gigantem]

gīgantmæcg m. *son of a giant*, GEN1268.

gigoð=geoguð; **gihsa**=geocsa

gihōa=gicða; **gihōu**=gehðu

gild=gield; **gild-**=gyld-

±**gilda** m. *member of a brotherhood of related persons*, v. LL2·378; 445.

gildan=(1) gieldan; (2) gyldan

gilddagas mp. *guild-days, festival-days*, WW107²².

gilde v. twi-g.

+**gilde** n. *membership of a guild*, TC.

+**gildheall** (y) f. *guild-hall*, KC4·277′.

gildlic adj. *of a guild, festival*, A41·106.

gildrǣden (y) f. *guild-membership*, Ct.

±**gildscipe** m. *guild, brotherhood*, Ct,LL. [*'guildship'*]

gildsester (y) m. *measure of bulk belonging to a corporate body*, TC606,611.

gillan=giellan

gillister n. gillistre f. *phlegm, pus, matter*, LCD. [=geolster]

gilm, gilma (e) m. *handful*, Lcd,OEG : *sheaf,* Æ. [*'yelm'*]

gilp I. *dust, powder*, WW521¹⁸. II.=gielp

gilt=gylt

gilte (y) f. *young sow*, WW119²⁵. [*'yelt'*]

gim=gimm; **gīm-**=gīem-

gimbǣre *gem-bearing, set with gems*, OEG.

gimcynn n. *precious stone, gem*, AA,Bo.

gimfæst (B1272)=ginfæst

gimm (y) m. (occl. nap. gimme) *precious stone, 'gem,' jewel*, Æ,Bl,VPs; CP : (†) *sun, star.* [*L.* gemma]

±**gimmian** *to adorn with gems*, ÆGR.

gimmisc *jewelled*, AA7⁶.

gimreced n. *bejewelled hall, palace*, MET8²⁵.

gimrodor? m. *draconite (precious stone)*, OEG (v. BTac).

gimstān m. *stone capable of being made into a gem, jewel*, Æ; AO. [*'gemstone'*]

gīmung=gēmung

gimwyrhta (y) m. *jeweller*, ÆH1·64⁹.

gin I. n. *yawning deep*, Ex430. II. adj.= ginn

gīn, gīna=gēn, gēna

gīnan I. *to yawn.* II. *to drive back*, ÆL25⁶³⁶.

gind=geond

ginfæst† *ample, liberal.* [ginn]

ginfæsten n. *great fastness, stronghold?* Ex524.

ging, gingest v. geong.

gingi-ber, -fer(e) f. *'ginger,'* Lcd.

gingra I. (Æ) v. geong. II.=geongra

gingre=geongre

ginian (eo, y) *to 'yawn,' gape*, AO,CP,GD, Gl,Lcd,Ps : *utter a sound*, WW. [gīnan]

giniend (e, eo, y) *'yawning,'* AO,BH,GD.

ginn† *spacious, wide, ample.*

ginnan=onginnan

ginnes f. *gap, interval*, Cp3731.

ginnfæst=ginfæst

ginnwīsed (y) *very wise*, Gu839? (or? ginn-wīse *of noble manners*, BTs).

ginung (e, eo, y) f. *opening of the mouth, howling, biting*, Gl. [*'yawning'*]

gīo=gēo; **giofol**=gifol

giohðhād=geoguðhād; **gīow**=gīw

giowian (RG)=giwian

gīp-=gyp-

gīr-=gearw-, geor-, gier-, gyr-

gird=gierd; **giren** (VPs)=grīn

girsandæg (VH15)=gierstandæg

girstbītung=gristbītung

girwan=gearwian

+**gīscan** *to close, bolt, bar*, GL.

gisclan *to sob*, Bo8⁸. [=geocsian]

gīse=gēse

gīsl, gīsel m. *hostage*, AO. [*'yisel'*]

gīsldu (-ðu) f. *the giving of hostages*, WW459⁷.

gīslhād m. *state of being a hostage*, Cp990.

gīslian *to give hostages*, CHR.

gist I. m. *'yeast,' froth*, Lcd. II.=giest

gist-=giest-; **gīst**=ӯst

gistran=geostran; **gīstung**=gītsung

git dual of pron. 2 pers. (ðu); g. incer; d. inc; a. inc(it) *you two*, B,Bl,G. git Johannis *thou and John.* [*'yit'*]

gīt, gīta=gīet, gīeta; **gitrife**=giðrife

gitsere m. *miser*, Æ,CP.

gītsian (ӯ) *to be greedy, long for, covet*, B,Bo, CP,G; Æ : (+) *obtain with greed*, CP364²². [*'yisse'*]

gītsiendlic *insatiable*, RPs100⁵.

gītsiendnes f. *avarice*, W188n.

gītsung (ӯ) f. *avarice, greediness, covetousness, desire*, CP.

glōcorn n. *a plant, spurge-laurel?* LCD,WW.

glōrife (y) f. *cockle*, LCD,WW.

giðu=gehðu

gīu (Æ)=gēo; glu-=geo-
Glūll (Bf 24)=Iūla, Gēola
Gīuling, Giūluling *July*, Cp 70 Q (A 20·137).
gīw (ēo) m. *griffin, vulture*, WW 258⁷.
±gīwian (ī? v. A 16·98) *to ask*, NG.
giwung f. *petition*, DR,NG.
glād pret. 3 sg. of glīdan.
glad- v. glæd.
gladian (ea) (†) *to gleam, glisten* : (±) intr.
be glad, rejoice, JnL,Lcd : (±) tr. *gladden,
rejoice, gratify, appease, Æ,VPs*. ['*glad*']
gladine=glædene
gladung f. *rejoicing*, RB : *gladdening*, W :
appeasing, LPs. ['*gladding*']
glæd I. (glad- in obl. cases) (†) *bright,
shining, brilliant, gleaming, Gen,Ph,Sol* :
cheerful, '*glad,' joyous, B,CP,Chr,Cr,G,
Ps; Æ : pleasant, kind, gracious, Æ,B*. II.
n. *joy, gladness*, Wy 68. ['*glad*']
glædene (a, e) f. *iris, gladiolus*, Gl; Lcd.
['*gladdon*']
glǣdestede=glēdstede
glædine (Gl)=glædene
glædlic *bright, shining*, Wid : *kindly,
pleasant, agreeable*, Ps. adv. -līce '*gladly,'
joyfully, kindly, willingly*, BH,Chr.
glædman '*hilaris*,' WW 171⁴⁰ : *kind, gracious*, B 367.
glædmōd *cheerful, joyous* : *kind, gracious*.
glædmōdnes f. *kindness, bounty*, CP 391⁶.
glædnes (e¹) f. '*gladness,' joy, BH*; Æ,DR
(+) : *good-nature*, WW 74²³.
glædscipe m. *gladness, joy*, JnR,Lcd.
['*gladship*']
glǣdstede=glēdstede
glǣm† m. *a brilliant light*, Gu : '*gleam,'
brilliance, brightness, splendour, beauty*,
Gen,Jul.
glæng=gleng
glæppe (a) f. *buck-bean*, Ct,Lcd.
glær m. *amber, resin*, WW.
glæren *vitreous, glassy* (Sievers 234a).
[glæs]
glæs I. n. nap. glasu, and (once) glæsas
(GPH 397) '*glass*,' Bo,Cr; Æ. II. *a glass
vessel*, BH,Lcd.
glæsen *of glass, glassy*, Bl. ['*glassen*']
glæsenēage *grey-eyed*, WW 416¹.
glæsfæt n. *glass (vessel)*, BH 398b,o³,GD
10¹⁶.
glæsful m. *a '*glassful,' BH 398t³.
glæsgegot? *poured or molten glass*, WE 63⁹.
glæshlūtor† *clear, transparent*.
glæterian *to glitter*, OEG,WW.
glæterung f. *shining*, RPs 48¹⁵.
glætlic=glædlic; glǣw=glēaw
glappe=glæppe
glasu v. glæs; glāw=glēaw
glēam m? n? *revelry, joy*, Gen 12.

glēaw (ā, æ, ē) *penetrating, keen, prudent,
wise, skilful, G,Gl,VPs*; Æ,AO,CP : (†)
good. ['*glew*'] adv. -e.
glēawferhð† *prudent*.
glēawhycgende* (Jul), glēawhȳdig† *thoughtful, wise, prudent*.
glēawlic (ǣ, ēo) *wise, prudent, skilful, diligent*. adv. -līce.
glēawmōd *wise, sagacious*, CP.
glēawnes (ǣ) f. *wisdom, prudence, skill,
penetration*, Æ : *diligence : sign, token*, Bf.
glēawscipe m. *wisdom, thoughtfulness, diligence : proof, indication, test*, Bf 156²⁴.
glēd (oe) f. *glowing coal, ember, fire, flame*,
LG,Ps; Æ. [glōwan; '*gleed*']
+glēdan *to make hot, kindle*, PPs 77²³.
gleddian *to sprinkle, throw over*, Lcd 3·292¹⁴.
glēde f. *glowing coal*, LPs 17⁹.
glēdegesa m. *fiery terror*, B 2650.
gledene=glædene
glēdfæt n. *chafing-dish*, Lcd 123b : *censer*,
WW.
gledine=glædene
glednes (KGl)=glædnes
glēdscofl (oe) f. *fire-shovel*, Cp 7 u.
glēdstede† m. *altar*, Gen.
glemm m? *blemish, spot*, W 67⁸.
glencan=glengan
glendran *to devour, swallow*, MtR.
+glendrian *to precipitate*, LkL 4²⁹.
gleng mf. (nap. gleng(e)as, glenge, glenga)
ornament, honour, splendour, CP.
±glengan (æ) *to adorn, decorate*, ÆL : *trim
(lamp)* : (+) *set in order, compose*.
+glengendlīce *elegantly*, OEG 1202.
glengful *decked out, adorned*, GPH 395.
glengista? (meaning doubtful) AA 1²⁰ (v.
BTs and ac).
glenglic *magnificent, brilliant*, WW 467²⁵.
glengnes f. *adornment*, MFH 123¹⁵.
glentrian=glendran
glēo=glīw; glēof=glēow II.
gleomu f. *splendour*, Ruin 34?
glēow I.=glīw. II. pret. 3 sg. of glōwan.
glēow-=glēaw-, glīw-
glēsan *to gloss*, ÆGr 293¹³. [L. glossa]
glēsing f. *glossing, explanation*, ÆGr 293¹⁴.
glēw=glēaw
glīa (OEG 3173)=glīga gp. of glīg.
glid *slippery*, CPs 34⁶.
glida (io) m. *kite, vulture*, Æ,Cp. ['*glede*']
±glīdan¹ *to '*glide,' slip, slide*, An,B; Æ,AO,
CP : *glide away, vanish*.
glidder *slippery*, VHy : *lustful*. ['*glidder*']
gliddrian *to slip, be unstable*, OEG 4104.
glider (W 239¹⁴)=glidder
gliderung (y) f. *phantom*, WW 401⁴⁰.
glīg=glīw
glind m. *hedge, fence*, BC 1·296'.

glioda (Cp)=glida

glisian *to glitter*, WW. [*'glise'*]

glisnian (y) *to 'glisten,' gleam*, Shr, Run.

glit pres. 3 sg. of glīdan.

glitenian *to glitter, shine* : *be distinguished*, Bf44⁶.

glitenung f. *coruscation, gleam*, SPs143⁸.

glitin-, glitn-=gliten-

glīw (ēo, īg, īo, īu, ēow) n. *'glee,' pleasure, mirth, play, sport*, Bas,Gl,Ph : *music*, Gn, Ps : *mockery*.

glīwbeam (īg) m. *musical instrument, harp, timbrel*, LRSPs149³.

glīwbydenestre (ȳ) f. *female musician*, LPs 67²⁶.

glīwcræft m. *music, minstrelsy*, GD62¹³.

glīwcynn? (ȳ) *a kind of music?* (BTs), LPs146¹⁰.

glīwdrēam (ēo) m. *music, mirth*, B3021.

glīwere m. *buffoon, parasite*, OEG.

glīwgamen (īg) n. *revelry*, W46¹⁶.

glīwgeorn (īg) *fond of sport*, LL.

glīwhlēoðriendlic *musical*, WW446³⁶.

glīwian (ēo) *to make merry, jest, play* (*music*), *sing*, BH,LL : *adorn*, Rᴅ27¹³. [*'glew'*]

glīwiend m. *performer, player*, SPs67²⁶.

glīwingman m. *debauchee?* OEG50⁹.

glīwlic *mimic, jesting*, GPH396.

glīwmǣden (īe) n. *female musician*, ERPs 67²⁶.

glīwman (ēo, īg) m. *'gleeman,' minstrel, player, jester*, B; CP,WW : *parasite*, HGL.

glīwre=glīwere

glīwstæf m. *melody, joy*, Wᴀ52.

glīwstōl m. *seat of joy*, Rᴅ88⁸.

glīwung f. *boisterous laughter, mockery*, OEG1472.

glīwword (ēow) n. *song, poem*, Mᴇᴛ7².

glōf, glōfe f. *'glove,' pouch*, B,Guth; LF60. foxes g. *foxglove*.

+glōfed *gloved*, AS43⁴.

glōfung f. *supplying with gloves*, LL450,10.

glōfwyrt f. *glovewort, dog's tongue, lily of the valley*, Lᴄᴅ.

glōm m? *gloaming, twilight*, Cʀᴇᴀᴛ71.

glōmung f. *'gloaming,' twilight*, DHy,WW.

gloria m. *doxology*, RB.

glōwan⁷ *to 'glow,'* Æ,OEG.

glōwende *'glowing,' burning*, Lcd80b.

gly-=gli-

gnād pret. 3 sg. of gnīdan.

gnægen=gnagen pp. of gnagan.

gnæt m. *'gnat,' midge*, AO,Lcd,Mt.

gnagan⁶ *to 'gnaw,'* Æ,Ct,DD.

-gnāst v. fȳr-g.

gnēad-=gnēað-

gnēað *niggardly*, B,BH : *frugal, sparing*, Sʜʀ. [v. *'gnede'*]

gnēaðlicnes f. *frugality*, OEG2437.

gnēaðnes (ē) f. *frugality* : *scarcity*, MH.

gnēðe *scanty, sparing*, WW. [*'gnede'*] adv. -līce, GD. [*'gnedely'*]

gnēðelicnes=gnēaðlicnes

gnidan¹ *to rub, grind together, crumble*, Lk; Æ,AO. [*'gnide'*]

gnidil m. *rubber, pestle*, Cp440 ᴘ.

gniding f. *rubbing*, Lᴄᴅ11b.

gnit pres. 3 sg. of gnīdan.

gnōgon pret. pl. of gnagan.

gnorn† I. *sad, sorrowful, troubled, depressed.* II. m. *sadness, sorrow, trouble.*

gnornan=gnornian

gnorncearig *sad, troubled*, Jᴜʟ529.

gnorngan=gnornian

gnornhof† n. *prison, cell*, Aɴ.

gnornian *to be sad, murmur, complain, mourn, lament, grieve*, CP.

gnornscendende *hastening away in sadness*, PPs89¹⁰. [scyndan]

gnornsorg† f. *sadness, sorrow.*

gnornung (e) f. *sadness, sorrow, lamentation, discontent*, Æ,AO,CP.

gnornword n. *lamentation*, Gᴇɴ767.

gnuddian *to rub*, OEG56³³.

gnyran=gnyrran

gnyrn† f. *sadness, mourning, calamity* : *wrong, insult, fault, blemish.* [gnorn]

gnyrnwracu f. *revenge, enmity*, Eʟ359.

gnyrran *to grind the teeth*, W138²⁹ : *creak*, Lcd. [v. *'gnar'*]

+gnysan=cnyssan; **gnȳðe**=gnēað

gōað 3 p. sg. pres. of gōian.

gōc=gēoc

God m. np. -as, -u a 'ɢᴏᴅ,' *image of a god*, Æ; AO : *God, the (Christian) Deity*, Æ; CP : *godlike person*, Bo.

gōd I. comp. bet(e)ra, bettra, superl. bet(e)st 'ɢᴏᴏᴅ' (*of persons or things*), *virtuous* : *desirable, favourable, salutary, pleasant* : *valid, efficient, suitable* : *considerable, sufficiently great.* II. n. *good thing, advantage, benefit, gift*, B,Bl,Mt; Æ, AO,CP : '*good,' goodness, welfare*, CP : *virtue, ability, doughtiness* : *goods, property, wealth*, CP.

godæppel m. *quince*, WW364¹⁶. [=coddæppel]

godbearn n. *divine child, Son of God* : *godchild*, W. [*'godbairn'*]

godborg m? *solemn pledge (given in church?)*, LL18·33; 66,33 and v. 2·232,1d.

godbōt f. *atonement*, LL258,51.

godcund *religious, sacred, divine, spiritual, heaven-sent*, Gen,Chr; Æ,CP. [*'godcund'*]

godcundlic *divine, of or from God, spiritual, celestial*, Æ,CP. adv. -līce *divinely*, Æ : *canonically.*

godcundmæht n? *divine majesty*, MtL.

godcundnes f. *divine nature, divinity, God-head, Æ,Lcd* : *divine service* : *oblation*, LL. ['*godcundness*']

godcundspēd f. *divine nature, godhead*, VH 14.

gōddǣd f. *good work, Cr* : *benefit, PPs*. ['*good deed*']

goddohtor f. '*goddaughter*,' *Ct*.

gōddōnd† m. (nap. gōddēnd), *benefactor*.

goddrēam† m. *joy of heaven*, Gu.

godě-=god-

godfæder m. *God the Father* : '*godfather*,' *Ct,LL*.

godfrecnes (BH 70¹²)=godwrecnes

gōdfremmend m. *doer of good?* B 299.

godfyrht (e, i) *godfearing, An,Chr*. ['*god-fright*']

godgeld=godgield

godgesprǣce (BH)=godsprǣce

godgield (e², i², y²) n. *heathen god, idol* : *heathen rite*, AO.

godgildlic *of idol-worship*, WW 466¹⁶.

godgim m. *heavenly jewel?* EL 1114.

godhād m. *divine nature*, CP 261¹⁷.

±gōdian *to improve, get better, Chr,Lcd* : *make better* : *endow, enrich, KC*; Æ. ['*good*']

Goding m. *Son of God*, LkR 4¹.

gōdlār f. *good teaching*, LL 304 B.

gōdlēas *bad, evil, BH*. ['*goodless*']

godlic *godlike, divine*, WW 220,221.

gōdlic '*goodly*,' *excellent, Gen* : *comely, fair*, GPH 394.

gōdlīf n. *good life*, CHR 1095.

godmǣgen n. *divine power, divinity*, AA 37,42.

godmōdor f. '*godmother*,' *Shr*.

gōdnes f. '*goodness*,' *virtue, Bo* : *good-will, beneficence, kindliness, Bo,Æ* : *good thing*, DA 90.

gōdscipe m. *kindness, DR*. ['*goodship*']

godscyld f. *sin against God, impiety*, JUL 204.

godscyldig *impious*, Gu 834.

godsibb m. *sponsor, W*. ['*gossip*']

godsibbrǣden f. *sponsorial obligations*, W 228³.

gōdspēdig† *rich, happy*.

godspel n. '*gospel*,' *glad tidings, Mt* : *one of the four gospels, An*; Æ,CP : *the gospel (for the day), Mt*.

godspelbodung f. *gospel-preaching, new dis-pensation, ÆL,ÆT*.

godspellbōc f. *book containing the four gospels, LL*. ['*gospel-book*']

godspellere m. '*gospeller*,' *evangelist, Bl*; Æ,CP.

godspellian *to preach the gospel, evangelize, Ps*; Æ,CP. ['*gospel*']

godspell-ic (Æ), -isc *evangelical*.

godspelltraht m. *gospel commentary, homily*, Æ.

godsprǣce (ē) n. *oracle*, BH.

godsunu m. '*godson*,' *BH,Chr,Ma*.

godōrymm m. *divine majesty*, GD.

godōrymnes f. *divine glory*, AS 9²?

godwebb I. n. *fine cloth, purple*, CP : *fine clothes* : *curtain* : *flag*. **II.**=godwebben

godwebbcyn? (gode-) n. *purple (cloth)*, SOL 152'.

godwebben *of purple*, BL 95¹⁹, LF 47¹⁵ : *of silk or cotton*, HGL.

godwebgyrla m. *cloth of purple*, W 197¹.

godwebwyrhta m. *weaver of purple*, AA 8¹⁸.

gōdwillende *well-pleased*, EHy 16⁶.

godwrǣc (e²) *wicked*, BL.

godwrǣclic *impious, sacrilegious*, GD 232¹³.

godwrece=godwrǣc

godwrecnes f. (-wyrc- WYN 45) *wickedness, impiety*, BHB 70¹² .

goffian *to be vain*, BYH 80¹¹.

gofol=gafol

gōlan *to lament, groan*, BH 88(v.also gēgan).

gōl pret. 3 sg. of galan.

gold n. '*gold*,' *Æ,OET*; CP.

goldǣht f. *wealth in gold*, B 2748.

goldbeorht *bright with gold*, RUIN 34.

goldblēoh *golden-hued*, WW 140²⁴.

goldblōma m. *golden bloom?* (v. BTs), W 251¹¹; BL 105¹⁸.

goldburg† f. *city in which gold is given? rich city?* AN,GEN.

golde f. '*solsequia*,' *marigold*, WW 301⁶. ['*gold*']

golde-=gold-

golden pp. of gieldan.

goldfæt† n. *golden vessel*.

goldfǣted *plated or adorned with gold*, LL 460,10 H.

goldfāg *variegated or shining with gold*.

goldfell n. *gold plate*, WW 358¹⁵.

goldfellen *of gilded leather*, ÆL 31²⁵².

goldfinc m. '*goldfinch*,' *WW*.

goldfinger m. *ring-finger*, LL.

goldfrætwe fp. *gold ornaments*, CR,W.

goldfyld *covered with gold*, WW 518⁴.

goldfyll? *gold leaf, gold foil*, ES 8·478 (v. BTs).

goldgearwe fp. *gold ornaments*, NC 298.

goldgewefen *woven with gold*, OEG 4297.

goldgeweorc n. *golden object*, MH 222.

goldgiefa† (i, y) m. *gold-giver, prince, lord*.

goldhilted *golden hilted*, RD 56¹⁴.

goldhladen *adorned with gold*, FIN 13.

goldhoma m. *gold-adorned coat of mail*, EL 992.

goldhord nm. *treasure of gold, treasury, El, VPs*; Æ,AO. ['*goldhoard*']

goldhordhūs n. *privy*, WW 184[14].
goldhordian *to collect treasure, hoard*, Sc 173[12].
goldhroden† *ornamented with gold*. [hrēo-dan]
goldhwæt *greedy for gold*, B 3074?
goldlæfer f. *gold plate*, HGL 431.
goldlēaf n. *gold leaf or plate*, W 263[6]. [=læfer]
goldmæstling (e) n. *brass*, WW. [v. 'gold']
goldmāðm m. *treasure*, B 2414.
goldmestling=goldmæstling
goldōra m. *gold ore*, OEG 1810.
goldsele† m. *hall in which gold is distributed*.
goldsmið m. *'goldsmith,'* Æ.
goldsmiðu f. *goldsmith's art*, WY 73.
goldspēdig *rich in gold*, JUL 39.
goldtorht *bright like gold*, CREAT 78.
goldðēof m. *stealer of gold*, LL 54,9[2].
goldðrǣd m. *gold thread*, WW 196[15].
goldweard m. *keeper of gold (dragon)*, B 3081.
goldwecg m. *a lump of gold*, OEG 451.
goldwine† m. *liberal prince, lord, king*.
goldwlanc† *brave with gold, richly adorned*.
goldwlencu f. *gold ornament*, BL 195.
goldwyrt f. *heliotrope, marigold*, OEG 26[26].
golfetung (LPs 78[4])=gaffetung
gōlon pret. pl. of galan.
golpen pp. of gielpan.
gom-=gam-
gōma m. (sg. or pl. used indifferently) *inside of mouth or throat, palate, jaws*, Lcd, Rd,VPs; Æ. ['gum']
gombe (a)† f. *tribute*.
gomor *Hebrew measure, omer*, Æ. ['gomer']
gon-=gan-; **gond-**=gand-, geond-
gōp m. *slave, servant*, RD 50[3]. [or ?=gēap]
gor n. *dung, dirt, filth*, Æ,Cp,Rd. ['gore']
gōr=gār III.
gorettan *to gaze, stare about*, OEG 5[3] : *pour forth, emit*, GPH 398.
gorettung f. *gazing*, OEG 5[3]n.
gorian *to gaze, stare about*, OEG 7[6].
gors (Cp?), gorst m. *'gorse,' furze*, MH,MrR: *juniper*, Lcd : 'rhamnus,' S[2]Ps 57[10].
gorstbēam m. *furze bush*, Mk 12[26].
gōs f. nap. gēs *'goose,'* LL,Rd,WW; Æ.
gōs-fugol m. nap. -fuglas *goose*, Ct.
gōshafoc (u[3]) m. *'goshawk,'* WW.
gost=gorst; **gōst**=gāst
+got n. *shedding (of tears)*, BH 376[12].
Gota sg. -an pl. *'Goth,'* BH.
goten pp. of gēotan.
-gotennes v. tō-g.
Got-isc (GD), -onisc (OEG) adj. *of the Goths*.
gōtwoðe f. *goatweed*, LCD. [gāt]
gōung (ēo) f. *groaning*, BH 76[15]. [gōian]
grād m. (Æ), grāde f. *step, grade, rank*. [L.]

grǣd m. *grass*, WW.
grǣda=grēada
grǣdan I. *to cry, call out*, Lcd : *crow*, CP,Rd. ['grede'] II. ds. of wk. adj. *grassy*, ÆL 18[245].
grǣde I. *grassy*, Æ. II.=grǣd
grǣde-, grǣdi-=grǣdig-
grǣdig (ē) *'greedy,' hungry, covetous*, Æ,B, Bl,Sol : *eager*, CP. adv. -līce, Æ,Bas.
grǣdignes f. *greediness, avarice*, Æ.
grǣdum adv. *greedily*, GU 710.
grǣf I. (a) n. *cave, 'grave,' trench*, Seaf; Mdf. [grafan] II. n? *style for writing*, WW. [L. graphium]
grǣfa m. grǣfe f. *bush, bramble, grove, thicket*, WW; Mdf : *brush-wood (for burning), fuel*, Chr. ['greave']
grǣfen pp. of grafan.
grǣfhūs n. *grave*, SAT 708.
grǣfsex n. *graving tool*, WW. [seax]
grǣft mfn. *graven image, carved object, sculpture*, Æ.
grǣftgeweorc n. *graven image*, DEUT 5[8].
grǣfð pres. 3 sg: of grafan.
grǣg *'grey,'* Æ,Ep,Gen,Met,WW.
grǣggōs f. *grey (wild) goose*, GL.
grǣghǣwe *grey*, WW 402[40].
grǣghama *grey-coated*, FIN 6.
grǣgmǣl *grey-coloured*, B 2682.
grǣgōs=grǣggōs
grǣm-, grǣn-=grem-, gren-; **grǣp**=grēp
+grǣppian *to seize*, MtL 14[31].
grǣs n. (nap. grasu) *'grass,'* Cp,CP. [v. also gærs]
grǣsgrēne (e[1], oe[2]) *'grass-green,'* Ep.
grǣshoppa v. gærshoppa.
grǣsmolde f. *greensward*, B 1881.
grǣswang† m. *greensward*, VH 14.
grǣt I.=pres. 3 sg. of (1) grǣdan, (2) grētan. II.=grēat
grǣtan=grētan; **graf**=grǣf
grāf nm. *'grove,'* BC; Mdf.
grāfa m. *grove*, KC.
grafan[6] *to dig, dig up*, Met,Rd,Rim : 'grave,' *engrave, carve, chisel*, PPs.
grafere m. *'sculptor,' graver*, WW 164[14].
grafet n. *trench*, EC 354; 355.
gram (o) adj. *angry, cruel, fierce*, B,G; AO : *oppressive, hostile* : (as sb.) *enemy*. ['grame']
grama I. m. *rage, anger*, Æ : *trouble*, Lcd. ['grame'] II. *devil, demon*, ÆL.
gramatisccræft=grammaticcræft
grambǣre *passionate*, CP 289[5].
grame adv. *angrily, fiercely, cruelly*.
gramfærnes f. *wrath*, LL (226[25]). [=*grambærnes]
gramhegdig=gramhȳdig
gramheort† *hostile-minded*, VH 14.

gramhycgende *hostile*, PPs 68²⁵.

gramhўdig† *hostile, malignant*, VH 14.

gramian *to anger, enrage*, W 199². **gramigende** *raging*, GPH 402.

gramlic *wrathful, fierce, cruel, severe*, Æ. adv. -līce, *Ps*. ['*gramely*']

grammatic *grammatical*, ÆL 35¹⁴.

grammaticcræft m. *art of grammar*, BH 258¹⁵.

grammaticere m. *grammarian*, BF 158¹⁷.

grammatisc=grammatic

grammōd *cruel*, BL 223³³.

gramword n. *evil speech*, PPs 74⁵.

grand pret. 3 sg. of grindan.

grandorlēas (o) *guileless*, JUL 271.

grānian² *to* '*groan*,' *lament*, Bl,Ps.

granu f. *moustache*, Cp 335 M (v. BTs).

grānung f. '*groaning*,' *lamentation*, Æ.

grāp I. f.† *grasp, grip*. [grīpan] II. pret. 3 sg. of grīpan.

±**grāpian** *to feel for, lay hold,of, seize, touch*, Æ,B,Bl,Rd,VPs : *attain, reach*, BF 144¹. ['*grope*']

grāpigendlic *tangible*, ÆH 1·230.

grāpung f. *sense of feeling, touch*, Æ. ['*groping*']

grāscinnen *made of grey skins or grey fur*, CHR 1075 D. [ON. grāskinn]

grasian *to* '*graze*,' Lcd.

grasu v. græs.

gratan (LCD 3·292²⁴)=grotan

graðul *gradual, antiphon*, CM 1020.

grēada m. *lap, bosom*, CP,Lk. ['*greade*']

grēat (æ) comp. grīetra '*great*,' *tall, thick, stout, massive*, A,Æ,Bo,Chr,WW : *coarse*, BC,Lcd.

grēatewyrt f. *meadow saffron*, WW 298⁷.

grēatian² *to become enlarged*, CP. ['*great*']

grēatnes (ē) f. '*greatness*,' RB 88¹⁵.

Grēcas mpl. *Greeks* (v. AB 40·342).

Grēcisc *Greek, Grecian*, Æ.

grēd=grǣd; **gref**-, grēf-=grǣf-, grǣf-

grēg-=grǣg-; **grem**-=grim-

gremet-=grymet-

±**gremian** *to enrage, provoke, irritate*, AO; Æ,CP : *revile*, Mk. ['*greme*']

gremman=gremian

gremung (æ) f. *provocation*, LPs 94⁹.

grēne '*green*,' Ct,Gl,Lcd : *young, immature*, Lcd : *raw* : *growing, living*, LkL (oe) : *as* sb., Lcd.

grēnhǣwen *green-coloured*, WW 379²⁴.

grēnian *to become* '*green*,' *flourish*, Met.

grēnnes f. *greenness*, BH ; CP : (in pl.) *green things, plants*, BF 82⁴.

grennian *to* '*grin*,' *gnash the teeth*, Jul,Sc.

grennung (æ) f. *grinning*, Cp 174 R.

grēofa m. *pot, pan*, WW. [Ger. griebe]

grēop=grēp

grēosn (īo) *gravel, pebble*, KGL 76³. [Ger. greiss]

grēot n. '*grit*,' *sand, earth*, An,B,Gen; Æ.

grēotan² *to cry, lament*, B,Sol. [v. '*greet*']

grēothord n. *body*, Gu 1240.

grēow pret. 3 sg. of grōwan.

grēp, grēpe f. *ditch, furrow, drain : privy*, ES 9·505 ; GL. [v. '*grip*']

gres-=græs-; **grēt**-=grēat-

grētan I. (±) *to* '*greet*,' *salute, accost, speak to, challenge*, B,Gl,Mk,Jul : (±) *to seek out, approach, visit*, AO,B,Gen,LG : *ill-treat, attack*, AO : *touch, take hold of, handle, deal with*, ÆGr : *have an effect upon*, ZDA 34·232 : *cohabit with*. hearpan grētan *play the harp*, Cra. **II.**† (ǣ) *to weep, bemoan, lament, deplore*, B,Cp,Cr. [v. '*greet*']

grēting f. '*greeting*,' BH,LkL (oe) : *present*.

grētinghūs n. *audience chamber*, WW 184³.

grētingword n. *word of greeting*, ÆGR 209¹⁴.

+**grētlic** *commendatory*, RBL 103⁶.

gretta=grytta

greðe '*sodalis*'? OEG 29². ·

grēwð pres. 3 sg. of grōwan.

griellan=grillan

grietra v. grēat.

grīghund m. '*greyhound*,' WW 276³.

grillan (ie, y) *to provoke, offend*, CP : *gnash the teeth*, GL. ['*grill*']

grim (CP)=grimm

grīma† m. *mask, helmet*, EL : *ghost*, RD.

grimena '*bruchus*,' *caterpillar*? EPs 104³⁴.

grimet-=grymet-

grimful *fierce, violent*, ES 39·348.

grimhelm† m. *helmet* (*with visor*).

griming *spectre*, WW 446²⁶.

grimlic *fierce, blood-thirsty, cruel, terrible, severe*, Æ,AO,B. adv. -līce. ['*grimly*']

grimm *fierce, savage*, B,Bl,Ma : *dire, severe, bitter, painful*, BH,Bl,Chr. ['*grim*']

grimman³† *to rage : hasten on*, B 306.

grimmān n. *terrible sin*, BHb 50⁸.

grimme *savagely, cruelly, severely*, AO,Gen. ['*grim*']

grimnes f. *ferocity, cruelty*, Bl,Gu,WW : *severity*. ['*grimness*']

grimsian *to rage*, BH.

grimsung f. *harshness, severity*, CP 125¹⁴.

grin '*ilium*,' *region of the groin*, LL.

±**grīn** (ī, ў; also short?) nf. *snare, gin*, PPs, VPs; Æ,CP : *halter, noose*, Mt. ['*grin*']

+**grind**† n. *impact, crash*.

±**grindan³** (y) *to rub together, grate, scrape*, Rd : *gnash*, Ps : '*grind*,' *sharpen*, Æ,Mt, pp. WW.

grinde f. *shingle*, BC (v. Mdf).

grindel m. nap. grindlas *bar, bolt*. pl. *grating, hurdle*, GEN 384 (v. BT).

grindere m. *grinder*, LCD 3·178¹.

grinde-tōð, grindig- m. *grinding tooth, molar*, WW 440²⁶.

grindle f. *herring*, WW 356¹².

gring=cring

+**grīnian** *to ensnare*, KGl. ['*grin*']

grint pres. 3 sg. of grindan.

grinu '*avidius*' (said of some colour), WW 163¹⁹,356²⁵.

grīosn=grēosn

gripa m. *handful, sheaf*, LCD.

±**grīpan** intr. (wᵢ d. g. on or tō) *to seek to get hold of, assail, attack, B,Bl,Gen*; CP : tr. (w. g.) *seize, snatch, take, apprehend, Sol,WW*. ['*gripe*']

gripe m. '*grip,*' *grasp, seizure, attack, B, WW*; Æ. gūðbilla g. *shield* : *handful, Lcd,Ps.*

grīpend m. *seizer, robber*, WW 516¹³.

+**gripennes** f. *seizing, snare, captivity*, EPs 34⁸.

±**grippan** (io) *to seize, obtain*, DR, LG.

gripu f. *kettle, caldron*, SOL 46.

gripul '*capax,*' WW 198³⁹. ['*gripple*']

-grīsan (ȳ) v. ā-g.

grislic '*grisly,*' *horrible*, HL 15¹⁸². adv. RWH 84.

grīst n. *action of grinding*, WW. ['*grist*']

gristan? *to gnash, grind*, HGL 513 (cp. OEG 4605 and n).

gristbāt-=gristbit-

gristbite m. *gnashing*, W 188⁵.

gristbitian *to gnash the teeth, rage*, Æ,BH, Mk,WW; Æ. ['*gristbite*']

gristbitung f. *gnashing of teeth*, Bl,Mt. ['*gristbiting*']

gristle f. '*gristle,*' Gl,WW.

gristlung (y) f. *gnashing*, Lk 13²⁸.

grīstra m. *baker*, WW.

gritta=grytta

grið n. *truce, (temporary) peace*, Ma : *protection of the person, asylum, sanctuary, guarantee of safety*, LL. ['*grith*']

griðbryce m. *breach of* 'grið,' LL : *penalty for such a breach*, LL. ['*grithbreach*']

±**griðian** *to make a truce or peace*, Chr : *protect*, LL. ['*grith*']

griðlagu f. *law of temporary or local peace*, LL 470,9.

griðlēas *unprotected*, W 158⁷.

groe-=grē-

grōf pret. 3 sg. of grafan.

grom=gram; **gron-**=gran-

grond pret. 3 sg. of grindan.

gronwisc (=a) '*acus,*' Cp 160A (v. AB 9·35).

grōp f. *ditch*, Ln 150.

gropa m. *a liquid measure*, WW 204³.

grōpian=grāpian; **-groren** v. be-g.

grorn I. m. *sorrow, sadness*, RIM 89. II. adj. *sad, agitated*, OET 127⁶. adv. -e.

grornhof n. *sad home, hell*, JUL 324.

grornian *to mourn, complain*, CR,Ps.

grorntorn *sadness*, RIM 66?

grornung f. *complaint*, NG.

grost *cartilage*, Ln 57.

grot I. n. *particle*, Bo; AO : *meal*. ['*grot*'] II. sbpl. (grotan) '*groats,*' *coarse meal*, Lcd.

grotig *earthy*, GPH 396.

±**grōwan**⁷ *to* 'GROW,' *increase, flourish* : *germinate*, CP : *become?* WW 441²⁸ (v. NP 15·272).

grōwende '*growing,*' Gen,KGl.

grōwnes f. *growth*, BH : *prosperity*, HL 124²⁵⁷.

grummon pret. pl. of grimman.

gruncian *to desire*, GPH 396.

grund m. 'GROUND,' *bottom* : *foundation* : *abyss, hell* : *plain, country, land, earth*:*sea, water*.

grundbedd n. *ground, soil*, RD 81²⁴.

grundbūend† m. *earth-dweller*.

grunddēope *depths of the sea*, APs 64⁸.

grunden pp. of grindan.

grundeswelge (i³, u³, v³) f. '*groundsel,*' Gl, Lcd.

grundfūs *hastening to hell*, MOD 49.

grundhyrde m. *keeper of the abyss*, B 2136.

grundinga=grundlinga

grundlēas *bottomless, unfathomable*, Bo : *boundless, vast*. ['*groundless*']

grundlēaslic *boundless, vast*, CP 417¹⁰.

grundling m. *groundling (fish)*, BC 3·525.

grundlinga (u³) adv. *from the foundation, completely*, Æ : *to the ground, prone, prostrate*, Æ.

grundon pret. pl. of grindan.

grundscēat† m. *region*, CR.

grundsele m. *abysmal dwelling*, B 2139.

grundsopa '*cartilago,*' GL (v. BTs).

grundstān m. *foundation-stone*, WW. ['*groundstone*']

+**grundstaðelian** *to establish firmly*, ÆL 8²¹.

grundwæg m. *earth*, AN 582.

grundwang† m. *(ground-plain), the earth*, B : *bottom (of a lake)*.

grundweall m. *foundation*, Æ,Lk. ['*groundwall*']

+**grundweallian** *to establish, found*, EPs 23².

grundwela m. *earthly riches*, GEN 957.

grundwiergen (y) f. *water-wolf*, B 1518.

grunian, grunnian, *to grunt* (OEG) : *chew the cud?* Sc 54'.

grunnettan *to* '*grunt,*' Cp.

grun(n)ung f. *grunting, bellowing*, OEG.

grut m. *gulf, chasm, abyss* : *stone, rock*, OEG 1814.

grūt f. (ds. grȳt, grūt) *groats, coarse meal,* Cp,Ct,Lcd : *grains, the spent grain after brewing,* Lcd. ['*grout*']

grutt, grutte=grut; gryllan=grillan

grym=grim(m)

grymet-(t)an, -tian (e, i) *to grunt, roar, rage,* Æ.

grymet(t)ung f. *grunting, roaring, bellowing,* Æ.

grymm=grimm

grymman I. *to mourn, wail,* LPs 37⁹ (gyrm-). ['*yarm*'] II.=gremian

gryn=gyrn; grȳn=grīn

+grynd n. *plot of ground,* TC 231²².

gryndan I. *to set, sink (of the sun),* WW. ['*grind*'; grund] II. (+) *to found (of a house),* MtL 7²⁵ (wry-). III.=grindan

grynde n. *abyss,* SAT 331.

grynel (WW 291³)=cyrnel

grȳnian=grīnian

grynsmið m. *worker of ill,* AN 919.

grȳpe (=ī) f. *ditch, drain,* OEG. [v. '*grip*']

gryre† m. *horror, terror : fierceness, violence,* DD 8 : *horrible thing.*

gryrebrōga† m. *terror, horror.*

gryrefæst *terribly firm,* EL 76a.

gryrefāh† adj. (used as sb.) *spotted horror,* B.

gryregæst (æ)? m. *terrible stranger,* B 2560.

gryregeatwe fp. *war-gear,* B 324.

gryrehwīl f. *terrible time,* AN 468.

gryrelēoð† n. *terrible song.*

gryrelic† *terrible, horrible,* B.

gryremiht f. *terrible power,* W 195²⁰.

gryresīð m. *dangerous expedition,* B 1462.

gryrran *to gnash,* DD 195.

grys-, grȳs-=gris-, grīs-

grȳt I. pres. 3 sg. of grēotan. II. v. grūt.

grȳtan *to flourish,* WW 240²⁹. [grēat]

grȳto f. *greatness,* AA 12⁷. [grēat]

grytt n. *dust, meal,* GL.

grytta, gryttan f. pl. *coarse meal, bran, chaff,* Ep,Lcd,WW. ['*grit*']

grytte f. *spider,* JLVPs 89⁹.

grȳttra (A4·151)=*grietra cp. of grēat. ['*greater*']

gryð-=grið-; gū=gēo

guldon pret. pl. of gieldan.

gullisc? (an attribute of silver), SOL 150⁹.

gullon pret. pl. of giellan.

gulpon pret. pl. of gielpan.

guma† m. *man, lord, hero,* B. ['*gome*']

gumcynn† sn. *human race, men, nation.*

gumcyst† f. *excellence, bravery, virtue, liberality.* adv. -um *excellently.*

gumdrēam m. *enjoyment of life,* B 2469.

gumdryhten m. *lord,* B 1642.

gumfēða m. *troop,* B 1401.

gumfrēa m. *king,* DA 651.

-gumian v. ofer-g.

gummann m. *man,* B 1028.

gumrīce† n. *kingdom, earth.*

gumrinc† m. *man, warrior.*

gumstōl m. *ruler's seat, throne,* B 1952.

gumðegen m. *man,* CRA 83.

gumðēod f. *folk, people,* GEN 226.

gund m. *matter, pus,* Lcd. ['*gound*']

gundeswilge (Ep,Erf,Ln)=grundeswelge

gundig *goundy, mattery,* Erf.

gung=geong; gung-=ging-

gungon pret. pl. of gangan.

gunnon (BH) pret. pl. of ginnan.

gupan '*clunibus, renibus, coxe,*' WW 205⁴¹ (v. A 31·522).

gurron pret. pl. of gyrran.

guton pret. pl. of gēotan.

guttas mp. '*guts,*' *entrails,* HGl 408.

gūð† f. *combat, battle, war.*

gūðbeorn m. *fighting-hero,* B 314.

gūðbill† n. *battle-bill, sword.*

gūðbord† n. *war-shield,* GEN.

gūðbyrne f. *corslet, coat of mail,* B 321.

gūðcearu f. *war-trouble,* B 1258.

gūðcræft m. *war-craft,* B 127.

gūðcwēn† f. *warrior queen,* EL.

gūðcyning† m. *warrior king,* B.

gūðcyst f. *troop, warrior band?* (Kluge) : *bravery?* (BT),EX 343.

gūðdēað m. *death in battle,* B 2249.

gūðfana m. *gonfanon, war-banner, ensign, standard,* Æ,AO.

gūð-flā? f., -flān? mf. *battle-arrow,* GEN 2063.

gūðfloga m. *winged fighter,* B 2528.

gūðfona=gūðfana

gūðfrēa m. *warlike prince,* AN 1335.

gūðfrec *bold in battle* (GK), *greedy for destruction* (BTs),AN 1119.

gūðfreca† m. *warrior.*

gūðfremmend† m. *warrior.*

gūðfugol m. *bird of war, eagle,* RD 25⁸.

gūðgeatwe† fp. *armour,* B.

gūðgelǣca m. *warrior,* EL 43.

gūðgemōt† n. *battle, combat.*

gūðgetāwe=gūðgeatwe

gūðgeðingu† np. *battle, contest,* AN.

gūðgewǣde† n. *war-dress, armour,* B.

gūðgeweorc† n. *warlike deed,* B.

gūðgewinn† n. *battle.*

gūðhafoc m. *war-hawk, eagle,* †CHR 937A.

gūðheard *bold in battle,* EL 204.

gūðhelm m. *helmet,* B 2487.

gūðhere m. *warlike host, army,* GEN 1967.

gūðhorn m. *war-horn, trumpet,* B 1432.

gūðhrēð m. *martial glory,* B 819.

gūðhwæt *fierce in battle,* AP 57.

gūðlēoð n. *war-song,* B 1522.

gŭð-mæcga, -maga m. *warrior*, SOL90.
gŭðmōdig? *of warlike mind*, B306.
Gūðmyrce pl. *Ethiopians*, EX69.
gŭðplega† m. *attack, battle*.
gŭðrǣs† m. *battle-rush, onslaught*, B.
gŭðrēaf n. *armour*, JUL387.
gŭðrēow *fierce in battle*, B58. [hrēow]
gŭðrinc† m. *warrior, hero*.
gŭðrōf† *brave in battle*.
gŭðscearu f. *slaughter in battle*, B1213.
gŭðsceaða m. *ravaging invader*, B2318.
gŭðsceorp n. *armour*, JUD329.
gŭðscrūd n. *armour*, EL258.
gŭðsearo† n. *armour*.
gŭðsele m. *hall of warriors*, B443.
gŭðspell n. *tidings of a war*, GEN2097.
gŭðsweord n. *sword*, B2154.
gŭððracu† f. *hostile attack*, GEN.
gŭððrēat m. *warlike troop*, EX193.
gŭðweard† m. *war-lord, king*.
gŭðweorc n. *warlike deed*, AN1068.
gŭðwērig *wounded*, B1586.
gŭðwiga m. *warrior*, B2112.
gŭðwine† m. *battle-friend, weapon*, B.
gŭðwudu m. *spear*, FIN6.
gy-=ge-, gi-; gyc-=gic-; gyd=gid(d)
gyden (AO), gydenu f. (occl. gs. gydenan)
 goddess. [god]
gydenlic '*vestalis*' (=*dealis?* A31·63), WW
 524³³.
gydig (i) *possessed* (*by a spirit*), *insane*,
 OEG5009. ['*giddy*']
gyf=gif; gyf-=geof-, gief-, gif-
gyf-=gif-
gyhða (Æ)=gicða; gyhðu=gehðu
gyld=gield; gyld-=gild-, gylt-
+gyld=gylden
±gyldan I. *to gild*, Ps,WW. ['*gilded*'] II.
 (AO)=gieldan
±gylden *golden*, B,Dan; Æ,AO,CP. ['*gilden*']
gyldenbēag (i) m. *crown*, LEV8⁹.
gyldenbend *golden band*, LEVC8⁹.
gyldenfeax *golden-haired*, WW348³⁵.
gyldenhilte *golden-hilted*, BC3·74'.
gyldenhīwe *golden-hued*, OEG43⁵.
gyldenmūða *golden-mouthed* (*Chrysostom*),
 GD94²⁴; ZDA31·7.
gyldenwecg (gylding-) m. *gold mine*, WW
 241¹⁷.
gylece (IM127¹⁴)?=pylece
gylian, gyllan *to yell, shout*. gyliende
 '*garrulus*,' OEG56¹³⁸.
gylm=gilm; gylp=gielp
gylt (e, i, ie) m. '*guilt*,' *sin, offence, crime,
 fault*, Bf,Bl,Chr,Mt,Ps; AO,CP.
±gyltan *to commit sin, be guilty*, CP,Mt,RB,
 VPs. ['*guilt*,' '*guilting*']
gyltend m. *sinner, debtor*, CP.

gyltig *offending*, '*guilty*,' Mt.
gylting (u¹) f. *sin*, DR.
gyltlic *sinful*, Mt26⁸⁶. adv. -līce *faultily*, Sc
 35³.
gyltwīte n. (gyld-) *fine for unpaid tax*, KC
 2·406 : *for a crime*, 6·240.
gylung? '*garrulitas*,' OEG56¹⁴¹.
gym=gimm; gym-=gim-
gȳm-=gīem-; gymian=gymmian
gymm=gimm
±gymmian *to cut the flesh*, OEG3799.
gyn-=geon-, gin-; gȳn-=gīn-
-gȳpe (=īe?) v. æ-g.
gypigend (=i) *yawning*, GPH398.
gypung (=i) f. *gaping, open mouth*, GPH
 402.
gyr I. m. *filth, mud, marsh*. II. *fir tree*, WW
 269¹⁴.
gyr-=geor-, gier-; gyra=gyr I.
±gyrdan (pret. gyrde), *to* '*gird*' (*sword*),
 Gen,PPs : *encircle, surround*, JnL : (+)
 invest with attributes, PPs.
gyrdel (e) m. '*girdle*,' *belt, zone*, Lcd,Mt;
 Æ : *purse*.
gyrdelbred n. *writing-tablet*, WW277¹³.
gyrdelhring n. *girdle, buckle*, WW432.
gyrdels, gyrder=gyrdel; gyrdil-=gyrdel-
gȳren=grīn
gyrman=grymman
gyrn† mn. *sorrow, misfortune*.
gyrnstafas mp. *injury, affliction*, JUL245.
gyrnwracu† f. *revenge for injury*.
gyrran³ [=gierran, georran] *to sound, chatter*,
 Æ : *grunt* : *to creak, grate, An,OEG*. ['*yerr*']
gyrretan *to roar* (*of lions*), LPs.
gyrsandæg (MFH97)=gierstandæg
gyrst *gnashing of teeth, anger*, HGl513.
 [v. '*grist*' and OEG4605n]
gyrstandæg (Æ)=gierstandæg
gyrtrēow n. *fir-tree*, WW138¹¹.
gyru I. (?) *muddy*, KC3·412. II. f.=gyr
gyrwan=gierwian
gyrwefenn n. *marsh*, ÆGR60¹⁰.
gȳse=gēse; gȳsel=gīsl
gyst=(1) giest, (2) gist
gyst-=giest-
gysternlicdæg=gierstandæg
gyt=git pron.
gȳt I. pres. 3 sg. of gēotan. II.=giet
gȳt-=gīet-, gīt-
gyte, gytt (NG) m. *pouring forth, shedding*,
 Æ : *flood*, Æ. [gēotan]
gytesǣl m. (dp. gytesālum) *joy at wine-
 pouring, carousal*, JUD22.
gytestrēam m. *running stream*, WW.
gytfeorm f. *ploughing-feast*, LL452,21⁴.
gyð-=giðð-; gȳu=gēo

H

h is often wrongly prefixed to words, or (conversely) dropped, as in Cockney English.
hā m. *oar-thole, rowlock.* æt hā *for each oar, or each oarsman,* CHR 1040 C. [*Icel.* hār]
habban anv. ptc. pres. hæbbende; pres. 1 sg. hæbbe, 2. hæfst, 3. hæfð, pl. hæbbað, habbað; pret. 3 sg. hæfde; subj. hæbbe; imperat. hafa; pp. (±)hæf(e)d *to* 'HAVE*,' AO,CP : *possess, own, hold,* AO,CP : *keep, retain : entertain, cherish : look after, carry on : esteem, consider,* AO,CP : *be subject to, experience : get, obtain,* Chr : *assert :* used as auxiliary to indicate past tense, *have,* Æ,Chr. h. for *consider :* (+) *hold, keep from, restrain, preserve,* Æ,CP. yfle +h. *afflict, torment.*
haca m. *hook, door-fastening,* Cp 311 P (v. BTs).
-haccian v. tō-h.
hacele (æ) f. *cloak, coat, vestment, cassock, 'pallium,'* AO,WW; Æ. ['hackle']
hacod (æ, e) m. *pike, mullet,* Cp,Ep,WW. ['haked']
hacole, hacule=hacele
hād m. (rare gs. hāda) *person, individual, character, individuality,* Æ,BH,Mt : *degree, rank, order, office (especially holy office),* Æ,BH,CP : *condition, state, nature, character, form, manner,* B,Sol : *sex,* BH, Chr : *race, family, tribe : choir.* ['had']
-hād masc. suffix; usu. denotes state or condition, as cildhād, mægðhād. [*Eng.* -hood]
+hada m. *brother monk,* LL.
hādārung f. *respect of persons,* LL 474,18.
hādbōt f. *compensation for injury or insult to a priest,* LL. ['hadbot']
hādbreca m. *injurer of one in (holy) orders,* LL.
hād-bryce, -brice m. *injury of one in (holy) orders,* LL.
hādelīce adv. *as to persons,* DHy 29⁶.
hādesmann m. *member of a particular order,* CHR 995 F.
hādgrīð n. *privilege (as regards peace) of holy orders,* LL 471,19.
±hādian *to ordain, consecrate,* BH,Chr; Æ. ['hade']
hādnotu f. *office of a priest,* LL 458 H.
hādor I. n. *clearness, brightness,* B 414 (or ? hador,=heaðor). II.† (æ) *bright, clear, fresh : distinct, loud.* [*Ger.* heiter] adv. hādre.
hādswǣpa m. *bridesman,* WW 174³⁵.
hādswǣpe (ā) f. *bridesmaid,* WW.
hādung f. *consecration, ordination,* LL. [v. 'hade'] hādunge underfōn *to take the veil.*

hādungdæg (i²) m. *ordination day,* ÆL 33⁵⁹.
hæb, hæb- (GL)=hæf, hæf-
hæbb-=habb-, hebb-
hæbbednes f. *continence,* BF 124²⁵.
hæbbendlic '*habilis,'* ÆGR 54⁵.
-hæbbere v. sulh-h.
hæbbung (e²) f. *constraint,* WW 372,503.
hæc-=hac-
hæc(c) I. fm. *grating,* '*hatch,' half-gate,* Ct. II.=hæcce I.
+hæcca *sausage,* WW 411²⁰. [haccian]
hæcce I. fn. *crozier.* II. (e) *fence,* BC 3·147'. III.=hæc
hæccelēas *without a fence? or hatch?* EC 389'.
hæcgeat (e²) n. *hatch-gate,* KC 5·376¹⁴.
hæcine (a) f. *a thin vinous drink,* '*posca,'* WW 129³ (v. A 8·451 and Ducange, s.v.).
hæcwer m. *hatch-weir, a weir in which fish were caught,* KC 3·450.
hǣdor=hādor
hædre† *straitly, anxiously,* SOL.
hǣdre=hādre
hæf I.† n. (heaf-, haf- in obl. cases) *sea, ocean,* WW. II. m. *leaven,* OEG.
hǣfd=hēafod
hæfde pret. sg. of habban.
hæfe I. m. *leaven,* Sc. [*Ger.* hefe] II.= hefe I.
hǣfed=hēafod
-hæfednes v. be-, for-h.
hæfegītsung? f. *covetousness,* EPs 118³⁶.
hæfen I. f. *the having, owning : property, possessions,* Æ. [*Ger.* habe] II. f. '*haven,' port,* Chr. III.=hefen. IV. pp. of hebban.
hæfen-=hafen-; **hæfenblǣte**=hæferblǣte
hæfene=hæfen II.
hæfer (e) m. *he-goat,* WW.
hæferbīte m. *forceps,* WW 198¹⁶. [v. hæfern]
hæferblǣte f? *bittern? snipe?* WW 116⁴¹; 361¹⁷.
hæfergāt=hæfer
hæfern m. *crab,* WW.
hæfig=hefig; **hæfne**=hæfen
hæfreblǣte=hæferblǣte; **hæfst** v. habban.
±hæft I. m. *bond, fetter : captive, slave, servant : bondage, imprisonment, affliction,* Æ : (±) *seizing, thing seized,* CLPs 123⁶. II. adj. *captive.* III. n. '*haft,' handle,* Lcd, WW; Æ. IV. pp. of hæftan.
±hæftan *to bind, fetter : arrest, detain, imprison : condemn,* DR 197¹³. [*Ger.* heften]
hæfte=hæft II.
hæfteclomm m. *fetter,* †CHR 942 A.
+hæftednes f. *captivity : snare,* Ps.
hæftedōm m. *slavery, captivity,* MET 25⁶⁵.
hæften f. *confinement,* CHR 1095.
+hæftend m. *prisoner,* MFH 136.
hæftenēod=hæftnīed

hæftincel (e²) n. *slave,* WW.

hæfting f. *fastening, lock,* NIC502²⁵.

hæftlic *captious,* OEG3208.

hæftling m. *prisoner, captive,* Æ.

hæftmēce m. *hilted sword,* B1457.

±**hæftnes** (RWH22²⁰, v. also MFH165)= hæftednes

hæftneð=hæftnoð

±**hæftnian** *to take prisoner : seize, detain.*

hæftnīed (ē, ȳ) f. *custody, imprisonment, bondage.* Æ,AO.

±**hæftnīedan** *to take captive,* GD135¹⁵.

hæftnīedling (ē², y²) m. *captive,* ÆL.

hæftnīednes (ē², ȳ²) f. *captivity,* GD346²², NC299.

hæftnoð (e²) m. *confinement, imprisonment,* CHR.

hæftnung f. *confinement, captivity,* Æ,CHR.

hæftnȳd (Æ)=hæftnīed

hæftung f. *fetter,* MFH166.

hæftworld f. *world under bondage,* BL9⁴.

hæfð pres. 3 sg. of habban.

hæfuc=hafoc; **hæg-**=hago-, hagu-, hege-

+**hæg** n. *enclosure, meadow,* OEG; Mdf.

+**hægan**? *to vex, harass?* Ex169 (GK). or ?=+hnægan (BTs).

hæghāl *safe and sound,* DR.

hægsugga m. *hedge-sparrow,* ZDA33·241.

hæg-tes(se), -tis f. *fury, witch, pythoness,* Æ,GL.

hægðorn (Æ)=haguðorn

hægweard m. *keeper of cattle in a common field,* LL452,20.

hæh-=hēah-; **hæhtis**=hægtes

hæl I. n. *omen,* B204,WW36². **II.**=hælu. **III.** adj.=hāl

hæl-; hæl-=hel-; hāl-, hēl-

hǣlan I. (±) *to ' heal,' cure, save,* Lcd,Mt,Ps; Æ,CP : *greet, salute,* GD36²⁷. +hǣl! *Hosanna!* [hāl] **II.** *to castrate,* LCD3·186²²: (+) ÆP106⁶.

+**hæld**=+hield

hælet m. *man, hero.*

hæle n.=hǣlu

±**hæle** *safe,* SPs7¹¹.

+**hæled**=hāl

+**hælednes** f. *healing,* GD247¹¹.

hǣlend (ē) m. *Saviour, Christ,* Æ,G. [' heal-end']

hǣlendlic *wholesome, salutary,* OEG153⁸.

hælet-=hālet-

hæleð† m. (nap. hæleðas, hæleð) *man, hero, fighter,* B. [' heleth']

hæleðhelm=heoloðhelm

hælf-ter, f. -tre, m. ' *halter,*' WW.

hǣlgere (a²) m. *sanctifier,* DR.

hælhiht=healhiht

hǣlig *unstable, inconstant,* Bo115³.

hæling f. ' *healing,*' NIC.

hælm=healm

hǣlnes f. *salvation, safety,* CP : *sanctuary.* [' healness ']

hǣlnesgrið n. *peace-privileges attaching to a sanctuary,* LL471,19.

hǣlotīd f. *prosperous time,* CHR1065D.

hǣls-=hāls-

hǣlð, hǣlðo f. ' *health,*' Æ : *salvation,* Lcd; Æ : *healing,* Æ.

hǣlu f. *health,* Cr,Lcd : *prosperity,* MtL : *safety, salvation,* KC,Lk; Æ,CP : *healing, cure.* [' heal ']

hǣlubearn† n. *Saviour, Christ,* CR.

hǣlwyrt f. ' *pulegium,' pennyroyal,* WW 300²⁴.

hǣlynd=hǣlend

hǣmæht (MkR1²²)=hēahmiht

±**hǣman** *to have intercourse with, cohabit with,* Æ,CP : *marry,* MtR.

hǣmed (ē) n. (nap. hǣmedru) *cohabitation,* Æ,CP : *marriage : adultery, fornication,* WW420¹⁰.

hǣmedceorl m. *married man,* LL.

hǣmedgemāna m. *matrimony,* WW441²⁴.

hǣmedlāc n. *coition,* RD43³.

hǣmedrīm m. ' *lenocinium,*' OEG5046. [=-drēam]

hǣmedru v. hǣmed.

hǣmedscipe m. *cohabitation, wedlock,* OEG.

hǣmedðing n. *coition, cohabitation,* ÆL : *marriage.*

hǣmedwīf n. *married woman,* WW450²⁴.

hǣmend m. *fornicator,* WW420¹³.

hǣmere m. *consort, bedfellow,* Æ.

hǣmet, hǣmeð=hǣmed; **hæn**=henn

hǣnan I. *to stone,* Jn; Æ. [' hene '] **II.**=hīenan

hænep (e) m. ' *hemp,*' Lcd,WW.

hænfugel=hennfugol; **hænn**=henn

hǣnðu=hīenðu

+**hæp,** +hæplic (GL) *fit, convenient.*

+**hæplicnes** (e) f. *convenience, opportunity,* OET122⁶.

hæppan? *to go by chance,* ÆL31⁴⁷⁷.

hæpse f. ' *hasp,' fastening,* Æ.

hæpsian *to ' hasp,' fasten,* Æ.

hæpte (pret. 3 sg.) *jumped,* ÆL31⁴⁷⁷.

hǣr (ā, ē) n. ' *hair,*' Lcd,Mk; Æ : *a hair,* Æ, Cp,Mk.

hær-=har-, hear-, her(e)-; **hǣr-**=hēr-

hǣre (ē) f. *sackcloth of hair,* Mt,VPs; Æ. [' haire ']

+**hǣre** *hairy,* AA33³.

hǣren *of hair,* Bl,Lcd. [' hairen ']

hærenfagol sb. *hedgehog,* SPs103¹⁹ (v. BTs).

hærfest (e) m. *autumn,* ' *harvest*'-time, Bf, Ct,WW; AO : *August,* A10·185. h. hand-ful *handful of corn* (*a due belonging to the husbandman on an estate*), LL450.

hærfestlic *autumnal* : *of harvest*, Æ (108¹⁹⁸).

Hærfestmōnað m. '*harvest-month*,' *September*, ÆGr 43⁸.

hærfest-tīd (BH) f., **-tīma** (BF) m. *autumn, harvest-time.*

hærfestwǣta m. *autumn rain*, AO 102⁷.

hǣrgripa (ē) m. *seizing by the hair*, LL 611.

hǣriht *hairy*, WW 513⁸.

hǣring (ē) m. '*herring*,' Gl,WW ; Æ.

hǣringtīma m. *herring season*, Ct.

hǣrloccas mp. *locks of hair*, HGl. ['*hairlock*']

hærmberg (N) = hearmbeorg

hærn I. f. *wave, tide* : (†) *sea, ocean.* II. *brain*, CHR 1137.

hǣrnǣdl f. *curling-pin*, OEG 1200.

hærnflota m. *ship*, Gu 1307.

hærsceard n. *hare-lip*, LCD.

hǣrsyfe (ē) n. '*hair-sieve*,' A 9·264.

hǣs f. '*hest*,' *bidding, behest, command*, Æ, Gen. [hātan]

hæsel m. '*hazel*' *shrub*, Gl,Lcd ; Æ ; Mdf.

hæselhnutu (a¹) f. '*hazel-nut*,' Gl,WW.

hæselrǣw f. *a row of hazels*, EC 445¹⁹.

hæselwrīd m. *hazel-thicket*, KC 2·250'.

hǣsere m. *master, lord*, LkLR.

hǣsl = hæsel

hǣslen *of hazel*, Lcd. ['*hazelen*']

hæsp = hæpse ; **hæssuc** = hassuc

hǣst† I. *violent, vehement.* adv. hǣst-e, -līce. II. (ē) f. *violence, strife.*

hǣswalwe (WW 7²⁸) = sǣswealwe?

hæt m. *head-covering*, '*hat*,' Cp,AO ; Æ.

hǣt pres. 3 sg. of hātan.

±hǣtan (ā) tr. *to* '*heat**,' Lcd,Shr : intr. *become hot*, Gl.

hǣtcole = hǣðcole

hǣte f. *heat*, Æ,AO. [hāt]

hǣteru np. *garments*, ÆH. ['*hater*']

hǣting f. *heating*, WW 281⁸.

hǣto = hǣtu ; **hǣts** (ÆL 18³⁵⁰) = hǣgtes

hǣtst pres. 2 sg. of hātan.

hætt = hæt ; **hǣtte** = hātte, v. hātan.

hǣttan = hettan

hættian I. (e) *to scalp*, LL 334,30⁵. II. = hatian

hǣtu (o², e²) f. '*heat*,' *warmth*, Bl,Lcd,Mt, VPs ; Æ : *fervour, ardour*, VHy.

hǣð I. mn. '*heath*,' *untilled land, waste*, Ex ; Mdf : *heather*, Gl,Lcd. II. f. (WW 317²⁴) = hǣða

hǣða m. *heat, hot weather* ÆL 14¹⁶⁸.

hǣðberie f. *whortleberry*, LCD.

hǣðcole f. *name of a plant*, WW.

hǣðen I. (ē) '*heathen*,' *heathenish, pagan*, Æ,Bl,Ct ; AO,CP. II. m. *gentile, heathen man (especially of the Danes)*, Æ,Mk.

hǣðena m. *heathen*, LkR 21²⁵.

hǣðencyning m. *heathen king*, DA 54.

hǣðencynn n. *heathen race*, GEN 2546.

hǣðendōm m. '*heathendom*,' *false religion*, LL.

hǣðenfeoh n. *heathen sacrifice?* JUL 53.

hǣðenfolc n. *heathen people*, W 223¹².

hǣðengield (i³, y³) n. *idolatry*, Æ : *idol*, Æ.

hǣðengilda (y³) m. *idolater*, Æ.

hǣðenhere m. *Danish army*, CHR.

hǣðenisc '*heathenish*,' *pagan*, AO.

hǣðennes f. *heathenism, paganism*, BH : *heathen country*, OET 175⁷. ['*heathenesse*']

hǣðenscipe (ē) m. *paganism, idolatry*, Æ, Chr. ['*heathenship*']

hǣðenstyrc m. *heathen calf (the golden calf of the Israelites)*, PPs 105¹⁷.

hǣðfeld m. *heath-land*, Bo,Ct.

hǣðiht *heathy*, KC.

hǣðīn = hǣðen-

hǣðstapa† m. *heath-stalker, wolf, stag.* [stæppan]

hǣðung f. *heating, parching*, ÆH 1·286. [= hǣtung]

hǣwe *iron-coloured, bluish, grey*, GL.

hǣwen (ē) *blue, purple, azure, green*, Gl. ['*haw*']

hǣwengrēne *cerulean*, WW 379²³.

hǣwenhydele f. *a plant*, LCD.

hafa, imperat. of habban ; hafast, hafað = hæfst, hæfð pres. 2 and 3 sg. of habban.

-hafa v. wan-h ; **hafala** = hafela

hafastu = hafast ðu

hafecere = hafocere

hafela† (ea¹, o², u²) m. *head*, LCD.

hafelǣst = hafenlēast

hafen pp. of hebban.

hafenian† *to hold, grasp.* [hebban]

hafenlēas *destitute, needy, poor*, Æ,WW. ['*haveless*' ; hæfen]

hafenlēast f. *want, poverty*, ÆH.

hāfern = hæfern

hafetian (i²) *to clap, flap*, Æ.

hafoc (ea) m. '*hawk*,' Gl,Wy.

hafoccynn n. *hawk-tribe*, Æ.

hafocere m. '*hawker*,' LL ; WW 235⁹,ÆP 140²⁴.

hafocfugel m. *hawk*, LL (162¹⁹).

hafocung f. *hawking*, BC 1·280'.

hafocwyrt f. *a plant*, LCD.

hafola = hafela ; **-hafol(nes)** v. wan-h.

hafuc = hafoc

hafudland (WW 147¹⁸) = hēafodland

haga I. m. *hedge, enclosure, curtilage*, WW ; Mdf : *fortified enclosure*, B : *homestead, house*, KC 4·86' : *game-enclosure?* GBG. ['*haw*'] II. m. '*haw*,' WW 204²⁰ : *trifle*, WW 138³⁹ ; 269⁵.

hagal = hagol

hagaðorn = haguðorn ; **hage-** = hago-

+**hagian** (impers.) *to please, suit.* gif him (hine) tō ðǣm +hagige *if he can afford it.*

hago- v. also hæg-.

hagol (æ¹, e¹, a², e²) mn. *'hail,' Æ,Gen,Met, Ph,VPs : hail-shower, hailstorm,Bo : name of the rune for* h.

hagolfaru (hægl-) f. *hailstorm,* Wa 105.

hagolian (a²) *to 'hail,' AO* 104²⁰.

hagolscūr (æ¹, e²) m. *hail-shower, An;* Men 35. [v. *'hail'*]

hagolstān m. *'hailstone,' Æ.*

hagorūn (ea) f. *spell,* Nar 50¹⁴.

hagospind (ea) n. *cheek,* Gl,Lcd. [haga]

hagosteald I. (hæg-, heh-) *unmarried, independent : military* (of young men). **II.** m. *unmarried man attached to a court, bachelor, young man, young warrior, liege man.* [*Ger.* hagestolz] **III.** n. *celibacy,* Rd 21³¹. **IV.** (heh-) *virgin,* LL,NG.

hagostealdhād (hægst-) m. *unmarried state,* NG.

hagostealdlic (heh-) *virgin,* DR 66¹.

hagostealdman (hægst-) m. *bachelor, warrior,* Gl,Rd.

hagostealdnes (heh-) f. *virginity,* Jnp 13.

hagu-=hago-

haguðorn (æ¹) m. *'hawthorn,' whitethorn, Gl,Mt,Lcd.*

ha ha interj. *'ha! ha!' ÆGr.*

hal=heal; **hal-**=heal(h)-; **hāl-**=hǣl-

±**hāl** *'hale,' 'whole'* (*'y-hole'*), *entire, uninjured, healthy, well, sound, safe, genuine, straightforward, Lcd,Mt;* Æ,CP. wes ðu h., h. westu, h. bēo ðu *hail!*

hala I. m. *after-birth,* Lcd. [helan (IF 48·256)] **II.** (+) (o) m. *counsellor, confidant, supporter,* ÆL 23²⁹⁰,WW 110²¹.

hālbǣre *wholesome, salutary,* Sc 32⁷⁸.

halc (OET 489)=healh

hald-=heald-

hāleg=hāleg-=hālig, hālg-

±**hālettan** (ǣ) *to greet, hail, salute,* GD.

hālettend m. *middle finger (used in saluting),* WW.

hālettung f. *greeting, salutation,* Bl.

hālfæst *pious? healthy?* RB 72⁶.

hālga I. wk. form of adj. hālig. **II.** m. *saint, Æ,Ct.* [*'hallow'*]

hālgawaras=hāligwaras

±**hālgian** *to 'hallow,' sanctify, Æ,Jn : consecrate, dedicate, ordain, BH,Bl,Chr; Æ : reverence,* †Hy,Mt : *keep holy, Bl.*

+**hālgigend** m. *sanctifier,* DHy 64².

±**hālgung** (ǣ) f. *'hallowing,' consecration, BH : sanctuary,* EPs 73⁷.

hālgungbōc f. *benedictional,* NC 299.

hālgungram m. *consecrated ram,* Ex 29²².

hāli-=hālig-

hālig *'holy,' consecrated, sacred, Bf,Lk : venerated, Æ,G,VPs : godly, saintly, CP, MkL : ecclesiastical : pacific, tame,* Gen 201. as sb. *what is holy, MtL.*

±**hāligan I.** *to heal up, get well, CP : save : be saved.* **II.**=hālgian

hāligdæg m. *holy day, Sabbath, MkL,LL.* [*'holiday'*]

hāligdōm m. *holiness, righteousness, sanctity, Æ; CP : holy place, sanctuary, chapel, Æ : relics, holy things, LL : holy office, CP 51¹ : sacrament : holy doctrines, CP* 383⁷. [*'halidom'*]

hāligdōmhūs m. *'sacrarium,'* CM 818.

hāligern n. *holy place, sanctuary : sacrament.*

hāliglice *holily,* Chrd 117⁴.

Hāligmōnað m. (*holy month*), *September,* MH.

hālignes f. *'holiness,' sanctity, religion, Bl, Ps; Æ : holy place, sanctuary, CP,W : holy thing, relic : sacred rites,* BH 136²⁴.

hāligportic m. *sanctuary,* CJVPs.

hālig-rift, -ryft, -reft n. *veil, Æ.*

hāligwæcca m. *vigil-keeper,* LL (224').

hāligwæter n. *'holy water,' BH.*

hālig-waras, -ware mp. *saints, N.*

hāligweorc n. *sanctuary,* APs 73⁷.

halm=healm

hālnes f. *'wholeness,' ANS.*

hālor† n? *salvation,* Jul. [hǣl]

hālp=healp pret. 3 sg. of helpan.

hals-=heals-

hāls f. *salvation,* Cr 587?

hālsere (ǣ) m. *soothsayer, augur,* Cp.

halsgang (WW 190³²)=healsgund

±**hālsian** (ǣ, ēa) *to adjure, Mt : (+) take oath, swear, Nic : call upon, VPs : convoke : implore, entreat, CP,OET : augur, WW : exorcise, LL.* [v. *'halse'* and healsian]

hālsi(g)end m. *exorcist, soothsayer, augur, Æ.*

halstān=healstān

hālsung f. *exorcism, LL, OET : augury, divination : entreaty,Bl,VPs.* [v. *'halsing'*]

hālsunggebed n. *prayer in a church service,* RBL 39⁶.

hālsungtīma m. *time of supplication,* Chrd 30².

hālswurðung f. *thanksgiving for safety,* Ex 581. [hāls]

halt=healt; **halō**=heald II.

hālwenda m. *Saviour, Æ : safety* RBL 12¹³.

hālwende *healing, healthful, salutary, Æ, CP : sanctifying, Æ.*

hālwendlic *salutary, wholesome.* adv. -līce, Æ,CP.

hālwendnes f. *salubrity,* BH 28³⁰ : *salvation,* LPs.

hālwynde=hālwende
ham I. m? *under-garment* ('*subucula*,' OEG), *WW*. ['*hame*'] **II.**=hamm
hām I. m. ds. hām *village, hamlet, manor, estate, Æ,BH,Chr,LG* : '*home,*' *dwelling, house, BH,Ct,G,LL* : *region, country,* AO. **II.** adv. '*home,*' *homewards, Chr,Jn;* Æ. **III.** '*cauterium,*' A30·258; 33·390.
hama m. *covering, dress, garment* : *womb,* '*puerperium,*' v. OEG : *slough of a snake,* NC299.
hāma m. *cricket,* WW.
hamacgian=āmagian? (or +m.)
hāmcūð *familiar,* MtKp11[1].
hāmcyme m. *home-coming, return,* Æ. ['*homecome*']
hamel? *rugged,* KC.
hamela=hamola
hamele f. *rowlock* (only in phr. æt ǣlcre hamelan *for every oar,* i.e. *rower,* CHR 1039E). [ON. hamla; v. also hā]
hamelian *to hamstring, mutilate, Chr.* ['*hamble*']
hamer=hamor; **-hamer** v. clod-h.
±**hāmettan** *to domicile,* Ct,LL : *bring debtors back to their home,* CHRD116[1].
hāmfærelt n. *going home,* AO146[21].
hāmfæst *resident, settled in or owning a house,* Æ.
hāmfaru f. *attack of an enemy in his house, housebreaking* : *fine for housebreaking.* [v. LL2·504]
hāmhenn f. *domestic fowl,* LCD92a.
+**hāmian** *to establish in a home,* JnL p188[7].
hamland (o[1]) n. *enclosed pasture,* EC208[11]. [hamm]
hāmlēas *homeless,* RD40[9].
hamm I. m. *piece of pasture-land, enclosure, dwelling, Ct;* ÆL; Mdf. ['*ham*'] **II.** f. '*ham*' (*part of leg*), *Lcd,WW;* Æ.
+**hammen** *patched?* (of shoes), GD37[13].
-hamod v. +fiðer-h.
hamola (o[1]) *man with cropped hair.* tō hamolan besciran *to shave the hair off* (*as insult*), LL68,35[3].
hamor (o[1], e[2]) m. '*hammer,*' *Jul,WW.*
hamorian (amer-) *to beat out, forge,* GPH 396.
hamorsecg m. *hammer-sedge,* LCD.
hamorwyrt f. *black hellebore, wall-pellitory, Lcd*1·374; WW300[22]. ['*hammerwort*']
hāmscīr f. *aedileship,* GL.
-hāmscyld v. riht-h.
hāmsittende *living at home,* LL.
hāmslō m. *return home,* HL10[273].
hāmslōian *to return home,* WW118[18].
hāmsōcn f. *offence of attacking a man in his own house, LL* : *the franchise of holding pleas of this offence and receiving the penal-*

ties for it : *the penalty itself, Ct.* ['*hame-sucken*']
hāmsteall m. *homestead, Ct.* ['*homestall*']
hāmstede m. '*homestead,*' *Ct.*
hamule (CHR1039E)=hamele
hamur=hamor
hāmweard *homewards, towards home, on the way home, Chr;* Æ,AO. ['*homeward*']
hāmweardes adv. '*homewards,*' *Chr.*
hāmweorðung f. *ornament of a home,* B2998.
hāmwerd (Æ)=hāmweard
hāmwerod (eo[2], u[3]) n. *household,* BH191[22].
hāmwyrt f. *house-leek, Lcd.* ['*homewort*']
hān I. f. (*boundary-*)*stone, BC.* ['*hone*'] **II.?**=hā
hana m. *cock,* Æ. [*Ger.* hahn]
hanasang m. *cock-crow,* MH4[16].
hancrēd (ǣ) m. *cock-crow,* Æ. [crāwan]
hancrēdtīd (o[1]) f. *time of cock-crow,* WW 413[35].
hand I. (o) f. (gds. handa) '*hand*',' *Jn,VPs, WW;* Æ,AO,CP : *side* (*in defining position*), Æ : *power, control, possession, charge, Ps,RB* : *agency, Ps,VPs* : *person regarded as holder or receiver of something.* brād h. *palm.* on h. gān *to yield.* swiðre h. *right, left, hand.* on gehwæðere h. *on both sides.* on h. āgiefan, tō handa lǣtan *to hand over* (*to*). on handa sellan, *to give a pledge, promise, bargain.* tō handa healdan *hold* (*land*) *of another.* wel on h. *favourably.* **II.** adv. *exactly,* RBL.
handæx f. '*dextralis,*' *a kind of axe,* WW 221[22].
handbæftian (ea[2], a[3]) *to lament,* NG.
handbana† m. *slayer by hand,* B.
handbelle f. '*hand-bell,*' *Ct.*
handbōc f. '*handbook,*' *manual, Bf,LL,WW.*
handbona=handbana
handbred n. *palm of the hand, breadth of the hand, span,* WW158[11]; ÆL. ['*handbrede*']
handclāð n. *towel,* Æ. ['*handcloth*']
handcops m. *handcuff, manacle, CPs,WW.* [v. '*cops*']
handcræft m. *manual skill, power of the hand, handicraft,* Æ,LL. ['*handcraft*']
handcwyrn f. *hand-mill,* ANS,JUD16[21]. [cweorn]
handdǣda m. *doer with his own hand,* LL.
handele=handle
+**handfæstan** *to betroth,* RWH135[14].
handfæstnung (e[2]) f. *joining hands in confirmation of a pledge,* WW.
handfang-=infang-
handful nf. '*handful,*' *Ep,LPs.*
handgang m. *submission, surrender,* GL.
handgemaca m. *companion,* ÆL23[421].
handgemōt† n. *battle,* B

handgesceaft f. *handiwork*, GEN 455.
handgesella (o[1]) m. *companion*, B 1481.
handgestealla† m. *companion*, B.
handgeswing n. *blow, stroke*, EL 115.
handgeweald n. *power, possession*, PPs 105[30].
handgeweorc n. '*handiwork*,' *creation*, Æ, Ps.
handgewinn n. *manual labour, work*, BH, HL : (†) *struggle, contest*.
handgewrit n. *handwriting, autograph, holograph, agreement, deed*.
handgewriðen *hand-woven*, B 1937. [wrī-ðan]
handgift f. *wedding present*, †Hy 10[18].
handgong=handgang
handgripe m. '*hand-grip*,' B 965?
handgrið n. *security, peace, protection given by the king's hand*, LL (v. 2·494). ['*hand-grith*']
handhabbend *red-handed* (*thief*), LL 172,6. ['*handhabbend*']
handhæf n. *burden*, LkL 11[46].
handhamur m. '*hand-hammer*,' WW 448[2].
handhrægl n. *napkin, towel*, WW 127[1].
handhrine m. *touch*, AN 1022.
handhwīl f. *instant*, Æ. ['*handwhile*']
handle f. '*handle*,' Cp,WW.
handlēan† n. *requital, recompense*.
handleng(u) f. *a hand's length*, IM 124[74].
±**handlian** *to* '*handle*,' *feel*, Æ,Lcd : *deal with, discuss*, Bf 56,72.
handlin n. *hand-cloth, napkin* : *maniple*, WW 124[34].
handlinga adv. *by hand*, ÆL 11[247] : *hand to hand, at close quarters*, Æ. ['*handlings*']
handlocen† *joined together by hand*, B.
handlung f. '*handling*,' Æ.
handmægen† n. *bodily strength*.
handmitta=anmitta
handnægl m. *finger-nail*, LCD 125a.
handplega† m. *fight, battle*.
handprēost m. *domestic chaplain*, Æ.
handræs m. *onrush, attack*, B 2072.
handrōf *famed for strength*, EX 247.
handscalu=handscolu
handscolu† f. *retinue*, B.
handscyldig *condemned to lose a hand*, LL 471,13[1].
handseald *given personally* (*by the king*), LL 637,12.
handseax (e[2]) n. *dirk, dagger*, Æ,BH.
handselen '*mancipatio*,' WW 449[29].
handseten f. *signature, ratification*, Ct.
handsex=handseax; **handslyht**=andslyht
handsmæll m. *blow with the hand*, '*alapa*,' JnLR 19[3].
handspitel m. *hand-shovel, spade*, WW 241[45].
handsporu f. *claw, finger*, B 986.

handstoc n. *cuff, sleeve*, v. ES 38·352.
handswyle m. *swelling on the hand*, WW 205[10].
handtam *submissive to handling*, ÆL 8[86] [v. '*hand-tame*']
handðegn m. *retainer, servant*, BH.
handðwēal n. *washing of the hands*, WW 146[9].
handweorc n. *handiwork*, Rd,LL. ['*hand work*']
handworht *made with hands*, Mk 14[58].
handwundor n. *marvel of handiwork*, E 2768.
handwyrm (o) m. *a kind of insect*, Cp,WW. ['*handworm*']
handwyrst f. *wrist*, WW. ['*handwrist*']
-hanga v. līc-h.
+**hange** (o) *disposed, inclined to*, RIM 42.
hangelle f. *a hanging object*, '*mentula*'? RD 45[6].
hangen pp. of hōn.
hangian (±) (intr.) *to* '*hang**,' *be hanged*, Æ, B,El,G ; CP : *depend, rest on*, Æ : (tr.) *hang, suspend*, Æ,Chr,G,Lcd.
hangra m. '*hanger*,' *wooded slope*, KC ; Mdf.
hangrǣd? (ES 39·348)=hancrēd
hangwīte? n. *penalty for miscarriage of justice*, EC. [v. '*hangwite*']
hār I. '*hoar*,' *An* : *hoary, grey, old*, B,Ct, Jud,Met,Wa. II.=hǣr
hara m. '*hare*,' Ep ; Æ.
haranhige *hare's foot* (*plant*), LCD.
haransprecel *viper's bugloss*, LCD 57b,WW 299[6].
hāranwyrt=hārewyrt
harasteorra m. *dogstar*, WW 198[34].
harað, harad m. *wood* (only in place-names, FTP 76)
hard=heard ; **hārehūne**=hārhūne
hāre-wyrt, hāran- (LCD) f. *a plant*, '*colocasia*,' WW 135[5].
hārhūne f. *horehound*, LCD.
hārian *to become hoary or grey*, Æ,Shr. ['*hoar*']
hārnes f. *hoariness*, WW. ['*hoarness*']
hārung f. *hoariness, old age*, ÆGR 295[14].
hārwelle, hārwenge (Æ) *hoary, grey-haired*.
hārwengnes f. *hoariness, old age*, WW 198[31].
hās '*hoarse*,' ÆGR,WW.
hāsæta m. *oarsman, rower*, CHR 1052 E. [hā]
hasewa=haswa wk. form of hasu.
hāshrīman (ȳ[2]) *to sound harshly*, GUTH 128[127].
hāsian *to be or become* '*hoarse*,' ÆGR 190[10].
haslhnutu (WW)=hæselhnutu
hāsnes f. '*hoarseness*,' WW ; Æ.
hassuc m. *coarse grass*, KC. ['*hassock*']
hāsswēge *sounding hoarsely*, GPH 391.
hasu† (ea) *dusky, grey, ashen*.

hasufāg *grey, ashen,* RD 12¹.

hasupād *grey-coated,* †CHR 937.

haswigfeŏre *grey-feathered,* PH 153.

hāt I. *'hot,' flaming, Gu,Lcd;* Æ,AO,CP : *fervent, excited,* Bl : *intense, violent, An, Gu,Ph : inspiring? attractive?* SEAF 64. **II.** n. *heat, fire.* **III.** (±) n. *promise, vow,* LkL; CP.

+hata m. *enemy, opponent,* WW 393³⁰.

±hātan⁷ active pret. hē(h)t, hē(h)ton; passive pret. (origly. pres.) hātte *(CP,Mt) to command, direct, bid, order,* Æ,Ct : *summon,* Dan : *vow, promise,* Jul : (w. nom.=voc.) *name, call,* AO; CP : *be called, CP,Gen,Mt;* Æ. [*'hight'*]

hāte adv. *hotly, fervidly,* Æ. [*'hot'*]

hātheort (y²) **I.** n. *anger, rage.* **II.** (±) *wrathful, furious, passionate,* Æ,CP : *ardent, whole-hearted.* adv. -līce.

+hātheortan=hāthiertan

hātheorte f.=hātheort I.

hātheortnes f. *rage, mania,* Æ,CP : *zeal.*

±hāthiertan (eo, i, y) *to be or become angry,* CP : *enrage.*

hāthige m. *anger,* PPs 89⁷. [hyge]

hāthort (KGL)=hātheort

±hat-ian, -igan *to 'hate,' treat as an enemy,* CP; Æ.

hātian *to be or get 'hot,'* VPs.

hatigend m. *enemy,* ÆGR 205⁸.

hātigende *becoming hot,* LCD.

hatigendlic *hateful,* ÆL 3⁶⁰⁵.

+hātland n. *promised land,* BH 346⁸.

hātlīce *ardently,* Sc.

hātnes f. *heat,* ES 58·478.

hatol *hostile, bitter,* Æ,WW (KGl) : *odious.* [*'hatel'*; cp. hetol]

hātte v. hātan.

hattefagol sb. *hedgehog,* APs 103⁸ (cp. hæren-f.).

hatung f. *hatred,* LPs; Æ. [*'hating'*]

hātung f. *heating, inflammation,* LCD.

hātwende *hot, burning,* Ex 74.

+haŏerian=heaŏorian

haŏoliŏa m. *elbow,* LCD 99a (v. AB 29·253).

-hāwe v. earfoŏ-h.

hāwere m. *spectator,* CP 229¹⁷.

±hāwian *to gaze on, view, look at, observe, notice,* Æ,CP.

hāwung f. *observation,* AS.

hē m., hēo f., hit n. (pers. pron.) 'HE*,' *she, it;* pl. *they* : (reflex. pron.) *himself, herself, itself.*

hēa I. np. and nsm. (wk.) of hēah adj. **II.**=hēah adv. **III.**=hēa, hī, nap. of hē.

hēa-=hēah-; **headorr**=heaŏor

hēador, hēadēor=hēahdēor

hēaf m. *lamentation, wailing,* AO. [=hēof]

hēafd-=hēafod-

hēafdian *to behead,* ÆL,MH.

+hēafdod *having a head,* WW 152⁴⁵

hēafed=hēafod; **heafela**=hafela

hēaflan (Æ)=hēofian

hēaflic *sad, grievous,* BL 123⁶.

heafo (B 2478) nap. of hæf.

heafoc=hafoc

hēafod n. gs. hēafdes *'head,'* Æ,JnR,VPs : *top,* OET : *source, origin : chief, leader,* CP, Chr : *capital (city),* AO. hēafdes ŏolian *to forfeit life.*

hēafodæcer (afu) m. *'a strip of land an acre in extent, lying at the head of a field'* (BTs), KC,WW 147¹⁹.

hēafodædre f. *cephalic vein,* LCD 95b.

hēafodbæŏ n. *a wash for the head,* LCD 57b.

hēafodbald (=ea³) *impudent,* WW 401¹⁹.

hēafodbān n. *skull,* LCD.

hēafodbēag m. *crown,* Bo 112²³.

hēafodbend m. *diadem, crown : head-bond, fetter about the head,* Æ.

hēafodbeorg I. f. *helmet,* B 1030. **II.** m. *prominent hill?* KC.

hēafodbeorht *with a splendid, shining head,* RD 20².

hēafodbiscop m. *high-priest,* ÆH 2·420³¹.

hēafodbolla m. *skull,* NC 300.

hēafodbolster n. *pillow,* LCD,WW.

hēafodbotl n. *ancestral seat,* Ct.

hēafodburh f. *chief city,* Æ,AO.

hēafodclāŏ n. *head-cloth, head-dress,* WW; Æ. [*'headcloth'*]

hēafodcwide m. *important saying,* LL : *chapter,* DR.

hēafodcyrice f. *cathedral,* LL 282 n19.

hēafodece m. *'headache,'* Lcd 7b; Æ.

hēafodfrætennes (e³) f. *hairpin, ornament for the hair,* WW.

hēafod-gemæcca, -gemaca (CP) m. *mate, companion, fellow-servant.*

hēafodgerīm n. *number by heads, greatest number,* JUD 309.

hēafodgetel n. *cardinal number,* ÆGR 283⁸.

hēafodgewǣde n. *face-covering, veil,* Æ,W.

hēafodgilt m. *deadly sin,* W : *capital offence,* LL 380,2.

hēafodgimm† m. *head's gem, eye,* AN.

hēafodgold n. *crown,* PPs,W.

hēafodhǣr n. *hair of the head,* WW.

hēafodhebba m. *beginning, starter,* BF 62¹² : *prime mover,* ÆL 23⁶⁵.

hēafodhrægl (u²) n. *an article of clothing or bedding,* RBL 93³, Sc 74².

hēafodhrīefŏo f. *scurfiness of the head,* LCD 85b.

hēafodiht (e³) *with a head or tuft,* LCD 86a.

hēafodleahter m. *capital crime, deadly sin,* Æ.

hēafodlēas *'headless,'* WW; Æ.

hēafodlic *capital, deadly* (crime), *Bl* : *at the top*, WW : *principal*, AO. ['*headly*']

hēafodling (u²) m. *equal, fellow-servant, MtL.* ['*headling*']

hēafodloca m. *skull*, LCD.

hēafodlond n. *strip of land in a field, left for turning a plough, Ct; WW.* ['*headland*']

hēafod-mǣg†, -māga (AN) m. *near blood-relation.*

hēafodmǣgen n. *cardinal virtue, ÆL* 16³¹².

hēafodmann m. '*head-man,*' *captain, WW; Æ.*

hēafodmynster n. *church, cathedral,* LL.

hēafodpanne f. *skull, Mt.* ['*headpan*']

hēafodport m. *chief town,* CHR 1086.

hēafodrīce n. *empire,* AO 58³¹.

hēafodsār m. *pain in the head,* LCD.

hēafodsealf f. *head-salve,* LCD 130b.

hēafodsegn m? n? *banner,* B2152 (v. eofor-h.).

hēafodsīen (ȳ³)† f. (*eyesight*), *eye,* GEN, WY.

hēafodslǣge (u²) m. *head of a pillar, architrave?* (BTs), WW 376¹⁵.

hēafodsmæl '*capitium,*' *part of a woman's dress,* WW 276¹⁸, 369¹⁹.

hēafodstede m. *chief place,* AO : *high place, sacred place,* LL 470,3⁵.

hēafodstocc m. *stake on which the head of a beheaded criminal was fixed,* Æ, KC.

hēafodstōl m. *capital,* AO 124,144.

hēafodstōw f. *place for the head,* BH 324³.

hēafodswīma m. *dizziness,* GEN 1568.

hēafodsȳn = hēafodsīen

hēafodsynn (æ¹) f. *deadly sin,* W 290²⁵.

hēafodðwēal n. *washing of the head,* WW 146⁸.

hēafodwærc m. *pain in the head,* Lcd; WW. ['*headwark*']

hēafodweard I. f. *watch over the head, death-watch,* B2909 : *body-guard,* LL 444,1. ['*headward*'] **II.** m. *chief protector, leader.* **III.** f. *chapter.*

hēafodweg m. *head-road* (v. BTs), Ct.

hēafodwind m. *chief wind (E, S, W or N wind),* LCD 3·274.

hēafodwīsa m. *chief, director,* GEN 1619.

hēafodwōð f. *voice,* RD 9³.

hēafodwund f. *wound in the head,* LL 20, 44.

hēafodwylm m. *tears,* EL 1133 : *burning pain in the head,* LCD 9b.

hēafodwyrhta m. *chief workman,* ÆH 2·530.

heafola = hafela; **hēafre** = hēahfore

hēafsang m. *dirge,* WW 430²². [hēofan]

heafu (B1862) nap. of hæf.

heafuc (VPs) = hafoc; **hēafud** = hēafod

hēag = hēah; **heaga-** = hago-

hēage (Æ) = hēah adv.

heago- = hago-, hagu-; **hēagum** v. hēah.

hēah I. (ē) gsm. hēas, asm. hēan(n)e, gp. hēar(r)a, dp. hēagum, hēam, comp. hīerra (ē, ēah, īe, ȳ) ; sup. hīehst (ēa, ē, ȳ) 'HIGH,' *tall, lofty, Æ : high-class, exalted, sublime, illustrious, important, CP : proud, haughty : deep : right* (hand). **II.** adv. '*high,*' *aloft, ÆGr.*

hēahaltāre m. *high altar,* W.

hēahbeorg m. *mountain,* PPs 94⁴.

hēahbiscop m. *archbishop, pontiff,* LL : (*Jewish*) *high-priest,* HL 10⁴³⁰. [v. '*high*']

hēahbliss f. *exultation,* PPs 118¹¹¹.

hēahboda m. *archangel,* CR 295.

hēahburg f. *chief city :* (†) *town on a height.*

hēahcāsere m. *emperor,* †Hy 7⁶⁰.

hēahcleofa m. *principal chamber,* AA 6¹⁵

hēah-clif n. nap. -cleofu *high cliff,* CR, W.

hēahcræft m. *high skill,* RD 36⁴.

hēahcræftiga m. *architect,* BH.

hēahcyning† m. *high king, B : God.* [v. '*high*']

hēahdēor n. *stag, deer,* CHR.

hēahdēorhund (hēador-) m. *deer-hound,* LL, TC.

hēahdēorhunta m. *stag-hunter,* Ct.

hēahdīacon m. *archdeacon,* BL, MH.

hēah-eald* superl. -yldest (CM 36) *excellent, distinguished.*

hēah-ealdor, -ealdormann m. *ruler, patrician.*

hēahengel m. *archangel,* Bf; Æ. [v. '*high*']

hēahfæder m. *God : patriarch,* Bl; Æ, CP : (*church*) *father.* [v. '*high*']

hēahfæst *permanent, immutable,* WID 143.

hēahfæsten n. *fortified town, city,* DR, WW.

hēahflōd m. *deep water,* GEN : *high tide,* WW.

hēahfore f. '*heifer,*' *Æ, BH, WW.*

hēahfrēa† m. *high lord,* CR.

hēahfrēols m. *great festival,* LL 344,47.

hēahfrēolsdæg m. *great feast-day,* LL 252,25.

hēahfrēolstīd f. *great festival,* LL 252,22².

hēahfru (WW) = hēahfore

hēahfȳr n. *towering flame,* WH 22.

hēahgǣst m. *Holy Ghost,* CR 358.

hēahgealdor n. *charm,* PPs 57⁴.

hēahgerēfa m. *high sheriff, chief officer, pro-consul, prefect, Æ.*

hēahgesamnung f. *chief synagogue,* Mk 5²².

hēahgesceaft f. *noble creature,* GEN 4.

hēahgesceap n. *fate,* B 3084.

hēahgestrēon† n. *rich treasure.*

hēahgetimbrad *high-built,* SAT 29.

hēahgetimbru† npl. *lofty edifice.*

hēahgeðrīng n. *whelming flood,* RD 4²⁷.

hēahgeðungen = hēahðungen

hēahgeweorc† n. *excellent work.*

hēahgnornung f. *deep grief,* PPs 101¹⁸.

hēahgod m. *Most High, God,* PPs 56². ['*high God*']

hēahgræft *carved in bas-relief,* WW348⁹.
hēahhād m. *holy orders,* LL(334⁶).
hēahhæf? n. *deep sea,* HU25 (Sedgefield).
hēahhelm *loftily crested,* ZDA33·238.
hēahheolode (ēh-) f. *elecampane,* LCD28b.
hēahheort *proud,* DA540.
hēahhlīð† n. *high hill.*
hēahhlūtor *very pure,* BH348B¹⁹.
hēahhwiolod (ē¹) *having high wheels,* WW
140³².
hēahhylte n. *a high-placed shrubbery,* Ct.
hēahhyrde m. *head abbot,* OEG910.
hēahhyrne=ēaghyrne
hēahlǣce (ē²) m. *learned physician,* MH.
hēahland n. *mountainous country,* Ex385.
hēahlārēow m. *head teacher,* WW.
hēahlēce=hēahlǣce
hēahleornere n. *high teacher, master,* OEG
910.
hēahlic=hēalic
hēahlufe f. *great love,* B1954.
hēahmægen n. *great force : power, virtue,*
ÆL.
hēahmæsse f. *high mass,* CHR.
hēahmæssedæg m. *high mass day,* NC300.
hēahmiht f. *high authority, great might,*
PPs150²,VH15 : *the Almighty,* VH15.
hēahmōd† *high spirited, exultant : proud,
haughty.*
hēahmōdnes f. *pride,* CP301¹.
hēahmōr m. *high moor,* BHB364⁴.
hēahnama m. *most exalted name,* †Hy7¹⁸.
hēahnes (Æ)=hēanes; **hēahra** v. hēah.
hēahreced† n. *high building, temple.*
hēahrodor m. *high heaven,* GEN151,BYH
124²⁸.
hēahrūn f. *pythoness,* WW493³⁸.
hēahsācerd m. *high or chief priest,* G,HL.
hēahsǣ f. *high sea, the deep,* Met166³. [v.
'*sea*']
hēahsǣl† f. *great happiness,* PPs.
hēahsǣðēof? m. *chief pirate,* WW.
hēahsangere m. *chief singer,* BH314³.
hēahsceaða m. *chief pirate,* OEG8²²⁸.
hēahscēawere (ē¹) m. '*pontifex,*' DR21¹.
hēahscīreman (ē¹) m. '*procurator,*' DR193⁶.
hēahseld n.† *throne : rostrum,* WW.
hēahsele m. *high hall,* B647.
hēahsetl (ē) n. *exalted seat, throne, judgment-
seat,* Æ,JnL. [v. '*settle*']
hēahsittende *sitting on high,* A8·368.
hēahsomnung (MkL; ē¹)=hēahgesamnung
hēahstēap *very high,* GEN2839.
hēahstede m. *high place,* B285.
hēahstefn† *having a high prow.*
hēahstrǣt m. *highway,* Ct. ['*high street*']
hēahstrengðu f. *strength,* PPs107⁷.
hēahsunne (ē¹) adj. mp. *very sinful,* MkR2¹⁵.
hēahsynn f. *deadly sin, crime,* DR,LL.

hēahtīd f. *holy day,* LL. ['*high tide*']
hēahtimber m. *lofty building,* CRA45.
hēahtorr m. *high mountain,* OEG2035.
hēahtrēow f. *solemn compact,* Ex388.
hēahðearf f. *great need,* PPs117.
hēahðegen m. *chief officer, captain,* Æ :
apostle, Æ : *angel.*
hēahðegnung f. *important function,* Ex96.
hēahðēod (ē¹) f. *great people,* GUTH.
hēahðrēa m. *great affliction,* GEN2545.
hēah-ðrymm m., -ðrymnest† f. *great glory.*
hēahðuf†=hīehðu
hēahðungen *of high rank, illustrious,* AO.
hēahweg m. *highway,* EC130' (hēi-).
hēahwēofod n. *high altar,* WW186²¹.
hēahweorc=hēahgeweorc
hēahwita m. *high councillor,* CHR1009.
hēahyldest v. hēaheald.
heal=(1) healh; (2)=heall
hēal (BL)=hāl; **hēal-**=hēl-
hēala m. *hydrocele,* CP65⁵.
healærn n. *hall-building,* B78.
healc=healoc
heald I. n. *keeping, custody, guard, protection,* Chr1036,KC : *observance, observation, watch : protector, guardian.* ['*hold*';
=hield] II. *sloping, inclined, bent.*
±**healdan⁷** (a) (tr. and intr.) *to '*hold*''*
('*i-hald*'), *contain, hold fast, grasp, retain,
possess, inhabit,* Æ,Chr; CP: *curb, restrain,
compel, control, rule, reign,* Chr,CP: *keep,
guard, preserve, foster, cherish, defend,* Æ,
Bl,Mt,Ps; AO: *withhold, detain, lock up :
maintain, uphold, support,* Æ,LL : *regard,
observe, fulfil, do, practise,* Bl; Æ : *satisfy,
pay: take care,* CP: *celebrate, hold (festival) :
hold out* (intr.), *last : proceed, go : treat,
behave to, bear oneself : keep in mind.*
ongēan h. *resist.* tō handa h. *hold (land,
etc.) of another.*
+**healddagas** mp. *kalends,* WW176²⁷.
+**healde** *contented? careful?* v. MFH162.
+**healden** f. *observance,* BHB468⁶.
healdend m. *protector, guardian, ruler, king,
lord, God: economical person,* LCD3·192²³.
+**healdendgeorn** (a¹) *continent,* DR45¹⁰?
+**healdfæst** *safe,* LCD.
healdiend m. *preserver,* CEPs114⁶.
healding (a) f. *keeping, observance,* VPs118⁹.
±**healdnes** f. *keeping, observance,* BH :
guard, watch, APs38² : *office of a bishop,*
WW400⁹.
healdsum (hal-) *careful,* ANS129·25.
+**healdsum** *provident, economical, frugal,*
CP : *virtuous, chaste, continent,* ÆL : *safe.*
±**healdsumnes** f. *keeping, observance, devotion,* Æ : *custody, preservation : restraint,
abstinence : continence, chastity.*
hēalēce (GL)=hēahlǣce

hēalede I. *suffering from hydrocele, ruptured,* CP72⁴. **II.**=hēlede
healf (a) **I.** adj. *'half,'* *Bf,Ct,Jud,Lcd*; Æ, AO. ðridde h., etc.=*two and a half, etc.* [*Ger.* drittehalb] **II.** f. *half, Æ,G,Chr* : *side, Gl,Mt,Ct*; Æ,AO : *part,* CP.
healfbrocen *half-broken,* BH436⁶.
healfclǣmed *half-plastered,* HL17²⁶⁷.
healfclungen (a¹) *half-congealed,* Cp265s.
healfclypigende adj. *semi-vowel,* ÆGR.
healf-cwic, -cucu *half-dead,* AO,CP.
healfdēad *half-dead,* LCD.
healfeald (a¹) *half-grown,* LCD92a.
healffers *hemistich,* ZDA31·10.
healffēðe *lame,* GPH396.
healffrēo *half-free,* W171⁴E.
healfgemet *'diametra,'* ZDA31·10.
healfhār *somewhat hoary,* A8·449.
healfhēafod n. *front of the head,* ÆGR74⁵.
healfhrūh *half-rough,* WW152¹⁴.
healfhunding m. *cynocephalus,* AA33¹⁴, WE54¹¹.
healfhwīt *somewhat white,* WW163⁷.
healfhȳd *half a hide (of land),* LL460,7¹.
healfmann m. *'half-man,'* ÆGr27.
healfmarc *half a mark* (v. marc), Ct,LL.
healfnacod *half-naked,* AA15³.
healfpenigwurð n. *halfpenny-worth,* LL,W.
healfrēad *reddish,* WW149³⁵.
healfrūh *half-rough,* WW152²⁴.
healfscyldig *partially guilty,* ZDA31·23.
healfsester m. *half a 'sester' (measure of bulk),* WW444⁴. [*L.* sextarius]
healfsinewealt *semicircular,* WW179²⁸.
healfslǣpende *half-asleep,* LV3; MH138¹.
healfsoden *half-cooked,* LCD,LL.
healfter=hælfter
healftryndel n. *hemisphere,* WW140⁷.
healfunga *to a certain extent, partially, imperfectly,* Æ,CP. ['halfing']
healfweg m. *half-way,* KC.
healfwudu m. *field-balm,* LCD44b.
healgamen m. *social enjoyment,* B1066.
healgian=halgian
healh m. (? n. at LHy6³¹) (nap. halas) *corner, nook, secret place,* CP,Guth,WW : *small hollow in a hill-side or slope,* Ct, (GBG). ['hale']
healhālgung (æa¹) f. *'ceremonia,'* WW180¹⁵.
healhihte *having many angles,* OEG121.
hēalic (ē) *high, elevated, exalted, lofty, sublime,* Æ; CP : *deep, profound, intense,* Æ, CP : *lordly, noble, great, illustrious, distinguished, notable, excellent,* Æ; CP : *proud, haughty : egregious, heinous,* W. adv. -līce *highly, aloft,* Æ : *in or to high position or rank, loftily,* BH : *intensely, very,* Bl. ['highly']

hēalicnes f. *sublimity, majesty,* Æ.
heall **I.** f. *'hall,' dwelling, house,* B,Mt; Æ, CP : *palace, temple, law-court.* **II.**=healh. **III.** *rock,* OEG4111.
heallic *palatial,* WW499²⁹.
heallrēaf n. *wall-tapestry,* TC530'.
heallreced n. *hall-building,* B68 (heal-).
heallsittend† m. *sitter-in-hall,* B (heal-).
heallðegn† m. *hall-officer,* B (heal-).
heallwāhrift n. *wall-tapestry,* TC530'.
heallwudu m. *woodwork of hall,* B (heal-).
healm **I.** (a, æ) m. *'haulm,' stalk, straw, stubble,* Lcd,MtL,VPs : *'culmen,' thatched roof? harvest-land?* (v. LL116,61; 3·79 and BTs). **II.**=helm
healmstrēaw n. *stubble,* SPs82¹⁴.
healoc, healc m. *cavity, sinuosity,* LCD.
healp pret. 3 sg. of helpan.
heals (a) m. *neck,* Gen : *prow of a ship.* ['halse']
hēals-=hāls-
healsbēag† m. *collar, necklace,* B.
healsbeorg f. *neck-armour,* OEG.
healsbōc f. *phylactery,* G. [hāls]
healsbrynige *corslet,* v. OEG2⁴¹⁸.
healsed (a¹; o²) mn. *head-cloth,* NG : *neck of a tunic,* WW514¹.
healseta m. *the neck of a tunic,* MH200¹.
healsfæst, *arrogant,* GEN2238.
healsfang n. *fine prescribed in substitution for capital and other punishments, preferential share of the 'wergeld,'* LL (v. 2·489 and BTs). ['halsfang']
healsgang m. *neck-tumour,* WW190³².
healsgebedda f. *beloved bedfellow, wife,* B63.
healsgund (a¹) m. *neck-tumour,* LCD,WW.
healsian *to entreat earnestly, beseech, implore,* CP; AO. [v. also hālsian]
healsi(g)endlic (ā) *that may be intreated,* APs89¹³ : *imploring,* GD17²³. adv. -līce *importunately.*
healsleðer n. *reins,* OET522.
healsmǣgeð f. *beloved·maid,* GEN2155.
healsmyne m. *necklace,* Æ : *neck-ornament.* [mene]
healsōme f. *neck-tumour,* LCD132b.
healsrefeðer (a¹) f. *feathers of a pillow, down,* RD41⁸⁰. [cp.*OHG.* halsare *'cervical'*]
heals-scod, -ed=healsed
healstān (a, e) m. *small cake,* WW.
healswærc m. *pain in the neck,* LCD113a.
healswriða m. *necklace,* RD5⁴.
healswyrt (a) f. *a plant, daffodil?* Lcd,WW; OEG. ['halswort']
healt (eo) *'halt,' limping, lame,* AO.
healt-=heald-
healtian (a) *to 'halt,' limp,* CP,VPs; Æ : *hesitate,* ÆL18⁹⁸ : *fall away,* BH.

healðegn† m. *hall-officer*, B.

healwudu m. *woodwork of hall*, B 1317.

hēam v. hēah.

hēam-ol, -ul *miserly*, Cp.

hēamolscipe m. *miserliness*, NC 300.

hēan I. *lowly, despised, poor, mean, bare, abject*, B, VPs; Æ,AO. ['hean'] adv. hēane. **II.** v. hēah. **III.** (±) *to raise, exalt, extol*, BH. [=*hīen, hȳn; 'high']

hēanes f. 'highness,' Bf (hēah-),CP : *something high, high place, height*, Mt(hēah-), VPs. on hēanissum *in the highest*, 'in excelsis,' Æ : *excellence, sublimity*, CP : *high rank : deep place*, LkL 5⁴.

hēanhād m. *difficulty*, WW 345²⁹, 488⁴.

hēanlic *abject, poor*, AO. adv. -līce.

hēanmōd† *downcast, depressed, sad*.

hēannes I. (ē) f. *treading down*, NG. **II.**= hēanes

hēanspēdig *poor*, CRA 26.

hēap mf. (*of things*) 'heap,' Cp,CP : *host, crowd, assembly, company, troop, band*, B, Bl; Æ,CP. on hēape *together*.

±hēapian *to 'heap' up, collect, bring together, accumulate*, Lk.

hēapmǣlum adv. *by companies, in troops, flocks*, Æ,CP; AO. ['heapmeal']

hēapum adv. *in heaps, in troops*.

hēapung f. *heap*, BH. ['heaping']

hear- (N)=heor-

hēara=hēahra (v. hēah).

heard I. (a) 'hard,' *harsh, severe, stern, cruel* (*things and persons*), B,Bl,Cr,Mt,Lcd : *strong, intense, vigorous, violent*, B,Bl : *hardy, bold*, B; AO : *resistant*, Bf 158². **II.** n. *hard object*.

heardcwide m. *harsh speech, abuse* (or ? hearmcwide), CR 1444.

hearde adv. 'hard,' *hardly, firmly, very severely, strictly, vehemently*, Æ : *exceedingly, greatly*, Æ : *painfully, grievously*.

heardecg I.† *sharp of edge*. **II.** f. *sword*, EL 758.

heard(ha)ra m. *a fish, mullet?* GL.

heardhēaw *chisel*, Cp 408 c.

heardheort *hard-hearted*, Æ : *stubborn*, Æ.

heardheortnes f. *hard-heartedness*, Æ,CP.

heardhicgende† *brave*, B.

±heardian *to be or become hard*, Lcd : *harden*, Lcd. ['hard']

hearding† m. *bold man, hero*.

heardlic *stern, severe, harsh, terrible : bold, warlike : excessive*. adv. -līce *harshly, resolutely, severely, sternly : stoutly, bravely*, Æ : *excessively : hardly* ('paulatim,' 'tractim'), ES 42·174.

heardlicnes f. *austerity*, GUTH 70¹⁵.

heardmōd *brave, bold, over-confident*, Æ : *obstinate*, ÆL 36³²⁶.

heardmōdnes f. *obstinacy*, ÆH 1·252¹⁸.

heardnebba m. *raven*, ÆH 2·144¹⁵.

heardnes f. 'hardness,' Ep,Mt,Lcd,RB.

heardra (OEG)=heardhara

heardrǣd *firm, constant*, GEN 2348.

heardsǣlig *unfortunate, unhappy*, Bo.

heardsǣlnes f. *calamity*, AO 104¹⁷.

heardsǣlð f. *hard lot, calamity, unhappiness*, AO : *misconduct, wickedness*, CP.

heardung f. *hardening*, LCD.

heardwendlice *strictly*, BH 365¹⁵.

hearg, hearga (æ, e) m. *temple, altar, sanctuary, idol*, AO,CP : *grove*, Az 110.

heargeard (herh-) m. *dwelling in the woods*, WIF 15.

hearglic (h) *idolatrous*, WW 236².

heargtræf (æ¹) n. *idol-temple*, B 175.

heargweard m. *temple-warden, priest* (herig-), AN 1126.

hearh=hearg

hearm (e) **I.** m. *damage, 'harm,' injury, evil, affliction*, B,Chr,Gen; Æ,CP : *grief, pain*, Gen : *insult, calumny*. **II.** adj. *harmful, malignant, evil*.

hēarm=hrēam

hearma m. *mouse? weasel?* OET ('mygale,' Ep,Erf; 'netila,' Cp). [OHG. harmo]

hearmascinnen *made of ermine*, CHR 1075 D.

hearmberg (æ) m. *mound of calamity*, FM 373, RUNE CASKET.

hearmcwalu f. *great suffering*, CR 1609.

hearmcweodolian (VPs)=hearmcwidolian

hearmcweðan⁵ *to speak evil of, revile*, NG.

hearmcweðend (e¹) m. *slanderer*, JPs 71⁴.

hearmcwiddian (y²) *to calumniate*, Bo,LPs 118²².

hearmcwide† m. *calumny, blasphemy : heavy sentence, curse*.

hearmcwidol *evil-speaking, slanderous*, Æ.

hearmcwidolian (eo², e³) *to speak evil, slander*, ARSPs 118¹²².

hearmcwidolnes f. *slander*, EPs 118¹³⁴.

hearmdæg m. *day of grief*, B 3153.

hearmedwīt n. *grievous reproach*, PPs 68²¹.

hearmful *hurtful, noxious*, OEG 46¹³.

-hearmgeorn v. un-h.

hearmheortnes f. *complaint*, WW 511¹⁶.

hearmian *to 'harm,' injure*, Æ,Rood.

hearmlēoð† n. *elegy, lamentation*.

hearmlic *harmful, grievous*, Æ.

hearmloca† m. *prison : hell*.

hearmplega m. *fight, strife*, GEN 1898.

hearmscaða m. *terrible enemy*, B 766.

hearmscearu† f. *affliction, punishment, penalty*, GEN. [scearan]

hearmslege m. *grievous blow*, CR 1435.

hearmsprǣc f. *calumny*, WW 198³.

hearmstæf† m. *harm, sorrow, tribulation*.

hearmtān m. *shoot of sorrow*, GEN 992.

hearpe (æ) f. '*harp*,' Æ,*VPs*; CP.
hearpenægel m. *plectrum*, ApT 17⁷.
hearpere (a) m. '*harper*,' *Bo,Ln*; Æ,CP.
hearpestre f. (*female*) *harper*, WW 190⁶.
hearpestreng m. '*harp-string*,' *ApT* 17⁸.
hearplan *to* '*harp*,' *Bo*; Æ.
hearpnægel (WW)=hearpenægel
hearpsang m. *psalm*, WW 129⁴⁰.
hearpslege m. *plectrum* (*instrument for striking the harp*), OEG : *harp-playing*.
hearpswēg m. *sound of the harp*, BLPs 150³.
hearpung f. '*harping*,' *Bo*.
hearra I.† (æ, e, ie, eo) m. *lord, master, Chr, Gen.* ['*her*'] **II.**=heorr
hēarra=hēahra (v. hēah).
hearstepanne=hierstepanne
hēarsum=hiersum
heart (NG)=heord, heorot
-hearwa v. Sigel-h.; **hēas** v. hēah.
heascan=hyscan; **heasu**=hasu
heaðo-=heaðu- (=*war*)
heaðor n. *restraint, confinement*, RD.
±heaðorian (e²) *to shut in, restrain, control.*
hēaðrym=hēahðrymm
heaðubyrne† f. *war-corslet.*
heaðudēor† *bold, brave*, B.
heaðufremmende *fighting*, EL 130.
heaðufȳr† n. *cruel fire*, B.
heaðugeong *young in war*, Fin 2.
heaðuglemm m. *wound got in battle*, RD 57³.
heaðugrim† *fierce.*
heaðulāc† n. *battle-play, battle*, B.
heaðulind f. *linden-wood shield*, †Chr 937.
hēaðullðende† m. *seafaring warrior*, B.
heaðumǣre *famed in battle*, B 2802.
heaðurǣs† m. *onrush, attack*, B.
heaðurēaf n. *war-gear*, B 401.
heaðurinc† m. *warrior.*
heaðurōf† *famed in war, brave.*
heaðusceard? *dinted in war*, B 2830? (or ? heaðuscearp *battle-sharp*).
heaðusōoc *wounded*, B 2754.
heaðusigel m. *sun*, RD 72¹⁶.
heaðustēap† *towering in battle*, B.
heaðuswāt† m. *blood of battle*, B.
heaðusweng m. *battle-stroke*, B 2581.
heaðutorht *clear as a battle-cry*, B 2553.
heaðuwǣd f. *armour*, B 39.
heaðuweorc n. *battle-deed*, B 2892.
heaðuwērig *weary from fighting*, Wald 2¹⁷.
heaðuwylm† (æ², e³) m. *fierce flame.*
hēaum=hēagum dp. of hēah.
+hēaw n. *gnashing, grinding*, HL,Sat.
hēaw-=hēaw- (hēawi, Cp 303 c=hǣwen).
±hēawan⁷ *to* '*hew*,' *hack, strike, cleave, cut, cut down, kill : make by hewing*, LL. æftan h. *to slander*, W 160⁴.
heawen (K)=heofon

-hēawere v. hrīðer-, wudu-h.
-hebba v. hēafod-h.
±hebban⁶ (æ) pres. 3 sg. hōf, pl. hōfon, pp. hafen (hæfen) (wk. forms in LWS, pret. hefde, pp. hefod) *to* '*heave**,' *raise, lift, lift up, exalt*, Æ,B,Bl,Ps; CP : intr. *rise*, W 100³.
hebbe=hæbbe (v. habban).
-hebbe, **-hebbing** v. ūp-h.
hebbendlic *exalted*, DR 181¹⁴.
hebeld=hefeld; **heben**=heofon
heber=hæfer; **hebuc**=hafoc
hecc=hæc; **heced**=hacod
hēcen (y²) n. *kid*, Bf 134¹⁷,ES 35·332.
hecg, hecge f. *enclosure, hedge.*
hecga-spind, -swind=hagospind
±hēdan I. (w. g.) *to* '*heed*,' *observe*, B,LL; Æ : *care for, guard, protect, take charge of*, LL : *obtain, receive, take*, Æ. **II.**=hȳdan
hōddern (ȳ) n. *storehouse, storeroom*, BH,Gl.
hēde pret. 3 sg. of hēgan.
hedeclāð m. *a coarse, thick, upper garment like a chasuble*, Lod 1·346¹⁷.
heden m. *robe, hood, chasuble*, LL.
hedendlic *captious*, OEG 3208. adv. -līce, WW 199¹.
hef-=heof-
hefaldian=hefeldian
hefde I. (VPs)=hæfde pret. 3 sg. of habban.
II. v. hebban.
hefe I. (æ) m. *weight, burden*, Æ : '*mina, talentum*,' GPH 396. **II.**=hæfe
+hefed *weighed down*, WW 251¹⁶.
hefeful *severe*, RB 49¹⁸.
hefeg=hefig
hefeld n. *thread* (*for weaving*), Gl. [v. '*heald*']
±hefeldian (a²) *to fix the weft, begin the web*, Gl.
hefeldōrǣd m. *thread* (*for weaving*), Gl,Lcd. [v. '*heald*']
hefelgyrd (e³) f. *weaver's shuttle*, Gl.
hefe-lic, -līce=hefig-lic, -lice
hefen I. (æ) f. *burden*, RB 49¹⁸. **II.**=heofon
hefetīme=hefigtīme
hefeð pres. 3 sg. of hebban.
hefgian=hefigian
hefig (æ) '*heavy*,' *Met,Mt* : *important, grave, severe, serious, Bf,Bl,Mt,Chr* : *oppressive, grievous, Ps,LL* : *slow, dull.* [hebban] adv. hefige, *Ps.*
±hefigian *to make`heavy, VPs* : *weigh down, oppress, afflict, grieve, BH,CP,Mt* : *aggravate, increase* : *become heavy, depressed, weakened, CP,Gu.* ['*heavy*']
hefiglic *heavy, weighty, serious, severe, burdensome, grievous, sad*, Æ. adv. -līce, *violently, intensely, CP,Lk* : *sorrowfully, Gen* : *sluggishly, Mt.* ['*heavily*']

hefigmód *oppressive*, ERPs54⁴ : *heavy-hearted*, NC300.
hefignes (æ) f. *'heaviness,' weight, burden, affliction*, MtL; CP : *dulness, torpor*, Bo.
hefigtýme (i³) *heavy, grievous, severe, troublesome, oppressive*, Æ. [tēam]
hefigtýmnes f. *trouble*, Æ.
hefod wk. pp., hefð pres. 3 sg. of hebban.
hefon=heofon; **heft-**=hæft-
hefug=hefigu pl. of hefig, CP285¹.
heg-=hege-; **hēg**=hīeg
±**hēgan**† *to perform, achieve* : *hold (a meeting)*, An : *exalt, worship*, Da207⁷.
hegdig=hygdig
hege (ea) m. *'hedge,' fence*, Æ,Ct,Gl. ['hay']
hegeclife f. *hedge-clivers*, Lcd20a.
hegegian=hegian
hegehymele f. *hop-plant*, WW302⁵.
hegel (VPs)=hægl, hagol
hegerǣw (e³) f. *'hedgerow,'* KC.
hegerife f. *cleavers, goose grass*, Lcd. ['hairif']
hegesāhl m. *hedge-stake*, GD24²⁸. [sagol]
hegessugge *hedge-sparrow*, WW131³⁴. [sucga; 'haysugge']
hege-steall m. -stōw f. *place with a hedge*, KC.
hegewege m. *road between hedges*, KC.
hegge f. (BC,Chr)=hege
±**hegian** *to fence in, hedge, enclose*, Sc. grep h. *to cut a grip*, LL455,13. ['hay']
hēgnes=hēanes
hegstæf m. *bar to stop an opening in a fence* (BTs),WW205³¹.
hegstald-=hægstealdhēh
hēh (VPs, N), hēh-=hēah, hēah-
+**hēhan** (VHy)=hēan III.
hē hē indicates laughter, ÆGr. ['he']
hēhst pres. 2 sg. of hōn.
hehstald=hagosteald
hēht pret. 3 sg. of hātan.
hēhðu=hīehðu; +**heige** (KGL83⁴⁰)=+hæg
hēlsta=hēhsta (v. hēah).
hēlweg=hēahweg
hel=hell, helle-
hēla (ǣ) m. *'heel,'* Gl,JnL,Lcd,OET,WW.
hēla-=hāle-
hēlade (ēa¹) *having large heels*, WW.
±**helan⁴** *to conceal, cover, hide*, AO,VPs, Æ (pp.); CP. ['hele']
hēlan I. (oe) *to calumniate*, MtR5⁴⁴. II.= hǣlan I.
held=hield
helde I. f. *tansy*, Lcd,WW; Æ. ['helde'] II.=hyldo
hele f. *subterfuge*, LL(320¹⁷). or ?=hāl (BTs). ['hele']
hele-=helle-, ele-
hēlend=hǣlend

helerung=heolorung; **heleð**=hæleð
helf-=healf-, hielf-
helfan *to halve*, Cp303B? (herbid).
helgod=hellgod; **helhrūne**=hellerūne
±**hellan** *to conceal, cover, hide*, Æ,LL. ['hele']
hēlic, hēlīce=hēahlic, hēalīce
hell (y) f. *Hades*, Æ,VPs : *'hell,' place of torment, Gehenna*, Bo,RB; Æ,AO,CP. [helan]
hell- v. also helle-.
hellbend mf. *bond of hell*, B3072.
hellcniht m. *devil, demon*, ÆL3³⁷².
hellcræft m. *hellish power*, An1104.
hellcund *of hell*, W254¹⁵.
hellcwalu f. *pains of hell*, Cb1190.
helldor† n. *gate of hell*, Gu. [v. 'hell']
helle m. *hell*, WW.
hellebealu n. *hell-bale*, Cr1427.
hellebrōga m. *terror of hell*, LPs,VH.
hellebryne m. *hell-fire*, Jud,W.
hellecǣgan pl. *keys of hell*, MFH128.
helleceafl m. *jaws of hell*, An1702.
hellecinn n. *hellish race*, Cr1620.
helleclamm m. *hell-bond*, Gen373.
helledēofol† mn. *devil*.
helle-dor n. -duru f. *gate of hell*.
helleflōr m. *floor of hell, courts of hell*, Sat70.
hellefýr n. *hell-fire*, GD.
hellegāst† (ǣ³) m. *spirit of hell*, B.
hellegeat n. *gate of hell*, ÆH1·288, MP 1·610.
hellegrund† m. *abyss of hell*, VH.
hellegrut m. *pit of hell*, OEG689.
hellegryre m. *horror of hell*, Sat433.
hellehæft(a), -hæftling† m. *prisoner of hell, devil*.
hellehēaf m. *wailings or howlings of hell*, Gen38.
hellehinca m. *hell-limper, devil*, An1173. [cp. Ger. hinken]
hellehund m. *hell-hound*, KC3·350¹⁸.
hellehūs n. *hell-house*, Gu649.
hellelic=hellic
helleloc n. *hell-prison*, GD325³⁰.
hellemægen n. *troop of hell*, MFH166,VH.
hellemere m. *Stygian lake*, WW.
hellenið m. *torments of hell*, Gen775.
hellerūne f. *pythoness, sorceress*, Æ : *demon*, B163.
hellescealc m. *devil*, Sat133.
hellesceaða=hellsceaða
hellesēað m. *pit of hell*.
hellestōw f. *infernal region*, GD332⁹.
hellesūsl n. *hell-torment*, Æ.
helletintreg *hell-torment*, MFH128¹⁹,VH.
helletintrega m. *hell-torment*, VH16.
helleðegn (hel-)† m. *devil*.
hellewīte n. *hell-pains, torment*, Æ,CP.

hellewïtebrōga m. *horror of hell-torment,* W 151²⁴.
hellfiren f. *hellish crime,* PART 6.
hellfūs† *bound for hell.*
hellgeðowing n. *confinement in hell,* GEN 696.
hellgod n. *god of the lower world,* Bo,WW.
hellheort *terrified,* NC 301.
hellheoðo f. *vault of hell, hell,* SAT 700 (or ? two words).
hellic *of hell, hellish, Æ.* [' *hellick* ']
hellsceaða m. *hell-foe, devil : grave.*
hell-træf, nap. -trafu n. *devil's temple,* AN 1693.
helltrega m. *hell-torture,* GEN 73.
hell-waran, -ware mp., -waru fp. *dwellers in hell, Æ.* [v. ' *hell* ']
hellwendlic (helw-) *infernal,* WW 437³¹.
hellwerod n. *host of hell,* W 25²¹.
hellwiht (hel-) fn. *devil,* W 186².
helm I. m. *protection, defence, covering, crown, Æ,Rd : summit, top (of trees), Æ, Bo,WW;* CP : *helmet, Cp,WW* : (†) *protector, lord.* ['*helm*'] II. (WW 279¹⁴)=elm
helma m. '*helm,' rudder, Bo,Cp,WW;* Æ.
helm-bǣre, -berende *leafy, WW.* [v. '*helm*']
helmberend m.† *helmeted warrior,* B.
±**helmian** (y) *to cover, crown, An* : *provide with a helmet, ÆGr.* ['*helm*'; '*i-helmed*']
-**helmig** v. lēaf-h.
helmiht *leafy,* WW 395⁵; 493²⁸.
helmweard (holm-) m. *pilot,* AN 359.
hēlo=hǣlu; **helor**=heolor
help (y) fm. '*help,' succour, aid, AO,B,Bl.*
±**helpan³** (w. g. or d.) *to* '*help*,' support, succour, Æ,CP,Ct,G,LL,Ps* : *benefit, do good to, Lcd*(intr.)*,LL* : *cure, amend, Mk.*
helpe f.=help
helpend m. *helper, Bl.* ['*helpend*']
helpendlic adj. *to be liberated,* GPH 402.
helpendrāp m. *helping-rope,* WW 463³⁵.
helrūn=hellerune
helrūna m. *hellish monster,* B 163.
helrӯnegu f. *sorceress, witch,* WW 472¹¹.
hōlspure f. *heel,* VPs.
helt I.=hilt. II. pres. 3 sg. of heldan. III. (KGL)=hielt pres. 3 sg. of healdan.
helto=hielto-
helðegn=helleðegn; **helur**=heolor
helustr (Ep,Erf)=heolstor
hem m. '*hem,' border,* WW 125¹³.
+**hēme?** *customary,* AS 33¹³n.
hemed (BC 2·522') v. hemman.
hēmed, hēmeð=hǣmed
hemeðe n. *under-garment,* OEG 3725. [*Ger.* hemd]
hemlic (Æ)=hymlic
hemman? *to stop up, close* (GK),PPs 106⁴². [*MHG.* hemmen]

hemming (i) m. *shoe of undressed leather,* WW 468³¹. [' *hemming* ']
hen=henn; **hēn**=hēan; **hēn-**=hīen-
hēnan=hīenan
+**hendan** *to hold,* PPs 138⁸ : *seize, catch,* LPs 58¹³. [hand]
+**hende** *near, at hand, Æ,Mk* : *convenient, AO.* adv. *near, at home, Æ* : *closely, in detail,* BF 72²³. ['*hend*']
-**hendig** v. list-h.
+**hendnes** f. *neighbourhood, proximity, Æ.*
henep=hænep
heng pret. 3 sg. of hōn.
hengeclif n. *overhanging cliff,* WW 180⁴.
hengen f. *hanging, Æ* : *cross, Æ* : *rack, torture, Æ* : *imprisonment.*
hengenwītnung f. *imprisonment,* LL 471,16.
hengest, hengst m. *stallion, steed, horse, gelding, Ct,WW;* Æ. ['*hengest*']
hengetrēow (enge-) n. *gallows,* GPH 395.
hengwīte n. *fine for not detaining an offender,* LL 496,4.
henn (æ) f. '*hen,' Bf,Mt,Lcd.*
henna m. *fowl,* LL (220¹³).
henneǣg n. *hen's egg,* LCD.
hennebelle (æ) f. *henbane, Lcd,WW.* ['*henbell*']
hennebroð n. *chicken broth,* LCD.
hennfugol m. *hen,* Ct.
hēnnis (LG)=hīennes
hentan *to pursue, attack, LL; Æ* : (±) *appropriate, seize, Chr.* ['*hent*,' '*i-hente*']
hēnð=hīenð; **henu**=heonu
hēo I. nasf. and nap. of pron. 3 pers. '*she,' they.* II.†=hīw
hēodæg adv. *to-day,* GEN 661. [*Ger.* heute]
hēof I. m. *wailing, mourning, grief, Æ,AO.* II. str. pret. 3 sg. of hēofan.
hēofan⁷⁹ (pret. hēof, hōf, hēofon) *to lament,* CP.
heofan, heofen=heofon
hēofendlic *dismal, mournful, WW.* adv. -līce.
hēof-ian, -igian *to lament, Æ.*
heofig-=hefig-
hēofigendlic *lamenting,* A 10·146; 188.
hēofod=hēafod; **heofog** (BL)=hefig
heofon (e¹, a², e², u²) mf. '*sky, firmament, Æ,Bo,Chr,Met,VPs* : '*heaven,' Æ,G* : *the power of heaven, Mt,Lk.*
hēofon I. f. *lamentation?* Ex 46. II. str. pret. pl. of hēofan.
heofonbēacen n. *sign in the sky,* Ex 107.
heofonbeorht† *heavenly bright.*
heofonbig(g)ende *chaste,* DHy. [ON. byggja]
heofonbȳme f. *heavenly trumpet,* CR 949.
heofoncandel† f. *sun, moon, stars.*
heofoncenned *heaven-born,* DHy 108⁴.

heofoncolu npl. *heat of the sun*, Ex 71.
heofoncund *celestial, heavenly*, CP.
heofoncundlic *heavenly*, W.
heofoncyning m. *king of heaven, Christ, Bl* 201. [' *heavenking* ']
heofondēma m. *heavenly ruler*, SAT 658.
hēofondlīce = hēofendlīce
heofondrēam† m. *joy of heaven*.
heofonduguð f. *heavenly host*, CR 1655.
heofone (Æ,W) = heofon
heofonengel m.† *angel of heaven*, CR.
heofonflēogende *flying*, JPs 103¹².
heofonflōd m. *torrent (of rain)*, BH 236¹⁷.
heofonfugol† m. *fowl of the air*, GEN.
heofonfȳr n. *fire from heaven, lightning*, W 262¹⁵.
heofonhæbbend m. *possessor of heaven*, WW 385²¹.
heofonhālig *holy and heavenly*, AN 728.
heofonhām† m. *heavenly home*, PPs.
heofonhēah *reaching to heaven*, Da 553. ['*heavenhigh*']
heofonheall f. *heavenly hall*, LL (382¹⁰). [v. '*heaven*']
heofonhlāf m. *bread of heaven, manna*, PPs 104³⁵.
heofonhrōf m. †*vault of heaven, heaven*, Ph: *roof, ceiling*. WW 432⁸? [v. '*heaven*']
heofonhwealf† f. *vault of heaven*, AN.
heofonhyrst f. *ornament of the heavens*, GEN 2189.
heofonisc (e²) *heavenly*, AO 1⁶.
heofonlēoht n. *heavenly light*, AN 976.
heofonlēoma m. *heavenly light*, AN 840.
heofonlic '*heavenly*,' *celestial*, Bl,Lk; CP : *chaste*, ÆGR 66³,WW 203²¹. adv. -līce, ÆGR 239⁷,WW 375²².
heofonmægen† n. *heavenly force*.
heofonrīce n. *kingdom of heaven*, Bl,Cr; AO. ['*heavenric*']
heofonsetl n. *throne of heaven*, DD 277.
heofonsteorra† m. *star of heaven*.
heofonstōl m. *throne of heaven*, GEN 8.
heofontimber n. *heavenly structure*, GEN 146.
heofontorht† *very bright, glorious*.
heofontungol† n. *heavenly luminary*, VH 16.
heofonðrēat m. *heavenly company*, SAT 222.
heofonðrymm m. *heavenly glory*, AN.
heofon-ware, -waran mp., -waru fp. *inhabitants of heaven*, Æ. ['*heavenware*']
heofonwealdend (e²) *the God (ruler) of heaven*, OEG 23¹⁰.
heofonweard† m. *heaven's keeper, God*, GEN.
heofonwerod n. *heavenly host*, W.
heofonwlitig *divinely fair*, NC 301.
heofonwolcen† n. *cloud of heaven*, VH 16.
heofonwōma† m. *terrible noise from heaven*.

heofonwuldor n. *heavenly glory*, †Hy 6¹².
hēofsīð m. *lamentable state*, RIM 43? [hēof]
heofun = heofon
hēofung f. *lamentation, mourning*, Æ.
hēofungdæg m. *day of mourning*, Æ.
hēofungtīd f. *time of mourning*, Æ.
heolan = helan
heolca m. *hoar-frost*, LPs 118⁸³.
heold pret. 3 sg. of healdan.
heoldan = healdan
heolfor† n. *gore, blood*, AN,B.
heolfrig† *gory, bloody*, JUD.
heolor (e¹, e², u²) f. *scales, balance*, GL.
heolorbledu (e¹, u²) f. *scale of a balance*, WW 427³⁵.
heolorian *to weigh, ponder*, GL.
heolorung (e¹, e²) f. '*momentum*,' *the turning of a scale*, WW 450¹².
heoloðcynn n. *denizens of hell*, CR 1542.
-heoloðe v. hēah-h, hind-h.
heoloðhelm† (æ) m. *helmet which makes the wearer invisible*.
heolp = healp; **heolr-** = heolor-
heolstor (e²) I. m. *darkness, concealment, cover, hiding-place, retreat*. [helan] II. adj. *dark, shadowy*, Æ.
heolstorcofa m. *dark chamber, grave*, PH 49.
heolstorhof n. *hell*, EL 764.
heolstorloca† m. *prison, cell*, AN.
heolstor-sceado (GEN 103) f., -scuwa (AN 1255) m. *concealing shade, darkness*.
heolstrig *shadowy, obscure*, WW.
heolstrung ? f. *darkness*, DR 182¹⁷.
heolt = healt
heom dp. of hē, hēo, hit.
heona (*LkL*) heonan *VPs*; heonane (*Gen*) = heonon(e)
heono (NG) = heonu
heonon(e) (a²) *hence, from here, away, Mt : from now.* h. forð *henceforth*. ['*hen*']
heononsīð m. *departure, death*, DOM 86.
heononweard *transient*, BL,GEN.
heonu (an(n)a, āne, eno, (he)ono) *if, but, therefore, moreover, whether*, ANS 91·205 : *lo! behold!* NG.
heonun (*Mt*) = heonon
hēop (LPs 67¹⁴) = hēap
hēopa m. *bramble*, LkL 20³⁷.
hēopbrēmel (ȳ²) m. *dog-rose, bramble, Lcd.* [v. '*hip*']
hēope f. '*hip*,' *seed-vessel of wild-rose, Cp, Lcd,WW*; Æ : *bush, brier*.
heor = heorr
heora gp. of hē, hēo, hit.
hēoran = hīeran
±heorcnian (e, y) tr. and intr. *to '*hearken*,' listen*, Æ,Guth.
heorcnung f. '*hearkening*,' *listening, power of hearing*, Æ.

heord I. (e, io) f. '*herd*,' *flock*, Æ,LL,Mt, WW; CP : *keeping, care, custody*, CP. **II.** *sycamore*, LkR19⁴. [heorot-?] **III.**= hīred. **IV.** (+) (S²Ps38²)=+heordung
heorde I. f. '*hards*' (*of flax*), *tow*, Cp,WW. **II.** (VPs)=hierde. **III.**=heord
±**heordnes** f. *custody, keeping, watch*, GD, Ps.
±**heordrǣden** (y¹) f. *custody, care, keeping, watch, ward*, ÆL : *keeping-place*, LPs78¹.
+**heordung** f. *guard, watch*, ERPs38².
hēore I.† (ȳ;=īe) *pleasant, secure*, B : *gentle, mild, pure*, Gen. ['*here*'] **II.**=hīere
heorl=eorl; **heoro**=heoru; **hēorod**=hīered
heorot (u²) m. '*hart*,' *stag*, Bo (heort), VPs.
heorotberge f. *buckthorn-berry*, WW.
heorotbrem(b)el m. *buckthorn*, Lcd. [v. '*hart*']
heorotbrembellēaf n. *leaf of the buckthorn*, Lcd119b.
heorotbrēr f. *buckthorn*, LkR17⁶(heart-).
heorotclǣfre f. '*hart-clover*,' *hemp agrimony*, Lcd.
heorotcrop m. *cluster of hartwort flowers*, Lcd.
heorotsmeoru n. *hart's grease*, Lcd45a.
heorotsol n. *stag's wallowing-place*, KC.
heorr mf. *hinge*, B,Bo,Cp,LPs : *cardinal point*, Lcd. ['*harre*']
heorra=(1) hearra; (2) heorr
heort I. (±) *high-minded, stout-hearted*, ÆL. **II.**=heorot
heortan=hiertan
heortancnys f. '(*com*)*pulsus cordis*'? v. ZDA31·13n.
heortbucc m. *roebuck*, WW119¹².
heortcoða m. *heart disease*, WW199³⁵.
heortcoðu f. *heart disease*, Lcd65b.
heorte f. '*HEART*' (*organ*) : *breast, soul, spirit* : *will, desire* : *courage* : *mind, intellect* : *affections*.
heortece m. '*heartache*,' Lcd.
heorten (y) *of a hart*, Lcd1·216¹⁵.
heortgesida pl. *entrails*, Lev3³.
heortgyre m. *terror of heart*, W86¹⁵.
heorthama m. *pericardium, internal fat*, Æ.
heorthogu f. *heart-care*, W177⁷.
heortlēas *dispirited*, DD124,W137²².
+**heortlufu** f. *hearty love*, †Hy9²⁹.
heortsārnes f. *grief*, GenC6⁶.
heortscræf n. *heart*, DD39.
heortsēoc *ill from heart disease* (Swt).
heortwærc m. *pain at the heart*, Lcd.
heorð (e) m. '*hearth*,' *fire*, Gl,Az : *house, home*, Æ,LL.
heorð-=eorð-
heorða m. *deer-* (*or goat-?*) *skin*, WW337³. [hyrð]

heorðbacen *baked on the hearth*, WW. [v. '*hearth*']
heorðcneoht m. *attendant*, CP361¹⁸.
heorðe=heorde
heorðfæst *having a settled home*, LL322'.
heorðgenēat† m. *retainer*, B.
heorðpening m. '*hearth-penny*,' *tax* (*for the Church*), *Peter's penny*, LL (v. 2·506).
heorðswǣpe f. *bridesmaid*, Cp701P.
heorðwerod† n. *body of retainers*.
heoru† m. *sword*, B.
heorublāc *mortally wounded*, B2488? (or ?hildeblāc).
heorucumbul n. *standard*, El107.
heorudolg n. *deadly wound*, An944.
heorudrēor† m. *sword-blood, gore*, B.
heorudrēorig† *blood-stained* : *deathly sick*, Ph217.
heorudrync m. *sword-drink, blood shed by the sword*, B2358.
heorufæðm m. *deadly grasp*, Ex504.
heoruflā f. *arrow*, LPs56⁵.
heorugīfre† *fierce, greedy for slaughter*.
heorugrǣdig† *bloodthirsty*, An.
heorugrimm† *savage, fierce*.
heoruhōciht *savagely barbed*, B1438.
heorung=herung
heoruscearp *very sharp*, Rd6⁸.
heorusceorp n. *war equipments*, Hell73.
heoruserce f. *coat of mail*, B2539.
heoruswealwe f. *falcon, hawk*, Wy186.
heorusweng† m. *sword-stroke*.
heorut=heorot
heoruwǣpen n. *sword*, Jud263.
heoruweallende *gushing with destruction*, B2781.
heoruwearg m. *bloodthirsty wolf*, B1267.
heoruword n. *hostile speech*, FT84.
heoruwulf m. *warrior*, Ex181.
hēow I. pret. 3 sg. of hēawan. **II.**=hīw
hēow-=hīw-; **hēowan**=hēofan
heplic=hæplic; **her-**=hear-, hier-, here-
hēr I. adv. '*here*,' *in this place*, Æ,G,VPs : *in this world*, Bl,LL : *at this point of time, at this date, now*, Chr,Ct : *towards this place, hither*, B. **II.**=hǣr
hēr-=hǣr-, hīer-, hȳr-
hēræfter (ȳ) adv. '*hereafter*,' *later on*, A,BH.
hērbeforan adv. *before, previously*, W52¹¹; FM361²³.
hērbeufan (u², iu²) adv. *here above, previously*, Ct; CP. [v. '*here*']
hērbūende† mp. *dwellers on this earth*.
herbyrg=herebeorg; **hercnian**=heorcnian
hērcyme m. *coming here, advent*, Cr250.
herd=heord; **herd-**, **hērd-**=hierd-, hīerd-
here (obl. cases usu. have herg-, herig-) m. *predatory band, troop, army, host, multitude*, Chr,Mt; AO,CP ('*se h.*' almost

always=*the Danish army* in CHR) : *battle, war, devastation.* ['*here*']

hère I. f. *dignity, importance?* MET 10⁵⁴? (Sedgef. reads 'here'). **II.** (VPs)=hǣre

here-bēacen, -bēacn n. *military ensign, standard : beacon, lighthouse.*

here-beorg, -byrg f. *lodgings, quarters,* NC 346. [*Ger.* herberge]

herebeorgian (y³) *to take up one's quarters, lodge,* CHR 1048F : RWH 137⁹. [*Ger.* herbergen]

herebléaŏ *cowardly,* Ex 453.

herebrŏga m. *dread of war,* B 462.

herebȳme f. *trumpet, sackbut,* Ex,OEG.

herebyrgian=herebeorgian

herebyrne f. *corslet,* B 1443. [v. '*here*']

herecirm m. *war cry,* GU 872.

herecist=herecyst

herecombol n. *standard,* EL 25?

herecyst† f. *warlike band,* Ex.

+heredlic (LPs 105²)=+hierendlic

herefeld† m. *battlefield, field.*

herefeoh n. *booty,* AO 118⁵.

herefēŏa m. *war-troop,* CR 1013.

hereflȳma (ē, ī) m. *deserter,* BR 23.

herefolc† n. *army,* JUD.

herefong m. *osprey,* WW.

herefugol m. *bird of prey,* Ex 161.

hereg-=herg-, herig-

heregang m. *invasion,* W 312¹ : *devastation,* BH 306B⁷. [v. '*here*']

heregeatland n. *heriot-land,* EC 220. [v. '*heriot*']

here-geatu fn. gp. -geat(w)e, -geat(w)a, -geatu *war-gear, military equipment, Bo, Ma* : '*heriot,*' *Ct,LL* (v. 2·500).

heregild (e, eo, y) n. *war-tax, Danegeld, Chr,Ct.* ['*heregeld*']

heregrīma† m. *helmet,* B.

herehand f. *violence of war,* BH 356²².

herehlŏŏ f. *war-host, troop,* GU 1042.

herehūŏ (ȳ³) f. *booty, prey, plunder,* Æ, AO.

herelāf f. *remains of a host,* Æ : *spoil,* Æ.

herelic *martial,* WW 374²⁶.

herelof mn. *fame, glory,* OEG : *trophy,* OEG.

heremæcg m. *warrior,* GEN 2483.

heremægen† n. *warlike force, multitude.*

heremann m. *soldier,* LkL 7⁸.

hèremann=hīeremann

heremeŏel n. *national assembly,* EL 550.

±herenes (æ) f. *praise,* BH,PPs.

herenett n. *corslet,* B 1553.

herenīŏ m. *warfare,* B 2474.

herenuma m. *prisoner,* LL (238¹¹).

herepāŏ† f. *corslet, coat of mail.*

her(e)-paŏ, -pæŏ m. *military road, highway,* v. CC 46 and Mdf.

hererǣs m. *hostile raid,* W 271².

hererǣswa m. *commander,* EL 995.

hererēaf f. *war spoil, plunder, booty,* Æ.

hererinc† m. *warrior.*

heresceaft m. *spear,* B 335.

heresceorp n. *war-dress,* FIN 45.

hereslŏŏ† m. *warlike expedition.*

herespēd f. *success in war,* B 64.

hèrespel n. *glorious discourse,* CREAT 37.

herestrǣl m. *arrow,* B 1435.

herestrǣt f. *highway, main road,* CP 375⁹ and N (LL 556,10²).

hereswēg m. *martial sound,* RUIN 23.

heresyrce f. *corslet,* B 1511.

heretēam m. *plunder, devastation,* GEN : *predatory excursion,* LL.

heretēma† (ȳ³) m. *general, king, ruler.*

here-toga, -toha m. *commander, general, chieftain,* Æ,BH ; AO,CP. ['*heretoga*']

hereŏ m. *booty,* GD 224²⁶. [hergaŏ]

hereŏrēat m. *war-band, troop,* Ex,WW.

hereŏrym m. *phalanx,* WW 411³⁴.

herewǣd f. *mail, armour,* B 1897.

herewǣpen n. *weapon,* PPs 34³.

herewæsma m. *prowess,* B 677.

herewǣŏa† m. *warrior,* JUD.

hereweg m. *highway,* WW 146³³.

hereweorc n. *war-work,* EL 656.

herewian=hierwan

herewic n. *dwellings, camp,* BL.

herewīsa† m. *captain, general.*

herewŏp m. *the cry of an army,* Ex 460.

hereword n. *praise, renown,* CHR 1009F.

herewŏsa† m. *warrior.*

herewulf m. *warrior,* GEN 2015.

herewurd (HGL 423)=hereword

herfest=hærfest ; **herg**=hearg

herg-=hereg-, heri(g)-

hergaŏ (here-, oᵌ) m. *harrying, devastation* : *booty,* GD.

hergere m. *one who praises,* DR. ['*heryer*']

±hergian *to ravage, plunder, lay waste,* '*harry,*' *AO,Chr* ; Æ,CP : *seize, take, capture.* ['*harrow*' ; here]

hergiend m. *plunderer,* GL.

hergoŏ=hergaŏ

hergung (AO), hergiung f. '*harrying,*' *ravaging, raid, invasion, attack,* BH,Chr : *plunder, booty* : '*harrowing,*' Æ.

herh=hearg

herian I. (æ) *to extol, praise, commend,* Æ,AO,BH,Bl,CP,VPs. ['*hery*'] **II.**= hierwan. **III.**=hergian. **IV.**=erian

herig=hearg ; v. also here.

herigend m. *flatterer,* Sc 205¹⁵.

±herigendlic *laudable, commendable,* Æ : *praising : excellent.* adv. -lice.

herigendsang m. *song of praise,* WW 335¹⁷.

hering=herung ; **hēring**=hīering

hĕrinne adv. '*herein*,' *Æ.*
herlic I. (æ) *noble*, MET. **II.**=herelic
hĕrnes=hīernes
hĕrof adv. '*hereof*,' *of this, A.*
hĕron adv. *herein, Ct*; LL. ['*hereon*']
hĕrongean adv. *contrariwise*, W 52⁸.
hĕrongemong *at this point, in this connection, meanwhile*, CP : *among others* CP.
her-pað, -poð=herepað
hĕrra=hēarra, hīerra (v. hēah).
hĕrrihte (æ) *at this point*, AS.
herst-=hierst-; **hĕrsum**=hīersum
hĕrtŏ *thus far*, OEG 56⁸⁰.
hĕrtŏĕacan *besides*, W.
herð=heorð
herðan pl. '*testiculi*,' LL 84,65.
herðbelig m. '*scrotum*,' WW.
herðland (NC 357)=yrðland
herung (eo) f. *praise, Æ,CP.* ['*herying*']
herutbeg (OEG 54²)=heorotberge
herw-=hierw-
herwið adv. '*herewith*,' *EC* 236.
hes-=hys-; **hĕst**=hæst
hĕt pret. 3 sg. of hātan.
hetan *to attack*, ÆL 35²⁸⁰.
hete (ea) m. '*hate*,' *envy, malice, hostility, persecution, punishment*, B,BH,VPs; Æ, AO,CP.
hetegrim† *fierce, cruel*, AN.
hetel=hetol
hetelic *hostile, malignant, horrible, violent, excessive*, AO,B. ['*hatelich*'] adv. -līce, *Æ.* ['*hately*']
hetend=hettend
hetenīð† m. *hostility, spite, wickedness.*
heterŏf *full of hate*, AN 1422.
heterūn f. *charm which produces hate*, RD 34⁷.
hetespræc f. *defiant speech*, GEN 263.
hetesweng m. *hostile blow*, B 2225.
heteðanc† m. *hostile design.*
heteðoncol *hostile*, JUL 105.
hetol *hating, hostile, evil, Æ,WW* : *savage* : *violent, severe*, RB 67¹⁶. [v. '*hatel*']
hetolnes (e²) f. *violence, fierceness*, OEG 11¹⁵².
hĕton pret. pl. of hātan.
hĕtt (AO)=hæt pres. 3 sg. of hātan.
hettan (æ) *to chase, persecute*, OEG 8³⁸⁸.
hettend† m. *enemy, antagonist.*
hettende pres. part. of hatian.
hĕðen=hæðen; **hĕwen**=hæwen
hī=hēo, hīe
hice *name of a bird*, '*parruca*,' WW 38².
hicemāse f. *blue titmouse*, WW 132²⁴.
hicgan=hycgan
hicol m. *woodpecker*, BC 1·47²⁵ (Mdf).
hīd I. fn. a '*hide*' *of land* (*about 120 acres, but amount varied greatly*), Chr,Ct,LL, v. EC pp 457–461 and LL 2·513. [hīwan] **II.**=hȳd

hīdan=hȳdan
hider adv. '*hither*,' *to this side, on this side, Æ,Cp,VPs.* comp. hideror *nearer*. h. and ðider (*Cp,CP*), hidres ðidres (*Bo*), *hither and thither.*
hidercyme m. *advent, arrival, BH.* ['*hithercome*']
hidere *hither*, WW 522³.
hidergeond adv. *thither, yonder*, Mt 26³⁶.
hiderryne adj. (i¹, i³) *of our country*, OET 115¹²¹.
hidertŏcyme=hidercyme
hiderweard adj. and adv. '*hitherward*,' *towards this place, Chr.*
hīdgild I. n. *tax paid on each hide of land, Ct.* ['*hidegeld*'] **II.**=hȳdgild
hīdir-=hider-
hīdmǣlum adv. *by hides*, KC 6·98⁴.
hidres v. hider.
hīe I. nap. of hē, hēo, hit. ['*HI**, *hy*']
II.=hēo nasf. of hē. ['*HI*, *hy*']
hieder=hider
hieftnīed (EPs 123⁶)=hæftnīed
hīeg (ē, ī, ȳ) n. '*hay*,' *cut grass*, G,Lcd,VPs. [hēawan]
hīeghūs (ē, ī) n. *hay store*, WW. ['*hayhouse*']
hīegian (CP)=hīgian
hīegsīðe (ē) m. *hay-scythe*, GD 37¹³.
hīehra, hīehst ['*highest*'] v. hēah.
hīehð(u) (ē, ēa, ȳ) f. (often indecl.) '*height*,' *highest point, summit, Gen,Sc* : *the heavens, heaven, Cr,El,Gu,Sc* : *glory.* [hēah]
±hīeld (æ, e, eo, i, y) f. (usu. +) *keeping, custody, guard, protection*, CP : *loyalty, fidelity, Chr,LL* : *observance, observation, watching* : *secret place* : *protector, guardian.* ['*held(e)*']
±hīeldan (e, y) intr. *to lean, incline, slope*, Bo : tr. *force downwards, bow or bend down*, B,Lk. ['*hield*']
hielde (e, y) f. *slope, declivity*, KC,WW. ['*hield*']
-hielde (y) v. earfoð-h.
+hīeldelīc (y) *safe*, GD 348¹⁰.
+hīeldnes (y) f. *observance*, PPs 18¹⁰.
hielfe (e, y) n. *handle*, CP,WW. ['*helve*']
hielfling (e) m. *mite, farthing*, LkL 12⁶. [healf]
hiellan *to make a noise*, EPs 82³.
hielpeð pres. 3 sg. of helpan.
hielt pres. 3 sg. of healdan.
-hieltan (y) v. ā-h. [healt]
hielto (e, y) f. *lameness*, MH 116¹⁰.
±hīenan (ǣ, ē, ȳ) *to fell, prostrate* : *overcome* : *weaken, crush, afflict, injure, oppress* : *abase, humble, insult*, B,LkL : *accuse, condemn*, CP. ['*hean*']
hiene as. of hē (*CP*). ['*hin*']

+**hīene** (ē) *ready to fall, frail,* DR 189[16].

hīenend (e[1]) m. *accuser,* JnL p 5[9].

hīennes (ē, ȳ) f. *crushing, destruction,* BH, LkR.

hīenð, hīenðo (ǣ, ē, ȳ) f. *humiliation, affliction, oppression, annoyance,* CP : *loss, damage, harm* : *act of hanging,* DHy 59[7].

hīera gp. of hē, hēo, hit. ['HER*']

hīera=hīerra v. hēah.

±**hīeran** (ē, ēo, ī, ȳ) tr. and intr. *to* 'HEAR' ('y-*here*'), *listen* (to), Æ : (w. d.) *obey, follow,* Æ; CP : *accede to, grant* : *be subject to, belong to, serve,* AO : (+) *judge.*

±**hīerdan** (i, y) *to harden, make hard* : *strengthen, fortify, confirm, encourage,* CP. [heard]

hīerde (eo, i, y) m. (f. at ÆGR 57[16]) *shepherd, herdsman,* CP,G; AO : *guardian, keeper,* B,Bl,Gen,Met,WW : *pastor,* Bl. ['herd']

hīerdebelig (e) m. *shepherd's bag,* Bl 31[17]. [v. 'belly']

hīerdebōc f. *pastoral book* (translation of the *Cura Pastoralis* of Pope Gregory), CP.

hīerdecnapa (y) m. *shepherd boy,* ÆL 23[418].

hīerdelēas (i, y) *without a shepherd or pastor,* Æ. ['herdless']

hīerdelic (y) *pastoral,* CP.

hīerdeman (y) m. *shepherd,* Æ. ['herdman']

hīerdenn (y) f. *hardening,* Sol 150'.

hīerdewyrt (i) f. *name of a plant,* Lcd.

±**hīerdnes** (eo, i, y) f. *custody, watch, guard.*

hīerdung (y) f. *strengthening, restoring,* WW 150[34].

hīere gds. of hēo. ['HER*']

hīered=hīred

hīereman (ē, ī, ȳ) m. *retainer, servant, subject, hearer, parishioner,* Mk; CP. ['hireman']

+**hīerend** m. *hearer,* CP.

+**hīerendlic** (e[1], y[1]) *audible,* LPs 142[8],ÆGR 152[6].

+**hīering** (ē) f. *hearing, hearsay,* LPs 111[7].

hīeringman (ē, ȳ) m. *subject,* RWH 96[5] : *hireling,* 126[35].

hīernes (ē, ȳ) f. (+) *hearing, report* : (±) *obedience, subjection, allegiance,* CP : *jurisdiction, district.*

hīerra=hearra

hīerra v. hēah, CP. ['HIGHER']

±**hīerstan** (e, i, y) *to fry, roast, scorch, pain,* CP. [cp. OHG. giharsten]

hīerste (e, y) f. *frying-pan* : *gridiron,* WW 214[40].

hīerstepanne (ea, y) f. *frying-pan,* CP.

hīersting (y) f. *frying, burning,* CP : *frying-pan?* ÆGR 175[3].

hīerstinghlāf (e) m. *crust,* WW 372[18].

±**hīersum** (ē, ēa, ī, ȳ) w. d. *obedient, docile,* BH,Gu. ['hearsum']

±**hīersumian** (ēa, ī, ȳ) w. d. *to obey, serve,* BH,Mt; AO : (+) *reduce, subject, conquer,* Chr. ['hearsum']

hīersumlic (ȳ) *willing,* GD 152[1].

±**hīersumnes** (ī, ȳ) f. *obedience, submission,* BH; CP : *service* : *humility.* ['hersumnesse']

±**hīertan** (e, eo, y) *to cheer, encourage,* CP; Æ : *be renewed, refreshed* : *revive* : *cherish.* ['heart'; heort]

hīerting (y) f. *soothing,* OEG 17[10].

±**hīerwan** (e, i, y) *to abuse, blaspheme, condemn, illtreat* : *to deride, despise.*

hīerwend (i) m. *blasphemer,* Lev 24[14].

hīerwendlic *contemptible.* adv. -līce (e) *with contempt.*

hīerwing (y) f. *blasphemy,* Sc 137[12].

hīerwnes (i, y) f. *contempt, reproach* : *blasphemy,* W 70[12].

hīew=hīw

hīewestān m. *hewn stone,* AO 212[10].

hīewet (ȳ) n. *cutting,* CP,WW. [hēawan]

hīewian=hīwian

hīewð (CP) pres. 3 sg. of hēawan.

hīf- (v. OEG 3913)=hīw-

hīg=hīe I.; **hīg**=hīeg

hīgan=hīwan; **hīge**=hyge

hīgendlīce *quickly, immediately,* RWH 25[13]. [hīgian]

higera m., higere f. *jay, magpie, jackdaw, woodpecker.* [Ger. häher]

higgan=hycgan

hīgian *to 'hie,' strive, hasten,* Bl,Bo,CP.

hīgid=hīd

hīglā 'heu!' RPs 119[5].

hīglēast=hygelēast; **hīgna** v. hīwan.

hīgo (N)=hīwan; **hīgora,** higra=higera

hīgre=higere; **hīgscipe**=hīwscipe

hīgð f. *exertion, effort,* ZDA. ['hight']

hīgung f. *effort,* GD 254[34].

hīhsan=hyscan; **hīht**=hyht

hīhting f. *exultation, gladness,* WW 233[42].

hīhðo=hīehðu; **hīlc**=hylc

hīlā=hīglā

hild I.† f. *war, combat.* II.=hield

hildbedd n. *deathbed,* An 1094.

hildebill† n. *sword,* B.

hildeblāc? *deadly pale, mortally wounded,* B 2488 (or ?heorublāc).

hildebord† n. *buckler,* B.

hildecalla m. *war-herald,* Ex 252.

hildecorðor n. *warlike band,* Ap 41.

hildecyst f. *valour,* B 2598.

hildedēoful n. *demon,* PPs 95[5].

hildedēor *war-fierce, brave,* Æ.

hildefreca† m. *warrior.*

hildegeatwe† fp. *war-harness,* B.

hildegesa m. *terror of battle*, EL 113.
hildegicel m. *battle-icicle* (*blood dripping from a sword*), B 1606.
hildegiest m. *enemy*, RD 54⁹.
hildegrāp† f. *hostile grip*, B.
hildeheard *bold in battle*, AP 21.
hildehlem† m. *crash of battle*, B.
hildelēoma† m. *Gleam of battle* (name of a sword), B.
hildelēoð n. *war-song*, JUD 211.
hildemēce m. *sword*, B 2202.
hildemecg m. *warrior*, B 799.
hildenǣdre† f. *war-snake, arrow*.
hildepīl† m. *dart, javelin*, RD. [v. '*pile*']
hilderǣs m. *charge, attack*, B 300.
hilderand m. *shield*, B 1242.
hilderinc† m. *warrior, hero*.
hildesǣd *battle-worn*, B 2723.
hildesceorp n. *armour*, B 2155.
hildescūr m. *shower of darts*, GU 1116.
hildeserce f. *corslet*, EL 234.
hildesetl n. *saddle*, B 1039.
hildespell n. *warlike speech*, EX 573.
hildestrengo f. *vigour for battle*, B 2113.
hildeswāt m. *vapour of battle?* B 2558.
hildeswēg m. *sound of battle*, GEN 1991.
hildetorht *shining in battle*, MET 25⁹.
hildetux m. *tusk* (*as weapon*), B 1511.
hildeðremma m. *warrior*, JUL 64.
hildeðrymm (AN 1034) m., hildeðrȳð (RD 20⁴) f. *warlike strength, valour*.
hildewǣpen m. *weapon of war*, B 39.
hildewīsa m. *commander*, B 1064.
hildewōma† m. *crash of battle*.
hildewrǣsn f. *fetter for captives*, SOL 292.
hildewulf m. *hero*, GEN 2051.
hildfreca=hildefreca
hildfrom *valiant in war*, AN 1204.
hildfruma† m. *battle-chief, prince, emperor*.
hildlata m. *laggard in battle, coward*, B 2846.
hildstapa m. *warrior*, AN 1260.
hildðracu f. *onset of battle*, GEN 2157.
hileð=hilð; **hilhāma**=hyllehāma
hill=hyll, hell
+hilmed (y) *helmeted*, WW 413²⁷ : *covered with foliage*, WW 405,526.
hilpestu=hilpest ðu (pres. 2 sg. of helpan and pron. 2 pers. sing.).
hilpeð, hilpð pres. 3 sg. of helpan.
hilt I.=hielt pres. 3 sg. of healdan. **II.** mn. =hilte
±hilte fn. *handle, 'hilt'* (*of sword*), B,WW ; (pl.=sg.) Æ,B,Sol.
hilt(e)cumbor n. *banner with a staff*, B 1022 (or ?hilde-).
hilted '*hilted,' with a hilt*, B.
hilting m. *sword*, OEG 758.
hiltlēas *having no hilt*, WW 142³⁴.
hiltsweord (y) n. *hilted sword*, BO 111¹⁶.

±hiltu np. of hilte.
hilð pres. 3 sg. of helan.
him ds. of hē, dp. of hē, hēo, hit. ['HIM']
himming (CP 1557)=hemming
hīna v. hīwan.
hīnan=heonon ; **hīnan**=hīenan
-hinca v. helle-h.
hind (y) f. '*hind*' (*female deer*), CHR,WW.
hindan *from behind, behind, in the rear*, Æ,AO. æt h. *behind*, Æ. [*Ger.* hinten]
hindanweard adv. *hindwards, at the end*, PH 298.
hindberge f. *raspberry*, CP,EP,LCD : *strawberry?* WW 409¹². ['*hindberry*']
hindbrēr m. *raspberry bush*, LCD 146b (hinde-).
hindcealf mn. *fawn*, WW. ['*hindcalf*']
hindema† superl. adj. *hindmost, last*.
hinder adj. *after* (*thought*), *sad, sinister* (*thought*)? MFH,RWH 143¹³. adv. *behind, back, after, in the farthest part, down.* on h. *backwards*, Æ.
hindergēap *wily, cunning, deceitful*, WW. ['*hinderyeap*']
hindergenga m. *one who walks backwards*, OEG 26²³ : *apostate*, OEG 5¹⁶.
hinderhōc m. *trick*, MOD 34.
hinderling I. m. *mean wretch, sneak*, LL 665'. **II.** adv. in phr. 'on hinderling' *backwards*, PPS. ['*hinderling*']
hindernes f. *wickedness, guile*, NC 301 ; MFH 166.
hinderscipe m. *wickedness*, DHY,OEG.
hinderðēostru np. *nether darkness*, PPS 85¹².
hinderweard *slow, sluggish*, PH 314.
hindeweard *reversed, wrong end first, from behind*, CP.
hindfalod n. *hind-fold*, KC 6·112³¹.
hind-hæleðe, -heoloð(e) f. '*ambrosia,*' *water agrimony*, WW. [v. '*hindheal*']
±hindrian *to 'hinder,' check, repress*, CHR, LL.
hindsīð (BL)=hinsīð
hine I. as. of hē. **II.**=heonon
hīne=hīwene
hinfūs† *ready to depart or die*.
hingang† m. *departure, death*, OET 149. [v. '*yong*']
hingrian (BL ; Æ)=hyngrian
hinn-=hin- ; **hinon**=heonon
hinsīð† m. *departure, death*. [heonon]
hinsīðgryre m. *fear of death*, SAT 456.
hīo v. he ; **hīo-**=heo-
hīonne? f. '*dura mater,*' LL 5,36.
hīor=heorr ; **hīored**=hīred
hīoro-=heoru-
hīowesclīce=hīwisclīce ; **hīp-**=hyp-
hīpsful (OEG 11¹⁸⁰)=hyspful
hīr=hȳr ; **hīr-, hīr-**=hier-, hēor-, hīer-

hira gp. of hē, hēo, hit; **hīrd-**=hīred-
hīre gds. of hēo. ['HER*']
hīred (ēo, īe, ȳ) m. *household, family, retinue,* AO,Bo,Mt,WW : *brotherhood, company,* Æ,Ct. ['hird']
hīredcniht m. *domestic, member of a household,* Æ.
hīredcūð *domestic, familiar,* So 203¹³.
hīredgerēfa m. 'ex-consul,' WW 110⁶.
hīredlic *pertaining to a household or court, domestic, familiar.*
hīredlōf (=lēof) *friendly,* A 13·445.
hīredman m. *retainer, follower,* Æ,Ma. ['hirdman']
hīredprēost (ȳ) m. *chaplain,* TC 571² : *regular priest,* EC 255.
hīredwīfman m. *female member of a household,* TC 531⁶.
hīredwīst f. *familiarity,* Sc 203¹².
hīru=hūru
his gs. of hē. ['HIS']
hīs (BH)=īs; **hisc-**=hysc-
hislic *suitable,* GD 183⁵.
hispan=hyspan; **hiss**=hos; **hisse**=hyse
hīt v. hē. ['IT']
hittan (y) *to fall in with, meet with, 'hit' upon,* Chr 1066. [ON. hitta]
hīð-=hȳð-; **hīðer**=hider
hīu (NG)=hēo
hīw I. (ēo, īe, īo, ȳ) n. *appearance, form, species, kind,* Æ,Bl,Cr,G,WW : *apparition,* WW 236⁸ : 'hue,' *colour,* Bf,Bl : *beauty : figure of speech.* **II.** (io) f. *fortune,* AA 11².
hīwan mp. (gen. hīwna, hī(g)na) *members of a family, household or religious house,* Chr, G; Æ. ['hind,' 'hewe']
hīwbeorht† *radiant, beautiful.*
hīwcund (hīl-) *familiar, domestic,* Gl.
hīwcūð (īe) *domestic, familiar, well-known,* Æ,CP.
hīwcūðlic *domestic, familiar.* adv. -līce.
+**hīwcūðlician** *to make known or familiar to,* NC 294.
hīwcūðnes f. *familiarity,* GD 71²⁴; 140⁷.
hīwcūðrædnes f. *familiarity,* WW 191²⁴.
hīwen n. *household,* Æ. ['hewen']
+**hīwendlic** *allegorical,* WW 354⁴.
hīwere m. *dissembler, hypocrite,* Æ.
hīwfæger *comely of form,* MFH 167.
hīwfæst *comely, fair,* OEG.
hīwgedāl n. *divorce,* G.
±**hīwian** I. *to form, fashion,* WW : *colour : dissimulate, feign, pretend,* Æ : *figure, signify,* Æ : (+) *transform, transfigure.* ['hue,' 'hued'] **II.** *to marry,* CP 318¹.
hīwisc n. *household,* Æ : *hide (of land* v. hīd). adv. -līce *familiarly.*
+**hīwlæcan** *to form, shape, fashion,* NC 294 : *colour,* Lcd 1·262¹⁴.

hīwlēas *shapeless,* WW : *colourless,* Lcd 11. ['hueless']
hīwlic I. *comely,* Lcd,OEG : *figurative,* HGl. **II.** *matronly?* WW 442².
hīwna v. hīwan.
hīwnes f. *hue, colour, appearance,* WE 65¹⁴.
+**hīwodlīce** *in form,* ÆGr 250,251.
hīwrǣden f. *family, household, religious house,* Æ.
hīwscipe m. *family, household : hide (of land),* CC 127.
hīwð pres. 3 sg. of hēawan.
hīwung I. (ēo, ȳ) f. (±) *appearance, likeness, form, figure : portrayal,* ByH 102³³ : *pretence, hypocrisy,* Æ : *irony,* WW 416³². **II.** f. *marriage,* AO 64²⁴.
hlacerian *to deride, mock,* LPs 24³.
hlacerung f. *unseemly behaviour, or words, mockery,* LPs 43¹⁴.
±**hladan**⁶ (æ, ea) *to 'lade,' draw, or take in water,* Æ,JnR : *heap up, lay on, build, load, burden,* B,Gen,Rd; CP.
hladung f. *drawing ('haustus'),* DHy 58⁶.
hlæ=hlæw
hlæd n. *heap? burden?* CP 21¹⁶⁰. ['lade']
hlædder (Bl), **hlæddre**=hlæder
hlæddisc m. *loaded dish?* WW 126³⁹.
hlædel m. 'ladle,' LL,ZDA.
hlæden I. m. *bucket,* WW 123⁵. **II.** pp. of hladan.
hlæder f. 'ladder,' *steps,* Æ,Bf,LL; CP.
hlæderstæf f. *rung of a ladder,* ByH 80³⁰.
hlæderwyrt f. *ladder-wort, Jacob's ladder,* Lcd.
hlædhweogl n. *water-wheel, wheel for drawing up water,* WW 347⁷.
hlædrede *having steps,* BC 3·492'.
hlædst=hlætst pres. 2 sg. of hladan.
hlædtrendel m. *wheel for drawing water,* OEG 502.
hlæfde 'sparsio panis,' WW 277⁶.
hlæfdige (ā, ē) f. *mistress (over servants),* LL,VPs,WW : *chatelaine, 'lady,' queen,* Chr,Ct : *the Virgin Mary,* Cr. sēo ealde h. *the queen dowager,* Chr 1051 c.
hlæfl=læfel
+**hlæg** n. *derision, scorn,* Dom 15.
hlægulian (Cp 317)=hlagolian
hlæhan (N,VPs)=hliehhan
hlæhter=hleahtor
hlænan I. *to cause to lean,* Jul 63. **II.**=lænan
-hlænan v. ā-hl.
hlæne 'lean,' Æ; AO.
±**hlænian** *to become lean,* CP : *make lean, starve,* CP. ['lean']
hlænnes f. 'leanness,' Æ,OEG.
±**hlænsian** *to make lean, weaken,* OEG. ['lense']

hlǽpewince (WW)=lēapewince

hlæst n. *burden, load, freight, B,Rd.* holmes h. *finny tribe.* ['*last*']

+hlǽstan (e) *to load, burden, BH* : *adorn,* JUD 36. [v. '*last*' vb.]

hlǣsting f. *toll on loading a ship,* TC 359, 411.

hlǣstscip n. *trading-vessel,* Cp 147 H.

hlǽt=lǽt

hlǽtst pres. 2 sg. of hladan.

hlǣw† (ā) mn. *mound, cairn, hill, mountain, B* : *grave-yard, barrow, Met* : *hollow mound, cave.* ['*low*']

hlāf m. '*loaf,*' *cake, bread, food, Bf,NG; Æ, AO,CP* : *sacramental bread, ÆP* 108²³.

hlāfǣta m. ('*loaf-eater*'), *dependant, LL* 4,25.

hlāfbrytta m. *slave in charge of the bread-store?* EC 255.

hlǣfdie (VPs)=hlǣfdige

hlāfgang m. *attendance at, or participation in, a meal, RB* : *partaking of the Eucharist,* LL 473,27.

hlāf-gebrecu f. (PPs), -gebroc (MH) n. *bit of bread.*

hlāfhwǣte m. *bread-wheat,* TC 144'.

hlāflēast f. *want of bread,* CAS 34²⁰.

hlāfmæsse f. '*Lammas*' (*August* 1), *AO; Æ.*

hlāfmæssedæg m. *Lammas-day.*

hlāfmæssetīd f. *Lammas-tide,* LCD 6a.

hlāfofn m. *baker's oven,* WW 411⁸.

hlāford m. '*lord,*' *master, ruler, AO,B,Bf, Chr,G; Æ,CP* : *husband, Ct* : *the Lord, God, Æ.* [hlāf, weard]

hlāforddōm m. *lordship, authority, CP* : *patronage.* ['*lorddom*']

hlāfordgift m? n? *grant (or appointment) by a lord,* HGL 412 (v. BTs).

hlāfordhold *loyal to a lord,* Bo 42²⁴.

hlāfordhyldo f. *loyalty, AO.*

hlāfording m. *lord, master,* W 298⁷.

hlāfordlēas *without a lord, leaderless, B.* ['*lordless*']

hlāfordlic '*lordly,*' *noble, OEG* 187¹.

hlāfordscipe m. '*lordship,*' *authority, rule, CP* : '*dominatio*' (*title of an order of angels*), ÆH 1·342'.

hlāfordsearu fn. *high treason, LL.*

hlāfordsōcn f. *act of seeking the protection of a lord, LL.*

hlāfordswica m. *traitor, Lcd; Æ.* ['*lord-swike*']

hlāfordswice m. *high treason, treachery,* W 160.

hlāford-swīcung (MFH 167; W 225²⁸), -syr-wung (LL 16 n 5) f. *betrayal of one's lord.*

hlāfordðrimm m. *dominion, power,* NC 302.

hlāfrǣce f. *oven-rake,* OEG 53⁴³ (hlāb-).

hlāfsēnung f. *blessing of bread (on Lammas-day),* MH 136¹.

hlāfurd=hlāford

hlāfweard m. *steward,* PPs 104¹⁷ (v. GK 884 s.v. healf-).

hlagol *inclined to laugh,* W 40⁸.

hlagolian (æ) *to sound,* Cp 317.

hlāmmæsse=hlāfmæsse

hlanc '*lank,*' *lean, thin, Jud,PPs.*

hland (o) n. *urine, Lcd.* ['*lant*']

hlaðian=laðian; hlāw=hlǽw

hleadan=hladan; hleahter=hleahtor

hleahterful *scornful,* GUTH.

hleahterlic *ridiculous,* Sc 38⁷.

hleahtor (e) m. '*laughter,*' *jubilation, B,Bl, CP,Sc* : *derision.*

hleahtorbǣre *causing laughter,* RB 18⁶.

hleahtorsmið m. *laughter-maker,* Ex 43.

hleahtrian (e) *to deride,* LPs 21⁸.

hlēapan⁷ *to* '*leap,*' *run, go, jump, dance, spring, Æ,B,BH,Chr,CP* : (+) *leap upon, mount (a horse).*

hlēapere m. *runner, courier, Chr* : *wanderer* : *horseman* : '*leaper,*' *dancer, WW* : *itinerant monk,* RB 135²⁰.

hlēapestre f. *female dancer,* WW 311³³.

hlēapettan v. *to leap up,* BH 390⁹.

hlēapewince f. '*lapwing,*' *WW.*

hlēapung f. *dancing, Æ.* ['*leaping*']

hlēat pret. 3 sg. of hlēotan.

hlec *leaky, CP,OEG.* [v. '*leak*']

hlecan⁵ *to cohere,* CP 361²⁰.

hlēda, hlēde (ȳ) m. *seat,* ÆGR 34³.

hlēf=hlǣw; -hlēfan (oe) v. ā-hl.

hlēga (LkL 6¹⁶)=lǣwa; hlehhan=hliehhan

hlēg(i)ende (æ¹, u²) *deep-sounding,* WW 9²⁷; 358¹⁹.

hleht-=hleaht-

hlem m. *sound,* CP 253¹⁷.

hlemman *to cause to sound, clash,* WH 61.

hlēnan=lǣnan

+hlencan *to twist, bend?* LCD.

hlence f. *coat of mail,* Ex 218.

hlennan=hlynnan

hlenortēar m. *hyssop,* LPs 50⁸.

hlēo† m? n? (hlēow), gs. hlēowes (no pl.) *covering, refuge, defence, shelter, protection, Cr,PPs* : *protector, lord.* ['*lee*']

hlēo-=hlēow-

hlēobord n. *book-cover,* RD 27¹².

hlēoburh† f. *protecting city, B.*

hlēod=hlōd

+hleodu pl. of +hlid.

hlēohrǣscnes f. '*supplantatio*'? LPs 40¹⁰.

hlēolēast† *without shelter, comfortless.*

hleomoc m. hleomoce f. *speedwell, Lcd.* [v. '*brooklime*']

hlēon=hlēowan; hleon-=hlin-

hlēonað m. *shelter,* GU 222.

hlēonian *to cherish*, WW377³².
hlēop pret. 3 sg. of hlēapan.
hlēor n. *cheek*, Lcd,WW : *face, countenance*, Ep,Gu. ['*leer*']
hlēoran (ÆL)=lēoran
hlēorbān n. (*cheek-bone*), *temple*, LPs131⁵.
hlēorberg? f. *cheek-guard, helmet*, B304?
hlēorbolster m. *pillow*, B688.
hlēordropa m. *tear*, Gu1315.
hlēorsceamu f. *confusion of face*, PPs68⁸.
hlēorslæge m. *a blow on the cheek*, CP 261⁶.
hlēortorht *beautiful*, RD69⁶.
hlēosceorp n. *sheltering robe*, RD10⁵.
hlēotan¹ *to cast lots*, Æ,AO : (±) *get by lot, obtain*.
hlēoð=(1) hlēowð; (2) pres. pl. of hlēowan.
hlēoð-=hlōð-
hlēoðor n. *noise, sound, voice, song : hearing*.
+**hlēoðor** *harmonious*, BH60¹⁸.
hlēoðorcwide† m. *speaking, words, discourse, song, prophecy*.
hlēoðorcyme m. *coming with trumpet-sound*, Da710.
hlēoðorstede m. *place of conference*, Gen 2399.
hlēoðrere (ō) m. *rhetorician*, OET180⁴.
hlēoðrian *to sound, speak, sing, cry aloud, resound, proclaim*, Æ.
hlēoðrung f. *sound*, MFH130 : *harmony, hymn*, Bf198⁵ : *reproof*, SPs37¹¹.
hleoðu v. hlið.
hlēow=hlēo
±**hlēow** I. (ī) *sheltered, warm, sunny*, Lcd, Nar. adv. hlēowe. [v. '*lew*'] II.=+hlōw
±**hlēowan** (ī, ȳ) *to warm, make warm, cherish*, Bl : *become warm or hot*. ['*lew*']
hlēowdryhten m. *protector, patron*, Wid94.
hlēowfæst *protecting, consoling*, Cr,RB.
hlēowfeðre fp. *sheltering wings*, Gen2740.
hlēowlora m. *one who has lost a protector*, Gen1953.
hlēowmǣg† m. *kinsman who is bound to afford protection*.
hlēownes f. *warmth*, A8·451.
hlēowon pret. pl. of hlōwan.
hlēowsian *to shelter, protect*, WW235²⁹.
hlēowstede m. *sunny place*, WW336³⁰.
hlēowstōl m. *shelter, asylum*, Gen2011.
hlēowð (ī, ȳ) f. *shelter, covering, warmth*, Æ, Hex. ['*lewth*']
±**hlēowung** (ē, ī, ȳ) f. *shelter, protection, favour*, CM,WW.
hlestan=hlæstan, hlystan
hlet (KGl) pres. 3 sg. of hladan.
hlēt (VPs; MkR)=hliet
+**hlēða**† m. *companion, denizen*. hlōð]
hlēðrian=hlēoðrian; **hlēw**=hlæw
hlēw-=hlēow-

hlēwesa (EPs139¹³)=lēwsa
hlēwð pres. 3 sg. of hlōwan.
hlid I. n. '*lid*,' *covering, door, gate, opening*, Æ. II.=hlið
+**hlid**† n. (nap. hlidu, hleodu) *covering, vault, roof*.
hlīdan¹ *to come forth, spring up*, PPs79¹¹?
hlidfæst *closed by a lid*, TC516⁴.
hlidgeat n. *swing-gate, folding-door*, BC, EC; Æ; Mdf. ['*lidgate*']
+**hlidod** (eo) *having a lid*, BH320¹⁰. ['*lidded*']
hliehhan⁶ (e, i, y) *to laugh*, Æ,CP : (±) *laugh at, deride*, Æ,MtL : *rejoice*.
hlīep (ȳ) mf., hlīepe f. '*leap*,' *bound, spring, sudden movement*, Cr,Lcd : *thing to leap from*, AO : *place to leap over?* v. CC54 : *waterfall*, Ct.
hlīepen pres. pl. of hlēapan.
hlīepgeat (ȳ) n. *a low gate*, KC. ['*leapgate*']
hliet (ē, ȳ) m. *lot, share : chance, fortune*, CP.
hlīfend (hlīb-) *threatening*, Cp223m.
hlīfian *to rise high, tower, overhang*, B,GD.
hlīgan¹ᵛ *to attribute (to)*, CP,Da.
hligsa (CP)=hlīsa
hlihan, hlihcan, hlihhan=hliehhan
hlimman³† (y) *to sound, resound, roar, rage*.
hlimme† f. *stream, torrent*, PPs.
hlin I. (=y) m. *maple-tree*, RD56⁹. [*Ger.* lehne] II.=hlynn
hlinbedd n. *sick-bed, couch*, B3034.
hlinc m. *ridge, bank, rising ground, hill*, EC, Ph; v. GBG and Mdf. ['*link*']
hlincrǣw f. *bank forming a boundary*, EC, KC.
hlinduru† f. *latticed door*.
±**hlinian** (eo, y) *to '*lean*,*' B; Æ : *recline, lie down, rest*, Jn,MkL; CP.
hliniend m. *one who reclines*, HGl414.
hlinrǣced† n. *prison*, An,Jul.
hlinscū(w)a† m. *darkness of confinement*.
hlinsian=hlynsian
±**hlinung** f. '*leaning*,' Lk : *seat, couch*.
hlīosa=hlīsa
hlīpð pres. 3 sg. of hlēapan.
hlīra=līra
hlīsa (īo, ȳ) m. *sound : rumour, fame, glory*, CP.
hlīsbǣre *renowned*, OEG.
hlīsēadig *renowned, famed*, Bo.
hlīsēadignes f. *renown*, Bo75²⁸.
hlīsful *of good repute, famous*, Æ. adv. -līce, Æ,AO.
hlīsig *renowned*, OEG8²⁵⁰.
hlīstan=hlystan; **hlīt**=hlyt
hlið I.† n. (nap. hleoðu) *cliff, precipice, slope, hill-side, hill*, An,B; Mdf. ['*lith*'] II.=hlid

hlīw=hlēow

hlīwe f. *shelter*, KC.

hloccetung f. *sighing*, HGL421[7].

hlōd pret. 3 sg. of hladan; **hlodd**=hlot

hlōgon pret. pl., hlōh pret. 3 sg. of hliehhan.

hlom (WW117[25]), hlond=hland

hlōse f. *pigsty*, LL454,10; NC302; Mdf.

hlosnere m. *listener*, OEG2333 : *disciple*, Bf56[11].

hlosnian *to listen* : *wait, Æ* : *be on the look out for, spy, Æ.* hlosniende '*attonitus,*' WW.

hlōsstede m. *site of a pigsty*, KC.

hlot, hlott n. '*lot*,' *part, portion, share, BC,LkL* : (+) *selection by lot, choice, decision, Æ,AO.* hl. sendan, weorpan *to cast lots, Bl,Mt.*

hloten pp. of hleotan.

+**hlotland** n. *allotted land, inheritance,* Jos 24[30].

hlōð f. *troop, crowd, band*, AO : *booty, spoil* : *complicity with a band of robbers*, LL 94,14.

hlōðbōt f. *penalty imposed on a member of a gang of malefactors*, LL64,29.

hlōðere m. *robber*, WW506[36]. [hlōð]

hlōðgecrod n. *mass of troops*, RD4[63].

hlōðian (ēo) *to spoil, plunder*, BH.

hlōðslīht m. *murder by a member of a gang of malefactors*, LL18,29.

+**hlōw** n. *lowing, bellowing, bleating, Æ.*

hlōwan[7] *to '* low,' *roar, bellow, Æ,El.*

hlōwung f. *lowing, bleating, bellowing*, WW 192[7]; 195[13].

hlūd adj. comp. hlūdre, hluddre '*loud,*' *noisy, sounding, sonorous, Bl,CP; Æ.*

hlūdclipol *loud, noisy*, RBL35[11] (hlūt-).

hluddre v. hlūd.

hlūde adv. *loudly, aloud, Bl; Æ,CP.* ['*loud*']

hlūdnes f. '*loudness,*' *clamour*, Bf176[23].

hlūdstefne *loud-sounding*, WW416[18].

hlūdswēge adv. *loudly, Æ.*

hlummon pret. pl. of hlimman.

hlupon pret. pl. of hlēapan.

hluton pret. pl. of hlēotan.

hlūtor, hlūttor (e[2]) gsm. hlūtres *pure, clear, bright, sincere, Æ,CP.* [*Ger.* lauter} adv. -līce.

hlūtorlīcnes=hlūtornes

hlūtornes f. *clearness, brightness, simplicity, purity, Æ.*

hlūtre I. adv. *clearly, brightly* : *untroubled,* PPs104[3]. II. ds. of hlūtor.

hlūtter, hlūttor=hlūtor

±**hlūttrian** *to clear, purify, make bright* : *to become clear.*

hlyd=hlid

±**hlȳd** fm. *noise, sound* : *tumult, disturbance, dissension.* [hlūd]

hlȳda=hlēda

Hlȳda m. *March*, Lcd. ['*Lide*'; hlūd]

hlȳdan *to make a noise, sound, clamour, vociferate, Æ,CP.* [hlūd]

hlȳde I. f. *torrent*, BC (Mdf). II. (LL455')= hlēde?

hlȳdig *garrulous*, OEG1418. [hlūd]

hlȳding f. *noise, cry*, MtL25[6] (lȳ-).

hlyhhan=hliehhan

hlymman=hlimman; **hlyn**=hlynn

hlynian=(1) hlynnan; (2) hlinian

±**hlynn** I. m. *sound, noise, din, tumult*, AO. II. f. *torrent*, JnR. ['*linn*']

hlynnan (e) *to make a noise, resound, shout, roar.*

hlynrian *to thunder*, WW519[34].

hlynsian† (i) *to resound.*

hlȳp=hlīep

hlȳrian (=īe) *to blow out (the cheeks)*, LPs 80[4]. [hlēor]

hlȳsa (Æ)=hlīsa

hlȳsfullīce=hlīsfullīce

hlysnan *to '* listen,' *MtL*; Cp.

hlysnere m. *hearer*, DR29[4] (ly-).

±**hlyst** f. *sense of hearing, Æ,Lcd* : *listening.* ['*list*']

±**hlystan** (e, i) *to listen, hear, CP,LL; Æ* : *attend to, obey, Lk.* ['*list*']

+**hlyste** *audible*, CHRD22[36].

+**hlystend**, hlystere m. *listener, Æ.*

+**hlystful** *attentive, gracious*, LPs89[13].

hlysting f. *act of listening*, RWH136[23].

hlyte m. *lot, portion*, WW40[13].

+**hlyta** m. *companion*, CPs44[9]. ['hlot']

hlȳtere m. *priest*, NC302. (v. BTs)

hlytm m. *casting of lots*, B3126? ·

hlytman *to decide by lot*, MFH167.

hlytta m. *diviner, soothsayer*, AO184[26] : (+) *partner, fellow*, RPs44[8]. [hlot]

+**hlytto** (e) *fellowship, lot*, DR.

hlȳttor (HGL418)=hlūttor, hlūtor

hlȳttrian *to purify*, ÆGr222[7].

hlȳttrung f. *cleaning, refining*, WW179[36].

-**hlȳðan** (=īe) v. be-hl.; **hlȳðre**=lȳðre

hlȳw=hlēow-; **hlȳwing**=hlēowung

hnacod=nacod

hnǣcan *to check, destroy, kill, Æ.* [=nǣcan]

±**hnǣgan** I. *to bow down, bend, humble, curb, vanquish.* [hnīgan] II. *to '* neigh,' *ÆGr.* III.=nǣgan

hnǣgung f. '*neighing,*' *ÆGr,Cp.*

hnæpp m. *bowl*, EC,OEG,WW. ['*nap*']

hnæpp-=hnapp-

hnæppan *to strike*, Bo130[19,20].

hnæsce=hnesce

+**hnǣst**, +hnāst† n. *collision, conflict, battle.* [hnītan]

+**hnǣstan** (næst-) *to contend with*, RD 28[10].

hnãg, hnãh **I.** *bent down, abject, poor, humble, lowly* : *niggardly.* **II.** pret. 3 sg. of hnīgan.

hnappian (æ, e, ea) *to doze, slumber, sleep,* CP,Mt,Sc,VPs; Æ. ['nap']

hnappung (æ, ea) f. *napping, slumbering,* VPs; CP.

hnǣt pret. 3 sg. of hnītan.

hneap- (VPs)=hnap-

-hnēapan v. ā-hn.

hnēaw *mean, niggardly, stingy, miserly,* CP. [Ger. genau] adv. -līce.

hnēawnes f. *meanness,* CP.

hnecca m. '*neck*,' Æ,CP.

hnēgan=(1) nǣgan; (2) hnǣgan

hneofule f.=hnifol

hneoton pret. pl. of hnītan.

hnep (GD 186²⁷)=hnæpp

hneppian (KGL)=hnappian

hnescan=hnescian

hnesce I. (æ, i, y) *soft, tender, mild,* CP : *weak, delicate,* Æ : *slack, negligent,* CP : *effeminate, wanton,* Æ. ['NESH'] **II.** n. *soft object.* **III.** adv. *softly,* ÆL37³⁰¹.

±hnescian *to make soft, soften,* Æ,EPs : *become soft, give way, waver,* CP,Lcd; ÆL. ['nesh']

hnesclic *soft, luxurious, effeminate,* AO. adv. -līce *softly, gently, tenderly,* CP. ['neshly']

hnescnes f. *softness, weakness, effeminacy,* CP,Lcd,MtL; Æ : *soft part of anything.* ['neshness']

hnett (MtL4¹⁸)=nett

hnexian (Æ)=hnescian

hnifol m. *brow, forehead,* LCD,WW.

hnifol-crumb, -crump *inclined, prone,* WW.

hnīgan¹ *to bow oneself, bend, bow down* : *fall, decline, sink.* [Ger. neigen]

±hnigian *to bow down (the head),* LCD 7a, LL.

hniglan=hnygelan

hnipend *bending, lowly,* HGL436.

hnipian *to bow down,* Met,OEG; Æ : *bow the head, look gloomy,* CP. ['nipe']

hnippan? *to bow down,* OEG 1579n.

hnisce (MkR13²⁸)=hnesce

hnītan *to thrust, gore, butt,* Æ : *knock, come into collision with, encounter.*

hnītol *addicted to butting (of an ox),* Æ,LL.

hnītu f. *louse-egg,* '*nit*,' Ep,Lcd; Æ.

hnoc m. *wether sheep,* WW 120³⁴.

hnoll m. *top, crown of the head,* Æ,VPs. ['noll']

hnoppian *to pluck,* WW480²⁷.

hnor? *sneezing* Ln65. [*hnēosan]

hnossian *to strike,* RD6⁷.

hnot *bare, bald,* '*close-cropped,*' ÆGr. ['not']

hnutbēam m. *nut tree,* Lcd; WW. [v. 'nut']

hnutcyrnel mn. *kernel of a nut,* LCD.

hnutu f. gs. and nap. hnyte '*nut*,' Erf,Lcd, MtR; Mdf.

+hnycned *wrinkled?* LCD 97a.

hnydele=hydele

hnygelan (i) pl. *clippings,* WW.

hnÿlung f. *reclining,* WW 153²⁴.

+hnyscan *to crush,* MtR21⁴⁴. [hnesce]

hnysce=hnesce

+hnyst *contrite,* PsC 127.

hnyte gs. and nap. of hnutu.

hō I.=hōh. **II.** pres. 1 sg. of hōn.

hōbanca m. *couch,* WW 280¹². [hōh]

hōc m. '*hook*,' BH,WW : *angle,* Mt,Nar.

hoc(c) m. *mallow,* Cp,Lcd. ['hock']

hōced *curved,* KC. ['hooked']

hocer=hocor; **hocg**=hogg

hōciht(e) *with many bends?* KC3·365', 6·227⁹.

hōcīsern n. *small sickle,* WW235¹.

hoclēaf n. *mallow,* LCD.

hocor n. *insult, derision,* W164¹⁷. ['hoker']

hocorwyrde *derisive, scornful,* W164¹³. [v. 'hoker']

hōd m. '*hood*,' Ep,WW.

hof n. *enclosure, court, dwelling, building, house, hall* : *temple, sanctuary.* [Ger. hof]

hōf I. m. '*hoof*,' Run,WW; Æ. **II.** pret. 3 sg. of hebban.

hofding m. *chief, leader,* CHR1076. [ON. höfðingi]

hōfe f. '*hove*,' *alehoof (plant),* Lcd,WW.

hofer (o²) m. *hump,* ÆL : *swelling,* GL.

hofer-ede, -od *humpbacked,* CP,Lcd,WW. ['hovered']

hoferiend, +hoferod (ÆL)=hoferede

-hōflan v. be-h.

hōflic *pertaining to a court,* OEG 2996.

+hōfod *hoofed,* ÆL25⁴⁴.

hōfon pret. pl. of hebban.

hofor=hofer

hōf-rec, -ræc n. *hoof-track, bridle-track,* LCD.

hofrede *bedridden,* WW162⁸.

hōfring m. *print of a horse's hoof (=hr.),* OEG18.

hofweard m. *ædile,* WW111²⁰.

hog-=hoh-

hoga I. *careful, prudent,* DR,MtL. ['howe'] **II.** m. *fear, care* : *attempt, struggle,* OEG 8²⁸³.

hoga-=hog-, hoh-; **hogade**=hogode

hogascipe (o²) m. *prudence,* DR,LkL.

hogde pret. of hycgan or hogian.

hogelēas *free from care,* RWH79³³.

hogg m. *hog,* NC302 (v. LF132).

±hogian (LWS for hycgan q.v.) *to care for, think about, reflect, busy oneself with,* G; Æ : *intend,* B : *strive, wish for.* ['how,' 'howe']

hogu f. *care,* Æ. ['how,' 'howe']

hogung f. *endeavour*, DHy8¹².
hōh m., gs. hōs, nap. hōas, hōs, dp. hōum *hough, heel*, Æ,*Jn,Ps.* on h. *behind : point of land*, *Ct,Gl,Nar*; Mdf. [' *ho*,' ' *hoe* '; v. also ' *hough* ']
hoh-fæst, hog(a)- (NG) *cautious, wise.*
hōhfōt m. *heel*, LPs55⁷.
hohful (hoga-, N) *careful, thoughtful*, Æ : *full of care, anxious, pensive, sad, Ct,Sc* : *persistent*, ÆL31¹⁰⁸⁴. [' *howful* ']
hohfulnes f. *care, trouble*, RBL, W.
hōh-hwyrfing, -hwerfing f. *heel-turning, circle?* v. OEG18n.
hōhing f. *hanging*, WNL294a¹².
hohlīce (hog-) *prudently*, LkL16⁸.
hohmōd *sad, sorrowful*, W72⁸.
hōhscanca m. *leg, shank*, LCD14a.
hōhsinu f. *sinew of the heel*, Æ,*Lcd*. [' *hough-sinew* ']
-hōhsnian v. on-h.
hōhspor n. *heel*, WW160²⁶.
hol I. *hollow, concave*, LCD : *depressed, lying in a hollow, CP,Ct,MH.* [' *holl* '] **II.** n. *hollow place, cave, hole, den, Ct,Lk,Met,Ps, WW*; Æ,AO : *perforation, aperture, Cp.* [' *hole*,' ' *holl* ']
hōl n. *calumny, slander*, ÆL,W.
-hola v. oter-h.
+hola=+hala
holc n? holca? m. *hole, cavity*, Lcd. [' *holk* ']
hold I. *gracious, friendly, kind, favourable, AO,B*; Æ : *true, faithful, loyal*, Æ,LL; CP : *devout : acceptable, pleasant.* [' *hold* '] adv. holde, *Ps.* [' *holde* '] **II.** n. *dead body, carcase, Mt*; Æ. [' *hold* '] **III.** m. *holder of allodial land, ranking below a jarl (Danish title)*, LL : *notable, chief*, MkR6²¹. [*ON.* holdr]
holdāð m. *oath of allegiance*, CHR1085.
holdelīce=holdlīce
holdhlāford m. *gracious lord, liege lord*, CHR 1014E.
holdian *to cut up, disembowel*, ÆL23⁷⁸. [hold II.]
holdingstōw f. *slaughterhouse*, KC.
holdlīc *faithful, friendly*, OEG50²⁹. adv. -līce *graciously*, Æ,WW : *faithfully, loyally : devoutly.* [' *holdely* ']
holdrǣden f. *faithful service*, ÆH2·150³⁰.
holdscipe m. *loyalty, allegiance*, CHR.
holecerse *a plant*, LCD29b.
holegn=holen I.
holen I. m. ' *holly*,' WW; Æ; Mdf. adj. *of holly.* **II.** pp. of helan.
hōlenga=hōlinga
holenlēaf n. *holly leaf*, LCD127a.
holenrind f. *holly bark*, LCD29b.
holenstybb m. *holly-stump*, KC3·338'.
holh (*CP*), holg n. gs. hōles *hole*, ' *hollow*.'

hollan *to hollow out, scoop out*, Æ : *to become hollow, be perforated*, Æ. [' *hole* ']
hōlian *to oppress*, LPs. [' *hole* ']
+hollan *to obtain*, CP209¹⁹.
holing f. *hollow place*, GD113¹¹.
hōlinga (o², u²) adv. *in vain, without reason*, BH,LL.
holl=hol II.
hollēac n. *a kind of onion*, WW270²⁹. [' *holleke* ']
holm m. †*wave, sea, ocean, water, B* : (in prose, esp. in place-names) *island* (esp. in a river or creek), *Chr.* [' *holm* ']
holmærn n. *ship*, GEN1422.
holmclift† n. *sea-cliff, rocky shore*, B.
holmeg adj. *of the sea*, Ex118.
holmmægen n. *force of the waves*, RD3⁹.
holm-ōracu† f., gs. -ōræce *restless sea.*
holmweall m. *wall of sea water*, Ex467.
holmweard (AN359)=helmweard
holmweg m. *sea-path*, AN382.
holmwylm m. *billows*, B2411.
holnes f. *hollow place*, GDo99²².
holoc=holc
hōlonga=hōlinga
holpen pp. of helpan.
holrian=heolorian
holstæf m. ' *apex*,' *tittle*, MtR5¹⁸.
holt nm. *forest, wood, grove, thicket*, Æ,B; CP; Mdf : *wood, timber, Jul.* [' *holt* ']
holt-hana, -ana m. *woodcock*, WW344³⁰.
hōltihte f. *calumny*, WW116²⁵,198³.
holtwudu† m. *forest, grove, Ph* : *wood (timber).* [v. ' *holt* ']
hōlunga=hōlinga; **hom**=ham
hōm=ōm; **hōman**=ōman
hōn I. (sv⁷) pret. heng, pp. hangen *to hang, suspend, crucify*, Æ : *put on (clothes)*, Bo 42¹⁵n. **II.** pl. *tendrils of a vine?* A4·143.
hon-=han-; **hona**=(1) heonu; (2) hana
hōnende *having heels*, WW161²⁶. [hōh]
+honge=+hange
hongen pp. of hōn.
hop n. *privet?* OEG36¹⁴ (but v. BTs) : *enclosed land in a marsh*, KC6·243¹⁴.
hōp m. *hoop?* NR22; v. NC303.
-hop v. fen-, mōr-h.
hopa m. ' *hope*,' Æ. [usu. tōhopa]
hōpgehnāst n. *dashing of waves*, RD4²⁷.
±hopian *to* ' *hope*,' *expect, look for*, Æ,Bf; CP : *put trust in*, Æ,Bo,Bl.
hōpig *eddying, surging*, PPs68².
+hopp n. *small bag, seed-pod*, WW405³.
hoppāda m. *upper garment, cope*, WW188¹⁴.
hoppe f. *a kind of ornament*, AO : *dog-collar*, LL194,8.
hoppestre f. *female dancer*, Æ. [' *hoppestere* ']
hoppetan *to hop, leap for joy : to throb.*

hoppian to '*hop*,' *leap, dance,* Æ : *limp,* ÆL21⁴¹⁷.

hopscȳte f. *sheet, counterpane,* Æ(9³⁰⁷).

hopsteort *train of a dress,* WW438¹⁶ (v. BTs).

hōr n. *adultery* (Swt).

hora-=horu-; **horas** v. horh.

hōrcwene f. *whore, adulteress,* LL.

hord nm. '*hoard*,' *treasure,* B,Chr,Cr,Gen, MtR,WW.

hordærn=hordern

hordburg f. *treasure-city,* B,BC,GEN.

hord-cleofa, -clyfa m. *treasure-chest, treasury, secret chamber,* Æ.

hordcofa m. *treasure-chamber, closet* : (†) *breast, heart, thoughts.*

hordere m. *treasurer, chamberlain, steward,* Æ,KC. ['*hoarder*']

hordern n. *treasury, storehouse,* B,LL.

horderwȳce f. *office of treasurer,* CHR 1137.

hordfæt n. *treasure-receptacle,* Æ.

hord-geat n., gs. -gates *door of a treasure-chamber,* RD43¹¹.

hordgestrēon† n. *hoarded treasure.*

hordian to '*hoard*,' Æ.

hordloca m. *treasure-chest, coffer* : (†) *secret thoughts, mind.*

hordmægen n. *riches,* DA675.

hordmāðm† m. *hoarded treasure,* B.

hordweard m. *guardian of treasure* : *king* : *heir, first-born.*

hordwela m. *hoarded wealth,* B2344.

hordweorðung f. *honouring by gifts,* B952.

hordwynn f. *delightful treasure,* B2270.

hordwyrðe *worth hoarding,* B2245?

hōre f. *whore, prostitute,* OEG.

horeht=horwiht

+**hor(g)ian** to *defile,* BK : *spit upon,* NG.

horh (horg) mn., gs. hor(w)es, instr. horu, nap. horas *phlegm, mucus,* Æ,El,Ep,Lcd : *dirt, defilement, uncleanness;* Mdf. ['*hore*']

horheht=horwiht

+**horian** (N)=+horgian

horig *foul, filthy,* Æ,ApT,LL. ['*hory*']

hōring m. *adulterer, fornicator,* W309²¹.

horn m. '*HORN*' (*musical instrument, drinking-horn, cupping-horn*), *beast's horn,* AO : *projection, pinnacle.*

hornbǣre *horned,* ÆGR27¹⁶.

hornblāwere m. '*horn-blower*,' *trumpeter,* Gl.

hornboga† m. *bow tipped with horn? curved like a horn?*

hornbora m. *horn-bearer, trumpeter,* WW.

hornede *having horns,* AA19¹³.

hornfisc m. *garfish,* AN370.

hornfōted *hoofed,* WW213²².

horngēap† *broad between the gables,* ES 64·207.

horngestrēon n. *wealth of pinnacles (on a house)?* [or ?=hordgestrēon], RUIN23.

+**hornian** to *insult,* MkL12⁴. [?=+horgian]

hornlēas *without horns,* ES39·349.

hornpic m. *pinnacle,* MtL. [v. '*pike*']

hornreced n. *hall with gables,* B704.

hornsæl n.=hornsele

hornscēað f. *pinnacle,* MtL4⁵.

hornscip n. *beaked ship,* AN274.

hornsele m. *house with gables,* GEN1821.

hornungsunu m. *bastard,* WW456¹⁰.

horo-=horu-

horpytt m. *mud-hole,* EC445¹⁵.

hors n. '*horse*,' OET,WW,VPs; Æ,AO,CP.

horsbǣr f. *horse-litter,* BH; ÆL. ['*horsebier*']

horsc I. *sharp, active, ready, daring* : *quick-witted, wise, prudent.* II. *foul,* KC3·456¹⁶.

horscamb m. '*horse-comb*,' *curry-comb, strigil,* WW.

horschwæl (=*horshwæl) m. '*walrus*,' AO 17³⁶. [v. '*horse*']

horsclic *squalid, foul,* OEG1789. [horh]

horsclīce *briskly, readily, promptly* : *prudently, wisely,* GL.

horscniht m. *groom, esquire,* Æ(8²⁴²).

horscræt n. '*biga*,' *chariot,* WW194²⁸.

horselene f. *elecampane,* WW. ['*horseheal*']

horsern n. *stable,* WW.

horsgærstūn m. *meadow in which horses are kept,* KC3·414'. [v. '*horse*']

horshelene=horselene

horshere m. *mounted force* (BTs).

horshierde (i², y²) m. *ostler, groom,* GL.

±**horsian** to *provide with horses,* AO,Chr. ['*horse*,' '*y-horsed*']

horslīce=horsclīce

horsminte *wild mint,* LCD187b.

horspæð m. *horse-track,* KC5·157'.

hors-ðegn, -ðēn m. *ostler, groom, equerry* : *muleteer.*

horswǣn m. *chariot,* WW140⁴.

horswealh m. *groom, equerry,* LL22; 132.

horsweard f. *care of horses,* LL445,2.

horsweg m. *bridle-road,* KC. ['*horseway*']

hortan sbpl. '*whortle*'-*berries,* v. OEG2⁴³³.

horu=horh

horusēað m. *sink, pit,* Bo112¹⁵.

horuweg (o²) m. *dirty road?* KC5·173¹⁷.

horweht=horwiht; **horwes** v. horh.

horwig=orweg

+**horwigian**=+horgian

horwiht (e²) *mucose, defiled, filthy,* GUTH 36⁹.

horwyll m. *muddy stream,* EC445¹⁹.

horxlic=horsclic

hos *shoot, tendril,* GL.

hōs I. f. *escort, company,* B924. II. v. hōh.

hosa m., **hose** f. '*hose*,' WW.

hosebend m. *hose-band, garter,* OEG 4822.
hosp m. *reproach, insult,* Æ : *blasphemy,* Æ.
hospcwlde m. *insulting speech,* EL 523.
hospettan *to ridicule,* Cp 697 s.
hosplic *insulting,* ÆH 2·232³¹.
hospsprǣc f. *jeer, taunt,* ÆH 2·514¹¹.
hospul *despised,* RPs 88³⁵.
hospword n. *abusive language, contemptuous expression,* Æ.
hoss=hos; **hosse**=hyse
hōstig (ÆL 35¹⁹²)=ōstig
hosu f. *hose,* RB : *pod, husk,* Cp 1867.
hotor=otor
hoðma† m. *darkness, the grave.*
hr-=r-
hrā=hrǣw
hraca? m. (*Lcd*)=hrace
hrāca (ǣ) m. *clearing of the throat* : *mucus.*
hracca (e, ea) '*occiput,*' WW 463²¹.
hrace, hracu (æ) f. *throat,* Æ, VPs : *gorge,* KC 3·440'. ['*rake*']
hrad- v. hræd-; **hrade**=hraðe
±**hradian** (ea, ð) *to be quick, hasten, come quickly* : *do quickly or diligently* : *put briefly,* BF 52⁸ : *further, prosper,* ÆL 20⁷⁸.
hradung (æ) f. *quickness, despatch, diligence.*
hræ-=hra-, hre-, hrea-
hrǣ=hrǣw; **hrǣ-**=hrēa-, hrēo-, rǣ-
hrǣcan tr. and intr. *to 'reach,' bring up* (*blood or phlegm*), CP,Lcd; Æ.
+**hrǣcan**=+reccan
hrǣcea m. *clearing of the throat,* LCD 9a. [=hrāca]
hrǣcetan *to eructate,* LCD 84a.
hrǣcetung f. *eructation,* LCD 69b.
hrǣcgebrǣc n. *sore throat,* WW.
hrǣcing=ræcing
hrǣctan=hræcetan
hrǣctunge f. *uvula,* LCD 17a.
hrǣcung f. *clearing of the throat,* Lcd : *phlegm,* WW 162³⁴. ['*reaching*']
hrǣd (e) (hrad- occly. in obl. cases) *quick, nimble, ready, active, alert, prompt,* Bo,CP, Gl,Mt. ['*rad*']
hrǣdbita m. *blackbeetle,* WW (hrǣð-).
hrǣdfērnes f. *swiftness,* Bo 72¹⁷.
hrǣdhȳdig *hasty* (Swt).
hrǣdhȳdignes f. *haste, precipitation,* CP.
hrǣding f. *haste.* on hrǣdinge *quickly,* Æ, W.
hrǣdlic (ð) *quick, sudden, premature,* Æ, AO,CP. adv. -līce *hastily, soon, forthwith,* B,Bo,DR; Æ,CP. ['*radly*,' '*rathely*']
hrǣdlicnes (e) f. *suddenness,* GUTH : *earliness,* EPs 118¹⁴⁷.
hrǣdmōd *hasty,* ÆL 16³⁴².
Hrǣdmōnað=Hrēðmōnað
hrǣdnes f. (eð) *quickness, promptitude* : *brevity.*

hrǣdrīpe (ræd-) *ripening early,* WW.
hrǣdtæfle *quick at throwing dice?* CRA 73 (v. ES 43·339).
hrǣdung=hradung
hrǣdwǣn m. *swift chariot,* MET 24⁴¹.
hrǣdwilnes f. *haste, precipitation,* CP.
hrǣdwyrde *hasty of speech,* WA 66.
hrǣfn I. hræfen (e) m. *raven,* Æ,B,G,Gl, Ma,VPs : *sign of the raven* (*the Danish banner*). II.=hæfern
hrǣfncynn (e) n. *raven-species,* Æ.
hrǣfnesfōt m. *ravensfoot, cinquefoil,* Gl, Lcd.
hrǣfneslēac *orchid,* LCD.
-hrǣgan v. ofer-hr.
hrǣge=rǣge; **hrǣgel**=hrǣgl
hrǣgelgefrǣtwodnes f. *fine clothing,* LL (396²⁷).
hrǣgelðegn m. *keeper of the robes.*
hrǣgl n. (e) *dress, clothing,* Gl,Jn; AO : *vestment,* CP : *cloth, sheet* : *armour* : *sail,* BF 14⁷. ['*rail*']
hrǣglcyst f. *clothes-box, trunk,* Ct.
hrǣglgewǣde n. *dress,* WW 430³³.
hrǣglhūs f. *vestry,* RB.
hrǣglscēara fp. *tailors' shears,* WW 241⁴⁰ (rægl-).
hrǣgltalu f. *clothing store,* KC,RB (v. BTs).
hrǣglung f. *clothing,* WW 151⁵.
hrǣglweard m. *keeper of vestments or robes,* WW 279¹⁹.
hrǣgnloca=brægnloca
hrǣmn, hrǣm=hræfn; **hrǣn**=hærn
hrǣron pret. pl. of hreran.
hrǣs v. hrǣw and rǣs.
hrǣscetung=ræscetung
-hrǣscian v. ā-hr.
hrǣtelwyrt f. *rattlewort,* WW 301³.
hrǣð=hrǣd. ['*rathe*']
hrǣw I. (ā, ēa) nm. gs. hrǣs *living body* : *corpse, carcase, carrion.* II.=hrēaw I.
hrǣwīc (hrēa-) n. *place of corpses,* B 1214.
hrāfyll m. *slaughter,* B 277.
hrāgīfre *deadly,* WW 408¹⁰.
hrāgra m. *heron,* GL.
hrālic=hrāwlic
hramgealla=ramgealla; **hrāmig**=hrēmig
hramma m. *cramp, spasm,* LCD,WW.
hram-sa (o) m., -se f. *onion, garlic,* Gl,Lcd, WW. ['*rams,*' '*ramson*']
hramsacrop m. *head of wild garlic,* GL.
hran (o) m. *whale,* GL.
hrān I. m. *reindeer,* AO. II. pret. 3 sg. of hrīnan.
hrand I.=rand. II. pret. 3 sg. of hrindan.
hrandsparwa (o¹) m. *sparrow,* MtL 10²⁹.
hranfix (o) m. *whale,* AA 33⁷,B 540.
hrānhund? m. *deerhound?* v. LL 2·117.

hranmere (o) m. *sea,* MET 5¹⁰.
hranrād† f. *(whale's-road), sea.*
hratele f. *'bobonica' (plant),* WW 296².
['*rattle*']
hratian *to rush, hasten,* OET (=hradian?).
hraðe (æ, e) I. *quick,* Bo,Chr,PPs. II. adv.
comp. hraðor, superl. hraðost *hastily,
quickly, promptly, readily, immediately,
soon,* Æ,B,Bo,Cr,G,Ps; CP : *too soon,* Bo.
swā h. swā *as soon as,* Æ. ['*rathe,*' '*rather,*'
'*rathest*']
hraðer=hreðer; **hraðian**=hradian
hrāw=hrǣw
hrāwērig *weary in body,* PH 554.
hrāwlic *funereal,* WW 406¹.
hrēa I. f. *indigestion?* LCD 94b. [hrēaw I.]
II.=hrēaw I. and II.
hrēac m. '*rick,*' *heap, stack,* TC,WW.
hrēaccopp m. *top of a rick,* LL 453,21⁴.
hrēacmete m. *food given to the labourers on
completing a rick,* LL 452'.
hrēad-=hrēod-
-hrēad v. earm-hr. [hrēoðan]
hrēaf=rēaf
hrēam m. *noise, outcry, alarm,* Æ,CP : *cry,
lamentation, sorrow,* B,Cr. ['*ream*']
hrēamig=hrēmig
hrēanes=hrēohnes
hrēas pret. 3 sg. of hrēosan.
hrēat pret. 3 sg. of hrūtan.
hreaðemūs (a²) f. *bat,* AA,LCD.
hreaðian (VPs)=hradian
hrēaw I. '*raw,*' *uncooked,* Æ,Lcd. II.=
hrǣw nm. III. pret. 3 sg. of hrēowan.
hrēaw-=hrēow-
hrēawan *to be raw,* WW 215⁴³ (rēaw-).
hrēawic=hrǣwīc
hrēawnes I. f. *rawness,* OEG 3283. II.=
hrēownes
+hrec=+rec; **hrēc-**=hrǣc-
hrecca=hracca
hred (KGl)=hrǣd; **-hreda** v. æfreda.
hreddan *to free from, recover, rescue, save,*
Cr; Æ : *take away.* ['*redd*']
hreddere m. *defender,* CHRD 94⁴.
hreddung (æ) f. *salvation, liberation,* Æ.
Hredmōnað=Hrēðmōnað
±hrēfan *to roof,* Æ. [hrōf]
hrefn=(1) hræfn; (2) hæfern
hrefnan=ræfnan
hrefncynn=hræfncynn
hregresi? *groin,* MLN 11·333; ZDA 33·244.
hrēh=hrēoh; **hrem**=hræfn I.
hrēman I.† *to boast.* [Ger. rühmen] II.=
hrīeman
hrēmig (ēa)† *boasting, vaunting, exulting :
clamorous, loud.*
hremm=hræfn I.
±hremman *to hinder, cumber,* Æ.

hremming f. *hindrance, obstacle,* GL,LCD.
hremn=hræfn I.
hrenian *to smell of, be redolent of,* SC 106⁵.
hrēo=hrēoh, hrēow; **hrēocan**=rēocan
hrēod n. '*reed,*'*rush,* Æ,BH,Gl,LG; CP; Mdf.
hrēodan² *to adorn* (only in pp. ±hroden).
hrēodbedd n. '*reed-bed,*' Æ.
hrēodcynn n. *kind of reed,* NC 303.
hrēod-ig, -iht, -ihtig (e²) *reedy,* KC,WW.
hrēodpīpere m. *flute-player,* WW 190⁷.
hrēodwæter n. *reedy marsh,* AA 30¹⁹.
hrēof *rough, scabby, leprous,* Wh; CP. as
sb.=*leper.* ['*reof*']
-hrēofian v. ā-hr.
hrēofl I. f. *scabbiness, leprosy,* CP. II. adj.
leprous.
hrēofla m. *roughness of the skin, leprosy,*
Æ : *leper,* Æ. [hrēof]
hrēof-lic, -lig (Æ) *leprous, suffering from
skin-disease.*
hrēofnes f. *leprosy,* NUM 12¹⁰.
hrēofol, hrēoful=hrēofl I.
hrēog=hrēoh
hrēogan *to become stormy,* AA 34¹⁹.
hrēoh (ē) I. adj. *rough, fierce, wild, angry,*
Met; Æ,AO,CP : *disturbed, troubled, sad*
(v. hrēow) : *stormy, tempestuous,* B,Bo,
Chr. ['*reh*'] II. n. *stormy weather, tempest.*
hrēohful *stormy,* ES 39·349.
hrēohlic *stormy, tempestuous,* W 136²⁷.
hrēohmōd† *savage, ferocious :* sad, troubled.
hrēohnes (ēa) f. *rough weather, storm,* Æ.
hrēol sb. '*reel,*' LL,WW ; Æ.
hrēon-=rēon-
hrēones=(1) hrēohnes; (2) hrēownes
hrēop pret. 3 sg. of hrōpan.
hreopian=hrepian
hrēorig adj. *in ruins,* RUIN 3. [hrēosan]
±hrēosan² *to fall, sink, fall down, go to ruin,*
Æ,B,Cr,VPs; AO,CP : *rush* : *rush upon,
attack.* ['*reose*']
hrēosendlic *perishable : ready to fall,* OEG.
hrēosian=hrēowsian
hrēoð (KGl) pres. 3 sg. of hrēosan.
-hrēoða (ē, ēa) v. bord-, scild-hr.
hrēoung (īu) f. *hardness of breathing,* LCD,
WW.
±hrēow I. f. *sorrow, regret, penitence, repentance, penance,* B,Bl,CP,Cr. ['*rue*'] II.
sorrowful, repentant, BH 352⁵. III. adj.=
hrēoh? IV. *raw,* Ex 12⁹. ['*row*']
±hrēowan² (often impersonal w. d. pers.)
to affect one with regret or contrition, Bo,
CP,Gen,LL : *distress, grieve,* Cr,Gen :
(intr.) *be penitent, repent,* MkL. ['*rue,*'
'*i-rew*']
hrēowcearig† *troubled, sad.*
hrēowende (ǣ) *penitent,* LkL. ['*rueing*']
hrēowesung=hrēowsung

hrēowian *to repent*, MkL 1¹⁵.

hrēowig *sorrowful, sad*, GEN 799.

hrēowigmōd† *sad, sorrowful*.

hrēowlic (ī, ȳ) *grievous, pitiful, sad, wretched, cruel*, Chr,Ps. adv. -lice, AO,Chr. ['*ruly*']

hrēownes (ēa) f. *penitence, contrition, repentance*, Gl,LL; CP. ['*rueness*,' '*rewniss*']

hrēowon=rēowon pret. pl. of rōwan.

hrēowsende=hrēosende, v. hrēosan

±hrēowsian (ȳ) *to feel sorrow or penitence*, AO,Mt; CP : *do penance*, HL 149¹²⁶. ['*reusie*']

hrēowsung f. *repentance, penitence, sorrow*, CP,Lk; Æ. ['*reusing*']

hrēpan *to cry out*, WW 375¹⁰.

±hrepian (eo), hreppan *to touch, treat (of)*, Mt; Æ : *attack*, BK 6. ['*repe*']

hrepsung (ÆL)=repsung

hrepung f. *sense of touch, touch*, Æ.

±hrēran (tr.) *to move, shake, agitate.* [hrōr; *Ger.* rühren]

hrēre *lightly boiled*, Lcd. ['*rear*']

hrērednes (ȳ) f. *haste*, LPs 51⁶.

hrēremus f. *bat*, WW. ['*rearmouse*'; hrēran]

hrēr(e)nes (ȳ) f. *disturbance, commotion, tempest*.

hresl=hrisil

+hresp n. *stripping, spoliation*, NC 294.

+hrespan *to strip, spoil*, PPs 43¹².

hrēst=hrȳst pres. 3 sg. of hrēosan.

hreð=hræd

hrēð† mn. *victory, glory*.

hrēða m. *covering of goat-skin, mantle*, GL.

hrēðan *to exult, rejoice*, Ex 573.

hreðe=hraðe; hrēðe=rēðe

hrēðeadig† *glorious, victorious*.

Hrēðemōnað=Hrēðmōnað

hreðer† (a, æ) mn. *breast, bosom : heart, mind, thought : womb*.

hreðerbealo n. *heart-sorrow*, B 1343.

hreðercofa m. *breast*, CR 1323.

hreðergleaw *wise, prudent*, Ex 13.

hreðerloca† m. *breast*.

-hrēðig v. ēad-, sige-, will-hr.

hrēðlēas *inglorious*, Gu 878.

Hrēðmōnað m. *month of March*, MH.

hrēðnes=rēðnes; hrēðor=hrēðer

hrēðsigor m. *glorious victory*, B 2583.

hricg=hrycg

hrician *to cut, cut to pieces*, ÆL 23⁷³.

hricsc *rick, wrench, sprain*, LCD 27a.

hriddel n. '*riddle*,' *sieve*, LL 455,17.

hridder(n), hrider n. *sieve* Æ,GL; GD. ['*ridder*']

hrīdrian *to sift, winnow*, Lk. ['*ridder*']

±hrīeman (ē, ī, ȳ) *to cry out : shout, rave*, Æ,CP : *bewail, lament*, JnL. ['*reme*']

+hriered *destroyed*, WW 496¹⁸.

hriewð pres. 3 sg. of hrēowan.

±hrif n. *belly, womb*, Æ,AO.

hrif (AA 8¹)=rif

+hrifian *to bring forth*, LPs 7¹⁵.

+hrifnian (ī?) *to tear off? become rapacious?* AO 142²⁶.

hriftēung f. *pain in the bowels*, WW 112²³.

hrifðo f. *scurfiness*, LCD 90b. [hrēof]

hrifwerc m. *pain in the bowels*, WW 112²³.

hrifwund *wounded in the belly*, LL 6,61.

hrig=hrycg

hrīm m. '*rime*,' *hoar-frost*, Cp,Ph; Æ.

hrīman=hrīeman

-hrīman v. be-hr.

hrīmceald *icy cold*, WA 4.

hrīmforst m. *hoar-frost*, LPs 77⁴⁷ (rīm-).

hrīmgicel m. *icicle*, SEAF 17.

hrīmig *rimy, frosty*, BL.

hrīmigheard *frozen hard*, RD 88⁷.

hrimpan (rim-) pp. (h)rumpen *to twist, coil*, WW 366⁴⁰.

+hrin n. *morsel*, EPs 147¹⁷.

+hrīn (NG)=+rīn=+rēn

±hrīnan¹ (w. a. g. or d.) *to touch, lay hold of, reach, seize, strike*, B,Ps : *have connection with*, DR 106'. ['*rine*']

hrincg=hring; hrind=rind

hrindan² *to thrust, push*, RD 55⁴.

±hrine m. *sense of touch : touch : contact*, AA 41²⁷.

±hrinenes f. *touch, contact*, BH.

hring I. m. RING, *link of chain, fetter, festoon*, CP : *anything circular, circle, circular group*, Ph : *border, horizon*, Gen : (†) (pl.) *rings of gold (as ornaments and as money)* : (†) *corslet : circuit (of a year), cycle, course : orb, globe.* II.† m. (only in wōpes hr.) *sound? flood? (of tears, v.* BTs).

hringādl (? br-) f. *a disease, ringworm?* MLR 19·201.

hringan *to '*ring*,' sound, clash*, B,Sol : *announce by bells*, RB.

hringbān n. *ring-shaped bone*, WW 157. ['*ringbone*']

hringboga m. *coiled serpent*, B 2561.

hringe f. *ring*, Æ,GL.

hringed† *made of rings*, B.

hringedstefna† m. *ring-prowed ship*, B.

hring-fāg, -fāh *ring-spotted, variegated*, GEN 37³.

hringfinger m. '*ring-finger*,' Lcd,WW.

hringgeat n? *ring-gate*, RUIN 4.

hringgewindla m. *sphere*, WW 426²⁵.

hringīren n. *ring-mail*, B 322.

hringloca m. *coat of ring-mail*, MA 145.

hringmǣl *sword with ring-like patterns*, B.

hringmǣled *adorned with rings (of a sword)*, GEN 1992.

hringmere n. *bath*, RUIN 455.

hringnaca m. *ring-prowed ship*, B1863.
hringnett n. *ring-mail*, B1889.
hringpytt m. *round pit*, KC.
hringsele† m. *hall in which rings are bestowed*, B.
hringsetl n. *circus*, OEG.
hringsittend m. *spectator, onlooker*, OEG65.
hringöegu† f. *receiving of rings*.
hringweorðung f. *ring-ornament, costly ring, rings*, B3017.
hringwīsan adv. *ringwise, in rings*, AA23¹⁴.
hringwyll m. *circular well*, KC.
hrīning f. *touch*, JnL. [v. '*rine*']
+hriorde (w)=+reorde; **hrīp-**=rīp-
hrīs I. n. *twig, branch*. II. *covered with brushwood?* KC.
hrīsc=risc; **hrīscan**=hrȳscan
hrīseht *bushy, bristly*, WW513⁸.
hrisel=rysel
hrīsel, hrīs(i)l f? *shuttle : bone of the lower arm, radius*. [hrisian]
hrisian (y) (tr. and intr.) *to shake, move, be shaken, clatter*, An,B,Ps,VPs : (+) *to shake together*, WW370,485. ['*rese*']
hrīsig (rȳsig) *bushy*, OEG8³³⁷.
hrīst pres. 3 sg. of hrēosan.
hrīstle f. *rattle*, WW391¹⁸.
hrīstlende *noisy, creaky*, WW504⁸.
hrīstung f. *quivering, rattling noise*, LCD 97a.
hrīð (u) m. *fever*, LCD80a.
hrīð I. f. *snow-storm, tempest*, WA102. II.= hrīðer
hrīðādl f. *fever*, LCD80a.
hrīðer (ȳ) n. *neat cattle, ox, bull, cow, heifer*, Bl,Ct,Lcd,WW. ['*rother*']
hrīðeren *of cattle*, Lcd. ['*rotheren*']
hrīðerfrēols (ȳ) m. *sacrifice of a bull*, OEG 4719.
hrīðerhēawere (ȳ) m. *butcher*, WW129¹⁶.
hrīðerheord (ȳ) *herd of cattle*, Æ. [v. '*rother*']
hrīðerhyrde (ȳ) m. *herdsman*, ÆH1·322'.
hrīðfald m. *cattle-pen*, WW195³⁴.
hrīðheorde (ie)=hrīðerhyrde
hrīðian *to shake, be feverish, have a fever*, Æ.
hrīðig (ȳ) *storm-beaten? ruined?* WA77.
hrīðing f. *fever*, LCD96b.
hrīung=hrēoung; **hrīw-**=hrēow-
hrīwð pres. 3 sg. of hrēowan.
hrōc m. '*rook*,' ÆL,Cp.
hrōd=rōd
hroden I. (±) *covered, adorned, ornamented* (pp. of hrēodan). II.=roden
hroder=rodor
hrōf m. '*roof*,' *ceiling*, Æ,B,Cr,G ; AO,CP : *top, summit*, Bo,Cr,Mk : *heaven, sky*, Cr.
hrōffæst *with a firm roof*, MET7⁶.
hrōflēas (rōf-) *roofless*, WW186³⁰.

hrōfsele m. *roofed hall*, B1515.
hrōfstān m. *roof stone*, ÆH1·508'.
hrōftīgel f. *roofing tile*, WW.
hrōftimber n. *material for roofing*, OEG 2256.
hrōfwyrhta m. *roof-maker, builder*, WW.
hrog *mucus from the nose, phlegm*, WW 290³²
hromsa=hramsa; **hron**=hran; **hrop**=rop
hrōp m. *clamour, lamentation*, Bl. ['*rope*']
hrōpan⁷† *to shout, proclaim : cry out, scream, howl*, Gu,Ps. ['*rope*']
-hrops v. ofer-hr.
hropwyrc=ropwærc
hrōr *stirring, busy, active : strong, brave*.
+hror n. *calamity, plague, ruin*, BH284⁴. [hrēosan]
±hroren pp. of hrēosan.
+hrorenes f. *downfall, ruin*, LPs31⁴.
+hrorenlic *perishable, transitory, unstable*, NC294; MFH147.
hrōse=rōse
hrōst m. *perch*, '*roost*,' LL454,11.
hrōstbēag m. *woodwork (of a roof)*, RUIN32.
hrot m. *scum*, LCD84a.
hrōðer=hrōðor
hrōðgirela m. *crown*, RPs20⁴.
hroðhund (A8·450)=roðhund
hrōðor† m. *solace, joy, pleasure : benefit*.
hrūm m. *soot*, MH,WW.
-hrūmian v. be-hr.
hrūmig *sooty*, WW362¹².
hrumpen v. hrimpan.
hrung f. *cross-bar, spoke*, Rd23¹⁰. ['*rung*']
hruron pret. pl. of hrēosan.
hrurul *deciduous*, BDS30·11⁶³.
hrūse† f. *earth, soil, ground*.
hrūt *dark-coloured?* (BTs),WW361¹³.
hrūtan⁶ *to make a noise, whiz, snore*, Æ,Cp. ['*rout*']
hruð=hrið; **hrūðer** (KC)=hrīðer
+hrūxl n. *noise, tumult*, v. ES39·344.
hrūxlian (rūx-) *to make a noise*, MtR9²³.
hryc=hrycg
hrycg (i) m. *back, spine*, Æ,CP,Lcd; AO : '*ridge*,' *elevated surface*, B,Ct,Lk,Ps ; Mdf.
hrycgbān n. *back-bone, spine*, Ps. ['*ridge-bone*']
hrycgbrǣdan (hrig-) pl. *flesh on each side of the spine*, LCD3·118'.
hrycghǣr n. *hair on an animal's back*, LCD 1·360¹⁹.
hrycghrægl (i) n. *mantle*, TC529¹⁰.
hrycg-mearg (i, -mearð) n. *spinal marrow*, WW292⁷.
hrycgme(a)rglið n. *spine*, WW265²³.
hrycgrib (i) n. *rib*, WW.
hrycg-rible, -riple *flesh on each side of the spine*, WW.

hrycgweg m. 'ridge-way,' road on a ridge, Ct.

hrycigan to plough over again, GPH 398.

hrȳding f. clearing, cleared land, WW 147¹².

hrȳfing f. scab, ·LCD 32b. [hrēof]

hryg=hrycg

hrȳman=hrīeman

hrympel? wrinkle, WW 531⁴ (hryp-). [v. 'rimple']

+hryne=+ryne

hryre I. m. fall, descent, ruin, destruction, decay, Æ,B,Bo; AO,CP. ['rure'] II. perishable, Æ.

hrȳre-=hrēr-, hrēre-

hrȳsc a blow, LCD 2b.

hrȳscan to make a noise, creak, v. ES 39·344.

hrysel=rysel; hryslan, hryssan=hrisian

hryst=hyrst

hrȳst pres. 3 sg. of hrēosan.

hrystan=hyrstan

hrȳte (y?) 'balidinus,' WW 163¹⁸ (cp. hrūt).

hrȳðer=hrīðer; hrȳðig=hrīðig

hryðða=ryðða; hrȳwlic=hrēowlic

hrȳwsian=hrēowsian

hrȳwð pres. 3 sg. of hrēowsian.

hū adv. 'HOW,' Æ,CP. hū gerādes; hū meta how. hū gēares at what time of year. hū nyta wherefore. hū ne dōð...? do not...? hū nys...? is not...? : (with comparatives) the : (±) in some way or other, Shr. hū ne nū 'nonne.'

hūcs, hūcx=hūsc

hūdenian to shake, CP 461¹⁶.

hūf=ūf I. and II.

hūfe covering for the head, Cp,WW. ['houve']

hūfian to put a covering on the head, LEV 8¹³.

+hugod minded, GEN 725.

hū-hwega, -hugu somewhere about. h. swā about.

hui! huig! interj.

huilpe=hwilpe

hulc m. I. 'hulk,' ship, LL,WW; Æ. II. hut, Æ,LL,WW.

hulfestre f. plover, WW 287¹⁴.

hūlic pron. of what sort, AO.

hulpon pret. pl. of helpan.

hulu f. husk, pod, WW. ['hull']

hūluco (AO)=hūlic; huma=uma

humele=hymele; hūmen (VHy)=ȳmen

hūmeta adv. in what way, how, Æ.

hun?=hunu

huncettan to limp, halt, RPs 17⁴⁶.

hund I. n. hundred, AO,Bf,G; Æ : (in comp.) decade. ['hund'] II. m. hound, dog, Bo, CP,Jud; Æ,AO : sea-beast (v. sǣhund), OEG.

hundæhtatig (VPs)=hundeahtatig

hundællef- (-ændlæf-)=hundendlufon-

hundeahtatig num. 'eighty,' AO.

hundeahtatigoða eightieth, GEN 5²⁵.

hundeahtatigwintere eighty years old, Æ.

hunden of dogs, canine, BLRPs 77⁴⁵.

hundend-lufontig, -leftig (æ²) hundred and ten, Ct.

hund-endlufontigoða, -ælleftiogoða hundred and tenth, CP 465²³.

hundesbēo (WW 380²¹)=hundespēo

hundescwelcan pl. colocynth berries, WW 364³¹.

hundesflēoge f. dog's parasite, AO,GL.

hundeshēafod n. snapdragon, LCD 2·395.

hundeslūs f. dog's parasite, WW 319⁴.

hundes-micge, -tunge f. cynoglossum (plant), LCD 3·333.

hundes-pēo (CPs), -pīe (VPs 104³¹) f. dog's parasite.

hundeswyrm m. dog's worm, parasite, WW 122²⁵.

hund-feald, -fealdlic hundred-fold, Æ. ['hundfold']

hundfrēa m. centurion, MtL 22¹⁹ mg.

hundlic of or like dogs, canine, Æ.

hundnigontēoða ninetieth, Æ.

hundnigontig ninety, Mt. [v. 'hund']

hundnigontiggēare ninety years (old), GEN 5⁹.

hundnigontigoða ninetieth, Æ,CP.

hundnigontigwintre ninety years old, GEN 17¹⁷.

hund-red, -rað n. 'hundred' (number), Bf, G,Ps,WW; Æ : hundred (political district), hundred-court, assembly of the men of a hundred, LL. hundredes ealdor, mann head of the hundred court, centurion.

hundredgemōt n. hundred-moot, LL.

hundredmann m. centurion, Æ : captain of a hundred, Ex 18²¹,DEUT 1¹⁵.

hundredpenig m. contribution levied by the sheriff or lord of the hundred for the support of his office, TC 432,433.

hundredseten f. rules of the hundred, LL.

hundredsōcn f. attendance at the hundred-moot : fine for non-attendance, Ct.

hundreð (MkR)=hundred

hundseofontig num. seventy, Mt; Æ. [v. 'hund']

hundseofontigfeald seventy-fold, ÆH.

hundseofontiggēare seventy years (old), GEN 5¹².

hundseofontigoða seventieth, CP (io², io⁴).

hundseofontigseofonfeald seventy-seven-fold, GEN 4²⁴.

hundseofontigwintre seventy years old, GEN 5³¹.

hundtēontig hundred, Æ,Gen,Shr. [v. 'hund']

hundtēontig-feald, -fealdlic hundred-fold. adv. -līce, W 237⁹.

hundtēontiggēare *a hundred years old*, Æ.
hundtēontigōða *hundredth*, ÆGR,RB.
hundtēontigwintre *a hundred years old*, NC 303.
hundtwelftig *hundred and twenty*, AO.
hundtwelftigwintre *aged a hundred and twenty*, DEUTC31².
hundtwentig *hundred and twenty*, ÆT.
hundtwentigwintre *aged a hundred and twenty*, DEUT31².
hundwealh (æ²) m. *attendant on dogs*, WW 111²⁵.
hundwelle *a hundred-fold*, MtL13⁸. [= -wille]
hundwintre *aged a hundred years*, Æ (GEN).
hūne f. *horehound*, LCD.
hū ne nū '*nonne*,' RPs52⁵; Hy6⁶.
hunger=hungor
hungerbiten *starving*, CHR1096.
hungergēar mn. *famine-year*, Æ,GEN41⁵⁰.
hungerlǣwe *famishing, starving*, LHy3⁵.
hungerlic *hungry, famishing*, WW.
hungor m. '*hunger*,' *desire*, *An,Cr,VPs, WW*; CP : *famine*, *Æ,Mt,Chr.*
hungrig '*hungry*,' *famishing*, *Gu,MtL*; Æ, AO : *meagre*, OEG.
hungur=hungor
hunig n. '*honey*,' *AO,VPs*; Æ,CP.
hunigæppel m. *pastille of honey?* *Ep,WW.*
hunigbǣre *honeyed*, OEG.
hunigbin f. *vessel for honey*, LL455,17.
hunigcamb f. '*honey-comb*,' Sc50⁹.
hunigflōwende *flowing with honey*, GU1250.
huniggafol n. *rent paid in honey*, LL448,4⁵.
hunigsūge f. *honeysuckle? clover? privet?* *Cp,WW.* ['*honeysuck*']
hunigswēte '*honey-sweet*,' *mellifluous*, Æ.
hunigtēar m. *honey which drips from the comb*, GL,LCD.
hunigtēar-en, -lic *nectar-like*, GL.
huni-sūge, -sūce=hunigsūge
hūnsporu mf. '*dolon*,' *pike?* Cp356D.
hunta m. *huntsman*, Æ,AO : *a kind of spider*, Lcd54a. ['*hunt*']
huntað=huntoð
huntaðfaru f. *hunting expedition*, LL252,22.
±huntian, huntgan *to '*hunt*'* (intr.), Lcd, WW; (tr.) Æ.
huntiege f. *huntress*, A6·188.
huntigspere n. *hunting-spear*, WW142¹².
huntigystre=huntiege
huntoð, huntnoð, huntnold, huntnað m. *hunting, what is caught by hunting, game, prey*. Æ,Ct,Lcd; AO. ['*hunteth*']
huntung f. '*hunting*,' *WW* : *a hunt, chase, DR* : *what is hunted, game*, ES37·188.
hūnðyrlu np. *holes in the upper part of a mast*, WW288¹⁵.
hunu? *a disease*, WW502³¹.

hūon=hwōn; hupbān, huppbān=hypbān
-hupian v. on-h.
hupseax=hypeseax
hurnitu=hyrnetu
hūru adv. *at least, at all events, however, nevertheless, yet, even, only, LL*; Æ : *about, not less than, AO* : *surely, truly, certainly, indeed, especially*, CP. h. swīðost *most particularly*. ['*hure*']
hūruðinga *at least, especially*, Æ.
hūs n. '*house*,' B,G,RB; Æ,AO,CP : *temple, tabernacle, G,Ps* : *dwelling-place, El,Ph* : *inn* : *household, JnL* : *family, racc, Ps.*
±hūsa m. *member of a household*, G.
hūsærn n. *dwelling-house*, CHRD102¹.
hūsbonda (ō²?) m. *householder, master of a house*, Mt,Chr. ['*husband*']
hūsbonde f. *mistress of a house*, Ex3²².
hūsbryce (e², i²) m. *housebreaking, burglary*, LL. ['*housebreach*']
hūsbrycel *burglarious*, WW205²⁸.
hūsbryne m. *burning of a house*, Ct.
hūsbunda=hūsbonda
hūsc n. *mockery, derision, scorn, insult*. Gen,WW. ['*hux*']
hūscarl m. *member of the king's body-guard*, Chr,KC. ['*house carl*'; ON.]
hūsclic *shameful, ignominious, outrageous*, Æ. adv. -lice.
hūscword n. *insulting speech*, An. [v. '*hux*']
+hūsed *furnished with a house*, WW121³².
hūsel n. '*housel*,' *Eucharist*, Æ,BH : *the Host*, LL : *a sacrifice*, MtL12⁷.
hūselbearn (-ul) n. *communicant*, GU531.
hūselbox *housel-box*, ÆP178⁶.
hūseldisc m. *housel-dish, paten*, GL,LCD.
hūsel-fæt n. nap. -fatu *sacrificial or sacramental vessel*, BH,LL.
hūselgang m. *going to, partaking of the Eucharist*, Æ,LL.
hūselgenga m. *communicant*, v. LL2·263.
hūselhālgung f. *attendance at the Eucharist, communicating*, Æ : *Holy Communion*, W34⁵.
hūsellāf f. *remains of the Eucharist*, ÆP27¹⁰.
hūselportic (u²) m. *sacristy*, BH94¹⁰.
hūselðēn m. *acolyte*, LL.
hūsfæst adj. *occupying a house*, Ct.
hūshefen m. *ceiling*, WW432⁸. [heofon]
hūshlāford m. *master of the house*, Æ.
hūshlēow n. *housing, shelter*, LL(282'); W74⁴.
±hūsian *to '*house*,' receive into one's house*, LL.
hūsincel n. *habitation*, DR,BJVPs.
±hūslian *to administer the sacrament*, A (pp.),LL. ['*housel*']
hūslung f. *administration of the sacrament*, Æ. ['*houseling*']

hūslwer (sel) m. *communicant*, Gu768.

hūsrǣden f. *household, family*, LPs.

±hūsscipe m. *house* (e.g. *of Israel*), *race*, Ps.

hūsstede m. *site of a house*, LCD.

hūsting n. *tribunal, court* (*esp. in London*), Chr. ['*husting*']

hūsul, hūsul=hūs(e)l

hūswist f. *home*, LPs5⁸.

hūð I. f. *plunder, booty, prey*, Æ. II. f., hūðe f.=hȳð

hūx=hūsc

hwā mf., hwæt n. pron. (interrog.) '*who*,' Æ,B,Met : '*what*,' Æ,Bo,Ps; AO,CP : (indef.) *any one, some one, anything, something*, Æ,AO,CP : *each*. swā hwā swā *whosoever*. swā hwæt swā *whatsoever*. tō hwǣm *wherefore*.

+hwā *each one, every one, any one, whoever*.

hwæcce v. hwicce.

+hwǣde *slight, scanty, small, young*, Æ.

hwæder (CP)=hwider

+hwǣdnes f. *smallness, fewness, insignificance*.

hwǣg (ē) n? '*whey*,' Cp,LL.

hwæl I. (usu. hwal- in obl. cases) m. '*whale*,' *walrus*, Æ,AO,Bf. II. pret. 3 sg. of hwelan. III.=hwall. IV. (Ex161)=wæl n?

hwælc (N)=hwilc

hwælen *like a whale*, SoL263.

hwælhunta m. *whale-fisher, whaler*, Æ,AO.

hwælhuntað m. *whale-fishery, whaling*, AO.

hwælmeret m. *sea*, An,Rd.

hwælweg (wæl-) m. *sea*, Seaf63.

hwæm=hwemm

hwǣm (LkL,VPs) ds. of hwā, hwæt. ['*whom*']

+hwǣmlic *each, every*, LkL9²³.

-hwǣnan v. ā-hw.

hwæne (G)=hwone, asm. of hwā.

hwǣne=hwēne

hwænne (G, Ps), hwæne ('*when*')=hwonne

hwær=hwer

hwǣr (ā) adv. and conj. '*WHERE*,' *whither, somewhere, anywhere, everywhere*, CP. wel h. *nearly everywhere*. swā hw. swā *wheresoever, wherever*. elles hw. *elsewhere*. hwǣr...hwǣr *here...there*.

+hwǣr *everywhere, in all directions*, Æ : *on every occasion, always*, Æ,B : *somewhere*. ['*y-where*']

hwærf=hwearf; hwærfan=hwierfan

hwærflung=hwyrflung

hwǣr-hwega, -h(w)ugu *somewhere*.

hwæs I. *sharp, piercing*, Cr1444. II. gs. of hwā, hwæt (CP,G,WW). ['*whose*']

hwǣst m. *blowing*, v. OEG2452n.

hwǣstrian (ā) *to murmur, mutter*, NG.

hwǣstrung (ā) f. *murmur, whispering, muttering*.

hwæt I. (neut. of hwā, which see) adv. *why, wherefore : indeed, surely, truly, for*. interj. '*WHAT*!' *lo!* (calls attention to a following statement) *ah! behold!* Æ. II. adj. (obl. cases have hwat-) *sharp, brisk, quick, active : bold, brave*, B,Cra; AO. ['*what*']
III. (CP) pres. 3 sg. of hwettan.

+hwæt (Cr) neut. of +hwā. ['*i-hwat*']

hwǣte (ē) m. '*wheat*,' *corn*, G,VPs; CP. [hwīt]

hwǣteadig *very brave*, El1195?

hwǣtecorn n. *corn of wheat*, Lcd13a. ['*wheatcorn*']

hwǣtecroft m. *wheat-field*, BC3·135'.

hwǣtecynn n. *wheat*, PPs147³.

hwǣtegryttan pl. *wheaten groats*, WW141²⁰.

hwǣtehealm m. *wheat-straw*, LCD49a.

hwǣteland n. '*wheat-land*,' KC3·159²¹.

hwǣtemelu n. '*wheat-meal*,' Lcd126a.

hwǣten '*wheaten*,' G,Lcd,OET; Æ.

hwǣtesmedma m. *wheat-meal*, LCD.

hwǣtewǣstm m. *corn, wheat*, CPs77²⁵.

hwæthwara=hwæthwugu

hwæt-hwugu, -hwigu, -hugu, -hwega, -hwegu, -hwygu adj. sb. pron. and adv. *somewhat, slightly, a little, something*.

hwæt-hwugununges (CP), -hweganunges, -huguningas adv. *somewhat*.

hwætlīce adv. *quickly, promptly*, Ps. ['*whatliche*']

hwætmōdt *bold, courageous*.

±hwætnes f. *quickness, activity*, Bf,Bo.

hwætrēd (=rǣd) *firm, determined*, Ruin20.

hwætscipe m. *activity, vigour, boldness, bravery*, AO,CP.

hwæðer (e) adj. pron. conj. (with subj.) and adv. '*whether*,' Æ,G : *which of two, 'whether*',' Æ,AO,G. swā hw. swā *whichever*. hwæðer...ðe *whether...or : each of two, both : one of two, either*, CP.

+hwæðer *both, either, each*.

hwæðere, hwæð(ð)re I. adv. *however, yet, nevertheless, still*, B,Lcd; Æ,AO,CP. ['*whether*'] II.=hwæðer adv.

+hwæðere *nevertheless*, Run10.

hwæðreðeah (RPs72¹⁸)=ðeahhwæðre

hwal- v. hwæl; hwalf=hwealf I.

hwall (=æ) *forward, bold*, WW. [hwelan]

hwām (B,Bl,G) ds. of hwā, hwæt. ['*whom*']

hwamm (o) m. *corner, angle, prominence*, Æ,CP : *porch*.

hwamstān (o¹) m. *corner-stone*, MtL21⁴².

hwan=hwon instr. of hwæt.

hwān=hwām; hwanan=hwanon

hwane (Bl)=hwone asm. of hwā.

hwanne (Bl)=hwonne

hwanon, hwanone adv. *whence*, Æ,B,Bo, LG,Mt. ['*when*']

+hwanon adv. *from every quarter*, Æ.

hwanonhwegu adv. *from anywhere*, Ep 1095.

hwǎr (*G*), hwāra (*AO*)=hwǣr

hwarne (*not*) *at all*, MtL8³⁰.

hwǎst-=hwǣst-

hwasta? m. *eunuch*, Mt,WW.

hwat- v. hwæt.

hwat-a I. m. *augur, soothsayer*, Æ. **II.** (æ), -an fpl. *augury, divination*, Æ,*Lev*. ['*whate*']

hwatend '*iris Illyrica*' (*plant*), WW.

hwatu f. *omen*, W.

hwatung f. *augury, divination*, LL.

hwaðer-=hweðer-

hwēal (WW162²⁵)=ðwēal

hwealf I. *concave, hollow, arched, vaulted*. **II.** f. *vault, arch*. [cp. *Ger*. gewölbe]

hwealhafoc=wealhhafoc

hwealp=hwelp

hwearf I.† m. *crowd, troop, concourse*, Gu. ['*wharf*'; hweorfan] **II.** (a, e, eo) m. *exchange* : *what is exchanged* : (+) *vicissitude* : *error*, MtR27⁶⁴ : *going, distance*, LkLR 24¹³. **III.** pret. 3 sg. of hweorfan. **IV.** m. '*wharf*,' *embankment*, Ct.

hwearfan=hwierfan

hwearfian (e, eo) *to turn, roll or toss about, revolve*, GD; Æ : *wave* : *change*, CP : *wander, move, pass by*, AO. ['*wharve*']

hwearflic (e³) *changing, transitory*, Bo 25¹⁰n : *quick, agile*, Fin35? adv. -līce *in turn*.

+hwearfnes f. *conversion*, CP447¹³.

hwearft m. *revolution, circuit, circle* : *lapse* (*of time*).

hwearftlian (y) *to revolve, turn round*, Æ : *wander, be tossed about*, OEG.

hwearfung f. *revolution* : *change, vicissitude* : *exchange*.

hwebbung=webbung; **hweder**=hwider

+hwēdnes (KGL)=+hwǣdnes

hwēg=hwǣg; **hwega** *about, somewhat*.

hwegl=hwēol

hwelan⁴ *to roar, rage*, An495.

hwelc (AO,CP)=hwilc

±hwelian, hwellan? *to suppurate, cause to suppurate, develop weals, come to a head*, CP,Lcd,Sc. ['*wheal*']

hwelp(a) (ea, y) m. '*whelp*,' *the young of an animal, cub*, Lcd,LG,Sc,VPs,WW ; AO.

hwelung f. *din*, WW423²⁰.

hwem=hwemm

hwemdragen *sloping, slanting*, Bl207¹⁷.

hwemm (æ) m. *corner, angle*, Æ. [hwamm]

±hwemman *to bend, turn, incline*, Chr 1052.

hwēne (ǣ) adv. *somewhat, a little*, Æ,AO,CP. [instr. of hwōn]

hweogl=hwēol

hwēol, hweogol, hweohl n. '*wheel*,' Bo,Lcd, MH,OEG : (*as instrument of torture*) ÆL, Bo : *circle*, Bo,DHy,MH.

hwēolfāg *having a circular border or decoration*, WW375³².

hwēolgodweb n. *robe with a circular border?* WW382³⁵ (hwegl-).

hwēollāst m. *orbit*, DHy93¹⁷.

hwēolrād f. *rut, orbit*, Cp2330.

hwēolrīðig n. *a brook that turns a wheel*, KC 3·289,381.

hwēolweg m. *cart-road*, KC3·386⁴.

hwěop pret. 3 sg. of hwōpan.

+hweorf I. n. *a turning*, Lcd91a. **II.** *converted*, MtR18³ (+werf) : *active?* Cra68.

hweorfa m. *joint* : *whorl of a spindle*, Lcd. ['*wharve*']

±hweorfan³ (o, u) *to turn*, Bo : *change*, CP : *turn out*, Bo : *move, go, come* : *wander about, roam, go about*, GD : *turn back, return, turn from, depart* : *die* : *be converted*. feohtan mid hweorfendum sigum *to fight with varying success*, AO. ['*wharve*']

hweorfbān (u, y) n. *joint, kneecap*, Lcd, WW.

hweorfian=hwearfian

hwěos pret. 3 sg. of hwōsan.

hweoða=hwiða

hweowl, hweowol=hwēol

hwer (æ, y) m. *pot, bowl, kettle, caldron*, Æ.

+hwěr=+hwǣr

hwerb (WW53¹³)=hweorfa

hwerbān=hweorfbān

hwerf=hwearf

hwerf-=hwearf-, hweorf-, hwierf-

hwergen adv. only in phr. elles hwergen *elsewhere*, B2590.

hwerhwette f. *cucumber*, Lcd,WW.

hwěst v. hwōsan; **hwět**=wǣt

hwěte (KGL)=hwǣte

hwete- (*Cp*), hwet-stān (*AO*) m. '*whetstone*.'

±hwettan *to* '*whet*,' *sharpen, incite, encourage*, B,Bl,CP.

-hwette v. hwer-h.; **hweðer**=hwæðer

hweðre=hwæðere; **hwī**=hwȳ

hwicce f. *locker, chest, trunk*, OEG18b¹¹. ['*whitch*']

hwicung f. *squeaking* (*of mice*), GD185⁴(c).

hwider (æ) adv. '*whither*,' Æ,Bl,Bo,LG; AO,CP. swā hw. swā *wherever, whithersoever*.

+hwider *in every direction, everywhere, anywhere, whithersoever*.

hwiderhwega *somewhither*, Lcd68a.

hwiderryne adj. *directed whither*, Ln43³³.

hwidre *whither*, Bo78¹.

hwīe=hwȳ

+**hwielfan** (e, y) *to arch, bend over, IM.* ['*whelve*']

±**hwierfan** (æ, e, ea, i, y) *to turn, revolve, change, transfer, convert, return, Bo,CP; AO : wander, move, go, depart, AO : exchange, barter :* (+) *overturn, destroy.* ['*wharve*'] For comps. see hwyrf-.

-**hwierfere** v. pening-hw.

hwig=hwȳ

hwīl f. '*while,*' *time, Bl,Bo,Gen,LG; Æ,CP : a long time : hour, NG.* nū hwīle *just now, a while ago.* ealle hwīle *all the while.* ōðre hwīle...ōðre hwīle *at one time...at another time, Hy.* adv. hwīle *once, Deor.* ðā hwīle (ðe) *while, whilst, meanwhile, Bl,RB.*

hwīlc (e, y) interrog. pron. and adj. WHICH*, *what, CP :* (indef.) *whosoever, whichever : any (one), some (one).* swā hw. swā *whosoever, whatever, Chr.*

+**hwīlc** *each, any, every (one), all, some, many, whoever, whatever.* anra +hw. *each one.*

hwilchwega=hwilchwugu

hwilc-hwene, -hwone, -hwegno pron. *some, some one, something, NG.*

hwilc-hwugu, -hugu (e²) (hwilc is declined) pron. *any, some, some one, AO,CP : not much, little : anything, something, NG.*

±**hwilcnes** f. *quality, Æ.*

hwīle v. hwīl.

hwīlen *passing, transitory, WH87 : temporal, GD181¹². ['*whilend*']*

hwīlend-e (*Sc; '*whilend*'),* -lic (CP)=hwīlwend-e, -lic

hwīleð pres. 3 sg. of hwelan.

hwīlfæc n. *a space of time, OEG1178.*

hwīlhwega adv. *for some time.*

hwīlon (Æ)=hwīlum

hwīlpe f. *curlew? SEAF21. [Du. wilp]*

hwīlsticce n. *interval, short space of time, odd moment, GD254²⁴,WW420²⁸.*

hwīltīdum adv. *sometimes, at times, Æ,CP.* hwīltīdum...hwīltīdum *at some times...at others.*

hwīlðrāg f. *period of time, GD243¹⁹.*

hwīlum adv. (dp. of hwil) '*whilom,*' *sometimes, once, Met; Æ,CP.* hwīlum... hwīlum *now...now, at one time...at another, MH.*

hwīlwende *transitory, temporary : temporal, Æ.*

hwīlwendlic *transitory, temporary, temporal, G; Æ.* adv. -līce, Æ. ['*whilwendlic*']

hwimpel=wimpel

hwīnan¹ *to hiss, whizz, whistle, Wid.* ['*whine*']

hwinsian *to whine, NC303.*

hwinsung f. *whining, NC303.*

hwirfan=hwierfan

hwirfð pres. 3 sg. of hweorfan.

hwīrlic (HGL434)=hwearflic

hwiscettung f. *squeaking (of mice), GD 185⁴ (o).*

hwisprian *to '*whisper,*' murmur, NG.*

hwisprung f. '*whispering,*' *murmuring, JnR 7¹².*

hwistle f. *reed, '*whistle,*' pipe, LG,WW.*

hwistlere m. '*whistler,*' piper, G.*

hwistlian *to '*whistle,*' hiss, Gl,Lcd.*

hwistlung f. '*whistling,*' hissing, piping, music, CP,Gu,LG,WW.*

hwīt I. '*WHITE*' : *bright, radiant, glistening, flashing, clear, fair.* II. n. *whiteness : white food : white of egg, Æ,Lcd.*

±**hwītan** *to whiten : brighten, polish, LPs, WW.*

hwītcorn n. *manna, JnL6³¹mg.*

hwīt-cwidu, -cudu m. *mastic, LCD.*

hwīte *white, LCD.*

hwīteclæfre f. *white clover, LCD.*

hwītegōs *white goose, WW259,351.*

hwītehlāf m. *white bread, TC474'.*

hwītel (ȳ) m. *blanket, cloak, Æ,BH.* ['*whittle*']

hwītelēac n. *white leek, WW353⁸.*

hwītfōt *white-footed, GL.*

hwītian *to whiten, become white, be white, Æ.*

hwītingmelu n. *whiting-powder, Lcd119b.* [v. '*whiting*']

hwītingtrēow n. '*whitten*' tree, WW139¹.*

hwītlēac n. *onion, WW353⁸.*

hwītling m. *a kind of fish, whiting? NC 303.*

hwīt-loc, -loccede *fair-haired, blonde, RD.*

hwītnes f. '*whiteness,*' Bl; Æ.*

hwīða m., hwiðu (eo) f? *air, breeze, Æ, CP.*

hwol? '*infigens,*' OEG37⁶.

hwomm=hwamm

hwon form of instr. case of hwā, only found in adverbial phrases like 'tō hwon, for hwon' *why, LG :* 'bi hwon' *how, Gu.* ['*whon*']

hwōn I. adj. *little, few.* II. n. *a little, trifle, Lcd,LG : somewhat : a little while. ['*whon*'] III. adv. *somewhat.*

hwonan=hwanon

hwone (CP) asm. of hwā.

hwōnlic *little, small, Æ.* adv. -līce, *moderately, slightly, little, Æ : cursorily, BF30¹².*

hwōnlotum (=-hlot-) adv. *in small quantities, GL.*

hwonne (a, æ, e) adv. '*when,*' then, at some time : at any time, Bl,Gu,Ps; CP : as long as, until.* nū hw. *just now.*

hwonon=hwanon

hwōpan⁷† *to threaten, Ex.*

hworfan=hweorfan

hwōsan 3pers. pres. hwēst; pret. hwēos *to cough*, Æ,LcD 96b.

hwōsta m. *cough, WW*. ['*hoast?*']

hwoðerian (a¹) *to foam, surge? roar?* ÆH 2·388¹⁹. [hwiða]

hwoðrung f. *a harsh sound*, OEG 26¹⁴.

hwu (LWS)=hū; **hwugu**=hwega

hwugudǣl m. *small part*, HL 18³⁴⁶.

hwurf-=hwearf-, hweorf-, hwierf-, hwyrf-

hwurfon pret. pl. of hweorfan.

hwurful *fickle*, CP 245⁷. [hweorfan]

hwurfulnes f. *inconstancy, mutability*, CP.

hwȳ (inst. of hwæt) adv. and conj. '*WHY*.' tō hwȳ *wherefore*.

hwyder (Æ)=hwider; **hwylc**=hwilc

hwylca (=e) m. *pustule, tumour, boil, WW* 161¹⁷. ['*whelk*']

hwylfan=hwielfan

hwȳlon=hwīlum; **hwylp**=hwelp

hwyr=hwer; **hwyrf-**=hweorf-, hwierf-

+hwyrfe(d)nes f. *inclination*, Æ : *conversion*, BH.

hwyrfel m. *circuit, exterior, higher part?* BL 125²¹ : (meaning doubtful), EC 328'.

hwyrfepōl m. *whirlpool, eddy*, WW 383³⁴.

hwyrflede *round*, v. OEG 23⁴².

hwyrfling m. *orb*, OEG 1992.

hwyrflung (æ) f. *change, turning, revolution*, BF,DR : *wandering, error*, MtL 24²⁴.

hwyrfnes f. *dizziness, giddiness*, LcD.

±**hwyrft** m. *turning, circuit, revolution, motion, course, orbit* : *way out, outlet*. +hw. gēares *anniversary*.

hwyrftlian=hwearftlian

+**hwyrftnes** f. *return*, Ps.

hwyrftweg m. *escape*, RD 4⁶.

hwystl-=wistl-; **hwȳtel**=hwītel

hȳ=hīe; +**hȳan**=hēan III.

±**hycgan** (i) *to think, consider, meditate, study* : *understand* : *resolve upon, determine, purpose* : *remember* : *hope*. h. fram *be averse to* (v. also hogian).

+**hycglic** *considerable*, GD 328¹⁶.

hȳd I. '*hide*,' *skin, Chr,LL*; Æ,AO,CP. hȳde ðolian *to undergo a flogging*. **II.**=hīd

+**hȳd** I. *furnished with a skin*, NAR 50⁵. **II.** pp. of hēan. **III.**=+hygd

±**hȳdan** I. *to* '*hide*' ('*i-hede*'), *conceal, preserve, CP* : (refl. and intr.) *hide oneself, CP,Ps* : *sheath* (a sword), *bury* (a corpse), Æ. **II.** *to fasten with a rope of hide* (BTs), WH 13. **III.**=hēdan

hȳddern=hēddern; **-hydele** v. hǣwen-h.

+**hȳdelicnes**=+hȳðelicnes

hȳdels m. *hiding-place, cave, MkR,LL*. ['*hidels*']

hyder=hider

hȳdesacc m. *leather sack or bag*, ANS 151·80.

hȳdgild (y²) n. *fine to save one's skin* (*i.e. instead of flogging*), LL. ['*hidegild*']

hȳdig I. *leathern*, WW 125³⁵. **II.**=hygdig

+**hȳdnes** I. f. *comfort*, Cp 210o : *security*, CP 387. **II.**=+hȳðnes

hȳdscip=hȳðscip

hȳf f. '*hive*,' *Cp,Lcd,WW*.

hȳg=hīeg

+**hygd** (i), hygd (PPs 120⁴,VH) fn. *mind, thought* : *reflection, forethought*.

hygdig (e¹) *heedful, thoughtful,. careful* : *chaste, modest*. adv. -līce *chastely*.

hygdignes f. *chastity, modesty*, DR.

hyge (i)† m. *thought, mind, heart, disposition, intention, Seaf,Da* : *courage* : *pride*, GEN 354. ['*high*']

hygebend mf. *heart-strings*, B 1878.

hygeblind *mentally blind*, JUL 61.

hygeblīðe† *blithe of heart, glad, joyful*.

hygeclǣne *pure in heart*, PPs 104³.

hygecræft† m. *power of mind, wisdom*.

hygecræftig† *wise, prudent*.

hȳgedriht f. *band of household retainers?* RIM 21. [hīw]

hygefæst *wise*, RD 43¹⁴.

hygefrōd *wise*, GEN 1953.

hygefrōfor† f. *consolation*.

hygegǣlsa *hesitating, slow, sluggish*, PH 314. [gǣlan]

hygegāl *loose, wanton*, RD 13¹².

hygegār m. *wile*, MOD 34.

hygegēomor† *sad in mind*.

hygeglēaw† *prudent in mind*.

hygegrim *savage, cruel*, JUL 595.

hygelēas (e, i) *thoughtless, foolish, rash*, Æ : *unbridled, extravagant*.

hygelēaslic (i) *unbridled*, OEG 3170. adv. -līce *thoughtlessly*.

hygelēast f. *heedlessness, folly*, Æ.

hygemǣðum (i) *reverently*, B 2909.

hygemēðe *sad. saddening*, B 2442.

hygerōf† *stout-hearted, brave*, GEN.

hygerūn f. *secret*, EL 1099.

hygesceaft f. *mind, heart*, GEN 288.

hygesnottor† *sagacious, wise*.

hygesorg† f. *heart-sorrow, anxiety*.

hygestrang (i) *brave*, MEN 42.

hygetēona† m. *injury, insult*, GEN.

hygetrēow f. *fidelity*, GEN 2367.

hygeðanc† m. *thought*.

hygeðancol† *thoughtful, wise*.

hygeðihtig (i¹) *courageous*, B 746.

hygeðrymm (i¹) m. *courage*, B 339.

hygeðrȳð (i) f. *pride, insolence*, GEN 2238.

hygewælm m. *mental agitation, anger*, GEN 980.

hygewlanc† *haughty, proud*, RD.

hyggean=hycgan; **hȳglā** (LPs)=hīglā

hyhsan=hyscan; **hȳhst** v. hēah.

hyht (e, i) mf. (±) *hope, trust, Bl,Ps;* Æ,CP : *joy, exultation* : (±) *desire, expectation* : (+) *comfort.* ['*hight*']

±**hyhtan** (i) *to hope, trust, Ps* : *rejoice, exult, be glad* : *soften (hardship),* GUTH 86⁸. ['*hight*']

+**hyhtendlic** *to be hoped for,* GD 269¹³.

hyhtful (e, i) *hopeful* : *full of joy, mirthful, pleasant, glad.*

hyhtgiefu f. *pleasing gift,* RIM 21.

hyhtgifa m. *giver of joy,* EL 852.

hyhting (i¹) f. *exultation,* WW 233⁴².

hyhtlēas (i¹) *unbelieving,* GEN 2387.

hyhtlic† *hopeful, joyful, pleasant.* adv. -līce.

hyhtplega† m. *joyous play, sport.*

hyhtwilla m. *hoped-for joy,* SAT 159.

hyhtwynn f. *joy of hope, joy,* JUD 121.

hyhðo=hiehðu; **hyl**=hyll

hylc (i) m. *bend, turn,* GL : *unevenness,* WW.

+**hylced** *bent, curved, bandy,* GPH 398.

hyld (*Gen*)=hield

hyldan I. *to flay, skin,* Æ,WW. ['*hild*'; hold II.] **II.** (+)=ieldan

hyldāð m. *oath of allegiance,* LL 396B.

hylde=hielde

hyldemǣg† m. *near kinsman,* GEN.

hyldere m. *flayer, butcher,* GL. [hold II.]

+**hyldig** *patient,* SPs 7¹².

hylding (=ie) f. *curve, inclination,* WW 382². [heald]

hyldo f. *favour, grace, kindness, protection* : *allegiance, loyalty, reverence,* AO,CP. [=hield]

hyldrǣden (e¹) f. *fidelity,* TC 610'.

hyldu (Æ)=hyldo

hylest pres. 2 sg. of helan.

hylfe (Æ)=hielfe; -**hylian** v. be-h.

hyll I. mf. '*hill*,' Æ; Mdf. **II.**=hell

hyllehāma (i) m. '*cicada,*' *cricket, grasshopper,* GL.

hyllic (i) *hilly,* BC 3·577.

+**hylman**=helmian; -**hylman** v. for-, ofer-h.

hylp=help

hylpð pres. 3 sg. of helpan.

hylsten *baked (on the hearth),* WW 393³¹.

hylsung (o²) f. '*tympanum,*' EPs 150⁴ ·(v. ES 53·359).

hylt=hielt pres. 3 sg. of healdan.

hylt-=hilt-

-**hylte** v. hēah-h.

hylto=hielto

hylu f. *a hollow,* KC 3·407.

hylwyrt f. '*hillwort,*' *pulegium, WW.*

hym=him; **hymblice** (GL)=hymlic

Hymbre sbpl. *Northumbrians,* OET 571.

hymele f. *hop plant,* WW; Mdf. [L.]

hymelic=hymlic; **hymen**=ymen

hym-lic (e) m., -līce f. '*hemlock,*' Gl,Lcd, WW.

hȳn=hēan; **hȳnan** (Æ)=hīenan

hynd=hind

-**hynde** v. six-, twelf-, twi-h.; of-hende.

hynden f. *community of 100 men,* LL.

hyndenmann m. *chief man in the community of 100 men,* LL 175; 178.

hyne=hine as. of hē.

±**hyngran,** hyngrian (i) *to be hungry,* '*hunger,*' (impers.) Æ,JnL; (intr.) Cr,Lk : (trans.) *hunger for,* Mt 5⁶.

hyngrig=hungrig

hȳnnes (=īe) f. *persecution, destruction,* BH 34⁵. [hēan]

hynnilǣc (Ep)=ynnilēac

hȳnð, hȳnðu=hīenðo

hyp-=hype-

+**hȳpan** (Æ)=+hēapian

hype m. '*hip*' *Bl,WW;* Æ,CP.

hȳpe (=īe) f. *heap,* Æ.

hypebān n. *hip-bone,* WW 159²⁵.

hypebānece m. *sciatica,* LCD.

hȳpel (=īe) m. *heap, mound,* GL.

hypeseax (hup-)† n. *short sword, dagger,* GL.

+**hypsan** (LPs 9²⁵)=hyspan

hypwærc (i¹, e²) n. *pain in the hips,* WW 113¹⁵.

hȳr (ī) f. '*hire,*' *wages,* Æ,LL : *interest, usury,* Æ.

hyra gp. of hē, hēo, hit.

hȳra (ē) m. *follower, mercenary* : *servant, hireling,* CP 88¹⁵ : *dependant,* BH 104¹⁹.

hyran *to spit,* MkR 14⁶⁵. [cp. +horian]

±**hȳran**=(1) hīeran; (2) hȳrian

hyrcnian=heorcnian

hyrd I. f. *door,* GEN 2695 (GK). [cp. *Ger.* hürde] **II.** *parchment?* GUTH 213¹⁰.

hyrd-, heord-=hierd-

hyrdel m. '*hurdle,*' *frame,* Æ,WW.

hyre gds. of hēo; **hȳre**=hēore

+**hȳre-**=+hīere-

hȳreborg (īe) m. *interest,* WW 515¹.

hȳred=hīred; **hȳrefter**=hēræfter

hȳre-geoc, -geoht=hȳrgeoht

hȳregilda m. *mercenary, hireling,* WW 111¹¹.

hȳremann=hīeremann

hyrfan (TC 611⁵)=yrfan

hȳrgeoht n. *hired yoke of oxen,* LL 24,60.

hyrian *to imitate,* Bo.

hȳrian *to* '*hire*' ('*i-hire*'), Æ,Mt,WW (pp.).

hȳrigmann m. *hireling.* [=hīeremann]

hyring (e¹) f. *imitation,* RB 128¹⁴.

hȳrling m. '*hireling,*' Mk 1²⁰.

hȳrmann=hȳrigmann

hyrnan *to jut out like a horn,* Ct.

hyrne f. *angle, corner,* CP,Mt; Mdf. ['*hern*']

±**hyrned** *horned, beaked,* Lcd; Æ. ['*i-horned*']

hyrnednebba† *horny-billed, horn-beaked,* BR,JUD. [horn]

hyrnen I. *of horn*, LRPs 97[6]. **II.** *angular*, OEG 7[20].

hȳrnes=hīernes

+**hyrnes** (VH 16)=+herenes

hyrnet, hyrenetu f. '*hornet*,' *Gl,WW* :*gadfly*, WW 121[12].

hyrnful *angular, with many angles*, OEG 121.

hyrnig *angular*, OEG 121.

hyrnstän m. *corner-stone, keystone*, ÆH 1·106.

hȳroxa m. *hired ox*, LL 116 B.

hyrra (KGL)=heorra, heorr

hȳrra I. v. hēah. **II.**=hȳra

hyrsian *to go on horseback?* BHB 194[35].

hyrst† **I.** f. (±) *ornament, decoration, jewel, treasure* : *accoutrements, trappings, armour*. [*Ger.* rüstung] **II.** m. *hillock, height, wood, wooded eminence*, *Rd,Ct.* ['*hurst*']

hyrst-=hierst-

±**hyrstan I.** *to decorate, adorn, ornament, equip*. [*Ger.* rüsten] **II.** (+) *to murmur*, LkLR 15[2]. **III.**=hierstan

hȳrsum=hīersum; **hyrtan**=hiertan

hyrten=heorten

hyrð f. *skin, hide*, ES 41·323.

hyröll (*Cp*)=hyrdel; **hȳru**=hūru

+**hȳrung** f. *hiring*, WW 213[12].

hyrw-=hierw-

hys=his

±**hyscan** (ea, i) (tr.) *to jeer at, reproach, Ps* : (intr.) *to rail*, W. ['*heascen*']

hyscend (i) m. *reviler*, GPH 398.

hyscild (WW 170[12])=hysecild

hyse† nap. hyssas m. *son, youth, young man, warrior*, GL : *shoot, scion*, HGL 419[69].

hysebeorðor n. *the bearing of male offspring*, GL : *boy, young man*, An.

hyse-berðling, -byrding m. *the bearing of male offspring*, GL.

hyseberðre f. *woman who bears a son*, DHy 50[17].

hysecild n. *male child*, Æ,AO.

hyserinc m. *young man*, GD 338[22].

hysewīse adv. *like young men*, WW 417[35].

hysope=ysope

hyspan (e, i) pret. hyspde and hyspte *to mock, scorn, deride, revile, reproach*, AO. [hosp]

hyspend m. *calumniator*, RPs 71[4].

+**hyspendlic** *abominable*, LPs 13[1].

hyspful *contumelious*, OEG 11[180].

hysp-nes (EPs), -ung (Bo) f. *contumely*.

hysse=hyse

hyt I. f. *heat*, B 2649. [*ON.* hita; or ? read hāt] **II.**=hit pron.

hȳt pres. 3 sg. of hȳdan.

hyttan=hittan

hȳð I. f. *landing-place, harbour, creek, port, Cp,Guth,Met,Ps;* Æ,CP. ['*hithe*'] **II.**=hȳðð

hȳðan (ī) *plunder, ravage*, BH,GD. [hūð]

+**hȳðe** *appropriate, convenient*, Æ.

±**hȳðegian** *to facilitate*, GPH,Sc.

hȳðegung f. *advantage*, Sc 12[6].

±**hȳðelic** *suitable, proper, convenient, advantageous*. adv. -līce.

+**hȳðelicnes** f. '*opportunitas*,' NC 345.

hȳðgild n. *harbour festival, sacrifice or service*, OEG.

hȳðlic *belonging to a harbour*, WW.

+**hȳðlic**=+hȳðelic

+**hȳðnes** f. *advantage*, ÆL 23b[252] : *occasion*, EPs 9[22].

hȳðscip (ī) n. *a light, piratical vessel*, GL.

hȳðð, hȳððo f. *gain, advantage*, Æ.

+**hyððo** n. *subsistence*, ÆL 23b[492].

hȳðweard m. *warden of a harbour*, B 1915.

hȳw=hīw; +**hȳwan**=+īewan

hyxan=hyscan

I

ia (Æ)=gēa; **iacessūre**=gēacessūre

iacinctus, īacintus m. *jacinth*, CP. [*L.* hyacinthus]

iagul=gēagl; **iara**=gearo

iarwan=gierwan; **īb-**=īf-

ic pron. (1st pers.) '*I*,' *Cp,Jn*. [*Ger.* ich]

īcan, īcean=īecan; **īce**=ȳce

īcend m. '*auctor*,' ÆGR 48[12]. [īecan]

īcestre f. '*auctrix*,' ÆGR 48[12].

icge only in phr. 'icge gold,' *treasure-gold? rich gold?* B 1108 (v. Klb p 168 and BTs).

idæges adv. *on the same day*, Æ.

idel (ȳ) **I.** (often īdl- in obl. cases) *worthless, useless, vain*, Æ,CP,Gen,Mt,VPs : *empty, desolate, bare, void, destitute, devoid* (*of*), Æ,B,VPs; CP : '*idle,*' *unemployed*, Mt. on ī. adv. *in vain*, Æ. **II.** n. *emptiness, frivolity, idleness*, *Lcd,LL,Sol* : *inattention, carelessness.*

idelgeorn *slothful, idle*, Bo : *useless*, W.

idelgielp (e[3], i[3]) n. *empty boasting, vainglory*, CP,DHy,WW.

idelgild n. *vain worship, idolatry*, Æ.

idelgildoffrung f. *offering to an idol*, Æ.

idelhende *empty-handed, empty*, Æ,CP.

idelinga (a[2]) '*frivola*,' GPH 389.

idellic *vain, idle*. adv. -līce, VPs. ['*idly*']

idelnes f. *frivolity, vanity, emptiness, falseness*, VPs; CP : '*idleness*,' *vain existence*, LL : *superstition*. in (on) īdelnisse *in vain*.

-idelspræce v. fela-ī.

ides *virgin* : (†) *woman, wife, lady, queen.*

idig *busy? active?* (BT) : *greedy for? desirous of?* (GK), PH 407?

idl- v. īdel.

±**Idlian** *to become empty or useless : profane,*
BH362¹¹.

Idol n. *idol,* LL. [*L.*]

ie v. ēa.

±**Iecan** (ǣ, ē, ī, ȳ) pret. īecte, īhte *to in-
crease, enlarge, add to, augment, prolong,
An,Lcd,Lk*; AO,CP : *fulfil, carry out,*
RSL11·486. ['*eche*'; ēac]

Iecinctus=īacinctus

Iecessūre=gēacessūre; **Iedel-**=īdel-

Ieg (īg) f. *island.* [ēa]

Iegbūend (ī) m. *islander,* CP.

Iegclif (ēg-) n. *sea-cliff,* B2893.

Iegland (ē, ī) n. '*island,*' *BH,Bo,Chr,Wh.*

Iegstrēam (ē¹)† m. *current, river, sea.*

Iehtan=ēhtan; **Ielc-**=ilc-; **Ield**=ieldo

±**Ieldan** (i, y) *to delay, put off, prolong,
hesitate, tarry, CP : connive at, dissimulate.*
['*eld*'; eald]

Ieldcian (CP)=elcian

Ielde† (e, ea, i, y) mp. *men.*

Ielden (æ) n. *delay,* BH400²⁰.

Ieldendlic (e) *dilatory,* WW441².

Ieldest (æ, e, y) superl. of eald '*eldest,*'
chief, Æ,Mt,CP.

Ieldesta (y¹) m. *chief,* Ex17⁵.

Ieldful (i, y) *dilatory, delaying,* OEG.

Ieldian (y) *to put off, delay, Æ.*

Ielding f. *delay, tarrying,* CP : *dissimulation.*

Ieldo (æ, e, i, y) f. *age, Æ,Gu,Lcd : period :
old age, old people, Æ,Bl;* CP : *an age of the
world, Æ,Gu.* ['*eld*'; eald]

Ieldra (y) (comp. of eald) used as sbpl.
parents, ancestors, Bl,El,Ct. ['*elder*']

Ieldrafæder (æld-) m. *grandfather,* WW7³⁴.

Ieldu=ieldo; **Ielf**=ælf

Iemung (WW277²²)=gēmung; **Ierd**=gierd

Ierf- v. also yrf-.

Ierfa m. *heir,* OET446⁸ (erba).

Ierfe (æ, e, i, y) n. *heritage, bequest, property,*
CP : *cattle.* [*Ger.* erbe]

Ierfian (i, y) *to inherit, possess :* (+) *to stock
with cattle,* TC158¹⁰.

Iergan *to dishearten, dismay,* Jos,W. [earg]

Iergð(u) f. *remissness, sloth, cowardice,* AO.
[earg]

Ierlic (i, y) *angry, vehement,* ApT.

±**Ierman** *to harass, vex, afflict,* CP. [earm]

Ierming (eo, e, y) m. *person of no account,
poor wretch,* AO,CP.

Iermð, iermðu (e, ea, eo, y) f. *misery, distress, poverty, B,Bo,Ps : disease : crime :
reproach,* CPs118¹³⁴. ['*ermth*'; earm]

Iernan³ (æ, i, y; rinnan) pret. 3 sg. arn,
orn, pl. urnon; pp. urnen (±) *to '* run*,'
move rapidly, hasten, flow, spread, Æ,AO,
CP,Lcd,VPs : pursue, Bo,Ps : cause to
move rapidly, turn, grind, AO,BH :* (+) *get
to, attain, meet with :* (+) *occur (to one's*

mind), GD : (+) *coagulate,* Lcd : (+) *grow
up.* [v. also '*ern*']

Iernes (eo, y) f. *anger,* BL123⁸,HL.

Ierning (e) f. *discharge, flow,* NG.

Ierre I. (i, y) *wandering, erring, perverse,
depraved, Ps,Sol : angry, fierce, Æ,Bl,Chr,
CP,G;* AO. II. n. *anger, Bl,CP,El,Lk.*
['*irre*']

Ierremōd (y) *wrathful, wild,* B726.

Ierrenga (eo¹, y¹, i², u²) adv. *angrily, fiercely,*
CP.

Ierreðweorh (y) *very angry,* SAT399?

Ierscipe (y) m. *anger,* LPs9²⁵.

±**Iersian** (i, io, y) *to be angry with, rage :
enrage, irritate,* CP.

Iersigendlic (y) *passionate, emotional, Æ.*

Iersung (i, y) f. *anger,* CP.

Ierð-=eorð-, yrð-

Iesca (Ep,Erf)=geocsa

Iesend, iesende *entrails,* WW. [=gesen]

Ieteð pres. 3 sg. of etan.

Ieð adv. comp. (=ēað) *easily, An,Met;* AO,
CP. ['*eath*'] For comps. v. also ēað-.

+**Ieðan** I. (ē) *to alleviate,* Gu1179 : *be
merciful,* GD. II. (ǣ, ē, ȳ) *to lay waste,
ravage, devastate, destroy, Æ.*

Ieðe I. *easy, good-natured, pleasant,* AO.
II. (ē)† *barren, waste, desolate.*

Ieðegean=ȳðgian

Ieðelic *easy,* CP : *moderate sized,* GD. adv.
-līce *easily,* AO,CP.

Ieðnes f. *ease, pleasure,* CP425¹¹.

+**Ieðrian** (ē) *to make or become easier,* GD,
Lcd.

Ieðrung? f. *amelioration, a making easier?*
(BTs), SOUL107 (MS edring *q.v.*).

Ieðtogen (ȳ) *easily brought about,* ÆL23³¹⁷.

±**Iewan** (ēa, ēo, ȳ) *to show, display, reveal,
disclose, point out,* CP. [ēage; cp. ēowan]

Ife? *a kind of plant,* WW301¹² (iue).

Ifegn (Cp)=īfig

Ifig n. '*ivy,*' *Gl,Lcd,Shr.*

Ifigbearo *ivy-grove,* CC50.

Ifig-crop, -croppa m. *cluster of ivy berries,*
Lcd,WW. [v. '*ivy*']

Ifiglēaf n. '*ivy-leaf,*' Lcd117b.

Ifigrind f. *ivy-bark,* LCD121b.

Ifig-tearo, -tara n. *ivy-tar, resin from tar,*
LCD.

Ifigtwig n. *ivy-twig,* LCD117a.

Ifiht *ivy-covered,* KC.

ig=ic; **Ig**=īeg; **igbūend**=īegbuend

Igdæges=īdæges; **igel**=īl; **igg**=īeg

iggað, iggoð, īg(e)oð m. '*ait,*' *eyot, small
island, Æ,Chr.* [īeg]

igil, igl (Æ)=īl

Igland=īegland

Igoð, īgð=iggað; **ih**=ic

Ihte pret. 3 sg. of īecan.

íl (igil) m. *hedgehog, porcupine, CP,Shr, WW.* [*'íl'*]
íland=īegland
±ílca (y) pron. (usu. wk) *the same, An,Bo, Chr,Ct;* CP. [*'ilk'*]
ílce adv. v. swā; **íld-**=ield-
íle (y) m. *sole of the foot, Æ* : *callosity, corn, Æ.* [cp. *Ger.* eilen]
ílfetu, ilfe(t)te (y;=ie) f. *swan,* GL; Mdf.
íll n.=ile; **íllca**=ilca
ílleracu f. *surfeit,* WW378¹⁵.
+**íllerocad** *surfeited,* CVPs77⁶⁵.
ílnetu (WW367²⁷)=ilfetu
ílugsecg v. eolhsecg; **ímb-** v. ymb-
ímberdling, imbyrdling=inbyrdling
ímpa? m., **impe?** f. *graft, shoot, scion, CP* 381¹⁷. [*'imp'*]
ímpian *to 'imp,' implant, graft,* LL454,12.
(+) *busy oneself with,* CP132²⁵.
ín I. prep. with a. and d. (instr.) (local) 'IN,' *into, upon, on, at, to, among* : (temporal) *in, at, about, towards, during* : (purpose) *in, to, for.* **II.** sb. and adv.=inn
ín- (v. BH xxxiii ff.)=on-, inn-
ínāberan⁴ (inn-) *to bring in,* Æ.
ínādl f. *internal disease,* LCD.
ínǣlan (VPs)=onǣlan; **ínāgān**=ingān
ínāgēode=inēode pret. 3 sg. of ingān.
ínāsendan *to send in,* Mk2⁴.
ínāwritting f. *inscription,* LkL20²⁴.
ínbǣrnednes (e²), inbærnes f. *burning, incense, frankincense.* [=onb-]
ínbecweðan⁵ *to inculcate,* WW429³⁶.
ínbelǣdan *to lead in,* LHy.
ínbelūcan² *to shut,* BL217²⁶.
ínbend mf. *internal bond,* GU928.
ínber-=on-, in-byr-
ínberan *to carry in,* LL386,1.
ínbernes (VPs)=inbærnes
ínbeslēan *to hack into (any one),* LL86,74.
ínbestingan *to penetrate,* LL7,64².
ínbetȳnednes f. *life of a recluse,* GD212⁵.
ínbewindan³ *to enfold, enwrap,* LkL (inn-).
ínbirdling=inbyrdling
ínblāwan⁷ *to inspire, breathe upon, JnR* : *inflate, puff up,* EC. [*'inblow'*]
ínboden *proclaimed.* [onbēodan]
ínbolgen *exasperated,* DR. [=onb-]
ínboren ptc. *indigenous, native, SR;* GPH390. [*'inborn'*]
ínborh m. *bail, security in cases of theft,* LL. [*'inborgh'*]
ínbrēdan³ *to burst in upon,* GPH393.
ín-brengan, -bringan *to bring in, present, Mk.* [*'inbring'*]
ínbryne (byr) m. *conflagration,* DR64⁶.
ínbryrd-=onbryrd-
±ínbūan *to inhabit,* MtL23²¹.
ínbūend m. *inhabitant,* WW210¹³.

ín-burg, -burh f. *hall,* WW.
ínbyrde (e²) *born on the estate,* TC.
ínbyrdling (e²) m. *slave born in a master's house, Æ* : *native,* OEG.
ínbyrne (DR)=inbryne
ínbyrð pres. 3 sg. of inberan.
ínc (*Mt,Mk*) da. of git, dual pers. pron. [*'inc'*]
ínca m. *question, scruple, suspicion, doubt* : *occasion,* RB : *grievance, quarrel, grudge,* BH. incan witan *to have a grudge.*
íncaðeode=ingeðeode; **ínce**=ynce
íncēgan (=īe) *to call upon,* DR119³.
íncēgung (=īe) f. *invocation,* DR.
íncempa m. *soldier of the same company,* WW207⁶.
íncer (y) **I.** gen. of git, dual pers. pron.
II. adj. pron. *of or belonging to both of you, MH,Mt.* [*'inker'*]
+**íncfullian** *to offend, scandalize,* MtR. [inca]
íncga=inca
íncit acc. of git, dual personal pronoun.
íncleofe (i, y) f. *chamber, closet* : *cave, den.*
íncniht m. *household servant,* Æ.
íncofa m. *inner chamber, ÆL* : *heart,* MET 22¹⁸.
íncoðu f. *internal disease,* Æ.
íncuman⁴ *to come in, go into, enter,* Æ. [*'income'*]
íncund *interior, internal, inward, secret,* Æ,CP. adv. -līce, Æ.
íncundnes f. *inward conviction, sincerity,* W105³⁰ : *inward part, recess,* DHy.
íncūð *strange, extraordinary.* adv. -līce, ÆT1104.
íncyme m. *entrance,* LV32.
índǣlan *to infuse,* DR.
índēpan (=īe) *to dip in,* LkL16²⁴.
índīegelnes f. *hiding-place,* RPs17¹².
índisc *Indian,* Æ.
índrencan *to steep, saturate* : *fill to overflowing,* VPs22⁵. [=ondrencan]
índrīfan¹ *to ejaculate, utter,* SAT80.
índrihten=indryhten
índrincan³ *to imbibe, drink.* indruncen *plied with drink.*
índryhten *distinguished, noble, excellent,* WW.
índryhto† f. *honour, glory.*
íneardian *to dwell in, inhabit,* VPs.
íneðdisc n. *household stuff, furniture,* WW 147³². [ȳddisc]
ínelfe=innelfe; **ínerfe**=innierfe
íneðung f. *inspiration, breathing,* APs17¹⁶. [ēðung]
ínfær n. *ingress, entrance, entry, admission,* Æ,WW. [*'infare'*]
ínfǣreld n. *in-coming, entrance, admission,* Æ : *interior* : *vestibule.*

infangene-ðéof, infangen-ðéf sb. *right of judging thieves caught within the limits of one's jurisdiction, and of taking the fines for the crime, Ct*; v. LL 2·523. ['*infangthief*']

infaran[6] I. *to enter, Æ,Jn.* ['*infare*'] II.= innefaran

infaru f. *incursion, inroad, CHR 1048.*

infeallan[7] *to fall in, VPs.*

infeccan *to fetch in, BL 175[1].*

inféran *to enter in, Æ.*

infiht n. *brawl in a house, LL 597'.*

infindan[3] *to find, discover, NG.*

inflǽscnes f. *incarnation, EC 161[23].*

infléde† *full of water.*

infléon[2] *to fly from, RIM 44.*

infóster n. *bringing up, rearing, LL 396'.*

infród† *very aged, experienced, B.*

ing I. *name of the rune for* ng. II.=ging, geong. III.=inn

-ing suffix, as in earming, lytling (originally patronymic).

in-gán anv. pret. -éode *to go in, enter, BH, Mt.* ['*ingo*']

ingang (eo[2]) m. *ingress, entrance, access, beginning, BH,Ps* (inn-) : *entrance-fee.* ['*ingang*']

ingangan[7] *to go in, enter, Æ.*

ingebed n. *earnest prayer, PPs 87[2].*

ingeberigan (NG)=onbyrgan

ingebringan[3] *to bring in, LL 150'.*

inge-cígan, -cégan '*invocare*,' VPs; CPs 90[15].

ingedón anv. *to put in, BH 434[20].*

ingedrincan (GPH 391)=indrincan

ingefeallan[7] '*incidere*,' Ps.

ingefeoht n. *internal war, BH.*

ingefolc n. *native race, Ex 142.*

ingehrif (-gerif) n. *womb, LPs 21[8].*

inge-hygd, -hýd (Æ), -híd f. *consciousness, mind, conscience, sense, understanding : meaning, intention, purpose, design.*

ingehygdnes f. *intention, LPs 48[5].*

ingelǽdan=inlǽdan

ingelaðian *to invite, Lk 14.*

ingemang v. ongemang prep.

ingemynd† fn. *recollection, memory, mind.*

ingemynde *well-remembered, EL 896.*

ingenga m. *visitor, intruder, B 1776.*

ingeongan (LG; v. '*yong*')=ingangan

ingéotan[2] *to pour in, fill, GUTH.*

ingéoting (yn-? =ymb-) f. *inpouring, OEG.*

ingerec n. *broil, BH.* [=ungerec]

ingerif=ingehrif

ingeseted *placed in, inserted, WW 427[17].*

ingesteald *household goods, B 1155.*

ingeswel n. *internal swelling, WW 113[5].*

ingeðanc mn. *thought, mind, conscience, intention, Æ,CP.*

ingeðéod† f. *nation, Ex,PPs.*

ingeðóht *conscience, GD 72[12].*

ingeweaxen *implanted, WW 427[8].*

ingewinn n. *civil war, AO 88[29].*

ingewitnes f. *consciousness, conscience, BH.*

ingong (CP)=ingang

ingyte m. *pouring in, infusion, inspiration, CM 424.* [géotan]

inhǽtan *to inflame, GD 29[9].*

inheald *in bas-relief, embossed, WW 423[28].*

inhebban (CR 313)=onhebban

inheldan=onhieldan

inheord f. *herd kept by the lord on his lands, LL 449,7.*

inhíred m. *family, household, Æ.*

in-híwan, -hígan sbpl. *members of a household or community, servants.*

inhold *loyal in heart, LCD 3·442'.*

inhýrnes f. *possession, EC 364'.*

inlífe=innylfe; **ininnan**=oninnan

inlád f. *right of water-passage inland, KC 4·209[5] : entrance-fee, Jn p 188[9].*

inlǽdan '*inducere*,' *to introduce, NG.*

inlǽnd-=inlend-

±inlagian *to reverse sentence of outlawry, Chr,LL.* ['*inlaw*']

inland n. *land in the lord's own occupation, domain, demesne, EC,LL.* ['*inland*']

inlaðian *to invite, G.*

inlaðigend m. *inviter, Sc 170[12].*

inlec=inlic; **inlégan** (VPs)=onlíegan

inléhtan=inlíhtan

inlenda m. *native, GL.*

in-lende, -lendisc (LCD) *native, indigenous.*

inléohtan=inlíhtan

inlic *internal, interior, inward, BH : native.* adv. -líce *inwardly : thoroughly, sincerely, heartily, BH,Bo.* ['*inly*']

inlíchomung f. *incarnation, DR.*

inlígian=onlígian

±inlíhtan *to illuminate, enlighten.*

inlíhtend m. *illuminator, DR 2[6].*

inlíhtian (NG)=inlihtan

inlíhtnes f. *illumination, VPs.*

inlíðewác=unleoðuwác

inlíxan *to become light, dawn, LkL 23[54].*

inlocast superl. adv.=inlícost

inlýhtan=inlíhtan

inmearg n. *marrow, GPH 397.*

inméde *close to one's heart, important in one's estimation, RB; BK 15.*

inn I. n. *dwelling, apartment, lodging, chamber, house, Æ,Mt*; AO : *quartering oneself (of soldiers).* ['*inn*'] II. adv. '*in*,' *into, inwards, within, inside of, Æ,AO,B, BL,G : inwardly.* inn on *into.* inn tó is used with words of granting to indicate the grantee, CC 125 (ES 57·4).

inn-=in-; **inna** (LkL)=innoð

innan I. prep. (w. a. g. d.) *from within* : *within, in, into, CP.* **II.** adv. *within, inside, in, AO.* ['INNE']
innanbordes adv. *at home, CP.*
innanburhware sbpl. *residents within the walls of a town,* TC510'.
innancund *inner, inward, internal,* LCD : *thorough, hearty,* PPs 118², ¹⁰.
innane=innan II.
innanearm m. *inner side of arm,* LCD 87b.
innantidernes (ie,ȳ) f. *internal weakness,* LCD.
innanweard=inweard
innanwund f. *internal wound,* LCD 3b.
innað=innoð
innāwritting (*LkL*)=onwriting
inne adv. *in, inside, within, in-doors, A, AO,BH,Chr,Ct,Lcd.* ['*inne*']
inne-=inn-, in-
innecund adj. *inward,* CP 139.
inne-faran, -foran *bowels,* LCD.
innefeoh n. *household goods,* LL 5,28; v. 3·9.
innelfe=innylfe
innemest (superl. of inne) adj. '*inmost,' Sc* : *most intimate, deep or close, CP.* adv.
innera, in(n)ra (compar. of inne) '*inner,' interior, GF,WW* : *mental, spiritual, BH, LL,Sc.*
inneð=innoð
inne-weard, -werd=inweard
innheardmann m. *one of the household troops,* MtL 8⁹. [inhīred]
innhere m. *native army,* CHR 1006 E.
innian *to go in, Bo* : (±) *put up, lodge, Chr* 1048 : (+) *include* : (+) *fill, restore, make good, Æ.* ['*inn*']
innierfe (e²) n. *household stuff, furniture, goods,* Bo 31¹⁹.
innifli (Cp 1151)=innylfe
±**inniwian** *to renew,* DR.
innon=innan
innor (*ÆGr*) compar. of inne. ['*inner*']
innoð mf. *inside, entrails, stomach, womb, breast, heart, BH,Bo,G; Æ,CP.*
innoðmægen (e³) n. *strength,* EHy 5¹⁶.
innoðtȳdernes f. *weakness of the bowels,* LCD 105a.
innoðwund f. *internal wound,* LCD 88b.
innra=innera
innung f. *dwelling* : *contents, takings, revenue, Bo,KC.* ['*inning*']
innweardlīce=inweardlīce
innweorud n. *retainers, household,* WID 111.
innylfe (e, i) n. *bowels, womb,* LCD.
inorf n. *household goods, furniture,* LCD,WW.
inra (Æ)=innera
inrǣcan '*ingesserunt,'* WW 420¹⁸ (v. A 31·532).
inrǣsan *to rush upon,* MtL.

inrēcels n. *incense,* LkR 1⁹.
insæglung=inseglung
insǣte adj. *dependent,* WW 185⁹.
insǣtnes=insetnes
inscēawere m. *inspector,* DR 194.
inscēawung f. *inspection, view,* NG.
insceðende=unscæððende
in-seg(e)l (æ) n. *seal, signet, Ct,WW.* ['*inseil*'; *L.*]
±**inseglian** (æ) *to seal, LL*; ÆL. ['*inseil*']
inseglung (æ²) f. *sealing, seal,* Æ.
insendan *to send in, put in,* VPs.
inseten f. *an institution,* DR.
insetnes f. *regulation,* DR.
insettan *to institute,* BH,JnL.
insigle n. *seal, signet,* DR,TC. [insegel]
insiht f. *narrative,* JnL.
insittende *sitting within,* RD 47⁷.
insmoh m. *slough,* MH 162¹¹.
insōcn f. *brawl in a house,* LL 597,80¹².
insomnian *to gather in,* BH 274¹.
inspīderwiht '*spider,' Lcd* 167b (very doubtful, v. BTac).
inspinn n. *spindle,* WW.
instæpe I. m. *entrance,* ÆH 1·84. **II.**= instæpes
instæpes (e²) adv. *forthwith, directly,* BL.
instæppan (Æ)=insteppan
instandan⁶ (o²) *to be present,* DR.
instandendlic (o²) *required for present use,* MtR 6¹¹.
instede (y) *immediately,* NG.
in-stepe, -stepes=instæpes
insteppan⁶ (æ) *to go in, enter,* Æ.
instice m. *internal stitching pain,* LCD.
instigan¹ *to climb in,* GD 24.
instihtian *to appoint, arrange,* LkL p 2⁶.
insting=onsting; **instyde**=instede
inswān m. *lord's swineherd,* LL 447.
inswōgan⁷ *to invade,* BH 278⁸.
inswōgennes (ēo²) f. *onrush,* BH 110³³.
intiga (KGL)=intinga; **intimb-**=ontimb-
intinga m. *matter, business, Æ* : *cause* : *fault.* butan intingan *in vain, emptily.*
intō prep. w. d. (instr.), a. 'INTO,' *to, against, in, Æ,Chr.*
intrahtnung f. *interpretation,* MtL p 2⁷.
intrepettan *to trip, dance,* Ln 37¹⁹⁷.
inðanc (ByH 132¹⁴)=ingeðanc
inðer adv. *apart,* MtR 17¹.
inðicce *crass, thick,* MtL 13¹⁵.
inðīnen f. *female servant,* GPH 401.
inðing (N)=intinga; **inðwēan**=onðwēan
in-wærc, -wræc m. *internal pain,* GD,LL.
inwǣte f. *internal humour,* LCD 97a.
inwaru f. *services due to the lord on his* '*inland,'* Ct.
inweard I. (innan-, inne-) adj. *internal, inward, inner, intrinsic, deep, sincere,*

earnest, Æ,*B,Bo,Cr.* as sbn. *inward parts,* Æ,*WW.* **II.** adv. *within* : *mentally, spiritually, LkL.* ['*inward*']
inweardlic (e, o, u) *internal, Lcd* : *inner,* RWH 136[17] : *earnest, sincere,* W. adv. *-lïce* '*inwardly,*' Æ : *deeply, thoroughly, heartily,* Æ,*Met.*
inwendan *to change,* VPs.
inweorc n. *indoor work,* LL 454,11.
inwerd-=inweard-; **inwid**=inwit
inwidda m. *adversary, evil one,* Jud 28.
inwise f. *condiment,* Lcd 69a.
inwit I. n. *evil, deceit.* **II.** adj. *wicked, deceitful.*
inwitfeng m. *spiteful clutch,* B 1447.
inwitflān m. *treacherous shaft,* Mod 37.
inwitful *wicked, crafty,* Ps,WW.
inwitgæst m. *evil guest,* B 2670.
inwitgecynd n. *evil nature,* Sol 329.
inwitgyren f. *treacherous snare,* PPs 139[5].
inwithlemm (id) m. *treacherous wound,* Rood 47.
inwithrōf m. *unfriendly roof,* B 3123.
inwitnet n. *net of malice,* B 2167.
inwitnīð† m. *cunning hostility.*
inwitrūn f. *evil, crafty counsel,* Jul 610.
inwitscear m. *murderous attack,* B 2478.
inwitsearo n. *artful intrigue,* B 1101.
inwitsorh† f. *sorrow.*
inwitspell n. *tale of woe,* Gen 2024.
inwitstæf† m. *wickedness, evil,* PPs.
inwitðanc† m. *evil thought, hostile intent.*
inwitwrāsn† f. *hostile fetter,* An.
inwræc=inwærc
inwrītere m. *writer, secretary,* ZDA 31·23.
inwritting f. *inscription,* MtK p 4[5]. [=onwr-]
inwudu m. *private woodland,* BC 3·189[2].
inwund f. *internal wound,* Lcd 70a.
inwunenes f. *persistence,* WW 426[5].
inwunung f. *residence in,* NC 304.
inwyrm m. *intestinal worm,* Lcd.
io-=geo-; **īo** (=īu)=gēo; **ioc**=geoc
iom=eom; **īong** (N)=geong, gang
īonna (N) adv. *within.*
ionnað=innoð
ïor m. *name of a river-fish (eel?)* : *name of the rune for* io, Run 28.
iorning=ærning
iornð=iernð pres. 3 sg. of iernan.
iorsian (Kgl)=iersian
Iotas mpl. *the Jutes,* Chr.
īow m.=īw; **iowan**=īewan
ippingīren=yppingīren; **iren**=īsen
irfe=ierfe; **irgian**=eargian
Irīnges weg m. *Milky Way,* WW 53[22].
irm-=ierm-; **irn-**=iern-, eorn-
irre=ierre; **irs-**=iers-
irsen-=īsen-; **irðling**=yrðling
is pres. 3 sg. of eom, anv.

Ïs n. '*ice,*' B,BH,*Met,PPs* : (pl.) *pieces of ice, BH* : *name of the rune for* ï.
īsærn (Gl)=īsearn
īsceald† *icy cold, Met,Seaf.* ['*icecold*']
īse (N)=gese
īsearn (æ, e) m. *halcyon, kingfisher,* Gl.
īsen I. (īsern, īren) n. '**IRON,**' Æ,*CP* : *iron instrument* : *fetter* : (†) *iron weapon, sword* : *ordeal of red-hot iron,* LL 230,6. **II.** adj. *o* *iron,* '**IRON,**' Æ,*CP.* **III.** (WW)=īsearn
īsenbend† (īr-) mf. *iron bond, fetter.*
īsenbyrne (īsern-) f. *iron corslet,* B 671.
īsend=īesend; **Isenesmið**=īsensmið
īsenfetor (īsern-) f. *iron fetter,* Gl.
īsengelōma (īr-) m. *iron instrument, weapon,* AA 13[16].
īsengræf m. *iron-mine,* KC 5·234'.
īsengrǣg (grēi) '*iron-grey,*' WW.
īsenheard (īr-) '*iron-hard,*' B 112.
īsenhearde f. ('*iron-hard*'), *black centaury, vervain, knapweed,* Lcd.
īsenhelm (irsen-) m. *iron helmet,* WW 142[2].
īsenhere (-ern) m. *iron-clad army,* Ex 348.
īsenhyrst adj. *with iron fittings,* KC.
īsenordāl (ȳ) n. *ordeal by iron,* LL.
īsenōre (īsern-) f. *iron mine,* WW 237[20].
īsen-panna m., -panne f. *frying-pan,* Gl.
īsenscofl f. *iron shovel,* Gl (īsernscobl).
īsenscūr f. *shower of arrows,* B 3116 (-ern).
īsensmið m. *blacksmith,* WW.
īsenswāt? m. *dross of iron?* (v. BT s.v. swāt). Lcd 108a.
īsentange f. *snuffers,* WW 327[14].
īsenðrēat m. *iron-clad troop,* B 330 (īr-).
īsenwyrhta m. *blacksmith,* WW 310[33].
īsern (Lcd)=īesend
īsern (1)=īsen; (2)=īsearn
īsgebind n. *fetters of ice,* B 1113.
īsgeblǣd (ȳ) n. *ice-blister, chilblain?* Lcd.
ïsig '*icy,*' Met : *covered with ice,* B 33.
ïsigfeðera *with frosted wings,* Seaf 24.
ïsiht *icy,* ÆL 23b[572].
ïslōes adv. *immediately,* LL (338[11]).
īsmere m. *icy lake,* Met 28[62].
±īsnian *to cover with iron.* pp. īsnod *iron-clad,* WW 236[19].
ïtest, itst pres. 2 sg., iteð, itt pres. 3 sg. of etan.
īð=īeð; **īu-,** iū=geo-, gēo; **īuc**=geoc
īūdēas sbmp. *the Jews,* G.
īūdēisc *Jewish,* G.
iugian=geocian; **īulh** (NG)=ēowic, ēow
Īūla (Men 221)=Gēola
īutan=Iotas
īuwian (AS 7[16] and n.)=īewan
ïw (ēow) m. '*yew,*' *yew-tree,* Cp,KC,*Rd* ; Æ; Mdf.
ïwberge (ēow) f. *yew-berry,* Lcd. [v. '*yew*']

K

Words beginning with **k** will be found under **c**.

L

lā interj. *lo! behold! oh! ah!* Æ. lā lēof *O Lord! O sir!* : *indeed, verily,* Æ. hwæt lā *what!* wā lā wā! *alas!*

label=(*lafel), læfel; **laber** (*Lcd*)=læfer

lāc nf. *play, sport* : (†) *strife, battle* : *sacrifice, offering,* Æ,CP : *gift, present, Mt*; Æ : *booty, B* : (†) *message.* ['*lake*']

+lac† n. *tumult, commotion.* sweorda +l. *battle* : *crowd, host,* CR 896.

lācan pret. 3 sg. leolc *to move up and down, leap, jump, swing, fly, Jul* : *play* (*instrument*) : *play upon, delude,* AO,Bo : (†) *fight, contend, B.* ['*lake*']

lācdǣd f. *munificence,* OEG 3833.

lacen? *a cloak,* WW 377²². [*Ger.* laken?]

lācfæsten *the offering of a fast,* BL 37¹⁸.

lācgeofa m. *generous giver,* PPs 67¹⁸.

+lācian *to present, bestow* : *accompany with gifts.*

lāclic *sacrificial,* ÆPD 116⁸.

±lācnian (ǣ, ē) *to heal, cure, treat, look after,* Æ,BH,*LkL*; AO,CP : *foment, dress* (*a wound*). ['*lechne*']

lācnigendlic *surgical,* HGL 478.

lācnimende only in bēon l. '*munerari*,' BHy 3¹⁹.

lācnung (ǣ) f. *healing, cure,* Æ : *medicament, remedy, Lcd*; RB. ['*lechning*']

lācsang m. *offertory hymn,* WW 130².

lac-tuc(e), m. -tuca f. *lettuce,* Æ,LCD. [*L.*]

lacu f. *stream, EC* : *pool, pond, Chr* 656 E. ['*lake*']

lād I. f. *course, journey, An,B* : (±) *way, street, water-way* : *leading, carrying, LL* : *maintenance, support.* ['*load*,' '*lode*'] **II.** f. *clearing from blame or accusation, purgation, exculpation,* CP.

ladan (NG)=hladan

±lādian *to exculpate oneself* : *let off, excuse,* Æ,AO,CP.

lādiendlic *excusable,* WW 233³¹.

lādmann m. *leader, guide,* Æ. ['*lodeman*']

lād-rinc? -rincman m. *conductor, escort,* LL 3,7 (v. 2·441 and 3·6).

ladsar=laser

lādscipe m. *leadership,* WW 481⁶.

lādtēow, lādðēow=lāttēow

lādung f. *exculpation, excuse, defence, apology,* Æ,CP.

lǣc=(1) lēac; (2) lāc; **lǣca**=lǣce

-lǣca v. āg-, ellen-l. etc.

+lǣca m. *a rival,* GPH 391.

lǣcan *to spring up, rise, flare up,* SAT 716.

+lǣcan *to emulate,* GPH 391 : *join with, make common cause with?* CPs 140⁴. [lāc]

±lǣccan *to seize, grasp, comprehend,* Æ : *capture, catch, Chr,G,LL* : *take, receive,* Æ. ['*latch*,' '*i-lecche*']

lǣccung (e) f. *reproach,* EPs 88³⁵.

lǣce (ē, ȳ) m. *physician, doctor, BH,LkL*; Æ,CP : '*leech*,' *WW*; Æ.

lǣcebōc f. *book of prescriptions,* LCD.

lǣcecræft m. '*leech-craft*,' *art of healing, Bo,Lcd*; Æ : *remedy, prescription,* Æ.

lǣcecræftig *skilled in medicine,* LCD 186b.

lǣcecynn n. *race of physicians,* RD 6¹⁰.

lǣcecyst f. *medicine chest,* GD 344¹⁷.

lǣcedōm (ē) m. *medicament, medicine, BH, WW* : *healing, salvation,* CP. ['*leechdom*']

lǣcedōmlic *salutary,* A 5·458.

lǣcedōmnes f. *cataplasm,* WW.

lǣcefeoh n. *doctor's fee,* LL (148¹⁹).

lǣcefinger m. ('*leech-finger*'), *fourth finger, Lcd,WW.*

lǣcegeatwa? (-getea) fp. *medical apparatus,* v. NC 304.

lǣcehūs n. *hostelry, hospital,* Lk 10³⁴.

lǣceiren n. *surgeon's knife, lancet,* GD 32.

lǣcesealf f. *medicinal ointment,* WW 514²¹.

lǣceseax n. *lancet,* CP 187⁹.

lǣcewyrt f. *medicinal herb, drug,* Æ : *ribwort* : *medical treatment.*

lǣcnian=lācnian

lǣdan (±) *to* '*LEAD*,' *guide, conduct, carry, lift, take, bring,* Æ,*Chr*; CP : (±) *produce, bring forth* : *pass, lead* (*life*) : *to mark or beat the bounds of land,* EC 155⁵ : *do* : *place, lay,* Æ : *sprout forth, grow, spread.* wīf l. *take a wife, marry.*

lǣde (BH 400²)=lǣwede

lǣden I. (ē, ēo) n. '*Latin*,' *Bf,BH,CP,LG* : *any foreign language, Lcd.* ['*leden*'] **II.** (ē, ȳ) adj. *Latin.*

lǣdenbōc (ē, ȳ) f. *Latin book,* Æ.

lǣdend I. m. *bringer,* CR. **II.** m. *excuser, apologist,* PPs 140⁵. [*lǣdan]

+lǣdendlic *ductile, malleable,* LRPs 97⁵.

lǣdengereord n. *Latin language,* LCD 3·440'.

lǣdengeðēode n. *Latin language,* CP 7.

lǣdenisc *Latin,* BH.

lǣdenlār f. *knowledge of Latin,* W 124¹².

Lǣdenlic *Latin,* NC 304.

+lǣdenlic (EPs 97)=+lǣdendlic

lǣdennama m. *Latin noun,* ÆGR 292¹⁸.

lǣdensprǣc (ē) f. *Latin language,* Æ,CP.

lǣdenstæfum (ē) adv. *in Latin,* Jn 19²⁰.

lǣdenware mpl. *Latin people, Romans,* CP

lǣdenword (ē) n. *Latin word,* ÆGR 122⁶.

lǣdere m. *leader,* S²Hy 6¹³.

lǣdnes f. *bringing forth,* BHo 76¹⁵.

lǣdtēow=lāttēow

lǣf=(1) lāf; (2) lēaf

±**lǣfan** (ē) I. to 'leave' ('yleft'), bequeath, B,Jn; Æ,CP : spare, leave behind, have left, G : remain, Æ. [lāf] II.=līefan

lǣfel (e) m. spoon, basin, vessel, bowl, cup. [Ger. löffel; L. labellum]

lǣfend (WW 168[17])=lǣwend

lǣfer f. rush, reed, iris, gladiolus, Lcd,WW; Æ : metal plate, Æ. ['laver'; 'levers']

lǣferbed n. reed-bed, WW 138[29].

lǣfnes=lēafnes

lǣg pret. 3 sg. of licgan.

lǣg=(1) lēag; (2) līeg

lǣgde=legde pret. sg. of lecgan.

lǣgon pret. pl. of licgan.

lǣgt=līget

lǣht pp., lǣhte pret. sg. of lǣccan.

lǣl (ē) f., lǣla m. rod, whip, switch : bruise, weal, stripe, Ex.

lǣlan? to be bruised, An 1445 (GK read lǣla m.).

lǣlian I. to become black and blue, WW 431[30]. II. (ē) to level, aim at, Lcd.

lǣmen (ē) of clay, earthen, Æ. [lām]

lǣmian=lēmian

lǣn (ā) I. nf. loan, borrowing, lease, grant, gift, present, benefit, Æ,CP. [lēon] II.= lǣnland

lǣn-=lēn-

±**lǣnan** (ē) to 'lend,' Æ,WW ; CP : give, grant, lease, Gen ; Æ.

lǣndagas† mpl. loan-days, transitory days, days of a man's life, B.

lǣnde-, lǣnden-=lenden-

lǣne (ē) lent, temporary, inconstant, transitory, CP : perishable, frail, poor : weak, sinful, CP. [lǣn]

lǣnelic passing, transitory, Bl 73[9].

lǣnend m. lender, WW. ['lenend']

lǣnendlic (W)=lǣnelic

lǣnere m. 'lender,' WW 189[21].

lǣng=leng; **lǣngten-**=lencten-

lǣnian=lēanian

lǣnland n. leased land, v. LL 2·323.

lǣnlic (LL)=lǣnelic; **-lǣnung** v. fēoh-l.

lǣpeldre f. dish, ÆH,WW. [lapian]

lǣpewince (e) f. lapwing, Gl.

lǣppa (a) m. lappet, piece, section, lobe, portion, district, CP,Lcd; Æ. ['lap']

-lǣppede v. fif-l.

+**lǣr** empty : empty-handed. [Ger. leer]

+**lǣran** (ē) to teach, instruct, guide, BH,LL : enjoin, advise, persuade, urge, preach : (+) convert : (+) †recall, ES 37·197. 1. forð hand down (to others). ±lǣred learned (opposed to lǣwed), CP. hence clerical (as opposed to lay), spiritual (as opposed to temporal), Æ,CP. ['lere,' 'ylere(d)']

+**lǣre**=lǣr

+**lǣrednes** f. learning, skill, Æ,BH.

lǣrend m. misleader, instigator, HL 154[71].

lǣrest=lǣst

lǣrestre f. instructress, Æ.

lǣrgedōfe adapted for instruction? FT 61.

lǣrig m. border? cover ? (of a shield), v. A 37·55 and LF 171.

-lǣrigian v. ymb-l.

lǣringmǣden n. female pupil, ApT 20[13].

lǣringmann m. disciple, RB 20[6].

lǣrnes f. emptiness, Lcd 22b. ['leerness']

lǣs pret. 3 sg. of lesan.

lǣs I. (ē) adv. and sbn. less, lest, Æ,AO,CP. ðȳ lǣs (ðe) conj. w. subj. lest. II. f. gs. lǣswe pasture, JnL,WW; Æ; Mdf. ['lease,' 'leasow'] III. f. (blood-)letting, Lcd.

lǣsboren of lower birth, LL (246').

lǣsest (MtR)=lǣst I.; **lǣsian**=lǣswian

lǣson pret. pl. of lesan.

lǣssa (ē) adj. (comp. of lȳtel) 'less,' smaller, fewer, Æ,Bo,Chr : inferior, MtL,MtR. sb. Æ,Bf. adv. BH.

lǣst f. fault, sin, NC 305. [ON.]

lǣst I. superl. of lȳtel 'least,' G,Gu,Lcd; CP, AO. ðe lǣste lest, CM. II. f. performance, fulfilment, Ex 308. III.=lāst

±**lǣstan** (ē) to follow, help, serve, B,Bl,Met, OET ; AO : perform, do, carry out, accomplish, B,Bo,Gen; AO : endure, last, continue, Cr,Met; Æ : furnish, pay, grant, W. ['last,' 'ylast']

lǣste f. 'last' (for the foot), WW.

lǣstend m. doer, performer, BH.

+**lǣstfullian** to testify, LPs 80[9].

+**lǣstwyrhta** (eo[2]) m. shoemaker, WW.

lǣswe v. lǣs II.

±**lǣswian** tr. and intr. to depasture, graze, feed, Æ,LkL. ['leasow']

lǣt I. (lat- in obl. cases) comp. lǣtra; sup. lǣtest, lǣtemest slow, B,Bl,CP,Lcd; Æ : slack, lax, negligent : 'late,' An,Lk. II. m. man of the class between the slave and the ceorl, LL (v. 2·564). ['laet']

lǣt pres. 3 sg. of lǣdan.

+**lǣt**=+lǣte II.

±**lǣtan**[7] pret. 3 sg. lēt, leort to allow to remain, leave behind, depart from, 'let' alone, Bl,CP : leave undone, BH : bequeath, EC : allow, Bl,LL : cause to do, BH : regard as, consider, BH,Chr,CP : suppose : conduct oneself : behave towards, treat : allow to escape, emit, let out, set free, Æ,Lcd : 'let' (on lease), BC : assert, pretend, Lk : allot, assign. 1. from refrain from. 1. ūt to put to sea. +1. nēah land approach the shore? (ES 37·191). on bæc 1. leave behind. 1. for to take (one) for. on trēowe +1. to entrust, WW 239[7].

lǣtania=lētania

lætbyrd f. *slow birth*, LCD 185a.

+**lǣte I.** n. *manners, bearing*, NC 295. [*ON.* lǣti] **II.** n. *junction of roads*, Æ,CHRD.

lætemest I. adv. *lastly, finally*, NG. **II.** v. læt. ['*latemost*']

læthȳdig *slow-minded, dull*, CRA 10.

lætlīce adv. *slowly, Gu.* ['*lately*']

lætmest=lætemest

lætnes f. *slowness*, ÆL 23b⁶⁴⁷ : *sloth*, GD 174²³.

lætra (*Æ,LL*) v. læt. ['*latter*']

lætrǣde *slow, deliberate*, CP 149¹⁴. ['*latrede*']

lætsum *backward, Chr.* ['*latesome*']

lætt f. (pl. latta) *beam*, '*lath*,' WW.

lǣttēow=lǣttēow

lǣttewestre f. *guide*, Æ 23b⁵⁰⁸. [lǣttēow]

lætting=letting; **-lǣttu** v. un-l.

lǣð n. *a division of a county containing several hundreds*, '*lathe*,' BC 3·162 : *landed property?* (*meadow*) *land?* LL 400,3².

lǣð-=lāð-

lǣðan *to abuse, revile, hate* : *cause to shun*, RB 11¹⁸. [lāð]

lǣðð, lǣððo (CP) f. *wrong, injury* : *hatred, malice, Bl.* ['*leth*'; lāð]

lǣuw=lēow

lǣw (ē) f. *injury*, W 165⁹.

lǣwa (ē) m. *betrayer, traitor, Lk*; Æ. [v. '*lewe*']

±**lǣwan** *to betray*, BL,Ps. [*Goth.* lēwjan]

-lǣwe v. druncen-, hunger-l.

lǣwede *lay, laic, unlearned.* as sb. *layman, BH*; Æ,CP. ['*lewd*']

lǣwel=læfel

lǣwend m. *betrayer, traitor*, GL.

lǣwerce=lāwerce; **lǣwil**=læfel

lǣx=leax

lāf f. *what is left, remnant, legacy, relic, remains, rest, Bl,Chr*; Æ : *relict, widow*, Æ,AO. tō lāfe *alone.* tō lāfe bēon *to remain over, Bl.* wǣpna, daroða l. *survivors of battle.* hamora lāfa *results of forging, swords.* ['*lave*'; līfan]

lāferce=lāwerce

±**laflan** *to pour water on, wash*, '*lave*,' *bathe, B,Lcd* : *ladle out, Lcd.*

lafor m. *leopard*, AA 22³.

lag-=lah-; **-laga** v. lund-l.

laga m. *law*, LL,WW.

lage-=lagu-

lagen pp. of lēan II.

±**lagian** *to ordain*, W. ['*law*,' '*i-lahen*']

lago-=lagu-; **-lagol** v. ǣ-l.

lāgon=lǣgon pret. pl. of licgan.

lagu I. f. (old neut. pl. lagu; CHR 1052D) '*law*,' *ordinance, rule, regulation*, Æ; *Chr, LL,RB,W* : *right, legal privilege*, LL : *district governed by the same laws.* **II.** m.

water, flood, sea, ocean, Gen,Mt : *name of the rune for* l. ['*lay*']

+**lagu** np. *extent, surface* (*of sea*), SEAF 64? [*OS.* gilagu]

lagucræftig *skilled in seafaring*, B 209.

lagufæsten† n. *sea, ocean.*

lagufæðm m. *enveloping waves*, RD 61⁷.

laguflōd m. *wave, stream, waters, flood, sea, ocean.*

lagulād† f. *water-way, sea.*

lagumearg m. *sea-horse, ship*, GU 1306.

lagusīð† m. *sea-journey*, GEN.

lagustrǣt f. *sea-path*, B 239.

lagustrēam† m. *water, sea, ocean.*

laguswimmend m. *swimming in the sea* (*fish*), SOL 289.

lāh pret. 3 sg. of lēon.

lah-=lag-

lahbreca m. *law-breaker, impious man*, SC 9¹⁰. [lagu]

lahbrecende *impious, profane*, SC 9⁹.

lahbryce m. *breach of the law*, LL.

lah-cēap, **-cōp** m. *money paid* (*by an outlaw*) *for restitution of legal rights*, LL.

lahlic *lawful, legal*, SC 46². adv. -lice.

lahmann m. *an official declarer of the law*, LL 376. ['*lawman*']

lahriht n. *legal right*, LL.

lah-slitt fn., **-slite** m. *fine for breach of the* (*Danish*) *law*, LL.

lahwita m. *lawyer*, LL (308¹³).

lām n. '*loom*,' *clay, earth*, Æ,WW; Mdf.

lama (o) wk. adj. and sbm. *crippled*, '*lame*,' *paralytic, weak*, Æ,BH,Cp,El,Mt,WW.

lamb (e, o) pl. lamb(e)ru, lambor (A) n. '*lamb*,' Æ,G,Gl,Gu,VPs.

lambyrd f. *imperfect birth*, LCD 185a.

lāmfæt n.† *vessel of clay* (*the body*).

lamp I. pret. 3 sg. of limpan. **II.** (KGL)= lamb

lamprede f. *lamprey*, WW 94¹⁷. [L.]

lāmpytt m. '*loampit*,' KC 3·252²⁴.

lāmsceall *tile*, APs 21¹⁶.

lāmsēað m. *loampit*, EC 448¹³.

lāmwyrhta m. *potter*, G.

lān=lǣn

lanan obl. cases of lanu.

land (o) n. *earth*, '*land*,' *soil*, B,BH,Gen,Sc, WW; Mdf : *territory, realm, province, district, Cp,Chr,Bl,VPs* : *landed property*, Æ,Bl : *country* (*not town*), Æ,BH : *ridge in a ploughed field.*

+**landa** (o) m. *compatriot, kinsman*, WW 211²⁰.

landādl=hlandādl?

landælf f. *land-elf*, WW 516²⁷.

landāgend m. *native*, BH.

landāgende *owning land*, LL.

landâr f. *landed property*, Æ.

landbegenga (i²) m. *husbandman, peasant, native*, CP.
landbegengnes (o¹) f. *habitation*, BPs 119⁵.
landbigong (o¹) m. *dwelling in a country*, BPs 118⁵⁴.
landbōc f. *'land-book,' written grant of land*, Ct,WW.
landbrǣce m. *first ploughing (after land has lain fallow)*, WW 105¹¹.
landbūend I. mf. *inhabitant, native : husbandman*. **II.** f. *colony*, WE 51¹.
landbūende *dwelling on the land*, CREAT 80.
landbūnes f. *colony, settlement*, WE 51¹².
land-cēap, -cōp m. *fine paid to the lord on the alienation of land*, BC. ['landcheap']
landcofa m. *land, district*, LPs 59⁸.
landefn(e) n. *measure or proportion of land*, CHR 1085.
landesmann (Æ,Chr) = landmann
landfæsten (o¹) n. *natural fortress*, AO 80¹⁴.
landfeoh n. *recognitory rent for land*, KC.
landfolc n. *'land-folk,' natives*, Æ.
landfruma m. *ruler, prince*, B 31.
landfyrd f. *army*, BH,CHR.
landfyrding f. *military operations on land*, CHR 999.
landgafol n. *land-tax, tribute*, LL. ['landgavel']
landgehwerf (=ea³) n. *exchange of land*, TC 191⁶.
landgemaca m. *neighbour*, OEG.
landge-mǣre, -mirce n. *boundary, limit, frontier*, AO.
landgesceaft f. *earthly creature*, DA 360.
landgeweorc n. *fortified place*, B 938.
landgewyrpe n. *heap of earth?* KC.
landhæbbende *owning or ruling land*, DR, LL.
landhæfen f. *real property*, LL 22,32.
landhere m. *native force : land force (opposed to naval force)*.
landhlāford m. *lord of a country, lord of a manor, 'landlord,'* EC,LL.
landhredding f. *redemption of land*, CC 9¹¹⁸.
landlagu f. *local law*, LL. ['landlaw']
landlēas *not owning land*, LL. ['landless']
land-lēod m., nap. -lēode, -lēoda, -lēodan *inhabitant of a country, native*, AO.
landlyre m. *loss of territory*, CHR 1105.
landmann m. *inhabitant of a country, native*, Ex,LL. ['landmann']
landmearc m. *boundary*, Jul,KC. ['landmark']
landmearca m. *land, country*, LPs 59⁸.
+**landod** *having landed property*, LL 182,11.
landopenung f. *first ploughing of land*, WW 147⁹.
landrǣden v. ealdlandrǣden.
landrest f. *grave*, AN 782.

landrica m. *landed proprietor*, LL.
landrice n. *territory*, AO,WW.
landriht n. *'land-right,' right to own or occupy land or connected with its occupation, B,Ex,Gen : that which is due from land or estates*.
landscearu (a²) f. *tract of land, province, country*, CP : *boundary, landmark*. [v. CC 48]
landscipe m. *region*, GEN 376.
landscoru = landscearu
landsēta m. *settler*, WW 111¹⁵. [sǣta]
+**landseten** f. *occupation of land*, Ct : *occupied land, estate*, LL.
landseðla m. *occupier of land*, TC 593⁶.
landsidu m. *custom of a country*, CP.
landsittende *occupying land*, CHR 1085.
landsōcn† f. *search for land to settle on*.
landspēd f. *landed property*, KC 3·349'.
landspēdig *rich in land*, ÆGR.
landsplott m. *plot of land*, KC,LPs.
landstede (o) m. *region*, WIF 16.
landstycce n. *small plot of ground*, GD,LL.
landwaru f. *inhabitants, population*, B 2321.
landweard m. *coast-warden*, B 1890.
landwela m. *earthly possessions*, PH 505.
lane = lanu
lang (o) comp. lengra, superl. lengest 'long,' tall, ÆGr,AO,BH,G,Lcd,Ma; CP : lasting.
+**lang** (usu. w. æt or on) *dependent on, attainable from, present in, belonging to*, Æ,AO,Gu. [v. 'along']
Langafrīgedæg m. *Good Friday*, LL.
langað = langoð
langbolster mn. *feather-bed*, WW 276³⁶.
lange (o) adv. comp. leng, lenge, superl. lengest 'long,' a long time, far, B,BH,Bl, Bo.
langfǣre *lasting, protracted*, Æ.
langfērnes f. *length, long duration*, Sc 29¹.
langfirst m. *long space of time*, GU 920.
langgestrēon n. *old store of wealth*, B 2240.
langian I. (o) (impers. with acc. of pers.) *to 'long,' yearn after, grieve for, be pained*, AO : *lengthen, grow longer*, Lcd : *summon*. **II.** *to belong*, KC 4·215⁴.
+**langian** *to send for, summon, call*, Æ : *apprehend, seize*, LL 202,6².
langieldo f. *advanced age* (Swt)
langlīce adv. *for a long time, long, at length*, Æ.
langlīfe *long-lived*, Æ.
langmōd *constant, patient*, Ps. adv. -lice.
langmōdig *long-suffering*, EPs 7¹².
langmōdnes f. *long-suffering*, Sc 10¹⁷.
langnes f. *length*, Æ. ['longness']
langoð† m. *longing, discontent*.
langsceaft *having a long shaft*, AA 23¹⁰.
langscip n. *man of war*, CHR 897 A.

langstrang '*longanimis*,' LPs 102⁸.
langsum (o¹) *long, lasting, tedious, protracted,* B,*Lcd*; Æ. ['*longsome*']
langsumlic (o) *tedious,* ÆH 1·362'. adv. -līce *long,* AO 58¹⁷ : *patiently,* ÆL 23b³⁹¹.
langsumnes f. *length,* Ps; Æ : *patience,* NC 305. ['*longsomeness*']
langswéored (ȳ²) *long-necked,* HExC 253, 279.
langtwidig *lasting, assured,* B 1708.
langung (o) f. '*longing*,' *Bl* : *weariness, sadness, dejection,* Æ : *delay,* CP. [langian]
langunghwīl f. *time of weariness,* AN 125.
langweb n. *warp* (*in weaving*), WW 187¹².
langwege (o¹, oe²) '*peregre*,' MkL 13³⁴.
langwyrpe *oblong,* NC 305³⁴⁷.
lánland=lǣnland
lann (o)† f. *chain, fetter.*
lanu (o) f. '*lane*,' *street, Bl.*
laplan *to* '*lap*' *up, drink, Lcd*; Æ.
lappa (GL)=lǣppa
lár f. '*love,*' *learning, science, art of teaching, preaching, doctrine, Bl*; Æ,CP : *study : precept, exhortation, advice, instigation, JnL*; AO : *history, story : cunning,* GEN 2693.
lárbóc f. *book containing instruction* (used of St Paul's Epistles, and Bede's works), Æ.
lárbodung f. *teaching, preaching,* CHRD 50¹⁰.
lárbysn f. *example,* WW 163⁴³.
lárcniht (e²) m. *disciple,* LkL p 2².
lárcræft m. *knowledge,* SOL 3 : *erudition,* CHRD 66³⁶.
lárcwide† m. *teaching, precept.*
lárdōm m. *teaching, instruction,* LL 258,51.
lár-éow, -ow, -uw(a) m. *teacher, master, preacher, BH,JnL,WW*; Æ,AO,CP. ['*larew*']
láréowdóm m. *function of teacher, instruction,* CP : *ecclesiastical authority,* Æ,CP.
láréowlic *like a teacher,* OEG,RB.
láréowsetl n. *teacher's seat, pulpit,* OEG,Mt.
láréwes=láréowes gs. of láréow.
lárfæsten n. *prescribed fast,* A 11·99.
lárhlystend m. *catechumen,* OEG 2881.
lárhús n. *school,* HGL 405.
lárléast (ē, ȳ) f. *want of instruction, ignorance,* LL,W.
lárlic *of or conducive to learning, instructive,* Æ : *learned : doctrinal : persuasive.* betwux lárlicum gefylcum *amongst soldiers in training,* Æ.
lársmiÐ† m. (nap. -smeoðas) *teacher, counsellor.*
lárspell n. *homily, treatise,* Æ. ['*lorespell*']
lársum *teachable,* NC 305.
lárswice m. *trickery,* W 309¹⁴.
lár-ðéaw, -ðéow (Jn 1³⁸; '*lorthew*')= láréow

láröegn m. *teacher,* NC 305.
láruw(a) (LG)=láreow
lárwita m. *learned man,* LL (308¹³).
láser (o²) m? *weed, tare,* BF 30¹⁶,GL.
lást (ǣ, ē, ēa) m. *sole of foot : spoor, footprint, track, trace,* B,*Bl*; Æ,CP : *gait, step.* on lást(e) *behind, after, in pursuit of.* on l. lecgan *to follow.* lástas lecgan *to go.* ['*last*']
±**lást** (ǣ, ē) n. *accomplishment, observance,* RB 5⁵ : *duty, due, obligation, vow.*
+**lástful** *helpful, serviceable, LL*; AO. ['*lastfull*']
lástweard m. *successor, heir, follower : pursuer.*
lástword n. *fame after death,* SEAF 73.
lasur=laser; **lat-** v. læt-; **lát**=lád
lata m. *slow person,* BL 163⁸.
late adv. comp. lator, sup. latest '*late*,' *Chr, Jul : slowly, Lcd :* at last, AO : *lately,* RB. [læt]
latemest=lǣtemest II.; **látéow**=lǣttéow
±**latian** *to be slow, indolent : linger, delay, hesitate,* Æ.
lator, adv. comp., latost (æ), superl. *slower, later, Bf;* AO,CP. ['*latter*,' '*last*']
latt=lætt
lattéh f. *guiding rein,* WW 120⁹. [lád]
láttéow, láttéowa (ǣ) m. *leader, guide, general, Bo,VPs* (lad-); AO,CP. ['*lattew*']
láttéowdóm m. *leadership, guidance, instruction,* CP.
látðéow, látuw=lǣttéow
latu f. *delay : (+) hindrance,* DR 96⁵?
latung f. *delay, hindrance,* OEG 7¹²⁹.
láð I. (±) *hated, hateful, hostile, malignant, evil,* AO,B : *loathsome, noxious, unpleasant, Chr,Ep;* CP. ['*loath*'] **II.** n. *pain, harm, injury, misfortune,* AO : *insult, annoyance, harmful thing, BH,Lcd;* CP. ['*loath*']
láðbite m. *wound,* B 1122.
láðe adv. *inimically, in detestation,* BH,PPs.
láðéow=lǣttéow
láðettan (ǣ) *to hate, loathe : make hateful or repulsive,* Æ.
láðgeníðla† m. *persecutor, foe.*
láðgetéona† m. *enemy.* B.
láðgewinna m. *enemy,* RD 16²⁹.
laðian *to invite, summon, call upon, ask,* Æ, CP. [Ger. laden]
láðian *to hate, be hated,* AO; Æ. ['*loathe*']
láðléas *inoffensive, innocent,* WW. ['*loathless*']
láðlic '*loathly*,' *hateful, horrible, repulsive, unpleasant, BH;* Æ. adv. -líce, Met.
láðscipe m. *misfortune,* GEN 2048.
láðsearu n? *hateful contrivance,* DA 436.
láðsíð m. *painful journey, death,* Ex 44.
láðspel n. *sad tidings,* AO.
láððéow=lǣttéow

±**laðung** f. *calling, invitation, CP : assembly, congregation, church,* Æ. ['*lathing*']
lāðwende† *hateful, hostile, bad.*
lāðwendemōd *hostile-minded,* GEN 448.
lāðwendnes f. *hostility,* LCD.
lāðweorc n. *evil deed,* PPs 105[26].
laur m. *laurel, bay, laver,* LCD.
laurbēam (lawer-) m. *laurel,* WE,WW.
laurberige f. *laurel-berry,* LCD.
+**laured** *laurel-flavoured,* LCD 84a.
laurice (*Cp*)=lāwerce
laurisc *of laurel,* AA 6[20].
laurtrēow n. *laurel-tree,* LCD.
lauwer, lawer=laur
lāwerce (ǣ) f. '*lark,*' WW; Mdf.
lawernbēam m. *laurel,* WE 6[12].
lēa I. (VPs)=lēo. II. gdas. of lēah.
lēac I. (ǣ, ē, ēo) n. '*leek,*' *onion, garlic, garden-herb,* Lcd; Æ. II. pret. 3 sg. of lūcan.
lēac-=lēah-
lēacblæd n. *leek leaf,* NC 305.
lēaccærse (e[2]) f. *cress, nasturtium, Erf*; LCD. [v. '*cress*']
lēac-trog, -troc *a bunch of berries,* GL.
lēactūn (lēah-, lēh-) m. *kitchen-garden, garden of herbs,* LkL,WW. ['*leighton*']
lēactūnweard (ē[1]) m. *gardener,* WW 127[14]. ['*leightonward*']
lēacweard (ē[1], o[2]) m. *gardener,* G,WW.
lēad (ē) n. '*lead,*' *BH*; Æ,CP : *leaden vessel, cauldron,* LL.
lēaden (ē) '*leaden,*' Æ,LL.
lēadgedelf n. *lead-mine,* KC 3·401[7].
lēadgewiht n. *lead-weight, a scale of weight,* v. CC 77.
lēadgota m. *plumber,* LL 455,16.
lēadstæf m. *loaded stick,* WW 441[20].
lēaf (ī) I. (±) f. '*leave*' ('*y-leave*'), *permission, privilege, BH,Chr,Sc*; Æ,CP. II. (ēo) n. '*leaf,*' *shoot,* pl. *foliage, MtL,VPs*; Æ : *sheet of paper, BH.* III. (+) *leafy,* WW 411[12].
±**lēafa** m. *belief, faith,* Æ,Bo,Mt; AO : *creed.* ['*leve,*' '*yleve*']
±**lēafe** (ǣ) f. *leave, permission, licence,* Æ.
±**lēafful** *believing, JnR : orthodox (Christian) : faithful, trustworthy, MtL.* ['*leafful*'] adv. -līce.
+**lēaffulnes** f. *faith, trust, faithfulness,* Æ.
lēafhelmig *leafy at the top,* GPH 390.
±**lēafhlystend** (e) m. *catechumen,* OEG.
+**lēaflēas** *unbelieving,* Æ.
+**lēaflēasnes** f. *unbelief,* W 294[2].
+**lēaf-lēast,** -lȳst f. *unbelief,* Æ.
lēaflēoht *easy to believe?* RB 5[19].
+**lēaflic** *credible, faithful,* Æ : *catholic,* WW 201[26]. adv. -līce.
lēafnes (ē, ȳ) f. *leave, permission,* BH.

+**lēafnesword** n. *password,* B 245.
lēafscead n. *leafy shade,* PH 205.
lēafsele m. *booth,* BYH 118[14].
+**lēafsum** (ǣ) *believing, faithful : credible.*
lēafwyrm (i[2]) m. *caterpillar,* ASPs 77[51].
lēag I. (ē) f. '*lye,*' *alkalized water, Ep,Lcd.* II.=lēah I. III. pret. 3 sg. of lēogan and lēon.
lēah I. lēage (CHR) m. *piece of ground,* '*lea,*' *meadow, BC*; v. GBG and Mdf. II.=lēag I. and III.
leahte pret. 3 sg. of leccan.
leahter=leahtor
leahtor (e[1]) m. *vice, sin, offence, crime, fault,* Æ,CP : *reproach : disease, injury,* LCD.
leahtor-=hleahtor-
leahtorcwide m. *opprobrious speech,* JUL 199.
leahtorful (e[1], e[2]) *vicious, seductive,* Æ.
leahtorlēas (e[2]) *faultless, blameless,* EL, LL.
leahtorlic *vicious, faulty,* GUTH 101[11]. adv. līce *foully, wickedly,* Æ.
-leahtorwyrðe v. un-l.
leahtras nap. of leahtor.
±**leahtrian** (e) *to accuse, revile, reprove, blame,* Æ; AO,CP : *corrupt.* ['*lehtrie*']
leahtric m. *lettuce,* LCD,WW. [*L.* lactuca]
lēahtrog=lēactrog
lēahtrung (ē) f. *derogation,* WW 150[1].
lēahtūn=lēactūn
lēan I. n. *reward, gift, loan, compensation, remuneration, retribution, B,Mt*; Æ. ['*lean*'] II. sv[6] (pret. 3 sg. lōg, lōh) and wv. *to blame, reproach,* AO,CP.
lēangyfa m. *rewarder,* LCD 3·436'.
±**lēanian** (ǣ) *to reward, recompense, repay, requite,* Æ,CP. [*Ger.* lohnen]
lēap m. *basket, W : basket for catching or keeping fish, WW : measure : trunk (body),* JUD 111. ['*leap*']
lēas I. adj. (w. g.) *without, free from, devoid of, bereft of* : (±) *false, faithless : untruthful, deceitful, WW*; Æ : *lax : vain, worthless.* II. n. *falsehood, lying, Bo*; CP : *untruth, mistake.* ['*lease*']
lēasbrēd (-bregd) I. *lying, false, deceitful,* Æ. II. m. *cheating, trickery,* LL,W.
lēasbrēda m. *trickster,* ES 43·306.
lēasbrēdende *wily, deceitful,* ÆGR 286[6].
lēasbrēdnes (ǣ[2]) f. *deception, falsehood,* ÆL.
lēasbregd=lēasbrēd
lēascræft m. *false art,* BL 25[12].
lēase *falsely,* BH 122[17].
lēasere m. *liar, hypocrite, MtL : buffoon, mime, jester, fool.* ['*leaser*']
lēasest (*MtL*)=lǣst I.
lēasettan *to pretend,* Æ,RB.
lēas-ferhð, -fyrhð *false,* NC 305.

lēasferðnes f. *levity, folly,* CP313¹⁰.
lēasfyrhte=lēasferhð
lēasgewlta m. *a false witness,* ÆH1·46'.
lēasgewltnes f. *false witness,* Æ.
lēasglelp m. *vainglory,* CP367²⁴.
lēaslan *to lie,* Ps. ['*lease*']
lēasllc *false, deceitful, sham, empty,* Æ,CP. adv. -līce, Æ,CP.
lēasllccettan *to dissemble,* WW388⁸³.
lēasllcettung f. *dissimulation,* GUTH12¹⁸.
lēasmōdnes f. *instability,* CP308⁶.
lēasnes f. *lying : levity,* BH322²³.
lēasōleccan *to blandish, flatter,* GD34²⁷.
lēasōlecung f. *empty flattery,* WW430²¹.
lēassagol (u²) *lying, false,* Æ.
lēasscēawere m. *spy,* B253.
lēasspell n. *lie, fiction, fable,* BH,WW.
lēasspellung f. *empty or false talk,* AO.
lēassponung f. *allurement,* WW452³.
lēast=lāst; lēast-=læst-
lēastyhtan *to cajole,* WW431⁴.
lēastyhtung f. *cajolery,* WW430²¹.
lēasuht (=wiht?) *enticer, seducer,* OEG4014.
lēasung f. '*leasing,*' *lying, false witness, deceit, hypocrisy, artifice,* JnL : *a lie,* Ps : *empty talk, frivolity, laxity.* II. f. *indemnity?* WW.
lēasungspell n. *idle tale,* AO40⁸.
lēaswyrcend m. *deceiver,* ÆH1·102.
lēat pret. 3 sg. of lūtan.
leatlan=latian; +leaðlan=+laðian
lēaðor n. *soap, soda,* Lcd,WW. ['*lather*']
lēaðorwyrt (lēoðo-) f. *soap-wort?* LCD16a.
lēawede=læwede
lēawfinger (=æ¹) m. *index-finger, forefinger,* PPs72¹¹.
leax (æ, e) m. *salmon,* Cp,Met,WW; ÆL. ['*lax*']
leb-=lef-, læf-; lec=hlec
+lec pret. 3 sg. of +lacan.
lēc I. m. *look, regard,* Æ; A11·118⁵⁰. II.= lēac I. and II.
+lecc-=+læcc-
leccan pret. 3 sg. leahte, le(o)hte *to water, irrigate, wet, moisten, slake,* CP. [cp. *Ger.* lechzen]
leccing f. *irrigation, watering,* WW (KGl). ['*leaching*']
lēce=lǣce; lēcetere (KGL65²⁹)=līcettere
lecg f. *part of a weapon?* (BT) *sheath?* (WC), TC527⁹.
±lecgan *to* '*lay,*' *put, place, deposit, set,* Æ, G,Gen,Lcd,Rd; CP : *dispose, arrange :* attach, W : *bury,* Jn,Chr : *put before, submit,* Æ : *betake oneself, go :* lay (egg), Lcd : *prostrate, cast down, lay low, kill,* Bo,Lk,LL. l. on (w. d.) *put upon, charge with,* Chr,Gu; CP. lāstas l. *go, journey,* Gen. on lāst l. *follow.* [causative of licgan]

lēclwyrt (Cp)=lǣcewyrt
lēcnlan (NG)=lācnian
lectrlc=leahtric; lēctūn-=lēactūn-
lecða m. *ship's bottom or hold,* Ep,WW46¹⁴.
+led '*catasta,*' WW (v. BTs).
lēd=lēad; lēdan=lǣdan
lēde=legde pret. 3 sg. of lecgan.
lēden=lǣden, lēaden
lēf I. (ī) *feeble, infirm, weak, injured.* II.=lēaf
lēf-=lēaf-; lēfan=(1) līefan; (2) lǣfan
+lēfed *weak, sickly, aged,* BH,W.
lefel, lefil=læfel
+lēfenscipe m. *justification,* JnL15²².
lēfmon m. *sick person,* GNE45.
lēfung f. *paralysis,* ÆH2·486¹⁸.
leg (=læg) pret. 3 sg. of licgan.
lēg=(1) līeg; (2) lēah; lēg-=līg-, lēog-
lēga (A)=lǣwa
legde pret. 3 sg. of lecgan.
+lege f? *lair, bed,* Mdf (or ?+legu (BTs)).
lēgelēoht n. *light (of flame),* MFH168.
legen pp. of licgan.
leger n. *lying, illness,* AO,B; Æ : '*lair,*' couch, bed, Wif : *grave,* LL; Æ. clǣne legere *consecrated grave.* on life ge on legere *in life and in death,* LL. [licgan]
lēgeræsc (RWH79,81)=līgetræsc
legerbǣre *sick, ill,* TC611²⁰.
legerbedd n. *bed, sick bed,* Æ : *grave.*
+leger-ed, -od *confined to bed,* Æ.
legerfæst *sick, ill,* RB64⁷.
+legergield n. '*lupercalia,*' WW437¹⁴.
legerstōw f. *burial place,* ÆH.
legertēam m. *cohabitation, marriage,* MH174⁹.
legerwlte fm. *fine for unlawful cohabitation,* LL. ['*lairwite*']
lēges=lēages gs. of lēah.
legeð pres. 3 sg. of lecgan.
legie f. *legion,* AO. [L.]
+legu v. +lege.
-legu v. ealdor-l.; leh-=leah-
lēh=lēah; lēh-=lēac-; lēhnan=lȳgnian
lēht=lēoht; lēhtan (Nar)=līhtan
lehte pret. 3 sg. of leccan.
lehtor=leahtor; lēl (KGL)=læl
leloðre f. *silverweed?* GL.
lemb=lamb
lēmen (KGL82⁴⁰)=lǣmen
±lemlan (æ) *to subdue,* CP303¹¹ : *lame, disable,* B905.
lempedu f. *lamprey,* WW438¹⁷. ['*limpet*'; L. lampreda]
lemphealt *limping,* Gl,WW. ['*limphalt*']
lemplt f. *dish, basin,* OET108'.
lēnan (KGL)=lǣnan
lencten (æ) I. m. *springtime,* Lcd,LL; Æ : *the fast of Lent,* W. II. adj. *pertaining to Lent,* Bf,RB. ['*lenten*']

lenctenãdl f. *spring fever, tertian ague, dysentery,* BH,Lcd.
lenctenbere m. *Lent barley,* ANS84[326].
lenctenbryce m. *breach of the Lenten fast,* LL344,47.
lenctendæg m. *day of Lent,* CHRD,W117[15].
lenctenerðe f. *land ploughed in spring,* WW 105[7]. [eorðe]
lenctenfæsten n. *Lent,* CHRD,RB.
lenctenhǣto f. *heat of spring,* AO102[6].
lenctenlic *of spring, vernal,* Æ : lenten, Æ.
lenctenlifen f. *Lenten fare,* CHRD 15[3].
lenctenmōnað m. *a spring month,* ExC34[18].
lenctensufel (længt-) n. *Lent food,* LL450,9.
lenctentid f. *spring, Lent,* Æ.
lenctentima m. *spring,* OEG 3837 : *Lent,* Æ.
lenctenwuce f. *a week in Lent,* Jn5[8] (rubric).
lenctin-=lencten-
+lend I. *furnished with land (by the lord),* LL448'. II.=+lynd
+lenda m. *one rich in land,* OEG3154.
lendan *to land, arrive,* Chr; Æ,AO,CP : *go* : (+) *endow with land,* Æ. ['*lend*'; land]
lende-=lenden-
lendenãdl f. *disease of the loins,* Lcd 87a.
lendenbãn n. *loin-bone,* WW159[13]. [v. '*lend*']
lenden-brǣde, -brēde f. *loin,* Lcd,LL.
lendenece m. *pain in the loins,* Lcd 24a.
lendensēoc *diseased in the loins,* Lcd.
lendensid *reaching to the loins,* NC306.
lendenu (æ) np. *loins,* Mt,WW; Æ. ['*lend*']
lendenwyrc m. *a disease of the kidneys,* WW 113[12]. [wærc]
-lendisc v. dūn-, up-, ūre-, ut-l.
lēne=lǣne
leng I. (æ) f. *length, height,* Æ. II. adv. (comp. of lange) *longer,* Æ,Lk. ['*leng*']
lengan I. (±) *to lengthen, prolong, protract, delay,* Da : *extend, reach, attain* : *belong.* on hornum gelengdum '*tubis ductilibus,*' CVPs97[6]. ['*leng*'] II. (+) *to call for,* DHy90[3].
lengcten-=lencten-
lenge (æ) I. adj. (±) *belonging, related* : *near (of time),* B83. II. v. lange. III.=lengu
+lenge *belonging to, related to,* Æ : *addicted to.*
lengest (Chr,Mk) superl. of lang(e). ['*longest*']
lengfære *more durable,* ANS 119·435.
lengian (impers. w. a.) *to long,* Sol 270.
lenglifra comp. of langlife.
lengo=lengu
lengra (BH) comp. of lang. ['*lenger*']
lengten=lencten
lengtogra comp. adj. *more prolix,* Sc 161[18].
lengðu f. '*length.*' on lengðe *at length, finally,* AO144[1].

lengu f. *length,* Bo,BH : *height,* Sol. ['*lengh*']
lent f. *lentil,* Gl. [L. lentem]
lenten=lencten
lēo mf. gdas. lēon, also ds. lēone, lēonan, asf. lēo, and dp. lēonum '*lion,*' *lioness,* AO,Lcd,VPs,WW ; Æ. [L.]
lēoc (WW283[21])=lēac
lēod I. m. *man,* LL14,25 : '*wergeld*' *for manslaughter,* LL (=lēodgeld) : (+) *fellow-countryman, compatriot* : (†) *chief, prince, king,* B. ['*lede*'] II. f. (usu. in pl. lēode) *people, nation,* An,B,Bl,Lk; Æ,AO. ['*lede*']
lēoda I.=+lēod I. II. (LWS)=lēode
lēodan[2]† *to spring up, grow* : *spring from.*
lēodbealu† n. *calamity to a people,* B.
lēodbiscop m. *suffragan bishop, provincial,* Chr; Æ. [v. '*lede*']
lēodburg† f. *town,* B,Gen.
lēodbygen f. *sale of one's compatriots, slave-traffic,* LL20,11Ld (v. 2·133).
lēodcyning m. *king, ruler,* B54.
lēode fp. *men, people, country,* B,Lk; AO (v. lēod).
lēoden (Lcd)=lǣden
lēodfruma† m. *prince, patriarch, chief.*
lēodgeard† m. *country,* Gen.
lēodgebyrga† m. *lord, protector, prince, king.*
lēodgeld n. '*wergeld*' *for manslaughter,* LL.
lēodgeðincð f. *order, rank,* LL.
lēodgewinn m. *strife,* Jul 201.
lēodgota=lēadgota
lēodgryre m. *general terror,* Sol 278.
lēodhata m. *persecutor, tyrant,* GD.
lēodhete† m. *popular hatred, hostility,* An.
lēodhryre m. *fall of a prince (or nation?),* B 2030,2391.
lēodhwæt *very valiant,* El 11.
-lēodisc v. ðider-l.
lēodmǣg† m. *relative, comrade.*
lēodmægen† n. *might of the people, host.*
lēodmearc† f. *domain, country,* An.
lēodrǣden f. *country, region,* GD 204[28].
lēodriht n. *law of the land,* An,KC.
lēodrūne f. *pythoness, sorceress,* Lcd 52b.
lēodscearu† f. *tribe, nation,* Ex 337.
lēodsceaða† m. *public enemy.*
lēodscipe m. *nation, people,* Æ : *country, region.*
lēodstefn m. *assembly,* PPs82[7].
lēodðēaw m. *popular usage,* AA,Gen.
lēodweard† f. *government.*
lēodweras† mp. *men, human beings.*
lēodwerod n. *host of people,* Ex 77.
lēodwita m. *wise man, elder, chief,* LL456.
lēodwynn f. *home joy,* †Hy4[89].
lēodwyrhta=lēoðwyrhta
lēof I. (±) adj. *dear, valued, beloved, pleasant, agreeable,* Æ,B,Chr,CP,HGl,LL. ['*yleof*']
II. m. *beloved one, friend* : (in addressing

persons) *sir! sire! Æ,EC : impure companion*, GPH394. [*'lief'*]
leofen=lifen; **leofian** (*Bl*)=libban
lēoffæst *dear, precious*, ÆP172[13].
lēofian *to be or become dear*, Gu110.
lēoflic *dear, lovable, pleasant, beautiful, delightful*, B,Cr : *precious, valued*. adv. -līce *lovingly, kindly, gladly, willingly*, BH. [*'liefly'*]
lēofspell n. *good news*, El1017.
lēof-tǣl, -tǣle *kind, lovable, loving, dear, grateful, agreeable*, CP.
lēofwende *kind, loving, gracious, acceptable, estimable, agreeable*.
lēofwendum *ardently*, Cr471.
±**lēogan**[2] *to 'lie,'* Bl,WW : *deceive, belie, betray*, Æ,CP : *be in error*, ÆGr. l. *on to charge falsely*.
lēogere (e[1], o[2]) m. *'liar,' false witness*, W, MtL; Æ : *hypocrite*, MkL7[6].
lēoht (ē, ī) **I.** '*LIGHT*,' *not heavy*, AO; CP : *slight, easy, trifling, inconsiderable*, CP : *quick, agile : gentle*. **II.** n. '*LIGHT*,' *daylight*, Æ : *power of vision : luminary*. **III.** *luminous, bright, 'light,' clear, resplendent, renowned, beautiful*, BH,Lcd,VPs ; AO,CP.
lēohtan=līhtan
lēohtbǣre *brilliant, luminous*, Cra,Lcd.
lēohtbēamede *bright-shining*, ÆH1·610.
lēohtberend m. *light-bearer, Lucifer*, Æ.
lēohtberende *light-bearing, luminous*, Æ (Gen).
lēohtbora m. *light-bearer*, LV36.
lēohtbrǣdnes f. *levity, frivolity, wantonness*.
leohte=lehte pret. 3 sg. of leccan.
lēohte I. adv. *lightly, easily, comfortably*, BH. [*'light'*] **II.** adv. *brightly, clearly, brilliantly*, Bl,Cr. [*'light'*]
lēoht-fæt n. nap. -fatu *lantern, torch, lamp, light*, Æ,CP.
lēohtfætels m. *lamp*, LPs17[29].
lēohtfruma† m. *source of light*.
lēoht-gesceot, -gescot n. *payment for providing lights in church*, LL.
lēohtian I. *to be lightened, relieved*. **II.** *to become light, dawn*, CM474 : *give light, illuminate*.
lēohting=līhting
lēohtīsern (ē[1]) n. *candlestick*, NG.
lēohtlēas *dark*, Æ. [*'lightless'*]
lēohtlic I. *light, of little weight or importance*, Æ,CP. adv. -līce *lightly, slightly*, BH, Lcd : *inconsiderately : easily, quickly : gently, softly, slowly*, CP; Æ. [*'lightly'*] **II.** *bright, radiant*, Rd.
lēohtmōd *easy-going*, GnE86.
lēohtmōdnes f. *inconstancy, frivolity*, CP.
lēohtsāwend *author of light*, GPH389[2].
lēohtscēawigend *light-seeing*, WW434[20].

lēohtsceot=lēohtgesceot
lēohtwyrhta=lēoðwyrhta
leolc pret. 3 sg. of lācan.
±**lēoma** m. *ray of light, beam, radiance, gleam, glare*, B; Æ : *lightning*. [*'leam'*]
+**lēomod** *having rays of light*, Lcd3·272[4]. [v. *'leam'*]
leomu nap. of lim.
±**lēon I.** (sv[1]) *to lend, give, grant*, B,LkL. [*Ger.* leihen] **II.** gdas. of lēo.
lēona mf. *lion, lioness*, Æ.
lēones? *league*, WE51.
lēonesēað m. *lions' den*, GD150[9].
lēonflǣsc n. *lion's flesh*, Lcd1·364'. [v. *'lion'*]
lēonfōt m. *lion's foot (plant)*, Lcd,WW.
lēonhwelp m. *lion's cub*, WW434[6].
±**lēoran** (wv., but rare pp. loren) *to go, depart, vanish, die* (A; v. JAW44).
±**lēorednes** f. *departure, transmigration : death*, ÆL : *anniversary of a death*, MH : *vision*.
lēorende, +lēorendlic *transitory*, DR.
lēorednes=lēorednes
lēorian=lēoran
leornan=leornian
leornere m. *'learner,' disciple*, Æ,CP : *scholar*, BH : *reader*.
leornes f. *learning*, BHo,CA162[20].
lēornes=lēorednes
±**leornian** *to 'learn,' read, study, think about*, Æ,Bf,BH,Bl,MkR; AO,CP.
leorningcild n., leorningcniht (Æ,CP) m. *student, disciple*.
leorningende *teachable*, W172[22].
leorninghūs n. *school*, WW.
leornung f., ds. leornunga *'learning,' reading, study, meditation*, CP; AO : *discipleship*, WW223[36].
leornungcræft m. *learning*, El380.
leornungmann m. *learner, disciple* (used even of women), Æ.
leornungscōl f. *school*, GD14[6].
leort pret. 3 sg. of lǣtan.
-**lēosan** v. be-l., for-l.
leoð=leoðu v. lið; **leoð-**=lið-
lēoð n. *song, lay, poem*, B,WW ; Æ,AO. [*'leoth'*]
lēoðcræft m. *poetic art : poem, poetry*, Æ.
lēoðcræftig *skilled in song*, Deor40.
lēoðcwide m. *lay, poem*, AO120[2].
leoðe-=leoðu-
lēoðgidding f. *lay, song, poem*, An1481.
leoðian†=liðian
lēoðlic *versified*, ÆH,Bf42[14].
leoðo-=leoðu-
lēoðorūn f. *wise counsel given in song*, El 522.
lēoðowyrt=lēaðorwyrt?

lēoðr-=hlēoðr-

lēoðsang m. *song, poem, poetry,* BH.

leoðu I. f. *retinue, following?* RIM 14 (GK).
II. v. lið.

leoðubend† mf. *chain, fetter, bond.*

leoðubīge (i¹, e²) *flexible, yielding,* Æ.
['*litheby*']

leoðubīgnes (i¹, o²) f. *flexibility of limbs,*
GUTH 90²¹.

leoðucǣga m. *limbs serving as a key,* CR 334.

lēoðucræft† m. *skill of hand,* B,CRA.

leoðucræftig *agile,* PH 268.

leoðufæst *able, skilful,* CRA 95.

leoðulic *appertaining to the limbs, bodily,*
AN 1630.

leoðusār n. *pain in the limbs,* WW 213⁸.

leoðusyrce† f. *corslet,* B.

leoðuwāc (i) *with supple limbs, flexible,
pliant,* CRA 84. ['*leathwake*']

+**leoðuwācian** (i) *to mitigate, soften,* Æ.

leoðuwācunga (liðe-)? '*compeditorum,*' EPS
78¹¹.

±**leoðuwǣcan** (i) *to be or become calm or
pliant : appease, mitigate : revive : soften :
adapt?* ÆL 31⁴⁸².

lēoðweorc n. *poetry,* WW 188³⁰.

lēoðwīse f. *verse, poetry,* Æ,BF.

lēoðword n. *a word in a poem,* AN 1490.

lēoðwrenc m. *trick in a poem? spurious
passage?* BF 186²⁷.

lēoðwyrhta m. *poet,* ÆGR.

lēow (ǣu) n. *ham, thigh,* KC.

-lēow (ē, ā) v. mund-l.

leowe f. *league* (*distance*), WW 147²².

lēower pl. of lēow.

lēowð (ÆGR 129 J)=hlēowð

lepewince=læpewince

leppan *to feed* (*hawks*), WY 89 (v. ES 37·195).

lēran (KGL)=lǣran

lere (KGL 83¹⁹)=lyre; **lērēow-**=lārēow-

+**les**=+lise

lēs-=līes-

lesan⁵ *to collect, pick, select, gather, glean,* Æ.
['*lease*']

lesca m. *groin,* HGL,OET.

-lesende, -lesendlic, -lesung v. ed-l.

lēst=lāst; **lesu**=lysu; **lēsw-**=lǣsw-

lēt I. pret. 3 sg. of lǣtan. **II.**=lǣt
pres. 3 sg. of lǣdan. **III.**=lēat pret. of
lūtan.

lētan=lǣtan

lētanīa m. '*litany,*' MH; BH,WW. [L.
litania]

letig (KGL)=lytig

±**lettan** (æ) *to* '*let,*' *hinder, delay, impede,
oppress,* Æ,Bo,Gu (w. g.),W; AO,CP.

lettend m. *hinderer,* ES 39·349.

letting (æ) f. '*letting,*' *hindrance, delay,* Chr,
RB; CP.

lǣð=lǣð; **-leðer** v. heals-, weald-l.

leðera=liðera

leðercodd m. *leather bag,* WW 117³. [v.
'*leather*']

leðeren=leðren

leðerhelm m. *leathern helmet,* WW 142¹.

leðerhosu f. *leathern gaiter,* WW.

leðern=leðren

leðerwyrhta m. *tanner, currier,* GL.

lēðr-=lyðr-

leðren (i) '*leathern,*' WW.

lēud=(1) lēod; (2) lǣwede

lēw f.=lǣw

+**lēwed** *weak, ill?* Æ (Ex 22¹⁰, cp. limlǣweo;
or ? read +lēfed).

lēwend=lǣwend; **lēwer**=lēower

lēwsa (=ǣ) m. *weakness,* EPS 87⁹.

lex=leax; **lēxnian** (WW 241²¹)=lācnian

līb-, libb-=līf-, lyb-

libban (y) pret. 3 sg. lif(e)de *to* '*LIVE,*' *experience, be, exist,* Æ; AO,CP.

lībr-=lifer-

līc n. *body,* B,Cr : *corpse,* AO,B; Æ,CP.
['*lich*']

+**līc I.** adj. (w. d.) *like* : '*alike*' ('*ylike*'),
similar, equal, B,BH,Jul,LL; Æ,CP :
suitable : likely, Mt. +līcost *double, twin.*
II. n. *something like another thing :
similitude.*

+**līca,** +līce wk. forms used as sb. *an equal,*
Æ,CP. adv. ±līce (usu. +; and +līc in
NG) *as, like, equally, similarly,* AO,Bl.
+līce and *like as if.*

līcam-=līcham-

līcbeorg f. *coffin, sarcophagus,* Cp 45 S.

+**līcbisnung** f. *imitation,* DR 76¹.

līcburg f. *cemetery,* Cp 433 C.

līccere, līccetere=līcettere

līcettan (Æ)=līcettan

līccian *to* '*lick,*' Æ,Ps : *lap, lick up,* Lcd.

līccung f. *licking,* ÆH 1·330²³.

līcema=līchama; **līcendlic**=līciendlic

līcettan *to feign, dissimulate,* CP : *flatter,* BH.

līcettere (ē) m. *deceiver, hypocrite,* CP.

līcettung, līcetung f. *feigning, deceit, hypocrisy, flattery.*

līcewyrðe=līcwyrðe

līcfæt† n. *body,* GU.

±**līcgan⁵** *to* '*LIE*,*' *be situated, be at rest,
remain, be,* Æ,AO,CP : *lie down, lie low,
yield, subside, fall, lie prostrate, fail, lie
dead,* Æ,AO,Chr : *lead, extend to,* Æ;
AO : *flow, go, run,* AO : *belong to : lie
along, border?* AN 334. l. for *take the part
of,* LL 152,3. l. mid *cohabit with.* l. on
cnēowum *to kneel.* wið licgendum fēo *for
ready money.*

līchama m. *body, corpse,* BO,Mt ; Æ,CP :
trunk, CR 628. ['*licham*']

+līchamian *to clothe with flesh*, RWH 136³³.
+līchamod *incarnate*, BL 33¹⁵.
līchamlēas *incorporeal*, ÆT.
līchamlic (o²) *bodily, carnal, physical, material*, *Bo,Lk*; Æ. adv. -līce *bodily, personally, in the flesh, BH*; Æ. ['*lichamly*']
-līchamung v. in-l.; līchom-=licham-
līchanga m. *gibbet?* KC 5·321' (BTac).
līchord† n. *interior of the body*, GU.
līchrægel n. *winding-sheet*, MH 76²⁶.
līchryre m. *bodily decay, death*, GEN 1099.
līchryst=līcrest; līchwamlic=lichamlic
līcian I. (±) (w. d. or impers.) *to please*, Æ, AO,Bl,Bo; CP : *be sufficient.* ['*like,*' '*ylike*'] II. (+) *to be or make like : seem likely*, AO.
līciendlic *agreeable, pleasant*, PPs. adv. -līce.
+līclǣtan⁷ *to liken, compare*, MkLR 4³⁰.
līclēoð n. *dirge*, OEG.
līclic *relating to the dead, funeral*, GPH 401.
+līclic *fitting, proper*, LCD. adv. -līce *equally.*
līcmann m. *bearer, pall-bearer*, Æ.
līcnes (±) f. '*likeness*' ('*i-likeness*'), *similarity : figure, stature, image, Æ,MtL :* (+) *parable.*
līcpytt m. *grave*, ÆGR 66¹⁰? (or ? dīc, pytt).
līcrest f. *sepulchre, tomb, Lcd*; Æ : *hearse*, ÆL 26¹⁸¹ : *cemetery*, OEG 4347. [v. '*lich*']
līcs-=līx-
līcsang m. *dirge*, OEG.
līcsār† n. *wound*, B,CR.
līcstōw f. *place of burial*, GD 340³⁵.
līcsyrce f. *corslet*, B 550.
līctūn m. *burial-ground*, LL.
līcðēnung f. *obsequies, funeral*, Æ : *laying out (of corpse)*, ÆL 31¹⁴²⁹.
līcðēote f. *pore*, WW 159¹³.
līcðrōwere m. *leper*, Æ.
līcðrūh f. *sepulchre*, GD 225.
līcum-=līcham-
±līcung f. *pleasure*, CP. ['*liking*']
līcwiglung f. *necromancy*, LL (248³).
līcwund f. *wound*, Ex 239.
±līcwyrðe (e, eo, o, u) *pleasing, acceptable*, *Bo*; CP : *estimable, praiseworthy : accepted, recognised, sterling.* ['*likeworth*']
līcwyrðlīce *pleasingly*, ÆL 23b⁵⁷.
līcwyrðnes f. *good pleasure*, LPs 88¹⁸.
līd† n. *ship, vessel.* [līðan]
līda m. *sailor*, GNE 104.
Līda=Līða; liden pp. of līðan.
līdeð pres. 3 sg. of lēodan.
līdmann† m. *seafarer, sailor, pirate.*
līdrin=lēðren
līdweard m. *ship-master*, AN 244.
līdwērig *weary of sea-voyages*, AN 482.

±līefan I. (ē, ī, ȳ) *to allow, grant, concede*, *Mt,CP.* ['*leve*'; lēaf] II. (ē, ēo, ī, ȳ) tr. and intr. *to believe, trust, confide in, Bl,Bo, Met,MH.* ['*leve,*' '*yleve*'] III. (+) *to be dear to*, CR 1645.
+līefed (ȳ) *believing, faithful, pious*, Æ.
+līefedlic (ȳ) *permissible*, LL (436').
+līefedlīce (ȳ) *trustfully, credulously*, AO.
+līefen (ē) *excused*, LkR 14¹⁹.
+līefenscipe m. *justification*, JnLR 15²².
līeffæstan=līffæstan
līeg (æ, ē, ī) mn. *fire, flame, lightning*, *B,Bl*; CP. ['*leye*']
līeg- v. līg-
līeget=līget
līegeð I.=legeð pres. 3 sg. of lecgan. II. pres. 3 sg. of licgan.
līeht-=lēoht-, līht-
līehð pres. 3 sg. of lēogan.
±līesan (ē, ȳ) *to loosen, release, redeem, deliver, liberate*, *Cr,LkR.* ['*leese*']
līesing I. (ī, ȳ) m. *freedman*, LL. II. (ē) f. *deliverance, release*, LkL. ['*leesing*']
+līesnes (ē) f. *redemption*, DR 12¹⁷.
līeð-=līð-; līexan=līxan
līf I. n. '*life,*' *existence*, Æ,B,Chr,JnL : *lifetime, RB.* on life, tō life, lifes *alive*, Æ, *BH : way of life* (e.g. *monastic*), *BH,Chr, Lk,W*; CP : *place where the life is according to rule, monastery*, CHR. II.=lēf. III.= lēaf I.
līf-=līef-
līfbrycgung f. *way of life*, DR 7¹⁵.
līfbysig *struggling for life*, B 966.
līfcearu† f. *care about life*, GEN.
līfdæg m. nap. līfdagas (usu. in plur.) '*life-day,*' *lifetime*, *B,Cr.*
līfde, lifede pret. sg. of libban.
līfen (eo) f. *sustenance*, AN,GL.
līfer n. f. '*liver,*' *Bo,WW*; Æ. II. f. *a weight*, WW 432²⁸. [*L.* libra?]
līferādl f. *liver complaint*, LCD,WW.
līferbȳl m. *protuberance of the liver*, LCD 76b.
līferhol n. *hollow in the liver*, LCD 76b.
līferlæppa m. *lobe of the liver*, WW.
līfersēoc *ill in the liver*, LCD.
līfersēocnes f. *disease of the liver*, LCD.
līferwærc m. *pain in the liver*, LCD 60a.
līferwyrt n. *liverwort*, ANS 84·326.
līfesn (BH 362¹⁶)=lybesn
līffadung f. *regulation of life*, LL 82²² (Wilk.).
līffæc n. *lifetime, life*, LL,W.
±līffæst *living, quickened, full of life, vigorous : settled.*
±līffæstan (īe, ȳ) *to quicken, endow with life*, Æ,CP.
+līffæstnian *to quicken*, RPs 142¹¹.
līffet-=lyffet-

líffrēa† m. *Lord of life, God.*

líffruma† m. *source of life (God).*

lífgan=libban

lífgedāl n. *death,* GD.

lífgesceaft† f. *life's conditions or record,* B.

lífgetwinnan mp. *twins,* Sol 141.

líflan (*LG,Nar*) ['*ylife*']=libban

líflende (y) *that lives or has life,* BH : *when alive, BH,VPs* : as sb. *the '*living*,' VHy.*

líflād f. *course of life, conduct, RB.* ['*livelihood*']

líflǣst=líflēast

líflēas *not endowed with life, '*lifeless*,' inanimate, Æ : dead, Æ.*

líflēast f. *loss of life, death,* Æ.

líflic *living, Æ : '*lively*' : long-lived : necessary to life, vital, DHy,Hex.* adv. -**líce** *vitally, so as to impart life, Æ.*

líflyre m. *loss of life,* LL466,2.

lífneru f. *food, sustenance,* An 1091.

lífnes (*BHCA* 362¹⁶)=lybesn

lífre gs. of lifer I.

lífre-=lifer-

lífrig *clotted,* A30·132.

líft=lyft

lífweard m. *guardian of life,* El 1036.

lífweg m. *way of life, way in life,* W.

lífwela† m. *riches.*

lífwelle *living (water),* JnL4¹⁰.

lífwraðu† f. *protection of life,* B.

lífwynn† f. *enjoyment of life.*

líg (Æ)=līeg; **líg-**=lyg-

lígbǣre, lígberende *flaming,* Gl.

lígberend m. *flame-bearer,* WW239²⁴.

lígbryne (ē)† m. *burning, fire.*

lígbysig (ē) *busy with fire,* Rd31¹.

lígcwalu f. *fiery torment,* El296.

lígdraca (ē)† m. *fiery dragon,* B.

lígegesa m. *flaming terror,* B2780.

lígen I. (ē) *flaming, fiery, Æ.* II. pp. of lēon.

lígenword=lygeword

+líg-ere n. -ernes f. *concubinage, fornication, adultery,* AO.

líget nm., līgetu (ē) f. *lightning, flash of lightning, BH,Bl,Mt; Æ,AO.* ['*lait*'; līeg]

lígetræsc (ē) m. *lightning, flash of light, coruscation,* Lk10¹⁸. [līget]

lígetsleht (ē¹, æ³) m. *lightning-stroke, thunderbolt,* GD,MH.

lígetung f. *lightning,* EHy6⁴¹.

lígeð pres. 3 sg. of licgan.

líg-fǣmende, -fāmblāwende *vomiting fire,* BH432⁷.

lígfȳr n. *fire,* Ex77.

lígge=līege ds. of līeg; **lígit**=líget

líglic (ē) *fiery,* Guth131¹⁹⁶.

líg-locc, -locced *having flaming locks,* WW.

lígnan (=īe)† *to deny.*

lígræsc (ē¹, e²)=lígetræsc

líg-ræscetung, -ræscung (ȳ¹) f. *lightning,* LPs.

lígspíwel *vomiting flame,* GPH,W.

lígð pres. 3 sg. of licgan.

líg-ōracu† f. gds. -ōrǣce *fiery onset, violence of flames,* Ph.

lígȳð f. *wave of fire,* B2672.

líh imperat. sg. of lēon.

líht=lēoht

líhtan (ē, ēo, ȳ) I. (±) *to make '*light*,' easy, relieve, alleviate, Lcd; CP : dismount, '*alight*,' BH.* II. (=īe; ȳ) *to lighten, illuminate, give light, shine, Æ,Jn : grow light, dawn, Da : '*light*,' kindle.*

líhtian=líhtan

líhting I. f. *relief, alleviation, release,* LL. ['*lighting*'] II. (ēo) f. *shining, illumination, light, Æ : dawn : lightning.* ['*lighting*']

líhtingnes f. *lightness of taxation,* LL(306²¹).

líhtnes f. *brightness,* W230¹². ['*lightness*']

líhð pres. 3 sg. of lēogan.

lílie f. '*lily,*' Bl,Lcd; Æ. [L. lilium]

lim (y) n. nap. leomu *'*limb*,' member, Æ, B,Bl; AO,CP : branch, B : agent, offspring? Bl33 : bone?* CPs6³.

lím m. *anything sticky, '*lime*,' mortar, cement, gluten, Æ,Ep,WW : bird-lime, snare,* BF144⁶.

+líman *to cement, join, stick together,* ÆGr.

límfín f. *lime-heap,* BC1·518'.

límgelecg n. *shape,* WW.

límgesihð f. *body,* RHy11⁴⁰.

limhāl *sound of limb,* Gu661.

+límian=+líman

líming f. *smearing, plastering,* WW. ['*liming*']

limlǣw f. *injury to limbs, mutilation,* LL (278n4).

limlǣweo *maimed,* LL132,10.

limlēas *without limbs,* Æ2·270²².

limmǣlum adv. *limb by limb,* WW. ['*limb-meal*']

limmlama *crippled,* W4¹².

limnacod *stark naked,* Gen 1566.

+limp n. *occurrence : misfortune, accident,* CP.

±limpan³ *to happen, occur, exist, B,Bo,Chr, Met; Æ,AO,CP : belong to, suit, befit, Ct : concern, CP.* ['*limp*,' '*i-limp*']

±limpful *fitting, convenient,* AS1²¹.

limplǣcan *to unite, connect,* OEG80.

+limplic *fitting, suitable, ÆL : happening : '*accidentia*,' ÆGr.* adv. -líce (±).

+limplicnes f. *opportunity,* VPs9¹⁰.

limrǣden f. *form? disposition of the limbs?* v. OEG2530.

limsēoc† *lame, paralytic.*

limwǣde n. *clothing,* PPs103².

limwæstm m. *stature,* Sat 130.

lïmwērig *weary of limb*, ROOD 63.

līn n. *flax, linen, cloth, napkin, towel*, Ct,Gl, JnR,MtR; CP. ['*line*']

līnacer m. *flax-field*, EC 239¹⁰.

lind I. f. *lime-tree, linden*, Ct, Gl; Æ; Mdf : (†) *shield (of wood)*. ['*lind*'] **II.**=lynd

līndcroda m. *crash of shields, battle*, GEN 1998.

līnde=lind I.

linden *made of 'linden'-wood*, GnE.

līndgecrod n. *shield-bearing troop*, AN 1222.

līndgelāc n. *battle*, AP 76.

līndgesteallat m. *companion in war*.

līndhæbbende† m. *shield-bearer, warrior*.

līndplega† m. *shield-play, battle*.

līndrycg m. *ridge where limes grow*, EC 447²³.

līndwered n. *troop armed with shields*, EL 142.

līndwiga m. *warrior*, B 2603.

lind-wīgend†, -wīggend† m. *shielded warrior*.

līne f. *line, cable, rope*, Sol,WW : *series, row* : *rule, direction*.

līnece (WW 286²¹)=līnete

līnen adj. '*linen,' made of flax*, CP,Ep; Æ.

līnenhrægl n. *linen cloth*, NG.

līnenweard *clad in linen*, ÆP 84¹⁹, RWH 66⁵.

līnete (-ece) f. *linnet*, WW 286²¹.

līnetwig(l)e f. *linnet*, Cp,Erf,WW. ['*lint-white*']

-līng suffix (1) for forming personal nouns (dēorling, ræpling). (2) for forming advbs. (hinderling).

līnhǣwen *flax-coloured*, LCD.

līnland n. *land in flax*, KC 3·19⁴.

līnlēag m. *flax ground*, EC 166².

linnan³ (w. instr. or g.) *to cease from, desist, lose, yield up (life)*, B. ['*lin*']

līnsǣd (e²) n. '*linseed,*' Lcd,LL.

līnwǣd f. *linen cloth or garment*, NG.

līnwyrt f. *flax*, LCD.

līo (WW 438²²)=lēo

lippa m., lippe? f. (LL 2·136) '*lip,*' Lcd,RB, WW.

līra m. *any fleshy part of the body, muscle, calf of the leg*, Lcd,WW. ['*lire*']

+**līre**=+ligere

līreht *fleshy*, LCD 91a.

līs=liss; **līs-**=līes-; **līsan** (GL)=lesan

+**līse** (e) nap. +leosu n. *reading, study*, BH.

+**līsian** *to slip, glide*, CP 437.

-līsnian, -listnian v. be-l.

liss (līðs) f. *grace, favour, love, kindness, mercy*, Æ : *joy, peace, rest*, Ph,W : *remission, forgiveness*, †Hy 10⁵⁴ : *alleviation*, Æ : *saving (of life)*. ['*liss*'; līðe]

lissan *to subdue*, Sol 294. ['*lisse*']

list mf. *art, cleverness, cunning, experience, skill, craft*, Cr,Gen. listum *cunningly, skilfully*. ['*list*']

listan=lystan

līste f. '*list,' fringe, border, Ep*.

listelīce adv. *carefully*, LCD 11a.

listhendig *skilful*, CRA 95. **listum** v. list.

listwrenc m. *deception*, W 81; 128n⁹.

līsð pres. 3 sg. of lesan.

līt *colour, dye*, RWH 141¹⁰.

līt=lȳt

lītan *to bend, incline*, MET 26¹¹⁹.

līte-, lītel=lytig-, lȳtel; **lītig**=lytig

lītigere m. *dyer*, RWH 141⁹.

lītl-=lȳtl-; **lītsmann**=liðsmann

lið I. nm. nap. leoðu, liðu *limb, member*, BH,Cr; Æ,AO,CP : *joint*, Lcd : *tip (of finger)*, Lk. ['*lith*'] **II.** n. *fleet*. [ON. lið]

līð I. n. *cider, native wine, fermented drink*, CP : *beaker, cup*. **II.** *mercy*, VH 16. **III.** pres. 3 sg. of licgan. **IV.**=līðe adj. **V.**=līhð

Līða m. *name of months June (ǣrra L.) and July (æftera L.)*, MEN,MH.

līðādl f. *gout*, LCD,WW.

līðan¹ I. (±) *to go, travel, sail*, B,BH : (+) *arrive*, WW. ['*lithe*'] **II.** *to be bereft of*, GnE 26? **III.** (CP)=līðigian

līðe I. adj. *gentle, soft, calm, mild*, ApT,B, Mt; Æ,AO,CP : *gracious, kind, agreeable, sweet*, Bo,Gen; Æ. ['*lithe*'] **II.** adv.

līðe-=leoðu-; **līðeg**=līðig

līðelīc *gentle, soft, mild*, CP. adv. -līce, CP. ['*lithely*']

+**līðen** (y) *having travelled much*, CAS 26¹³. [līðan]

līðercian *to smooth down, flatter*, GL.

līðere f., liðera m. *sling, slinging pouch*, BH, Cp; Æ. ['*lither*'; leðer]

līðeren=leðren

līðerlīc *of a sling*, WW 247⁴.

līðgeat=hlidgeat

līðian (CP; Æ)=līðigian

±**līðian** (eo) *to unloose, release*, GD.

līðig *lithe, flexible, bending, yielding*, Æ,W. ['*lithy*']

līðigian (±) *to soften, calm, mitigate, assuage, appease*, CP; Æ : *be mild*. ['*lithe*']

līðincel n. *little joint*, WW.

līðlīc=līðelic; **līðmann**=lidmann

līðnes f. *mildness, softness, gentleness, kindness*, Æ,CP.

līðo-=leoðu-; **līðre**=liðere

līðre=lȳðre; **līðrin**=leðren; **līðs**=liss

līðsēaw n. *synovia*, LCD.

līðsmann m. *seafarer, pirate*, CHR.

līðu v. lið.

līðule m? *synovia*, LCD. [lið, ele]

līðung f. *alleviation, relief*, LCD 1·112² : '*venia,' 'miseratio,*' OEG 8³⁹⁸.

līðwǣge n. *drinking-cup*, B1982.
līðwǣrc m. *pain in the limbs*, LCD49b.
līðwyrde *mild of speech*, NC348.
līðwyrt f. *dwarf elder*, LCD,WW.
līxan (=īe) *to shine, flash, glitter, gleam*.
līxende *splendidly*, LkL16¹⁹.
līxung f. *brilliance, brightness*, DR.
-lō pl. -lōn v. mæst-, sceaft-l.
lob (GL)=lof
lobbe f. *spider*, LPs. ['lob']
loc I. n. 'lock,' *bolt, bar*, Æ,BH; AO : *enclosure, fold, prison, stronghold*, CP : *bargain, agreement, settlement, conclusion* : *clause*, OEG7¹⁹⁵. [lūcan] II.=locc I.
lōc, lōca interj. 'look,' *see, look you*. l. hū *however* : *whatever*, Gen16⁶. l. hwænne, hwonne *whenever*. spel l. hwænne mann wille *a discourse for any occasion you please*, Æ. l. hwǣr *wherever*. l. hwǣðer *whichever*. l. hwā, l. hwæt, *whoever, whatever*. l. hwylc *whichever*. l. nu *observe, note, behold*, ÆGr.
loca I. m. *enclosure, stronghold*. II. m. *lock (of wool)*, GL.
lōca-hū v. lōc interj.
locbore f. *one who wears long hair, free woman*, LL7,73.
locc I. m. 'lock' (*of hair*), *hair, curl*, Bl,CP, Ep; Æ. II.=loc I.
loccetan (MtL)?=rocettan (JAW77).
±loccian *to attract, entice, soothe*, CP
loccod *hairy, shaggy*, OEG56¹³.
locen I. pp. of lūcan. II. (SAT300?)=loc
locer=locor
locfeax n. *hair*, WW379⁴².
locgewind n. *hair*, WW199⁷.
lōc-hū, -hwænne etc. v. lōc hū, lōc hwænne, etc.
lochyrdel m. *hurdle for sheepfolds*, LL454,9.
lōcian (±) *to see, behold, look, gaze*, Bl,G, Met; AO : *observe, notice, take heed*, CP; Æ : *belong, pertain*, Æ. l. tō *regard with favour*, CP.
locor m. *plane (tool)*, GL.
locstān m. *stone closing an entrance*, ÆL 23³⁴⁵.
-lōcung v. ðurh-l.
loddere m. *beggar*, Æ; Mdf. [lyðre]
+lodr f. *backbone, spine*, LCD65a.
lodrung f. *rubbish, nonsense*, WW478⁸.
+lodwyrt f. *silverweed*, LCD,WW.
loerge (Ep) np. of lorg.
lof I. n. (m. B1536) *praise, glory, repute*, Cp; Æ,CP : *song of praise, hymn*. ['lof'] II. n. *protection, help?* AN991 (v. also lōf).
lōf 'redimicula,' OEG5241=glōf (?), v. ES 37·186, or ?*fillet, band*, at AN991 (BTs).
lofbǣre *praising, giving praise*, VHy.
lofdǣd f. *praiseworthy deed*, B24.

lofgeorn *eager for praise*, ÆL16³⁰² : *lavish? ostentatious?* RB54⁹; 55³.
lofherung f. *praising*, LPs55¹².
loflan *to praise, exalt*, Gen,PPs; CP : (±) *appraise, value*. ['love']
loflāc n. *offering in honour of any one*, W 107⁶.
loflǣcan *to praise*, LPs118¹⁷⁵.
loflic *laudable*, HGL498. adv. -līce *gloriously*, BL165¹⁶.
lofmægen n. *praise*, PPs105².
lofsang m. *song of praise, canticle, hymn, psalm*, BH; Æ : *lauds*. ['lofsong']
lofsealm m. *the 148th Psalm, lauds*, RB36¹⁹.
lofsingende *singing hymns of praise*, OEG 4912.
lofsum *praiseworthy*, GEN468.
lofte (on) adv. phr. *in the air, aloft*, Hex, MLN. ['loft']
lofung f. *praising, laudation* : *appraising*, Æ.
lōg pret. 3 sg. of lēan.
-loga v. āð-, trēow-, wed-, word-l. [leogan]
+logendlic adj. *to be kept in order*, RBL63⁵.
lōges v. lōh; logeðer=logðer
±lōgian *to lodge, place, put by*, Æ : *put in order, arrange, collect, settle*, Æ : *discourse*, Æ : *divide, portion out*. +l. ūp *lay by, deposit*, +lōgod *interpolated*, BF70²². +lōgod sprǣc (*well*)-*ordered speech, style*.
logðer (o²) *cunning, artful*, WW.
+lōgung f. *order*, CM599.
lōh I. n., gs. lōges *place, stead* (only in phr. on his lōh), CHR779E. II. pret. 3 sg. of lēan II.
lōhsceaft m. *bolt, bar? stick with a strap to it?* (BTs), AS1².
loma=lama
±lōma m. *tool, utensil, article of furniture*, BH; GL. ['loom']
lomb, lomber=lamb
±lōme (1) adj. *frequent*, ÆL31¹⁰¹⁹; (2) adv. *often, frequently*, Gen. oft (and) +l. *constantly, diligently*. ['ylome']
+lōmed=+lēomod; lōmelic=lōmlic
±lōmlǣcan *to frequent*, Æ : *be frequent*.
+lōmlǣcende *frequent*, Æ : *frequentative (vb)*, ÆGR213⁷.
+lōmlǣcing f. *frequency, frequenting*, ÆGR 213⁷.
+lōmlǣcnes f. *a numerous assembly*, Ps.
+lōmlic *repeated, frequent, numerous*, AO, CP. adv. -līce.
+lōmlīcian *to become frequent*, BL109².
+lōmlīcnes f. *repetition*, BF174²¹ : *a numerous assembly*, CPs117²⁷.
lomp pret. 3 sg. of limpan.
+lomrǣde *frequent*, TC.
lond=land
londádl f. *strangury?* LCD108a. [hland]

lone=lane; **long**=lang
Longbeard-an, -as sbmpl. *Lombards*, AO.
lonn, lonu=lann, lanu
loppe f. *spider*, Bo,WW. ['lop']
loppestre f. '*lobster*,' WW; Æ : *locust*, MkL.
lopust, lopystre=loppestre
lor n. (in phr. tō lore, tō lose) *loss, destruction*, Bl; CP. ['lore']
-lora v. hlēow-l.
loren pp. (str.) of lēoran.
lorg, lorh fm. *pole, distaff, weaver's beam*, GL,WYN 168.
los=lor ['loss']; **losewist**=loswist
losian (u) wv. (±) *to be lost, fail, perish*, Bo, CP; Æ : (±) *escape, get away* : '*lose*,' LkL 15⁴ : *destroy*, LkL 17²⁷.
losigendlic *ready to perish*, ÆH.
losing, loswist f. *loss, destruction*, NG.
lot n. *fraud, guile*, ÆL,CP.
loten pp. of lūtan.
lotwrenc m. *deception, deceit, cunning, artifice, trick*, Æ,AO,CP.
lotwrencceast f. *cunning*, Mk 12¹⁵.
loða m. *upper garment, mantle, cloak*, CP.
lox m. *lynx*, BH,WW. [*Ger.* luchs]
luba-, lube-=lufe-
lūcan² I. (±) (tr.) *to lock, close, enclose, fasten, shut up*, An : (intr.) *close up, form one mass*, Ph : *interlock, intertwine, twist, wind*, CP : *conclude*. ['louk'] II. *pluck out, pull up*, Met. ['louk'²]
-lucor v. MFB n30.
ludgæt n. *side-gate, postern gate*, GL.
ludon pret. pl. of lēodan.
lufelic=luflic
lufen f. *hope?* (BT; GK), DA 73, B 2886.
lufestice f. *lovage (plant)*, LCD. [*L.* levisticum]
lufestre f. *female lover*, OEG.
luffendlic=lufiendlic
luffeorm f. *hospitality*, AB 34·10.
±**lufian** *to 'love,' cherish, show love to*, Æ, Chr,JnL,VPs; CP : *fondle, caress* : *delight in, approve, practise*.
lufiend m. *lover*, Æ.
lufiende *affectionate*, ÆGr. ['loving']
lufi(g)endlic *lovely, beautiful*, Æ : *lovable*, Æ.
luflic *amiable, loving*, Lcd : *lovable*, Ps. adv. -līce *kindly*, CP : *willingly, gladly*, BH. ['lovely']
lufrǣden f. *love*, LPs. ['lovered']
lufsum *loving, lovable, pleasant*, Cr. ['lovesome']
lufsumlic *gracious*, BH 248¹⁷. adv. -līce
lufsumnes f. *pleasantness, kindness*, WW 218³⁴. ['lovesomeness']
luftācen n. '*love-token*,' B 1863.
luf-tȳme (Æ), -tēme (RB) *pleasant, sweet, grateful, benevolent*.

luftȳmlic *pleasant*, OEG 56²⁵⁴.
lufu f. 'LOVE,' *strong liking, affection, favour*, Æ; AO,CP : *desire* : *kind action* : *love (of God)*, JnR : *amicable settlement*, LL 392'.
lufung f. *action of loving*, GD 73¹⁴.
lufwende *lovable, pleasant*, BF,LCD.
lufwendlic *friendly*, KGL 73³⁴. adv. -līce *gently*, KGL 80²¹.
lugon pret. pl. of lēogan.
luh n. *loch, pond*, NG; Mdf. [*Keltic*]
+**lumpenlic** *occasional*, A 10·143 : *suitable*, A 10·141. [limpan]
lumpon pret. pl. of limpan.
luncian? *to limp* LPs 17⁴⁶. [cp. *Norw.* lunke?]
lundlaga m. *kidney*, Æ,LCD,WW.
lungen f. '*lung*,' Lcd,WW.
lungenādl f. *lung-disease*, LCD.
lungenǣder f. *vein of the lungs*, LCD 40b.
lungensealf f. *lung-salve*, LCD 141a.
lungenwyrt f. '*lung-wort*,' Lcd.
-lunger v. cēas-l.
lungre† adv. *soon, forthwith, suddenly, quickly*.
lunnon pret. pl. of linnan.
lūs f. nap. lȳs '*louse*,' Æ,Cp,Hex.
lusian (GPH)=losian
lust I. m. *desire, appetite*, Æ,BH,JnL : *pleasure*, Bo,Lk (pl.) : *sensuous appetite, lust*, Jul,Lcd,WW. II. adj. *willing*, W 246¹⁰.
lustbǣre I. *desirable, pleasant, agreeable, cheerful, joyous*, Æ,AO : *desirous*, ÆL 4¹¹⁶. II. adv. *gladly, willingly*.
lustbǣrlic *pleasant*, AO. adv. -līce.
lustbǣrnes f. *enjoyment, pleasure, desire*, CP.
lustful *wishful, desirous*, AO 100²⁷ : (+) *desirable*, WW 220⁵. ['lustful']
±**lustfullian** *to rejoice, enjoy*, Æ : *desire*, BF 4¹⁸ : *be pleasing to*, CP 70²⁴.
±**lustfullice** *gladly, heartily*, Bl. ['lustfully']
±**lustfullung** f. *desire, pleasure, delight*, Æ.
±**lustfulnes** f. *desire, pleasure*, BH; CP. ['lustfulness']
lustgeornnes f. *concupiscence*, G.
lustgryn f. *snare of pleasure*, SOUL 23.
+**lustian** *to delight in*, Sc.
lustlice *willingly, gladly*, Bl; Æ,AO.
lustmoce f. *lady's-smock (plant)*, LCD.
lustsumlic *pleasant*, AO. adv. -līce *willingly*.
lustum adv. *with pleasure, gladly*, CR,PPs.
lūsðorn m. *spindle-tree*, EC 445'.
±**lūtan²** *to bend, stoop, decline*, Æ,AO.
+**loten dæg** *after part of day* : *bow, make obeisance, fall down*, Bl,VPs : (+) *lay down*, MtL 8²⁰ : *entreat*. ['lout']

±lūtian *to lie hid, hide, lurk,* Æ,*VHy*; AO, CP. ['*lout*'²]
lūtter, lūttor=hlūttor, hlūtor
lūðer-=lȳðer-
lybb n. *drug, poison, charm,* LCD,GL.
lybban=libban
lybbestre f. *sorceress,* WW 200²⁵.
lybcorn n. *a medicinal seed, wild saffron?* GL.
lybcræft m. *skill in the use of drugs, magic, witchcraft,* BL.
lybesn (i) f. *charm, amulet, knot,* BH,GL.
lyblāc nm. *occult art, use of drugs for magic, witchcraft,* LCD,LL.
lyblǣca m. *wizard, sorcerer,* GL.
lybsin, lybsn=lybesn
lȳc-=lǣc-, līc-; lycce=lyge II.
lȳcð pres. 3 sg. of lūcan.
lȳden (LWS)=lǣden; lȳf=lif
lȳf-=lēaf-, lēf-, lief-, lif-
lyfde, lyfede pret. 3 sg. of libban.
lyfesn=lybesn
lyffetere m. *flatterer,* Æ,GL.
lyffet-tan, -tian *to flatter,* Æ.
lyffetung f. *adulation, flattery,* Æ.
lyflan=lifian, libban
lyft fmn. *air, sky, clouds, atmosphere,* B, *Lcd*; Æ,AO,CP. on lyfte *on high, aloft.* ['*lift*'; *Ger.* luft]
lyftādl f. *paralysis, palsy,* BH,LCD.
lyftedor m. *clouds,* Ex 251.
lyften *of the air, aerial,* ÆH,HEX.
lyftfæt n. *vessel in the air (moon),* RD 30³.
lyftflēogend m. *flier in the air, bird,* SOL 289.
lyftfloga m. *flier in the air, dragon,* B 2315.
lyftgelāc† n. *flight through the air,* AN.
lyftgeswenced *driven by the wind,* B 1913.
lyfthelm† m. *air, mist, cloud.*
lyftlācende† *sporting in the air, flying.*
lyftlic (u¹) *aerial,* ByH 118².
lyftsceaða m. *aerial robber (raven),* WY 39.
lyftwundor n. *aerial wonder,* Ex 90.
lyftwynn† f. *pleasure in flying.*
lyge I. (i) m. '*lie,' falsehood,* BH,*Sat.* II. *lying, false* (MtR 26⁶⁰; =*lygge, JAW 25). III. '*sicalia,' secale? corn? rye?* WW 301².
lygen (i) f. *lie, falsehood,* GEN,PR.
lygenian=lygnian
lygesearu† n. *lying wile, trick.*
lygespell (i) n. *falsehood,* WW 449².
lygesynnig (i) *lying, false,* EL 899.
lygetorn (i) *feigned anger or grief,* B 1943.
lygeword (i)† n. *lying word, lie.*
lygewyrhta (i) m. *liar,* LEAS.
lygnes (i) f. *falseness : false things,* WW 239⁹.
±lygnian (i) *to give one the lie, convict of falsehood,* Æ. +lygnod *perjured,* Æ.
lȳht-=līht-
lyhð pres. 3 sg. of lēan.

lȳhð pres. 3 sg. of lēogan; lym=lim
lȳman *to shine,* GD 171⁵.
lymp-=limp-
±lynde, lyndo (i) f. *fat, grease,* LCD.
+lyndu np. *joints of the spine,* WW 159²².
-lynian v. ā-l., tō-l.
lynibor n. *borer, gimlet,* WW 273¹³.
lynis m. '*linch'-pin, Ep,WW.*
lypenwyrhta m. *tanner,* WW.
lyre (e) m. *loss, destruction, damage, hurt,* WW; Æ. ['*lure*'; lēosan]
lyrewrenc m. *hurtful intrigue,* MFH 169.
-lyrtan v. be-l.; lȳs v. lūs; lȳs-=līes-
lysferht=leasferhð
lysnan, lysnere=hlysnan, hlysnere
lȳssa (KGL)=lǣssa; lyssen=lyswen
±lystan *impers. w. a.* (d.) *of pers. and g. of thing or inf. to please, cause pleasure or desire, provoke longing,* Æ,Bl,Bo,Met; AO, CP. +lysted *desirous of.* ['*list*'; lust]
lystere (OEG 4674)=? lyftere, lyffetere
+lystfullīce=lustfullīce
lysu I. *base, false, evil,* AN 1222. II. n. *evil deed,* LL.
lyswen I. *purulent, corrupt,* LCD. II. n. *pus, matter,* LCD.
lȳt *adv. and adj. and indecl. sb. little, few,* B, DD,*Gen,Run*; Æ,AO. ['*lite*']
lȳtan=lūtan; lȳteg=lytig
lȳtel I. adj. 'LITTLE,' *not large,* Æ,AO : *unimportant, mean : short (distance, time),* B : *not much, Mt,Ps.* II. adv. *little, slightly, Ps.* III. sb. AO,*Lcd,Ps.*
lȳtelhȳdig *pusillanimous,* CRA 10.
lyte-lic, -līce=lytig-lic, -līce
lȳtelmōd *pusillanimous,* CP.
lȳtelne=lȳtesne
lȳtelnes f. *smallness,* ÆGr 228¹⁴. ['*littleness*']
lȳtesnā (JUL), lȳtes(t)ne (BH) adv. *nearly, almost.*
lȳthwōn adv. and sb. (w. g.) *little, but little, very few,* Æ,CP.
lytig (e) *crafty, cunning,* AO : *prudent,* KGL.
lytigian *to feign, act crookedly,* MA 86.
lytiglic *deceitful, crafty.* adv. -līce, CP.
lytignes f. *cunning,* CP 237²².
lȳtle f. *female slave,* Æ (9⁴⁰¹).
±lȳtlian *to lessen, decrease, diminish,* Bo, JnL; CP : *shorten, curtail, abrogate ⸬ fall out of use,* LL 267,37 : *belittle.* ['*little*']
lȳtling m. *little one, infant, child,* Æ,CP : *unimportant person,* CHRD 2⁴.
lȳtlum adv. (d. of lȳtel) *little by little, gradually,* Æ; CP. ['*litlum*']
lȳtlung (i) f. *diminution :* (+) *insufficiency, want,* Sc 57¹ (cp. EHy 5¹²).
lyttl-=lȳtl-

lyttuccas mpl. *particles, small pieces*, GPH 400.

lyð=lið; **lyða**=liða; +**lyðen**=+liðen

lyðerful *evil, vile*, W40⁵.

lyðerlic *bad, sordid, mean, vile*, AO. adv. -līce (ū¹), *WW* 178²⁷. [*'litherly'*]

lyðernes (ū¹) f. *wickedness*, HL18⁸.

lyðran (ē;=īe) *to anoint, smear, 'lather,'* *JnL,Lcd.* [lēaðor]

lyðre=liðere

lyðre I. (ē, ī) adj. *bad, wicked, base, mean, corrupt, wretched,* Æ,AO,Lk,WW. [*'lither'*] adv. SAT 62. II. comp. of līðe.

lyðwyrt=līðwyrt; **lyxan**=līxan

M

mā I. (ǣ) adv. [comp. of micle] *more, rather, longer, hereafter, further,* Æ,CP. ðe mā ðe *more than.* II. sb. (indecl.) *more,* Æ. III. adj. *more,* Æ. [*'mo'*] IV.=man I.

mabuldor=mapulder; **maca**=+mæcca

macalic *convenient,* MkR 6²¹.

macian *to 'make,' form, construct, do, A,Æ : prepare, arrange, cause,* Æ,Gen,Mt : *use,* Æ : *behave, fare,* Æ,Bo; CP : *compare : transform,* ÆP204¹¹. macian ūp *to put up,* Æ.

mācræftig (=mægencr-)† *mighty.*

macung f. *making, doing,* CHR 1101.

+**mād** *silly, mad,* WW.

mādm=māðm

mādmōd n. *foolishness,* MOD 25.

mǣ (*VPs*)=mā

±**mǣc** *well-suited, companionable : similar, equal.*

mæcan=mecgan, mengan

+**mæcca** (a, e) mf. *mate, equal, one of a pair, comrade, companion,* ÆGr,MtR : (±) *husband, wife,* Æ,Bl,Ct,Mt : pl. *pair,* CHRD 48²⁶. [*'match'*]

mæcefisc=mecefisc

mæcg† m. *man, disciple : son.*

mæcga m. *man,* Wy 52.

mæcian=mecgan, mengan

+**mæclic** *conjugal,* Sc.

+**mæcnes** f. *cohabitation,* BH.

+**mæcscipe** m. *cohabitation,* CR 199.

mǣd (ē) f. ds. (EWS) mēda; nap. mǣd(w)a, mǣdwe *'mead,' 'meadow,' pasture,* BC, OEG; Æ,AO; Mdf.

+**mǣdan** *to make mad or foolish.* pp. +mǣd(ed), *Cp,Rd,WW.*

mæddre f. *'madder,'* Lcd; Æ.

mǣden (Æ,AO,CP)=mægden

mǣdencild n. *female child, girl,* AO; Æ. [*'maiden-child'*]

mǣdenhēap m. *band of virgins,* DD 289.

mǣdenlic *maidenly, virgin,* Æ.

mǣdere=mæddre

mǣderecīo m. *sprig of madder,* LCD.

+**mǣdla** m. *madness,* LCD 122b.

mǣdiacu f. *meadow-stream,* KC.

mǣdland m. *meadow-land,* KC.

mǣdmǣwect (=-wett) *mowing of a meadow,* LL448,5².

Mǣdmōnað (e¹) *July,* MEN (Hickes).

mǣdrǣden f. *mowing, tract of mown grass,* KC6·153¹⁰.

mǣdsplott m. *plot of meadow-land,* KC 4·72⁷.

mǣdwa m., mǣdwe f.=mǣd

mǣdweland=mǣdland

mæg I. pres. 3 sg. of magan. II. (Sc4¹⁹ ; 12¹⁷)=mægen

±**mǣg** (ē) I. m. nap. māgas (v. LL2·651) *male kinsman, parent, son, brother, nephew, cousin,* B,Ep; Æ,AO,CP : *compatriot,* A 46·76. [*'may'*] II.† f. *female relation, wife, woman, maiden,* Rd10⁹. [*'may'*]

mǣgbana m. *destroyer of kinsfolk,* W242⁵.

mǣgbōt f. *compensation paid to the relatives of a murdered man,* LL.

mǣgburg f. *family, tribe, race, people, nation : genealogy.*

mǣgcild n. *young kinsman,* Ct,Lcd.

mǣgcnafa m. *youthful kinsman,* BC2·329'.

mǣgcūð *related,* OEG.

mǣgcwalm (ē) m. *murder of a relation,* Cp 179P.

mægden (ǣd) n. *maiden, virgin,* LL; Æ : *girl,* Mt : *maid, servant,* Bl.

mægden- see also mǣden-.

mægdenǣw f. *marriage with a virgin,* LL (1·332').

mægdenhād m. *'maidenhood,'* Cr; CP.

mægdenman m. *'maid,' virgin,* AO,Lcd. [*'maidenman'*]

mǣge=māge

mægen I. (e) n. *bodily strength, might, 'main' force, power, vigour, valour,* B; Æ,CP : *virtue, efficacy, efficiency,* Lcd : *good deed : picked men of a nation, host, troop, army,* An,Chr; AO : *miracle.* [magan] II. subj. pl. of magan.

mægenāgende *mighty,* B2837.

mægenbyrðen† f. *huge burden,* B. [v. *'main'*]

mægencorðor n. *strong troop,* GEN 1986.

mægencræft† m. *main force, great strength, might.*

mægencyning† m. *mighty king,* Cr. [v. *'main'*]

mægendǣd f. *mighty deed,* CRA 12.

mægenēaca m. *succour,* Az 138.

mægenēacen† *mighty, vigorous.*

mægenearfeðe† n. *great misery or trial.*

mægenellen n. *mighty valour*, B659.
mægenfæst *vigorous, strong, steadfast*, Æ.
mægenfolc n. *mighty company*, Cr 877. [v. '*main*']
mægenfultum m. *mighty help*, B 1455.
mægenhēap m. *powerful band*, Ex 197.
mægenheard *very strong*, Run 5.
mægenian (gn-) *to gain strength* : (+) *establish, confirm*, BH 306¹⁸.
mægenig? (mēn-) *strong*, Ex 6¹ (BTs).
mægenlēas *powerless, feeble, helpless*, WW; Æ. ['*mainless*'] adv. -līce.
mægenlēast f. *weakness, feebleness*, Æ : *inability*, RB.
mægenrǣs m. *mighty onslaught*, B 1519. [v. '*main*']
mægenrōf† *powerful*, Ex,RD.
mægenscype m. *might, power*, Da 20.
mægensibb f. *great love*, VH 16.
mægenspēd† f. *power, virtue*.
mægenstān m. *huge stone*, Met 5¹⁶. [v. '*main*']
mægenstrang† *of great virtue or strength*.
mægenstreng-o, -ðu f. *great might*.
mægenðegen m. *mighty minister*, Gu 1099.
mægenðīse f. *violence, force*, Rd 28¹⁰.
mægenðrēat† m. *mighty host*.
mægenðrymm m. *power, might, majesty, greatness, glory*, Mt; Æ,CP : *virtue*, Bf : *heavenly host* : (†) *Christ* : (†) *heaven*. [v. '*main*']
mægenðrymnes f. *great glory, majesty*, Æ.
mægenweorc† n. *mighty work*, PPs.
mægenwīsa m. *general*, Ex 553.
mægenwudu m. *strong spear*, B 236.
mægenwundor n. *striking wonder*, Cr 927.
mæger *meagre, lean*, Guth,Lcd.
mægerian *to macerate, make lean*, WW. [*Ger.* magern]
mægester=magister
mægeð, mægeð=mægð, mægð
mǣggemōt n. *meeting of kinsmen*, AO 248¹⁸.
mǣggewrit n. *genealogy, pedigree*.
mǣggieldan³? *to contribute towards the fine for manslaughter by a kinsman*, LL 122,74².
mǣghǣmed n. *incest*, BH 280¹.
mǣghand (mēg-, mēi-) f. *natural heir, relative*, Ct.
mægister=magister
mǣglagu f. *law as to relatives*, LL 266,25.
mǣglēas *without relatives*, LL.
mǣglēast (RWH 29⁷)=mægenlēast
mǣglic *belonging to a kinsman*, ÆH.
mǣglufu f. *love*, Jul 70.
mǣgmorðor n. *murder of a relative*, GL.
mǣgmyrðra m. *murderer of a relative, parricide*, OEG,GD 239⁴.
mægn=mægen; mægnan=mengan
mægon=magon pres. pl. of magan

mǣgracu f. *generation, genealogy*, Æ.
mǣgrǣden f. *relationship*, AO.
mǣgrǣs m. *attack on relatives*, W 164⁴.
mǣgsclr [mēg-] f. *division of a people containing the kinsmen of a particular family* (BT), DR 193¹⁰.
mǣgsibb f. *relationship : affection of relatives*.
mǣgsibbung f. *reconciliation, peace-making*, JGPh 1·63.
mǣgsiblic *related*, WW 375¹⁷.
mǣgslaga m. *slayer of a relative, parricide, fratricide*, Æ.
mǣgsliht m. *murder of a relative*, W 130².
mægster=magister
mǣgð† f. gp. mǣgða, dp. mǣgðum, otherwise uninflected *maiden, virgin, girl, woman, wife*. [*Goth.* magaðs]
±mǣgð I. (ȳ) f. *family group, clan, tribe, generation, stock, race, people*, Æ,AO : *province, country*, Æ. II. *longing, ambition*, Gl,Lcd : *greed*, Bo.
mægða m. *mayweed*, Lcd,WW.
mǣgðblǣd (geð) n. *pudendum muliebre* GPH 400⁶.
mǣgðbōt f. *fine for assault on an unmarried woman?* LL 7,74.
mǣgðhād m. *virginity, chastity, purity*, MH ; Æ,CP : *band of young persons : relationship*, Æ. ['*maidhood*']
mǣgðhādlic *maidenly*, OEG 1469
mǣgðlagu=mǣglagu
mǣgðlēas *not of noble birth*, WW 219⁸.
mǣgðmann m. *maiden, virgin*, LL 8,82.
mǣgðmorðor (ē¹) nm. *murder of kin*, OEG 2⁴¹³.
mǣgðmyrðra m. *murderer of kin*, OEG 2³³⁵.
mǣgðrǣden f. *friendship, relationship*, OEG.
mǣgðsibb (ȳ²) f. *kindred*, HGl 523.
mǣgwine† m. *friendly relative, clansman*.
mǣgwlite (ā, ē) m. *aspect, species, form*.
mǣgwlitian (ē¹) *to fashion*, MtL 17².
mǣgwlitlīce (ē¹) *figuratively*, MkL p 4¹⁰.
mæht=meaht, miht
mǣhð (AS 38¹¹)=mǣgð II.
mǣl I. (ā, ē) n. *mark, sign, ornament : cross, crucifix : armour, harness, sword : measure*, Lcd : (†) *time, point of time, occasion, season : time for eating, 'meal,' meals*, CP; Æ. II. f. (†) *talk, conversation : contest, battle*. [mæðel] III.=māl
+mǣl *stained, dyed*, An 1333.
+mǣlan *to mark, stain*, Jul 591.
±mǣlan† *to speak, talk*, Gen,Ps. ['*mele*,' '*i-mele*'; mæðlan]
mǣlcearu f. *trouble of the time*, B 189.
mæld-=meld-
mǣldæg† m. *appointed time, day*, Gen.

mældropa m. *phlegm, saliva, mucus*, WW 240⁹.

mældropiende *running with mucus*, WW 161³³.

mæle I. m. (ē) *cup, bowl, bucket, Ep,Lcd.* ['*meal*'] II. *marked*, KC.

mælgesceaft f. *fate*, B2737.

mælsceafa (æ?) m. *canker, caterpillar, WW.* ['*malshave*']

mæltan (VPs)=meltan

mæl-tang m., -tange f. *pair of compasses*, WW.

mæl-tīd f., -tīma m. *meal-time*, NC348.

mæn=menn nap. of man.

mæn-=man-, men-

±**mænan** I. (ē) *to '*mean,*' signify, intend, Æ, Bo,Sol;* CP : *consider.* II. *to tell : mention, relate, declare, communicate to, speak of, B : speak (a language).* III. *to complain of, lament, bewail, sorrow, grieve, Bo; Æ,AO, CP.*

mæne I. (±, usu. +) *common, public, general, universal, Mt;* AO : *owned in common, WW : catholic : lower (clergy) : mutual.* habban +m. *to have or hold in common.* ['*i-mene*'] II. (+) n. *fellowship, intercourse.* III. *false, mean, wicked.* [mān] IV. (+) *subdued, overpowered,* GEN,GNE. [=*+mægne, ES43·308]

±**mænelic** (usu. +) *common, ordinary : mutual : public, general, universal, Æ.* adv. -līce.

+**mænelicnes** f. *generality,* OEG.

mænibræde *relating to many things,* WW 115⁸.·

mænlic=mænelic

+**mænnes** f. *community, fellowship, intercourse, union, Shr : sharing : land held in common,* BC1·597'. [v. '*i-mene*']

+**mænscipe** m. *community, fellowship : union,* W248²³ : *common ownership,* RB 103²⁰.

±**mænsumian** *to impart : partake of, participate in, have fellowship with : live with, marry : communicate : administer Eucharist, Æ.*

+**mænsumnes** f. *fellowship, participation (in Eucharist),* BH.

mænsumung f. *fellowship, participation, ÆH : (+) administration of the Eucharist,* CM,RBL.

mænu=menigu

+**mænung** f. *marriage,* HL.

mærāc f. *boundary-oak,* KC3·379'.

mæran (ā) I. (±) *to declare, proclaim, celebrate, glorify, honour.* II. (+) *to determine, fix limits,* WID42.

mærapeldre f. *apple-tree on a boundary,* KC3·390⁵.

mærbrōc m. *boundary-brook,* KC.

mærc (1)=mearc; (2)=mearg

mærcnoll m. *boundary-knoll,* EC445.

mærcumb m. *border valley,* KC.

mærdīc f. *boundary-dike,* KC.

mære⸗(1) mare; (2) mere I.

mære I. (ē) *famous, great, excellent, sublime, splendid, Æ,B,Ep;* AO,CP. ['*mere*'] II. *pure, sterling (of money).* [v. '*mere*' adj.] III. (±, usu. +) *boundary, border, Mk,VPs;* AO; Mdf : *balk of a plough-land,* GBG : *end.* IV. *declaration,* TC646,648 (v. A 46·214). ['*mere*' sb.]

mærelsrāp m. *ship's rope, cable,* WW.

mæretorht=meretorht

mærflōde *border channel,* EC370⁵.

mærford *border ford,* KC5·126'.

mærfurh *border furrow,* KC.

mærgeard *border fence,* KC3·462³.

mærgen=morgen

mærh (Cp,Ep), mærh-=mearg, mearh-

+**mærhaga** (ē) m. *boundary-hedge,* EC388¹⁰.

mær-hege m. *boundary-hedge,* EC447.

mærhlinc *border ridge,* KC.

mærhlīsa m. *notoriety,* WW382¹⁰.

mærian *to be distinguished,* DHy.

+**mærian**=+mǣrsian II.

mæringcwudu n. *mastic of sweet basil?* LCD131a.

+**mærlacu** f. *boundary-stream,* EC387'.

mærlic (ȳ) *great, splendid, glorious, famous, Æ,AO,CP.* adv. -līce, Æ.

mærnes f. *greatness, honour, fame,* LPs, WW.

mær-pōl, -pul m. *boundary-pool,* EC445⁸, KC5·198'.

mærpytt m. *pit on a boundary,* KC.

mærsc=mersc

mærsere (ē) m. *herald,* DR56¹⁷.

±**mærsian** (ē) I. *to make or become famous, proclaim, declare, announce, Æ,CP : celebrate : glorify, honour, exalt, praise, Æ : spread (fame) : enlarge.* II. *to mark out, bound, limit.*

mærsīc *border rivulet,* KC6·60¹⁷.

mærstān m. *boundary-stone,* BC3·154. ['*merestone*']

mærsung (ē) f. *fame, report, renown : celebration, festival, Æ : exalting, magnifying : (±) magnificence, celebrity.*

mærsungtīma m. *time of glorifying,* ÆH 2·360²⁵.

+**mærtrēow** *boundary-tree,* KC3·342'.

mærð=mearð

mærð f. *glory, fame : famous exploit, Æ, AO,CP.*

±**mær-ðorn**, -ðyrne *boundary-hawthorn,* KC.

mærðu=mærð

mæru=mearu

+mǣrung? _ending_, RHy5¹⁰.

mærw-=mearu-

±mǣrweg m. _boundary-road_, Ct.

mǣrweorc m. _noble work_, PPs110⁴.

+mǣrwyll m. _boundary-stream_, KC3·193⁹.

mæscre (ǣ?) f. _mesh_, WW450¹⁰.

mæsen _brazen_ (Earle): _of maple_ (BT), EC 250.

mæslere m. _sacristan_, GD228¹⁵.

mæsling, mæslen (_MkL_)=mæstling

mæssanhacele=mæssehacele

mæsse (e) f. _'mass,' Eucharist, celebration of Eucharist_, Æ,BH,Ct; CP : _special mass-day, festival of the church_. [_L_. missa]

mæsseǣfen m. _eve of a festival_, CHR,LL.

mæsse-bōc f. nap. -bēc _'mass-book,' missal_, LL.

mæssecrēda m. _creed said at mass, Niċene creed_, LL. ['_mass-creed_']

mæssedæg m. _'mass-day,' festival_, Bl.

mæssegierela m. _mass-vestment, surplice_, CP87¹⁹.

mæssehacele f. _mass-vestment, cope, chasuble_, LV40,WW327²².

mæssehrægl n. _vestment, surplice_, CP.

mæsselāc n. _mass-offering, host_, WW

mæsseniht f. _eve of a festival_, CHR,W.

mæsseprēost m. _'mass-priest,' clergyman, high-priest_, Æ,AO; CP. [v. also '_priest_']

mæsseprēosthād m. _office or orders of a mass-priest_, BH.

mæsseprēostscīr f. _district for which a mass-priest officiated_, LL.

mæsserbana m. _murderer of a priest_, W 165²⁸.

mæssere m. _priest who celebrates mass_, Az. ['_masser_']

mæsserēaf n. _mass-vestments_, Æ.

mæssesang m. _office of mass_, BH,LL.

mæssesteall m. _seat in a church choir_ (Napier), _place from which the priest said mass?_ (BTs), v. NC307,348.

mæssetīd f. _time of saying mass_, LL(140²⁰).

mæsseðegn m. _mass-priest_, LL460,5.

mæsseðēnung f. _service of the mass, celebration of mass_, A11·8¹⁵, BYH76¹⁵.

mæsseūhta m. _hour, or service, of matins on a feast-day_, NC307.

mæssewīn (e) n. _wine used at mass_, WW.

mæssian (±) _to celebrate 'mass,'_ Æ : (+) _attend mass_.

mæssung f. _office of mass_, CHRD35¹³.

mæst I. m. (_ship's_) _'mast,'_ B; Æ,AO. **II.** m. _'mast,' food of swine, acorns, beech-nuts_, BC.

mǣst (ā, ē) **I.** adj. (superl. of micel), _AO, Chr,Bo,Mt_. ['_most_'] **II.** adv. _mostly, for the most part, in the greatest degree, chiefly_,

especially, very much. eal m., m. eal _almost, nearly_. m. ǣlc _nearly every one_, Æ,AO, CP. **III.** n. _most_.

±mǣstan _to feed with 'mast,' fatten_, BC; _anoint_, RPs22⁵,Æ,CP.

mæstcyst f. _mast-socket_, WW.

mæstelberg m. _fattened hog_, MtL6⁷. [bearg]

mæsten n. _mast, pasture for swine_, Ct,LL.

mæstenrǣden f. _right of feeding swine in mast-pastures_, KC3·451¹⁰.

mæstentrēow n. _tree yielding mast_, WW 137²³.

mæstland f. _land yielding mast_, TC140².

mǣstlīcost adv. (superl.) _particularly_, CM 1169.

mæstling I. n. _brass_, WW : _brazen vessel_, Mk. ['_maslin_'] **II.** _fatling_, OEG61²⁹.

mæstlingsmið m. _brass-worker_, WW539⁶.

mæstlōn sbpl. _pulleys at the top of a mast_, WW199³⁰.

mæstrǣden=mæstenrǣden

mæstrāp m. _mast-rope_, Ex82.

mæsttwist m. _rope supporting a mast_, WW.

mǣt I. pret. 3 sg. of metan. **II.**=mete m.

±mǣtan _to dream_ (impers.), Æ; (trans.) _Lcd_. ['_mete_']

mǣte=mete

mǣte (ē) _mean, moderate, poor, inferior, small, bad_. also adv.

+mǣte _suitable_, RB; ÆL. ['_meet_']

mǣtfæst-=metfæst-

+mǣtgian (ÆL)=+metgian

mǣting f. _dream_, Lcd. ['_meting_']

mǣton pret. pl. of metan.

mǣð I. f. _measure, degree, proportion, rate_, Æ; AO : _honour, respect, reverence_, LL : _what is meet, right, fitness, ability, virtue, goodness_, Æ,CP : _lot, state, rank_, Æ. ['_methe_'] **II.** n. _cutting of grass_, BC. ['_math_']

mǣð-=mægð-

±mǣðegian _to honour, respect, spare_, W; ÆT. ['_methe_']

mǣðel (e) n. _council, meeting, popular assembly_ : (†) _speech, interview_.

mǣðelcwide† (e) m. _discourse_.

mǣðelern n. _council-house, prætorium_, WW.

mǣðelfrið (ðl) mn. _security_ ('frið') _enjoyed by public assemblies_, LL3,1 (v. 2·464 and 3·4).

mǣðel-hēgende†, -hergende _holding conclave, deliberating_.

mǣðelstede† (e) m. _place of assembly : battle-field_.

mǣðelword (e) n. _address, speech_, B236

mǣð(e)re m. _mower_, WW235,237.

mǣðful _humane_, ÆGr. ['_metheful_']

mǣðlan=mǣðegian; **mæðl**=mæðel
mǣðlan (*Cr*)=maðelian
mǣðlēas *rapacious, Æ.* ['*metheless*']
mǣðlic *moderate, proportioned, befitting, Ct,
LL.* adv. -*līce humanely, courteously,
ÆGr.* ['*methely*']
mǣðmēd f. *pay for haymaking,* LL 452'.
mǣðre=mǣðere
±**mǣðrian** *to honour,* LL.
mǣðung f. *measuring, adjudication,* CHRD
35¹⁸.
mǣw (ea, e) m. '*mew,*' *sea-gull, An,Cp,Shr.*
mǣwpul (ā) m. *sea-gulls' pool,* Ct.
māfealdra comp. of manigfeald.
maffian *to go astray, wax wanton,* CHRD
74²,77².
mag-=mæg-
maga I. m. '*maw,*' *stomach, Cp,Lcd,WW;
Æ,CP.* **II.** *powerful, strong : able, competent, having means.*
māga I.† m. *son, descendant, young man,
man.* **II.** gp. of mæg.
magan swv. pres. 1, 3 sg. mæg; 2, meaht,
miht; pl. magon; pret. 3 sg. meahte *to be
able, Bo,G,WW : have permission or power
(I '*may*,*' I can), DD,G : to be strong,
competent, avail, prevail, Æ,B,BH,Gl,
VPs;* CP. mæg wið *avails against, cures,*
LCD.
māgas v. mǣg; **magaðe**=mageðe
magaðiht *strong of stomach,* LCD 3·68¹⁷.
magdalatrēow n. *almond-tree,* WW 139¹¹.
[*L.* amygdala]
mage f. (WW 159¹⁴)=maga
māge (ā) f. *female relative, B; Æ.* ['*mowe*']
māgeēct ptc. *augmented,* WW. [īecan]
mageðe (æ¹, o²) f. *camomile, mayweed,* Lcd,
WW. ['*maythe*']
magian *to prevail,* ERPs 12⁵; NC 348 : (+)
recover (health), LCD 3·184²¹? (BTac; or
?āmagian).
magister (æ) m. *leader, chief, 'master,'
teacher, Æ,Bo;* AO,CP. [*L.* magister]
magisterdōm (mægster-) m. *office of a master
or teacher, Sc* 120⁹. ['*masterdom*']
±**māglic**=±mālic
mago† (magu) m. gs. maga, nap. mæcgas
*male kinsman, son, descendant : young
man, servant : man, warrior.*
magodryht f. *band of warriors,* B 67.
magogeoguð f. *youth,* CRI 1429.
magorǣdend m. *counsellor of men,* AN
1463.
magorǣswa† m. *chief, prince.*
magorinc† m. *youth, man, warrior.*
magotimber† n. *child, son,* GEN : *increase
of family, progeny,* GNE.
magotūdor† n. *descendant, offspring.*
magoðe, magoðe=mageðe

magoðegn† m. *vassal, retainer, warrior, man,
servant, minister.*
magu=mago; **māgwlite**=mægwlite
±**māh** *bad, wanton, shameless, importunate.*
mahan=magon pres. pl. of magan.
+**māhlic** *importunate : wanton, shameless :
wicked.* adv. -*līce impudently.*
+**māhlicnes** f. *importunity,* CP : *wantonness,
shamelessness : time of need,* SPs 9²².
+**māhnes** f. *importunity, persistence : shamelessness : boldness : contumacy,* WYN 57.
maht (VPs)=miht
Māius '*May,*' *Bf.*
māl I. n. *suit, cause, case, action, terms,
agreement, covenanted pay, Chr.* hē scy-
lode ix scypa of māle *he paid nine ships
out of commission,* CHR 1049c. ['*mail*']
II. n. *spot, mark, blemish, Æ.* **III.**=mǣl n.
māl-=mǣl-, māhl-
mālscrung f. *enchantment, charm, Cp,Lcd.*
['*maskering*']
mālswyrd (u²) n. *sword with inlaid ornament,* TC 560'. [mǣl]
malt (Gl)=mealt; **malwe** (WW)=mealwe
mamme f. *teat,* GPH 401⁷⁷. [*L.* mamma]
mamor, mam(e)ra m. *lethargy, heavy sleep,*
GL.
mamrian *to think out, design,* PPs 63⁵.
man I. pron. indef. *one, people, they, B,Mt;
Æ.* ['*man*'] **II.**=mann. **III.** pres. 3 sg.
of munan.
mān I. n. *evil deed, crime, wickedness,
guilt, sin, B,Ps; Æ : false oath, ÆP*
216¹⁴. **II.** adj. *bad, criminal, false, Ps;*
AO. ['*man*']
+**man** (o) *having a mane,* WW 492²⁰.
man-=mann-
+**māna** m. *community, company, Æ : common property : communion, companionship, intercourse, Bo,BH;* CP : *cohabitation, LG.* tō +mānan *in common,* CP.
['*mone,*' '*ymone*']
manað pres. 3 sg. of manian.
mānāð m. *false oath, perjury,* LL; HL.
['*manath*']
mānāðswaru f. *perjury,* LL.
mānbealu n. *crime, cruelty,* DA 45.
manbōt (o¹) f. *fine paid to the lord of a man
slain,* LL (v. 2·576). ['*manbote*']
mānbryne m. *fatal, destructive fire,* CHR
962A.
mancgere=mangere
-**mancian** v. be-m.
man-cus, -cas, -cos, -cs m. gp. mancessa
(CP) *a 'mancus,' thirty silver pence, one-
eighth of a pound, Æ,BC.*
mancwealm m. *mortality, pestilence, destruction, Chr;* AO. ['*manqualm*']
mancwealmnes f. *manslaughter,* NG.

mancwyld (o) f. *mortality, pestilence,* BH 190⁸.

mancynn n. *mankind, Æ,B,Bl : inhabitants, people, men,* CP. ['*mankin*']

mancyst f. *human virtue,* MFH 169.

mand (o) f. *basket, Cp,MtL,WW.* ['*maund*']

mándǣd f. *sin, crime,* Ph; Æ,AO,CP. [v. '*man*']

mándǣda m. *evil-doer,* NC 329.

mándǣde *evil-doing, wicked,* LL,W.

mándeorf *bold in evil?* ÆPD120³¹.

mandrēam† m. *revelry, festivity.*

mándrinc m. *poison,* RD 24¹³.

mandryhten† m. *lord, master,* B.

+**máne** *having a mane,* WE 57¹⁶.

maneg=manig

mánfæhðu f. *wickedness,* GEN 1378.

manfaru f. *host, troop,* GU 257.

mánfeld m. *field of crime,* AO 108²⁰.

mánfolm f. *evil-doer,* PPs 143⁸.

mánfordǣdla m. *evil-doer,* B 563.

mánforwyrht n. *evil deed, sin,* CR1095.

mánfrēa† m. *lord of evil, Devil.*

mánfremmende† *sinning, vicious.*

mánful *wicked, evil, infamous, degraded,* Æ : *fearful, dire.*

mánfullic *infamous, evil, sinful,* Æ. adv. -líce, Æ.

mánfulnes f. *wickedness,* Æ.

manfultum (o¹) m. *military force,* AO 216⁸.

+**mang** I. n. *mixture, union : troop, crowd, multitude,* Jud : *congregation, assembly : business : cohabitation.* in +m. *during.* on +m. *in the midst of.* ['*ymong*'] II. prep. (w. d. or a.) *among,* AO,G; Æ,CP. ['*ymong*']

mángenga m. *evil-doer,* BH 36⁵.

mángenīola m. *evil persecutor,* AN 918.

+**mang(en)nes** f. *mingling, mixture,* OEG.

mangere m. *trader, merchant, broker,* Æ.

mángewyrhta m. *sinner,* PPs 77³⁸.

±**mangian** *to gain by trading,* Æ,CP.

mangung f. *trade, business,* Æ.

mangunghūs n. *house of merchandise,* Jn 2¹⁶.

mánhūs n. *home of wickedness, hell,* Ex 535.

±**manian** I. (o) *to remind,· admonish, warn, exhort, instigate,* Æ,CP : *instruct, advise,* Æ : *claim, demand, ask.* II. (+) *to be restored to health?* GD 338³⁰.

mánidel *vain and bad (words),* PPs 143.

maniend m. *admonisher,* CP 407¹³ : *collector : creditor.*

manif-=manigf-

manig (æ¹, e¹, o¹, e²) nap. manega '*many,*' *many a, much,* Æ,AO,B,BH,Ps; CP.

manigean=manian; **manigeo**=menigu

manigfeald (æ, e, o¹) '*manifold,' various, varied, complicated,* Æ,WW; CP : *numerous, abundant : plural,* ÆGr. adv. -fealde.

±**manigfeald(l)an** (æ¹, a³, y³) *to multiply, abound, increase, extend,* OEG; CP : *reward.* ['*manifold*']

manigfealdlic *manifold.* adv. -líce *in various ways,* LG,VPs; CP : (gram.) *in the plural number.* ['*manifoldly*']

manigfealdnes f. *multiplicity, abundance, complexity,* LG,WW. ['*manifoldness*']

manigsīðes (mani-) adv. *often,* W 144¹¹.

manig-tēaw (æ¹), -tīwe, -tȳwe *skilful, dexterous,* Æ.

manigtēawnes (mænitȳw-) f. *skill, dexterity,* OEG.

manlēas (o) *uninhabited,* WW. ['*manless*']

mánlic *infamous, nefarious,* Æ. adv. -líce *falsely, wickedly.*

manlíca m. *effigy, image, statue,* GEN,BL.

manlíce adv. *manfully, nobly,* B. ['*manly*']

manlufu f. *love for men,* GU 324.

manm-=mannm-

mann (o) m., nap. men(n) *person (male or fem.),* Æ,Bl,Lcd,G,VHy; AO,CP : *man : mankind,* Mk,VPs : *brave man, hero : vassal, servant : name of the rune for* m. *used indefinitely, like Mod. Eng. 'one,'* v. man I.

mann-, see also man-.

manna I. m. *man,* Æ. II. n. '*manna*' *(food),* Æ,CP. [L.]

mannbǣre *producing men,* ÆH 1·450.

mannēaca (mon-) m. *progeny,* AO 158²⁰.

mannhata (o¹) m. *man-hater,* ByH 38³².

mannian *to 'man,' garrison,* Chr 1087E.

mannmægen (o) n. *troop, force, cohort,* JnL 18².

mannmenigu (o) f. *multitude,* AO.

mannmyrring f. *destruction of men,* CHR1096.

mannmyrðra m. *a homicide,* LL.

mannsylen (i²) f. *traffic in men, sale of men unlawfully as slaves,* LL,W. [selen]

manrǣden f. *dependence, homage, service, tribute, due,* Æ. ['*manred*']

manrím† n. *number of men.*

mánsceatt m. *usury,* PPs 71¹⁴.

mánsceaða† m. *enemy, sinner.*

mánscild f. *crime, fault, sin,* †Hy 8²³.

manscipe m. *humanity, courtesy,* BC. ['*manship*']

mánscyldig† *criminal, guilty.*

manslen=mannsylen

manslæht=manslieht

manslaga m. *man-slayer, murderer,* Æ.

mánslagu f. *cruel blow,* AN 1218.

manslēan *to kill, murder,* RB 16¹⁸ (or ? two words).

manslege m. *manslaughter, homicide,* BL, LL.

manslieht (e², i²) m. *manslaughter, murder,* CP. ['*manslaught*']

manslot *share in ownership of land? measure of land?* v. NC307. [*ON.* mannshlutr]
-mānsumian, -mānsumung v. ā-m.
manswǣs *meek*, RPs 24⁹.
mānswara (o²) m. *perjurer*, Bl. ['*manswear*']
mānswaru f. *perjury*, LL,WW. [swerian]
mānswerian⁶ *to forswear, perjure oneself*, LL. ['*manswear*']
mānswica m. *deceiver, traitor* (mann-? v. LL2·142).
mansylen (i²) f. *traffic in men, act of selling men as slaves*. [sellan]
manðēaw† m. *habit, custom* (? sometimes mānðēaw *sinful custom*).
manðēof m. *man-stealer*, v. L2·542.
manðrymm m. *troop of men*, MFH 97¹¹.
manðwǣre (o) *gentle, kind, humane, mild, meek*, ÆL,CP. [*OHG.* mandwāri]
+**manðwǣrian** *to humanize*, CP362²¹.
manðwǣrnes (o¹, y²) f. *gentleness, courtesy, weakness*, ÆL,CP.
manu f. '*mane*,' Erf1182; WE54¹³.
manung f. *admonition*, CP : *claim* : *place of toll* : *district for purposes of tribute or taxation* : *residents in a taxing district*.
mānwamm (o²) m. *guilty stain*, CR1280.
mānweorc I. n. *crime, sin*. II. adj. *sinful*, EL.
manweorod (o) m. *collection of men, troop, congregation, assembly*, AO.
manweorðung f. *adoration of human beings*, LL (248³).
manwīse† (o) f. *manner or custom of men*.
mānword n. *wicked word*, PPs58¹².
mānwrǣce *wicked*, WW426¹⁹.
mānwyrhta† m. *evil-doer, sinner*, PPs.
manwyrð n. *value or price of a man*, LL.
mapulder (o²) m. *maple tree*, Ct,LCD.
mapuldern *made of maple*, Ct,WW.
mapul-dre, -dor, -dur f., -trē(ow) m. (Mdf)= mapulder
māra m., māre fn. (compar. of micel) *greater, 'more,' stronger, mightier*, Æ,Bl, CP,LL. adv. *in addition*, Mt.
māran=mǣran
mārbēam (VPs)=mōrbēam
marc n. *a denomination of weight* (usu. half a pound), *mark* (money of account), CHR, Ct.
marcian=mearcian
mare (e) f. *nightmare, monster*, Ep,Lcd. ['*mare*']
māre v. māra; **mārels**=mǣrelsrāp
marenis=mearuwnes; **margen-**=morgen-
+**mārian** *to increase*, Sc40¹⁶.
market n. *market*, TC422²⁰ (v.l.). [*L.* mercatum]

marma m. *marble*, LCD1·154¹⁴. [*L.* marmor]
marman-stān (marmel-, marm(or)-) m. *marble, piece of marble*, Æ,Bl. ['*marmstone*']
marmstāngedelf n. *quarrying of marble*, ÆH1·560³².
-marod v. ā-m.
martir, martyr(e) m. '*martyr*,' BH,Men; Æ,AO. [*L.*]
martirlogium m. *martyrology*, IM122⁴⁵.
martr-=martyr-
martyrcynn m. *race of martyrs*, ÆL23⁸⁵.
martyrdōm m. '*martyrdom*,' BH; Æ,CP.
martyrhād m. *martyrdom*, BH,GD.
+**mar-tyrian**, -trian *to* '*martyr*,' *torture*, AO, BH.
martyrracu f. *martyrology*, ÆL23³³⁴.
martyrung f. *passion* (*of Christ*), AO254²⁴. ['*martyring*']
mārðu=mǣrð
masc=max
māse f. *name of a small bird*, GL. [*Ger.* meise]
-maslan v. ā-m.
massere m. *merchant* : *moneylender*, BK 10.
māst=mǣst; **matt**, matte (*CP*)=meatte
mattuc (æ¹, ea¹, e¹, eo¹, o²) m. '*mattock*,' AO,Gl,LL; Æ : *fork, trident*.
māð pret. 3 sg. of mīðan.
maða m. *maggot, worm, grub*, WW. ['*mathe*']
maðal-=maðel-
+**maðel** n. *speech, talking*, NIC507²⁰. [=mæðel?]
maðelere m. *speaker, haranguer*, WW. [v. '*mathele*']
maðelian† (æ¹, e¹, a², o²) *to harangue, make a speech, speak*, An,B,Cp,Cr. ['*mell*,' '*mathele*']
maðelig *talkative, noisy*, KGL75²³.
maðelung f. *loquacity*, OEG. [v. '*mathele*']
māðm=māðum
māðm- see also māððum.
māðmǣht† f. *valuable thing, treasure*, B.
māðmcleofa (mād-) m. *treasure-chamber*, Æ (9²⁷⁷).
māðmcyst f. *treasure-chest*, Mt27⁶.
māðmgestrēon n. *treasure*, B,MFH.
māðmhord n. *treasure-hoard*, Ex368.
māðmhūs n. *treasure-house, treasury*, AO, CP.
māðmhyrde m. *treasurer*, Bo64¹³.
maðolian=maðelian
māððum=māðum, māðm
maððum-fæt n., pl. -fatu *precious vessel*, Æ.
māððumgesteald n. *treasure*, JUL36.
māððumgifu f. *gift of treasure*, B1301.

māððumgyfa m. *giver of treasure, prince, king*, WA 92.
māððumsele m. *hall of treasure*, SOL 189.
māððumsigle n. *costly ornament*, B 2757.
māððumsweord n. *costly sword*, B 1023.
māððumwela m. *valuables*, B 2750.
maðu f.=maða
māðum m., gs. māðmes *treasure, object of value, jewel, ornament, gift*, Gn,Met; CP. ['*madme*']
māðum-=māðm-, māððum-
māwan[7] *to* '*mow*,' AO,BH.
māwpul=mǣwpul
max n. *net*, WW. ['*mask*']
mǣxwyrt f. *mash-wort (malt soaked in boiling water)*, LCD. [v. FTP 322]
me I. das. of pers. pron. ic *me*. II. (RB 35[9]; 127[13])=menn
meagol (e[1]) *mighty, strong, firm, emphatic, impressive*. [magan]
meagollīce adv. *earnestly*, BL.
meagolmōd *earnest, strenuous*, A 11·97[3].
meagolmōdnes f. *earnestness*, BL.
meagolnes f. *earnestness, strength of will*, BL,HL.
meaht I.=miht. II. pres. 2 sg. of magan.
meahte pret. 3 sg. of magan.
mealc pret. of melcan.
mealclīðe?=meolclīðe; mealehūs=meluhūs
mealewe=mealwe; mealm=mealmstān
-meallian v. ā-m.
mealmeht *sandy? chalky?* KC 3·394[13]. [v. '*malm*']
mealmstān m. *soft stone, sandstone? limestone?* AO 212[28]. [v. '*malm*']
mealt I. n. *steeped grain*, '*malt*,' Ct,Ep. [meltan] II. *sour*, LCD 3·6[17]? III. pret. 3 sg. of meltan.
mealtealoð n. *malt-ale*, ANS 84[325].
mealtgescot n. *payment in malt*, W 171[2].
mealthūs n. '*malt-house*,' WW.
mealtwyrt (u[2]) f. '*malt-wort*,' WW.
mealu=melu
mealwe f. '*mallow*,' Lcd,WW. [L. malva]
mear=mearh
mearc (ǣ, e) f. (±) '*mark*,' *sign, line of division*, Æ,MkL,RB : *standard*, ÆGr : (±) *boundary, limit, term, border*, BC,Gen; CP; Mdf : *defined area, district, province*, AO. tō ðæs +mearces ðe *in the direction that*.
mearca m. *space marked out*, GD 197[4].
mearcdīc (e) f. *boundary-ditch*, BC 1·295[7].
mearcere (ǣ) m. *writer, notary*, OEG.
mearcford *boundary-ford*, EC 382[1].
mearcgemot *court for settling boundaries of properties?* v. LL 2·143.
mearcgrǣfa m. *boundary-thicket*, KC 3·135'.
mearchlinc m. *boundary-ridge*, KC 6·33[22].

mearchof n. *dwelling*, Ex 61.
±mearcian *to* '*mark*,' *stain, brand, seal*, BC, LL,MtL,Ph; Æ : *mark a boundary, measure, define, describe, designate*, Æ, Gen : *mark out, design*, Bo : *create* : *note, observe*. +mearcod *baptized*, BF 124[14].
mearc-īsern, -īsen n. *branding-iron*, GL,MH.
mearcland n. *border-land, march, moor* : (†) *province, country, district* : *sea-coast*, RD 4[23].
mearcpæð† m. *road, path*, AN,EL.
mearcstapa† m. *march-haunter*, B.
mearcstede m. *border-land, desolate district*, SOL 217.
mearcðrēat m. *army, troop*, Ex 173.
mearcung (æ, e) f. *marking, branding* : *mark, characteristic* : (±) *description, arrangement* : *constellation* : *title, chapter*, NG.
mearcweard m. *wolf*, Ex 168.
mearcweg m. *border-road*, BC,KC.
mearcwill m. *boundary-spring*, EC 293'.
meard=(1) meord, mēd; (2) mearð
mēares v. mearh I.
mearg (æ, e) nm. I. '*marrow*,' *pith*, Lcd. II. *sausage*, GL. [=mærg] III.=mearh I.
mēargealla (e[1], e[2]) m. *gentian*, LCD. [mearh] +meargian *to be rich, marrowy*, LPs 65[15].
mearglic (e) *marrowy, fat*, VPs.
mearh I.† m. gs. mēares *horse, steed*. II.=mearg
mearhæccel n. *sausage-meat*, WW 411[20].
mearhcofa m. *bone*, PPs 101[3].
mearhgehǣc n. *sausage-meat*, WW 427[30].
mearmstān=marmanstān
mearn pret. 3 sg. of murnan.
+mearr I. n. *stumbling-block, obstruction, error*, CP : *emptiness, vanity*, RPs 88[48]. II. *wicked, fraudulent*, LL 140,1[5].
mearrian *to err*, Bo 55[23].
mearð (æ, e) m. *marten*, Ep,AO. ['*mart*']
mearu (æ, e, y), mear(u)w- in obl. cases *tender, soft*, Lcd,MtR : *callow*, OEG : *delicate*, RB : *frail*, GD 119[17]. ['*meruw*']
mearulic (merwe, mærw-) *frivolous, delicate, luxurious*, GD. adv. -līce *weakly*.
mearuwnes f. *tenderness, frailty*, CP 211[18].
mēast=mǣst
meatte (a) f. '*mat*,' *mattress*, Gl. [L.]
mēaw=mǣw
mec as. of ic pers. pron.
+mec=+mæc
mēce m. *sword, blade*, GL. [Goth. mēkeis]
mēcefisc (ǣ) m. *mullet*, ÆGR 308[5].
mecg=mæcg
mecgan *to mix, stir*, LCD.
mech=mesc
mechanisc *mechanical*, ÆL 5[251]. [L.]
mēd I. f. '*meed*,' *reward, pay, price, compensation, bribe*, ÆL (gs. mēdes), B,BH, Bl; CP. II.=mǣd

med- in comp. principally indicates mediocrity, but often comes to have a distinct negative value; see, *e.g.*, medtrum, medwīs. [midde]

mēda v. mǣd; **-mēdan** v. on-m.

medder=mēder; **mēdder-**, mēddr-=mēdr-

meddrosna fp. *dregs of mead*, LCD 48a.

+mēde I. n. *consent, good-will, pleasure*, Ct : *covenant*. II. *agreeable, pleasant : suitable*.

medel=mæðel

medema (eo¹) m. *treadle*, WW.

medeme (eo¹) *middling, average, mean, little : sufficient, considerable, respectable, proper, fit, worthy, trustworthy, perfect*, CP.

±medemian (eo¹) *to mete out, allot, assign, place : moderate : (+) humble : respect, honour*, Æ : (+) *condescend*, Æ : (+) *advance, promote, deem worthy*, Æ.

medemlic *moderate, mediocre : intermediate : simple : worthy*. adv. **-līce** *slightly, moderately, incompletely : suitably, worthily, kindly*.

medemlicnes f. *mediocrity*, OEG.

medemmicel (Æ)=medmicel

medemnes f. *dignity, worth*, Æ,CP : *benignity, condescension*, BL.

medemung f. *measuring, measure*, Ct,LL.

mēden=mægden

mēder ds. and LWS gs. of mōdor.

mēderce=mȳderce; **medere**=mæddre

mēderen, mēdern=mēdren

mēderwyrhta=mēterwyrhta

medewyrt=meduwyrt

mēdgilda (ǣ) m. *pensioner, hireling*, Æ.

mēdian *to reward*, GD 237²³.

mēdl-=mǣðl-; **-mēdla** v. an-, ofer-m.

medlen=midlen

medm-=medem-

medmicel I. *moderate-sized, short, small, limited, unimportant, slight, mean, poor*. II. n. *a little*.

medmicelnes f. *smallness (of mind)*, SPs 54⁸.

medmicle comp. medmāre, adv. *humbly, meanly, slightly*.

medo=medu; **medom-**=medem-

+mēdred=+mēdren I.

+mēdren I. *maternal, of a mother*. II. n. *the mother's side (by descent)*, LL 156,11.

+mēdren *born of the same mother*, AO 114¹³.

mēdrencynn n. *mother's kindred*, CR 246.

mēdrengecynd n. *mother's nature*, W 17⁷.

mēdrenmǣg m. *maternal kinsman*, LL.

mēdrenmǣgð f. *maternal kindred*, LL 392,3.

medrīce *of low rank*, WW 115²⁶.

mēdsceatt m. *payment, fee, reward, bribe, gift*, Æ,CP.

medsēlð (ǣ) f. *ill-fortune*, AO 164²⁸.

medspēdig *poor*, CRA 9.

medstrang *of middle rank*, BL 185¹⁶.

medtrum *weak, infirm, sickly, ill*, CP : *of lower rank*. [cp. medmicel]

medtrumnes (met-; y²) f. *weakness, infirmity, sickness, illness, disease*, AO,CP.

medu (eo) mn. gs. med(e)wes *'mead'* (drink), B,Rd; AO.

+mēdu=+mēde

meduærn (o²) n. *mead-hall, banqueting-house*, B 69.

medubenc† f. *bench in a mead-hall*, B.

meduburg† *mead-city, rejoicing city*.

medudrēam† m. *mead-joy, jollity*, B.

medudrenc (eo¹) m. *mead*, W 245⁴.

medudrinc (o²) m. *mead-drinking*, SEAF 22.

meduful† n. *mead-cup*, B,WY.

medugāl† *mead-excited, drunk*.

meduheall† f. *mead-hall*.

medum-=medem-

medurǣden (eo¹) f. *strong drink?* (BT), *dealing out of mead?* (GK), GNE 88.

meduscenc (eo¹) m. *mead-cup*, B 1980.

meduscerwen (ea¹) f. *deprival of (mead-) joy, distress, mortal panic?* AN 1526.

meduseld n. *mead-hall*, B 3065.

medusetl n. (eo¹, o²) *mead-seat*, B 5.

medustīg f. *path to the mead-hall*, B 924.

meduwērig† *overpowered with mead, drunk*.

meduwong (eo¹, o²) m. *field (where the mead-hall stood)*, B 1643.

meduwyrt (eo¹, e²) f. *meadow-sweet*, LCD : *'rubia', madder*, OEG 56⁴⁰. ['*meadwort*']

medwīs *dull, stupid, foolish*, CP. [cp. medmicel]

mēdwyrhta m. *a hireling*, SC 123¹².

meg=mæg

mēg=(1) mǣw; (2) mǣg

mēg-=mǣg-; **megol**=meago

meh=mec, me, as. of ic

meht=meaht, miht; **mēl**, mēig=mǣg

meige (KGL 81³²)=mǣge pres. 3 sg. subj. of magan.

meiðhād (KGL 56⁷)=mægðhād

mēl=mǣl n.

mela=melu

±melcan³ (i) *to milk*, ÆGR,LCD.

melcingfæt=meolcfæt

meld f. *proclamation*, DA 648.

melda m. *reporter, informer, betrayer*, Æ.

meldan (Rd)=meldian

melde f. *orache (plant)*, LCD. ['*milds*']

meldfeoh n. *informer's reward*, LL 96,17.

±meldian *to announce, declare, tell, proclaim, reveal*, Ps; Æ : *inform against, accuse*. ['*meld*']

meldung f. *betrayal*, BH 240⁴.

mēle=mǣle

meledēaw mn. *honey-dew, nectar*, Ph,WW (mild-). ['*mildew*']

melewes=melwes gs. of melu.

-melle, -melnes v. ǣ-m.

melo=melu; melsc=milisc

±meltan I. (y) (sv³) *to consume by fire,* '*melt*,' *burn up,* B,MH,Ps,WW; Æ : *dissolve, digest.* II.=mieltan

meltestre=myltestre

meltung f. *digestion,* LCD.

melu (ea, eo) n., gs. mel(u)wes '*meal,*' *flour,* Lcd; Æ.

melugescot n. *payment in meal,* W171.

meluhūdern n. *meal-house,* LL455,17.

meluhūs (ea¹, e²) n. *meal-house,* WW 185²⁷.

meluw (LWS)=melu

men v. mann; mĕnan=mǣnan

mend-=mynd-; +mĕne-=+mǣne-

mene (y) m. *necklace, collar, ornament, jewel,* Æ. [v. KLED s.v. māhne]

menegian=myndgian; menego=menigu

menen=mennen

menescilling m. *moon-shaped ornament, coin worn as ornament,* GL.

±mengan (æ) tr. and intr. *to mix, combine, unite,* Lk,Sat,WW; CP: (±) *associate with, consort, cohabit with,* BH,Ps : *disturb,* B : (†) *converse.* ['*meng*']

+mengedlic *mixed, confused,* Cp1542. adv. -līce? GL.

+mengednes, +meng(d)nes f. *mingling, mixture, connection,* Æ,BH : *sexual intercourse,* CP.

mengeo, mengo, mengu=menigu

mengung f. *mixture, composition,* ZDA : *fellowship,* GD : (+) *confusion.* ['*menging*']

meni (LWS)=manig; menian=mynian

menig (LWS)=manig; mĕnig v. mægenig.

menigdu f. *band of people,* WW448²⁷.

menigu (a¹, æ¹, eo³) f. usu. indecl. in sg. *company, multitude, host,* Æ,AO,CP. [manig]

menio, meniu (LWS)=menigu

menisc=mennisc

menn v. mann.

mennen, mennenu (æ¹, i¹) nf. *handmaiden, slave,* GD,LL.

mennesc=mennisc

mennisc I. adj. *human, natural,* Bo,CP; Æ. II. n. *mankind, folk, race, people,* Bl; Æ, CP. ['*mannish*']

mennisclic *human,* Æ,CP : *humane,* Bo, RB. adv. -līce, Æ.

mennisc-licnes (EHy15³⁵), -nes f. *state of man, human nature, incarnation,* BH; Æ : *humaneness, humanity.* ['*mannishness*']

menniscu f. *humanity, human state,* CP39²⁴.

mentel (æ) m., gs. mentles *mantle, cloak,* CP. [*L.* mantellum]

mentelprĕon m. *mantle-pin, brooch,* TC533'.

menung=(*mynung), mynegung

mĕo mf? gs. and nap. mĕon *shoe-sole, sock? sandal?* RB,WW.

meocs=meox

+meodnes f. *dignity,* DR192'. [=medemnes]

meodo, meodu=medu; meodom-=medem

meodoma=medema; mĕodren=mĕdren

meodum-=medem-

meolc I. *giving milk, milch.* II. (i) f '*milk,*' BH; Æ,AO.

meolcdĕond (i; -tĕond) m. *suckling.* JVPs 8³.

meolcen (i¹, y¹) adj. *of milk,* LCD

meolcfæt n. *milk-pail,* WW123²⁸.

meolchwīt '*milk-white,*' GPH.

meolcian (i, y) *to* '*milk,*' Lcd,Shr : (±) *give milk, suckle,* Bl.

meolclīðe (ea) *soft as milk,* CM49.

meolcsūcend m. *suckling,* WW.

meolo (Bo)=melu; meoloc (CP)=meolc

meolu=melu; meoluc=meolc

mĕon v. mĕo.

mĕoning m. *garter,* WW234²² (wĕon-).

meord f. *reward, pay,* BH GD. ⌈Goth. mizdō]

meoring f. *danger?* Ex62?

meorð=meord

mĕos I. m. *moss,* BH. ['*mese*'] II. adj. *mossy.*

mĕose=mēse; meotod, meotud=metod

meottoc (Cp)=mattuc

+meotu=+metu nap. of +met.

meotud-=metod-

meoðon (BH)=miðon pret. pl. of mīðan.

mĕowle† f. *maiden, virgin* : *woman.* ⌈Goth. mawilō]

meox (e, i, y) n. *filth, dirt, dung,* Æ,Bo,Lk. ['*mix*']

meoxbearwe f. *dung-barrow,* WW336⁸.

meoxen=mixen

meoxforce (y¹) f. *dung-fork,* WW106³⁹.

meoxscofl (e¹) f. *dung-shovel,* LL455,17.

meoxwille (cs) f. *dung-basket,* LPs807'.

mĕr-=mǣr-

mera m. *incubus,* GL.

merc (A)=mearc; merce=merece

+merce=+mierce; mercels=mircels

Mercisc=Miercisc

mercong (NG)=mearcung

mere I. m. (†) *sea, ocean,* An : *lake, pond, pool, cistern,* B,Ep,Jn; CP; Mdf. ['*mere*'] II.=mare. III.=miere

mĕre (VPs)=mǣre I.

merebāt m. *sea-boat, vessel,* AN246.

merecandel f. *sun,* MET13⁵⁷.

merece n. *smallage, wild celery,* Æ,Gl,Lcd.

mereciest f. *sea-chest, ark,* GEN1317.

meredĕað† m. *death at sea,* Ex.

meredĕor n. *sea-animal,* B558.

merefara m. *sailor*, B502.
merefaroð† m. *surging of the waves*.
merefix m. *sea-fish*, B549.
mereflōd† m. *sea, body of water, deluge*.
mere-grot (Æ) n., -grota (BH) m. *pearl*. [v. '*margarite*']
meregrund† m. *lake-bottom, depths of the sea*.
merehengest† m. *sea-horse, ship*.
merehrægl n. *sail*, B1905.
merehūs† n. *sea-house, the ark*, GEN.
merehwearf m. *sea-shore*, Ex516.
mērehwīt *pure white, sterling (of silver)*. [mǣre II.]
merelād f. *sea-way*, Hu27.
merelīðende† m. *seafaring (man), sailor*.
mere-menn(en), -menin n. *mermaid, siren*, Cp,WW. ['*mermin*']
mere-nǣddra m., -nǣddre, -nǣdre f. '*murena*,' *sea-adder, lamprey*, GL.
meresmylte *quiet as the sea, calm*, MET21¹².
meresteall m. *stagnant water*, MFH169.
merestrǣt† f. *sea-path*.
merestrēam† m. *sea-water*.
merestrengo f. *strength in swimming*, B523.
mereswīn n. *porpoise, dolphin*, Cp,Lcd. ['*mereswine*']
meretorht (æ)† *(rising) bright from the sea*.
meretorr m. *towering wall of the (Red) sea*, Ex484.
mereðyssa† m. *ship*, AN.
mereweard m. *sea-warden*, WH53.
merewērig *sea-weary*, SEAF12.
merewīf n. *water-witch*, B1519.
merg (Cp195M)=mearg
merg-=mearg-, meri-, morg-, myrg-
merian *to purify, cleanse*, Sol : *test*. ['*mere*']
merice (GL)=merce; **merien**=morgen
merig=(1) myrge; (2) mearg
merig-=myrg-; **merigen** (Æ,AO)=morgen
merisc=mersc
merne=mergenne ds. of mergen
merr-=mierr-; **mērs-**=mǣrs-
mersc (æ) m. '*marsh*,' *swamp*, Gl; CP.
merschōfe m. *marsh-hove*, LCD35b.
merschop n. *high ground in fenny country*, BC2·526.
merscland n. '*marsh-land*,' Chr1098.
merscmealwe f. '*marsh-mallow*,' Lcd.
merscmeargealla m. *gentiana pneumonanthe*, LCD.
merscmylen f. *mill in a fen*, KC6·100¹².
merscware pl. *inhabitants of marshes*. (1) *Romney marsh*, CHR796. (2) *the fens?* CHR838.
mertze f. *merchandise*, WW32²⁵ : *trading dues*, 145²⁸. [*L*. mercem]
merð=mearð
merðern *made of skins of martens*, CHR 1075D.

mērðu (N)=mǣrð; **meru** (MtR)=mearu
meruw-, merwe-=mearu(w)-
mēs (K)=mȳs, v. mus.
mesa fpl. *dung*, LCD37a (v. NP15·272).
mēsan *to eat*, RD41⁵². [mōs]
mēse (ēo, ī, ȳ) f. *table*, Æ : *what is placed on a table*, GL. [*L.*]
mēshrægel (ȳ¹) n. *napkin*, RBL93¹⁰.
mess-=mǣss-
mēsta (KGL)=mǣsta superl. of micel.
±**met** (usu. +) *measure (vessel or amount)*, Æ : *act of measuring, appointed share, quantity*, Mt : *space, distance*, LL : *boundary, limit*, Bo,Met : *manner, degree, way : ability, adequacy, capacity : rule, law : mood* (gram.) : *metre : moderation*, MtR. ealle +mete *in all respects.* on +m. *in vain*, RPs88⁴⁸. nānum +m. *by no means, on no account.* ['*met*,' '*i-met*']
+**met**† *fit, proper, apt, meet.* adv. -mēte.
+**mēt**=+mōt; **-mēt** v. wēa-m.
meta (Sc153)=mete; **metærn**=meteærn
±**metan**⁵ *to measure*, '*mete*' *out* ('*ymete*'), *mark off*, Æ,Ex,Mt,VPs : *compare*, Bo; CP : *estimate*, Bl : *pass over, traverse*, B.
±**mētan** I. *to* '*meet*,' *find, find out, fall in with, encounter*, Bo,Bl; Æ,AO,CP : *obtain*, CP. II. *to paint, design*, ÆGr. ['*mete*']
metbælg m. *wallet*, LkR22³⁵. [v. '*belly*']
met-cund, -cundlic *metrical*, GL.
mete (æ) m. nap. mettas '*meat*,' *food*, BH, CP,Lk,Sc; Æ,AO.
mēte=mǣte
meteærn n. *refectory*, GD,WW.
meteāflīung f. *atrophy*, WW.
meteāwel *meat-hook?* LL455¹⁷.
meteclyfa m. *food-store, pantry*, OEG56²⁷⁰.
metecorn n. *allowance of corn to dependants*, TC. ['*metecorn*']
metecū f. *cow for killing*, LL450',451.
metecweorra m. *surfeit, indigestion*, LCD 3·60⁴.
+**mētednes** f. *finding, discovery*, LPs27⁴
metefæt [met-] n. *dish*, GPH403.
metefǣtels m. *cupboard for food*, WW107⁵. ['*metefetill*']
meteg-=metg-
metegafol n. *payment in food*, LL448,4⁵.
metegearwa fp. *preparations of food*, LCD 78b.
metegyrd=metgeard
metelǣst=metelīest
metelāf f. *leavings of a meal*, Æ,LL.
metelēas *without food*, Æ.
mete-līest (AO), -lē(a)st, -līst, -lȳst f. *lack of food, starvation*.
metend m. *measurer*, WW398²⁸ : *God*, GEN 1809.
+**mētend** '*inventor*,' GPH391.

metenēad f. *requisites in the way of food*, LL 383'? (v. 2·145).

mēter n. '*metre*,' *versification, Bf,BH.* [*L.*]

meterædere m. *reader at meal-times*, NC309.

mētercræft m. *art of versifying*, BH258¹⁵.

mētercund *relating to metre*, WW.

mētere m. *painter*, Ct,WW.

mēterfers n. *hexameter verse*, BH.

mētergeweorc n. *verse*, BH484⁹.

mēterlīc *metrical*, OEG124.

metern=meteærn

mēterwyrhta m. *metrician, poet*, WW.

metesōcn f. *craving, appetite*, Lcd65a.

metesticca m. *spoon*, WW126³⁵.

metestwamm m. *edible mushroom*, WW.

metetīd f. *meal-time*, GD277²⁴.

meteðearfende† *needing food, destitute*, AN.

meteðegn m. *seneschal, steward*, Ex131.

meteðīht *well-nourished*, Lcd3·68¹⁷.

meteðīng n. *operation connected with cooking*, CHRD19¹⁹.

meteūtsiht f. *dysentery*, WW.

+metfæst *moderate, reasonable, modest, meek.*

+metfæstan (æ¹, e²) *to compare*, LPs48²¹.

+metfæstlīc *moderate : modest, gentle.* adv. -līce *modestly, humbly, meekly.*

+metfæstnes f. *moderation, modesty, sobriety*, BH.

metfæt=metefæt

+metfæt n. *a measure (vessel)*, Æ,WW.

+metfest-=metfæst-

metgeard f. *measuring-stick, rod, pole, perch*, WW147²⁰. ·

±metgian *to moderate, control, govern*, Æ, CP : *weigh in mind, consider : assign due measure to : prepare : regulate.*

+metgiend m. *ruler, governor*, AS11².

±metgung f. *moderation, temperance*, AO, CP : *reflection, meditation : rule, regulation.*

metgyrd=metgeard

metian I. *to provision*, CHR1013. II.= metgian

mēting I. (±) f. *meeting (friendly or hostile)*, Æ,AO : *assembly, congregation*, Ps,RB : *finding, discovery : agreement*, GD. II. *painting, picture*, Æ.

+metlǣcan *to moderate*, CP101¹².

+metlic *measurable : fitting, suitable : moderate*, CP : *mild, discreet*, CP. adv. -līce.

+metlicung f. *adjustment, regulation*, Lcd 60b,86a.

+metnes f. *moderation*, RWH7¹⁹.

+mētnes (MH136²³)=+mētednes

metod† m. *fate : Creator, God, Christ.*

+metodlīce *inevitably*, ByH40²⁵.

metodsceaft† f. *decree of fate, doom, death.* gewītan m. sēon, tō metodsceafte *to die*, B.

metodwang (meotud-) m. *battlefield*, AN 11.

metrāp m. *measuring-rope, sounding-line*, Cp178B.

mētsceat=mēdsceatt

metscipe m. *feeding, meal*, LL178,8¹. ['*meteship*']

metseax n. *meat-knife*, AO244¹⁸.

±metsian *to supply with food*, Æ.

metsung f. *feeding, provisioning*, CHR.

+metta m. *sharer in food, guest*, Æ. ['*mette*']

mettac=mattuc; mettas v. mete.

mette-=mete-

mētte pret. 3 sg. of mētan.

metten f. *one of the Fates*, Bo102²².

mettian=mētan I.; +metting=+mēting

-mētto v. wēa-m.; mettoc (*Ep*)=mattuc

mettrum=medtrum; metud (N)=metod

mōðe (†) *tired, worn out, dejected, sad : troublesome.* [*Ger.* müde]

meðel=mæðel; meðema=medema

+mēðgian *to exhaust, tire out*, Gu950.

mēðian *to grow weary*, Lcd57a.

mēðig *tired, weary*, AO86,134.

meðl=mæðl, mæðel; meðl-=mæðl-, maðel-

mēðnes f. *fatigue*, OET(Bd²).

+mēðrian *to honour*, LL(1·384⁴).

mēw=mǣw; mexscofl=meoxscofl

micel-=micel-, micl-

micel (y) adj. comp. māra, superl. mǣst(a) *great, intense, much, many*, Æ,BC,Bo,Chr, Lcd,MH ; AO,CP : (of time) *long : loud.* sb. with gen. *much*, AO,CP. adv. *greatly, much*, CP,Gen. ['*mickle*']

micelǣte (y) *greedy*, SHR16²⁰.

miceldōend (i²) *doing great things*, DR45⁷.

micelhēafdede *big-headed*, WW380¹².

micelian=miclian

micellic *great, splendid, magnificent.* adv. -līce *grandly : very, exceedingly.*

micelmōd *magnanimous*, PPs144³.

micelnes (y) f. *greatness, size*, Æ,CP : *mass : quantity : multitude, abundance : magnificence : great deed.*

micelsprecende *boasting*, LPs11⁴.

micelu (y) f. *largeness, size*, Lcd.

micg=mycg

micga m., micge f. *urine*, Lcd. ['*mig*']

micgern (y) *internal fat, suet*, WW. ['*midgern*']

micgða=migoða; micl-=micel-

micle, micles, miclum adv. (obl. cases of micel) *much, very, greatly.*

±miclian (y) *to become great, increase*, AN; AO : *make great, make larger, magnify, extol, Bl.* ['*mickle*']

±miclung (y) f. *the doing of great things, great deeds, greatness*, Ps.

micul=micel

mid I. prep. w. d. inst. (WS) and a. (A only) *with, in conjunction with, in company with, together with*, Æ,*Chr* : *into the presence of* : *through, by means of, by* : *among, in* : *at* (time) : *in the sight of, opinion of*, Æ. m. ealle, eallum *altogether, completely, entirely*, Æ, *Chr*. m. ðám *with that, thereupon*. m. ðám ðe *when*. m. ðám ðæt *through that, on that account, because, when*. m. ðȳ (ðe) *when, while*. **II.** adv. *at the same time, together, simultaneously, likewise, Lcd*. ['MID'] **III.**=midd

midd superl. mid(e)mest *mid, middle, midway, BH,CP,Lcd*. tó middes adv. *in the midst*. ['*mid*']

middæg m. '*mid-day*,' *noon, Lcd* : *one of the canonical hours, sext, WW*. fram middæge oð nón *from noon to 3 p.m.*, Æ.

middæglic adj. *mid-day, meridian*, BH,Ps.

middægsang m. *mid-day service, sext*, RB, LL.

middægtíd f. *noon*, WW450⁵.

middægðénung f. *dinner*, NC309.

middan (on) v. onmiddan.

middandægllc=middægllc

middan(g)eard m. *the globe, world, earth, B, Jn*; Æ,AO,CP : *mankind*. ['*middenerd*']

middan(g)earden *worldly*, Sc16¹⁶.

middangeardllc *earthly*, BH118¹⁹.

middansumer m. *midsummer* (24 *June*).

middanwinter m. *midwinter, Christmas*.

midde I. adj. *mid, middle*. **II.** f. *middle, centre* (only in phr. on middan).

middel I. n. '*middle*,' *centre, El,Mk,Ps, WW* : *waist, Bl*. **II.** adj. (superl. midlest) *middle, intermediate, BH,LL*.

middelædr f. *median vein*, LCD.

middeldæg m. *mid-day, noon*, LCD.

middelǽl m. *middle*, AO10⁶.

middelfinger m. *middle finger*, LL,WW.

middel-flēra m., -flēre f. *partition, septum*, WW.

middelfót m. *instep*, WW160²⁵.

middelgemǽru npl. *central region*, SOL255.

middelgesculdru np. *part of the body between the shoulders*, WW159¹⁷.

middelhrycg m. *middle ridge*, Ct.

middelniht† f. *midnight*.

middelríce n. *the middle kingdom*, CHR887A.

midden-=middan-

midde-niht, -neaht, middernæht (*LkL*) f. '*midnight*.' [v. ES39·350]

middesumer=middansumer

middeweard I. adv. *in the middle of, through the midst*. **II.** adj. *middle*, AO. **III.** sb. *middle, LPs*. ['*midward*']

middewinter=middanwinter

middun- (N)=middan-

mideard=middangeard

midel=middel; **midemest** v. midd.

midfæsten m. *mid-Lent*, CHR1047.

mid-feorh, -feorwe (CP), -ferh(ð) mn. *youth, middle age* ('*juventus*' GL).

midfyrhtnes f. *middle age* BL163.

midgearwung f. *preparation*, MkL p5¹⁰.

midgeslð n. *companion*, OEG680? (v. BTs).

midhelp [mið-] f. *help, assistance*, DR 29¹⁸.

midhilte f. *middle of the hilt*, WW199²¹.

midhlȳt m. *fellowship*, TF103⁷.

midhrif nm. '*midriff*,' *diaphragm, Lcd* : *bowels*.

midhriðre (y²) n. *diaphragm, Cp,WW*. ['*midred*']

-midian v. ā-.

midl n. *bit* (*of a bridle*), Æ : *oar-thong*, WW.

midle=middele, ds. of middel.

+midleahtrian *to reproach*, Sc200⁶.

midlen I. (e) n. *middle, centre, midst*. **II.** adj. *midmost*, ÆGR14²¹.

midlencten n. *mid-Lent*, CHR.

midlest superl. of middel.

mídlhring m. *ring of a bit*, WW456¹⁴.

+midlian *to halve, divide*, CPs54²⁷.

±midlian *to bridle, curb*, CP : *muzzle*, W191.

midligend m. *mediator*, BH206²⁶.

midlung f. *middle, midst*. adv. -lunga *to a moderate extent*.

midmest v. midd; **midmycel**=medmicel

midnedæg m. *mid-day*, Æ,MH.

midnes f. *middle, midst*, HL.

midniht f. *midnight*, Æ.

midor compar. of midd, adj.

midrád f. *riding in company*, LL175,4.

midrece=mȳderce; **midrif**=midhrif

midsingend m. *one who sings with another*, WW129²⁵.

±midsíð(eg)ian *to accompany, associate with*, GL.

midspecend m. *interlocutor, advocate*, MP 1·592⁶.

midsp(r)eca m. *advocate*, ÆH : '*liberator*,' *excuser*, CHRD62²⁶.

midsprecende *speaking for*, NIC.

midstréam m. *mid-stream*, KC5·380.

midsumer (o³) m. '*midsummer*,' *Bf,BH*.

Midsumermónað *June*, MEN (Hickes).

midswégan *'concinere*,' EPs57³.

midðám, midðȳ=mid ðám, mid ðȳ

midðeahtian *to consent*, RHy6²⁷.

midðolian *to sympathise*, Sc.

midðrówung f. *compassion*, Sc.

midweg m. '*midway*,' *CP*; GD314¹¹.

midwinter m. '*midwinter*,' *Christmas, Chr, Lcd*.

Midwintermónað *December*, MEN (Hickes).

midwist f. *presence, society* : *cooperation, participation*, LL378⁶.

midwunung f. *living in company, fellowship*, Æ.

midwyrhta m. *cooperator*, CP.

midyrfenuma m. *coheir*, Sc 148⁴.

mieht=miht

±**mieltan** (i, y) (tr. and intr.) *to* '*melt*,' El, Lcd; Æ: *digest*, CP: *refine, purge* : *exhaust*, MH 54³.

Mierce, Miercan pl. *Mercians* : *Mercia*, CHR (lit. *borderers*; cp. mearc).

+**mierce** (e) n. *boundary, limit*, AA 3³ : *sign, token*, MkL 16¹⁷.

Miercisc (e) *Mercian*, LL 464,1.

miere (e, i, y) f. '*mare*,' BH,WW. [mearh]

mierra (e) m. *deceiver*, MtL 27⁶³.

±**mierran** (e, i, y) *to* '*mar*,' *disturb, confuse*, CP : *scatter, squander, waste* : *upset, hinder, obstruct*, Æ; AO : *err*, MtL.

mierrelse (y) f. *cause of offence*, JUL 338.

mierrend (y) *prodigal, wasteful*, NC 311.

mierring (e, i, y) f. *hindering : squandering, waste*, CP.

±**migan**¹ *to make water*, LCD,ÆGR.

migeða=migoða; **migga** (Æ)=micga

miggung, mīging f. *making water*, WW.

migol *diuretic*, LCD.

migoða m. *urine*, LCD.

miht (a, æ, ea, e, ie, y) **I.** f. '*might*,' *bodily strength: power, authority, ability*, BH,Bl, Lcd; Æ : *virtue*, Lcd : *mighty work, miracle*, G. pl. *Gods*, OEG : *angels*, Æ. **II.** adj. †*mighty, powerful : possible*.

mihte pret. sg. of magan.

mihteleas=mihtleas

mihtelic, mihtlic *possible*. adv. -lice *mightily, powerfully, by might, miraculously*, Æ,BH. ['*mightly*']

mihtesetl n. *seat of power*, EETS 34·301.

mihtful *powerful*, HL 15¹³⁷.

mihtig (æ, ea) '*mighty*,' *important*, BH,CP, VPs : *able, effective*, Lcd : *possible*. adv. -līce, Bo. ['*mightily*']

mihtleas *powerless, weak, exhausted*, Æ.

mihtloc (ea¹) *belt of might*, CREAT 88.

mihtmod n. *violent temper, passion*, Ex 149.

mihtu=miht ðu

mil I. f. '*mile*,' Bl,WW; AO. [L.] **II.** n. *millet*, WW. ['*mile*']

milc (VPs)=meolc; **milcan**=melcan

milde I. adj. '*mild*,' *merciful, kind, generous, gentle, meek*, B,Bl,Gu,LL; AO,CP. **II.** adv. *mercifully, graciously*, Cr.

mildeaw=meledeaw

mildelic *propitious*. adv. *graciously, affably, kindly*, AO; Æ. ['*mildly*']

+**mildgian** *to mitigate, make mild or calm*, Ps. [mildian]

mild-heort, -heortlic *merciful, clement, compassionate*, MtL (milt-); Æ,AO. ['*mildheart*'] adv. -lice, Æ,CP.

mildheortnes f. *loving-kindness, mercy, pity*, LL; Æ,AO. ['*mildheartiness*']

mildian *to become mild*, GPH 399.

mildnes f. *mildness, mercy*, NC 309.

milds=milts

milgemæt m. *mile-measure, milestone?* KC 3·252²¹.

milgemearc n. *measure by miles*, B 1362.

milgetæl n. *mile*, WE 51,59.

milisc (e, y) *sweet, mild, mulled*, GL,LCD.

milite *soldiers*, NC 309.

militisc *military*, GD. [L. miles]

milpæð† m. *distance reckoned by miles? road with milestones on it?* EL,EX,RUN.

+**milscad** *honeyed, mixed with honey*, WW.

milscapuldor f. *sweet apple tree*, GL.

milt m. (LCD 87a)=milte; **milt-**=mild-, milte-

milt-coðe, -coðu f. *disease of the spleen*, LCD.

milte mf. '*milt*,' *spleen*, Gl,Lcd; Æ.

miltesöoc *splenetic*, LCD,WW.

miltestre=myltestre

miltewærc m. *pain in the spleen*, LCD.

milts f. *mercy, compassion, benevolence, kindness, favour*, B,VPs; CP : (†) *joy*. ['*milce*']

±**miltsian** (w. d.) *to compassionate, pity, show mercy*, Bo,Mt,Ps; Æ,CP : *soften, make merciful*. ['*milce*,' '*i-milce*']

±**miltsi(g)end** m. *pitier*, Æ,Ps.

miltsigendlic *pardonable, venial*, GPH.

miltsung f. (±) *mercy, sympathy, pity, indulgence, pardon*, Æ,CP : *moderation, reduction (of punishment)*, LL 468,10.

miltwræc=miltewærc; **milz**=milts

mima m. '*mime*,' MH.

+**mimor** (w. d.) *well-known*. adv. -lice *by heart*.

min†? *evil, harmful*. [v. BTs, and NED s.v. '*min*']

min I. pron. *my*, '*mine*,' Æ,B,G. mīnes ðances *by my will*. **II.** gs. of ic *of me*.

mind I. *diadem*, DR 92⁵ (v. LF 160). **II.**= mynd

mindom† m. *state of exile*, PPs 54⁷.

mine=myne; **minet-**=mynet-

minlic *petty* (Swt).

minlice adv. *in my manner*, WW 449¹⁶.

minnæn '*manipulos*,' *sheaves?* EPs 128⁷; '*magnalia*,' 105²¹.

minne I. nap. of min? **II.**=myne

minnen=menen

±**minsian** *to diminish*, W.

minsung f. *parsimony*, OEG 3748.

mint? (MtR), minte f. '*mint*,' G; CP; Mdf. [L.]

minthamm m. *field of mint*, KC 5·374'.

mio-=meo-

mircapuldur (Cp)=milscapuldor?

Mirce, Mircan=Mierce

mirce I. (y;=ie) adj. *murky, dark, black, uncanny, evil, B,Ph.* **II.** adv.? AN 1315. **III.** n. *murkiness, darkness, Da*448. ['*murk*']

mircels (e, y;=ie) mf. *sign, token, seal, signet* : *mark, marked place,* ÆL : *trophy,* Gu 429. [mearc]

mire=miere; **mīre**=mīnre gdfs. of mīn.

mirg-, mīrig-=myrg-

mīrgŏ, mirhŏ=myrgŏ; **mirr-**=mierr-

misbegān anv. *to disfigure,* MtL6¹⁶.

misbēodan² (w. d.) *to ill-use, injure, do wrong to, LL,W.* ['*misbede*']

misboren *abortive,* Lcd : *degenerate.* ['*misborn*']

misbrōden *drawn aside,* WW224²¹.

misbyrd f. *abortion,* GL.

misbyrdo f. *malformation,* LCD.

misbysnian *to set a bad example,* ÆH 2·50⁴.

miscalfian *to cast a calf,* WW456¹².

miscenning f. *a mistake or variation in pleading before a court* : *a fine exacted for this, EC,LL* (v. 2·148). ['*miskenning*']

miscian *to mix, apportion,* Bo,LCD. [L.]

miscrōcettan *to croak or shriek horribly,* GUTH36¹. [crācettan]

miscwēman *to displease,* ÆL23²⁸⁷.

miscweŏan⁵ *to speak ill, curse,* NG : *speak incorrectly.*

miscyrran (=ie) *to pervert,* MET2⁸.

misdǣd f. '*misdeed,*' *evil deed, sin, CP;* Æ.

misdōn anv. *to do evil, transgress, do amiss, err, JnL,LL,W.* ['*misdo*']

mīse=mēse

misefesian *to cut the hair amiss,* LL(254¹³).

misendebyrdan (i⁴) *to arrange amiss,* LL 382.

misenlic, misendlic=missenlic

misfadian *to order amiss,* LL.

misfadung f. *misconduct, irregularity,* RB, WW.

misfaran⁶ *to go wrong, transgress, CP* : *fare ill, Æ,W.* ['*misfare*']

misfēdan (oe) *to nourish ill,* EVPs.

misfeng m. *misdeed, sin,* NC309.

misfēran *to do wrong, err,* Æ. ['*misfere*']

misfōn⁷ *to make a mistake, be deceived* : *fail to get.*

misgedwield n. *error, perversion,* JUL326.

misgehygd fn. *evil thought,* AN772.

misgelimp n. *misfortune,* W211³⁰.

misgemynd f. *evil memory,* SOL495.

mis(ge)widere m. *bad weather, storm,* LCD, VH.

misgrētan *to greet amiss, insult,* Ct.

misgȳman *to neglect,* LL. ['*misyeme*']

mishæbbende *being ill,* MtL8¹⁶.

mishealdan⁷ *not to keep, to neglect,* Æ (9¹³⁰).

mishealdsumnes f. *carelessness,* LL(196³):

mishērnes (=īe²) f. *act of disobedience,* W.

mis-hweorfed, -hwyrfed, -hworfen *perverted, inverted,* Bo,GL.

mishȳran (=īe²) *to hear amiss, not to listen to, disobey, RB,W.* ['*mishear*']

mislǣdan *to* '*mislead,*' Æ.

mislǣran *to teach amiss, give bad advice to,* ÆL5·119. ['*mislear*']

mislār f. *ill teaching, evil suggestion,* Sc.

mislēc-=mislic-

mislic *unlike, various, manifold, Bl,Bo;* Æ, CP : *wandering, erratic.* ['*mislich*'] adv. -lice *in various ways, diversely, aimlessly, Bo,Chr.* ['*misliche*']

mislician (w. d.) *to displease, disquiet, Æ, CP.* ['*mislike*']

mislicnes f. *variety, diversity,* Æ.

mislicum *variously,* AS54⁴.

mislimp n. *misfortune,* VHY,WW.

mislimpan³ impers. w. d. *to go wrong, turn out badly,* AO.

mislybban (=i²) *to lead a bad life,* Æ. ['*mislive*']

mismacian *to mar,* BYH64³.

mismicel *of varying sizes?* EX373.

misrǣcan *to abuse,* ÆH 2·590'.

misrǣd m. *misguidance,* Æ : *misconduct,* Æ.

misrǣdan *to advise wrongly,* RB : *read wrongly,* APT3¹¹.

miss n. *absence, loss,* ÆL23²⁷¹.

miss-=mis-

missan (w. g.) *to* '*miss*' (*a mark*), B : (w. d.) *escape the notice of a person.*

missare=missere

misscrence *distorted, shrivelled,* GUTH.

misscrȳdan *to clothe amiss,* ÆH 1·530'.

misse-=mis-

missenlic *various, manifold, different, diverse,* AO. adv. -lice, CP.

missenlicnes f. *variety, diversity* : '*qualitas*'? GD46⁹.

misseret n. *half-year, year.*

misspōwan⁷ *to fare badly,* AO82³⁴.

missprecan⁵ *to grumble, murmur,* JnL6⁴¹,⁴³.

mist m. '*mist,*' *Æ,Bo,Met,WW* : *dimness (of eyesight),* Lcd.

mist-=mis-

mistǣcan *to teach amiss,* Æ. ['*misteach*']

mistel m. *mistletoe, Cp,Ep* : *basil,* Lcd. ['*missel*']

mistellām n. *birdlime,* WW279¹⁵.

misteltān (i²) m. '*mistletoe,*' *WW.*

mistglōm m? *misty gloom,* WH47.

misthelm m. *covering of mist,* JUL470.

misthlīŏt n. *misty cliff, cloud-capped slope.*

mistian *to be or grow misty,* ÆGr. ['*mist*']

mistīd f. *evil time,* FM360¹².

mistīdan (impers.) *to miscarry, fail*, LL 348'. ['*mistide*']

mistīg '*misty*,' B.

mistīhtan (=y²) *to lead astray, dissuade*, Æ.

mistīhtendlic *dehortative*, ÆGR 225¹².

mistil-=mistel-

mistīmian [impers. w. d.] *to happen amiss*, Bas. ['*mistime*']

mistlic=mislic

mistran *to grow dim*, DEUT 34⁷.

mistrīwan *to mistrust*, DR 39¹⁶.

mistūcian *to ill-treat*, CHR 1083,GD 15.

misðēon³ *to mis-thrive, degenerate*, CHRD,GL.

misðyncan (impers.) *to be mistaken*, APT 14²⁵.

misweaxan⁶ *to grow improperly*, ÆH 2·74¹². miswendan *to pervert, abuse*, Æ : *be perverted, err*, Æ.

miswende *erring, ill-behaving*, Æ.

miswenian *to misuse, abuse*, Sc 224¹⁰ (?= miswerian, MLN 25·80).

misweorc n. *misdeed*, JnR 3¹⁹.

misweorðan³ *to turn out amiss*, W 240⁴.

miswidere=misgewidere

miswissian *to mislead*, LL 130; 381.

miswrītan¹ *to write incorrectly*, ÆGr. ['*miswrite*']

miswurðian (=eo²) *to dishonour, ill-treat*, LL 381,25.

miswyssigan=miswissian

mīte f. '*mite*' (*small insect*), WW 122⁶ (v. BTs).

mitta m., mitte f. *a measure, bushel*, Ct, WW; Æ,CP. ['*mit*'; metan]

±mittan *to meet, meet with, find*.

mitte=mitta

±mitting f. *meeting, convention*, AO.

mittȳ=mid ðȳ; mið (LkL)=mid

mīðan¹ *to hide, conceal* (tr. and intr.), *keep to oneself, dissemble*, BH,Bo,WW; CP : *conceal oneself, remain concealed*, Lcd : (†) *avoid, shun, refrain from*. ['*mithe*']

mīðgian *to conceal*, GD 122³.

mīðl=midl; mix=meox

mixen (y) f. *dung-heap, dung*, Æ,LkL. ['*mixen*']

mixendynge (y¹) f. *dung*, LL 454,9.

mixenplante f. *nightshade* (*plant*), LCD.

mixian=miscian

mōd n. (±) *heart, mind, spirit*, '*mood*,' *temper*, B,BH,Bl; Æ,AO,CP : *courage*, B; AO : *arrogance, pride*, AO : *power, violence*. +mōd *of one mind, harmonious, peaceful*, CP.

mōdblind† *blind, undiscerning*.

mōdblissiende *exulting*, PPs 67¹⁷.

mōdbysgung f. *anxiety*, DOM 84.

mōdcearig *sorrowful of heart*, WA 2.

mōdcearu† f. *sorrow, grief*.

mōdcræft† m. *intelligence*.

mōdcræftig *intelligent*, CRA 62.

mōddor=mōdor

mōddren *of mothers*, APT 4¹².

mōddri(g)e=mōdrige; mōde-=mōdig-

mōdearfoð n. *grief of mind*, †Hy 4⁸⁷.

mōdeg=mōdig; mōder=mōdor

mōdercynd=mēdrengecynd

mōderge=mōdrige

mōdful *proud, haughty*, LCD 3·188'.

mōdgehygd† n. *thought*.

mōdgemynd† n. *mind, thought*.

mōdgēomor† *sad, dejected*.

mōdgeðanc m. *thought, understanding, mind*.

mōdgeðōht m. *thought, understanding, mind*.

mōdgeðyldig *patient*, AN 983.

mōdgewinna m. *care*, GEN 2797.

mōdgian=mōdigian

mōdgidanc (N)=mōdgeðanc

mōdglæd *joyous*, GU 1311.

mōdglēaw *wise*, SOL 180.

mōdhæp? *brave*, EX 242 (GK).

mōdhete m. *hatred*, GEN 1756.

mōdhord n. *secret thoughts*, AN 172.

mōdhwæt† *brave, bold*.

mōdig (CP), mōdi *spirited, daring, bold, brave, high-souled, magnanimous*, B; Æ : *impetuous, headstrong*, Æ; CP : *arrogant, proud*, Æ,CP. ['*moody*']

mōdigan, mōdigian *to grow proud or overbearing, be high-minded, glory, exult, show bravery*, Æ : *take offence through pride*, Æ.

mōdiglic (mōde-) *high-souled, lofty, proud* : *brave, bold* : *splendid, magnificent*. adv. -līce, Ma (mōde-). ['*moodily*']

mōdignes f. *greatness of soul* : *pride, arrogance, haughtiness*, Æ. ['*moodiness*']

mōdilic=mōdiglic

mōdlēas *spiritless*, KGL 66⁴⁰ : *senseless*, CHRD.

mōdlēast f. *want of courage, despondency*, Æ.

mōdlēof *dear, precious*, FT 28.

mōdlufu† f. *heart's affection, love*.

mōdnes (RWH 2³⁶)=mōdignes

+mōdod *disposed*, ÆH 1·524¹⁸.

mōdor (e²) f., ds. mēder '*mother*,' WW; (*of animals*), LL; AO,CP.

mōdorcild (mōð-) n. *a child of one's* (*own*) *mother*, PPs 68⁸.

mōdorcynn n. *maternal descent*, CHR 1067 D.

mōdorhealf f. *mother's side*, CHR 1076 D.

mōdorhrif n. *womb*, PPs.

mōdorlēas (e²) *motherless*, W 228²².

mōdorlic (e²) *maternal*, ÆGr. ['*motherly*'] adv. -līce.

mōdorlufu f. *love for a mother*, NC 309.

mōdorslaga m. *matricide*, WW 335⁶.

mōdrige, mōdrie f. *mother's sister, maternal aunt,* Æ,AO : *cousin.* [mōdor]

mōdrōf *valiant,* An 1493.

mōdsefa† m. *heart, mind, spirit, soul : thought, imagination, purpose, character.*

mōdsēoc *sick at heart,* Gen 1235.

mōdsēocnes f. *disease of the heart,* WW 199³⁵.

mōdsnotor† *wise.*

mōdsorg† f. *heart-sorrow.*

mōdstaðol m. *principle, character,* LL (318n1).

mōd-staðolnes, -staðolfæstnes f. *firmness of mind,* W 53¹⁰.

+mōdsum *accordant, in agreement,* CP 360¹³.

+mōdsumian *to agree,* CP.

+mōdsumnes f. *agreement, concord,* CP.

mōdswīð *resolute,* PsC 89.

mōd-ðracu f. gs. -ðræce *courage,* B 385.

mōððrēa m. *anguish,* Rd 4⁵⁰.

mōðōwǣre *meek,* LPs 24⁹.

mōðōwǣrnes f. *patience, meekness,* W.

mōdur=mōdor

mōdwǣg m. *proud wave,* Ex 499.

mōdwelig *gifted, talented, wise,* CP 9¹².

mōdwlanc† *stout-hearted : haughty.*

mōdwyn f. *heart's joy, property,* Rd 87⁷.

moetan (Cp)=mētan

mohða, mohðe (N)=moððe

molcen n. *coagulated or curdled milk,* Lcd, WW. [*Ger.* molke]

+molcen *milked,* Lcd 34a.

molda? m. v. molde II.

moldærn (e²)† n. *grave.*

moldcorn n. *granular tuber of saxifraga granulata, and the plant itself,* Lcd.

molde I. f. *sand,* 'mould,' *dust, soil,* Cp,BH, GK; Æ : *land, country : world.* **II.**? f. *top of the head,* Lcd 3·42 (or molda?). ['*mould*']

moldern=moldærn

moldgewind n. *top of the head,* NC 310.

moldgræf† n. *grave.*

moldhrērende *moving upon earth,* Creat 27.

moldhȳpe f. *heap of dust,* ÆH 1·492'.

moldstōw f. *site, sepulchre,* GPH 391.

moldweg† m. *earth.*

moldwyrm m. *earth-worm,* Soul 72.

molegn n. *curds,* Gl.

molegnstycce n. *piece of curd,* Gl.

moling=molegn

molsn n? *decay,* NC 310.

±molsnian *to moulder, decay,* Æ.

molten pp. of meltan.

momra=mamera, mamor; **mon**=man

mōna m. '*moon,*' Bo,Lcd; Æ,AO,CP.

mōnanǣfen m. *Sunday evening,* LL.

mōnandæg m. '*Monday,*' Bf,Jn.

mōnanniht f. *Monday eve, i.e. Sunday evening,* LL.

mōnað m. nap. mōn(e)ðas, mōnað '*month,*' BH,Bo,Lk,Lcd; AO,CP. [mōna]

mōnaðādl f. *morbus menstrualis,* BH.

mōnaðādlig *menstruous,* BH 78⁵.

mōnaðblōd n. '*menstruum,*' WW.

mōnaðbōt f. *penance for a month,* LL (278¹¹).

mōnaðfylen f. *time of full moon,* OEG.

mōnaðgecynd f. '*menstruum,*' Lcd.

mōnaðlic *monthly, lunar,* Gl : as sb.= mōnaðādl, Lcd.

mōnaðsēoc I. *menstruous,* Æ. **II.**=mōnsēoc

mōnaðsēocnes (o²) f. *lunacy,* Lcd 1·170⁴.

moncus=mancus; **mond**=mand

mōndæg=mōnandæg; **mōne** f.=mōna

mōnelic *lunar,* Æ,Lcd.

+mong=+mang; **monig**=manig

mōnlic=mōnelic; **monn**=mann

mōnoð=mōnað

mōnsēoc '*moonsick,*' *lunatic, epileptic,* MtR.

mont=munt; **mōnð**=mōnað

monuc=munuc

mōr m. '*moor,*' *morass, swamp,* B; Mdf : *hill, mountain,* AO.

morað (ō?) n. *sweet boiled wine with herbs,* Gl,Lcd. [*L.* moratum]

mōrbēam (ā, ū) m. *mulberry tree, bramble,* VPs. [v. '*more*']

mōrberie f. *mulberry (fruit),* ÆL 25⁵⁷⁶.

more f. *carrot, parsnip,* Lcd,WW. ['*more*']

moreð=morað

mōrfæsten n. *moor-fastness,* Chr.

mōrflēoge f. '*cariscus,*' *a kind of fly,* NC 310.

morgen (a, e) m. ds. morgenne '*morn,*' *morning, forenoon,* B,MtL,VPs : *sunrise,* B : *morrow,* Æ,B; CP. on mor(gen)ne (1) *in the morning,* (2) *to-morrow.*

morgenceald *chill at morn,* B 3022.

morgencolla m. *morning terror,* Jud 245.

morgendæg (e¹) m. *morrow,* Bl,Guth.

morgendlic=morgenlic

morgendrenc m. *morning drink,* Lcd.

morgengebedtīd f. *morning prayer,* Guth 40²⁵.

morgengifu f. *gift by a husband to his wife the morning after the wedding,* BC,WW. ['*moryeve*']

morgenlēoht n. *dawn, morning,* B.

morgenlic *matutinal, morning : of the morrow.* morgenlica dæg *to-morrow.*

morgenlong *lasting a morning,* B 2895.

morgenmæsse f. *morning mass, first mass,* ANS 84·2.

morgenmete m. *morning meal,* Sol 192¹⁹.

morgenrēn m. *morning rain,* Az 82.

morgensēoc *sad at morn,* An 241.

morgenspǣc f. *regular meeting of a guild on the morrow after the guild-feast,* TC. ['*mornspeech*']

morgenspell n. *news published at morn*, EL 970.

morgensteorra m. *morning star*, Bo. ['*mornstar*']

morgenswēg m. *cry at morn*, B 129.

morgentīd (a¹, e¹) f. *morning*, CHR,Ps.

morgentīdlic *matutinal*, BPs 129⁶.

morgentorht *bright at morn*, AN 241.

morgenwacian *to rise early*, WW.

morgenwlǣtung f. *morning sickness*, LCD 169b.

mōrhǣð f. *mountain-heath*, PPs 82¹⁰.

mōrheald *heathy, marshy?* EX 61.

mōrhop n. *moor-swamp*, B 450.

mōrig *marshy*, GEN 41².

mōrlǣs *marshy pasture*, KC 3·408²².

mōrland n. '*moor-land,*' *mountain-waste*, LkL.

morne ds., mornes gs. of morgen.

morod, moroð=morað

mōrsceaða m. *robber*, NG.

mōrsecg mn. *sedge*, LCD 3·140'.

mōrseohtre f. *marshy ditch*, CHRD 96²⁸.

mōrslǣd n. *marshy valley*, KC.

mōrstapa m. *traverser of moors*, RUN 2.

mortere m. *a mortar*, LCD,WW. [*L.* mortarium]

morð nm. *death, destruction, homicide,* '*murder,*' AO; Æ : *deadly sin.* ['*murth*']

morð-=morðor-

morðcrundel mn. *barrow raised over a dead body? deadly pool? corpse-pit?* KC 3·23'.

morðdǣd f. *murder, deadly sin, crime,* Æ.

morðor nm., gs. morðres (mp. morðras) *deed of violence,* '*murder,*' *homicide, manslaughter,* B,Bl : *mortal sin, crime* : *injury, punishment, torment, misery.*

morðorbealu† n. *violent death, murder.*

morðorbed n. *bed of death (by violence)*, B 2436.

morðorcofa m. *prison*, AN 1006.

morðorcræft m. *murderous crime*, AN 177.

morðorcwalu f. *murder*, NC 310.

morðorcwealm m. *murder, death*, GnE 152.

morðorhete m. *blood-feud*, B 1105.

morðorhof n. *place of torment*, EL 1303.

morðorhūs n. *house of torment*, CR 1625.

morðorhycgende *with murderous thoughts*, WIF 20.

morðorlēan n. *retribution for sin*, CR 1612.

morðorscyldig *guilty*, AN 1601.

morðorslaga m. *homicide, murderer*, NG.

morðorslagu f. *homicide, murder*, NG.

morðorslege m. *homicide, murder*, LL (148¹⁴).

morð(or)slīht (e²) m. *slaughter, murder.*

morð(or)wyrhta m. *murderer*, W.

morðslaga (Æ)=morðorslaga

morðslīht=morðorslīht; **morður**=morðor

morðweorc n. *deadly work, act which causes death, murder*, LL.

morðwyrhta=morðorwyrhta

moru f. *parsnip, carrot* (=more).

mōrwyrt f. *moor-wort*, LCD 48b.

mōs n. **I.** *bog, marsh*, BC. ['*moss*'] **II.** n. *food, victuals.* [*Ger.* mus]

mōst, mōste v. *mōtan.

mot n. '*mote,*' *speck, atom, Mt,WW.*

mōt **I.** (±, usu. +) n. '*moot*' ('*gemot*'), *society, assembly, court, council, synod, Chr,MtL;* Mdf. +m. *counsel : litigation,* Bo : (+) *conflict, encounter.* **II.** f. *toll, tribute,* MkL. [*Ger.* maut] **III.** pres. sg. of *mōtan.

±mōtærn (e²) n. *courthouse*, AO.

mōtan* swv. pres. 1, 3 sg. mōt, pres. 2 sg. mōst, pres. pl. mōton, pret. mōste (*may*). *to be allowed, be able to, have opportunity to, be compelled to, must,* B,Gen; AO,CP. mōste ic *would that I might!* ['*mote*']

+mōtan=mētan

mōtbell f. *bell for summoning a moot*, LL. [v. '*moot*']

±mōtbeorh m. *hill of meeting*, BC.

mōtere m. *public speaker*, WW. ['*mooter*']

mōtern=mōtærn

mōtgerēfa m. *moot-reeve, chairman of a moot*, EC 342'.

±mōthūs n. *moot-hall, place of assembly*, WW; W. ['*moothouse*']

±mōtian *to speak to or about, converse with, address, harangue,* Æ : *argue, plead, discuss, dispute,* Hex. ['*moot*']

mōtlǣðu sbpl. *courts, assemblies?* TC 433²¹ (v. BTs).

+mōtlēah m. *meadow of meeting*, BC.

+mōtmann m. *orator, counsellor*, WW 164³⁵; 310²⁹.

+mōtstede m. *place of meeting*, SOUL 152.

±mōtstōw f. *place of meeting, forum*, EPs, GL.

mōtung f. *conversation, discussion*, OEG. ['*mooting*']

mōtweorð (u²) *qualified to attend the moot*, EC 343'.

mōðfreten *moth-eaten*, ÆL 23⁴³⁷.

mōðor=mōdor

mōððe f. '*moth,*' Lk,MtL (mohðe).

mucgwyrt f. *artemisia,* '*mugwort,*' Lcd, WW.

mucxle=muscelle; **mūdrica**=mȳderce

mūga m. '*mow,*' *heap of corn,* Æ.

mugan*=magan; **mugwyrt**=mucgwyrt

mūha (Cp)=muga

mūl m. '*mule,*' Ps; ÆL. [*L.* mulus]

mūlhyrde m. *mule-keeper*, ÆGR 35⁵.

multon pret. pl. of meltan.

+**mun** (w. g.) *mindful, remembering,* AO 48¹¹.

±**munan** (usu. +) pres. 1, 3 sg. man (mon), 2 manst, pl. munon, pret. munde swv. *to think about, be mindful of, remember, mention, Bl,Jul,Lk;* Æ,AO,CP : *consider.* ['*i-mune*']

mund f. I.† *hand : palm (of the hand, as a measure)* : *trust, security, protection, guardianship,* Æ : *protector, guardian : the king's peace : fine for breach of the laws of protection or guardianship of the king's peace,* v. LL2·555; 641. [cp. *Ger.* vormund] **II.** m. *money paid by bridegroom to bride's father, bridegroom's gift to bride,* CR93. **III.**=mynd

mundbeorg m. *protecting hill,* PPs124².

mundberd=mundbyrd

mundbora m. *protector, preserver, guardian, advocate,* Æ : *prefect.*

mundbryce (i²) m. *breach of the laws of protection or guardianship,* LL : *fine for the breach of such laws.*

mundbyrd f. *protection, patronage, help* : *fine for a breach of the peace,* LL.

±**mundbyrdan** *to protect,* Bo,VH.

mundbyrdnes f. *protection : security, independence : protector, guardian, advocate.*

mundbyre=mundbyrde (ds. of mundbyrd).

mundcræft m. *protecting power,* LCD 1·384¹³.

munde v. munan; +**munde**=+mynde

mundgripe† m. *hand-grasp,* B.

mundheals f. *protection?* CR445.

±**mundian** *to protect, watch over, act as guardian of,* Æ.

mundiend m. *protector,* TC525⁸.

mund-lēow, -lēu, -lāu f. *wash-hand basin,* WW. [*ON.* munnlaug]

mundrōf *strong with the hands,* RD84³.

mundwist f. *guardianship, protection,* NC 310.

munec=munuc

munetere=mynetere

mungung=mynegung

+**muning** f. *remembrance,* CM378.

munt m. *mountain, hill,* Æ,AO,CP. [*L.*]

muntælfen f. *mountain nymph,* WW189⁴. [v. '*elven*']

muntclȳse f. *mountain prison,* W84H.

muntland n. *hill-country,* Lk1³⁹.

munuc (e²) m. '*monk,*' BH,RB : (used also of women, A27·255). [*L.* monachus]

munucbehāt n. *monastic vow,* HL18⁸¹,⁹⁵.

munuccild n. *child intended for monastic life,* Æ,BF102¹⁶.

munuccnapa m. *young monk,* GD.

munucgegyrela m. *monastic garb,* BH34²⁷.

munuchād m. *monastic orders, the monastic life,* Æ,BH; CP. ['*monkhood*']

munuchēap m. *company of monks,* BF150¹⁹.

munucian (e²) *to make a monk of,* LL. ['*monk*']

munuclic *monkish, monastic, BH;* Æ. adv. -līce. ['*monkly*']

munuclīf n. *monastic life,* Æ : *cloister, monastery,* Æ,AO.

munucrēaf n. *monk's garb,* GD27¹⁷.

munucregol m. *monastic rule, mode of life,* Æ : *a body of monks under a certain rule,* TC544¹².

munucscrūd n. *monk's garb,* ÆP142⁵.

munucstōw f. *place of monks,* BH236²⁵.

munucðēaw m. *monastic rule,* ANS84·7.

munucwīse f. *fashion of a monk,* ÆL 6·247.

mūr m. *wall,* CR1143. [*L.* murus]

mūr-bēam, -berie=mōr-bēam, -berie

murc *dismal, wretched,* PPs145⁶. [myrce]

murcian *to complain, repine, grieve,* CP.

murcnere m. *complainer,* RB21⁵.

murcnian=murcian

murcung f. *complaint, sorrow,* CP.

murge=myrge

murnan³ (and wv.) *to care, be anxious or fearful about, An,Bo,Wald* : *hesitate* : '*mourn,' sorrow, bemoan, Wy* : *long after, An37.*

murnung f. *complaint, grief,* Bo18¹⁹ (v.l. murcnung), LCD,VH.

murra, murre=myrra, myrre

mūs f. gs. mūs, mūse, nap. mȳs '*mouse,' Bo;* Æ; Mdf : *muscle (of the arm),* WW158⁶.

mus-celle, -cule f. *shell-fish,* '*mussel,' Gl.* [*L.*]

muscflēote f? *a small fly found in wine* (mustflēoge? BT), WW121²².

muscle=muscelle

mūsepise f. *mouse-pea, vetch,* WW148³⁵.

mūsfealle (a²) f. *mouse-trap,* WW.

mūsfealu *mouse-coloured,* WW448⁹.

mūshafoc n. *mouse-hawk, buzzard,* WW.

musle=muscelle; **musscel** (GL)=muscelle

must m. '*must,' new wine, Bo;* Æ. [*L.*]

-**mūtian** v. be-m.

mūtung f. '*mutuum,' loan,* WW449³⁰.

mūð m. '*mouth,' opening, door, gate, Æ,BH, CP,Mt.*

mūða m. *mouth (of a river), estuary,* AO, CHR : (†) *entrance to a house, door.*

mūðādl f. *mouth-disease,* WW.

mūðberstung f. *eruption of the mouth,* WW.

mūðbona m. *devourer,* B2079.

mūðcoðu f. *mouth-disease,* WW.

mūðettan *to blab out, let out,* Æ (6¹⁶⁰).

mūðfrēo *free to speak,* PPs11⁴.

mūðhæl f. *wholesome speech,* Ex552.

mūðhrōf m. *palate,* OEG332.

mūðlēas *mouthless,* RD61⁹.

mūðsir *pain in the mouth*, LL.
mūðsealf f. *mouth-salve*, LCD 18ŀ
mūwa (WW 348⁶)=mūga
muxle=muscelle
myce? (ES 43·309), mycel (LW Ṩ=micel
mycg (i) m. '*midge*,' Cp,Lcd,WW.
mycgern=micgern
mycgnet (i) n. *mosquito-net*, WW 183¹³.
mycl-=micl-; myd-=mid-
mydd n. *bushel*, AO 190¹². [L. modius]
mȳderce f. *money storing-place, chest*, ÆGR
  (IF 48·267).
mygg (GL)=mycg; mȳgð=mǣgð
myhtig=mihtig
mȳhð pres. 3 sg. of mīgan.
myl n. *dust*, JAW 32; ES 41·163. [Ger.
  müll]
mylc=meolc
myldan=miltan; -myldan v. be-m.
myle-=mylen-
mylen mf. '*mill*,' KC,LL,RB; Mdf.
mylendīc f. *mill-dike*, Ct.
mylenfeld m. *mill-field*, KC 5·381'.
mylengafol n. *mill-tax, mill-rent?* NC 310.
mylengear m. *mill-yair*, Ct (v. A 46·228
  and BTs).
mylenhwēol n. '*mill-wheel*,' Lcd.
mylenpull m. *mill-pool*, Ct.
mylenscearp *sharpened on a grindstone*, BR
  24.
mylenstān m. *grindstone*, WW. ['*mill-
  stone*']
mylen-steall, -stede m. *mill*, KC.
mylenstīg f. *path to a mill*, KC 3·389⁸.
mylentroh n. *mill-trough, mill-conduit*, WW.
mylenwaru f. *mill-weir*, KC 3·454⁷.
mylenweg *road to a mill*, KC 6·31'.
myle(n)wer m. '*mill-weir*,' *mill-dam*, KC
  4·92'.
mylenwyrd, myleweard m. *tenant of a
  (manorial) mill, miller*, WW. ['*millward*']
mylestrēam m. '*mill-stream*,' BC 2·377.
myller (EC 179¹)=myle(n)wer?
mylisc, mylsc=milisc
mylma m. *retreat?* GPH 398¹⁵⁰.
myln=mylen
myltan=(1) meltan; (2) mieltan
myltenhūs n. *brothel*, ES 9·39.
myltestre (e, i) f. *prostitute*, Æ. [L.
  meretricem]
myltestrehūs n. *brothel*, WW 186².
myltestrern? (=ærn) *brothel*, v. OEG 8²²⁵.
mymerian *to remember*, W 74¹⁵.
+mynan=+munan
±mynd (usu. +) fn. *memory, remembrance*,
  Æ,BH,Met : *memorial, record*, Æ : *act of
  commemoration*, Bl,MH : *thought, purpose*,
  Bl : *consciousness, mind. intellect.* on
  +m. niman *to recollect*. ['*mind*']

+myndblīðe (i¹) *memorial*, EP 101¹³; 134¹³.
+mynddæg f. *anniversary, BH*. [v. '*mind*']
+mynde I. *mindful*, EL 1064. II. *river-
  mouth*, BH 398¹⁷ (v. JAW 31).
+mynde-=myndig-
+myndewyrðe *worth mentioning or remembering*, BH 486¹².
+myndful (e¹) *of good memory*, LCD 3·186.
±myndgian *to remember, be mindful of* :
  (w. g.) *remind*, W; CP : *intend : com-
  memorate, mention*, PPs : *exhort, impel,
  warn : demand payment*, LL 206,1².
  +myndgod *aforesaid*. ['*ming*']
myndgiend m. *one who reminds*, B 1105.
±myndgung f. *admonition*, CP : *remembrance, memorandum*, LL 453²¹ (mynġ-) :
  memorial, AO 98²ᵇ.
±myndig *mindful, recollecting*, Mk : *memorable : thoughtful, wise*, HELL 77. se
  +myndiga *the aforesaid*. ['*mindy*']
+myn-diglic, -delic *memorable : hortatory*.
  adv. -līce *by heart*, Æ : *thoughtfully*,
  MFB 103.
+myndiglicnes f. *remembrance*, SPs 101¹³.
±myndlēas *foolish, senseless*, Æ. ['*mind-
  less*']
+myndlȳst f. *madness*, ZDA 31·22.
+myndstōw f. *monument, tomb*, G,RPs.
+myndwyrðe=+myndewyrðe
myne I.† m. *memory, remembrance : feeling,
  affection, love, favour : purpose, desire,
  wish*, B : *memorial.* m. witan *to love*.
  ['*min*'] II. m. *minnow*, WW. III.=mene
+myne I. *mindful*, MtR 5²³. II. pres. subj.
  of +munan.
mynecen, mynecenu f. *female monk, nun*,
  WW; Æ. ['*minchen*'; munuc]
mynegian=myndgian
mynegiendlic *hortatory*, CM 30.
±mynegung f. *warning, admonition, exhortation*, Æ : *claim*. (=+myndgung)
mynelic *desirable*, WID 4.
mynescilling=menescilling
mynet n. *coin, money*, Cp,Lcd,MtR. ['*mint*';
  L. moneta]
mynetcȳpa m. *money-changer*, ÆH 1·412.
mynetere m. '*minter*,' *coiner*, Æ : *money-
  changer*, Mt; Æ.
±mynetian *to coin*, LL 158,14; BC 3·75.
mynetīsen n. *coinage? die for stamping
  coin?* (BTs), ÆL 23⁴⁴⁷.
mynetslege m. *minting, coinage*, ÆL 23⁴⁷⁵.
mynetsmiððe f. *mint*, LL 158,14¹.
myng-=myneg-, myndg-
mynian (e) *to intend, be impelled : direct
  oneself towards an object*, AS 1⁹.
mynig-=myneg-; mynit=mynet
mynle f. *desire*, MET 26⁶⁷.
mynnan=mynian

mynster (æ²) n. *monastery, nunnery, BH : mother-church, 'minster,' cathedral, LL.* [*L.* monasterium]

mynsterbōc f? *minster-book,* NC310.

mynsterclǣnsung f. *purification of a minster,* LL.

mynsterclūse f. *monastic enclosure, stall, cell, monastery,* CM22.

mynsterfæder m. *abbot,* GD293¹.

mynsterfǣmne f. *nun,* BH20¹⁹.

mynstergang m. *act of joining an order of monks,* LL(146').

mynstergēat n. *monastery gate,* GD145².

mynsterhām m. *monastery,* LL,TC.

mynsterhata m. *persecutor of monasteries,* W165²⁸.

mynsterland n. *land owned by a monastery,* KC3·60'.

mynsterlic *monastic,* Æ. adv. -līce.

mynsterlīf n. *monastic life,* Æ : *monastery.*

mynstermann m. *monk,* Æ,Bғ.

mynstermunuc m. *monk who lives in a monastery (i.e. not an anchorite),* ÆH.

mynsterprafost m. *provost of a monastery,* TC434⁴.

mynsterprēost m. *priest of a church or minster,* LL(254⁸).

mynsterscīr f. *control of a monastery,* BH 458¹¹.

mynsterstede m. *monastic buildings,* GD 182¹⁹.

mynsterstōw f. *place of a minster, town,* BH 160¹⁶.

mynstertimbrung f. *building of a monastery,* GD147¹¹.

mynsterðēaw m. *monastic custom,* BH452¹².

mynsterðegnung f. *monastic service,* RB85¹⁷.

mynsterwīse f. *monastic custom,* GF110²⁷.

+mynt n. *intention,* RWH135¹⁵.

±myntan *to intend, determine, resolve,* Æ, B,Bo : *destine : think,* Jud : *bring forth,* Sc215¹ : *give up to,* LL400,3. ['*mint,*' '*i-munte*']

myranhēafod n. *mare's head* (a nick-name), Chr1010e.

Myrce, Myrcan=Mierce; **myrce**=mirce

myre (Æ,AO)=miere

myrenæddra=merenæddra

myrgan *to be 'merry,' rejoice,* PPs.

myrge adj. (e, i, u) *pleasing, agreeable,* Æ,Bo,Met : *pleasant, sweet,* DHy. ['*merry*'] adv. myrge (AS,W), myriglīce *pleasantly, melodiously,* GD286¹. ['*merry*']

myrgelēoð n. *epitaph?* BHв94¹².

myrgen I. f. *joy, pleasure,* Met(Introd.)5. II.=morgen

myrgnes f. *melody,* WW33³¹.

myrgð (e, i), myrhð f. '*mirth,*' *joy, pleasure, sweetness (of sound),* Æ,Bo.

myrig-=myrg-; **mȳrlic**=mǣrlic

myrr-=mierr-

myrra m., myrre f. (u) '*myrrh,*' *Æ,MtR,VPs.*

myrrelse f. *offence, scandal, stumbling-block,* Jul338.

myrten I. n. *flesh of an animal which has died of itself, carrion,* LL. II. adj. *dead* (of animals which have not been killed), LL.

myrð=myrgð, v. also myrðu.

myrðra m. *homicide, murderer,* LL,W.

-myrðran, -myrðrian v. ā-, for-, of-m.

myrðrung f. *parricide, murder,* WW467²¹.

myrðu (=ie) f. *mischief, trouble,* B810.

myrw-=mearuw- (v. mearu); **mȳs** v. mūs.

±myscan *to injure, afflict,* PPs : *offend,* OEG17⁴⁷.

mysci sbpl. *flies,* PPs104²⁷.

mȳse=mēse; **mytting**=mitting

+mȳðe n. (usu. pl.) *mouth, confluence, junction of two streams,* BH,Ct.

myx=meox; **myx-**=mix-

N

nā (ō) adv. conj. *not, 'no,' not at all, not even, never, by no means,* Bl,Cr,Met,VPs; Æ,AO,CP. nā ðæt ān *not only.* nā...nā *neither...nor.* ne nā *nor.* nā mā *no more,* ÆGr,Bl. ['*no mo*'] nā māre sb. *nothing more,* Bo,Mk. ['*no more*']

nab-=naf-

nabban anv. pres. 1 sg. næbbe, 2 næfst, 3 nafað, næfð, pl. nabbað, næbbað; pret. næfde (v. habban) *not to have, to lack, be without,* Bo(+næfd), Jn; AO,CP. [v. '*have*']

naca† m. *vessel, boat, ship.* [*Ger.* nachen]

+naced=nacod; **naclan**=nacodian

nacod=nacod, nacud (æ) (+) I. adj. '*naked,*' *nude, bare,* Æ,CP : *empty : not fully clothed.* II. f. *nakedness.*

+nac(od)ian *to lay bare, strip,* BH,MkL.

næ adv.=ne

næbbað, næbbe v. nabban.

nǣbre=nǣfre

næcad (Cp499e '*exserta*')=nacod

±nǣcan (Æ)=hnǣcan

nǣced=nacod

nǣcednes f. *nakedness,* Æ.

nǣcedu f. *nakedness,* MFH169.

næct=niht; **nǣdder-**=nǣder-

nǣddre (CP)=nǣdre

nǣddrewinde f. *adder-wort,* WW287¹⁶.

nǣderbita m. *ichneumon,* WW.

nǣdercynn n. *snake-tribe,* Lcd : *a kind of snake,* AA.

nǣderfāh *spotted like a snake,* HL15¹⁸³.

nǣdl (ē) f. '*needle,*' *G,Soul;* Æ.

nǣdre (ē) f. ' adder,' snake, serpent, viper, Mt; AO,CP.

nǣdrewyrt (der) f. adder-wort, LCD,WW.

nǣfde pret. 3 sg. of nabban.

nǣfebor auger, A 9·263³. [nafu]

nǣfig (NG)=næftig; **nǣfne**=nefne

nǣfre (ē) adv. ' never,' B,Bl,Bo,Chr,G,LL; CP. [ne, æfre]

nǣfst v. nabban.

nǣft f. need, want, poverty, Sc 157³,⁷.

nǣftcyrrend not returning, CP 77³⁹. [ne eft]

nǣftig poor, Sc 190¹.

±nǣgan I.† (ē) (often followed by wordum) to approach, accost, speak to : attack. II.= hnǣgan

nǣgel=nægl; **nǣgen**=ne mægen

nǣgl m. ' NAIL,' peg, AO; Æ : finger-nail, toe-nail, claw, Æ : plectrum, WY 84 : spear, WW 377¹⁵ : (in comp.) handle.

nǣgledbord† with nailed sides.

nǣgledcnearr m. nail-fastened vessel, †CHR 937.

nǣgledcræt n. iron chariot (Swt).

nǣgledsinc n. studded vessel, B 2023.

±nǣglian ' to nail,' fasten with nails, MtLR; Æ.

nǣglsex n. knife for cutting the nails, WW. [seax; v. ' nail']

nǣh=nēah; **nǣhsta**=nīehsta

nǣht (NG,VPs)=niht; **nǣht**=nāht

nǣlēacan (S²Ps 54²²)=nēalēcan

nǣllǣs=nealles; **nǣm**=neom

nǣm f. taking, receiving, NC 311.

+nǣman to take away, GUTH 14¹¹.

nǣmel receptive, NC 311. [' nimble']

nǣming f. bargain, contract, WW 180¹⁷.

nǣmne=nemne

+nǣmnian (LL 455')=nemnian

nǣmniendlic=nemniendlic

nǣnig pron. no one, none, not any, no (used as sb. w. gen. and as adj.). nǣnige ðinga adv. not at all, in no wise. [ne, ǣnig]

nǣnig-wuht, -uht in no wise, nothing, ANDR 119⁶.

nǣniht (NG)=nānwiht

nǣnne v. nān.

nǣp m. turnip, rape, Cp,Lcd. [' neep']

nǣpsǣd n. rape seed, LCD.

nǣpte=nefte

nǣre, nǣron (Æ,AO,CP)=ne wǣre, ne wǣron

nǣrende ptc. not being. [ne, wesan]

nǣrra=nēara

nǣs I. (AO,CP)=ne wæs. II. adv. not, not at all, CP. [=nalæs] III.=næss. IV. pret. 3 sg. of nesan.

nǣsc fawn-skin, GL,LCD.

nǣse (NG)=nese

nǣsgristle f. nose-gristle, GL.

nǣs-hlið n. dp. -hleoðum declivity, slope (of a headland), B 1428.

nǣss (e), nǣssa m. ' ness,' cliff, headland, cape, An,B,Chr,Ct : (†) earth, ground.

nǣstan=hnǣstan

nǣster ' caucale' (=caucalia?), lipped vessel, WW 202¹ (v. A 49·378 and IF 48·266).

nǣsðyrl n. nostril, Æ,LCD.

±nǣtan to annoy, afflict, press upon, subdue, injure, destroy, CP.

nǣting f. blaming, CP 353¹¹.

nǣðl=nǣdl

nafa I. m.=nafu. II.=ne hafa imperat. of nabban

nafað pres. 3 sg. of nabban.

nafela m. ' navel,' AO,Gl,Lcd; Æ.

nafeða m. nave (of a wheel), WW 106²⁷.

nafogār m. ' auger,' Gl,WW.

nafu f. nave (of a wheel), Bo,WW

nafula=nafela

nafulsceaft f. navel, LCD 3·124'.

+nāg striking, pressing? RIM 57?

nāgan* pres. 3 sg. nāh; pret. nāhte, nāhton not to owe, not to be bound, not to be allowed, to have no right to, not to own, not to have, to lose, be unable to, AO. nāhte ought not. [ne, āgan]

nāht (ǣ, āu, āw, ō) I. n. ' NAUGHT,' nothing, CP : wickedness, evil-doing, CP. instr. nāhte w. comparatives=nothing. II. useless, bad, poor, Æ. III. adv. not, not at all, Æ, CP. [nā, wiht]

nāhte v. nāgan.

nāhtfremmend m. evil-doer, PPs 58².

nāhtgītsung (āu¹) f. wicked avarice, CP 333⁵.

nāhtlic worthless, of no avail, CHR 979 E. adv. -līce (ō¹) wickedly, badly. VPs. 36⁸,⁹. [' noughtly']

nāhtnes f. worthlessness, CHR 449a.

nāhtscipe f. worthlessness, CHR 449 E.

nāh-wǣr, -wǣrn (o¹) adv. ' nowhere,' in no case, never, not at all, Æ,Bf,Bl,GD.

nāhwǣðer neither, Bo,Bl; CP. [' nauther']

nāhwǣr=nāhwǣr

nāhwider ' no-whither,' nowhere, Bo,RB.

nāhwonan adv. from nowhere, Bo 89².

nalǣs, nalas, nales (AO,CP), nalles (CP), nals=nealles

nalde (N,VPs)=nolde pret. of *nyllan.

nam I. pret. 3 sg. of niman. II. (N)=ne eom

nām f. (legal) seizure, LL.

nama (o) m. ' NAME,' Æ; AO,CP : reputation : noun, ÆGR.

nambōc (o) f. register of names, WW 342¹¹.

nambred (o) n. register of names (on a tablet), WW 499⁴⁰.

namcūð well-known, LL : celebrated, HL; (nome-), Æ. [' namecouth']

namcūðlīce adv. *by name, individually,* Æ.
namcyging (=ie²) f. *naming,* CHRD 9²⁹.
±namian *to ' name,' Gen* : *mention,* Æ : *call, Scr* : *nominate, appoint,* Æ,LL.
nammǣlum adv. *by name,* LF 55¹⁴, OEG.
+namn adj. *of the same name,* RD 53³; 54¹³?
namnian *to address, invoke,* ÆT 683.
nāmon pret. pl. of niman.
nāmrǣden f. *learning,* WW 431⁸.
nān as. nǣnne, nānne **I.** pron. and adj. 'NONE,' *not one, no.* nāne ðinga *on no account.* **II.** sb. w. g. *none, no one, nothing.* [nē, ān]
nān-wiht, -(w)uht **I.** n. (often w. g.) *nothing, naught,* AO,CP. **II.** adv. *not at all, in no wise.*
nāp pret. 3 sg. of nīpan.
nard m. *spikenard, unguent,* LCD. [*L.* nardus]
nart (*JnL*)=neart; naru=nearu
nas=næs=ne wæs
nāst (=ne wāst) v. nytan.
nasōyrl=næsðyrl; nasu=nosu
nāt (*Bo,Jn*)=ne wāt, v. nytan.
nāteshwōn (Æ), nāteðæshwōn adv. *not, not at all, by no means.*
nāthwā adj. pron. *some one* (=*L.* nescio quis).
nāthwǣr adv. *somewhere or other,* RD.
nāthwæt pron. *something or other,* RD.
nāt-hwīlc, -hwylc adj. pron. (indef.)† (*I know not which), some one or other.*
nātōhwōn, nātōðæshwōn=nāteshwōn
nāðēlǣs (AO)=nāðȳlǣs
nāðer (Æ,AO,CP), nāðor (Æ)=nāhwæðer
nāðinc n. *nothing,* HL 18⁴⁸.
nāðȳlǣs (ō¹, ē²) *nevertheless,* AO.
nāuht=nāht
nāwa adv. *never,* LCD 94b. [ne, āwa]
nāwer=nāhwǣr
nāwērn [=nāhwǣrn] adv. *nowhere,* WW.
nāwht, nāwiht=nāht; nāwðer=nāhwæðer
nāwuht (*CP*)=nāwiht, nāht
ne **I.** adv. *not, no,* Æ,CP. **II.** conj. *neither, nor,* Æ,CP.
nēa-=nēah-
nēad=nīed; nēad- v. also nīed, nȳd-.
nēadclamm n. *necessity, extremity,* LPs 106²⁸.
nēadcofa m. *prison,* AN 1311.
nēadgafol n. *tax, tribute,* LL.
nēadgewuna m. *enforced custom,* WW 221⁸.
nēadgylda m. *debtor,* WW 221¹⁰.
nēadhād m. *compulsion, force,* WW 480²¹.
nēadhǣs f. *order which one must obey,* LL 12.
±nēadian **I.** *to compel, force, constrain, urge, impel,* Æ. **II.** v. nēodian.
nēadignes f. *obligation,* OEG 2106.

nēadinga (AO), nēadlunga=nēadunga
nēadnēod f. *unavoidable necessity,* CHRD 61⁹.
nēadprin? n. *necessary equipment,* ÆP 13⁷ (or ?=nēadðing).
nēadðing n. *necessary thing,* RB 57; ÆP 13⁷?
nēadung f. *compulsion,* Æ.
nēadunga, nēadunge adv. *forcibly,* Æ.
nēadwīs *needful, fitting, due,* Æ. adv. *of necessity,* Æ.
nēadwīsnes f. *necessity,* OEG 2396.
nēadwīte n. *inevitable punishment,* MFH 170.
nēadwraca m. *avenger by necessity,* TC 611'.
nēah **I.** (ē, ī) [comp. nēara, superl. nīehsta q.v.] adj. 'NEAR' ['NAR'], 'NIGH,' *close,* AO,CP : *late.* **II.** adv. 'NEAR,' 'NIGH,' *AO* : *about, almost, nearly, lately, CP.* nēar and nēar *nearer and nearer.* æt nīehstan *next, at length, finally.* **III.** prep. w. d. *near, close to : according to,* AO.
+nēah **I.**† *sufficiency, abundance.* **II.** (ē) *closely, seriously,* BL 101³². **III.** pres. 3 sg. of +nugan.
nēahbūend m. *neighbour,* RD 26².
nēahceaster f. *nearest town,* BH 52²⁷ (nēh-).
nēahcyrice f. *neighbouring church,* GD.
nēahdǣl m. *neighbourhood,* GD 71³⁰.
nēahdūn f. *neighbouring hill,* AA 20¹⁷.
nēahēa f. *neighbouring river,* AA 33⁷.
nēahēaland n. *neighbouring island,* MH 84¹⁷.
nēahfæder m. ' *vicinus pater,*' GD 179⁷.
nēah-feald, -fealdlic (GD) *intimate.*
nēahfrēond (ē¹) m. *near friend, near kinsman,* GUTH 56²².
nēahgangol (w. d.) *placed near,* ÆL 23¹³¹.
nēahgebūr (ē) m. ' *neighbour,*' Bf,CP,HL, Lk.
nēahgebȳren (nēhhe-) f. *neighbour,* Lk 15⁹.
nēahgebȳrild (nēhe-) m. *neighbour,* LkL 15⁹.
nēahgehūsa (ē) m. *neighbour,* JVPs.
±neah-he, -hi(g)e (usu. +) *sufficiently : abundantly : often, frequently : earnestly.*
nēahhebūr=nēahgebūr
+neahhelīce (nehl-) *sufficiently, frequently, usually,* LL,GUTH.
nēahhergung f. *warring close at hand,* HL 200¹⁷⁴.
neah-hie, -hige=neahhe
+nēahian *to draw near to,* LPs 90¹⁰.
nēahlǣcan=nēalǣcan
nēahland n. *neighbourhood,* GD 69²⁸.
nēah-mǣg m. nap. -māgas *near relation,* LL.
nēahmǣgð f. *neighbouring tribe,* BH.
nēahmann (ē¹) m. *neighbour,* BH.
nēahmunt m. *neighbouring mountain,* AA, GD.
nēahnes (ē¹) f. *nearness, neighbourhood,* BH.

nēahnun(n)mynster *neighbouring convent,* BH 254¹⁰.

nēahslbb I. adj. *related,* LL. **II.** f. *affinity, near relationship,* W.

nēahsta=nīehsta

nēahstōw f. *neighbourhood, place near,* Bo, MH.

neaht (*Met*)=niht

nēahtīd f. *approaching time,* BH 290²⁹.

nēahtūn (ē) m. *neighbouring town or village,* HL 199¹⁵⁷.

nēahōēod f. *neighbouring nation,* AO 46,96.

nēahwæter n. *neighbouring piece of water,* AA 34².

+**nēahwian** (ē) *to draw near, approach, cleave to,* NG.

nēahwudu m. *neighbouring wood,* GD 229²⁰.

±**nēalǣcan** (w. d.) *to come or draw near, approach,* BH,Bl,LG; Æ,AO,CP : *be near,* GD 85⁹ : *be like : cling to,* CPs 136⁶. [' *nehleche* '; nēah, lǣcan]

nēalǣcung f. *approach, access,* Æ,RB. [' *nehleching* ']

nēalic (ē) *near, neighbouring.* adv. -līce *nearly, about, Bl*; CP. [' *nighly* ']

nealles adv. *not, not at all, by no means,* CP.

neam=neom; **nēam-**=nēahm-

nēan adv. *from near by : close at hand, near : nearly, about.*

+**nēan**=+nēahwian; **neap**=hnæpp

nēar comp. of nēah, adv. *near, nearer,* AO.

+**near**=+ner

nēara, nēarra (AO), comp. of nēah, adj. *later, latter, nearer.*

neara-=neparo-; **nearo** (AO)=nearu

nearobregd f. *crafty trick,* Jul 302.

nearocræft m. *skill in enclosing?* B 2243.

nearofāh *intensely hostile,* B 2317.

nearogrāp f. *close grasp,* RD 81⁶.

nearolic *oppressive, straitened,* EL 913. adv. -līce ' *narrowly,' closely, briefly, accurately,* Æ,CP : *strictly, stringently, oppressively : evilly.*

nearonēd f. *urgent need,* An 102.

nearones f. *strait,* AO : *small space : scantiness : oppression : distress, anxiety, trouble.*

nearosearu† (u²) f. *dark cunning.*

nearosorg (u²) f. *crushing distress,* EL 1261.

nearoðanc (u²) m. *wickedness,* OEG.

nearoðancnes f. *wickedness,* LPs 27⁴.

nearoðearf f. *dire need,* CR 69.

nearowrenc (u²) m. *evil trick,* Mod 44.

neart *art not,* Bo. [' *nart* '; ne eart]

nearu I.† f? n? gs. nearu, near(o)we *strait, danger, distress, difficulty.* n. ðrōwian *to be in straits : confinement, imprisonment : prison, hiding-place.* **II.** adj. ' *narrow,' constricted, limited, petty,* AO,B,Bo,G : *causing*

or accompanied by difficulty, hardship, oppressive, Bl,Rd : *strict, severe,* CP.

nearu-=nearo-

nearwe adv. *narrowly, closely, strictly,* B, Met : *carefully, exactly,* El; CP : *oppressively, forcibly : artfully : anxiously.* [' *narrow* ']

nearwelīce=nearolīce

nearwian (±) *to force in, cramp, confine, afflict : crowd : become smaller, shrink.*

nearxnewang=neorxnawang

nēasian (VPs)=nēosian

nēat n. *animal, beast, ox,* CP,VPs; pl. *cattle,* Met,VPs. [' *neat* ']

+**nēat** m. *companion, follower* (esp. *in war*), Chr,WW : *dependant, vassal, tenant who works for a lord,* v. LL 2·427. [v. ' *geneat* ']

nēaten=nīeten

±**nēatland** n. *land of a dependant or vassal,* LL 196,1¹.

+**nēatmann**=+nēat

+**nēatriht** n. *regulations as to the tenure of* ' genēatland,' LL 445,2.

+**neatscolu** f. *band of comrades,* Jul 684.

nēawest (AO,CP), nēawist (Æ) fm. *neighbourhood, nearness, presence : society, cohabitation.* [nēah, wesan]

nēawung f. *nearness,* MtL 13²⁸.

neb(b) n. *bill, beak, beak-shaped thing,* Cp, Ph : *nose,* LL : *face, countenance, complexion,* Æ,CP. n. wið n. *face to face,* RWH 138³⁸. [' *neb* ']

nebb-=neb-

nebbian *to retort upon, rebuke, confront,* ÆH 1·256.

nebcorn n. *pimple,* Lcd 1·118'.

nebgebrǣc n. *nasal mucus,* WW.

nebsealf f. *antimony, face-powder,* OEG.

nebwlātful *barefaced, shameless,* OEG 2²¹⁷.

nebwlātung f. *impudence,* OEG 4306.

neb-wlite, -wlitu m. *face, countenance,* Æ.

nechebūr=nēahgebūr; **nectl-**=nihte-

ned=net(t); **nēd**=(1) nīed; (2) nēod

nēd- (A)=nēad-, nīed-, nȳd-; **nēdl**=nǣdl

nēdre (VPs), nēddre=nǣdre

nefa m. (±) *nephew,* Æ,AO : *stepson : grandson : second cousin.*

nefene f. *granddaughter : niece,* WW 173³¹.

nefne=nemne; **nēfre**=nǣfre adv.

nefte f. *cat's mint,* Lcd,WW. [L. nepeta]

nēfugol m. *bird of prey,* Gen 2158. [cp. nēobedd]

nēgan=nǣgan; **negled-**=nægled-

nēh=nēah; +**nehe**, +nehh(ig)e=+neahhe

nēhst, nēhsta=nīehst, nīehsta

neht=niht

neirxnawong (N)=neorxnawang

nēista=nīehsta

nele (AO,CP)=nelle (Æ) pres. 1, 3 sing., nelt=pres. 2 sg. of nellan. [v. 'will']

nellan=*nyllan

nem-nan, -nian (±) to name, call, Bl,Bo, Lcd,MkL; Æ,AO,CP : enumerate : address, speak to : nominate : invoke : mention, relate, Bo; Æ. ['nemn']

nemne (A;=WS nymðe) conj. and prep. unless, except, save, only.

nemnian=nemnan

nemnl(g)endlic naming, nominative, ÆGR 22¹⁰.

nemning (æ) f. name, ÆL23⁸⁶⁴.

nemðe=nymðe

nenä (WW252¹)=ne nā v. nā.

nĕnig (KGL)=nænig

nĕobeddt n. corpse-bed, bed of death, GEN, PH. [cp. Goth. naus]

nĕod I. f. (ē, īe, ȳ) desire, longing : zeal, earnestness : pleasure, delight. [FTP299] **II.**=nīed

nĕode adv. (instr. of nēod) eagerly, zealously, diligently.

nĕodfracu f. yearning, greed, MET31¹⁵ (v. ES39·335).

nĕodfrēond m. kinsman, friend, HL18¹⁵⁰. [nīed]

nĕodful I. zealous, earnest, JUL720. **II.**= nīedful

nĕodhūs (NC312)=nīedhūs

±**nĕodian** (=ēa; impers. w. g.) to be necessary, require, be required, RB. ['need']

nĕodlaðu f. wish, B1320.

nĕodlīce adv. eagerly, carefully, zealously, diligently, Æ : (†) greatly, PPs.

nĕodlof n. zealous praise, PPs148¹².

nĕodspearuwa m. (restless?) sparrow, PPs 123⁶.

nĕodðearflic necessary, GD148⁶.

nĕodweorðung f. zealous honouring, PPs 142¹¹.

neofa=nefa; **nĕol**=neowol

nĕo-lǣcan (VPs), -lēcan (MtL)=nēalǣcan

neom=ne eom (am not).

neoman=niman

nĕomian to sound sweetly? WYRD84.

nĕon=nīwan

+**nĕopan²**? to engulf, overwhelm, Ex475.

nĕor adv.=nēar

+**neorð** contented, Cp544. [from Nerthus? IF48]

neorxnawang m. Paradise, Æ,CP; v. A 53·337 and IF48·267.

neorxnawanglic adj. of Paradise, GD179¹.

nĕosan, nĕosian (Æ) to search out, find out, inspect : (±) visit, go to : attack, visit with affliction.

nĕoslð m. death, MoD55.

neosu=nosu

±**nĕosung** f. access : visitation, visit, Æ.

nĕotan² (usu. w. g.) to use, have the use of, enjoy, employ. [Ger. geniessen]

nĕoten=nīeten

neoð-an, -ane (i) adv. below, down, beneath, from beneath, Æ,Bl,Bo (-on). ['nethen']

neoðe-=niðe-; **neoðon**=neoðan

neoðor, neoðor-=niðor, niðer-

neoðoweard=niðeweard; **neoðra**=niðera

nĕow-=nīw-; **neowel**=neowol

nĕowĕrno (WW454²⁸)=nāwĕrn

neowol (i) precipitous : headlong : prone, prostrate, Æ,Bo : obscure, deep down, abysmal. ['nuel']

neowollic (i¹, e²) profound, deep, ÆL7⁶⁶.

neowolnes (i¹) f. depth, abyss, chasm, Æ.

nĕp only in phr. forðganges n. without power of advancing? Ex469.

nĕpflōd m. 'neap'-tide, ebb, low tide, Gl,MH.

nepte=nefte

±**ner** (ea) n. refuge, protection, ÆL,AO.

nĕr=nēar

+**ner-ednes** (BH), -renes (GD) f. deliverance.

nergend m. saviour, preserver (Christ, God).

nergendlic that should be preserved? (BTs).

±**nerian** to save, rescue, liberate, Æ,AO,CP : preserve, defend, protect. [Ger. nähren]

neriend, nerigend=nergend

nĕrra=nēar(r)a

+**nerstede** m. refuge, sanctuary, WW186²³.

nerung f. guard, protection, OEG5395.

nerw-=nearw-, nirew-; **nerx-**=neorx-

±**nesan⁵** (usu. +) to escape from, survive, be saved.

nese (æ) adv. no, Æ,CP. [ne, sī]

ness=næss

nest I. n. 'nest,' MtL,Ph; Æ : young bird, brood. **II.** n. food, provisions, victuals.

nĕst, nēsta (VPs)=nīehst, nīehsta

nestan to spin, NG.

nestig=nihstig

nestlian to make a nest, LPs103¹⁶. ['nestle']

nestpohha m. wallet, MtL10¹⁰.

net=nett; **net-**=nyt-

neta m. caul, WW266²⁰.

netan=nytan

netel, netele f. 'nettle,' Lcd.

netenes=nytennes; **nĕtl** (Cp)=nǣdl

netle (Cp)=netele

neton=nyton

netrǣp m. snare, gin, WW.

nett (y) n. 'net,' Bo,LG,WW : netting, network, Ex,WW : spider's web, PPs. [Goth. nati]

nette (y) f. the net-like caul, WW.

neutgern n. *knitting yarn*, EC377¹⁴. [gearn]

+nettian *to ensnare*, OEG4596.

±**nēðan** *to venture on, dare, risk*, AO. [nōð]

+nēðedlic=+nīededlic

+neðerian=+niðerian

nēðing f. *boldness, daring*, GU: *risk*, AO.

nēðl (A)=nǣdl

neurisn f. *aneurism*, LCD.

newesēoða (i¹) m. *pit of the stomach? bowels?* GL,LCD.

nēwest=nēawest

nēxt (LWS)=nīehst; **nī-**=nīg-, nīw- **nic**, nicc adv. *not I* (=no). [ne, ic]

niccan *to say 'no,' refuse*, KC6·201⁶.

nicor (e²) m. nap. nicras *water-sprite, sea-monster*, B,Bl: *hippopotamus, walrus*, Nar. ['*nicker*']

nicorhūs n. *sea-monster's dwelling*, B1411.

nīd=nīed; **nīd-**=nēad-, nīed-, nȳd-

nīed I. (ē, ēa, ēo, ī, ȳ; see NED) fn. '*NEED*,' *necessity, compulsion, duty*, AO; CP : *errand, business*, Æ : *emergency*, Æ : *hardship, distress, difficulty, trouble, pain*, AO : *force, violence* : *what is necessary* : *inevitableness* : *fetter*, DEOR5 : *name of the rune for* n. **II.**=nēod

nīed- v. also nēad-, nȳd-.

nīedan (ē, ī, ȳ) *to compel, force, urge, press*, Æ,Bo,Bl,LG,VHy; AO,CP. ['*need*']

nīedbād (ē, ȳ) f. *toll, exaction, blackmail* : *bodily torment*, ES49·350.

nīedbādere (ē) m. *toll-collector*, TC29¹⁰.

nīedbehǣfdlic *necessary*, BH396²⁴.

nīedbehǣfednes (ē¹) f. *necessity*, Æ.

nīedbehǣfnes (ȳ¹) f. *requisite*, ÆL30⁸.

nīedbehēfe (y¹) *needful, necessary*, Æ.

nīedbe-hof (Æ), -hoflic (BH) (ȳ) *necessary.*

nīedbeðearf (y³) *necessary*, CP7⁷.

nīede, nīedes (ēa, ēo, ī, ȳ) adv. (instr. and gs. of nīed) *of need, needs, necessarily, compulsorily*, CP.

+nīededlic (ē) *compulsory*, BH62²³(v.l.).

nīedenga, nīedunga adv. *necessarily, by force, forcibly*, CP.

nīedfaru f. *compulsory journey, death*, OET149.

nīedful (ēo) *needful*, CM377.

nīedhǣmed (ē, ȳ) n. *rape*, LL.

nīedhiernes (ē¹, ē²) f. *slavery*, DR6⁵.

nīedhūs (ēo) *needed room*, CHRD21¹⁸.

nīedling m. *slave*, AO : *captive*, GD : *sailor*, BH.

nīedmicel (ē) *urgent*, BL233¹¹? (MS med-).

nīednǣm f. *seizure*, BH,LL.

nīedscyld f. *moral necessity*, CP57⁶.

nīedsibb (ēa) f. *relationship*, OEG,WW.

nīedðearf I. f. *need, necessity, compulsion, force*, CP : *distress* : *want, thing needed*. **II.** adj. *necessary*.

nīedðearflic (ē, ēa, ȳ) *necessary, useful.* adv. -līce, ÆGR,GD.

nīedðearfnes (ēa, ē, ȳ) f. *need, necessity* : *compulsion* : *trouble* : *time of need*, EPs9²¹.

nīedðēow (ē, ȳ) m. *slave*, LL,W.

nīedðrafung f. *reproof*, CP297²².

nīedwǣdla m. *poor wretch*, GEN929.

nīehst (ē) **I.** adv. (superl. of nēah) *most nearly, in closest proximity* : *last (in time)*, Bl,Gen. **II.** adj. *latest, last*, Æ : *nearest*, '*NEXT*,' CP,Chr. æt nīehstan *at last, next.*

nīehsta mf. *closest friend*, CP : (±) *neighbour*, MkL,VPs : *next of kin*, LL. ['*next*']

nīeht (CP)=niht

±**nīer-wan**, -wian (i, y) *to confine, repress* : *beset, rebuke, chasten*. [v. '*narrow*']

nīeten (ē, ēo, ī, ȳ) n. *small animal, beast, cattle*, Bo,Lcd,VPs; AO,CP. ['*neten*'; nēat]

nīetencynn n. *kind of animal*, Æ.

nīetenlic (ē, ȳ) *animal, brutish*, Bo35²⁸. adv. -līce *like an animal*, W55¹⁶.

nīetennes (ȳ) f. *brutishness*, Æ.

nieðemest=niðemest; **nieðer**=niðer

nīewe=nīwe

nīfara (nīw-) m. *newcomer, stranger*, PPs38¹⁵.

nifol *dark, gloomy*. [=neowol]

nift f. *niece*, BH,Ep,TC : *granddaughter* : *step-daughter*. ['*nift*']

nīg-=nīw-; **nigan**=nigon; **nige-**=nigo-

nīgecyrred *newly converted*, OEG3447.

nīgefara=nīfara

nīgehalgod *newly consecrated (of a king), newly crowned*, ÆL18³²⁶.

nīgehwyrfed *newly converted*, ÆL5¹²⁶.

nigend(e) (KC)=nigoða

nīghworfen *newly converted*, ÆH2·130'.

nigon (e²) '*nine*,' Bf,Bl,Chr,Ct,G; AO,CP.

nigonfeald '*nine-fold*,' ÆGr.

nigongylde *entitled to nine-fold compensation*, LL470,7.

nigonnihte *nine days old*, ANS129·22.

nigontēoða '*nineteenth*,' Chr,MH : '*nine-tieth*,' OEG2521 (nigen-).

nigontīene (ȳ³) '*nineteen*,' Bf,Men.

nigontig '*ninety*,' Lk; CP.

nigontȳnlic *containing the number nineteen*, BH470²⁰.

nigonwintre *nine years old*, AO186¹⁰.

nigoða (y) '*ninth*,' Bl,KC,LG,MH : *ninth part*, Bl.

nigoðe *ninthly*, LL181,9.

nigslȳcod ptc. *freshly smoothed, glossy*, MH206²⁷. [v. '*slick*']

nigun=nigon; **nīh** (KGL55²⁵)=nēah

nihold (GL), nihol=neowol

nihst, nīhsta=nīehst, nīehsta

nihstig *fasting*, LCD. [ne, wist]

niht (æ, e, ea, ie, y) f. (gs. also nihtes) 'NIGHT' (often used in enumerations where mod. Eng. uses days), *darkness*, AO,CP.

niht-=nyht-

nihtbealu n. *destruction by night*, B 193.

nihtbutorflēoge f. *beetle or moth which flies by night*, WW 121¹³; A 8·450.

nihtēage *that can see at night*, WW.

nihteald *that happened yesterday*, LL.

nihtegale (a, æ, e) f. *nightingale*, Cp : *night-jar*. ['*nightgale*']

nihtēge=nihtēage

nihtegesa m. *nocturnal terror*, PPs 90⁵.

nihtelic=nihtlic

nihterne adv. *by night* : *during a night*, LCD.

nihternnes f. *night season*, LCD 3·288'.

nihtes (æ) adv. (gs. of niht) *by night*, Æ.

nihtfeormung f. *shelter at night*, GEN 2433.

nihtgenga† m. *night-goer, goblin*.

nihtgenge f. *night-prowler, hyæna*, WW.

nihtgerīm† n. *number of nights*.

nihtgild n. *night sacrifice or service*, GL.

nihtglōm m? *gloom of night*, GU 916.

nihthelm† m. *shades of night*.

niht-hræfn, -hrefn, -hremn m. *night-raven, night-jar*, GL,Ps.

nihthrōc m. *night-raven*, LPs 101⁷.

nihthwīl f. *space of a night*, W 147⁹.

+nihtian *to become night, grow dark*, NC 295.

nihtlang *lasting through the night*, Æ. adv. -langes, Æ.

nihtlic *nocturnal, of the night, at night*, Æ, CP.

nihtnihstig (ea¹, e²) *having fasted for a night*, LCD.

nihtremn=nihthræfn

nihtrest f. *couch*, GEN 2863.

nihtrīm=nihtgerīm

nihtsang m. *compline* : *book of service for compline*, Ct.

nihtscada *night-shade (plant)*, WW 135³ (v. MP 24·217).

niht-scūa† m., gs. -scū(w)an *shades of night*.

nihtslæp m. *night's sleep*, ÆL 23⁴⁴².

nihtsum=nyhtsum

nihtwacu f. *night-watch*, Seaf 7. ['*night-wake*']

nihtwæcce f. '*night-watch,' vigil*, Lk.

nihtwaru f. *clothing for night*, RB 90⁴.

·nihtweard m. *guardian at night*, Ex 116.

nihtweorc n. *deed done at night*, B 827.

nihð (MP 1·613) pres. 3 sg. of nēahwian.

nīhwyrfed (OEG 3138)=nīgehwyrfed

nīlæred *newly initiated*, OEG 3138.

nile=nyle, pres. 1 sg. of *nyllan.

±niman⁴ (eo, io, y) *to take, assume, undertake, accept, receive, get, obtain* : *hold, seize, catch, grasp, pluck up, carry off* : *occupy* :

adopt, appropriate : *bear, carry, bring* : *betake oneself, go* : *contain* : *experience* : *suffer, tolerate* : *give* : (+) *grasp, comprehend* : (+) *take to wife*. friÐ +n. *make peace.* hē hine genam *he collected himself, reflected.* sige n. *gain victory.* on n. *take effect*, LCD. se nimenda dæl *the participle*, BF 94²². ['NIM*']

-nimend, -nimendnes v. dæl-n.

niming f. *action of taking*, LkL. ['*nimming*']

nimðe=nymðe; **niol**=neowol

niow-=nēow-

nip? sb. *rope*, GPH 399⁴⁵¹.

+nip *darkness, mist, cloud, obscurity*, Æ.

±nīpan¹† *to grow dark, obscure*.

+nipful *dark, gloomy*, ES 39·347.

nirewett (nirw-) n. *narrowness* : *narrow place, defile, pass*, AO : *hardness of breathing*.

nirwan=nierwan

nirwð (=ie) f. *prison house*, WW 399⁵.

nis (Æ,Bo,VPs)=ne is (*is not*). ['*nis*']

nisēoða=newesēoða

nīsoden ptc. *newly-boiled*, OEG 326 (=nīw-).

nistan (VPs), nistian (SPs) *to build nests*. ['*nest*']

nistig=nihstig

nist-lan (PPs), -lian (EPs) (y) *to build nests*. ['*nestle*']

nit-=nyt-; **nīten**=nīeten

niton (Bo,RG)=nyton; v. nytan. ['*niten*']

niÐ n. *abyss*, SAT 634?

nīÐ m. *strife, enmity, attack, war* : *evil, hatred, spite, Bl,Cr,VPs*; AO,CP : *oppression, affliction, trouble, grief*, AO. ['*nith*']

nīÐan=neoÐan

nīÐan *to envy, hate*, GD 117⁵.

nīÐas=niÐÐas

nīÐcwalu f. *violent death, destruction*, CR 1258.

nīÐcwealm m. *violent death*, PPs 77⁵⁰.

nīÐdraca m. *hostile dragon*, B 2273.

nīÐemest (Bo,Bl) v. niÐera.

niÐer (eo, io, y) adv. *below, beneath, down, downwards, B,Bo*; AO,CP. ['*nether*']

niÐera (eo, y) (comp.) adj. niÐemest, nyÐemest (superl.; positive not found) *lower, under, lowest, Bl,Bo,VPs,WW*; CP. ['*nether*']

niÐerāscūfan (ēo⁴) *to push down*, Æ.

niÐerāstīgan¹ *to descend*, Æ,CP.

niÐerbogen ptc. *bent down*, KC 4·72¹.

niÐerdæl m. *lower part, PPs 138¹³*. [v. '*nether*']

niÐere adv. *below, down, low down, Bo,Cr*. ['*nether*']

niÐerecg f. *lower edge*, KC.

niÐerflōr f. *lower story*, GD 170¹⁷.

niðergān (y¹) *to descend,* Æ.

niðergang (y) m. *descent,* Lcd 3·246⁶. [v. 'nether']

niðerheald *bent downwards,* Met 31²³.

niðerhrēosende (y) *falling down,* Æ.

niðerhryre (y¹) m. *downfall,* Sc 229¹².

±niðerian (e, y) *to depress, abase, bring low, oppress,* Jud,Lk,VPs; AO,CP : *accuse* : *condemn.* +nyðred *ignominious,* ÆL 23b¹⁴. ['nither']

+niðerigendlic (y) *deserving condemnation,* Sc 162¹⁸.

niðerlecgung (y) f. *deposition, entombment,* CM 421.

niðerlic *low, low-lying, inferior, lowly,* CP.

niðernes (y) f. *deepness, bottom,* BH 212²¹.

niðeronwend *downwards,* GD.

niðerra=niðera

niðerscēotende (y) *rushing downwards,* OEG.

niðerscyfe m. *rushing downwards, descent,* HGL 468.

niðersīge (y¹) m. *going down,* LPs.

niðerstīgan=niðerāstīgan

niðerstīge (y¹) m. *descent,* RB. [v. 'nether']

niðerstīgende *descending,* RB. [v. 'nether']

niðertorfian *to throw down,* GPH 390.

±niðerung (y) f. *humiliation, abasement, downthrow, condemnation,* BH,LG,OEG; Æ. ['nither']

niðerweard adj. *directed downwards.* adv. -weardes, Æ,OEG,RG. ['netherward(s)']

niðeweard *situated beneath, low, nethermost,* Æ,Ph. ['netheward']

nīðful *envious, quarrelsome, ill-disposed, evil,* Æ. ['nithfull']

nīðfullīce *maliciously,* ÆH 1·46'.

nīðgæst† (y²) m. *hostile alien, fell demon.*

nīðgetēon n. *attack,* Gen 2068.

nīðgeweorc n. *evil deed,* B683.

nīðgrama m. *anger, malice,* W 180⁹.

nīðgrim† *fierce, hostile,* B,PPs.

nīðgripe m. *fierce grasp,* B976? [or ?nȳd-]

nīðheard† (and EPs 27⁴) *bold, brave in battle.*

nīðhell f. *hateful hell,* HL 15¹⁵⁰.

nīðhete† m. *hostility, evil intent : affliction, torment : foe,* An 833?

nīðhycgende† *evil-scheming.*

nīðhȳdig (ē²) *valorous,* B3165.

nīðlg *envious, malicious,* OEG p 224n.

nīðing m. *wretch, villain, coward, outlaw,* Chr,LL. ['nithing']

+nīðla† m. *enemy : enmity, fierceness* (?+nīðle).

nīðlīce adv. *abjectly,* OEG 744.

nīðloca m. *place of torment,* Hell 64.

nīðor=niðer

nīðplega m. *battle, fight,* An 414.

nīðr-=niðer-

nīðscēaða m. *foe, persecutor,* RD 16²⁴.

nīðscipe m. *wickedness,* LPs 7¹⁰.

nīðsele m. *hall of conflict,* B1513.

nīðsynn f. *grievous sin,* Sat 180.

nīððas† mpl. *men.*

nīðweorc n. *battle,* †Chr 973.

nīðwracu† f. *severe punishment.*

nīðwundor n. *dire wonder, portent,* B1365.

nīwan (ēo) adv. *newly, lately,* Æ,AO.

nīwanācenned *new-born,* MH 170¹².

nīwancumen (WW)=nīwcumen

nīwane=nīwan

nīwbacen (nīg-) *newly baked,* Jos 9¹².

nīwcend *new-born,* BH 144²³ (nīc-).

nīwcilct *newly whitewashed,* AO 286³⁰.

nīwcumen (nī(g)-) *new-comer, neophyte,* RB.

nīwe (ēo, īe) I. (nīg-, nī-, in compounds) adj. 'new', *fresh, recent, novel, unheard of, untried, inexperienced,* Æ,AO; CP. nīwan *stefne again.* II. adv. (Bl)=nīwan. ['new']

nīwel=neowol

nīwerne (ȳ) *tender,* ÆH 1·566⁵.

nīwesēoða=newesēoða

nīwian *to renew, restore,* Chr,El,Lcd. ['new']

nīwiht=nāht

nīwlic (ȳ) *fresh.* adv. -līce *lately, recently,* Æ,AO,Ps. ['newly']

nīwlinga (ēo) *anew,* GD 266²⁸. ·

nīwnes (ēo, īo) f. 'newness,' *novelty,* BH, Lcd.

nīwol=neowol

nīwtyrwed *newly tarred,* B295.

nīwung f. *rudiment,* OEG 914.

nīwunga (eo) adv. *newly, anew,* An,NG.

nixtnig (RB 138³)=nihstig

nō (CP)=nā

noctern n? n? *nocturn* (religious service), CM 220⁵⁶¹. [L.]

+nōg, +nōh I. adj. 'enough,' *sufficient, abundant,* An,Bo,RB; CP : *much, many.* II. adv. *sufficiently,* Bo : *fully, quite, abundantly,* Bo.

+nōgian *to be abundant,* NC 345.

nōh-=nāh-

nolde (Æ) v. *nyllan and 'will.'

nom pret. 3 sg. of niman.

nom-, nome-=nam-

non m. *title of senior monks,* RB.

nōn fn (m. RB 73¹⁴) *the ninth hour* (=3 p.m.), B,BH,Lcd : *nones* (service held at the ninth hour), RB,WW. tō nōnes *till three o'clock.* ['noon'; L. nona (hora)]

nōnbelle f. *noon-bell,* LL (436').

nōngereord n. *meal after nones, dinner,* RB 74⁸.

nōnhring m. *ringing of the noon-bell,* TF 114¹⁴.

nōnmete m. *afternoon meal, Sol,WW.*
['*noonmeat*']
nonne=nunne
nōnsang m. *service at* 3 *p.m., nones,* ÆP.
nōntīd f. *ninth hour,* Æ,*Bl.* ['*noontide*']
nōntīma m. *ninth hour,* Btk 216³¹.
norð I. adj. comp. norð(er)ra, superl.
norðmest *northern,* AO. II. adv. comp.
norðor *northwards, Chr,Met* : *in the north,*
'*north,*' *AO,B,Bl.*
norðan adv. *from the north,* AO. be...
norðan prep. (w. d.) *north of,* AO.
norðanēastan adv. *from the north-east,
north-easterly,* AO.
norðanēastanwind m. *north-east wind,* WW.
Norð(an)hymbre mp. *Northumbrians, Chr* :
Northumbria. ['*Northumber*']
norðanweard *northward,* Bl,Chr.
norðanwestan adv. *from the north-west,
north-westerly,* AO.
norðanwestanwind m. *north-west wind,* WW
8¹⁰.
norðanwind m. *north wind,* Bo,WW.
norðdǣl m. *north quarter, northern part,
north,* Æ,*AO,Chr.* ['*northdeal*']
norðduru f. *north door,* Bl 203.
norðēast m. (and adv.) '*north-east,*' BC,
Chr.
norðēastende m. *north-east end,* AO 14¹⁴.
norðēasthyrne f. *north-east corner,* LV 71.
norðēastlang *extending north-eastwards,* AO.
norðēastrodor m. *north-east quarter,* BH
424²⁰.
norðefes f. *northern border,* KC 5·221².
norðemest=norðmest
norðende m. *northern quarter,* Chr,Met.
norðerne '*northern,*' *Northumbrian, Scan-
dinavian,* Æ,*Chr,Met.*
norðerra (*BC,Chr*) comp. adj. v. norð.
['*norther*']
norðeweard adj. *northward, north,* AO.
norðfolc n. *northern folk* : *people of Nor-
folk.*
norðgemǣre n. *northern limit,* AO 10'.
norðheald *inclined northwards,* BC 2·246'.
norðhealf f. *north side, north,* AO,*Bl.*
['*northhalf*']
norðhere m. *army from the north,* Chr 910A.
norðhylde f. *north slope,* KC 3·418'.
Norðhymbre=(1) Norðanhymbre; (2)
Norðhymbrisc
Norðhymbrisc *Northumbrian,* Æ (SR 15⁵⁸).
norðhyrne f. *north corner,* KC 3·449²⁰.
norðland n. *northern land or shore,* AO,*Chr.*
['*northland*']
norðlang *north-along,* KC.
norðlanu f. *north lane,* Ct.
norðlēode mp. *northern folk, Angles,* LL.
norðlic *northern,* WW 361¹.

Norðmann m. *dweller in the north, Scandi-
navian,* Æ,*AO,Chr.* ['*Northman*']
norðmest (*AO,Met*) superl. of norð adj. and
adv. ['*northmost*']
norðor (*AO*) v. norð. ['*norther*']
norðportic m. *north porch,* BH 106².
norðra v. norð.
norðrihte (y; AO 17), -rihtes (KC 3·450⁵)
direct northwards, due north.
norðrodor m. *northern sky,* Gu 1253.
norðryhte=norðrihte
norðsǣ f. *northern sea, Bristol Channel,
Chr* : *Baltic,* '*North Sea,*' Æ.
norðscēata m. *northern point, promontory,*
AO 28³.
norðsciphere m. *Danish fleet,* Chr 980c.
norððēod f. *northern people,* BH 50¹².
norððunor m. *thunder from the north,* ES
39·351.
Norð-wēalas, -wālas mp. *North Welsh (i.e.
not Cornish)* : *Wales.*
Norðwēalcynn n. *inhabitants of* (*North*)
Wales, Chr.
norðweard adj. and adv. *north,* '*northward,*'
Chr; AO.
norðweardes adv. '*northwards,*' *Chr.*
norðweg m. *a way leading northwards,* Ex
68 : *Norway.*
norðwest adv. '*north-west,*' *AO,BC.*
norðwestende m. *north-west end,* AO.
norðwestgemǣre m. *north-west boundary,*
AO 8³¹.
norðwind m. *north wind,* WW 378⁸.
nōse† f. *ness, promontory,* B.
nosgrisele (WW 427)=nosugrisle
nosle (*WW* 153)=nostle
nostle f. *fillet, band,* CP,WW. ['*nostel*']
nos-ðirl, -ðyr(e)l, -terl (*WW*) n. '*nostril,*'
Æ,*Lcd.*
nosu f. gds. nosa, nose '*nose,*' Æ,*Chr,
CP.
nosugrisle f. *nose-gristle,* WW 290³⁰.
nōt m. *mark, note,* Bf 182²⁴. [L. *nota*]
nōtere m. *scribe, writer,* OEG 2846. [L.]
nōteðæshwōn=nāteshwōn
notgeorn *industrious,* W 72⁹. [nēotan]
±notian I. *to enjoy* : *use, employ,* Bo,RB,
WW; Æ,CP : *discharge an office.* ['*note*']
II. (+) *note,* Mt p 12².
notu f. *enjoyment, use, advantage, utility,*
AO,RB : *employment, office, discharge of a
duty,* Æ,*RB;* CP. ['*note*'; nēotan]
notwierðe (u²) *useful,* ANS 129·18.
notwrītere m. *one who makes notes, scribe,*
WW 451³⁵.
nōð† f. *daring, boldness* : *booty, plunder*
(GK), Wh 28?
nōðer (*CP*)=nāhwæðer. ['*nother*']
nōwend m. *shipmaster, sailor,* OEG.

nōwēr=nāhwēr

nōwiht (CP,VPs) (u², y²)=nāht. ['nought']

nōwðer (BC)=nāhwæðer. ['nouther']

nū I. adv. 'now,' at present, at this time, immediately, Æ,AO,Bl,VPs; CP : very recently, Bf,Bo : introducing commands, requests (Bl,Cr,Ps) and arguments (Æ,Bo, CP). nū gēn still. nū ʒīet as yet, still. nū ðā now, already, Æ ('nowthe'). II. conj. now that, inasmuch as, because, since, when, Bl,Bo,VPs; AO,CP. III. interj. lo! behold! come! Æ. nū lā now.

+nugan* swv. impers. pres. 3 sg. +neah to suffice, not to lack.

nūhwīlum now-a-days, Bo 123⁶.

numen I. pp. of niman. II. 'vulsio,' MkL p 2¹⁷ (v. A 16·74).

numol (æ¹, e², u²) 'capax,' holding much, quick at learning, ÆGr,WW : 'mordax,' biting, CHRD 74²⁰. ['nimble']

nūna adv. now, WW 254²⁴.

nunfǣmne f. nun, GD 50,340. [v. 'nun']

nunhīred m. nunnery, TC 232⁶.

nunlīf n. life of a nun, GD 199¹⁶.

nun(nan)mynster n. convent, nunnery, Ct, GD.

nunne f. 'nun,' Æ,BH : pagan priestess, vestal, AO.

nunscrūd n. nun's dress, TC 538¹².

nusēoða=neweseoða; nūðā v. nū.

nuton (DR)=nyton (v. nytan).

nybðe (VHy)=nymðe

+nycled (GL)=+cnycled

nȳd I.=nīed. II.=nēod

nȳd-=nēad-, nīed-

nȳdbebod n. command, CREAT 72.

nȳdboda m. messenger of evil? Ex 474.

nȳdbrice (ē) m. requirement, need, ÆH 2·144'.

nȳdbysgu f. toil, trouble, RIM 44.

nȳdbysig distressed, JUL 423.

nȳdcleofa† m. prison, EL, JUL.

nȳdcosting f. affliction, Gu 1126.

nȳddǣda m. one who acts under compulsion, LL 36,26.

+nȳdenlic compulsory, BH 62²³B.

nȳdfara m. fugitive, exile, Ex 208.

nȳdgedāl† n. forced dissolution, death, Gu.

nȳdgenga m. wretched wanderer, DA 633.

nȳdgestealla m. comrade in need, B 882.

nȳdgewald m. tyranny, CR 1451.

nȳdgild n. exaction, tribute, W 162¹¹.

nȳdgrāp f. (RIM 73), nȳdgripe m. (B 976) coercive grip.

nȳdhǣmedre m. adulterer, OEG.

nȳdhǣmestre (ē) f. mistress? concubine? adulteress? OEG 4451.

nȳdhelp mf. help in trouble, LL (278²).

nȳdlic (ēo) necessary, Sc.

±nȳd-mǣg m., -māge f. blood-relation, cousin, LL.

nȳdmægen (ē¹) n. force, DR 117¹³.

nȳdnǣman to force, ravish, LL.

nȳdnes f. necessity, LL (158¹⁰).

nȳdnima (ē) m. one who takes by force, NG.

nȳdniman³ (ēa) to take by force, abduct, LL 360, 73, 2.

nȳdnimend (ē¹) f. rapine, MtR 23²⁵.

nȳdnimu (ē) f. rapine, forcible seizure, DR.

nȳdnimung f. rapine, abduction, WW 116²⁹.

nȳdriht n. duty, office : due, tribute, LL.

nȳdðēowetling m. bond-slave, TC 628¹³.

nȳdðēowigan to reduce to servitude, exact service from (an ecclesiastical establishment), LL 381,21.

nȳdwracu† f. violence, distress.

nȳdwrǣclīce violently, ÆL 23b⁴⁰⁴.

nȳdwyrhta m. involuntary agent, LL.

+nyhe=+neahhe

nȳhst=niehst; nyht=niht

+nyht fn. abundance, fulness, sufficiency, CP. [+nugan]

+nyhtful abundant, plentiful, WW 40³⁴.

+nyhtlīce abundantly, WW 3².

±nyhtsum abundant, abounding : (+) satisfied, contented. adv. -līce, VPs.

+nyhtsumian to suffice, abound, Æ.

+nyhtsumnes f. abundance, plenty, VPs.

+nyhtsumung (-ihð-) f. abundance, RPs 77²⁵.

+nyhð (W 1)6²¹)=+nyht?

nyllan* anv. pret. nolde to be unwilling, Æ, CP; AO : refuse, prevent, PPs 5⁸. ['NILL*'; ne, willan]

nyman=niman; -nyme v. fore-n.

nymne=nemne

nymðe (e, i) conj. unless, except : nor, EPs 130¹.

+nyp=+nip

nypel m. trunk (of an elephant), Æ (4²⁸⁶).

nȳr=nēar=nēah adv.

nyrgend=nergend; nyrðra=norðerra

±nyrwan v. nyrwian=nierwan

nyrwett=nirewett; nys=nis=ne is

nysse, nyste (Bo,Bl,VPs)=ne wisse, ne wiste v. nytan. ['nist']

nystlan=nistlan; nyt=(1) nytt; (2) nett

+nȳt fn. 3 sg. of +nīedan

nytan (e, i) anv. pres. 1, 3 sg. nāt, 2 nāst, pl. nyton, pret. nyste, nysse not to know, to be ignorant, Æ,AO,CP. [ne, witan]

nyten ignorant, ÆH 1·62¹⁴. [ne, witan]

nȳten (Lcd)=nīeten

nytende adv. ignorantly, Æ.

nytendnes=nytennes

nytenlic ignorant, ÆH 2·134².

nytennes (e, i) f. ignorance, laziness, ignominy, Æ : unknown state, ÆL 33²⁶⁰

nytlic *useful, profitable*, AA,LCD. [*Ger.* nützlich] adv. -līce.

nytlicnes f. *utility*, LCD 1·314[8].

nytnes f. *use, benefit, convenience*, BH,GD.

nyton v. nytan.

nytt I. f. *use, utility, advantage*, AO,CP : *duty, office, employment*, B : *supervision, care*, GD 180[28]. **II.** adj. *useful, beneficial, helpful, profitable*, AO,CP. [nēotan]

nytte=nette

±**nyttian** *to enjoy, use*, Lcd : *eat*. ['*nutte*']

nyttnes=nytnes

nytto=nytt I.

nyttol *useful*, LCD 32b.

nyttung (i) f. *profit, advantage*, WW 116[37].

nytu (*MtR* 7[16])=hnutu

nytun=nyton=ne witon

nytweorð-=nytwierð-

nyt-wierðe (CP), -wirðe, -wyrðe (Æ) *useful, profitable*.

nytwierðlic *useful, profitable*. adv. -līce, CP.

nytwierðnes (eo, y) f. *utility*, WW.

nytwurð-, nytwyrð-=nytwierð-

nyðan=neoðan

nyðe-, nyðer-=niðer-, niðr-; **nȳw-**=nīw-

nywel, nywol=neowol; **nȳxt**=nīehst

nyxtnig (LCD)=nihstig

O

o=on; **ō** (N)=ā; **ob**, ob- (K)=of, of-

obet (*Cp,Ep*)=ofet; **obst** (Cp 217 E)=ofost

oc=ac

ōc pret. 3 sg. of acan.

ōcon pret. pl. of acan.

ōcusta m. *armpit*, GL.

ōden (o?) f. *threshing-floor*, AS,Sc.

ōdencole *hollow serving as a threshing-floor*, EC 121[2].

+**ōdon**=+ēodon; **oe-**=a-, e-, ē-

oeg (N)=woeg=weg

ōeg-hwēr, -hwelc (Cp)=ǣg-hwǣr, -hwilc

oeht- (N)=ēht-; **oembeht** (Cp)=ambiht

oemseten (=ymb-) f. *shoot, slip?* (Swt), *row (of vines)?* (BT), Cp 534A.

oexen=exen v. oxa.

of I. prep. w. d. '*OF*,' *from, out of*, Æ,AO, etc. : *among, concerning, about*, AO : *by*, Chr : *derived from, made of, belonging to*, Æ,AO,CP. **II.** adv. '*off*,' *away, absent*, Bl, Chr,LL,Mt.

of-=æf-

ofācēapian *to buy off*, LL 122,74.

ofāceorfan[3] *to cut or prune off*, AO,CP.

ofācsian *to find out by asking, be informed, hear of, learn*, Æ.

ofādōn anv. *to pull out, tear out*, LL 86,70[74] : *leave out, except*, LL 182,10.

ofādrincan[3] *to drain*, Æ : *quench*, AO.

ofādrygan *to dry off, wipe off*, CP 71[11]

ofæt=ofet

ofǣte? f. *food*, HEX 194.

ofāhēawan[7] *to cut off*, ÆL 29[293].

ofāniman *to take away*, GUTH 19[26].

ofāsceacan[6] *to shake off*, CM 993 : *excuse*.

ofāsciran (e, y) *to cut off*, LL 68,35[5].

ofāsēoðan[2] *to purge, purify*, BH 288[9].

ofāslēan[6] *to smite off*, CHR.

ofāsnīdan *to cut off*, LCD.

ofātēon[2] *to pull out, withdraw*, CP.

ofāweorpan *to cast aside, throw off* (or ? two words), VH 17.

ofāxian (Æ)=ofācsian

ofbēatan[7] *to beat to death, kill*, AO.

ofblindian *to blind*, JnLR 12[40].

ofcalan[6] *to chill, make or grow cold*, Æ,W.

ofcliplan *to obtain by calling, call for*, Æ.

ofcuman[4] *to spring from, be derived from*, Æ.

ofcyrf m. *a section, cutting*, Æ : *amputation*, Æ.

ofdæl *inclined (downwards)*, Bo 53[14].

ofdæle (e[2]) n. *decline, declivity, descent, abyss*. CP.

ofdōn anv. *to put out, put off, take off (clothes)*.

ofdrǣdan[7] (but wk. pp. ofdrædd) *to fear, be afraid, terrified*, Æ,CP.

ofdrincan *to intoxicate*, LL.

ofdruncnian *to get drunk (on)*, CHRD 74[7].

ofdūne adv. *down*, AO,CP.

ofdūneheald adv. *directed downwards* (Swt).

ofdūneonwend *downwards*, GD 24[28].

ofdūnesettan *to set down*, VHy.

ofdūnestīgan[1] *to descend*, VPs.

ofdūneweard(es) adv. *downwards*, GD.

ofdūnrihte *downwards*, MFH 170.

ofe-=ufe-

ofearmian *to be pitiful*, RSPs 36[22],76[9].

ofearmung f. *compassion*, BLPs 102[4].

ofēhtan *to persecute*, RPs 43[17].

ofelēte=oflǣte

ofen m., gs. ofnes *furnace*, MH,MtLR : '*oven*,' Æ.

ofenan=ufenan

ofenbacen *baked in an oven*, Æ.

ofen-raca m., -racu f. *oven-rake*, WW.

ofer I. prep. [w. d. (rest) and a. (motion)] '*OVER*,' *beyond, above, upon, in, across, past*, Æ,AO,CP. ofer bæc *backwards, back* : *throughout* : *against, in contravention of, contrary to, beyond*, AO,CHR : *of* : (*time*) *after, through, during, at the end of*, AO, Chr : *more than* : *in addition to, besides, beyond*. **II.** adv. *above, on high* : *to or on the other side*, AO : *from side to side, across*, AO : *beyond, above* (quantity).

ōfer (o²) m. (gs. ōfres) *border, margin, edge* : *brink, river-bank, sea-shore,* Æ,B,Lcd; AO. ['*over*'; v. Mdf]

oferǣt m. *gluttony, feasting, excess, CP*; Æ : *feast.* ['*overeat*']

oferǣte *gluttonous,* RB17¹⁵.

oferāhebban=oferhebban

oferāwrit-=oferwrit-

oferbǣcgetðung f. *tetanus,* WW112²⁰.

oferbebēodan² *to rule,* WW178³⁷.

oferbecuman⁴ *to supervene,* CM133,1060.

ofer-bēon anv. pres. 3 pl. -sind *to be over, command,* CM112; WW178³⁷.

oferbīdan¹ *to outlast, outlive, TC.* ['*over-bide*']

oferbiternes (y³) f. *excessive bitterness, SPs.* ['*overbitterness*']

oferblica m. *surface,* OET181⁴⁴.

oferblīðe *too light-hearted,* CP.

oferbrǣdan *to spread over, suffuse, be spread over, overshadow, cover over, CP*; Æ. ['*overbrede*']

oferbrǣdels m. *outside, surface, covering* : *coverlet, veil, garment,* Æ,CP : *cerecloth,* MFH153.

oferbrǣw m. *eye-brow,* LCD3·188⁵. [brǣw]

oferbrecan⁴ *to transgress, violate,* AO.

oferbrēdan=oferbregdan

oferbrǣdels (KGL)=oferbrǣdels

oferbregdan³ *to draw over, cover, overspread* : *be covered over, show a film over.*

oferbrū f. *eye-brow,* GL.

oferbrycgian (i³) *to span as by a bridge,* Æ. ['*overbridge*']

ofercæfed *overlaid with ornament,* GPH394.

oferceald *excessively cold, Run*11. ['*overcold*']

ofercīdan *to chide sharply,* EPs,LL.

ofercīdung f. *chiding, reproof,* EPs149⁷.

ofercierr (e) m. *passing over,* MtL1¹¹.

ofercierran (e) *to cross over,* LkL16²⁶.

oferclif n. *steep place, overhanging cliff,* WW480².

oferclimban³ *to climb over, AO*134¹³. ['*over-climb*']

oferclipian *to cry out,* LkL23¹⁸.

ofercostung f. *great tribulation,* JnL16³³.

ofercræft m. *fraud,* LL(166²⁰).

ofercuman⁴ *to overcome, subdue, compel, conquer, AO,B,Lcd,WW*; CP : *obtain, attain, reach, overtake, BH,Cp.Jud,WW.* ['*overcome*']

ofercwealm *great mortality,* A3·113.

ofercyme m. *arrival,* BH436²⁰.

ofercymend (mm) m. *assailant,* LkL.

ofercyðan *to outdo by preponderance of oaths,* v. LL2·689.

oferdōn anv. *to '*overdo,' *do to excess,* Æ. oferdōne ðing *excesses,* Æ.

oferdrenc (Æ)=oferdrync

oferdrencan *to make drunk,* AO,CP : *give copiously to drink,* GEN43³⁴.

oferdrīfan¹ *to overcome, defeat, dispense, Æ, DR* : *confute, Æ* : *cover (by drifting sand),* AO40¹ : *outvote,* LL. ['*overdrive*']

oferdrinc=oferdrync

oferdrincan³ *to drink too much, get drunk, CP,LL.* ['*overdrink*']

oferdrincere m. *drunkard,* HL12⁹⁵,¹²⁴.

oferdruncen I. n. *drunkenness,* LL. **II.** ptc. *drunk.*

oferdruncennes f. *drunkenness,* Æ,CP.

oferdrync m. *over-drinking, drunkenness, CP* : *revelry, feasting.* ['*overdrink*']

oferdyre n. *lintel,* WW280¹⁶.

ofere *over, across,* v. LV8 : *from above,* RPs.

oferēaca m. *surplus, overplus, remainder, addition, increase,* Æ.

ofereald (y) *very old,* RB61¹².

oferealdormann m. *chief officer,* BH264¹ (v.l.).

ofereall *anywhere,* BF138²¹.

oferēca=ofereaca

ofereldu (HL11⁶⁰N)=oferyldu

oferēt=oferǣt

ofer-etol (CP), -eotol, -ettol *gluttonous.*

oferetolnes f. *gluttony,* CP317¹⁸.

oferfær n. *passing over,* NG.

oferfæreld n. *passage, journey over or across,* Æ,AO.

oferfǣt *too fat,* WW. ['*overfat*']

oferfæðman† *to envelop, overshadow.*

oferfaran⁶ (intr.) *to pass, cross, go over, Ps* : (tr.) *traverse, go through, penetrate, Gen,W*; Æ,AO : *come across, meet with, overtake* : *pass through, withstand, overcome.* ['*over-fare*']

oferfeallan⁷ *to attack,* BL203.

oferfeng I. m. *fibula, buckle, clasp,* GL. **II.** pret. 3 sg. of oferfōn.

oferfeohtan³ *to conquer,* Æ,CP.

oferfēran *to traverse, cross, pass along, over, by, or through,* Æ,AO : *come upon, meet with.*

oferferian *to carry over, transport,* OEG3680.

oferfērnes f. *fordable place,* BH58¹.

oferfēðre *overloaded,* v. ES43·312.

oferfil=oferfyll

oferflēdan *to overflow, flood,* LCD3·252'.

oferflēde *in flood,* LCD3·252'.

oferflēon² *to fly over, Æ* : *flee from, yield to,* B2525.

oferflēwednes=oferflōwednes

oferflītan¹ *to overcome, beat, confute,* AO.

oferflōwan *to flow over, run over, '*overflow,' *AO,Lk.*

ofer-flōwed(līc)nes, -flōwen(d)nes (Æ) f. *excess, superfluity.*

ofer-flōwend (*RB*), -flōwe(n)dlic *superfluous* : *excessive*, VH 17. [*'overflowing'*] adv -līce. .

oferflōwnes f. *superfluity*, CP.

oferfōn[7] *to seize, take prisoner*, AO.

oferfrēcednes f. *oppression*, V²Ps 31⁷.

oferfroren *frozen over*, AO.

oferfull *too full*, LPs. [*'overfull'*]

oferfunden *tested*, AO 296⁹.

oferfundennes f. *trial, experiment*, OEG 543.

oferfylgan *to pursue, attack*, CP.

ofer-fyll, -fyllo, -fyllu f. *surfeit, gluttony, excess*, Bo,Lcd; Æ,CP : *overplus, resulting liquor*, LCD 47a. [*'overfyll'*]

oferfyllan *to cram*, RB,WW.

oferfylnes f. *surfeit, excess*, GD 339³.

oferfyrr f. *excessive distance*, AO 24²¹. [feorr]

ofergǣgan *to transgress*, Æ.

ofergǣgednes f. *transgression*, Æ.

ofergǣgend m. *transgressor*, ÆL 30⁴¹¹.

ofer-gān anv., -gangan⁷ *to pass over, beyond, across, traverse, cross*, Æ,Lcd,VPs; AO, CP : *transgress, overstep*, Met, MtL, Ps : *overrun, overcome, overspread, conquer*, Chr,Ex,Lcd,Rd; Æ : *come upon, overtake, seize, attack*, Æ,An : *pass off, pass away, end*, AO,CP : *overreach*, CHRD 110³⁴. [*'overgo,' 'overgang'*]

ofergaplan *to be forgetful of, neglect*, RB 112².

ofergēare *old*, LCD 19a.

ofergeatu f. *oblivion*, PPs 128⁶.

ofergeatul=ofergitol

ofergedrync n. *excess in drinking*, BL 99²¹.

ofergedyre=oferdyre

ofergemet I. n. *excess*, AS,CP. II. *excessive*, VH 17 (or ? two words).

ofergēmnes f. *watching for*, NG. [gīeman]

ofergenga m. *traveller*, LCD.

ofergenihtsumian *to superabound*, Sc 131¹⁵.

ofergeong (=gang) m. *going across*, MtK p 12¹³.

ofergeot-=ofergi(e)t-

ofergēotan² *to pour upon, suffuse, flood, overwhelm*, Æ.

ofergeotende *forgetful*, BH 114²². [ofergietan]

ofer-geotol, -geottol=ofergitol

ofergesāwan=ofersāwan

ofergesettan *to set over*, CP,VPs.

ofergestondan⁶ (=a⁴) *to stand over*, BH.

ofergetilian *to overcome*, ÆL 23b¹⁸⁵.

ofergetimbran *to erect*, BL 205.

ofergetol-=ofergitol-

ofergeðyld *intolerable state*, SOL 84²⁴.

ofergeweorc n. *superstructure : sepulchre*, Æ.

ofergewrit n. *superscription, inscription*, G, WW.

ofergietan⁵ *to forget, disregard, neglect*, CP.

ofergīfre *gluttonous*, CP 177,308.

ofergildan=ofergyldan

ofergīman *to neglect, disregard*, RB,SAT.

ofergitan=ofergietan

ofer-gitol, -gittol (ea, eo, y) *forgetful*, Ps.

ofergitolian (e, eo) *to forget*, JVPs.

ofergitolnes (e, eo, y) f. *forgetfulness*, BL,Ps.

oferglenged (æ³) *over-adorned*, ÆPD 134¹¹.

oferglēsan (oe) *to write glosses over*, Jn p 188⁷.

oferglīdan¹ *to glide over, traverse, pass over, overshadow*, Æ.

ofergrǣdig *too covetous*, W. [*'overgreedy'*]

ofergrōwan⁷ *to overgrow*, CP 336⁸.

ofergumian *to neglect, disregard*, RB 113².

ofergyld *gilt*, Æ.

ofergyldan (i) *to encase, overlay or adorn with gold*, Æ,CP.

ofergylden *overlaid with gold*, LL 460,10.

ofergȳman=ofergīman

ofergyrd ptc. *girt*, GPH 394.

ofergytan=ofergietan

ofergytnes f. *oblivion, forgetfulness*, LkR, PPs.

oferhacele f. *hood*, LL (140²²).

oferhangen *covered*, GD 202¹⁹.

oferhāt *over-hot*, LCD 4a.

oferhēafod adv. *in each case*, ÆH 1·30⁴.

oferhēah *very tall, lofty*, Run 26. [*'overhigh'*]

oferhealdan *to overcome, overtake*, VH : *'supertenere,'* LL (198¹¹)?

oferhealfhēafod n. *crown of the head*, WW 156¹¹.

oferheargian=oferhergan

oferhebban⁶ *to pass over, omit, neglect*, AO, LL; CP. [*'overheave'*]

oferhebbendlic *highly exalted*, DR.

oferhelian *to cover over, conceal*, Sc; CP. [*'overhele'*]

oferheling f. *covering*, Sc. [v. *'overhele'*]

oferhelmian *to overshadow*, B 1364.

oferheortnes f. *vehemence of feeling*, AO 166²⁰.

oferhergean *to overrun, ravage*, AO,CHR.

oferhīd-=oferhygd-

oferhīeran (ēo, ȳ) *to overhear,' hear*, AO : *disobey, disregard, neglect*, AO.

oferhīernes (ē, ī, ȳ) f. *neglect, disobedience : fine for transgression of law or legal orders* (=*'superauditio'*), LL.

oferhīgd=oferhygd

oferhige? m. *pride*, PPs 87⁷. [hyge]

oferhigendlīce *daringly, presumptuously*, BYH 102¹⁶.

oferhigian *to delude, turn the head of*, B 2766.

oferhīran (AO)=oferhīeran

oferhīwian *to transfigure : paint over*, NG.

oferhlæstan *to overload*, AO.

oferhlēapan⁷ *to jump over, surmount, overcome*, BH : *pass over*, Lcd. [*'overleap'*] oferhlēapend m. *over-leaper*, WW 190².

oferhlēoŏrian *to surpass in loudness*, AA, SOL 152¹².

oferhlēoŏur *failing to hear*, PPs 93⁹.

oferhlīfan¹ (OEG), oferhlīfian (Æ,CP) *to tower over, overtop, excel, exceed, surpass*.

oferhlīfung f. *loftiness, sublimity*, GL.

ofer-hlūd, -hlȳde *clamorous, noisy*, WW. ['*overloud*'] adv. -hlūde.

oferhlȳp m. *a jump, leap (over something)*, BF 72,112.

oferhlyttrian *to clarify, strain*, ÆGR 222⁶.

oferhoga m. *despiser, proud man*, W.

oferhogian *to despise*, Bl,Bo. ['*overhow*']

oferhogiend m. *despiser*, RB 48⁶.

oferhogodnes f. *pride, disdain*, GD 144³.

oferholt n. *phalanx of shields*, Ex 157.

oferhrǣgan (w. d.) *to tower above?* SOL 35.

oferhrēfan *to roof over, cover*, BL,LCD.

oferhrēred *overthrown*, WW.

oferhrops *greediness*, WW 102¹⁹.

oferhrȳfan = oferhrēfan

oferhrȳred = oferhrēred

oferhycgean *to despise*, AO,CP.

oferhȳd = oferhygd

oferhygd (i) I. fn. *pride, conceit, arrogance*, CP : *highmindedness*, AS. II. adj. *haughty, proud*.

oferhygdgian *to be proud*, CVPs 9²³.

oferhygdig I. n. *pride*, MFH,PPs. II. adj. *haughty, proud*, Æ.

ofer-hygd(ig)līce, -hīdlīce *arrogantly*, GD.

oferhygdnes f. *excessive pride, arrogance*, VH 18.

oferhygdu. = oferhygd I.

oferhylmend m. *dissembler*, PPs 118¹¹⁹.

oferhȳran = oferhīeran

oferhȳre *heedless, neglectful*, LL (244').

oferhyrned *having horns above*, RUN 2.

oferhȳrnes f. *heedlessness, neglect, disobedience*, LL.

+oferian *to elevate*, HGL 428 (= uferian).

oferīdyllīce *vainly, emptily*, CPs 30⁷.

ofering f. *superabundance*, Bo.

oferlād f. '*translatio*,' *solemn removal of the body or relics of a saint to a shrine*, DR 62⁹.

oferlǣdan *to oppress*, Bl : *translate*. ['*overlead*']

oferlǣfan *to leave over : be left over, remain*, LkLR. ['*overleave*']

oferlagu f. *cloak*, GL.

oferlecgan *to place over*, CM 899 : *overburden, surfeit*, HL 11⁹⁹; 12⁷³.

oferlēof *very dear*, RUN 23.

oferlēoran *to pass over, or by : transgress, prevaricate*.

oferlēornes f. *transgression*, CPs 100³.

oferlibban *to survive*. ÆGr,TC. ['*overlive*']

oferlīce *excessively*, W. [v. '*overly*']

oferlīfa (y³) m. *excess*, NC 348.

oferlīfian = oferhlīfian

oferlīhtan *to light upon*, ÆL 23b⁵⁵⁸ : *excel in brightness*.

oferlīŏan¹ *to pass over, sail over*, GUTH,MH.

oferlufu f. *too great love*, W. ['*overlove*']

oferlyfa = oferlifa

oferlyftlic *above the air*, NC 314.

ofermǣcga m. *very illustrious being*, GU 664.

ofermægen† n. *overpowering might*.

ofermǣstan *to over-fatten*, BH (Wheloc 228').

ofermǣte *excessive, immoderate*, AO,CP. ['*overmete*']

ofermǣtlic *vast*, AO 52¹⁰.

ofermǣto = ofermětto

ofermagan swv. *to prevail*, Sc 97¹⁹.

ofermāŏum m. *costly treasure*, B 2993.

ofermearcung (e³) f. *superscription*, MkL p 5¹.

ofermēde I. n. *pride*, CP. II. adj. *proud, arrogant*. [mōd]

ofermēdla m. *haughtiness, pride*, LL.

ofermēdu (CP) = ofermētto

ofermete m. *gorging, gluttony*, CP.

ofermětto f. (often in pl.) *pride*, Æ,AO, CP.

ofermicel *over-much, excessive*, AO,RB. ['*overmickle*']

ofermicelnes f. *excess*, Sc 50¹³.

ofermōd I. n. *pride, insolence*, Gen,Ma. ['*overmod*'] II. adj. *proud, overbearing, insolent*, Bl; Æ,CP.

ofer-mōdgian (CP), -mōdig(i)an *to be proud, arrogant*.

ofermōdgung f. *pride*, CP 109¹¹.

ofermōdig *proud, arrogant*, Lcd; AO. adv. -līce. [v. '*overmod*']

ofermōdignes f. *pride, haughtiness, arrogance*, Mk. [v. '*overmod*']

ofermōdlic *proud, haughty, insolent*, CP. adv. -līce.

ofermōdnes = ofermōdignes

ofernēod f. (ī³) *extreme need*, LL,W. II. *very necessary*, CM.

oferniman⁴ (y) *to take away, carry off, seize, ravish : come over*, BH 410B¹².

ofernōn fn. *afternoon (after 3.0 p.m.)*, WW 175⁴⁷.

oferorn = oferarn pret. 3 sg. of oferyrnan.

oferprūt I. '*over-proud*,' *presumptuous, arrogant, haughty*, Sc. II. f. *excessive pride*, W 81'.

oferrǣdan *to read over*, Æ : *consider, infer*. ['*overread*']

oferranc *too luxurious*, W 46¹. ['*overrank*']

oferreccan *to confute, convince, convict*, CP.

oferrencu f. *extravagance*, W 46².

oferrīcsian *to rule over*, CP 119¹⁹.

oferrīdan[1] *to ride across,* BH 196[8]. ['*over-ride*']

oferrōwan[7] *to row over,* Æ.

ofersǣlic *on the other side of the sea,* BH 246[3].

ofersǣlig *excessively happy,* DD 246.

ofersǣlð f. *excessive pleasure,* MET 5[27].

ofersǣwisc *from across the sea, foreign,* LCD, MH.

ofersāwan[7] *to sow* (*over*), Mt 13[25]. ['*over-sow*']

oferscēadan[7] *to scatter over, sprinkle over,* LCD 67b.

ofer-sceadian (CP), -sceadewian *to over-shadow.*

ofersceatt m. *usury, interest,* MtR 25[27].

oferscēawian *to superintend,* LL.

oferscēawigend m. *overseer, bishop,* LL.

oferscīnan[1] *to illuminate,* BF, BL : *excel* (*in brightness*), ByH 112'.

oferscūwian *to overshadow,* MtR 17[5].

ofersēam m. *bag,* LkL 12[33].

ofersēcan *to overtax,* B 2686.

ofersegl m. *top-sail,* WW 7[4].

oferseglian *to sail across,* Mt. ['*oversail*']

ofersēgon=ofersāwon pret. pl. of ofersēon.

ofersendan *to transmit,* ÆGR 172[13].

ofersēocnes f. *great illness,* LL.

oferseolfrian (y) *to cover over with silver,* AO.

ofersēon[5] *to see over, overlook, survey, observe, see,* Bo : *despise, neglect,* W. ['*over-see*']

ofersettan *to set over,* VPs : *overcome,* GD 347[30].

ofersittan[5] *occupy, possess,* Bo, VPs : *forbear, desist, refrain from,* Æ, B. ['*oversit*']

oferslǣge=oferslege

oferslǣp m. *too much sleep,* LCD 1·342[13].

oferslēan[6] *to subdue, overcome,* RB 32[15].

oferslege n. *lintel,* Æ, BF.

oferslop n. *loose upper garment, surplice, stole,* Lcd, LkL. ['*overslop*']

oferslype m. *over-garment, surplice,* Æ.

ofersmēaung f. *too exhaustive consideration,* CP 97[17].

ofersmītan *to smear over,* LCD 67b.

ofersprǣc f. *loquacity,* CP.

ofersprǣce *talkative, tale-bearing,* Æ, CP.

ofersprǣdan *to overlay, cover,* RB 84[23].

oferspreca m. *one who talks too much,* OEG 28[9].

ofersprecan[5] *to say too much,* LPs : *be abusive.*

ofersprēce=ofersprǣce

ofersprecol *talking too much, tattling, indiscreet,* CP.

ofersprecolnes f. *talkativeness,* CP 308[16].

oferstǣlan *to confute, convict, convince,* Æ, CP.

oferstæppan[6] *to* '*over-step,*' *cross,* LPs : *exceed,* KC.

oferstandan[6] *to stand over,* BH 308[25].

ofersteall m. *opposition,* ÆH 1·534[20].

oferstealla m. *survivor,* MH 210[28].

oferstellan *to jump over,* BH 400[22].

ofersteppan=oferstæppan

oferstīgan[1] *to climb over, mount, scale, surmount, overcome,* AO; Æ, CP : *surpass, excel, exceed,* BH; Æ, CP. ['*oversty*']

oferstige m. *astonishment,* ÆL 23[555].

oferstīgendlic *superlative,* ÆGR 15[18].

oferstīgennes *passing over,* OEG 405.

oferswimman[3] *to swim over or across,* B 2367. ['*overswim*']

oferswingan[3] '*transverberare*'! GD 344[33].

oferswīðan (ȳ) wv. and sv[1] *to overpower, overcome, conquer, vanquish,* Æ, AO, CP : *excel, surpass.*

oferswīðe adv. *over-much, excessively,* Chr. ['*overswithe*']

oferswīðend m. *vanquisher,* ÆL 30[126].

oferswīðestre f. '*victrix,*' WW 224[39].

oferswīðnes f. *pressure, distress,* NG.

oferswīðrian *to prevail, conquer,* LPs, RB.

oferswīðung f. *pressure, distress,* NG.

oferswōgan[7] *to cover, choke,* BL 203[9].

oferswȳðan=oferswīðan

ofersylfrian (AO)=oferseolfrian

ofersȳman (=īe) *to overload, oppress,* RB.

ofertæl n. *odd number,* LCD 1·288[8].

ofertǣle *superstitious,* Sc 218[10].

ofertalian *to confute, convince,* RWH 3[28].

oferteldan[3] *to cover over,* Ex 81.

ofertēon[2] *to draw over, cover,* Æ : *finish,* WW 209[35].

ofertogennes f. *the condition of being covered.*

ofertrahtnian *to treat of,* ÆH 1·202'.

ofertredan *to tread down,* GPH. ['*over-tread*']

ofertrūwa m. *over-confidence,* LL 180,8[7]. ['*overtrow*']

ofertrūwian *to trust too much,* CP, W.

oferðearf f. *great need, extreme distress,* W.

oferðearfa m. *one in great need,* CR 153.

oferðeccan *to cover over, hide,* Æ.

oferðencan *to think over, reflect,* GD.

oferðēon[1, 3] *to excel, surpass,* Æ, CP.

oferðōht *thought over, considered,* GD 316[20].

oferðrēawian (ā[3]) '*increpare,*' EPs 67[31].

oferðryccednes (i) f. *pressure,* CPs 31[7].

oferðrymm m. *excessive power,* DD 52.

oferufa *upon, above,* NG.

oferwacian *to watch over,* Æ. ['*overwake*']

oferwadan[6] *to wade across,* AO 72[33]. ['*over-wade*']

oferwealdan[7] *to get the better of,* LL 454,7.

oferwealdend m. *over-lord, ruler,* EL 1236.

oferweaxan[6] *to overgrow, overspread,* Æ, Bl. ['*overwax*']

oferweder n. *storm, tempest,* CHR 794 E.

oferwelig *very rich*, NC314.

oferwenian *to be proud, become insolent or presumptuous*, Sc,Gl.

oferweorc n. *sarcophagus, tomb*, Æ,OEG. ['*overwork*']

oferweorpan[3] *to throw over, overthrow*, CP, Lcd : *throw down, assault*, LL56,11[1] : *cast something over another, sprinkle : stumble?* B1543. ['*overwarp*']

oferwīgan *to overcome*, Sol299.

oferwillan[7] *to boil down : boil over*, Lcd. [weallan]

oferwinnan[3] *to contend with, overcome, subdue*, Æ,AO; CP. ['*overwin*']

oferwintran *to go through the winter*, WW 97[11]. ['*overwinter*']

oferwist f. *gluttony, excess*, CP,LL.

oferwistlic *supersubstantial*, MtL6[11].

oferwlencan *to be very wealthy*, AO44[12]. [wlanc]

oferwlencu f. *excessive riches*, Gu389.

oferwrecan[5] *to overwhelm*, WW35[14].

oferwrēon[1,2] *to cover over, conceal, hide*, VPs : *clothe*, Mt. ['*overwry*']

oferwrigels n. *covering*, Gl.

oferwrit n. *epistle*, MtLp10[1] : *superscription*, LkR23[38].

oferwriten *superscription*, Mtp12[2].

oferwrīðan *to wrap round*, Lcd49a.

oferwyllan=oferwillan

oferwyrcan *to cover over, overlay*, Sol; Æ, AO. ['*overwork*']

oferwyrðe *very worthy*, A11·171.

oferyld (W147[17])=oferyldu

oferyldu (=ie) f. *extreme old age*, MFH170.

oferyrnan[3] (=ie) *to go or run over*, Æ,Lcd : '*overrun*,' *cover over, overwhelm*, Æ,BH : *run past, cross.*

oferyð f. *overwhelming wave*, SPs54[25].

ofesc f. *border?* KC3·393[10].

ofest=efest, ofost

ofestan (e[1]) *to hasten*, RBL.

ofetrip? n. *harvest*, ZDPh36·550.

ofet(t) (æ) n. *fruit, legume*, Gen,Gl. ['*ovet*']

ofeweard=ufeweard; offǣran=āfǣran

offaran[6] *to intercept, overtake, fall upon, attack*, Æ,AO. hindan o. *to intercept from behind, cut off retreat*, AO.

offeallan[7] *to fall upon, cut off, kill, destroy, end*, Æ,Chr; AO : *fall away from, be lost to*, LL144,6. hine offēoll *committed suicide*, Chr962a. ['*offall*']

offellan=offyllan

offēran *to overtake (an enemy)*, Æ,Chr.

offerenda m. *psalm or anthem sung during the offertory*, ÆP168[15]; ANS84·5[29].

offerian *to carry off*, B1583.

offēstre f. *nurse not living in the house? foster-mother?* CC10[22].

offlēogan[3] *to fly away* (Swt).

±offrian *to 'offer,' sacrifice, bring an oblation*, Æ,AO,VPs; CP. [L. offerre]

offringclāð m. *offertory cloth*, NC314.

offringdagas mpl. *offering days*, OEG40[23].

offringdisc m. *offering-dish, paten*, Ct.

offringhlāf m. *shew-bread*, Mt12[4].

offringsang m. *hymn while an offering is made*, ÆH1·218[9]; ÆP214[23].

offringsceat m. *offering-napkin*, KC. [v. '*offering*']

offrung f. *presenting to God, oblation, sacrifice*, Æ,Mt : *thing presented, 'offering,'* Æ. [offrung- v. also offring-]

offrunghūs n. *house of sacrifice*, NC 314.

offrungspic n. *sacrificial bacon*, ÆL25[92].

offyligan *to follow up*, LkLR1[3].

offyllan (e;=ie) *to strike down, destroy, kill*, BH.

of-gān anv., pret. -ēode; -gangan[7] *to demand, require, exact, extort*, Æ : *attain, obtain, acquire, gain*, Æ : *start from, begin.* ['*ofgo*']

ofgangend-e, -lic *derivative*, ÆGr.

ofgefen (Cp)=ofgifen pp. of ofgiefan.

ofgeorn *elated*, HGl.

ofgēotan[2] *to moisten, soak, steep*, Æ : *quench*, Æ : *pour out*, JnL2[25].

ofgestīgnes f. *descent*, MtLp6[1].

ofgiefan[5] (i, y) *to give up, resign, leave, quit, desert*, AO. [giefan]

ofhabban *to hold back*, Ex9[3].

ofhæccan *to hack off*, LL.

ofhagian *to be inconvenient*, W275[5].

ofhealdan[7] *to withhold, retain*, Chr1035c. ['*ofhold*']

ofhearmian (impers.) *to cause grief*, Jud11[1].

ofhende *lost, absent*, Met25[34].

ofheran (RWH59[16])=ofhieran

ofhingrian (=y[2]) *to be hungry*, Æ(3[551]). ['*ofhungered*']

ofhnītan *to gore to death*, LL32,21.

ofhrēosan[2] *to overwhelm, cover over*, Æ : *fall down, fall headlong*, Æ.

ofhrēowan[2] *to cause or feel pity*, Æ. ['*arewe*']

ofhwylfan *to roll away*, ARHy2[12]. [v. '*whelve*']

ofhyrian *to imitate*, GD120[14].

ofirnan[3] *to overtake*, Æ,Bo : *tire with running*, Æ. ['*ofrun*']

oflǣtan[7] *to let go, lay aside, leave behind : let flow*, Bo66[29].

oflǣte (ā, ē) f. *oblation, offering*, Ps : *sacramental wafer*, Æ,Lcd. ['*oflete*'; L. oblata]

oflǣthlāf m. *bread used for the sacrament*, GD343[15].

oflangian *to long*, Æ. ['*oflonged*']

oflāte (VPs)=oflǣte

oflecgan *to lay down*, PPs 68[1].
oflēogan[2] *to lie, be false*, PPs 17[43].
oflēte=oflǣte
oflicgan[5] *to overlay (a child)*, LL. ['*oflie*']
oflician (w. d.) *to displease, be displeasing to*, Æ.
oflinnan[3] *to cease, stop*, BL 247[8] : *desist (from)*.
oflongian=oflangian
oflystan *to fill with desire, please*, Æ,Bo. pp. of-lysted, -lyst *desirous of, pleased with*. ['*oflust*']
ofmanian *to exact (a fine)*, LL 201,1.
ofmunan swv. *to remember, recollect*, CP.
ofmyrðrian *to murder*, CHR 979 E.
ofn=ofen
ofnēadian *to obtain by force, extort*, TC 295[22].
ofnet n? *closed vessel?* (BT), *small vessel?* LCD 11b. [ofn]
ofniman[4] *to fail*, LL (170[6]).
ofor=(1) eofor; (2) ufor; (3) ofer; **ōfor**=ōfer
ofost f. *haste, speed, zeal*, Æ. adv. -līce. on ofoste, of(e)stum *speedily, hastily*.
ofr (GL)=hofer
ofrǣcan *to reach, obtain*, LL 333 col 2. [v. '*ofreach*']
ōfres gs. of ōfer.
ofrian, ofrung (AO)=offrian, offrung
ofrīdan[1] *to overtake by riding, overtake*, Æ, Chr. ['*ofride*']
ofsacan[6] *to deny a charge*, LL 108B, n 5. ['*ofsake*']
ofscacan[6] *to shudder*, OEG 4160. [v.'*shake*']
ofsceamian (a) *to put to shame*, Æ,Bo. ['*ofshame*']
ofscēotan[2] *to shoot down, hit, kill*, Æ,AO, CP. pp. ofscoten *elf-struck (of cattle seized with sudden disease)*.
ofscleacnes (APs 43[22])=ofslegennes
ofscotian *to shoot down*, AO : *spear*, AA 23[11].
ofsendan *to summon*, Chr 1048. ['*ofsend*']
ofsēon[5] *to see, behold*, Æ. ['*ofsee*']
ofsetenes f. *siege*, WW 458[28] : *sitting down*, EPs 138[1] (ob-).
ofsetnian *to besiege*, NC 349.
ofsettan (æ) *to beset, oppress, afflict*, Hept, Lcd; Æ. ['*ofset*']
ofsettung f. *pressure*, Sc 143[5].
ofsittan[5] *to press down, repress, oppress*, Æ, CP : *occupy*, Hept,Bo; CP : *hedge in, compass about, besiege*. ['*ofsit*']
ofslēan[6] *to strike off or out, cut off, destroy* : *strike down, kill*, AO,BH,Lcd; Æ,CP. ['*ofslay*']
ofslegennes f. *slaughter*, JRVPs 43[22].
ofslītan[1] *to bite (of a serpent)*, NUM 21[9] (GR).
ofsmorian *to suffocate, strangle*, AO.
ofsnīðan[1] *to cut off, kill*, Æ.

ofsprǣc f. *locution, utterance*, HGL 460.
ofspring m. '*offspring*,' *descendants, posterity*, Æ,KC.
ofspyrian *to trace out*, LL 96,17.
ofst=ofost
ofstǣnan *to stone, kill*, APT 26[24].
ofstæppan[6] *to trample upon*, JOS 10[24].
ofstan=ofestan
ofstandan[6] *to remain, persist, continue*, Lcd; Æ : *restore, make restitution*. ['*ofstand*']
ofstede adv. *immediately*, Sc 193[12].
ofstende *hastening*, CM 186.
ofstician *to pierce, stab (to death), transfix*, AO.
ofstig *swift*, GPH 392.
ofstīgan *to descend*, NG : *ascend*, MtL : *depart*, MtL.
ofstingan[3] *to pierce, stab (to death)*, AO,Chr; Æ,CP. ['*ofsting*']
ofstint (=ofstent) pres. 3 sg. of ofstandan.
ofstlīce=ofostlīce
ofstofen *impelled*, PPs.
ofstum v. ofost.
ofswelgan[3] *to swallow up*, Bo 46[15]n.
ofswerian *to abjure, deny on oath*, LL.
ofswingan[3] *to scourge (to death)*, AO 154[8].
ofswȳðan (=ī) *to overcome*, LHY.
oft adv. comp. oftor, superl. oftost *often, frequently*, CP,G; Æ. oftost symle *continually*. o. and gelome *diligently*. ['*oft*']
oftacan[2] *to overtake*, NC 325.
oftalu f. *rejoinder, verdict against a claim*, TC 302[22] (v. LL 3·226).
oftēon[2] *to withhold, take away, withdraw*, Æ, CP.
oftfēðre *requiring many journeys to carry*, v. ES 43·312.
ofthrǣd-=oftrǣd-
oftige m. *withholding*, LL.
oftorflan *to stone to death*, Æ,AO.
oftrǣde *often or always available : frequent*, Bo 136[17].
oftrǣdlic *frequent*, AO. adv. -līce, CP.
oftredan[5] *to tread down, trample on*, Æ. ['*oftread*']
oftreddan *to tread to death*, AO 260[18]. ['*oftread*']
oftsīð m. *frequent occasion*, AO 290[29]. on oftsīðas *frequently*, CHR 979 C.
oftðwēal n. *frequent washing*, NC 314.
oftyrfan *to stone*, AO 172[28].
ofðǣnan *to be too moist*, LCD.
ofðe or, OEG 11[177] and n. [=oððe]
ofðecgan *to destroy*, GEN 2002.
ofðēflan *to dry up?* ÆL 34[144].
ofðencan *to recall to mind*, CP 349[10]; VH 18.
ofðennan=ofðǣnan
ofðincð pres. 3 sg. of ofðyncan.
ofðīnan *to be too moist*, HL 204[319].

of-ðreccan (KGL), -ðriccan=ofðryccan

ofðringan⁸ *to throng, press upon,* ÆH,Mk.

ofðryccan (e, i) *to press, squeeze,* Æ: *oppress, afflict, repress, destroy,* Æ: *occupy forcibly.*

ofðryc(oed)nes f. *trouble, oppression,* CP.

ofðryscan *to repress, subdue,* CP.

ofðrysm(l)an *to choke, stifle,* Mk4¹⁹. [ðrosm]

ofðylman *to choke, suffocate,* NC314.

ofðyncan (impers.) *to give offence, insult, vex, displease, weary, grieve,* Æ,AO,B,Bo, CP,LL. ['ofthink']

ofðyrstan *to suffer from thirst, be thirsty, thirst (for),* Hept,Soul; Æ. ['athirst,' 'of- thirst']

ofðȳstrian *to obscure,* SPs73²¹. [ðēostrian]

ofunnan swv. *to begrudge, deny, envy,* Æ, CP.

ofweard (MFH170)=æfweard

ofweorpan⁸ *to stone (to death), kill by a missile,* Æ,AO.

ofworplan *to kill (by stoning),* LL.

ofwundrian *to be astonished,* Æ.

ófȳrit (WW385³⁹)=āfȳred pp. of āfȳran.

öga m. *fear, terror, dread,* Æ: *terrible object,* Æ. [ege]

ögengel m. *bar, bolt,* WW459¹⁰.

ö-hilde (e², y²), -heald *sloping, inclined,* GL.

öhsta=ōcusta

öht I. f. *persecution, enmity.* öhte grettan *to profane,* GD235⁶. [FTP9,558] **II.**= āwuht

ohtrip v. ofetrip.

ö-hwǣr, -hwæðer=ā-hwǣr, -hwæðer

öhwanon=āhwonan; **öhylde**=öhilde

öl pret. 3 sg. of alan.

ölǣc-=ōlecc-

ölǣcung f. 'conspiratio,' OEG4955 (=ān-?).

olbend=olfend

±**öleccan** (æ, i) *to soothe, caress, flatter : please, charm, propitiate,* CP. [leccan]

öleccere, ōlecere m. *flatterer,* CP,WW.

öleccung (æ) f. *soothing, flattery, persuasion, allurement, charm,* CP.

ölectend m. *flatterer,* Cp1519. [=öleccend]

ölehtung f. *flattery,* GD : *indulgence,* MFH 170 (ölect-).

ölfæt=ālfæt

olfend m., olfenda m., olfende f. *camel,* Bl, Mt; CP. ['olfend'; L. elephantem]

olfendmyre f. *she-camel,* GEN32¹⁵.

öliec-=ōlecc-

oll n. *contumely, contempt, scorn, insult,* Æ. on oll 'nequicquam,' OEG2000.

ollonc, ollunc, ollung (LWS; A)=andlang

ölðwong m. *strap,* WW379³².

ölyhtword n. *flattering speech,* BL99²⁶. [öleccan]

m m. *rust,* Æ.

m-=am-

oma? m. ome? f. *a liquid measure,* v. NC 314. [L. (h)ama]

öman fp. *eruptions of the skin, erysipelas,* LCD. [cp. healsōme]

omb-=amb-

ömcynn n. *corrupt humour,* LCD31a.

omer (a¹, e¹) *a bird, 'scorellus,'* GL.

ömian *to become rusty,* Sc196⁵.

ömidda=onmidda

ömig *rusty, rust-eaten, rust-coloured : in- flammatory,* LCD.

ömihte *inflammatory,* LCD.

ompella=ampella; **ompre**=ampre I.

on I. prep. (w. d., instr., and a.) (local, etc.) 'ON,' *upon, on to* (but ofer is more com- mon), *up to, among,* AO,CP : *in, into, within,* Æ : (temporal) *in, during, at, on, about,* Æ,AO : *against, towards,* AO : *ac- cording to, in accordance with, in respect to,* Æ : *for, in exchange for.* **II.** adv. *on,* CP : *forward, onward : continuously,* Æ (forð on). on riht *rightly.* on ǣr adv. *formerly.* on ān *continuously, in concert : at once, forthwith.* **III.** pres. 3 sg. of unnan. **IV.** (M)=ond, and

on- I. often meaningless, and only rarely= prep. on. **II.**=an-. **III.**=un-. **IV.**=in-

onāðön anv. *to put on,* ÆL7¹⁵⁶.

onǣht f. *possession,* CVPs2⁸.

onǣlan *to set fire to, ignite, heat, inspire, incite, inflame, burn, consume,* Chr (an-), Gen,Sol; Æ,CP. ['anneal(ed)']

onǣlend m. 'incensor,' GPH399.

onǣlet n. *lightning,* LPs143⁶.

onǣr adv. *formerly.* [on, ǣr]

onǣðele (w. d.) *natural to,* MET13⁵¹.

onāfæstnian *to make fast, bind,* LPs9¹⁶.

onāhebban⁶ *to lift up, exalt,* CP56¹⁹.

onāl n. *burning : incense, what is burnt,* Ps.

onārīsan¹ *to rise up (against),* ERPs.

onarn pret. 3 sg. of oniernan.

onāsāwan⁷ *to implant, instil,* MFH170.

onāscunung=onscunung

onāsendan *to send into, implant in, impart to,* CM203.

onāsendednes (æ⁸) f. 'immissio,' LPs77⁴⁹.

onāsetednes f. *a laying on (of hands),* NC 349.

onāsettan *to set upon, place on, impress upon,* Æ,CM.

onāslagen *beaten (of metal),* LPs97⁶.

onāswēgan *to sound forth,* LPs28³.

onāwinnan⁸ *to fight against,* LPs34¹; 55².

onbæc adv. *backwards, back, behind,* G,Ps.

onbæcling (e) adv. *backward, behind.* o. gewend *having one's back turned,* Æ.

onbærnan *to kindle, ignite, heat, excite, in- spire, inflame, burn,* AO,CP.

onbærn-ing (JPs65¹⁵), -nes (SPs) f. *incense.*

onbǣru f. *self-restraint?* Gu 1027.
onbāsnung f. *expectation*, DR 4³⁴.
onbeblāwan¹ *to blow upon*, LPs 104¹⁹
onbecling (EPs)=onbæcling
onbecuman=oncuman
onbecyme m. *approach*, Sc 211⁸.
onbēgan=onbīgan
onbēgnes (=īe) f. *bending, curvature*, WW.
onbeht=ambiht
onbelǣdan *to inflict upon*, WW 90.
onbēn f. *imprecation*, BH 104³.
onbēodan² *to command, order*, AO : *announce, proclaim*, Æ,AO.
onbeornan³ *to set fire to*, Ex : *inflame*, LCD.
onbēotend *threatening, impending*, DR 53².
onberan⁴ I. *to carry off, plunder : diminish, weaken.* II. *to be situated?* GD 98¹⁴.
onbergan=onbyrgan
onbescēawung f. *inspection, examination*, Sc 66¹⁰.
onbescēofan² *to thrust out*, WW 220¹⁹, ²¹.
onbeslagen *inflicted*, Æ.
onbestǣlan *to convict of crime*, LL 30,15.
onbestingan=inbestingan; **onbid**=anbid
onbīdan¹ *to remain, wait*, B : w. g. *wait for, await, expect*, AO : *attend upon, wait on.* ['onbide']
onbīgan (ē;=īe) *to subdue, subjugate*, BL, Ps.
onbiht=ambiht
onbindan³ *to unbind, untie, loosen : release*, CP : *disclose.*
onbirgan=onbyrgan
onbitan¹ (w. g.) *to taste of, partake of, feed upon*, AA,LL.
onblǣst m. *onrush, attack*, EHy 5⁸.
onblǣstan *to break in*, WW 428¹.
onblandan³ *to mingle*, An 675.
onblāwan⁷ *to blow on or into, inspire, breathe : puff up.*
onblāwing f. *breathing upon*, JnL p 8⁶(in-).
onblāwnes f. *inspiration*, BL 7²⁶.
onblinnan (MFH 118)=āblinnan
onblōtan⁴ *to sacrifice, kill a victim*, GEN 2933.
onborgian *to borrow*, CC 9¹¹⁷.
onbran=onbarn pret. 3 sg. of onbeornan.
on-bregdan, -brēdan³ tr. and intr. *to move, start up : burst open.*
onbring m. *instigation*, LL.
onbringelle f. *instigation*, ÆL 23b²⁹¹.
onbrosnung f. *decay, corruption*, EPs 29¹⁰.
onbryce m. *inroad*, OEG 2480.
±onbryrdan (āb-, inb-) *to excite, inspire, incite, encourage*, Æ,CP. onbryrd *excited, fired, ardent : contrite.* [brord]
onbryrding f. *incitement*, WW 419⁴².
onbryrdnes (e²) f. *inspiration, incitement, ardour*, Æ : *remorse, contrition.*

onbūgan²,¹ *to bend : bow, submit, yield to, agree with*, Bl,Mt; Æ,AO : *bend aside, deviate.* ['onbow']
onbūtan prep. (w. d. a.) and adv. 'about,' *round about*, Æ : *round, around*, CP. adv. phr. west o. faran *to go west about.* [=ābūtan]
onbyhtscealc=ambihtscealc
onbyrdan=anbyrdan
onbyrgan I. (e, i) *to taste, eat*, Æ. II. *to be surety*, v. OEG 7⁹⁹.
onbyrging f. *tasting*, LCD 1·136¹².
onbyrhtan *to illuminate*, BL 105³¹.
onbyrignes f. *tasting*, BL 209¹².
oncelg- (N)=oncīg-
oncennan *to bear, bring forth*, ÆT,KGL.
oncer=ancor
oncierran (e, i, y) *to turn, alter, change, transform : turn off or away, avert, prevent : turn oneself, go.*
oncīgan (ei²;=īe) *to call upon, invoke*, DR.
oncīgnes, oncīgung (ei) f. *invocation*, DR.
onclēow=anclēow
onclifian (eo, y) *to adhere, stick to, persist in*, GD,RPs.
onclyfiende *sticking to, tenacious*, Ct.
onclypian *to call upon*, GEN 4²⁶ (GR).
on-cnǣwe, -cnāwe *known, recognised*, EPs 31⁵.
oncnāwan⁷ *to understand, know, perceive, observe*, Ma ; Æ,CP : *acknowledge, confess, disclose*, Æ. ['acknow']
oncnāwednes (RWH 92⁹)=oncnāwennes
oncnāwend m. *one who knows*, A 11·119.
on-cnāwennes(Æ),-cnāwnes(CP),-cnāwung (Sc) f. *acknowledgment, knowledge.*
oncnyssan *to cast down, afflict*, CPVPs.
oncnyttan=uncnyttan
oncor=ancor; **ōncra**=āncra
oncunnan swv. *to know*, GL : *reproach, blame, accuse*, CP.
oncunnes f. *accusation*, JVPs ; BH 212¹⁵.
oncunning f. *accusation*, BH 212¹⁵(B).
oncwealdan *to slay*, EPs 61⁴.
oncweðan⁵ *to answer, resound, echo*, Æ : *protest.*
oncyrran=oncierran; **oncyrrāp**=ancorrāp
oncȳðan *to make known*, TC 117¹.
oncȳðdǣd f. *hurtful deed*, An 1181.
oncȳðig *conscious, understanding*, EL 725 : *known*, ZDA 33·73¹².
oncȳð† f. *pain, distress of mind*, B.
ond=and
ondǣlan *to infuse*, DR,LkL.
ondǣlend m. *one who imparts, infuser*, LkL.
onde-=ande-; **onder-**=under-
onderslic, ondeslic (DR)=ondrysenlic
ondesn, ondesnes f. *fear*, DR.
ondgit=andgiet; **ondlēan**=andlēan

ondliota=ondwleota, andwlita
ondlong=andlang; **ondo** (NG)=anda
ondōn anv. **I.** *to undo, open.* [=un-] **II.** *to put on (clothes),* CM390; Sc83⁶.
ondōung f. *injection,* LCD97b.
on-drǣdan⁷ (and wv.) pret. 3 sg. -drēd, -drǣd, -dreord (A), also -drǣdde, pp. -drǣd (tr.) *to dread, fear,* B,Chr,Mt : (refl.) *be afraid,* El,Lk. [' adread']
ondrǣdendlic *fearful, terrible,* Æ.
ondrǣding f. *dread, fear, terror,* AO.
ondrencan *to intoxicate,* GUTH62²⁰ : *fill with water,* JPs64¹¹.
ondresn=ondrysnu
ondrincan³ (w. g.) *to drink,* BH.
ondrislic=ondrysenlic
ondruncnian *to become intoxicated,* EPs35⁹.
on-drysenlic, -drys(n)lic *terrible,* BH,MH. adv. -līce *reverently, with fear,* VH18.
ondrysne (and-) *terrible,* AO : *feared, venerated, venerable.*
ondrysnlic=ondrysenlic
ondrysnu (and-) f. *fear,* CP : *respect, reverence,* BL : *etiquette,* B1796.
ondrystlic=ondrysenlic
onds-=ands-
ondūne *down,* MH214¹¹.
ondw-=andw-
one=ono
onealdian *to grow old,* SPs31³.
oneardian *to inhabit,* CSPs (=in-).
oneardiend *inhabitant, indweller,* GD,PPs.
onefen, onefn=onemn
on-ēgan, -ēgnian (oe) *to fear, dread.* [ōga]
onēhting f. *persecution,* OEG2974.
onemn I. prep. (w. d.) *abreast of, alongside of, by, near, during,* Æ,B,Ma; AO. [' anent'] **II.** adv. *together, exactly, directly.* o. ðǣm *at the same time.*
onemnōrōwigan *to sympathise,* ÆL23b²⁴³.
onerian *to plough up,* Æ,CP.
onerning f. *attack,* DR36¹. [iernan]
ōnettan *to hasten, hurry forward, be quick,* Æ : *be busy, brisk* : *anticipate,* Æ,CP : (+) *get quickly, seize, occupy.*
ōnettung f. *precipitation,* CP455¹⁵.
oneða†=anda
onēōgung f. *breathing on,* ERPs17¹⁶.
onfægnian *to fawn on,* Bo102¹⁵.
onfæreld n. *going on, progress, journey* : *going in, entrance* : *attack, assault,* Sc212⁵.
onfæstan *to make fast,* GD224¹⁶.
onfæstnian (e²) *to pierce,* Jn,SPs.
onfæðmnes f. *embrace,* BL7²⁶.
onfangend m. *receiver,* ES9·37.
onfangennes f. *reception, acceptance,* Æ.
onfealdan⁷ *to unfold,* GD,MH.
onfeall (e) m. *swelling,* Lcd. [' onfall']
onfeallende ptc. *rushing on, overwhelming.*

onfehtan (VPs)=onfeohtan; **onfell**=onfeall
onfeng I.=andfeng. **II.** pret. 3 sg. of onfōn.
onfeohtan³ (e) *to attack, assault, fight with,* CHR.
onfillende (WW420¹⁹)=onfeallende
onfilte (WW)=anfilte
onfindan³ (but occl. wk. pret. onfunde) *to find out, learn, perceive, feel, notice, observe, discover,* CP : *experience, suffer.*
onfindend m. *discoverer,* GPH391.
onflǣscnes f. *incarnation,* BL81²⁹; BHy2⁴¹.
onflyge m., onflygen n. *infectious disease* (BT), LCD.
onfōn⁷ *to take, receive, accept,* BH,Lcd,Mt; Æ : *stand sponsor,* Chr : *harbour, favour unrighteously,* LL : *take hold of* : *undertake,* (a duty) *undergo* (a rite), Bl : *begin* : *conceive,* Ps. onfangenum gebede *after engaging in prayer,* Æ. [' fang,' ' onfang']
onfōnd m. *undertaker, supporter,* Ps,AS14⁶?
onfōndlic (an-) *to be received,* CHRD110⁸.
onfongenes=onfangennes
onforan I. prep. *before* (time), *at the beginning of,* Chr. **II.** adv. *before, in front of,* Ps. [' afore']
onfordōn ptc. *destroyed,* LPs101²¹.
onforeweard-um, -an adv. *in front, in the first line, in the fore part, above all,* Æ; A5·455.
onforht=anforht
onforhtian *to be afraid, fear,* Æ,GL.
onforwyrd n. *destruction,* CSPs.
onfundelnes f. *experience,* LCD.
onfunden *experienced,* AS14⁶.
onfundennes f. *explanation* : *trial, experiment, experience.* [onfindan]
onga=anga; **ongægn,** ongǣn=ongēan
ongalan⁶ *to recite* (a charm), LCD3·42¹⁸, S²Ps57⁶.
ongalend m. *enchanter,* BLPs57⁶.
ongalnes f. *song,* BRPs70⁶.
ongān I.=ongēan. **II.** anv. *to approach, enter into,* ES38·20 : *attack,* ES41·325.
ongang (o²) m. *entrance, incursion, assault, attack* : *worship,* BH106¹⁴.
ongangan⁷=ongān; **onge**=enge
on-gēan (ā, ē), -geagn (æ, e) **I.** prep. *towards, against, opposite to, contrary to,* Æ; AO,CP : *against, in exchange for.* **II.** adv. *opposite, back,* Æ : 'AGAIN.' eft o. *back again.* o. ðæt *on the other hand, on the contrary.*
ongēancyme m. *return,* Æ.
ongēancyrrendlic *relative,* ÆGR231¹⁷.
ongēanfealdan⁷ *to fold or roll back,* Sc148¹¹.
ongēanfēran (agēan-) *to return,* CHR1070.
ongēanflōwende *ebbing and flowing,* v. OEG 2363.
ongēanhworfennes f. *obstacle,* OEG2713.

ongēanhwyrf (ag-) m. *return*, HGL419.
ongēanhwyrfan (ag-) *to turn again, return*.
ongēanlecgan *to lay up, store up*, Sc156[6].
ongēansprecend m. *one who reproaches*, RSPs43[17].
ongēanweard *going back or towards*, AO : *near*, BK4. adv. -weardes, Æ.
ongēanweardlic *adversative*. adv. -līce, ÆGR.
ongēanwerian *to revile in return*, RB17[13]. [wyrigan]
ongēanwinnende *resisting*, APT2[4].
ongēanwiðerian *to oppose*, Sc33[20].
ongēanwyrdnes f. *opposition*, OEG3975.
ongeboren *in-born*, OEG4648,2[360].
ongebringan *to bring upon : impose*, CM36 : *enjoin*, CM1185 : *incline, induce*, ÆL25[549].
ongebyrigean (V[2]Ps33[9])=onbyrgan I.
ongecīgan *to call upon, invoke*, RHy1[4].
ongecīgung (ei[3]) f. *invocation*, DR99[13].
ongecoplīce=ungecoplīce
onge-fæstnian, -festnian (Ps)=onfæstnian
ongefeht n. *attack*, DR. [feoht]
ongeflogen *attacked by disease*, LCD1·86'. [cp. onflygen]
on-gegen, -gegn=ongēan
ongehrēosan[2] *to rush upon, fall upon*, WW419[6].
ongehȳōnes f. *advantage, profit*, LL476,12.
ongel, Ongel=angel I.
ongelǣdan=ingelǣdan
ongelic (NG) I. *like*. II. *likeness*. adv. -līce, AO.
ongelīcnes f. *form, pattern*, Mt p14[20].
ongelīhtan (AS2[2])=onlihtan
on-gemang, -gemong prep. (w. d.) and adv. *among, during*, CP : *meanwhile*, CM. o. ðisum, ðǣm *meanwhile*.
ongemet=ungemet
ongēn, ongein=ongēan
ongenǣman *to take away (from)*, GUTH14[11].
ongeotan=ongietan
ongēotan *to infuse, impregnate*, GD51[14].
ongēotung f. *pouring in*, LCD88a.
on-gerwan, pp. -gered (VPs)=ongierwan
ongesēon=onsēon
ongesetenes f. *knowledge*, BH474[15].
ongeslēan[6] *to slay*, BH44[17].
ongespanan[1] *to draw on, allure*, WW421[22].
onget-=ongiet-
ongetǣcan *to enjoin*, CM363.
ongetimbran *to build up*, AO.
ongeðwǣre=ungeðwǣre
ongewinn n. *assault*, Sc33[17].
ongewiss=ungewiss
ongewrigennes (GD139[1])=onwrigennes
ongieldan[3] (i) *to atone for, be punished for, pay (the penalty) for*, AO : *pay, offer (gifts, sacrifice)*. [Ger. entgelten]

ongien=onginn
ongierwan (e, i, y) pret. -girede I. *to unclothe, divest, strip*, Æ (=un-). II. *to clothe*, EPs131[16].
ongietan[5] (e, eo, i, y) *to grasp, seize : understand, learn, recognise, know, distinguish, judge, consider*, Mt ; AO,CP : *see, perceive : discover : hear : feel, experience : know carnally*. ['anget']
ongietenes f. *knowledge, understanding*, BH : *meaning*, GUTH80[22].
ongifan[5] (æ) *to give back*, Æ : *forgive*.
ongildan=ongieldan
onginn=anginn
onginnan[3] *to begin, attempt, endeavour, try hard*, Æ,G ; AO,CP (This vb. is often used periphrastically w. another vb. in the inf., to denote the simple action of the latter. The compound is best translated by the historical aorist of the second vb.) : *attack, assail : act*, ÆL (āg-). ['ongin']
onginnendlic *inchoative*, ÆGR.
onginnes f. *undertaking*, BH,WW.
on-girwan=ongierwan
ongit=andgiet ; **ongit-**=ongiet-
Ongle (AO), Onglisc=Angle, Englisc
ongnora? ongnere=angnere
Ongol=Angel ; **ongong**=ongang
ongrataō? '*arridet*,' OEG33[2] (v. BTs).
ongris-, ongrys-=angris-
ongrynt? '*arridet*,' OEG33[2] (v. BTs).
ongrype m. *attack*, W187[2].
ongryrelic *horrible*, GUTH36[24].
ongseta=angseta ; **ongunnenes**=onginnes
ongy-=ongi-
ongyrdan *to unbuckle, unfasten*, ÆL ; BH196[28]. ['ungird']
ongyrnō '*inrogat*,' Sc10[4].
ongytan=ongietan
ongyte f. *inpouring*, ÆH1·362'.
onhādian (LL66,21)=unhādian
onhǣldan (VPs)=onhieldan
onhǣle *secret, concealed, hidden*, CR896.
onhǣtan *to heat, inflame*, AO,CP.
onhagian (impers.) *to be possible or convenient, be fitting, suit, please*, Æ,CP : *be at leisure*.
onhātan[1]† *to promise*, JUL.
onhātian *to become hot*, WW.
onhāwian *to behold*, ÆL3[261].
onhealdan[7] (an-) *to keep (peace)*, MET11[42].
onhēaw m. *trunk of tree, block of wood for hewing on*, WW.
onhebban[6] (occl. wk. pret. onhefde) *to raise up, erect, lift up, exalt*, Bl ; Æ : *leaven : begin : take away*. ['onheave']
onhefednes (an-) f. *exaltation*, RB23[2].
onheld-=onhield-
onhergian *to harass*, CP73[18].

onheri-=onhyri-

onhetting f. *persecution*, OEG 2¹³⁰.

onhicgan=onhycgan

onhieldan (CP) (i²) *to bend, bend down, lean, recline, incline* : *decline, sink* : *fall away*, CPs 118¹⁰².

onhieldednes (e², y²) f. *declining*, CVPs 72⁴.

onhigian *to attack, despoil*, OEG.

onhindan, onhinder adv. *behind, backward*.

onhinderling adv. *back*, PPs.

onhiscan=onhyscan

onhlīdan¹ *to open, reveal, unclose* : *appear*.

onhlinian *to lean on*, GL.

onhnīgan¹ *to bend down, bow, worship*.

onhnigenes f. *adoration*, LF 56⁵.

onhōhsnian *to detest?* (BT), *put an end to?* B 1944.

onhōn⁷ *to hang, crucify*, AO.

onhrēran=onhrēran; **onhrǣs**=onr.ēs

onhrēodan² *to adorn* (or? onrēodan=*redden*), GEN 2931.

onhrēosan² *to fall upon, rush upon*, GD,Ps.

onhrēran *to move, disturb, arouse, excite*, CP.

onhrīnan¹ (w. g. or d.) *to touch, lay hold of*, Æ,CP.

onhrine m. *touch, contact*, LCD 1·328¹.

onhrōp m. *importunity*, Æ : *reproach*, LPs 68²⁰.

onhryre *attack*, OEG 50⁷² (onri-).

onhupian *to step back, retire*, CP 441²⁸.

onhwelan⁴ *to bellow back, resound*, WW 528³⁹.

onhweorfan³ *to change, turn, reverse*, CP.

onhwerfan (y²;=ie) *to turn, change, turn round*.

onhwerfednes (æ) f. *change*, AS 9³.

onhycgan (i²) *to consider*, DA 473.

onhyldan=onhieldan

onhyrdan† *to strengthen, encourage.* [heard]

onhyrenes f. *imitation*, CP,GD.

onhyr-gend, -iend (e, i;=ie) m. *emulator, imitator*, GD,GL.

onhyrian (e) *to emulate, imitate*, CP.

onhyring (e) f. *imitation, zeal*, Æ,CP.

onhȳrsumian *to be busied with*, RB 71¹⁷.

onhyscan (i) *to mock at, vilify, reproach* : *detest* : *deceive.* [husc]

oniernan³ (y²) (†) *to give way, open* (*of a door*) : '*currere*,' BPs 118³² : '*incurrere*,' LL 410,3⁵ : *pour forth*, VH 18.

oninnan prep. (w. d.) and adv. *within, into, among*.

onlǣc (Cp 1725)=onlēac, pret. 3 sg. of onlūcan.

onlǣccan *to reproach*, EPs 105⁷.

onlǣdan=inlǣdan

onlǣnan *to lend, grant, let, lease*, CP.

onlǣpnes (BH 128²³)=ānlīpnes

onlǣtan (an-) *to relax, permit*, RB.

onlang=andlang; **onlēc**=anlēc

onlecgende (*salve*) *to be applied*, LCD.

onlegen f. *poultice*, LCD.

onlēoht-=onlīht-

onlēon¹† *to lend, grant, give*, WW.

onlēoðlan=onlīðigan

onlēs-=onlīes-

onlic (an-) *like, resembling, similar, Mt*; CP adv. -līce, AO,CP. ['*anlike*']

+**onlician** (an-; -līcan, GD 75⁴) *to compare make like, simulate*.

onlicnes f. *resemblance, likeness, similitude*, Gen. : *picture, image, idol*, WW ; AO,CP : *parable* : *stature, form.* ['*anlikeness*']

+**onlicung** (an-) f. *likeness*, CHRD 71¹³.

onliesan (ē, ȳ) *to loosen, set free, release*, CP.

onliesednes (ī²) f. *remission* (*of sins*), AHy 9⁷⁷.

onliesend (ē, ȳ) m. *liberator*, CPs 39¹⁸ : *redeemer*, GD.

onliesendlic (ȳ) *absolvable*, GD 345².

onliesnes (ē) f. *deliverance*, BL,GD.

onligan (in-) *to inflame*, JPs 104¹⁹.

onlihtan (ēo, ȳ) *to illuminate, give light to, enlighten*, Bl,Bo; CP : *restore to sight* : *shine.* ['*onlight*']

onlihtednes=onlīhtnes

onlihtend m. *enlightener*, PPs 26¹.

onlihting f. *illumination, enlightenment*, Æ.

onlihtnes f. *illumination*, BH,Ps.

onlīðian (eo) *to loosen, relax*, GD.

onlīðigan *to become pliant, yield*, SOL 356.

onlōcian *to look on, behold*, Æ,CP.

onlōciend m. *onlooker, spectator*, Æ.

onlong=andlang

onlūcan³ (=un-) *to unlock, open, unfold, reveal, disclose*, CP.

onlūtan² *to bow, incline, bend down*, CP.

onlūtung f. '*involucrum*,' GPH 402.

onlȳ-=onlī-; **onlȳs-**=onlīes-

onmǣdla=onmēdla

onmǣlan *to speak to*, DA 210.

onman v. onmunan.

onmang (Æ)=ongemang

onmearca m. *inscription*, MkL 12¹⁶ (MkR in-).

onmearcung (e²) f. *inscription*, NG.

onmēdan *to presume, take upon oneself?* RD 56¹⁵.

onmēdla=anmēdla

onmeltan³? *to soften*, PPs 88³⁸.

onmētan I. *to paint, cover over?* PPs 88⁴⁶. II. *to come upon, find out*, EPs 114³.

onmiddan prep. (w. d.) *amid, in the midst, at the middle of*, Æ.

onmitta=anmitta; **onmōd**=anmōd

onmunan swv. pres. 3 sg. onman, pret. onmunde *to esteem, think worthy of, consider entitled to*, CP : refl. *care for, wish* : *remember* : *remind*, B 2640.

onmyrran *to mar, disturb,* TC390'.
onn=ann, pres. 3 sg. of unnan.
onnhīgan (WW255¹¹)=onhnīgan
onnīman⁴ *to receive, take,* PPs.
onnytt=unnytt
ono=heonu
onoeðung (VPs)=oneðung
onōrettan† *to perform with effort, accomplish.*
onorðung f. *inspiration, inbreathing,* LPs, Sc.
onoða (WW)=anda
onpennian *to open,* CP277⁸.
onrād f. *riding on horseback,* Lcd 68b.
onræfniendlic=unræfniendlic
onrǣs m. *onrush, assault, attack,* Æ,CP.
onrǣsan I. *to rush (on),* VPs. ['*onrese*']
II. nap. of wk. sb. *irruptions,* WW.
onrǣsend m. *attacker,* LPs17⁴⁰.
onrēaflian *to strip (of),* A12·505 (=un-).
onred m. *name of a plant,* Lcd.
onrēodan v. onhrēodan; **onrettan**=orrettan
onrīd n. *riding horse,* CC23²⁵.
onrīdan¹ *to ride (on a raid, etc.),* Chr871A.
onriht *right, lawful, proper : owned by?*
Ex358. adv. *aright,* Æ. also -līce, Bl43¹⁶.
onrihtwīsnes=unrihtwīsnes
onrīptīd f. *harvest-time,* ES39·352.
onrīsan (Æ)=ārīsan ['*onrise*']
onryne m. *course : incursion, assault,* Lcd.
onsacan⁶ *to contest, dispute, strive against, resist, repel : (†) attack : refuse, deny, contradict, refute : exculpate, excuse oneself : renounce.*
onsæc I. *denying : denied : excused.* II. (LL24,41Ld)=andsæc
onsǣgan† *to prostrate,* DD,Gu.
onsǣgd-=onsæged-
onsǣge *assailing, attacking,* B,CC,W. [sīgan]
onsǣgednes (e) f. *sacrifice, offering,* Æ : *oblation, (sacrificial) victim.*
onsǣgnes f. *holocaust, sacrifice,* BLPs65¹⁵.
onsǣgung f. *sacrifice,* WW.
onsǣlan *to untie, loosen,* B,Bl. [=unsǣlan]
onsæt I. pret. 3 sg. of onsittan. II.=onset
onsǣtnes f. *snare,* DR121¹⁹.
onsǣtnung f. *snare,* DR147⁷.
onsagu f. *affirmation, accusation, reproach,* Mt; Æ. ['*onsaw*']
onsand f. *sending against,* VPs. ['*onsand*']
onsang m. *incantation,* GD73²⁶.
onsāwan⁷ *to sow : introduce into, implant,* CM658.
onsceacan⁶ (a) *to shake, shake off, remove,* Gl.
onsceacnes f. *excuse,* EPs. [=onsacnes, Swt]
onsceamian=ofsceamian
onscendan *to confound, put to shame,* GD.

onsceon-=onscun-
onsceortian *to grow short,* MH104²³.
onscēotan² (un-) *to open,* Gl.
onscillan (=y²) *to give back a sound, resound,* OEG8²⁶⁵.
onscōgan (an-) *to unshoe,* CP. pp. onscōd *unshod.* [=un-] ˙
onscrȳdan *to clothe,* EPs,Sc.
onscunian (a¹, eo², y²) *to shun, avoid, fear, detest, hate,* LL; Æ,CP : *put away, reject, despise : irritate.* ['*ashun*']
on-scuniendlic (CP), -scunigendlic (Æ), -scunodlic *hateful, detestable.*
onscunigend m. *hater,* Bl111²⁹.
onscunung f. *execration, abomination : exasperation,* Ps.
onscynian=onscunian
onscyte m. *attack, assault,* Æ.
onseacan (Cp665)=onsceacan
onsēcan *require, exact,* Jul. ['*onseek*']
onsecgan *to renounce, deny : offer sacrifice,* AO : *impute,* Æ : *inform,* Æ.
onsecgend m. *sacrificer,* LL.
onsēgednes=onsǣgednes
onsēn (VPs)=ansīen
onsendan *to send out, send forth, transmit, yield up,* AO,CP : *offer to,* VH.
onsēon I. (sv⁵) *to see, look on, behold, regard, take notice of,* AO. II. (A)=ansīen
on-set, -setl, n. *a sitting on, riding on,* GD 183.
onset(e)nes f. *laying on (of hands),* MH84² : *constitution, founding.*
onsettan *to impose,* CP : *oppress, bear down.*
onsīcan¹ *to sigh, groan,* Bo.
onsīen I. (ȳ)† f. *lack, want.* II.=ansīen
onsīgan¹ *to sink, decline, descend : approach, impend,* Æ : *assail,* Æ.
onsit=onset
onsittan I. sv⁵ *to seat oneself in, occupy,* Æ : *oppress.* II. sv⁵ *to fear, dread* (=ond-).
onsittend m. *rider,* CHy4¹.
onslǣge m. *blow,* WW. [slege]
onslǣpan⁷ and wv. *to go to sleep, sleep,* BH.
onslāpan=onslǣpan
onslūpan⁷ *to unloose,* GD221²³. [=un-]
onsmyrung f. *anointing,* Chrd80¹⁹.
onsnǣsan (LL69,36) v. snǣsan.
onsnīðan¹ *to cut up,* Lcd (ES43·321).
onsond=onsand
onspǣc f. *imputation, charge, claim,* LL.
onspannan⁷ *to unfasten, unbind, unloose, open, disclose, release.* [=un-]
onspeca (an-) m. *accuser,* Chrd62²⁶ : *claimant,* LL138,1³.
onspecend m. *accuser, plaintiff,* TC169.
onspillend m. *player,* A13·28,29.
onspornan=onspurnan
onspornend (=un-) *not stumbling,* Sc187⁸.

onspræc f. *speech, discourse,* GD332⁹ (an-).
onspreccan *to enliven,* RIM9?
onsprecend=onspecend
onspringan³ *to spring forth, originate, rise, burst forth, burst asunder.*
onsprungennes f. *eclipse,* WW225³⁹.
onspurnan³ *to strike against, stumble,* WW 420³⁹.
onstæl m. *order, arrangement,* GU796.
onstǣlan *to impute to, accuse of,* MFH170.
onstæpe (e) m. *ingress,* ESPs67²⁶ (=in-).
onstæppan⁶ *to walk, go,* LCD,SPs (=in-).
onstal (=ea?) m. *provision, supply,* CP4¹.
onstǎl m? *charge, reproof,* OEG.
onstandende *urgent, persistent,* Sc111¹⁴.
onstede=unstede
onstellan *to institute, create, originate, establish, give the example of,* Bl; AO,CP. [' onstell']
onstēpan (=īe) *to raise,* †Hy4³⁸.
onstīgend m. *mounted man,* VHy4¹.
onsting m. *claim, authority, jurisdiction, right of intervention,* Ct.
onstingan *to be angry (with)?* RBL115¹⁶.
onstǐōlan *to harden,* JnLR12⁴⁰.
onstregdan³ (and wk.) (i²) *to sprinkle,* BJVPs 50⁹.
onstydfullnes f. *instability,* DR. [=uni-]
onstȳran *to govern,* BH276¹¹ (v.l.).
onstyr-ednes, -enes f. *movement,* BH,Ps.
onstyrian *to move, rouse, disturb, stir, agitate, excite,* CP.
onsund=ansund
onsun-dran, -dron, -drum adv. *singly, separately, apart, Gen,Mk : privately : especially.* [' asunder']
onsundrian=āsyndrian
onswāpan⁷ *to sweep on, blow on,* GL : *sweep away, banish.*
onswarian=andswarian
onswebban *to put to sleep, bury,* WW.
onswīfan¹ *to swing forward, turn against : push off, put aside, turn away.*
onswīŏlic *mighty, loud,* ÆL31²⁸¹.
onswōgan=inswōgan
onswornod *confused,* NC315.
onsymbelnes f. *celebration (of mass),* BH 112⁶.
onsȳn=ansīen, onsīen I.
onsyngian=unsyngian
ontalu f. *claim at law,* TC302²² (v. LL 3·226).
ontēnan (KGL65⁵)=ontȳnan
ontendan *to kindle, set fire to, inflame,* Æ, Lcd,LL. [' tind,' ' ontend']
ontendnes (y) f. *burning, fire,* Æ : *inflammation,* Æ : *incitement, fuel,* Æ : *passion.*
ontēon² *to draw to oneself, assume, undertake,* CP : *pull, pull out : untie* (=un-).

ontēona m. *injury, oppression,* ERPs102⁶.
ontige m. *claim, usurpation,* RB140⁹.
ontiht-=ontyht-
ontimber *material,* Æ : *cause, occasion,* Æ.
ontimbernes f. *material,* MFH171 : *teaching, edification.*
ontimbr-an, -ian, *to instruct,* BH.
ontre=antre
ontrēowan *to entrust, confide,* DA269?
ontrym-ian, -man ' *invalescere,*' NG.
ontȳdran *to nourish, foster,* AO182²⁶.
ontȳdre ' *sine foetu,' effete,* WW. [=ortȳdre?]
ontygnes f. *accusation,* LL22,37.
ontyhtan (i) *to urge on, incite,* B3086 : *be intent on.*
ontyhting (i) f. *attention, application, aim, intention, instigation,* Sc.
ontȳnan (ē) *to open, reveal, display,* CP. [tūn]
ontyndnes=ontendnes
ontȳnnes f. *opening,* BL93²⁴.
onŏæslic (Sc33²⁰)=unŏæslic
onŏenian *to stretch,* EPs63³.
onŏēon¹,³† *to be useful, succeed, prosper.*
onŏēowigan *to serve,* CM473.
onŏicgan *to eat of, partake of,* VH18.
±onŏracian (a-, an-, and-) *to fear, dread,* Æ.
onŏracung (an-) f. *fear, awe,* LPs34²⁶.
on-ŏræce, -ŏræclic (an-) *formidable, dreadful,* Æ.
onŏrēagung f. *reproach,* ÆL23b⁶⁷².
onŏrecan⁵ refl. *to fear,* GUTH132²⁰⁸.
onŏringan³ *to press on or forward,* AO : *move, be moved?* GU1300.
onŏunian *to swell up? move round?* RD41⁹¹ : *exceed bounds.*
onŏwægennes f. *washing,* HL13¹³⁸,¹⁵⁴.
onŏwēan⁶ (in-) *to wash,* BH,GD.
onu=heonu
onufan prep. (w. d.) and adv. *above, upon, on, Jud*; AO : *beyond, after.* [' anoven']
onunder (an-) *under,* MFH171.
onuppan I. prep. (w. d.) *upon, on,* CP. **II.** adv. *in addition, besides.*
onūtan *out of doors,* LCD106b.
onwacan⁶ *to awake,* AO : *arise, be born.*
onwaccan f. *incitement, arousing,* DR74¹².
onwacnian=onwæcnian
onwadan⁶ *to penetrate into, attack, seize, occupy.*
onwǣcan *to weaken, shake (a resolution), soften, mollify,* CP. [wāc]
onwæcenes f. *arousing,* GD337³³.
on-wæcnan, -wæcnian (e) *to awake, CP : arise, spring, be born* (=āwæcnan). [' awaken']
onwǣld (N)=onweald
onwæmme=unwemme; **onwær-**=unwær-

onwæstm m. *increase*, DR69[9] : *branch*, PPs. [ōwæstm]

onwæterig=unwæterig

onwald, onwalh=onweald, onwealg

onwarian *to guard oneself against*, MFH 171.

onwealcan[7] *to roll, roll round*, LCD 1·246[10].

onweald (a[1], a[2]) **I.** mfn. *authority, power, rule, sway, command, AO,Lk*; CP : *jurisdiction, territory*, CP. **II.** adj. *mighty, powerful*. ['*onwald*']

onwealda (an-) m. *ruler, governor, sovereign* : *the Lord, God*.

+**onwealdian** (an-; æ[2]) *to have dominion over, get possession of*, LPs,LkLR.

onwealdig (a[1], a[2]) *powerful*, Bo 108[18].

onwealdnes f. *power, possession*, ERPs 2[8].

onwealg, onwealh *whole, sound, entire, uninjured, safe*, AO.

onwealglīce (an-) *wholly, completely*, CP 220[22].

onwealhnes f. *soundness, wholeness, purity, modesty, chastity*.

onweard (=and-) adj. *acting against, opposed to*, Æ.

onwecnian=onwæcnian

onweg (aweg) adv. '*away*,' *forth, out, off, onward, along*, B,Chr.

onwegācyr(red)nes (=ie[4]) f. *apostasy*, BH 176 (v.l.).

onwegādrīfan[1] *to drive away*, VPs.

onwegādrifennes f. *a driving away*, GD 185[13].

onwegāfirran *to remove away*, VHy.

onwegālǣdnes f. *removal*, BH446[16].

onwegāscūfan[2] *to push away*, VPs.

onwegāwendan *to remove*, VPs.

onwegfæreld n. *departure*, GD 119[26].

onweggewit n. *mental aberration*, VPs 115[11].

onweggewitennes f. *departure*, BH170[10].

onwegoncernes=onwegācyrrednes

onwegpullian *to pull away*, ES43·339.

onwemme=unwemme

onwendan *to change, exchange* : *upset, end, overturn, turn aside, avert*, VPs : *change for the better, amend* : *change for the worse, pervert* : *transgress* : *deprive* : *return*.

onwendedlic *changeable*, LCD 3·164[8].

on-wendednes, -wendnes f. *movement, change, alteration*, VPs.

onweorpan[3] (in-) *cast in one's teeth, accuse* : *turn or throw aside* : *begin the web*.

onweorpnes f. *onpouring*, BH118[6].

onwēstan=āwēstan

onwīcan[1] *to yield, give way*, WW.

onwille *wished for, agreeable*, GU 700.

onwindan[3] *unwind, loosen* : *retreat*, AN 531.

onwinnan[3] *to attack, assail*, Æ.

onwist f. *habitation*, Ex 18.

onwlite=andwlite

onworpennes f. *enticement, allurement, inspiration*, HL200[164].

onwrecan=āwrecan

onwrēon[1,2] *to uncover, unfold, display, explain, reveal*, Æ,CP.

on-wrig(en)nes, -wrihnes f. *revelation, exposure, exposition*, Æ. [wrēon]

onwrīting f. *inscription*, Lk20[24]. ['*onwriting*']

onwrītung=onwrīðung

onwrīðan *to unbind, unwrap* (JUD173)= unwrīðan.

onwrīðod pp. *supported*, BF198[23].

onwrīðung f. *ligament, bandage*, WW439[13] (onwrīt-).

onwunian *to inhabit, remain*, Ps.

onwunung f. *dwelling-place* : *assiduity*, OEG75.

onwurpan=onweorpan

onwyllan *to cause to boil, inflame*, GU 362.

onwylwan *to roll up, roll together*, EHy 2[12].

onȳðan *to pour in*, SC200[7].

onȳwan (=īe) *to show, manifest* : refl. *appear*.

open '*OPEN*,' *exposed, AO* : *evident, well-known, public, manifest, plain, clear, AO* : *open to re-trial*, LL10,9.

openærs m. *medlar*, WW137[36]. ['*openarse*']

openere m. *opener*, BF152[3].

±**openian** *to 'open,' open up, disclose, declare, reveal, expound*, Æ,BH,Ps; CP : (+) intr. *become manifest* : (+) *be open to, exposed to*.

openlic *open, public*, WW. adv. -līce '*openly*,' *manifestly, plainly, clearly, unreservedly*, Bl,Bo,RB.

opennes f. *openness, publicity*, OEG : *manifestation*, ÆL23b[43].

±**openung** f. *opening, disclosure, manifestation*, BL,W.

oportanie=aprōtane

ōr† n. *beginning, origin* : *front, An,B.* ['*ore*,' cp. ord]

or prefix (lit. '*out of*'=L. ex-) is privative, as in orsorg, orwēna; or denotes origin, antiquity, as in oreald. [*Ger.* ur-]

ōra I. m. *border, bank, shore*, CHR; Mdf. **II.** m. '*ore*,' *unwrought metal, BH,Ps,WW* : *brass, ÆGr,Cp,CP*. **III.** *a coin of Danish origin, LkL,LL* (v. 2·601). ['*ora*']

orað=oroð

orblēde *bloodless*, WW397[29]. [blōd]

orc I. m. *pitcher, crock, cup*, B,GL. [*Late L.* orca; *L.* urceus] **II.** m. *demon*, GL. [*L.* orcus] or-cēape, -cēapes, -cēapunga, -cēapungum adv. *gratis, without cause.*

orc-eard, -erd (Æ,*Lcd*)=ortgeard

orcēas *inviolable, unimpugned, unassailed,* GL.

orcēasnes f. *immunity, purity,* GL.

orcerdlēh f. *orchard,* HGL. [ortgeard, lēah]

orcerdweard m. *gardener,* WW 333²⁵.

orcgeard, orcird=ortgeard

orcnǣwe (ā) *evident, well-known.*

orcnēas mp. *monsters,* B112. [*L.* Orcus]

orcðyrs m. *monster of hell, Orcus,* WW.

orcyrd=ortgeard

ord m. *point, spear-point, spear,* Æ,B,*CP* : *source, beginning,* Æ,*CP* : *front, vanguard,* Æ : *chief, prince;* in pl. *first men, the flower.* ['*ord*']

ordǣle *not participating, free from,* WW.

ordāl (ē) mn. '*ordeal,' LL.* [*Ger.* urteil]

ordālīsen n. *iron used in an ordeal,* LL388,1.

ordbana m. *murderer,* GEN 1097.

ordceard=ortgeard; ordēl=ordāl

ordfruma m. *fount, source,* Æ : *author, creator, instigator,* AO : (†) *chief, prince.*

ordfrymm (e²) *original,* ES49·352.

ordstæpe m. *spear-stab, wound,* RD71¹⁶.

ordwyga m. *warrior,* WALD1⁶.

-ōre v. īsen-ō.

oreald *very old,* Bo102¹⁸. [*Ger.* uralt]

ōred-=ōret-

orel n. *robe, garment, mantle, veil,* Æ,GL. [*L.* orarium]

oreldo=oryldu

orene I. *excessive,* v. SF157 : *harmful.* II. n. *excess : injury?* LCD3·16⁵ (orne).

orenlīce *excessively,* MFH171.

ōret† m. *contest, battle.*

ōret-=orret(t)-

ōretfeld m. *place of contest,* OEG8⁵⁰.

ōretla m. *contumely, insult,* GD200¹⁶.

ōretlof n. *triumph,* CM497.

ōret-mæcg† (e³), -mæcga (WW) m. *champion, warrior.*

ōretstōw f. *wrestling place, place of contest,* OEG.

ōrett-=ōret-

ōretta† m. *champion, warrior, hero.*

oreð=oroð; oreðlan=orðian

orf n. *cattle, live stock,* Æ,*Chr*,LL. ['*orf*']

orfcwealm (a²) m. *cattle-plague, murrain,* CHR,W.

orfcynn (i²) n. *cattle,* Æ.

orfeorme (y) (†) *destitute of, lacking :* (†) *empty, useless : squalid, filthy.*

orfeormnes f. *squalor, filthiness,* Cp488s.

orfgebitt n. *grazing,* WW149³³.

orfiermu f. *squalor,* OET96⁹³³.

orfyrme=orfeorme

orfyrmð *refuse,* OEG609.

organ m. *canticle, song, voice,* SOL.

organa? organe? f., organ-an, -on pl. *musical instrument,* Æ,A*pT*,Ps. ['*organ*'; *L.* organum]

organdrēam (APs150⁴)=orgeldrēam

organe f. *marjoram,* Lcd. ['*organ*'; *L.* origanum]

organian=orgnian

organystre *player on an instrument,* GEN4²¹.

orgeate=orgyte

orgel (o²) *pride,* WW. ['*orgel*']

orgeldrēam m. *sound of a musical instrument,* Bl. [v. '*orgle*']

orgellic *ignominious,* CP. adv. -līce *proudly, insolently, scornfully,* Æ.

orgello (A11·98)=orgel

orgelnes f. *pride,* OEG1108. [v. '*orgel*']

orgelword n. *arrogant speech,* ÆH2·248¹¹.

orgete=orgyte

orgilde *not having discharged a payment (of* '*wergeld*'), LL.

orgilīce=orgellīce

orgnian *to sing to an instrumental accompaniment,* ÆGR181².

orgol=orgel

orgyte (ea, e) *well-known, manifest,* AO.

orh-=org-; orhlættre=orleahtre

orhlȳte *without lot or share in, destitute of,* Æ.

oriege *out of sight, not visible,* ANS98·128.

orl m.=orel n.

orlæg† (e) n. *fate,* DA,DD.

orleahter m. '*discrimen,' lack of vice or defect,* v. ES37·179 : *danger,* CHRD2⁸.

orleahtre *blameless,* B,BL.

orleg=orlæg

orlegcēap m. *battle-booty?* GEN1994.

orlege I. n. *strife, war.* II. adj. *hostile.*

orlegfrom *keen in battle,* RD21¹⁵.

orleggīfre (æ) *fond of strife,* GEN2287.

orleghwīl† f. *war-time,* B.

orlegnīð† m. *war, hostility,* GEN.

orlegsceaft f. '*supplicium'?* SOL456? (GK).

orlegstund f. *time of adversity,* SOL374.

orlegweorc n. *battle,* GEN2020.

ormǣte I. (ā, ē) adj. *boundless, huge, excessive, intense,* Æ,*Chr*; AO. II. adv. ['*ormete*'; metan]

ormǣtlic *excessive,* CHR1117 : *tremendous,* WYN148. adv. -līce.

ormǣtnes f. *excess, immensity,* Æ.

or-mēte, -mette=ormǣte

ormōd *despondent, despairing, hopeless,* Bo, Hept; Æ,CP. ['*ormod*']

ormōdnes f. *desperation, despair,* CP.

orn=arn pret. 3 sg. of iernan.

orn-=oren-

ornest n. *trial by battle,* LL.

oroð n. *breath, breathing, snorting,* B,GL.

orped *adult, active, Bf.* ['*orped*'] adv. -līce *boldly* : *clearly, definitely.*

orrest f. *battle, combat,* CHR. [ON. orrusta]

orretscipe m. *infamy,* WW.

±orrettan *to put to confusion, disgrace.*

orsāwle *lifeless, dead,* ÆL.

orsceattinga *gratuitously,* BH 242⁷.

orsorg (w. g.) *unconcerned, without care or anxiety, safe,* CP. [OHG. ursorg]

orsorglic (w. g.) *secure,* CP. adv. -līce *carelessly, rashly,* Æ,CP : *without anxiety or hindrance* : *securely, safely,* CP.

orsorgnes f. *security, prosperity,* CP : *carelessness,* CHRD 50⁴.

orsorh=orsorg

ortgeard (*CP*), orce(a)rd (*Æ*) m. *garden,* '*ORCHARD*'.'

ortgeard-=orcerd-; ortrēowe=ortrīewe

ortrēownes (ȳ) f. *diffidence, mistrust,* BL, GD.

ortrīewan (y) *to despair* (*of*) : (+) *doubt, disbelieve.*

ortrīewe (ēo, ȳ) *despairing, hopeless,* AO,W : *treacherous, faithless.* ['*ortrow*']

±ortrūwian w. g. *to despair, doubt,* Æ. ['*ortrow*']

ortrūwung f. *despair,* Sc 131³,⁴.

ortrȳw-=ortrīew-

ortȳdre *barren,* A 11·2⁴².

orð (KGL)=oroð

orðanc I. mn. *intelligence, understanding, mind : cleverness, skill : skilful work, mechanical art,* Æ. [OHG. urdank] II. adj. *ingenious, skilful.*

orðancbend (o²) f. *cunning band,* RD 43¹⁵.

orðances *thoughtlessly,* SOL 164.

orðanclic *ingenious,* GD 269¹³.

orðancpil (o²) m. *ploughshare?* RD 22¹².

orðancscipe m. *mechanical art,* GL.

orðancum *skilfully,* B,GL.

orðian *to breathe, gasp,* Æ : *long for, aspire to,* Æ. [oroð]

orðonc (CP)=orðanc

orðung f. *breathing, breath,* Æ : *pore.*

oruð=oroð

orwearde adv. *unguarded,* B 3127.

orweg *trackless?* A 19·110.·

orwegnes f. *inaccessibility,* WW 220³⁴.

orwegstig f. *out-of-the-way track,* WW.

orwēna (indecl. adj.)=orwēne

+orwēnan *to despair,* Æ,GD.

orwēne (w. g.) *hopeless, despairing of,* Æ : *despaired of, desperate.*

orwēnnes f. *despair,* Æ,LL.

orwīge *not fighting, unwarlike, cowardly* : *not liable to the legal consequences* (*of homicide*), LL 76,42⁵,⁷.

orwīte=orwīge

orwurð n. *ignominy,* CPs 82¹⁷.

orwyrð (VPs), orwyrðu f. *shame, dishonour* : *abuse.*

+orwyrðan *to disgrace,* GL.

+orwyrðe (-de) *traduced,* WW 51²³.

orwyrðlic *shameful,* MH 156²¹.

oryldu f. *great age.* [ieldo]

ōs m., gp. ēsa *a divinity, god : name of the rune for* o.

oser '*vimen,*' *osier,* OEG 10².

ōsle f. '*merula,*' '*ouzel,*' *blackbird,* Cp,Ep, WW. [amsel]

ōsogen (WW 501³³)=āsogen pp. of āsugan.

ōst m. *protuberance, knot, lump,* GL,MH.

osterhlāf m. *oyster-patty,* LCD 79a.

osterscyll (o²) f. *oyster-shell,* LCD 1·338¹⁶.

ōstig, ōstiht *knotty, rough, scaly,* GL.

ostre f. *oyster,* WW. [L. ostrea]

ostor-=oster-

ot I. (VPs)=æt. II.=oð

oter (KC)=otor

oterhola m. *otter's hole,* KC 3·23'.

otor, otr (Ep), ottor m. '*otter,*' WW.

otsperning (KGL 70¹⁶)=ætspornung

oð I. prep. w. a. and (rarely) d. *to, up to, as far as* : *until,* Æ,AO,CP. oð ðisum *up to now,* ES 43·166. II. conj. *until.* III. as prefix. usu. denotes departure, separation, as in oðfeallan, oðwendan.

oðberan† *to bear away, carry off* : *bring.*

oðberstan³ *to break away, escape,* KC,LL.

oð-brēdan, -bregdan³ *to snatch away, carry off, rescue, remove, withdraw,* Gu; AO. ['*atbraid*']

oðclīfan¹ *to cleave to, stick, adhere,* CR 1267.

oðcwelan⁴ *to die,* LL 112,53.

oðcyrran (=ie) *to be perverted,* JUL 338.

oðdōn anv. *to put out* (*eyes*), LL 32,19.

oðēawan=oðīewan

oðēacan *to add to,* VPs 68²⁷. [ēac]

oðēhtian *to drive away? dispossess?* LCD 1·384¹⁵ (A 52·118).

oðel=ēðel; oðēowan=oðīewan

ōðer I. (+ at KC 6·155⁹) pron. sb. or adj. (always strong) *one of two,* Æ,AO : *second,* Æ : '*OTHER*' : *something else, anything else : alternate, next : remaining, rest,* AO : *further, existing besides,* Æ : *another* : (in pl.) *the rest, the others.* ōðer...ōðer *the one...the other,* Æ, CP : *other...than,* CP. ōðer oððe...oððe *either...or.* ōðer *healf one and a half.* II. ('*aut*')=āhwæðer. comp. adv. ōðerlīcor *otherwise,* RB 87¹⁹. ['*otherliker*'] III. *word, speech* ('*eloquium*'), PPs 118³⁸. [ON. ōðr]

ōðergēara adv. *next year,* LCD.

ōðerhwīle *sometimes,* BF 118²⁹.

ōðerlucor (RWH 77⁷)=ōðerlīcor

oðēwan=oðīewan

oðfæstan† *to inflict upon*, El,Sat : *set to (a task), entrust, commit*, CP.

oðfaran⁶ w. d. *to flee from, Ex.* ['*atfare*']

oðfeallan¹ *to fall off, decline, decay*, CP : *fall away from, be lost to, be wanting, fail* : *cease to concern.*

oðfēolan³ *to cleave, adhere*, WW416²⁴.

oðfeorrian *to take away*, Lcd 1·384⁴.

oðferian *to take away, bear off* : *save (life).*

oðflēogan² *to fly away*, Ph347.

oðflēon² (w. d.) *to flee away, escape*, Æ,AO.

oðflītan¹ *to gain by legal process*, TC169′.

oðgān anv. *to go away, escape*, B2934.

oðglīdan¹ *to glide away, escape*, Sol401.

oðgrīpan¹ *to rescue*, BH408²⁷.

oðhealdan⁷ *to keep back*, CP. ['*athold*']

oðhebban⁶ *to raise, exalt, lift up*, CP.

oðhelde=oðhylde

oðhlēapan⁷ *to escape*, LL218,1¹¹.

oðhrīnan¹ *to touch*, HL16²²⁸.

oðhȳdan *to hide from*, AO94¹¹.

oðhylde (e) *contented*, Lcd.

ōðian=ēðian

oðiernan³ *to run away*, LL,Met.

oðīewan (ē, ēa, ēo, ī, ȳ) tr. *to show, Gen*; CP : *show oneself, appear, El.* ['*atew*']

oðīewodnes f. *manifestation*, RWH67² (=ætēow-).

oðlǣdan *to lead away, carry off, snatch from, withdraw, Ps.* ['*atlead*']

oðlengan *to belong, pertain*, Wyn49,68.

oðrān=oðhrān pret. 3 sg. of oðhrīnan.

oðrīdan¹ *to ride, proceed*, Hell40.

oðrinnan³ *to run off, escape*, Met20¹³⁸. [v. '*atrin*']

oðrōwan⁷ *to escape by rowing*, Chr897A.

oðsacan⁶ (w. g.) *to deny, abjure*, AO.

oðscacan⁶ *to escape*, LL177,6³.

oðscēotan² *to escape, slip off, turn aside*, Æ.

oðscūfan² intr. *to move off*, Ph168.

oðsperning f. *stumbling-block*, KGl.

oðspurnan³ (eo) *to dash against*, Bl,KGl.

oðstandan⁶ *to stand fixed, remain, cease*, AO : *stand behind*, Æ : *perplex, hinder.*

oðstillan *to stop*, Lcd1·82⁶.

oðswerian⁶ *to abjure, deny on oath*, AO,LL.

oðswīgan *to become silent*, OET631.

oðswimman³ (y) *to escape by swimming*, Chr915D.

oðtēon² *to take away*, Lcd87a.

oððæt conj. *until* (or two words).

oððe, oðða conj. *or* : *and*, ANS151·79. oððe...oððe *either...or*, BH ['OTHER'] : (=oð ðe) *until.*

oððēodan *to sever, dismember*, An1423.

oððet (KGl61¹⁹)=oððæt

oððīcgan⁵ *to take away*, Ex338.

oððingian *to obtain by unfair means, usurp*, LL(412⁹).

oððo (BH66²⁰), oððon (HL,LL) conj. *or.* [=oððe]

oððringan³ *to deprive of*, AO : *drive out*, GD.

oðwendan *to turn away, divert, deprive of*, Gen403. ['*atwend*']

oðwindan³ *to escape, get away*, Chr897A.

oðwītan¹ *to charge with, blame, reproach with, taunt*, AO,CP.

oðwyrcan *to harm*, Lcd1·384⁶.

oðȳwan=oðīewan

ōwæstm m. *shoot, branch, twig*, Gl,Ps.

ōwana (N)=āhwonan

ō-web, -wef (ā) n. *woof, weft*, Cp,WW. ['*abb*']

ōwer, ōwern (BH)=āhwær; ōwiht=āwiht

ōwisc f. *edge*, KC3·388²⁵.

ōwðer=āhwæðer; ōwul=āwel

oxa m. nap. oxan, œxen, exen, dp. ox(n)um '*ox*,' Ct,JnL,Rd,VPs,WW ; CP.

oxancealf n. *ox-calf*, LevC1³.

oxangang m. *an eighth of a 'plough-land,' hide*, BC3·370. ['*oxgang*']

oxanhyrde m. *herdsman*, OEG,WW.

oxanslyppe f. '*oxlip*,' Lcd.

ōxn f. *arm-pit*, WW.

oxnahyrde=oxanhyrde

oxnalybb n. *ox-heal (plant)*, Lcd.

ōxta=ōcusta; oxum v. oxa.

P

pād f. *covering, coat, cloak*, WW.

paddanlēg f. *toad-meadow, frog-island*, BC 2·246⁶.

padde, pade f. *toad, frog*, Chr1137 ; BC 2·377¹⁶. ['*pad*']

pǣca m. *deceiver*, Bas40²¹.

pǣcan *to cheat, deceive*, RB,W.

pægel n. *gill, small measure, wine vessel*, WW124² (A8·450). [v. '*pail*']

pǣl m. *javelin* (v. OEG19³).

pæll (e) m. *silk robe, cloak*, ÆGr : '*pall*,' *hanging, covering*, ÆH : *purple garment, purple*, BH,WW. [L. pallium]

pællen (e) *of costly stuff, purple*, Æ. ['*pallen*']

pællerēad v. fellerēad ; pǣlm==palm

pǣneg, pǣning=pening ; -pǣran v. for-p.

pǣrl? '*enula*' ('*gemmula*'? Wülker), ÆGr 304⁷.

pǣtig=(prætig), prættig

pæð (a) mfn. nap. paðas '*path*,' *track*, Ct, Ex,Gl,Ps ; Æ : *valley*, LkL.

pæððan *to traverse, travel over, pass along*, Met,Rd. ['*path*']

pāl m. '*pole*,' *stake, post*, WW334² : *spade.* [L. palus]

palendse (AO), palentse, pal(l)ente f., palent (Æ) m. *palace.* [Late L. palantium]

palentlic *of a palace, palatial,* WW 342⁷.
palester=palstr
pallium m. *pallium,* CHR 804 : *splendid garment,* ÆL 36¹⁶⁰. [*L.*]
palm (æ), palma (ea) m. *'palm'-tree, Æ, DR,JnL,VPs : palm-branch,* Æ.
palm-æppel, -appel m. *date,* WW.
palmbearu m. *palm-grove,* WW 488¹³.
palm-dæg (Æ), -sunnandæg (*Lk* 19²⁹) m. *'Palm Sunday.'*
palm-trēo, -trēow m. *'palm-tree,' Æ,JnL.*
palmtwig n. *palm-twig, palm-branch,* Æ.
+**palmtwigian**† *to deck with palm-branches.*
palmwuce f. *week of which Palm Sunday is the first day.*
palstr, palster sb. *prick, point, spike,* GL.
palðer (AA 39¹⁵), pandher (PA 12) m. *panther.*
panic m. *a kind of millet,* LCD.
panmete m. *cooked food,* WW 409⁹.
panne (o) f. *'pan,' CP,WW.*
pāpa m. *'pope,' BH;* Æ,CP. [*L.* papa]
pāpanhād m. *papal office, Æ.* [*'popehood'*]
pāpdōm m. *papacy,* CHR 592.
paper m? *papyrus,* WW 523⁷.
papig=popig
papolstān (o¹, e²) m. *pebble,* Æ,OEG. [*'pebblestone'; L.* papula]
pāp-seld, -setl n. *papacy,* BL 205²⁰.
paradis m. *Paradise,* HEX 512.
paralisin ds. of sb. *paralysis,* ÆL 25⁷²⁴.
-parian v. ā-p.
part m. *'part,' ÆGr.* [*L.* partem]
passion f. nap. passione *the part of the gospel containing the account of Christ's passion,* OET 444³⁷.
pað, paðu=pæð
pāwa m. pāwe f. *peacock, peahen, ÆGr,Ep, Lcd,WW.* [*'po'; Lat.* pavo]
pēa m. *peafowl,* Ph 312. [*'pea'*]
peall *'defrutum'* (sc. *vinum*), OEG (v. ES 37·184).
peaneg=pening
pear-roc, -ruc m. *'clatrum,' fence by which a space is enclosed,* Gl : *enclosure, enclosed land, Bo,Chr,KC;* ÆL. [*'parrock'*]
pecg m? *pig?* BC 3·223²² (pygg? v. SKED).
pell, pellen=pæll, pællen
pellican m. *'pelican,' Ps* 101⁵.
pen=penn
pending, pene(n)g, penig=pening
pening m. *'PENNY*,' coin, money, Æ,LL* (v. 2·614) : *pennyweight,* Lcd.
pening-hwyrfere, -mangere m. *moneychanger,* WW.
peningslæht (=i³) m. *coining money,* MtL 17²⁵.
peningwǣg f. *pennyweight,* LCD 47b.
peningweorð (u³) n. *pennyworth, Lcd,KC;* Æ.

penn m. *'pen,' fold, BC;* Mdf. [*L.*]
pennig, penning=pening
pentecosten m. *'Pentecost,' Æ,Bf,Chr.*
pēo=pīe
peonie f. *'peony,' Lcd* 1·168¹⁴. [*L.*]
peorð m. *name of the rune for* p, *chessman?* RUN 38.
peose (piose, pyose)=pise; **pere**=peru
perewōs n. *pear-juice, perry,* WW 128²⁰.
perfince=perwince
pernex m. *a supposed bird?* (mistranslation of *L.* pernix), RD 41⁶⁶.
per-sic, -soc, -suc m. *peach,* LCD. [*L.* persicum]
Persisc *Persian, Æ.*
persoctrēow n. *peach-tree,* WW 138¹.
peru f. *'pear,' ÆGr.* [*L.* pirum]
perwince f. *'periwinkle' (plant),* WW.
petersilie f. *'parsley,' Lcd.* [*Ger.* petersilie]
pētig=(prǣtig), prættig; **peððan**=pæððan
philosoph m. *philosopher,* AO.
pic n. *'pitch,' Ep,Sc;* Æ. [*L.* picem]
pic m. *point, pointed tool, pick, pickaxe, Cp,WW.* [*'pike'*]
picen *pitchy, of pitch,* BL,DHY.
picgbrēad? (picbred) *'glans,' mast, pig's food,* WW 139³⁵. [v. *'pig'*]
+**pician** *to cover with 'pitch,' Lcd* 10a.
picung f. *'stigmata,' pricking, Cp* 572s. [*'picking'*]
pie f. *parasite,* GL.
pierisc *Pierian,* A 31·535.
pigment, pihment (y) *drug,* LCD. [*L.*]
pihten *part of a loom,* OEG. [*L.* pecten]
pil m. *a pointed object, spike, nail, shaft, stake, Æ,Chr : arrow, dart, javelin :* pl. *hairs of plants, Lcd* 1·304¹. [*'pile'; L.* pilum]
pilce=pylece; **pile**=pyle
pile f. *mortar,* CP. [*L.* pila]
pilece=pylece
+**piled** *spiked, spiky,* ÆH.
pilere m. *one who pounds in a mortar,* WW 141¹⁹.
pilian (y¹) *to peel, skin,* LCD 3·114¹³.
±**pilian** *to pound in a mortar,* Ex 16¹⁴,WW 114²⁵.
pilsāpe f. *'silotrum,' soap for removing hair?* WW 127³⁶,(NP 8·204).
pilstæf m. *pestle,* CP 267².
pil-stampe f., -stocc m., pilstre f. *pestle,* WW.
pin f. *pain, anguish, torture.* [*L.* poena]
pinbēam m. *pine-tree, Æ.* [v. *'pine'*]
pinca=pynca
pinecwalu m? n? *torture,* W 241¹³.
pinere m. *tormentor,* GPH,NG.
pinewincle=winewincle
pingan=pyngan
pin-hnutu f. ds. -hnyte *fir-cone, Lcd.* [*'pine-nut'*]

±pīnian *to torture, torment, AO,MtL*; Æ,CP.
['*pine*'; *L.* poena]
pinn sb. '*pin,*' *peg, Bf : pen,* Mt p2¹⁷.
pinnan obl. case of wk. sb. pinne? *flask,
bottle,* WW97¹⁰.
pīnnes f. *pain, torture,* TC369'.
pinsian *to weigh, consider, examine, reflect,*
CP. [*L.* pensare]
pintel '*penis,*' WW292¹ᵛ ['*pintle*']
pīntrēow n. '*pine-tree Lcd*; ÆL.
pīn-trēowen, -trȳwen *of or belonging to a
pine-tree,* Lcd.
pīnung f. *torment, punishment,* Æ,AO.
pīnungtōl n. *instrument of torture,* Æ.
pionie (OEG56⁴¹⁸)=peonie; piose=pise
pīpdrēam m. *piping,* Lcd3·208²².
pīpe f. '*pipe,*' *tube, Lcd*; Mdf : *wind instrument, W,WW : channel,* KC3·380². [*L.*]
pipeneale f. *pimpernel* (Swt).
piper=pipor
pīpere m. '*piper,*' *MtR,WW.*
pīpian *to '*pipe*' (blow an instrument), NC*
(ZDA34·234).
piplian (y) *to show eruptions, break out in
pimples,* Lcd.
pīplic *musical,* OEG1644.
pipor (e²) m. '*pepper,*' *Æ,Lcd.* [*L.* piper]
piporcorn n. '*pepper-corn,*' *Lcd.*
piporcwyrn f. *pepper mill,* ANS84·325.
piporhorn (e) m. *horn for pepper,* LL455,17.
±pip(o)rian *to season with '*pepper,*' *Lcd.*
Pirenisc *Pyrrhenian,* A31·535.
pirge (Gl)=pirie
pirgrāf m. *pear-orchard,* KC5·284'.
pirie, pirige (Æ) f. *pear-tree.*
pīs *heavy,* NG. [*L.* pensum]
pise f. (eo, io, y) *pea, Cp,Lcd,WW.*
['*pease**']
pisle f. *warm chamber?* WW186¹⁰. [*Low L.*
pisalis]
pīslic *heavy,* NG. adv. -līce.
pistel=pistol
pistol m. *letter,* Æ : *apostolic letter,* Æ.
['*pistle*'; *L.* epistola]
pistolbōc f. *book of the epistles,* LL. [v.
'*pistle*']
pistolclāð m. *vestment worn by the epistoler,*
BC3·366'.
pistolrǣdere m. *epistle-reader, sub-deacon,*
CM.
pistolrǣding f. *a lesson in the church service,*
Æ. [v. '*pistle*']
pistolrocc (e²) m. *vestment worn by the
epistoler,* TC429²².
pitt=pytt
pīða wm. *inward part, '*pith,*' Bo*; CP.
placunis (wlacunis)=wlæcnes
plǣce f. *open space, street, DR,MtLR.*
['*place*'; *L.* platea]

plæg-=pleg-; plǣse, plǣtse=plǣce
plǣtt m. *slap, smack,* ÆH2·248'.
plǣttan *to buffet, smack,* Jn19³. ['*plat*']
plagian=plegian
planēta *chasuble* (BTs). [v. '*planet*']
plante f. '*plant,*' *shoot, CP,VPs.* [*L.* planta]
±plantian *to '*plant,*' *Æ,CP,VPs.*
plantsticca m. *dibble,* WW106¹⁷.
plantung f. '*planting,*' *WW : plant, Mt.*
plaster I. n. '*plaster*' (as medicament), DDₗ
Lcd. [*L.* emplastrum] II.=palster
-platian v. ā-pl.
+platod *plated* (of gold), OEG11⁶¹.
platung f. *metal plate,* WW196²⁴. [v. '*plate*']
pleagian=plegian
plega (a, æ) m. *quick motion, movement,
exercise, Chr,Cp,Cr,Gen,WW : '*play,*'
festivity, drama, game, sport, AO,Bl*; Æ :
battle, B : gear for games, ApT12¹⁷ : *ap-
plause.*
plegan, ±plegian (a, æ, eo) (pres. occly.
strong) *to move rapidly, An,Gen : exercise,
occupy or busy oneself, Bo,Bl,LL : '*play,*'
sport with, amuse oneself, dance, CP,MtL :
contend, fight : play on an instrument, Ps :
clap the hands, applaud, El,VPs : make
sport of, mock, Æ : cohabit* (with), Rd43².
plegemann=plegmann
plegende '*playing,*' Shr.
plegere m. '*player,*' WW108⁹.
plegestōw=plegstōw
plegestre f. *female athlete,* OEG4735.
pleghūs n. '*playhouse,*' *theatre,* OEG1752.
plegian=plegan
pleglic (Gl) *athletic : scenic : comic.*
plegmann m. *gymnosophist, athlete,* Gl.
plegol *playful, jocular,* ÆL21²⁹² : *wanton,*
Chrd54²³.
plegscip n. *small vessel,* WW181⁴⁰.
plegscyld (e²) m. *play-shield, small shield,*
Gl.
plegstede m. *playground,* KC6·244⁸.
plegstōw f. *playground, gymnasium, amphitheatre, Lcd,WW.* ['*playstow*']
plēo ds. of pleoh.
pleogan=plegan
pleoh n. gs. plēos *danger, risk, harm,* Æ,AO,
CP : *responsibility,* LL70,36².
plēolic *dangerous, hurtful, hazardous,* Æ,
AO.
plēon⁵ (w. g.) *to expose to danger, adventure
oneself,* CP.
plett f? *fold,* NG. [*L.* plecta]
plice v. plyccan.
plicettan? *to play with,* v. NC315.
plicgan *to scrape, scratch,* GPH396.
pliht m. *peril, risk, danger, damage,* VPs,
WW; Æ. tō plihte *dangerously.* [plēon;
'*plight*']

plihtan *to imperil, compromise, LL.* [*'plight'*]
plihtere m. *look-out man at the prow,* OEG.
plihtlic *perilous, dangerous,* LCD,WW.
ploccian=pluccian
plōg, plōh m. *what a yoke of oxen could plough in a day, a plough-land, Lcd.* [*'plough'*]
plont-=plant-
plot *'plot' of ground,* LL400,3 (v. 3·237).
pluccian *to 'pluck,' tear,* Æ,Mt,WW.
plūm f. *down?* Cp1600 (v. A47·248).
plūmblǣd f. *plum,* LCD86a.
plūme f. *'plum,'* Æ,Cp : *plum-tree,* Cp,Ep, Erf; Mdf.
plūmfeðer f. *down,* ES9·39. [*L.* pluma]
plūmsēaw (ē²) n. *plum-juice,* LCD3·114'.
plūmslā f. *wild plum, sloe,* WW139⁴.
plūmtrēow n. *'plum-tree,' Lcd;* ÆGR.
plyccan *only in* plice 2 sg. subj. (*IM* 122) *and* plyce (imperat.) (*IM* 127) *to pluck, pull, snatch,* NC315. [*'plitch'*]
plyhtlic=plihtlic
plȳme f. *plum, plum-tree,* GL. [*L.* *prunea]
pocādl f. *eruptive disease, pox,* LCD.
pocc m. *'pock,' blister, pustule, ulcer, Lcd.*
pocca (*LkL*)=pohha
pohha, poh(ch)a m. *pocket, bag,* CP,MkL. [*'pough'*]
pohhede *baggy, RB.* [*'pough'*]
pōl m. *'pool,'* CP,JnL; Æ; Mdf.
pōlbǣr f. *pasture-land by a pool,* KC (MLR 19·203).
polente? f. *parched corn,* Æ. [*'polenta'; L.*]
pollegie f. *pennyroyal,* LCD. [*L.* pulegium]
pollup m. *scourge?* (BT), LL(278').
pon-=pan-; **pond**=pynd
popæg (Cp)=popig
popelstān (*OEG* 1815)=papolstān
popig m? *'poppy,'* Gl,WW.
popul *poplar?* KC3·219⁸ (v. BT).
por, porr, porlēac n. *leek,* Æ. [*L.* porrum]
port I. mn. *'port,' harbour, AO* : *town (esp. with market rights or with a harbour),* BH, Chr,LG,LL; Mdf. [*L.* portus] II. m. *portal, door, gate, entrance,* MtL,Ps; Mdf. [*'port'; L.* porta]
portcwēne f. *prostitute,* NG.
porte f.=port II.
portgeat n. *city gate,* Æ,WW.
portgerēfa m. *'port-reeve,' mayor,* Æ,Ct,LL, WW.
portgeriht n. *town-due,* KC3·138¹⁰.
portherpað *main road to a town,* KC3·453'.
±portian *to bray (in a mortar),* CP.
portic mn. *portico, porch, vestibule, sanctuary, chapel,* BH,Jn; Æ. [*'portic'*]
portmann m. *townsman,* Æ,WW. [*'portman'*]
portstrǣt f. *public road,* KC.

portweall m. *city wall,* Æ.
portweg *public road,* KC6·81¹.
port-wer (DR), -weora (KC) m. *citizen* (=-wara).
±pos n. *cold in head, Lcd.* [*'pose'*]
posa (NG)=pusa
poshlīwe *a kind of shelter?* KC3·82².
posl, postling m. *pellet, pill,* LCD.
post m. *'post,'* Æ,WW. [*L.* postis]
postol m. *apostle,* LkR. [*'postle'*]
potian *to push, butt, goad,* Æ,W. [*'pote'*]
pott m. *'pot,' Lcd* 1·378' (v. late).
pottere m. *'potter,'* BC3·49'.
prætt m. nap. prattas *trick, craft, art,* Æ,W, ZDA. [*'prat'*]
prættig (e) *tricky, sly, cunning, wily, astute,* WW; Æ. [*'pretty'*]
prafost (ā¹? o¹, a², e²) m. *officer, 'provost' (of a monastery),* KC,MH,RB; Æ. [*L.* propos(i)tus]
prafostfolgoð m. *order or rank of provost,* RB126⁶.
prafostscīr f. *provostship,* RB124¹⁶.
pranga v. wranga.
prass m. *noise, tumult,* ÆL.
prattas v. prætt; **prēan**=prēon
prēde=prȳte
prēdicere m. *preacher,* ÆGR276¹.
prēdician *to preach,* Lk8¹.
prēdicung f. *preaching,* NC315.
prēon m. *'fibula,' pin, brooch,* TC,WW. [*'preen'*]
prēost (ēa, ē, īo) m. *'priest,' presbyter,* BH, LL,Mt,Nic,WW; AO,CP.
prēostgesamnung f. *community of priests,* NC315.
prēosthād m. *'priesthood,'* BH,OEG; Æ,CP.
prēosthēap m. *body of priests,* GD302²⁵.
prēosthīred (ȳ²) m. *body of priests,* CHRD.
prēostlagu f. *ecclesiastical law, canon law,* LL380,2³.
prēostlic *'priestly,' canonical,* Chrd89³⁷; CM667.
prēostlīf n. *priests' quarters, monastery,* ÆL 31⁸⁴⁶.
prēostrēaf n. *priestly garment,* CHRD64²⁷.
prēostregol m. *canonical rule,* CHRD.
prēostscȳr f. *parish,* LL. [*'priestshire'*]
prēowthwīl f. *twinkling of an eye, moment,* Æ.
press f. *press (for clothes),* LL455,15.
prica m., price f. *'prick,' point, spot, dot,* Æ, Lcd,Mt : *small portion of space or time,* Æ, Bf.
-priccan v. ā-p.
pricel, pricels m. *'prickle,' goad, point,* Lk, OEG : *jot, tittle,* MtL,LkL.
±prician tr. *to pierce,* Æ : *prick out* : intr. *'prick,' sting,* Sc : (+) *point out,* BF.

pricmælum adv. *point by point*, Bf 112³⁰.

pricðorn m. *thorn-tree*, KC 3·436¹⁶.

pricung f. *'pricking,' remorse*, Æ 2·88²².

prīm n? *the first hour* (6 *a.m.*) : *the service held at* 6 *a.m.*, *'prime,' RB,WW.* [*L.* prima (sc. hora)]

prīmsang m. *prime-song, service of prime*, Chrd,LL.

princ? *twinkling of an eye, moment*, v. OEG 2369.

prior m. *'prior,' Chr,TC.* [*L.*]

prīt=prȳt

-prīwan v. be-pr.

prodbor (prot-) n. *auger?* MtR.

profast=prafost

prōfian *to assume to be, take for*, LL. [*L.* probare]

profost=prafost

prūd, prūt *'proud*,' arrogant*, OEG,Sc.

prutene (ū?) f. *southern-wood, wormwood*, Lcd. [*L.* abrotanum]

prūtian *to be 'proud,' Chrd.*

prūtlic *haughty.* adv. -līce *proudly, pompously, magnificently*: *confidently*, Bf 150¹⁴.

prūtscipe m. *arrogance, pride*, Gl,Ps.

prūtswongor *overburdened with pride*, W 257¹² (v.l.).

prūtung f. *pride, arrogance*, OEG. [v. *'proud'*]

prȳde=prȳte; **prȳdecere**=prēdicere

prȳt(o), prȳte f. *'pride,' haughtiness, pomp*, Æ,LL,OEG,W.

psaltere (*Lcd*)=saltere

psealm (*WW*), psalm=sealm

pūca m. *goblin*, OEG 23². ['*puck*']

pūcel m. *goblin*, GPH 394²⁴². ['*puckle*']

pucian *to poke, creep*, GPH 397.

pudd m. *ditch*, GPH 399.

puduc m. *wart*, GPH 396.

pull mf. *pool, creek*, KC (v. GBG). [*Keltic*]

pullian *to 'pull,' draw, AA* : *pluck off* (*wool*), Lcd 3·176.

pūlsper n. *reed*, MtL 11⁷ (v. A 39·364).

pumic m? *pumice*, Lcd 38a. [*L.* pumicem]

pumicstān m. *pumice-stone*, WW 148³.

pund n. *'pound'* (*in weight or in money*), *pint*, Bf,Ct,G,Lcd; Æ,AO : *weight*, Wyn 43. [*L.* pondo]

pundar, pundor=pundur

pundere m. *one who weighs*, MtL p 2³.

pundern n. *pair of scales* : *plumb-line*, OEG.

punderngend m? *one who weighs* (BTs), KGl 545.

pundfald a *'pinfold,' pound*, BC.

pundmæte adj. *of a pound weight*, RB 63¹⁶.

pundur n. *weight, plumb-line*, Cp 264 D. [*L.* pondere]

pundwǣg f. *pound weight, measure* (*of corn*),

pūnere m. *'pounder,' pestle*, Sc 95¹⁹.

pung m. *purse*, Cp. ['*pung*']

pungetung f. *pricking*, Lcd. [pyngan]

±pūnian *to 'pound,' beat, bruise*, Lcd,Sc.

punt '*punt*,' WW. [*L.* ponto]

pūr *bittern? sea-gull?* WW 116,285. ['*purre*']

purlamb n. *lamb without blemish*, Ex 12⁵.

purpl, purple (*JnL*)=purpure

purpure f., purpur (WW 152²⁰) *purple, a purple garment*, AO,Mk; CP. ['*purpur*']

purpuren *purple*, WW 151²⁴. ['*purpurine*']

purs '*purse*,' OEG 18ʙ³⁶. [*late L.* bursa]

pusa (o) m. *bag, scrip*, NG.

puslian *to pick out*, Lcd 127a.

-pūte v. ǣle-p.

pūtung f. *instigation*, Chrd 62²⁷. ['*putting*']

pȳcan *to 'pick,' Chr* 796 f?

pyff m. *a 'puff' of wind*, Bo 47²⁶ (Napier).

pyffan, pret. pyfte *to puff, blow*, v. OEG 1886.

pyhment=pigment; **pyl-**=pil-

pylce (*A* 7·30)=pylece

pyle (i) m. *'pillow,' Æ,AO,CP,Lcd.* [*L.* pulvinum]

pylece f. *a warm fur garment, robe, pelisse*, A,WW. ['*pilch*']

pylewer *pillow*, OEG 56¹⁶. ['*pilliver*']

pyll=pull

pylu (OEG 29⁴), pylwe=pyle

pynca (i) m. *point*, OEG 3683. [pyngan]

pynd? sb. *cistern? lake?* Rim 49.

+pyndan *to impound, shut up*, CP 276. ['*pind*']

pynding f. *dam*, CP 276. [v. '*pind*']

pyngan (i) *to prick*, CP. ['*ping*'; *L.* pungere]

pypelian=piplian

pyretre f. *pellitory*, Lcd 3·12¹⁹. [*L.* pyrethrum]

pyrie, pyrige=pirie, pirige

pyrtan *to strike, beat*, GPH 401.

pyse (Æ)=pise

pysecynn n. *sort of pea*, Lcd 71a.

pȳtan *to put out* (*eyes*), Chr 796 f?

pytt m. *'pit,' hole, well, grave*, AO,Ct,G,LL; CP; Mdf : *pustule*. [*L.* puteus]

pytted '*pitted,' dented, marked* (*of a sword*), EC 225'.

pyttel (i) m. *hawk, kite*, WW.

Q

qu- is usually written cw-, which see.

R

rā m. nap. rān '*roe,' roebuck*, BH,Gl,Lcd; Mdf.

rabbian *to rage*, W 84¹¹.

raca m. '*rake*,' Bf, Gl; GD 192.

racca m. *part of the rigging of a ship*, WW.
racente f. *chain, fetter*, Bl,Bo,Sc; AO. ['*rackan*']
+**racentēagian** *to chain*, ÆL31⁸⁵.
racen-tēah f. gs. -tēage *chain, fetter*, Bl; Æ. ['*rakenteie*']
racete=racente
racetēage (*Mk*)=racentēah
racian (w. d.) *to rule, govern, control* : *go forward, move*, CP,W : *hasten*, NR28²⁵. ['*rake*']
raciend m. *speaker, orator*, GD265¹².
rācing (*JnL*)=rǣcing
racu I. f. *exposition, explanation, observation* : *reason, argument* : *account, narrative*, Æ,CP : *rhetoric* : *comedy*. [reccan] II. f. (LL455¹⁵)=raca
rād I. f. *ride, riding, expedition, journey*, BH, Bo,Lcd : *raid*, Chr,LL : *modulation*, Run5 : *name of the rune for* r. ['*road*'; rīdan] II. pret. 3 sg. of rīdan. III. m.=rǣd
+**rād** I. n. *reckoning, account* : *condition, stipulation*, AO : *intention* : *reason, wisdom, discernment*, Æ,AO : *accuracy*. ðus +r. *such, of this kind*. hū +rādes *how*. II. adj. *conditioned, circumstanced, disposed, adapted*, CP : *wise, clever, skilful*, Bo; AO : *straight*, Guth. +rāde sprǣc *prose*.
-**rād** v. brand-r.
rādcniht m. *tenant holding subject to service on horseback*, v. LL1·73. ['*radknight*']
rade=hraðe; +**rādegian**=+rādian
rādehere, rādhere=rǣdehere
radelod *having straight branches?* BC3·44.
rādhors n. *riding-horse*, HL. ['*roadhorse*']
radian=hradian
+**rādian** (eg, ig) *to reckon with, arrange*, Bo 96¹⁵ : *call to account*.
+**rādlic** *proper, fitting*, Æ. adv. -līce, *intelligently, clearly*.
+**rādod** *intelligent*, Lcd3·196⁷.
rador=rodor
radost=hraðost, v. hraðe.
rādpytt m. *draw-well?* Rd59¹⁵.
+**rādscipe** m. *discretion*, Met22⁴⁸.
rādstefn f. *message taken by a mounted man*, LL456,3. [cp. rādcniht]
rādumbel=rāradumbla
rādwērig *weary of travelling*, Rd21¹⁴.
ræc=rec; **rǣcan**, ræccan=reccan
rǣcan I. *to* '*reach*' *out, stretch out*, Æ,CP : *offer, present, give, grant*, Æ : *procure?* (Lieb), LL447⁶ and 3·249 : *extend* (intr.). II.=hrǣcan
+**rǣcan** '*reach*,' *attain, overtake*, Bl,Sat : *give* : *obtain, seize, take, get, gain*, Chr; AO : *address, speak to*, AO : *handle, deal with* : *strike*.
ræcc m. *setter* (*dog*), WW276⁴. ['*rache*']

rǣce f. (*Cp*)=raca; **rǣced**=reced
rǣcing f. '*reaching,*' *holding out, presenting*, JnL : *seizing, capture*, DR (hr-).
rǣd=hrǣd
rǣd I. (ā, ē) m. *advice, counsel*, Æ : *resolution, deliberation, plan, way, design*, Æ, AO : *council, conspiracy*, Æ : *decree, ordinance*, CP : *wisdom, sense, reason, intelligence*, Æ : *gain, profit, benefit, good fortune, remedy*, Æ : *help* : *power, might*. tō rǣde +niman *resolve*, AO. tō rǣde ðincan *seem advisable*. ['REDE'] II. adj. =rēad. III. (ē) n. *reading lesson*, NG.
±**rǣdan** (ē) pret. 3 sg. reord, rēd; also wv. *to advise, counsel, persuade*, Æ : *consult, discuss, deliberate, plot, design*, Æ, AO : *decree, decide*, Æ : *rule, guide, have control over, possess* : *arrange* : *equip, provide for* : *bring, deliver* (*goods*) : *have an idea, guess, forebode*, Æ : *read, explain*, Æ : *learn by reading* : *put in order*, BH : *help*. ['READ,' 'REDE']
rǣdbana (ē) m. *accessory to a murder*, LL.
rǣdbora (ē) m. *adviser, counsellor*, Æ : (*Roman*) *consul*.
rǣdda m. *robin*, WW44¹⁸. [rēad]
rǣdde wk. pret. 3 sg. of rǣdan.
rǣde (ē) I. adj. (±) *prepared, ready, ready for riding* (*horse*), PPs : *skilled, simple*. ['*i-rede*'] II. n. (+) *trappings, armour, accoutrements, ornaments*. III. f. *reading, lesson*, RB18⁹. IV. (+) *design, device?* El1054,1108.
rǣdecempa m. *horse-soldier*, WW228³⁹.
rǣdefæsting f. *entertainment of the king's visitors, or of his messengers when riding on his business*, KC2·60'.
rǣdegafol n. *rent paid in one payment* (*in money or in kind*), LL118,67.
rǣdehere m. *mounted troop, cavalry*, AO.
+**rǣdelīce**=+rǣdlīce; **rǣdelle**=rǣdelse
rǣdels mf., rǣdelse (ē) f. *enigma, 'riddle,'* Æ : *consideration, discussion* : *imagination, conjecture, interpretation*.
rǣdemann m. *horseman*, PPs32¹⁵.
rǣden (ē) f. *condition, terms, stipulation*, Æ : *rule, government, direction* : *estimation*, WW.
±**rǣdend** m. *controller, disposer, ruler* : *diviner*, Sc75¹².
rǣdendlic *relating to a decree*, WW387, 494.
rǣdengewrit n. *written agreement*, TC168¹².
rǣdere m. '*reader,*' '*lector*' (*ecclesiastical order*), Bf,RB,LL : *scholar, diviner, expounder, interpreter*, OEG.
rǣdescamol m. *couch, reading-desk?* WW.
rǣdesmann m. *counsellor, adviser* : *steward*, EC. ['*redesman*']

rǣdewiga m. *horse-soldier*, WW 228[38].
rǣdfæst *resolute, wise*, Æ.
rǣdfæstnes f. *reasonableness*, LL (306[19]).
rǣdfindende *giving counsel*, WW 383[6].
rǣdgeðeaht n. *deliberation, counsel*, EL, W.
rǣdgifa m. *counsellor, councillor*, CHR,LL : *consul*.
rǣdgift '*consulatus*,' '*senatus*,' GL.
rǣdhors n. *riding-horse*, Æ (8[233]).
rǣdhycgende *knowing, wise*, FT 26.
rǣdic (e) m. '*radish*,' Lcd,WW. [L. radicem]
rǣdin=rǣden
rǣding I. f. '*reading*,' *a reading (passage read), lesson, narrative*, Æ,CP,RB : *consideration, consultation, counselling*, Æ (100[270]); (+) WW 383[25]. **II.**=rǣden
rǣdingboc f. *lectionary, book of the lessons*.
rǣdinggewrit (WW 115[10])=rǣdengewrit
rǣdinggrād m. *steps to lectern*, NC 316.
rǣdingscam-ol (-ul) m. *ambo, rostrum, lectern, reading-desk*, OEG (=rǣdescamol).
rǣdistre f. *female reader*, GL.
rǣdlēas (ē) *ill-advised, unwise, helpless, rash, in disorder*, Chr,Da : *wretched, bad, miserable*. ['*redeless*']
rǣdlic *expedient, advisable, wise*, AO,CP. adv. -līce *wisely, prudently, skilfully, cunningly*, CP,HL : *deliberately, on purpose : fully, explicitly*, GD 102[19]. ['*redly*']
rǣdlīce=hrǣdlīce
rǣdmægen n. *productive force*, RIM 10? (or? rādmægen).
rǣdnes=hrǣdnes
±rǣdnes f. *agreement : decree : condition : definition, decision*.
rǣdo f. (RB 62[15]n)=rǣd III.
+rǣdod *harnessed, caparisoned*, Æ (cp. +rǣde).
rǣdrīpe=hrǣdrīpe
rǣdsnotter *clever, sage*, AN 473.
rǣdðeahtende† ptc. *taking counsel*, EL.
rǣdðeahtere m. *counsellor*, AO 72,256.
rǣdðeahtung f. *counsel, advice*, AO 154[27].
rǣdwǣn (AO)=hrǣdwǣn (or ? rǣd-=rād-).
rǣdwita m. *counsellor, adviser*, DD 299.
rǣdystre=rǣdistre; **rǣf**=rēaf
+rǣf *brought home to, convicted of*, LL 66,32.
rǣfen=hrǣfn
rǣfn-an, -ian (GD) *to perform, do : undergo*.
rǣfs-=reps-
rǣfter (e, ea) m. *rafter, beam*, BH,GL.
rǣge (ā) f. *roe*, GL,LCD. [rā]
rǣgel=hrægl
rǣgerēose f. *spinal muscles*, LCD.
rǣghār *grey (with lichen)*, RUIN 10. [ragu]
rǣgl=hrægl; **rǣgn**=rēgn
rǣgolfæst=regolfæst; **rǣgu**=ragu

rǣhte pret. 3 sg. of rǣcan.
rǣm=hrǣfn; **-rǣman** v. ā-r.
rǣnc=renco; **rǣng-**=reng-·
rǣp pret. 3 sg. of repan.
rǣpan (ȳ) (±) *to bind, fetter, capture, enslave : yoke together*, ÆL 31[785].
rǣping=rǣpling
rǣpling m. *prisoner, criminal*, Æ. [rǣpan]
rǣplingweard (ē) *warder*, WW 111[10].
rǣps=reps
+rǣptan *to bind, fetter*, Bo 112[1].
rǣran *to* '*rear,*' *raise, build, create*, BH,Gen : *lift up, elevate, promote*, Bl : *establish, begin, commit, do*, Cr,W; CP : *arouse, excite, stir up*, Rd. [rīsan]
rǣs m. *rush, leap, jump, running*, Æ,Cr, LG (hr-) : *onrush, storm, attack*, Æ,B. ['*rese*']
rǣsan *to rush, hasten*, CP : *enter on rashly : rush upon, attack*, B,Bl,MH. ['*rese*']
rǣsbora† m. *counsellor, leader, guide*.
rǣsc m. *shower*, OEG 3974.
rǣscan *to vibrate, quiver*, DHy 94[1].
rǣscettan *to crackle, creak, coruscate*, DD, WW. ['*reschette*']
rǣslan=rǣswian
rǣsn n. *plank, beam, wall-plate, raising piece*, Æ,WW. ['*rasen*']
rǣst=rest
rǣswa† m. *leader, counsellor, ruler, guide : chief, prince, king*.
rǣswan, rǣswian *to think, consider, conjecture, suspect*, CP.
rǣswum dp. of *rǣs? or rǣsu? f. or *rǣswa? *suggestion, deliberation, counsel*, Az 126.
rǣswung f. *reasoning, conjecture*, GL.
rǣt m. '*rat*,' WW 118[41].
rǣt pres. 3 sg. of rǣdan.
ræð-=hræð-; **ræðe**=hraðe
ræðe=rēðe
+rǣðe=+rēde
rǣw I. (±) (ā, ēa) f. *row, line : succession*, LCD : *hedgerow*. [v. '*rew*' and Mdf] **II.**=hrǣw
+rǣwed, +rǣwe(n), +rǣwod *arranged in rows*, WW.
-rāflan v. ā-r.; **rāge**=rǣge
raggig *shaggy, bristly, rough*, OEG. ['*raggy*']
ragofinc=ragufinc
ragu (æ) f. *lichen*, Æ,LCD.
ragufinc (ea[1]) m. *name of a bird, kind of finch*, WW.
rāha=rā
rāhdēor n. *roe-buck*, Æ,Lcd. ['*roedeer*']
rāhhege m. *deer-fence*, KC 3·77'.
rāhte=rǣhte pret. sg. of rǣcan.
ram=ramm; **ramesa**=hramsa
ramgealla m. *ram-gall (plant)*, LCD.

ramm (o) m. *'ram' (sheep)*, *Æ,VPs* : *(engine of war)*, *Æ,CP* : *(zodiacal sign)*, *Bf.*

ran pret. 3 sg. of rinnan.

rān I. n. *open robbery, rapine.* [*ON.*] **II.** pret. 3 sg. of rīnan. **III.** nap. of rā.

ranc *froward, proud, overbearing*, *Æ* : *noble, brave, strong*, *Chr* : *ostentatious* : *full-grown, mature*, *ÆL* 35²². [*'rank'*] adv. -līce *boldly, confidently* : *ostentatiously, showily*, *LL.* [*'rankly'*]

rancstrǣt f. *straight road? splendid road?* GEN 2112.

rand (o) m. *border, edge? KC* : (†) *boss of shield, rim of shield* : (†) *shield, buckler*, *B.* [v. *'rand'*]

rand-bēag, -bēah m. *boss (of a shield), shield*, *Æ,*GL.

randburg f. *fortified city?* JUL 19 : *shield-wall of waves (in the Red Sea)*, EX 463?

randgebeorh n. *protecting shield of waves (in the Red Sea)*, EX 296.

randhæbbend (o¹) m. *shield-bearer, warrior*, B 861.

rand-wīga†, -wīgend†, -wīggend m. *shield-warrior, man at arms.*

rānn=rān III.

rāp I. m. 'ROPE,' *cord, cable*, AO,CP. **II.** pret. 3 sg. of rīpan.

rāpgenga m. *rope-dancer*, WW 408²⁵.

rāpincel n. *(small rope), cord, string*, GL.

rāplic adj. *of rope*, GPH 399.

+**rār** n. *roaring, howling*, MH 16²⁰.

rāradumbla m., rāredumle f. *bittern*, GL. [*Ger.* rohrdommel]

rārian *to 'roar,' bellow, cry, lament, mourn*, *Æ,MH,MtL.*

rārung f. *'roaring,' howling, bellowing*, WW.

rās pret. 3 sg. of rīsan.

rāsettan† *to rage (of fire)*, CR, MET. [rǣsan]

rāslan *to explore*, B 2283.

ratlan=hratian

raðe=hraðe

rāw (*Lcd* 89b)=rǣw [*'row'*]

+**rāwan** *to arrange in line*, WW.

raxan *to stretch oneself*, Guth. [*'rax'*]

rēac pret. 3 sg. of rēocan.

rēad I. 'RED,' *Æ,CP*; *(of gold)*, *Æ.* **II.** pret. 3 sg. of rēodan.

rēada pl. *small intestines*, WW 159³⁸ : *tonsil*, LCD. [*'read'*]

rēadbasu (e²) *reddish purple*, LL.

rēade adv. *with red colour*, LCD.

rēadfāh *red of hue*, RUIN 10.

rēadgoldlǣfer f. *plating of (red) gold*, OEG 1070.

rēadian *to be or become 'red,'* Lcd,MtR; *Æ.*

rēadlēaf *red-leaved*, BC; Mdf.

rēadlesc *'rubricata' (pellis)*, v. OEG 5324.

rēadnes f. *'redness,'* BH,Bl; *Æ.*

rēadstalede *red-stalked*, LCD 1·378'.

rēaf (ē) n. *plunder, booty, spoil*, LkL,Ps : *garment, armour, vestment*, Mt; *Æ.* [*'reaf,' 'reif'*]

+**rēafa**=+rēfa

rēafere m. *robber, plunderer*, *Æ,Bo,Lk*; AO, CP. [*'reaver'*]

-**rēafetian** v. wīn-(h)r.

rēafgend m. *robber*, KC 3·350²⁶.

±**rēaflan I.** *to rob, plunder, take by force, waste, ravage*, *Æ,Bo,B,G,VPs,W*; AO : *carry off, remove, transport*, CP : (+) *strip*, NG. [*'reave'*] **II.** *to robe*, ÆP 126¹⁰.

rēafigende *rapacious*, ÆL. [*'reaving'*]

rēaflāc nm. *robbery, rapine*, ÆH : *plunder, booty*, Bo. [*'reflac'*]

rēafol *rapacious*, LCD,GL.

rēafolnes f. *rapacity*, OEG.

reafter=ræfter

rēafung f. *spoliation, plundering*, AO 84²¹.

reagufinc (GL)=ragufinc

reahte pret. 3 sg. of reccan.

reahtigan *to dispute, discuss*, AO 130²⁶.

rēam I. m. *cream*, Lcd 113b. [*'ream'*] **II.**=hrēam

rēama=rēoma

rēamwīn? n. *a kind of wine*, OEG. [cp. *Fr.* vin crémant]

rēat pret. 3 sg. of rēotan.

rēaðe=rēðe; **rēaw**=rǣw

rēawde=hrēawde, pret. of hrēawan.

rēc m. *smoke*, Gen,Ps. [*'reek'*]

+**rec I.** n. *rule, government* : *decree* : *explanation.* **II.** n. *tumult*, MtL 27²⁴ (? for ungerec). **III.** *a small vessel, brigantine?* WW 30,432.

recan⁵ *to bring, convey*, WW 420¹⁸ : (+) *go, move, rush.*

±**rēcan I.** pret. 3 sg. rēhte *to fumigate, expose to smoke*, Lcd : *burn incense*, GL. [v. *'reek'*] **II.**=reccan II.

reccan I. *to stretch, tend, go*, CP : *extend, hold out to, give* : (±) *instruct, explain, interpret*, *Æ* : *tell, narrate*, B,Bo,G : *quote* : *correct, reprove*, AO : (+) *to wield (authority), give judgment, decide, direct, control*, *Æ,CP* : (+) *prove* : (+) *count, reckon*, *Æ.* [*'recche'*] **II.** (rēcan) *to take care of, be interested in*, *Æ,B,Bo,Cr* : *care for*, Mk : *care, desire (to do something)*, Bo, Lcd,LL,MkL,WW. [*'reck'*]

recce- (CP), **recci-**=rēce-

-**recce** v. earfoð-r.

+**reccelic**=+reclic

rēcceliest (e³, ea³, i³) f. *carelessness, negligence*, CP.

reccend m. *ruler, guide*, *Æ,*AO.

reccend(d)ōm m. *governance, oversight*, CP.

reccenes=+recenes

reccere m. *teacher, ruler, director,* CP : *interpreter,* MtLp2[13].

reccing f. *narrative,* ÆL30[375].

reced nm. *building, house, palace, hall* : '*triclinium,*' OEG.

recedlic (æ) *palatial,* WW.

±**recednes** f. *narrative, history,* Æ : *interpretation* : *direction, correction.* ānfeald +r. *prose.*

recedōm=reccendōm

rēcel (v. MFH 171)=rēcels

rēcelēas '*reckless,*' *careless, negligent,* BH, Bo,Cp,W.

rēcelēasian *to neglect,* W. ['*reckless*']

rēcelēaslīce adv. *heedlessly, carelessly, inattentively,* CP (rēcce-), HL. ['*recklessly*']

rēcelēasnes f. '*recklessness,*' *carelessness, negligence,* LL,W ; Æ.

rēce-lēast, -līestu=rēccelīest

rēcels (ī, ȳ) m. *incense, frankincense,* MtL, Lcd,Lk ; Æ. ['*rekels*'; rēc]

rēcelsbūc (ȳ) m. *censer,* WW.

rēcelsfæt (i) n. *censer,* Æ. ['*rekelsfat*']

rēcelsian *to perfume with incense,* LCD.

rēcelsrēocè f. *burning of incense,* FBO75[19].

recen *ready, prompt, quick,* Wa : *rapid, violent,* Cr,Ps. ['*reken*']

recendōm=reccendōm

recene (i, y) adv. *instantly, quickly,* Æ.

+**recenes** f. *narrative, interpretation* : *direction, correction.*

recenian *to pay* : (+) *explain, recount, relate,* Ex525. ['*reckon*']

recenlīce (o²) adv. *immediately, forthwith,* G. ['*rekenly*']

recennes *coming together?* WW381[7] : *going?* BHB436[15].

rēcetung (VPs)=hrǣcetung

+**reclic** *circumstantial,* CPc193[15]. adv. -līce *directly, straight* : *methodically* : *smoothly.*

+**recnes** f. *direction, inclination,* EPs138[3].

recnian=recenian

recon I. *remuneration,* GL. **II.**=recen

recse=risce ; **recyd**=reced

+**recu**=+rec-

rēd I.=rǣd. **II.** pret. 3 sg. of rǣdan.

red-; rēd-=rǣd-; rǣd-; **rēde**=rēðe

redestān m. '*synophites,*' *red ochre?* WW47[15].

+**redian** (æ) *to reach* : *discover,* W : *effect.*

rēdon pret. pl. of rǣdan.

±**rēfa** (usu. +) m. *high official,* '*reeve,*' *steward, sheriff, count* ('*comes*'), *prefect, consul,* BH,Ct,Mk,MH.

+**rēfærn** n. *court-house,* MH124[13].

+**rēfland** n. *land held by a reeve,* BC.

+**rēfmǣd** f. *reeve's meadow,* Ct. [v. '*reeve*']

+**rēfmann** m. *official, courtier,* GD308·315.

refsan=repsan

+**rēfscipe** m. *reeve's office, stewardship,* Æ : *consulate,* WW371,495. ['*reeveship*']

+**rēfscīr** f. *steward's office, prefecture,* OEG.

refter (ē?)=ræfter

regellic=regollic; **regen-**=regn-, rēn-

regn (rēn; Æ,MH) m. '*rain,*' VPs : *showers of rain,* Bl.

regn-=rēn-; **regnan**=rīnan

regnheard *very hard,* B326. (cp. regnðēof)

regnian I. *to* '*rain,*' MtR5[45]. **II.**=rēnian

regnðēof† m. *downright thief.* [FTP335]

regol (eo) m. *rule, regulation, canon, law, standard, pattern,* Æ : *monastic code of rules,* Æ : *ruler (instrument).* [L. regula]

regolbryce m. *breach of rules,* W166[22].

regolfæst (æ) *rigid, strict, adhering to monastic rules,* MEN44.

regolian *to draw lines with a ruler,* NC316.

regollagu f. *monastic law,* LL266,25.

regollic *according to rules, canonical, regular.* adv. -līce.

regollīf (eo) m. *life according to ecclesiastical rules,* BH,LL.

regolsticca m. *rule, ruler (instrument),* Æ.

regolðēaw m. *discipline of (monastic) rule,* A10·144[125].

regolweard m. *regulator, director, ruler, abbot, provost,* BH.

regul=regol; **reht** (VPs)=riht

rehte pret. 3 sg. of reccan.

rēhte pret. 3 sg. of rēcan II.

relicgang m. *visiting of relics,* MH62,72.

reliquias. mpl. *relics of saints* (reliquium is used in sg.), MFH171.

reliquiasōcn f. *visit to a shrine,* MFH172.

rēman=rȳman

remian *to mend,* v. NC317.

Rēmisc *Roman,* JnL18[12].

remm-=hremm-; **remn**=hræfn

rempan *to be hasty, precipitate,* CP149[12].

rēn (AO,CP)=regn

+**rēn** (ī) n. *ornament,* CP : *building,* NG.

rēnboga m. '*rainbow,*' Æ.

renc, renco (æ) f. *pride, ostentation,* LL,W.

rendan *to* '*rend,*' *tear, cut down,* LG.

rendegn (Erf1137)=ærnðegn

+**rendrian** *to peel,* LCD25a.

rēndropa m. '*raindrop,*' Lcd3·278'.

rene=ryne

+**rēne I.** (ī) n. *ornament,* CP : *instrument* : *building,* NG. **II.** (±)=±ryne

renel (KGL)=rynel; **reng**=regn

renge (y) f. *spider, spider's web,* Ps. [L. arānea]

rengwyrm (æ) m. *intestinal worm,* LCD.

±**rēnian** *to prepare* : (+) *arrange, set in order, mend, set (trap)* : (+) *adorn.* +r. tō bismere *humiliate, degrade,* AO. [*reg-nian; Goth. raginōn]

rēniend m. *revealer*, EL880.

rēnig (*Lcd,Rd*), rēnlic (Æ) '*rainy.*'

+**rennan** *to coagulate*, EPs67¹⁶.

rēnscūr m. '*rain-shower,*' Æ.

rēnsnægl m. *snail*, OEG23²⁰.

+**rēnung** (regn-) f. *arranging*, WW371¹⁹.

rēnwæter n. '*rain-water,*' Lcd.

renweard m. *house-guardian*, B770. [ærn]

rēnwyrm m. *earthworm*, WW. ['*rainworm*']

rēo (1)=rēowe; (2)=hrēoh

rēoc *savage, furious*, B122.

rēocan I. sv² intr. *to emit vapour, steam or smoke*, '*reek,*' Lcd,Ps; Æ : *stink.* **II.** (WW 244³⁶)=rēcan

rēocende (ē) *smoking, steaming*, Æ,Jud, MtL. ['*reeking*']

rēod I. '*red,*' *ruddy*, Æ,Erf,MH. ['*reod*'] **II.** n. *red colour*, WW. **III.**=hrēod

rēodan² *to redden, stain with blood* : (†) *kill?*

reodian *to sift? search out?* (=redian? ES 51·184), EL1239.

rēodian=rēadian

rēodmūða m. '*faseacus*' (*bird*), WW234²⁵

rēodnæsc (WW38¹³)?=rēadlesc

rēofan² (only in pp. rofen) *to rend, break*, Ex463.

reogol=regol

reohhe f. '*ray,*' *thornback?* WW181⁶.

+**rēohnung**=+rēnung; **reoht**=riht

rēol=hrēol; **reoma**=rima

rēoma (ēa) m. *membrane, ligament*, Lcd, WW. ['*rim*']

rēon I.=rēowon pret. pl. of rōwan. **II.** *lament*, HELL6.

rēone asm. of rēo(we).

±**rēonian** *to conspire, plot*, Æ.

rēonig† *mournful, sad, gloomy*, EL.

rēonigmōd† *mournful, weary.*

±**rēonung** f. *whispering, muttering, conspiracy*, ÆL,AO : *astrology*, OEG. [rūn]

reopa m. *bundle of corn, sheaf*, VPs. ['*reap*']

reopan (VPs)=repan; **reopian**=ripian

±**reord† I.** fn. *voice*, B,Cr,Ps : *language, speech*, ÆL. ['*rerde*'] **II.** f. *sustenance, food* : *meal, feast.* **III.** pret. 3 sg. of rædan.

reordan=reordian II.

reordberend† m. *man*, CR.

+**reorddæg** m. *feast-day*, ÆL23b⁷⁵³.

+**reordglēawnes** f. *skill in singing*, LPs32³.

reordhūs n. *eating room, refectory*, MkL14¹⁵.

reordian I. *to speak, discourse*, B,Cr,Gen : *read.* ['*rerde*'] **II.** (±) *to feed, refresh, entertain, feast.*

+**reordnes** f. *food, feasting, banquet* : *satiety.*

±**reordung** f. *refection, meal*, Æ.

+**reordunghūs** n. *refectory*, WW328³².

+**reordungtīd** f. *meal-time*, GD145¹³.

reosan '*pissli,*' *name of a plant?* WW300⁵.

+**rēosan**=+hrēosan; **-rēose** v. ræge-r.

rēost *rest* (part of a plough), CP,WW. ['*reest*']

rēotan²† *to weep, mourn, wail.*

rēote v. rētu.

rēotig *mournful, sad, tearful*, RD1¹⁰.

rēow I.=hrēoh. **II.** pret. 3 sg. of rōwan.

rēowe f. *covering, rug, blanket, mantle*, BH, LL. [=rȳhe]

rēowlic=hrēowlic; **rēowot**=rēwet

rep-=hrep-

repan⁵ *to reap*, CHR,VPs.

repel m. *staff, rod*, GD20²⁶ (v. ES37·192).

reps m. *response* (*in a church service*), Æ, RB. [L. responsorium]

repsan (æ) *to reprove, blame*, GL.

repsung (æ) f. **I.** *a division of the night*, BF 122²¹ (hr-). **II.** *reproving*, GL. [=*ræfsung]

repung=hrepung; **rēran**=ræran

+**rerding**=+reordung; **resce**=risce

rēsele f. *answer, solution*, RD40²⁸. [=*ræsele]

rēsian=ræswian

+**resp** *convicted of*, LL (v.l. for +ræf).

respons *response*, LL(140²¹).

rest (æ) f. '*REST,*' *quiet, repose, sleep*, Æ : (±) *resting-place, bed, couch* : *grave.*

±**resta** f. *bedfellow, consort, wife*, Æ.

restan (absol. and refl.) *to* '*REST,*' *repose*, Æ : (+) *give rest to, lodge* : (w. g.) *rest from, remain, lie*, Æ.

rēstan *to rejoice, exult?* PPs113⁴.

restbedd n. *bed, couch*, PPs131³.

rest-dæg (æ), reste-, resten- (Æ) m. *day of rest, Sabbath day*, CP,G. ['*restday*']

restengēar n. *year of rest from work*, LEV 25⁵.

restgemāna m. *cohabitation*, BL,LCD.

resthūs n. *chamber*, APs,BH.

restlēas '*restless,*' *without rest*, RB121¹⁴.

+**restscipe** m. *cohabitation*, BH76²⁷.

rēsung (CP)=ræswung

±**rētan** *to delight, cheer, comfort*, CP. [rōt]

rētend m. *comforter*, W257⁴.

rētu f. (only in d. rēote) *joy*, B2457.

reðe *righteous, just*, PPs (or ?=rēðe).

rēðe (of persons) *fierce, cruel, violent, harsh, severe*, Æ,B,BH : (of things) *terrible, dreadful*, Bl,Bo,CP : *zealous*, CP. ['*rethe*']

rēðegian=rēðian

rēðehygdig *right-minded*, ALM2.

rēðeman m. *usurer* (GK), PPs108¹¹. [Goth. raðjo?]

rēðemōd† *savage, cruel, fierce, indignant.*

rēðen *wild*, ÆL10¹⁰² (cp. AS96).

rēð-ian, -igian *to rage, be fierce*, Æ,GD.

rēðig *fierce*, WW402²³.

rēðigmōd *savage, fierce*, MET25¹⁷.

rēðlic *fierce, cruel, deadly.* adv. -līce *violently.*

rēðnes f. *cruelty, severity, harshness, Bl,CP*; AO : *savageness, ferocity, BH,Lcd*; CP : *zeal*, CP : *storminess*, LkL8²⁴ (hr-). ['*retheness*']

±**rēðra** m. *rower, sailor*, GL.

+**rēðre** *constant*, CP306¹⁵.

±**rēðru** np. *oars*, GD,HL.

rēðscipe m. *fury, anger*, WW245¹⁷.

rēwet, rēwut n. *rowing*, Æ : *rowing-boat, vessel*, Æ. [rōwan]

rex m. inserted for 'cyning' at EL610, 1042.

riaht (K)=riht I.

rib, ribb n. '*rib*,' *Æ,Cp,MH,Soul*; AO.

ribbe f. *hound's-tongue, ribwort*, Ep,Lcd, WW. ['*rib*']

ribbspāca np. *rib-spokes, the brisket?* (BT), WW265²⁴.

rīca m. *influential man, ruler*, Æ.

rīcan (BDS16³⁶⁷)=rēcan (*riecan)

rīcceter, rīccetere (Æ)=rīceter

rīce I. *strong, powerful*, Da; LCD : *great, mighty, of high rank*, Æ,BH,MH; AO,CP : '*rich*,' Æ,BH,Bo,Lk. II. n. *rule, reign, power, might, authority, empire*, Æ,Bl,Cr, MH; AO. fōn tō rīce *to ascend the throne* : *kingdom, nation, diocese*, B; AO,CP : *reign (period of time)*. ['*riche*']

rīcedōm n. *kingly rule*, W125⁹. ['*richdom*']

rīcels=rēcels; **rīcen-**=recen-

rīceter, rīcetere n. *force, might, power, rule, dominion, glory, greatness*, CP : *ambition*, Æ : *tyranny, oppression, violence* : *arrogance*, ÆL32²³³.

rīcg, ricig=hrycg

rīclic *sumptuous*, AS39⁴. adv. -līce *powerfully*, Æ,CP : *sumptuously*, Lk. ['*richly*']

rīcone=recene; **rīcs**=risc

rīcsere m. *ruler*, DR113³.

rīcsian *to bear rule, reign, govern, tyrannize*, Æ,AO,CP : *dominate, prevail*.

rīcsiend ᷓ. *ruler*, DR102⁸.

rīcsung f. *domination*, DR174¹⁰.

+**rīd** n. *riding*, WW229².

-**rīda** v. brand-r, tot-r.

rīdan¹ (±) *to* '*ride**,' AO : *move about, swing, rock, ride (at anchor)* : *float, sail*, Gen : *chafe (of fetters)* : (+) *ride over, occupy (a country), seize* : (+) *ride up to*, tō handa gerīdan *to bring into a person's power or possession*.

ridda m. *rider, horseman, horse-soldier*, Æ.

-**rīdel** v. for(e)-r.

rīdehere m. *mounted force*, OEG2⁴⁴⁴.

rīdend m. *rider, cavalier*, B2457.

rīdere m. '*rider*,' *trooper, knight*, Chr1085L.

rīdesoht f? *fever*, NG. [hriÐ? suht?]

rīdusende *swinging*, GL.

rīdwiga m. *horse-soldier*, WW110²⁸.

rīece=rīce; **rīeht**=riht; **rīf**=hrif

rīf *violent, fierce, ravenous, noxious*, AA.

+**rīf** n. *seizing, catch (of fish)* : *number caught*.

+**rīf** *garment*, WW107¹¹ (v. NC295).

-**rīfe** v. hege-r.

rīfe *abundant*, Lcd3·164²¹. ['*rife*']

rīfelede *wrinkled*, OEG18b⁷⁸. ['*rivelled*']

rīfeling m. *shoe or sandal of raw hide*, WW 125. ['*rivelling*']

rīfelung f. *wrinkle*, A32·506.

+**rīfian** *to wrinkle*, ÆH1·614¹⁴.

rift, rifte (y) n. *cloak, veil, curtain*, Æ,Cp, MtL. ['*rift*']

rifter m. *reaping-hook, sickle, scythe*, GL.

riftre, riftere (y) m. *reaper*, Æ,GL.

rige=ryge; **rignan**=rīnan

rīhsian=rīcsian

±**riht** (æ, e, eo, y) I. n. *(what is straight),* '*RIGHT*,' *equity, justice, law, canon, rule*, Æ,CP : *cause, legal action*, Æ : *a right, privilege*, CP : *correctness, truth*. on r.; mid rihte *rightly, correctly, properly* : *what is due, duty, obligation*, CP : *reckoning, account*. II. adj. *straight, erect, direct* : '*RIGHT*,' *proper, fair, just, equitable, lawful, permissible* : *upright, righteous* : *true, correct* : *fitting, appropriate* : *real, genuine* : *right (as opposed to left)*.

rihtæðelcwēn f. *lawful wife*, W298¹⁸.

rihtæðelo (y) npl. *true nobility*, Bo,MET.

rihtǣw f. *lawful wedlock*, W : *lawful wife*, LL.

±**rihtan** (e, y) *to make straight* : *set right, amend, correct, rebuke*, Æ : *guide, govern, direct, rule* : *set up, assign, restore, replace, erect*. ['*RIGHT*']

rihtandaga m. *proper (fixed) day*, LL.

rihtandswaru f. *retort, reproof*, PPs37¹⁴.

rihtcynecynn (y¹) n. *legitimate royal family*, AO.

rihtcyning m. *lawful king*, BH360¹⁴.

rihtcynn n. *true stock*, W13⁶.

rihtdōm *just judgment*, LL320,15b.

rihtdōnde ptc. *doing what is right*, BL.

rihte adv. '*RIGHT*,' *due, straight (of direction, as in right on, due east), outright*, CP : *precisely, exactly, just*, AO : *rightly, duly, well, correctly, truly, properly, fairly, justly* : *directly, immediately*, Æ. ðǣr rihte *thereupon, straightway*.

+**rihte** n. *right, due*, Æ,Chr(1074L) : *religious rite, office*, ÆL. +rihtu pl. *last offices*. on +r. *straight on*. up on +r. *upright*. ['*i-riht*']

rihtebred n. *measure, rule, square*, WW.

rihtend m. *director, ruler, leader, guide*, Bo, GD.

rihtendebyrdnes f. *right order*, NC317.

rihtere m. *director, ruler*, Bo. ['*righter*']

rihtes (e) adv. *right, straight*, KC3·392⁶.

rihtfædrencynn (e, y) n. *direct paternal descent or pedigree.*

rihtfæsten n. *duly ordained fast*, LL 132,8.

rihtfæstendæg m. *duly appointed fast-day,* Æ.

rihtfæstentíd f. *duly appointed time of fasting,* Æ.

rihtfremmende (y)† *acting rightly.*

rihtful '*rightful*,' *honourable,* CHR 1100 L.

rihtgebroðru mpl. *brethren,* DR 57⁴.

rihtgefég n. *proper joint,* GD 248²⁶.

rihtgefremed *catholic, orthodox,* BH 456¹⁵.

rihtgegylda m. *duly appointed member of a guild,* TC 606¹⁴.

rihtgehātan⁷ *to pledge oneself, swear,* RPs 14⁴.

rihtgehíwan pl. *lawfully married persons,* LL 22 n16.

rihtgeléafful *orthodox,* BH,LL.

rihtgeléaffulnes f. *right belief,* ÆL 23b⁶⁹⁷.

rihtgeléaflíce adv. *in an orthodox manner,* CM 1167.

rihtgelýfed (ē³) ptc. *orthodox, catholic.*

rihtgelýfende *believing rightly, faithful,* BL.

rihtgemæcca m. *lawful husband,* LL.

rihtgemǣre=rihtlandgemǣre

rihtgemet n. *proper measure,* NC 317.

rihtgesamhíwan pl. *lawfully married persons,* LL 22,38.

rihtgescéad n. *right understanding,* GD 56².

rihtgeset *duly appointed, canonical,* CM 412.

rihtgesetednes f. *right ordinance,* NC 317.

rihtgesetnes f. *rightful office,* Bo 12¹³.

rihtgesinscipe *lawful wedlock,* LL.

+**rihtgeswinc** *lawful work,* CHRD 70³.

rihtgeðancod *right-minded,* LPs.

rihtgewitt (y) n. *right mind,* MH 192²².

rihtgewittig *in one's right mind,* GD 245²².

rihtgifu f. *irrevocable gift,* LL 366,81; 385.

rihthǣmed (y¹) n. *lawful wedlock,* CP.

rihthāmscyld m. *legal means of protection to a homestead?* LL 5,32 and v. ANS 115·389 (but v. BTs).

rihthāmsōcn f. *actual* 'hāmsōcn' (v. hāmsōcn), LL 614,49⁵⁸.

rihthand f. *right hand,* NIC 492; 508.

rihthanddǣda m. *actual perpetrator,* LL 188,1³.

rihtheort *righteous, just,* CPVPs.

rihthíwa (y¹) m. *lawful consort,* CP.

rihthláford m. *rightful lord,* LL.

rihthláforddōm m. *lawful authority,* CHR 918 C.

rihthláfordhyldo (e⁶) f. *loyalty,* W.

rihting f. *action of guiding aright, direction, order, rule, guidance,* Æ,RB : *correction, reproof,* Æ : *body of rights, privilege? privileged district?* CHR 963 E : '*regularis*' (*in computation*), BF 30¹⁹. [*'righting'*]

±**rihtlǣcan** *to make straight, put right, rectify, set in order,* RB,W : *direct.* [*'rightleche'*]

rihtlǣce m. *duly qualified physician,* W 12¹².

rihtlǣcung (y) f. *criticism, correction,* Æ,CP.

rihtlagu f. *regular legal ordinance,* W.

rihtlandgemǣre n. *lawful boundary (of land),* KC.

rihtlic (y) *right, proper, just, fit, righteous,* Æ⁻ : *adapted, fitted.* adv. -líce *justly, uprightly, virtuously,* Æ : *properly,* 'RIGHTLY,' *regularly : correctly, precisely,* CP.

rihtlícettere m. *downright hypocrite,* W 54¹⁴.

rihtlíf n. *right life, regular union (of married people),* LCD 3·176'.

rihtlíflǣd m. *right way of life,* GD 336¹.

rihtlíðlic *articulate,* WW 355⁸.

rihtmédrencynn (e¹, oe²) n. *direct mother's line,* OET 651.

rihtméterfers n. *correct hexameter verse,* BF 100⁷.

rihtmunuc m. *true mónk,* RB 73¹⁹.

rihtnama m. *correct name,* ÆL 23⁵⁴⁷.

rihtnes (e) f. '*rightness,' rectitude, equity,* Ps : *perpendicularity, straightness,* WW : *reckoning, account,* MtL : (+) *correction.*

rihtnorðanwind (y¹) m. *north wind,* AO 17¹⁷.

rihtraciend m. *expounder of righteousness (the preacher, Ecclesiastes),* GD 264²⁷.

rihtracu (y) f. *correct account,* TC 170⁴ : *right reason,* GD 262.

+**rihtreccan** *to guide, show rightly,* AS 26¹⁶.

rihtregol m. *right rule, canon,* LL,OEG.

rihtryne m. *right or straight course,* Bo, MET.

rihtscír (LL 252,21)=rihtscriftscír

rihtscrífend m. *jurisconsult, lawyer,* WW.

rihtscriftscír f. *properly assigned district of a confessor, parish,* LL 240,12¹.

rihtscylling m. *shilling of sterling money,* LL (222⁷).

rihtscytte (y) *sure of aim,* CRA 51.

rihtsinscipe *lawful wedlock,* Æ (1·148).

rihtsmēaung (e¹) f. *right reasoning or argument,* MtL p 9¹⁰.

rihtspell (y) n. *true discourse,* CP 9¹⁰.

rihtstefn f. *ordinary voice,* GD 28²⁸.

riht-tíd (BH 206²⁰) f., -tima (Bo 12¹³) m. *proper time.*

riht-ðéow, -ðēowa m. *lawful slave,* GD 180⁶.

rihtungōrēd m. *plumb-line,* WW 150⁴¹.

rihtweg m. *right way,* W.

rihtwer m. *lawful husband : legally correct* 'wergild,' LL 466; 467.

rihtwestende (y¹) m. *extreme western limit,* AO 8³².

rihtwíf n. *lawful wife,* LL 348,54¹.

rihtwillende *wishing to do right,* Bo 11¹⁷.

rihtwís '*righteous,' just,* Bl,Bo,Chr,VPs; CP : *right, justifiable,* Bl.

rihtwīsend m. *Sadducee*, Mt 3⁷.

±**rihtwīsian** *to make 'righteous,' justify*, Lk, VPs; Æ : *direct aright, rule.*

rihtwīslic (y¹) *righteous*, CP. adv. -līce *rightly, reasonably*, Bo. ['righteously']

rihtwīsnes f. *'righteousness,' justice*, Mt; CP : *rightness, reason : righteous acts*, Æ.

+**rihtwīsung** (e) f. *justification*, VPs 88³².

rihtwrītere m. *correct writer*, GL.

rihtwuldriende *orthodox*, BHB 310³³.

rihtwyrŏe *proper, fitting*, AS 13²².

rihtymbren n. *duly appointed Embertide*, W117.

rihtymbrendagas mp. *duly appointed Ember days*, W117.

rīm-=hrīm-

±**rīm** n. *number, counting, reckoning*, Chr, Cr,VPs; Æ,AO,CP. ['rime']

rīma m. *'rim,' verge, border, coast*, Cp,WW.

rīman (±) *to count, number, reckon*, AO,Ps; Æ : *tell, enumerate, relate*, CP : *account, esteem as.* ['rime']

rīmāŏ m. *oath by a number of persons*, LL 154,9.

+**rīmbōc** *calendar*, ÆH 1·98'.

±**rīmcræft** m. *arithmetic, reckoning, computation : calendar*, ÆL 10¹.

rīmcræftig *skilled in reckoning*, BF.

rīmcræftiga m. *one skilful at figures*, BF 42¹².

-**rīme** v. earfoŏ-r.; **rīmforst**=hrīmforst

rīmge-tæl, -tel† n. *number*, GEN.

+**rīmian** *to calculate*, A 8·307⁴⁰ (v.l.+rūnian at BF 70²⁴).

rīmpan v. hrimpan.

rīmre m. *reckoner, calculator*, BF 70¹⁷.

+**rīmtæl** (HR 13¹¹)=rīmgetæl

rīmtalu f. *number*, EL 820.

+**rīn** (NG)=+rēn

rīnan¹ (and wv.) impers. and intr. *to rain*, Æ,Bl,Mt : *to send down, or fall, like rain*, Lk,VPs : (+) *to wet with rain*, WW 379¹⁵. ['rine']

+**rīnan**=+hrīnan

rinc m. *man, warrior, hero*, B,Cr,Met. ['rink']

rincgetæl n. *number of men*, Ex 234.

rincsetl (HGL 489)=hringsetl

rind, rinde f. *'rind,' bark, outside*, Bo,Cr, Lcd; CP : *crust*, Æ.

-**rindan**, -rindran v. be-r.

rindeclifer f. *wood-pecker? nut-hatch?* WW 427²⁹.

rinden *of bark*, GPH 390.

rindlēas *havı ıg no bark*, WW 190³¹.

rīne=rȳne; **ring**=hring; **rīning**=hrīning

±**rinnan³** *to 'run*,' flow*, Chr,Cr,Ps,Sat : (+) *run together, blend, coagulate*, Cp. [=iernan]

rinnelle f. *runnel, rivulet, stream.* [=rynele]

rinning (y) f. *rennet*, WW 128⁴³ : (+) *coagulation*, LCD 1·292⁸. ['running']

±**rīp** (ȳ) n. *harvest*, BH,Chr,Mt : *cut corn, sheaf : ripeness, maturity*, PPs 118¹⁴⁷. ['ripe,' 'reap']

rīpan I. (±) (ēo, ȳ) *to 'reap*,' Æ,AO,Chr, CP,G. II. (AS 10⁵)=rīpian

+**rīpan** (hr-) *to rob*, G,W.

rīpe *'ripe,' mature*, BH,Bo.

rīpemann m. *reaper*, MtL (hr-). ['reapman']

rīpere m. *'reaper,'* Mt.

rīpian (ēo) *to become 'ripe,' ripen*, Æ,Bf.

rīpīsern n. *sickle*, MtLR 4²⁹.

rīpnes f. *'ripeness,' harvest*, LPs.

rippel? *a coppice?* (BTs), Ct.

riptere=riftere

rīptīma m. *time of harvest*, Mt. ['reaptime']

rīpung f. *ripening, ripeness, maturity*, Bf, RB,VPs. ['riping']

+**rīs** n. *fury*, WW 43⁶.

±**rīsan¹** I. (usu. +) *to 'rise,' stand up*, Ps : *rise together*, DR 25¹ : *be fit, be proper*, Æ, Gu. ['irise'] II. *to seize, carry off.*

risc, risce (e;=y) f. *'rush,'* Cp; Mdf. [L.]

riscbedd n. *bed of rushes*, EC. [v. 'rush']

riscen *made of rushes*, Æ. ['rushen']

rischealh (y¹) *rushy corner? rushy slope?* BC 1·183². [v. 'rush']

risciht *rushy*, KC.

risclēac n. *rush leek, rush garlic*, WW 356³⁶.

riscrīŏig *rushy stream*, KC.

riscōŷfel m. *rush-bed*, Ct,GL.

risen-=risn-

+**risen** *seizure*, GUTH 78⁵. [rīsan]

rīsende? *rapacious*, BL 225¹⁷.

+**risenlic** *convenient, suitable, becoming, honest, honourable*, AO,CP. adv. -līce.

risiendum *'odorato'?* OEG 23⁴.

+**rislic** *equal to, like*, BHCA 450³.

±**risne** I. *fit, meet, proper, convenient.* II. n. (usu. pl.) *what is fitting, dignity, honour*, AO.

+**risnes** f. *congruity*, WW 383¹⁶.

+**risnian** *to agree, accord*, WW 336³⁷.

risoda m. *rheum*, LCD (Harl) 1b.

rīt pres. 3 sg. of rīdan.

riŏ f. *favour, indulgence*, Sc 224⁷.

riŏ fm. (±) riŏe f. *rivulet, stream*, Æ,Bo, CP; Mdf. ['rithe']

riŏfald m. *cattle-pen, cow-shed*, WW 195³⁴. [hriŏ-]

rīŏig n. *streamlet*, Mdf.

rīŏŏa=ryŏŏa; **rix** (Æ,BH)=risc

+**rīxian**=rīcsian; **rō**=rōw II.

rocc m. *over-garment, rochet*, LCD,WW. [Ger. rock]

roc(c)ettan *to eructate, belch forth, utter*, NG, VPs.

roccian *to rock (a child)* RWH 137¹².

rōd I. f. '*rood*,' *cross, gallows*, *Æ,Bl,G,MH, VHy*; CP : *crucifix*, *Chr* : *rood (land measure)*, BC : *plot of land of a square rod, BC,EC* (v. GBG and Mdf).

rōdbīgenga m. *worshipper of the cross*, WW 216¹⁶.

rōdbora m. *cross-bearer*, GPH 389.

rodd m? '*rod*,' *stick (to beat with)*, HL 15¹¹⁹.

rōdehengen f. *hanging, crucifixion*, Æ.

roden (B 1151?) pp. of rēodan.

roder = rodor

rōdetācen n. *sign of the cross*, Æ.

rōdewyrðe *deserving hanging*, HL 18³⁸⁹.

+rōdfæstnian *to crucify* (BT).

rodor (a) m., gs. rod(o)res *ether, sky, heavens, firmament*, Æ,CP.

rodorbeorht *heaven-bright*, DA 369.

rodorcyning† m. *king of heaven*, EL.

rodorlic *of the heavens, heavenly, celestial*, Æ.

rodorlīhtung (roder-) f. *dawn*, LPs.

rodorstōl (a¹) m. *heavenly throne*, GEN 749.

rodortorht *heavenly-bright*, GEN 1416.

rodortungol n. *star of heaven*, GEN 1667.

rōdwurðlend m. *cross-worshipper*, HGL 403³⁰.

roeðe (Cp,NG) = rēðe

rōf I. † *vigorous, strong, brave, noble, renowned*. II. ? *array, number*, BH (Sch) 699 n 83.

rofen pp. of rēofan; **rōflēas** = hrōflēas

roglan *to flourish*, GNE 119.

rōhte pret. 3 sg. of rēcan.

rom = ramm

Rōm (*Bl,Bo*), Rōmeburg (*AO*) f. '*Rome*.'

Rōmān-e, -an pl. *Romans*, AO.

rōmānisc *Roman*, Æ,AO.

romēl *sooty*, WW 10³¹ (BTs). [= hrūmig]

Rōm-feoh, -gesceot (*LL*) n., -penig (*LL, Shr,W*) m. '*Rome-penny*,' '*Romescot*,' *Peter's pence*.

rōmian (w. g.) *to possess?* GEN 350.

romm = ramm

Rōmwalh (u¹) m. *Roman*. [wealh]

Rōm-ware (AO), -waran pl. *inhabitants of Rome, Romans*.

rond = rand

rop I. ? *broth*, WW 272⁹. II. = ropp

rōp *liberal*, RD 58³.

rōpnes f. *liberality*, WW.

ropp m. *intestines*, Lcd,WW (hr-). ['*rope*']

ropwærc m. *colic*, WW 211¹².

rōrend = rōwend

rōsbedd *rose-bed*, OEG 23⁸.

+rōscian (o? FTP 353) = rōstian

rōse, rose f. '*rose*,' *Æ,Bf,Bl,Bo,MH*. [L. rosa]

rōsen *made of roses*, Lcd : *rose-coloured, rosy*, *Æ,ZDA*. ['*rosen*']

+rōsod *of roses*, OEG 3278.

rōst = rūst

+rōstian *to roast, dry*, WW.

rot = hrot

rōt *glad, cheerful, bright*, RIM : *noble, excellent*, Æ.

rōt(e)? '*root*,' NC 318.

rōtfæst ('*root-fast*'), *firmly established*, Chr 1127.

rōthwīl f. *time of refreshing*, PPs.

±rotian *to '*rot*,' putrefy*, *Æ,Bf,CP,Lcd*.

rōtlīce *gladly, cheerfully*, BH 348³.

rōtnes f. *gladness*, DR : *refuge, protection*, Pss.

+rōtsian *to comfort, gladden*, CP 417⁹.

rōtsung f. *refuge, protection, comfort*, EPs 9¹⁰.

rotung f. *corruption, ulcer*, WW 114¹⁴. [rotian]

rōðer I. m. *rower, sailor*, CP. [rōwan] II. = rōðor

roðhund m. *mastiff*, WW. [ryðða]

rōðor n., gs. rōðres *oar, scull*, CP,WW. ['*rudder*']

rōðra = rēðra

rōw I. *quiet, calm, gentle, soft, mild*, CP. II. f. *quietness, rest*, Gu. ['*row*']

±rōwan⁷ pret. pl. rēowon, rēon *to go by water*, '*row*,' *sail, swim*, LkL (hr-), WW; Æ.

rōwend m. *rower*, CP : *sailor*, Æ.

rōwett = rēwet

rōwing f. '*rowing*,' NG.

rōwnes f. *rowing*, BH 384²².

rudduc m. *robin*, WW. ['*ruddock*']

rūde I. m. *scabbiness, scab*, WW 161¹⁴ (= *hrūda? A 30·253). II. f. *rue*. [L. ruta]

rudig *rubicund*, '*ruddy*,' OEG 2932.

rudon pret. pl. of rēodan.

rudu f. *red colour*, ApT : *ruddy complexion*, WW : *red cosmetic*, ÆL. ['*rud*']

rues = ryges gs. of ryge; **rūg** = rūh

rugern m. *month of rye-harvest, August?* LL 12 Pro.

rūh gs. rūwes '*rough**,' Guth,Rd; Æ : *coarse (of cloth)*, DHy,WW : *hairy, shaggy*, Æ : *undressed, untanned*, WW.

ruhha? m. *ray (fish)*, NC 324 (suhha). ['*rough*']

rūm I. adj. (±) *roomy, wide, long, spacious, ample, large, liberal*, B,Bo,Mt,VPs; Æ, CP : *unoccupied : unfettered, open, unrestricted, loose : noble, august*. II. m. (±) *space (extent or time)*, '*room*,' Gen,Lk : *scope, opportunity*, B,Met. on +rum *at large, apart*.

rūma *stumbling-block*, A 41·102²⁰.

+ruma† m. *space, place*.

rūman = rȳman

rūme (once +) adv. *widely, spaciously, roomily, amply, liberally, extensively, abundantly, Gen,Lcd* : *light-heartedly* : *in detail,* JUL314. ['*room*']

rūmed-=rūmmōd-

rūmgāl *revelling in release from confinement* (*Noah's dove*), GEN 1466. adv. -*līce widely,* NC318.

rūmgifa (eo²) m. *bountiful giver,* BH 194³³.

rūmgiful (y²) *bountiful,* Æ,CP.

rūmgifulnes (eo², y²) f. *liberality, bounty, profusion,* Æ.

rūmheort *large-hearted, generous,* B : *free from care,* RB. adv. -*līce,* VH.

rūmheortnes f. *liberality,* LL,W.

rūmian *to become clear of obstructions,* Lcd 1·76¹³. ['*room*']

rūmlic *benign, liberal* : *plentiful,* Æ. adv. ±rūmlīce *at large, fully, kindly, liberally, abundantly,* Æ,Bl,MtL. ['*roomly*']

rūmmōd *liberal, lavish, kind,* CP.

rūmmōdlic *ample, large, full, liberal, gracious.* adv. -*līce.*

rūmmōdnes f. *large-heartedness, liberality, kindness,* CP.

rūmnes f. *breadth, abundance,* Æ.

rūmōd=rūmmōd

rūmor adv. comp. *still further,* GEN.

+rumpen=+hrumpen v. hrimpan.

rūmwelle *spacious,* MtL7¹³.

rūn f. *mystery, secrecy, secret, El,JnL* : *counsel, consultation, B,KC,Wa* : (*secret*) *council* : *runic character, letter, BH* : *writing, An,Da.* ['*roun*']

+rūna m. *counsellor, confidant,* GL.

rūncofa m. *chamber of secrets, breast, bosom,* MET 22⁵⁹.

rūncræftig *skilled in mysteries,* DA 734.

rūnere m. *whisperer, tale-bearer,* Æ. ['*rouner*']

rūnian (+at BF70²⁴) *to whisper, murmur, talk secrets, conspire,* Æ,Ps,Sol. ['*round*']

rūniende *whispering,* WW 441. ['*rouning*']

runl *foul? running?* LCD 3·36¹⁷. [?=*hrunol]

rūnlic *mystical,* MtL p5¹¹.

-runn v. cȳs-gerunn.

+runnen pp. of +rinnan.

+runnenes f. *that has been cooled or congealed,* GPH 398.

rūnstæf m. *runic letter, rune,* Æ,B. ['*runestave*']

rūnung f. *whispering, wheedling,* Æ. ['*rouning*']

rūnwita† m. *adviser, counsellor, wise man.*

rūst m. '*rust*,' Cp,MtL,RB : *moral canker,* CP,HL.

rūstig '*rusty*,' AO 251²¹.

rūte=rūde

rūwa m., rūwe f. *covering, tapestry,* W.

rūwes v. rūh.

rūxlan (MtR 9²³)=hrūxlian

rȳan=rȳn

ryc-, rȳc-=rec-, rēc-

rȳcð pres. 3 sg. of rēocan.

rȳd (LL 192,2B)=rād I.

+ryddan *to clear* (*land*), AS 39⁵.

+rȳde *prepared, ready? easy?* RD 64¹⁵.

ryden n. *name of a plant,* LCD 122a.

rȳderian v. ā-r.

rȳe=rȳhe

rȳfe '*rife*,' *frequent,* Lcd 3·164²¹.

ryft (i, e) n. *covering, veil, curtain, cloak,* CP.

ryge (i) m. '*rye*,' Cp.

rygen (i) *made of rye,* Lcd. ['*ryen*']

rȳhe f. *rug, blanket,* GL. [=rēowe]

ryht=riht; **rȳm-**=rīm-

±rȳman (ē) *to clear, open up, An,B,Lk,Met, W* : *widen, extend, prolong, enlarge,* Æ,CP : *make room, retire, yield,* Æ. ['*rime*'; rūm]

rȳmet n. *room, space, extent,* Æ : *comfort, benefit.*

rȳmetlēast f. *want of room,* ÆH 1·34²².

rȳmð f. *amplitude,* CM 18.

rȳn, rȳnan *to roar, rage,* Bo.

ryne (e) mn. *running, onward course,* Æ,Bf, Bo,VHy; AO : *flux, flow* (*water, blood*), Lk; Æ : *period of time, cycle, course of life* : *expanse, extent* : *orbit.* ['*rune*']

±rȳne n. *mystery, dark saying* : *mystic rite* : *sacrament* : *sacramental elements,* Æ.

rynegiest m. *running spirit* (=*lightning*)? *rain-foe?* (Tupper), RD 4⁵⁸.

-rȳnegu v. hel-r.

rynel I. (e) m. *runnel, stream,* Bl,GD,VPs. ['*rindle*'] II. *runner, messenger,* Æ.

rynele f.=rynel I.

±rȳn(e)lic *secret, mystical* : *figurative, sacramental.* adv. -*līce.*

rynelīce? '*cursim*,' OEG 7⁹⁰.

rȳnemann m. *one skilled in mysteries,* RD 43¹³.

rynestrong *strong in running,* RD 20⁷.

ryneswift† *swift in running,* MET.

ryneðrāg f. *space of time,* GU 184.

rynewǣn† m. *swift vehicle, chariot,* PPs 19⁷.

ryng-=reng-

±rȳnig *good in counsel?* CRA 51. [rūn]

ryniga? m. *liquid that runs off?* LCD.

rynning f. *rennet,* WW 128⁴³.

+rynning=+rinning

rȳnstæf (RWH 119³⁶)=rūnstæf; **rȳp**=rīp

+rynu (Æ)=+ryne

+rȳpan I. *to spoil, plunder, rob, Chr,MtL, LL,W.* ['*ripe*'] II. pl. *sheaves,* CSPs. III.=rǣpan. IV.=rīpan.

rȳpere m. *robber, plunderer,* LL,W.

rȳping m. *plunder, spoliation,* OEG 3149. ['*riping*']

ryplen? *made of broom*, GPH399 (A31·536).
ryps=reps; **-rȳrlc** v. sǽ-r.; **rysc-**=risc-
rysel, rysl (Æ), rys(e)le (hl-) m. *lard, fat* :
resin, LCD210¹³ : *abdomen*, WW159⁶ (cp.
ryselwærc).
ryselwærc *pain in the stomach*, LCD115b.
+rysen-, +rysn-=+risn-
rȳslg (OEG8³³⁷)=hrīsig
ryt *rubbish for burning, underwood*, LL
36,27 (v. 3·46).
rȳð I.=rīð. II. pres. 3 sg. of rȳn.
rȳðer=hrīðer
ryðða (i) m. *a species of dog, mastiff*, Æ,
WW. [*Ger.* rüde]

S

sā m. *tub, bucket*, Gl. [*ON.* sār; v. '*say*']
saban m? *sheet*, WW502³³.
sac=(1) sacu; (2) sæc
saca nap. of sacu.
±**saca** m. *opponent, foe*, B,BH.
sacan⁶ *to struggle, dispute, disagree, wrangle,
fight* : *accuse, blame, bring a criminal or
civil action against any one, lay claim to,*
LL.
sacc (æ) m. '*sack,*' *bag*, Æ. [*L.* saccus]
sācerd mf. *priest, priestess*, Æ,CP. [*L.*]
sācerdbana m. *priest-slayer*, W.
sācerdgerīsne *befitting a priest*, BH206¹².
sācerdhād m. *priesthood*, CP.
sācerdland n. *land allotted to priests*, GEN
47²⁶.
sācerdlic *sacerdotal, priestly*, Æ,BH.
sācerhād=sācerdhād
sacful *quarrelsome, contentious*, Æ. ['*sak-
ful*']
saclan *to wrangle, strive*, Æ.
saclēas *innocent*, LL : *unmolested, safe*, Chr,
KC,MtL. ['*sackless*']
sacu f. (oblique cases often have sæc-) (±)
*conflict, strife, war, battle, feud, sedition,
dispute*, Æ,B,LL; AO : *reproof : affliction,
persecution, trial : sin, fault, B,Ph :
prosecution, lawsuit, action.* s. and sōcn
*jurisdiction, right of holding a court for
criminal and civil matters*, LL (v. 2·455).
['*sake*']
sad- v. sæd.
sāda m. *snare, cord, halter*, NG,PPs. [cp.
Ger. saite]
sadel=sadol
±**sadellan** *to '*saddle,*'* Æ, KC. ['*saddled*']
sadlan *to be sated, get wearied*, Bo : (+)
satiate, fill, Ps. ['*sade*'; sæd]
sadol (e², u²) m. '*saddle,*' *B*; GD.
sadolbeorht *with ornamented saddle*, B2175.
sadolboga (u²) m. '*saddle-bow,*' *WW*.

sadolfelg f. *pommel of a saddle*, GL.
Saduceīsc *Sadducean*; as sb. m. *Sadducee.*
sadul=sadol
sǣ mf. often indecl. but also gs. sǣs, sǽwe,
sēo; nap. sǣs, gp. sǽwa, dp. sǽwum,
sǣ(u)m *sheet of water, '*sea,*' lake, pool*, Æ,
B,Bo,G,Lcd,VPs.
sǣǣl m. *sea-eel*, WW447³⁶.
sǣælfen f. *sea-elf, naiad*, WW.
sǣbāt† f. '*sea-boat,*' *vessel, ship*, B.
sǣbeorg m. *cliff by the sea : mountain of
waves?* AN308.
sǣbrōga m. *sea-terror*, SOL84¹³.
sǣburg f. *seaport town*, MtL4¹³.
sǣc I. *offensive, odious : guilty.* II. (KGL
61²²)=sacc
sǣc-, sǣc-=sec- (and v. sacu), sēc-
sǣcce I.† f. *strife, contest.* [sacan] II. m.
sackcloth, Æ. ['*sack*';=sacc]
sǣcce pres. 1 sg. of sācan.
sǣccing m. *sacking, pallet*, Mk6⁶⁵ (v. NED).
sǣcdōm=sceacdōm
sǣceaster f. *seaport town*, MtR4¹³.
sǣceosol m. *sea-sand, shingle*, GEN32¹²,
WW147⁴¹.
sǣcerd=sacerd; **sǣcgen**=segen
sǣcir m. *sea-ebbing*, EX291.
sǣclian (Chr)=sīclian
sǣclif n. *cliff by the sea*, Bo. ['*seacliff*']
sǣcocc m. *cockle*, WW94¹⁴.
sǣcol n. *jet*, WW416². ['*seacoal*']
sǣcyning m. *sea-king*, B2382.
sǣcysul=sǣceosol
sǣd (occl. sad- in obl. cases) w. g. *sated with,
weary of, satiated, filled, full*, Ps,Rd. ['*sad*']
sǣd (ē) n., nap. sǣd, sǣdu '*seed,*' Mk,VPs;
Æ,CP : *fruit, offspring, posterity*, MkL,
VPs : *sowing*, Met; Æ : *growth.*
sǣdberende *seed-bearing*, Æ.
sǣdcynn n. *kind of seed*, LL,WW.
sǣde pret. 3 sg. of secgan.
sǣdēor m. *sea-monster*, LCD,MH.
sǣdere m. *sower*, Æ,MkL. ['*seeder*']
sǣdian *to sow*, MtL13⁸ : *provide seed*, LL
450,10.
sǣdlēap m. *sower's basket*, Bf. ['*seedlip*']
sǣdlic *belonging to seed, seminal*, DR146⁸.
sǣdnað m. *sowing*, WW147⁴.
sǣdnes f. *satiety*, GPH391.
sǣdraca m. *sea-dragon*, B,GL.
sǣdtīma m. *seed-time*, HEXC226.
sǣearm m. *arm of the sea*, AO22⁴.
sǣelfen=sǣælfen
sǣfǣreld n. *passage of the (Red) sea*, AO
38³³.
sǣfǣsten f. *watery stronghold, ocean*, EX127.
sǣ-faroð, -fearoð† m. *sea-coast.*
Sǣfern f. *Severn*, CHR. [*L.* Sabrina]
sǣfisc m. '*sea-fish,*' *Cr.*

sǣflōd mn. *tide, inundation, flood, flow of the sea, flood-tide*, AO : *flow of a river*, VH : (†) *sea.* ['*seaflood*']

sǣflota m. (*sea-floater*), *ship*, AN381.

sǣfōr f. *sea-voyage*, SEAF42.

±**sǣgan** *to cause to sink, settle : cause to fall, fell, destroy.* [sīgan]

sægd-=sæged-

sǣgde pret. 3 sg. of secgan.

sǣgdig (N)=sægde ic

sǣgēap *spacious* (*ship*), B1896 (v. ES 64·211).

±**sǣgednes** f. *sacrifice*, MkLR12³³; APs 65¹³ : *mystery*, MtL13¹¹ (gd-).

sǣgemǣre n. *sea-coast*, G.

±**sǣgen**=+segen

sǣgenga m. *ship*, B : *sailor*, BF156³¹.

sǣgeset m. *coast region*, GL.

sægl=sigel; **sægnian**=segnian

sǣgon pret. pl. of sēon.

sǣgrund m. *sea-bottom, abyss*, Æ,CP.

sǣh=seah

sǣhealf f. *side next the sea, seaside*, Æ,CHR.

sǣhengest m. *sea-horse, ship*, AN488 : *hippopotamus*, WW.

sǣhete m. *surging of the sea*, BH384²⁴.

sǣholm m. *ocean*, AN529.

sǣht=seht

sǣhund m. *sea-dog, sea-beast*, OEG26⁶¹.

sǣl n. nap. salu *room, hall, castle*, B,Rd. ['*sale*']

sǣl (ē) **I.** mf. (occl. dp. sālum) *time, season, opportunity, occasion, condition, position*, Lcd; Æ,AO : *prosperity, happiness, joy*, B. on sǣlum *happy*; '*gaudete*,' GD202⁶. tō sǣles *in due time*, NR39. ['*sele*'] **II.**= sēl II.

sǣlāc† n. *sea-gift, sea-spoil*, B.

sǣlād† f. *sea-way, sea-voyage.*

sǣlāf f. *sea-leavings, jetsam*, Ex584.

±**sǣlan I.** (ē) *to take place, happen*, CP : *succeed*, GD202⁶. [sǣl I.] **II.**† *to tie, bind, fetter, fasten : curb, restrain, confine.* [sāl]

sǣland n. *coast, maritime district*, TC308¹.

sǣld=seld

sǣlen I. *made of willow*, WW518⁶. [sealh] **II.**=selen

sǣleoda=sǣlida

sǣlēoð n. *song at sea, rowers' song*, WW 379⁹.

-sǣleða v. sealt-s.

sǣlic *of the sea, marine*, Æ.

sǣlida m. *seafarer, sailor : pirate.* [līðan]

±**sǣlig** (+ exc. at LL300A) *fortuitous*, OEG 4185 : *happy, prosperous*, AO,Bo,Gen; CP. ['*i-seli*']

+**sǣlige** *happily*, WW407²³.

+**sǣliglic** (ē) *happy, blessed, fortunate.* adv. -līce, Bo,DR. ['*seelily*']

+**sǣlignes** f. *happiness*, (*good*) *fortune*, CP : *occurrence.*

sǣ-līðend, -līðende† m. *sailor.*

+**sǣllic**=+sǣliglic

sǣlmerige f. *brine*, ÆGR192¹⁸. [L. *salmoria; Gk. ἁλμυρίς]

+**sǣlnes** f. *occurrence*, GL.

+**sǣltan** (NG)=syltan

sǣltna m. *name of a bird, bunting? robin?* WW44¹⁷.

sǣlð f. *dwelling, house*, GEN785.

±**sǣlð** (ȳ) f. (usu. in pl.) *hap, fortune : happiness, prosperity, blessing*, Bo; Æ,CP. ['*i-selth*']

sǣlwang (o²)† m. *fertile plain.*

sǣm v. sǣ; **sǣma**=sēma

+**sǣman**=+sīeman

sǣmann m. '*seaman*,' *pirate, viking*, B.

sǣmearh† m. *sea-horse, ship*, E2.

sǣmend=sēmend

sǣmest superl. (of *sǣme?) *worst.*

sǣmestre=sēamestre

sǣmēðe *weary from a sea-voyage*, B325.

sǣminte f. *sea-mint*, WW.

sǣmninga=samnunga

sǣmra comp. (of *sǣme?) *worse, inferior, weaker.*

sǣmtinges=samtinges

sǣn (ē) *maritime, marine*, OEG6²³, 8¹²⁸.

sǣnaca m. *sea-vessel, ship*, HU26.

sǣnæs m. *cape, promontory*, B,GL.

sǣncgan=sengan; **sǣndan**=sendan

sǣne (often w. g.) *slack, lazy, careless, negligent, dull, cowardly.*

sǣnet n. *net for sea-fishing*, WW336²⁰.

sǣngan=sengan; **sǣnian**=segnian

sǣnig *maritime, marine*, A13·32.

sǣostre f. *sea-oyster*, WE63¹⁷.

sǣp n. '*sap*,' *juice*, Cr,WW.

sǣp (ÆL3¹⁶²)=sēap

sǣpig '*sappy*,' *juicy, succulent*, OEG16¹.

sǣppe f. *spruce fir*, WW269¹⁴. [L. *sappinum; Fr. sapin]

sǣpspōn f. *a shaving with sap in it*, LCD 106b.

sǣre=sāre

sǣrima m. *sea-shore, coast*, Chr. ['*searim*']

sǣrinc† m. *seaman, pirate, viking.*

sǣrōf *hardy at sea*, CRA56.

sǣrwian=searwian

sǣrȳric m. *sea-reed?* (GK); *an ait?* (BT), WH10.

sǣs=sess; **sǣs** v. sǣ.

sǣsceaða m. *pirate*, WW469⁶.

sǣscell f. '*sea-shell*,' MH18²³.

sǣslð m. *sea-voyage*, B1149.

sǣ-snægl, -snǣl m. '*sea-snail*,' WW.

sǣsteorra m. *guiding star* (*for sailors*), HL. ['*seastar*']

sæster=sester

sǣstrand n. '*sea-strand*,' *foreshore*, *ÆH*.

sǣstrēam, as mpl. *waters of the sea*, *An*. ['*seastream*']

sǣswalwe (hǣ-) f. *sand-martin*, WW7²⁸.

sǣt pret. 3 sg. of sittan.

sǣt f. *lurking-place* : *snare, gin?* LL445,2. [sittan]

+**sæt** n. *act of sitting*, MkL p5¹⁴.

sǣta m. *holding of land*, EC447¹⁸.

-sǣta (ē) v. burg-s.

sǣtan=sǣtian; **-sǣte** v. an(d)-s.

sǣte f. *house*, KC3·79¹⁵.

+**sǣte** (ē) n. *snare, ambush*, DR37¹⁰.

Sæterdæg=Sætern(es)dæg

sǣt-ere, -nere (ē) m. *waylayer, robber* : *spy* : *seditious one, seducer* (*the devil*), CP.

Sætern-dæg, Sæter(n)es- m. '*Saturday*,' *BH,Bl,Lk*. [*L*. Saturni dies]

Sæterniht f. *Friday night*, ÆH1·216²⁷.

sǣtian (ē) (w. g.) *to lie in wait for, plot against*, CP. [sittan]

sǣtil, sætl=setl; **sǣtn-**=sǣt-

+**sǣtnes**=+setnes

sǣton pret. pl. of sittan.

sǣtung (ē) f. *ambush, trap, plot, snare*, CP : *sedition*.

sǣð (ÆL36²⁹⁵)=sēað

sǣðēof v. hēahsǣðēof.

sǣðerie=saturege; **sǣðnes**=sēðnes

sǣðrenewudu = sūðernewudu; **sǣum** v. sǣ.

sǣūpwearp *jetsam*, TC421'.

sǣwǣg m. *sea-wave*, DA384.

sǣwæter n. '*sea-water*,' *Lcd*10b.

sǣwan=sāwan

sǣwār n. *sea-weed*, WW135²¹. ['*seaware*']

sǣwaroð n. *sea-shore, beach*, Az,Bo.

sǣwe v. sǣ.

sǣweall† m. '*sea-wall*,' *sea-shore, beach, cliff*, B : *wall of water* (*in the Red Sea*).

sǣweard m. *coast-warden*, B,LL.

sǣweg m. *path through the sea*, Ps8⁸. ['*seaway*']

sǣwērig† *weary from a sea-voyage*, *An*. ['*seaweary*']

sǣwet n. *sowing*, BH. [sāwan]

sǣwīcing m. *sea-viking*, Ex333.

sǣwiht f. *marine animal*, BH26⁶.

sǣwinewincle f? *periwinkle* (*shell-fish*), Lcd90a.

sǣwong m. *sea-shore, beach*, B1964.

sǣwð pres. 3 sg. of sāwan.

sǣwudu m. *vessel, ship*, B226.

sǣwum v. sǣ.

sǣwylm m. *sea-surf, billow*, B393.

sæx (GL)=seax

sǣӯð f. *sea-wave*, RUN,WW.

safene, safine f. *savine* (*a kind of juniper*), Lcd. [*L*. sabina]

saftriende ptc. *rheumy*, WW161³⁴ (MLR 19·203).

sāg I. *a sinking*, RD79⁵ (or ?sagol). II. pret. 3 sg. of sīgan.

saga I. imperat. of secgan. II. m. *story, narrative*, ÆL7¹⁹³. III. m.=sagu II.

+**saga** n. *narrative*, LkL1¹.

sagast pres. 2 sg., sagað pres. 3 sg., sagode pret. 3 sg. of secgan.

sāgol (e²) m. (sāgl- in obl. cases) *club, cudgel, stick, staff, pole*, AO,GD,Mt; Æ,CP. ['*sowel*']

-sagol v. lēas-, sōð-, wǣr-s.

sagu (±) I. f. '*saw*,' *saying, report, story, tradition, tale*, Lk,WW; Æ : *presage, prophecy* : *witness, testimony*. [secgan] II. f. '*saw*' (*tool*), Bf,WW.

sāh I. pret. 3 sg. of sīgan. II. pret. 3 sg. of sēon II.

sahl-=sealh-; **sāhl**=sāgol; **saht**=seht

sāl mf. *bond, rope, cord, rein, collar*, B,Gen. ['*sole*'; *Ger*. seil]

sala m. *act of selling*, '*sale*,' WW.

salb (*Ep*)=sealf; **salch**=sealh

salde=sealde pret. 3 sg. of sellan.

salf (Cp)=sealf

salfie, salfige f. *sage*, Lcd. [*L*. salvia]

salh (*Gl*), salig=sealh

salletan *to sing psalms, play on, or sing to, the harp*, PPs104². [*L*. psallere]

salm-=sealm-

sālnes f. *silence*, Bf122²². [cp. *Goth*. silan]

salo=salu; **salor**=solor

salowigpād=salwigpād

salt=sealt

saltere (ea) m. '*psalter**,' *collection of psalms, service-book containing the psalms*, Æ,BH,Ct,LL : *psaltery*, Lcd (ps-). [*L*. psalterium]

salthaga m. *robin redbreast?* WW286¹¹.

salu I. (ea) *dark, dusky*, Rd. ['*sallow*'] II. nap. of sæl.

salubrūn (ea¹, o²) *dark brown*, FIN37.

sālum v. sǣl.

saluneb *dark-complexioned*, RD50⁵.

salupād *dark-coated*, RD58³.

saluwigpād=salwigpād

salwed ptc. *darkened, painted black* (*with pitch*), GEN1481.

salwigfeðera *having dark plumage*, GEN1448.

salwigpād† *having dark plumage*.

sālwong=sǣlwang

sam conj. *whether, or*. sam...sam *whether... or*, AO. sam ge...sam ge; sam ðe...sam ðe *whether...or*.

sam- (=*together*) denotes union, combination, or agreement. [*ON*. sam-]

sām- (=*half-*) denotes a partial or imperfect condition. [*L*. semi-]

sama=same v. swā.
samad-=samod-
sāmbærned *half-burnt*, OEG.
sāmboren *born out of due time*, WW356².
sāmbryce m. *partial breach (of rules, laws, etc.)*, LL468,9.
sām-cwic, -cucu (o¹) *half-dead*, Æ,AO
same only in swā s. (swā) *in like manner also, as*, CP.
samed=samod
samen (o¹) adv. *together*, JnR.
sāmgrēne *half-green, immature*, WW405⁴.
sāmgung *young*, CM123. [geong]
sāmhāl *unwell, weakly*, W273¹⁰.
samheort *unanimous*, PPs149¹.
±**samhīwan** pl. *members of the same household, married persons*, CP.
samhwylc pron. *some*, BL,LL.
sāmlǣred *half-taught, badly instructed*, Æ.
samlīce *together, at the same time*, SOL 148¹⁸.
samlinga=samnunga
sāmlocen *half-closed*, NC318.
sammǣle *agreed, accordant, united*, CHR, LL.
sāmmelt *half-digested*, LCD69b.
±**samnian** *to assemble, meet, collect, unite, join, gather together*, (tr.) Da,Lcd; (refl.) CHR : (intr.) Ps : *glean*. ['sam']
samninga=samnunga
±**samnung** (o) f. (but occl. gs. samnunges), *union, congregation, meeting, assembly, council*, MkL; Æ,CP : *collection* : *union in marriage*. ['samening']
samnunga (æ, e, o) adv. *forthwith, immediately, suddenly*. [=semninga]
samnungewide (o¹) *collect*, DR2¹.
samod (o¹) I. adv. *simultaneously, at the same time, together*, Æ,AO : *entirely*, Æ : *also, as well, too*. II. prep. (w. d.) *together with, at* (of time), Æ. [Ger. sammt]
samodcumend *flocking together*, CM282.
samodeard (o¹, u²) m. *common home*, GU 1346.
samodfæst *joined together*, CR1581.
samodgang *continuous*, GD170²³ (v. NC 318).
samodgeflit (o¹) n. *strife*, WW382³⁸.
samodgeslō m. *comrade*, GPH400.
samodherian (o¹) *to praise together*, RPs 116¹.
samodhering f. *praising*, ES40·302.
+**samodlǣcan** *to bring together*, RPs112⁸.
samodlīce adv. *together*, CHR1123.
samodrynelas mpl. 'concurrentes,' BF46¹.
samodsīōlan *to accompany*, MFH137¹⁸.
samodsprǣc f. *colloquy, conversation*, CM 511.
samodswēgende *consonantal*, ÆGR5¹⁷.

samodtang *continuous, successive*, v. NC 318.
samodðyrlic (o¹) adj. *concordant*, WW378⁴⁰.
samodwellung (o¹) f. *welding together*, WW 380⁴⁴. [weallan]
samodwist f. *a being one with*, GD224⁴.
samodwunung f. *common residence, living together*, LL(422').
samodwyrcende *co-operating*, WW384¹².
sāmra=sǣmra
samrād *harmonious, united*, MET11⁹⁶.
samrǣden f. *married state*, CP19¹⁸.
sāmsoden *half-cooked*, LL(166²n).
sāmstorfen *half-dead*, GPH401.
sāmswǣled *half-burnt*, OEG4388.
samswēge (u¹) adj. *sounding in unison*.
samtinges (æ¹, e¹, e²) adv. *all at once, immediately, forthwith*, Æ.
samðe conj. in phrase samðe...samðe...as well...as... ('tam'... 'quam'...), CM,Sc, etc. [sam]
sāmweaxen *half-grown*, NC319.
samwinnende ptc. *contending together*, WW 211⁷.
sāmwīs *stupid, dull, foolish*, CP. adv. -līce.
samwist† f. *living together, cohabitation*, GL.
sāmworht *unfinished*, CHR.
samwrǣdnes f. *union, combination*, Bo114⁴.
sāmwyrcan *to half do a thing*, LL350,61¹.
sanc I. pret. 3 sg. of sincan. II.=sang
sanct m. *holy person, saint*, Æ. [L. sanctus]
sand (o) I. f. *action of sending, embassy, mission, deputation*, Æ : *message* : (also m.) *messenger, ambassador*, KC : *sending, service, course of food, repast, mess, victuals*, Gl; Æ. ['sand'; sendan] II. n. 'sand,' *gravel*, Æ,MtR,VPs; AO; Mdf : *sandy shore, sea-shore, beach*.
sandbeorg m. *sand-hill, sand-bank*, Bo,KC.
sandceosol m. *sand, gravel*, Æ.
sandcorn n. *grain of sand*, Æ.
sandful *sandy*, Sc223¹³.
sandgeweorp (u²) n. *sand-bank, quicksand*, WW.
sandgewyrpe n. *sand-heap*, KC6·228'.
sandgrot n. *grain of sand*, HELL117.
sand-hlið n., nap. -hleoðu *sandy slope, hillock*, AN236.
sandhof n. *sand-house, barrow, grave*, GU 1169.
sandhricg m. *sand-bank*, ÆGR75⁸.
sandhyll (o¹) m. 'sand-hill,' Cp.
sandig 'sandy,' Lcd.
sandiht (o) *sandy, dusty*, AO.
sandland (o¹, o²) n. *sandy shore*, GU1308.
sandpytt m. *sand-pit*, ÆL35³²⁵.
sandrid n. *quicksand*, WW183⁷.
sandsēað m. *sand-pit*, KC.

sang (o) **I.** m. *noise, 'song,' singing,* B,Bo, Cr,LkL : *psalm, poem, lay,* Bl,CP,VPs. **II.** pret. 3 sg. of singan.

sangbōc f. *singing-book, service-book,* KC, LL. ['*songbook*']

sangcræft m. *art of singing, composing poetry, or playing an instrument,* BH,PH.

sangdrēam m. '*cantilena,' song, music,* CM 638.

sangere (o) m. *singer, poet,* BH,Bl. ['*songer*']

sangestre f. *songstress,* ÆGr. ['*songster*']

sangpīpe f. *pipe,* GPH 389²⁶.

-sānlan v. a-s. [sæne]

sann pret. 3 sg. of sinnan.

sāp f? *amber, unguent,* GL.

sāpbox m. *resin-box? soap-box?* LL455,17.

sāpe f. '*soap,' salve,* Lcd,WW; Æ.

sār I. n. *bodily pain, sickness : wound, 'SORE,' raw place : suffering, sorrow, affliction,* Bo,Chr. **II.** adj. *sore, sad, grievous, painful, wounding,* CP.

Sar(a)cene (o², i³) pl. *Saracens,* AO,DR.

Saracenisc adj. *Saracen,* Æ.

sārbenn† f. *painful sore or wound.*

sārbōt f. *compensation for wounding,* LL 500,10¹.

Sarc-=Sarac-

sārclāð m. *bandage,* WW.

sārcrene (ē²?) *sore, tender,* Lcd 65b.

sārcwide† m. *taunt, reproach : lament.*

sāre (ǣ) adv. *sorely, heavily, grievously, bitterly,* B,Cr,Gen,Ps : *painfully,* B. ['*sore*']

sārege *grief, trouble,* RWH 88¹³.

sārettan *to grieve, lament, complain,* CP.

sārferhð *sorrowful,* GEN 2244.

sarga m. *trumpet, clarion,* GL.

sārgian (±) *to cause pain, afflict, wound, grieve : be pained, suffer, languish,* CP. [sārig]

sārgung f. *lamentation, grief,* Sc,W.

sārian *to become painful,* CP : *grieve, be sad, feel sorry for,* BH.

sārig '*sorry,' grieved, sorrowful,* Æ,B,Bo, Cr,Ps.

sārigcierm (e³) m. *wailing,* MFH 128⁸.

sārigferhð† *sad-hearted.*

sāriglic *sad,* GD 290⁶.

sārigmōd *dejected, mournful,* B. ['*sorry-mood*']

sārignes f. *sadness, grief,* Æ,Chr. ['*sorriness*']

sārlic *grievous, sad, doleful, painful, lamentable, bitter,* Æ,B,Bo,Bl. adv. -līce '*sorely,' grievously, mournfully, bitterly, painfully,* Æ,Bl,Bo,Jul; CP.

sārnes f. *affliction, distress, suffering, pain, grief,* Æ. ['*soreness*']

sārsēofung f. *complaint,* WW 488³⁶.

sārslege† m. *painful blow,* JUL.

sārspell n. *sad story, complaint,* MH 16³.

sārstæf m. *cutting word, abuse,* GU 205.

sārung=sārgung; **sarw-**=searw-

sār-wracu† f., gds. -wrǣce *grievous persecution, sore tribulation.*

sārwylm m. *pain, illness,* GU 1123.

saturege f. *savory (plant),* Lcd 147a,WW. ['*satureie*'; L.]

sāul=sāwol

±**sāwan⁷** *to 'sow*,' strew seed, implant,* Æ : *disseminate,* CP.

sāwel=sāwol

+**sāwelod** *having a soul,* G : *endowed with life,* LL.

sāwend, sāwere (Mt) m. '*sower.*'

+**sawenlic**=+sewenlic

sāwl (CP), sāwle=sāwol

sāwlian *to expire,* Æ.

sāwlung (e²) f. *dying,* Shr. ['*souling*']

sā-wol (-wel, -wul, -wl) f., gs. sāwle '*soul,' life,* Æ,B,Bl,Bo,Ps; CP : *spirit,* Bl,Chr : *living being,* Æ.

sāwolberend m. *human being,* B 1004 (wl).

sāwolcund (e) *spiritual,* GU 288.

sāwoldrēor† n. *life-blood.*

sāwolgedāl† n. *death.*

sāwolgesceot=sāwolscot

sāwolhord (e², wl)† n. *life, body.*

sāwolhūs† n. (*soul-house), body,* GU.

sāwollēas *soulless, lifeless,* Æ.

sāwol-sceat (e²), -scot m. *payment to the church on the death of a person,* LL.

sāwolðearf f. *soul's need,* TC 474 (wl).

sāwon pret. pl. of sēon.

sāwul=sāwol

sca-, scā-, v. also scea-, scēa-.

scāda m. *crown of head,* PPs 67²¹. ['*shode*']

+**scādwyrt** (ēa) f. *oxeye,* LCD 103a, WW 50².

scæ-; scǣ-=scea-, sce-; scēa-

scæc (e) *fetters,* JGPh 1·329. [Du. schake]

scæftamund=sceaftmund

scæfð=sceafoða

scæm-=scam-

scǣnan I. (±) (ē, ēa) *to break, wrench open, shatter,* Æ. ['*shene*'] **II.** (+) *to render brilliant?* SOL 222 (GK).

+**scǣninges** f. *collision,* WW 384¹⁰.

scēp=scēap; **scæptlō** (Cp)=sceaftlō

scær=scear I. and II.

scæron pret. pl. of scieran.

scæð I. (*Gen*)=scēað. **II.**=scegð

scafa m. *plane,* Ep,LL. ['*shave*']

±**scafan⁶** (a, æ, ea) *to 'shave,' scrape, polish,* Cp,BH.

scæffōt *splay-footed,* GL.

scalde=sceolde pret. 3 sg. of sculan.

scaldhūlas pl. *reed, sedge*, WW37¹⁵ (v. ES 43·320).

scaldōȳfel=scealdōȳfel

+scaldwyrt (WW278²⁵)=+scādwyrt

scamel=scamol

scamfæst '*shamefast,' modest, CP.*

scamful (eo) *modest*, DR. ['*shameful*']

scamian (ea, eo, o) (w. g.) *to be ashamed, blush*, B,CP : (impers., w. a. of pers. and g. of thing) *cause shame*, Æ,CP. ['*shame*']

scamlēas '*shameless,' impudent, immodest,* CP.

scamlēaslic *shameless,* CP. adv. -līce '*shamelessly,'* CP.

scamlēast (ea¹) f. *impudence, shamelessness, immodesty,* GL,Mk.

scamlic (æ, ea) *shameful, disgraceful,* OEG ; AO : *modest.* ['*shamely*'] adv. -līce, CP.

scamlim n. *private member,* GPH390, WW 535³¹?

scamol (æ¹, e¹, ea¹, eo¹, o¹ ; e², u²) m. *stool, footstool, bench, table (of money-changers),* Bl,VPs. ['*shamble*']

scamu (ea, eo, o) f. '*shame,' confusion,* Cp, Lk : *disgrace, dishonour,* Cr : *insult,* MkR : *shameful circumstance,* WW : *modesty,* CP : *private parts,* Gen,WW. s. dōn *to inflict injury.*

scamul=scamol

scamung (ea) f. *disgrace,* LRPs68²⁰.

scān pret. 3 sg. of scīnan.

scanca m. '*shank,' shin, leg,* G,Ph,Gl,Sol, WW : *ham?* LL (sconc).

scancbend (scang-) m. *garter,* WW152³⁹.

scancforad (e³) *broken-legged,* CP,Lcd.

scancgebeorg f. *leg-greave,* WW535⁹.

scancgegirela m. *anklet, garter,* WW467²⁹.

scanclīra m. *calf of the leg,* WW266⁴.

scand I. (ea, eo, o) f. *ignominy, shame, confusion, disgrace,* Chr,Cr : *scandal, disgraceful thing,* CP. II. m. *wretch, impostor, recreant, buffoon,* Æ,WW. III. f. *bad woman,* ÆL. ['*shond*']

scandful *shameful, disgraceful,* MH. ['*shondfull*']

scandhūs m. *house of ill fame,* MH26²⁴.

scandlic (ea, o) *shameful, disgraceful, vile, unchaste,* Bo ; Æ,AO. ['*shondly*'] adv. -līce *shamefully, obscenely : insultingly.*

scandlicnes (o) f. *shame, disgrace,* CP : *disgraceful act.*

scandlufiende *loving shamefully,* Lcd 1·lxi⁴.

scandword (ea) n. *abusive, blasphemous or obscene language,* W255¹⁵.

scandwyrde *slanderous,* AB34¹⁰.

scang-=scanc- ; +scāp-=+scēap-

+scapen pp. of scieppan.

scapu-lare n., -larie f. *scapulary,* RB.

scar-=scear- ; scaþ-=sceaþ-

scēab (Cp)=scēaf ; sceaba=scafa

sceabb (æ, e) m. '*scab,'* CP,Lcd. ['*shab*']

sceabbede *purulent, having sores or scabs,* OEG. ['*shabbed*']

sceacan⁶ (tr. and intr.) *to* '*shake,' move quickly to and fro, brandish* : *go, glide, hasten, flee, depart,* Æ : *pass from, proceed,* CP.

sceacdōm (æ) m. *flight,* Gen31²⁰.

sceacel (e) m. '*shackle,'* WW : *plectrum.*

scēacere m. *robber,* NG. [*Ger.* schächer]

sceacga m. *rough hair, wool, etc.,* WW. ['*shag*']

sceacgede *hairy, shaggy,* WW.

sceaclīne (WW182²⁶)=sceatline

sceacnes f. '*excussio,'* EPs140⁴.

sceacul=sceacel

scead (a, æ, e) n. *shadow, shade : shelter, protection : stye,* Cp1954 (ES43·326).

+scēad (ā) I. n. *separation, distinction,* LkL : *discretion, understanding, argument,* Æ ; CP : *reason,* ÆP142¹¹ : *reckoning, account, statement,* Mt : *accuracy : art, manner, method.* ['*shed*'] II. *reasonable, prudent : calculated,* GL.

±scēadan⁷ (ā, ē) (tr. and intr.) *to divide, separate, part,* Soul ; Lcd : *discriminate, decide, determine, appoint : differ : scatter,* '*shed,' Lcd : expound : decree : write down.*

sceadd m. '*shad' (fish),* KC6·147¹⁹.

sceaddgenge *seasonable for shad,* KC6·147¹⁸.

scēadelīce=scēadlīce

+scēadenlīce *severally,* WW491³⁶.

scēadenmǣl *damascened (sword),* B1939.

scēadesealf f. *salve or powder (for the head?),* Lcd.

sceadew-=sceadw-

sceadiht *shady,* CVHy5³.

sceadlic *shady,* OEG2885.

+scēadlic *reasonable, discreet, wise, accurate,* CP. adv. -līce.

+scēadnes '*auctoritas,'* Chrd13¹⁸.

sceadu (a) f., gs. scead(u)we, sceade '*shade,' shadow, darkness,* Ex,Ps,Sol ; CP : *shady place, arbour,* Lcd : *shelter : scene,* v. OEG 2885.

sceadugeard m. *shady place,* Cp79т.

sceadugenga m. *wanderer in darkness,* B 703.

sceaduhelm (a¹) m. *darkness,* B650.

sceadwian (a¹) *to protect,* LPs90⁴. ['*shadow*']

sceadwig *shady,* RHy5³.

±scēadwīs (ā) *sagacious, intelligent, rational, reasonable, wise,* Æ. adv. -līce, *clearly,* AO60⁹.

+scēadwīslic (RBL14¹)=+scēadwīs

scēadwīsnes f. *sagacity, reason : discrimination, discretion : separation,* VH : *reckoning.*

sceadwung f. *overshadowing, Lcd; Æ : something giving shade,* OEG438. ['*shadowing*']

scēaf I. m. '*sheaf,*' *bundle, Æ,Lcd;* CP. **II.** pret. 3 sg. of scūfan.

sceaf-=scaf-

scēafmǣlum adv. *into bundles,* Mt13³⁰.

sceaf(o)ða m. *chip, shaving, slip, scraping,* BH.

sceaft (æ, e) m. *staff, pole, '*shaft,' *Met,WW : spear-shaft, spear, Æ;* CP.

±sceaft fmn., nap. -tu, -ta, -te, tas *created being, creature, Bo; Æ,CP : origin, creation, construction, existence, Bo; Æ,CP : (+) dispensation, destiny, fate,* CP : (+) *condition, nature.* ['*shaft*']

sceaft-lō, pl. -lōn *spear-strap,* Cp (sce(a)pt-).

sceaftmund (æ) f. *span, LL.* ['*shaftment*']

sceaftriht(e) adv. *in a straight line,* CC54.

sceafð=sceafoða

sceaga (a) m. *copse, Ct;* Mdf. ['*shaw*']

sceagod=sceacgede

sceal pres. 1 and 3 sg. of sculan.

scealc m. *servant, retainer, soldier, subject, member of a crew, Ps : man, youth,* B. ['*shalk*']

sceald *shallow, BC*1·593 (v. PST1895–8, 532 and '*shoal*').

scealde=sceolde pret. 2 sg. of sculan.

scealdðȳfel (a¹) m. *thicket,* GD100; 212.

scealfor f., scealfra (Æ) m. *diver (bird), cormorant.* [cp. *OHG.* scarbo]

scealga (y) m. *a fish, roach? rudd? WW.* ['*shallow*']

-scealian v. ā-s.

sceall=sceal pres. 1 and 3 sg. of sculan.

sceallan pl. '*testiculi,*' Lcd.

scealtu=scealt ðu (pres. 2 sg. of sculan, and pron. 2 pers.).

scealu (a) f. *shell, husk, Ep : scale (of a balance), Æ : dish, KC.* ['*shale*']

scēam m. *pale grey or white horse?* RD23⁴. [*Ger.* schimmel]

sceam-=scam-

scēan pret. 3 sg. of scīnan.

scēanan=scǣnan

sceanc-=scanc-

sceand=scand

+sceandnes (ÆL)=+scendnes

scēanfeld=scīnfeld

scēap (ǣ, ē, ī) n. '*sheep,*' *CP,G,RB,VPs, WW.*

+sceap (a) n., nap. -pu '*shape,*' *form, created being, creature, El,Gen,WW : creation : dispensation, fate : condition : sex,* DR51⁴ : (±) '*genitalia,*' A11·2.

-sceap v. for-s.

scēapǣtere (ǣ¹, ī¹; e²) m. *sheep's carcase,* LL449,8.

sceapen pp. of scieppan.

scēapen adj. *of a sheep,* Lcd.

+sceapennes f. *creation, formation, Æ.*

scēaphām m. *sheepfold,* EC373′.

scēapheord (y²) f. *flock of sheep,* Ex12³².

scēapheorden n. *shed,* WW185¹⁵.

+sceaphwīl (æ) f. *fated hour,* B26.

scēaphyrde (i) m. '*shepherd.*' (*W;* Æ).

scēaplic *of a sheep,* OEG11¹⁸⁷.

+sceaplīce ably, fitly, BHCA324⁴.

scēapscearu (ē) f. *sheep-shearing,* GEN38¹².

-sceapung v. for-s.

scēapwæsce f. *place for washing sheep,* Ct.

scēapwīc n. *sheepfold,* KC3·405⁵.

scear I. (æ, e) mn. *ploughshare, Cp,Sc.* ['*share*'] **II.** pret. 3 sg. of scieran.

scēara=scēarra

scearbēam m. *wood to which the ploughshare is fixed,* WW196²⁸. [v. '*share*']

sceard I. n. *incision, cleft, gap, Ct : potsherd, GPH.* ['*shard*'] **II.** adj. *cut, mutilated, gashed, notched, hacked* : (w. g.) *bereft of.*

±scearfian *to cut off, scrape, shred,* Lcd, LkL.

scearflian *to scrape,* Lcd1·184′.

scearfung f. *scraping, scarifying,* Lcd.

scearian (a) *to allot,* KC.

scearn (æ, e) n. *dung, muck, Æ,Lcd,VPs.* ['*sharn*']

scearnbudda m. *dung-beetle,* ÆGr308¹n. ['*sharnbud*']

scearn-wibba (æ, e) -wifel (-fifel, WW) m. *dung-beetle.*

scēaron=scǣron pret. pl. of scieran.

scearp (a, æ) '*sharp,*' *pointed, prickly, Lcd, Soul,VPs : acute, keen, active, shrewd, Æ, Bo,Lcd : severe, rough, harsh, AO,Hell, Lcd : biting, bitter, acid, Lcd : brave.* [scieran]

scearpe I. adv. *sharply, keenly, Hex,Ps;* Æ. ['*sharp*'] **II.** f. *scarification,* Lcd.

scearpecged '*sharp-edged,*' Æ.

scearpian *to score, scarify,* Lcd.

scearplic *sharp, severe, effectual.* adv. -līce '*sharply,*' *acutely, keenly,* CP : *painfully, severely, OET,W : effectually,* CM192 : *attentively, Bf : quickly, WW.*

scearpnes f. '*sharpness,*' *acuteness, keen observation, Bo,Cp,CP; Æ : tartness, pungency, acidity, Lcd,W; Æ : effrontery,* GD : *efficacy.*

scearpnumol *effective,* Lcd.

scearpsīene *keen-sighted,* Bo72,73.

scearpsmēawung f. *argument,* G.

scearpðanc(ful)līce adv. *efficaciously,* Sc.

scearpðancol *quick-witted, keen,* Lcd3·440′.

scearpung f. *scarifying,* Lcd.

scēarra fpl. *shears, scissors, CP,Gl,LL.* ['*shear*']

scearseax (e, i, ie, y) n. *razor,* CP.

scearu I. (a, æ, y) f. *shearing, shaving, tonsure,* Æ. **II.** (a) f. '*share'-bone, groin,* Lcd,WW.

scearwund? *wounded in the groin,* LL6, 63.

scēat I. m. *corner, angle, edge, point, promontory,* Mdf : *quarter, district, region, surface (of the earth)* : *lap, bosom, fold,* CP : *napkin, sheet, covering, cloak, garment,* CP : *inlet, creek,* BH90²⁷. [*Ger. schoss*] **II.** pret. 3 sg. of scēotan.

scēata m. *angle, corner,* AO : *bosom, lap, lower part of a sail* : *napkin.* [*Ger.* schote]

scēatcod m. *wallet,* WW107⁵. [codd]

sceatlīne f. *sheet by which a sail is trimmed to the wind,* WW288²⁴.

sceatt (æ,. e) m. *property, treasure, coin, money, wealth,* LL : *payment, price, tribute, bribe, reward,* Æ : *rent, mortgage-money* : *money of account, denarius, twentieth part of a shilling* (Kent), v. LL2·634. ['*sceat*']

sceatwyrpan *to make the payment to the bridegroom on which the bride passes into his power from that of the father,* WW386¹ (v. ES42·170).

scēað (æ, ē) f. '*sheath,*' Æ,Gen,JnL (ēæ) : *spike, nail,* JnL20²⁵? [cp. hornscēað]

sceaða (a) m. *injurious person, criminal, thief, assassin,* B Mt; Æ : (†) *warrior, antagonist* : *fiend, devil* : *injury,* Gen549. ['*scathe*']

sceaðan=scēððan

sceaðe f. *injury,* VH19.

sceaðel f. *shuttle? weaver's slay?* LL455,15,1 (v. ANS115,165).

sceaðenes=sceðnes

sceaðful *hurtful,* GD209. ['*scatheful*']

±**sceaðian** *to injure, spoil, steal,* Æ.

sceaðig (æ) *injurious,* ÆGr63¹⁵.

sceaðōīgnes f. *injury, harm,* WYN35.

sceaðung f. *injury, damage,* TC138¹⁸,VH.

scēawendsprǣc f. *buffoonery,* WW533⁴.

scēawendwīse f. *buffoon's song,* RD9⁹.

scēawere m. *spectator, observer, watchman, spy,* B; Æ,CP : *mirror,* NC. ['*shower*']

±**scēawian** *to look, gaze, see, behold, observe,* B; Æ,AO,CP : *inspect, examine, scrutinize,* Chr,Lk; Æ,AO,CP : *have respect to, look favourably on,* Æ : *look out, look for, choose,* Æ : *decree, grant, exhibit, display,* Gen. ['*show*']

scēawigend m? *spectator,* OEG,AA2¹⁴.

scēawung (ā) f. *seeing, surveying, inspection, scrutiny, examination, contemplation,* AO, CP : *respect, regard* : *show, spectacle, appearance,* Bl,MkL : *toll on exposure of goods.* ['*showing*']

scēawungstōw f. *place of observation,* Æ (1·210).

sceb=sceabb; **scēb**=scēaf; **scec**=scæc

scecel=sceacel; **sced**=scead

scēd pret. 3 sg. of scēadan.

scef-=sceaf-, scyf-

scegð (æ, ei) mf. *vessel, ship,* CHR,MH (v. WC137n). [*ON.* skeið]

scegðmann (æ) m. *sailor, pirate, viking,* Æ.

scehð=scegð; **scelð-**=scegð-

scel=(1) sceal; (2) sciell

sceld=(1) scield; (2) scyld I.

sceld-=scild-, scyld-; **scele**=scelle

scelēge (GL)=sceolhēge

scelfan³ (=ie) *to totter, shake,* LL. [*ON.* skialfa]

scelfor=scealfor

scell I.=sceal. **II.**=sciell

scelle (=ie) *cutting off, separation* Cp777c: *discretion* RWH145⁴ (v. FM100).

scemel=scamol; **scēnan**=scǣnan

scenc (æ) m. (±) *drink, draught,* Lcd,MtL : *cup,* CM959. ['*shench*']

±**scencan** (æ) *to pour out, give drink,* B,LPs, Sc; Æ,CP. ['*shench*']

scencingcuppe f. *jug,* TC536⁷.

scendan I. (±, i, ie, y) *to put to shame, confound, discomfit,* AO,VPs; CP : *blame,* CP : *corrupt, injure,* Cr,DR : *disgrace, insult.* ['*shend*'] **II.**=scyndan I.

scendle f. *reproach,* LkLR11⁸.

+**scendnes** (æ, e, ea, i, y) f. *shame, confusion,* Æ,Ps. ['*shendness*']

+**scendð** f. *confusion,* VPs108²⁹.

scendung f. *reproach, affliction,* DR,LkL.

scēne=scīene; **scēnfeld**=scīnfeld

scennum dp. of sb. *pommel of sword-hilt? plate of metal on pommel?* B1694.

+**scento,** +**scendðo** (VPs) f. *shame, confusion.*

scēo I. *cloud?* RD4⁴¹. **II.**=scēoh, scōh

sceo-; scēo-=scͻ-, scu-; scō-, scū-

scēoc pret. 3 sg. of sceacan.

scēod I.=scōd pret. 3 sg. of scēððan. **II.** pp. of scōgan.

scēofan=scūfan; **scēogan** (CP)=scōgan

scēoh I. '*shy,*' *timid,* Rim43. **II.**=scōh

scēohmōd *timid,* JUL672.

sceol (*scēolh) *squinting, awry,* WW. [*Ger.* scheel]

sceolan=sculan; **sceoldan**=scieldan

sceolh-ēge, -ē(a)gede (y) *squinting,* Æ.

sceolu=scolu; **sceom-**=scam-

scēon (±) I.† *to fall (to), occur, happen* : *go quickly, fly.* **II.**=scōgan

sceon-=scīen-

scēona gp. of scēoh.

sceonc-=scanc-; **sceond**=scand

sceop=scop

scēop pret. 3 sg. of scieppan.

sceoppa m. *booth,* Lk21¹. ['*shop*']

sceoppend=scieppend
sceopu nap. of scip.
scēor=scūr; **sceoran**=scieran
sceorf (u, y) n. '*scurf*,' *BH* : *a skin disease*, *Lcd* : (+) *irritation of the stomach*, LCD.
sceorfan³ *to scarify, gnaw,* AO : (+) *scrape, shred.*
sceorfe(n)de (u¹) *rough, scabby,* LCD 56a, 65b.
sceorian=scorian
sceorp (o) n. *ornament, clothing,* AO : *equipment, fittings (for a ship?),* LL 444,1.
±**sceorpan³** *to scrape, gnaw,* LCD.
sceort=scort
scēos gs., nap. of scēoh, scōh.
sceot=scot
±**scēot** *ready, quick,* RB 97¹⁶.
sceota m. '*shoat,*' *trout,* WW 94.
±**scēotan²** *to* 'SHOOT,' *hurl missiles, cast,* Æ : *strike, hit, push, thrust, AO* : *run, rush, dart, press forward,* Æ : *contribute, pay* : *refer to, appeal to,* Æ : *allot, assign* : *befall, fall to, happen,* CHRD.
scēotend† m. *bowman, warrior.*
sceoton=scuton pret. pl. of scēotan.
sceoða=sceaða
scep=scyp I.; **scep-**=sciep-
+**scep**=+sceap; **scēp** (*VPs*)=scēap
scepen I. pp. of scieppan. **II.**=scipen. **III.** (N)=scieppend
sceppe f. *a dry measure,* NC 319. [*ON.* skeppa].
sceptlōh, sceptōg (GL)=sceaftlō
scer=scear; **scer-**=scear-, scier-, scir-
scerero (OET)=scēarra
scer(n)icge (=ie) f. *actress, female jester,* A, MH, RD (sciren-).
+**scert** (OEG 130)=scyrt, pp. of scyrtan.
sceruru=scēarra
-**scerwen** v. ealu-s, medu-s.
scēt=scēat pret. 3 sg. of scēotan.
scēte=scȳte; **scetel** (KGL)=scyttel
scett=sceatt; **scēð**=(1) scēað; (2) scegð
sceðdǣd (æ) f. *injurious deed, crime,* WW.
sceð-nes, -enes f. *hurt, injury,* BH.
±**sceððan⁶** and wv. (ea, y) *to scathe, injure, hurt, crush, oppress, disturb.* [sceaða]
sceððend† m. *adversary,* DR.
+**sceððendlic** *hurtful,* DR 118¹⁶.
sceððu f. *hurt, injury,* LCD 1·342'.
sceōwrǣc *hurtful, wicked,* BL 161³³.
sceu-, scēu-=scu-, scū-
scēwyrhta=sceowyrhta
scīa m. *shin, leg,* GL.
sciccels, sciccel (y) m. *coat, mantle, cloak,* Æ.
sciccing m. *mantle, cloak, cape,* GL.
scīd n. *thin slip of wood, shingle, billet,* Gl. ['*shide*']

scīdhrēac m. *rick or heap of firewood,* EC 351¹⁰.
scīdweall m. *wooden palings,* WW 146²⁸
+**scīe**=+scȳ
-**scīelan** (ȳ) v. be-s.
scield (e, i, y) m. '*shield,*' *B,VPs* : *protector, Bl,Ph* : (±) *protection, defence,* AO,CP : *part of a bird's plumage?* PH 308.
scield- v. also scild-.
±**scieldan** (i, eo, y) *to protect,* '*shield*' ('*i-shield*'), *guard, defend, defend oneself,* Æ,B,Bl,Bo,Lcd,VPs; AO,CP. +scieldod *furnished with shields,* Bl.
sciele (CP) pres. sg. subj. of sculan.
sciell I. f. '*shell,*' *Cp,MH,OEG* : *shell-fish* : *scale,* Æ,AO,CP. [scalu] II. (y) *sonorous, shrill,* Rim 27. ['*shill*']
sciellfisc (i, y) m. '*shell-fish,*' *Bo.*
-**sciellig** (y) v. stān-s.
scielliht (e) *having a shell,* LCD.
sciendan=scendan
scīene (ē, ēo, ī, ȳ) *beautiful,* B,Cr,Gen,Pa, Ph : *bright, brilliant, light,* Cr. ['*sheen*']
scīenes (ēo, ī, ȳ) f. *suggestion, instigation,* CP. [scȳan]
scienn=scinn, scīn
scīenð pres. 3 sg. of scīnan.
±**scieppan⁶** (e, i, y) *to create, form,* '*shape*' ('*i-shape*'), *make,* Gen : *order, destine, arrange, adjudge, assign,* B,Wy; AO.
±**Scieppend** (y) m. *Creator,* B; CP. ['*sheppend*']
±**scieran⁴** (æ, e, eo, i) *to cleave, hew, cut,* An, B : *cut hair,* Æ,CP : *receive tonsure,* Guth : '*shear*' *sheep,* BC. pp. scoren *abrupt,* CP 215⁸.
scierden (e) adj. *of sherds,* GPH 400. [sceard]
sciering (e) f. *shearing, shaving,* CM 610.
±**scierpan** (e, y) I. *to deck, clothe, equip,* ÆL. [sceorp] II. *to sharpen,* LL,VPs : *rouse, invigorate, strengthen.* +scierpt *acute* (*accent*), BF 184¹. ['*sharp*']
+**scierpla** (i, y) *clothing, garments,* AN, BL.
+**scierpendlīce** (y¹) *fittingly,* BHB 324⁴.
scierseax=scearseax
scīet pres. 3 sg. of scēotan.
scīete (ē, ī, ȳ) f. *cloth, towel, shroud,* Æ,BH, Cp,Mk,WW. ['*sheet*']
scīfe=scyfe
±**scīftan** (y) *to divide, distribute, allot, appoint,* LL : *place, order, arrange,* LL,W. ['*shift*']
scilbrung=scylfrung
scild=scield; **scild-**=scyld-
scildburh† (e, y) f. *shield-wall, phalanx* : *roof of shields, testudo* : *place of refuge,* SAT 309.
scilden f. *protection,* WW 52¹⁷.

±**scild-end**, -ere (ie, y) m. *protector, defender*, Ps.

scildfreca (y¹) m. *warrior*, B1033.

scildhete m. *foe*, AN85. [scyld]

scildhrēoða (y¹, e², ea²) m. *shield, buckler : testudo, phalanx.*

±**scildnes** (ie) f. *defence, protection*, CP.

scildtruma (y¹) m. *testudo, phalanx, company (of troops)*, Æ,OEG. ['sheltron']

scildung (y¹) f. *protection*, Æ,DR.

scildweall (y¹) m. *wall of shields*, B3118.

scildwiga (y¹) m. *warrior*, B288.

scildwyrhta (y¹) m. *shield-maker*, Ct,LL.

scile (CP) pres. subj. of sculan.

scilfix=sciellfisc

scilfor *yellow, golden*, OEG.

scill=sciell

scilling (y) m. *'shilling' (consisting of a varying number of pence), silver coin*, Æ, G,LL (v. 2·640),WW.

scillingrīm n. *count of shillings*, WID92.

scīma m. *ray, light, brightness, effulgence, splendour*, CP : *twilight, gloom*. [scīnan]

scimerian (y) *to 'shimmer,' glisten, shine*, NC319; OEG23⁵¹.

scīmian *to shine, glisten*, ÆGr,LkL : *grow dusky, dim, be dazzled, bleared*, Æ. ['shim']

scīn=scinn

scīnan¹ (ȳ) *to* SHINE, *flash*, Æ,CP : *be resplendent* : (+) *shine upon, illuminate.*

scinbān n. *'shin-bone,'* WW.

scinccing (OET p. 26)=sciccing

+**scincio** np. *the fat about the kidneys*, LCD.

scind-=scend-

scindel m. *a shingle*, KC6·33'.

scīndlāc=scīnlāc

scīnefrian *to glitter*, WW348¹⁹.

scīnelāc=scinnlāc

scīnende (ȳ) *'shining,'* MH,WW : *eminent, distinguished*, BH.

scīnendlic *shining*, LPs18⁹.

scīnfeld (ēa) m. *Elysian fields, Tempe.*

scīnhosu f. *greave*, OEG.

scinn I. n., scinna m. *spectre, illusion, phantom, evil spirit*, CP : *magical image*, ÆL36⁴⁰⁴. II. n. *skin*, CHR1075,WW 427²⁷?

scinncræft (y) m. *sorcery, magic*, AO.

scinncræftiga m.*sorcerer*, GD27¹⁵; LL248,7.

scinnere m. *magician*, GL.

scīnnes I. f. *radiance*, MKL13²⁴. II.= scīenes

scinngedwola m. *phantom*, WW455¹¹.

scinngelāc n. *jugglery, magical practices*, AN767.

scinnhīw n. *spectre, illusion, phantasm*, Æ.

scinnlāc I. n. *sorcery, magic : apparition, spectre, delusion, superstition : frenzy, rage*, AO. II.=scinnlǣce I.

scinnlǣca (ā²) m. *wizard, magician*, AO.

scinnlǣce I. *magical, spectral*, AO. II. f. *sorceress, witch.*

scinnlic (y) *spectral*, NC320.

scinnsēoc *spectre-haunted*, LCD1·364⁴.

scinu (y) f. *'shin,'* WW.

scip (y) n. *'ship,'* BH,Bo,Chr,Cp; AO,CP.

scīp=scēap

scipāc f. *oak for shipbuilding*, KC.

scipbroc n. *hardship on ship-board*, BL173⁶.

scipbrucol (y) *destructive to shipping*, GPH 401⁹.

scipbryce m. *right to claim wreckage*, KC 4·208. ['shipbreche']

scipbȳme (y) f. *ship's trumpet*, GPH391.

scipcræft m. *naval force*, CHR1048D.

scipdrincende *shipwrecked*, DR61¹⁶.

scipe I. m. *pay, wage*, WW; ÆL31⁵⁵ : *position, rank.* ['shipe'] II. (+) n. *fate*, B2570?

scipehere=sciphere

scipen (e, y) f. *'shippon,' stall, cattle-shed*, BH,LL.

scipere (y) m. *shipman, sailor*, Chr. ['shipper']

scipfǣreld n. *voyage*, Æ,GD273¹⁸.

scipfæt n. *a vessel in the form of a ship*, WW124⁸.

scipfarend (y) m. *sailor*, BH(Sch)261²

scipfērend m. *sailor*, AN250.

scipfierd f. *naval expedition, fleet*, AO.

scipflota m. *sailor, pirate*, CHR937A.

scipforðung f. *equipment of ships*, LL314'.

scipfultum m. *naval aid*, CHR1049C.

scipfylleð *private jurisdiction exercised over a group of three hundreds*, KC6·240 (v. BT).

scipfyrd=scipfierd

scipfyrdung f. *fleet, naval expedition*, CHR, LL.

scipfyrð(r)ung f. *equipment of ships*, LL.

scipgebroc n. *shipwreck*, AO,CP.

scipgefeoht (y) n. *naval battle*, GPH389.

scipgefēre n. *sailing*, BH150².

scipgetāwu f. *tackling of a ship*, WW181²⁴.

scipgyld n. *ship-tax, ship-money*, TC307²⁴.

sciphamor m. *hammer for giving a signal to rowers*, WW.

sciphere m. *naval force, fleet (usu. hostile), squadron*, AO,CHR : *crew of a warship.*

scipherelic *naval*, HGL406⁴⁰.

sciphlǣder f. *ship's ladder*, WW.

sciphlæst (y) m. *ship-load, crew*, AO,CP : *ship of burden.*

sciphlāford m. *ship-master, skipper*, WW 181²¹.

sciplan *to take 'ship,' embark* : (±) *man or equip a ship*, Chr.

scipincel n. *little ship*, WW.

sciplād (y) f. *journeying by sea*, BH198²⁰.

sciplæst=sciphlæst

sciplic naval, GL,HL 199¹²⁷.

scipliŏ n. naval force, CHR 1055 c.

scipliŏend m. seaman : voyager, ÆL 33¹⁸⁸.

scipliŏende ptc. sailing, WW.

scipmærls m. ship's rope, cable, WW.

scipmann (y) m. 'shipman,' sailor, rower, BH,Chr : one who goes on trading voyages.

scipp-=sciepp-

scippräp m. ship's rope, cable, AO.

sciprēŏra (y¹) m. rower, sailor, GPH.

sciprōŏor n. ship's oar or rudder, WW 455¹⁸.

sciprōwend m. rower, sailor, WW 455¹⁴.

scipryne m. passage for ships, TC 341¹⁶.

scipsetl n. bench for rowers, WW.

scipsōcn f. (KC 6·240') i.q. scipfylleŏ.

scipsteall (y) m. place for ships, BC 3·316¹⁶.

scipstēora m. steerman, pilot, CP.

scipsteorra m. pole-star, LCD 3·270'.

scip-stiera, -stȳra=scipstēora

scip-tearo, -ter, n., gs. -tearos; scip-t(e)ara, -te(o)ra m. (ship-tar), bitumen, pitch, LCD.

sciptoll n. passage money, ÆL 30¹⁶⁷.

scipwealh m. servant whose service is connected with ships? (BT); one liable to serve in the fleet? (Swt), EC 376¹⁵.

scipweard m. ship-master, AN 297.

scipwered n. crew, WW 451¹⁷.

scipwïsan (on) adv. like a ship, AA,Æ.

scipwræc jetsam, KC 4·146.

scipwyrhta m. 'shipwright,' WW 112⁵.

scïr I. (ȳ) f. office, appointment, charge, authority, supremacy, AO,Cp,LL (+ at DR 187⁹); CP : district, diocese, see, province, 'shire,' parish, AO,Gl,LL; Æ : tribe. **II.** adj. bright, gleaming, shining, resplendent, B, Bo : clear, translucent, Cr, WW : pure, unmixed, B,Bo : white, Jn 4³⁵. ['shire']

scïran=scïeran

scïran (ȳ) to make clear, say, tell, declare, B, CP : arrange, determine, decide, decree, act in authority, CP, (+) LkL 16² : (±) clear from, get rid of, AO,CP.

scïrbasu bright purple, WW 193¹².

scïrbisceop m. bishop of a diocese, WW 173³⁰.

scïre I. adv. brightly, An : clearly : mightily, Cr 1142. ['shire'] **II.** 'peribolum,' enclosure, curtilage, WW 184²².

scïre-=scïr-

scïrecg keen-edged, LCD 1·390⁷.

scïrenicge (RD 9⁹)=scernicge

scïresmann=scïrmann

scïrfemūs (=ie) f. shrew (mouse), WW 477¹⁶. [sceorfan]

scïrgemōt n. shire-moot, LL,TC.

scïrgerēfa m. 'sheriff,' KC.

scïrgesceat (ȳ) n. property of a see, KC 3·327².

scïrham clad in bright mail, B 1895.

±**scïrian** (e, y) to ordain, appoint : allot, assign, grant : (+) mark off, count, reckon.

scïriendlic (y) derivative, WW 222²³.

scïrigmann=scïrmann

scïrlett n. piece or measure of land, EC 239⁹.

scïrmæled brightly adorned, JUD 230.

scïrmann (ȳ) m. governor of a shire, prefect, sheriff, steward, procurator, official, KC; Æ,CP; v. LL 2·649 : inhabitant of a district, Æ. ['shireman']

scïrnes f. elucidation, WW 279²³.

scïrp-=scierp-; **scïrseax**=scearseax

scïrŏegen m. thane of a shire, BC 1·544⁸.

scïrung f. separation, rejection, RB 109²¹.

scïr-wæter (scyr-) n. water forming a boundary, CHR 656 E. [scieran]

scïrwered bright? GU 1262.

scïrwita m. chief man of a shire, W.

-scïtan¹ v. be-sc.

scïte=scȳte; **scïtefinger**=scytefinger

scïtol purgative, LCD 66a.

scïtte f. purging, Lcd. ['shit']

scïttels (Æ)=scyttels

scl-(GL)=sl-

scmēgende (VPs)=smēagende pres. ptc. of smēagan.

scnïcend (GL)=snïcend pres. ptc. of snïcan.

scō=scōh; **sco-**=sceo-

scōas=scōs v. scōh; **scobl**=scofl

scōc pret. 3 sg. of sceacan.

scocca=scucca

scocha (=scohha) 'lenocinium,' Ep 579.

scōcnyll m. signal for putting on shoes, ANS 84·10.

scōd I. pret. 3 sg. of sceŏŏan. **II.** v. scōgan.

scōere m. shoemaker, Gl. ['shoer']

scōf pret. 3 sg. of sceafan.

scofen pp. of scufan.

scofettan to drive hither and thither, CP 169¹³.

scofl f. 'shovel,' Cp,Ep,LL.

scōgan pp. sc(ē)od to 'shoe,' Æ,CP.

scōh, scō, scēo m. gs. nap. sc(ē)os, gp. sc(ē)one, dp. sc(ē)on, scōum 'shoe,' Bf,G, Mt,WW.

scōhere=scōere

scōhnægl m. shoe-nail, WW.

scōhŏēn (ēo) m. shoe-cleaner, RBL 91⁹.

scōh-ŏwang, -ŏong m. 'shoe-thong,' bootlace, Jn.

scōhwyrhta (ēo, ēoh) m. shoemaker, leatherworker, GD 322, WW 97⁵.

scōian=scōgan

scōl f. 'school,' Æ,BH,Lcd; AO.

+**scola I.** m. debtor, WW 15²⁸. [sceal] **II.** companion, OEG 2271n. [scolu]

+scōla m. *fellow-student*, OEG 2271.
scolde pret. 3 sg. of sculan.
scōlere m. '*scholar*,' *learner*, Bf,LL.
scolh (WW 241¹³)=seolh
scōlere (Bf 54²⁷)=scōlere
scōlmann m.. *scholar*, WW 314²⁹ : *client*,
163⁴⁴.
scolu I. (eo) f. *troop, host, multitude* : *shoal*
(of fishes), A 13·418. II.=scōl
scom-=scam-
scōmhylte (scomm-?) n. *brushwood, copse,
thicket*, WW 411³.
scōmlic *short*, MH 98¹³.
scōn=scēon v. scēoh; scon-=scan-
scop (eo) m. *singer, poet, B,Bo*; AO. ['*scop*']
scōp pret. 3 sg. of scieppan.
scopcræft m. *poetry*, ÆGR 215⁹.
scopgereord (eo¹) n. *poetical language*, BH.
scoplēoð n. *poem*, AO.
scoplic *poetic*, OEG 119.
scora m. *hairy garment*, WW 278¹.
scoren pp. of scieran.
scorian (eo) I. *to refuse*, Æ. II. *to jut out,*
GD 213⁵.
scorp=sceorp
scort (eo, y) '*short,*' *not long, not tall*, Bo,
GD,Lcd : *brief*, Æ,Bf,Bl,Bo,CP.
scortian (eo) *to become* '*short,*' *shorten*, Lcd :
(±) *run short, fail.*
scortlic (eo) *brief*, Sc 214¹⁶. adv. -līce
'*shortly,*' *briefly, soon*, AO,LPs,ZDA; Æ.
scortnes (eo) f. '*shortness,*' *small amount* :
summary, abstract, ÆGr : *short space of
time.*
scortwyrplic (eo) *shortly coming to pass*,
Lcd 3·156².
scoru a '*score*,' NC 320. [scoren; scieran]
scōs gs. of scōh.
±scot (eo) n. '*shot,*' *shooting*, OEG; AO· :
darting, rapid motion, Men : *what is shot
forth*, AO,CP : (+) *scot, payment* : *private
apartment, sanctum, chancel*, Æ.
+scota m. *fellow-soldier*, WW 15,207.
scoten pp. of scēotan.
+scotfeoht n. *shooting, battle*, PPs.
scotfrēo *scot-free, free of tribute*, KC.
±scotian (eo) (tr. and intr.) *to move rapidly,
shoot, hurl a javelin*, Æ.
scotlīra m. *calf of the leg*, Lcd.
scotspere n. *dart, javelin*, HGL 405.
Scottas mpl. *the Scots*, BH,Chr; Æ,CP.
['*Scot*']
scotung (eo) f. *missile* : *shooting* : *darting,
flashing*, Lcd 3·280'.
scōum v. scōh.
scōung f. *provision of shoes*, LL 450,10.
-scrād v. scrīðend-s.
scrādung=scrēadung
scræb m. *cormorant? ibis?* Cp 1311.

±scræf (ea, e) n. [obl. cases occly. have
scraf-] *cave, cavern, hole, pit*, Æ,CP : *hovel,*
Æ : *den*, MtR 21¹³.
+scræpe=+scrēpe
scræette f. *adulteress, prostitute*, GL. [L
scratta]
scrǣwa=scrēawa
scrāf pret. 3 sg. of scrīfan.
scraf- v. scræf.
scrallettan† intr. *to sound loudly.*
scranc pret. 3 sg. of scrincan.
scrapian *to scrape*, IM. ['*shrape*']
scrāð pret. 3 sg. of scrīðan.
scrēad(e) f. '*shred,*' *cutting, scrap*, WW.
±scrēadian *to* '*shred,*' *peel, prune, cut off*, Æ.
scrēadung (ā) f. *shred, cutting, fragment*,
MtL : *pruning, trimming*, WW. ['*shredding*']
scrēadungīsen n. *pruning-knife*, WW. [v.
'*shredding*']
scrēaf=scræf
scrēawa m. '*shrew*' *(mouse)*, Gl.
screb=scræb; scrēc=scrīc
scref=scræf
scremman *to cause to stumble*, Lev 19¹⁴.
±screncan *to cause to stumble, ensnare,
deceive*, CP,Ps : (+) *cause to shrink or
shrivel*, MtL 13⁶. ['*shrench*']
+scrence *withered, dry*, LkL 6⁸.
+screncednes f. *tripping up*, CVPs 40¹⁰.
screodu v. scrid; +scrēope=+scrēpe
screopu=screpu
screpan⁵ (i,y) *to scrape, scratch*, Cp,Lcd,
MkR : *prepare*, LF 47'. ['*screpe*']
scrēpan *to become dry, withered*, MkR 9¹⁸.
scrēpe (ǣ, ēo) I. n. (+) *advantage*. II. (±)
suitable, adapted, fit. adv. -līce.
+scrēpnes (oe) f. *convenience*, Cp 568.
screpu (eo) f. *strigil, curry-comb*, GL.
scrēwa=scrēawa; scrīban (GL)=scrīfan
scrīc (ē, ū) *shrike, missel-thrush?* GL.
scrid I. n. nap. screodu *vehicle, chariot,
litter*. II. *quick, fleet*, An 496.
scrīdan=scrȳdan
scrīde m. *course, orbit*, Met 28¹¹.
scridon pret. pl. of scrīðan.
scridwǣn m. *chariot* : *curule chair*, Bo.
scridwīsa m. *charioteer*, WW 150¹⁴.
+scrif n. *judgment, edict*, WW : *ceremony,*
WW.
±scrīfan¹ *prescribe, ordain, allot, assign,
impose (punishment)*, LL; Æ : *hear confession*, '*shrive,*' LL : *receive absolution* :
have regard to, be troubled about, care for, CP.
scrifen ptc? *painted?* Rim 13.
scrift m. *prescribed penalty or penance*, LL :
absolution, LL : *confessor*, CP,Cr; Æ :
judge. tō scrifte gān *to go to confession,*
LL,W. ['*shrift*']

scriftbōc f. *book of penances, or on penance*, LL,W.

scriftscīr f. *confessor's area of jurisdiction* : *diocese*, LL 164,26.

scriftsprǣc f. *confession*, LL.

scrimman³ *to shrink*, Lcd 2b. ['*shrim*']

scrīn (ȳ) n. *chest, coffer, ark*, Æ,Jn : '*shrine*,' Æ : *cage (for criminals)*. [L. scrinium]

±**scrincan³** *to 'shrink,' contract, shrivel up, wither, pine away*, Æ,AO,Lcd.

scrind f. *swift course?* PPs 103²⁴.

scringan=scrincan; **-scripel** (y) v. ēar-s.

scrīpen, scrīpende '*austerus*,' LkLR 19²¹.

scripeð (Cp) pres. 3 sg. of screpan.

scritta m. *hermaphrodite*, WW 161¹¹. (v. FTp 473).

scrīð (v. OEG 2185)=scrid I.

scrīðan¹ *to go, move, glide*, B,Gu. ['*scrithe*']

scrīðe m. *course*, Met 28¹¹.

-scrīðol v. wīd-s.; **scroepe**, scrōpe=scrēpe

scrofel n? *scrofula*, Lcd 182a.

scrūc=scrīc

scrūd n., ds. scrȳd *clothing, dress* : *garment, vestment*, Æ,Chr,WW. ['*shroud*']

scrūd-=scrūt-

scrūdelshūs n. *sacristy, vestry*, ANS 84¹⁵. [scrȳdan]

scrūdfeoh n.*money for buying clothes*, NC 320.

scrūdfultum m. *grant towards providing clothes*, Ct.

scrūdland n. *land bequeathed as provision for clothing*, TC 329¹⁹.

scrūdwaru f. *garb*, LL.

scruf [Lcd]=sceorf

scruncon pret. pl. of scrincan.

scrūtnere (ūd) m. *examiner*, Chrd 88³³.

scrūtnian (ūd) *to examine, scrutinize, consider*, Æ.

scrūtnung (ūd) f. *search, investigation*, Lcd, ERPs.

scrybb d. *scrub, brushwood*, TC 525²².

scrȳd v. scrūd.

±**scrȳdan** (ī) *to clothe, dress*, Æ,Bl,Lk,Mt. ['*shride*']

scryft=scrift

scrynce *withered*, JnL 5³.

scrypan=screpan

scua m. *shadow, shade, darkness* : *protection*.

scucca (eo) m. *sprite, evil spirit, demon*, B, Bo,Mt : *the devil*. ['*shuck*']

scuccen (eo) *devilish*, NC 319.

scuccgyld (eu¹) n. *idol*, PPs 105²⁶.

scūdan² *to run, hurry?* Gu 828.

scūfan² (ēo) *to* '*shove*,*'* *thrust, push*, Æ : *push with violence, urge, impel*, CP : *push out, expel, deliver up* : (†) *display* : (intr.) *to move, go.*

sculan anv. pres. 1 sing. sce(a)l(l), scal, pl. sculon (eo), pret. sc(e)olde, sc(e)alde *to be*

obliged ('SHALL*,' *have to, must, must needs, am bound to, ought to*), Æ,AO,CP : *owe*.

scul-dor, -dra m., nap. -dru, -dra, +scyldru, -dre '*shoulder*,' Bl,Ep,Lcd,LG.

sculdorhrægl n. *cape*, WW 327²⁴.

sculdorwǣrc m. *pain in the shoulders*, Lcd.

sculdur=sculdor

scule pres. subj. of sculan.

sculthēta (WW)=scyldlǣta

±**scunian** (y) *to 'shun,' avoid*, Guth : *be afraid*, DR : (tr.) *abhor*, TC.

scunung f. *abomination*, LHy 6²³ (? for on-s.).

scūr (ēo) m. (f) '*shower*,' *storm, tempest, trouble, commotion, breeze*, An,LkR,Ps; CP : †*shower of blows or missiles*, El,Jud 79.

scūra† m. *shower (of rain)*.

scūrbeorg f. *roof*, Ruin 5.

scūrboga m. *rainbow*, Gen 1540.

±**scurf**=sceorf

scūrfāh *rainy, stormy*, A 9·369; MFH 172.

scūrheard† *made hard by blows (epithet of a sword)*.

scūrsceadu f. *protection against storms*, Gen 813.

scutel I. m. *dish, platter*, WW 280²². ['*scuttle*'] II.=scytel

scuton pret. pl. of scēotan.

scuwa=scua

+**scȳ** npl. *pair of shoes*, Æ,Ps.

scȳan? scȳn? *to suggest, persuade, prompt, incite, tempt*, BH,MtR.

scyccel, scyccels=sciccels

scydd m. *twist on a hill-side?* (Earle): *alluvial ground?* (BT),KC.

scȳde pret. 3 sg. of scēon and scȳan, scȳn.

scyfe (e, i) m. *shove, pushing, precipitation, furtherance, instigation*, CP. tō +sc. *headlong*.

scyfel(e) f. *woman's hood, head-dress*, GL.

scȳft pres. 3 sg. of scūfan.

scyftan=sciftan

+**scȳgean** *to furnish with shoes*, TC 616'.

scyhhan (ES 43·318)=scyn I.

scyhtan *to impel, prompt, urge*, Gen 898; Gu 98.

scyl=sciell

scylcen f. *female servant, slave, concubine*, ÆH 2·162'. [scealc]

±**scyld** I. (e) fm. *offence, fault, crime, guilt, sin*, CP : *obligation, liability, due, debt*, CP. [sculan; Ger. schuld] II.=scield

scyld-=scield-, scild-

+**scyldan** *to accuse*, LL 156,11.

scyldfrecu f. *wicked craving*, Gen 898.

scyldful *sinful, guilty*, Æ.

scyldg-=scyldig-

scyld-hata, -hetet m. *enemy.*
scyldian=(1) scyldigian; (2) scyldan
scyldig (e, i) (usu. w. g.) *guilty, criminal, sinful,* Æ,B; CP : *liable, responsible, in debt to,* CP. ealdres sc. *having forfeited his life.* [' *shildy* ']
scyldigian *to sin* : (+) *place in the position of a criminal, render liable to punishment.*
scyldignes f. *guilt,* DR42,103.
scyldigung f. *sum demanded as* 'wergeld,' LL156,11.
scyld-læta [-hæta? cp. sculthēta] m. *bailiff,* WW230²⁰.
scyldlēas *guiltless,* LCD.
scyldo=scyld I.
+scyldru v. sculdor; **scyldu**=scyld I.
scyldung=(1) scildung; (2) scyldigung
scyldwīte n. *fine for a crime of violence,* LL567,38.
scyldwreccende ptc. *avenging sin,* CR 1161.
scyldwyrcende† *evil-doing.*
scyle pres. subj. of sculan.
scylēagede=sceolhēgede
scylf m. *crag, ledge, shelf,* Mdf : *pinnacle, turret, tower,* Æ.
-scylfan v. ā-s.
scylfe m. *shelf, floor,* GEN1306.
scylfig *rocky,* OEG (scylp-).
scylfisc=sciellfisc; **scylfor**=scilfor
scylfrung (i) f. *shaking, swinging?* BL99³⁴; WW516¹⁶ (-brong).
scylfð pres. 3 sg. of scelfan.
scylga=scealga
scylian (=ie) *to separate, part, divide off.* sc. of māle *to pay off, discharge,* Chr1049. [' *shill* ']
scyll=sciell
scyllan (=ie) *to resound, sound loudly,* WW; OEG4890. [' *shill* ']
scylling=scilling; **scylp**=scylf
scyltumend m. *helper,* PPs27⁸.
scylun (N)=sculon pres. pl. of sculan.
scymrian=scimerian
scȳn I. *to* ' *shy,*' ÆL31⁹⁷¹. **II.** v. scȳan.
scȳn-=scīn-, scinn-
±scyndan I. (e) (tr., intr.) *to hurry, hasten, drive forward, impel* : *incite, exhort,* CP. **II.**=scendan
scyndel m. *disreputable person,* BF130²².
scyndendlīce adv. *hastily,* WW.
scyndnes f. *persuasion, prompting,* GD.
+scyndnes=+scandnes; **scȳne**=scīene
scȳnes, scȳnnes=scīenes
+scynian (DR32⁵)=scunian
scynn n. *skin, fur,* CHR1075D. [*ON.*]
scynu (*WW*307²⁷)=scinu
scyp I. m. *patch,* v. ES43·316. **II.** (*Chr* 1048)=scip

scypen=scipen
scypian *to take shape,* LCD3·146¹⁵.
scypp-=sciepp-
scyr-=scear-, scier-, scir-; **scȳr**=scīr
±scyrdan *to harm, injure, destroy,* AN,LL. [sceard]
+scȳrdan=+scrȳdan; **scyrf**=sceorf
scyrft *scarifying? scraping?* Cp130s.
scyrfð pres. 3 sg. of sceorfan.
scȳrmǣlum adv. *stormily,* Bo47²⁵. [scūr]
scyrp-=scierp-
±scyrtan (e) tr. *to shorten,* AO : intr. *run short, decrease, fail.* [sceort]
scyrte f. *skirt,* GPH393. [' *shirt* ']
scyrtest superl. of scort.
scyrting f. *shortening, abstract, epitome,* ÆH 2·460⁶.
scyrtra comp. of scort.
scȳt pres. 3 sg. of scēotan.
scyte (ē) m. *shooting, hurling,* AO : *stroke, blow,* ZDA : *dart.* [' *shute* '; scēotan]
scȳte f. (ē;=īe) ' *sheet,*' *linen cloth,* BH,Cp, Mk. [scēat]
scytefinger m. *forefinger,* LL,WW.
scyte-heald, -healden *inclined, sloping, precipitous,* GL.
scytel I. (u) m. *dart, arrow,* Erf,Ps : *tongue of a balance.* [' *shuttle* '] **II.** (=i) m. *excrement.* [scītan]
scytelfinger=scytefinger; **scytels**=scyttel
scyterǣs m. *headlong rush,* WW426⁷.
scytere m. *shooter,* KC.
scytheald=scyteheald
scytta m. *shooter, archer,* Æ,AO.
scyttan (usu. for-sc.) *to bolt,* ' *shut* ' *to,* Æ : *discharge, pay off.*
scyttel, scyttels (e, i) m. *bolt, bar,* Æ,Bl,W, ZDA. [' *shuttle* '; scēotan]
Scyttisc I. *Scotch, Irish.* **II.** *Irish or Scotch language.* [Scottas]
scyððan=sceððan
sē m., sēo f., ðæt n. pers. (dem.) pron. *he, she, it, that, this* : rel. pron. *who, which* : def. art. ' THE*.' **II.**=sǣ. **III.**=swā
sēa (*OET*)=sēaw; **sēad** (NG)=sēod
sēada=sēaða; **seaflan** (NG)=seofian
seah pret. 3 sg. of sēon.
seaht=seht I.; **seal**=sealh
sealde pret. 3 sg. of sellan.
±sealdnes (a) f. *act of giving,* WW389³⁵ : *grant, gift,* KC2·5³².
sēales gs. of sealh.
sealf (a) f. ' *salve,*' *ointment, unguent, medicament,* Lcd,Mk; CP.
sealfbox (e) m. *salve-box,* G,BK.
sealfcynn n. *an unguent,* WW351³⁰.
sealfe=sealf; **sealfer-**=seolfor-
±sealfian *to* ' *salve,*' *anoint,* Erf,WW.
sealfie=salfie

sealf-læcnung, -læcung *(WW* 114¹⁶) f. *curing by unguents, pharmacy.* [v. *'leeching'*]

sealh (a) m., gs. sēales *willow, Gl,Lcd,Ps;* Mdf. [*'sallow'*]

sealhangra m. *willow-hanger,* KC6·234¹⁷.

sealhrind f. *willow-bark,* LCD.

sealhyrst m. *willow-copse,* KC5·256'.

seallan=sellan

sealm (a, eo) m. *'psalm*,'* song, RB,Ps;* Æ, CP.

sealma (e) m. *bed, couch,* B,GL.

sealmcwide m. *psalm,* LPs97⁵.

sealmfæt n. only in phr. 'on sealmfatum,' *'in vasis psalmorum'!* PPs,70²⁰.

sealmgetæl n. *number of psalms,* RB.

sealm-glīg, -glīw n. *psaltery, psalmody,* LRPs.

sealmian *to play an accompaniment on the harp, Ps* 107¹. [*'psalm'*]

sealmlēoð n. *psalm,* BLPs56⁹.

sealmlof n. *psalm,* LPs.

sealmloflan *to sing psalms,* LPs 104².

sealmsang m. *psalm : composition or singing of psalms, Æ : psaltery,* CPs32² : *one of the canonical hours,* GD.

sealmsangere m. *psalmist,* CHRD112¹².

sealmsangmǣrsung f. *psalm-singing in the canonical hours,* ÆL23b³⁶.

sealmscop (eo²) m. *psalmist,* Æ,CP.

sealmtraht m. *exposition of psalms,* Æ (3²⁹⁷).

sealmwyrhta m. *psalmist, Æ.* [*'psalm-wright'*]

sealobrūn=salubrūn

sealt I. n. *'salt,' Lcd,MtL;* CP. II. adj. *salt, briny, Cr;* AO,CP. [v. Mdf]

sealtan⁷ (a) *to 'salt,' Æ,G,IM,Lcd.*

sealtbrōc (a) m. *brook running from salt-works?* KC3·206³⁰.

sealtere I. m. *'salter,' salt-worker, WW;* Æ. II. (CM362,679)=saltere

sealtern n. *salt-works,* BC. [*'saltern'*]

sealtfæt n. *salt-cellar,* LL,WW. [*'saltfat'*]

sealthālgung (a) f. *consecration of salt,* OET 587.

sealtherpað (a) m. *road to salt-works,* KC 3·206'.

sealthūs n. *'salt-house,' WW.*

sealtian (a) *to dance,* Lk7³². [*L.* saltare]

sealticge f. *dancer,* MH156¹⁴.

sealting f. *dancing,* CHRD79¹.

sealtlēaf n. *'mozicia,'* WW (?-lēap, NP 7·215).

sealtmere m. *brackish pond,* EC449'.

sealtnes (a) f. *'saltness,' VPs.*

sealtrod *track with willows,* KC3·236'.

sealtsǣleða (y¹) m. *saltness,* LPs106³⁴; RPs.

sealtsēað m. *saline spring,* BH26²².

sealtstān m. *rock-salt,* Lcd1·374¹⁴ : *pillar of salt, Gen;* Æ. [*'saltstone'*]

sealtstrǣt f. *road to salt-works,* KC.

sealtwīc n. *a place where salt is sold,* KC.

sealtwylle (a) f. *salt spring, KC,LG.* [*'saltwell'*]

sealtȳð† f. *salt wave, sea-wave.*

sēam I. (ēo) m. *burden, load, Æ,LkL,LkR :* *bag : harness of a beast of burden,* Æ : *duty of furnishing beasts of burden.* [*'seam'*] II. m. *'seam,' suture, junction,* Æ,WW.

sēamere I. m. *beast of burden, mule,* WW. [*L.* sagmarius] II. m. *tailor,* Æ. [sēam II.]

sēamestre f. *sempstress, (also of males) sewer, tailor, Æ,KC,WW.* [*'seamster'*]

sēamhors n. *pack-horse,* WW119⁴².

sēampending m. *toll of a penny a load,* KC.

sēamsadol m. *pack-saddle,* WW119⁴¹.

sēamsticca m. *an appliance used in weaving.* LL455,15¹.

sēap pret. 3 sg. of sūpan.

sēar *dry, 'sere,' barren, GPH*402⁶⁹.

seara-, seare-=searo-; **sēargian**=sārgian

sēarian *to become sere, wither, Shr.* [*'sear'*]

searo (searu) n. *art, skill, cleverness, cunning : device, trick, snare, ambuscade, plot, treachery,* Æ,AO,CP : *work of art, cunning device, engine (of war) : armour, war-gear, trappings.*

searobend m. *artistic clasp,* B2086.

searobunden *cunningly fastened,* RD56⁴.

searocǣg f. *insidious key,* Gu1118.

searocēap n. *artistic object,* RD33⁷.

searocēne *very bold,* PPs100¹⁰.

searocræft m. *artifice, treachery, wile,* Æ : *artistic skill, art : engine, instrument (of torture),* Æ.

searocræftig† *skilful, cunning.*

searo *fears secret path?* RIM65 (ES65·189).

searofāh *variegated, cunningly inlaid,* B 1444.

searogemme=searogimm

searogimm m. *curious gem,* B,Ps.

searogrim *fierce, formidable,* B594.

searohæbbend† m. *warrior.*

searohwīt n. *brilliant whiteness,* RIM67.

searolic *artistic, ingenious.* adv. -līce.

searomete m. *dainty, delicacy,* NC321.

searonet n. *armour-net, corslet,* B406 : *ensnaring net,* AN64; 945.

searoniō† m. *treachery, strife, battle,* B.

searopīl m. *artistic javelin,* RD87².

searorūn f. *mystery,* CREAT15.

searosǣled *cleverly bound,* RD24¹⁶.

searoðanc m. *sagacity, ingenuity, skill,* CP : *cunning, artifice.*

searoðancol† *shrewd, wise,* JUD.

searowrenc (y¹, a²) m. *artifice, trick,* AO.

searowundor n. *strange object,* B920.

searu=searo; **searw-** v. searo.

searwian (a, æ) *to be deceitful, dissimulate, cheat.*

searwum (dp. of searo) *skilfully.*

searwung=sierwung

seatul, seatl (NG)=setl

sēað I. (ǣ) m. *hole, pit, MkL*; CP; Mdf : *well, cistern, spring, fountain, lake,* Mdf. ['*seath*'; sēoðan] **II.** pret. 3 sg. of sēoðan.

sēaða m. *heartburn?* LCD 21a.

sēaw m. *sap, juice, moisture, Gl,Lcd.* ['*sew*']

+**sēaw** *succulent,* LCD 95b : *soaked,* LCD 86²⁰.

seax (æ, e) n. *knife, hip-knife, short sword, dirk, dagger, Æ,B,Cp*; CP. ['*sax*']

seaxbenn (siex-) f. *dagger-wound,* B 2904.

Seaxe, Seaxan mpl.(gp. Seaxna) *Saxons,* AO.

Seaxland (e) n. *England,* SHR 16⁴.

±**sēcan I.** *to search for,* '*SEEK*' ('*i-seche*'), *inquire, ask for, look for,* Æ : *try, strive after, long for, wish, desire,* CP. s. on, tō *look to for, expect from,* CP : *visit, go to,* AO; Æ : *approach, attain to* : *get* : *attack, pursue, follow,* Chr; AO : *go, move, proceed,* Æ. **II.** (KGL)=sȳcan

secce (B 600)=sæcce, gs. of sacu.

secful (KGL)=sacful

secg I. m. (n) '*sedge*,' *reed, rush, flag, Gl, Lcd,WW*; Mdf. **II.**† f. *sword.* **III.**† m. *man, warrior, hero,* B. ['*segge*'] **IV.** m. *ocean,* OET.

secga m. *sayer, informant,* LL 396,4.

±**secgan** (æ) *to* '*SAY*' ('*i-seggen*'), *speak, inform, utter, declare, tell, recite,* Æ; AO, CP : *signify, mean,* Æ : *explain, discuss* : *attribute to* : (+) *avoid?* LkL p 3⁸. s. on *accuse of, charge with,* Æ.

secge f. *speech,* CR 190.

secgend m. *speaker, narrator,* CP,BH.

secggan=secgan

secggescēre? f. *grasshopper,* Cp 464.

secgihtig *sedgy,* WW 200²⁷.

secglēac n. *sedge-leek, rush-garlic,* LCD.

secgplega m. *sword-play, battle,* AN 1355.

secgrōf *brave?* (GK), *troop?* (FTP 347), RUIN 27.

secgscāra? m. *landrail, corncrake,* WW 287¹¹ and N.

sēcnes f. *visiting,* LkR 19⁴⁴ (oe).

sēd (VPs)=sǣd

+**sēdan** *to satisfy,* PPs 106⁸. [sæd]

sēde=sægde pret. 3 sg. of secgan.

sedinglīne=stedinglīne

±**sedl** (NG)=setl

sefa (eo) m. *mind, spirit, understanding, heart,* †CP 9¹⁰.

sēfer-=sȳfer-; **sēflan**=seofian

sēfre=sȳfre

sēft comp. adv. *more softly.*

±**sēfte** *soft, pleasant, comfortable, easy* : *gentle, mild* : *effeminate, luxurious.*

sēftēadig *prosperous,* SEAF 56.

sēftllc *luxurious,* AS 39⁴.

sēftnes f. *rest, quietness, peace,* Æ,AO.

segc-=secg-; **segel**=segl

segen I. (æ) (±) f. *conversation, speech, statement,* Æ,AO : *premonition, prophecy,* AO : *report, story, legend.* sēo hālga +s. *Holy Writ.* **II.**=segn

+**segenlic**=+sewenlic; **segg**=secg

segl I. mn. '*sail,*' *AO,Bo,MH*; Æ : *veil, curtain,* CR 1139 : *pillar of cloud,* Ex. **II.**=sigel

±**seg-lan,** -lian *to* '*sail*' : (+) *equip with a sail.*

seglbōsm m. *bellying sail,* GL.

seglgerǣde n. *sail-tackle,* TC 549¹⁷.

seglgyrd (e²) mf. *sail-yard, yard, cross-pole,* Cp,WW.

seglian=seglan

seglrād f. (*sail-road*), *sea,* B 1429.

seglrōd f. *sail-rod, sail-yard.* [v. '*rood*']

seglung f. '*sailing,*' BH.

segn mn. *sign, mark, token,* Gen : *ensign, banner, B,BH.* ['*senye*'; *L.* signum]

segnberend m. *warrior,* RD 41²⁰.

segnbora m. *standard-bearer,* BL,WW.

segncyning m. *king before whom a banner is borne* (BT), Ex 172.

segne f. '*seine,' drag-net, Ex,JnL.*

+**segnes** f. *expression,* ÆL 23b⁷⁸.

±**segnian** (ǣn) *to make the sign of the cross, cross oneself, consecrate, bless,* Æ,BH. ['*sain*']

segnung f. *blessing, consecration,* BH,GD.

sēgon=sāwon pret. pl. of sēon.

seh (VPs)=seoh imperat. of sēon.

seht I. (ea) mf. *settlement, arrangement, agreement,* KC : *friendship, peace, BH.* **II.** adj. *reconciled, agreed, at peace, BC.* ['*saught*']

±**sehtian** *to conciliate, settle,* LL. ['*saught*']

±**sehtlian** (a, æ) *to reconcile, to come to an agreement,* CHR.

±**sehtnes** f. *agreement, reconciliation, peace,* Æ,Chr. ['*saughtness*']

sēhð=sēcð pres. 3 sg. of sēcan.

±**sehðe** [=seh ðu] interj. *behold!*

seigl, seign=segl, segn

seim *fat,* EPs 62⁶. ['*seam*'; *Late L.* sagimen]

seista=siexta; **sel** sn.=sǣl

sēl I. adj. comp. sēlra (*Mt*), sēlla (*B*), sȳlla (*B*), superl. sēlest (*Lk*), sēlost *good, great, excellent, clever, skilful,* AO : *noble, honourable* : *fitting, fit, advisable* : *sound, healthy, happy, prosperous.* [v. '*sele*'] **II.** (ǣ) comp. adv. (also sēlor) superl. sēlost *better, more effectually, rather, sooner, in preference,* Æ,CP. [sæl]

sēlan (OET,Ct)=sǣlan I. **selcūð**=seldcūð

seld† (æ) I. n. *hall, palace, residence.* II. n. *seat, throne, daïs, VPs.* ['*seld*']
+selda† *comrade, retainer.*
seldan adv., comp. seld(n)or, superl. seldost '*seldom*,' *rarely, CP;* Æ.
şeldcüð *unusual, rare, strange, novel, Bo;* Æ : *various, WW.* ['*selcouth*']
seldcyme m. *infrequent coming,* RD 1¹⁴.
selde f. *vestibule,* WW 183⁹⁹.
selden *few, rare,* Sc 197¹⁸.
seldguma m. *retainer?* B 249.
seld-hwanne (CP), -hwænne (Æ) adv. *seldom, rarely.*
seldlic *rare, strange, wondrous, B* (syll-), *Met* (sell-) : *select, choice, excellent.* adv. -līce, *Sol;* Æ. ['*selly*']
seldnor, seldor, seldost v. seldan.
seldon=seldan
seldsīene *rare, extraordinary, unfamiliar, AO,KC?* (-sȳnde). ['*seldseen*']
seldun (*CP*), seldum (*Sol*)=seldan
sele† m. *hall, house, dwelling, prison,* KC. [*Ger.* saal]
+sele m. *tabernacle,* EPs 14¹.
seledrēam† m. *hall-joy, festivity.*
seleful n. *hall-goblet,* B 619.
selegesceot n. '*tabernaculum*,' *tent, lodging-place, nest,* M. [*Ger.* geschoss]
selegyst m. *hall-guest,* B 1545.
selen (y) f. *grant, gift* : *tribute,* MkL p 5¹ : *munificence,* OEG. [sellan]
±selenes f. *tradition* : (+) *giving,* DR.
selerædend† m. *hall ruler or possessor.*
selerest f. *bed in hall,* B 690.
selescot=selegesceot
selesecg m. *retainer,* WA 34.
selest pres. 2 sg., seleð pres. 3 sg. of sellan.
sēlest v. sēl.
seleðegn m. *retainer, attendant,* B 1794.
seleweard m. *hall-warden,* B 667.
self I. (eo, i, y) pron. (str. and wk.) 'SELF,' *AO,CP* : *own.* mid him selfum *by himself.* adj. *same, CP.* II.=sealf
selfæta (y) m. *cannibal,* AN 175.
selfæte f. *a plant, wild oat?* LCD.
selfbana (o²) m. *a suicide,* GL.
selfcwala (y) *a suicide,* MFH 172.
selfcwalu (y) f. *suicide,* WY 56.
selfdēma, self-dēmere (RB), -dēmende (OEG 58¹⁹) (y) m. '*sarabaita*,' *monk living subject only to his own rules.*
selfdōm m. *independence* (Swt).
selfe v. swā.
selflic (y) *spontaneous, voluntary,* OEG.
selflīce I. n. *self-love,* '*amour propre*,' *pride, vanity, CP* : *egotism,* CP 25⁷. II. adj. *egotistic, puffed up, vain, CP.*
selfmyrðra (y) m. *one who takes his own life,* WW 424²⁵.

selfmyrðrung (y) f. *suicide* (*action*).
selfren=seolfren
selfsceafte *not begotten,* GEN 523.
selfswēgend (y) m. *vowel.*
selfwealdlīce (eo¹, e²) *arbitrarily,* GD 289⁵, v.l.
selfwendlīce=selfwillendlīce
selfwill n. *own will, free-will,* Bo,Met. ['*selfwill*']
selfwille (y) *spontaneous, voluntary.* adv. -willes, Æ,RB. ['*selfwill*']
selfwillende *voluntary,* LPs 67¹⁰.
selfwillendlīce (eo¹) *following one's own will, arbitrarily,* GD 289⁵.
selian=sylian; **sēlig**=sælig
sēlla=sēlra, v. sēl.
±sellan (ea, i, ie, y) (w. d. pers. and a. thing) *to give, furnish, supply, lend,* Æ,B, Mt; AO,CP : *surrender, give up, betray,* Æ, JnL : *entrust, deliver to, appoint, allot* : *lay by, hide,* WW 212⁴¹ : '*sell**,' Æ,Jn : *promise.* āð s. *make oath, swear,* LL.
sellen=selen
sellend (y) m. *giver,* Æ : *betrayer,* MkLR 14⁴⁴.
sellendlic adj. *to be given,* CHRD 102.
sellic=seldlic; **selma** (GL)=sealma
selmerige=sælmerige; **selnes**=selenes
sēlor, sēlost, sēlra v. sēl; **selt-**=sylt-
sēlð pres. 3 sg. of sellan; **sēlð**=sǣlð
+sēm n. *reconciliation,* LL 10,10.
sēma (ī, ȳ) m. *arbitrator, judge,* ÆGR, GD.
±sēman I. *to smooth over, put right, settle, reconcile, pacify,* AO,Chr,LL. ['*seem*,' '*i-seme*'] II.=sīeman
sēmann (RUN 45)=sǣmann
sēmend (ǣ) m. *conciliator, arbitrator,* LL.
sēmestre=sēamestre
semian=seomian; **semle**=simble
semnendlic *sudden,* GD 235⁴. adv. -līce *by chance.*
semninga (M)=samnunga
semtinges=samtinges; **senap**=senep
±sencan, tr. *to sink, plunge* (*in water*), *submerge, drown.* [sincan]
send f. *gift,* RB 87¹¹.
sendan I. (±) *to '*send*'* ('*i-send*'), *send forth, despatch, B,BH,Bl,CP,MtL;* Æ,AO : *impel, drive,* MkL : *throw, hurl, cast, VPs* : *put, place, lay* : *utter.* II. *to feast,* B 600? [sand]
senderlīce (KGL 74²⁷)=synderlīce
senderlīpe (HGL)=synderlīpe
sendlic adj. *about to be sent* (*on a journey*), RBL 113⁴.
sendnes f. *sending,* WW.
+sēne=+sīene
senep m. *mustard,* Gl,LCD. [*L.* sinapi]

senepsǣd n. *mustard-seed*, LCD 3·88¹⁵.
sengan (æ) *to 'singe,' burn slightly*, LL
449,6² : *afflict*, RPs30¹⁰.
sēnian=segnian; **senn** (HGL519)=synn
senop=senep; **senoð** (CHR)=sinoð
senscipe=sinscipe
senst, **sent**=sendest, sendeð pres. 2 and
3 sg. of sendan.
senu=seonu
sēo I. f. gas. sēo(n) *pupil (of eye)*, Æ.
II. pron. v. sē. [v. *'she'*] III. gs. of sǣ.
IV. pres. 1 sg. of sēon. V. pres. 2 sg.
subj. of bēon (wesan).
sēoc *'sick,' ill, diseased, feeble, weak*, Bl,Bo,
Chr; Æ,CP : (†) *wounded : morally sick,
corrupt*, Jul,RB : *sad, troubled*, FAp,Gu.
sēocan I. *to be ill, fall ill*, ANS117·25;
GD. [*'sick'*] II.=sēcan
sēoclian=sīclian
sēocmōd *infirm of mind*, CHRD23⁹.
sēocnes f. *'sickness,' disease*, LL,W : *a
disease*, Lcd3·126'.
sēod (ēa) m. *scrip, purse, bag*, Æ,GL.
seodo, seodu=sidu; **seofa**=sefa
seofafald (DR)=seofonfeald
seofan, seofen=seofon; **seofeð-**=seofoð-
seofian (e, ea, i, y) *to sigh, lament*, CP.
seofon *'SEVEN,'* Æ,AO.
seofonfeald *'seven-fold,'* Æ,Bf,RB.
seofonfealdlīce adv. *seven times*, VPs.
seofongetel (e²) *the number seven*, OEG1533.
seofonlēafe f. *tormentilla, setfoil (plant)*,
LCD 1·232¹.
seofonnihte adj. *seven days old*, LCD :
lasting seven days, Æ.
seofon-tēoða (AO), -te(o)g(e)ða *'seven-
teenth,'* BH.
seofontiene (y³) *'seventeen,'* BH ; AO.
seofontienenihte *seventeen days old*, LCD
3·180.
seofontienewintre *seventeen years old*, AO
190³⁰.
seofontīne=seofontiene
seofonwintre (y) *seven years old*, Æ,B,BH.
seofoða I. *'seventh,'* Bl,Mt ; Æ,AO,CP.
II.=sifeða
seofoðe *seventhly*, LL158,18.
seofung f. *lamentation*, Bo,MET. [seofian]
seoh imperat. of sēon.
seohhe f. *sieve*, LL,WW. [sēon II.]
seohhian *to drain, filter*, ÆP172²¹, (+) ES
49·353.
seohter m., seohtre (i) f. *drain, ditch*, Ct
(Mdf).
seolc, seol-oc, -uc (io) m. *'silk,' silken cloth*,
Bo,Lcd.
-seolcan v. ā-s.
seolcen (i) *'silken,' made of silk*, Bo,WW ;
Æ.

seolcwyrm m. *'silkworm,'* WW.
sēoles v. seolh; **seolf** (VPs)=self
seolfer=seolfor; **seolfern**=seolfren
seolfor (i, io, u, y) n., gs. seolfres *'SILVER,'*
CP ; Æ.
seolforfæt n. *silver vessel*, BH252¹⁶.
seolforgewiht (y) m. *silver-weight*, LCD
3·92¹⁴.
seolforhammen *plated with silver*, EC225'.
seolfor-hilt, -hilted (TC) *'silver-hilted.'*
seolforsmið m. *'silversmith,'* WW.
seolforstycce m. *piece of silver*, A11·8³.
seolfren (e, i, y) *made of silver, 'silvern,'*
Bo,Chr,Met.
seolfring (y) m. *silver coin*, Æ.
seolh m., gs. sēoles *'seal,'* AO,Lcd,WW.
seolhbæð n. *seal's bath, sea*, RD11¹¹.
seolhpæð? n? *seal's path, sea, ocean*, AN1710.
seolm (WW101¹⁶)=sealm
seoloc, seoluc=seolc; **seolofr-**=seolfr-
seoloð (io¹, e²) m. *sea*, B2367?
seolufr-=seolfor-, seolfr-; **sēom**=sēam I.
seomian† (e) *to be tired, lie at rest, tarry,
continue, stand : hang, swing, sway : lower
(as a cloud) : lay wait for*, B161.
sēomint (WW136³¹?)=sǣminte
sēon I. (±) sv⁵ *to 'see*'* (*'i-see'*), *look, behold*,
B,G,Ps,Rd : *observe, perceive, understand,
know*, Cr,Ps : *inspect, visit : experience,
suffer*, B,Cr : *appear*, BF86⁸ : (pass)
seem : (+) *provide*, OET175¹³. sih ðe lo!
behold! II. sv¹ (tr.) *to strain, filter*, Æ,AO :
(intr.) *run, ooze, trickle, drop, drip*, Æ,AO,
Lcd. [*'sye,' 'sying'*] III.v. sēo. IV.=sīen
seon-=sin-
seondon=sind pres. pl. ind. of wesan.
sēonian *to languish*, GD284² . [OHG.
siunōn]
seono (e¹, i¹; io¹, u²) f. *'sinew,'* B,Lcd ; AN.
seonobend f. *sinew-band?* DEOR6.
seonobenn f. *injury to a sinew*, WY19.
seonod=sinoð
seonodolg n. *injury to a sinew*, AN1408.
seonoð=sinoð
seonu=seono; **seonwe** gs. of seono.
seorðan² *to lie with*, MtL5²⁷. [ON?]
seorwum (Cp)=searwum, dp. of searo.
sēoslig *afflicted*, GU899. [sūsl]
sēota=sǣta; **seotl**=setl
seotol=(1) setl; (2) sweotol
seotu nap. of set.
±sēoðan² (ȳ) *'seethe,' boil*, Lcd : *be troubled
in mind, brood*, B : *afflict, disturb*.
seoððan=siððan
-sēoung (ēu) v. eag-s.
sēow pret. 3 sg. of sāwan.
sēowan, sēowian (ī, īo, ȳ) *to 'sew,' knit
together, link, unite*, Æ,Cp,Mk.
seox=siex; **seoxter**=sester

sep (*GPH* 391)=sæp
sēpan† *to instruct.*
serc m., **serce** f. (y) '*sark,*' *shirt*, B,WW : *corslet, coat of mail.*
serede=sierwde pret. 3 sg. of sierwan.
Sēremōnað *June*, MEN. [v. '*siere*']
serew-, serw-=searw-, sierw-
serð=seorð, imperat. of seorðan.
sescle f. *sixth part*, BF 192².⁴. [*L.* sextula]
sess m. *place for sitting, seat, bench*, B,Cp.
sessian *to grow calm*, AN 453.
sesta=siexta
sester (eo, y) m. *a certain measure of bulk*, Æ : *vessel, pitcher*, Æ. [*L.* sextarius]
-sestre v. twī-s.
±set n. *seat, habitation : entrenchment, camp, stall, fold : setting (of the sun).* [sittan]
sēt-=sǣt-
sete imperat. of settan.
+setednes=+setnes; **setel** (CP)=setl
seten I. f. *set, shoot, slip*, VPs : *plantation : occupied (tilled?) land*, LL 118,68. **II.** pp. of sittan.
+setenes=+setnes
+setennes f. *sitting*, VPs 138².
sētere=sǣtere; **Seterndæg**=Sæterndæg
setgong=setlgang
sethrægl n. *covering for a seat*, Ct,WW.
sētlan=sǣtian; **setln** (GL)=seten
setl (æ, ea, eo, i, o) n. *seat, stall, sitting, place, residence*, Æ,B,BH,CP : *throne*, see : *siege*, AO. tō setle gān *to set (of the sun)*, Æ. ['*settle*']
+setl n. *assembly*, OEG 1753.
+setla (æ) m. *one sitting beside*, ÆL 2²³⁷ : *assessor, fellow-judge*, OEG 56²⁰.
setlan *to '* *settle' (cause to sit), place, put, Whale.*
setlgang m. *setting, sinking*, Æ.
setlgangende ptc. *setting*, BH 476¹³.
setlhrægel n. *seat-cover*, Ct.
setlrād f. *setting, sinking*, Ex 109.
setlung f. *sitting, setting*, Æ,Ps.
sētn-=sǣt(n)-
±setnes (+ exc. in N) f. *foundation, creation, construction*, MtL : *position, size, extent : institution, law, ordinance, decree, will*, Æ, BH,Mk : *instruction : record, narrative : sentence, paragraph, figure of speech, composition.* ['*i-setness*']
setol=setl
sēton=sǣton pret. pl. of sittan.
setrægel (IM)=sethrægl
settan (±) *to make to sit*, '*SET,*' *lay, put, deposit, place, fix*, Æ; CP : *occupy, set or put down*, Æ : (±) *appoint, assign, institute, prepare, ordain, create, form, make, found, build*, Æ,AO : *sow, plant*, Cp,Cr,Gen,

MtL : *settle* (tr. and intr.), *abate, subside, sink* : *compose, compile, write*, Æ : *add* : *translate* : (+) *people, garrison* : *be situated* : *set off* : *lay in wait*, LPs 9³⁰. s. ūt *issue, send forth, dismiss.* s. of *displace, depose.* sīð s. *travel, journey.* ±s. wið, ongean *compare.* s. tō gafole *let land.* [sittan]
+settednes (CHRD)=+setnes
settend m. *creator, ordainer*, DA 333.
+settendlic *appointed, canonical*, CM 362.
sēttere=sǣtere
setðorn m. *a kind of tree*, EC 291'.
+setu† np. v. +set.
±sēðan *to affirm, testify*, Æ : *prove.* [sōð]
seðel (NG)=setl
±sēðend m. *asserter, affirmer*, WW.
+sēðnes (ǣ) f. *affirmation*, ByH 8'.
seððe=sehðe
±sēðung f. *affirmation, proof*, Æ.
sēw=sēow pret. 3 sg. of sāwan.
sēw-=sǣw-
sewen=sawen pp. of sēon.
+sewenlic *visible*, Æ,Bo. adv. -līce *evidently.*
sex (NG)=(1) siex; (2) seax
Sexland=Seaxland; **sexta**=siexta
sī 3 p. sg. pres. subj. of wesan.
sibæðeling m. *related noble*, B 2708.
sibb (y) (v. LL 2·651) f. *relationship*, AO,B, Chr; Æ : *love, friendship : peace, happiness*, BH,Chr,VPs; AO,CP. ['*sib*']
±sibb *related, akin*, B,LkL,W. as sb. *kinsman, kinswoman*, W,Soul. ['*sib,' 'i-sib*']
sibb-=sib-
sibbecoss m. *kiss of peace*, ES 33·176.
sibbegedriht=sibgedryht
±sibbian (y) *to bring together, conciliate, reconcile*, Æ,CP.
sibbs-=sibs-
sibcwide (y) m. *pacific speech*, LEAS 29.
sibfæc n. *degree of affinity*, LL.
sibgebyrd f. *blood-relationship*, GEN 1901.
sibgedryht† f. *related band : peaceful host.*
sibgemāgas mpl. *blood-relations*, Ex 386.
sibgeornes f. *pacific disposition, friendship, love*, W.
sibge-sihð, -syhð f. *vision of peace* (lit. trans. of '*Hierosolyma*'), Ps.
sibi (GL) sibian=sife, seofian
sibleger n. *incest*, LL,W.
siblic *of peace, peaceable*, Æ : *related.* adv. -līce.
±sibling m. *relative, kinsman*, Æ. ['*sibling*']
siblufu† f. *friendship, love.*
+sibnes f. *affinity, relationship*, WW 345¹⁶.
sibrēden f. *affinity, relationship*, Chr 1127. ['*sibred*']
±sibsum *peace-loving, peaceable, friendly*, CP. adv. -līce. [v. '*i-sibb*']

+**sibsumian** *to reconcile, be reconciled*, Æ.
sibsumnes f. *peace, concord, Chr*; CP : *brotherly love*. ['*sibsomeness*']
+**sibsumung** f. *peace-making*, WW 172⁴¹.
sibun (Cp)=seofon
sīc n. *small stream, BC*; Mdf. ['*sitch*']
sīcan I. (sv¹) *tō sigh, yearn for, AO,PPs*. ['*siche*'] II.=sȳcan
siccet-, siccett-, siccit-=sicett-
siccclian=sīclian
sīce m. *sigh, Lcd* 1·388¹¹. ['*siche*']
sicel=sicol; **sīcelian**=sīclian
sicer-=sicor-
sicerian *to trickle, penetrate, ooze, CP* 437¹⁴. ['*sicker*']
sicettan *to sigh, groan, mourn*, CP.
sicettung f. *sighing, sigh, sob, lamentation*, Æ.
sīcle *sick, ill*, ANS 129·21.
±**sīclian** (æ, ē, ēo, ȳ) *to sicken, become ill or weak, Lcd*; ÆL. ['*sickle*'; sēoc]
sicol (u²) m. '*sickle,*' Bf,Mk,WW.
sicor *sure, certain, trustworthy, A* : *secure, CP*. ['*sicker*']
sicorlīce (e²) *with full certainty, NC* 321 (=RWH 145¹²); FM 99. ['*sickerly*']
sicornes f. *certainty, NC* 321. ['*sickerness*']
sīd *ample, wide, broad, large, vast, An,B, Gen,LL*. ['*side*']
sīdādl f. *pain in the side, pleurisy*, WW 112³².
sīdan adv. wīdan and s. *far and wide*, BC. [v. '*side*']
sīde I. adv. *amply, widely, extensively*, OEG. s. and wīde *far and wide*, El. ['*side*'] II. (±) f. '*SIDE,*' Æ,CP. III. f. *silk*. [L. seta]
sīdece m. *pain in the side*, LCD 172a.
sideful (y) *decorous, modest, pure, virtuous, honest*, Æ. ['*sedeful*'] adv. -līce.
sidefulnes f. *virtue, modesty*, ÆL.
sidelic *sober, discreet*, GPH 389.
sidelīce adv. *fitly, suitable*, CP 153.
siden v. ælf-s.
sīden *made of silk*, OEG 3161,2.
sīdewāre f. *zedoary*, LCD 137b. [*Late L.*]
sīdfæðme, sīdfæðmed† *wide-bosomed, capacious (of a ship)*, B. [v. '*side*']
sīdfeaxe, sīdfeaxode *long-haired*, Æ. [v. '*side*']
sīdfolc† n. *great people or number of people*.
sīdhealf f. *a large place*, APs 17²⁰.
sīdian intr. *to extend?* RIM 65. [sīd]
+**sīdian** (y) *to arrange, set right, order*. [sidu]
sīdland† n. *extensive land*, GEN.
sīdlingweg m. *sidelong way, road that runs obliquely?* (BT), KC 3·446′.
sido=sidu
sīdrand m. *broad shield*, B 1289.

sidu (eo) m., gds. sida *custom, practice, manner, habit, rite, CP* : *manners, morality, good conduct, purity*, CP. [*Ger*. sitte]
sidung (y) f. *rule, regulation*, GPH 398.
sīdung (ȳ) f. *augmentation, growth*, BF 64²⁹.
sīdwǣrc m. *pain in the side*, GD,LCD.
sīdweg† m. *long road* : (in pl.) *distance*.
sīdwyrm (ȳ) m. *silk-worm*, WW.
sīe pres. 1 sg. subj. of wesan (bēon).
siehst pres. 2 sg., siehð pres. 3 sg. of sēon.
+**siehð**=+siht; **sielf**=self; **siellan**=sellan
siellic=seldlic
±**sīeman** (ǣ, ē, ȳ) *to load, burden*, Æ,LkL. ['*seam*']
siemble=simble
sīen I. (ēo, ī, ȳ) f. *power of sight, sight, vision, Jul,Lcd* : *pupil, eye*. ['*sene*'] II. (=sīn) pl. pres. subj. of wesan.
siendon, sient (=sindon, sind) pl. pres. of wesan.
+**sīene** (ē, ī, ȳ) *seen, visible, evident, plain, B*. ['*sene*'] adv. *plainly*.
+**sīenelic** (ē, ȳ) *visible*, BH 216¹⁴,VH. adv. -līce.
sierce=serce
siere '*sere,*' *dry, withered*, BC 1·515²². [sēarian]
sierian=sierwan
±**sierwan** (i, y) *to plan, devise, contrive* : *plot, lay snares for, entrap*, CP : *put on armour* : (+) *fit out, arm, equip*, MA 159. [searu]
sierwung (ea, y) f. *plotting, artifice, trap, snare, treachery*, Æ.
sieððan=siððan
siex (e, eo, i, y) 'six,' AO. For comps. v. also six-.
siexbenn=seaxbenn
siexfeald '*six-fold,*' WW.
siexhund *six hundred*, AO; WID. [v. '*six*']
siexta (e, i, y) '*sixth,*' AO,Chr,LG,MH.
siexte (y) *sixthly*, LL 158,17.
siextig (e, i, y) '*sixty,*' AO,Bl,LG.
sife (y) n. '*sieve,*' Cp,Lcd,WW.
sifeða (eo, y) m. and fpl. *siftings, chaff, bran* : *tares, rubbish*.
sifian=seofian; **sifiða**=sifeða; **sīfre**=sȳfre
siftan (e, y) *to* '*sift,*' Æ,Bo,Cp.
sifun=seofon
sig=sī 3 p. sing. pres. subj. of wesan (bēon).
+**sig** n. *victory*, DR 28².
sīgan¹ I. (±) *to sink, set (of the sun), B,Bo, Chr* : *decline, CP* : *descend, fall, fall down*, Æ : *move, advance, go, go to, approach, B, Chr*. sāh ūt *came out*, Æ. II.=sēon II.
sigbēh (NG)=sigebēah; **sigdi** (*Ep*)=sīðe
sige I. (y) m. *victory, success, triumph*, Æ, AO,CHR. II. m. *sinking, setting (of the sun)*, MET 13⁵⁶. [sīgan]

sige-bēacn, -bēacen n. *banner, Æ : emblem of victory, trophy, cross (of Christ),* EL.
sigebēah m. *victor's circlet, crown,* BH.
sigebēam† m. *tree of victory, cross.*
sigebearn† n. *victor-child (Christ),* EL.
sigebeorht *victorious,* BL203'.
sigebeorn m. *victorious hero,* FIN 38.
sigebrōðor m. *victorious brother,* AN 183.
sigebȳme f. *trump of victory,* Ex 565.
sigecempa m. *victorious champion,* PPs 50¹⁰.
sigecwēn† f. *victorious queen,* EL.
sigedēma† m. *victorious judge.*
sigedryhten† m. *lord of victory, God.*
sigeēadig *victorious,* B 1557.
sigefæst *victorious, triumphant, Æ.*
±**sigefæstan** (e³) *to triumph : crown as victor.*
sīgefæstnes f. *triumph, victory,* Ps.
sigefest=sigefæst
sigefolc† n. *victorious people.*
sigegealdor (y¹) n. *victory-bringing charm,* Lcd 1·388¹³. ['sigalder']
sigegefeoht n. *victory,* BH 158⁶.
sigegyrd f. *victory-bringing rod,* LCD.
sigehrēmig† (ǣ) *rejoicing in victory.*
sigehrēð f. *fame gained by victory? confidence or joy of victory?* B490 (v. Klb 143).
sigehrēðig† *victorious, triumphant.*
sigehwīl f. *hour of victory,* B 2710.
sigel I.† (æ, e) m? n? *sun : name of the rune for* s. **II.**=sigil. **III.** f.=sigle I.
sigelbeorht† *sun-bright, brilliant,* MEN.
sigele=sigle
sigelēan n. *reward of victory,* EL,HGL.
sigelēas† *not victorious, defeated.*
sigelēoð† n. *song of victory.*
Sigelhearwa m. *Ethiopian,* VPs.
sigel-hweorfa m., -hwe(o)rfe f. *heliotrope.*
sigelic *victorious,* WW.
sigeltorht *radiant,* AN 1248.
Sigel-waras, -ware pl. *Ethiopians,* MH.
sigemēce m. *victorious sword,* CR 1531.
sīgend m. *wave,* WW. [sigan]
sīger m. *glutton,* OET 72⁵⁶⁸.
siger-=sigor-
sigerēaf n. *triumphal robe,* WW 153¹⁵.
sigerian I. *to be gluttonous,* WW 489¹⁴. **II.**=sigorian
sigerīce† *victorious, triumphant,* Ex.
sigerōf† *victorious, triumphant.*
sigesceorp n. *ornament of victory,* GN 136.
sigesīð (i²) m. *successful expedition,* OET.
sigespēd† f. *success,* AN,EL.
sigetācen n. *emblem of victory, sign.*
sigetīber n. *sacrifice for victory,* Ex 402.
sigetorht *brilliant in victory,* SAT 240.
sigetūdor n. *dominating race,* GU 838.
sigeðēod† f. *victorious people,* B.

sigeðrēat m. *victorious troop,* CR 844.
sigeðūf? m. *triumphal banner,* JUD 201.
sigewǣpen n. *victorious weapon,* B 804.
sigewang† m. *field of victory.*
sigewīf n. *victorious woman,* LCD 1·384'.
+**sigfæstnian** *to be crowned as victor,* G.
sigi-=sige-
sigil, sigl n. *fibula, buckle, brooch, gem.* [cp. sigle]
sigirian=sigorian
siglan *to 'sail,'* AO.
sigle I. n. *necklace, collar.* II. f. *rye, black spelt,* LCD 48a. [L. secale]
sigor (y) m. *victory, triumph, Æ.* [sige]
sigorbēacen n. *emblem of victory,* EL 985.
sigorbeorht *triumphant,* CR 10.
sigorcynn n. *victorious race,* EL 755.
sigorēadig† *victorious.*
sigorfæst *victorious,* GD,GU.
sigorfæstnes (siger-) f. *victory,* A 11·173.
sigorlēan† n. *reward of victory.*
sigorlic *triumphal,* GL.
sigorspēd† f. *good fortune in war.*
sigortācen n. *convincing sign,* GU 1089.
sigortīfer n. *offering for victory,* JUL 255.
sigorweorc m. *deed of victory,* Ex 316.
sigorwuldor n. *glory of victory,* GU 93.
sigrian=sigorian
sigrīend m. *victor,* DHy 38³.
sigsonte f. *a plant,* LCD 27b, 39a.
sigðe=sīðe; **sih**=seoh; **sihsta**=siexta
+**siht** (ie, y) f. *faculty or act of sight, Æ,Bo, Mk* : CP : *aspect : what is seen, vision, apparition.* ['i-sight']
-**siht,** -sihte v. blōd-, ūt-s.
sihte *marshy?* KC 3·430'.
+**sīhte**=+sȳhte pret. 3 sg. of +sȳcan.
sihtre=seohtre
sihð I. f. *thing seen, vision,* JnL,MkL. ['sight'] II. pres. 3 sg. of sēon. III. (+)= +siht
sīhð pres. 3 sg. of sīgan.
+**sihðe** (BPs 53⁶)=+sehðe
+**sihðnes** f. *vision,* MtL p7⁷.
silcen=seolcen; **silf**=self, seolf
-**silfran** v. be-s.
Sīlhearwa (Æ)=Sigelhearwa
sillan=sellan; **silofr**=seolfor
sīma I. m. *band, chain,* GEN 765. **II.**=sēma
simbel I. (on) adv. *always, continually,* AO. [cp. simbles] **II.**=simble
simbelfarende *roving, nomadic,* AO 26¹⁶.
simbelgefēra (y¹) m. *constant companion,* MET 11⁵⁰.
simble (e, y) adv. *ever, for ever, always, constantly, continually, continuously.* oftost s. *continually.*
simbles adv. *ever, always,* AN 64.

simblian (y) *to frequent*, DR 15¹⁰.
simb-lunga, -linga (siml-) *continually, constantly*, DR.
simel=(1) simbel adv.; (2) symbel
simeringwyrt=symeringwyrt
siml, siml-=simbel, simbl-
sīn I. (ȳ) refl. possess. pron. *his, her, its, their*. II.=sīen. III. plur. pres. subj. of wesan.
sin- (y) prefix, *perpetual, permanent, lasting, infinite, immense*.
sinað-=seonoð-, sinoð-
sinbyrnende *ever burning*, MET 8⁵².
sinc (y)† n. *treasure, riches, gold, valuables, jewel*.
sincald *perpetually cold*, Ex 472.
sincaldu f. *perpetual cold*, PH 17.
±**sincan³** *to ' sink,' become submerged*, MtR : *subside*, Gen : *digest easily, act as aperient?* Lcd 81b.
sincbrytta m. *distributor of treasure, prince*, A 3·71¹⁷.
sincfæt† n. *precious vessel, precious setting*.
sincfāg† *richly adorned*.
sincgestrēon† n. *treasure, jewel*.
sincgewǣge n. *abundance of treasure*, RIM 17.
sinc-giefa, -gifa† m. *giver of treasure, ruler, chief, lord, king*.
sincgifu f. *gift of treasure*, AN 1511.
sincgim m. *valuable gem, jewel*, EL 264.
sincgyfa=sincgiefa
sinchroden† ptc. *adorned with costly ornaments*.
sincmāððum m. *treasure*, B 2193.
sincstān m. *precious stone*, MET 21²¹.
sincðego† f. *receipt of treasure*. [ðicgan]
sincweorðung† f. *costly gift*.
sind plur. pres. indic. of wesan.
sinder (y) n. *' cinder,' dross, scoria, slag*, Cp,WW ; CP.
sinder-=sundor-; **sinderlīce**=synderlīce
sinderōm m. *rust*, WW 402⁴¹.
sindon plur. pres. indic. of wesan.
sindor=sinder
sindorlīpes (RB)=sundorlīpes
sindrēam† m. *everlasting joy*.
sindrig (Æ)=syndrig; +**sīne**=+sīene
sineht *sinewy*, LCD 91a. [seono]
sine-wealt, -weald (eo¹, y¹, æ²), *round, globular, concave*, Æ : *circular, cylindrical*. [sin-]
sinewealtian *to be unsteady*, WW 515³¹.
sinewealtnes f. *roundness, globularity*, LCD, WW.
sinewind *artery*, WW 352²⁵. [seonu]
sinfrēa m. *overlord, husband*, B 1934.
sinfulle f. *house-leek*, LCD,WW.
singal *perpetual, everlasting*, Æ,CP : *continuous, constant*, Æ : *daily*.

singala, singale(s) adv. *always, continually*.
singalflōwende ptc. *ever-flowing*, WW 177³⁶.
+**singalian** (y) *to continue*, ACPs 88⁶¹.
singallic *incessant, continual*, CP 61²¹. adv. (±) -līce.
+**singallician** *to continue*, JPs 88⁶¹, 140⁶.
singalnes f. *perseverance, assiduity*, OEG.
singalrene m. *constant flow*, HGL 418. [ryne]
±**singan³** (y) *to ' SING,' celebrate in song*, AO, CP : *crow, sing (of birds)*, Æ : *chant, intone : read, recite, narrate : (of things) sound, resound, ring, clank*, CP.
+**singe** (=+sinie?) f. *wife*, JUL 54. [cp. sinig]
singendlic *that may be sung*, LVPs 118⁵⁴.
sing-ere, -estre=sang-ere, -estre
singian (Æ)=syngian
singrēne (y) I. f. *house-leek, periwinkle*, Lcd. ['sengreen'] II. adj. *evergreen : uncooked (of vegetables)*.
singrim adj. *exceeding fierce*, JUL 230.
sinhere m. *huge army*, B 2936.
sinhīg-=sinhīw-
±**sin-hīwan**, -hīgan npl. *wedded couple*, Æ, CP.
+**sinhīwen** (synn-) *married*, HL,W.
sinhīwscipe m. *permanent tie (marriage)*, Bo 50¹.
sinhwurf-=sinhwyrf-
sinhwyrfel *round*, BL.
sinhwyrfende ptc. *round*, OEG 114.
+**sinig** *marriage*, DR 108⁷.
+**sinigan**, sinigian *to marry*, NG.
+**sinigscipe**=sinscipe
+**sinlīce** (y) adv. *often*, RB 127⁹ : *diligently*, 97¹⁴.
sinn=synn
sinnan³† (w. g.) *to meditate upon, think of, care about : cease?* [Ger. sinnen]
sinnig=synnig
sinnihte† (y¹, ea²) n. *eternal night*. adv. -nihtes *in continual night, night after night*.
sinnīð m. *perpetual misery*, RIM 52.
sinop=senep
sinoð (e, eo, y) f. *synod, council, meeting, assembly*. [L. synodus]
sinoðbōc (e, eo, y) f. *record of the decrees of a synod, canon law*, LL 46,49⁸.
sinoðdōm (eo) m. *decree of a synod*, EL 552.
sinoðlic *synodical*, BH.
sinoðstōw (eo¹, a²) f. *meeting-place, place where a synod is held*, BH 102⁵.
sinowalt=sinewealt
sinrǣden f. *(continuing state), marriage*, CP.
±**sinscipe** (e, y) m. *cohabitation, marriage*, Æ,CP : (+) *married couple*, CP.
+**sinsciplic** (y) *conjugal*, CHRD,LL (440⁶).
+**sinscippend** *married*, GD 218⁴.

sinsnǣd f. *large piece*, B743.
sinsorg f. *perpetual grief*, WIF45.
sint=sind plur. pres. indic. of wesan.
sintre(n)dende ptc. *round*, OEG. [v. '*trend*']
sintryndel (y¹, æ²) adj. *circular, globular*, LCD,WW.
sinðyrstende ptc. (w. g.) *ever-thirsting*, AO 130³¹.
sinu=seono
sinuwealt, sinwealt=sinewealt
sinwrǣnnes (y) f. *constant lechery*, WW 113²².
sīo=sēo; **slodo**=sidu; **sioía**=sefa
siogor (AA)=sigor
siol-=seol-, sel-
sioloð m? *water? sea?* B2367 (v. Klb).
sion '*laber*,' *a marsh plant?* Lcd 1·254. ['*sion*']
sīon=sēon II.; **sipian**=sypian
sīpian *to sink low, wane, decline*, LCD 3·151 (v. A31·538).
sīr=siger; **sirew-**, sirw-=searw-, sierw-
sisemūs f. *dormouse*, WW.
sīst=sīhst pres. 2 sg. of sēon I.
sit pres. 3 sg. of sittan.
sitl=setl
±**sittan⁵** *to* 'SIT,' *sit down, recline, rest*, Æ; AO,CP : *remain, continue, be situated*, AO : *settle, encamp, dwell, occupy, possess*, Chr : *abide, reside*, AO : *lie in wait, besiege, invest*, Chr : *preside over*, Æ; CP : †*perch, roost* : (+) *sit out, finish*. on cnēowum s. *kneel*, AO. wið earm +s. *lean*. on s. (1) *assail, attack*; (2) *press on, weigh down*, Æ.
sīð (ȳ) I. m. *going, motion, journey, errand* : *departure, death* : *expedition, undertaking, enterprise* : *road, way* : *time, turn, occasion*, Æ; AO. on ānne s. *at one and the same time*. ōðre sīðe...ōðre sīðe *on one occasion ..on another* : *conduct, way of life, manner*, Æ : *fate, destiny, experience, hap, fortune*, Æ. ['SITHE'] II. adv. *late, afterwards*, G. comp. sīð, sīðor *later*. ǣr and s. *always*. ne ǣr ne s. *never*. ǣr oððe s. *ever* : a comp. adj. sīðra *late, later*, and a superl. sīð(e)mest, sīðest *latest, last* are formed from sīð. æt sīðestan *at last, finally*. ['*sithe*'] III. prep. and conj. *after*. s. ðam *after, afterwards*. [*Ger*. seit] IV. (±)=±sihð pres. 3 sg. of sēon I.
+**sīð** I. m. (rare ds. +sīðan) *comrade, companion* : (†) *follower, retainer, warrior* : *count, thane*, Æ. II. n. *company*, v. LL 2·427; 446.
sīðberend m. *reaper*, WW235³. [sīðe]
sīðbōc f. *itinerary*, OEG 2023.
sīðboda m. *herald of departure (the pillar of cloud)*, Ex250.

sīðboren ptc. *late-born*, VPs,WW.
+**sīðcund** *fit to rank as a thane*, BH,LL.
+**sīðcundlic** *intimate*, BH120³³ (v.l.).
sīðdagas mpl. *later times*, EL639.
sīðe m. '*scythe*,' Æ,Gl.
sīðemest, sīðest v. sīð II.
sīðfæt (Æ,CP), sīðfat mn. *way, journey, voyage, expedition* : *path, road, course*, Æ : *experience, conduct* : *period of time*.
sīðfrom† *ready for a journey*.
sīðgeomor *travel-weary*, FAP1.
sīðian *to go, depart, travel, wander*, Æ,B. ['*sithe*']
+**sīðlic**=+sīðcundlic
sīðlice adv. *lately, after a time*, ÆH.
+**sīðmægen** n. *band of warriors*, GNE89.
+**sīðmann**=+sīð
sīðmest, sīðor, sīðra v. sīð II.
+**sīðrǣden** f. *troop*, WW206²¹.
+**sīðscipe** m. *fellowship, society*, BH.
sīðstapel *step, track*, LPs16⁵.
sīðð=sīð
sīðða adv. and conj. *afterwards*, JnL,LkL. ['*sith*']
sīððan, sīððon (eo, y) I. adv. *since, afterwards, from now on, hereafter, further, then, thereupon, after, later*, Æ. II. conj. *as soon as, when, since, after that, inasmuch as*. sīððan...sīððan *when...then*. III. prep. (w. a.) (LWS) *after*. ['SITHEN'; sīð, ðam]
sīðweg (GU859)=sīdweg
sīðwerod n. *travelling troop*, GEN2114.
±**sīðwīf** n. *noble lady*, GD,MH.
sīwan=sīwian
siwen pp. of sēon II.
siwen-ige, -igge, -ēge *blear-eyed*, GPH,CP 67.
±**sīwian** (ēo, ȳ) *to sew, mend, patch* : *knit together, unite*.
six=siex; **six-**; v. also siex-.
sixecge *six-sided, hexagonal*, WW.
sixfēte (y) adj. *of six (poetical) feet*, BF 192⁸.
sixgylde *entitled to six-fold compensation*, LL3,1.
sixhynde *belonging to the class whose 'wergeld' was 600 shillings*, LL.
sixhyndeman (e¹, y¹) m. *one of the* sixhynde *class*, LL30,39.
sixhyrnede (e²) *having six angles*, WW179¹³.
sixnihte *six days old*, LCD.
sixteogoða '*sixtieth*,' ÆGr,RB.
sixtēoða (e¹, ȳ²) '*sixteenth*,' MH,ÆGr.
sixtigǣre *60-oared ship*. [ār]
sixtigfeald '*sixty-fold*,' ÆGr.
sixtigwintre *sixty years old*, Æ (GEN).
sixtȳne (y¹, e²) '*sixteen*,' Bf,MH.
sixtȳnenihte *sixteen days old*, LCD.
sixtȳnewintre *sixteen years old*, MH 190,192.

slā=slāh
slacful (=æ) *lazy*, GL,LCD.
slacian=sleacian
slād pret. 3 sg. of slīdan.
slæ-=slea-; **slǣ**=slēa
-slæccan v. ā-sl.
slæd (a, e, ea) n. *valley, glade, AO*; Mdf. ['slade']
-slǣfan v. tō-s.
slæg-=sleg-
slæge m., slæget n.=slege
slægen pp. of slēan.
slǣgu (ē) f. *lethargy*, GL (v. A33·387).
slæht=slieht
slæhtan *to strike, slay*, NG. [*Ger.* schlachten]
+slæhte pret. 3 sg. of +sleccan.
slæhðo=sliehð pres. 3 sg. of slēan.
slǣp I. (ā, ē, ēa) m. 'SLEEP,' *Æ,CP : sleepiness, inactivity, CP : death.* II. m? *slippery place?* KC.
±slǣpan[7] (ē, ā) pret. 3 sg. slēp, slēap; also wk. slǣpte, slēpte, slēpde *to* 'SLEEP,' CP : *be benumbed, motionless, inactive, Æ,CP : lie with, Æ : rest in the grave, die, Æ.*
slǣpbǣre *soporific*, LCD 1·284'.
slǣpdrenc (æ²) m. *sleeping draught*, LCD 146b.
slǣpere m. *sleeper*, ÆL 1·23¹.
slǣpern (ā, ē, y²;=æ²) n. *dormitory*.
slǣping *sleeping*, APs 3⁶.
slǣplēas *sleepless*, GPH 399.
slǣplēast f. *sleeplessness, Æ.*
slǣpnes f. *sleepiness*, HL 14¹⁰⁶.
slǣpor *drowsy, sleepy*, SOL 258¹.
slǣpwērig *weary and sleepy*, RD 5⁵.
slǣpyrn=slǣpærn
slǣt=sliehð pres. 3 sg. of slēan.
slǣtan *to bait (a boar)*, ÆL 12⁷². ['sleat']
slǣting f. *right of hunting*, Chr 1087. ['sleating']
slǣw=slāw; **-slǣwan** v. ā-s.
slǣwð (ē) f. *sloth, indolence, Æ,Bo*; CP. ['sleuth'; slāw]
slāg=slāh
slaga m. *slayer, homicide, Æ,CP : executioner*, ÆL 12²³?
slagen pp. of slēan.
slagu=slægu
slāh, slāg f. 'sloe' *(fruit of the blackthorn), Cp,Lcd,WW*; Mdf.
slahe=slēa
slāhðorn m. *blackthorn, Cp,Lcd*; Mdf. ['sloethorn']
slāhðornragu f. *blackthorn, lichen*, LCD 54a.
slāhðornrind f. *blackthorn bark*, LCD.
slān I. (K,N)=slēan. II. gs. of slā (slāh).
slanc pret. 3 sg. of slincan.
slang pret. 3 sg. of slingan.

slǣp=slæp; **slāpel**=slāpol
slāpfulnes f. *lethargy*, WW 541⁴²?
slāpian *to become sleepy*, CP.
slāpol *somnolent, lethargic*, RB,ÆGR 305⁷.
slāpolnes (e²) f. *somnolence, lethargy, Æ.*
slāpornes f. *lethargy*, A 11·98.
slāpul=slāpol
slar-ege, -ie f. 'clary' *(plant), Lcd,WW.*
slāt pret. 3 sg. of slītan.
slāw 'SLOW,' *sluggish, torpid, lazy, CP.*
slāwerm (KGL 80²²)=slāwyrm
slāwian *to be slow, sluggish, Æ.*
slāwlīce adv. 'slowly,' *sluggishly, A,CP.*
slāwyrm m. 'slow-worm,' *snake, Gl,Sc.*
slēa f. 'slay,' *weaver's reed, WW.* [slēan; cp. slege]
sleac (v. A 39·366) 'SLACK,' *remiss, lax, sluggish, indolent, languid, Æ,CP : slow, gentle, easy, Æ.*
sleacian *to delay, retard, slacken, relax efforts, Æ.* ['slake']
sleaclic *slow, languid, idle*, HGL 472. adv. -līce.
sleacmōdnes f. *slackness, laziness*, BYH 40²⁷.
sleacnes (e) f. *slowness, Æ,Bf,Lcd : remissness, laziness, CP.* ['slackness']
sleacornes f. *laziness*, A 11·98⁴⁰.
sleaht=slieht
slēan⁶ *to strike, beat, stamp, coin (money), forge (weapons), Æ : throw, cast : sting (snake) : pitch (tent), Æ : strike across (country), dash, break, rush, come quickly, Æ : 'SLAY*,' kill, Æ,AO,CP. wæl +s. to slaughter : cast into chains : (+) strike down : play (harp, etc.) : (+) gain by fighting, win, conquer.*
slēap I. pret. 3 sg. of slǣpan. II. pret. 3 sg. of slūpan. III.=slǣp
slēaw=slāw; **slēbescōh**=slēfescōh
slec-=sleac-
+sleccan *to weaken, disable*, CR 149. [sleac]
slecg f. ('sledge'-)*hammer, mallet, Nar,WW*; Æ.
slecgettan *to beat, throb*, LCD 82b.
slecgwyrhta m. *metal-worker*, GENC 4²².
sled=slæd; **slēf**=slīefe
slēfan *to slip (clothes) on, Guth.* +slēfed *furnished with sleeves.* ['sleve']
slēfescōh m. *slipper*, GL (slēbe-).
slēflēas=slīeflēas
slege (æ) m. *beating, blow, stroke, Æ : slaying, slaughter, murder, Æ,AO,CP : crash, impact, clap (of thunder) : destruction, defeat, AO : (weaver's) 'slay,' WW 188⁵.* [slēan]
slegebȳtl m. *beetle, hammer*, LCD 122b.
slegefǣge *doomed to perish*, JUD 247.
slegel m. *plectrum*, WW 466²⁸.

slegen pp. of slēan.

sleghrȳðer (slægr-) n. *cattle for slaughter*, NC321.

slegnēat (æ¹, ǣ²) n. *cattle for slaughter*, TC 105⁴.

slēgu=slǣgu

sleh=sleah imperat. of slēan.

sleht=slieht

slehð=sliehð pres. 3 sg. of slēan.

slēow=slīw

slēp I. (VPs)=slǣp. **II.** pret. 3 sg. of slǣpan.

slēp-=slǣp-

slēpan=(1) slǣpan; (2) (MET9⁵⁵). slȳpan

sleð (VPs)=sliehð pres. 3 sg. of slēan.

slēwð=slǣwð; **slī** (GL)=slīw

slic (ī?) n. *beater, mallet, hammer*, LL455,15. WW75¹⁶.

-slicod (y) v. nīg-s.

slid (APs34⁶)=slidor I.

slīdan¹ *to ' slide*,' glide, slip, fall, fall down*, Guth : *fail, err, lapse*, Sol : *pass away, be transitory or unstable.*

sliddor=slidor

slide m. *sliding, slip, fall*, Æ,CP.

sliderian=slidrian

slidor I. *slippery, Ps,Run.* ['slidder'] **II.** n? *slippery place*, WW.

slidornes f. *slippery place, slipperiness*, BlPs. ['slidderness']

slidrian *to slip, slide, CP,PPs.* ['sliddern']

slīefe (ē, ī, ȳ) f. '*sleeve,*' Æ,Bl,LL,RB.

slīeflēas (ē, ȳ) '*sleeveless,*' RB,WW.

slieht (æ, ea, e, i, y) m. *stroke, slaughter, murder, death, AO,HL* : *animals for slaughter* : (+) †*battle.* ['sleight'; slēan]

sliehtswȳn (y¹) n. *pig for killing*, LL.

sliehð pres. 3 sg. of slēan.

slīf, slife=slīefe; **-slīfan** v. tō-s.

slifer *slippery*, HGL405.

sliht (AO,Æ)=slieht

-slihtes v. eorð-s.

slihð pres. 3 sg. of slēan.

slīm n. '*slime,*' CPs,WW.

slincan³ *to slink, creep, crawl*, AA,DD.

slincend mn. *reptile*, Æ (GEN).

slingan³ *to worm, twist oneself, creep into.* [Ger. schlingen]

slipa=slypa

slipeg, slipig *slimy*, LCD.

slipor *slippery, filthy, Sc* : *unsteady, shifty*, Æ. ['slipper']

slipornes f. *filthiness*, DHy36⁸. ['slipperness']

+slit n. *rending, biting, bite*, Æ : *something to be torn or rent : backbiting, calumny.*

±slītan¹ *to slit, tear, split, shiver, rend to pieces, divide : bite, sting, wound*, CP : *backbite*, CP. [v. 'slit,' 'slite']

slitcwealm m. *death by rending*, LL(166n).

slite I. m. *slit, rent, tear, bite.* **II.** f? *cyclamen.*

sliten m. *schismatic, heretic*, MtLp8⁹.

slītendlic *gorging*, WW437⁵.

slītere m. *gorger, glutton*, WW : *destroyer*, W235²⁴.

+slītglīw n. *raillery*, WW372³².

slītnes f. *desolation, destruction, tearing up*, LL,MtL.

slītol *biting, pungent*, GPH394.

slītung f. *tearing, biting*, DEUT,LCD.

slīðan¹ *to injure, wound*, GnE202.

slīðe† I. adj. *savage, fierce, dire, cruel, hard, hurtful, perilous.* **II.** adv. *savagely.*

slīðelic *abominable*, EPs105¹⁹.

slīðen *cruel, hard, evil*, B,Bo.

slīðheard† (e²) *cruel, severe, savage.*

slīðhende *with fell paw*, GnE177.

slīðnes f. *abomination?* EPs105³⁶.

slīw m. *a fish, tench, mullet*, GL.

slōg I. pret. 3 sg. of slēan. **II.**=slōh I.

slōh I. mfn., gs. slō(ge)s, slō; das. slō(h) '*slough,' mire*, BH,W. **II.** pret. 3 sg. of slēan.

-slop v. ofer-s; **slopen** pp. of slūpan.

slota m. *morsel*, Sc153¹².

slūma m. *slumber*, DD,Gu. ['sloom']

slūmere m. *sleeper*, NC322.

sluncon pret. pl. of slincan.

slūpan² *to slip, glide, move softly*, Ex,LL.

slȳf=slīef; **slyht**=slieht

slyhð=sliehð pres. 3 sg. of slēan.

slypa m. *slime, paste, pulp*, Lcd. ['slip']

slȳpan (ē,=īe) *to slip (on or off)*, A9·32¹⁵⁸.

slȳpescōh m. *slipper*, WW277²⁹.

slyppe f. *paste*, LCD163a.

slypræsn n. *sliding beam?* WW237¹. [ræsn]

slȳpð pres. 3 sg. of slūpan.

±smacian *to coax, flatter, allure, seduce*, HGL476; OEG3005.

smæc m. '*smack,' taste, WW* : *scent, odour*, WW.

±smæccan *to taste*, ÆGr. ['smatch']

smæl I. (often smal- in obl. cases) sup. smalost, smælst 'SMALL' : *thin, slender, narrow, AO* : *fine*, CP. **II.** v. hēafodsmæl.

smæle=smale

smæleðerm (A13·323)=smælðearme

smæll (=ie) m. *slap, smack, JnL.* ['small']

smælðearmas (y²) mp. *small intestines*, LCD.

smælðearme n. *lower abdomen*, CP.

smǣr (smǣre?) m. *lip*, GL,LCD.

smǣre-=smeoru-

smǣte *pure, refined, Cp,MH* ; Æ. ['smeat']

smǣtegold n. *pure gold*, WW.

smǣtegylden adj. *of pure gold*, WW.

smal- v. smæl.

smale *finely, into small pieces, Bo* : *softly (not loudly).* ['small']

smalian *to become thin*, LCD 2a (Harl.).
smalum *little by little*, OEG 1553.
smalung f. *reducing (of flesh)*, LCD 98a.
smāt pret. 3 sg. of smītan.
smēac pret. 3 sg. of smēocan.
smēade pret. 3 sg. of smēagan.
smēag- v. smēah.
±**smēagan**, smēan (ē) *to think, think out, reflect, meditate on, deliberate*, Æ,CP : *examine, penetrate, scrutinize, look closely into*, Æ : *suppose : seek (opportunity).*
smēagelegen (? v. OEG 4142n) f. *syllogism.*
smēagendlic *meditative*, ÆGr 211[6]. adv. -līce *accurately*, GD 172[14].
smēagung=smēaung
smēah I. adj. (smēag- in obl. cases) *sagacious, acute, subtle : penetrating.* II. pret. 3 sg. of smūgan.
+**smēah** n. *intrigue*, CHR 1094.
smēalic *searching, exhaustive, careful*, CP : *exquisite, choice.* adv. -līce *closely, thoroughly, accurately*, Æ,CP : *subtlely.*
smēalicnes f. *subtlety*, CHRD 98[35].
smēamete m. *delicacy (food)*, BHCHRD.
smēan, smēang=smēagan, smēaung
smearcian (e) *to smile*, Bo; Æ. ['*smirk*']
smeart *smarting, painful*, W 295[10]. ['*smart*']
smeartung (e) f. *tickling*, A 8·450.
smēað I. f. *meditation*, SPs 118[77]. II. pres. 3 sg. of smēagan.
smēaðanclīce adv. *in detail*, BF 78[12].
smēa-ðancol, -ðancollic *subtle.* adv. -e, -līce *exactly, thoroughly, studiously*, Æ.
smēaðancolnes f. *strictness*, ÆH 2·80′.
±**smēaung** (ē) f. *reflection, thought*, CP : *inquiry, search : intention, effort : intrigue : interpretation*, RWH 21[29].
smēawrenc m. *cunning device*, TC 339[8] (smēh-).
smēawung=smēaung
smēawyrhta m. *skilled artisan*, LL 455,16.
smēawyrm m. *intestinal worm*, LCD.
smec=smæc; **smēc**=smīc
smedma (eo) m. *fine flour, pollen meal*, Gl, Lcd; Æ. ['*smeddum*']
smedmen adj. *of fine flour*, Sc 154[1].
smēgan=smēagan
smēgawyrm=smēawyrm
smēh=smēah
smelt I. (y) m. *sardine*, '*smelt*,' Cp. II.= smolt
smelting (i, y) f. *amber*, ÆL.
smēocan[2] *to emit smoke*, Æ,Lcd WW : *fumigate*, Lcd. ['*smeek*']
smeoduma=smedma
smēoh=smēah; **smeolt**=smolt
smeortan[3] *to '*smart*,'* AO 36[30] (or ? fȳr-smeortende=*smarting like fire*).
smeortung (e) f. *smarting*, WW 114[3].

smeoru (e), smeoruw n. *ointment, fat, grease, lard, tallow, suet*, CP,VPs. ['*smear*']
smeorumangestre (e[1], e[2]) f. *butter-woman*, LL.
smeorusealf (e[1], a[2]) f. *unguent*, LCD 55b.
smeoruðearm (æ[1], e[1]) m. *entrail*, WW.
smeoruwig (e[1], e[2]) *rich, fat*, LCD 79a.
smeoruwyrt f. '*smearwort*,' Cp,Lcd.
smeoðlan=smiðian
smer-=smear-, smeor-, smir-, smier-
smēr=smǣr; **smera**=smeoru
smere-=smeoru-
smerian *to laugh to scorn*, MtL 9[24].
smeringwyrt f. *name of a plant*, '*crispa, victoriola*,' WW 135[1]. [cp. smeoruwyrt]
smeruwan=smierwan
smerwung=smirung; **smēte-**=smǣte-
±**smēðan** *to smooth, soften, polish*, CP : *appease, soothe*, CP.
smeðe (RB)=smiðHe
smēðe *smooth, polished, soft*, Cp,JnL,Lk; Æ,AO,CP : *suave, agreeable*, CP : *not harsh (of the voice)*, VHy : *lenitive.* ['*smeeth*']
±**smēðian** *to smoothen*, Lcd,OEG : *become smooth.* ['*smeeth*']
smēðnes f. *smoothness, smooth place*, Æ, WW. ['*smeethness*']
smēung=smēaung
smīc (ē, ȳ) m. *vapour, smoke*, Æ,AO,Bo, PPs,VHy. ['*smeech*'; '*smitch*']
smīcan (ē) *to smoke, fumigate*, LCD,Ps. [smēocan]
smicer *beauteous, elegant, fair, tasteful*, Cp, Shr,TC. ['*smicker*'] adv. -ere, CP.
smicernes f. *smartness*, WW 416[31].
+**smicerod** *well-fashioned*, WW 406[21].
smicor=smicer; **smidema**=smedma
smiec=smīc
±**smierwan** (e, i, y) *to* '*smear*,' *anoint, salve*, Bf,Bl,G,VPs (smirian); CP. [smeoru] For comps. v. smir-.
smilte=smylte
smilting=smelting
smirels (e, y) m. *ointment, salve*, Æ,LL. ['*smerles*']
smirenes (e, y) f. *ointment, unguent*, LCD, LG.
smirewan, smirian=smierwan
smiringele (y[1]) m. *anointing oil*, Ex 29[21].
smirung (e, y) f. *ointment, unguent*, HL, Lcd : *unction : smearing, greasing.* [smeoru]
smirwan=smierwan; **smirwung**=smirung
smītan[1] *to daub, smear, soil, pollute, defile*, Æ,Cp,Lcd. ['*smite*']
smitte f. *smudge, smut, blot*, OEG,RB : *pollution.* ['*smit*']
±**smittian** *to befoul, pollute*, WW : *infect*, OEG. ['*smit*']

smiÐ m. *handicraftsman, 'smith,' black-smith, armourer, carpenter, Æ,B,MtL.*
smiÐbelg (y²) m. *smith's bellows,* SOL85¹³.
smiÐcræft m. *manual art,* BH442¹⁶.
smiÐcræftega m. *skilled workman,* GEN 1084.
smiÐian (eo) *to forge, fabricate, design, Æ, OEG.* ['smith']
smiÐlīce adv. *dexterously,* WW.
smiÐÐe (smeÐe) f. *smithy, forge, Æ,BH,RB.* ['smithe']
smoc m. *'smock,' shift, WW.*
smoca m. *'smoke,' LPs,Nar* (cc).
smocen pp. of smēocan.
smocian *to emit 'smoke,' Æ,LPs : fumigate, Lcd.*
-smogu v. ǣ-s.; **-smoh** v. in-s.
smolt I. (e, eo) *mild, peaceful, still, gentle, MtL.* ['smolt'] **II.** *lard, fat, CM,NC.* ['smolt']
smolte=smylte
smoltlīce adv. *gently,* RWH146²⁶.
smorian *to strangle, choke, suffocate, Cp, MtR.* ['smore']
smōÐ *'smooth,' serene, calm, Sc*6'; ES9·40.
smucon pret. pl. of smēorcan.
smūgan² *to creep, Æ.* [Ger. schmiegen]
smūgendlic *creeping,* LPs68³⁵.
smȳc=smīc
smȳcÐ pres. 3 sg. of smēocan.
smygel, smygels m. *retreat, burrow,* GL.
smyllan (=ie) *to crack (a whip),* GPH 388.
smylt=smelt
+**smyltan** *to appease,* BH386¹² : *assuage,* LCD.
smylte I. *mild, peaceable, calm,* CP : *cheer-ful : prosperous.* **II.** adv. *softly.* [smolt]
smyltelic=smyltlic
smylting (Æ)=smelting
smyltlic *tranquil, serene,* DR,MH.
smyltnes f. *tranquillity, peace, quiet, silence, CP : gentleness, smoothness, mildness, com-posure, placidity, CP : evening calm.*
smyr-=smier-, smir-
smytte=smitte; **snā**=snāw
snaca m. *'snake,' serpent, Lk,W.*
snacc m. *a small vessel, war-ship, Chr.* ['snack']
snād=snǣd II.
-snæcce v. twī-s.
snǣd I. m. *handle of a scythe, ÆH*2·162. ['snead'] **II.** (ā) m. *detached area of wood-land,* Ct (Mdf). **III.** f. *piece, morsel, slice, portion of food, Æ,Lcd.* ['snede'; snīdan]
±**snǣdan I.** (ē) *to cut, slice, lop off, hew, Ln,CP,MtR.* ['sned'; snīÐan] **II.** *to eat, take a meal,* CHR1048.
snǣdel (GL)=snǣdelÐearm

snǣdelÐearm m. *great gut,* GL,LCD.
snǣding f. *meal, snack,* CM,RBL.
snǣdinghūs n. *cook's shop,* WW185¹.
snǣdingscēap n. *sheep for slaughter,* PPs 43²³.
snǣdmǣlum adv. *bit by bit,* LCD127a.
snægl (e), snægel m. *'snail,' Cp,Lcd,WW.*
snǣl=snægl; **snǣs**=snās
snǣsan (or? onsnǣsan) *to run through, pierce, spit,* LL69,36. [snās]
snǣÐfeld m. *a defined tract of pasture or woodland* (v. Mdf). [snǣd]
snās (ǣ) f. *spit, skewer,* WW237¹⁷ and N.
snāÐ I. pret. 3 sg. of snīÐan. **II.**(?) n? *killing* (v. OEG3070).
snāw, snāwa (MkL9³) m. *'snow,' Bl,Chr, Met,VPs : snow-storm, Bo.*
snāwceald *icy-cold,* MET29⁸.
snāwgebland n. *snow-storm,* AO186³⁴.
snāwhwīt *snow-white, Æ.*
snāwig *'snowy,' Lcd.*
snāwīt=snāwhwīt
snāwlic *snowy,* LCD,WW.
sneare, snearh f. *'snare,' OEG.*
snēdan=snǣdan; **snēl,** sneg(e)l=snægl
snell *smart, ready, rapid, keen, fresh, brisk, active, strong, bold, An,B,Cra,Ph;* AO. ['snell']
snellic *smart, ready, quick, rapid, bold.* adv. -līce, Wy. ['snelly']
snellscipe m. *quickness, boldness,* CHR1057D.
snelnes f. *agility,* ApT13⁷.
snēomet adv. *quickly, speedily, swiftly : immediately, at once.*
+**sneorcan³** (e) *to shrivel, dry up,* VPs30¹³.
snēowan⁷ (ō)† *to hasten, go.*
snērt f. *harpstring,* Ln. [cp. Ger. schnur]
+**snerc** pret. of sneorcan.
snīcan¹ *to sneak along, creep, crawl, CP,Lcd.* ['snike']
snid I. (±) n. *slice : cutting : slaughter.* [Ger. schnitt] **II.** m. *saw,* CP.
snide I. m. *incision : slaughter,* ES13·27⁹. **II.**=snid II.
sniden pp., snidon pret. pl. of snīÐan.
snidīsen n. *lancet,* LCD78a.
snirian=snyrian
snīte f. *snipe, Cp,WW.* ['snite']
±**snīÐan¹** *to cut, lance,* CP : *cut off, amputate, CP : hew down, slay, kill, Æ; CP : mow, reap.* ['snithe']
sniÐstrēo *carline thistle?* (BT), *chopped straw?* (JGPh1·328),Cp358s.
sniÐung f. *incision, wound,* LCD : *slaughter,* WW.
snīwan *to snow, AA,BH,Cp; Æ.* ['snew']
snōca m. *nook? inlet?* BC3·141' (v. Mdf).
snōd f. *hood, head-dress, fillet, Æ.*
snoffa m. *'nausea,' CM*50.

snofl *phlegm, mucus*, LCD 9a.
snoflig *full of phlegm*, BF 12¹⁸.
snofol=snofl
snoru f. *daughter-in-law*, Æ,AO. [*Ger.*
schnur]
+snot n. *mucus*, LCD 20b.
snotor, snoter *clever, prudent, intelligent,
discerning*, Bl,Chr,MtL; Æ,CP. ['*snoter*']
snotorlic (e²) *philosophic, wise, clever.* adv.
-līce.
snotornes (e²) f. *wisdom, prudence*, Æ.
snotorscipe m. *ratiocination, reason, reasonableness*, OEG 3215; 2¹⁷².
-snotorung (e²) v. word-s.
snotorwyrde *wise of speech, plausible*, W
107¹.
snotter, snottor, snottra (wk.)=snotor
snōwan=snēowan
snūd I. adj. *quickly approaching*, CR 842.
II. n? *speed*, AN 267.
snūde† adv. *quickly, at once*, NG.
snyflung f. *mucus from the nose*, NC 322.
['*snivelling*']
snyrian† *to hasten, hurry.*
snyring *sharp rock*, WW 371²².
snȳtan *to blow the nose*, NC 322. ['*snite*']
-snȳtels v. candel-s.
snyteru=snyttru
snȳting f. *blowing of nose*, WW 162.
['*sniting*']
snytre *clever, wise*, GEN 2808.
snytrian *to be clever, wise*, SOL.
snytro, snytru=snyttru
±snyttru f. (often in pl.) *wisdom, cleverness,
prudence, sagacity, intelligence*, AO,CP.
snyttrucræft† m. *wisdom, sagacity.*
snyttruhūs n. *house of wisdom*, PPs 77⁶⁰.
snyttrum adv. *cunningly, wisely*, B,PPs.
snyðian *to go nose or beak forwards* (*of a
plough*), RD 22⁶.
-snyðian, -snyððan v. be-s.
soc I. (±) n. *suck, sucking*, Æ. ['*sock*']
II. m. *soakings*, Mdf.
sōc I. pret. 3 sg. of sacan. **II.**=sōcn
socc m. '*sock,*' *light shoe, slipper*, Cp,RB.
[*L.* soccus]
socian *to* '*soak,*' Lcd. [sūcan]
sōcn f. *seeking, question, inquiry, case,
cause* : *visit, resort*, Æ,W : *attack*, B 1777 :
refuge, asylum, sanctuary, Æ : *the exercise
of judicial power, jurisdiction, right of
inquisition, right of taking fines, revenue*
(v. sacu), KC,LL (v. 2·454) : *district in
which a* '*socn*' *was exercised* (EHR 27·20).
['*soken*']
sōcnes=sēcnes
+sod n. *cooking, boiling*, GL : *trial*, CP 267¹⁹.
soden pp. of sēoðan.
sodomitisc *sodomitish*, A 11·101³².

sōfte I. (=sēfte) adj. '*soft,*' *mild, gentle*, Æ :
quiet, calm, tranquil, undisturbed, Æ :
luxurious : *agreeable*, A 9·28. **II.** adv.
Gen,Lcd,Met.
sōftnes f. *ease, comfort* : '*softness,*' *luxury*,
Æ.
sogeða (o²) m. *hiccough, eructation*, LCD.
sōht pp., sōhte pret. 3 sg. of sēcan.
sol I. n. *mud, wet sand, wallowing-place,
slough*, CP. **II.** *a wooden halter or collar
for beasts*, WW 462³¹. [v. '*sole*']
sōl n. *sun*, PPs 120⁶.
solar=solor
sōlate f. *sunflower, heliotrope*, LCD.
sole f. *shoe, sandal*, WW 125²⁵. [*L.*]
solere=solor
solian *to soil, become defiled*, Rim 67. ['*sole*']
sōlmerca m. *sundial*, NC 350.
Solmōnað m. *February*, MEN,MH.
solor m. *loft, upper room*, CP,Ph : '*pala-
tium,*' *hall, dwelling*, GD 248¹⁴ : *raised
platform*, OEG 2²¹¹. ['*sollar*'; *L.* solarium]
solsece (æ²) f. *heliotrope*, LCD,WW. [*L.*
solsequia]
som=sam ; **sōm**-=sām-
sōm f. *arbitration, agreement, reconciliation*,
Æ,LL. ['*some*']
+sōm *unanimous, peaceable, friendly*, Æ.
somn-=samn- ; **somod**=samod
somw-=samw-
sōn m. *sound, music*, CP. be sōne *aloud,
loudly*. [*L.* sonus]
sōna adv. '*SOON,*' *directly, forthwith, immediately, at once*, Chr,CP. s. swā *as
soon as, when*, CP.
sonc=sanc pret. of sincan.
sōncræft m. *music*, A 13·38³⁰⁶.
sond=sand
song I.=sang pret. 3 sg. of singan. **II.** sb.
bed, NG. [*ON.* sæng] **III.** *grape*, EHy 6³².
sonwald (NG)=sinewealt
sopa m. '*sup,*' *sip*, Lcd. ['*sope*']
sopcuppe f. *sop-cup*, TC.
sopp '*offula,*' '*sop,*' OEG 61¹⁰.
soppian *to soak*, '*sop,*' Lcd 86a.
sore *mote*, MtL 7³.
sorg f. (occl. gs. in -es) '*sorrow,*' *pain, grief,
trouble, care, distress, anxiety*, B,Bl,Bo,Cr;
CP.
sorgbyrðen f. *load of sorrow*, AN 1534.
sorgcearig† *anxious, sorrowful*, B.
sorgcearu f. *sorrow, anxiety*, GU 939.
sorgful '*sorrowful,*' *sad, anxious, careful*,
Æ,B,CP : *distressing, doleful*, B,Ph.
sorgian (pres. ptc. sorgende) *to* '*sorrow,*'
care, grieve, be sorry for, be anxious about,
B,Bl,Bo; CP.
sorglēas *free from sorrow or care*, CR,LL.
sorglēast (h) f. *security*, LCD.

sorglēoð† (h) *dirge*, B.
sorglic *miserable*. adv. -līce, CAS. ['*sorrowly*']
sorglufu f. *sad love*, DEOR 16.
sorgstafas mp. *anxiety, care*, JUL 660.
sorgung f. '*sorrowing*,' W 114⁴.
sorgwīte (h) n. *grievous torment*, W 187².
sorgword (h) n. *lamentation*, GEN 789.
sorgwylm (æ²)† m. *wave of sorrow*.
sorh=sorg
sorig *sorry*, CP 227⁸.
sot=sott
sōt n. (*what settles down*), '*soot*,' Cp,Lcd.
sotel, sotl, sotol=setl
sotman m. *foolish man*, ÆLD 17¹⁰¹.
sotscipe m. *dulness, folly*, WW 171³³. ['*sotship*']
sott I. adj. *foolish, dull, stupid*. II. m. *dullard, fool*, Bf. *open sott downright fool*, Æ. ['*sot*']
sottian *to be foolish*, ByH 80¹¹.
sōð I. n. *truth, justice, righteousness, rectitude*, CP : *reality, certainty*. tō sōðe, tō sōðum *in truth, truly, truthfully, accurately*. tō sōðan, ðurh sōð *verily, in truth*. II. adj. *true, genuine, real*, AO,CP : *just, righteous*. ['SOOTH'] III.=L. *pro-* in compounds, in DR and NG.
sōðbora? m. *soothsayer, astrologer*, CHR 975A.
sōð-cwed, -cweden *veracious*, NG.
sōðcwide m. *true speech, truth, just saying : proverb*, NG.
Sōðcyning† m. *King of truth, God*.
sōðe adv. *truly, really, accurately, truthfully, rightly*, B,PPs. ['*sooth*']
sōðes adv. *verily*, Mt. [v. '*sooth*']
Sōðfæder m. *Father of truth, God*, CR 103.
sōðfæst (e²) *true, trustworthy, honest*, Bl, Chr,Cr,OET,VPs : *just, righteous, JnL, PPs*. ['*soothfast*']
±**sōðfæstian** *to justify*, NG.
sōðfæstlic (e) *true, sincere*, AN 876. adv. -līce *truly, honestly*, OET 452. ['*soothfastly*']
sōðfæstnes f. *truth, truthfulness, fairness, fidelity*, Bf,Bl,Bo,CP,VPs : *justice*. ['*soothfastness*']
sōðfest=sōðfæst
sōðfylgan '*prosequi*,' DR 29¹⁸.
sōðgid (ie²)† n. *true report*.
sōðhweðere conj. *nevertheless*, NG.
±**sōðian** *to prove true, bear witness to*, LL, NG. ['*soothe*'; '*i-sothe*']
sōðlic adj. *true, truthful, real, genuine, right*, Bo. -līce adv. *indeed, really, certainly, Bl,El,G,VPs*. conj. *for, now, then, but*, CP. ['*soothly*']
sōðlufu f. *lovingkindness*, RWH 93²².
sōðsagol *truthful*, ÆGR,GD.

sōðsagu f. *truth*, W : *true story*, MtL. ['*soothsaw*']
sōðsecgan *to speak the truth*, BL.
sōðsecgendlīce *truly, genuinely*, GD 185¹⁷.
sōðsegen (æ²) f. *true statement*, ÆH.
sōðspǣce *truthful*, W 72¹⁶ E.
sōðspell n. *true story, history*, MtL p 7².
sōðsprǣc f. *true saying*, DR 171¹⁸.
sōðtācen n. *prodigy*, DR 43¹⁶.
sōðða (*JnL,LkL*)=siðða
sōðword† n. *true word*, PPs.
spāca m. '*spoke*' (*of wheel, etc.*), Bo : '*spoke-bone*' (*radius*), WW.
spade=spadu ; **spādl**=spātl
spadu (æ) f. '*spade*,' Æ,Gl,LL. [L. spatha]
spæc I. pret. 3 sg. of specan. II. n. *small branch, tendril*, WW.
spǣc=sprǣc
spǣclēas '*speechless*,' GPH 398⁷².
spænð pres. 3 sg. of spanan.
spær *sparing*, Sc 52⁶.
spær-=spear-
spǣren adj. *of plaster*, GL.
spǣrhende (y²) *sparing*, ÆGR.
spǣrian (N)=sparian
spǣrlic (e) adj. *sparing*, HGL 494. aðv. -līce.
spǣrlīra (e, ea, eo) m. *calf of leg*, Æ. ['*sparlire*']
spærlīred *with a thick calf*, WW 161²⁷.
spærnes f. *frugality, nearness*, DR,GL.
spærstān m. *gypsum, chalk*, WW. ['*sparstone*']
spǣtan *to* '*spit*,' *spew*, G; Æ,CP. ['*spete*']
spǣtl=spātl
spǣtl(l)an *to spit*, BH : *foam at the mouth*, WW.
spǣtung f. *spitting*, LCD 65a.
spala m. *substitute*, LL 484,2¹.
spāld (El)=spātl. ['*spold*']
spaldur *balsam*, GL (v. ES 37·186).
span=spann
+**span** n. *suggestion, persuasion, allurement*, CP.
±**spanan**⁷ *to draw on, allure, seduce, mislead, persuade, instigate*, Æ,AO,CP.
span-e, -u, pl. -a, -an f. *teat*, LCD,WW.
spanere (o) m. *seducer, enticer*, WW.
±**spang** fn. *clasp, buckle*, GEN. [Ger. spange]
spann I. f. '*span*' (*measure*), BH,WW. II. pret. 3 sg. of spinnan.
+**spann** n. *fastening, band, buckle, yoke*, CP.
±**spannan**⁷ *to join, link, fasten, attach*, CP.
spannung f. *span*, WW.
-spanung (i²) v. for-, lēas-s.
sparcian=spearcian
±**sparian** *to* '*spare*,' *be indulgent or merciful to, save, BH,CP,Shr,VPs : use sparingly, not to use*, Æ : *forbear, abstain from*, BH, CP.

+**sparrian** *to shut, bar*, MtL6⁶.
sparwa=spearwa
spātl (ǣ) n. *spittle, saliva*, CP,Lcd,NG.
['*spattle*']
spātlian *to spit out*, WW162. ['*spattle*']
spātlung f. *what is spit out, spittle*, WW162.
['*spattling*']
spāōl=spātl
spāw pret. 3 sg. of spīwan.
speaft (MkL8²³)=speoft; **speara**=spearwa
spearca (æ,e) m. '*spark*,' Bf,Bo,Cp,MH;CP.
spearcian *to throw out sparks, sparkle*, SAT
78? (v. OEG4029).
spearewa=spearwa
spearhafoc m. *sparrow-hawk*, Cp,WW.
['*spar-hawk*']
spearlīr-=spærlīr-
spearn pret. 3 sg. of spurnan.
spearnes=spærnes
spearnlian *to spurn, kick, sprawl*, Æ,GL.
spearwa I. m. '*sparrow*,' BH,Chr,Cp,Ps.
II. m. *calf (of the leg)*, GL (cp. spærlīra).
spec=spic; **spēc**=spēæc, sprēæc
specan=sprecan
specca m. '*speck*,' *spot*, Cp,Lcd,WW.
specfāh *spotted, blotched*, Cp22.
sped '*glaucoma*,' *sticky moisture, phlegm,
rheum*, Cp,OEG. ['*spade*']
spēd f. *luck, success, prosperity*, Cp,El,
PPs : *riches, wealth, abundance*, Cr,Gen;
AO : *opportunity, power, faculty*, Bl,PPs :
(only in dp. spēdum) '*speed*,' *quickness,
Gen.* on s. *fluently, skilfully* : *offspring?*
PPs103¹⁶. [spōwan]
±**spēdan** w. d. *to prosper, succeed*, Chr,Ma.
['*speed*']
spēddropa m. *useful drop (ink)*, RD27⁸.
spedlende *suffering from* 'sped,' WW.
spēdig *lucky, prosperous, rich*, AO : *plen-
teous, abundant : powerful.*
+**spēdiglīce** adv. *prosperously*, LPs44⁵.
spēdignes f. *opulence*, OEG3605.
spēdlīce adv. *effectually, effectively*, PPs.
+**spēdsumian** *to prosper*, OEG3630.
spēdum v. spēd; **spel**=spell
spelc m? *splint*, Lcd. ['*spelk*']
spelcan *to fasten with splints*, Lcd. ['*spelk*']
speld n., nap. speld, speldru *ember, torch*,
OEG,WW. ['*speld*']
+**spelia** m. *vicar, substitute, representative,
deputy.*
spelian *to be substitute for, represent*, Æ,RB.
['*spele*']
speliend m. *substitute, representative*, Æ,GR.
speling f. *deputyship*, RB10¹².
spell n. *narrative, history, story, fable*, Bo :
speech, discourse, homily, Æ,B,Bo,Da,Lcd;
AO,CP : *message, news : statement, observation.* ['*spell*' and v. Mdf]

spellbōc f. *book of sermons*, TC430²¹.
spellboda m. *messenger, ambassador, angel
speaker : prophet.* [beodan]
spellcwide m. *historical narrative*, AO100¹².
±**spellian** *to speak, discourse, talk*, Bo,Lcd,
LkL; Æ : *announce, relate, proclaim*, Met :
conspire, GD106¹. ['*spell*']
spellstōw f. *place of proclamations*, Ct.
spellung f. *speech, conversation, narrative,
discourse*, Æ.
spelt I. m. '*spelt*,' *corn*, WW. [L.] II.
'*planca*,' *board of a book*, WW164. ['*spelt*']
spelter (LCD3·136)=spaldur
-spendan v. ā-, for-s.
spendung f. '*spending*,' ÆH556²⁹.
spenn (=spēonn) pret. 3 sg. of spannan.
spennels m. *clasp*, WW238³⁴.
spenst pres. 2 sg., spenð pres. 3 sg. of
spanan.
speoft (MkR8²³; MtL27³⁰) redupl. pret. of
spatan? to spit. [v. ANS141·176]
+**speoftian** *to spit upon*, LkL18³². [ES
38·34]
spēon pret. 3 sg. of spanan, spannan.
Spēonisc *Spanish*, ÆL37¹.
speoru (GL) nap. of spere.
speorulīra=spærlīra
spēow pret. 3 sg. of spōwan.
spēow-=spīw-; **sper-**=spær-, spear-, spyr-
spere n., nap. spe(o)ru '*spear*,' *javelin,
lance*, Æ,AO,Chr,CP,Cp,LG : *stitching
pain*, LCD175a.
sperebrōga m. *terror at spears*, RD18⁴.
sperehand f. *male line of descent*, BC3·340¹⁹.
sperehealf f. *male line of descent*, TC491²⁰.
sperelēas *without a (spear-)head*, WW143⁷.
sperenīð n. *battle*, GEN2059.
speresceaft (æ³) m. '*spear-shaft*,' GD14²⁷.
sperewyrt (speru-) f. '*spearwort*,' *elecampane*, Lcd,WW.
speriend (WW66²⁰)=spyrigend
+**sperod** *armed with a spear*, ÆGR,BL.
spic n. *fat bacon*, Lcd,OET; Æ. ['*spick*']
spīce f., spīca m. *aromatic herb, spice?* BL,
LCD. [L. *species*]
spichūs n. *larder*, GL,LCD.
spīcing m. *spike, nail*, ANS125⁵¹.
spicmāse f. *titmouse*, WW286¹⁵.
spigettan *to spit*, Æ,Bo.
spilǣg '*spilagius*' (*spalangius?*), *a venomous
insect*, DR125¹⁶.
spilc=spelc
spild m. *annihilation, ruin*, CP.
spildan *to waste, ruin, destroy*, AN,JnL.
spildsīð m. *destructive expedition*, EX153.
spilian *to sport, play*, LL,W. ['*spile*']
±**spillan** *to destroy, mutilate, kill*, LG :
waste, DR : '*spill*' (*blood*), NIC.
spillere m. *parasite, jester*, OEG679.

spilling f. *waste*, CHR999E.
spilð (GL)=spild
spind sb. *fat*, WW.
spindel=sprindel
spinel f., gs. spinle '*spindle*,' *Cp,LL* : *the thread on a spindle?* OEG17³⁷.
spinelhealf (nl) f. *female line of descent*, TC491²¹.
spinge=spynge; **spinil**, spinl=spinel
-spinn v. in-s.
±**spinnan³** *to* '*spin*,' *Æ,Cp,Lcd,MtR* : *twist, writhe, Æ.*
spir *spike, blade*, LCD99b.
spircan (y) *to sparkle, Æ,*GL.
spircing (y) *sprinkling*, GPH398.
spitel m. *small spade, dibble, LL* ; GD201²⁰.
['*spittle*']
spittan *to dig in with a spud*, LL454,10.
±**spittan** *to* '*spit*,' *LkR,MtR,MkL.*
spittian *to spit* (*for cooking*) (Swt).
spitu f. '*spit*' (*cooking*), *Æ,HL.*
spiðra? m. *spider*, LCD53b.
spiwan¹ *to spit, spit out, '*spew*,' vomit, Æ, Bl,Chr,CP,Jul,MH.*
spiwdrenc (i²) m. *liquid emetic*, LCD.
spiwe m. *vomiting*, LCD22b.
spiwedrenc=spiwdrenc
spiwere m. *one who spews*, WW108⁴. ['*spewer*']
spiweða=spiwða
spiwian (io) *to spew, spit up* (w. d.), JUL476.
spiwing (ēo) f. '*spewing*,' WW.
spiwol *emetic*, LCD.
spiwða (eo) m. *vomiting, vomit, Æ.*
splatan? *to split*, v. ES49·156.
splin=spinl
splott m. *spot, blot* : *patch* (*of land*), *Æ.*
+**splottod** *spotted*, TC537'.
spōn I. m. *sliver, chip, shaving, BH,Cp,Lcd.* ['*spoon*'] II. pret. 3 sg. of spanan.
+**spon**, spong=+span, spang
sponge f. '*sponge*,' *Mt.*
sponn=spann
spor n. *spoor, track, trail, footprint, CP* : *trace, vestige.* [*Ger.* spur]
spor-=spur-
sporettan¹ *to kick*, CVHy6¹⁵.
sporetung f. *kicking*, EHy6¹⁵.
spornettan *to spurn, kick*, WW.
sporning f. *stumbling-block*, Sc134⁵. [v. '*spurning*']
sporwrecel? m. *what is tracked after being driven off?* (BT), TC172'.
±**spōwan⁷** *to succeed, thrive, Æ,AO,CP* : (impers.) *profit, avail, help, Æ.*
spōwendlice adv. *prosperously*, PPs.
spracen n. *berry-bearing alder*, LCD,WW.
spræc I. n. *shoot, slip*, WW44²⁹. II. pret. 3 sg. of sprecan.

spræc (ē) f. *language, Æ* : '*SPEECH*,' *power of speech, CP* : *statement, narrative, fable, discourse, conversation, Æ,CP* : *eloquence, Æ* : *report, rumour* : *decision, judgment* : *charge, suit, CP* : *point, question* : *place for speaking*, NG.
spræcan=sprecan
spræccyn n. *mode of speech*, BH486¹.
spræce f. *talk, discourse*, Bo137¹.
+**spræce** *eloquent, affable, Æ,*BH.
+**spræcelic** *incapable of being used alone* (*of the inseparable prepositions*), ÆGR.
spræcful *talkative*, LPs139¹².
spræchūs n. *senate-house, curia* : *auditorium, WW* : *guest-quarters* (*in a monastery*), ÆL 31⁸⁴⁷. ['*speech-house*']
spræcon pret. pl. of sprecan.
sprædan *to spread* : (+) *stretch forth, extend.*
sprædung f. *propagation*, DR109².
sprængan=sprengan
spranc=sprang
spranca m. *shoot, slip, branch*, Gl. ['*spronk*']
sprang pret. 3 sg. of springan.
sprangettan *to quiver*, MP1·610; WW 473².
spreawlian *to* '*sprawl*,' *move convulsively*, GPH,OEG.
+**sprec** n. *faculty of speech* : *talk, discussion.*
sprec=spræc
±**spreca** m. *spokesman, councillor, Æ.*
±**sprecan¹** *to* '*SPEAK**,' *say, utter, make a speech, Æ,AO,CP* : *converse, converse with, Æ* : *declare, tell of* : (+) *agree*, AO. sp. on *lay claim to.*
+**sprecendlic** (spec-) *that should be spoken*, Sc123².
sprecern n. *place for speaking*, NG. [spræc, ærn]
sprecolnes (spec-) f. *loquacity*, Sc170¹⁵.
sprecul *talkative*, SPs139¹².
sprengan (æ) (±) *to scatter, strew, sprinkle, sow, Æ,LL* : *spring, break, burst, split.* sp. on *administer a clyster.* [causative of springan; '*sprenge*']
sprenging (i) f. *sprinkling*, CM388.
sprēot m. *pole, pike, spear, Cp,TC,WW.* ['*sprit*']
spretting=sprytting
spreullan (OEG50³⁴)=spreawlian
spreut (GL)=sprēot
spricð pres. 3 sg. of sprecan.
sprincel m. *basket-snare* (*for catching fish*), WW (v. ES43·322; FM200).
sprind *vigorous, strong*, OEG,Sol. ['*sprind*'; springan]
-sprindlad v. ā-s.
sprindlice adv. *vigorously*, OEG738.
spring (y) m. '*spring*,' *source*, BC : *sprinkling* : *ulcer* : *flux.*

±**springan**[3] *to jump, leap, 'spring,' burst forth, rise,* B,Bo,G,Ma,MH; Æ : *spread, be diffused, grow,* Æ,Bf : *want, lack,* VH.
springd=sprind; **springing**=sprenging
springwyrt f. *caper-plant,* LCD.
+**sprintan** *to emit, utter,* JnL p 187[12].
spritting=sprytting
sprota m., sprot(t) n. *sprout. twig,* OEG, WW : *peg.* ['*sprote*']
sprott m. *sprat,* ÆL,Bf,NC. ['*sprot*']
sprungen pp., sprungon pret. pl. of springan.
-**sprūtan** v. ā-, geond-s.
sprycŏ pres. 3 sg. of sprecan.
spryng=spring; **sprȳtan**=spryttan
sprytle f. *chip,* BH 204[56] (v.l.).
spryttan *to sprout, come forth, spring, germinate, yield fruit,* BH,Lcd; Æ : *incite.* ['*sprit*']
sprytting (e, i) f. *shoot, sprout : increase,* CM 381.
spunnen pp., spunnon pret. pl. of spinnan.
spur-=spor-
spura (o) m. *spur,* Æ,Gl.
spure f. *heel,* EPs 48[5].
spurleŏer n. *spur-strap,* WW 97[10].
±**spurnan**[3] (o) *to strike against, kick,* PPs : '*spurn,' reject,* Æ : *stumble.*
spurnere (o) m. *fuller,* ÆGR 35[2].
spurul (=*spurnul?) *given to kicking or trampling?* OET.
spylian v. ā-s.
spynge (i), spyncge f. *sponge,* AO. [L. spongia]
spyrc-=spirc-
spyrd m. '*stadium,' race-course,* NG.
spyremann (e[1]) m. *tracker,* TC 172'.
±**spyrian** (i) *to make a track, go, pursue, travel, journey,* CP : *follow out, ask about, investigate,* BH,Bo. ['*speer*'; spor]
spyrigend m. *investigator, inquirer,* SOL 140.
spyrnan *to stumble,* RWH 94[22].
spyrran (e;=ie) *to strike,* AA 22[8].
spyrring f. *striking,* OEG.
spyrte (e, i) f. *wicker basket, eel-basket,* Æ. [L. sporta]
spyrung f. *asking, investigation,* OEG 5214.
staca m. *pin, 'stake,'* AO,Lcd; Æ.
stacan (stagan) *to pierce with a stake, spit* (or ?*roast,* ES 40·242), IM 124[71].
stacung f. *the piercing of an effigy by a 'staca' (a method of injury by witchcraft),* LL.
stæde-=stede-
stæf m., nap. stafas '*staff,' stick, rod,* Æ,Bo, Cp,LPs,CP : *pastoral staff :* (often in pl.) *letter, character, writing,* Æ,Bo,WW : *document :* (in pl.) *letters, literature, learning.*
stæfad=stafod

stæfcræft m. *grammar,* Æ : (in pl.) *learning,* BH.
stæfcræftig *lettered,* OEG.
stæfcyst f. *letters, learning from books,* Æ.
stæfgefēg n. *syllable,* ÆGR : *letters,* LSPs 70[15].
+**stæflǣred** *instructed, lettered,* LCD.
stæfleahtor m. *grammatical fault,* OEG 5467.
stæfleornere m. *student,* OEG 3126.
stæflic *literary : literal,* Æ. ['*staffly*']
stæfliŏere f. *sling, 'balista,'* GL.
stæfn=stefn
stæfplega m. *literary game,* GL.
stæfrǣw f. *row of letters, line of writing,* ÆL 23b[767] : *alphabet,* BH 484[27].
stæfröf *alphabet,* WW 397[14].
stæfsweord n. '*dolon,' lance? javelin?* WW. ['*staffsword*']
stæfwīs (e) *lettered, learned,* LCD 3·186'.
stæfwrītere=stærwrītere
stæg n. I. '*stay' (rope),* WW 288[26]. II. *pool, pond.* [L. stagnum]
-**stǣgan** v. ā-st.
stǣgel *steep,* CR,GL. [stīgan]
stǣger I. fn? '*stair,' staircase,* Æ,WW. [stīgan] II. (ByH 110[18])=stǣgel
stǣgl=stǣgel
stæl I. n. *place, spot.* on stale *in place of, instead of.* on stale bēon *stand in (good) stead, be a help to,* AO 232[23] : *situation, condition.* [Ger. stelle] II. pret. 3 sg. of stelan.
stǣl=staŏol; **stǣla**=stela
±**stǣlan** *to found, institute, carry on :* *confess, admit,* VH. synne st. *to institute sin,* i.e. *enter on a conflict,* MEN 287 : (w. d.) *put upon, impute to, accuse of, charge with :* (†) *avenge.* [=*stæŏlian=staŏolian]
stǣle=stale ds. of stalu.
stǣlg=stǣgel
stǣlgiest m. *thievish stranger,* RD 48[5].
stǣlherige m. *predatory army,* CP,CHR. [stelan]
stǣlhrān m. *decoy-reindeer,* AO 18[11].
stæll=steall; **stællan**=stiellan
+**stǣllan** *to stall, stable,* MH 20[1].
stǣlon pret. pl. of stelan.
stǣltihtle f. *charge of stealing,* LL.
stǣlŏing n. *theft,* CHRD 19[16]. [stelan]
stǣlwierŏe *serviceable,* CP,Chr,Shr. [staŏol; '*stalworth*']
stǣlwyrt f. *water-starwort,* WW 299[5].
+**stǣn-**=+sten-
stǣn-=stǣnen-, stān-
stǣnan (±) *to stone,* Mt; Æ,CP : *adorn with precious stones,* EL 151. ['*steen*']
stænc=stenc
stǣne f. *pitcher, jug,* WW 415[18]. ['*stean*']

stǣnen *made of stone, stony, Bl,G,MH*; Æ, AO,CP. ['*stonen*']

stǣner *stony ground*, NG.

stǣng=steng

stǣnilic *stony*, LCD 1·216'.

stǣning f. *stoning*, Æ,MH.

stæpe (a, e) m. usu. nap. stapas (stæpan, RPs139⁵) *going, gait, 'step,' pace, Ps,Rd, W*; Æ,CP : *spoor : power of locomotion : short distance, measure of length, MtR,WW* : *step, stair, Æ,VPs* : *pedestal, socket, HL* 199 : *grade, degree, Æ.* in stæpe *instantly*.

stæpegong (e) m. *stepping, going*, RIM 22.

stæpmǣlum adv. *step by step, by degrees, gradually*, CP.

±stæppan⁶ (e) *to 'STEP,' go, advance, Æ,CP*; AO.

stæppescōh (e) m. *slipper*, WW.

stær m., nap. staras *starling, Cp,MtL.* ['*stare*']

stǣr (ē) n. *story, history, narrative*, BH. [v. A37·56 and LF161]

stærblind *stone-blind, Cp.* ['*stareblind*']

stǣrcedferhð=stercedferhð

stǣreblind (*Shr*)=stærblind

stǣrleornere? m. *student of history*, v. OEG 4145n.

stǣrlīce adv. *historically*, OEG 2³¹⁰.

stǣrling m. '*starling*,' ZDA 33·241⁵⁴.

stærn=stearn

stǣrtractere m. *commentator, historian*, WW 207¹.

stǣrwrītere m. *historian*, AO.

stæð n. occl. gds. staðe, nap. staðas *shore, river-bank, AO,Chr*; Æ,CP. ['*staith*']

stæðfæst *firm, stable*, CR 981.

stæðhlȳpe I. (ē) *sloping, precipitous.* II. f. *a steep place*, GD 95¹⁶.

stæðhlȳplīce adv. *steeply*, BL 207²⁰.

stæðswealwe f. *sand-martin*, LCD,WW.

stæððah *to support*, RD 4⁷⁴.

±stæððolg *staid, serious*, Æ.

±stæððolgnes f. *staidness, seriousness*, Æ,CP.

stæðweall m. *barrier of the shore*, GEN 1376.

stæðwyrt f. *a plant*, LCD 29a.

stafas nap. of stæf.

stafian *to dictate*, Æ.

stafod (æ, e) *striped*, Ep,Erf.

stāg pret. 3 sg. of stīgan.

stagan=stacan?

stagga m. *stag*, LL 624,24. ['*stag*']

stāh pret. 3 sg. of stīgan.

stal=steall

+stāl n. *plaint, accusation, confession?* MFH 163,VH : *contention*, GD 329¹⁵.

+stala m. *accessory in theft*, LL 100,25¹.

stalað=staðol

stald=steald; stale v. stæl.

stālern n. *court of law*, WW.

staleð-=staðol-

stalgong m. *stealthy going*, GU 1113.

stalian *to go stealthily*, AO : (±) *steal*, Æ.

±stāllan *to establish, confirm, strengthen* : *make an accusation*, LL 110B¹. [=staðolian]

stall=steall

stalu I. (±) f. *stealing, robbery, theft, Bl, MtL*; Æ : *stolen article : fine for stealing.* ['*stale*'] II. *wood to which harp-strings are fixed?* WW 203³⁶. [v. '*stale*']

stalung f. *stealing, robbery*, AO.

stam (o) *stammering*, GL.

stamera m. *stammerer*, EC 226'.

stamerian (omr-) *to 'stammer,' GPH,HL.*

stammetan (o) *to stammer*, WW 447³⁰.

stamor *stammering*, GL.

stān m. (and n. in NG) '*STONE*,' *rock : gem*, CP : *calculus : milestone* (v. Mdf).

stānæx (e²) f. *stone-workers' axe?* WW.

stānbæð n. *vapour bath made by water poured on to heated stones* (BT),LCD.

stānbeorg m. *rocky elevation*, B,Ct.

stānberende *stony*, WW 427³⁶.

stānbill n. *tool for working stone*, WW 447³³.

stānboga† m. *rocky arch*, B.

stānbrycg f. *stone bridge*, Ct,WW.

stānbucca m. *mountain goat*, ÆGR 68⁵.

stānburg f. *town or fort of stone*, GEN; Mdf.

stanc I. pret. 3 sg. of stincan. II. sb. *sprinkling*, WW.

stāncarr m. *rock*, DR 19¹¹.

stānceastel (i²) m. *walled enclosure? heap of stones?* Ct (v. GBG).

stānceosel (i², y²) m. *sand*, GENC 22¹⁷,OEG.

stān-clif n., nap. -clifu, -cleofu (B) *rock, cliff, crag*, GD.

stānclūd m. *rock*, Æ,CP.

stāncnoll m. *rocky knoll*, EC 248¹⁷.

stāncræftiga m. *clever stone-worker*, MH 202¹⁴.

stāncrian *to sprinkle*, WW 162⁴⁶.

stāncrop m. '*stone-crop*' (*plant*), LCD.

stāncynn n. *kind of stone*, VH,ZDA 34·233.

stāncysel=stānceosel

stāncyst(en) *chestnut-tree*, KC 4·8²². [L. castanea]

stand (o) m. *delay*, MkLR 6³⁵. [v. '*stand*']

±standan⁶ (o) *to 'STAND*' ('*i-stand*'), *occupy a place, stand firm, Æ,AO,CP* : *congeal*, LCD 35b : *remain, continue, abide*, AO, CP : *stand good, be valid, be, exist, take place, Æ,CP : oppose, resist attack : reprove* : *stand still, stop, Æ* : (†) *appear, flash out* : *arise, come* : (†) *be present to, come upon (of fear).* ne s. tō ahte *be of no account*, W 82n. (+) *stand up, keep one's feet*, BO : (+) *attack, assail, ÆL* : (+) *perform.* s. on *consist : depend on.*

stāndenu *stony valley,* KC3·383.
stāneht=stānihte; **stānex**=stānæx
stān-fæt n., nap. -fatu *stone vessel,* G, WAL.
stānfāh† *stone-paven.*
stānflōr m. *paving-stone, tessella,* OEG 14³. [cp. flōrstān]
stang pret. 3 sg. of stingan.
stāngaderung f. *stone wall,* ERPs 61³.
stāngeat n. *opening between rocks,* Ct.
stāngedelf n. *stone-quarry,* KC.
stāngefeall n. *heap of stones,* MH 212²¹.
stāngefōg n. *stone-laying,* EL 1021.
stāngella (i²) m. ' *staniel,' pelican, VPs,WW.*
stāngetimbre n. *masonry,* WW 441⁶.
stāngeweorc n. *art of building : stone-work, masonry,* Æ.
stān-gripe m., dp. -greopum *handful of stones?* EL 824.
stānhege m. *stone fence, wall,* LPs 79¹³.
stānhlīet (Ct)=stānhȳwet
stānhlinc m. *stony ridge,* KC.
stān-hlīð† n., nap. -hliðu, -hleoðu *rocky slope, cliff, rock.*
stānhof n. *stone building,* RUIN 39.
stānhol n. *hole in a rock,* AA 8,33.
stānhricg m. *rocky ridge,* OEG 5465.
stānhȳpe f. *stone-heap,* KC 3·431⁹.
stānhȳwet n. *stone-quarry,* WW 112¹⁰.
stānig (ǣ) ' *stony,' rocky, MtR* ; AO.
stāniht (ǣ) **I.** adj. *stony, rocky,* AO. **II.** n. *stony ground* (Swt).
stānincel n. *little stone,* A 13·31⁸⁶.
stānlesung f. *building with loose stones,* WW 117³⁴. [lesan]
stānlīm m. *cement, mortar,* WW 205⁹.
stānmerce m. *parsley,* WW.
stānrocc m. *high rock, obelisk,* GL.
stānscalu f. *shale,* EC 306¹⁸.
stānscræf n. *rocky cave,* MH.
stānscylf m. *rugged rock,* HGL 449.
stānscylig *shaly, stony,* Mk 4⁵. [sciell]
stānsticce n. *bit of stone,* WW 376¹⁸.
stānstrǣt f. *paved road,* TC 525²¹.
stāntorr m. *stone tower : crag, rock,* GD 12.
stānweall m. ' *stone wall,' VPs* ; Æ.
stānweg m. *paved road,* BC 1·417'.
stānweorc n. ' *stone-work,' RWH 43¹⁷ : stone structure,* Æ.
stānwong m. *stony plain,* RD 88⁶.
stānwurma m. *mineral colour,* OEG 1061.
stānwurðung f. *worship of stones,* LL.
stānwyrht? f. *stone structure,* WW 341¹⁰.
stānwyrhta m. *stone-mason,* GL.
stapa m. *grasshopper, locust,* WW.
stapas v. stæpe; **stapel**=stapol
stapela m. *post, stake,* LL 387,4².
stapen pp. of steppan.

stapol m., nap. stapolas, staplas *basis, trunk of a tree, post, prop, support, stay, pillar, column, An,MtL,WW : threshold? B* 926 : *market and court?* (v. EC 466n) : *steps up to a house door,* WW 126⁸. [' staple'; v. Mdf]
stapolweg m. *staked-out road?* KC 5·281²³.
-stapplian v. under-s.; **stapul**=stapol
staras v. stær; **starc**=stearc
stareblind=stærblind
±**starian** *to* ' *stare,' gaze,* ÆL,B.
stað- v. stæð; **staðel**=staðol
staðol (ea¹, e², u²) m. *base, foundation, support, BH,WW* ; AO,CP : *station, position, state, condition,* CP : *stability, security : firmament, heavens : underside of a turf,* Lcd : *estate, farm,* GD 222. [' staddle'; standan]
staðolǣht f. *real estate,* RIM 22.
staðolfæst *fixed, firm, steadfast, Bo,MtL.* [' stathelfast']
staðolfæstlic *steadfast, firm,* Æ. adv. -līce.
staðolfæstnes (ea) f. *stability,* Æ,GD.
+**staðol-fæst(n)ian,** -festian (ea¹, u²) *to make firm, establish.*
staðolfæstnung f. *foundation,* LPs 136⁷.
±**staðolian** (e²) *to fix, found, establish, Bl : confirm, make steadfast, strengthen.* [' stathel']
+**staðoliend** (e²) m. *founder,* LPs 47².
±**staðolung** f. *foundation, settlement : ordinance,* RB 112²⁴.
staðolwang† m. *settling place.*
staðul=staðol; **steaf-**=stæf-
+**steal** n. *structure, frame,* WA 110.
stealc† *lofty, steep, precipitous,* RD.
-stealcian v. be-s.
stealcung f. *act of going stealthily,* ÆH. [' stalking']
steald pret. 3 sg. of stellan.
+**steald†** n. *dwelling, habitation.*
stealdan⁷ *to possess, own,* RIM 22.
steall (a) mn. *standing, place, position, state, WW* : ' *stall' (for cattle), stable,* Cp; Æ : *fishing ground.*
-stealla v. eaxl-, hand-, ofer-s.
steallere (a) m. *marshal, constable,* CHR, KC.
-steallian v. forð-s.
stēam (ē, īe) m. ' *steam,' moisture, exhalation,* Æ,Lcd,Pa : *steaming fluid, blood,* ROOD 62.
stēap I. *precipitous, deep : high, lofty, B, Rd : prominent, projecting,* Æ : *upright? B* 2566 : *bright, brilliant, Gn,Sol.* [' steep'] **II.** (ēo) m. *stoup, beaker, flagon.*
stēap-=stēop-
stēaphēah *very high,* RD 26⁴.
stēapol m. *cairn?* Ct (Swt).

stearc (a) *stiff, rigid, obstinate, Æ,El : stern, severe, hard, Æ : harsh, rough, strong, violent, impetuous, WW.* ['*stark*']

stearcferð *harsh, stern,* JUL636.

stearcheard *excessive,* DD200?

stearcheort† *stout-hearted,* B.

stearcian *to stiffen, become hard,* GPH402⁵⁶. ['*stark*']

stearclīce adv. *stoutly, strongly, vigorously, Chr* 1016D : *strictly,* CHRD54²⁶. ['*starkly*']

stearcmōd *stubborn,* CHRD8²⁷.

stearm (NG)=storm

stearn (æ, e) m. *sea-swallow? tern? Gl,Seaf.* ['*stern*']

stearra (DR)=steorra

steartlian *to kick, struggle,* OEG. ['*startle*']

stea-ðel, -ðul=staðol

steb=stybb; **stebn** (GL)=stefn

stēda m. *stud-horse, stallion, Æ : entire camel.* ['*steed*']

stede (y) m. *place, site, position, station, Æ, Bo,Ct,Lcd,RB*; CP; Mdf : *firmness, standing, stability, steadfastness, fixity, Æ : strangury.* of s. *immediately.* [standan; '*stead*']

stedefæst '*steadfast,' steady, firm, Ma,LL*; ÆL.

stedefæstnes (styd-) f. *constancy,* DR50².

stedeheard† *firm, strong,* JUD223 (or ?steðe-).

stedelēas *unsteady, unstable,* ÆL.

stedewang† m. *field, plain.*

stedewist f. *steadiness,* HGL530⁴.

+stēdhors n. *stud-horse, stallion,* BH 138CA¹.

stedig *sterile,* Æ,LPs.

+stedigian (e²) *to stand still,* ÆL31²⁴².

stedignes f. *sterility,* ERSPs34¹².

stedinglīne f. *stay (ship's rope),* WW.

stef-=stæf-, staf-; **stefen**=stefn I.

stefn (æ) I. f. *voice, sound,* Æ,CP. II. m. *message, summons, turn (of military service), time : a body of men who take a turn at work, the English military force?* (BT), KC5·121'. nīwan stefne *anew, again.* III. m. '*stem,' trunk, Bo,Sol :* foundation, root, Bo : *prow or stern of a vessel,* B,WW. [stæf]

stefna† (æ) m. *prow or stern of a ship,* An. ['*stem*']

stefnan I. (±) *to institute, arrange, regulate : alternate.* II. (+) *to provide with a fringe,* CM288.

stefnbyrd f. *control,* CREAT45.

stefnelof n. '*vociferatio,'* LPs26⁶.

stefnettan (mn) *to stand firm,* MA122.

stefnhlōw (mn) *vocalic,* BF100¹⁶.

±stefnian (w. d.) *to summon,* CHR, MFH 163.

stefning (mn) f. *border, hem,* WW : turn, shift, CHR894.

stefnmǣlum (mm) *alternately,* CM280.

stela (æ, eo) m. *stalk : support,* ÆT.

±stelan⁴ *to '* steal,' rob, Æ,Cp,LG,LL.

stēle (GL)=stȳle

stellan I. (y) *to place, put, set (example), AO,CP.* +stelled bēon mid *have an attack of,* GD. ['*stell*'] II.=stiellan

stelmēle m. *handled vessel,* LL455,17.

stelscofl (eo¹) f. *shovel with (long) handle?* GPH400⁴⁹⁸.

stem-=stefn-

stēm=stēam; **stēm-**=stīem-

steming=stemning

stemn (CP)=stefn

stempan *to pound,* LCD1·378'.

stempingīsern n. *stamping-iron,* WW.

+sten (æ) n. *groaning,* PPs30¹¹.

stenan *to groan,* PPs37⁹ : *rattle, clash,* EL 151.

stēnan=stǣnan

stenc m. *odour,* Æ,BH,Bl : *scent, fragrance,* CP : '*stench,' stink,* Æ,AO,BH. [stincan]

±stencan I. *to scatter :* afflict? PPs43³. II. *to stink,* JnL. ['*stench*'] III.? *to pant,* HGL.

stencbǣre *stinking,* BH48¹⁷.

stencbrengende *odoriferous,* DR77'.

+stence (æ) *odoriferous,* LCD1·282'.

stencfæt n., pl. -fatu *smelling bottle,* OEG 8²⁹⁹.

±stencnes f. *odour,* DR.

stenecian *to pant,* OEG6⁵. [stenan]

steng m. *stake, pole, bar, rod, staff, cudgel, Cp,LG,MH*; CP. ['*sting*'; v. Mdf]

stent pres. 3 sg. of standan.

steol-=stel-

stēold pret. 3 sg. of stealdan.

stēop=stēap

stēopbearn n. *orphan, Æ.* ['*stepbairn*']

stēopcild (ē, ēa) n. *orphan, unprotected one, Bl,Jn.* ['*stepchild*']

stēopdohtor (ē) f. '*step-daughter,' WW,* RWH139¹².

stēopfæder m. '*step-father,' AO,Ep.*

stēopmōdor f. '*step-mother,' AO,Cp.*

stēopsunu m. '*step-son,' AO,Cp,WW.*

stēor I. (ȳ) f. *steering, direction, guidance, Æ,BH : rule, regulation, Æ : restraint, discipline, correction,* Æ,CP : *penalty, fine, punishment,* Æ,CP. ['*steer*'] II. m. '*steer,' bullock, young cow,* Gl.

stēora (īe, īo, ȳ) m. *steersman, pilot, guider, director,* CP. ['*steer*']

stēoran=stīeran

stēorbord n. '*starboard,' AO.*

stēore f. *direction, discipline,* LL.

stēorend (ȳ) m. *corrector, director, ruler,* AN.

stēorere m. *steersman,* CP431³¹.

stēoresmann (*LL*)=stēormann ['*steers-man*']

steorfa m. *pestilence* : *carrion*, LL.

steorfan³ *to die*, ÆH. ['*starve*']

steorglēaw *clever at astronomy*, OEG.

stēorlēas *not under control or rule, wild, profligate, foolish*, Bo. ['*steerless*']

stēorlēaslic *unmanageable*, GD 289¹⁰.

stēormann m. *pilot, master of a ship*, Æ. ['*steerman*']

stēornægl m. *handle of a helm*, WW 312⁴?

steornede *having a bold forehead?* WW. [cp. *Ger.* stirn]

stēoroxa m. *steer*, WW 120²⁶.

steorra m. '*star*,' Chr,Lcd,VPs.

stēorrēðra m. *steersman, master of a ship*, BL.

stēor-rōðer, -rōðor n. '*rudder*,' Cp; CP.

steorscēawere m. *astronomer, astrologer*, WW.

stēorscēofol f. *rudder*, WW.

stēorsetl n. *steersman's seat, after-part of a ship*, Æ.

stēorsprēc (=ǣ) *reproof*, RPs 37¹⁵.

stēorstefn m. *stern (of ship)*, WW 482¹⁵.

steort (e) sm. *tail*, Cp,Bo : *spit of land, cape* : *plough-tail*. ['*start*']

stēor-weorð, -wierðe *blameworthy, reprehensible*, CP 194,195³.

steorwigle n. *astrology*, GL.

steorwiglere m. *mathematician, astrologer*, OEG 55⁸.

steorwiglung f. *astrology*, A 13·33¹⁴¹.

step-=stæp-; stēp-=stēop-

stēpan† I. (±) *to erect, raise* : *elevate, exalt, honour, adorn, enrich* : (+) *help, support*. [stēap] II. (±) *to initiate, consecrate*, WW.

stēpel=stīpel

stēr=stǣr

stēran I. *to burn incense* : *fumigate*, Æ,Lcd. ['*stere*'] II.=stīeran

stercedferhð† (æ) *stout of heart, determined, bold, brave*.

stēring f. *incense*, OEG 1512.

stermelda m. *informer? complainant?* LL 9,5; v. 2·202.

stern=stearn; sterra (N)=steorra

stert=steort; sterung=styrung

stēða (WW)=stēda

steðeheard? *hardened on the anvil*, JUD 223 (v. ES 64·212).

stēup- (Ep)=stēop-

stī-=stig-; stic-=stycce-

sticādl f. *pain in the side, stitch*, WW 112²².

sticca m. '*stick*,' Lcd : *peg, pointer* : *spoon*, Lcd.

sticce I. n. *sticky matter*, LCD. II.=stycce

sticcian=stician

±stice m. *sting, prick, puncture, stab*, CP, LL : '*stitch*,' *pain in the side*, Lcd.

sticel I. m. *prick, goad, thorn*, CP. II.=sticol

sticels (Æ)=sticel

sticfōdder n. *case for spoons? or made of twigs?* LL 455,17.

stician (y) (±) tr. *to '*stick*,' prick, stab, transfix, goad, gouge out*, AO,BH,MH; CP : *kill* : intr. *stick, inhere, be placed, lie, remain fixed, be hampered*, Æ,Bo; CP : *project*, KC.

sticmǣlum (Æ)=styccemǣlum

stic-ol, -ul *lofty, sharp, abrupt, steep*, Æ : *arduous, rough* : *scaly* : *biting*, GPH 417.

sticolnes (y²) f. *height*, OEG 4437.

stictǣnel m. *basket*, WW 403².

sticung f. *pricking, goading, stabbing*, AO.

sticwærc m. *stitch in the side*, WW 112²¹.

sticwyrt f. *agrimony*, WW 136²¹.

stīegan=stīgan

stiell m. *jump, leap, spring*, CR 720–736.

±stiellan I. (æ, e, i, y) *to leap, rush* : *attack*, GD. II. (y) *to make stalls for cattle? or to put them in stalls?* LL 454,11¹³.

stiem=stēam

stieman (ē, ȳ) *to emit vapour, '*steam*,' exhale (odour)*, Æ,Ph. [stēam]

stieme (ī) *a plant?* LCD 3·32¹⁹?

stieming (ē) f. *fragrance*, OEG.

stiep m. *downfall?* GEN 60?

-stiepan (ē, ēa, ēo, ȳ) v. ā-s.

stiera=stēora

±stieran (ēo, ī, ȳ) *to '*steer*,' guide, direct, govern, rule*, Æ,BH,Bo,CP : (w. d. or g.) *restrain, correct, reprove, punish*, Bl,Lcd, MkL; Æ,AO,CP. [stēor]

-stierfan (æ, e, y) v. ā-s.

stiern-=styrn-

stiernes (ȳ) f. *discipline*, Æ.

stiernlice (CP) v. styrnlice.

stif *rigid, '*stiff*,'* GPH 394.

stifearh m. *little pig (kept in a sty)*, LL 449,7. [stig]

stifian *to be or become rigid*, ÆGR.

stific|an=stȳfecian

stifig *steep*, BC (Mdf).

stig n. *sty, pen* : *hall*, Ct,GL.

stig fm. *narrow path, way, footpath, track, road, course, line*, B,G,Ps. ['*sty*']

±stigan¹ *to move, go, reach* : *go up, spring up, ascend, rise, mount, scale*, Bo,VPs; AO,CP : *go down, descend*, Æ,CP. ['*sty*']

stige m. *ascent, descent*, MEN 64.

stig-el (-ol) f. '*stile*,' Ct,GD 24.

stigelhamm m. *enclosure reached by a stile*, KC 5·289².

stīgend I. m. *stye (on the eye)*, WW 114¹⁰. ['*styan*'] II. m. *sailor*, v. OEG 32n.

stigian *to shut into a '*sty*,'* Bf.

stīgnes f. *descent*, LkL 19³⁷.

stigrāp m. 'stirrup,' WW.

stigu=stig

stig-weard, -wita=stī-weard, -wita

stihl=stigel

+stiht n. dispensation, provision, VH 20.

stihtan (±) to rule, direct, arrange, order, ordain, AO,CP : instigate. [Ger. stiften]

stihtend (y) m. disposer, JUL 419 : protector, RPs 58¹².

stihtere m. director, ruler, CP 391²² : steward, GD 221¹⁹.

stihtian (CP)=stihtan

±stihtung f. arrangement, direction, dispensation, providence, AO.

stīhð pres. 3 sg. of stīgan.

stileð=stylð pres. 3 sg. of stelan.

±stillan (y) I. to be still, have rest, Ma : (w. d. or a.) 'still' ('i-still'), quiet, calm, appease, hush, An,BH,Gen,LL : stop, restrain, abate, relieve, Lcd. II.=stiellan

stille adj. adv. 'STILL,' quiet, calm, stable, fixed : gentle, Æ; CP : silent, Æ : secret.

stilles=stilnes

stillīce adv. silently, CM 266.

stil(l)nes (AO,CP) f. 'stillness,' quiet, Æ, Bo : silence, HL : peace, AO,CP : release, relaxation, CP.

stīme=stīeme

stincan³ to emit a smell, 'stink,' exhale, ÆGr, Cp,Lcd; AO : sniff, B 2289 : rise (of dust, vapour, etc.), RD 30¹².

+stincan³ tr. to smell, CP : have the sense of smell, PPs. ['i-stink']

sting (y) m. 'sting,' puncture, thrust, BH, Guth.

stingan³ I. to 'sting,' stab, pierce, push through, thrust, Bo,Ma; CP. st. on lay claim to, usurp. II.=stincan

stintan=styntan; stīora=stēora

stiorc=stirc

stīpel (ē, ȳ) m. 'steeple,' tower, Æ,Mt. [stēap]

stīpere m. post, prop, WW 126¹¹.

+stīr-=+stȳr; stir-=styr-

stīran=stīeran; stīrāp=stigrāp

stirc (io, y) n. calf, Æ,GL.

stirgan=styrian; stītian=stihtan

stīð stiff, thick, rigid, hard, firm, strong, CP : resolute, brave, Æ : stubborn, unrelenting, austere, strict, fierce, harsh, cruel, CP; Æ. ['stith']

stīðe I. adv. very much, strongly, well : harshly, strictly, severely, bitterly, Gen; Æ. ['stith'] II. f. name of a plant, LCD 160b.

stīðecg stiff-edged, RD 88¹⁴.

stīðferhð† determined, stern.

stīðhycgende† (-hug-) determined, resolute, brave : stern, obstinate.

stīðhȳdig† determined, resolute.

stīðhygd determined, resolute, JUL 654.

+stīðlan to become hard : become strong, grow up, mature, Æ : make firm, CP.

stīðlic firm, stout, strong, hard : decided : harsh, stern, severe, Æ,CP. adv. -līce forcibly, BF 94¹³.

stīðmægen n. powerful force, DD 114.

stīðmōd† resolute, brave, firm, unflinching, stubborn, stern, severe.

stīðnes f. hardness, rigidity, strictness, severity, rigour, Æ : firmness, constancy, Æ.

stīðweg m. rough way, RD 4³⁵.

stīweard m. 'steward,' housekeeper, guardian, WW. [stig-]

stīwita m. housekeeper? householder? GEN 2079; RD 4¹⁰.

stoc n. place, house, dwelling, GD (v. ES 37·191). ['stoke']

stocc m. 'stock,' stump, stake, post, log, Æ, Bl,OET ; Mdf : stocks : trumpet, MtL 6².

stoccen made of logs? KC 3·73'.

stoclīf n. dwelling-place, city, AS.

stocweard m. citizen, OEG 5272.

stocwīc n. dwelling-place, GD 172⁴.

stod mf. post, WW 106³³.

-stod v. wealh-s.

stōd I. f. 'stud' (of horses), KC,WW; Mdf. II. pret. 3 sg. of standan.

stōdfald m. stud-fold, paddock, Ct.

stōdhors n. stud-horse, stallion, BH 138¹. [v. 'steed']

stodla m. (weaver's) slay, LL 455,15¹.

stōdmyre (e²) f. brood-mare, LL 58,16. ['studmare']

stōdon pret. pl. of standan.

stōdðēof m. horse-stealer, LL 54,9².

stofa, stofu, mf. bath-room, GL. [v. 'stove']

stofbæð (u¹) n. vapour-bath, LCD.

stofn mf. trunk, stem, branch, shoot, OEG, WW : progeny, OEG : station, position. ['stoven']

+stogen pp. of +stīgan at MFB 208.

stōl m. 'stool,' chair, seat, CP,Cp,G,Gen, Lcd,LL : throne : bishop's see.

stole fn. 'stole,' long outer garment, DR, NG. [L.]

stolen pp. of stelan.

stom=stam

stonc=stanc pret. 3 sg. of stincan.

stond=stand

stōp pret. 3 sg. of steppan.

stōpel m. footprint, BL 127.

stoppa m. bucket, pail, GD,Gl. ['stop']

-stoppian v. for-s. ['stop']

stōr I. m. incense, frankincense, Æ. [L. storax] II. strong, great, Chr 1085. ['stour']

storc m. 'stork,' Æ,Gl.

stōr-cille, -cyl(le) f. censer, Æ.

stōrfæt n. *censer*, IM 120¹⁴.

storm m. *tempest*, '*storm*,' *Lcd,LG,VPs* : (†) *rush, onrush, attack, tumult, disturbance, An,B*; CP.

stormig *stormy*, OEG?,RWH 66¹⁵ (storem-).

stormsǣ *stormy sea*, Bo 115²².

stōrsæp n. *resin*, OEG 4027.

stōrsticca m. *rod for stirring the incense in the censer?* (BT), EC 250,21.

stot m. *a kind of horse*, v. *NC* 323. ['*stot*']

stōw f. *spot, site, station, locality, position, B,Bo*; Æ,AO,CP; Mdf : (*holy*) *place*, LL. ['*stow*']

stōwigan *to retain, restrain*, Cp 1713.

stōwlic *local, limited by space*, Æ. adv. -līce *as regards place*, Æ.

strāc pret. 3 sg. of strīcan.

strācian *to* '*stroke*,' *CP,Lcd*.

strācung f. *stroking*, WW 179⁹.

strād (1) pret. 3 sg. of strīdan; (2)=strēad

strǣc (ǣ? e) I. *firm, strict, severe, stern, rigid, obstinate, hard*, Æ,CP : *strenuous, vehement, violent*, Æ. [streccan] II. n. *rigour* : *violence, force*, Æ.

strǣclic *strict*, CP. adv. -līce *strictly, severely, vehemently, violently*, CP.

strǣcnes (e) f. *pertinacity* : *rigidity, rigour*, GD.

strǣde f. *pace*, MtL 5⁴¹.

strǣdon pret. pl. of strēdan.

strǣgd pret. 3 sg. of stregdan.

strǣgdnes f. *aspersion*, BH 446¹⁵.

strǣgl=strǣl II.

strǣl I. fm. *arrow, dart, missile*. [Ger. strahl] II. f. *curtain, quilt, matting, bed, Gl*. ['*strail*']

strǣlbora m. *archer*, WW.

strǣle f.=strǣl I.

strǣllan *to shoot* (*an arrow*), RPs 63⁵.

strǣlwyrt f. *name of a plant*, LCD 36b.

strǣngō (VPs)=strengō

strǣt I. f. '*street*,' *high road, B,Ct,G,OET*; Æ,CP; Mdf. [*L. strata (via)*] II. f. *bed*, CPs. [*L. stratum*]

strǣtlanu f. *street*, NC 323.

strǣttweard (ē) f. *waywarden*, LL.

strand n. '*strand*,' *sea-shore, G,KC*; Æ.

strang (o) comp. strengra, superl. strengest (from strenge) '*STRONG*,' *powerful, able, firm, bold, brave*, Æ,CP : *constant, resolute, strenuous* : *strict, severe, AO* : CP : *arduous* : *violent*.

strange adv. comp. strangor, superl. strangost *strongly, violently, furiously, severely, BH,Met*. ['*strong*']

stranghynde *strong of hand*, ÆT 473.

±**strangian** *to strengthen, confirm*, Æ,Bl; AO,CP : *be strong, prevail*, Æ,VPs : *press* (*after*) RWH 86²⁵. ['*strong*']

stranglic *strong, stout, firm, solid, sound, robust*, Æ : *severe*. adv. -līce *strongly, firmly, stoutly, boldly, bravely*, Æ,CP : *fiercely, violently, MH*.

strangmōd *resolute*, RB 138²⁸.

strangnes f. *strength, power, force*, Lk, Ps.

±**strangung** f. *strengthening, quickening, nourishing*, Æ : *vigour*, Æ.

strapulas mp. *breeches*, WW 125².

strāwberige=strēawberige

strē (N), strēa=strēaw

streac=stearc

strēad pret. 3 sg. of strūdan.

streaht pp. of streccan.

strēal=strǣl

strēam m. '*stream*,' *flood, current, river, Bl, Bo,G,GD,Lcd*; AO,CP : (†) pl. *sea*.

strēamfaru f. *rush of water*, AN 1578.

strēamgewinn n. *strife of waters*, RD 4²⁶.

strēamlic *of water*, ÆH 1·444¹⁰.

strēamracu f. *water-course, channel*, AN, WW.

strēamrād f. *course of a stream*, GL : *sea-path*, CRA.

strēamrynes adv. *flowing like a stream*, Æ.

strēamstæð n. *shore*, GEN 1434.

strēamweall m. *shore*, GEN 1494.

strēamwelm m. *surging stream*, AN 495.

strēaw (ē, ēo) n. '*straw*,' *hay*, Æ,Lcd.

strēaw-berige, -beriewīse f. '*strawberry*,' *Lcd,WW*.

strēawian=strewian; **strec** (Æ)=stræc

strec-=stræc-

streccan (±) *to stretch* ('*i-stretche*'), *spread out, prostrate, BH,G,Lcd* : *reach, extend*, Æ.

streccanmōd *persistent*, ÆP 80¹⁰.

strecednes f. *bed, couch*, LPs.

streclic=stræclic

strēdan³ (and wv; pret. 3 sg. strēdde, pp. strēded, strēd)=stregdan

strēgan *to strew*, Seaf 97. ['*stray*']

stregdan³ (and wv.) pret. strǣgd, strugdon (wk. stregde), pp. strogden (wk. stregd, strēdd) *to strew, sprinkle, disperse, scatter, straggle* : *to spread, extend*.

strēgl=strǣl II.

strehte pret. 3 sg. of streccan.

strēl=strǣl; **strēn**=strēowen

strēnan=strīenan

streng I. m. '*string*,' *cord, rope, ligature, sinew, An,AS,B,G,Lcd*. in pl. *tackle, rigging* : *lineage, race*. II.=strengu

±**strengan** *to strengthen*, LkL. +strenged *formed, made*, OEG 46⁸.

strenge *severe*, GEN 60. [v. strang]

strengel m. *ruler, chief*, B 3115. [strang]

strengest (AO,CP) v. strang.

strenglic *strong, firm*, GEN 273. adv. -līce.

strengra (*Bo*; Æ,AO,CP) v. strang. ['*strenger*']

strengð, strengðu f. 'STRENGTH,' *force, vigour* : *ability, superiority* : *firmness, fortitude, Æ* : *manhood, mature years* : *violence, ApT.*

strengu f. *strength, power, vigour, ability, B,VPs*; CP : *firmness, fortitude,* CP : *virtue.* ['*strengh*']

strenð (KGL)=strengð

strēon I. (±) n. *gain, acquisition, property, treasure, AO,LG,WW*; Æ,CP : *traffic, usury* : *procreation, Æ.* ['*i-streon*,' v. '*strain*'] II.=strēowen

strēonan=strīenan

+**strēones** (ēu) f. *petty gain,* GPH 389.

+**strēonful** *costly, valuable, precious, Æ.*

strēow=strēaw

strēowen (ē) f. *resting-place, couch, bed,* BH.

strēowian=strewian

strēownes f. *mattress, bedding,* BL 227.

strēt I. pres. 3 sg. of strēdan. II.=strǣt

strēw=strēaw; **strēwen**=strēowen

±**strewian** (ēa, ēo) *to* '*strew*,' *scatter, Bl*; CP.

strewung f. *what one lies on, bedding,* LPs 131³.

±**stric** n. *plague? strife? sedition?* LCD,LL,W.

strica m. *stroke, line, mark, Æ.* ['*streak*']

±**strīcan¹** *to pass lightly over the surface, stroke, rub, wipe,* Lcd : *move, go, run,* Met. ['*strike*']

stricel m. I. *fount, breast,* GL. II. *implement for smoothing corn in a measure? rope?* (ES 43·325), Cp 266 т.

strīchrægl n. *a cloth for wiping?* CC 23²¹.

+**strician** *to knit together, mend,* MtL 4²¹.

strīdan¹ *to* '*stride*,' *Gl.* up on s. *mount (a horse),* GD 81²⁰.

stride m. '*stride*,' *step,* Cp 134 P.

±**strīenan** (ēo, ī, ȳ) *to acquire, gain, amass,* CP : *beget, AO,Mt*; CP : *increase, augment?* CP. ['*strene*']

+**strīenendlic** (e, y) *begetting,* OEG : *genitive,* ÆGR.

strigdeð pres. 3 sg. of stregdan.

strīman⁴ *to resist, oppose,* Cp.

strīna (=īe) m. *acquirer,* v. OEG 27¹.

strīnan=strīenan

strīnend (ēo;=īe) m. *acquirer,* ES 39·352.

-**strīpan** (y) v. be-s.

stripligan '*perfringere*'? v. OEG 46²¹.

strīð m. *strife, struggle, fight, contest, dispute, contention* : *opposition, antagonism,* HEXC 328 D. [OS.]

stroccian *to stroke,* NC 323.

+**strod** n. *plunder, robbery,* BH : *confiscation,* WW.

strōd n. *marshy land (covered with bushes or trees?)* BC (Mdf); PST 95/98,537.

stroden pp. of strūdan.

strōden, strogden pp. of stregdan.

±**strogdnes** f. *scattering, sprinkling,* DR.

strong=strang

strop '*struppus*,' (*oar-*)*thong, strap,* WW 181⁴². ['*strop*']

strosle (GD 100¹⁹)=ðrosle

-**strowennes** v. ā-s.

+**strud** (GD 162³²)=+strod

±**strūdan²** *to ravage, spoil, plunder, carry off.*

strūdend m. *robber* : *money-lender,* WW.

strūdere m. *robber,* GL,VH.

strūdgendlīce *greedily,* CHRD 108¹⁸.

±**strūdian** *to plunder,* NC 296,324.

strūdung f. *spoliation, robbery,* LL,W.

strugde (NG) wk. pret. 3 sg. of stregdan.

strūta (WW)=strȳta

strūtian *to stand out stiffly, struggle,* ÆL 32²⁰⁸. ['*strut*']

strūtnian (ÆL 23²⁶⁸)=scrūtnian

+**strȳdan** *to rob, deprive,* LL.

+**strȳdd**=+strēdd pp. of stregdan.

strȳdere=strȳndere

strȳn-=strīen-, strīn-

strȳnd (=īe) f. *generation, line of inheritance, race, stock, tribe, BH,DR,LG* : *gain,* WW 488³⁰. ['*strind*']

strȳndan *to waste,* WW.

strȳndere m. *squanderer, prodigal,* WW.

+**strynge** m. *wrestler,* WW 465⁴⁰.

strȳta (ū) m. *ostrich,* WW 48⁸⁷. [*L.* struthio]

stubb=stybb

stūc *heap,* ES 11·512.

studdian *to look after, be careful for,* RWH 136¹⁷.

studding f. *care, trouble, labour,* MFB 107 and n.

studu f., gs. stude, ds. styde (also indecl. in sg.), nap. styde *column, pillar, post, buttress, BH,WW.* ['*stud*']

stufbæð=stofbæð

stulor *stealthy, stolen, Æ.* adv. -līce, Æ.

+**stun** n. *din, crash, whirlwind,* CR,WW.

stuncen pp., stuncon pret. pl. of stincan.

stund f. *short space of time, moment, period, time, An,Met* : *hard time, Rd* : *hour* : *signal.* stunde *now, at once, from time to time* (v. also stundum). ['*stound*']

+**stund** n. *noise,* GUTH 36²⁸ (=+stun).

-**stundian** v. ā-s.

stundmǣlum adv. *from time to time, gradually, Æ* : *time after time, alternately, Æ,ZDA.* ['*stoundmeal*']

stundum adv. *from time to time, at times, Æ* : *with effort, laboriously, eagerly, fiercely, Æ.* [dp. of stund]

stungen pp., stungon pret. pl. of stingan.

stunian *to crash, resound, roar* : *impinge, dash.*

stunra (KGL69³¹)=stuntra gp. of stunt.
stunt *dull, stupid, foolish,* Æ.
stuntlīc *stupid, foolish,* Æ. adv. -līce, Æ.
stuntnes f. *stupidity, folly,* Æ.
stuntscipe m. *foolishness,* Mk7²².
stuntspr̄ēc f. *silly talk* (BT).
stuntspr̄ēce *talking foolishly,* Sc97¹⁰.
stuntwyrde *talking foolishly,* W72¹⁷.
stūpian *to 'stoop,' AO : slope,* Lcd.
sturtende (DR57¹²)=styrtende
stūt m. *gnat,* WW. ['*stout*']
stuðansceaft m. *prop,* AS1¹,¹⁰.
stuðu=studu
stybb m. *stump,* ÆGr,KC,WW; Mdf. ['*stub*']
stycce (i) n. *piece, portion, bit, fragment,* Æ : *mite (small piece of money).* ymbe st. *after a short time.* [*Ger.* stück]
styccem̄ēlum adv. *piecemeal, little by little, by degrees, gradually : to bits, to pieces,* AO : *here and there,* AO.
stycian=stician
styde I.=stede. II. v. studu.
styfician (i¹) *to root up, extirpate,* Lcd3·184'.
styficlēah *a clearing in a wood,* BC3·694¹⁰ (v. PST95/98·541).
styficung (e²) f. *clearing (land)?* Ct.
styhtan=stihtan
stȳlan (=īe) *to harden, attemper,* Cr679. ['*steeled*']
stȳle (ē) n. *'steel,' B,Gl.*
stȳlecg *steel-edged,* B1533.
stȳlen† *of steel, hard as steel,* Sol; VH. ['*steelen*']
styll=stiell
styllan (1)=stiellan; (2)=stillan
±styltan *to be amazed, dazed, hesitate,* NG.
stylð pres. 3 sg. of stelan.
stȳman=stīeman; **styng**=sting
stynt=stent pres. 3 sg. of standan.
styntan *to make dull, stupefy,* Cp89H. [stunt]
+stynðo *coercion,* NC296.
stȳpel=stīpel
stȳr=stēor; **styra**=styria
stȳran=(1) stīeran; (2) stēran
styrc=stirc; **stȳrend**=stēorend
styrenes f. *power of motion, movement : disturbance, tumult :* (+) *tribulation,* DR.
styrfig adj. *belonging to an animal which died of disease,* LL. [storfe]
styrfð pres. 3 sg. of steorfan.
styrgan=styrian
styria, styr(i)ga (i) m. *name of a fish, sturgeon,* Gl. [*Ger.* stör]
±styrian (i) *to 'STIR,' move* (tr. and intr.), *rouse, agitate, excite, urge,* CP : *cause : tell, rehearse,* B873.
styric=stirc
styrigendlic *moving,* Æ : *mobile,* GD149³¹.

styring=styrung
styrman *to storm, roar, rage, cry out, shout,* B,BH,Bo. ['*sturme*']
styrne (=ie) *'stern,' grave, strict, hard, severe, cruel,* Gen,Gl,W.
styrnenga adv. *inexorably,* Sol282.
styrnlic (ie) *hard, severe, harsh.* adv. -līce, CP.
styrnmōd *stern of mood,* Jud227.
styrtan *to 'start,' leap up.* only in pres. ptc. sturtende (=styrtende), DR57¹².
styrung (e) f. *moving, motion,* Bf,Bo,G; CP : *disturbance, commotion,* G : *exercise.* ['*stirring*']
styðe ds. and nap. of stuðu (studu).
sū f. *sow.* [=sugu]
suā=swā
subdīacon m. *subdeacon,* Æ,BH.
sūcan² *to 'suck,'* Æ,Lk,PPs,VHy.
sucga=sugga; **sucht-,** suct-=suht-
sudon pret. pl. of sēoðan.
sue-=swe-
sufel, suf(o)l n. *relish eaten with bread* (v. LL2·754), Jn,RB. ['*sowl*']
+sufel, sufl adj. *with a relish added to it? (of bread),* Ct,LL.
suflmete m. *delicacy, relish,* GD201²⁶.
sufon (Bf48⁹)=seofon
sūftlēre=swiftlēre
sūgan² *to suck, suck in,* CP : *have hiccough?* Lcd.
sugga m. *a kind of bird, titlark? wagtail?* Gl.
±sugian *to be or become silent,* AO. [cp. swīgian]
sugu f. *'sow,'* Cp,CP; Æ.
suht (y) f. *illness,* Gen472.
suhterga† m. *brother's son, nephew : uncle's son, cousin,* WW.
suhtergefædera̧n, suhtorfædran† mp. *uncle and nephew.*
suhtriga=suhterga
suindr- (NG)=syndr-
sūl (Æ), sulh (AO) sfm., gs. sūle(s), ds. sylg (CP), syl(h), as. sūl, sulh; nap. sylh, syll (Æ), gp. sūla, dp. sūlum *plough,* Lcd,LG : *furrow, gully : a measure of land* (Mdf). ['*sullow*']
sūlerēost *rest (part of a plough),* WW219⁶.
sulf=sufl
sulfer, sulfern (DR)=seolfor, seolfren
sulhæcer m. *a strip of land for ploughing,* LL450,9¹.
sulhælmesse f. *ecclesiastical tax on ploughed land,* LL.
sulhandla m. *plough tail,* WW. [v. '*sullow*']
sulhbēam m. *plough tail,* WW. [v. '*beam*']
sulhgang m. *the land which can be gone over by one plough in a day,* W170³⁷.
sulhgesīdu np. *ploughing tackle,* LL455¹⁷.

sulhgetēog n. *ploughing implements*, LCD 1·400¹⁹. [cp. *Ger.* zeug]
sulhgeweorc n. *plough-making*, GEN 1086.
sulhhæbbere m. *ploughman*, WW 495¹⁹.
sūlincel n. *small furrow*, WW 348³³.
sull, suluh=sūl
sulung n. *in Kent, the fiscal unit corresponding to the hide (or carucate in other counties)* (NED) *Ct,LL*. ['*suling*']
sum indef. pron. (used substantively w. g.) *a certain one, some one, something, one.* sixa s. *one of six* : (used adjectivally) *a certain*, 'SOME,' *any, Æ,AO*. sume...sume *some...others*. hit...sum...sum...*part of it...the rest...* : (used adverbially) *about*. s. hund *about a hundred*. sumes, s. on dǣle *to some extent, somewhat*.
sumar, sumer=sumor
sumdǣl *somewhat, some portion. Cp.* ['*somedeal*']
sūmnes f. *delay*, MtL 25¹⁹. [cp. *Ger.* versäumnis]
sumor m., gs. sumeres, ds. sumera, sumere '*summer*,' *Bo,Chr,Gn,Ph,VPs*; AO.
sumorbōc=sumorrǣdingbōc
sumorhāt n. *summer heat*, RIM 67.
sumorhǣte f. *summer heat*, AO,RB.
sumorhūs n. *summer-house*, ÆL 36⁹⁸.
sumorlǣcan *to draw on towards summer*, ÆH 1·614.
sumorlang† *summer-long, of the length of a summer's day.*
sumorlic *of summer*, *Lcd,WW*. ['*summerly*']
sumorlida I. m. *summer army or expedition (one which only comes for the summer)*, CHR 871. [līðan] **II.** (=-loda) m. *shoot, twig*, WW 450³⁰ (v. A 13·330).
sumormæsse f. *midsummer* (Swt).
sumorrǣdingbōc (e²) f. *summer lectionary*, TC 430¹⁶.
sumorselde f. *summer-house*, WW 184¹.
sumsende *swishing (of rain)*, RD 4⁴⁷.
sumswēge=samswēge
sumur=sumor
sunbēam mf. '*sunbeam*,' *Æ* : *sunshine*.
sunbearu m. *sunny grove*, PH 33.
sunbeorht *bright with sunshine*, PH 436.
sunbryne m. *sunburn*, LCD.
suncen pp., suncon pret. pl. of sincan.
sund n. *swimming, Æ,B,AO* : *capacity for swimming* : (†) *sea, ocean, water*. ['*sound*']
+sund *sound ('i-sound'), safe, whole, uninjured, healthy, prosperous, Æ,B*.
sundampre (o²) *dock (plant)*, LCD 44a.
sund-būende†, -buend mp. *sea-dwellers, man, mankind*.
sundcorn n. *saxifrage*, LCD,WW.
sundēaw *rosemary? sundew?* WW 301⁷.

+sundelic (WW 496²⁴)=+syndiglic
sunder=sundor
sunderanweald m. *monarchy*, ES 11·66.
sunderboren *reckoned apart*, OEG 26¹⁷.
sunderfolgoð m. *official teachership*, AO 286⁵.
sunder-frēodōm, -frēols m. *privilege*, Ct.
sunderlīpes *separately, specially*, *OEG,RBL*. ['*sunderlepes*']
sundermǣlum *separately, singly*, OEG.
sundermēd f. *private meadow*, Ct.
sunderstōw f. *special place*, Bo 80².
+sundful *sound, whole, healthy* : *prosperous, Æ,Ps*. ['*i-sundfull*']
+sundfullian *to prosper*, Ps.
+sundfullic *sound, safe, sure*. adv. -līce *safely, prosperously, Æ*.
±sundfulnes f. *health,prosperity, Æ,Bo,CP* : *safety*, BYH 126⁸.
sundgebland n. *commingled sea, surge*, B 1450.
sundgyrd (e²) f. *sounding-rod*, WW.
sundhelm† m. *covering of water, sea*, RD.
sundhengest† m. *sea-horse, ship*, CR.
sundhwæt *good at swimming*, WHALE 57.
+sundig (y) *favourable*, BH 386¹³Ca.
+sund(ig)lic (y) *prosperous*, BH : *safe*, GD 348¹⁰ : *healthy*. adv. -līce.
sundlīne f. *sounding-line, lead*, WW.
sundmere m. *swimming-bath*, WW.
sundnytt f. *use of the power of swimming*, B 2360.
sundor adv. *asunder, apart* : *severally* : *differently*.
sundor- v. also sunder-, synder-.
sundorcræft m. *special power or capacity*.
sundorcræftiglīce *with special skill*, BHCA 324³.
sundorcȳððu f. *special knowledge* LL (322³²).
sundorfeoh n. *private property*, Ct.
sundorgecynd n. *special quality*, PA 30.
sundorgenga m. *solitary (animal)*, BL 199⁵.
sundorgerēfland n. *land reserved to the jurisdiction of a 'gerēfa'?* WW 421¹¹.
sundorgifu f. *special gift, privilege*, Bo,GL.
sundorhālga m. *Pharisee, Æ*.
sundorland n. *private property*, GD,WW.
sundorlic *special*, Bo; CP 409¹⁰. adv. -līce *apart, Æ,Bo,LG*. ['*sunderly*']
sundorlīf n. *life in seclusion*, BH 294⁴.
sundormæsse f. *separate mass, special mass*, BK 27'; RSL 11·486.
sundornotu f. *special office*, LL 456,2.
sundornytt f. *special use, office, or service*, CP.
sundorriht n. *special right, privilege*, WW.
sundorseld (u²) n. *special seat, throne*, VPs.
sundorsetl n. *hermitage*, GUTH.

sundorsprǣc f. *private conversation, private conference,* Æ,AO,CP.

sundor-weorðung, -weorðmynt f. *special honour, prerogative.*

sundorwíc n. *separate dwelling,* BH262¹⁴.

sundorwine m. *bosom friend,* FT29.

sundorwís *specially wise,* EL588.

sundorwundor n. *special wonder,* MOD2.

sundoryrfe n. *private inheritance,* PPs 67¹⁰.

sundplega† m. *sporting in the waves, bathing.*

sundrǣp m. *sounding line, lead,* WW358¹⁷.

sundreced n. *sea-house, ark,* GEN1335.

+**sundrian**=+syndrian. ['*sunder*']

sundrum (on) adv. *singly, separately, apart: continuously,* CM211.

sundur=sundor

sundwudu† m. (*sea-wood*), *ship.*

suner (MtR)=sunor

sunfeld m. *Elysian fields,* SOL(K),WW.

sunfolgend '*solisequia*,' *marigold? heliotrope?* GL.

sunganges adv. *moving with the sun,* LL.

sungen pp. of (1) singan; (2) swingan.

sungíhte *solstice,* MH104¹⁹,²¹.

sungon pret. pl. of singan.

sunhät '*soliflua*,' OEG56²⁰⁵.

sunlíc *solar, of the sun,* Æ.

sunna m. '*SUN*,' Æ.

Sunnadæg (N)=sunnandæg

Sunnanǣfen m. *eve of Sunday, Saturday.* [*Ger.* Sonnabend]

sunnancorn *gromel* (*plant*), LCD1·314¹⁸?

Sunnandæg m. '*Sunday**,' Bl,G,LL; Æ.

sunnanléoma m. *ray of light, sunbeam,* GD 171,172.

Sunnanmergen m. *Sunday morning,* ÆL 31¹³⁷¹.

Sunnanniht f. *Saturday night,* Æ : *Sunday,* LL52,5⁶.

sunnanscíma m. *sunshine,* MFH173.

sunnansetlgong m. *sunset,* CHR773.

Sunnanúhta m. *Sunday morning* (*early*), *early service time,* Æ,LL.

sunnb-=sunb-

sunne f. '*SUN*,' Æ,AO,CP.

sunnebéam=sunbéam

sunneléoma (RWH147¹¹)=sunnanléoma

sunnon pret. pl. of sinnan.

sunnu=sunne

sunor (e²) fn. *herd of swine,* NG.

sunsceadu f. *veil,* WW239¹⁹.

sunscíene *radiant,* JUL229.

sunscín *mirror,* WW519⁴.

sunset n. *west,* NG.

sunstede m. *solstice,* BF,LCD.

sunsunu? m. *grandson,* v. LL460,11n.

sunu m., gds. suna '*SON*,' *descendant,* Æ : *the Son : young of animals.*

sunucennicge f. *mother,* DR.

sunusunu=sunsunu

sunwlitig *fair with sunshine,* GNC7.

±**súpan²** *to swallow, sip, taste,* '*sup*,' *drink,* Æ,CP,Lcd,LG,Ps : (+) *sop up, absorb.*

súr '*sour*,' *tart, acid,* BC,Lcd : *made sour, fermented,* Lcd,WW.

súre f. *sorrel,* LCD,GL.

súr-éagede, -ég(ed)e, -íge *blear-eyed,* Æ.

-súrian v. á-s.

súr-milsc, -melsc, -melst adj. *half sour and half sweet* (*apple*).

súrnes f. '*sourness*,' WW347³⁵.

súsel=súsl

súsl nf. *misery, torment, torture,* Æ,AO.

súslbona m. *devil,* SAT640.

súslcwalu (-sel-) f. *painful death,* W.

súslhof n. *place of torment,* †Hy10³¹.

súslstede (sel-) m. *place of torment, hell,* OEG56¹⁸⁴.

suster=sweostor; **sutel**=sweotol

sútere m. *shoemaker,* Æ. ['*souter*'; L.]

-sútian v. be-s.; **sutol**, sutul=sweotol

súð* I. adj. comp. súð(er)ra, sýðer(r)a, superl. súðmest '*SOUTH*,' *southern,* AO. II. adv. comp. súðor, sýð *southwards, south,* AO,CP.

súðan adv. *from the south,* CP : *on or in the south,* AO. be s. (w. d.), wið s. (w. a.) *south of.*

súðanéastan adv. *in or from the south-east: to the south-east,* AO.

súðanéastanwind m. *south-east wind,* WW 144.

súðanéasterne *south-eastern,* LPs.

Súðanhymbre mp. *Mercians,* CHR.

súðanweard=súðeweard

súðanwestan adv. *from the south-west,* WW.

súðanwestan-wind, -winda m. *a south-west wind.*

súðanwesterne *south-western,* Bo10¹³.

súðanwind m. *south wind,* WW.

súðdǣl m. *southern region, the south,* Æ, VPs; AO. ['*southdeal*']

súðduru f. *south door,* BL201¹⁵.

súðéast adv. '*south-east*,' AO,Chr.

súðéastende m. *south-east end,* Bo67³¹.

súðéasterne *south-eastern,* ÆGR8².

súðecg f. *southern edge,* KC.

súðende m. *south end,* KC5·86'.

Súðengle pl. *South Anglians, people of southern England,* LL.

súðerige '*satirion*' (*plant*), WW137¹. [L. satureia?]

súðerne '*southern*,' *southerly,* Æ,Bo,Lcd, MtL.

súðernewudu m. '*southernwood*,' *wormwood,* Lcd.

súðerra v. súð.

sūðeweard adj. *southward, south, southern,*
AO.

sūðfolc n. *southern nation or people, Suffolk,*
Chr,Lcd.

sūðfōr f. *journey south, pilgrimage to Rome,*
BC 1·446.

sūðgārsecg m. *southern ocean,* AO.

sūðgemǣre n. *southern border,* AO.

sūðheald† *inclining southwards.*

sūðhealf f. *south side, AO;* Æ. ['*southhalf*']

Sūðhymbre mpl. *Mercians,* Chr.

sūðland n. *southern land or shore, Æ,Chr.*
['*southland*']

sūðmǣgð f. *southern province,* BH.

sūðmann† m. *man from the south,* Gen.

sūðmest '*southmost,*' *AO.*

Sūðmyrce (e) pl. *southern Mercians,* BH
238³⁴.

sūðor v. sūð.

sūðportic m. *south porch,* Chr 1036.

sūðra v. sūð.

sūðrihte (y) adv. *due south,* AO.

sūðrima m. *south coast,* Chr.

sūðrodor (a²) m. *southern sky,* Ph.

Sūðsǣ mf. *south sea, English Channel,*
Æ.

Sūð-seaxan, -seaxe pl. *South-Saxons, people
of Sussex : Sussex,* Chr.

sūðstæð n. *south coast,* Chr 897a.

sūðwāg m. *south wall,* Æ,Bl.

sūðweard adv. *towards the south, southwards, AO,Lcd.* ['*southward*']

sūðweardes adv. '*southwards,*' Met.

sūðweg m. *southern country,* Ex 155.

sūðwest I. m. *the south-west, Chr.* II. adv.
'*south-west,*' *AO.*

sūðwesterne '*south-western,*' ApT.

sūðwind m. *south wind,* Ex 289.

suwian (LWS)=sugian

swā (ǣ, ē) I. adv. and conj. (w. ind. or subj.)
*so as, consequently, just as, so far as, in
such wise, in this or that way, thus, so that,
provided that,* Æ. swā swā *so as, just as,
so that.* swā same (swā) *in like manner :
therefore, on that account : as, like :* (w.
comparatives) *the.* swā...swā *the...the :
where : when, so soon, as soon : although,
unless, yet : if, as if.* II. pron. '*so*,' *the
same, such, that.* swā hwā swā *whosoever.*
swā hwǣr swā *wherever.* bi swā hwaðerre
efes swā *on whichever side.* swā ilce=
swilce. swā selfe *in the same way.* ēac swā
also. swā hwilc swā *whosoever.* swā...ne
though...not. swā...swā *whether...or; either
...or.* swā ðeah *nevertheless, yet, however.*

swāc pret. 3 sg. of swīcan.

swǣ=swā

swæc (CP), swæcc (e) m. *flavour, taste :
smell, odour, fragrance.*

+swæccan (e) *to smell* (tr.), DD 206; (intr.)
ARPs 113¹⁴; ÆGr 221 т⁹.

swæcehēow '*insania*'? RPs 39⁵ (v. ES
38·22).

swæf pret. 3 sg. of swefan.

swǣfan? *to burn,* Met 8⁴⁷.

swæfen=swefn; swæflen=sweflen

swǣg=swēg; swægl=swegl

±swǣlan (tr.) *to burn, Cr,LPs.* ['*sweal*']

swælc=swilc

swǣm m. *trifler, idler,* Bf : *vain object,*
Chrd.

-swǣman v. ā-s.; swæncan=swencan

swǣp *enticement, persuasion, deceit* (v.
OEG 2894n).

+swǣpa (ā, ē) pl. *sweepings, rubbish,* Gl.
[swāpan]

swǣpels (VPs) m? swǣpelse f. *robe, garment.*

swǣpig *fraudulent,* OEG 2894.

swǣr I. (ā, ē) *heavy, sad, Ps : oppressive,
grievous, Cr,Gen : sluggish, inactive, weak,
Cp,LG.* II. n. *sadness, trouble,* MFH 173.
['*sweer*']

swǣrbyrd? f. *difficult birth?* Lcd 185a.

swǣre† (ā) *grievously, oppressively.*

+swǣre=swǣr

+swǣred *oppressed, weighed down,* Lcd
3·120'.

swǣrlic (ā) *grievous, heavy, Æ.* adv. -līce, Æ.

swǣrmōd *indolent, sluggish,* W 257.

swǣrmōdnes (ā) f. *dulness, stupidity,* CP
149¹⁵.

swǣrnes (ā) f. *heaviness, Æ : sluggishness,
Bo.* ['*sweerness*']

swǣrt (WW 257³)=sweart

±swǣs (ē) *intimate, special, favourite, dear,
beloved : own : agreeable, gentle, benevolent :
sweet, sugary.*

+swǣse *blandly, pleasantly,* WW 196¹².

swǣsenddagas mpl. *ides* (in Roman calendar), WW.

swǣsende (ē) n. (mostly used in pl. swǣ-
sendu) *food, meal, dinner, banquet, dainties :
blandishments,* WW 61²⁶.

swǣsing-=swǣsend-

±swǣslǣcan (ē¹) *to wheedle,* WW 61,196.

swǣslic *kind, friendly, agreeable, pleasant.*
adv. -līce *kindly : properly : plausibly.*

±swǣsnes f. *wheedling, Æ : pleasure.*

+swǣsscipe m. *companionship,* NC 296.

swǣsung f. *lenitive, soothing application,*
WW 241²⁴.

swǣswyrde *fair spoken,* WW 190³⁵.

±swǣtan *to sweat, exude, Æ,AO,BH,Lcd,
Nar : labour, toil, CP : bleed,* Cross 20 : *weld,*
A 22·395 : (+) *oppress,* CPs 93⁵. [swāt]

swǣð (e) n., nap. swaðu *footprint, track,*
CP : *trace, vestige,* CP. [cp. swaðu f.]

swæðel=sweðel

swæðelyne 'pinguis,' OEG 27³².

swæðer pron. whichever, whosoever, CP. [swā, hwæðer]

+swæðian to trace out, investigate, EPs 138³.

swæðlǣcan to search out, visit, CHy 9⁶⁸.

swæðorian=swaðrian, sweðrian

swæðu=swaðu

swāf pret. 3 sg. of swīfan.

swāhwætswā pron. whatsoever.

swāhwæðer pron. whichever, LL.

swal(e)we=swealwe; swālīc=swilc

swaloð=sweoloð

swāmian to become dark, Gu 1069.

swamm (o) I. m. fungus, mushroom, Æ : sponge. [Ger. schwamm] II. pret. 3 sg. of swimman.

swan (o) m. 'swan,' Ep,Ph,WW.

swān m. herdsman, swineherd, peasant, Chr, Ep : (†) swain, youth, man, warrior. ['swon']

swanc pret. 3 sg. of swincan.

swancor† slender, trim, lithe, supple : languishing, weak, PPs 118⁸¹.

swang pret. 3 sg. of swingan.

swāngerēfa m. swineherd, reeve, officer set over the depasturing of swine in forests, Ct.

swangettung f. movement, agitation, NC 324.

swangor (o) heavy, inert, BH,W.

swangornes (o) f. sloth, laziness, CP.

swanrād f. swan's-road, sea, B 200.

swānrīht n. law as to swineherds, LL 449,6¹.

swānsteorra m. evening star, Cp 145 u.

+swāpa=+swǣpa

±swāpan⁷ to sweep, drive, swing. rush (of wind), ÆGr,Bo,Ex,LPs : sweep up, take possession of, AO. ['swope']

swār=swǣr

swarc-=swearc-

-swarian (e, eo, o) v. and-s.

swarn-=sworn-; swart=sweart

swās=swǣs

swāt I. (ō) m? n? (+ at LCD 3·98¹⁷) 'sweat,' perspiration, exudation, Æ,CP,Lk : (†) blood : foam, LkR 9³⁹ : toil : labour, Bl; Æ. ['swote'] II. (+) sweaty, sweating, LCD.

swatan (ā?) pl. beer, WW.

swātclāð m. 'sudarium,' napkin, ÆP 178².

swātfāh† blood-stained, bloody.

swātig sweaty, AO : (†) gory. ['swoty']

swātighlēor with sweaty brow, GEN 934 (or ? two words).

swātlīn n. napkin, CP.

swātswaðu f. gory track, B 2946.

swātðyrel n. pore of the skin, WW 159¹³.

swāðēah adv. however, yet, nevertheless.

swāðēahhwæðre adv. however, Æ.

swaðer=swæðer

swaðian to swathe, wrap up, RWH 137¹³.

swaðorian, swaðrian=sweðrian

swaðu (æ, e) f. footstep, track, pathway, B Bo,MH : trace, vestige, BH : scar, Shı ['swath'; cp. swæð]

swaðul m? flame, B 782.

swaðum (in) dp. bandages, WW 484¹ ['swathe']

swē=swā; swealewe=swealwe

swealg, swealh pret. 3 sg. of swelgan.

swealt pret. 3 sg. of sweltan.

swealwe (a, o) f. 'swallow,' Ep,Gu,Lcd.

swearc pret. 3 sg. of sweorcan.

swearcian to become dark, ÆH 2·258¹⁵.

swearcmōdnes (a) f. pusillanimity, LPs 54⁹.

swearcung (a) f. darkness, RPs 17²⁹.

sweard m. hide, rind, skin, Gl. ['sward'] +swearf (LCD)=+sweorf

swearm m. 'swarm,' multitude, Gl.

sweart swarthy, black, dark, B,Lcd; Æ : gloomy : evil, infamous, Æ,Jul. ['swart']

sweartbyrd (æ¹) a dismal birth, LCD 3·66'.

swearte† adv. miserably, evilly.

swearthǣwen dark-blue, purple, violet, WW 376²⁴.

±sweartian to become black, Æ,Lcd : make black. ['swart']

sweartlāst with black tracks, RD 27¹¹.

sweartnes f. blackness, black substance, Gl. ['swartness']

sweartung f. darkness, EPs 17²⁹.

swearð (G)=sweard ['swarth']

±swebban to put to sleep, lull, G : (†) kill, Æ,B. ['sweve']

swec (KGL)=swæc

swefan⁵ to sleep, slumber, rest, B,Cp : (†) sleep in death : cease, Ex. ['sweve']

swefecere m. sleeper, CHRD 26².

swefecung f. sleep, CHRD 31⁴.

swefed pp. of swebban.

swefel (æ) m. sulphur, Æ. [Ger. schwefel]

swefelrēc m. sulphurous smoke, VPs 10⁷.

swefen=swefn

swefet=sweofot

swefeð pres. 3 sg. of swebban.

+swefian to put to sleep, lull, appease, Æ. ['sweve']

swefl=swefel

sweflen sulphurous, of brimstone, Æ,AO.

sweflennes (eo) f. sulphurousness, MFH 123³.

sweflenrēc (APs)=swefelrēc

sweflsweart sulphurous? WW 49²⁰.

sweflðrosm m. sulphurous smoke, ERSPs 10⁷.

swefn n. (often pl.) sleep, Gen; Æ,AO : dream, vision, CP,Da,LG. ['sweven']

swefnian (w. nom. pers.) to dream, Lcd : (+)(w. acc. pers.) appear in a dream. ['sweven']

swefnl(g)end m. *dreamer*, GEN 37¹⁹.
swefnracu f. *interpretation of dreams*, LL (154²⁹).
swefnreccere m. *interpreter of dreams*, WW 366¹².
swefot=sweofot
swēg (ǣ) m. *sound*, Æ,AO,CP : *noise, clamour, tumult* : *melody, harmony, tone*, Æ : *voice* : *musical instrument* : '*persona*,' Sc. [swōgan]
swēgan *to make a noise, sound, roar, crash*, Æ : *import, signify*, Æ. ['*swey*']
swēgcræft m. *musicians' art, music*, APT 16.
swēgdynn m. *noise, crash*, CR 955.
±swēge *sonorous, harmonious*, ÆL.
swegel=swegl
swēgendlic adj. *vocal, vowel*, ÆGR 6¹⁵.
sweger f. *mother-in-law*, Æ. [*Ger.* schwieger]
swēgesweard m. *organist* (*!*) JGPh 1·64.
swēghlēoðor† m. *sound, melody*.
swēging f. *sound, clang, roar*, Lk,WW.
swegl† (æ) I. n. *sky, heavens, ether* : *the sun* : *music?* II.=segl
sweglbefalden *ether-begirt*, SAT 588.
sweglbeorht *ether-bright, radiant*, GU 1187.
sweglbōsm m. *heaven, sky*, GEN 9 (pl.).
sweglcondel f. *heaven's candle, sun*, PH 108.
sweglcyning† m. *King of heaven*.
swegldrēam† m. *music*.
swegle† I. adj. *bright, ether-like, clear, brilliant, splendid.* II. adv. *clearly, brightly.*
sweglhorn m. *kind of musical instrument*, GL. [cp. *Goth.* swiglōn]
swēglic *sonorous*, CM 675.
sweglrād f. *modulation, music*, RIM 29.
swegltorht† *heavenly-bright.*
sweglwered (gel-) *ether-clad*, B 606.
sweglwuldor n. *heavenly glory*, GU 1160.
sweglwundor n. *heavenly wonder*, GU 1292.
swegr=sweger
+swegra=+swigra
+swēgsumlīce? *unanimously*, HL 18¹⁶².
swehor (GL)=swēor
sweig (KGL 88⁴)=swēg
sweigð=swēgeð pres. 3 sg. of swēgan.
+swel=+swell
swelan⁴ *to burn, be burnt up* : *inflame (of wound).*
swelc (*Bo,LG,OET* ; AO,CP)=swilc. [v. '*such*']
swelca m. *pustule*, WW 112¹⁷.
swelce=swilce
+swelg n. *abyss, whirlpool*, GL. ['*swallow*']
±swelgan³ *to* '*swallow*,' *incorporate, absorb, imbibe, devour*, Lcd,LL.
swelgend (y) fmn. (±) *whirlpool, vortex, gulf, abyss*, CP : *glutton, drunkard, debauchee*, AO.

swelgendnes f. *whirlpool*, WW 373².
swelgere m. *glutton*, WW 102¹⁵. ['*swallower*']
swelgnes f. *whirlpool*, WW 510¹⁸.
swelhð=swelgð pres. 3 sg. of swelgan.
swellend=swelgend
+swell n. *swelling, tumour, boil*, Æ,LCD.
±swellan³ *to* '*swell*,' B,Lcd.
swellende *burning*, OEG 377⁸.
swelling f. *swelling*, EL 245.
±sweltan³ (i, y) *to die, perish*, Æ,B,Bo ; AO, CP. ['*swelt*']
sweltendlic *about to die*, Lk,Sc.
-swemman v. be-s.
±swenc m. *trouble, tribulation, toil* : (+) *temptation*, LkL,Nar. ['*swench*']
±swencan (æ) *to vex, distress, trouble, afflict, torment, oppress*, B,Bl,Bo,G ; Æ,CP. [causative of swincan; '*swenche*']
+swenc-ednes, -ennes, -nes (AA) f. *trouble, affliction, toil*, Æ.
sweng m. *stroke, blow, cut, thrust*, B,El. ['*sweng*']
swengan *to shake, shatter*, Gl : *swing, rush, fly out*, HL. ['*swenge*'; causative of swingan]
sweocol (CP)=swicol; sweofl-=swefl-
sweofot (e) n. *sleep*, B. ['*swevet*']
swēogian=swīgian; sweolce=swilce
Swēoland n. *Sweden*, AO 19².
sweoloð (a, o) m. *burning heat, glow, fire, flame.* [swelan]
sweoloðhāt (o¹) *burning hot*, OEG 56²⁰².
sweolung? f. *inflammation*, LCD 76b (sweop-).
Swēon pl. *Swedes*, AO,B,CHR.
swēop pret. 3 sg. of swāpan.
sweop-=swip-
sweopung v. sweolung.
swēor I. (ē, ȳ) mf. *pillar, column, prop*, CP : *bolt, bar*, ES 37·183. II. m. *father-in-law*, Æ,AO,CP : (±) *cousin.* [*Ger.* schwäher] III.=swōr pret. of swerian.
swēora (ī, īo, ū, ȳ) m. *neck, nape*, Bo,Bl,G ; AO,CP. ['*swire*']
swēorbān n. *neck-bone, neck*, VHy. ['*swirebone*']
swēorbēag (u) m. *neck-band, necklace, collar, torque*, Æ.
+sweorc (o) n. *cloud, darkness, mist*, GEN, VPs.
±sweorcan³ *to grow dark, darken* (intr.), *become overcast, be obscured*, An : *be troubled, sad, become grievous, troublesome, angry*, B,Met; ÆL : *fall out (of mind)*, JPs 30¹³. ['*swerk*']
sweorcendferhð *sombre, sad*, JUD 269.
+sweorcenes (o, cn) f. *gloom*, LL (400⁹).
swēorclāð m. *neckcloth*, WW 210³⁶.

sweorcops m. *yoke, pillory, Gl.* [v. 'cops']

sweorcoðu f. *quinsy,* LCD.

sweord (o, u, y) n. 'sword,' *Æ,B,Bl,Fin,G;* AO,CP.

sweordbealo n. *sword-bale,* B1147.

sweordberende 'sword-bearing,' *Gen* 1060.

sweordbite m. *sword-wound,* JUL603.

sweordbora (u, y) m. *sword-bearer, swords-man, Æ.*

sweordfætels m. *sword-belt,* ÆL23¹⁷⁸.

sweordfreca m. *swordsman, warrior,* B1468.

sweordgenīðla m. *sworded foe,* EL1181.

sweordgeswing (y¹) n. *sword-brandishing,* JUD240.

sweordgifu (y¹) f. *gift of swords,* B2884.

sweordgripe m. *sword-attack,* JUL488.

sweordhwīta (u, y) m. *sword-furbisher,* LL.

sweordlēoma (u¹) m. *flashing of swords,* FIN35.

+sweordod (u) *provided with a sword, ÆGr, NC.* ['sworded']

sweordplega m. *fighting,* Wal22. ['sword-play']

sweordrǣs m. *attack,* AP59.

sweordslege m. *sword-thrust,* JUL671.

sweordtige m. *sword-drawing,* LPs9⁷.

sweordwegende (u¹) *sword-bearing,* LCD 3·204'.

sweordwīgend m. *warrior,* Ex260.

sweordwund *wounded with the sword,* WAL7.

sweordwyrhta (u¹) m. *sword-maker?* LCD 3·194¹⁰.

+sweorf (ea, y) n. *filings,* LCD.

±sweorfan³ *to file or grind away, polish, wipe, rub, scour.*

sweorhnitu f. *nit which lives on the neck of animals, tick,* WW.

Swēorīce n. *Sweden,* B.

swēorracentēh (ū¹) f. *neck-chain,* WW107³⁴.

swēorrōd (ū¹) f. *cross worn on the neck, EC* 250¹¹. [v. 'rood']

swēorscacul m. *yoke, pillory,* WW116⁹.

swēortēag (ē) f. *collar,* GL.

+swēoru (ī, ȳ) np. *hills,* PPs.

swēorwærc m. *pain in the neck,* LCD.

sweostor (e, i, u, y) f. indecl. in sg., nap. sweoster, sweostra, sweostru 'SISTER,' *Æ,AO : nun.*

+sweos-tor, -tra, -tru fp. *sisters,* AO.

+sweosternu bearn *children of sisters, cousins.*

sweostorbearn n. *sister's child, nephew, niece,* WW452².

sweostorsunu m. *sister's son, nephew, BH, Chr.* [v. 'sister']

swēot† n. *troop, army, company, body, swarm.*

sweota? sweote? 'scrotum,' LCD, v. A 30·134.

sweotel=sweotol

sweotol (i, u, y) *distinct, clear, evident, manifest, open, public, B,Bl,CP,OEG;* AO. ['sutel']

sweotole (e, o, u) adv. *clearly, precisely, plainly, openly, visibly,* CP.

±sweotolian (e, u, y) *to show, reveal, make manifest, Mt; Æ : become manifest, GK : state, explain, prove.* ['sutele']

sweotollic (u¹, y¹) *clear, distinct.* adv. -līce *clearly, precisely, plainly, visibly, openly, Æ,BH.* ['suteliche']

±sweotolung (i, u, y) f. *manifestation, Epiphany : definition, explanation, exposition, declaration, Æ : written testimony, evidence.*

±sweotolungdæg (e, u) m. *Epiphany, Æ.*

sweotul=sweotol

Swēoðēod f. *Swedes, Sweden,* B,CHR.

sweoðerian=sweðrian

sweoðol I. m? *heat, flame,* B3145. [cp. swaðul] II.=sweðel

swēowian=swīgian; +swēpa=+swæpa

swēr=(1) swār; (2) sweger; (3) swēor

±swerian⁶ (but occl. wk. pret. swerede) *to 'SWEAR,' Æ;* AO,CP : *swear in (to an office) : speak?* SOL425. [Ger. schwören]

swerigendlic *jurative, used in swearing (of certain adverbs),* ÆGR227.

swertling m. *titlark? warbler?* WW131¹⁵.

swēs=swǣs; swester (N)=sweostor

±swētan *to make sweet, sweeten,* Jul,Lcd; Æ,CP.

swēte I. adj. 'SWEET,' *pure, fragrant, pleasant, agreeable, AO,CP : beloved, dear : fresh (not salt).* II. n. *sweetness, sweet.* [swōt]

swetelian (KGL)=sweotolian

swētian *to be sweet,* CP425¹⁴.

+swētlǣcan *to batten,* RPs65¹⁵.

swētlīce *sweetly, pleasantly,* BH486⁴.

swētmete m. *sweetmeat, dainty,* CP41¹⁵.

swētnes f. *sweetness, fragrance, BH,CP : pleasantness, BH : kindliness, goodness, Ps : something sweet, Cp*524A.

swetole=sweotole

swētswēge *agreeable (of sound),* DHy58⁸.

swētwyrde *smooth-spoken,* WW : *stuttering,* WW.

sweð=swæð

sweðel (æ, eo) m. *swaddling band, bandage, binding, G,Gl.* ['sweddle']

sweðerian=sweðrian; -sweðian v. be-.

sweðolian *to relent, be appeased,* CHR1123.

±sweðrian (a, æ, eo, i) *to retire, vanish, melt away, abate, dwindle, decrease, subside.*

+sweðrung (æ) f. *failure,* LCD.

sweðu=swaðu

sweðung f. *poultice*, CHRD,LCD.

swic n. *illusion*, CM441 : *deceit, treachery*, AO. ['swike']

+swic n. *offence*, MtR,WW : *snare*, OEG 127² : *cessation*.

swica m. *deceiver, traitor, betrayer*, Chr,G. ['swike']

±swīcan¹ (†) *to wander* : (†) *depart* : (w. g.) *cease from, yield, give way*, AO,CP : (w. d.) *fail, fall short, be wanting, abandon, desert, turn traitor*, AO : *deceive*, Æ. ūt s. *go forth*. from s. *fall off, rebel*. ['SWIKE,' 'I-SWIKE']

swicc m. (BH430⁴)=swæcc

swiccræft m. *treachery*, G,LL.

swicdōm m. *fraud, deception, deceit*, AO, Chr; Æ : *betrayal, treason : scandal, offence*. ['swikedom']

swice I. m. (†) *escape, end* : (†) *procrastination, delay*, GU1007 : *offence, snare, treachery, deceit*, AO. ['swike'] II. adj. *fallacious, deceitful*. III. f. *trap, snare*, GL. ['swike'] IV.=swicc

+swicednes=+swicennes

swīcend m. *deceiver*, HL18³⁹,⁸⁷.

+swicennes f. *abstention, cessation*, Æ : *repentance*.

swicful *fraudulent, deceitful*, OEG. ['swikeful']

swician *to wander : be treacherous, deceive, cheat*, Æ : *blaspheme : cause to offend*.

+swicing f. *intermission, cessation*, CM 103.

±swicn f. *purgation, clearance, discharge*, LL.

+swicnan *to clear (of a charge)*, LL.

swicol *guileful, false, deceitful*, Æ,Lcd. ['swikel']

swicollic *fraudulent, deceiving, deceptive, causing to stumble*. adv. -līce.

swicolnes f. *deceit*, W. ['swikelness']

+swicu f. *cessation*, RB148¹²³n.

swicung f. *deceit, fraud, deception*, A,Lcd : *stumbling-block, offence*. ['swiking']

swīfan¹ *to revolve, sweep, wend : intervene*, EC164. [Ger. schweifen]

+swifornes=+swipornes

swift (y) 'swift,' *quick*, Æ,B,Bo,CP,GD; AO. adv. -līce, Æ,LPs,W. ['swiftly']

swiftlēre (u, y) m. *slipper*, Æ. [L. subtalaris]

swiftnes f. *swiftness, speed*, Bo,Ps.

swiftu f. *swiftness*, MET28³.

swīgan=swīgian

swīgdagas mp. *days of silence (last three days of Holy Week)*, Æ. [v. 'swie']

swīge, swigge I. f. *silence, stillness, rest*, Æ, CP. II. adj. *still, quiet, silent, taciturn*, CP.

swīgen f. *silence*, ÆH2·532⁴.

swīgeniht f. *night of silence*, ÆP154³ (v. swīgdagas).

±swīgian (ȳ; ī, ēo, ū) *to be or become silent, keep silence, be quiet, still*, B,BH; CP. ['swie']

swīgendlīce adv. *silently*, HL18³¹¹.

swīglīce *silently*, GENC24²¹.

swīglung f. *silence*, ANS84·3. (or ? swīglunga *silently*)

swīgmæsse f. *silent mass*, NC324. ['swimesse']

swīgnes f. *time of silence*, WW211⁴².

+swīgra (e) m. *sister's son, nephew, cousin*.

swīgtīma (swīt-) m. *silent time, eventide, early part of the night*, BF122²².

swīgūht m. *dawn of the days of silence* (v. swīgdagas), ANS84·7.

±swīgung f. *silence : time of silence : delay*, NG.

swilc (æ, e, y) pron. (used substantively) *such a one, he, the same*, Æ : (used adjectivally) 'SUCH,' CP : (as relative) *which*, Æ. swilc...hwilc *such...as; so...as*. swilc...swilc *so much (many)...as; as much (many)...as*, Æ. ['swilk,' v. 'such']

swilce (e, eo, y) adv. and conj. (w. ind.) *just as, as, in like manner, in such manner, likewise, resembling, thus* : (w. subj.) *as if, as though* : *also, moreover, too*, Bo. ['such']

swilchwugu *some...or other*, ÆL23b⁷⁸⁶.

swilcnes f. 'qualitas,' *nature*, Lcd,RB. ['suchness']

swile=swyle

swilian, swillan *to 'swill,' wash, wash out, gargle*, Cp,Lcd,Ps.

s⁻ꝥl(l)ing f. 'swilling,' *wash, gargle*, Lcd.

swilt=swylt

swiltan=sweltan

swilð pres. 3 sg. of swellan.

swilunge=swīglunga

swīma m. *vertigo, dizziness : swoon*, Cr,Jud, Lcd; Æ. ['swime']

swimæsse=swīgmæsse

±swimman³ (y) *to 'swim,' float*, AA,Æ,B, Lcd,Rd,Wa.

swimmendlic (y) *able to swim*, ÆGR55³.

swīn (ȳ) n. *wild-boar, pig, hog*, pl. 'swine,' Bo,Cp,G,Rd; CP; Mdf : *boar-image (on a helmet)*, B.

+swin n. *song, melody*, PH137.

±swinc n. *toil, work, effort*, Æ,Ps : *hardship*, Gen : *the produce of labour*, W229⁷. ['swing,' 'swink,' 'i-swinch']

±swincan³ *to labour, work at, strive, struggle*, Æ,B; CP : *be in trouble : languish*. ['swink']

+swincdagas mp. *days of tribulation*, SEAF 2.

+swincednes (EPs17¹⁹)=+swencednes

±swincful *toilsome, painful, disastrous*, Bo; Æ. ['swinkful']

+**swincfulnes** f. *tribulation*, LPs 33⁷ : *trouble*, Sc 60¹¹.

±**swincléas** (y) *without toil*, ÆH 2·364⁹. ['*swinkless*']

swinclic *laborious*, W 294¹⁸.

+**swincnes** f. *hardship, trial*, CHRD,GUTH.

swind=spind

swindan³ *to vanish, consume, pine away, languish, BH,Ps*. ['*swind*']

swīnen adj. *pig's, swine's*, LCD,Ps.

+**swing†** I. n. *surge, fluctuation*. II.= +swinc

swingan³ I. *to beat, strike, smack, whip, scourge, flog, chastise, afflict*, Æ,B,Bl,Cp, Lcd; AO,CP. '*swing*' *oneself, fly*, B 2264. sw. on twā *to divide by a blow*. II. (Æ,Ps)= swincan

swinge (y) f. *stroke, blow, stripe* : *chastisement*, CP.

swingell f. (often swingel-, swingl- in obl. cases) ; swingel(l)e f. *whip, scourge, rod*, Æ : *stroke, stripe, blow* : *affliction*, CP.

swingere m. *striker, scourger*, RD 28⁷.

swinglung f. *dizziness*, Lcd,WW. ['*swingling*']

swīnhaga m. *pig-pen*, KC.

swīnhyrde (ī) m. '*swineherd*,' ZDA 33·239²¹.

swīnin (GL)=swīnen

swīnlic *swinish*, WW 508²⁹?

swīnlic n. *boar-image* (*on a helmet*), B 1452.

swinn m. *melody*, OEG.

swīnnes f. *pork food*, EPs 16¹⁴.

swīnsceadu *pannage*, TC 263⁷ (v. BTs).

swinsian (y) *to sound melodiously, make melody, sing*.

swinsung f. *sound, melody, harmony*, BH, GL.

swinsungcræft m. *music*, WW 442¹².

swinsweg? *melody* (v. OEG xxxiii).

swipa m., swipe f.=swipu

swipian† (eo) *to whip, scourge, beat*.

±**swipor** *cunning*, BH,SOL.

+**swipor-e**, -līce *cunningly*, Ps.

+**swipornes** (e²) f. *wile, cunning*, HL,MkR.

swippan=swipian

swipu (eo, o) f. *whip, stick, scourge*, Gl,RG, Sol : *chastisement, affliction*. ['*swepe*']

swir-, swīr-=sweor-, sweor-

+**swirga**, +swiria=+swigra

swirman (=ie) *to swarm*, LCD 1·384'.

swister=sweostor

swital, switel, switol=sweotol

swītīma=swīgtīma

swīð (ȳ) *strong, mighty, powerful, active* : *severe, violent*. comp. swiðre *right* (*hand, side, etc.*).

±**swīðan** [wv. and sv¹? cp. unforswiðen] *to strengthen, establish, support* : *use force against*, Æ (v. A 36·66).

swīðe (ȳ) adv. *very much, exceedingly, severely, violently, fiercely*, B,Bl,Chr,G; AO,CP. comp. swīðor *more, rather*. superl. swīðost *most, especially, exceedingly* : *almost, nearly*. for swīðe, swīðe swīðe *very much, very severely*, CP. ['*swith*']

swīðfæstnes f. *violence*, LL (138 n4).

swīðfeorm *rich, fruitful* : *violent*, RD.

swīðfeormende *becoming violent*, WW 374¹¹.

swīðferhð† (y) *bold, brave, rash*.

=**swīðfrom** *very strong, vigorous*. adv. -līce.

swīðhrēownes f. *remorse*, MFH 173.

swīðhwæt *very active*, RUN 5.

swīðhycgende (i)† *bold-minded*, B.

swīðian *to become strong* : *prevail* : *fix*, WW.

swīðlæt *very lax*, LL (318').

swīðlic *intense, excessive, severe, violent*, Æ : *immense*, Æ : *effective*. adv. -līce, Bo,G, ['*swithly*']

swīðlicnes f. *excess*, RBL 73⁷.

swīðmihtig *very mighty*, PPs 85¹³.

swīðmōd† *stout-hearted, brave* : *insolent, arrogant*.

swīðmōdnes f. *magnanimity*, A 11·173, SOL 150⁴.

swīðnes f. *excess, violence*, CM 458.

swīðor comp. of swīðe.

swīðra comp. of swīð, Lcd,LG. ['*swither*']

swīðrian=sweðrian

swīðrian *to avail, become strong, prevail*, Æ.

swīðsnel *very quick, agile*, CRA 82.

swīðspecende (ȳ) *talkative*, OEG 56¹⁴⁰.

swīðsprecel *talkative*, LPs 11⁴.

swīðstincende *strong-smelling*, WW 408¹⁸.

swīðstrang *very strong*, BH 38⁶B.

swīðstrēme *having a strong current, rapid*, BH 38⁶.

swīðswēge *strong-sounding, heroic*, OEG.

swīður=swīðor comp. of swīðe.

swiung f. *spasm, cramp*, WW 112¹⁹.

swiung=swīgung

swodrian *to be fast asleep*, SPs 3⁵. ['*swother*']

swoeg=swēg ; **swoesendu**=swǣsendu

swoetnes (GL,VPs)=swētnes

swōg (VPs)=swēg

swōgan⁷ *to sound, roar, howl, rustle, whistle, rattle*, Cr,Gen. ['*sough*']

+**swogen** *in a swoon, silenced, dead*, Æ,Lcd. ['*swow*(*n*)']

+**swogennes** v. in-s.

+**swōgung** f. *swooning*, Lcd. ['*swowing*']

swol n. *heat, burning, flame, glow*. [swelan; Ger. schwül]

swoleð=sweoloð

swolgen pp. of swelgan.

swolgettan *to gargle, wash the throat*, LCD.

swolig f. *burning*, LCD,WW.
swollen (*Ep*) pp. of swellan.
swoloð, swoloða (OEG 23⁵⁵)=sweoloð
swolten pp. of sweltan.
swoluð (*Æ*)=sweoloð; swolwe=swealwe
swom=swamm I. and II.; swon=swan
swoncor=swancor
swong=swang pret. 3 sg. of swingan.
swongor=swangor; swonrād=swanrād
+swōpe *sweepings, refuse*, Ln 111¹⁵.
swopu (NG)=swipu
swor (Ex 239)=spor
swōr I. pret. 3 sg. of swerian. II.=sār.
III.=swēor
swōra=swēora; sworc=sweorc
sworcen pp. of sweorcan.
sword=sweord
sworen pp. of swerian.
swōretendlic *short-winded*, WW 355⁹.
swōrettan *to breathe hard, pant, yawn, sigh,*
Æ.
swōret-ung, -tung f. *hard breathing, panting,
sobbing, sighing, moaning*, Æ.
sworfen pp. of sweorfan.
swornian (a) *to coagulate*, GL.
swōron pret. pl. of swerian.
swostor=sweostor
swōt I. *sweet*, *JnL,Nar,OEG*. adv. swōte
ÆGr. ['*soot*'] II.=swāt
swōtlic *savoury, sweet*, CP 311⁸. adv.
-līce.
swōtmete m. *sweetmeat, dainty*, Bo 33²³.
swōtnes f. *sweetness*, *DR,Shr*. ['*sootness*']
swotol=sweotol
swōt-stence (WW 341⁵), -stencende (DR)
sweet-smelling.
swoðung=sweðung
+swōwung=+swōgung
swūgian (CP)=swīgian; swulc=swilc
swulgon pret. pl. of swelgan.
swulton pret. pl. of sweltan.
swulung=sulung
swuncon pret. pl. of swincan.
-swundennes v. ā-s.
swur-, swūr-=sweor-, swēor-
swust-er, -or, -ur (*Æ*)=sweostor
swut-el-, -ol-, -ul-=sweotol-
swūwian=swīgian; swyc-=swic-
swyft=swift; swȳg-=swīg-
swȳge=swīge; swyl-=swil-
swyle (i) m. *tumour, swelling.* [swellan]
swyliend=swelgend
swylt† (i) m. *death.* [sweltan]
swylt-=swelt-
swyltcwalu† f. *agony of death*, AN.
swyltdæg† m. *death-day.*
swyltdēað m. *death*, PPs 55¹¹.
swylthwīl† f. *hour of death*, PH.
swym-=swim-; swȳn=swīn

swyn-=swin-; swyp- (N)=swip-
swȳr=swēor; swyrd=sweord
+swyrf=+sweorf
swyrfð pres. 3 sg. of sweorfan.
+swȳsnes=+swǣsnes; swyster=sweostor
swytel, swytol=sweotol; swȳð=swīð
swȳwian=sūgian, swīgian
sȳ=sīe pres. subj. of bēon.
syb, sybb=sibb
±sȳcan (ē, ī) *to suckle : wean*, ASPs 130².
[sūcan]
syce (i, ī?) *sucking*, OEG 57⁸.
sȳclian=sīclian
sycomer m. *sycamore*, BK 4.
sȳcð pres. 3 sg. of sūcan; sȳcan.
+syd n. *wallowing-place*, WW 146¹⁵. [sēo-
ðan]
sȳd=sīd; +sydian=+sidian
syde m. *a decoction*, LCD 1·280³. [sēoðan]
syfan=seofon; syfe=sife
sȳferǣte *abstemious*, RB 119²⁵.
sȳferlic (ē) *neat, cleanly, pure, sober,
moderate.* adv. -līce.
sȳferlicnes f. *purity*, VH 20.
sȳferne asm. of sȳfre.
sȳfernes f. *cleanliness, purity, sobriety,
moderation*, Æ.
syfeða=seofoða; syfian=seofian
+syflan *to provide with relishes, flavour*, TC,
W. [sufl]
syflige (RBL), syfling (*Æ*) f. *food, pap,
broth, soup : seasoning, relish.*
syfol=sufel; syfon=seofon
sȳfre (ē, ī) *clean, pure, chaste, sober,
abstinent, temperate*, Æ. [*Ger.* sauber]
syftan=siftan
syge I. m. *sight, aspect*, FT 64? II.=sige I.
sygel=sigel; sygor=sigor
syh=seoh imperat. of sēon; syht=suht
syhð pres. 3 sg. of sēon I. and II.
+syhð=+sihð
+syhðe (BPs 120⁴)=+sehðe; syl=syle
sȳl I. f. *column, pillar, support*, AO. [*Ger.*
säule] II. ds. of sūl, sulh.
sȳla m. *ploughman*, OEG 2357. [sulh]
sȳlæx f. *a kind of axe*, WW 379³³ (v. ES
43·327).
syle, sylen *miry place, wallowing-place*,
OEG. [sol]
sylen=selen
syleð pres. 3 sg. of syllan; sylf=self
sylfer, sylfor, sylfur (M)=seolfor
sylfren (*Æ*)=seolfren
sylfwill- (*Æ*)=selfwill-
sylg ds., sylh ds. and nap. of sūl, sulh.
Sȳlhearwa=Sigelhearwa
±sylhð(e) n. *team of oxen.* [sulh]
syllan (e) *to sully, soil, pollute*, CP,Met.
['*sule*']

syll I. f. 'sill,' threshold, foundation, base, basis, Æ,B,CP. II. nap. of sulh.
sylla m. giver, RBL25⁶. [sellan]
sȳlla (Deor6)=sēlla (sēlra) v. sēl I.
syllan (Æ)=sellan; sylle=syll I.
syllend (Æ)=sellend; syllic=seldlic
sylofr, sylofren=seolfor, seolfren
sȳlra=sēlra v. sēl I.
±syltan (æ, e;=ie) to salt, season, Æ. [sealt]
sylu f. bog, miry place, Ct.
sȳma=sēma; sȳman=sīeman
symbel I. n. feast-day, festivity, revel, feast, AO : (†) festival, holy day : solemn office. II.=simbel
symbelcalic (i) m. chalice, TC515¹⁸.
symbelcennes f. feast of a nativity, DR.
symbeldæg m. feast-day, festival, holiday, Æ.
symbele=simble
symbelgāl wanton with feasting, drunk, DD 79.
symbelgereord n. feasting, carousal, Sol 407.
symbelgifa m. giver of feasts, An 1419.
symbelhūs n. guest-chamber, LkLR22¹².
symbelian=symblian
symbellic festive : solemn. adv. -līce solemnly, DR,RBL.
symbelmōnaðlic adj. of a festival month? WW375³⁸.
symbelnes f. festival, feasting, festivity, Æ : festal character, Bf84² : solemn assembly, solemn office.
symbeltīd f. festival-time, DR.
symbelwērig weary with feasting, Gen 2640.
symbelwlonc elated with feasting, Mod 40.
symbelwynn f. joy of feasting, B1782.
symblan to feast, banquet, CP.
symble (Æ)=simble adv.
symblian (i) to feast, carouse, CP.
symel=symbel
symeringwyrt f. violet, WW322⁹.
syml=symbel I.; syml-=simbl-
ˈsymnenlic=semnendlic; syn=synn
sȳn I.=sīen f. II.=sīn, sien pres. pl. subj. of wesan (bēon). III.=sīn I.
syn- v. also sin-, synn-.
syna=suna gs. of sunu.
synbend m. bond of sin, Nic504²³.
synbōt f. penance, LL(316').
synbryne m? burning ardour of sin, MFH 143¹⁸.
synbyrðen f. burden of sin, Bl,Cr.
synbysig guilt-haunted, B2227.
syncræft m. evil art? ByH102³⁰.
synd=sind pres. pl. ind. of wesan (bēon).
+synd-=+sund-

syndǣd f. sinful deed, PPs,W.
syndan=sendan
synder-=sundor-
synderǣ (u²) f. special law, DR190¹⁰.
synderlic (e¹, i¹) singular, separate, special, peculiar, private, Bo,CP : remote. adv -līce Æ, BH, Bo, MkL. [' sunderly ']
synderlicnes f. separateness, separation seclusion, OEG : singularity, special ex cellence, GD286¹¹.
synder-līpe, -lȳpe, -lȳpig peculiar, special. adv. -līpes (ȳ), OEG,RB. [' sunderlepes ']
+syndgian to make to prosper, BH320¹².
syndig skilled in swimming, Cra58.
+syndig favourable, BH386¹³.
+syndiglic (del-) prosperous, BH388¹⁸.
syndir-=synder-
+syndlǣcan (synt-) to cause to prosper, RPs117²⁵.
syndolh n. deadly wound, B817 (or=sin-?).
syndon=sindon pres. pl. ind. of wesan (bēon).
Syndonisc Indian, MFH173, Nic592. [L. Gk.]
syndra? m., syndre? f.=sinder
±syndrian (u) to ' sunder,' separate, divide, KC,LG,Sc.
syndrig (i) separate, single, PPs : ' sundry,' various, distinct, Æ,BH : special, private, peculiar, exceptional, particular, Æ; AO, CP : characteristic : (distributive) one each. [sundor]
syndrige adv. separately, specially, apart, alone, LG. [' sundry ']
syndrigendlic discretive, ÆGr229⁷.
syndriglic special, peculiar, BH. adv. -līce specially : separately, BH. [' sundrily ']
syndrung v. ā-s.
syndurǣ=synderǣ
synew-=sinew-; and v. seonu.
synfāh sin-stained, Cr1083.
±syngian to sin, transgress, err, Æ,CP.
syngrigendlic=syndrigendlio
syngrin (y²) f. snare of sin, harm, W.
syngung f. transgression, HL12¹³⁷. [' sin ning ']
synleahter m. stain of sin, W134²⁴.
synlēas ' sinless,' guiltless, innocent, CP,Jn, W.
synlēaw injury caused by sin, W165²⁵.
synlic sinful, foul, wicked. adv. -līce.
+synlīce=+sinlīce
synn (e, i) f. (†) injury, mischief, enmity, feud : ' sin,' guilt, crime, Bl,Bo,Chr,G,Sc, VPs; CP.
synn- see also syn-.
synnadæg (N)=sunnandæg
synnecge f. female sinner, MH126⁴.
synneðōht sinful thought, ByH136¹³.

synnful '*sinful*,' *guilty, wicked, corrupt, Bl, LG,VPs*; CP.

synnglend m. *sinner*, EPs 111¹⁰.

+synnian *to commit adultery*, NG.

synnig *guilty, punishable, criminal* : *sinful*, CP.

synnlust m. *desire to sin*, Æ.

synoð=seonoð

synræs m. *temptation*, LL (284⁹).

synrūst m. *canker of sin*, Cr 1321.

syn-sceaða, -scaða† m. *sin-stained wretch, sinful outrager*, VH 20.

synscyldig *wicked*, DD 168.

synt=sind pres. pl. ind. of wesan (bēon).

+synt-=+synd-

±synto f. *soundness, health* : *prosperity, welfare, salvation.* [gesund]

synwracu† f. *punishment for sin.*

synwund f. *wound of sin*, Cr,LL.

synwyrcende† *sinning.*

sypan=sypian

sype m. *wetting, act of soaking through*, Bo. ['*sipe*']

sypian (i) *to absorb, drink in, Lcd* 94b. ['*sipe*']

sȳpian=sīpian; **sypo**, syppo=swipu

syrc m., syrce f.=serc, serce

syre=searwe, v. searo; **sȳre**=sīere

syredon=sier(w)edon pret. pl. of sierwan.

syretung f. *lurking place*, WW 440⁶. [searu]

syrewrenc=searwrenc

syrewung=searwung

syrfe f. *service-tree*, EC 373¹¹. [*L.* sorbus]

syrftrēow n. *service-tree*, KC 3·379'.

syric, syrice=serc, serce

sȳring f. *sour milk, buttermilk*, LL,WW. [sūr]

Syrisc *Syrian*, ÆL 18⁴⁰².

syrode=sierwde pret. 3 sg. of sierwan.

syru=searo

syrwa=searwa gp. of searo.

syr-wan, -wian (Æ)=sierwan

Syrware mpl. *Syrians*, Ph 166.

syrwung=sierwung

syrwwrenc=searowrenc; **syster**=sester

syt-=sit-

sȳð I.=sīð. II. v. sūð adv. III. pres. 3 sg. of sēoðan.

sȳð-=sīð-; **sȳðan**=siððan

sȳðerra (BC,Lcd) v. sūð. ['*souther*']

sȳðst pres. 2 sg. of sēoðan.

sȳððan=siððan; **sȳwian**=sēowian

syx, syx-=siex, siex-, six-

T

tā I. f. '*toe*,' *Cp,LL,WW*. II. f. (Æ)=tān m.

tabele, tablu, tabul, f., tabula m.=tabule

tabule f. '*table*,' *BH* : *a wooden hammer, or piece of wood struck as a signal for assem-*

---

ling monks, CM : *writing tablet, Bf* : *gaming table, Gl* : *table of the law.* [*L.*]

tacan⁶ *to* '*take*,' *seize, Chr* 1072,1076. t. on *to touch.*

+tacclan *to tame, subdue*, GPH 402 (= +ðaccian).

tācen, tācn n., nap. tācen, tācnu 'TOKEN,' *symbol, sign, signal, mark, indication, suggestion, Æ,CP* : *portent, marvel, wonder, miracle* : *evidence, proof* : *standard, banner.*

tācen-=tācn-

tācencircol m. *indiction*, TC 126³.

tācnan (Cp)=tæcnan

tācnberend m. *standard-bearer*, ÆGr 27¹⁵.

tācnbora m. *standard-bearer* : *guide*, ApT.

±tācnian *to mark, indicate* : *betoken, denote, signify, represent, Bl,Bo*; AO,CP : *symbolise, ÆH,Bl* : *portend* : *demonstrate, express.* ['*token*']

+tācni(g)endlic *typical, emblematic, ÆH* 2·278¹⁴; ÆP 122¹⁷.

±tācnung f. *sign, presage, token, signal, Bo* : *manifestation, signification, type, Bo,BH* : *indication, symptom, proof* : *dispensation, AO* 60¹ : *phase* (*of moon*), *zodiacal sign,* ANS 145·256. ['*tokening*']

tācon, tācun=tācen

tācor, tācur m. *brother-in-law*, Æ.

tāde, tādi(g)e f. '*toad*,' *WW.*

tæbere *a weaving tool? tenterhook?* WW 294¹⁷.

tæcan, pret. tæhte *to transfer, translate*, Æ. [*ON.* taka]

±tæcan *to show, declare, demonstrate, Æ, AO* : 'TEACH*' ('*i-tæche*'), *instruct, train, Æ*; CP : *assign, prescribe, direct, Æ,CP* : *warn* : *persuade*, MtR 28¹⁴. +t. fram *dismiss*, LL 162,22.

tæcing f. *teaching, instruction, Æ* : *doctrine* : *direction, injunction, command, rule.*

tæcnan *to mark by a token, denote, designate, mark out.* [*Ger.* zeichnen]

-tæcne v. earfoð-t.

tæcnend m. *index-finger*, A 13·329, WW 426³⁸.

tæcnian=tācnian

tæcning f. *demonstration, proof*, Bo 90¹.

tæfl, tæfel (e²) fn. *cube, die, game with dice or tables, Gl,Wy.* [*L.* tabula; v. '*tavel*']

tæfl-an, -ian *to gamble, Gl.* ['*tavel*']

tæfle adj. *given to dice-playing*, GnE 185.

tæflere m. *gambler*, WW. [v. '*tavel*']

tæflstān m. *gambling-stone, die, Gl.* [v. '*tavel*']

tæflung f. *gaming, playing at dice*, NC 325.

tæg (A)=tēag

tægel, tægl (e) m. '*tail*,' *LL,WW*; Æ.

tæglhær n. *hair of the tail*, Lcd 1·360'.

tægðian (M)=teogoðian

tæherian (*NG*)=tēarian
tæhher (NG)=tēar
tæhte pret. 3 sg. of tæcan.
tæl (a, e) n. *number, Æ.*
tǣl (ā) f. *blame, reproach, calumny, abuse,* CP,WW : *blasphemy : disgrace.* ['*tele*']
+**tæl** I. (e, ea) n., nap. +talu *number, series,* Æ,LG : *numeral,* ÆGR : *number of people, tribe* : *catalogue,* WW418³⁶ : *reckoning, estimation, opinion.* ['*tel*,' '*i-tel*'] II. adj. np. +tale *swift, ready,* PPs56⁵ : *competent,* WW505³. [v. '*tall*']
tæla=tela
±**tǣlan** (ē) *to blame, censure, scold, reprove, reproach, accuse,* Æ,AO,CP : *speak ill of, slander, insult, deride,* Bo,LRG,LL,WW : *despise, maltreat: dispute.* ['*tele*']
tælberend=telgberend
+**tælcircul** m. *cycle, series,* WW204⁴².
+**tælcræft** (e) m. *arithmetic,* OEG3117.
+**tæld**=+teld; -**tǣle** v. lēof-, un-t.
tǣlend m. *slanderer, backbiter* : *mocker, scoffer* : *reprover.*
tǣlende *censorious, slanderous,* Bl,LL.
tǣlere (ē) m. *derider, scoffer,* KGL75¹⁶.
+**tælfæst** *measurable,* LPs38⁶.
tælfers (e¹) n. '*versus catalecticus*,' OEG127.
+**tælful** *numerous,* Sc231¹⁰.
tǣlful (ā) *blameworthy,* CHRD67³⁶.
tælg=telg
tǣlhlehter m. *derision,* WW172⁴. [hleahtor]
tælian=talian
tæling f. *reproof,* CP : *derogation : slander, derision.*
tælla (GPH394)=telga; **tællan**=tellan
tǣllēas *blameless,* CP. adv. -līce, CP.
tǣllic (ā) *blameworthy : slanderous, blasphemous.* adv. -līce *reprehensibly : shamelessly?* CHRD70⁵.
tælmearc f. *date, period,* Gu849. [talu]
tælmet n. *measure, portion,* AN113. [talu]
tǣlnes (ē) f. *blame, reproof,* CP : *derogation : slander, calumny, insult.*
+**tælrīm** n. *order, succession,* SOL38.
±**tælsum** *in numbers, rhythmic,* OEG.
tǣlweorð=tǣlwierð-
tǣl-wierðe, -wierðlic *reprehensible, blameworthy,* CP. adv. -līce.
tǣlwierðlicnes (eo²) f. *blameableness,* CP 52¹⁵.
+**tælwīs** (e) *skilled in arithmetic,* BF112⁹, WW207⁴⁰.
tǣlwyrd-, tǣlwyrð-=tǣlwierð-
tǣman=tīeman
tæmespīle f. *sieve-frame, sieve-stand? sieve-stake?* LL455,17 and 3·255. [v. '*temse*']
tæmian (GD11⁹)=temian
tǣnel (ē¹, ī²) m. *wicker basket,* Æ,Gl. ['*teanel*'; tān]

tǣnen *made of twigs,* OEG. [tān]
tæng-=teng-; **tǣnil**=tǣnel
tæppa m. '*tap*,' *spigot, IM.*
tæppe f? *strip of stuff or cloth,* '*tape*,' WW 107³³.
tæpp-ed, -et n. *figured cloth, tapestry, carpet,* TC,WW. ['*tapet*']
tæppelbred n. *footstool,* NG.
tæppere m. *tapster, tavern-keeper,* Sc,WW. ['*tapper*']
tæppestre f. *tapstress, female tavern-keeper,* ÆGr. ['*tapster*']
tæppet=tæpped
tæpplan *to open* (*a cask*)? *furnish it with a tap or spout? IM*125. ['*tap*']
tæppilbred=tæppelbred
tær pret. 3 sg. of teran; **tǣr**=tēar
tǣsan (±) *to pull, tear, comb, card,* Lcd : (†) *wound, injure, assault:* (+) *influence,* CP 297¹⁸. ['*tease*']
±**tǣse** I. *pleasant,* Met : *convenient, suitable,* B. ['*i-tase*'] II. (+) n. *advantage, convenience,* CP387 : *useful thing, implement.*
tǣsel f. '*teasel*' (*plant*), Lcd1·282¹⁵.
+**tǣslic** *convenient.* adv. -līce *conveniently : gently, softly, smoothly,* CP.
tǣslice (NG)=ðæslice
+**tǣsnes** f. *advantage, convenience,* WW.
tǣso=tēosu
+**tǣsu**=+tǣse II.
tǣtan *to gladden, cheer,* WY4.
tætteca m? *rag, tatter, shred?* Æ,KC (v. BT).
tǣð=tēð, v. tōð.
-**tǣwe** (ēo) v. æl-t.
tāh pret. 3 sg. of tēon II.
+**tāh** n. *teaching,* RIM2 (ES65·188).
tāhe (GL)=tā
tāhspura m. *spur, tip of toe?* WW197¹⁴.
tāhte=tǣhte pret. 3 sg. of tǣcan.
tal (N)=talu; **tāl**=tǣl; **tala**=tela
tald=teald pp. of tellan.
+**tale** v. tæl.
talente f. '*talent*' (*money of account*), AO. [L.]
±**talian** (æ) *to count, calculate, reckon, account, consider, think, esteem, value,* BH,CP,LG,W : *argue,* CP : *tell, relate,* LG; Æ : *impute, assign,* Æ,BH. (=tellan.) ['*tale*']
+**talscipe** m. *multitude,* NG.
talt-=tealt-
talu f. '*tale*,' *series, calculation : list,* WW : *statement, deposition, relation, communication, narrative,* Æ,KC : *fable, tale, story* : *accusation, action at law* (v. LL3·226).
+**talu** v. +tǣl.
tālwyrð-=tǣlwierð-
tam '*tame*,' Æ,Bo,WW : *tractable, gentle, mild,* Bo,Gn.

tama m. *tameness*, Bo,MET.
tamclan *to tame, soothe*, CHRD 96[18].
-tamcol v. un-t.
tān I. m. *twig, rod, switch, branch* : *rod of divination.* **II.** *shooting? spreading?* GEN 2360. **III.** pl. of tā.
tānede *diseased in the toes?* WW 161[28].
±**tang**, tange (o) f. (sg. and pl.) *pincers, 'tongs,' forceps, Æ,BH,Bf,Gl; Æ.*
+**tang** (w. d.) *in contact with* (=pret. 3 sg. of +tingan). adv. +tange (o), RIM 42?
+**tanglīce** *together*, RB 47[15].
tānhlyta m. *soothsayer, augur, diviner*, WW 189[3]. [tān, hlot]
tānhlytere m. *soothsayer, diviner*, WW 183[32].
+**tanned** *tanned*, WW 118[7]. ['*tanned*']
tannere m. '*tanner*,' KC 2·411'.
taper (*Lcd,WW*)=tapor
taperæx f. *small axe*, CHR 1031A, CC 28[16]. [*ON.* taparöx]
tapor (ea[1]; e[2], u[2]) m. *lamp-wick, 'taper,' candle*, CP : *a feeble light*, PH 114. [*Keltic?*]
taporberend m. *acolyte*, GL.
taran v. teoru.
targa? m., **targe?** f. *small shield, buckler*, KC. [v. '*targe*']
+**targed** *furnished with a shield*, OEG 2259.
taru? f. *tear, rent*, WW 416[27]. [teran]
tasol, tasul (GL)=teosel; **-tāwere** v. flæsc-t.
±**tāwian** *to prepare, make ready, make* : *till, cultivate, BH* : *harass, afflict, insult, Æ, AO*. t. tō bysmore *outrage, profane, Æ,W.* ['*taw*']
+**tāw-u**, -a np. *apparatus, implements* : *genitalia*, LCD 26a.
te-=tō-; **tēa** (NG)=tīen
+**tēad** (ē) pp. of +tēon and +tēagan.
tēafor I. n. *red, red lead, vermilion, purple, WW.* [v. '*tiver*'] **II.** meaning doubtful, or ? tēaforgēap (v. GK), RUIN 31.
tēag (æ, ē) **I.** f. *cord, band, thong, fetter, Cr, WW.* ['*tie*'] **II.** *case, chest, Æ,WW* : *enclosure, BC.* ['*tye*']
+**tēagan** (ē) pret. +tēde, pp. +tēad *to make, prepare, dress, till.*
teagor (*Gu*)=tēar
tēah I. pret. 3 sg. of tēon I. and II. **II.**= tēag
teal-=tal-, tæl-, tel-
tēal-=tæl-; +**teald**=+teld
tealde pret. 3 sg. of tellan; **tealgor**=telgor
tealt *unstable, precarious, Run,W.* ['*tealt*']
tealt(r)ian (a) *to totter, shake, stumble, waver* : *be untrustworthy* : *amble*. [cp. *Ger.* zelter]
tēam (ē) m. *descendant, family, race, line, Æ,Mk,TC* : *child-bearing, Æ* : *brood, Æ* : *company, band, Æ* : '*team*' (*of horses, oxen,*

etc.), *WW* : *vouching to warranty, right of jurisdiction in matters of warranty, EC,LL.*
+**tēama** (ȳ) m. *warrantor, surety*, LL.
tēaman=tīeman
tēamful *fruitful, LPs,WW.* [v. '*teemful*']
tēamian=tīeman
tēampōl m. *breeding pool*, EC 322'.
tēan- (A)=tēon-; **teaper** (K)=tapor
tēapor (*Lcd*)=tēafor
tēar m. *drop, Cr,Lcd* : '*tear*,*' *B,Bl*; CP : *what is distilled from anything in drops, 'nectar,' WW*; CM.
tearflian *to turn, roll, wallow*, Mk 9[20].
tēargēotende *tear-shedding, tearful*, NIC 508[15].
tēarian (tæherian, ē[1]) *to weep*, JnL. ['*tear*']
tēarig *tearful*, HGL : *watery*, LCD 125a.
tēarighlēor *with tearful cheeks*, GEN 2274.
tearn (WW 286[7])=stearn; **tearos** v. teoru.
teart *sharp, rough, severe, Æ,OEG.* ['*tart*'; tær pret. of teran]
teartlic *sharp, rough, Æ.* adv. -līce, OEG. ['*tartly*']
teartnes f. *sharpness, roughness, hardness, OEG; Æ.* ['*tartness*']
teartnumol *biting, effectual*, LCD 1·152[3].
teaslīce (NG)=ðæslīce
tēað=tēoð pres. pl. of tēon I. and II.
tebl, tebl-, tebil-=tæfl, tæfl-
tēc-=tæc-; **tēd-**=tīed-; +**tēd**=+tēad
tēde pret. of tēagan.
tēder=tȳder; **tēdr-**=tīed(e)r-, tȳdr-
tefel, tefil=tæfl
tēfrung (=īe) f. *picture*, AS 21[4].
tēg=tēag; **tēgan**=(1) tīegan; (2) tēagan
tēge=tīge; **tegl**=tægl; **tēgð-**=tēoð-
tēh=tēah pret. 3 sg. of tēon.
teherian (A)=tēarian
tehher, teher (*NG*)=tēar
tēhton pret. pl. of tǣcan.
teissu (LkL)=teosu; +**tel**=+tæl; **tēl-**=tǣl-
tela (i, ea, eo) **I.** adv. *well, fitly, properly, rightly, very, good, CP* : *prosperously, beneficially.* **II.** interj. *well! good!*
±**teld** n. *tent, pavilion, tabernacle, Æ,BH, TC.* ['*teld*']
+**teldgehlīwung** f. *tabernacle*, BF 74[14].
teldian *to spread* (*net*), *set* (*trap*), *Cp,PPs* : *entrap.* ['*teld*']
teldsticca m. *tent-peg*, JUD 4[21,22].
+**teldung** f. *tabernacle*, EPs 18[5]; 77[60].
+**teldwurðung** f. *feast of tabernacles*, WW 107[17].
teldwyrhta m. *tent-maker*, ÆH 1·392'.
telede=tealde pret. 3 sg. of tellan.
+**telfers** (OEG)=tælfers
telg (æ) m. *dye, colour, tincture*, BH,GL.
telga m. *twig, branch, bough, shoot, CP* : *pole, stock*, EC 95'.

+**telg-an**, -ian *to dye*, WW.

telgberend *yielding a dye*, WW462¹⁹.

telge f.=telga

telgestre (æ¹) m. *dyer*, GD342³.

telgian I. *to put forth branches*, RIM34. **II.**=talian. **III.**=telgan

telgor mf., telgra m., telgre f. *twig, branch, shoot*, Æ,*Gl*,*Lcd*. [v. '*tiller*']

telgung f. *dye, purple dye*, WW.

telian=tilian

±**tellan** (æ, ea) *to* 'TELL' ('*i-telle*'), *reckon, count, number, compute, calculate*, Æ : *account, estimate, consider, think, esteem, believe*, CP : *charge against, impute to* : *assign*: *state, recount, enumerate, announce, relate*, Æ. t. gelīc *compare*. [talu]

-**tellendlic** v. un-t.

teltrē, teltrēo n. *weaving-tool? tenterhook? tent-peg?* WW.

+**telwīs** *skilled in reckoning*, BF112⁹.

tēm=tēam ; **tema**=tama

tēman=tīeman

tēmbyrst m. *failure to secure a voucher*, EC 202¹. [tēam]

Temes, Temese f. *river Thames*, AO. [*L.* Tamisia]

±**temesian** (i²) *to sift*, MkL. ['*temse*']

±**temian** *to tame, subdue*, Æ,CP,*Lcd*,LG : (+) *suffer, permit*, ÆL23⁸¹⁰. ['*teme*']

tempel, templ n. '*temple*,' Æ,*Bl*,CP,G,VPs. [*L.* templum]

tempel-=templ-

tempelgeat n. *temple-door*, W49²⁵.

tempelhūs n. *temple*, ByH118²⁴.

templgeweorc n. *structure of the temple*, W277²⁵.

templhālgung f. *dedication of the temple*, OEG40³⁶.

templic adj. *of a temple*, OEG.

±**temprian** v. *to* '*temper*,' *moderate*, Æ,*Gl*, Sc : *cure, heal*, Æ : *control, curb*, Æ (refl.), *Lcd*. [*Lat*.]

temprung f. *tempering, moderation*, Sc.

tēn (VPs)=tīen ; **tēnan**=tȳnan

-**tendan** (y) v. ā-, for-, on-t.

tender=tynder

tend-ing, -ling f. *burning, stinging*, NC,GD. [v. '*tind*']

tēne=tīen ; **tēnel** (*Ep*)=tænel

±**tengan** (æ) *to press towards, hasten*, Æ. āweg t. *get away, get off*. +t. on *assail*, AO.

+**tenge** *near to, resting on* : *oppressing, burdensome*, AO.

tēnil=tænel

tennan *to lure, coax?* WY4?

tēo pres. 1 sg. of tēon I. and II.

teochian=teohhian

tēode pret. of tēon III., tēogan, teohhian.

teofenian† *to join, put together*, CREAT.

tēofor=tēafor

tēofrian *to appoint?* PPs117²¹.

tēogan=teohhian

teogeða, teogoða=tēoða

teogoðian *to* '*tithe*,' *grant or pay tithes*, Æ, CP,G : *divide by ten*, Æ.

teoh fm., gds. teohhe *race* : *band, troop, company, society*. [*Ger*. zeche]

tēoh imperat. of tēon.

+**tēoh** n. *matter, material, universe?* RIM2.

teohhe v. teoh.

±**teohhian** (i, io) *to determine, intend, propose*, Æ,CP : *consider, think, judge, estimate*. [*OHG*. gizehōn]

+**teohhung** f. *arrangement, ordering*, HL 13⁶⁹.

teohian=teohhian ; **teol-**=tel-, til-

teolōyrl n. '*foramen*,' '*fenestra*,' OEG.

teom (MtR21⁵)=tam

tēon I. (±) sv² *to pull, tug, draw, drag, row* (*boat*), CP : *draw together* : *withdraw, take*, LL356,70 : *entice, allure, induce, lead, bring*, CP : *bring up, educate*, Æ : *bring to, attract*, AO : *arrogate*, CP : *bring forth, produce*, Æ : *restrain*, LL : *betake oneself to, go, roam* : (+) *dispute*, NG : (+) *string up, play* (*instrument*). +togen *lengthened, long* (*of vowels*), ÆGR49¹⁴. ['TEE*,' '*i-teon*'; *teohan] **II.** sv¹ (but forms belonging to tēon I. often found) *accuse, censure*, Æ,LL ; AO : *proceed against successfully*, ANS144·253. ['*tee*'; *tīhan] **III.** wv. (±) *to prepare, furnish forth, arrange, adorn, deck* : *produce, work, do, create, make*, Æ : *settle, fix, establish, constitute, ordain*. [=teohhian] **IV.** num.= tīen. **V.** n.=tēona. **VI.**=dēon (v. JAW19).

tēona m. *injury, hurt, wrong*, *Bl*,*Mt* ; AO : *accusation, reproach, insult, contumely*, Æ, AO,CP : *anger, grief* : *malice*, Æ : *enmity, hostility*. ['*teen*']

tēoncwide† m. *hurtful speech* : *blasphemy*.

tēoncwidian *to slander, calumniate*, GL.

tēond I. m. *accuser*, LL. **II.** *drawer*, BH 288¹⁴.

tēone f.=tēona

tēonere m. *slanderer*, LPs71⁴.

tēonful *slanderous, evil, rebellious, painful*, SPs,W ; Æ. ['*teenful*']

tēonhete† m. *malicious hate*.

tēonian (ȳ) *to injure, irritate*, LPs : *slander*. ['*teen*']

tēonlēas *free from suffering*, MFH174.

tēonlēg† m. *destroying flame*.

tēonlic *destructive, shameful, hurtful*. adv. -līce.

tēonrǣden (e²) f. *abuse, wrong, injury, humiliation*, Æ.

tēonsmið m. *evil-doer*, Gu 176.
tēontig=hundtēontig
tēonword n. *reproach, abuse, calumny*, Æ, Lcd.
±**tēorian** *to fail, cease, become weary, be tired, exhausted, Gl,Lcd,LL,PPs* : '*tire*,' *weary, exhaust, PPs.* [teran]
±**tēorigendlic** *failing, defective*, Sc 181[4], ByH 56[15].
teoro=teoru
+**tēorodnes** f. *debility, weariness*, Gl.
teors m. '*calamus*,' '*veretrum*,' *Lcd,WW.* ['*tarse*']
teoru (e) n., occl. gs. tearos and wk. a. taran '*tar*,' *bitumen, distillation from a tree, resin, gum, balsam, Gl,Lcd* : *wax from the ear.*
±**tēorung** f. *exhaustion, weariness*, Æ.
teosel (a, e) m. *die* ('*tessera*'). [L.]
teosu (æ, e) f. *harm, injury, ruin, wrong.*
teosusprǣc f. *harmful speech*, PPs 139[11].
teosuword (teso-) n. *calumny, harmful speech*, NC.
teoswian (e) *to injure, harm*, Sol 94.
tēoð pres. pl. of tēon I. and II.
tēoða (ē) '*TENTH*,' *Æ,AO,Chr.* tēoðan dæl *tenth part.* [teogeða]
tēoðe *tenthly*, LL 181,10.
±**tēoðian** *to divide by ten, tithe, Æ* : *take a tenth* : *give tithes*, Æ,BC,CP,G.
tēoðing=tēoðung
tēoðingdæg m. *tithing day, tenth day*, Æ.
tēoðingealdor m. *ruler over ten, dean, captain of ten*, RB.
tēoðingmann m. '*tithing-man*,' *headborough, LL* : *captain of ten*, Æ.
tēoðung f. *division into ten, decimation, tenth part, tithe, 'tithing*,' *Æ,Lk,LL* : *band of ten men, LL.*
tēoðungcēap m. *tithe*, Bl 39[11].
tēoðunggeorn *diligent in paying tithes*, A 12·518[26].
tēoðungland n. *land set apart for tithes*, LL 2·750.
tēoðungsceatt m. *tithing-money, tithes*, Bl, LL.
tēowlic=tōwlic
teped (*KGl*), tepet=tæpped; **tēr** (*Lcd*)=tēar
+**ter** n. *tearing, laceration* : *thing torn* : *tumult, discord.*
±**teran**[4] (ea, eo) *to 'TEAR*,' *lacerate.*
terdnes (A 13·34)=teartnes
tergan=tirgan
termen (i[2]) m. *term, end*, Bf,Lcd. [L.]
tero, teru (*Ep,WW*)=teoru
tes-=teos-; +**tēse**=+tǣse
teter m. '*tetter*,' *skin eruption, eczema, ring-worm*, CP,Gl,Lcd,Sc.
teting=tyhting; **tēð** v. tōð.
tēða=tēoða; **-tewestre** v. wull-t.

+**tēðed** *toothed*, AA 31[7].
Tī=Tīw; **tīan** (N)=tēon III.
tīber† n. *offering, sacrifice, victim*, Gen.
tībernes f. *sacrificing, destruction*, AO 50[18].
ticcen (y) n. *kid, Æ,MtL.* ['*ticchen*']
ticgen (NG)=ticcen
ticgende *proudly adorned*, OEG.
ticia m. '*tick*' (*insect*), Gl.
tictator m. *dictator*, AO 70[3]. [L.]
tīd f. *time, period, season, while* : *hour* : *feast-day, festal-tide* : *canonical hour or service.* on tīde *at the proper time.* ['TIDE']
tīdan (±) *to betide, happen, Bo,LL* : *fall to* (*one's lot*), *BC.* ['*tide*,' '*i-tide*']
tīdanðēnung=tīdðēnung
tidd-=tīd-, tȳd-
tīddæg† m. *lifetime.*
tīdelīce=tīdlīce
tīdembwlātend=tīdymbwlātend
tīder=tīedre
tīdfara m. *one who travels at his own convenience?* Cr 1674 (or ? two words).
tīdgenge *having a monthly course, periodical*, GPH 392.
tīdlic *timely, seasonable, opportune*, AO : *temporal* : *temporary.* adv. -līce.
tīdlicnes f. *opportunity, fit time*, NG.
tīdran=tȳdran
tīdre=tīedre
tīdrēn m. *timely rain*, Deut 28[12].
±**tīdrian** (ȳ) *to become feeble, weak* : *decay.*
tīdsang mn. *canonical hours, lauds*, Æ.
tīdscēawere m. *astrologer*, WW 176[4].
tīdscriptor m. *chronographer, chronicler*, WW 204[17] (hybrid word).
tīdðēnung f. *service at one of the canonical hours*, FBO.
tīdum adv. *at times, occasionally.*
tīdung f. (usu. pl.) *event, tidings, news, Chr.* ['*tiding*']
tīdwrītere m. *chronicler*, Gl.
tīdwurdung f. *service at one of the canonical hours*, HL 11[67].
tīdymbwlātend (e[2]) m. *astrologer*, Lcd.
tīeder=tīedre
tīederlic (ē, ī, ȳ) *weak*, CP.
tīedernes (ē, ī, ȳ) *frailty* (*of body or soul*), CP.
tīedran=tȳdran
tīedre (ē, ī, ȳ) *weak, frail, infirm, CP* : *faint-hearted* : *fleeting.*
±**tīegan** (ē, ī, ȳ) *to 'tie*,' *bind, Æ*; *CP* : *join, connect, ÆGr.* [tēag]
tīegle=tigle; **tieht-**=tyht-
tīehð pres. 3 sg. of tēon I. and II.
tīel-=til-; **tīema**=tīma
tīeman (ǣ, ē, ī, ȳ) *to bring forth, engender, beget, propagate, Æ,W* : *make answerable for another person, call as witness, Æ,Bas* : (±) *vouch to warranty, LL.* ['*teem*'; tēam]

+**tīeme I.** (ē, ȳ) *suitable.* **II.** (ȳ) *team, yoke,* Æ.
tīen (ē, ī, ȳ) num. 'TEN,' *CP.*
tīenambre (ȳ) *holding ten ambers,* LCD 32b.
tīenbebod (ē) n. *decalogue,* OEG 11[108]
tīenfeald (ȳ) *ten-fold,* Æ.
tīengewintred (ȳ) *ten years old,* LL 19,27 H.
tīennihte (ȳ) *ten days old,* BF 162[13].
tīenstrenge (ē, ī) *ten-stringed,* VPs.
tīenwintre (ȳ) *ten years old,* Æ : *ten years long,* AO.
tīer *heap?* (GK), *drop?* (Sedgef.), MET 20[81].
tīfe f. *bitch,* LCD 64a.
tīfer=tīber
-**tīg** (ē, ȳ) v. *fore-,* forð-t.; **Tīg**=Tīw
tīgan=tīegan; **tīge**=tyge
tigel, tigele (o²) f. *earthen vessel, crock, pot, potsherd :* '*tile,*' *brick,* AO; Mdf : *slabs for roofing,* Cp,Lcd,VPs.
tigelærne f. *tile kiln? house of brick?* KC 3·130'.
tigelen *made of pot, earthenware,* SPs 2⁹.
tigelfāg *tile-adorned,* AN 842.
tigelgetel n. *tale of bricks,* Ex 5[18].
tigelgeweorc n. *brick-making,* Æ.
tigellēah m *brick-field,* KC 5·267[21].
tigelstān m. *tile,* ES 11·66. ['*tilestone*']
tigelwyrhta (y) m. *brick-maker, potter.*
tigen pp. of tēon II.
tiger pl. tigras '*tiger,*' Æ,Nar.
tīging f. *tie, connection,* ÆGR 14[14]. [tīgan]
tigl=(1) tigel; (2) tygel
tigle f. '*muraenula,*' *sea-mullet?* WW 180[30].
tigle, tigol(e)=tigel, tigele
tigon pret. pl. of tēon II.
tīgrisc *of a tiger,* A 4·161.
tigðian (AO)=tīðian
-**tigu** v. egeðgetigu [egðe]; **tigule**=tigele
tīhian=teohhian
tiht (y) m. *charge, crime,* LL,WW. [tēon II.]
tihtan I. (y) *to accuse,* LL. [tēon II.] **II.**= tyhtan
tihtbysig *involved in accusations, of bad reputation,* v. LL 2·305 and ANS 144·253.
tihtle (y) f. *accusation, suit, charge,* AO.
tihtlian *to accuse, charge,* LL.
tīhð pres. 3 sg. of tēon II.
til I. *good, apt, suitable, useful, profitable : excellent : brave : abounding.* **II.**† n. *goodness, fitness.* **III.** n.=till. **IV.** prep. *to,* MtL,OET. ['*till*']
tila=tela
tilen (eo) f. *endeavour,* GD 194[12].
tilfremmende *well-doing,* RD 60⁷.
tilgan=tilian; **till** (OET)=twilic
tilia, tilig(e)a (y) m. *tiller, workman, hind, labourer, farmer, husbandman,* Mt; Æ. ['*tilie*']

tilian (eo, y) *to aim at, aspire to, strive after, try, endeavour,* Æ; CP : (±) *procure, obtain, gain, provide,* Æ : *exert oneself, work, make, generate,* Æ,CP : *tend, cherish, cultivate,* '*TILL,*' *plough,* CP : *trade, traffic,* Æ : (±) *treat, cure.*
tiligea=tilia
tiling=tilung
till† n. *station, standing-place.*
till-=til-, tyll-
+**tillan** *to touch, attain,* Æ.
tillic† adj. *fit, good,* RD. adv. -līce.
tilmōdig† *well-disposed, kind, good.*
±**tilð,** tilðe (y) f. '*tilth,*' *labour, husbandry,* LL,W : *crop, harvest,* LL : *gain, profit,* OEG.
tilung (eo, ie, io, y) f. *acquisition, procuring : care, solicitude : occupation, work, performance,* CP : *tending, culture, husbandry,* Æ : *produce, gain, income,* Æ.
tīma m. 'TIME,' *period, space of time,* Æ, AO : *lifetime,* Æ : *fixed time,* Æ,AO,CP : *favourable time, opportunity,* CP : *a metrical unit,* Bf.
tīman=tīeman
±**timber** n. '*timber,*' *building material,* LL : *act of building : building, structure,* BH, Lcd,MtL,VPs : *trees, woods,* AO. [v. Mdf]
timbergeweorc n. *cutting timber,* BC 1·344⁹.
+**timberhālgung** f. *feast of tabernacles,* OEG 56[287].
timberhrycg m. *wooded ridge?* KC.
timberland (y¹, o³) n. *land given for repairing and maintaining buildings : land on which to grow timber* (BTs), KC 5·236[12].
+**timbernes** f. *building up, edification,* MFH 124.
timbor I. *a revolving borer, auger?* WW 273⁸. **II.** =timber
±**timbran,** timbrian *to build, construct, erect,* BH,CP,G,Gen,LL : *effect, do,* AO,CP; Æ : *edify, instruct : cut* '*timber.*'
+**tim-bre** n., -bru f. *building, structure,* Æ, AO.
timbr(i)end mf. *builder,* BH,GD.
±**timbrung** f. *act of building,* Æ : *structure : edification.*
+**tīmian** (ȳ) *to happen, fall out,* Æ,BF.
tīmlīce *quickly, soon,* ÆT 12.
timpana m. *timbrel,* Æ,CP,VPs. ['*tympan*']
timpestre f. *female timbrel-player,* LPs 67[26].
timple f. *a weaver's instrument,* LL 455,15¹ (cp. ātimplian).
tin I. n. '*tin,*' *CP.* **II.** f. *beam, rafter,* GL. **III.**=tinen
tīn num.=tīen
tinclian *to tickle,* Sc 52,88.
+**tinclic**=+tyngelic

tind m. *spike, beak, prong, tooth of a fork, Cp,Ep,Sol.* [' *tine* ']

tindig *spiked,* WW 116¹².

tindiht *forked, jagged, beaked,* GL,MH.

tindre=tyndre

tinen *made of tin,* ÆGr. [' *tinnen* ']

+**ting,** tinge=+tyng, tynge

+**tingan³** *to press against,* AN 138.

+**tingcræft** m. '*mechanica,*' *rhetoric,* HGL 479.

-**tining** v. gafol-t.

tinn *beam,* A 19·491.

tinnan *to stretch,* GL : *desire, long for? burn?* RIM 54.

tinnen=tinen

tinstrenge=tīenstrenge

tinterg=tintreg

tinterðegn=tintregðegn

tintreg (*AO*; Æ) n., tintrega m. *torture, torment, punishment,* AO,Lk,W. [' *tintregh* ']

tintreganlic=tintreglic

tintregend (terg) m. *torturer,* WW 341¹⁹.

±**tintregian** *to torment, torture, punish,* Æ, AO.

tintreglic *full of torment, infernal,* BH 346¹².

tintregstōw f. *place of torment,* GUTH 38⁴.

tintregðegn m. *torturer, executioner,* MtR, WW.

tintregung f. *torture, punishment,* Æ,WW.

tintrian (AO)=tintregian

tio-=teo-; **tiol-**=tel-, til-

tīr (ȳ) m. (†) *fame, glory, honour, ornament : name of the rune for* t : *name of a planet and a god (Mars),* RUN 17.

tīrēadig† *glorious, famous.*

tīrfæst† *glorious, famous.*

tīrfruma m. *prince of glory,* CR 206.

tīrgan (e, y;=ie) *to worry, exasperate, pain, provoke, excite,* Gl,Gu. [' *tar* ']

tīrging (y) f. '*zelus,*' *provocation,* BLPS.

tīrlēas *inglorious, infamous,* B 843.

tīrmeahtig† *of glorious might.*

tirð pres. 3 sg. of teran.

tīrwine m. (*famous*) *follower, retainer,* MET 25²¹.

tit, tite=titt

±**tītelian** *to indicate by a written mark, entitle, ascribe,* Æ : *appoint,* LL. [*L.*]

tītelung f. '*recapitulatio,*' *a giving of titles or headings,* OEG 1153.

titolose '*tidulosa*' (*plant*), OEG 56⁴²⁵.

titt m. '*teat,*' *nipple, breast,* Lcd,LkLR.

tittstrycel m. *teat,* WW 158⁴⁴.

tītul m. '*title,*' *superscription,* MkL 15²⁶. [*L.*]

tīð I. f. *assent, permission : giving, grant, boon, favour, concession,* Æ,BH (tigð). tīðe fremian *to grant.* [' *tithe* '] II. pres. 3 sg. of tēon I. and II.

tīða m., tīðe f. (only in phr. t. bēon, weorðan) *sharer in, receiver, grantee,* BH,Mt. [' *tithe* ']

±**tīðian** (often w. g. thing and d. pers.) *to give, bestow, grant, permit,* Æ,AO. [' TITHE ']

tīðing=tēoðung

tīðrian (ȳ) *to be favourable (to),* RWH 66¹³.

+**tīung** f. *preparation, arrangement,* Cp 684A.

tīurung=tēorung

Tīw *Tiw (northern god of war), Mars,* GL, MH : *name of the rune for* t.

Tīwesdæg m. '*Tuesday,*' *Bf*; RB.

Tīwesniht f. *Monday night,* LCD.

tō I. prep. **α** (w. d.) (motion) 'TO,' *into,* Æ,AO,CP. tō emnes *abreast of* : (rest) *at* : (figurative direction, object of verb) *conducing to, to.* fōn tō rīce *to ascend the throne* : (definition, destination) *for, as a.* wyrcan tō wīte *to contrive as a punishment* : *in accordance with, according to* : (time) *at.* tō midre niht *at midnight.* tō dæg *to-day.* tō langum fyrste *for a long time* : (with gerunds) *to express purpose, etc.* **β** (w. g.) (of time) *at.* II. adv. *besides, also,* Bo : '*too,*' *excessively, Bl,Cr* : *thereto : towards, in the direction of : in addition, besides.* adverbial phrases;—tō ðām (ðǣm), tō ðæs (1) *so* (adeo), *to such an extent.* (2) *to that end.* (3) *moreover, however.* tō hwæs *whither.* tō ðām ðæt, tō ðȳ ðæt *in order that.* tō ðon ðæt *until.* tō ðæs ðe *when, where.* tō hwon, tō hwȳ *for what, wherefore.* tō sōðum *truly.* tō ðearfe *according to what is needed.* ðær tō ēacan *in addition thereto.* ne tō wuhte *by no means.* tō him *next or nearest to him.*

tō- prefix I. with accent (stress) it has the meaning of adv. tō (as in tōcweðan, tōbringan, tōcuman). [*Ger.* zu-] II. without accent=*asunder* (as in tōbrecan). [*Ger.* zer-]

tōætȳcan (ē³) *to increase,* BH 112¹. [ēac]

tōætȳcnes f. *increase,* BH 226 CA³¹.

tōāmearcian *to mark out, assign,* SC 29⁵.

tōbǣdan *to elevate, exalt,* BF 144²,LPs 36³⁵.

tōbēatan⁷ *to beat severely, destroy by beating,* AO,Chr. [' tobeat ']

tōbefealdan⁷ *to fold together,* WW 343¹⁰.

tōbeflōwan⁷ *to flow up to,* LPs 61¹¹.

tōbegietan⁵ *to acquire, purchase,* EHy 4¹⁶.

tōbelimpan³ (impers.) *it belongs, behoves,* BL 49¹.

tōberan⁴ *to carry, remove, carry off, purloin, Bl* : *scatter, dissipate, distract, destroy : swell,* CP : *separate.* [' tobear ']

tōberennes f. *difference,* WW 390²⁷.

tōberstan[3] (intr.) *to burst apart, go to pieces,* Æ,AO : (tr.) *cause to burst apart, shatter,* Æ. ['*toburst*']

tōberstung f. *bursting,* LCD 74a.

tōbīgend *bowing down, tottering,* WW 386[30].

tōblǣdan *to inflate, puff up,* Sc 82[10] : *dilate, enlarge,* LHy 3[1].

tōblāwan[7] *to blow to pieces, blast, scatter,* Æ : *puff up, inflate, distend,* Lcd. ['*toblow*']

tōblāwennes f. *inflation,* ÆH 1·86[13].

tōborstennes f. *abscess,* LCD 1·322'.

tōbrǣdan *to spread abroad, disperse, scatter,* AO,CP : *spread out, extend,* Bo,Mt; Æ : *open, dilate : multiply.* ['*tobrede*']

tōbrǣd(ed)nes f. *broadness, breadth,* Ps.

tōbrecan[4] *to break in pieces, break up, shatter, destroy, ruin, wreck, overthrow, annul,* Æ, Bo,Lcd; AO,CP : *diffuse : break through, violate, force,* KC ; Æ,AO : *interrupt.* ['*tobreak*']

tōbrēdan I.=tōbregdan. II.=tōbrǣdan

tōbregdan[3] *tear in pieces, wrench apart, rend, lacerate,* AO,MtR : *distract : cast off, shake off : turn to, turn about.* slǣpe tōb. *awake, wake up.* ['*tobraid*']

tōbrengnes f. *oblation, offering,* EPs 39[7].

tōbrittlan=tōbrȳtan

tōbrocenlīc *brittle, fragile,* W 263[13].

tōbrȳs-an, -ian *to bruise, shatter, crush, break to pieces,* Mt; Æ. ['*tobruise*']

tōbrȳtan *to break in pieces, destroy,* Æ : *be repentant.* ['*tobryt*']

tōbrȳtednes f. *contrition, sorrow,* LPs.

tōbrȳtendlīc *brittle, fragile,* WW 242[12].

tōbrȳting f. *crushing, contrition,* Sc 82[12].

tōbryttlan=tōbrȳtan

tōc pret. 3 sg. of tacan.

tōceorfan[3] *to cut, cut to pieces, cut off, cut away,* Æ,MkL. ['*tocarve*']

tōcēowan[2] *to bite to pieces, chew, eat,* Æ. ['*tochew*']

tōch=tōh

tōcīnan[1] *to split open, cleave asunder, splinter, crack,* Cp,Lcd ; Æ. ['*tochine*']

tōcirhūs n. *lodging-house, inn,* WW 147[25].

tōclǣfan *to split, cleave,* OEG 18b[38].

tōclēofan[2] *to cleave asunder, split, divide,* Æ,Bo. ['*tocleave*']

tōcleoflan=toclifian

tōclifian *to cleave to, adhere, stick to,* BPs.

tōclifrian *to be torn in pieces, scratched about,* Æ.

tōclīp-=tōclyp-

tōclypigendlīc *vocative, used in calling,* ÆGR 241[15].

tōclypung f. *calling upon, invocation,* Æ.

tōcnāwan[7] *to know, acknowledge, recognise, distinguish, discern,* Æ,CP.

tōcnāw(en)nes f. *understanding, discernment,* ÆH 2·362' ; GD 311[11].

tōcnyssan *to shake,* RB 121[6].

tōcuman[4] *to come, arrive,* CP.

tōcwæs-cednes (RPs 105[30]), -tednes (SPs) f. *trembling, shaking, shattering.*

tōcweðan[5] *to forbid, interdict,, prohibit,* Æ.

tōcwīsan=tōcwȳsan

tōcwylman *to torment,* HL 12[56].

tōcwȳsan *to crush utterly, grind to pieces, bruise, destroy : be crushed,* Æ.

tōcwȳsednes f. *crushed condition,* Æ : *contrition,* GD 125[11].

tōcyme m. *coming, advent, arrival,* Æ,Bl, CP. ['*tocome*']

tōcyrcanweard *towards church,* ÆL 31[902].

tōcyrran (intr.) *to part, separate,* CHR.

tōdæg, tōdæge adv. '*to-day,*' Æ,CP ; AO.

tōdǣl=tōdāl

tōdǣlan (ē) tr. and intr. *to divide, separate, scatter, disperse,* Æ,AO,Bo,Chr,W : *dismember, cut off, destroy : distribute,* Æ : *discriminate, distinguish : be divided : express, utter,* CPs. ['*todeal*']

tōdǣledlīce adv. *separately, distinctly, diversely,* ÆGR.

tōdǣlednes f. *division : severance, separation : difference, intermission, respite, cessation,* Æ.

tōdǣlendlīc *separable, distinct.* adv. -līce.

tōdǣlnes f. *division, separation,* CP.

tōdāl n. *partition, division, separation,* Æ : *difference, distinction, discretion,* Æ : *dispersion* : '*comma,*' *dividing point, clause, section, period.*

tōdēlan (KGL)=tōdǣlan

tōdēman *to decide, judge, sentence, determine.*

tōdihtnian *to dispose, arrange,* BLPs 82[6].

tōdōn anv. *to apply, put to, add,* LCD : *divide, separate, distinguish,* Hex,LL : *undo, open, unbind,* PPs. ['*todo*']

tōdrǣfan *to scatter, disperse, separate, drive out or apart,* BH,Mt; Æ. ['*todreve*']

tō-drǣfednes (Æ), -drǣfnes (JnL) f. *dispersion, scattering.*

tōdrēosan[2] *to be destroyed, perish, decay,* MH. ['*todrese*']

tōdrīfan[1] *to scatter, disperse, drive away,* B, JnL ; Æ : *destroy, repel.* ['*todrive*']

tōdwæscan† *to put out, extinguish.*

tōēacan prep. and adv. *besides, moreover, also,* Æ,AO,CP.

tōēcan=tōēacan; **tōēcnes**=tōīecnes

tōefenes, tōemnes (AO) prep. (d.) *alongside.*

tōendebyrdnes f. *order, series,* BH 216[20].

tōeð (VPs)=tēð

tōēðlan *to inspire,* GD 270[13].

tōfæng=tōfeng

tōfǣr n. *departure, decease,* LkL 9[31].

tōfaran[6] intr. *to be scattered, disperse, separate, disappear, Gen,Lcd*; AO. ['*tofare*']

tōfealdan[7] *to come to land* (trans. of *L.* 'applicare'), ÆGR 138[9].

tōfeallan[7] *to fall down, collapse, AO : fall apart, fall off, Æ.* ['*tofall*']

tōfeng I. (?) m. *grip, seizure,* LPs 123[6]. II. pret. 3 sg. of tōfōn.

tōfēran *to go in different directions, separate, disperse, Æ : deal out, distribute, Æ.*

tōferian *to scatter, disperse, get rid of : put off : digest,* RB 32[14].

tōfēsian *to drive away, rout,* W 132,133.

tōflēam m. *refuge,* RPs 93[22].

tō-flēon, -flēogan[2] *to be dispersed, fly apart, burst, Lcd.* ['*tofly*']

tōflēotan[2] *to carry away by a flood, Chr* 1097. ['*tofleet*']

tōflōwan[7] *to flow down or apart, be split, melt, Æ,CP : flow away, ebb : flow to, pour in : distract,* CP.

tōflōw-(ed)nes, -en(d)nes f. *flowing, flux, Æ : diffusion,* GD 94[21].

tō-foran (e[3], o[3]) prep. (w. d.) (time and place) *before, BH,Chr,G : (superiority) above, over, beyond, Æ,Bo : besides, ÆH* 2·584'. ['*tofore*']

tōforlǣtan[7] *to dismiss,* OEG 605.

tōforlǣtennes f. *intermission, ÆH,RBL.*

toft m. *homestead, site of a house, Ct,Lcd*; LL 400. ['*toft*']

tōfyllan *to smite in pieces,* PPs 67[21].

+tog n. *tugging, contraction, spasm, cramp,* LCD : pl. *traces (of a horse),* ÆL 31[973].

tōgædereweard adv. *towards one another,* AO.

tō-gædre, -gædere, -gadere adv. '*together,*' *An,BC,Mt.* tōg. gān, fōn, cuman *to engage in battle,* CHR. [*gaderian*]

tōgægnes=tōgegnes, tōgēanes

tōgǣlan *to profane, defile,* LPs 88[32].

tōgǣnan *to say, affirm,* LPs 93[4].

tōgān anv. pret. 3 sg. tōēode *to go to or into :* (impers. w. g.) *come to pass, happen : separate, part, depart, Æ,HR.* ['*togo*']

tōgang m. *approach, access, attack,* CM,LCD.

tōgangan[7] *to go away, pass away, BH,Rd.* ['*togang*']

tōgēan prep. w. d. *towards, MkL* (-eægn). ['*togains*']

tōgēanes prep. w. d. and a.; adv. *in opposition to, against, B,Chr,SPs : towards, to, Æ,Bl,MkL : before, CP : in return, in reply.* him tōg. *to meet him, Chr,MtL.* ['*togains*']

tōgēare adv. *in this year,* BF 156[17].

tōgeclifian (eo, y)=tōclifian

tōgecorennes f. *adoption,* DR 29[14].

tōgeēcan=tōgeīecan

tōgeefnan? *to associate with, join oneself to?* AS 39[6]. [MS tōgeenan]

tōgegnes=tōgēanes

tōgehlytto f. *fellowship, union,* DR 109[15].

tōgeīecan *to add to, increase,* BF,GD.

tōgeīecendlic (ī[3]) *added to, adjectival, adjective,* ÆGR.

tōgeīht pp. of tōgeīecan.

tōgeīhtnes f. *addition, increment,* BF 46[33].

tōgeladung f. *assembly,* MFH 174.

tōgelǣstan (e[3]) *to accompany,* WW 365[41].

tōgelan[4] *to diffuse,* GD 192[18].

tōgelaðung f. *concourse,* MFH 173.

tōgelēstan=tōgelǣstan

tōgelicgende *belonging,* KC 3·350[1].

togen pp. of tēon I. (and occly. II.).

tōgenēalǣcan=tōnealǣcan

tōgēnes=tōgēanes

tōgengan *to separate,* GEN 841.

-tōgennes v. ofer-t., ðurh-t.

tōgēotan[2] *to pour away, spill : spread : exhaust.*

tōgescēadan[7] *to expound, interpret,* LkR 24[27].

tōgescofen (CP) pp. of tōscūfan.

tōgesettan *to put to,* RPs 9[39].

tōgetēon[2,1] *to draw towards, attract,* BPs.

togettan impers. *to twitch, be spasmodic,* LCD 81a. [*togian*]

tōgeðēodan (īe, ȳ) *to adhere, cling to : adjoin,* BH 56[30].

tōgewegen *applied,* BH.

tōgewunod *accustomed,* AS 23[19].

tōgeȳcan=tōgeīecan

togian *to draw, drag,* HL 15[308]. ['*tow*']

tōgife, tōgifes adv. *freely, gratis.*

toginan[1] *to be opened, split, gape, yawn.* [cp. *Ger.* gähnen]

tōglīdan[1] *to glide away, split, slip, fall asunder, vanish, B,Met.* ['*toglide*']

tōgolen pret. of tōgelan.

tōgotennes f. *pouring out, effusion, shedding, spreading,* LCD.

+togu np. *traces (of a horse),* ÆL 31[973].

togung f. *tugging, twitch, spasm,* LCD.

tōh '*tough,*' *Cp,Ep : tenacious, sticky, Lcd.*

tōhacclan *to hack to pieces, Æ* (31[86]). ['*tohack*']

tōhǣlan *to emasculate, weaken,* MFH 174.

tōheald (a[2], y[2]) adj. and adv. *inclined, forward, in advance.*

tōhēawan[7] *to hew in pieces, Æ,Chr.* ['*tohew*']

tōhīgung f. *result, effect,* DR.

tōhīht=tōhyht

tohl=tōl

tōhladan[6] *to scatter, disperse, destroy* (or ? *tōhlacan*), GEN 1693.

tōhlēotan[2] *to divide by lot*, BL,PPs.

tōhlic *tough, tenacious.* adv. -lice, GL.

tōhlīdan[1] *to split, open, spring apart, burst, gape, break*, AO.

tohlīne f. *tow-line*, WW. [togian]

tōhlocen=tōlocen pp. of tōlūcan.

tōhlystend m. *listener*, CP 96.

tōhnescan *to soften*, LCD 94a.

tōhopa m. *hope, Bo,PPs*; CP. ['*tohope*']

tōhopung f. *faith, trust*, ÆL 23[155].

tōhrēosan[2] *to fall to pieces, decay, BH,W*; ÆL. ['*toreose*']

tōhrēran *to break, shake to pieces, destroy*, GL.

tōhricod ptc. *cut off, dispersed*, GPH 398, 399.

tōhrȳran *to shake in pieces*, v. OEG 2261.

+toht n. *battle array, battle*, MA 104.

tohte† f. *fight, conflict, battle, campaign.*

tōhuntian *to hunt*, WE 65[7].

tōhwega adv. and sb. *somewhat, some, a little.*

tōhweorfan[3] *to go away, separate, scatter, disperse*, CHR.

tōhwon adv. *wherefore, why* : *to which (point), to what extent, how far, how long* : *to which end, for what purpose or reason.*

tōhwyrfan (=ie[2]) *to overturn*, LPs 117[13].

tōhyht m. *hope, refuge, consolation*, RUN.

tōhyld=tōheald

tōīecan (ē[2], ȳ[2]) *to increase*, BH 112[1]B.

tōīecnes (ē[2]) f. *increase*, BH 226[31].

tōiernan[3] *to run to, run together* : *flow away, be dispersed* : *run hither and thither, wander about.*

tōirnan=tōiernan; tol=toll

tōl n. '*tool,' instrument, implement, Æ,Bo, LL* : *weapon*, ZDA 9·424.

tōlǣgon pret. pl. of tōlicgan.

tōlǣtan[7] *to disperse, relax, release*, CP.

tōlǣtennes f. *despondency*, LCD 1·262[3].

tolcendlīce adv. *wantonly*, GPH 401.

tolcettende '*indruticans,*' v. OEG 1218.

tolcetung f. *wanton excitement*, OEG.

tōleoðlan=tōliðian; tōlēs-=tōlȳs-

tolfrēo '*toll-free,*' KC 4·209[19].

tolgetung=tolcetung; tōlic=tōhlic

tōlicgan[5] *to lie or extend in different directions, separate, part, divide*, AO,BC. ['*tolie*']

tōliðlan (eo) *to dismember, separate, Æ* : *relax, cancel*, GD 349[28].

toll mn. *impost, 'toll,' tribute, Chr,EC,G, Gl* : *passage-money, Æ* : *rent, Æ* : *act or right of taking toll, Æ.*

tollere m. *tax-gatherer, publican, Æ,WW.* ['*toller*']

tollsceam-ol, -ul m. *seat of custom, treasury,*

tollscīr f. *taxing district*, ÆH 2·468'.

toln f. *toll, custom, duty*, TC. ['*tolne*']

tolnere m. *tax-gatherer*, WW. ['*tolner*']

tōlōcian *to belong to*, CC 22[7].

tolsetl n. *place of toll or custom, Æ.*

tōlūcan[2] *to pull apart, dislocate, destroy, BH.* ['*tolouk*']

tōlȳsan (ē;=īe) *to dissolve, loosen, relax, Æ* : *unhinge, separate, break open.*

tōlȳs(ed)nes (ē) f. *loosing, dissolution, dispersion, destruction, release, dismissal* : *desolation*, GD : *death.*

tōlȳsend m. *destroyer*, WW 220[13].

tōlȳsendlic *destructive*, LPs 119[4].

tōlȳsing (ē) f. *loosing, release, redemption* : *destruction*, LCD 3·206[20].

tom=tam

tōm adj. w. g. *free from*, Cr 1211. ['*toom*']

tōmǣldan *to hinder by speech*, DD 26. [meldian]

tōmearcian *to distinguish, describe, note down, enrol*, G,SPs.

tōmearcodnes f. *enumeration, census, enrolment*, Lk 2[2].

tō-mergen, -merigen (Æ)=tōmorgen

tōmetan[5] *to mete out*, LPs 107[8].

tōmiddes prep. (w. d.) *amidst, among, in the midst of, Æ,Jn*; AO,CP. adv. *into the midst, B,Lcd.* ['*tomids*']

tōmorgen adv. *to-morrow, Bf,CP.* ['*to-morn*']

tōn dsmn. of tōh.

tōnama m. *surname, MkL*; Æ. ['*toname*']

+tōnamian *to name besides, surname*, LKL 6[14] (tor-).

tōnēalǣcan *to approach*, Pss.

tōnemnan *to distinguish by name, name*, AO.

tōnēolīcan=tōnēalǣcan

tong, tonge=tang, tange

tonian *to thunder*, ÆGR 138[3].

tonice=tunece

tōniman[4] *separate, take apart* : *take away.*

tōnom-=tōnam-

top I. m. '*top' (highest part)*, WW 143[25] : *tassel, tuft.* II. '*top' (plaything)? ball? ApT* 13[13].

toppa m. *thread, tuft?* OEG 23[45].

tor=torr

tōrǣcan (pret. 3 sg. tōræhte) *to join, put together*, OEG 4489.

tōrǣndan=tōrendan; toranēage=torenīge

tōrbegete (o?) *hard to get*, LCD 43b.

torcht, torct-=torht, torht-

torcul n. *wine-press*, MtR 21[33]. [L.]

torcyrre *hard to convert*, MH 110[15].

tord n. *piece of excrement, dung, filth*, LCD.

tordwifel m. *dung-beetle*, LCD.

toren pp. of teran.

tōrendan (æ) *to rend apart, tear in pieces,* MkL,PPs. ['*torend*']

toren-ēage, -īg(g)e, -īege *blear-eyed,* CP.

tōrēosan=tōhrēosan

±**torflan** *to throw, cast missiles, shoot, stone,* Mk; Æ : *be tossed,* NC326. ['*torve*']

torfung f. *throwing, casting* (*of stones*), AO.

torht I. n. *clearness, brightness.* II. adj. *bright, radiant, beautiful, splendid, noble, illustrious,* Ph. ['*torht*'] adv. -e *brightly, clearly : beautifully, splendidly.*

torhtian *to show,* Cp216I.

torhtlic† *bright, clear, radiant, glorious.* adv. -līce.

torhtmōd† *glorious, noble.*

torhtnes f. *radiance, splendour,* GL,Lcd.

tōrinnan (CP)=tōiernan

torn I. n. *anger, indignation : grief, misery, suffering, pain.* [*Ger.* zorn] II. adj. *bitter, cruel, grievous.*

+**tornamian**=+tōnamian

torncwide† m. *offensive speech.*

torne† adv. *indignantly, insultingly, bitterly, grievously.*

torngemōt n. *battle,* B1140.

torngenīōla† m. *angry opponent.*

tornīge=torenīge

tornlic *sorrowful, grievous,* PPs125⁵.

tornmōd *angry,* Gu621.

tornsorg f. *sorrow, care,* FT76.

tornword n. *offensive expression,* Cr172.

tornwracu f. *revenge,* Gu272.

tornwyrdan *to be incensed?* AO54².

toroc *grub, weevil?* WW224³⁸ (ES41·164).

tōroren=tōhroren pp. of tōhrēosan.

torr m. '*tower,*' *watch-tower,* CP,MtL; AO : *rock, crag,* Mdf. [*L.* turris; v. ES41·102]

torrian *to tower,* ByH130¹³.

tōryne m. *running together, concourse,* ES 39·353.

tōrȳpan *to scratch,* EC164¹⁸.

tōsǣlan (impers., w. d. pers. and g. thing) *to be unsuccessful, fail : lack, want.*

tōsamne=tōsomne

tōsāwan⁷ *to strew, scatter, spread,* Æ.

tosca m. *frog, toad,* DR,PPs.

tōscacan=tōsceacan

tōscād-=tōscēad-

tōscǣgde v. tōscecgan.

tōscǣnan *to break in pieces, break,* Æ,JnL, MkLR. ['*toshene*']

tōscarian=tōscearian

tōsceacan⁶ (a) *to shake in pieces, WW : drive asunder, drive away, shake off,* Æ. ['*to-shake*']

tōscēacerian *to scatter,* ÆL23²⁴.

tōscēad n. *distinction, difference,* Æ,CP.

tōscēadan⁷ (ā) *to part, separate, scatter, divide : set at variance,* CP : *discern, discriminate, distinguish, decide,* Æ,Bo; CP : *differ : express,* LPs. ['*toshed*']

tōscēadednes f. *separation,* MFH101.

tōscēadend m. *divider, separator,* WW223³⁰.

tōscēadenes (ā) f. *separation, distinction,* HL158¹⁶².

tōscearian (a²) *to scatter,* APs67².

tōscecgan (æ) *to be separate, differ,* BH 160²⁵n.

tōscelian=tōscylian

tōscendan *to destroy,* GD121²⁴.

tōscēotan² intr. *to spring apart, disperse,* Æ. ['*toshoot*']

tōscerian (KGL)=tōscirian

tōscirian (e, y) *to divide, distribute,* MFH : *detach, separate,* GL : *distinguish,* CHRD.

tōscrīōan² *to flow apart, disperse,* MET20⁹³.

tōscūfan² *to push apart, scatter : impel, incite,* CP : *do away, remove.*

tōscyftan (=i) *to divide, distribute,* Chr. ['*toshift*']

tōscyl-ian, -ian (e) tr. and intr. *to separate, divide,* NC351.

tōscyrian=tōscirian

tōsendan (tr.) *to send to : send apart, send out, disperse.*

tōsēoōan² *to boil thoroughly,* Lcd.

tōsetednes f. *disposition,* EPs72⁷.

tōsettan *to dispose,* Pss,Bl.

tōsēōan? *to test, prove,* AS7¹¹.

tōsīgan¹ *to wear out, be threadbare,* Æ.

tōsittan⁵ *to be separated,* AO14¹⁸.

tōslacian *to slacken, relax,* WW73¹⁰.

tōslǣfan *to cut up,* NR32².

tōslēan⁶ *to strike in pieces, destroy,* Æ,AO. Gl : *drive away,* RB18³,⁴. ['*toslay*']

tōslīfan¹ *to split,* WW.

tōslītan¹ *to tear asunder, rend, wound, break open, open,* Æ,CP : *interrupt : separate, scatter, destroy,* CP : *distract : be different,* NG.

tōslitnes (y²) f. *laceration,* BH : *division,* NG.

tōslūpan² *to slip away, be relaxed, fall to pieces, open, dissolve,* Æ,CP : *melt* (*with fear*) : *be paralysed.* tōslopen *relaxed, loose, dissolute.*

tōslūping f. *dissolving, dissolution,* Sc68⁸.

tōsmēagan *to inquire into, consider,* Bo148⁵.

tōsnǣdan *to cut up,* NR28⁵.

tōsnīōan¹ *to cut asunder, cut up : cut off amputate.*

tōsōcn f. *visiting,* CHRD67³⁶.

tōsōcnes f. *pursuit,* DR28¹⁸.

tōsōcnung f. *pursuit,* DR81⁷.

tōsomne adv. *together,* Æ,AO,Bl; CP. t. cuman *to engage in battle.* ['*tosame*']

tōsomnian *to collect together, bring together,* BH 230⁷.

tōsōðan adv. *in sooth, in truth* (or ? two words).

tōsprǣc f. *speaking to (another), conversation,* Æ,CP.

tōsprǣdan *to spread out, IM;* Æ. ['*tospread*']

tōspringan³ *to spring apart, fly asunder, crack,* Æ. ['*tospring*']

tōsprytting f. *inciting,* CHR 1101.

tosta=tosca

tōstæncan=tōstencan

tōstandan⁶ *to be put off, not to occur : stand apart, differ from, be discordant,* Æ.

tōstencan (æ) *to scatter, disperse, drive apart, drag along,* Æ,CP : *nullify, destroy : perish,* SPs 82⁹.

tō-stencednes (Æ), -stenc(en)nes, f. *dispersion, dissolution, destruction.*

tōstencend m. *prodigal,* LCD.

tōsteng-=tōstenc-

tōstician *to pierce,* AO 128¹⁴.

tōstihtan *to order, arrange,* CPs 111⁵.

tōstincan³ *to distinguish by smell,* ÆH 2·372'.

tōstingan³ *to thrust in, pierce,* LCD.

tō-stregdan, -strēdan³ (and wv.) *to scatter, dissipate, disperse,* CP : *distract : destroy.*

tōstrēt (CP) pres. 3 sg. of tōstregdan.

tōsundrian *to separate,* LHy 7⁸.

tōswāpan⁷† *to disperse.*

tōswellan³ *to swell out,* Æ. ['*toswell*']

tōswengan *to drive asunder, destroy.* [swingan]

tōsweorcan³ *to obscure,* OEG 1737.

tōswīfan¹ intr. *to separate,* MET 11³⁶.

tōsyndrian *to sunder, separate, divide : discriminate.*

+**tot** n. *pomp, parade, vainglory,* ÆH.

tōtalu f. *reputation,* DR 102³.

tōtellan *to distinguish,* MET 16¹⁵.

tōtēon²,¹ *to draw asunder, pull apart, rend, destroy,* AO : *take to oneself, claim for oneself,* LL (or ? tō prep.).

tōteran⁴ *to tear in pieces, bite, lacerate, cut out,* Æ,AO,CP : *destroy : harass (mind).*

tōtian *to peep out, stick out, CP* 105⁵. ['*toot*']

tōtihting f. *instigation,* CHR 1094.

tōtorfian *to cast about, toss,* Mt 14²⁴.

tōtræglian *to pull to pieces, strip,* GPH 396²⁶⁷.

tōtredan⁵ *to tread to pieces?* GL.

totrida m. *swing?* GL,WW 276²⁷.

tōtwǣman (ē, ēa, ȳ) *to separate, divide, dissever, AO : distinguish : break up, break in pieces, dissolve : scatter : defer, postpone,* LL 298,17² : *divorce,* CHR 958 D. ['*totweme*']

tōtwǣmednes f. *separation, distinction,* W 194²².

tō-twē(a)man, -twȳman=tōtwǣman

tōð m., ds. and nap. tēð, occl. ds. tōðe and nap. tōð(as) '*tooth*,' *Cp,Guth,Lcd,LL, MtR,VPs;* AO : *tusk,* WW 397²⁷. tōðum ontȳnan *to utter.*

tōðece (æ²) m. *toothache,* AS 41⁴.

tōðenednes f. *stretching, distension,* OEG 5452.

tōðēnian *to attend upon, serve,* Sc 102⁹.

tōðening f. *distension,* OEG 2⁴⁷⁶.

tōðenung f. *administration,* CM 1185.

tōðerscan³ *to dash in pieces,* CHR 1009.

tōðgār m. *tooth-pick,* LCD 13b.

tōðindan³ *to swell up, inflate, puff up,* Æ : *be arrogant.*

tōðlēas *toothless,* GPH 394.

tōðmægen n. *strength of tusks,* GNC 20.

tōðrǣstan *to crush, destroy,* CPs 106¹⁶.

tōðreoma=tōðrima; **tōðrescan**=tōðerscan

tōðrima (eo²) m. *enclosure of teeth, gum,* LCD.

tōðringan *to drive asunder,* RD 4²⁷.

tōðsealf f. *tooth-salve,* LCD.

tōðsticca m. *tooth-pick,* WW 219³.

tōðunden pp. of tōðindan.

tōðundenes f. *the state of being puffed up, arrogance,* Æ.

tōðundenlic *arrogant.* adv. -līce, RB.

tōðunian *to astonish,* WW 346²².

tōðwǣrc m. *toothache,* LCD.

tōðwīnan¹ *to disappear,* HL 15²⁰⁰. [dwīnan]

tōðwyrm m. *a worm in the teeth,* LCD 19a.

tōwǣlede pret. sg. of *tōwieltan *to roll to,* MkL 15⁴⁶.

tō-ward, -wardes=tō-weard, -weardes

towcræft m. *spinning,* HL 10³³⁹.

tōweard I. adj. *facing, approaching, impending, BH,Bl,Lcd : future, Æ,Bl,Bo, Mk.* **II.** prep. (w. d., g.) *towards, AO,CP.* **III.** adv. *towards, forwards.* ['*toward*,' '*towards*']

tōweardes=tōweard II., III.

tōweardlic *in the future,* Æ. adv. -līce, BH 368²¹.

tōweardnes f. *future, time to come,* BH,Bl.

tōweaxan⁷ *to grow apart,* NR 22.

tōweccan *to arouse, excite,* B 2948.

tōwegan⁵ *disperse, scatter,* PH 184.

tōwendan *to overthrow, subvert, destroy,* Æ, AO. ['*towend*']

tōweorpan³ (e, u, y) *to cast down, break in pieces, dissipate, blot out, destroy, Æ,Bo, Mt;* AO,CP : *throw out,* CP. ['*towarp*']

tōwerd=tōweard; **tōwerpan**=tōweorpan

tō-wesnes (CP), -wesenes, -westnes (BH) f. *dissolution : separation, discord, dissension.*

towettan *to associate with,* LL (322').

towhūs n. *tow-house, spinning-house or chamber,* WW 186²⁹. [FTP 166]
tōwieltan v. tōwælede
tōwītan *to depart, pass away,* ByH 90².
tō-wiðere, -wiðre prep. (w. d., a.) *against,* Ex : *in answer to,* Cʀ.
towlic *belonging to thread.* t. weorc *material for spinning,* WW.
towmȳderce f. *tow-chest? work-box?* TC 538²¹.
tōword (VPs)=tōweard
tōworpednes=tōworpennes
tōworp(en)nes f. *subversion, destruction, desolation,* Æ,CP : *dispersion : expulsion.*
tōwrecan † *to drive asunder, scatter, dissipate.*
tōwrītan⁵ *to describe,* OEG 1065.
tōwritennes f. *writing down, description,* Æ.
tōwrīðan¹ *to twist apart, distort,* ÆGʀ 155¹⁵.
towtōl n. *spinning implement,* LL 455,15¹.
tōwunderlic '*admirabilis,*' SPs 41⁴.
tōwurpan (Æ)=tōweorpan
tōwyrd I. f. *opportunity,* BH 52²¹. II.= tōweard
tōwyrpan=tōweorpan
tōwyrpendlic *destructible,* GPH 394.
tōwyrpnes=tōworpennes
toxa (OEG 1858)=tosca
tōȳcan=tōīecan; **tōyrnan**=tōiernan
tracter *funnel,* NC 351. [*L.* trajectorium]
træd pret. 3 sg., trǣdon pret. pl. of tredan.
træf n., nap. tr(e)afu *tent, pavilion : dwelling, building,* Aɴ 844.
trǣglian *to pluck, pull,* GPH 398.
trændel=trendel; **træppe**=treppe
trafu v. træf.
trāg I.† adj. *evil, mean, bad.* II. f. *evil, affliction,* Eʟ 668.
trāge adv. *evilly, cruelly,* PPs 108²⁰.
-trāglīce v. un-t.
traht m. *text, passage : exposition, treatise, commentary,* Æ. [*L.* tractus]
trahtað m. *commentary,* WW. [*L.*]
trahtbōc f. (*religious*) *treatise, commentary,* Æ. [trahtian]
traht-ere, -nere (Æ) m. *expounder, commentator, expositor.*
±**traht-ian,** -nian (Æ) *to treat, comment on, expound, consider : interpret, translate,* NG. [*L.*]
trahtnung, trahtung f. *explanation, exposition, commentary,* Æ.
trāisc *tragic,* BH 154³.
tramet m. *page* (*of a book*), ÆGʀ.
trandende (o¹) *precipitous, steep,* Cp 805ᴘ.
trappe=treppe; **tratung**=trahtung
trē (NG), trēa (VPs)=trēow I.
treaflīce *grievously,* PPs 102⁶.
treafu v. træf.

±**trēagian** *to sew together, mend,* OEG.
treaht-=traht-; **trēawa**=trēowa
+**tred** n. *crowd,* WW 209¹⁰.
±**tredan⁵** (eo) tr. and intr. *to* '*tread*,*' *step on, trample,* B,CP,G,PPs; Æ,AO : *traverse, pass over, enter upon, roam through,* B.
treddan *to tread on, trample,* WW ̄ : *investigate,* PPs.
tredde f. *press* (*for wine, etc.*), GD.
treddian† *to tread, step, walk,* B.
trede *fit to tread on, firm,* Cʀ 1166.
tredel m. *step,* WW 117⁶ : *sole of foot,* LL 438,21. ['*treadle*']
tredend m. *treader,* WW 197⁹.
trefet '*trivet,*' *tripod,* BC 3·367'.
trēg (WW 281³⁵)=trīg
trega m. *misfortune, misery, trouble, grief, pain,* Gen,Met,RB. ['*tray*']
tregian *to trouble, harass, vex,* EPs,W.
+**tregian** *to feel repugnance at,* A 2·358.
treht-=traht-; **trem**=trym
tremegan=trymian, trymman
tremes=trymes; **tremm-**=trymm-
-tremman v. wið-t.
trendan *to turn round, revolve, roll,* A 1·285. ['*trend*']
trendel (æ, y) n. *sphere, circle, ring, orb,* Æ,Bf,Chr,Lcd : *circus.* ['*trendle*']
trendeled (y¹, y²) *made round,* WW 152⁵. [v. '*trindle*']
trendelnes f. *circuit, surrounding space,* RPs 11⁹ (u¹).
-trendlian v. ā-t.; **trēo**=trēow
treodan (VPs)=tredan; **trēoð**=trēowð
trēow I. n. (nap. trēowu, trēow) '*tree*,*' Æ, BH,CP,VPs; Mdf : *wood, timber,* BH : *beam, log, stake, stick,* AO,Bl; CP : *wood, grove : tree of the cross, cross, Rood.* II. f. (ū, ȳ) *truth, fidelity, faith, trust, belief : pledge, promise, agreement, treaty : favour, grace, kindness.* [*Ger.* treue] III.=trēowe
trēowa (AO,CP)=trūwa
trēowan=trīewan
trēowan (ē, ī, īe, ȳ) trans. w. d. *to believe, trust in, hope, be confident, rely* (*on*), B,Bo, Gen : intr. *trust,* PPs : refl. *exculpate oneself,* LL : (+) *persuade, suggest,* AO : *make true or credible : be faithful* (*to*) : *confederate* (*with*), Gʟ. ['*trow*']
trēowcynn n. *species of tree,* Æ.
trēowe I. (ē, ī, īe, ū, ȳ) '*true*' ('*i-treowe*'), *faithful, honest, trustworthy,* B,Chr,Gen, Gu,LL,WW ; AO : *genuine.* II.=trēow II.
trēowen (ī, ȳ) *of a tree, of wood, wooden,* Lcd,WW 125²⁸ ; Æ. ['*treen*']
±**trēowfæst** *true, faithful,* MtL,PPs ; Æ. ['*truefast*']
+**trēowfæstnian** *to be trusty,* MtL p 4¹².

trēowfēging f. *joining together (of boards)*, WW 206³⁴.

trēowfugol m. *forest bird*, Gu 707.

±**trēowful** *faithful, trusty, true.* adv. -līce.

+**trēowfulnes** f. *'Israel'!* RPs 21²⁵; Hy 7⁸³.

trēowgeðofta† m. *faithful comrade*, AA 45⁴.

trēowgeweorc n. *wood-work, a structure of timber*, BH 272⁵.

trēowgewrid n. *thicket of trees*, Guth 20⁷.

trēowian=trēowan

±**trēowlēas** *faithless, treacherous, false*, CP : *unbelieving.*

trēowlēasnes f. *treachery, faithlessness*, BH : *unbelief, heresy*, GD.

trēowlic *true, faithful, trusty : safe.* adv. -līce, PPs : *confidently*, GL. ['*truly*']

trēowloga m. *pledge-breaker*, B 2847.

trēowlufu f. '*true love*,' Cr 538.

±**trēownes** (ē) f. *object of trust*, Bo 149²⁵,VH. ['*trueness*']

trēowrǣden f. *state of fidelity*, Gen 2305.

±**trēowsian** (ȳ) *to plight one's faith*, Chr, LL : *exculpate oneself.* ['*treouse*']

trēowsteall n. *grove, plantation*, EC,KC.

trēowstede m. *grove*, WW 149¹⁷.

trēowteru (trēot-) n. *tree-tar, resin*, WW.

±**trēowð** (īe, ȳ) f. '*truth*,' *veracity*, AO : *troth, faith, fidelity*, Æ,AO : *pledge, covenant*, Æ.

trēowðrāg f. *time for faithfulness, fidelity*, Rim 57.

trēowufæst=trēowfæst

trēowwæstm m. *produce of trees*, Chr.

trēowweorðung f. *tree-worshipping*, LL.

trēowwyrhta (ȳ) m. *wood-worker, carpenter*, Æ.

trēowwyrm m. *cankerworm, caterpillar*, CJVPs 77⁴⁶.

treppan I. *to 'trap*,' KGl 211. II. *to tread*, KGl 144.

treppe (a, æ) f. '*trap*,' *snare*, WW.

tret (KGl) pres. 3 sg. of tredan.

trēu=trēo, trēow

trēw=trēow

tribulian=trifulian

+**tricce** *contented*, RB 109⁷.

trideð, triedeð=tredeð, tritt pres. 3 sg. of tredan.

trīew-=trēow-

trifelung f. *grinding, pounding, stamping*, WW 423²⁵.

trifet (KGl), trifot (GL) sb. *tribute*. [*L.* tributum]

±**trifulian** *to break, bruise, stamp*. [*L.* tribulare]

trig (ē) n. *wooden board, 'tray*,' Lcd.

trilidi=ðriliðe; **trim-**=trym-

trimilchi=ðrimeolce

trinda? m., **trinde?** f. *round lump, ball*, Lcd 139b.

trindhyrst m. *circular copse?* (Swt), KC 2·411' (? place-name).

tringan³ *press*, APs 103³³ (?*twingan, BT).

trīo-=trēo-, trēow-

trit, tritt pres. 3 sg. of tredan.

trīw=trēow

trochscip=trogscip

trod n., trodu f. *track, trace*, B,LL. ['*trod*'; tredan]

trog m. *hollow vessel, 'trough*,' *tray*, BC,Gl, JnL,Lcd : *canoe, boat*, AO.

trōg (NG)=drōg pret. 3 sg. of dragan.

troghrycg *ridge where there is a water-trough?* EC 447²⁰.

trogscip n. *a kind of boat*, WW.

troh (LWS)=trog; **trōh**=ðrōh

trondende *precipitous, steep*, Cp 805 P.

tropere m. *a book containing verses sung at certain festivals before the Introit*, IM,TC. [*Late L.* troparium]

trūa=trūwa, trēowa

±**trucian** *to fail, run short*, Æ : *deceive, disappoint.* ['*troke*']

trūg-=trūw-

trūgon (NG)=drōgon pret. pl. of dragan.

trūht (u?) *trout*, Æ. [*L.* tructa]

trum *firm, fixed, secure, strong, sound, vigorous, active*, Æ,CP : *trustworthy*, Bf 172²⁰.

+**trum**† n. *legion, army, host*, WW.

truma m. (±) *legion, troop*, AO; Æ : *regular order, array*, AO. ['*trume*']

±**trumian** *to grow strong, recover health, amend*, BH : *make strong.*

truming=trymming

trumlic *firm, durable, substantial, sound*, CP : *confirming, exhorting.* adv. -līce, *considerably*, Bf 80².

trumnað m. *confirmation*, Gu 729.

trumnes f. *soundness, health*, CP : *firmness, strength, stability*, Æ : *sureness, reliability : the firmament, heavens : confirmation, support.*

trundulnes=trendelnes

trūs (u?) m. *brushwood (for fuel)*, KC. ['*trouse*']

trūð m. *trumpeter, buffoon, actor*, Æ.

trūðhorn m. *trumpet, clarion*, GL.

trūw=trēow

±**trūwa** (ēo, ȳ) m. *fidelity, faith, confidence, trust, belief : pledge, promise, agreement, covenant : protection.*

+**trūwe**=+trēowe

±**trūwian** (ȳ) occl. pret. trūwde *to trust*, Æ,CP : *inspire with trust*, WW 243⁶ : *persuade*, AO : *exculpate oneself*, LL. ['TROW']

+**trūwung** f. *prop, stay, confidence*, CPs 88¹⁹.
+**tryccan** *to confide, trust*, JnL 16³³.
tryddian=treddian
trydeð=tredeð, tritt pres. 3 sg. of tredan.
trym† (e) n. *small piece, short length.* fōtes t. *a foot's length.*
trym-=trum-, trymm-
+**trym** n. *firmament*, PPs 71¹⁶.
+**trymednes** (LPs 104¹⁶)=+trymnes
try-mes (*Mt*) mf., -messe f., -messa m. *a drachm weight : an English coin* (v. LL 2·683) : *a Roman coin* ('*tremissis*'=3 *denarii*), LG. ['*thrimsa*']
trymian, trymman (e) *to strengthen, fortify, confirm, comfort, exhort, incite*, CP,Chr : *set in order, arrange, prepare, array, arm*, AO : *become strong : be arrayed : give* (hostages) : *testify, attest.* ['TRIM']
-**trymig**, -trymmig v. un-t.
trymmend m. *supporter*, PPs : *one who makes an agreement*, GL.
trymmendlic *hortatory, encouraging*, BH,GL.
±**trymming** f. *confirmation, strengthening, encouragement*, Æ : *support, prop : edification*, Æ : *ordinance* : (+) *fortress*, KGL 67⁴.
±**trymnes** f. *firmness, solidity : firmament, prop, support : confirmation, strengthening, encouragement : exhortation, instruction : arrangement, setting in order.* [trumnes]
tryms=trymes
trymð (i) f. *strength, support, staff, prop*, AS,LPs.
tryndel=trendel
trȳw=trēow; **trȳw-**=trēow-
tu=ðu; **Tū**=Tīw; **tū**=twā
tua=tuwa; **tuā**=twā
tube f. *trumpet*, GPH 391. [*L.* tuba]
±**tūcian** *to disturb, ill-treat, torment, punish*, Æ,Bo,Met : (+) *bedeck*, PPs 44¹¹ (? a mistake for +tunecian, IF 48·262). ['*tuck*']
tud? mn., tudu f? *shield*, OEG 5025 (cp. 747n).
tūdder, tūddor=tūdor
tūddorfōster m. *nourishment of offspring*, WW 219¹⁷.
tūddorful *prolific, fruitful*, GL.
tūddorspēd f. *fertility*, GEN 2752.
tūddortēonde† *begetting issue.*
tūddres gs. of tūddor.
tūdor, tūder n. *offspring, descendant, issue*, Æ,CP,Lcd,WW : *fruit.* ['*tudder*']
tūdorfæst *fertile*, WW 400³⁵.
tūdornes f. *offspring*, OEG 3849 (tydder-).
tugon pret. pl. of tēon.
tui-=twi-
tulge comp. tylg, superl. tylgest *strongly, firmly, well.*
tumbere m. *tumbler, dancer, player*, ÆGR 35⁶.

tumbian *to tumble, leap, dance*, G. ['*tumb*']
tumbing f. *dancing*, CHRD 79¹.
tūn m. *enclosure, garden, field, yard*, Chr, Gl,G,Lcd : *farm, manor*, BC,LL : *homestead, dwelling, house, mansion*, BH,MH; AO,CP : *group of houses, village*, '*town*,' Æ,Gl,JnL,KC,MH, v. LL 2·352. on tūn gān *to appear to men*, BF,MEN. [v. Mdf]
tūn-cerse (æ²) f., -cressa m. *garden-cress, nasturtium*, Cp,Ep,Lcd. ['*towncress*']
tūncirce f. *church in a '*tūn*,'* TC.
tunder=tynder
tunece f. *under-garment, tunic, coat, toga*, Æ,AO. [*L.* tunica]
+**tunecod** *clothed in a toga*, GPH 393 (v. also IF 48·262).
tūnesman (*LL*)=tūnmann. ['*townsman*']
tunge f. (m) '*tongue*,' Æ,BH,CP,Lcd : *speech, language*, CP,Mk,RB.
tūngebūr m. *inhabitant, resident*, GL.
tungel=tungol
tungele? *talkative*, OEG 56¹³⁹.
tūngerēfa m. *town-reeve, bailiff*, Æ : *prætor.*
tungeðrum *tongue-ligament*, Lcd. [v. '*thrum*']
tungful *talkative*, Sc 81⁹.
tungilsinwyrt=tunsingwyrt
tungle ds. of tungol.
tunglen *starry*, DHy. [tungol]
tunglere m. *astrologer*, GL.
tungol (e², u²) nm., nap. tunglu, tungol and (late) tunglan *luminary, star, planet, constellation*, Æ,AO.
tungolǣ (e²) f. *astronomy*, OEG.
tungolbǣre (e²) *covered with stars*, OEG.
tungolcræft (e²) m. *star-craft, astronomy*, Æ.
tungolcræft(i)ga (e², u²) m. *magician, astrologer.*
tungolcræftwīse (e²) f. *astronomy*, WW 346².
tungolgescēad (e²) n. *astrology*, GL.
tungolgim m. (*bright*) *star*, CR 1151.
tungolsprǣc f. *astrology*, HGL.
tungolwītega m. *star prophet, astrologer*, Æ.
tungul=tungol
tungwōd *sharp-tongued*, Sc 223¹³.
tūnhōfe f. *ground ivy*, Lcd 123a. ['*tunhoof*']
tunice=tunece
tūnincel n. *small property, small farm*, GL.
tuningwyrt=tunsingwyrt
tūnland n. *land forming a '*tūn*' or manor*, EC 445⁶.
tūnlic *rustic*, WW 127¹⁵.
tūnmann m. *villager, rustic, villein*, Æ,WW. ['*townman*']
tūnmelde f. *orach* (*plant*), WW 215³³.
tunne f. '*tun*,' *cask, barrel*, BC,Cp; Æ.
tunnebotm m. *bottom of a cask, drum?* WW 123¹⁰.
tūnprēost m. *village priest*, CHR 870 F.

tūnrǣd m. *town council*, ÆL30²⁹⁷.

tūnscipe m. '*township*,' *population of a village*, BH,LL.

tūnscīr f. *administration of an estate, stewardship*, Lk16.

tunsingwyrt f. *white hellebore*, LCD.

tūnsōen f. '*villarum jura regalia*,' *legal jurisdiction over a village*, TC308⁷ (v. LL 2·455)

tūnsteall m. *farm-stead, farm-yard?* KC.

tūnstede m. *farm-stead?* WW144²⁶.

tunuce=tunece

tūnweg m. '*privata via*,' *by-road*, KC, WW.

tūnyncel=tūnincel

tūr m. '*tower*,' *fortress*, Chr1097.

turf f., gds. tyrf '*turf*,' *sod, soil*, Chr,Cp, Guth,Lcd : *greensward*, BH,WW.

turfhaga m. *grassy plot* (or ?=tyrfhaga A 35·141), EL830.

turfhlēow n. *covering of turf*, KC3·15'.

turflan=torfian

turl *ladle*, Cp290T. [*L.* trulla]

turnian *to turn, revolve*, Æ,LCD.

turnigendlic *revolving*, A6·12n.

turning f. *rotation*, W253¹⁴.

turtla m., turtle f. '*turtle*'-*dove*, G,Ps; Æ. [*L.* turtur]

turtur m. *turtle-dove*, Bl,LG,VPs. ['*turtur*']

tūsc m. *grinder, canine tooth*, Guth,Lcd,LL. ['*tusk*']

tuu=tū, twā; Tuu=Tīw

tuwa (Æ,AO,CP), tuwwa (=twiwa) adv. *twice.*

tūx=tūsc

tūxel, tūxl m. *tusk, canine or molar tooth*, Lcd. ['*tuscle*']

twā I. (tū, v. twēgen), Æ,AO. ['*two*'] II. adv. *twice.* tū swā lang(e) *twice as long.*

twa-=twi-

twaddung? twædding f. *adulation*, CHRD.

twǣde num. *two parts out of three, two-thirds*, LCD. [twā]

+twǣfan w. g. *to separate from, deprive of* : *hinder* : w. a. *put an end to.*

twǣgen (M)=twēgen

twælf (M)=twelf

twǣm v. twēgen.

±twǣman (ē) *to divide into two, separate*, Bf,W : *cause to cease, adjust, settle* : *defer, postpone*, LL242¹⁹. ['*tweme*']

twǣmendlīce adv. *alternately, separately*, OEG1368.

twǣming f. *parting, division, separation*, Æ : *distinction*, Æ.

twǣonung=twēonung; twām v. twēgen.

+twanc n. *collusion, deception*, OEG1517.

twānihte *two days old*, LCD.

twe-=twi-

twēgen num. nom. m.; nom. f. twā; nom. n. tū, twā; gen. mfn. twēg(e)a, twēgra; dat. twǣm, twām *two*, Æ; AO,CP. tū swā lang *twice as long.* t. and t., twām and twām *in parties of two each.* ['TWAIN']

twēgentig (oe; NG)=twēntig

twelf 'TWELVE,' CP.

twelffeald *twelve-fold*, ÆH.

twelfgylde *twelve-fold*, LL3,1.

twelfhund *twelve hundred*, LL.

twelfhynde adj. *belonging to the class whose* '*wergild*' *was* 1200 *shillings*, LL.

twelfnihte *twelve days old*, LCD3·178'.

twelfta I. '*twelfth*,' An,Lcd,MH; AO. II.= Twelftadæg

Twelftadæg m. *Twelfth day*, LL296,17.

Twelftamæsseǣfen *Eve of the Epiphany*, CHR1066.

twelfte, *twelfthly, in the twelfth place*, LL 182,12.

twelftig=hundtwelftig

twelfwintre *twelve years old*, CP.

twēman=twǣman

twengan *to pinch*, IM. ['*twinge*']

twēntig 'TWENTY,' Æ,AO.

twēntigfeald *twenty-fold*, ÆGR.

twentiggēare *twenty years old*, ÆL32³⁷.

twēntigoða (io³, o³, u³) '*twentieth*,' Lcd,MH; Æ,AO.

twēntigwintre *twenty years old*, W3¹.

±twēo m. *doubt, ambiguity*, Æ,AO,CP.

tweo-=twi-, twy-; twēogan=twēon

twēogende *doubting*, BH.

twēogendlic *doubtful, uncertain*, AO. adv. -līce.

tweolf=twelf

twēolic (ī, ȳ) *doubtful, ambiguous, equivocal.* adv. -līce, AO,CP.

±twēon I. pret. sg. twēode *to doubt, hesitate*, AO,CP : (impers. w. a. of pers.) *seem doubtful.* II. (ī, ȳ) m. *doubt*, Bo.

twēona m. *doubt*, VH21.

twēonelēoht n. *twilight*, WW175²⁴.

±twēonian (ȳ) (pers. and impersonal) *to doubt, be uncertain, hesitate*, CP.

twēonigend, twēoniendlic (ī, ȳ) *doubtful, expressing doubt*, Æ. adv. -līce *perhaps*.

twēonol (ȳ) *doubtful*, Sc,WW.

twēontig=twēntig

twēonullēoht (WW175³⁹)=twēonelēoht

twēonum in phr. '*be* (sǣm, etc.) twēonum,' *between* (*the seas*, etc.).

twēonung (ī, ȳ) f. *doubt, scruple*, Æ.

+tweosa=+twisa; twēoung=twēonung

tweowa=tuwa; twi, twia=tuwa

twī=twig n.

twi- prefix with meaning *two, double*. [*Ger.* zwie-]

twibēte adj. *subject to double compensation*, LL.

twibill n. *(two-edged) axe*, Guth,*WW* ; Æ. ['*twibill*']

twibille *double-edged*, WW 141²⁷.

twiblēoh *twice-dyed, double-dyed*, CP : *biform*, CHRD 78⁶.

twibōte (adj. and adv.)=twibēte

twibrowen (y) *twice-brewed*, LCD 45b.

-twicce (æ) v. angel-t.

twiccen=twicen

twiccere m. *one who divided up the food in a monastery*, WW 127³³.

twiccian *to pluck, gather : catch hold of*, Lcd, Shr,*WW*. ['*twick*']

twi-cen, -cene, -cyne (y¹) f. *junction of roads.*

twicere=twiccere

twidæglic (a², y²) *lasting two days*, BH 350³².

twidæl m. *two-thirds*, LCD.

twidǣlan *to divide into two : differ*, Sc.

twidēagod *twice-dyed*, OEG 1060.

-twidig v. lang-t.; **twie-**=twi-

twi-ecge, -ecgede *two-edged*, BH,Ps.

twiendlīce *doubtingly*, GUTH 70. [twēon]

±**twi-feald** (Æ), -fald (CP) *two-fold, double, ambiguous*, BH,CP. ['*twifold*']

±**twifeald-an**, -ian (y¹, y²) *to double*, Æ.

twifealdlic (a) adj. *two-fold, double.* adv. -līce, Æ,*Mt*. ['*twifoldly*']

twifealdnes (ie) f. *duplicity*, CP : *irresolution*, CP 307³ : *duplication*, BF 174¹⁶.

twifēre *accessible by two ways*, WW 194³⁰.

twiferlǣcan (y) *to dissociate*, Sc 6⁸.

twifēte (eo, y) *two-footed*, ÆGR.

twifeðerede *as if with two wings, forked*, ÆGR 288¹¹.

twifingre (y) *two fingers thick*, LL 110, 49³.

twifyldan=twifealdan

twifyrclian (y¹, e²) *to branch off, deviate from*, ÆGR 288¹⁰ : *split into two.*

twifyrede *two-furrowed*, ÆGR 288¹¹.

twig n. '*twig*,' *branch, shoot, small tree*, LG; Æ,CP.

twig-=twi-; **twiga**=(1) twig; (2) tuwa

twigǣrede (y) *cloven*, ÆGR 288¹¹.

twigan=twēogan, twēon

twigea=tuwa; **twigedēagod**=twidēagod

twigilde (adj. adv. and ?sb.) *paying double, liable to a double fine*, LL.

twīh num. (acc.) only in phrase 'mid unc twīh' *between us two*, GEN 2253. [cp. Goth. tweihnai]

twihēafdede (y) *double-headed*, ÆGR.

twiheolor f. *balance*, Cp 140B.

twihinde=twihynde

twihīw(ed)e (ēo) *of two colours or shapes.*

twihīwian *to dissimulate*, Sc 44⁸.

twihlidede *having two openings*, ÆGR 288⁶ (y).

twihwēole *two-wheeled*, LCD.

twihwyrft m. *double period*, OEG 2513.

twihynde I. *having* '*wergild*' *of* 200 *shillings*. **II.** *a* '*wergild*' *of* 200 *shillings*, LL.

twihyndeman m. *man of the* '*twihynde*' *class*, LL 601,87⁴.

twiicce=twiecge

twilæpped *with two lappets*, WW 153¹⁷.

twilafte *two-edged*, WW 194³⁵.

twilībrocen *woven of threads of two colours?* TC 537²³ (v. WC 113⁷). [twilic]

twilic *double, woven of double thread*, Gl. ['*twilly*']

twīlic=twēolic

twimylte *twice-melted*, OEG 4462.

twīn I. n. *double thread, twist*, '*twine*,' *linen-thread, linen, (byssus)*, CP,Gl,Lk. **II.**= twēon II.

twinclian *to* '*twinkle*,' *wink*, Bo,CP.

twinebbe (y) *having two faces*, GPH 397⁴⁴⁶.

twinen *of linen*, OEG.

twing? sb. *cluster*, HGL 496.

twingan v. tringan.

twīnigend-=twēonigend-

twinihte (y) *two days old*, LCD 27b.

twinn '*twin*,' *two-fold, double, two by two*, Gl.

+**twinn** m. *twin.* pl. '*twins*,' *triplets*, MH, SHR.

+**twinnes** (y) f. *junction*, BF 176⁴.

twīnung=twēonung

twīnwyrm, m. '*buprestis*,' *small insect*, WW 122²⁷.

twio-=tweo

twirǣde (io, y) *uncertain : disagreeing*, Bo, *Mt*. ['*twirede*']

twirǣdnes (y¹, e²) f. *disagreement, discord, sedition*, Æ.

+**twis** *having the same parents*, GL.

+**twisa** m. *twin*, Æ.

twisceatte adv. *to the extent of a double payment*, LL 84,66¹.

twiscyldig *liable to a double penalty*, LL 90 H.

twiseht (y) *disunited, discordant*, Sc 192¹³.

twisehtan (y) *to disagree*, LCD 3·204', ANS 125·56²⁹⁵.

twisehtnes f. *dissension, disagreement*, Sc 6¹².

twiseltōð *with forked teeth?* WW 108¹⁵.

twisestre *containing two sesters*, JnL 2⁶(mg).

twisla m. *confluence, junction*, BC; KC 5·198'. ['*twisel*']

twislian *to fork, divide into two*, KC. ['*twisel*,' '*twisled*']

twisliht *forked, branched*, KC.

twislung f. *division, partition*, Lcd 3·436³ : *difference*, CHRD. ['*twisling*']

twisnæcce *double-pointed, cloven*, ÆGR 288¹¹.

twisnēse *double-pointed, cloven*, GPH393⁷³.
twisprǣc f. *double speech, deceit, detraction*.
twisprǣce *double-tongued, deceitful, detracting*, Æ.
twisprǣcnes (y) f. *double speech, detraction*.
twisprecan *to murmur*, NG.
twispunnen *twice-spun*, CP83²³.
-twist v. candel-, mǣst-t.
twistrenge *two-stringed*, ÆGR288¹⁰.
twitǣlged *double-dyed*, GL,VPs.
twi-ōrāwen, -ōrǣwen *twice thrown or twisted, twice woven*, CP.
twiwa=tuwa
twiwǣg f. *pair of scales*, WW194²⁸.
twiweg m. *junction of two roads*, WW177¹³.
twi-wintre, -winter adj. *two years old*, Æ.
twiwyrdig *ambiguous*, AO.
twoelf=twelf
twōgon=ōwōgon pret. pl. of ōwēan.
twuga, twuwa, twuwu=tuwa
twux=tusc; **twy-**=twi-
twȳ=twēo
twȳgean=twēogan, twēon I.
twȳlic (Æ)=twēolic; **twȳn**=twēon
twynihte=twinihte
twyspēcnes=twisprǣcnes
tȳ pres. 1 sg. of tȳn.
tyccen=ticcen; **tycht-**, tyct-=tyht-
tȳd (1)=tīd; (2) pp. of tȳn.
tȳd-=tīd-
+**tȳd**, tydd *skilled, learned*.
tydd-=tīd-, tūd-, tȳd-
tȳdde I. pret. 3 sg. of tȳn. **II.**=tiōde pret. 3 sg. of tīōian.
tȳde pret. sg. of tȳn.
tȳdernes (ydd) f. *branch*, OEG3849.
+**tȳdnes** f. *edification*, CHRD58³.
±**tȳdran** *to bring forth, produce, beget, propagate : be prolific.* [tūdor]
tȳdred *provided with offspring*, PPs143¹⁷.
tȳdrian=(1) tīdrian; (2) tȳdran
tȳdriend m. *propagator*, WW238²².
tȳdrung f. *propagation, production : branch*, ÆGR216¹⁵. [tūdor]
tyg-=tig-
tȳg=tēag
tyge (i) m. *drawing together, pulling, tug, pull* Æ : *leading (water) : draught (of water) : inference, statement*, Æ. [tēag, tīegan]
tygehōc (i¹) m. *hook for pulling*, LL455,15.
tygehorn (i) m. *cupping-horn*, LCD46a.
tygel m. *pulling-rope, rein*, Æ,WW. ['*tial*']
tygele f. '*murenula*,' *lamprey?* WW.
tygōlan=tīōian; **tyhhian**=teohhian
tȳhst pres. 2 sg. of tēon.
tyht I. (i) m. *instruction, training, habit*, Bo : *going, course, motion, progress*, El : *region*, GU1255. ['*tight*'; tēon] **II.**=tiht

tyht-=tiht-
±**tyhtan I.** (i) (+) *to stretch, draw, pull*, CM : *invite, incite, instigate, provoke, talk over, persuade, attract, lead astray, seduce*, Æ : (+) *teach, train*, PPs. ['*tight*'; tēon I.]
II.=tihtan
tyhten f. *incitement, excitement*, GL. [tēon I.]
tyhtend m. *inciter, instigator*, GL.
tyhtendlic (i) *persuading, hortatory*, Æ.
tyhtere (i) m. *inciter, enticer*, WW.
tyhting (i) f. *incitement, impulse, instigation, exhortation, suggestion, instruction, advice,* Æ : *enticement, allurement*, Æ. ['*tighting*']
tyhtnes (i) f. *inward impulse, instinct, conviction*, WW.
tȳhō pres. 3 sg. of tēon.
tyl=til
tyldsyle f. *tent*, WW187⁴. [teld]
tylg, tylgest v. tulge; **-tyllan** v. for-t.
tȳm=tēam; **tȳm-**=tēam-, tīm-; **tyma**=tama
tȳman (Æ)=tīeman
tymb-=timb-
±**tȳn I.** *to instruct, teach*, Æ,AO. **II.** (Æ)=tīen
tȳn-=tīen-
±**tȳnan I.** *to hedge in, fence, enclose, shut*, A,BH,LG,LL. ['*tine*'] **II.** (=īe) *to irritate, vex, trouble*, Bas,Bl,LL : *insult, revile*, Æ. ['*teen*']
tyncen n. *bladder?* AO72³⁰.
tynder (e, i, u) f. '*tinder*,' *fuel*, Bo,Gl,Sc; Æ : *cautery*. [tyndan]
tyndercynn n. *combustible*, WW.
tyndig=tindig; **tyndre**, tyndren=tynder
+**tȳne** n. *entrance, court*, PPs115⁸.
±**tynge I.** adj. *fluent, eloquent : skilful*. **II.** adv. (also -līce) *courteously*, OEG2853.
+**tyng(e)lic** *polished, elegant, rhetorical*. adv. -līce.
+**tyngnes** (i) f. *fluency, eloquence*, Æ,CP : *skill*, BF14²².
-tȳning v. æcer-t.; gafol-t.
tyntreg=tintreg
tyr-, tȳr- v. also tir-, tīr-.
-tyran (=īe) v. be-t.
tȳran (=īe) *to shed tears*, Æ : *run with water (eyes)*, LCD. [tēar]
tyrdelu, tyrdlu npl. *droppings, small pieces of excrement*, Lcd. ['*treddle*']
tȳrende *having watery eyes*, Lcd. ['*tear*']
tyrewa=tyrwa; **tyrf** v. turf.
+**tyrfan** *to strike, afflict*, GD29⁹. [torfian]
tyrfhaga f. *hoe, mattock*, Ln17².
tȳrgan=tēorian
tȳriāca m. (*treacle*), *sovereign remedy*, LCD, WW. [L. theriacum; Gk. θηριακός]
tȳrian=tēorian
tyrnan *to turn, move round, revolve*, Æ. [L. tornare]

tyrngeat n. *turnstile*, KC3·405⁴.
tyrning (u) f. *turning round, rotation*, OEG : *rotundity, roundness*, OEG : *crookedness, deceit*, OEG 56⁸⁶.
tyro=teoru
tyrð pres. 3 sg. of teran.
tyrwa m., tyrwe f. *'tar,' resin, Æ.* [=teoru]
tyr-wan. -wian I. (e, i;=ie) *to harass, vex*, *LPs.* ['*tar*'] II. *to 'tar,' B* 295 : *to make like tar*, LCD 140a.
tysca m. *buzzard*, WW 259¹².
tyslian *to put on*, CM 260, ES 8·62⁵.
tyslung f. *dressing*, ES 8·62⁶.
tysse f. *coarse cloth*, JGPh 1·63. [*OHG.* zussa]
tȳtan *to sparkle, shine*, DD 45.
tytt=titt; **tȳð**=tīð; **tȳw-**=tīw-

Ð

ðā I. adv. and conj. *then, at that time, Æ, AO,CP : after that time, thereupon, AO, Jul : when, at the time that, whilst, during, AO,B,Bl,Ps : there, where,* CHR : *seeing that, inasmuch as, if, when, since, as, because.* ðā ðā *when.* ðā...ðā *then...when.* ðā hwīle ðe *while, whilst, so long as.* ðā gīet v. ðāgīet. ['*tho*'] II. asf. and nap. of sē. ðā ðe *which.*
ðaca I. (±) m. *roof, covering.* II. gp. of ðæc.
±**ðaccian** *to clap, pat, stroke, touch gently*, *CP,Shr : smack, beat*, GD : *tame?* GPH 402. ['*thack*']
ðacele=ðæcele
ðacian *to thatch*, LL 454,10. ['*thack*']
ðacum dp. of ðæc.
ðadder (*JnL* 7³⁵)=ðider
ðæc I. (ea) n. *covering, roof of a building*, *Chr,MtR,PPs : thatch, Æ,BH.* ['*thack*'] II.=ðec pron. (das. of ðu).
ðæccille (N)=ðæcele; **ðæce** f.=ðæc I.
ðæcele (e) f. *torch, lamp, light*, AA,NG. [=fæcele]
ðæcen=ðecen; **ðæcile**=ðæcele
ðæctigile f. *roof-tile*, Cp 571.
ðæder, ðædres=ðider
ðæderlendisc (MH 178²⁵n)=ðiderlēodisc
+**ðæf** w. g. *agreeing to, consenting to, admitting : contented.*
ðǣf (*JnR*)=ðēof; **ðæfet-**=ðafet-
ðæge mnp. pron. *they, those, them, Lk,Jn, Sol.* ['*thaie*']
ðægen, ðægn=ðegen, ðegn
ðǣgon pret. pl. of ðicgan.
ðǣh (N)=ðēah I. and II.
ðæht (N)=ðeaht
ðǣm (ā, ē) dsmn. and dp. of sē pron. be ðǣm, on ðǣm *thereon, therein.* ēac ðǣm *in addition to this, besides this, also, moreover.* ǣr ðǣm ðe *before.* æfter ðǣm *after,*

later, next, after that (fashion). for ðǣm (ðe) *therefore, on that account, for that reason, because.* on ðǣm ðe *in this, in that.*
ðǣn=ðegn
ðǣnan *to moisten*, GD,LCD.
ðæncan=ðencan; **ðæncung**=ðancung
ðǣne=ðone asm. of sē.
ðǣnian=ðānian
ðænnan=ðennan; **ðænne**=ðonne
ðǣr (ē) adv. and conj. 'THERE*,' *thither, yonder : where, whither : then : when : though, if, so far as, whilst, provided that : in that respect.* ðǣr ðǣr *where, wherever.* ðǣr...of *therefrom.* ðǣr wið *in regard to that.*
ðǣra gp. of sē, sēo, ðæt.
ðǣrābūtan *about that place, ÆL.* ['*thereabout*']
ðǣræfter adv. '*thereafter*,' *CP,Lcd,Mt.*
ðǣræt '*thereat*,' *BH* 282⁶.
ðǣran *to dry*, HL 13¹⁰³.
ðǣr-big, -bie adv. '*thereby*,' *thus, CP* 42,43¹⁴.
ðǣrbinnan (o³) adv. *therein, Æ,AO.*
ðǣrbufan *besides that*, CP 52¹⁰.
ðǣre gdf. of sē.
ðǣrf=(1) ðearf; (2) ðeorf; **ðærf-**=ðearf-
ðǣrforan conj. *before that, Æ.*
ðǣrh=ðurh
ðǣrin '*therein*,' *wherein, Met.*
ðǣrinne (ē) *therein*, CP. ['*thereinne*']
ðærle=ðearle
ðǣrmid adv. *therewith, Æ,Bo.* ['*theremid*']
ðǣrnēhst *next to that*, LL 280,2¹.
ðǣrnian *to lose?* CHR 1119 (v. MFH 174).
ðǣrof adv. '*thereof*,' *of that, Lcd.*
ðǣrofer *over or above that, CP,G.* ['*thereover*']
ðǣron adv. *therein, Æ,CP : 'thereon,' Bl : thereinto, thereof.*
ðǣronbūtan (*Chr*)=ðǣreābūtan
ðǣronemn *alongside, ÆP* 164¹⁸.
ðǣrongēn adv. *on the contrary*, *W* 248²¹. ['*thereagain*']
ðǣronuppan adv. *thereupon, Æ.*
ðǣrrihte, ðærrihtes (ā, ē) adv *thereupon, forthwith, instantly, immediately, straightway, Æ,Bl,DHy.* ['*thereright(s)*']
ðǣrsc pret. 3 sg. of ðerscan.
ðǣrscan (NG)=ðerscan
ðærsc-wald, -wold=ðerscold
ðǣrst (SPs 74⁸)=dærst
ðǣrtō adv. '*thereto*,' *to it, to that place, Æ : besides, Æ,BH : for that purpose, Æ : belonging to, Æ.*
ðǣrtōēacan adv. *besides, in addition to that*, *ÆH* 2·84⁸. ['*thereteken*']
ðǣrtōgēanes adv. *on the contrary, in opposition thereto, Æ : in exchange for, TC* 436¹⁷. ['*theretoyens*']

ðærðær adv. *wherever, Æ.*

ðærunder adv. *beneath, CP.* ['*thereunder*']

ðæruppan *thereon, ÆL30²⁰⁰.* ['*thereup*']

ðærūt, ðærūte adv. *outside, without, AO, CP,Mk.* ['*thereout*']

ðærwið adv. *against, in exchange for, Æ :* '*therewith,*' *Bo.*

ðærymbe adv. *thereabout, on that point, W* 273¹.

ðærymbūtan *thereabouts, Bн,Bo.*

ðæs I. adv. (gs. of ðæt) *afterwards, AO,Chr: thence : accordingly, according as, Æ : therefore, because, CP : therefore, wherefore, because, that : as, according as; provided; (to express proportion) the (more, etc.), CP.* tō ðæs *to that point, to that degree.* ðæs ðe *since, after, afterwards, the more, CP,Mt.* ['THES'] **II.** gs. of sē and ðæt.

±ðæslǣcan *to agree with, be suitable, GL.*

ðæslīc I. adj. *suitable, congruous, Æ : harmonious : fair, elegant.* **II.**=ðyllic

ðæslīce adv. *opportunely, suitably, aptly, after this manner, similarly, thus, Æ,AO.*

ðæslicnes f. *fitness, convenience, ÆH* 1·326'.

ðæsma m. *leaven, yeast, RB10¹⁸.*

ðæsternes=ðēostornes

ðæsðe=ðæs ðe v. ðæs.

ðæt I. conj. and adv. 'THAT,' *so that, in order that, after that, then, thence.* ðæt ðe *that.* **II.** nas. of sē, ðæt. ['THAT*']

ðætte I. pron. *which, that which.* **II.** conj. *that, so that, in order that.* tō ðon ðætte *so that.* [ðæt ðe]

+ðafa I. m. *favourer, supporter, helper, CP.* **II.** adj. (cpve +ðafera) *agreeing, consenting, acquiescing.*

ðafetere, ðafettere m. *one who acquiesces in, or condones, what is wrong, CP.*

+ðafettan (æ, ea) *to consent, EHy6²⁷.*

±ðafian (ea) *to allow, suffer, endure, permit, tolerate, BH,Bo,Ct,G,LL,W ; CP : approve, consent to, submit to, AO,CP.* ['(i)-thave']

ðaforlic=ðaroflic, ðearflic

+ðafsum *consenting, agreeing, MtL5²⁵.*

+ðafsumnes f. *consent, agreement, Mt pref.* 14¹⁴.

±ðafung f. *permission, consent, Æ.*

ðāg, ðāh pret. 3 sg. of ðicgan, ðēon.

ðage=ðæge

ðāgēn=ðe āgēn *who again, Bl167⁶.*

ðāgīet, ðāgȳt adv. *still : yet.*

ðāgon pret. pl. of ðicgan.

ðāh=ðēah; ðām=ðǣm

ðamettan *to clap (the hands)? APs97⁸.*

ðan=ðon adv.

ðān I. adj. *moist, irrigated, WW.* **II.** n. *irrigated land.* [ðīnan] **III.** (LWS)=ðǣm

ðanan=ðanon

±ðanc (o) m. *thought, reflection, sentiment, idea, Æ : mind, will, purpose : grace, mercy, favour, pardon : thanks, gratitude, CP; AO, CP : pleasure, satisfaction, CP : reward, recompense, Gu442.* Gode ð. *thanks (be) to God.* Godes ðances *through the mercy of God.* Drihtnes ðances *according to the will of the Lord.* mīnes ðances *by my favour, of my own will.* on ð. *willingly, gladly.* an ðance *acceptable, pleasant, AO.* dēofla ðonces *in honour of devils, AO.* tōðance *for the sake of* ['THANK']

+ðanc mn. *thought, mind, Lk.* ['i-thank']

ðances adv. *thankfully, gladly : voluntarily, gratis, BC,Bo,Chr.* [v. 'thank']

ðancful adj. (+) *thoughtful, ingenious, clever :* '*thankful,*' *Bl : contented, satisfied, BH,WW : pleasing, agreeable, CM : energetic, spirited.* adv. -līce '*thankfully,*' *ÆL30¹⁴⁴.*

ðanchycgende *thoughtful, B2235.*

±ðancian (o) (w. g. thing and d. pers.) *to thank, give thanks, Æ; CP : recompense, reward :* (w. i.) *rejoice.* ['THANK']

+ðancmetian *to think over, deliberate, GEN* 1917. [metgian]

ðanc-metung (o¹, eo²), -metegung f. *deliberation, thought, BH88⁴* (v.l.).

±ðancol *thoughtful, mindful : prudent, wise :* (+) *desirous :* (+) *suppliant.*

ðancolmōd† *thoughtful, considerate, prudent, wise, attentive.*

ðanc-snot(t)or† *wise, prudent, ingenious.*

ðancung f. '*thanking,*' *thanksgiving, Æ,AO, JnL.*

ðanc-weorð, -weorðlic (u², y²) *thankworthy, acceptable : thankful, grateful : memorable.* adv. -līce *gladly, willingly, CP.*

ðancword n. *thanks, WID137.*

ðanc-wurð, -wyrð(e)=ðancweorð

ðand pret. 3 sg. of ðindan.

ðane (KGL)=ðone

ðanēcan ðe (o¹) adv. *whenever, as often as, Bo.*

+ðang n. *growth, SOL180¹²* (or ?=+ðanc, BTac).

ðānian (æ) *to be or become moist, moisten, WW.*

ðanne=ðonne

ðanon (CP)́, ðanone (o¹, a²) adv. *from that time or place, thence, away : whence, from which, of which, CP.* ðanon...ðanon *thence...whence : then, thereupon, henceforth : by which, through that.* ['THENNE']

ðanonforð (o¹, a²) adv. *after that, then, thenceforward, OET,W.*

ðanonweard adv. *departing thence, Bo103⁷.*

ðanun=ðanon

ðar-=ðear-, ðer-; **ðār**=ðǣr

ðára I.=ðǽr. II. gp. of sē, sēo, ðæt.
ðas=ðæs gsmn. of sē.
ðás I. afs. and nap. of ðēs. ['those'] II. nap. of ðǽw=ðēow
ðassum (N)=ðissum, dmns. of ðēs.
ðat=ðæt; ðáðá v. ðá.
ðǽw I.=ðēaw I. II.=ðēow
+ðáwenian=+ðwǽnan
ðáwian to 'thaw,' Lcd3·274'.
ðe I. rel. pron. (when govd. by a prep. the prep. follows) who, which, that. ðe is often associated by attraction with pers. pronouns. ðe ic I. ðe we we. ðe...his whose. sē ðe his he whose. II. conj. when : or : (=ðá) then : (=ðǽr) where, EL717 : (with comparatives) than. hwǽðer ðe...ðe whether...or. ðe...ðe the...or, either...or. III. art. the (indecl.), CHR963E and late. IV. particle added to ðēah, for ðǽm, ðæs, etc., without affecting their meaning. V. das. of ðu. ['THEE']
ðē=ðȳ; ðēa (NG)=ðēow
ðeac=ðæc; ðeaca=ðaca
ðēada (VPs)=ðēoda gp. of ðēod I.
ðēadōm (DR)=ðēowdōm
ðēaf (NG)=ðēof; ðeaflan=ðafian
ðeah pret. 3 sg. of ðicgan.
ðēah I. (ē) conj. and adv. 'though*,' although, even if, that, however, nevertheless, yet, still, Bl,Bo : whether, Bo. ð. ðe although. swā ð. nevertheless, yet. ð....ð. although, still, yet. II. pret. 3 sg. of ðēon.
ðēah-hwæðere, -hweðre adv. yet, moreover, however, nevertheless, but, Bl,CP. swā ð. yet, nevertheless. ['thoughwhether']
ðeaht n. counsel, advice, design, Æ. [ðencan]
+ðeaht fn. thought, consideration, counsel, advice, direction : design, contrivance, scheme, Æ,CP : council, assembly, Æ.
+ðeahta m. adviser, counsellor, WW99⁵.
ðeahte pret. 3 sg. of ðeccan.
+ðeahtend m. counsellor, WW.
+ðeahtendlic deliberative, LL12.
±ðeahtere m. counsellor, BH.
±ðeahtian to ponder, consider, deliberate upon, take counsel, Æ,CP : agree, MtL18¹⁹.
±ðeahtung (æ) f. counsel, consultation, GD, NG.
ðeahðe=ðeah ðe
ðēana adv. nevertheless, yet. swā ð. however, ever.
ðēara=ðára, gmfp. of ðæt.
ðearf I. (a, e, y) f. need, necessity, want, behoof, B,Lcd; CP. tō ðearfe as is needed, according to what is needed : benefit, profit, advantage, utility, Æ : trouble, hardship, privation, distress, danger : duty, employment. ['tharf'] II. needful, necessary. III.=ðeorf. IV. pres. 3 sg. of ðurfan.

ðearfa (æ, eo) I. m. poor man, pauper, beggar, Æ,CP. II. destitute, poor, needy, Æ.
+ðearfan to be in want, SOL268⁷³.
ðearfednes f. poverty, BH.
ðearf-end, -igend (o) m. poor man, BK.
ðearfende needy, in want, poor, CP.
ðearfendlic needy, poor, miserable, APT, GD.
ðearfendnes=ðearfednes
ðearflan to starve, be in need, want, PPs 71¹³. [Ger. darben]
+ðearflan to impose necessity, B1103.
ðearflēas adj. without cause or need, Æ. adv. -lēase.
ðearflic profitable, useful, convenient, necessary, Æ. adv. -līce.
ðearflicnes f. want, poverty, GL,SC.
ðearl adj. vigorous, strong, severe, strict, harsh, violent, heavy, excessive. adv. ðearle. swīðe ðearle with all their might.
ðearlic severe, cruel, harsh, violent, grievous. adv. -līce, CP.
ðearlmōd† stern, severe, violent, strong, mighty, JUD.
ðearlwīs strict, severe, relentless, CP.
ðearlwīslic severe, GD. adv. -līce, CP.
ðearlwīsnes f. severity, strictness, BH,GD.
ðearlwȳs-=ðearlwīs-
ðēarm (a, e) m. gut, entrail, Æ,Gl. ['tharm']
ðearm(ge)wind n. windpipe (=windðearm), OET509 (v. ES43·332).
ðearmgyrd m. girdle, belt, WW220¹.
ðearsc=ðærsc pret. 3 sg. of ðerscan.
ðearsm (BH426²⁴)=ðrosm
ðēat pret. 3 sg. of ðēotan.
ðēatan=ðēotan
ðēater m? theatre, AO154².
ðēatscipe (N)=ðēodscipe
ðēaw I. m. usage, custom, habit, conduct, disposition, AO,B,JnL; CP : (in pl.) virtues, (good) manners, morals, morality, Æ,AO,Bo,Bl; CP. ['thew'] II.=ðēow
+ðeawe customary, usual, GD142³³.
ðēawfæst decorous, moral, virtuous, honourable, LL : gentle, CRA.
ðēawfæstlīce correctly, ÆL5²²².
ðēawfæstnes f. obedience, discipline, Æ.
ðēawful moral, virtuous, W250⁴.
ðēawian I.=ðēowian. II. (+) to bring up well, Æ.
ðēawlēas ill-mannered, ÆH2·380¹¹.
ðēawlic customary, Æ : decent, moral, Æ : figurative. adv. -līce.
+ðēawod well-mannered, moral, Æ.
ðēb- (GL)=ðēof-
ðec das. of ðu. ['thee']
ðeccan (±) to cover, cover over, conceal, B, Gen,Lcd,PPs : (†) swallow up? ['thatch']
ðeccbryce m. tile, HGL459⁴².

ðeccend m. *protector, defender*, PPs 70.
ðecele=ðæcele
ðecen f. *thatch, tile, covering, roof* : (fig.) *house*, Æ. [ðeccan]
ðecest pres. 2 sg. of ðeccan.
ðecgan I. *to consume*, LCD. II. obl. case of sb? *receptacle?* (BT) or=ðeccan? (Lieb.), LL454,10.
+ðēd=+ðēod
ðēde pret. of ðēon (ðȳwan).
ðēf=ðēof
ðēfanðorn, ðefonðorn (APs57¹⁰), ðēfeðorn =ðȳfeðorn
ðefel *mulled wine?* OEG104.
ðēfel=ðȳfel
ðeflan *to pant, heave, palpitate*, HGL.
ðeften (HGl461⁵⁶)=ðyften; ðēfð=ðīefð
ðegan *to serve*, GU140.
ðegen I.=ðegn. II. pp. of ðicgan.
ðegen-=ðegn-, ðēn-
ðegeð 3 p. sg. pres. of ðecgan.
ðegh (GL)=ðēoh; ðegin=ðegn
ðegn (æ) [v. LL456; 2·680] m. *servant, minister, retainer, vassal, follower, disciple*, AO,CP : *freeman, master (as opposed to slave)* : *courtier, noble (official, as distinguished from hereditary)*, Æ : (†) *military attendant, warrior, hero*, AO. ['THANE']
ðegn- v. also ðēn-.
ðegnboren (ðegen-) *well-born*, LL.
ðegngylde n. *legal money value of a thane*, W162¹⁰.
ðegnhyse m. *attendant, retainer*, WW.
±ðegnlan (æ, ēn) (w. d.) *to serve, minister, wait on*, B,BH,Bl,G; CP : *supply another with anything* : *perform (an office)*. ['theine']
ðegnlagu f. *rights, duties or privileges of a thane*, LL,W.
ðegnlic *noble, brave, loyal*, Æ. adv. -līce.
ðegnrǣden f. *thaneship, service*, BL,GL.
ðegnriht n. *rights or privileges of a thane*, LL.
ðegnscipe m. *service, duty* : *ability*, AO : *manliness, valour*, AO : *body of retainers*.
ðegnscolu f. *band of vassals*, WW371⁷.
ðegnsorh f. *sorrow for loss of thanes*, B131.
ðegnung=ðēn-ung, -ing
ðegnweorud n. *band of followers*, CR751.
ðegnwer m. *thane's 'wergild,'* LL.
ðego=ðegu
ðēgon=ðǣgon pret. pl. of ðicgan
-ðegu v. bēah-, wīn-ð.; ðeh (A)=ðec
ðēh I.=ðēoh I. II. (A,K)=ðēah
ðeht=ðeaht
ðel, ðell n. *board, plank, (metal) plate*, AA, W. [Ger. *diele*]
ðelbrycg f. *bridge of planks*, Ct.
ðelcræft=ðylcræft

ðellfæsten n. *fastness made of planks, ship, ark*, GEN1482.
ðellian=ðilian
ðelma m. *noose, snare*, HGL429¹⁷.
-ðelu v. buruh-, benc-ð. ['theal']
ðēm=ðǣm; ðēn=ðegn
±ðencan I. *to* 'THINK*' ('*i-thenche*'), *imagine, think of, meditate, reason, consider*, Æ; AO,CP : *remember, recollect, CP* : *intend, purpose, attempt, devise*, AO : *learn* : *wish, desire, long for*. [ðanc] II. =ðyncan
ðencendlic *thoughtful*, MFH174.
ðende=ðenden; ðēnde=ðēonde
ðenden conj. and adv. *meanwhile, while, as long as, until*.
ðene=ðone
ðēnest f. *service, entertainment*, CHR1054D. [Ger. *dienst*]
ðēnestmann (ēo¹) m. *serving-man, retainer*, CHR656E.
ðēnestre f. *servant, handmaiden*, OEG1358.
ðeng=ðegn
ðengel† m. *prince, king, lord, ruler*.
ðenian=ðennan
ðēnian (Æ,CP)=ðegnian
ðēnigmann=ðēningmann
ðēningfæt n. *serving-vessel*, RB59.
ðēninggāst m. *ministering spirit*, ÆH 1·510¹⁵.
ðēninghūs n. *workshop*, GPH394.
ðēningmann m. *serving-man*, Æ,CP.
ðēnisc (*religious*) *service*, EC265⁷?
±ðennan (æ) *to stretch out, extend*, Lcd, PPs : *prostrate* : *exert oneself* : *spread the fame of, magnify*, OEG. ['thin']
ðenning f. *stretching, extension*, A11·172.
+ðēnsum *obedient, helpful, useful*, Æ. [ðegen]
ðēnung (ðegn-) *service, ministry*, BH,Bl, Bo; CP : (pl.) *attendants, retinue* : *use* : *church service, mass-book* : *meal-time, meal*, Æ. ['theining']
ðēnungbōc f. *book for divine service, mass-book*, ÆH1·98' : *Leviticus*, ÆT286².
ðēnungwerod n. *body of serving-men*, MH 218¹².
ðēo I.=ðēow m. II. ds. of ðēoh. III.= sēo II. IV. pres. 1 sg. of ðēon.
ðēod I. f. *people, nation, tribe*, Chr,Hy,Lk; AO,CP; Mdf : *region, country, province*, Bo : *men, war-troop, retainers* : (in pl.) *Gentiles*, Æ,MtR : *language*. ['thede'] II. *fellowship*, RB.
+ðēod pp. of +ðēon, ðȳwan.
±ðēodan (ī, īe, ȳ) *to join, associate (with), attach or subject oneself to*, Æ,CP : *come to, be near* : (+) *engage in* : (+) *translate*. ð. fram *separate*.

ðēodbealu† n. *public calamity.*
ðēodbūende† mp. *earth-dwellers, mortals.*
ðēodcwēn f. *queen, empress,* EL 1156.
ðēodcyning m. *monarch* : (†) *God.*
ðēode pret. 3 sg. of ðēon.
+ðēode n. *speech, language,* AO,CP : *nation* : *translation,* Æ : *meaning.*
ðēodegsa m. *general terror,* CR 834.
ðēoden m. *chief of a tribe, ruler, prince, king* : *God, Christ.* [ðēod]
ðēodend m. *translator,* OEG 15[6].
+ðēodendlic *copulative,* ÆGR 259[1].
ðēodengedāl n. *separation from one's lord (through his death),* Gu 1324.
ðēodenhold† *faithful to one's lord.*
ðēodenlēas *without a ruler or chief, lordless,* B 1103.
ðēoden-māðm (-mādm) m. *treasure given by a prince,* GEN 409.
ðēodenstōl† m. *throne.*
ðēodeorðe f. *inhabited earth,* W 240[15].
ðēodfēond m. *public enemy,* W.
ðēodfruma m. *prince, ruler,* MET 29[94].
ðēodgestrēon n. *people's treasure, great possession.* B 44; 1218.
ðēodguma† m. *man, warrior, retainer,* JUD.
ðēodhere m. *national army, host,* GEN 2160.
-ðēodig, -ðēodig-lic, -nes v. el-ð.
ðēodisc I.† n. *speech, language,* MET. II. adj. *Gentile,* OEG 8[360]. [Ger. *deutsch*]
+ðēodlǣcan *to adhere, cleave to,* LPs 24[21].
ðēodland n. *inhabited land, district, country, empire* : *the continent.*
ðēodlic *national,* ÆGR 65[6].
+ðēodlic *social, intimate,* WW 212[6].
ðēodlicetere m. *public deceiver, arch-hypocrite,* W 54[18].
ðēodloga m. *arch-liar,* W.
ðēodmægen n. *troop, host,* Ex 342.
±ðēodnes f. (+) *joining, suture* : *conjunction, association, society* : (+) *conjugation,* ÆGR : (+) *translation.*
±ðēodrǣden f. *intercourse, fellowship,* Æ.
ðēodsceaða† m. *public pest, criminal,* W.
ðēodscipe (+ in VH) m. I. *nation, people, community, population.* II. *connection, association* : *discipline, training, teaching, instruction, testimony* : *learning, erudition,* CP : *administration, law, authority* : *conduct.*
ðēodstefn m. *tribe, nation,* PPs 83[10].
+ðēodsumnes f. *agreement,* LkL p 8[1].
ðēodðrēa f? m? *general distress,* B 178.
ðēodwiga m. *great warrior,* PA 38.
ðēodwita m. *learned man* : *senator,* Æ.
ðēodwundor n. *great wonder,* CR 1155.
ðēof I. (ǣ, ēa) m., *criminal, 'thief,' robber,* G,LL,OET. II. f. *theft,* RBL 19[12].

ðēofdenn n. *robber's cave,* KC 3·15'.
ðēofend (only found in pl.?) f. *thieving, theft.*
ðēofet=ðiefð
ðēofeðorn=ðӯfeðorn
ðēoffeng m. *seizure of thieves by an owner on his own land* : *right to fines payable on conviction for theft?* TC (v. BT).
ðēofgild n. *payment for theft,* LL.
±ðēoflan *to 'thieve,' steal,* LL,TC.
ðēofmann m. *robber, brigand,* AO,ÆP.
ðēofsceaða m. *robber,* v. ANS 129·24 n 6.
ðēofsceolu=ðēofscolu
ðēofscip (ðeb-) n. *pirate-ship,* Ep. [v. 'thief']
ðēofscolu f. *band of robbers,* Bo 33[10].
ðēofscyldig f. *guilty of theft,* LL 226'.
ðēofslege m. *slaying of a thief,* LL 97.
ðēofsliht m. *slaying of a thief,* LL 104B.
ðēofstolen ptc. *stolen,* LL.
ðēofð=ðiefð
ðēofung f. *thieving,* NC 327.
ðēofunt (NG)=ðēofend
ðēofwracu f. *punishment for theft,* LL 174.
ðēoging f. *increase, profit* : *advance, progress.*
ðēoh I. (ē, ī) n. (gs. ðēos, ds. ðēo; gp. ðēona) *'thigh,' hip,* AO,Gl,Lcd,MH. II. imperat. of ðēon.
ðēohece n. *pain in the thigh,* LCD.
ðēohgelǣte n. *thigh-joint,* LCD.
ðēohgeweald np. *'genitalia,'* LCD.
ðēohhweorfa m. *knee-cap,* LCD.
ðēohscanca m. *thigh-bone,* LCD,WW.
ðēohseax (æ[2]) n. *hip-sword, short sword, dirk,* WW.
ðēohwræc m. *pain in the thigh,* LCD 1·354'.
±ðēon I. (sv[1,3]) *to thrive, prosper, flourish, grow, increase, ripen,* Æ,B,Bl,Bo,Lk,Sc : *be profitable, to become or be great, succeed, excel,* CP : *lengthen (of days).* +ðogen *adult.* ['*thee*,' '*i-thee*'] II. (wv.)=ðӯwan. III. (wv.)† *to perform, do.* IV. (+) *to receive, take.*
ðēona v. ðēoh; ðeonan=ðanon
ðēonde pres. ptc. of ðēon I.
ðēonen=ðanon; ðēonest=ðēnest
ðēonӯð=ðēownӯd
ðēor m? *inflammation?* LCD.
ðēorādl f. *inflammation? blistering heat?* LCD.
ðēorcung=deorcung
ðēordrenc m. *a drink used for inflammation,* LCD.
ðēorf (æ, e, o) I. adj. *unleavened,* Æ,G,WW : *fresh? skim? (milk),* LCD. II. n. *unleavened bread,* Æ. ['*tharf*']
ðēorfa=ðearfa
ðēorfdagas mp. *days of unleavened bread,* BF 168[33].

ðeorfhlāf m. *loaf of unleavened bread*, Æ.
ðeorfling m. *unleavened bread*, WW348²⁸.
['*tharfling*']
ðeorfnes f. *freedom from leaven, purity*,
Æ.
ðeorfsymbel n. *feast of unleavened bread*,
Ex23¹⁴.
ðeorgerid n. *inflammation?* Lcd 187a.
ðeorscwold=ðerscold
ðeorwærc m. *inflammatory disease?* Lcd
45b.
ðeorwenn f. *inflammatory tumour or blister,
carbuncle*, Lcd 123a.
ðeorwyrm m. *inflammatory (parasitic)
worm*, Lcd 45a.
ðeorwyrt f. *fleabane*, Lcd.
ðēos I. dem. pron., nom. fem. *this.* v. ðēs.
II. gs. of ðēoh. III. gs. of (ðēo=)ðēow.
ðeossa, ðeossum=ðissa, ðisum
ðēoster=ðēostor
ðēostor, ðēostre (īe, ī, ȳ) *dark, gloomy*, B,
BH,PPs : *sad, mournful.* ['*thester*']
ðēostorcofa† m. *dark chamber.*
ðēostorful (ȳ) *dark, dusky*, Æ,Mt. [v.
'*thester*']
ðēostorfulnes (ē, ȳ) f. *darkness*, OEG.
ðēostorlic (e²) *obscure, dark*, Æ. ['*thesterly*']
ðēostorloca m. *tomb*, El485.
ðēostornes (ǣ, ī, ȳ) f. *darkness*, AO,Bo.
['*thesterness*']
ðēostre=ðēostor, ðēostru
±ðēostrian (ȳ) *to grow dark, become dim, be
eclipsed*, Æ,BH : *darken, obscure*, Bo,MkL.
['*thester*']
ðēostrig (ȳ) *dark, obscure, blinded*, GD,Mk.
['*thestri*']
ðēostru f. (ī, īe, ȳ), ðēostre n. (often in pl.)
darkness, gloom, B,BH,CP,Mt; Æ. ['*thester*']
ðēostrung (ȳ) f. *twilight, gloom*, Guth36¹⁴.
ðeosum=ðisum
+ðēot I. n. *howling*, Guth48⁴. II. pres.
3 sg. of +ðēodan.
ðēotan² (ēa, ū) *to roar, howl*, Æ,Bo,Met :
sound forth, resound, murmur, WW.
['*theoten*']
ðēote f. *torrent, fountain, cataract, waterfall* :
conduit, pipe, Æ. [ðēotan]
ðēow I. fm. *servant, slave*, AO,CP,DR,G.
II. adj. *servile*, Æ,AO,Bo,W. ['*theow*']
ðēowa m. (Æ,CP)=ðēow I.
+ðēowa m. *enslaved person*, v. MFH 104.
ðēowǣt=ðēowot
ðēowan I. (ē, ī, ȳ) *to press, impress, force*,
Æ : *thrust, pierce, stab : crush, push,
oppress, check : threaten.* II.=ðēowian
ðēowatdōm=ðēowotdōm
ðēow-boren, -berde *not free-born, born in
servitude.*

ðēowcnapa m. *bondservant*, ÆH2·510'.
ðēowdōm (ēa) m. *slavery, servitude, service,
vassalage, subjection*, Æ,AO,DR; CP :
divine service. ['*theowdom*']
ðēowdōmhād m. *service*, BH480¹⁰.
ðēowe f. *female slave, handmaiden*, BH,
MtL (ī). ['*theow*']
ðēowen, ðēowene=ðēowe
ðēowet (Æ)=ðēowot, ðēowt-
ðēowhād m. *servitude, service*, BH.
ðēowian I. (±) (ē, ēa) (w. d.) occl. pret.
ðēowde *to serve, minister to, be subject to*,
Bo,Lk,Mt; AO,CP : *enslave, give over into
slavery*, Æ. ['*theow*'] II.=ðȳn. III. (+)
V²Ps140⁴=+ðēodan
ðēowin=ðēowe
ðēowincel (īo) n. *little servant*, CVHy3³.
ðēowing (ȳ) f. *threat, reproof*, GD238¹⁷.
ðēowlic *servile*, ÆGr55¹n.
ðēowmann m. *servant*, ByH134²⁰.
ðēowne as. of ðēowen.
ðēownȳd (ē²)† f. *serfdom, slavery*, Da.
ðēowot n. *service, ministry, servitude, bondage*, Æ,AO,CP.
ðēowotdōm m. *service*, CP2¹⁰.
+ðēowtian *to bring into captivity*, RWH
141¹⁶.
ðēowracian *to threaten, menace*, SPs102⁹.
ðēowracu (Æ)=ðēowwracu
+ðēowrǣden (RB)=ðēodrǣden
ðēowtlic *of a slave, servile*, Æ.
ðēowtling (wet) m. *servant, slave*, Æ.
ðēowtscipe m. *service*, ÆL23b²⁶.
ðēowð=ðēofð, ðīefð
ðēowu=ðēowe; ðēowut=ðēowot
ðēowwracu f. *commination, threat, threatening*, Æ.
ðeox *hunting-spear*, HGL423.
ðēr=ðǣr
ðeran *to rush*, Cp150j.
ðerc-, ðercs-=ðersc-
ðerc(c)an (WW)=ðerscan
ðerexwold=ðerscold; ðerf=ðeorf
ðerflicnes (KGL)=ðearflicnes
ðerh (NG)=ðurh
ðerinne=ðǣrinne; ðerrihte=ðǣrrihte
+ðersc n. *thrashing, beating*, GD.
±ðerscan³ (a, æ, ea, i, y) *to thresh*, 'THRASH*,
beat, strike*, CP.
ðerscel (y) f. *flail*, WW. ['*threshel*']
ðerscelflōr f. *threshing-floor*, Mt3¹².
ðerscing f. *thrashing*, DR40¹⁵.
ðersc-old, -wald, -wold, ðerx(w)old (æ, eo,
i, y) m. '*threshold,' border, limit*, Æ,BH,
Bl,Bo,Lcd,WW.
ðes=ðæs
ðēs (e?) m., ðēos f., ðis n. dem. pron.
'THIS.' beforan ðissum, ǣr ðissum *before
this, formerly.*

ðēster-=ðēostor-; ðēstrian=ðēostrian
ðet, ðette=ðæt, ðætte
ðēw-=ðēow-; ðī=ðȳ
ðīada (VPs 134¹⁶)=ðēoda gp. of ðēod.
+ðīan=+ðēon IV.
ðīcce I. adj. 'THICK,' viscous, solid, AO : dense, stiff, CP : numerous, abundant, AO : hazy, gloomy, Æ : deep, AO. II. adv. thickly, closely, Bo,Lcd,WW : often, frequently, Gen 684. III. (VPs 28⁹)=ðiccet.
ðīccet n. thick bushes, 'thicket,' SPs. [ðicce]
ðīccian tr., intr. to thicken, Æ,WW : crowd together, Shr. ['thick']
ðīccnes=ðicnes
ðīccol, ðiccul fat, corpulent, WW.
ðīcfeald dense, OEG 278.
+ðīcfyldan to make dense, GL.
±ðīcgan⁵ (and wv. in WS) (a, æ, e, ea) to take, receive, accept, Chr,Lcd : partake of, consume, taste, eat, drink, Mk; AO,CP. ['thig']
ðīclīce thickly, often, continually, frequently, in large numbers, AO.
ðīcnes f. 'thickness,' density, viscosity, hardness, GD,Lcd, SPs : depth : anything thick or heavy (as clouds or rain), LPs,ZDA : darkness : thicket.
ðīd-=ðēod-; ðīdan=ðyddan
ðīder (æ, y) adv. on that side, 'THITHER*,' whither, Æ; AO,CP. hider and ð. or. hidres ðidres (ðædres) hither and thither, CP : where, wherever.
ðīdercyme m. a coming hither, NC 327.
ðīdergeond thither, Æ.
ðīderinn (y¹, y²) adv. therein, into that place.
ðīderlēodisc to that people, native, MH 178²⁶.
ðīderweard, ðiderweardes adv. 'thitherwards,' thither, Æ,AO,Bo.
ðīdres=ðider; ðīed-=ðēod-
ðīeder (CP)=ðider; ðīef-=ðēof-
ðīefefeoh n. stolen goods, LL 100,25¹.
ðīefð (ē, ēo, ȳ) f. 'theft,' Lcd,LL : stolen goods, LL (ðēoft). [ðēof]
+ðīegen=+ðigen; ðīen=ðȳn
ðīende=ðēonde; ðīenen=ðīnen
ðīenga=ðinga gp. of ðing.
ðīestr-=ðēostr-; ðīf-=ðīef-, ðȳf-
ðīgde, ðigede pret. 1, 3 sg. of ðicgan.
ðīgen I. f. receiving, taking (of food or drink), eating, Æ : food or drink, Æ. [ðicgan] II. pp. of ðēon I. and ðicgan.
ðīgeð pres. 3 sg. of ðicgan.
ðīgnen=ðīnen
ðīgon pret. pl. of ðēon I.
ðīh=ðēoh
ðīhsl=ðīsl
-ðīht v. maga-ð., mete-ð. and 'thight.'
ðīhtig=ðyhtig
ðīhð pres. 3 sg. of ðēon I.

ðīll-=ðyl-
ðīllian (e, y) to lay with planks, board over, Æ. [Ger. dielen]
ðīllic=ðyllic
ðīlling f. boarding, floor : table, GD 97⁴.
ðīlle n. thin board, plank, flooring, GL. [Ger. diele]
ðīllian=ðilian; ðīllic=ðyllic
ðīmiama m. incense, Æ. [L. thymiama]
ðīn I. gs. of ðu. II. adj. pron. 'THINE,' thy. III.=ðigen I.
ðīnan to grow moist, Lcd 13b.
ðīnc=ðing
ðīncan=(1) ðyncan; (2) ðencan
+ðīncðo=+ðyncðo
+ðīnd n. swelling, Lcd,WW.
ðīndan³ to swell, swell up, Æ : (wrongly, through confusion betw. 'tabescere' and 'tumescere') melt, pass away, PPs 111⁹, 118¹⁵⁸ : be angry.
ðīnen f. maid-servant, handmaid, Æ : midwife, Æ. [ðegn]
ðīng n. 'THING,' creature, Æ : object, property, Æ : cause, motive, reason, Æ : lawsuit : event, affair, act, deed, enterprise, Æ, CP : condition, circumstances, Æ : contest, discussion, meeting, council, assembly : court of justice, v. LL 2·449 : point, respect. mid nānum ðingum adv. not at all. for his ðingum for his sake. for ðisum ðingum for this reason. be fullum ðingum abundantly. ænige ðinga anyhow, in any way, somehow. raðost ðinga at the earliest. ælces ðinges entirely, in every respect.
ðīngan to invite, address? GL.
+ðīngan I. sv³ to thrive. II.=ðingian
+ðīnge n. meeting, council : arrangement, agreement, covenant : intercession : fate.
±ðīngere m. advocate, intercessor, mediator, priest, GL,CP.
ðīngestre f. female advocate, mediatrix, HL 10⁶⁹⁸.
ðīnggemearc n.† reckoning of time, allotted time.
ðīngian (w. d.) to beg, pray, ask, intercede for, LL,Sat; CP : covenant, conciliate, compound with, settle : prescribe : (refl.) reconcile oneself (with) : determine, purpose, design, arrange : talk, harangue. ['thing']
ðīnglēas free (from sin or crime), LL 412.
ðīngrǣden f. intercession, pleading, mediation, intervention, Æ.
+ðīngsceat m. ransom, CP 339¹⁰.
ðīngstede† m. place of assembly.
ðīngstōw f. meeting-place, place of council : place where ways meet, village : market.
+ðīngð f. intercession, agreement : court where claims are settled? (BTs), LL 228,1¹.
+ðīngðo=+ðyncðo

ðingum adv. (instr. pl. of ðing) *purposely*.

±ðingung f. *advocacy, intercession, mediation*, Æ,CP.

ðinn-=ðynn-

ðinne asm. of ðin II.

ðinnen=ðinen

ðinra=ðynra comp. of ðynne.

ðinra gp. of ðin II.

ðint pres. 3 sg. of ðindan.

ðio, ðio-=ðeo, ðeo-

ðir f. *a female servant*, JnLR18¹⁷. [*ON.* ðir]

ðird- (*NG*)=ðrid-

ðire=ðinre gdsf. of ðin II.

ðirel=ðyrel; ðirl-=ðyrl-

ðirnet=ðyrniht

ðirsceflōr, ðirscelflōr=ðerscelflōr

ðirsceð pres. 3 sg. of ðerscan.

ðirscwald=ðerscold; ðirst=ðurst

ðis v. ðes; ðisa=ðissa gp. of ðes.

ðisan=ðisum dsmn. of ðes.

ðises gsmn. of ðes.

ðisl f., ðisle f. *waggon-pole, pole, shaft*. [*Ger.* deichsel]

ðislic=ðyllic; ðism=dism

ðisne as. of ðes.

ðison=ðisum dsmn. of ðes.

ðissa gp., ðisse, ðissere gdsf.; ðisson, ðissum dsmn. and dp. of ðes.

ðistel (y¹) m. '*thistle*,' *Gl,WW*; Mdf.

ðistelgeblǣd n. *blister caused by thistle*, LCD 162b.

ðistellēag m. *thistle-covered meadow?* KC 5·265²².

ðisteltwige f. *a kind of bird, goldfinch? linnet?* GL.

ðisternes (CP)=ðeostornes

ðistr-=ðeostr-

ðistra m. *trace, article of harness?* WW.

ðisum dsmn. and dp. of ðes.

ðiðer=ðider

ðiustra '*ambulas*' (*amplas?*) Cp535A.

ðīw-=ðȳw-, ðēow-; ðixl (GL)=ðisl

ðō f. *clay, loam*, GL. [*Ger.* ton]

ðocerian, ðocrian *to run up and down*, WW.

ðoddettan *to strike, push*, W.

ðoden (ō?) n. *whirlwind, high wind, whirlpool*, Æ,Cp,CP,Chr. ['*thode*']

ðōdor=ðōðor

ðoft, ðofte f. *bench for rowers*, WW. ['*thoft*']

+ðofta m. *comrade, mate*, Æ,AO : *follower, client*.

+ðoftian *to join, unite, associate* (wið), AO.

±ðoftrǣden f. *fellowship*, Æ.

±ðoftscipe m. *companionship*, W : *alliance* CP : *intimacy*, CHRD 67³⁴.

+ðogen *adult : virtuous, excellent*. [pp. of ðēon]

ðōh (GL)=tōh

ðōhe f. *clay*, GL (=ðō).

±ðōht (+exc. N) mn. *process of thinking* '*THOUGHT*' : *mind : a thought, idea, purpose : decree : compassion*, '*viscera*,' LkLH 1⁷⁸. [ðencan]

+ðohta=+ðofta

ðōhte pret. 3 sg. of ðencan.

+ðōhtung f. *counsel*, ZDA21·189.

ðōiht *clayey*, WW348¹¹.

ðol m. '*thole*,' *oar-pin*, Cp,WW.

ðolebyrde *patient*, Sc. ['*tholeburde*']

ðolebyrdnes f. *endurance*, Sc3⁸(i²). ['*thole burdness*']

ðolemōd=ðolmōd

±ðolian *to suffer, endure, undergo*. B,CP, Gen,MkL ; AO : *allow*, KC : *persevere, hold out* (intr.), *remain, survive* : (w. g.) *to lose, lack, forfeit, dispense with*, Æ. ['*thole*']

ðoll=ðol

ðolle f. *saucepan*, OEG 4115.

ðolmōd I. *forbearing, patient*, Æ,HL,Sc, OEG. II. m. *patience?* ÆL16³³⁴ D. ['*thole-mode*']

ðolmōdnes f. *forbearance, patience*, Æ. ['*tholemodeness*']

ðolo-=ðol(e)-

ðolung f. *passion*, Sc.

ðon I. instr. sing. of sē. II. adv. *then, now : thence* : (in negative clauses, with comparatives) *in comparison with : inasmuch as, when*. æfter ðon *after that*. ǣr ðon *before that* (antequam). nō ðon lange... *not long until...*. tō ðon *to that extent, so that, after that*. III. (VPs)=ðonne

ðōn=ðǣm; ðonan=ðanon; ðonc=ðanc

ðone asm. of sē *the, that*.

ðonēcan=ðanēcan; ðonen=ðanon

ðong=ðanc

ðonne (a, æ) adv. and conj. *THEN**, AO; CP : *therefore, wherefore : yet : while, when : thereafter, henceforth : rather than*, Ps : *since : although* : (with comparatives) '*than*,' Æ,CP. ðonne...ðonne *when...then*. ð. hwæðere *yet, nevertheless*. ð. gȳt *as yet, even*. ð. ǣr *be since*.

ðonon=ðanon

Ðor m. *Thor*, W ; LCD.

ðorf (NG)=ðeorf

ðorfæst *useful*, DR,LkR. [ðearf]

ðorfend=ðearfend

ðorfnian v. ðornian.

ðorfte pret. 3 sg. of ðurfan.

ðorh (VPs)=ðurh; ðorhniht=ðorniht

ðorlēas *useless*, NG. [ðearf]

ðorn m. '*thorn*,' *thorn-bush*, Æ,Bo,Cr,G,Gl; CP; Mdf : *name of the rune for* ð, *Run*.

ðorngeblǣd n. *blister caused by a thorn*, LCD 162b.

ðornian *to lose*, v. MFH174. [for ðorfnian?]

ðornig 'thorny,' Æ,W.

ðorn-iht, -eht(e) thorny, Gl,KC.

ðorning m. thorny place, BC1·480⁸ (Mdf).

ðornrind f. thorn-bark, Lcd 19a.

ðorof (MtL)=ðeorf

ðorp (ðrop) m. farm : village, Chr,Gl. ['thorp']

ðorscen pp. of ðerscan.

ðost m. dung, Lcd. ['thost']

+ðōt=+ðēot

ðoterian (o²) to cry, howl, lament, Æ.

ðoterung f. groaning, wailing, Æ.

ðotor-, ðotr-=ðoter-

ðōð (Chr 1135)=ðēah I.

ðōðor, ðōðer m. ball, AS,Gl.

ðox=dox; ðrā=ðrēa

+ðracen hardy, WW108²⁵.

ðracian to fear, dread, shun, RHy9⁵⁰.

ðracu† f., gs. ðræce pressure, fury, storm, violence : onrush, attack.

±ðræc (usu. +) n. throng : pressure, force, violence : equipment, OEG.

ðræcful? (e) strong, RPs58⁴.

ðræcheard brave in battle, El123.

ðræchwīl f. time of misery, Jul554.

ðræcian=ðracian

ðræcrōf keen in fight, Gen2030.

ðræcswald=ðerscold

ðræcwīg m. violent combat, Ex182.

ðræcwudu (e¹) m. spear, B1246.

ðrǣd (ē) m. 'thread,' Bo,Cp,Lcd; Æ.

+ðrǣf n. pressure, Chrd12⁶. (or +ðrafu)

+ðrǣf (on) unanimously (Swt).

ðrǣft n. contentiousness, Mod42.

ðrǣgan† to run, El.

ðrǣging=ðrēagung

ðrǣl (ēa) m. serf, 'thrall,' LL,NG.

ðrǣlriht n. serf's right, W158¹⁵.

ðrǣs (ē) fringe, hem, Gl.

ðrǣscan=ðrǣstan; ðræsce (Cp)=ðrysce

ðrǣst=dærst

±ðrǣstan to writhe, twist, press, force, BH : crush, oppress, torment, constrain, bind, Gl : destroy. [v. 'threst,' 'i-thrast']

+ðrǣstednes f. contrition, GD : crushing, WW.

ðrǣstnes f. trouble, pain, grief : (+) contrition.

ðrǣstung f. affliction, torment, CP317⁷.

ðrǣwen=ðrāwen pp. of ðrāwan.

ðrǣwung=ðrēagung; ðræxwold=ðerscold

ðraflian to restrain, reprove, CP : urge, push, press, Æ : demand, Chrd12¹⁰.

+ðrafu? f. compulsion, Chrd12⁶.

ðrafung f. reproof, correction, CP.

ðrāg f. space of time, time, while, period, season, Gen,Jul : occasion, B,Bl,Bo : evil times : paroxysm. ðrāge for a time, some time, long time. ðrāgum at times, some-

times. ealle ðrāge all the time, continually. ['throw']

ðrāgbysig long busy? Rd5¹.

ðrāglic (ðrah-) long-continued, MFH175.

ðrāgmǣlum† at times, sometimes.

ðrāh=ðrāg; ðrāll=ðrēal, ðrǣl

ðrang pret. 3 sg. of ðringan.

+ðrang n. throng, crowd, tumult, Ma299.

±ðrāwan⁷ to turn, twist, curl, Æ,Gl; CP : rack. ['throw']

ðrāwere m. perverse person, APs17²⁷.

ðrāwingspinl f. crisping-pin, OEG.

ðrāwu (Gl)=ðrēa; ðrē=ðrēo

ðrēa I. mfn. threat, menace, abuse, CP : rebuke, castigation : oppression, attack : calamity, throe. [ðrēowan] II. imperat. of ðrēagan.

ðreacs=ðreax

ðrēade pret. 1, 3 sg. of ðrēagan.

±ðrēagan, ðrēawian (ē) to rebuke, chastise, correct, punish, CP,Mt; Æ : threaten, menace : attack, oppress, torture, afflict, vex, harass. ['threa']

ðrēagend m. reprover, OEG5380.

ðrēagung (ǣ, ēaw-) f. threatening, reproof, correction, Æ,CP.

ðreahs=ðreax

ðrēal I. f. discipline, correction, punishment, Æ : reproof : threat. II.=ðrǣl

ðrēalic† severe, terrible, calamitous, Gen.

ðrēan (Æ)=ðrēagan; ðrēanēd=ðrēanīed

ðrēang=ðrēagung

ðrēanīed (ē², y²)† f. affliction, misery, distress, calamity.

ðrēaniedla (ē², ȳ²)† m. affliction, misfortune.

ðrēanīedlic calamitous, Jul128.

ðrēanȳd=ðrēanied

ðrēap m. troop, band, DD,DHy,OEG.

ðrēapian to reprove, correct, CP165¹⁷. ['threap']

ðrēapung f. reproof, CP167¹⁴. ['threaping']

ðrēaswinge f. chastisement, APs37¹⁸.

ðrēat I. (ēo) m. press, crowd, throng, host, troop, B,El,Mk : oppression, coercion, calamity, Bl,Jul : threatening? Æ. ['threat'] II. pret. 3 sg. of ðrēotan.

ðrēatend m. violent person, MtL.

ðrēatian to urge, press, force, attack, harass, Æ,Cp,MH,MtL : threaten, PPs : reprove, rebuke, check, PPs; Æ,CP. ['threat']

ðrēatmǣlum (ē) adv. in swarms, WW31²⁷.

ðrēatnes f. affliction, tribulation, MFH117.

ðrēatnian (Æ)=ðrēatian ['threaten']

ðrēatung f. threatening, compulsion, illusage, AO : correction, reproof, CP.

ðrēaung=ðrēagung

ðrēaw pret. 3 sg. of ðrēowan.

ðrēawend=ðrōwend

ðrēaweorc n. misery, Gen737. [OS.]

ðrēawian, ðrēawung=ðrēag-ian, -ung

ðreax (e) rottenness, rubbish, refuse, BAS
48²⁰; ÆL35¹⁵⁰. [ON. ðrekkr; v. ES43·332]

ðrec=ðræc

ðrece m. force, violence, W : weariness, LPs.
[ðracu]

ðrecswald=ðerscold; ðrēd (Cp)=ðræd

ðrefe a measure of corn or fodder, BC3·367.
['thrave']

+ðrēgan=+ðrēan; ðrēgian=ðrǣgan

ðrehtig=ðrohtig; ðremm=ðrymm

ðrēo v. ðrīe; ðreo-=ðri-

ðreodian (y) to think over, deliberate :
meditate : (+) resolve, GD.

ðreodung (i) f. deliberation, consideration,
BH : scruple, hesitation, W.

ðreohtig=ðrohtig

ðrēohund n. three hundred, Æ.

ðrēohundwintre of the age of three hundred
years, GEN5¹³.

ðreom v. ðrīe.

ðrēoniht f. period of three days, PA38.

ðrēora v. ðrīe

ðrēostru=ðēostru; ðrēot=ðrēat

ðrēotan² to vex, weary, AS47².

ðrēotēoða (ȳ) 'thirteenth,' Æ,MH (-tegða),
Mt; AO.

ðrēotīne (ē², ȳ²) 'thirteen,' BH,Men.

ðrēotīnegeare thirteen years old, MH216¹⁶.

ðrēott-=ðrēot-

ðrēow I. pret. 3 sg. of ðrāwan. II.=ðrīe

ðrēowian=ðrōwian; ðreoxwold=ðerscold

ðrep? 'fornix,' Ln34⁵⁹ (drep).

ðrepel=ðrypel; ðrerēðre=ðrirēðre

ðrēs=ðrǣs; ðrescan=ðerscan

ðrescold, ðrescwald=ðerscold

ðrēst-=ðrǣst-; ðrēt=(1) ðrēat; (2) ðrǣd

ðrēung=ðrēaung; ðrex=ðreax

ðrex-=ðersc-; ðrī=ðrīe; ðrīa=ðriwa

ðrībeddod (y) three-bedded, having three
couches, WW184²⁴.

ðriccan=ðryccan

ðridæglic (eo, y) lasting three days, BH
350³².

ðridǣled (eo, y) tripartite, OEG.

ðridda (y) num. adj. 'third*,' Bl,Cr,Lcd,
LG; AO,CP. ðridde healf two and a half.

ðriddandǣl m. third part, LL.

ðridung=ðreodung

ðrīe (ī, ȳ) num. nam.; nafn. ðrēo; gmfn.
ðrēora; dmfn. ðrim (ðreom) 'THREE*.'

ðrie-=ðri-; ðrīeste=ðrīste adv.

ðrietan to weary : force, Bo.

ðrifeald 'three-fold,' Æ,RB.

ðrifealdlīc three-fold, triple. adv. -līce in
three ways, LL. ['threefoldly']

ðrifeoðor=ðrifeðor

ðrifēte 'three-footed,' ÆGr.

ðrifeðor triangular, GL.

ðrifingre (y) three fingers broad or thick, LL
110,49³.

ðriflēre (y) three-storied, ÆH2·70¹⁷.

ðri-fotede, -fotad (y) 'three-footed,' WW.

ðrifyldan (=ie) to triplicate, ÆGR287⁴.

ðrifyrede three-furrowed, ÆGR288¹²n.

ðrig=ðrīe; ðriga=ðriwa

ðrigǣrede (eo¹) three-pronged, ÆGR288¹⁰.

ðrigēare three years old : space of three years.

ðrigylde I. adj. subject to three-fold payment,
or compensation, LL. II. adv. LL.

ðrihēafdede (y) 'three-headed,' ÆGr67¹¹.

ðrihing=ðriðing

ðrihīwede (y) having three forms, ÆGR
287¹⁰.

ðrihlidede (y) having three openings, ÆGR
288⁶.

ðri-hyrne, -hyrnede (eo) three-cornered, Æ,
LCD.

ðrilēfe (y) three-leaved. as sb.=trefoil?
wood-sorrel? WW133²². ['threeleaf']

ðrilen (WW151³⁴, y), ðrilig, ðrili adj. woven
with three threads, Gl; LV. ['thrile']

ðrilic (y) triple, three-fold, VHy.

ðrillöe n. year with an extra month (a third,
named liða), v. BT.

ðrim I.=ðrymm. II. v. ðrīe.

ðrim-=ðrym-

ðrimen (y) a third part, LCD47a.

Ðri-meolce, -milce n. May, MH.

Ðrimilcemönað (y¹, y²) m. May, MEN (v.
CHR p276).

ðrims, ðrimse=trymes; ðrindan=ðrintan

ðrinen (y) three-fold, CM.

Ðrines f. Trinity, Æ,BH,Bl,Cr,DR. ['three-
ness,' 'thrinness']

+ðring (y) n. crowd, pressure, commotion,
An; ÆL. ['thring']

±ðringan³ to press, squeeze, crowd upon,
throng, press forward, rush on, hasten,
advance, AO : oppress : (+) pinch (with
cold) : gain (by force). ['THRING*']

ðrinihte three days old, LCD.

ðrinlic three-fold, NC327.

ðrinna three-fold, three times, LL. ['thrin']

Ðrinnes (Æ)=Ðrines

ðrintan³ to swell, MOD24.

ðrīo=ðrēo, v. ðrīe.

ðrīostr- (KGL)=ðēostr-

ðrirēðre with three rows of oars. as sb.
trireme, AO (īe).

ðrisce=ðrysce; ðriscelflōr=ðerscelflōr

ðriscȳte (y¹) triangular, AO. [scēat]

ðrislite (ie) tripod, three-forked, A4·151.

ðrisnæcce (y¹, e²) three-forked, ÆGR288¹²

ðrīsnes=ðrīstnes

ðrīst, ðrīste I. adj. daring, rash, bold : audacious, shameless, CP,W. II. adv. boldly,
daringly. ['thriste'; Ger. dreist]

ðrístelic=ðrístiglic
ðrístful *presumptuous*, CM369.
ðrísthycgende† *brave-minded*.
ðrísthȳdig† *bold, valorous*, B.
+ðrístian *to dare, presume*, BH,LL.
ðrístiglic *rash, bold, daring*. adv. -līce.
±ðrístlǣcan *to presume, dare*, CP.
ðrístlǣcnes f. *boldness*, GD.
+ðrístlǣcung f. *presumption*, MFH164.
ðrístlēasnes f. *want of boldness?* A11·101.
ðrístlic *bold*, MFH. adv. -līce.
ðrístling m. *bold person?* (BT), *thrush* (Mdf),
  EC450¹⁵.
ðrístlong *very long?* (or=ðristling?) BC
  3·618.
ðrístnes f. *rashness, boldness*, CM,Sc.
ðrístra=ðīstra
ðrístrenge (eo, y) *three-stringed*, ÆGr288¹⁰.
ðrít (Æ) pres. 3 sg. of ðrīetan.
ðrítig 'THIRTY,' Æ; AO,CP.
ðrítigfeald 'thirty-fold,' Mt.
ðrítigoða (ēo, ȳ, tt) 'thirtieth,' ÆGr,BH,Mt.
ðrítigwintre *thirty years old*, Æ.
ðrittēoða=ðrēotēoða
ðrittig=ðrītig; ðrīð=ðrȳð
ðrīðing *third part of a county*, 'riding,'
  LL.
ðrīðinggerēfa m. *governor or sheriff of a*
  'ðrīðing,' LL.
ðriwa adv. *thrice*, Mk,RB; AO. ['thrie']
ðriwin-tre, -tra, -ter *three years old*, WW.
  [v. 'thrinter']
ðroc n. *table*, Mk11¹⁵ : *piece of wood on*
  which the ploughshare is fixed, WW219⁶.
  ['throck']
ðroehtig=ðrohtig
ðrōh I. 'rancor,' GL. II. 'rancidus,' OEG.
ðroht† I. m. *exertion, labour, endurance, toil,*
  trouble, suffering. II. adj. *dire, trouble-*
  some, tormenting.
ðrohtheard† *strong in enduring*, AN,EL :
  hard to endure, EL.
ðrohtig (e? eo) *enduring, persistent, per-*
  severing, laborious.
ðrong=ðrang pret. 3 sg. of ðringan.
ðrop=ðorp; ðrosle=ðrostle
ðrosm m. *smoke, vapour*, Æ.
ðrosmig *vaporous, smoky*, W138²⁶.
ðrostle (ō?) f. 'throstle,' *thrush*, BC,Cp,GD.
ðrota (WW306¹³)=ðrote
ðrotbolla m. *gullet, windpipe, larynx*, Æ,
  Gl,LL. ['throatboll']
ðrote, ðrotu f. 'throat,' Æ,Bo,WW.
ðroten pp. of ðrēotan.
ðrotu (Æ)=ðrote; ðrōung=ðrōwung
ðrōwend m. *serpent, scorpion, basilisk*, Æ.
ðrōwend-=ðrōwiend-
ðrōwere m. *sufferer, martyr*, DR,LCD.
ðrōwerhād, ðrōwethād m. *martyrdom*, GD.

±ðrōwian (o?) *to endure, suffer, die*, Æ,B,
  Bl,Bo; AO,CP : *pay for, atone for* : *sym-*
  pathise. ['throw']
ðrōwiendhād (e²) m. *martyrdom*, GD231⁸ c.
ðrōw-lendlic, -igendlic *suffering, enduring,*
  passive, Æ. ð. dēað *apoplexy*.
ðrōwung f. *suffering* : *passion, martyrdom*,
  Æ,CP : *painful symptom* : *anniversary of*
  martyrdom. ['throwing']
ðrōwungrǣding f. *reading about martyrs,*
  martyrology, CM286.
ðrōwung-tīd f., -tīma n. *time of suffering*, Æ.
+ðrūen pp. of ðweran.
ðrūh fmn. *pipe, trough*, Gl,MH : *chest* :
  tomb, coffin, Æ,BH ['through']
ðrum=ðrim v. ðrīe.
-ðrum v. tunge-ð. ['thrum']
ðrungen pp., ðrungon pret. pl. of ðringan.
ðrustfell n. *leprosy*, Cp103B.
-ðrūt v. fisc-ð.
ðrūtigende *strutting, bouncing*, Æ : *threaten-*
  ing, ÆL10²⁷³.
ðruton pret. pl. of ðrēotan.
ðrūtung *anger, pride* : *threatening*, ÆL7⁷⁶.
ðrūðhorn=truðhorn; ðrȳ=ðrīe, ðrī
ðrȳan=ðrȳn
±ðryccan pret., ðrycte, ðryhte (tr.) *to*
  trample on, crush, oppress, afflict, repress,
  Bo; CP : (intr.) *press, push*, Gu. ['thrutch']
±ðryccednes f. *distress, trouble*, RWH67³².
ðrycnes f. *tribulation, affliction*, MtR.
ðryd-=ðrid-, ðreod-; ðrȳd-=ðrȳð-
+ðrȳde pret. 3 sg. of +ðrȳn.
ðrȳh=ðrūh
ðryhte pret. 3 sg. of ðryccan.
ðryl=ðyrl, ðyrel
+ðrȳl n. *crowd, multitude*, ÆL23⁹². [ðrȳn]
ðrym=ðrymm
ðrymcyme m. *glorious coming*, Gu1230.
ðrymcyning† m. *glorious king, king of glory,*
  God.
ðrymdōm m. *glory*, W254¹⁴D.
ðrymen=ðrimen
ðrymfæst† *glorious, illustrious, noble,*
  mighty.
ðrymful† *glorious, majestic, peerless*.
ðrymilce=ðrimeolce
ðrymlic *glorious, magnificent*, AO : *powerful,*
  mighty. adv. -līce.
ðrymm m. *multitude, host, troop*, ÆL,Cr :
  torrent : *force, power, might, ability* : *glory,*
  majesty, splendour, Bl. ['thrum']
ðrymma m. *brave man, hero*, AN1141.
ðrymme, ðrymmum adv. *powerfully, vio-*
  lently.
ðrymrīce n. *realm of glory, heaven*, BL105¹¹.
ðrymsa=trymes
ðrym-seld n., -setl (Æ) n. *seat of honour,*
  throne.

ðrymsittende† ptc. *sitting in glory, dwelling in heaven*, An.

ðrymwealdend I. adj. *all-ruling*, Æ. II. m. *lord of glory.*

+ðrȳn *to press, bind*, v. NC328 : *repress* : *express.*

ðrync (AO76³⁴)=drinc imperat. of drincan.

ðrynen=ðrinen; Ðrynes=Ðrines

ðryng sb. *conduit, channel?* (=ðring?) WW 198¹⁴.

Ðrynnes (Æ)=Ðrines; ðryosm=ðrosm

ðrȳpel (ē) m. *instrument of torture, cross?* WW225⁴¹. [ðrēapian].

ðrȳpelūf '*eculeus,*' '*catasta,*' WW180¹³.

+ðryscan·*to weigh down, afflict, oppress*, CP. [ðerscan]

ðrysce (æ, i) '*thrush,*' WW.

ðryscel-=ðerscel-

±ðrysman, +ðrysmian *to press, oppress, stifle*, AO. [ðrosm]

ðryssce=ðrysce; ðrȳst=ðrīst

ðrȳst-=ðēost-

ðrȳt pres. 3 sg. of ðrēotan.

ðrȳð† f. (often in pl.) *might, power, force, strength : majesty, glory, splendour : multitude, troop, host.*

ðrȳðærn n. *noble house, palace*, B657.

ðrȳðbearn n. *strong youth*, An494.

ðrȳðbord n. *strong shield*, El151.

ðrȳðcyning m. *king of glory, God*, An436.

+ðrȳðed *mighty*, Ph486.

ðrȳðful (†) *strong, brave : splendid, glorious*, VH.

ðrȳðfullian (ðrȳd-) *to fill up*, RPs130¹.

ðrȳðgesteald n.*noble dwelling, palace*, CR354.

ðrȳðig *mighty, strong*, Gen1986?

ðrȳðlic *strong, valiant*, B. adv. -līce (?), B.

ðrȳðo=ðrȳð

ðrȳðswȳð† n. *mighty, powerful*, B.

ðrȳðu=ðrȳð

ðrȳðum† *very, violently.*

ðrȳðweorc n. *mighty work*, An774.

ðrȳðword n. *lofty discourse*, B643.

ðū (ū) pron. 2 pers., gs. ðīn, das. ðe, ðec; dual n. git, gīt, g. incer, d. inc, a. incit, inc; np. gē, gīe. gp. ēower, dp. ēow, ap. ēowic, ēow '*thou*.'

ðūf m. *tuft : banner, standard, crest.* [L. tufa]

+ðūf *thriving, luxuriant*, WW.

ðūfbære *leafy*, OEG2222.

ðūfeðistel=ðūðistel

ðūfian *to shoot forth, grow luxuriantly*, WW 408².

ðūfig *leafy*, WW408³.

ðūft m. *thicket*, WW408¹⁴.

ðugon pret. pl. of ðēon.

+ðūhslan *to make misty, dark*, W137⁹.

ðūhte pret. 3 sg. of ðyncan.

+ðūhtsum *abundant*, MH138¹⁵.

ðullic=ðyllic

ðūma m. '*thumb,*' Ep,Lcd,LL.

ðumle sbpl. *entrails*, Cp210ʋ.

+ðun n. *loud noise*, PPs,WW.

ðunar=ðunor

ðunden pp. of ðindan.

ðunelic=ðunorlic

ðuner, ðuner-=ðunor, ðun(o)r-

ðung m. *a poisonous plant, wolf's-bane, aconite, nightshade?* Gl.

+ðungen *full grown, thriven : competent, excellent, distinguished, virtuous*, ÆL. as sb. *notable, king's thane.* [pp. of ðēon]

+ðungenlīce adv. *virtuously, soberly*, WW.

±ðungennes f. *growth, maturity : goodness, excellence, virtue, perfection.*

ðunian *to stand out, be prominent : be proud : roar, thunder, crash, groan.*

ðunnung=ðūnung; ðunnur=ðunor

ðunor (e², u²) m., gs. ðun(o)res '*thunder,*' AO,Cp,Jn,Rd : *thunder-clap*, Lcd : *the god Thunder, Thor : Jupiter.*

ðunor-=ðunr-

ðunorbodu f. *sea-bream?* WW180³⁴.

ðunorclæfre f. *bugle (plant)*, Lcd.

ðunorlic (e²) *thundery*, OEG.

ðunorrād f. *thunder, thundering*, Æ.

ðunorrādlic *thundering*, HGL451⁴⁶.

ðunorrādstefn f. *voice of thunder*, PPs76¹⁴.

ðunorwyrt f. *thunder-wort, houseleek*, Lcd.

Ðunresdæg m. '*Thursday,*' LL.

ðunreslege m. *thunder-clap*, RWH83,85.

Ðunresniht f. *Thursday eve, Wednesday night.*

±ðunrian *to* '*thunder,*' Bo,Jn (impers.); PPs (pers.).

ðunring f. *thundering*, CHR1085.

ðunung f. *creaking, noise, din*, WW.

ðunur, ðunur-=ðunor, ðun(o)r-

ðun-wang (e, o), -wange (æ, e) f. (n?) *temple (of the head)*, Æ,WW. ['*thunwang*']

Ður=Ðor

ðuren=ðworen pp. of ðweran.

Ðuresdæg=Ðunresdæg

ðurfan swv. pres. 1, 3 sg. ðearf, pl. ðurfon; pret. sg. ðorfte; subj. pres. ðurfe, ðyrfe *to need, be required : must, have occasion to*, CP : *want, be needy : be under an obligation, owe.* ['*tharf*'; ðearf]

ðurg=ðurh prep.

ðurh (e, o) I. prep. (w. d. a. g.) (space) '*through*' ('*thorough*'), G : (time) *through, during*, PPs : (causal : agent, means, instrument) *through, by, by means of, in consequence of, because of.* ðurh ealle *entirely* : (manner) *in, with, by, in conformity with : for the sake of, in the name of :* (end, aim) *with a view to, on behalf of.* II. adv. *through, throughout.*

ðūrh=ðrūh

ðurharn pret. 3 sg. of ðurhiernan.

ðurhbeorht _very bright, transparent, radiant, clear_, Æ.

ðurhbiter _very bitter, sour, perverse_, CERPs 77⁸.

ðurhblāwan⁷ _to inspire, animate_, CM370.

ðurhborian _to bore through_, AA29¹⁷.

ðurhbrecan⁴ _to break through_, Æ,B.

ðurhbregdan³ _to draw through, transport_.

ðurhbrengan _to bring through_, LPs77¹³.

ðurhbrūcan² _to enjoy fully_, WW98¹.

ðurhburnen _thoroughly burnt_, Lcd 165b.

ðurhclǣnsian _to cleanse thoroughly_, MtR3¹².

ðurhcrēopan² _to creep or pass through_, Bo93⁵.

ðurhdelfan³ _to dig through, pierce_, Æ.

ðurhdrencan (æ²) _to saturate_, RWH138¹⁷.

ðurhdrēogan² _to work through, accomplish, pass (time)_, CM.

ðurhdrīfan¹ _to drive or push through, strike : pierce, perforate : penetrate, imbue_.

ðurhdūfan² _to dive through_, B1619.

ðurhendian (e¹) _to accomplish, perfect_, LL 411,2².

ðurhetan⁵† _to eat through, consume_, WW.

ðurhfær n. _secret place_, Sc39².

ðurhfæreld '_transitus_,' V²Ps143¹⁴.

ðurhfæstnian _to transfix_, JnLR19³⁷.

ðurhfaran⁶ _to pass through, traverse, penetrate, pierce_, CP.

ðurhfarennes f. _inner chamber_, ASPs104²⁸.

ðurhfēran _to pass through, traverse, penetrate_, BH. ['_thoroughfare_']

ðurhfēre I. _penetrable_. II. n. _secret chamber_, MkL24³⁶.

ðurhflēon² _to fly through_, BH136¹.

ðurhfōn⁷ _to penetrate_, B1504.

ðurh-gān anv., pret. -ēode _to go through, pass through, penetrate_, Æ. ['_throughgo_']

ðurhgangan⁷=ðurhgān

ðurhgefeht (o¹) n. _war_, Cp205P.

ðurhgēotan² _to fill entirely, imbue, saturate, impregnate_, BH,W.

ðurhglēdan _to heat through_, DA244.

ðurhhǣlan _to heal thoroughly_, Lcd.

ðurhhālig _most holy_, Chrd,Gl.

ðurhhefig _very heavy_, GD104²⁶.

ðurhholod _bored through_, OEG4035.

ðurhhwīt _quite white_, WW163⁶.

ðurhiernan³ _to run through, pierce_, Æ,WW.

ðurhlǣran _to persuade_, Sc38¹².

ðurhlǣred _very learned, skilled_, WW118²³.

ðurhlāð _very hateful_, WW130²⁸.

ðurhlēor-an, -ian _to penetrate_, GD : _pass through_, JVPs.

ðurhleornian _to learn thoroughly_, GD136⁴.

ðurhlōcung f. _preface, introduction_, WW 172³⁸.

ðurhrǣsan _to rush through_, RD4³⁶.

ðurhscēotan² _to shoot through, pierce_, Æ,AO.

ðurhscīnan (ȳ) _to shine through, be transparent_, WW148⁷. ['_throughshine_']

ðurhscīnendlic _illustrious, splendid_, LPs 15⁶.

ðurhscrīðan¹ _to go through, traverse_, Bf4³⁰ : _examine, consider_ : _þry into_, Bf142¹¹.

ðurhscyldig _very guilty_, ÆL11³²¹.

ðurhscȳne _transparent_, WW148⁷.

ðurhsēcan _to search through, inquire thoroughly into_, Sc209³. ['_throughseek_']

ðurhsēon⁵ _to look through, examine : penetrate_, Bo. ['_thoroughsee_']

ðurhslēan⁶ _to strike or pierce through_, Æ : _attack, afflict, kill_.

ðurhsmēagan _to search thoroughly, investigate, think out_, Chr,MH.

ðurhsmūgan² _to pierce, bore through, eat through_ : _go through carefully or slowly_.

ðurhsmyrian _to smear, anoint_, W229³.

ðurhspēdig _very rich_, ÆH1·502⁸.

ðurhstandan _to continue_, GD200⁸.

ðurhsticcian (o¹) _to transfix_, JnL19³⁷.

ðurhstingan³ _to pierce through, thrust through, prick_, Æ; CP. ['_throughsting_']

ðurhstrang _very strong_, OEG50²⁵.

ðurhswimman³ _to swim through_, WW52¹.

ðurhswīðan _to prevail_, LPs51⁹.

ðurhswōgan _to penetrate_, BH430⁵ (v.l.).

ðurhsȳne (=īe) _limpid, transparent_, OEG 23³⁵.

ðurhtēon² _to carry or put through : finish, fulfil, carry out, effect_, Æ,AO,CP : _draw, drag : continue : afford : undergo_.

ðurhtogennes f. _a religious reading at monastic meal-times_, RBL118⁷.

ðurhtrymman (e¹) _to confirm_, JnLR10²⁵.

ðurhðrāwan _to twist through_, Lcd.

ðurh-ðyddan, -ðȳn _to pierce, thrust through_, Æ.

ðurhðyrel (i²) _pierced through, perforated_, LL.

ðurh-ðyrelian (CP), -ðyrlian _to pierce, penetrate_.

ðurhunrot _very sad_, ZDA33·238¹¹.

ðurhūt prep. (w. a. Chr) adv. _right through_, Æ. ['_throughout_']

ðurhwacian _to keep vigil_, BL227⁷.

ðurhwacol (e³, u³) _wide-awake, sleepless_, Æ.

ðurhwadan⁶ _to penetrate, go through, bore, pierce_.

ðurhwæccan _to keep vigil_, LkL6¹².

ðurhwæcendlic _very vigilant_, ÆL23b⁴³.

ðurhwǣt _thoroughly wet_, ÆP172¹⁸.

ðurhwerod _quite sweet, very sweet_, Gl.

ðurhwlītan¹† _to look through, see_, Cr.

ðurhwrecan⁵ _to thrust through_, HL,WW.

ðurhwundian *to pierce through, wound badly,* LL 82,61[1].

ðurhwunenes f. *perseverance,* MFH 176.

ðurhwunian *to abide continuously, remain, continue, settle down,* Æ,AO,CP : *persevere, hold out, be steadfast,* CP.

ðurhwunigendlic *constant, continued.* adv. -līce.

ðurhwunol *perpetual,* CHRD 92[17].

ðurhwunung f. *perseverance, persistency,* RB,Sc : *continued residence,* RB.

Ðurresdæg=Ðunresdæg

ðurruc m. *small ship? hold of a ship? WW* 181[36]. [v. '*thurrock*']

ðurscon pret. pl. of ðerscan.

Ðursdæg (*Jn*)=Ðunresdæg

ðurst (y) m. '*thirst,*' Bf,Lcd ; Æ,AO,VPs.

ðurstig (y) '*thirsty,*' PPs,Mt ; Æ : *thirsting after, greedy,* Bo.

ðuru=duru ; ðuruh=ðurh

ðus adv. 'THUS,' *in this way* : *as follows* : *to this extent* (qualifying adjs.), Æ.

ðūsend num. (sbn., always followed by gen.) '*thousand,*' Æ,AO,Chr ; CP.

ðūsend-ealdor, -ealdorman m. *captain of a thousand men,* v. OEG 4747.

ðūsendfeald '*thousand-fold,*' Æ,W.

ðūsendgerīm n. *computation by thousands,* SOL 290.

ðūsendgetel n. *a thousand,* ÆGR 284[4].

ðūsendhīwe *multiform,* WW 101[1].

ðūsendlic adj. *of a thousand,* BL,WW.

ðūsendmǣle? adj. *a thousand each, a thousand,* PPs,WW.

ðūsendmǣlum† adv. *in thousands,* SAT.

ðūsendmann m. *captain of a thousand,* Æ.

ðūsendrīca m. *chief of a thousand,* WW 110[11].

ðūsent-=ðūsend- ; ðuslic=ðyllic

ðuss=ðus ; ðūtan=ðēotan

ðūðistel m. *sow-thistle, Gl.* ['*thowthistle*']

+ðūxsian (DOM 105)=+ðūhsian

ðwā (NG)=ðwēa pres. 1 sg. of ðwēan.

ðwægen pp. of ðwēan.

ðwæl=ðwēal

ðwǣle? (ē) f. *fillet? towel?* v. OEG 53[26].

±ðwǣnan *to soften, moisten,* BH,CP,LCD.

ðwæng=ðwang ; ðwǣr-=ðwēr-

±ðwǣre (usu. +) *united, concordant, harmonious,* Æ : *compliant, obedient* : *agreeable, pleasant, gentle* : *peaceful* : *prosperous.* adv. -līce.

±ðwǣr-ian, -lǣcan[1] (ē) *to agree, consent to* : *reconcile* : *suit, fit.*

+ðwǣrlic *agreeing, harmonious* : *symmetrical,* BF 180[1]. adv. -līce *gently.*

±ðwǣrnes f. *concord, peace,* CP : *gentleness.*

+ðwǣrung f. *consent,* SC 228[12].

ðwagen rare pp. of ðwēan.

ðwāh (A)=ðwēah imperat. of ðwēan.

ðwang (æ, e) mf. '*thong,*' *band, strap, cord,* Æ,G,WW : *phylactery,* MtL,R.

ðwār-=ðwǣr- ; ðwarm=ðwearm

ðwastrian *to whisper,* HL 18[381].

ðwāt pret. 3 sg. of ðwītan.

ðwēa pres. 1 sg. of ðwēan.

ðwēal (ǣ, ē) n. *washing, bath, laver,* CP,JnL 12[3] : *soap,* ES 43·334 : *ointment.* [*Goth.* ðwahl]

±ðwēan[6] *to wash, cleanse,* Æ,CP : *anoint,* MtL 6[17].

ðwearm m? *cutting tool,* GL.

ðwēhl=ðwēal ; ðwēle=ðwǣle

ðwēnan=ðwǣnan ; ðweng (NG)=ðwang

ðwēor, ðweorg=ðweorh

+ðwēor v. buter-geð.

ðwēora m. *depravity* : *perversity,* CP 222[8].

ðwēores adv. (gen. of ðweorh) *athwart, transversely, obliquely,* AO : *perversely.*

ðweorh adj., gmn. ðwēores *cross, transverse, bent, crooked* : *adverse* : *angry* : *perverse, depraved,* CP.

ðweorh-fero, -furu, -fyri *cross-furrow,* GL.

ðweorhtēme=ðwēortīeme

ðweorian=ðweran

±ðwēorian *to oppose, thwart, be opposed to or far from.*

ðwēorlic *perverse, contrary, adverse,* Æ : *reversed, out of order.* adv. -līce *insolently,* GD.

±ðwēornes (ȳ) f. *perversity, frowardness, obstinacy, depravity,* Æ.

ðwēorscipe m. *perversity,* CP 269[6].

ðwēortīeme (ē[2], ī[2], ȳ[2]) *contentious, perverse, wicked,* CP.

ðweoton (BH 204[32])=ðwiton pret. pl. of ðwītan.

ðwēr, ðwerh=ðweorh

±ðweran[4] *to stir, churn* : (†) *beat, forge, render malleable, soften.*

ðwēre (æ) f. *pestle,* OET 102,103.

ðwihð (ie) pres. 3 sg. of ðwēan.

ðwīnan *to decrease, lessen,* LCD.

+ðwinglod *fastened up? (BT),* HL 18[218].

ðwīr=ðweorh

ðwiril m. *handle of a churn, whisk,* WW 280[31]. [ðweran]

+ðwit n. *cuttings,* BH 204[32] (v.l.). [ðwītan]

ðwītan[1] *to cut, whittle, cut off, cut out,* BH, Lcd. ['*thwite*']

ðwōg, ðwōh pret. 3 sg., ðwogen pp. of ðwēan.

ðwong=ðwang

ðworen pp. of ðweran.

+ðwōrnes=+ðwēornes ; ðwurh=ðweorh

ðwyhð pres. 3 sg. of ðwēan.

ðwȳr (Æ), ðwȳr-=ðweorh, ðwēorðwȳrs=ðwēores

ðȳ I. pron. (instr. sing. of sē, ðæt). æfter ðȳ *after (that), later.* II. conj. and adv. *because, since, on that account : therefore, CP, Lcd : then :* (with comparatives) *the.* ðȳ... ðȳ *the...the.* mid ðȳ *while, when.* tō ðȳ ðæt *for the purpose that, in order that.* for ðȳ ðe *because.* ðȳ læs (ðe) *lest.* ['*thy*']

ðȳan=ðȳn; ðyc-=ðic-

ðȳdan=ðēodan

ðyddan *to strike, stab,* Æ,*CP : thrust, press,* Æ. ['*thud*']

+ðȳde (īe) *good, virtuous,* CRA 68.

ðyder=ðider; ðȳf=ðēof

ðȳfel m. *shrub, bush, copse, thicket,* Æ,*Lcd, LPs,WW.* ['*thyvel*'; ðūf]

ðȳfeðorn y? (ē, ēo, ī) m. *hawthorn? bramble?* Gl,*Lcd.* ['*thevethorn*']

ðȳflen? (or ? ryplen) *bushy,* GPH 399⁴⁵⁷.

ðyften f. *handmaid,* OEG. ['*thuften*']

ðȳfð=ðīefð; ðȳgan=ðȳn

+ðyht *pleasing,* RIM 18.

ðyhtig (i) *strong,* B 1558.

ðȳhð pres. 3 sg. of ðēon.

ðȳlæs conj. *lest.* ðȳ læs ðe *lest.*

ðylc=ðyllic

ðylcræft (e) m. *elocution, rhetoric,* OEG.

±ðyld (usu. +) nf. *patience,* LkLR. ['*thild*']

±ðyldelic *patient.* adv. -līce *patiently, quietly.*

+ðyld-ian, -(i)gian *to be patient, bear, endure,* CP : *give in, agree,* OEG 3237 : *wait for,* Ps.

±ðyldig (usu. +) adj. *patient,* DR; Æ,*CP.* [v. '*thild*'] adv. -līce.

+ðyldmōd *patient,* W 72⁷.

+ðyldmōdnes f. *patience,* NC 297.

+ðyldo (u²)=+ðyld

+ðyldum *patiently, steadfastly,* B 1705.

ðyle m. *speaker, orator : jester,* WW 385³.

ðylian (Æ)=ðilian; ðyling=ðiling

+ðyll n. *air, breeze,* DR 121¹⁸.

ðyllan *to calm, assuage,* BH.

ðyllic pron. *such, such a,* Æ,*AO,CP.* ['*thellich*']

+ðylmed '*densus*,' OEG 5⁴ (?=+ðiclic; or +ðȳllic, from ðȳn).

+ðylmed *brought down, abashed,* LPs 19⁹.

ðȳmel m. *thumbstall, '* thimble,*' Lcd.*

ðȳmele adj. *of the thickness of a thumb,* LL 110,49³.

ðȳn (1)=ðīn; (2) (±)=ðȳwan, ðēowan

±ðyncan (i) (impers. w. d.) pret. 3 sg. ðūhte *to appear, seem, CP;* AO. mē ðyncð *methinks.* him ðūhte *it seemed good to him.* ['THINK*']

±ðyneðo (i) f. *dignity, rank, office,* Æ,*CP :* *meeting, assembly, court of justice,* LL : *private arrangement (to defeat justice),* LL 112,52.

ðynden=ðenden

+ðynge=+ðinge

±ðyngo *progress, promotion,* N.

ðynhlæne *wasted, shrunk,* WW 446²⁴.

ðynne (i) '*thin*,' BH,*Lcd,RB : lean, Lcd, WW : not dense,* Æ,*BC : fluid, tenuous,* BH,*Lcd,Met : weak, poor,* BH,*Lcd.*

ðynnes (i) f. *lack of density, tenuity, fluidity,* Lcd 73b : *poverty, feebleness (of sight),* Lcd 1·134. ['*thinness*']

±ðynnian (i) *to '* thin,*' make thin, lessen, dilute,* Æ,*Gl,Lcd : become thin,* ÆL.

ðynnol (u²) *lean, thin,* WW 172¹⁶.

ðynnung, ðynung f. '*thinning*,' *act of making thin,* Lcd 98a.

ðynwefen *thin woven,* WW 439³⁴.

ðyrel (ȳ?) I. n. *hole, opening, aperture, perforation,* BH,*MtL,Sc,WW.* II. adj. *pierced, perforated, full of holes,* CP. ['*thirl*']

ðyrelhūs n. *turner's workshop,* WW 185³¹ (ðryl-).

ðyrelian=ðyrlian

ðyrelung f. *piercing,* CP 153²⁵.

ðyrelwamb *with pierced belly,* RD 79¹¹.

ðyrf=ðearf

ðyrfe subj. pres. sing. of ðurfan.

ðyrl=ðyrel

ðyrlian (i) *to perforate, pierce, excavate,* Æ, WW. ['*thirl*']

-ðyrlic v. samod-ð.; ðyrn=ðorn

ðyrne f. *thorn-bush, bramble,* Æ; Mdf.

ðyrnen *thorny, of thorns,* Æ,*CP.* ['*thornen*']

ðyrnet n. *thorn, bramble, thorn-thicket,* OEG.

ðyrniht, ðyrnihte *thorny,* LCD.

ðyrran *to dry, render dry,* RD 29⁴.

ðyrre *withered : dry,* Lcd. [Ger. dürr]

ðyrs m. *giant, demon, wizard,* B,*Cp*; Mdf. ['*thurse*']

ðyrscel=ðerscel

ðyrscð pres. 3 sg. of ðerscan.

ðyrscwold=ðerscold

ðyrst=ðurst

+ðyrst *thirsty,* MH 170⁶.

ðyrstan (pers. and impers.) *to '* thirst,*' thirst after,* AO,*CP,G,Lcd,Sc.* [ðurst]

+ðyrstgian=+ðrīstian

ðȳs instr. smn. of ðēs.

ðys-=ðis-; ðyslic=ðyllic

ðysma=disma

-ðyssa v. brim-ð.

ðȳster=ðēostor; ðȳstr-=ðēostr-

ðȳt, ðȳtt pres. 3 sg. of ðēotan.

-ðȳtan v. ā-ð. [OHG. dōzðn]

ðȳðel (LPs 79¹¹)=ðȳfel

ðȳðer=ðider; ðȳw-=ðēow-

±ðȳwan *to press, impress,* Æ : *stab, pierce : crush, push, oppress, check : threaten.*

+ðȳwe=+ðēawe

ðȳwð=ðīefð

U

uce, ucu=wuce, wucu

ūder n. *'udder,'* WW61[16].

udu (N)=wudu

ūf I. m. *owl,* GL : *vulture,* ÆGR48[17]n. **II.** m. *uvula,* WW.

ufa=ufan

ufan (o) adv. *from above,* Æ,AO,CP : *over, above, on high,* CP. on u.; u. on ðæt *besides.* on u. hærfest *in late autumn.* on u. midne winter *after Christmas.* [*Ger.* oben]

ufancumende *coming from above,* GD285[6].

ufancund *from above, supreme, divine,* CP.

ufane=ufan

ufanweard adj. (often used w. d. as a prep.) *highest, topmost,* Æ. ufanweardum *above, at the top.*

ufemest (superl. of uferra, ufor) *highest, uppermost, topmost,* Æ. ['*ovemest*']

ufen=ufan

ufenan, ufenon **I.** adv. *from above,* Chr,Jn, W. **II.** prep. *over and above,* DD. on ufenan *upon the top of.* ['*ovenon*']

ufera=uferra

±uferian (of-) *to delay, put off,* Æ : (+) *raise up, elevate,* Bk8 : *extol, honour,* Æ. [ufor]

uferor (u[3]) *higher,* OEG5058.

uferra comp. adj. *above, higher, upper,* BH : CP : *outer,* Lcd,WW : *after* (of time), *later, future,* AO,Lcd; CP. ['*over*,' '*uver*']

ufeweard I. adj. *upward, ascending, upper, higher up,* Æ,CP : *later.* **II.** sb. *upper part, outside,* Æ.

ufewerd=ufeweard; **uffrian**=uferian

ufon=ufan

ufor adv. *higher, further away, further up,* Æ,CP : *later, posterior, subsequent.*

ufora=uferra; **ufur**=ufor

uf-weard, -werd=ufeweard

uht=wuht=wiht fn.

ūht m., ūhte f. *twilight, dusk, early morning, dawn,* Lcd : *nocturns.* on ūhtan *at daybreak,* B,Bl. tō ūhtes *towards dawn.* ['*ughten*']

ūhtantīd=ūhttīd

ūhtantīma m. *time of nocturns,* Btk194[14].

ūhtcearu f. *sorrow at dawn,* Wif7.

ūhtentīd=ūhttīd

ūhtfloga m. *twilight-flier, dragon,* B2760.

ūhtgebed n. *morning prayer, matins,* Guth, WW.

ūhthlem m. *crash at dawn,* B2007.

ūhtlic I. *morning, matutinal, of matins,* BH. **II.**=ūtlic

ūhtsang m. *morning song, matins,* BH,RB : *nocturns.* ['*uhtsong*']

ūhtsanglic *nocturnal, used at nocturns,* CM 1014.

ūhtsceaða m. *twilight foe,* B2271.

ūhttīd f. *twilight, early morning, dawn,* BH. [v. '*ughten*']

ūhtðegnung f. *matins,* WW129[33].

ūhtwæcca f. *night watch, vigils,* RB40[10].

ūle f. '*owl*,' *Æ,Cp.*

ulf (JnL10[12])=wulf

ulmtrēow n. *elm tree,* WW138[12]. ['*ulmtree*'; L.]

ultur m. *vulture,* Bo102[33].

ūma m. *a weaver's beam,* WW.

umb, umbe=ymb, ymbe

umbor n. *infant,* GnE31.

umborwesende† *being a child,* B.

un- **I.** negative or pejorative prefix. **II.** occasionally=on- (prefix expressing reversal of a previous action) as in unbindan.

unābeden neg. ptc. *unbidden,* Æ.

unābēgendlic=unābȳgendlic

unāberendlic *unbearable,* Æ,CP. adv. -līce.

unāberiende *unbearable,* Lcd3·260[23]n.

unābēt=ungebēt

unābindendlic *indissoluble,* Bo.

unāblinn n. *irrepressible state, unceasing presence,* Guth46[10].

unāblinnend-e, -lic *unceasing, perpetual.* adv. -līce, Æ,AO,CP.

unāboht=ungeboht

unābrecendlic *inextricable,* WW419[2].

unābȳgendlic (ē) *inflexible,* WW421[30].

unācenned *unbegotten,* ÆH1·464'.

unācnycendlic *that cannot be untied or loosened,* DR108[10]. [cnyccan]

un-ācumendlic (Æ), -ācumenlic *unbearable, unattainable, impossible.*

unācumenlicnes f. *unbearableness,* RBL 114[9].

unācwencedlic *unquenchable,* G.

unādrūgod *undried, not dried, not hardened,* CP383[32].

unādrysn-ende, -en(d)lic *unquenchable,* NG.

un-ādwǣsced, -ādwǣscendlic, -ādwēscedlic *inextinguishable, unquenchable,* Æ.

unǣaðe=unēaðe

unǣfastlīce=unǣwfæstlīce

unǣm(et)ta m. *want of leisure, work, occupation, hindrance,* Chrd,LL.

unǣmtigian *to deprive of leisure,* AS36[19].

unǣrh=unearg

unǣsecgenlic (EPs100[4])=unāsēðendlic?

unǣt f. *gluttony,* Deut21[20].

unǣtspornen *not hindered,* GD60[26].

unǣðelboren *not of noble birth, low-born,* Æ.

unǣðele *of low birth, ignoble, base,* CP.

unǣðelian (an-) *to degrade, debase,* Bo,Met.

unǣðelīce adv. *ignobly, basely,* BH442[11].

unæðelnes f. *ignobility*, GD 151²⁴.
unǣwfæstlīce adv. *irreverently* : *unlawfully*.
unǣwisc (ē) '*pudicus*,' WW 291²⁵.
unāfandod *untried*, AS 32¹⁹.
unāfe(o)htendlic (æ³) *what cannot be contended against, inevitable*, DR,WW.
unāfīled *undefiled*, LPs 17³¹.
unāfūliende=unfūliende
unāfunden *undiscovered*, Æ : *untried*.
unā-fylledlic, -fyllendlic *that cannot be filled, insatiable*, Æ. adv. -līce.
unāga m. *one who owns nothing*, PPs 112⁶.
unāgǣledlīce *unremittingly*, Bl 121⁵.
unāgān adj. *not lapsed, in force*, KC.
unāgelȳfed=unālȳfed
unāgen *not one's own or under one's control, precarious*, CP.
unāgifen *unpaid*, TC 201'.
unāgunnen *without a beginning*, ÆH.
unāhefendlic *unbearable*, MFH 176.
un-ālīef-, -lē(a)f-=unālȳf-
unālogen *not false, true*, NC 328.
un-ālȳfed (CP), -lȳfe(n)dlic (īe) *not allowed, unlawful, illicit*. adv. -līce *unlawfully, without permission*, Sc.
unālȳfednes (ē³;=īe) f. *what is forbidden, licentiousness*, BH.
unālȳsendlic *without remission*, ÆH 1·500'.
unāmælt *unmelted*, Gl.
unāmānsumod *not excommunicated, in church fellowship*, Æ.
un-āmeten, -metenlic, -metgod *unmeasured, unbounded, immeasurable, immense*, Æ, RPs.
unan-=unon-
unandcȳðignes (o²) f. *ignorance*, JVPs 24⁷.
unandergilde *irreplaceable, invaluable*, Bo 27²⁰.
unandett *unconfessed*, W 71⁷.
unand-gittol, -gytful *unintelligent, incapable, ignorant, foolish*.
unandhēfe (-hoife) *insupportable*, MtR 23⁴.
unandweard *not present, absent*, ÆH 1·128¹⁷.
unandwendlic=unāwende(n)dlic
unandwīs *unskilful*, WW.
unānrǣdnes f. *inconstancy*, Bl 31³⁴.
unāpīnedlīce adv. *with impunity*, DR 113¹⁵.
unār f. *dishonour*, AO.
un-āræf(n)ed, -āræfne(n)dlic *not permissible, impracticable*, Æ : *intolerable*. adv. -līce.
unāreccendlic *unexplainable, wonderful*, Sc 26¹⁵.
unārefnendlic (VPs)=unāræfnendlic
unāreht *unexplained*, Bo 77¹⁶.
+unārian *to dishonour*, AO,CP.
unārīmed adj. *unnumbered, countless, innumerable*, AO.

unārīme(n)dlic *innumerable, immeasurable*, AO. adv. -līce, AO.
unārlic *dishonourable, dishonest, disgraceful* : *contrary to what is fitting, unnatural (of a will)*, WW. adv. -līce *dishonourably* : *unmercifully*.
unarodscipe f. *remissness, cowardice*, CP 149¹⁵.
unārwurðian (eo) *to dishonour*, ÆH 1·442'.
unārwurðlic *dishonourable*, Chrd 63²⁴.
unārwyrðnes f. *irreverence, indignity*, Sc 224¹.
unārȳmed=unārīmed
unāsæcgendlic=unāsecgendlic
unāsædd=unāsedd
unāscended *unhurt*, DR.
unāscruncen *not withered, undecayed*, DR 24¹⁶.
unāscyrigendlic *inseparable*, ÆH 1·326²⁷.
unāscyrod *not separated*, WW 253³.
unāsecgende *unspeakable, ineffable*, BH 264³⁰.
unāsecgendlic *indescribable, unspeakable, ineffable*, Æ. adv. -līce.
unāsedd *unsatisfied, unsatiated*, Gl.
unāsēðenlic (KGl), -āsēðendlic *insatiable*.
unāsīwod (ēo) *unsewed, without seam*, Jn 19²³.
unāsmēagendlic *inconceivable, inscrutable, unsearchable*, Æ.
unāsolcenlīce *diligently*, RB 20¹⁹.
unāspring-ende, -endlic (GD) *unfailing*.
un-āspyriendlic (e³, o³) *unsearchable*, GD, WW.
unāstīðod *not hardened, not firm*, CP 383³².
unāstyr-ed, -od *unmoved*, GD.
un-āstyriende, -āstyri(g)endlic adj. *immovable, firm* : *motionless*, Æ.
unāsundrodlic *inseparable*, DR.
unāswundenlīce adv. *diligently*, BH.
unātaladlic (N)=unātellendlic
unāteald (Scr 28³²)=unteald
unātellendlic (ea) *innumerable*, Chr.
unātemed *barbarous*, BH.
unātemedlic *untameable, wild, fierce*, BH 162²⁸.
unātēoriende *indefatigable*, OEG.
unātēorigendlic *lasting, permanent, unceasing*, Æ : *indefatigable, unwearied*. adv. -līce.
unātēorod *unwearied*, OEG 2373.
un-ātēriend-, -toriend-=unātēorigend-
unātwēogendlīce=untwēogendlīce
unāðrēotend *unwearied, assiduous, persistent*, Cr 388.
unāðroten *unwearied, indefatigable, vigorous*, CP 171⁹. adv. -līce, CP.
unāwægendlic *unshaken*, TC 319⁹.
unā-wæscen, -waxen *unwashed*, WW 190, 439.

unāwemmed (ALRSPs), -lic (DR) *un-stained, spotless.*

unāwemmednes f. *incorruption,* BF168²¹.

unā-wend, -wended(lic) *unchangeable, un-changed, inviolate : unmoved.*

unāwendend-e (MET), -lic (Æ) *unchange-able, unceasing.* adv. -līce.

unāwerded (oe;=ie) *unhurt,* N.

unāwīdlod *undefiled,* DR24¹⁶.

unāwriten *unwritten,* Æ.

un-bæ̆ldo, -bæ̆ldu=unbieldo

unbǣrende=unberende; **unbald**=unbeald

unbealaful *guiltless, innocent,* W.

unbeald (a) *cowardly, timid, weak, irre-solute, distrustful, CP,Jul.* ['*unbold*']

unbealu n. *innocence,* PPs100².

unbeboht *unsold,* AO18¹⁰.

unbebyriged *unburied,* GD,W.

unbecēas *incontestable,* LL112,53¹.

unbecrafod *unquestioned, not subject to claims,* LL358,72.

unbecweden *unbequeathed,* TC.

unbeden '*unbidden,*' *LL* (386).

unbe-fangenlic, -feonglic (BHCA224¹⁹) *un-intelligible, incomprehensible,* Æ.

unbefliten *undisputed,* EC69'.

unbefohten *unopposed, unattacked,* MA57.

unbefōndlic *incomprehensible,* BHo224¹⁹.

unbegān *untilled,* LCD : *unadorned,* HGL435.

unbegrīpendlic *incomprehensible,* BL.

unbegunnen *without a beginning,* Æ. ['*un-begun*']

unbehēafdod *not beheaded,* ÆL23¹⁸⁵.

unbehēfe *not suitable, inconvenient,* WW 508³⁴.

unbehelendlīce adv. *without concealment,* W138³.

unbehelod *uncovered, naked,* GENC9²¹.

unbehrēowsigende *unrepenting,* ÆH1·500¹⁵.

unbelimp=ungelimp

unbeorhte (y) *not brightly,* Bo.

unberēafigendlic *never to be taken away,* ÆL23b²⁴³.

unberende *unbearable : unfruitful, barren,* Æ,LG,VPs. ['*unbearing*']

unberendlic *unbearable,* LCD3·260²³.

unberendnes (eo²) f. *barrenness,* DR,VPs.

unbermed *unleavened, unfermented.* [beorma]

unbesacen (æ²) *undisputed,* LL.

unbesænged=unbesenged

unbescēawod *improvident, inconsiderate,* GL,Sc. adv. -līce.

unbescoren *unshorn,* RB135²⁹.

unbesenged *not singed, unburnt,* W25¹⁹.

unbesēondlic (BH224¹⁹)=unbefōndlic?

unbesmiten *undefiled, pure, spotless,* Æ.

unbesorh *unconcerned, not interested,* ÆH 2·486⁹.

unbēted *uncompensated, unexpiated, un-atoned,* CR1312.

unbeŏ̄ōhte adv. *unthinkingly,* CP434².

unbeweddod *unbetrothed, unmarried,* Æ.

unbewelled *not boiled away,* LCD93b. [weallan]

unbiddende *not praying,* ÆH1·156⁴.

unbieldo (æ) f. *want of boldness, diffidence, timidity,* CP.

unbilewit (y²) *harsh,* OEG56²³².

unbindan³ *to '* unbind,' *loosen, LG ;* Æ : *pay* (NG; trans. of '*solvere*'). [=onbindan]

unbiscopod *not confirmed by a bishop, LL, W.* ['*unbishoped*']

unblŏyrfe† *useless, idle, vain.*

unblēoh *clean, bright,* DD, PPs.

unbletsung f. *curse,* LL(310').

unblinnendlīce *incessantly,* BH34⁶.

unbliss f. *sorrow, affliction,* Æ.

+unblissian *to make unhappy,* NC297.

unblīŏe *joyless, sad, sorrowful,* CP : *un-friendly.*

unblīŏemēde *sad of heart,* MtL26³⁷.

unblŏdig *bloodless,* GPH395¹⁶.

unblonden *unmixed,* DR68¹⁵.

unboht '*unbought,' free,* NG.

unboren '*unborn,*' Æ,CP.

unbrād *narrow,* Ct,LCD.

unbræ̆ce† *unbreakable, indestructible.*

un-brece, -brice=unbryce; **unbrīece**=un-brȳce.

unbrocheard *delicate, tender,* Bo,WW.

unbrosn-igendlic (Æ), -endlic (GD) *inde-structible, incorruptible.*

unbrosnodlīce *incorruptibly,* GD348²³.

unbrosnung f. *incorruptibility,* Æ.

unbryce† *unbreakable : indestructible, ever-lasting.* [brecan]

unbrȳce (īe) *useless,* GL,PPs. [brūcan]

unbrȳde *honestly,* LL400,2.

unbunden (*LL, Rd*) pp. of unbindan.

unbȳed *uninhabited desert,* NG.

unbȳergo np. *uninhabited places,* DR1⁹ (? for unbȳencg, MLR18·273).

unbyrged '*unburied,*' MH28²¹.

unbyrhte=unbeorhte

unbyrnende *without burning,* B2548.

unc pers. pron. (d. a. dual) *us two.*

uncænned=unācenned

uncǣfscipe m. *sloth, neglect,* CHR47.

uncamprōf *unwarlike,* GPH399.

uncapitulod *without headings (to chapters),* LL(204¹).

uncēap(ed) *gratuitous, gratis,* MtL10⁸.

uncēapunga *gratuitously,* DA746.

uncēas(t) n? *oath of reconciliation,* LL104,35.

uncenned=unācenned

uncer I. g. dual of pers. pron. *of us two.* II. poss. pron. *belonging to us two.*

uncet=unc

unclǣmod *unsmeared*, GPH398.

unclǣne '*unclean*,' BH,Bl,Cr,LG,WW.

unclǣnlic *unclean, impure*, DR. adv. -līce, ÆH. ['*uncleanly*']

unclǣnnes f. *uncleanness, impurity*, AO, CP,DR,Mt,OEG.

unclǣno f. *uncleanness*, NG.

±unclǣnsian *to soil, pollute*, AO,CP.

unclǣnsod *unpurified*, CP. ['*uncleansed*']

unclēn-=unclǣn-

uncnyttan *to unbind, untie, loosen*, Lk; Æ. ['*unknit*']

uncoren *evil, reprobate*, VH21.

un-coða m., -coðu f. *disease*, Æ : *plague*, CHRD70[7].

uncrǣft m. *evil practice*, LL,W.

uncrǣftig *helpless*, DD239.

uncrafod (LL232,14)=unbecrafod

uncre gdf. of uncer II.

uncristen *infidel*, BHo306[23]. ['*unchristian*']

uncumlīðe *inhospitable*, W257[14].

uncūð *unknown, strange, unusual*, Æ,AO : *uncertain*, Æ,CP : *unfriendly, unkind, rough*. ['*uncouth*']

uncūða m. *stranger*, Jn10[5].

uncūðlic *unknown*. adv. -līce *in an unfriendly manner, unkindly*, LL. ['*uncouthly*']

uncūðnes f. *strangeness*, GD278[15].

uncwaciende *firmly*, CP41[7].

uncweden (*unsaid*), *revoked*, WW114[45].

uncwēme *not pleasing*, MFH176. ['*unqueme*']

uncweðende *speechless, dumb*, Bo,SolK.

uncwisse *dumb*, BH290[12].

uncwyd(d) *uncontested, undisputed*, LL.

uncȳme *unseemly, mean, paltry, poor*, BH, BL.

uncynde *unnatural*, Bo91[21]B.

un-cynn, -cynlic (Bo) *unsuitable, improper*.

uncȳpe *gratuitous*, WW514[31].

uncȳped=uncēaped

un-cyst, -cyste f. *mistake, error : vice, wickedness, crime*, Æ,CP : *stinginess, parsimony*, Æ : *disease*, LCD. [cēosan]

uncystig *mean, stingy, niggardly*, Æ, CP.

uncȳð=uncūð

uncȳðig *ignorant, unacquainted with : devoid of*, Gu1199.

un-cȳðð, -cȳððu f. *ignorance*, Æ,CP : *foreign country*.

undǣd f. *wicked deed, crime*, W.

undǣftelīce=ungedǣftlice

un-dǣled, -dǣld *undivided*, Bo.

undēaded *not deadened*, LCD3a.

undēadlic *immortal, for all eternity*, Æ,DR. adv. -līce. ['*undeadly*']

undēadlicnes f. *immortality*, Æ. ['*undeadliness*']

undēagollīce=undēogollīce

undearnunga adv. *openly*, LL.

undēað-=undēad-

undēaw *without dew*, LCD35a.

undeclīnigendlic *indeclinable*, ÆGR.

undēd=undǣd

undēogollīce (ēa, ī) adv. *plainly, clearly*, CP.

undēop *shallow, low*, CP.

undēopðancol *shallow, silly*, ÆH1·286'.

undēor=undēore I.

undēore I. adj. *cheap*, CP,WW. ['*undear*'] II. adv. *cheaply*.

undeornunga=undearnunga

under I. prep. w. d. and a. '*UNDER*,' *beneath*, Æ : *among*, AO : *before, in the presence of : under the shelter of*, CHR : *in the service of, in subjection to, under the rule of*, Æ,AO,Chr : *during*, AO,Chr : *by means of, by*. swerian u. God *to swear by God*. u. bæc=underbæc. II. adv. *beneath, below, underneath*, Æ,B,Chr,MH.

underāgendlic adj. '*submixus*,' DR182[16].

underandfōnd (o³, oe⁴) '*susceptor*,' DR 193[6].

under-bæc, -bæcling adv. *backwards, back, behind*, Æ,CP.

underbēgan *to subject*, DR. [bīegan]

underbeginnan³ *to undertake, purpose*, ÆT 76[7].

underberan⁴ *to support, endure*, DR,Sc. ['*underbear*']

under-brǣdan, -bregdan *to spread under*, WE.

underbūgan² *to submit (to)*, Æ.

underburg f. *suburb*, DEUT32[32].

underburhware mp. *dwellers in a suburb* (BT).

undercerran *to overturn, subvert*, LkLR23[2]. [cierran]

undercing=undercyning

undercrammian *to stuff between, fill out underneath*, ÆH1·430[4].

undercrēopan² *to be secretly grasped, seized by something*, Æ : *penetrate, undermine*, GD.

undercuman⁴ *to assist*, DR.

undercyn(in)g m. *under-king, viceroy*, Æ.

underdelf n. *undermining*, ASPs79[17].

underdelfan³ *to dig under, undermine, break through*, Æ,Lk. ['*underdelve*']

underdīacon m. *subdeacon*, LL.

underdōn anv. *to put under*, Lev1[12].

underdrencan *to choke by drowning*, MkL 5[13].

underdrīfennes f. *subjection*, LkLp6[16].

undereāde (N)=undereōde, pret. 3 sg. of undergān.

undereoton (Ruin 6)=undereten pp. of underetan.

underetan[5] *to eat underneath, undermine, subvert,* Bo 27².

underfang '*susceptor,*' SPs.

underfangelnes=underfangenes

underfangen (pp. of underfōn) *neophyte,* ÆL31⁷³⁰.

underfang-enes, -elnes f. *undertaking, assumption* : *reception, hospitality,* GD 76²².

underfealdan '*subdere,*' EHy 6³⁰.

underfeng I. m. *undertaking, taking in hand,* CP23²². **II.** pret. 3 sg. of underfōn.

underflōwan[7] *to flow under,* Rd 11².

underfolgoð m. *subordinate office,* AO 286⁵c.

underfōn *to receive, obtain, take, accept,* Æ, AO,CP : *take in, entertain* : *take up, undertake, assume, adopt,* Æ,AO,CP : *submit to, undergo,* Æ : *steal.* ['underfo']

underfōnd m. *one who takes anything in charge,* LPs.

underfōnlic *to be received,* RBL97⁸.

underfyligan '*subsequi,*' LkL23⁵⁵.

undergān anv. *to* '*undergo*' : *undermine, ruin,* Lcd.

undergangan[7]=undergān

undergend-=under(i)gend-

undergeoc *under the yoke, tame,* MkL21⁵.

undergerēfa m. '*proconsul,*' *deputy-governor,* Æ.

undergereord=underngereord

undergesett *placed under,* GD307¹².

undergestandan[6] *to stand under,* LL108,44.

undergeðēoded *subject,* LL88'.

undergeðēodnes=underðēodnes

undergietan[5] (i, y) *to note, mark, understand, perceive,* Æ,AO,Chr,Mt. ['underyete']

underginnan[3] *to begin, undertake,* ÆT76⁷n.

undergitan (Æ)=undergietan

undergynnan=underginnan

undergytan (Æ)=undergietan

underhebban[6] *to bear, support, lift,* NG.

underhlystan '*subaudire,*' *to supply an omitted word,* ÆGR151.

underhlystung f. *the act of supplying an omitted word,* ÆGR151.

underhnīgan[1] *to submit to, undergo,* Æ,CP : *succumb to, sink under.*

underholung f. '*suffossum,*' LV²Ps79¹⁷.

underhwītel m. *under-garment,* WW187²¹.

underhwrǣdel=underwrǣdel

underi-ende, -gende, -gendlic *inoffensive, harmless,* AO.

underiernan[3] *to run under* : '*succurrere,*' DR43⁸.

underlǣttēow m. *consul,* AO68²c.

underlecgan *to* '*underlay,*' *prop, support,* Æ,CP.

underlicgan[5] *to* '*underlie,*' *to be subject to, give way to,* Æ,CP,RB.

underlihtan *to alleviate,* DR.

underling m. *underling, inferior,* HL,KC.

underlūtan[2] *to bow or bend under* : *support, sustain,* CP.

undermete=undernmete

undern m. *morning (from 9.0 a.m. to 12.0 noon)* : *the third hour* (=9.0 a.m.; later, 11.0 a.m.), Lcd; Æ : *service at the third hour,* RB. ['undern']

underne=undierne

underneoðan (y³) adv. *underneath,* AO.

underngereord m. *morning meal, breakfast,* AO.

underngeweorc n. *breakfast,* GD66¹².

underngi(e)fl n. *repast, breakfast,* CP322¹⁹.

underniman[4] *to take in, receive, comprehend, understand,* Æ : *blame, be indignant at* : *take upon oneself,* Æ : *steal,* Lcd. ['undernim']

undernīðemest *lowest of all,* Met 20³⁵.

undernmǣl n. *morning-time,* Æ,B. ['undernmeal']

undernmete m. *morning meal, breakfast,* AO.

undernrest f. *morning rest,* MH42⁶.

undernsang m. *tierce (religious service about 9.0 a.m.),* RB,LL.

undernswǣsendu np. *early meal,* BH164³⁰.

underntīd f. *the third hour* (=9.0 a.m.), *noon, morning-time,* BH,Mt; Æ : *tierce.* ['underntide']

undernyðan (Æ)=underneoðan

underondfōnd=underandfōnd

underplantian '*supplantare,*' Sc,SPs.

undersang=undernsang

underscēotan[2] *to prop up, sustain, support,* CP : *intercept, pass under.*

underscyte m. *passage underneath, transit,* Æ : *brake, drag-chain,* OEG50¹⁵.

undersēcan *to examine, investigate, scrutinize,* CP. ['underseek']

undersettan '*supponere,*' LPs36²⁴?

undersingan[3] '*succinere,*' ÆGR181².

undersittan[5] '*subsidere,*' ÆGr157⁵.

undersmūgan[2] *to creep under, surprise,* RB.

understandan[6] (o³) *to* '*UNDERSTAND,*' *perceive,* Æ; CP : *observe, notice, take for granted,* ÆL23b¹⁸⁶ : '*subsistere,*' DR.

understandennes (o³) f. '*substantia,*' DR 31²⁰.

understanding f. '*understanding,*' Sc221¹³.

understapplian '*supplantare,*' LPs16¹³.

understaðolfæst=unstaðolfæst

understingan[3] *to prop up, support,* CP113¹¹.

understond-=understand-

understrēdan *to strew under,* MH18²¹.

understrēowed *underlaid,* ÆL37²⁰¹.

undersyrc m. *undershirt*, WW379³⁰. [serce]

undertīd (*Chrd*)=underntīd

undertōdal n. *secondary division*, ÆGR291⁵.

undertunge f. '*sublingua*,' *part under or behind the tongue, tongue-ligament*, WW 264¹⁷ (or ? two words, Cp,LPs9²⁸; 65¹⁷).

undertungeðrum *tongue-ligament*, Lcd. [v. '*thrum*']

underðencan (æ³) *to consider*, CP49²³ : (refl.)´*change one's mind, repent*, LL438,22.

underðēnian *to serve under*, Sc5⁶.

underðēod *subjected, subject* : *assistant, suffragan*.

underðēodan (īe, ȳ) *to subjoin, add* : *subjugate, subject, subdue, reduce, degrade*, Æ, CP : *support*, OEG4339.

under-ðēodendlīc, -ðēodenlic *subjunctive*, ÆGR.

underðēodnes (ī³) f. *subjection, submission, obedience*, Æ : '*supplantatio*,' EPs40¹⁰.

underðēow m. *subject, slave*, AO.

underðīedan (AO,CP)=underðēodan

underðīednes (ī³)=underðēodnes

underðȳdan=underðēodan

underweaxan⁶ '*succrescere*,' Sc104⁸.

underwedd n. *deposit, pledge*, Æ.

underwendan '*subvertere*,' Sc196⁶.

underweorpan '*subicere*,' EPs143².

underwrǣdel m? *waistband*, WW153¹.

underwreðian (eo, i, y) *to support, sustain, uphold, strengthen, establish*, Æ,CP.

underwreðung f. *propping up, support, sustentation*, Sc,WW.

underwrītan *to write at the foot of, subscribe*, BH312³⁰.

under-wrīðian, -wryðian=underwreðian

underwyrtwalian '*supplantare*,' EPs17⁴⁰.

underȳcan (īe) *to add*, CM385²⁹².

underyrnan=underiernan

undierne (e, i, y) **I.** *open, manifest, clearly known* : *public, nuncupatory*. **II.** adv.

undīgollīce=undēogollīce

undīlegod *unerased*, CP423²³.

undolfen *untilled*, GD202⁴.

undōm m. *unjust judgment, injustice*, W.

undōmlīce *indiscreetly*, Sc202¹⁵.

undōn anv. *to* '*UNDO*,' *open, loosen, separate*, Æ,AO : *cancel, discharge, abrogate, destroy*, LG.

undrēfed *untroubled, undisturbed, undefiled*, CP31³.

undrifen *not driven or tossed*, LL222,2.

undruncen *sober*, CP295⁸.

undrysnende *inextinguishable*, MtL3¹².

undȳre=undēore

undyrne=undierne

unēacen (ē) *barren*, OEG27³¹.

unēacniendlīc *unfruitful, sterile*, OEG1030.

unearfoðlīce adv. *without difficulty*, OEG.

un-earg, -earh (Æ), -earhlic (Æ) *not cowardly, dauntless, bold, brave*.

unēaðe (y) **I.** adj. *not easy, difficult, hard, disagreeable, grievous*, Æ,An,WW. **II.** adv. *not easily, hardly*, Bo,Chr,LG, WW : *unwillingly*, Æ,BH : *scarcely, only just*, Æ. ['*uneath*']

unēaðelic *difficult, hard, impossible* : *troublesome*, Nic611´. adv. -līce.

unēaðelicnes (ā², ǣ², ē², ȳ²) f. *difficulty*, BH 296²¹.

unēað-lǣ(c)ne, -lācne *not easily cured*, Lcd.

unēaðmylte *indigestible*, Lcd82b.

unēaðnes (ē, īe) f. *difficulty, inconvenience, trouble, worry*, Æ : *severity, harshness*.

unēawfæstlīce=unǣwfæstlīce

un-efn, -efen(lic) *unequal, unlike*, Cr : *anomalous, irregular*, ÆGR. adv. -efne, Ps. ['*uneven*']

un-ēmetta, -ēmota=unǣmta

unemn=unefn

unendebyrdlīce *in a disorderly manner*, CP.

unered—*unploughed, uncultivated*, WW147³.

unēstful *ungracious*, WW191¹⁷.

unēð-=unēað-, unīeð-

unēwisc=unǣwisc

unfǣcne (ā) *without malice, sincere, honest, faithful*, B,LL.

unfæderlīce adv. *in an unfatherly manner*, W106⁶.

unfǣge† *not fated to die*, B.

unfæger *not beautiful, unlovable, deformed, ugly, hideous*, B,Bo,Bl. ['*unfair*']

unfægernes (e) *ugliness, disfigurement*, GD 279¹⁵ : *abomination*, MtL24¹⁵.

unfǣglic *not fatal*, Bo107²⁹.

unfægre (ǣ) adv. *unfairly, foully*, Gen. ['*unfair*']

unfǣhð f. *peace* (*dropping of a feud*), LL 100,28.

unfǣle *wicked, unlovely, unholy, evil*, Gen, Mk,WW. ['*unfele*']

unfæst *not fixed, not firm, loose, unsteady, tottering*, Bo,CP. ['*unfast*']

unfæstende *not fasting*, LL(252¹).

unfæstlīce adv. *not firmly, vaguely, indistinctly*, CP156¹³.

+unfæstnian *to unfasten*, MFH165.

unfæstrǣd *unstable, inconstant*, CP.

unfæstrǣdnes f. *inconstancy*, CP.

unfæsð-=unfæst-

unfāh *exempt from hostility, not under a ban*, LL186,1¹.

unfealdan⁷ *to unfold, open*, G,GD : *explain*, Sc.

unfeax *without hair, bald* (Swt).

unfēcne=unfǣcne

unfēferig *not feverish*, Lcd1·164´.

unfeger-=unfæger-

unfēlende '*unfeeling*,' *insensible*, Lcd 99a.
unfenge *not acceptable*, MFH 176.
un-feor, -feorr adv. *not far from, near*.
unfeormigende (on-) *inexpiable*, ÆL 23b⁴²⁶.
unfēre *disabled, invalided*, CHR 1055.
unfērnes f. *impotence, infirmity*, RWH 137¹²
unflitme? *unreservedly?* B 1097.
un-flycge, -fligge *unfledged*, OEG 28¹³.
unforbærned *unburnt*, Æ,AO.
unforboden *unforbidden, lawful*, Æ.
unforbūgendlīc *unavoidable*. adv. -līce *without turning away*, ÆL 23b⁴³¹.
unforburnen *unburnt*, ÆH 2·480⁷.
unforcūð *reputable, good, honourable, noble, brave*, CP. adv. -līce. [fracoð]
unfordytt *unobstructed*, OEG 3613.
unforebyrdig *impatient*, Sc 8¹³.
unfored (od) *unbroken*, Æ.
unforedlīc (o³) *indissoluble*, OEG.
unforescēawod *hasty, unconsidered*, HEXC 387.
unforescēawodlīc *hasty, precipitate*, WW 426⁸. adv. (v. unforsc-).
unforfeored *unbroken?* WW 231³³.
unforgifen *unforgiven*, CP : *not given in marriage*.
unforgifende (y³) *unforgiving*, GD 320¹.
unforgitende *unforgetting, mindful*, GUTH 76²².
unforgolden *unpaid*, LEV 19¹³.
unforhæfednes (fd) f. *incontinence*, CP.
unforhladen *unexhausted*, WW 255³⁹.
unforht adj. *fearless, bold*. adv. -e, -līce.
unforhtigende *fearless*, ÆH 2·140'.
unforhtlēasnes? *fear, timidity*, VH 21.
unforhtmōd *fearless*, ÆH.
unforlǣten (ē) *not left*, NG.
unformolsnod neg. ptc. *uncorrupted, undecayed*, Æ.
unformolten *unconsumed*, ÆH 1·488⁷.
unforod=unfored
unforrot-edlic (HGL), -iendig (ÆP 14⁷), -iendlic (OEG) *incorruptible*.
unforscēawodlīce *unawares*, WW 92¹⁰ : *inconsiderately, hastily*, ÆH.
unfor-spornen, -spurned *not hindered*, GD 60²⁸.
unforswǣled *unburnt*, ÆH 2·20¹⁵.
unforswīgod *not passed over in silence*, ÆL 23b³⁵.
unforswȳðed *unconquered*, AA 3¹¹.
unfortredde sb. *the plant which cannot be killed by treading, polygonum aviculare, knot-grass*.
unfortreden *not destroyed by treading*, LCD 3·299'.
unforwandigendlīce adv. *unhesitatingly, boldly*, APT 21⁹.

unforwandodlīc adj. *unhesitating, fearless*, CP. adv. -līce *recklessly*, CP : *unswervingly*.
unforwealwod *unwithered*, BL 73²⁵.
unforwordenlīc (u³) *undecayed*, OEG 60.
unforworht I. *innocent*. II. *unrestricted, free*, KC.
unforwyrded *undecayed*, NC 351.
un-fracodlīce, -fracoðlīce *honourably, becomingly, fitly*, Bo.
unfratewod *unadorned, unpolished*, GPH 396. [frætwian]
unfremful *unprofitable*, Æ,GL.
unfremu f. *damage, hurt*, GEN.
unfrēondlīce *unkindly*, Gen 2689. ['unfriendly']
unfricgende *unquestioning*, GEN 2649.
unfrið m. *breach of peace, enmity, war*, AO : *state of being outside the king's peace*.
unfriðflota m. *hostile fleet*, CHR 1000 E.
unfriðhere m. *hostile army*, CHR.
unfriðland n. *hostile land*, LL 222,3¹.
unfriðmann m. *alien enemy*, LL 222,3³.
unfriðscip n. *hostile ship*, CHR,LL.
unfrōd *young, inexperienced*, B 2821.
unfrōforlīce *uncontestably*, OEG 56¹⁸⁷?
unfrom† *inert*, B,PPs.
unfūl '*insulsum*' MkLR 9⁵⁰.
unfulfremed *imperfect*, Æ.
unfulfremednes f. *imperfection*, CP.
unfulfremming f. *imperfection*, LPs 138¹⁶.
un-fūliende (HGL), -fūliendlic (OEG) *incorruptible*.
unfullod *unbaptized*, LL.
unfulworht *imperfect, unfinished*, RB 20³.
unfyrn adv. *not long ago*, BL : *soon*, GD.
ungænge *useless, vain*, MtR 15⁶.
ungan=ongan pret. 3 sg. of onginnan.
ungeǣndod=ungeendod
ungeǣsce *unheard of*, GD 284²⁰.
un-geǣwed (-iǣwed) *unmarried*, OEG 5248.
ungeandett *without confession*, W 135³².
ungeaplīce *carelessly, unskilfully*, CHRD 123⁹.
ungēara adv. *not long ago, lately, recently* : *soon, shortly*.
ungearo=ungearu
ungearu, gsm. ungear(o)wes *unready, disinclined, unprepared, untilled*, AO,CP. on ungearwe *unawares*, AO.
ungearuwitolnes f. *dulness of mind*, GD 331¹⁵.
ungearwyrd *not respected*, WW 421³².
ungēaðe=unēaðe
ungeǣxod *unasked*, ÆH 1·428⁶.
ungebarde=ungebierde
ungebēaten *unbeaten, unwrought*, Ln 23⁵.
ungebēgendlīc=ungebīgendlic
ungebeorhlīce *rashly? intemperately?* ÆH 2·322²⁶.
unge-bēt(ed), -bett *unatoned for*, CP : *unacquitted*, EC 217¹⁰.

ungebierde (a, y) *beardless*, GL.
ungebīged *unbent*, OEG 2977.
ungebīgendlic *inflexible, rigid : indeclinable*, ÆGR.
ungebleoh *of different colours, unlike*, ÆGR.
ungeblētsod *unblessed*, JUL 492.
ungeblȳged *intrepid*, GU 913. [blēoh]
ungeboden *without being summoned*, TC.
ungeboht *unbought, unbribed*, LL 398,8.
ungeboren *yet unborn*, LL 126 Pro.
ungebrocen *unbroken*, WW 398³².
ungebrocod *uninjured*, ÆH 1·464⁶.
ungebrosnendlic *undecaying*, BH,GD.
ungebrosnod *uncorrupted, undecayed*, Æ.
ungebrosnung f. *incorruption*, SC 71².
ungebunden *unbound*, ÆGR 14¹³; GD 214¹⁶.
ungebyrde I. *uncongenial*, BO 92²². **II.**=ungebierde
ungebyrded *inviolate*, GD 199⁴.
ungebyredlic *incongruous*, DR 179¹⁷.
ungecindelic=ungecyndelic
ungeclǣnsod *unclean, impure*, Æ.
ungecnāwen *unknown*, APT 17¹³.
ungecnyrdnes f. *negligence, indifference, idleness*, ÆH 2·552'.
ungecoplic *unsuitable, unbefitting, troublesome*. adv. -līce, SC 80¹⁴.
ungecoren *reprobate*. u. āð *oath taken by a body of persons generally* (*opposed to* cyreāð), LL.
ungecost *reprobate*, BH 480⁴.
ungecwēme *unpleasing, disagreeable*, SC 38¹⁵.
ungecyd *unsaid, not declared*, LL 212,9.
ungecynde *unnatural*, BO : *alien*, CHR.
unge-cyndelic, -cyndlic, -cynelic *unnatural, monstrous, terrible*. adv. -līce.
ungecyrred *unconverted*, LCD 3·442¹.
ungedæftelīce=ungedæftlīce
ungedæftenlic=ungedafenlic
ungedæftlīce adv. *unseasonably*, CP 97¹⁶.
ungedæftnes f. *untimely intervention or interruption*, CP 97¹⁹.
ungedafenlic *improper, unseemly*, Æ : *unseasonable, troublesome*, CP (v. A 33·272). adv. -līce *improperly, unduly, unreasonably, unjustly, unsuitably*.
ungedafenlicnes f. *unfitness, inconvenience*, CP s 9²².
ungedafniendlic (HGL 492)=ungedafenlic
ungedallic *infinite, without end*, GD 337¹¹.
ungedēfe *improper, not fitting, disagreeable*. adv. -līce.
unge-dēfelic, -dēflic=ungedafenlic
unge-dered, -derod (Æ) *unhurt, uninjured, unmolested*.
ungederstig=ungedyrstig
ungedrehtlīce adv. *indefatigably*, WW 428³.

ungedrȳme *inharmonious, discordant*, CHRD 57¹². [drēam]
ungedwimorlīce *clearly, without any delusion*, NC 328.
ungedyrstig *timid*, CP 209¹⁰.
ungeeahtendlic (a³, æ³) *estimable*, BH,GD.
ungeended=ungeendod
ungeendigendlic *infinitive*, ÆGR : *infinite*.
unge-endod (CP), -endodlic *unending, endless, infinite, boundless*.
ungefǣd (a) *indiscretion*, CHRD 13¹⁴.
ungefǣglic=unfǣglic; **ungefǣr-**=ungefēr-
ungefandod *untried, having no experience*, CP 407,409.
ungefaren *impassable, without a road*, BLPs.
ungefēa m. *unhappiness*, NC 328.
ungefēalīce *miserably*, CHR 755.
ungefēge *unfit, improper*, WW 191²².
unge-fēle, -fēled *without feeling*, LCD.
ungefēre I. *impassable : impenetrable, inaccessible*, CP. **II.** adv. *impassably*.
ungefēred *inaccessible*, AA 30⁷.
ungefērenlic *difficult, trackless*, AA 25⁹.
ungefērlic *unsocial, internecine*. adv. -līce *in civil war*.
ungefērne *impassable*, VPs (oe).
ungefeðered *not feathered*, WW 427¹⁶.
unge-fōg, -fōh I. *immoderate, excessive*, Æ : *overbearing, presumptuous, unbending*, Æ. **II.** n. *excess*, CHRD 70¹⁶. adv. -fōge *excessively*, AO.
unge-fōglic (AO), -fōhlic *fierce, strong : immense*. adv. -līce.
ungefrǣg-e, -elic *unheard of, unusual, inconceivable*. adv. -līce.
ungefrætwod *unadorned*, WW 419¹¹.
ungefrēdelīce adv. *callously*, CP 265¹⁶.
ungefrēglīce=ungefrǣglīce
ungefremed *unfinished*, LL,WW.
ungefremmung (on-) f. *imperfection*, RPs 138¹⁶.
ungefullod I. *unfulfilled*, RD 60¹⁴. [fullian] **II.**=ungefulwod
ungefulwod *unbaptized*, Æ,BL.
unge-fyld (BO), -fylle(n)d(lic) *insatiable*.
ungefynde *worthless, barren?* CP 411¹⁹.
ungefyrn adv. *not long hence, not long ago, not long after*, Æ.
ungegearwe=ungearwe v. ungearu.
unge-gearwod (DR), -gerad (MtR) *not clothed*.
ungeglenged *unadorned*, OEG 1210.
ungegrēt *ungreeted*, GUTH 22²⁰.
ungehādod *not ordained, not belonging to an order* (used of men and women), IM 127¹⁸.
un-gehǣlendlic, -gehǣledlic *incurable*, VHy.
ungehǣmed *unmarried*, OEG 1174.
ungehǣplic *unsuitable, unfit*, A 8·452.
ungehālgod *unhallowed, unconsecrated*, Æ.

ungehāten *unpromised, unbidden,* BL189²⁷.
ungehēafdod *not having come to a head,* LCD1·92′.
ungehealdsum *unchaste,* Æ. adv. -līce.
ungehealdsumnes f. *incontinence, unchastity,* KC,LL.
ungehealtsum=ungehealdsum
ungehefegod *not pregnant,* OEG27³¹.
ungehende (æ³) *remote,* HL12⁸.
ungehendnes f. *remoteness, distance,* ÆGR 14¹⁹.
ungeheort *disheartened,* ÆL23⁶².
ungehēred=ungehȳred
unge-hīersum (CP), -hīrsum (Æ) *disobedient, rebellious.*
ungehīrsumnes (ȳ) f. *disobedience,* Æ,VH.
ungehīrsumod (ȳ) *disobedient,* RBL12⁸.
unge-hīwod, -hīwodlic *unformed, not fashioned, unshapen : unfeigned, genuine.*
ungehlēoðor *inharmonious,* WW224⁷.
ungehrepod *untouched,* Æ.
ungehrinen *untouched,* BH,GD.
ungehwǣde *much,* LCD53b.
ungehwǣrnes=ungeðwǣrnes
ungehȳr-=unge-hīer-, -hīr-
ungehȳred (ē³) *unheard of, untold,* BH40³³.
ungehȳrnes f. *hardness of hearing, deafness,* LCD.
ungehyrt *disheartened, fearful,* W192²⁴.
ungel m. *fat, tallow, suet,* Æ.
ungelācnod *unhealed,* GUTH66¹⁶.
ungelādod *not acquitted,* EC217¹⁰.
ungelæccendlic *unreprovable,* Sc119¹¹.
ungelǣred *untaught, illiterate, unlearned, ignorant, rude,* Æ,CP. adv. -līce.
ungelǣredlic *unteachable,* GD110²¹.
ungelǣrednes f. *unskilfulness, ignorance,* CP.
ungelaðod *uninvited,* ÆH1·128¹⁸.
ungelēaf *unbelieving,* PPs67¹⁹.
ungelēafa m. *unbelief,* BL,CHR.
ungelēafful *unbelieving,* CP : *incredible,* OEG.
ungelēaffullic *unbelieving : incredible.* adv. -līce.
ungelēaffulnes f. *unbelief,* BL,G.
ungelēaflic *incredible,* Æ.
ungelēafsum *unbelieving,* BH.
ungelēafsumnes f. *unbelief, infidelity, heathenism,* BH70²⁵.
ungelēf-=ungelīf-; **ungelēofa**=ungelēafa
ungelic *unlike, different, dissimilar, diverse,* Æ,Bo,Bl,OEG; CP. adv. -līce. ['*uniliche,*' '*unilike*']
ungelica m. *one unlike others,* ÆL7²⁸.
ungelician *to displease,* Æ(94⁶⁶).
ungeliclic *improper,* GUTH12¹⁷. adv. -līce, LCD59a.
ungelicnes f. *unlikeness, difference,* CP.

ungelīef-=ungelīf-
ungelīfed (ȳ) I. *unbelieving,* Æ. II. *illicit,* BH2·229.
ungelīf-edlic, -endlic (īe, ȳ) *incredible, extraordinary.* adv. -līce.
unge-līfen, -līfende (e³, y³) *unbelieving,* NG.
ungelīfend (ē) m. *unbeliever,* NG.
ungelīfnes (ē) f. *unbelief,* NG.
ungeligen=ungelygen
ungelimp nm. *mishap, misfortune,* Æ.
ungelimplic *inconvenient, unfortunate, disastrous,* Æ : *abnormal, unreasonable.* adv. -līce.
ungelȳf-=ungelīf-
ungelygen *not lying, true,* LL.
ungēm-=ungȳm-
ungemaca m. '*impar,*' *not a match,* ÆGR.
ungemǣc *unlike,* GD91¹⁵; WW223³⁵.
ungemǣt=ungemet
ungemǣte I. *immense, extraordinary,* CHR 1115. ['*unimete*'] II. adv. *immensely.*
ungemǣtlic *excessive,* AO28²⁷.
ungemēde *unbearable, unpleasant,* MOD25.
ungemēdnes f. *adversity,* DR63¹³.
ungemeltnes f. *indigestion,* LCD68b.
ungemenged *unmixed, pure,* Bo100³¹.
ungemet n. *excess, superfluity : immensity : want of moderation,* Bo,Lcd. ['*unimete*']
ungemēt *not met with, unknown,* OEG2488.
ungemete I. adj. *huge,* GD12⁹. II. adv. *excessively, immeasurably, immoderately, extremely,* B,Ps. ['*unimete*']
ungemetegod (Æ)=ungemetgod
ungemetelice=ungemetlice
ungemetes=ungemete II.
ungemetfæst *not moderate, intemperate, excessive : very firm,* MET7³³.
ungemetfæstnes f. *excess, intemperance,* Bo 109⁹.
ungemetgod *out of due proportion, excessive,* CP : *unbridled, intemperate.*
ungemetgung f. *excess,* Æ,CP.
ungemetigende *intemperate, unrestrained,* VH22.
ungemetlic *immeasurable, immense,* AO : *excessive, immoderate, violent.* adv. -līce, AO,CP.
ungemetnes f. *extravagance,* OET180³.
ungemetum adv.=ungemete
ungemidlod *unrestrained, unbridled,* Æ, CHRD.
ungemiht *without strength, weak,* Bo108⁵n.
ungemihtig=unmihtig
ungemindig=ungemyndig
ungemōd *discordant, dissentient, quarrelsome,* CP.
ungemōdignes f. *contentiousness,* W8¹⁵n.
ungemōdnes f. *strife,* CP344⁹.
ungemolsnod *undecayed,* MH78¹.

ungemunecod *not made a monk*, LL(142⁴).
ungemylt *undigested*, LCD 2a (Harl).
ungemynd f. *madness*, LCD.
ungemyndig (w. g.) *unmindful, forgetful, heedless (of)*, Æ.
ungenæmnendlic *unknown?* GD 341¹³.
ungenĭdd (ē, īe) *uncompelled*, AO,CP.
ungeocian *to 'unyoke,'* ÆGr 277³.
ungeonbyrded=ungebyrded
ungeorne *negligently : unwillingly*, AO.
ungeornful *indifferent, remiss, slothful*, CP.
ungerād I. (w. g.) *ignorant, foolish, unskilled, unfit*, Æ,CP : (w. d.) *at variance, wrong, discordant, dissentient*, Æ,AO : *illconditioned, rude*, Æ. **II.** n. *discord*, CP : *folly*, Æ.
ungerādnes (æ) *disagreement*, LCD.
ungerǣd=ungerād
ungerǣde *foolish*, MFH 176.
ungerǣdlic *unteachable, ignorant, rough*, GD 110¹¹. adv. -līce *sharply, roughly, violently*.
ungerǣdnes f. *disagreement, sedition*, AO.
ungerǣdod *without harness*, KC.
ungerec n. *tumult*, BH,MtR 27²⁴.
ungereccan *to clear oneself of an accusation*, LL 168,1².
ungereclic *unruly, unrestrained*, BL 19⁶. adv. -līce *confusedly, recklessly*.
ungerĕdelīce=ungerǣdlīce
ungerĕnod *not ornamented*, TC 515'. [regn-]
ungereord *uninstructed, barbarous*, WW 193³.
ungereord(ed)lic *insatiable*, CVPs 100⁵.
ungereordod *unfed, empty*, ÆL 19⁹¹.
ungerepod=ungehrepod
ungerian=ungierwan; **ungeriht**=unriht
ungeriht *uncorrected, unreformed*, CHRD.
ungerīm I. n. *countless number, host*, Æ. **II.** *countless, untold*, Æ.
unge-rīmlic, -rīmed(lic) *countless, untold*.
ungerinen=ungehrinen
ungerinselīce=ungerisenlīce
ungerĭped *immature, too early*, Æ.
ungerisedlīce=ungerisenlīce
ungerīsende *indecent*, OEG 3673.
ungerisene I. *unseemly, improper : incongruous, inconvenient.* **II.**=ungerisnu
ungerisenlic *unbecoming, improper*, CP. adv. -līce, CP.
ungerisnes (uni-) f. *impropriety*, HGL 507.
ungerisnu n. (often pl.) *inconvenience : impropriety, indignity, disgrace*, AO.
ungerŏtsian=unrōtsian
ungerwan=ungierwan
ungerȳde I. *rough, boisterous*, W 137⁷. **II.** n. *rough place*, Lk 3⁵.
ungerȳdelic *rough, violent*, GD 265²; LV 47. adv. -līce *suddenly, impetuously*, Æ.

ungerȳdnes f. *noise, tumult*, Sc 82².
ungesadelod=unsadelod
ungesǣlig *unhappy, unfortunate*, Æ,AO, CP. adv. -līce *unhappily : wickedly*.
ungesǣlignes f. *unhappiness, misfortune*, BH,BL.
ungesǣllīce=ungesǣliglīce
ungesǣlð f. *trouble, misfortune, unhappiness, sorrow*, CP.
ungesawen=ungesewen
ungescaðignes=ungescéððignes
ungescéad I. n. *want of intelligence, senselessness.* **II.** adj. *unreasonable*, LCD : *excessive*, VH. **III.** adv. *exceedingly*, DA 243.
ungescéadlic *unreasonable, indiscreet.* adv. -līce *unreasonably, absurdly*.
ungescéadwīs(lic) *unintelligent, irrational, imprudent, foolish*, Æ,CP. adv. -līce.
ungescéadwīsnes f. *want of intelligence, indiscretion, folly, ignorance*, CP.
ungesce(a)pen *uncreated, unformed*, Æ.
ungescended *unhurt*, DR 146¹¹.
ungesceðóed *unhurt*, BH 218²⁵.
ungesceðóignes (a, æ) f. *innocence*, ÆH.
ungescrēpe (ǣ) **I.** n. *an inconvenience*, BH 382⁹. **II.** *inconvenient, useless*, BH,WW.
ungescrēpnes (ǣ) f. *discomfort*, BH 322³⁰.
ungescrōp n. *an inconvenience* BHc 382⁹.
ungesegenlic=ungesewenlic
ungeseht adj. *at variance*, FM 358²⁸.
ungesēl-=ungesǣl-; **ungesēne**=ungesȳne
ungesēnod *not signed with the cross*, SOL 148¹⁰. [segn]
ungesēonde *blind*, LCD 1·368'.
ungeseowenlic=ungesewenlic
unge-sewen, -sewen(d)lic *unseen, invisible*, Æ,CP. adv. -līce.
ungesibb *not related*, RD,SOL : *unfriendly, hostile*, BL,BH.
ungesibsum *quarrelsome, contentious*, CP.
ungesibsumnes f. *quarrelsomeness, discord*, CP 351¹.
ungesilt=unsealt
ungesoden *unsodden, unboiled*, LCD.
ungesom *at variance*, ÆH 1·478'.
ungespēdig=unspēdig
ungestæðóe-=ungestæðóig-
ungestæðóig *unsteady, inconstant, unstable, fickle*, CP. adv. -līce.
ungestæðóignes f. *inconstancy, frivolity*, CP.
ungestrēon n. *ill-gotten treasure*, W 183⁹.
ungestroden *not subject to confiscation*, LL 12,4¹.
ungesund *unsound, faulty*, RWH 105².
ungesundlīce *excessively, exceedingly*, GD 15².
ungeswēge *inharmonious, dissonant, discordant, out of tune, harsh*, GL.
ungeswenced *unceasing*, NC 329.

ungeswencedlic *unwearying*, BH 436[16].
ungeswicende *unceasing*, A 2·357.
ungeswicendlíce *incessantly*, Sc.
ungeswuncen *not laboured over, not well done*, WW 430[11].
ungesylt=unsealt
ungesýne (ē) *unseen, invisible*, WW 17[46].
ungesýnelic *invisible*, BL,W.
ungetǽse I. n. *trouble, hardship, severity*, CP. II. adj. *troublesome, inconvenient*.
ungetǽslíce adv. *inconveniently*, AS 30[10].
ungetǽsnes f. *unsuitableness, inconvenience*, WW 419[38].
ungetel *innumerable* (BT).
ungetemed=unātemed
ungetemprung f. *inclemency*, CM 461.
ungetēori(g)endlic *inexhaustible*. adv. -líce *incessantly*, LL.
ungetēorod *unfailing*, Æ : *unwearied*, CHRD.
ungetēse=ungetǽse II.
unge-tīmu f? -tíme n? *evil time, adversity, mishǽp*, AO,GD.
ungetinge (Æ), ungetingful (GPH) *not eloquent*. [tunge]
ungetogen *uneducated*, Æ. ['untowen']
ungetrēowe (ī, īe, ū, ý) *untrue, faithless*, Æ.
ungetrēownes f. *unbelief*, CP 447[6] : *faithlessness*, GD 160[5].
ungetrēowsian=untrēowsian
ungetrēowð f. *unfaithfulness, treachery*, W 160[6].
ungetrum *weak, infirm*, Bo 132[32].
unge-trūw-, -trýw-=un(ge)trēow-
ungetwǽre (WW 248[17])=ungeðwǽre
ungetwēogendlíce (GD 231[21]) = untwēogendlíce.
unge-týd, -týdd *ignorant, untaught, unskilful*, CP.
ungetýred=ungetēorod
ungeðǽslic *unfit, improper, unseemly*, WW 191[23].
ungeðanc mn. *evil thought*, W.
ungeðancful *unthankful, ungrateful*, W 241[4].
ungeðeaht n. *evil counsel*, RB 118[10].
ungeðeahtendlíce *hastily*, BH 124[13].
ungeðēawe adv. *not customary*, GUTH 72[17].
ungeðēawfæst *ill-regulated*, RBL 14[16].
ungeðēod *disunited, separate*, GEN 1698.
ungeðīnged *unexpected*, CP 317[13],VH.
ungeðungen *base*, NAR 42[12].
ungeðwǽre I. *disagreeing, quarrelsome, troublesome, stubborn, vexatious, undutiful, irreverent*, Æ,CP. II. n. *disturbance*, MtR 26[5].
ungeðwǽrian *to ɔe discordant, disagree, be at variance with*, Æ.
ungeðwǽrlic *inharmonious, discordant*, RB 19[2] : *hostile*, GD 349. adv. -líce *peevishly*.

ungeðwǽrnes f. *disturbance, quarrel, discord*, AO : *violence*, BH 44[27].
ungeðwēre=ungeðwǽre
ungeðyld fn. *impatience*, CP. [ðolian; *Ger*. ungeduld]
ungeðyldelíce adv. *impatiently*, Bo.
ungeðyldig *impatient*, Æ,CP.
ungeðylð=ungeðyld
ungeðyre '*discensor*'? Cp 283 D.
ungewǽder=ungewider
ungewǽm-=ungewem-
ungewǽpnod *without weapons, unarmed*, Æ.
ungewealden *disordered (of the stomach)*, LCD : *involuntary, unwilling*, VH.
un-gewealdes, -gewaldes adv. *involuntarily, by chance*, CP.
ungeweaxen *immature*, WW 352[27].
ungeweder=ungewider
un-gewemmed (Æ), -gewemmedlic *unspotted, unblemished, undefiled, uninjured*. adv. -líce *uncorruptly*, BH 276[20].
ungewem(med)nes f. *freedom (from stain)*.
ungewende(n)dlic *immovable*, GD,LCD.
ungewendnes f. *unchangeableness* (Swt).
ungewēned *unexpected*, LCD.
ungewēnedlic *unhoped for*, GD 347[14].
ungewēnendlic *incalculable*, GD 284[20].
un-gewērged, -gewērigod *unwearied, untiring*.
un-gewidere n., gs. -gewidres *bad weather, storm*.
ungewiderung f. *bad weather*, CHR 1086.
ungewild (y) *unsubdued*, OEG.
ungewilde (y) *not subject to, independent of*, AO : *untamed, unbridled*. [geweald]
ungewildelic (y) *unyielding*, ÆH 2·92[2].
ungewill *displeasing*, CHR.
ungewilles *undesignedly*, LL 31,21[13].
ungewintred *immature, young*, LL 18,26.
ungewirhtum=ungewyrhtum
ungewis=ungewiss
ungewislic *unaccustomed*, Bo 15[22]n.
ungewísnes f. *uncertainty, ignorance*, BH.
ungewiss I. n. *uncertainty, ignorance*, Æ, AO : *unconsciousness* : *ignominy, shame*, SPs 82[15]. II. adj. *uncertain*, Æ,CP : *unwise, ignorant, inexperienced* : *doubtful*, Æ : *causing shame, shameful*, KGL 75[10].
ungewisses *unconsciously, involuntarily*, CP.
ungewítendlic *permanent, imperishable*, ÆL 34[298]. adv. -líce *permanently, perpetually*, CP 441[21].
ungewitfæstnes f. *madness*, LCD 82b.
ungewitful *unwise, senseless, mad*, CP.
ungewitfulnes f. *madness*, CP 185[1].
ungewitlic *stupid, foolish*, LCD 65a.
ungewitnes f. *folly*, GD 95[23] (v. BTs).

ungewītnigendlīce *freely, with impunity,* ÆGR 233⁶n.

ungewītnod *unpunished,* Æ,CP.

ungewitt n. *folly, madness,* Æ.

ungewittig *irrational, foolish, mad,* Æ.

ungewittiglīce (-witte-) *unwisely, foolishly, madly,* GD 2; 104.

ungewittignes f. *folly, madness,* GD 163; 247.

ungewlitig *not bright, dull,* AS 31¹⁹.

±**ungewlitigian** *to disfigure,* AS.

ungeworht *unformed, unfinished,* Æ.

ungewriten *unwritten,* WW.

ungewuna I. m. *evil habit, vice,* CP 169⁹. II. *unusual,* Æ : *uninhabited,* Æ.

ungewunelic *unusual, strange,* Æ. [*Ger.* ungewöhnlich] adv. -līce, Æ.

ungewuniendlic *uninhabitable,* LCD.

ungewyder=ungewider

ungewyld-=ungewild-

ungewylles=unwilles

ungewynelic=ungewunelic

ungewyrded *uninjured,* PH 181.

ungewyrhtum (be) adv. phr. *without a cause,* CVPs.

ungier-wan, -ian (e, i, y) *to unclothe, divest of.*

ungifre *pernicious,* GEN 2470.

ungifu f. *evil gift,* W 52,58.

unginne *not great or broad,* GnE 206.

ungl=ungel; **unglad**=unglæd

unglæd (a) *cheerless, dull,* Bo 14¹⁴. ['*un-glad*']

unglædlic *implacable,* GPH 392 : *cheerless,* VH 22.

unglædnes f. '*imperitia*,' WW 423²⁹. [mistake for ungléawnes?]

ungléaw=ungléaw

ungléaw *ignorant, foolish, unwise,* Æ. adv. -līce, CP.

ungléawnes f. *want of discernment, folly, ignorance,* PA 70.

ungléawscipe m. *folly,* Sc 83¹⁶.

unglenged=ungeglenged

ungnýðe (ē) *not niggardly, not sparing, liberal.* adv. -līce, GD.

ungōd I. adj. *not good,* Lcd. ['*ungood*'] II. n. *evil.*

ungor=hungor

ungrædiglīce *abundantly,* GD 175¹.

ungrāpigende *not grasping,* ÆH 1·366′.

ungréne *not green, bare of grass,* GEN 117.

ungrīpendlic *irreprehensible,* EPs 18⁸.

ungrund *vast,* Ex 508.

ungrynde *bottomless,* RIM 49.

ungyleðe *unaccorded,* B 2921.

un-gyld, -gylde n. *excessive tax,* CHR. [gieldan]

ungylda m. *one who is not a member of a guild,* TC 606¹⁶.

ungylde adv. *not entitled to compensation,* LL.

ungyltig *innocent,* AO 184⁹.

un-gýmen, -gýming f. *carelessness,* BH.

ungýmende (ē) *careless,* BH 434⁵.

ungyrdan=ongyrdan

ungyrian=ungierwan

ungystlīðe (=ie) *inhospitable,* NC 329.

unhādian (on-) *to unfrock, divest of holy orders,* LL.

unhādod=ungehādod

unhādung f. '*exordinatio*,' RBL 110⁸.

unhæl=unhāl, unhælu

+**unhǣlan** *to weaken, debilitate,* Sc 51¹⁰.

unhǣlð f. *ill-health, weakness, infirmity.*

unhǣlu f. *sickness, unsoundness,* AO,Chrd, LL,MtL : *mischief, evil,* B,BF. ['*unheal*']

unhǣmed *unmarried,* WW 530¹⁹.

unhǣr=unhār

unhāl *sick, ill, weak,* Æ,Bo; CP. ['*un-whole*']

unhālgod *unhallowed, unconsecrated,* Æ.

unhāllan *to pine away,* BPs 118¹³⁹.

unhālig (ǣ) '*unholy,' profane,* ELPs 42¹.

un-hālwende (RHy), -hālwendlic (Æ) *incurable, deadly* : *unprofitable.*

unhandworht *not made with hands,* Mk 14⁵⁸.

unhār (=an-) *hoary, grizzled,* B 357.

unhéah (ē) *not high, low,* Æ.

unhéanlīce *valiantly,* CHR 755 : *not inadequately,* GD 43²⁵.

unhearmgeorn *inoffensive,* ÆH 2·44²⁰.

unhéarsumnes=unhiersumnes

un-hég, -héh=unhéah

unhelde (CHR 1095)=unhyldo

unhelian *to uncover, reveal,* Lk 12². ['*un-hele*']

un-héor-, -hér-=unhier-

unhered *unpraised, not celebrated,* Bo 68²⁴.

unherigendlic *not praiseworthy,* ÆH 2·406¹⁷.

unhetol *peaceable,* NC 329.

unhiere (ē, ēo, ý) I. *horrible, monstrous, fierce, wild, tempestuous.* II. adv. *horribly.*

unhierlic *wild, fierce, savage, gloomy.* adv. -līce (GD 161¹⁰).

unhiersum (ý) *disobedient,* GUTH 12¹⁴. adv. -līce.

unhiersumnes (ý) f. *disobedience,* CP.

unhierwan (y²) *to calumniate,* WC 70¹⁵.

unhiredwist f. *unfamiliarity,* Sc 203¹³.

unhiwe *formless,* GPH 399²⁵⁹.

unhiwed *not feigned,* OEG.

unhléowe *unfriendly, chill,* Ex 494.

unhlīdan (Æ)=onhlīdan

unhlīs(e) *infamous, disreputable,* KGL 68⁴².

unhlīsa m. *ill-fame, discredit, dishonour,* Æ.

unhlīsbǣre *disreputable,* WW 354¹⁷.

unhlīsēadig *infamous*, WW420¹⁵.
unhlīsful *infamous*, GL.
unhlīsig *infamous*, KGL56⁵.
unhlītme *very unhappily*, B1129 (or ?= unflitme).
unhlūd *not loud*, GD85⁵.
unhlȳs-=unhlīs-
unhnēaw† *generous, liberal*.
unhoga *foolish*, MkL7¹⁸.
unhold *disloyal, unfriendly, hostile*, Æ,BH. ['*unhold*']
unholda m. *monster, devil*, CR762.
unhrǣdsprǣce *slow of speech*, Ex6³⁰.
unhrēofilg *not leprous*, ÆH1·124'.
unhrōr *without motion*, Bo146²⁶.
unhūfed *bareheaded*, OEG4466.
unhwearfiende *unchangeable, fixed*, Bo20²⁹.
unhwīlen† *eternal*.
unhȳdig *ignorant, foolish*, An,Bo.
unhȳhst=unhēhst superl. of unhēah.
unhyldo (e) f. *displeasure, disfavour, unfriendliness*, CP. [*Ger.* unhuld]
unhyr-=onhyr-
unhȳr-=unhīer-
unhȳðig† *unhappy*, An, Gu.
uni-=unge-
unīeð adv. (comp.) *with greater difficulty, more hardly*, CP. [ēað]
unīeð-=unēað-
unin-seglian, -sæglian (Æ) *to unseal*.
unīðe=unīeðe; **uniucian**=ungeocian
unlāb=unlāf
unlācnigendlic *incurable*, LCD1·262¹.
unlācnod *unhealed*, CP61⁴.
unlǣce m. *bad physician*, LCD60b.
un-lǣd, -lǣde *poor, miserable, wretched, unhappy, unfortunate* : *accursed, wicked* : *straying? (of cattle)*.
unlǣdlic *miserable*, NC329. adv. -līce.
unlǣgne=unlīegne
unlǣne *permanent*, W264¹⁸.
unlǣred *unlearned, untaught, ignorant*, CP.
unlǣrednes=ungelǣrednes
unlæt *unwearied, indefatigable*, WW.
unlǣttu f. *sin*, GD289. [unlǣd]
unlāf f. *posthumous child*, WW.
unlagu f. *abuse of law, bad law, oppression, injustice*, LL. æt unlagum *unlawfully*. ['*unlaw*']
unland m. *desert, waste* : *counterfeit, supposed land*, WH13.
unlandāgende m. *not owning land*, LL112.
unlār f. *bad teaching*, LL,W.
unlaðod (ByH26²³)=ungelaðod
unlēafful=ungelēafful
unleahtorwyrðe *not culpable*, PPs18⁷.
unlēanod *unpaid*, EC148⁴.
unlēas *not false, true* : *truthful*. adv. -līce.
unlēcð=unlȳcð pres. 3 sg. of unlūcan.

unlēfedlic=unlȳfendlic; **unlēgne**=unlīegne
unlēof† *not dear, hated*.
unleoðuwāc (e³) *inflexible, rigid, stubborn*.
unleoðuwācnes f. *inflexibility*, WW.
unlēsan=unlīesan; **unlīb-**=unlyb-
unlic=ungelic
unlīchamlic *incorporeal*, Æ,GD.
unlīcð (Æ)=unlȳcð pres. 3 sg. of unlūcan.
unlīcwyrðe *displeasing*, ÆL23b³⁷⁴.
unlīefed=unālȳfed
unlīegne (ǣ, ē) *not to be questioned*, LL.
unlīesan (ē, ȳ) *to unloose*, Æ : *set free, put on a free footing*.
unlīf n. *death*, MFH176.
unlīfes *dead*, ÆL18²⁰³.
unlifi(g)ende (y) *lifeless, dead*. [libban]
unliss? (hl-) *disfavour*, OET464 (v. ANS 142·254).
unlītel=unlȳtel
unlīðe *ungentle, harsh, severe*, Æ.
unlīðowāc=unleoðuwāç
unlofod *unpraised*, PR62.
unlond=unland
unlūcan² *to unlock, open*, Chrd; Æ. ['*unlouk*']
unlust m. *evil desire, lust, sensuality*, Æ : *disinclination, weariness, laziness*, Æ,Sol : *nausea*, Lcd. [*Ger.* unlust]
+unlustian *to loathe*, BL59⁸.
unlyb-ba m., -be f. *poisonous drug, poison*, Æ : *witchcraft*, Æ. [lybb]
unlybbende (MH164²¹)=unlifigende
unlybwyrhta m. *worker with spells or poisons, wizard*, Æ.
unlȳfednes=unālīefednes
unlȳfendlic *illicit, unlawful*, ZDA31⁸.
unlȳfigende=unlifigende
unlyft f. *bad air*, LCD6a.
unlygen *unlying, truthful*, LL156,12.
unlȳsan (Æ)=unlīesan
unlȳt n. *a great deal*, PPs61⁹.
unlȳtel *not small, much, great, very large*.
unmǣdlīce=unmǣðlice
unmǣg? m. *evil kinsman? alien?* WALD2²³.
unmǣge *not akin*, PPs68⁸.
unmǣgel=unmeagol
unmǣgnes f. *weariness*, WW224¹⁴.
unmǣgðlīce=unmǣðlice
unmǣht- (N)=unmiht-
unmǣle *unspotted, immaculate, pure, virgin*.
unmǣne *not criminal, honest, innocent, truthful* : *free (from)*.
un-mǣre, -mǣrlic *inglorious*, Bo.
unmǣte *excessive, immense, great, vast*, BH; Æ : *countless, innumerable*. ['*unmeet*']
unmǣtlic (ē) *enormous*, AA6³,22⁴.
unmǣtnes f. *vastness, excessive greatness*, BH.
unmǣð f. *transgression, sin*, HL13·234.

unmǣ̆ðful *immoderate, excessive,* NC329.
unmǣ̆ŏlic *excessive,* Æ. adv. -līce *excessively,* Æ : *unmercifully, cruelly,* Æ.
un-maga m., -magu f. *needy person, dependant, orphan,* LL.
unmanig *not many, few,* GUTH,BH.
unmann m. *monster, wicked man,* Æ : *hero,* GUTH 12²⁷.
un-meagol, -meahl *insipid,* WW.
unmeaht=unmiht
unmedome (e³, u³) *incompetent, unfit, unworthy,* Æ,CP.
unmedomlīce adv. *negligently, carelessly,* LL.
unmeht=unmiht
unmeltung f. *indigestion,* LCD 95a.
unmendlinga=unmyndlinga
unmēne=unmæ̆ne
unmenged *unmixed,* WW.
unmenn nap. of unmann.
unmennisclic *inhuman,* Bo 70²⁶.
unmēt-=unmæ̆t-
unmicel (y²) *little, small,* GD.
unmīdlod *unrestrained, unbridled,* CP.
unmidome=unmedome
unmiht (ie) I. f. *weakness,* CP. ['*unmiht*']
II. (æ) *impossible,* MtL.
+**unmihtan** *to deprive of strength,* ÆL 25⁷⁷¹.
un-mihtelic, -mihtlic *impossible,* G.
unmihtig (æ, e) *weak, powerless,* Æ,Bo : *impossible,* NG. ['*unmighty*']
unmihtiglic (æ) *weak,* LCD : *impossible,* LkLR.
unmihtignes f. *weakness,* LCD.
unmilde *not meek, harsh,* BH 100²⁹. ['*unmild*']
unmildheort *merciless,* Æ.
unmilts f. *severity, anger,* Ct.
unmiltsigendlic *unpardonable,* ÆT 78⁶³. [milts]
unmiltsung f. *hardness of heart,* AO 64¹⁶.
unmirigð=unmyrhð
unmōd n. *depression,* LCD 65a.
unmōdig *humble,* CP : *timid.*
unmolsniendlic *uncorrupted,* OEG 60.
un-monig, -moneg=unmanig
unmurn *untroubled,* PPs 75⁴.
unmurnlīce† adv. *unpityingly, without sorrowing.*
unmycel=unmicel
unmyhtig=unmihtig; **unmylts-**=unmilts-
unmyndgian=unmynegian
unmynd-linga, -lenga, -lunga adv. *unawares, unexpectedly,* Æ,AO : *undesignedly.*
unmynegian *to overlook, not to demand,* LL 382,43.
unmyrge *unpleasant? sad?* WW 211¹⁶.
unmyrhð f. *sadness,* W 148⁹,VH.
unna m.=unne

±**unnan** pres. 1 sing. an(n), on(n), pl. unnon; pret. sg. ūðe, pp. ±unnen swv. w. d. pers. and g. thing *to grant, allow, bestow, give,* B,Bo,CP,Chr,G,Ps; AO,Æ : *be glad to see, wish, desire,* AO,Ps. unnendre handa *voluntarily.* ['(*i*)-*unne*']
unne f. *favour, approval, permission, consent* : *grant* : *liberality.*
unnēah adj. adv. *not near, far, away from.*
un-nēde, -nēdig=unnīedig
unnēdelīce (GD 346⁹; JAW 55,56)=ungnȳð-elīce
unnēg, unnēh=unnēah
unnend m. *one who grants,* DR 5⁵.
unnet=unnyt
unnīed-ig, -enga adv. *without compulsion or restraint, willingly,* CP. [nēad]
unnit=unnyt II.
unnīðing m. *honest man (not an outlaw),* CHR 1087; v. ANS 117·22.
un-nyt, -nytt I. adj. *useless, unprofitable,* Æ,CP. II. m. *unprofitableness, emptiness, vanity, folly : useless thing.*
unnytenes=unnytnes
unnytlic *useless, unprofitable, foolish,* CP. adv. -līce.
unnytlicnes f. *uselessness,* LCD.
unnytnes f. *unprofitableness, frivolity, emptiness,* LL,W.
unnytwyrðe *unprofitable, useless,* Æ,CP. adv. -wurðlice, Æ.
unnȳðnes? f. *peace, freedom from hate,* VH 23.
unofercumen *unsubdued,* GL.
unoferfēre (oe⁴) *impassable,* GL.
unoferhrēfed *not roofed in,* BL 125²¹.
unoferswīð-ed, -edlic, -ende, -endlic *unconquerable, invincible.*
unoferwin-nene (WW), -nendlic (AO) *invincible.*
unoferwrigen *not covered,* ÆL 23b²⁰⁹.
unoferwunnen *unconquered,* AO 156²⁸.
unoferwunnendlic=unoferwinnendlic
unoflinnedlice *unceasingly,* NC329.
unofslegen *not killed,* ÆH 2·544′.
unondcȳðignes f. *ignorance,* JVPs 24⁷.
unondgetful=unandgittol
unongunnen *without a beginning,* ByH 80²³.
unonlȳsendlic *unpardonable,* GD 348⁴.
unonstyred *unmoved,* GD 270⁹n.
unonstyrigendlic *motionless,* GD 225⁴.
unonwend-endlic, -edlic *unchangeable, constant, immovable.* adv. -līce.
unorne *old, worn out, decrepit,* Ma 256. ['*unorn*']
unornlic *old, worn,* Jos 9⁵.
unplēolic *not dangerous, safe,* Æ. adv. -līce.
unrǣd m. *folly, foolish plan : crime, mischief, injury, plot, treachery,* Æ,AO.

unrǣden f. *ill-considered act*, GEN982.

unrǣdfǣst *unreliable, incompetent*, ÆP 212¹⁵.

unrǣdfǣstlīce *unwisely, rashly*, ÆL18⁴⁵⁶.

unrǣdlic *thoughtless*, BL99²¹. adv. -līce, Æ.

unrǣdslō m. *foolish enterprise*, RD12⁴.

unrǣfniendlic *intolerable*, SPs123⁴ (on-).

unreht=unriht

unrehthǣmdere=unrihthǣmere

unreordlic v. ungereordlic

±unrētan *to make sad*, AO. [rōt]

unrētu f. *sadness, disquiet, anxiety*, AA46⁹.

unrēöe *not cruel, gentle*, ÆH2·44'.

unrīce *poor*, LL,RB.

unriht (e, y) I. n. *wrong, sin, vice, wickedness, evil*, Æ,B,Bo,Chr : *injustice, oppression*, Bo,LL; Æ : *wrong act*, Bo. II. adj. *wrong, unrighteous, wicked, false* : *unlawful*, Bo,Ps. ['unright']

unrihtcræfing f. *unjust claim*, TC.

unrihtcyst f. *vice*, LL(262').

unrihtdǣd f. *evil doing*, BH,W.

unrihtdǣde *iniquitous*, LPs9²⁴.

unrihtdēma m. *unjust judge*, W.

unrihtdōm m. *iniquity*, DA183.

unrihtdōnd m. *evildoer*, BL63¹⁵.

unrihte *unjustly, wrongly*, B,Ps. ['unright']

unrihtfēoung f. *unrighteous hate*, MET27¹.

unrihtful *unrighteous, wicked*, NC329.

unrihtgestrēon n. *unrighteous gain*, BL63⁸.

unrihtgestrod n. *ill-gotten booty*, NC330.

unrihtgewill n. *evil desire*, Bo9²³.

unrihtgewilnung (y)=unrihtwillnung

unrihtgilp m. *vainglory*, LL(262').

unrihtgītsung f. *wrongful greed*, BL,Bo.

unrihthǣman *to fornicate, commit adultery*.

unrihthǣmdere (VPs49¹⁸)=unrihthǣmere

unrihthǣmed I. n. *fornication, adultery*. II. adj. *adulterous*.

unrihthǣmedfremmere m. *adulterer*, NC 330.

unrihthǣmend m. *adulterer*, BL63.

unrihthǣmere m. *fornicator, adulterer*, Æ.

unrihthǣmeð=unrihthǣmed I.

unrihthǣmere (KGL)=unrihthǣmere

unrihtlic (e, y) *unrighteous, wrongful, wicked*, Æ. adv. -līce, MH,RB. ['unrightly']

unrihtlust m. *unlawful desire*, Bo19²⁰,VH.

unrihtlyblāc nm. *unlawful magic*, W253¹¹.

unrihtnes (e²) f. *wrong, wickedness*, BL.

unrihttīd f. *improper occasion*, MFH177.

unrihtweorc n. *secular work done on Sunday*, LL(130²⁵).

unrihtwīf n. *unlawful consort, mistress*, TC 373'.

unrihtwīfung f. *unlawful wedlock*, BH116³.

unrihtwillend (y²) m. *evil-disposed person*, CP89²².

unrihtwillnung f. *unlawful desire, lust, ambition*, CP.

unrihtwīs '*unrighteous,' wrong, unjust*, Bl, Bo,G,VPs; Æ,CP. adv. -līce, CP. ['unrighteously']

unrihtwīsnes (e, y) f. *injustice, 'unrighteousness,' iniquity*, Bf,VPs; Æ,CP.

unrihtwīsu f. *unrighteousness*, BL,Ps.

unrihtwrīgels n. *covering of error*, BL105³⁰.

unrihtwyreend m. *evildoer*, BL.

unrihtwyrhta (y) m. *evildoer*, CP.

unrīm I. n. *countless number, huge host, large quantity, mass.* II.=unrīme

unrīme *countless, innumerable*, BH.

unrīmfolc n. *countless number (of people)*, CP51¹².

unrīmgōd? n. *incalculable good*, BH94¹⁹.

unrīpe *immature, 'unripe,'* WW.

unrōt *sad, dejected*, Æ,CP : *displeased, angry.*

unrōtian *to become sad* : (±) *make sad.*

unrōtlic *sad, gloomy*, MtL. adv. -līce, MtR 16³.

unrōtmōd *sad-hearted*, BL113¹².

unrōtnes f. *sadness, contrition, disquietude*, Æ,CP.

±unrōtsian *to be or become sad, be grieved*, Æ : *make sad.*

unrūh *smooth, without seams*, JnLR19²³.

unryht (AO,CP)=unriht

unrȳne m. *diarrhœa*, LCD1·172¹².

unsac *not accused, innocent*, LCD3·288⁶.

unsadelod *not saddled*, LL.

unsǣd *unsated, insatiable*, PPs100⁵.

unsǣd I. n. *evil seed*, W40²³. II. *not said*, ÆH. ['unsaid']

unsǣht=unseht

unsǣl m. *unhappiness*, W236²⁶. ['unsele']

unsǣlan *to untie, unfasten*, WW.

unsǣle *wicked*, WW421²³. ['unsele']

unsǣlig *unfortunate, unhappy, wretched*, Jul,W : *mischievous, pernicious*, Gen637 : *wicked, An.* ['unseely']

unsǣlð f. *unhappiness, misfortune, adversity, misery*, Bo,Ps; CP. ['unselth']

unsǣpig *sapless*, ÆH1·102⁴.

unsalt=unsealt

unsamwrǣde *contrary, incongruous*, Bo 106⁶.

unsār *painless*, AO,CP.

unsāwen *unsown*, LL450,10.

unscæðed=ungesceðed

unscæðful (e, ea) *innocent*. adv. -līce, CP.

unscæðfulnes (ea, e) f. *innocence*, CP.

unscæðð-ednes, -ignes (e) f. *harmlessness, innocence*, Æ.

unscæðð-ende (e²), -ig *innocent, harmless*, Æ,BH.

unscamfæst *impudent, shameless*, GL.
unscamfulnes (eo²) f. *shamelessness, immodesty*, MkL7²⁰.
unscamig *unashamed*, JUL552.
unscamlic *shameless, immodest*, Æ. adv. -līce.
unscað-=unscæð(ð)-
un-scēad(e)līce *unreasonably*, RB54¹³.
unscēadwīslic *unreasonable*, ÆH2·210'.
unsceaft f. *monster?* RD88³².
unsceam-=unscam-
unsceapen *uncreated, unformed*, ByH72²⁰, RHy54¹³.
unscearp *not sharp (of wine)*, LCD.
unscearpnes f. *dulness*, BH402²⁹.
unscearpsȳne *not sharp-sighted*, LCD11b.
unsceað-=unscæð-
unscelleht (=ie) *not having a shell*, LCD33b.
unscellīce *without discrimination, recklessly?* RWH141³ (v. scelle).
unscende (y)† *blameless, glorious*.
un-scende, scendende *uninjured, uncorrupted*.
unscennan *to unharness*, WW91¹³.
unscēod=unscōd pp. of unscōgan.
unscēogan=unscōgan
unsceom- (NG)=unscam-
unscēotan (WW190³⁰)=onscēotan
unsceð-=unscæð-; unscildig=unscyldig
unscirped *unclothed*, MtL22¹¹.
unscōgan (ēo) *to unshoe*. pp. unscōd *'unshod,'* Æ,CP.
unscom-=unscam-
unscoren *unshorn*, CM,WW.
unscortende *not failing*, LkLR12³³.
unscrȳdan (ē², ī²) *to put off (clothes), undress, uncover, strip, deprive of*, Æ. unscrȳdd pp. *naked*. [scrūd]
unscyld f. *innocency*, SPs40¹³.
unscyldgung f. *innocence*, ERPs17²⁵.
unscyldig (i) *guiltless, innocent*, Æ,CP : *not responsible*.
unscyldiglic *excusable*, BL189³². adv. -līce *innocently*, BK12.
unscyldignes f. *innocence*, Ps.
unscynde=unscende
unscȳrdan=unscrȳdan
unscyttan *to undo, unbolt*, ÆL31⁸⁶³.
unscyðende=unscæððende
unseald *ungiven*, HL10⁴⁹⁵.
unsealt (a, y) *unsalted, insipid*, G,WW.
unsēfernes=unsȳfernes
unsefful *senseless*, RHy6³¹. [sefa]
unsegenlic (ByH6,8)=unsewenlic
unseglian *to unseal*, RWH78³³.
unseht I. mfn. *discord, disagreement, quarrel.* II. adj. *not agreed, hostile*, Chr. ['unsaught']
unsehtnes f. *discord, quarrel*, NC330. ['unsaughtness']

un-seldan, -seldon (Æ) *not seldom, repeatedly, frequently*, LL. ['unselde']
unsēofene *not sighing*, MFH177.
unsewenlic *invisible*, Bo138².
unsibb f. *dissension, contention, war, strife*. AO.
unsibbian *to disagree*, WW.
unsibsumnes f. *anxiety*, JnL p6¹.
unsideful *immodest, unchaste*, WW.
unsidefulnes f. *immodesty*, OEH300'.
unsidelīce *immodestly, indecorously*, CHRD 60³⁴.
unsidu m. *bad custom, vice, impurity, unseemliness.* [*Ger.* unsitte]
unsif-=unsȳf-
unsigefæst *not victorious*, ÆL18⁴⁴.
unsingian=unsyngian
unsīð m. *unfortunate journey or expedition, misfortune, mishap*, Æ.
unslǣpig *sleepless*, WW427¹⁵.
unslāw (ǣ, ēa) *not slow, active*, Æ,W. ['unslow'] adv. -līce, CP381¹.
unsleac *not remiss, active, diligent*, WW. adv. -līce, RB20¹⁸.
unslēaw=unslāw
unslid? unslit (Cp33s) n. *fat, grease, tallow.* [*Ger.* unschlitt; or ?=unsylt]
unslitten *untorn*, JnL19²³.
unslȳped *open, loosed*, W83⁹.
unsmǣðe=unsmēðe
unsmeoruwig *notgreasy*, LCD106b (smerig).
unsmēðe *not smooth, uneven, rough, scabby.*
unsmēðnes f. *roughness*, WW.
unsmōð=unsmēðe
unsnotor (e³) *unwise*, ÆGR. adv. -līce.
unsnotornes (y², e³) f. *folly : wickedness*, LPs.
unsnott-=unsnot-
unsnyttru† f. *folly, ignorance.*
unsnyttrum† adv. *foolishly.*
unsoden *uncooked*, Lcd. ['unsodden']
unsōfte *harshly, bitterly, severely, violently*, Gu,Lcd; Æ : *with difficulty, hardly, scarcely : uncomfortably.* ['unsoft']
unsōftlīce *harshly*, ÆH1·434⁷.
unsōm f. *disagreement*, LL.
unsorh *free from care*, BL217²⁹.
unsōð I. adj. *untrue, false.* II. n. *falsehood.*
unsōðfæst *untruthful : unjust, unrighteous.*
unsōðfæstnes f. *injustice, unrighteousness.*
+unsōðian *to falsify, disprove*, LL202,320.
unsōðsag-ol, -ul *untruthful*, Æ.
unspannan⁷ *to unfasten*, WW231³⁵.
unspecende=unsprecende
unspēd f. *want, poverty*, LG,Ps. ['unspeed']
unspēdig *poor*, Æ,AO : *not fertile*, GEN 962.

unspiwol *that stops vomiting?* LCD.

unspornend=onspornend

unsprecende *not able to speak*, Æ.

unstæfwis *illiterate*, GPH393.

unstæðöïg *unstable, irregular, weak, fritol ous, wanton*, Æ.

unstæðöïgnes f. *instability, inconstancy, wantonness*, Æ.

unstaðolfæst *unstable, unenduring, weak, fickle*, Æ.

unstaðolfæstnes f. *instability, weakness, fickleness*, Æ.

unstenc m. *stench, stink*, DD,W.

+unstill-an, -ian *to disturb, agitate*, RB.

unstille *moving, changeable, restless, inquiet, uneasy*, CP.

unstil(l)nes f. *agitation, restlessness, disturbance, disquiet, trouble, disorder, tumult*, Æ,AO.

unstrang *weak, infirm, feeble, MH,RB*; Æ. ['*unstrong*']

unstrenge *weak*, ÆH 2·390'.

unstydful *inconstant, apostate*, DR 121[10]. [=unstede-]

unstydfulnes (on-) f. *instability*, DR.

unstyrendlic *immovable, hard to carry*, MtL 23[4].

unstyriende *immovable, stationary*, Bo.

unswǣs *unpleasant, disagreeable, uncongenial*. adv. -swǣse.

unswǣslic *ungentle, cruel*, JUD 65. [swǣs]

unswefn n. *bad dream*, LCD 3·288'.

unsweotol *imperceptible, indistinct*, Bo, MET.

unswēte *not sweet : foul*, GD,Lcd. ['*unsweet*']

unswicen *unbetrayed, unharmed, safe*, CHR 1048.

un-swicende, -swiciende *true, faithful*, CHR.

unswicol *trustworthy, true*, GL,W.

unswīð *not strong*, LCD. adv. -swīðe *sluggishly*, OEG 56[83].

unsydeful=unsideful

unsyferlic *impure*, BL43[17].

unsyfernes f. *impurity, foulness*, BH.

unsyfre (ī) I. adj. *impure, unclean, filthy.* II. adv. *filthily*, CR1484?

unsylt=unsealt

unsyngian *to exculpate*, LL98,21[1].

unsynnig *guiltless, innocent*, Æ : *undeserved*.

unsynnum adv. *guiltlessly*, B1072.

untǣle *blameless, faultless*, Æ.

untǣled *unblamed*, CP351[20].

untǣllic (ā) *blameless, immaculate, undefiled, praiseworthy*. adv. -līce, Æ,CP.

untǣl-wierðe (y³) *blameless*, CP. adv. -wierðlice.

untæslic=unðæslic; untāl-=untǣl-

untala (NG)=untela

untamcul *untameable*, GPH397.

unteala=untela

unteald *uncounted*, LCD 3·264[11].

untealt *stable, steady*, CHR 897D.

untela adv. *not well, amiss, badly, ill, improperly, wrongly*, CP.

untellendlic *indescribable* (Swt).

untemed *untamed, CPs,WW*. ['*untemed*']

untēmende=untȳmende

untēnan (KGL)=ontȳnan

untēogoðad *untithed*, CP439[29].

unteola=untela

untēorig *untiring, unceasing*, MET 28[17].

untīdǣt *untimely eating*, NC330.

untīdfyl f. *untimely eating or drinking*, W46[14].

untīdgewidere n. *unseasonable weather*, CHR 1095.

untīdlic *unseasonable*, AO. adv. -līce.

untīdspǣc f. *untimely speech*, LL(322⁹).

untīdweorc n. *work at an improper time (e.g. on Sunday)*, W.

untīena (AO)=ontēona

untīgan *to 'untie,' loosen, unchain, G*; Æ. [tēag]

untilad *destitute*, Bo 16[12].

untīma m. *unseasonableness, wrong time*, Æ,CP : *bad time, misfortune*, W297⁷. ['*untime*']

untimber *worthless material?* (BTs), MFH 176 (or ?=on-t.).

untīme *ill-timed, unfortunate*, Æ. ['*untime*']

untīmnes f. *evil times*, W207[18].

untīnan=ontȳnan

untōbrocen *unbroken*, Æ.

untōclofen *uncloven*, ÆL25[45].

untōdǣled *undivided, individual, indivisible, inseparable*, BF,Bo.

untōdǣl(ed)lic *inseparable, indivisible*, Æ. adv. -līce.

untōdǣl(ed)nes f. *undividedness*, BF118[1].

untō-dǣl(end)-, dāl-, -dēlen-=untōdǣled-

untogen *untied, loose*, GD222[3].

untōlǣtendlic *incessantly*, GD117[23].

untō-lēsende, -lȳsende *that cannot be loosed, inextricable*, WW.

untōlȳsendlic *unforgivable*, GD342[26].

untōsceacen *unshaken*, TC.

untōslegen *unshattered*, AS22[23].

untōsliten *untorn, uninjured*, CP.

untōsprecendlic *ineffable*, TC.

untōwǣmed *undivided*, ÆH.

untōworpenlic (e², a⁴) *inviolable*, OEG11[163].

untrāglīce *frankly*, EL410.

untrēow=untrēowð

untrēowe (ī, ȳ) '*untrue,*' *unfaithful*, LL.

untrēowfǣst (ī, ȳ) *unfaithful, unreliable*, GPH,NIC475[28].

untrēowlīce *faithlessly*, AO. ['*untruly*']
untrēownes f. *unfaithfulness*, GD 160⁵.
untrēowsian *to defraud, deceive*, CP : *offend*, G.
untrēowŏ f. *unfaithfulness, treachery*, AO.
untrum *infirm, weakly, sick, ill*, BH,Bl, VPs; Æ,CP. ['*untrum*']
untrumhād m. *infirm state*, BH 78²⁸.
untrumian *to be or become sick or infirm* : *make weak*, Æ.
untrumlic *infirm, weak*, NUM 13²⁰.
untrumnes f. *weakness, sickliness, infirmity, illness*, Chr,CP,Mt; Æ,AO.
untrymed *unconfirmed (by a bishop)*, LL (140¹⁹).
un-trymig, -trymmig *sick, infirm*, NG.
untrymigan *to become weak*, JnL 6².
untrymmigo f. *illness*, MtL 10¹.
untrymnes=untrumnes
untrymŏ f. *weakness, illness*, LL,PPs.
untrȳw-=untrēow-
untwēgendlīce=untwēogendlīce
untwēo m. *certainty*, CR 961.
untwēod *undoubting*, AN 1244.
untweofeald=untwiefeald
untwēogende *unhesitating, not doubting*, CP.
untwēogendlīc *indubitable, certain*. adv. -līce *indubitably, unhesitatingly, undoubtingly*, AO,CP.
untwēolic (ī) *undoubted*, OEG. adv. -līce *certainly, with certainty*, Æ.
untwēonde=untwēogende
untwēon(d)līce=untwēogendlīce
untwēonigend (ȳ) *undoubting*, A 9·115⁴⁵.
untwī-, untwȳ-=untwēo-, untwīe-
untwīe-feald, -feld *not double*, CP : *not double-minded, without duplicity, sincere*, CP.
untȳd *unskilful, inexperienced*, CP.
untyddre=untȳdre; untȳdlic=untīdlic
untȳdre I. *firm, unbending*, AN 1254. II. m. *monster*, B 111.
untȳdrende *barren*, LCD 33b.
untȳgian=untīgan
untygŏa *unsuccessful (in getting one's wish)*, CP 257¹⁸.
untȳmende *barren, unfruitful*, Æ. [tīeman]
untȳnan=ontȳnan
untȳned *unfenced*, LL 106,40.
unŏærfe in phr. 'unŏærfe ŏing' '*nequaquam*,' MtL 2⁶. [unŏearf]
unŏæslic *inappropriate, unseemly, unbecoming, absurd*, Æ.
unŏæslicnes f. *impropriety*, ÆH 2·316⁸.
unŏæslicu f. *incongruity*, RB 124¹³.
unŏanc m. *ingratitude, disinclination, displeasure*, AO,Sol; Æ,CP : *evil intention, an ill turn*, ApT,Chr,CP; Æ. unŏances

unwillingly, compulsorily, AO, Chr,LL. ['*unthank*']
unŏancful *unthankful*, CP,GD.
unŏanc-ol, -ul *ungrateful*, NC 330.
unŏanc-wurŏe, -wyrŏe *ungrateful* : *not acceptable, disagreeable*, Æ.
unŏancwyrŏlīce *ungratefully*, NC 330.
unŏearf f. *damage, hurt, detriment, ruin*, Æ.
unŏearfes *without a cause*, PPs 13⁶.
unŏēaw m. *vice, sin, fault*, CP; Æ. ['*unthew*']
unŏēawfæst *disorderly, ill-mannered, dissolute*, Æ. adv. -līce.
unŏēawful *uncontrolled, disorderly*, WW.
unŏinged *unexpected, sudden*, CP.
unŏingod *unatoned for*, CP 423³⁵.
unŏolemōdnes f. *impatience*, A. ['*untholemoodness*']
unŏoligendlic *intolerable*, Sc 208¹⁴.
unŏorfæst *unprofitable*, DR 179¹⁷.
un-ŏrīste, -ŏrīeste *diffident*, CP.
unŏrōwendlicnes f. *impassibility*, ZDA 31·14.
unŏrōwigendlic *unsuffering*, Æ.
unŏurhscēotendlic *impenetrable*, LCD.
unŏurhtogen *unperformed*, CP 329¹⁴.
unŏwægen=unŏwogen
unŏwǣre=ungeŏwǣre
+unŏwǣrian *to disagree*, Æ,CP.
unŏwǣrnes f. (ē) *discord, division*, CHR.
un-ŏwean, -ŏwagen, -ŏwægen, -ŏwegen, -ŏwēn=unŏwogen
unŏwērnes=unŏwǣrnes
unŏwogen *unwashed*, G.
unŏyhtig *weak*, OET 107.
unŏyldig=ungeŏyldig
unŏyldlicnes f. *difficulty*, BH 2·340.
unwāclic† *steadfast, strong, noble, splendid*. adv. -līce.
unwǣded (ē) *not clothed*, MtL 22¹¹.
unwǣder=unweder
unwǣlgrim *gentle, merciful*, GD 133⁶.
unwǣm-=unwem-
unwǣr (-war- in obl. cases) *incautious, careless, unthinking, foolish*, Æ,Bl,CP : *unaware, unexpected*. on un-wǣr, -waran, -warum *unawares, unexpectedly*, Chr. ['*unware*']
unwǣres (o¹, a²) *unawares, suddenly*, Chr. ['*unwares*']
unwǣrlic *unwary, heedless*, CP. adv. -līce, AO,Bl,Chr; CP. ['*unwarely*']
unwǣrnes f. *heedlessness*, W 299⁷.
unwǣrscipe m. *folly*, ÆH 1·68⁴.
unwǣscen '*unwashen*,' Lcd 41b.
unwǣstm mfn. *barrenness*, W : *tare, weed*, NG.
unwǣstmbǣre *unfruitful, barren*, Æ,CP.

unwæstm-bærnes (Æ,AO), -berendnes (Æ) f. *unfruitfulness, barrenness, sterility.*
unwæstmberendlic *sterile*, WE 54⁹.
unwæstmfæst *barren*, BL 163⁶.
unwæstmfæstnes f. *barrenness*, BL 163¹⁷.
unwæterig *dry, desert, Lk.* ['*unwatery*']
unwandiende *unhesitating*, CP 381²⁵.
unwar- v. unwær.
unwarnod '*unwarned*,' LL 382³³.
unwealden *involuntary*, VH 23.
unwealt *steady, stable*, CHR 897.
unwearnum† adv. *irresistibly : suddenly, in a moment.*
unwearð=unweorð
unweaxen† *not grown up, young.*
unwēded=unwæded
unweder n. *unfavourable season, bad weather, storm, Chrd, LG; Æ.* ['*unweather*']
unwederlīce adv. *tempestuously*, Mt 16³.
unweg=onweg
unwegen *not weighed*, LCD 1·376⁷.
unwemlic *unsullied, pure*, WW 522³⁵.
un-wemme(d) *unblemished, unstained, uninjured, Æ,DR,Ps : inviolate.* ['*unwemmed*']
unwemmend m. *innocent man*, REPs 36¹⁸ (on-).
unwemming f. *incorruptibility, incorruption*, Sc 41¹⁰.
unwemmu (æ²) f. *spotlessness*, RWH 136³⁵.
unwemnes f. *purity*, HL 18⁴²².
unwended=unāwended
+**unwendnes**=onwendnes
unwēne *unexpected : hopeless, Æ.*
unwēned *unexpected, unhoped for*, AA,Sc.
unwēnlic adj. *unpromising, hopeless, desperate*, AO,CP. adv. -līce *unexpectedly, by chance*, GD 88¹⁷.
unwēnunga *unexpectedly*, Bo 140¹⁰.
unwēod n. *ill weed*, W 92¹⁹.
unweoder=unweder
unweorcheard *delicate, weakly, infirm*, RB 75⁸.
unweorclic (o) *unsuitable for work*, BF 122²⁴.
un-weorð (u, y), -wierðe (u) adj. adv. *unworthy, Æ : poor, mean, of low estate, AO, Chrd,RB : worthless : contemptible, ignoble, Bo.* ['*unworth*']
±**unweorðian** (o, u) *to slight, treat with contempt, dishonour, Æ,LG; CP : become worthless, vile, dishonour oneself.* ['*unworth*']
unweorðlic (u) *unworthy, dishonourable, AO : unimportant, humble, CP.* adv. -līce *unworthily, dishonourably, ignominiously, AO,CP : indignantly.*
unweorðnes f. *slight, contempt, disgrace*, AO,CP.

unweorðscipe m. *dishonour, disgrace, Bo : indignation*, CP 222⁹. ['*unworship*']
unweorðung (u) f. *disgrace : indignation*, CP 222¹² : *dishonouring*, CHRD 40.
unweotod=unwitod
unwer (KGL)=unwær
unwered *unprotected*, GEN 812.
unwērig *unwearying, indefatigable, persistent, AO, Lcd; Æ.* ['*unweary*']
unwerlīce=unwærlīce
unwerod *not sweet*, CP 447¹⁹.
unwestm=unwæstm; **unweðer**=unweder
unwīd *not wide*, NC 330.
unwidere n. *bad weather*, W.
unwidlod *unpolluted*, DR 90¹⁷.
unwierðe=unweorð
unwīese=unwīse, unwīslīce
unwilla m. *repugnance, displeasure, Æ,AO, LL,Sol,WW.* ['*unwill*']
unwillan=unwillum
unwillende '*unwilling*,' *involuntary, CP : averse (to), HL.*
unwilles adv. *unwillingly, involuntarily, reluctantly, Æ.*
unwillum adv. *unwillingly, reluctantly.* his unwillum *against his will*, AO : *involuntarily, unintentionally.*
unwilsumlīce adv. *involuntarily, against one's will*, BH 442²³.
unwindan³ (=on-) *to unwind, uncover, Æ.*
unwine m. *foe, enemy*, CHR,Ct.
unwinsum=unwynsum
unwīs '*unwise*,' *foolish, ignorant, uninformed, Bl,VPs; CP : insane*, GD.
unwīsdōm m. '*unwisdom*,' *imprudence, folly, ignorance, CP,VPs.*
unwīse=unwīslīce
unwīslic *foolish.* adv. -līce, CP,Lcd; Æ. ['*unwisely*']
unwīsnes f. *ignorance : wickedness*, DR.
unwita m. *witless person, ignoramus*, LL.
unwitende '*unwitting*,' *ignorant, AO.*
unwītnigendlice *without punishment, with impunity*, ÆGR 233⁶.
unwītnod *unpunished*, CP.
unwītnung f. *impunity*, Sc 235⁵.
unwitod (io, u) *uncertain*, DR,GNE.
unwittig *unconscious, ignorant, stupid, Æ.* ['*unwitty*']
unwittignes f. *folly*, GD 163³⁴.
unwittol *ignorant*, Sc 80¹².
unwitweorc n. *evil work*, BL 111². [?inwit-]
unwiðerweard *friendly*, CP 361²⁰.
unwiðerweardlic *not discordant*, NC 330.
unwiðmetenes f. *incomparability*, OEG 587.
unwiðmetenlic *not comparable, incomparable, Æ.* adv. -līce.
unwlite m. *dishonour*, WW.
unwliteg=unwlitig

±**unwlitegian** *to become disfigured*, CP : *disfigure, transform*, CP.
unwlitegung f. *disfigurement*, WW391[5].
unwlitig *unsightly, deformed, disfigured, ill-favoured*, Æ.
unwlitignes f. *disfigurement*, BH384[4].
unworclic=unweorclic
unword n. *abuse, slander*, AB34·10.
unworht v. ungeworht.
unworðian=unweorðian
unwrænc=unwrenc
unwrǣne *not lustful*, LCD.
unwrǣst(e) (ē) *feeble, weakly, evil*, AO, Chr : *unsteady, untrustworthy*, Chr. ['unwrast']
unwrǣstlīce adv. *incongruously, inaccurately*, BF186[25]. ['unwrastly']
unwrecen *unpunished, unavenged*, B,Bo.
unwrenc (æ) m. *vice, evil design*, CP,W. ['unwrench']
unwrēon[1],[2] *to uncover, reveal*, Æ,Bf,G,VPs. ['unwry']
unwrēst=unwrǣst
unwrig-ednes, -ennes f. *uncovering, revelation*, RBL42[16].
unwrigen *open, unconcealed*, MFH101[7] (pp. of unwrēon).
unwriten *unwritten*, Bo.
unwrītere m. *incorrect copyist*, ÆGR3[24](=ÆT80[120]).
unwrīðan *to untwist, unbind*, CP.
unwunden I. *not wound*, WW187[30]. II. pp. of unwindan.
unwundod '*unwounded*,' Gen183.
unwuniendlic *uninhabitable*, LCD3·262[2].
unwurð=unweorð; **unwuted**=unwitod
unwynsum *unpleasant*, Æ.
unwynsumnes f. *unpleasantness*, Æ.
unwyrcan *to undo, destroy*, A11·113.
unwyrd f. *misfortune, trouble*, Bo,LCD.
unwyrht f. *ill-doing*, Bo123[32].
unwyrtrumian *to root out*, MtL13[29].
unwyrð-=unweorð-; **unwyrðe**=unwierðe
unymb-fangen, -fangenlic *incomprehensible*, GD.
unymbwendedlic *unalterable*, DR164[16].
unymbwriten *not circumscribed*, GD268[24].
unyð-=unēað-
unyðgian *to trouble*, EPs34[15].
ūp adv. '*UP*,' Æ,CP : *up stream, up country (inland)*, AO,Chr : *upwards*. lǣtan ūp *to put ashore*. ūp forlǣtan *divide*.
ūpāblāwan[7] *to blow up, be in eruption (of a volcano)*, ÆL8[222].
ūpābrecan[4] *to break out or through, boil up*, Æ.
ūp-ābregdan, -ābrēdan[3] *to lift up, raise up, exalt*, Æ,CP : *expand*, BF70[11].
ūpāfangnes f. *reception, assumption*, A5·464.

ūpāhæf-=ūpāhaf-
ūpāhafenlīce (æ) adv. *arrogantly*, OEG667.
ūpāhafennes f. *exultation, presumption, arrogance, pride*, CP : *uplifting, elevation*, Æ.
ūpāhafu *lifting up*, CHRD30[21].
ūpāhebban[6] *to lift up, raise up, exalt*, Æ,CP : *rise in the air, fly*.
ūp-āhefednes (Æ), -āhefennes=ūpāhafennes
ūpāhōn[7] *to hang up*, Æ.
ūpāmȳlan? *to come to light, appear*, HGL463 (v. OEG4784).
ūpārǣran *to raise up, lift up, exalt*, AO,CP : *excite : introduce*, BF122[16].
ūpāreccan *to erect, raise, build*, VPs.
ūpārīsan[1] *to rise up*, CP.
ūpārisnes f. *resurrection*, EHy14[6].
ūpāspringan[3] *to spring up, arise*, BF84[11].
ūpāspringnes (u[3]) f. *uprising*, BF,LPs102[12].
ūpāspryttan *to sprout forth, germinate*, BF58[1].
ūpāstīgan[1] *to rise, ascend*, Æ,CP.
ūpā-stīgen(nes), -stīgnes f. *ascent, ascension, means of going up*.
Ūpāstīgnestīd f. *Ascension-tide*, VH23.
ūpāstreccan *to uplift*, CM38.
ūpātēon[2],[1] *to draw up, bring up, rear : draw out, pull out, pluck up : lift up, place in an upright position*, Æ.
ūpāðenian *to elevate, lift up*, CP.
ūp-āweallan, -āwallan[7] *to well up, steam up, boil up*, Æ.
ūpāwegan[5] *to lift up, support*, Æ.
ūpāwendan *to turn upwards, raise*, Æ. pp. ūpāwend *supine*, ÆGR.
ūpbrēdan[3] *to reproach with, upbraid*, W248[9].
ūpcuman[4] *to come up, arise*.
ūpcund *from above, heavenly*, CP.
ūpcyme m. *rising, origin, source*, DA,VPs.
ūpeard m. *land above, heaven*, GU1051.
ūpende m. *upper end*, Bo,KC.
ūpengel† m. *heavenly angel*.
ūpēode pret. 3 sg. of ūpgān.
ūpfǣreld n? *ascension*, ÆH1·444[1].
ūpfeax *bald in front*, WW276[32].
ūpfēgan *to erect*, CP.
ūpfēran *to go forth, spring forth*, GPH401.
ūpferian *to carry up, to raise*, Sc130[7].
ūp-flēogan (Æ), -flēon[2] *to fly up*.
ūpflēring f. *upper floor (of house)*, Æ.
ūpflōr fm., ūpflōre f. *upper chamber or story, garret*, Æ.
ūpflugon pret. pl. of ūpflēogan.
ūpgān anv. *to go up : make to go up, raise : rise (of sun)*, GUTH148[41].
ūpgang m. *rising, sunrise*, Æ : *going up, approach, ascent : landing, going inland*.

úpganga m. *landing,* MA 87.
úpgebrēdan (W 249³)=úpbrēdan
úpgemynd n. *contemplation of things above,* AN 1066.
úpgēotan² *to well up,* GUTH 131¹⁹⁹.
úpgodu np. *the gods above, heathen gods,* WW 497²⁵.
úpgong=úpgang
úphafenes=úpāhafennes
úphēafod n. *upper end,* KC 6·79¹⁰.
úphēah *uplifted, tall, high, elevated : sublime, noble, upright.*
úpheald n. *support,* KC 4·232⁵. ['uphold']
úphebban (JRsVPs)=úpāhebban
úphebbe f. *water-hen, coot,* PPs 103¹⁷.
úphebbing f. *uprising,* LkL 8⁸.
úp-hefenes (VPs), -hefnes=úpāhafennes
úpheofon m. *heaven above, sky,* BH,W.
úphladan⁶ *to draw up,* HGL 418.
úphūs n. *upper room,* WW 384³.
úpland n. *country (as opposed to town),* CHR 1087.
úplang (o²) *upright, erect : tall,* AA 33⁴.
úplegen f. *hair-pin,* WW 223¹⁶.
úplendisc *from the uplands, rural, rustic, from beyond the town,* Æ. [úpland]
úplic *upper, supreme, lofty, sublime, heavenly, celestial,* Æ,CP.
úplyft fnm. *upper air, ether, sky,* BTK 196,198.
úpnes f. *height,* LPs 103³.
úpniman⁴ *to raise up,* EHy 3⁸.
upon=uppan; upp=úp
uppan (o³) prep. (w. d. and a.) *on, upon, up to, against,* Æ,Chr,G,RB : (time) *on, after,* Chr,G : *in addition to.* wið u. *above.* on u. *against.*
+uppan=+yppan
uppe I. adv. *above, aloft, up, inland,* CP. u. on *upon.* II.=yppe
uppe-=úp-
uppian *to rise up, swell,* CP 277⁷.
uppl-=úpl-
uppon=uppan
úprador=úprodor
úprǣcan *to reach up,* BL 223¹⁰.
úpriht *upright, erect,* Æ : *face upwards,* OEG 2157. adv. -rihte *straight up,* KC.
úprine=úpryne
úprocettan *to belch up,* EPs 118¹⁷¹.
úp-roder, -rodor† m. *upper heavens, ether, firmament,* EX.
úpryne m. *ascent, rising (of sun),* BH,Bo.
úpsittan⁵ *'residere,'* ÆGR.
úpspring (u²) m. *rising up, origin, birth,* Æ : *what springs up.*
úpsprungennes f. *eclipse,* BH 240²⁰B.
úpstandende *'upstanding,' erect,* Lcd,WW 154.

úpstīgan¹ *to move up, rise, ascend,* Cr,Jn 1⁶¹. ['upsty']
úpstīge m. *ascent, ascension,* Æ : *staircase,* GD 170²⁴.
úpstīgend m. *one who mounts up, rider,* DR; CHy 4¹.
úptēon² *to draw up,* AA 24¹³.
úpðyddan *to swell up,* GUTH 131¹⁹⁷.
úpwæg=úpweg
úpwæstm m. *stature,* STC 68¹⁸.
úpware mp. *inhabitants of heaven,* WW 355²⁹.
úpweallan⁷ *to boil up,* AO.
úpweard, úpweardes adv. *up, 'upward(s),'* Æ : *towards heaven : backwards (in time),* Bf 156¹⁶.
úpweg† m. *ascent, ascension.*
úpyrnan³ (eo;=ie) *to run up, grow, increase : rise.*
úpyrne=úpryne
úr m. *bison, aurochs : name of the rune for* u. [*Ger.* auer]
úre I. possess. pron. 'OUR,' *ours,* Æ,AO, CP. II. gp. of ic.
úrelendisc *of our country,* ÆGR 93¹⁷.
úrigfeðere† *dewy-winged.*
úriglāst *leaving a damp track,* WY 29.
úrne asm. of úre I.
urnen pp., urnon pret. pl. of iernan.
úron=úrum dsmn. and dp. of úre I.
ús dap. of pers. pron. ic 'US.'
úser I. poss. pron. gen. ússes *our.* II. gp. of ic.
úsic, úsig, úsih=ús; ússe=úre; ússer= úser
ússes v. úser; ússic=úsic, ús
ússpīung f. *expectoration,* WW 113⁹. [út, spīwung]
ússum dsn. of úser.
út adv. *'out,'* AO,BH,Bo,G,Lcd : *without, outside.*
úta- (N)=útan-
útāberstan³ *to burst out, burst forth,* CP.
útābrecan⁴ *to break out,* Æ.
útācnyssan *to drive out,* ERPs 35¹³.
útacumen=útancumen
útacund *extraneous, external, foreign,* NG.
útacunda m. *stranger,* LkL 17¹⁸.
útacymen=útancymen
útādelfan³ *to dig out,* ÆGR.
útādōn anv. *to do out, put out,* Æ.
útādrǣfan *to drive out, expel, destroy,* Æ.
útādrīfan¹ *to drive out, disperse, dispel,* LL.
útæðmian (ē) *to breathe out,* MFH 122⁸.
útāfaran⁶ *to come forth, go out, depart,* CP.
útāflōwan=útflōwan
útālǣdan *to lead out,* LL,VPs : *produce : release,* VH.
útālēoran *to cause to depart, flee away,* CVPs 51⁷.

ûtāmǣr-an, -ian *to drive out, expel, de-populate,* BH.

utan=wuton

ûtan adv. *from outside, An,Chr* : *on the outside, without, Bo,Gen.* ūtan *landes abroad, PPs*64⁸. ['*outen*']

ûtanbordes adv. *from abroad,* CP3¹¹.

ûtan-cumen, -cymen I. *foreign, strange, AO, W* ; Æ : *belonging to another.* ['*outcome*'] II. m. *stranger, foreigner.*

ûtane adv. *from without, outwards, outside, externally,* CP : *abroad,* AO164¹⁴.

ûtanlandes v. ūtan.

ûtanweard *external, outside, WW.* ['*outward*']

ûtānȳdan *to drive out, expel,* RPs43³.

ûtanymbstandnes (o⁴) f. *surrounding,* JPs 140³.

ûtascēotan² *to sprout forth, burst forth,* CP : *to pierce out,* AO.

ûtāsellan *to grant outright,* KC6·154'.

ûtāslēan⁶ *to strike outwards, break out,* CP.

ûtāslīdan¹ *to slip forwards, fall (into),* GPH 388.

ûtāspīwan⁴ *to spew forth,* CP447¹⁷,¹⁹.

ûtātēon²,¹ *to draw out,* Æ.

ûtātȳnan *to exclude,* VPs.

ûtāðȳdan *to thrust out, cast out,* Æ.

ûtaweard (NG)=ūtanweard

ûtāwindan³ *to slip forwards, fall (into),* GPH388.

ûtberstan=ūtāberstan

ûtcumen=ūtancumen

ûtcwealm (a, æ) m. *utter destruction, extirpation,* Cp461ı.

ûtcȳðan *to promulgate, announce,* A4·166.

ûtdrǣf f. *decree of expulsion,* ÆL21⁸⁵.

ûtdrǣfere m. *driver out,* WW172⁴⁶.

ûtdragan⁶ *to remove,* LL454,9.

ûtdrīfan¹ *to drive out or away, expel, scatter, disperse.*

ûte adv. *out, without, outside, abroad,* BH, *Chr,LL,Mt* ; Æ : *out.* ['*oute*']

ûtemest=ȳtemest

ûten, ūtene=ūtan, ūtane

ûtera, ūterra adj. (ȳ) (comp.) *outer, exterior, external,* BH,LL,Ps,Sc ; AO,CP. superl. ȳtemest *uttermost, utmost, extreme, last.*

ûterlic (o²)*external,* MFB102:*material,*125.

ûtermere m. *outer sea, open sea,* CHR897A.

ûteweard adj. *external, 'outward,' outside, extreme, last, Chr.* as sb. *outward part, exterior, LG.* on ūteweardan *on the outside, outwardly.*

ûteweardum *outwards, Chr*893. ['*outward*']

ûtfær n. *going out, exit, departure,* Æ.

ûtfæreld n. *exodus, going out,* Æ,AO.

ûtfangeneðēof *right of judging thieves caught outside one's jurisdiction, and of taking fines for the crime, Ct.* [v. '*outfangthief*']

ûtfaru f. *going out,* Æ,RB. ['*outfare*']

ûtflōwan⁷ *to flow out,* Æ,CP : *scatter, be dispersed,* EHy5⁶.

ûtfōr f. *evacuation (from body),* LCD6a.

ûtforlǣtan *to cast out,* Æ,AO,CP.

ûtfūs *ready to start,* B33.

ûtgān anv. *to go out,* CP.

ût-gānde, -gangende *outgoing,* CD.

ûtgang (eo, o) m. *going out, departure, exit, exodus : latter part,Guth,MtL,VPs : privy : dejecta, excrement,* LCD : '*anus.*' ['*outgang*']

ûtgangan⁷=ūtgān

ûtgārsecg m. *remotest sea,* CREAT70.

ûtgefeoht n. *external war,* BH47² (Schipper).

ûtgegān=ūtgān ; **ûtgelǣdan**=ūtlǣdan

ûtgemǣre n. *extreme or remotest limit,* PPs.

ûtgenga m. *exit,* MtR22⁹.

ûtgēð (KGL) pres. 3 sg. of ūtgān.

ûtgong=ūtgang

ûthealf f. *outer side,* WW153⁴⁵.

ûthere m. *foreign army,* CHR.

ûthlēap n. *fine for a man escaping from his lord,* TC.

±**ûtian** *to put out, expel,* LL : *alienate (property).* ['*out*']

ûtirning (io) f. *flux,* MkL5²⁵.

ûtlād f. *right of passage outwards by water,* EC344 : *assembling (of material)?* AS2⁷.

ûtlǣdan *to lead out, bring out,* LL54,8¹.

ûtlǣdnes (ē) f. '*abductio,*' EHy6³⁶.

ûtlǣnda=ūtlenda ; **ûtlǣndisc**=ūtlendisc

ûtlǣs f. *out-pastures,* KC6·214.

ûtlaga m. '*outlaw,*' Æ,W.

±**ûtlagian** *to 'outlaw,' banish, Chr.*

ûtlagu? f. *outlawry,* LL. [ON. útlagi]

ûtlah *outlawed,* CHR,LL.

ûtland n. *foreign land, PPs* : *outlying land (granted to tenants),* TC502. ['*outland*']

ûtlec=ūtlic

ûtlednes=ūtlǣdnes

ûtlenda m. *foreigner, stranger, alien,* GL.

ûtlende=ūtlendisc

ûtlendisc (æ) I. *strange, foreign,* Æ,*Chr.* II. m. *foreigner, stranger.* ['*outlandish*']

ûtlēoran *to go out, pass,* GD.

ûtlic *foreign,* BH : *remote,* CHRD61.

ûtmǣran *to proclaim, announce,* AA49¹⁰.

ût-mǣst, -mest=ȳtemest

uton=wuton ; **ûton**=ūtan

ûtone=ūtane

ûtor (comp. of ūte) adv. *beyond, outside.*

ûtrǣsan *to rush out,* CHR.

ûtre=ūterre f. and n. of ūterra.

ûtrīdan¹ *to ride or go away,* LL210,8.

ûtrine=ūtryne

ūt-roccettan, -roccian *to belch out*, EJPs.
ūtryne m. *running away, issue, exit, outlet*,
Ps,Sc : *what runs out*, LCD.
ūtsang=ūhtsang
ūtscēotan² *to abut on*, EC121⁸ : *suffer to
escape, aid the escape of*, LL194,6¹.
ūtscūfan² *to push out, shut out, exclude*,
Æ.
ūtscyte m. *outfall, outlet, exit*, Æ.
ūtscytling m. *stranger, foreigner*, Sc200⁴.
ūt-sīht, -sihte f. *flux, diarrhœa*, Æ,AO.
ūtsihtādl f. *diarrhœa, dysentery*, LCD.
ūtsīon¹ *to issue out*, AO38⁷.
ūtsīð m. *going out, departure : death*, GU.
ūtspīwung v. ūsspīung.
utter, uttor=ūtor; **uttermæst**=ȳtemest
utun=wuton
ūtwǣpnedmann m. *stranger*, BH354²⁵.
ūtwǣrc m. *dysentery?* LCD.
ūtwald m. *outlying wood*, EC289¹⁷.
ūtwaru f. *foreign defence*, LL.
ūtweallan⁷ *to well out, flow forth*, AA41¹⁷.
ūtweard adj. *outside of, going away, striving
to get out*, B. ['*outward*']
ūtweardes adv. '*outwards,*' CP.
ūtweorc=ūtwærc
ūtwīcing m. *sea-rover*, CHR1098.
ūtyrnende *diuretic, purgative, diarrhœic*,
LCD.
ūtyrning (io²) f. *flux*, MkL5²⁵.
ūð- intensitive prefix.
ūðe pret. sg. of unnan.
ūðgende=ūðgenge
ūðgenge *fugitive, alien, fleeting, vanishing,
departing*, B,BH.
ūðmǣte *huge*, MH76¹n.
ūðon pret. pl. of unnan.
ūðuta=ūðwita; **ūðweot-**=ūðwit-
ūðwita (eo², u²) m. *scholar, sage, philosopher, scribe, Pharisee*, Æ.
ūðwitegung f. *philosophy*, Æ.
ūðwitelīc=ūðwitlic
ūðwitian *to study philosophy*, ÆGR146².
ūðwitlic *philosophical, academical*, WW.
ūðwuta (NG)=ūðwita; **ūðwyt-**=ūðwit-

V

vīpere f. *viper*, MtR23³³.

W

wā I. (see also wēa) m. '*WOE*,' *affliction,
misery, evil*, AO,CP; Æ. **II.** interj. (occly.
governs d.) *woe! alas!* CP. wā lā, wā lā
wā, wei lā wei *ah! oh! alas!* Æ,Bo,LPs.
['*wellaway*,' '*wellawo*']

wāc I. adj. *weak, soft, feeble, effeminate,
cowardly, timid, pliant*, Æ,CP,Wa :
*slender, frail : insignificant, mean, poor,
TC*; Æ : *bad, vile*. ['*woke*'] **II.** n. *weakness*, LL. **III.** pret. 3 sg. of wīcan.
wac-=wǣc-
wacan⁶† *to awake, arise, be born, originate*.
[v. '*wake*']
waccor=wacor
wāce *weakly, slowly, negligently*, LL.
wacel=wacol
wacen (æ¹, ea¹, a², o², u²) f. *wakefulness :
watching, vigil : division of the night*, NG :
incentive, DR63¹⁵.
wacian (æ, e) *to be awake or active, keep
awake, watch*, Æ,CP. ['*WAKE*']
wācian *to become weak, languish* : (±) *waver,
be cowardly, flinch, Chr,Ma*. ['*woke*']
waciende *watching, vigilant*.
wāclic *weakly, mean, vile, insignificant,
trifling*, Æ. adv. -līce, Æ,Met. ['*wokely*']
wācmōd n. *faint-hearted, cowardly*, CP :
weak-minded, irresolute, Æ.
wācmōdnes f. *weakness (of mind or body),
cowardice*, CP.
wācnes f. *weakness, insignificance*, Æ,
OEG. ['*wokeness*']
wacnian=wæcnan
wacol *awake, vigilant, watchful, attentive*,
Æ. adv. -līce, Æ.
wacon=wacen
wacor *watchful, vigilant, LL*; CP. ['*waker*']
adv. -līce, CP.
wacsan=wascan
wācscipe m. *weakness, slackness*, LL208,1⁵.
-wacu v. niht-w.; **wacul**=wacol
wǣcung f. *vigilance*, GD.
wād I. n. '*woad*,' ÆGr,Gl,Lcd; Mdf. **II.** (?)
drag-net, OEG61¹⁵ (v. A31·528).
wad- v. wæd.
wadan⁶ *to go, move, stride, advance, An,B :
'wade,' Ma*; AO : (+) *traverse, pervade, Ma*.
wadom=waðum
wādsǣd n. *woad-seed*, LL454,12.
wādspitl m. *woad-dibble, LL455,15*. [v.
'*spittle*']
wadu? v. wād II.
wadung f. *travelling, going*, Æ.
wǣ (N,VPs)=wā; **wǣarhrōd**=weargrōd
wǣb, wæbb=webb; **wǣc-**=wāc-
±**wǣcan** *to weaken, oppress, trouble*, BH.
[wāc]
wǣccan (±) *to 'watch,' wake*, DR. [=
wacian]
wǣcc(e) f. '*watch,' vigil, wakefulness*, Æ,Bo,
Bl,Lcd,Lk; CP.
wǣccen=wacen
wǣccende *watchful, awake*, B,Bl,Chrd,LL.
['*watch(ing)*']

wæccendlìce *watchfully*, GD 242¹⁴.

wæccer=wacor

+wǽcednes f. *weakness*, ÆH 2·552′.

wæcen=wacen; **wæcg** (GL)=wecg

wæclan=wacian

wæcnan, wæcnian [v. also wacan] *to come into being, awake, come forth, spring from, arise, be born*, B. ['waken']

±**wæd** n. [usu. pl.; wad- in obl. cases] *ford, water, sea, ocean*.

wǽd f. *robe, dress, apparel, clothing, garment, covering*, Æ,Bo,Da : *sail*, ES 40·326. ['weed']

wǽd-=wēd-

wǽdbrēc (ā) fp. *breeches*, GEN 3⁷.

wædd=wedd; ±**wǽde** n.=wǽd f.

wǽdelnes (ē) f. *poverty*, CP.

wæden=waden pp. of wadan.

wǽden *of woad, bluish, purple*, OEG. [wād]

wæder=weder

wǽderǎp m. *stay, halyard*; pl. *rigging*, WW 515¹⁵.

+wǽdian *to clothe, dress, equip, furnish*, G.

wǽdl (ē, ēð) f. *poverty*, Bo; CP : *barrenness*, AO. ['waedle']

wǽdla (ē) *poor, destitute*, VPs. as sb.= *beggar, poor man*, VPs; Æ,CP. ['waedle']

wǽdle=wǽdl

wǽdlian *to be poor, destitute, beg*, Æ.

wǽd-lìg (Æ), -ligend (GD) *poor*.

wǽdling m. *poor person*, JPs 87¹⁶.

wǽdlnes=wǽdelnes

wǽdlung f. *poverty, want*, Æ : *begging*, Æ.

wǽdo=wād

wæf pret. 3 sg. of wefan.

+wæf=+wef

wǽfan *to clothe*, W 119⁶.

wǽfels (ē) mn. *covering, mantle, cloak, dress, clothing, garment*, Æ.

wæfergange f. *spider*, CPs 89⁹. [wefan]

wǽfergeornnes f. *eagerness for sight-seeing*, LL (wǽfereorn-).

wǽferhūs n. *amphitheatre*, ÆL 24⁴⁹.

wǽferlìc *of a theatre, theatrical*, OEG 62.

wǽfernes f. *show, pomp, pageant*, OEG 4465.

wǽfer-sēn, -sēon=wǽfersȳn

wǽfersolor m. 'pulpitum,' *stage*, OEG 3458.

wǽferstōw (ēa) f. *theatre*, LCD.

wǽfersȳn (ē³, ēo³, ī³, īe³) f. *spectacle, sight, show, display*, Æ. [wāfian]

wæflian *to speak foolishly*, v. NC 333.

wǽfon pret. pl. of wefan.

wǽfre *unstable, unsteady, wavering, wandering, restless* : *flickering, expiring*.

wæfs=wæps

wæfð, wæft f. *show, spectacle*, Bo,MET.

wǽfung (GL)=wāfung

wæg I. m.=weg. II. pret. 3 sg. of wegan.

wǽg (ā, ē) I. m. *motion* : *water* : *wave, billow, flood, sea*. [wegan] II. (±)=wǽge. III.=wǽg. IV.=hwǽg

wægan=wegan

±**wǽgan** (ē) *to trouble, afflict*, CP : *deceive, falsify*, Æ : (+) *frustrate*, DOM 115.

wǽgbora m. *child of the waves?* B 1440.

wǽgbord n. *ship, vessel*, GEN 1340.

wǽgdēor n. *sea-animal*, CR 988.

wǽgdropa m. *water-drop, tear*, GU 1030.

wǽge I. f. *weight, scales, balance*, Æ,Sc, VPs,WW ['weigh'] : 'wey' (*of cheese, wool, etc.*), BC,LL : 'pensum,' *burden*. II.† (ē) n. *cup, chalice*.

+**wǽge** n. *weight, measure*, LCD.

wægel (WW 124²)=pægel?

wægen=wægn; **wægenðìxl**=wægneðìxl

wǽgescalu=wǽgscalu

wǽgetunge f. *tongue of a balance*, WW 148¹⁹.

wǽgfær n. *sea-voyage*, AN 925.

wǽgfæt n. *water-vessel, clouds*, RD 4³⁷.

wǽgfaru f. *track in the sea*, EX 298.

wǽgflota† m. (*wave-floater*), *ship*.

wǽghengest† m. *ship*.

wǽgholm m. *sea, ocean*, B 217.

wæglǽst=weglēast

wǽglìðend† m. *sea-farer, sailor*.

wǽglìðende† *seafaring*.

wægn (wægen, wǽn) m. *carriage*, 'wain,' *waggon, chariot, cart, vehicle*, B,Cp. Carles wǽn; wǽnes ðìxl *the constellation of the Great Bear*, Bo. [wegan]

-wægnan v. be-w.

wægnere (ǽn) m. *waggoner*, WW.

wǽgnere m. *enticer*, WW 436¹². [wǽgnian]

wægnest=wegnest

wægnfaru f. *chariot-journey*, WW.

wægngehrado (ǽn) *waggon-plank*, WW 267³³.

wægngèrefa (ǽn) m. 'carpentarius,' *waggon-master?* WW.

wægngewǽde (ǽn) n. *waggon-cover*, LL 455,17.

+**wǽgnian** *to deceive* : *condemn*, CHRD 97.

wægnscilling m. *tax on waggons*, TC 138¹².

wægntrēow (ǽn) n. *log given to the carter of a load of wood*, LL 453,21⁴.

wægnðìxl (ǽn) *cart-pin?* WW 343³⁹.

wægnweg (ǽn) m. *cart-road*, KC.

wægnwyrhta (ǽn) m. 'carpentarius,' *cart-wright*, WW. ['wainwright']

wǽgon pret. pl. of wegan.

wǽgpundern n. *weighing-machine*, LL.

wǽgrǎp? m. *wave-rope, wave-bond* (*ice*), B 1611. [or? wǽlrāp]

wǽgryft=wāgrift

wǽgscalu f. *scale of a balance*, WW 437¹⁹. [scealu; Ger. wagschale]

wǣgstæð n. *sea-shore*, RD 23².
wǣgstrēam m. *current*, Ex 311.
wǣgsweord n. *sword with wavy pattern*, B 1489.
wǣgðel† n. *ship, vessel*.
wǣgðrēa f. *peril of the sea*, GEN 1490.
wǣgðrēat m. *deluge*, GEN 1352.
+wǣht pp. of +wæcan and +wǣgan.
wæl I. n. [nap. walu] *slaughter, carnage*, BH; AO. w. +slēan *to slaughter* : *field of battle* : (usu. in pl.) *dead bodies*, AO. ['*wal*'] II. m.=wiell. III.=wel
wǣl mn. *whirlpool, eddy, pool*, Æ,CP : *ocean, sea, river, flood*. ['*weel*']
wæl-=wel-; wǣl-=wēal-
wæla=wela
±wǣlan *to afflict, vex, torment*, GU,MtR.
wælbedd† n. *slaughter-bed*.
wælbend f. *band of destruction*, B 1936.
wælbenn f. *deadly wound*, Ex 491.
wælblēat *deadly-pale?* B 2725.
wælceald *deadly-cold*, SOL 468.
wælcēasega m. *carrion-picker (raven)*, Ex 164.
wælclomm m. *deadly fetter*, GEN 2128.
wælcræft m. *deadly power*, RD 87¹¹.
wælcwealm m. *violent death*, RD 2⁸.
wæl-cyrige, -cyrie f. *(chooser of the slain), witch, sorceress*, Gl,Nar. ['*walkyrie*']
+wældan (MkLR)=+wieldan
wældēað m. *death in battle, violent death*, B 695.
wældrēor† n. *blood of battle, battle-gore*, GEN.
wælegian=weligian; wæler=weler
wælfǣhð f. *deadly feud*, B 2028.
wælfæðm m. *deadly embrace*, Ex 480.
wælfāg *blood-stained*, B 1128.
wælfeall=wælfill
wælfel *greedy for corpses, ghoulish*, EL 53.
wælfeld m. *battlefield*, CHR 937.
wælfill m. *slaughter, death, destruction*, GEN.
wælfūs *awaiting death*, B 2420.
wælfyll=wælfill
wælfyllo f. *fill of slaughter*, B 125.
wælfȳr† n. *deadly fire* : *funeral pyre*, B.
wælgǣst† m. *murderous sprite*, B.
wælgār† m. *deadly spear*.
wælgenga m. *sea-monster?* OEG 5⁴¹; 8³⁰⁵.
wælgīfre† *bloodthirsty, murderous*.
wælgimm m. *death-bringing gem?* RD 21⁴.
wælgrǣdig *flesh-eating, cannibal*, AN 135.
wælgrim *fierce, violent, bloody, cruel* : *fateful, dire*. adv. -līce, AO.
wælgrimnes f. *cruelty, torture*, GD.
wælgryre m. *deadly horror*, Ex 137.
wælhere m. *slaughtering army*, GEN 1983.
wælhlem m. *death-stroke*, B 2969.
wælhlence† f. *coat of mail*.

wælhrēow (ēa²) *cruel, fierce, savage, bloodthirsty*, CP.
wælhrēowlic *cruel*, VH. adv. -līce.
wælhrēownes f. *cruelty, ferocity, atrocity, slaughter*, Æ,CP.
wælhwelp m. *destroying hound*, RD 16²³.
wælig=welig; wǣlisc=wīelisc
wæll=weall; wæll-=wæl-
wælla=willa II.; wællan (N)=willan
wælle (VPs)=wille; wælm=wielm
wælmist† m. *mist of death*.
wælnett n. *death-net*, Ex 202.
wælnīð† m. *deadly hostility, war*.
wælnot m. *baleful inscription*, SOL 161.
wælpīl m. *deadly arrow, dart*, GU 1127.
wælrǣs† m. *deadly onslaught*, B.
wælrǣst=wælrest; wælrēow=wælhrēow
wǣlrāp? m. *flood-fetter (ice)*, B 1610?
wælrēaf n. *spoil from the slain* : *act of spoiling the slain*, LL.
wælrēc m. *deadly reek*, B 2661.
wælregn (ll) m. *deluge*, GEN 1350.
wælrēow=wælhrēow
wælrest (æ²)† f. *bed of slaughter, grave*.
wælrūn f. *murderous song?* EL 28.
wǣlsc=wīelisc
wælscēaft m. *deadly spear*, B 398.
wælscel n? *carnage*, JUD 313.
wælseax n. *dagger*, B 2703.
wælslíht (ea, i, y) m. *slaughter, carnage*, Chr : (†) *combat*. [v. '*wal*']
wælslíhta m. *murderer, slayer*, GD 254²².
wælslītende *corpse-biting*, W 187¹⁴ : *deadly-biting*, W 241¹².
wælspere n. *deadly spear*, Ma 322; LCD 175b. [v. '*wal*']
wælsteng m. *spear-shaft*, B 1638.
wælstōw f. *place of slaughter, battlefield*, AO. āgan wælstōwe geweald *to obtain possession of the battlefield, conquer*.
wælstrǣl mf. *deadly shaft*, GU 1260.
wælstrēam m. *deadly flood*, GEN 1301.
wælsweng m. *deadly thrust*, GEN 987.
wælt *part of thigh, sinew*, LL 7,68. [weald]
wæltan=wyltan
wælwang m. *field of the slain*, AN 1227.
wælweg (SEAF 63)=hwælweg
wælwulf† m. *warrior*, MA : *cannibal*, AN.
wǣlwyrt=wēalwyrt (or ? wæl- v. '*wallwort*').
wǣm=(1) wamm; (2) hwamm
wǣm-=wem-
wǣmbede *big-bellied*, WW 161²². [wamb]
wǣmman=wemman
wǣmn (LWS)=wǣpen
wǣmnian=wǣpnian; wǣmst-=wæstm-
wǣn=wenn; wǣn-=wen-
wǣn=wægn; wǣnan=wēnan
wǣnes=(1) wācnes; (2) wōhnes

wæng, wænge=wang, wange

wǣnunga=wēnunga; **wǣpan**=wēpan

wǣpen n. (nap. wǣp(e)n, wǣp(e)nu) '*weapon,*' *sword, B,Chr*; pl. *arms, Bo, Gu,VPs*; Æ,AO,CP : *membrum virile, WW.*

wǣpenbora m. *weapon-bearer, warrior, knight, Æ.*

wǣpend, wǣpened=wǣpned

wǣpen(ge)tæc n. *wapentake' (subdivision of a riding), LL.*

wǣpengeðræc n. *clash of spears?* DR 168³.

wǣpengewrixl(e) n. *hostile encounter,* CHR, W.

wǣpenhād=wǣpnedhād

wǣpenhete m. *armed hate,* AP80.

wǣpenhūs n. *armoury,* WW348¹³.

wǣpenlēas *unarmed, Æ,OEG.* ['*weaponless'*]

wǣpenlic *male,* WW.

wǣpenstrǣl fm. *arrow,* PPs56⁵.

wǣpentæc=wǣpengetæc

wǣpenðracu† f. *storm of weapons.*

wǣpenðrǣge *weapon, equipment?* CRA61?

wǣpenwīfestre=wǣpnedwīfestre

wǣpenwīga m. *armed warrior,* RD15¹.

wǣpmann (Æ, '*wapman'*)=wǣpnedmann

wǣpn=wǣpen; **wǣpnahūs**=wǣpenhūs

wǣpned I. adj. *male,* AO. II. m. *male person.*

wǣpnedbearn n. *male child,* BH76⁸.

wǣpnedcild n. *male child,* Æ,LCD.

wǣpnedcynn n. *male sex, Æ.*

wǣpnedhād m. *male sex, Æ* : *sexual power,* GD26³⁰.

wǣpnedhand f. *male line,* TC491'.

wǣpnedhealf f. *male line,* TC491¹⁶.

wǣpnedmann m. *male, man,* AO.

wǣpnedwīfestre f. *hermaphrodite,* WW.

±**wǣpnian** (mn) *to arm, Æ,Chr*; CP. ['*weapon'*]

wǣpnmann=wǣpnedmann

+**wǣpnu** np. *arms,* LPs45¹⁰.

±**wǣpnung** f. *armour, Æ* : *army.*

wǣps m. '*wasp,' Gl; Æ.* [*L.* vespa]

wǣr I. (napm. ware) *wary, cautious, prudent, Æ,CP* : (w. g.) *aware of, Æ,Chr* : *ready, prepared, attentive.* ['*ware'*] II.† n. *sea, ocean.* [*ON.* verr] III.=wer. IV.= wearr

wǣr I. adj. *true, correct,* GEN681. II. f. *faith, fidelity* : *keeping, protection* : *agreement, treaty, compact, pledge, covenant* : *bond (of friendship).*

+**wǣr** wg. '*aware' (of), watchful, on one's guard, Chr*1095.

wǣr-=war-, wear-, wer-, wier-, wyr-

wǣran=werian

wǣrc (wræc) m. *pain, suffering, anguish, BH,Lcd* (A; often confused with WS. weorc. v. JAW52). ['*wark'*]

wǣrcan *to be in pain,* Lcd. ['*wark'*]

wǣrcsār (e) n. *pain,* MkR13⁸.

wǣre=wer II.

wǣre I.=wǣr II. II. pret. 2 sg. of wesan.

wǣrfæst† (e²) *honourable, faithful, trusty.*

wǣrg=wērig

wǣr-genga, -ganga (ē¹)† wm. *one seeking protection, stranger* (or ?=wer-).

wǣriglan=wērgian

+**wǣrlǣcan** *to warn, Æ.*

±**wǣrlan** *to go, pass by,* DR,NG.

wǣrlēas† *faithless, perfidious.*

wǣrlic I. *careful, wary, circumspect, El,LL, WW.* ['*warely'*] adv. -līce, Æ,CP. II.= werlic

wǣrlīce adv. *truly,* GEN652?

wǣrlicnes f. *wariness,* HL13²⁶³. ['*wareliness'*]

wǣrloga† m. *troth-breaker, traitor, liar, devil.* ['*WARLOCK*'; lēogan]

wǣrlot n. *craftiness, deceit,* WW354³¹.

wǣrna=wrenna

wǣrnes I. f. *wariness, caution, Bl.* ['*wareness'*] II.=weargnes

wǣron pret. pl. of wesan.

wǣrnung=wiernung

wǣrsagol *cautious in speech,* W72¹⁷.

wǣrscipe m. *cunning, caution, prudence, Bo;* AO,CP. ['*warship'*]

wǣrstlic=wrǣstlic

wǣrword n. *word of warning,* WW.

wǣrwyrde *cautious in speech,* FT57.

wǣs pret. 1, 3 sg. of wesan.

wǣsc f. *ablution, washing,* CM441. [v. '*wash'*]

+**wǣsc** n. only in wǣtera +w. '*alluvium,'* WW179³⁵,187⁸. [v. '*wash'*]

-**wǣsce** v. scēap-w.

wǣscen=wascen pp. of wascan.

wǣscern n. *washing-place,* WW185².

wǣscestre f. *washer, house-keeper,* '*presbytera,' GD*276. m. at *GD*191²³ ('*fullo').* ['*washester'*]

wǣschūs n. '*wash-house,' bath-house,* ZDA 31·13³²³.

wǣscing m. *washing, ablution,* Ct.

wǣsend=wāsend; **-wǣsma** v. here-w.

wǣsp=wǣps; **wǣst**=west

wǣst-=wēst-; **wǣstem-**=wǣstm-

wǣstling m. *sheet, blanket,* GL.

wǣstm (e) mn. (nap. wǣst-mas, -me) *growth, increase* : *plant, produce, offspring, fruit, Bo,Bl,G;* Æ,CP : *result, benefit, product* : *interest, usury* : *abundance* : *stature, form, figure, B,G.* ['*wastum'*]

wǣstmaseten f. *planting,* Mt15¹³.

wæstmbǣre *fruitful,* Æ,CP.
+**wæstmbǣrian** *to be or make fruitful,* WW.
wæstmbǣrnes (io) f. *fruitfulness,* Æ.
wæstmbǣro f. *fruitfulness,* AO 58²⁰.
wæstmberende *fertile,* AO.
wæstmberednes f. *fertility,* BH 74³⁰ᴮ.
wæstme f.=wæstm
wæstmfæst *fruitful,* ANS 122²⁴⁷.
wæstmian *to grow, increase, bear fruit,* BL, LG.
wæstmlēas *unfruitful, RG;* Æ. ['*wastum-less'*]
wæstmlic *fruitful,* DR 18¹³.
wæstmsceatt m. *interest, usury,* Ps,WW.
wæsōm=wæstm
wǣt (ā, ē) **I.** adj. 'WET,' *moist, rainy,* Æ; AO. **II.** n. *moisture, Bo : liquid, drink,* RB; Æ. ǣt *and* w. *food and drink,* Æ.
wǣta m. *wetness, moisture, humours, fluid, water, CP,Bl,G;* Æ : *drink,* Æ : *sap : urine.* ['*wete'*]
±**wǣtan** *to 'wet,' moisten, water, Gu,Lcd, Rd : become wet : bedew, VPs.*
wǣte f.=wǣta m.
wæter (e) n. (gs. wætres, wæteres) 'WATER,' Æ,CP; Mdf : *sea.*
wæterādl f. *dropsy,* LCD.
wæter-ǣdre, -ǣddre f. *spring of water, source,* Æ.
wæterælfādl f. *a disease,* LCD.
wæterælfen f. *water-elf,* WW 457⁸.
wæter-berend (OEG 871), -berere (WW) m. *water-bearer, sutler, camp-follower.*
wæterbōh m. *succulent shoot, sprig,* WW 149²⁵.
wæterbolla m. *dropsy,* LCD.
wæterbrōga† m. *frightful flood,* AN.
wæterbūc m. *water-pot, pitcher,* Æ.
wæterbucca m. *water-spider,* WW 122⁴.
wæterburne f. *water-stream,* DD 3.
wæterbyden f. *bucket, cask,* WW 503¹⁴.
wæterclāð m. *towel,* RB 59⁷.
wætercrōg m. *water-pot,* WW 484²⁸.
wætercrūce f. *water-pot,* Cp 283 U.
wætercynn n. *water, form or kind of water,* VH 23.
wæterdrinc m. *a drink of water,* NC 331. [v. '*water'*]
wæter-egsa, -egesa† m. *water-terror.*
wæterelfen=wæterælfen
wæterfæsten n. *water-fastness, place protected by water,* CHR 894ᴬ.
wæter-fæt n., nap. -fatu *water-pot, flagon, Jn;* Æ. [v. '*water'*]
wæterflaxe f. *water-pitcher, Mk* 14¹³. [v. '*flask'*]
wæterflōd m. '*water-flood,' inundation, deluge, AO;* Æ.

wæterfrocga m. *water-frog,* CHRD 96²⁷. [v. '*water'*]
wæterful *dropsical,* WW.
wæterfyrhtnes f. *hydrophobia,* WW 112²⁴.
wætergāt f. *water-spider,* WW 122⁴.
wætergeblǣd n. *watery pustule?* LCD 162b.
wætergefeall n. '*waterfall,' CC* 116.
wætergelād n. *conduit,* WW 339⁴.
wætergelǣt n. *aqueduct,* WW 211¹³.
wætergesceaft f. *nature of water,* GD 220¹⁷.
wætergewǣsc n. '*alluvium,'* WW 187¹.
wætergrund m. *sea-bottom, depth,* PPs 106²³.
wætergyte m. '*Aquarius' (sign of the Zodiac),* LCD 3·246⁴.
wæterhæfern m. *crab,* LCD 16b.
wæterhālgung f. *consecration of water,* DR 117¹.
wæterhelm m. *covering of ice,* GNE 74?
±**wæterian** *to 'water,' moisten, irrigate, supply water (to),* Æ,Ps,CP : *lead (cattle) to water,* Æ *(Gen).*
wæterig '*watery,' watered,* Æ,Lcd,WW.
wæterlēas '*waterless,'* Æ *(Gen),*LG.
wæterlēast f. *want of water,* Æ (9¹⁷⁷).
wæterlic *aquatic,* GPH 394.
wætermēle (ǣ³) m. *bowl, basin,* ÆGR.
wæternǣdre f. *water-snake,* WW.
wæterordāl n. *water-ordeal,* LL 388,2.
wæterpund n. '*norma, libella aquatica,'* WW 150³⁷.
wæterpytt m. '*water-pit,' well,* Æ.
wæterrīðe? f. *conduit* (v. OEG 1714n).
wæterscēat m. *napkin, towel,* WW 127³.
wæter-scipe (Æ,CP), -scype m. *sheet of water, waters : conduit.*
wæterscȳte f. *towel, napkin,* Æ.
wætersēað m. *cistern : pool, lake,* GD 112¹⁷.
wætersēoc *dropsical, G;* Æ. ['*watersick'*]
wætersēocnes f. *dropsy,* Æ,LCD.
wæterslæd n. *watery glade,* KC.
wæterspryng m. *water-spring,* DA 386.
wætersteall m. *standing water, pond,* GUTH 20⁵.
wæterstefn f. *voice of waters,* PPs 92⁴.
wæterstoppa m. *bucket,* GD 11²².
wæterstrēam m. *river, OEG,Ps.* ['*water-stream'*]
wætertīge m. *canal, aqueduct,* HGL 418⁵⁰.
wæterðēote f. *conduit, flood-gate, torrent, cataract,* Æ.
wæter-ōīsa, -ðissa m. *whale,* WH 50 : *ship,* GU 1303.
wæterðrūh f. *water-pipe, conduit,* GL.
wæterðrȳð f. *rush of waters,* PPs 106²².
wæterung f. '*watering,' providing with water, carriage of water,* Æ.
wæterwǣdlnes f. *dearth of water,* ÆL 23b⁶³⁸.
wæterweg m. *watercourse, KC,WW.* ['*waterway'*]

wæterwrīte f. '*clepsydra*,' *water-clock*, WW 378³⁹.

wæterwyll m. *spring, fountain*, LL312,5¹.

wæterwyrt f. *water star-wort*, *LCD*. ['*water-wort*']

wæteryð f. *billow*, B2242.

wǣtian *to be wet*, WW447¹.

wǣtig (GPH389)=pætig

wǣtla *swathe, bandage*, LCD78a.

wǣtnes (ē) f. *moisture*, *LkL*8⁶. ['*wetness*']

wætrian=wæterian; **wætter** (N)=wæter

wǣtung f. *wetting, moisture*, LCD.

wæð n. *ford*, CHR1073D. [*ON.* vað]

-wæða v. here-w.

wǣðan *to wander, roam about* : *hunt*. [wāð]

wǣðeburne f. *fishing stream?* BC (Mdf).

wǣðelnes=wǣdelnes; **wǣðl**=wǣdl

wǣwærðlic *serious?* BF192³⁰. adv. (e², y²) -līce *confidently? plausibly?* BF6¹⁸,W169¹.

wæx (N)=weax

wēx=weox pret. 3 sg. of weaxan.

wæxð pres. 3 sg. of wascan.

waflan *to* '*wave*,' Æ,*Lcd*.

wāflan *to be agitated, astonished, amazed, gaze at, wonder at, admire*, Æ : *hesitate*.

wāflende '*theatralis*,' '*visibilis*,' OEG233.

wāforlic=wǣferlic

wāfung (ǣ, ē) f. *spectacle, display, pageantry, sight*, Æ : *astonishment*, Æ. [wāfian]

wāfungstede m. *place for shows, theatre*, WW.

wāfungstōw f. *place for shows, theatre*, LCD 3·206¹⁶.

wāg I. (ǣ) m. *wall*, Æ,*AO*,*B*,*Bl*; CP. ['*wough*'] II.=wǣg I.

wāghrægel n. *tapestry, vail*, NG.

waglan *to move, shake, swing, totter*, Æ,*Bo*, *Cp*,*Rd*. ['*waw*']

wagn=wægn

wāgon=wǣgon pret. pl. of wegan.

wāgrift (e, y) n. *tapestry, vail, curtain*, Æ.

wāgðeorl *doorway?* LPs61⁴. [ðyrel]

wāgðyling (wāh-) f. *wainscoting*, WW147³¹. [wāg, ðille]

wagung f. *moving, shaking*, LCD.

wāh I. *fine*, LCD101b (IF48·264). II. (Æ,*Bo*)=wāg

wāh-=wāg-

wahsan=wascan; **wal**=wæl I.

wal-=wæl-, weal-; **wala** (N)=wela I.

wālā! wālāwā! interj. (w. g.) v. wā.

walan v. walu I.; **Wālas**=Wēalas

walc-=wealc-

wal-crigge, -cyrge=wælcyrige

walcspinl (o¹) f. *curling-iron, crisping-pin*, WW198¹; OEG26⁷⁰.

wald (*BC*,*Jud*) ['*wold*']=weald

wald-=weald-

walde (CP443¹¹)=wolde

waldenīge *blue or grey-eyed, wall-eyed*, Erf 1166.

waldmora=wēalhmora

Wāle (=ēa) f. *Welshwoman, female slave*, RD.

waled *striped*, WW416²³. ['*waled*']

waler (DR)=weler; **walh**=wealh

wālic *woful, lamentable*, SAT100.

wall (VPs)=weall

wallað (DR)=pres. pl. of wællan, willan.

walm (N)=wielm

walu I. f. *ridge, bank*, KC : *rib, comb* (*of helmet*), B1031? : *weal, mark of a blow*, OEG. ['*wale*'] II. v. wæl I.

wālwyrt=wēalwyrt; **wam**=wamm

wamb (o) f. *belly, stomach*, LG,*Ps*,*Rd*,*WW*; Æ,CP : *bowels*, *Lcd* : *heart*, VHy : '*womb*', LG,*VPs* : *hollow*, BC,*Rd*.

wambādl f. *stomach-ache*, LCD81a.

wambhord n. *contents of the belly*, RD18¹⁰.

wambscyldig? *gluttonous?* v. NC331.

wambsēoc *having pain in the stomach*, LCD.

wamcwide (o)† *shameful speech, curse, blasphemy*.

wamdǣd (o)† f. *deed of shame, crime*.

wamfreht (o) n. *sinful divination*, WW.

wamful† *impure, shameful, sinful, bad*.

wamlust (o) m. *allurement, enticement*, A 13·28; OEG7³⁷.

wamm (o) I. mn. *stain, spot, scar*, B,*KGl* : *disgrace, defect, defilement, sin, evil, crime* : *injury, loss, hurt, misfortune*. ['*wam*'] II. adj. *shameful, bad*.

wamsceaða (o)† m. *sin-stained foe, devil*.

wamscyldig (o) *sinful, criminal*, GEN949.

wamwlite (o) m. *wound in the face*, LL.

wamwyrcende (o) *worker of sin*, CR1093.

wan I. (o) (usu. undecl. and used predicatively) *wanting, deficient, lacking, absent*, BH,*Bl*,*Cr*,*VPs*; CP. ānes wan ðe ðritig *or* ānes wana ðrittigum *twenty-nine*. ['*wane*'] II. pret. 3 sg. of winnan. III.= wann

wan- expresses *privation or negation*.

wana I. m. *lack, want, deficiency*, Bo,*Gl*; Æ. w. bēon *to lack, fail*, Æ. ['*wane*'] II.= wan I.

+wana *lacking, wanting*, MtL19²⁰. ['*wane*']

wanǣht (o) f. *want, poverty*, †Hy4¹⁰³.

wananbēam m. *spindle-tree*, GL.

wancol (e) *unstable, unsteady, tottering, vacillating, weak*, Bo. ['*wankle*']

wand I. pret. 3 sg. of windan. II. f? *mole* (*animal*), Gl. ['*want*']

+wand n. *fear*, RB68⁸ : *hesitation, scruple*. būtan gewande '*incunctanter*,' CHRD52²⁵. [windan]

wandeweorpe (u³) f. *mole* (*animal*), Æ.

wandian (o) *to hesitate, flinch, desist from, omit, neglect, Æ,Bl,CP : fear, stand in awe, Æ : have regard to, care for.* ['wonde']

wandlung f. *changeableness,* Bo 15²⁷.

-wandodlīce v. unfor-w.

wandrian *to 'wander,' roam, fly round, hover, Bo,CP,Fin,LL : change : stray, err.*

wandung f. **I.** *feeling of respect,* CHRD 61³⁴. **II.** *turning aside,* CHRD 99¹⁹.

wand-wurp, -wyrp=wandeweorpe

wanfāh (o) *dark-hued,* RD 53⁶.

wanfeax (o) *dark-haired,* RD 13⁸.

wanfōta m. *pelican,* WW 287¹⁰.

wanfȳr (o) n. *lurid flame,* CR 966.

wang I. (o) m. *plain, mead, field, place, B, Bl,Ph : world.* ['wong'] **II.** m.=wange

wangbeard m. *whisker,* LCD 73a.

wange (e, o) n. *jaw, cheek, Æ,Lcd,RG.* ['wang']

wangere m. *pillow, bolster, BH,WW.* ['wanger']

wangstede† m. *place, locality,* RWH 67¹².

wangtōð m. *molar, grinder, LL,WW.* ['wangtooth'] .

wangturf f. *meadow-turf,* LCD 1·400⁷.

wanhæf-=wanhaf-

+wanhǣlan *to weaken,* Æ.

wanhǣlð f. *weakness, sickness,* Sc 54¹⁹.

wanhǣw (o) *bluish,* WW 376²³.

wanhafa m. *poor man,* SPs 85¹.

wanhafol *needy,* ÆL.

wan-hafolnes, -haf(e)nes (æ²) f. *want, hunger.*

wanhāl *unsound, weak, ill, maimed,* Æ, CP.

+wanhālian *to make weak,* HL 12⁵¹.

wanhālnes f. *weakness, ill-health,* RB,Sc.

wanhlȳte *having no share in, free from,* WW 398³³.

wanhoga m. *thoughtless one, fool,* SOL.

wan-hygd, -hȳd† f. *carelessness, recklessness, daring.*

wanhygdig (hȳdig)† *careless, rash.*

±wanian *to diminish* (tr.), *lessen, curtail, injure, impair, take from, Ct,Rd; Æ,AO : infringe, annul : diminish* (intr.), *dwindle, decline, fade, decay, B,Chr,Chrd,Jn; Æ, CP : 'wane'* (moon), *Bl.*

wānian *to complain, bewail, lament, bemoan, B,Cr,Jul; AO.* ['wone']

wan-iendlic, -gendlic *diminutive,* ÆGR.

wann I. (o) *dark, dusky, lurid, B,Gl,Met.* ['wan'] **II.** pret. 3 sg. of winnan.

wannhāl=wanhāl

wannian *to become dark-coloured, turn black,* NC 332 : *become discoloured?* ÆP 178¹¹ ['wan']

wanniht *wan, pale, livid,* WW 431²¹.

wansǣlig (o¹)† *unhappy.*

wansceaft (o¹)† f. *misery, misfortune.*

wansceaf-ta m. (or -te f.) *a disease,* LCD.

wanscrȳd *poorly clad,* ÆH 2·500¹⁷.

wansēoc *'commitialis'?* v. OEG 4937.

wansian *to diminish,* Chr 656 E. ['wanze']

wanspēd f. *poverty, want, AO,Sc.* ['wanspeed']

wanspēdig *poor, indigent,* Æ. ['wanspeedy']

wanung (o) f. *waning, decrease, deprivation, diminution, loss, injury, weakening,* Æ, BH,Lcd.

wānung f. *howling, lamentation, Æ,LG.* ['wonung']

wanwegende *waning* (moon), LCD.

wāpe (a²?) *napkin, towel?* IM 122²³.

wapelian, wapolian *to bubble, froth, exhale, emit, pour forth,* GL.

wapul m? *bubble, froth,* WW.

war=wearr

wār I. n. *sea-weed, Gl : sand.* ['ware'] **II.**=wǣr

wara, gs. of waru.

-waran v. burg-, ceaster-, eorð-w.

waras (N)=weras nap. of wer I.

-waras v. burg-, eorð-w.

warað=waroð

ward=(1) weard; (2) wearð (weorðan)

-ware v. burg-, eorð-, ceaster-w.

waren-=warn-; **warht**=worht

warian I. *to be wary, beware, Gen,KGl,LL :* (±) *guard, protect, defend : warn, Gl;* CP : (†) *hold, possess, attend :* (†) *inhabit.* ['ware'] **II.** *to make a treaty* (with), BH.

wārig *weedy, dirty,* GnE 99.

wāriht *full of sea-weed,* GL.

waritrēo=weargtrēow

warnian (ea, are) (±) *to 'warn,' caution, Æ, Chr,Lcd,W :* (±) *take warning, take heed, guard oneself against, Æ,Lk;* CP : *deny* (oneself, etc.). [wearn]

warnung (ea) f. *'warning' : foresight, caution, Æ,Cr,Sol.*

waroð (a¹, ea¹, e¹, a², e², u²) n. *shore, strand, beach, B,Met,Ps.* ['warth']

wāroð n. *alga, sea-weed,* RD 41⁴⁹.

waroðfaruð m. *surf,* AN 197.

waroðgewinn (u²) n. *surf,* AN 439.

warp=wearp I.; **warr**=wearr

warpenig v. weardpening

warscipe=wærscipe

warð I. (N)=waroð. **II.** (N)=wearð pret. 3 sg. of weorðan.

waru I. f. *'ware,' article of merchandise,* Æ, WW. **II.** f. *shelter, protection, care, custody, guard, defence, vindication, AO,Gu;* Æ. ['ware']

-waru v. burg-, ciric-, eorð-w.

waruð, wāruð=waroð, wāroð

was=wæs; **-wāsa** v. wudu-w.

wascan⁶ (æ; acs, a(c)x) *to 'wash,' cleanse, Æ,BH,G,TC : bathe, lave.*

wāse (v. OEG 1818) f. *mire, marsh, Gl.* [*'ooze'*]

wāsend (ǣ) m. *'weasand,' windpipe, gullet, Gl,Lcd.*

wāsescite f. *cuttlefish*, WW 181⁷. [wāse, scēotan]

wāst pres. 2 sg. of witan.

wāt I. pres. 3 sg. of witan. **II.** pret. 3 sg. of wītan. **III.**=wǣt

watel (o², u²) m. *'wattle,' hurdle, covering :* (pl.) *thatching, BH,Gl,LkL.*

water=wæter; **watol**=watel

watr-=wætr-, wæter-

watul=watel

wāð† f. *wandering, journey : pursuit, hunt, hunting, chase,* MET 27¹³.

wāðan? *to wander, flee,* GUTH 113n.

waðema=waðuma

wāðol *wandering?* or m. *full moon?* FIN 8?

wað-um, -uma† m. *wave, flood, stream, sea.*

wāwa [*'wowe'*; ÆGr,Gen]=wēa

wāwan⁷ *to blow (of wind),* RD 41⁸¹.

waxan=(1) wascan; (2) weaxan

waxgeorn=weaxgeorn

we (ē) pron. (1st pers. plur.) g. ūser, d. ūs, acc. ūs(ic) 'WE.'

wēa m. *misfortune, evil, harm, trouble : grief, woe, misery : sin, wickedness.*

weacen=wacen

wēacwānian *to lament,* SAT 320.

wēadǣd† f. *evil deed.*

wēadhōc (Ep 887)=wēodhōc

weadu (K)=wudu

wēafod=wēofod; **weag**=weg

wēagesīð m. *companion in trouble,* W.

weagian=wagian

weahte pret. 3 sg. of weccan.

weahxan=weaxan

weal=(1) weall; (2) wæl

wēal=wealh; **weal-**=weall-, wel-

wēalāf† f. *wretched remnant.*

wēaland=wēalland

Wēalas (pl. of wealh) *the 'Welsh,' Chr,LL : Wales.* West Wē(a)las *West-Welsh, Cornish.*

+wealc n. *rolling, tossing motion : attack,* CHR 1100.

wealca (a) m. †*billow, rolling wave : light floating garment.*

wealcan⁷ (±) *to move round, revolve, roll, toss, Gl;* CP : *fluctuate : revolve in one's mind, discuss, scheme, reflect, Æ,CP : roll together :* (+) *go, traverse, Gl.* [*'walk'*]

wealcere m. *fuller,* WW 407²⁹. [*'walker'*]

±wealcian (a) *to curl,* OEG 26⁶⁹ : *roll up,* HGL 489⁵⁶.

wealcol *mobile, not firmly fixed,* GPH 399⁴⁴¹.

wealcspinl (a, o) f. *crisping-pin,* OEG,WW.

Wēalcynn n. *the Welsh kin,* EC 146′.

weald I. (a) m. *weald, forest, wood, grove, BC,Chr,Jud;* AO : *bushes, foliage,* GEN 846. [*'wold'*] **II.** m. *power, dominion, mastery,* AO (usu. +) : *groin,* LCD 1·12⁹. **III.** *powerful,* RB 117⁵. **IV.** conj. *in case.* w. ðeah *perhaps, possibly, ÆH.* [*'wald'*]

+weald (a) n. *might, power, possession, A, B,Rood : control, command, dominion, AO, Bl : bridle : protection : subjection : groin : pudenda : muscles of the neck?* LL 88,77. (his) gewealdes *of his own accord, intentionally, LL.* [*'wield'*]

±wealdan⁷ (a) w. g. d. (instr.) and a. *to rule, control, determine, direct, command, govern, possess, AO,CP :* 'WIELD*' (*a weapon*), *exercise : cause, bring about, CP.*

wealdbǣr f. *place affording mast for swine,* EC 60²³.

+wealden I. adj. *subject (to), easily controlled : inconsiderable, small, AO,CP.* **II.** adv. *moderately.*

wealdend (a) **I.** m. *leader, controller, ruler, lord, king* (often of God), *B,Bo.* [*'wald-end'*] **II.** f. *female ruler.*

±wealdende *ruling, powerful, Æ,Cr.* [*'wielding'*]

Wealdendgod m. *Lord God,* PPs.

+wealdendlīce *powerfully,* PPs 135¹⁶.

wealdendras late nap. of wealdend.

+wealdenmōd *self-controlled,* CRA 70.

wealdes (usu. +) *of one's own accord, voluntarily,* CP 198²².

wealdgenga m. *robber, thief,* ÆT 1089.

±wealdleðer n. *rein, bridle, Æ.*

wealdmoru=wēalhmoru

wealdnes (a) f. *rule,* VPs 144¹³.

wealdswaðu (a¹) f. *forest-track,* B 1403.

weale=wale; **wēales** v. wealh.

wealfæsten=weallfæsten

wealg *nauseous?* CP 447¹⁸. [*'wallow'*]

wealgat=weallgeat

wealh (a) m. (gs. weales) *foreigner, stranger, slave : Briton, Welshman : shameless person,* HGL 527²².

wealhāt *boiling hot, red-hot,* Lcd 96a. [*'wallhot'*]

wealhbaso f. *foreign red, vermilion,* GL.

Wealhcynn n. *men of Wales, Britons,* CHR.

wealhen=wīelen

wealhfǣreld (a) n. *a force which patrolled the Welsh border?* KC 2·60′.

wealh-gefēra, -gerēfa m. *commander of the 'wealhfǣreld,'* CHR 897A.

wealhhāfoc m. *foreign hawk, falcon,* AA, GL.

wealhhnutu (a) f. *'walnut,'* WW 452³⁴.

wealhisc=wīelisc

wealh-moru, -more (a¹) f., -mora m. *carrot, parsnip*, Lcd,WW.

wealhstod m. *interpreter, translator*, Æ,CP : *mediator*, CP.

Wealhðēod f. *Welsh nation*, LL.

wealhwyrt [v. '*wallwort*']=wēalwyrt

weallan *to be defiant*, ÆL12⁴⁸.

wēalic *woeful, sorrowful*, Wy12.

weall I. (a, æ) m. 'WALL,' *dike, earthwork, rampart, dam*, Æ; AO,CP; Mdf : (†) *rocky shore, cliff.* **II.** f. *fervour*, HGL465. **III.**= wæl. **IV.**=wiell

weallan⁷ (±) *to be agitated, rage, toss, well, bubble, seethe, foam, be hot, boil*, AO,B, Lcd; CP : *swarm*, Æ,WW : *flow*, Æ. ūp w. *to rise (of a river)*, AO. ['*wall*']

wēalland n. *foreign country*, Gen2706 (weal-) : *Normandy*, Chr1040e. [wealh]

Wēallas=Wēalas

weallclif n. *sea-cliff*, B3132.

wealldīc f. *a walled ditch?* KC5·346¹⁹.

wealldor n. *door in a wall*, Cr328.

+wealled=+weallod

weallende *boiling, raging*, Æ,B : *fervid, ardent, energetic, fiery : swarming (with vermin)*, Æ,WW. [v. '*wall*,' '*walling*']

weallfæsten n. *walled place, rampart, fortification, fortress.*

weallgeat† n. *rampart-gate, postern.*

weallgebrec n. *wall-breaking, act of making a breach*, AO134³⁰.

weallgeweorc n. *building of a wall*, Æ : *destruction of walls*, ÆGr12⁵.

weallian *to go abroad, travel, wander : go as pilgrim*, LL. ['*wall*']

weallīm m. *cement, mortar*, Gen11³.

wēallisc=wīelisc

+weallod *walled, Num.* [v. '*wall*']

weallstān† m. *stone used in building*, Cr, Ruin. ['*wallstone*']

weallstaðol (e³) m. *interpreter, translator*, RWH41³³ (wealh-?).

weallsteall m. *wall-place, foundation?* Wa88.

weallstēap† *steep as a wall*, Gen.

weallstilling (y) m. *repair of walls* (v. BT).

weallstōw=wælstōw

weallōrǣd (a¹) m. *plumb-line*, WW522²⁷.

weallung (a, y) f. *agitation, fervour, zeal.*

weallwala† m. *part of a house-wall? foundation?* Ruin21.

weallweg (a¹) m. *walled road?* Ct.

weallwyrhta m. *mason*, Gl.

weallwyrt=wealhwyrt

wēal-mora, -more=wealhmoru

wealnes (CPs)=wealdnes

wealowian=wealwian

wealsāda m. *cord (for binding captives)?* PPs139⁵. [wealh]

weallstilling (y²)=weallstilling

wealstod=wealhstod

wealt=wielt pres. 3 sg. of wealdan.

wealte f. *a ring*, Erf1105.

wealweorc n. *masonry*, Æ.

wealwian I. (a, y) *to roll* (intr.), Bo,BH, CP : *roll* (tr.). ['*wallow*'] **II.** *to dry up, shrivel, wither, decay*, Bo. ['*wallow*']

wealword n. *defiant word*, A11·98⁸⁷. [wealh]

wealwyrt (a, æ) f. *dwarf elder*, Cp,Lcd. ['*wallwort*']

wēamēt, wēamētto f. *passion, anger*, Æ.

wēamōd *ill-humoured, angry*, CP. ['*wemod*']

wēamōdnes f. *anger, impatience*, Æ,CP.

weaps=wæps

wear=(1) wearr; (2) hwer

wear-=wær-

wearas=weras npl. of wer.

wearc=wærc

weard I. fm. *watching*, '*ward,*' *protection, guardianship*, Æ,B; AO,CP : *waiting for, lurking, ambuscade.* **II.** m. *keeper, watchman, guard, guardian, protector*, B,Bl; AO : (†) *lord, king* : (†) *possessor.* **III.** adv. *towards, to.* wið... weard *towards.* **IV.**=wearð. **V.** '*sandix,*' v. A30·249.

weardian *to watch, guard, keep, protect, preserve*, LL,Ps : *hold, possess, occupy, inhabit : rule, govern*, Da665. lǣst w. *keep the track of, follow closely.* swaðe w. *remain behind.* leger w. *keep one's bed.* ['*ward*']

weardmann m. *watchman, guard, patrol*, Æ.

weardpening? (warp-) m. *rent paid in lieu of military service*, Ct1087? ['*wardpenny*']

weardseld, weardsetl (Æ) n. *guardhouse, watch-tower.*

weardsteall m. *watch-tower*, WW.

weardwīte n. *penalty for not keeping guard*, TC411³¹. ['*wardwite*']

wearf I. (EC202¹⁵)=wearp pret. 3 sg. of weorpan. **II.**=hwearf

wearg (e) **I.** m. *(wolf), accursed one, outlaw, felon, criminal, Rood,WW*; Æ. ['*wary*'] **II.** (-erig, -yrig) adj. *wicked, cursed, wretched.* [ON. vargr]

weargberende *villainous*, WW407²⁷.

weargbrǣde (-geb-) f. *a warty eruption, impetigo, stye in the eye, tetter, ringworm, mole, freckle*, Lcd,WW. ['*waribreed*']

wearglīc (ere-, eri-) *wretched.* adv. -līce (y¹).

weargnes (æ, e, y) f. *evil*, MtL,PPs.

weargrōd f. *scaffold, gallows*, Gl.

weargtreafu (rht) np. *hell*, El927.

weargtrēow (ari-) n. *gallows*, KC. ['*warytree*']

weargung (e) f. *misery*, EPs 87¹⁹.
wearh I.=wearg. II.=wearr
wēarīht=wearrīht
wearm '*warm*,' *Bo,Met,Rd*; Æ,CP. adv. -e, *Lcd*.
wearmelle=wurmille
±wearmian *to become or make* '*warm*,' *Æ, BH,G,HL,Ph,Rd*; CP.
wearmlīc *warm*, DA 350.
wearmnes f. *warmth*, ÆL 11¹⁶⁰. ['*warmness*']
wearn I. f. *reluctance, repugnance, refusal, denial*, CP : *resistance* : *reproaches, abuse.* [waru] II.=worn
wearn-=warn-, wearrn-
wearnmǣlum (ē) adv. *in troops*, WW 25¹. [worn]
wearnwīslīce adv. *obstinately*, WW.
wearod, wearoð=waroð
wearp I. (a) m. '*warp*,' *threads stretched lengthwise in a loom, Cp,Rd* : *twig, osier.* II. pret. 3 sg. of weorpan.
wearpfæt n. *basket*, WW. ['*warpfat*']
wearr (a, æ, eo) m. *callosity, Cp,Lcd.* ['*warre*']
wearrig (Æ), wearrīht *warty, knotty.*
wearrīhtnes f. *roughness (of skin)*, GL.
wearrnes (wearn-) f. *knottiness* (Swt).
wearscipe (AS 69¹⁵)=wærscipe?
weart, wearte (a, e) f. '*wart*,' *Cp,Lcd.*
weartere (æ) m. *occupier, dweller*, CHR 565. [weard]
wearð I. n.=weorð. II. pret. 3 sg. of weorðan. III.=waroð
wearð-=weorð-
wēas adv. *by chance, accidentally*, CP. mid w. *by chance.*
weasc-=wæsc-
wēasgelimp n. *chance occurrence*, WW 410¹⁰.
wēaspell n. *evil tidings*, B 1315.
weastern (CHR 1015)=western
weastm=wæstm
wēatācen† n. *sign of grief.*
wēaðearf f. *woeful need*, WIF 10.
weax (e) n. '*wax*,' *BC,Bl,Ps*; AO.
weaxæppel m. *ball of wax*, SOL 150³³.
±weaxan (e) I. sv⁷ *to* '*WAX*,' *grow, be fruitful, increase, become powerful, flourish, Æ, CP*; AO. II.=wascan
weaxberende m. *candle-bearer, acolyte*, DR 195⁸ (io²).
weaxbred (e) n. *writing-tablet, Æ,RB* : *diagram, table*, BF 180³⁰. ['*waxbred*']
weaxcandel (e¹, o²) f. '*wax candle*,' *Cp,WW.*
weaxen (e¹) I. *waxen, made of wax?* LCD. II. pp. of weaxan.
weaxgeorn (a) *very greedy*, WW 102¹³.
weaxgesceot n. *payment in wax*, W 171¹.

weaxhlāf m. *wax tablet*, LCD.
weaxhlāfsealf f. *wax salve*, LCD 92b.
±weaxnes f. *increase, growth* : *interest, usury.*
weaxscot=weaxgesceot
weaxsealf (e) f. *wax salve*, LCD,WW.
weaxung f. *growth, increase*, Bf 138¹⁹. ['*waxing*']
web, webb n. '*web*,' *weft* : *woven work, tapestry, B,Cp,Sc*; Æ. [wefan]
webba m. *weaver*, WW. ['*webbe*']
webbēam m. *weaver's beam*, WW : *treadle of a loom*, WW. ['*webbeam*']
webbestre f. *female weaver*, WW 188¹¹. ['*webster*']
webbgeweorc n. *weaving*, HL,MH.
webbian *to contrive, devise*, AN,BL,EL.
webbung (hw) f. *plotting, conspiracy*, OEG 2975 : '*scena*' (=wāfung? v. OEG 2920).
webgerēðru np. *weaver's tool*, WW 294¹⁶.
webgerod n. *weaver's implement*, Cp 1988.
webhōc m. *weaver's comb, reed?* WW.
weblīc *pertaining to a weaver*, GL.
websceaft m. *weaver's beam*, WW 293³⁹.
webtāwa m. *thread, line*, WW 433⁸.
web-tēag (æ¹, ǣ²) f. *weaving-thread*, OET 615.
wēbung (Cp 180s)=wāfung
webwyrhta m. *fuller*, MH.
wecca=wēoca
weccan (±) *to awaken, arouse*, B,BH,CP, Cr : *call up, bring forth, produce* : *recall* : *exhort, encourage* : *move, set in motion* : *kindle.* ['*wecche*']
weccend m. *instigator*, GPH 393.
wēce=wāc I.
wecedrenc m. *emetic*, LCD.
wecg m. '*wedge*,' *Cp,Sc* : *mass of metal, lump, Æ* : *piece of money, Æ,BH,WW.*
wecgan *to move, agitate, drive hither and thither, Met,Ps* : *be moved.* ['*weigh*']
wecian (VPs)=wacian
wecnian=wæcnian
wed=wedd
wēd=wǣd
+wēd I. n. *fury, rage, foolishness, madness.* [wōd] II. (ZDA 31·9¹⁶⁸) pp. of wēn.
±wēdan (ǣ) *to be or become mad, rage, Æ, BH,G*; AO,CP. ['*wede*']
wēd-beorge, -berge=wēdeberge
wedbrice=wedbryce
wedbrōðor m. *pledged brother (in a brotherhood of compact, not of blood)*, CHR. [wedd]
wedbryce m. *treachery*, W. [? v. '*wed*']
wedd n. *pledge, agreement, covenant, security, B,Bl,Chr*; Æ,AO,CP : *dowry*, WW. ['*wed*']
+weddian *engage, pledge oneself, covenant, promise, vow, Lk,LL* : *give to wife, betroth* : '*wed*,' *marry*, Chrd,LL.

weddung f. *pledging, betrothal, Nic*474³³. ['*wedding*']

wēde I. *raging, mad,* Lcd,LkL. [wŏd] **II.** (A)=wǣde

+**wēde** n. *fury, rage, madness,* Æ. [wŏd]

wēdeberge f. *hellebore,* Lcd,Gl.

wēdehund m. *mad dog,* Lcd,Met.

wēdelnes (VPs)=wǣdelnes

wēden (MFH178)=wǣden

wēdend *raving, Bo,Cp.* [v. '*wede*']

wēden(d)sēoc *mad,* GD135n; 223.

wēdenheort I. *mad, insane,* WW. **II.** n. *madness.*

wēdenheortnes f. *madness, frenzy,* CP.

weder I. n. 'WEATHER,' *air, AO : sky, firmament : breeze, storm, tempest.* **II.**=weðer

+**weder**=+wider

wederblāc *bleached by the weather,* A8·449.

wederbūrg f. *exposed town,* An 1699.

wedercandel f. *sun,* Ph 187.

wederdæg m. *day of fine weather,* Az 96.

wederfest *weather-bound,* Chr 1046 E.

wederian *to exhibit a change of weather,* Lcd.

wedertācen n. *sun,* Gu 1267.

+**wederu**=+wideru

wederung (æ) f. (*bad*) *weather, Chr* 1085. ['*weathering*']

wederwolcen n. *cloud,* Ex 75.

wedewe=wuduwe

+**wedfæstan** (wet-) *to pledge,* Cp 635 s.

wēding f. *madness,* GD 164²⁷; WW 409³⁸.

wēdl-=wǣdl-

wedlāc n. *pledge, plighted troth,* '*wedlock*,' Gl.

wedloga m. *violator of agreement, traitor.*

+**wef** n. *woof, web,* WW 490³⁸ : *text, context?* Bf 172¹¹.

wēf-=wāf-, wǣf-, wēof-

wefan⁵ (eo) (±) *to* '*weave*,' *BH,LPs, WW;* Æ : *devise, contrive, arrange.*

wefl I. f. *woof, warp,* Gl : *an implement for weaving, shuttle?* LL455,15 and 3·254. **II.**=wifel

weft, wefta m. '*weft*,' *A* 9·263.

weg I. (æ) m. 'WAY,' *direction, AO;* Æ : *path, road, highway,* Mdf : *journey,* Æ : *course of action,* CP. ealne w. (ealneg) adv. *always.* on w. (āweg) adv. *away.* be...wege *on the way* (*to*). **II.**=wæg II.

wēg=(1) wǣge; (2) wīg

weg-=onweg-; **wēg**-=wǣg-

wegan⁵ (±) *to carry, B,Nar : support, sustain, bear, bring,* CP : *move : wear, BH, CP* : (±) '*weigh*,' *measure,* ÆGr,Lcd,W.

+**wegan** *to fight,* B 2400.

weg-brāde, -brǣde (Æ) f. '*way-bread*,' *plantain, dock, Gl,Lcd.*

wegfarende (ǣ, ē) '*wayfaring*,' *ÆL.*

wegfērend m. *wayfarer, traveller,* Bo,GD.

wegfērende *wayfaring, ÆH,GD.* ['*wayfering*']

wegfōr f. *travel, journey,* WW 423³³.

wegg=wecg

weggedāl n. *road-dividing, cross-way,* Gl.

weggelǣte fn. *junction of roads, Gl.* ['*wayleet*']

weggē-slŏ? -sīða? (v. OEG 861) *travelling companion.*

weggewit n. *aberration* (*of mind*), CPs 115¹ᵇ.

weg-lā interj. '*euge!*' PPs 69⁴. [=wā lā]

weglēas *out of the way, erroneous : without a road,* WW. ['*wayless*']

weglēast (ī²) f. *trackless place, wilderness,* ARSPs 106⁴⁰.

wegnest (æ¹) n. *food for a journey,* HL : *viaticum,* BH.

wegrēaf n. *highway robbery,* LL.

wegtwiflung f. *branching of roads,* WW 179¹⁶. [=-twislung]

wegu f. *vehicle,* GD 314²⁵.

wegur (WW 143¹³)=wīgār

wehsan=weaxan

wehte pret. 3 sg. of weccan.

wei v. wā; **weig**=weg

wel I. adv. (comp. bet) 'WELL,' *abundantly,* Æ,CP : *very, very easily, very much : fully, quite,* Æ : *nearly : pleonastic* (as in ēac w.=*also*), *sometimes*=*indeed, to be sure.* tō w. *too well.* w. nēah *nearly, almost.* w. hwǣr, w. gehwǣr *for the most part, nearly everywhere.* wella *alas!* (cp. wā lā). **II.**=wæl. **III.**=wiell. **IV.**=wiel

wel-=hwel-, wæl-, weal-, wiel-

wela (a, ea, eo) m. '*weal*,' *prosperity, happiness, riches* (often in pl.), *BH,Bo,Bl,G, Gen; AO,*CP.

Wēland m. *the Smith-God, Northern Vulcan.*

welbescēawod *discreet, considerate,* RB, WW.

welboren '*well-born*,' *noble, Æ,*LG.

welcn=wolcen

weldǣd (ē²) f. *good deed, benefit, kindness,* Ph. ['*weldede*']

weldōn anv. *to do well,* CP : *benefit, satisfy, please,* MtL 15¹⁵.

weldōnd (ōe) m. *benefactor,* Gl,DR.

weldōnnes f. *well-doing, kindness,* DR 13¹⁷.

weleg=welig

welena gp. of wela.

weler (eo) mf. *lip, Æ,*CP.

weleðig *rich,* ANS 128·299.

welfremming f. *good deed, benefit,* DR 187¹⁷.

welfremnes f. *benefit,* DR.

welg=welig

welga=weliga wm. of welig adj.

welgā interj. *hail!* WW 25²³.

welgeboren=welboren

welgecwēme *well-pleasing,* SPs,VH.

welgecwēmedlic *well-pleasing,* SPs.
welgecwēmnes f. *favour,* DR.
welgedōn *well-done, good, beneficent,* CP.
welgehwǣr=welhwǣr
welgelīcian *to please well : be well pleased,* AO,CVPs.
welgelīcwirðe *well pleased, acceptable,* VPs 118¹⁰⁸.
welgelīcwirðnes f. *good pleasure,* VPs 140⁷.
welgespring=wyllspring
welgestemned *having a good voice,* ANS 84·6.
welgetȳd *well-instructed,* ES 39·354.
welgewende *thriving,* MFH 178.
welgian=weligian
welhǣwen *beautifully coloured,* CP 411²⁸.
welhrēowlīce=wælhrēowlīce
welhwā †pron. *each, every.*
±**welhwǣr** adv. *(nearly) everywhere,* CP.
±**welhwilc**† (e, y) pron. *each, any, nearly every.*
welig I. *well-to-do, rich, prosperous,* AO,B, WW; CP. ['*wealy*'] **II.** m. '*willow,*' LCD, LG.
±**weligian** *to be prosperous, abound : enrich,* Æ. [v. '*awelgien*']
weligstedende (woegl-) *making rich,* DR 98⁹.
well=(1) will; (2) wel; **wella**=wiella
wellā=wā lā; **welle**=wille
wellende (VPs)=willende pres. ptc. of willan.
wellere *bosom, fold, hollow,* WW.
wellibbende (y²) *living well, well conducted, reputable,* CP.
wellīcian *to please well,* MFH 178.
wellīcung f. *agreeableness,* EPs 68¹⁴.
wellīcwyrðe (u³) *well-pleasing,* BCPs 146¹⁰.
wellyrge (GL)=wælcyrige
welm(a)=wielm(a)
-welm v. fōt-w.; **Wēlond**=Wēland
welor=weler; **welp**=hwelp
welrēab (Ep,Erf 642)=wælrēaf
welrūmlīce adv. *graciously,* DR.
welrūmmōd *gracious,* DR 12²⁰.
wel-spring, -sprynge (CP)=wyll(ge)spring
welstincende *fragrant,* CP 439³³.
welswēgende *melodious,* SPs 150⁵.
welt, welð=wielt, wielð pres. 3 sg. of wealdan, weallan.
welðungen† *honoured, in high repute.*
weluc=weoloc
welung f. *revolution (of a wheel),* OEG 28³⁰. [wielwan]
welweorðe *of high esteem,* LCD 3·432'.
welwilled-=welwillend-
welwillende *well-wishing, benevolent, kindly, good,* Æ,Chrd; CP. ['*well-willing*']
welwillendlīce *benevolently, lovingly, kindly.*

wel-wille(n)dnes, -wilnes f. *benevolence, good-will, kindness,* Æ. ['*wellwillingness*']
wel-wyll-, -wylle(n)d-=welwillend-
welwyrcend m. *well-doer,* BL 137¹⁴.
welwyrcende *well-doing,* AS.
wem=wamm
wēman *to sound, be heard,* AN 740 : *announce,* AN 1480 : (±) *persuade, convince, lead astray.*
wēmend m. *herald, declarer,* EL 880.
wēmere m. *procurer,* WW 171²⁸.
±**wemman** (æ) *to defile, besmirch, profane, injure, ill-treat, destroy,* BH,Lk,LL,Ps; Æ, CP : *abuse, revile.* [v. '*wem,*' '*awem*']
+**wemmedlic** *corruptible,* ÆL 2·348⁸. adv. -līce, WW.
+**wemmednes** f. *defilement,* Æ.
±**wemmend** m. *adulterer, fornicator,* OEG.
+**wemmendlic** *seducing, corrupting,* OEG 2912.
±**wemming** m. *defilement, blemishing, spoiling,* OEG : (+) *profanation.* ['*wemming*']
+**wemmodlīce** (æ) adv. *corruptly,* WW 89².
wemnes=wemmednes
wen=(1) wynn; (2) wenn
wēn I. fm. (n?) *belief, hope, opinion, expectation, supposition,* Bo : *probability,* B : *estimation.* w. is ðæt *perhaps,* Bl,CP : *name of the rune for* w. ['*ween*'] **II.**= wægn
+**wēn** *to bend, twist,* NC 297 (A 14·139).
wēna m. *hope, opinion, expectation, idea, fancy,* CP.
±**wēnan** (w. g. or a.) *to '* WEEN,*' fancy, imagine, believe, think,* Æ; CP : *expect, hope,* Æ,AO,CP : *fear (for), despair (of)* : *esteem : wonder,* ES 37·191.
wenbȳl m. *boil, carbuncle,* LCD.
wencel I. (i) n. *child,* Bas,GD. ['*wenchel*'] **II.**=wancol
wend m. *what turns up, an event,* Bo,TC.
+**wend**=+wind
±**wendan** *to turn, direct,* Æ,CP : ' WEND' *one's way, go,* Æ,AO : *return : change, alter, vary, restore,* Æ : *happen : convert : translate,* CP. w. on *to turn against.* [windan]
wēnde pret. 3 sg. of wēnan.
Wendelsǣ mf. *Mediterranean Sea,* AO.
-wenden v. ed-w.
wendend m. *that which turns round,* WW 489¹².
wendende *movable, revolving,* Sc 97⁴.
wendere m. *translator, interpreter,* OEG 5259.
Wendle† mp. *Vandals.*
wendung f. *change, turning, rotation,* CP, Sc. ['*wending*']
+**wēne** *perhaps,* MkR 14² (oe).

wēnendlic *to be hoped for,* GD269¹⁴.

wēnere=wægnere

wēnestu=wēnstu; **weng**=wang

±**wenian** *to accustom, habituate, inure, train,* Æ,CP : *entertain, treat* : (+) *tame* : *break off,* '*wean*' *from,* RB. w. mid wynnum *treat kindly.* w. tō wiste *feast, entertain.*

wēninga=wēnunga

wēnlic *comely,* Æ : '*conveniens,*' MkL. adv. -līce *handsomely,* BF44⁸.

wenn I. mf. '*wen,*' *tumour,* Lcd,WW. II. (K)=wynn

wennan=wenian

wenncīcen n. *little wen,* ZDA31·46.

wennsealf (wen-) f. *wen-salve, ointment for a tumour,* LCD.

wenspryng m. '*nævus,*' *mole,* WW451¹⁹.

wēnstu=wēnst ðu, pres. 2 sing. of wēnan.

wensum=wynsum

went pres. 3 sg. of wendan.

Wentas, Wente, Went-Sæte, -Sætas mp. *people of Gwent* (roughly=Monmouthshire).

wēnð pres. 3 sing. of wēnan.

wēnung f. *expectation, hope,* BH; AO112¹² : *doubt.* ['*weening*']

wēn-unga, -unge (æ) adv. *possibly, perhaps, by chance,* Æ.

wenwyrt f. *crowfoot? lesser celandine? darnel?* LCD.

wēo (RD57⁵)=wōh? or wēa?

wēobed, wēobud=wēofod

wēoce f. *lamp or candle-'wick,*' IM.

wēocs=wēox pret. 3 sg. of weaxan.

wēocson pret. pl. of wacsan (=wascan).

wēocsteall (ES11·64)=wēohsteall

weocu=wucu

wēod n. *herb, grass,* G; CP : '*weed,*' Bo.

weodewe=wuduwe

wēodhōc m. '*weed-hook,*' *hoe,* Cp; LL 455,15.

wēodian *to* '*weed,*' LL454,9.

wēodmōnað m. *August,* MEN,MH.

weodo, weodu=wudu

weoduma=weotoma

wēodung f. '*weeding,*' WW105³.

weofan (VPs)=wefan

wēofod (e²) nm. *altar,* CP,Mt,RB. ['*weved*']

wēofodbōt f. *fine for injuring a priest, which was applied in support of the altar,* v. LL 2·276.

wēofodheorð (wībed-) m. *altar-hearth,* GD.

wēofodhrægl (wīgbed-) n. *altar-cover,* BH 90².

wēofod-scēat (Æ), -scēata m. *altar-cloth.*

wēofodsteall m. *place of the altar,* LL (254n).

wēofod-ðegn, -ðēn m. *altar-attendant, priest.*

wēofodðēnung f. *altar-service,* LL380,2.

wēofodwiglere (wigbed-) m. *soothsayer,* WW108¹⁰.

+**weofu** pl. of +wef.

wēofud=wēofod

weofung f. *weaving,* WW490³⁸.

wēog=wīg

weogas=wegas nap. of weg.

wēoh=wīg

wēohse=wēox pret. 3 sg. of weaxan.

wēohsteall m. *place of the altar, sanctuary, choir,* LL.

weol=weoll; **weol-** (A)=wel-

weolc I. pret. 3 sg. of wealcan. II.=weoloc

weolcen=wolcen

weolc-rēad, weolcen-=weolocrēad

weold pret. 3 sg. of wealdan.

weoll pret. 3 sg. of weallan.

weolm=wielm

weolme (=ea) f. *choice, pick of one's fellow-creatures,* CR445.

weoloc (e, i, y) m. '*whelk,*' *cockle, murex,* BH,Gl : (*purple*) *dye from the murex.*

weolocbasu *purple,* GL.

weolocrēad *shell-fish red, scarlet, purple,* BH,GL.

weolocscyll (e³) f. *whelk, cockle, shell-fish,* BH.

weoloctælg m. *purple dye,* WW. [telg]

weolt pret. 3 sg. of wealtan.

weoning (WW234²²)=meoning

wēop pret. 3 sg. of wēpan.

wēop-=wēp-; **weor**=wer I.

weorad=werod

weorc (e, o) n. '**WORK**,' *labour, action, deed,* Æ,CP : *exercise* : (†) *affliction, suffering pain, trouble, distress* (v. JAW52) : *fortification.* weorcum *with difficulty.*

+**weorc** n. *work, workmanship, labour, construction* : *structure, edifice,* Æ : *military work, fortification.*

weorc- v. also wyrc-.

weorccræft m. *mechanics,* OEG55⁶.

weorcdǣd (oe¹, ē²) f. *action, operation,* DR 125¹⁸.

weorcdæg m. *work-day,* CM,RB.

weorce I.† adj. *painful, bitter, difficult, hard.* II. adv. *hardly, with difficulty,* JUL.

weorcful *active,* Sc169¹ : *industrious,* OEG 55⁶.

weorcgerēfa m. *foreman, overseer,* Æ.

-**weorcheard,** -weorclic v. un-w.

weorchūs (e) n. *workshop,* WW.

+**weorclic** *pertaining to work,* OEG1042.

weorcmann (e) m. '*workman,*' Bo,LG.

weorcnȳten n. *working cattle,* LL26n.

weorcrǣden f. *corvée-work,* EC377¹.

weorcsige m. *success in work,* LCD1·388'.

weorcstän m. *hewn stone*, Æ.

weorcsum *painful*, GEN594.

weorcðeow† mf. *servant, slave*, GEN.

weorcuhta m. *hour of matins on a non-festival day*, NC332 (cp. mæsseuhta).

weorcum v. weorc.

weorcwyrðe *fit for work, able-bodied*, MFH 178.

weord=wyrd

weordungdæg (WW206³²)=weorðungdæg

weored=werod I.; **weoreld**=woruld

weoren pp. of weosan.

weorf n. *beast of burden* (v. CC129), *cattle*.

weorf-=hweorf-

weorfemeoluc? f. *milk from wild cattle?* LCD 102a (MS ðeorfe-).

weorftord (-oruf-) m. *dung of cattle*, PPs112⁶.

weorht=worht pp. of wyrcean.

+**weorht**=+wyrht; **weorian**=werian

weorld (BL)=woruld; **weorm**=wyrm

weormian=wearmian; **weorn**=worn

weornan=wiernan

±**weornian** (u) *to pine away, become weak, fade, wither, destroy*, Æ.

weorod=werod I. and II.

weorold=woruld

+**weorp** n. *throwing, dashing, tossing*, AN 306 : *what is thrown up*.

±**weorpan** (o, u, y) **I.** sv³ *to throw, cast, cast down, cast away*, Bo,G; Æ,AO,CP : *throw off, out, expel* : *throw upon* : *open*, ÆL : *drive away*, Jn : *sprinkle*, B,Lcd : *hit*, Bo : (+) *reach by throwing*, CP. w. tō handa *to hand over*. w. handa on *lay hands on (a person)* : (w. d. pers.) *charge with, accuse of*. ['*warp*'] **II.**=wierpan

weorpere m. *thrower, caster*, Rd28⁷. ['*warper*']

weorpian *to pine away*, ERPs38¹².

weorras (Cp161c)=wearras, nap. of wearr.

weort=wyrt; **weorteard**=ortgeard

weorð **I.** (e, ea, i, o, u, y) n. '*worth,*' *value, amount, price, purchase-money, ransom*, AO,G,VPs; CP. **II.** (ie, o, u, y) adj. *worth*, LL : *worthy, honoured, noble, honourable, of high rank*, Æ,BC,Bo; CP : *valued, dear, precious*, AO,CP : *fit, capable*. **III.**= worð I.

±**weorðan**³ (u, y) *to become, get, be* (passive auxiliary), *be done, be made*, CP : *happen, come to pass, arise, take place, settle* : (+) impers. *get on with, please, agree*, AO,Chr : *think of, occur to*. ['WORTH,' '*i-worth*']

weorðe=weorð, wierðe

weorðere m. *worshipper*, JnL.

weorðful (u¹) *worthy, honourable, honoured, glorious, good*, B,G,Chr,Lcd. ['*worthful*']

weorðfullic (u) *worthy, honoured, honourable, distinguished*, CP. adv. -līce, AO.

weorðfulnes f. *dignity, honour*, AO.

weorðgeorn *desirous of honour, high-souled*.

±**weorðian** (o, u, y) *to esteem, honour, worship, distinguish, celebrate, exalt, praise*, AO,CP : *adorn, deck* : *enrich, reward*. ['WORTH,' '*i-wurthi*']

-**weorðiend** v. rōd-w.

weorðig=worðig

weorðléas (u) *worthless*, WW130²⁰.

weorðlic (u, y) *important, valuable, splendid*, Æ '*O,Chr,Jul* : *worthy, estimable, honourable, distinguished, exalted*, Bo,Chr : *fit, becoming*. adv. -līce. ['*worthly*']

weorðlicnes f. *worthiness, honour, estimation*.

weorðmetednes (u¹) '*adinventio,*' SPs76¹².

weorð-mynd, -mynt (u) fmn. *honour, dignity, glory*, AO,CP : *mark of distinction*.

weorðnes (e, ie, o, u, y) f. *worth, estimation* : *splendour, rank, honour* : *integrity*.

weorðscipe (o, u) m. *worth, respect, honour, dignity, glory*, Æ; AO,CP : *advantage, good* : *distinction* (*in behaviour*), LL. ['*worship*']

weorððearfa (u¹, y¹) *poor man*, BK12.

weorðung f. *honouring, distinction, honour, glory*, CP,LG : *celebration, worship*, Æ : *excellence* : *ornament*. ['*worthing*']

weorðungdæg m. *day for bestowal of honours or offices, festival*, BK23.

weorðungstōw f. *place of worship, the Tabernacle*, Æ.

weoruc=weorc; **weorud**=werod

weoruf=weorf; **weoruld**=woruld

wēos gs. and nap. of wēoh.

weos-=wes-

weosnian=wisnian

weot-=wit-; **weotod**=witod

wēoðel=wēðel, wædl

weoðerweard=wiðerweard

weoðo-, wēoðo-=wiðo-, wiðo-

wēox pret. 3 sg. of weaxan.

weoxian *to cleanse?* A9·261,262.

±**wēpan**⁷ *to '* weep,' *complain, bewail, mourn over, deplore*, Æ,BH,CP,G,MH.

wēpen=wǣp(e)n

wēpende adj. '*weeping,*' Æ,BH,Ps.

wēpendlic *deplorable, mournful*, CHR. adv. -līce.

wēpman=wǣpnedmann

wēpn, wēpned=wǣpen, wǣpned

wēpnian=wǣpnian

wer **I.** m. *male being* : *man* : *husband*, Æ, AO : (†) *hero*. ['WERE'] **II.** m. *the legal money-equivalent of a person's life, a man's legal value* (=wergild), LL. **III.** m. '*weir,*' *dam, fish-trap*, CP,Ct; Mdf : *catch, draught*. [werian] **IV.** (or were?) *troop, band*, WW, ÆL30¹⁹⁵.

wĕr=wǣr II.; weran=werian
werbēam m. *warrior*, Ex486.
wer-borg, -borh m. *pledge for the payment of* 'wergild,' LL.
werc (GL,VPs)=weorc
wercan=wyrcan
wercyn n. *human race, tribe*, RIM61.
werdan=wierdan; were=wer
wēre (M)=wǣre II.
wered=werod; wĕreg=wĕrig
weregan (KGL)=wiergan
werfǣhðo f. *feud by which* 'wer' *is incurred, breach of the peace*, LL.
werfan=hwierfan
werg=(1) wearg; (2) wyr(i)g
wergan (A)=(1) wiergan; (2) werian I.
wĕrgan wk. ds. of wĕrig.
wergeld=wergild; wergend=weriend
wĕrgenga=wǣrgenga; werglan=wiergan
±wĕrgian *to* 'weary,' *exhaust, be or become tired*, BH,GD; Æ,AO,CP.
wergild (æ¹, e², i², y²) n. *compensation, value of a man's life* (v. LL2·731). ['*wergeld*']
wergildðēof m. *thief who might be redeemed by payment of his* 'wergild,' BC,LL. ['*wergeldthief*']
wergnes=weargnes
wergulu f. *crab-apple*, LCD3·34¹⁴ (v. BTs and MP24·220).
wĕrgum dsmn. of wĕrig.
wergyld=wergild
werhād m. *male sex, virility, manhood*, Æ.
werhbrǣde=weargbrǣde
werhta=wyrhta
wĕrî=wĕrig
±werian (æ) I. *to guard, keep, defend*, AO : *ward off, hinder, prevent, forbid : restrain : occupy, inhabit*, GU322 : *dam up*, CP469². ['*WERE*'] II. *to clothe, cover over : put on,* '*wear*,' *use*, AO,Chr,LL : *stock* (*land*). III. (+) *to make an alliance*, BH52¹⁹.
wĕrian=wĕrgian
weriend m. *defender*, Æ,W.
werig=wearg, wyrig
wĕrig '*WEARY*,' *tired, exhausted, miserable, sad*, AO,CP : *unfortunate*. [wōr]
werigcweðan=wyrgcweðan
werigen=werian
werigend=weriend
wĕrigferhð† adj. *weary, cast down*.
wĕrigian=wĕrgian
wĕrigmōd† *weary, cast down*.
werignes=wyrignes
wĕrignes f. '*weariness*,' BH.
werilic=werlic; wĕrines=wĕrignes
wering f. *weir, dam*, CP277⁸.
werlād f. *clearing by the oaths of a number of men according to a man's* 'wer,' LL.
werlēas *without a husband*, LL.

werlic *male, masculine*, ÆGR : *manly* : *marital*. adv. -līce, Æ.
wĕrloga=wǣrloga; werm-=wearm-
wermǣgð† f. *tribe, nation*, GEN.
wermet n. *man's measure, stature*, WW.
wermōd m. *wormwood, absinthe*, Æ.
wern-=wearn-, wiern-
werna (Cp)=wrenna
wernæg(e)l m. (*man's nail?*), *wart, tumour*, Æ. ['*warnel*']
werod (eo¹, e²) I. n. [nap. werodu, werod] *throng, company, band, multitude*, Bl,Cp, G; Æ : *host, army, troop, legion*, Æ,AO. ['*wered*'] II. *sweet*, Æ. III.† n. *sweet drink, mead*.
werodian *to grow sweet*, Bo51⁴.
+werodlǣcan (e²) *to make sweet or pleasant*, Sc196⁵.
werodlēst f. *lack of fighters*, EL63.
werodlīce adv. *sweetly*, CM887.
werodnes f. *sweetness, pleasantness*, Æ.
werold=woruld
wĕron (M)=wǣron pret. pl. of wesan.
weroð=waroð
werp f. *recovery* (*from sickness*), CP457¹⁶. [=wyrpe]
werpan=weorpan
werrēaf n. *civil clothing*, CHRD.
werrest (BL)=wierrest
werscipe=wǣrscipe
werse, werst=wierse, wierrest
werstede m. *place of a weir*, EC246¹⁰.
wert (KGL)=wyrt; werte=wearte
wer-tihtle, -tyhtle f. *charge involving the penalty of* 'wer,' *homicide*, LL.
werð=wierð pres. 3 sg. of weorðan.
werðēod† f. *folk, people, nation*.
werðnes (K)=weorðnes; werud=werod
weruld=woruld; wĕrun (NG)=wǣron
werwulf (-rew-) m. '*werewolf*,' *fiend*, LL.
wes (VPs)=wæs pret. 3 sg. of wesan.
wĕsa m. *drunkard*, WW84⁵. [wōs]
wesan anv. pres. 1 sg. eom, bēo, 2 eart, bist, 3 is, bið; pl. sind(on); bēoð; pret. wæs, wǣron; subj. pres. sīe, sȳ, bēo; sīn, bēon; pret. wǣre, wǣren *to* '*BE*'* : *happen*. v. also bēon.
+wesan *to strive, contend*, SOL181. [cp. +wosa]
±wĕsan *to soak, macerate : ooze*, Lcd : *dye*, OEG5196. ['*weese*']
wesand=wesend; wesc=wæsc
wĕse *moist, macerated*, LCD3·292⁶. [wōs]
wesend (eo) m. *bison*, GL.
wesendhorn m. *bison's horn*, TC536¹.
wesendlīce *essentially*, GD336; 337.
wesing f. '*confectio*,' '*debilitatio*,' v. OEG 1857.

wesle, weosule (*Gl*) f. '*weasel*,' *Æ,LL.*
+wesnes f. *dissension,* BH 274⁵.
wesp=wæps
west adv. *westwards,* '*west*,' *in a westerly direction, Bo,Chr,Ct,Ma*; AO.
westan, westane adv. *from the west, Gen, Lcd*; AO. be westan (prep. w. d.) *west of.* ['*westan*']
±**wēstan** *to lay waste, ravage, AO,PPs.* ['*weste*']
westanhealf=westhealf
westannorðan *north-west* (*wind*), OEG.
westansūðan *south-west,* AO.
westansūðanwind m. *south-west wind,* CVPs 77²⁶.
westanweard *westward,* AA 38¹⁶.
westanwind m. *west wind,* AO 17¹⁵.
West-Centingas mp. *people of West Kent,* CHR 999.
westdǣl m. *west quarter, western part, Bl, VPs*; AO. ['*westdeal*']
West-Dene mp. *West Danes,* B.
wēste *waste, barren, desolate, deserted, uninhabited, empty, B,BH,G,VPs.* wēste land *waste land, desert,* EHR 1912. ['*weste*']
westem (VPs)=wæstm
westema v. westerne
wēsten I. nmf. *waste, wilderness, desert, Æ, AO,CP.* **II.** adj. *waste, desolate, Æ.*
westende m. '*west end*,' *AO,Chr.*
wēstengryre m. *terror of the desert,* Ex 117.
wēstensetla m. *hermit, anchorite,* MH,RB.
wēstenstaðol m. *waste place,* RUIN 28.
westenwind=westanwind
wēstern (*LG*; '*western*')=wēsten
westerne '*western*,' *westerly, BH,Chr,Gl.* wester(r)a *more westerly*; westema, westmest (AO) *most westerly.*
westeweard=westweard
westhealf f. *west side, AO,Chr.* ['*westhalf*']
wēstig (oe) *waste, deserted, desert, NG,RG.* ['*westy*']
westlang adv. *extending westwards,* KC.
westm (VPs)=wæstm
westmearc f. *western boundary,* OET 484.
westmest (*AO,BC,KC*; '*westmost*') v. westerne.
wēstnes f. *desolation : desert place,* EPs 77¹⁹.
westnorðlang adv. *extending north-westwards,* AO 22¹⁷.
westnorðwind m. *north-west wind,* WW.
westra (*BC*; '*wester*')=westerra; v. westerne.
westrīce n. *western kingdom,* AO,CHR.
westrihtes (y²) adv. *due west, westwards,* AO.
westrodor† m. *western* (=*evening*) *sky.*
westsǣ f. *western sea,* AO,BH.

West-Seaxe, -Seaxan mp. *West Saxons : Wessex.*
westsūðende m. *south-west extremity,* AO 8²³.
westsūðwind m. *south-west wind,* WW.
westu=wes ðu, 2 pers. imperat. of wesan.
West-Wēalas mp. *Cornishmen,* CHR.
westwe(a)rd I. adv. *westwards, Chr,Lcd.* ['*westward*'] **II.** adj. *westerly, AO,Ct.*
westweg m. *western way,* PPs 74⁶.
westwind m. '*west wind*,' *BH* 458¹⁷.
wesule=wesle
wēt I. pres. 3 sg. of wēdan. **II.** adj.=wǣt
wet-, wēt-=wæt-, wǣt-
weterǣdre=wæterǣdre
+wetfæstan=+wedfæstan
wetma=wituma
wēðan *to assuage, make calm,* PPs 106²⁸.
wēðe *sweet, mild, pleasant,* BH,CR.
weðel *swathe, bandage,* WW 22¹⁴.
wēðel=wēðl, wǣdl; **wēðelnes**=wǣdelnes
weðer I. m. '*wether*' *sheep, ram, Æ,GD.* **II.**=weder I.
weðerwynde=wiðewinde; **wēðl**=wǣdl
±**wēðnes** f. *suavity, mildness,* DR,PPs.
wex (VPs)=weax; **wexe**=weax
wēxon=wēoxon pret. pl. of weaxan.
wh-=hw-
wī I.=wīg. **II.** (K)=weg
wiaht (K)=wiht
wiarald, wiaruld (K)=woruld
wibba m. *crawling thing, beetle,* WW 121²⁵.
wībed (VPs)=wēofod
wiber=wifer; **wibil** (GL)=wifel
wibora=wīgbora
wīc nf. *dwelling-place, lodging, habitation, house, mansion, B,BH,Gen*; CP : *village, town, Bl,Mk* : in pl. *entrenchments, camp, castle, fortress : street, lane : bay, creek.* ['*wick*'; v. Mdf]
wīc-=wuc-
±**wīcan¹** *to yield, give way, fall down,* B,Ex.
wīcbora=wīgbora
wicca I. m. *wizard, magician, soothsayer, astrologer, LL,WW.* ['*witch*'] **II.**=wicga
wicce (y) f. '*witch*,' *Æ,OEG.*
wiccecræft m. '*witchcraft*,' *magic, OEG,LL.*
wiccedōm m. *witchcraft,* BK 20; *HL* 11¹²³. ['*witchdom*']
wiccian *to use witchcraft, LL.* ['*witch*']
wiccræft (CRA 70)=wiccecræft? or wicgcræft (*skill with horses*)? (BT).
wiccung f. *enchantment, LL.* ['*witching*']
wiccungdōm m. *witchcraft,* DA 121.
wicdæg=wucdæg
wice I. mf. '*wych*'-*elm, Gl,Lcd.* **II.** (*Chr, BH*)=wuce. **III.**=weoce
wīce f. *office, function, Æ* : *officer,* CHR 1120. ['*wike*']
wīceard m. *dwelling-place,* GU 907.

wīceng=wīcing

wīcfreoðu f. *protection of a dwelling*, GnE129.

wīcg (y) n. *horse*, B (v. rare in prose). ['*widge*']

wīcga m. *insect, beetle*, Lcd,WW.

wīcgefēra (Chr897a)=wīcgerēfa

wīcgerēfa m. *bailiff, reeve of a '*wīc*' or vill*, Chr897bcd : '*publicanus*,' *tax-gatherer*, WW.

wīcgung=wiccung

wīcherpað m. *a public road to a '*wīc*'* (BT), KC3·418²⁶.

±**wīcian** *to dwell, lodge, rest in*, WW; Æ, AO : *encamp, bivouac*, CP : *harbour, anchor*, AO. ['*wick*']

wīcing m. *pirate, viking*, AO.

wīcingsceaðe f. *piracy*, Gl.

wīcnera, wīcnere (Æ) m. *steward, bailiff*, A, ZDA. ['*wickner*']

wīcnian *to attend upon*, Æ,RB127³.

wīcscēawere m. *provider of a home*, Bl163¹².

wīcsteall m. *camping-place*, Ex92.

wīcstede† m. *dwelling*, B.

wīcstōw f. *dwelling-place, residence : camp, encampment*, Æ,AO.

wīctūn m. *vestibule, court*, PPs.

wicðēn=wucðegn; **wicu**=wucu; **wid**=wið

wīd '*WIDE*,' *vast, broad, long*, Æ; AO,CP. w. and sīd *far and wide*. tō wīdan ealdre, tō wīdan fēore, wīdan fyrhð *for ever*.

wīdan adv. *from far* (v. also wīd), KC. ['*widen*']

wīdbrād *wide-spreading*, Gen643.

wīdcūð adj. *widely known, celebrated*, Æ.

wīde (once+) adv. *widely, afar, far and '*wide*,'* Æ,AO,CP. sīde and w. *far and wide*. ['*WIDE*']

wīdefeorh†=wīdeferð

wīdefeorlic (wider-) *eternal*, WW117²¹.

wīde-ferhð†, -fyrhð **I.** mn. (*long life*), *long duration, long time*. **II.** adv. *always*.

wider-=wiðer-

+**wī-dere** pl. -d(e)ru n. *weather (good or bad), storm, tempest*, AO. [weder]

+**widerian** (impers.) *to be fine weather*, LL 454,12.

wīdewe=wuduwe

wīdfæðme† *ample, extensive*, An.

wīdfarend m. *wanderer*, CP315⁴.

wīdfeorh=wīdeferhð

wīdfērende† *coming from afar*.

wīdferhð=wīdeferhð

wīdfloga† m. *wide-flier (of a dragon)*, B.

wīdfolc n. *great nation*, Gen1638?

wīdgal=wīdgil

wīdgangol *wandering, roving*, CP.

wīdgenge *wandering (monk)*, OEG58¹⁰.

wīd-gil, -gill (e, ie) *wide-spread, broad, extensive*, Æ,CP : *wandering*, GD.

wīdgilnes f. *amplitude, spaciousness*, Æ.

wīdgongel=wīdgangol; **wīdgyl**=wīdgil

wīdhergan *to extol*, CP439³⁴.

wīdlan *to become wider*, GD315.

wīdl mn? *impurity, filth, defilement*, GD, WW.

wīdland† n. *extensive country*, Gen.

wīdlāst† **I.** *far-wandering*. **II.** m. *long wandering, long way or road*, Rd.

±**wīdlian** *to defile, pollute, profane*, LL, NG.

±**wīdmǣran**=±wīdmǣrsian

wīdmǣre *celebrated, well-known*, AO,CP.

±**wīdmǣrsian** (tr., intr.) *to spread abroad, divulge*, Æ : *celebrate*.

wīdmǣrsung f. *proclamation*, Sc96¹¹.

wīdmērsian=wīdmǣrsian

wīdnes f. *width*, WE60¹⁸.

wīdobān=wiðobān

widor=weder; **wīdor-**=wider-

wīdor comp. of wīd.

wīdrynig *far-flowing*, An1509.

wīdsǣ mf. *open sea, ocean*, Æ,AO.

wīdsceop adj. *widely distributed*, Pa6.

wīdscofen *scattered far and wide*, B936.

wīdscriðol *erratic, wandering*, Chrd,LL.

wīdsīð† m. *long journey : far-traveller*.

wīdðil (DR98¹²)=wīdl; **widu**=wudu

widuw-, **wīdw-**=wuduw-

wīdwegas† mp. *distant regions*.

wiebed=wēofod; **wiebel**=wifel

wiece=wuce; **Wieht**=Wiht

wiel (e) m. *slave, servant*, Æ.

wiel- v. also wil-, wyl-.

+**wield** (i, eo) *power, control*, AO. ['*wield*']

±**wieldan** (æ, i, y) *to have power over, control*, CP : *tame, subdue, conquer, seize*, Chr,CP : (+) *compel*, LL265,15 : (+) *temper*. [v. '*WIELD*']

wielde I. (±) (y) *powerful, victorious*, Æ,AO, GD. **II.** *in the power of, under the control of*, Æ.

+**wieldend** (y) *subduer*, GPH391.

wielding (y) f. *domination, rule*, LPs.

wielede pret. 3 sg. of wielwan

wielen (i, y) f. *foreign woman, female slave*, AO.

wielincel n. *little servant, slave*, GPH401.

wielisc (æ, e, ea, i, y) *foreign : British (not Anglo-Saxon)*, BC,Chr,LL : '*Welsh*' : *not free, servile*. [wealh]

wiell, wiella m., wielle (AO) f. (e, i, y) '*WELL*,' *fountain, spring*, CP; Mdf. [weallan] For comps. v. wyll-.

wielle=wille pres. 3 sg. of willan.

wielm (a, æ, e, eo, i, y) m. *boiling, swelling, sur, billow, current, stream*, An,B,BH,CP, Jul : *burning, flame, inflammation : fervour ardour, zeal*, CP. ['*walm*'; weallan]

wielma (e) m. *inflammation*, Lcd31a (v. A46·227).

wielmfȳr (æ) n. *blazing fire*, Cr932.

wielmhāt (y) *burning hot*, Gen2584. [v. *'walm'*]

wieln-=wiln-

wielt I. pres. 3 sg. of wealdan. II.=wielð

wielð pres. 3 sg. of weallan.

wien-=win-

wieoldon=weoldon pret. pl. of wealdan.

±**wierdan**, +wierdlian (e, i, y) *to spoil, injure, destroy, violate, obstruct,* Bo,Cp, LG,Ps. [*'werde'*]

wierding (oe, y) f. *bodily injury*, DR, LL410,3⁵ : *blemish*, OEG649.

wierdnes (oe) f. *injury, vice*, DR.

wiergan (æ, e, i, iri, yri, y) *to abuse, outlaw, condemn, curse, proscribe,* Æ,CP,G,Gl : *blaspheme,* Æ : *do evil.* [For compounds v. wyrg-, wyrig-] [*'wary'*]

wiergen v. grund-w.

wiernan (e, i, y) (w. g. of thing and d. of pers.) *to withhold, be sparing of, deny, refuse, reject, decline,* AO,CP : *forbid, prevent from.* [*'WARN'*]

wiernung (æ) f. *refusal*, LL152,3. [*'warning'*]

wierp m. *cast, throw, shot, blow*, AO.

±**wierpan** (æ, y) *to recover from illness, get better,* CP.

wierpð pres. 3 sg. of weorpan.

wierrest (superl. of yfel) *'worst,'* Æ,Bl,Bo, CP,G,Ps.

wiers (y) adv. *'WORSE,'* CP.

wiersa m., wierse fn. (comp. of yfel *'WORSE,'* CP. [For comps. v. wyrs-]

wierst=wierrest

wierð pres. 3 sg. of weorðan.

wierðe (Bl,CP,G; *'wurthe'*)=weorð

wiese=wīse pl. of wīs.

wieste=wiste, v. witan.

wiet-, wiet-=wit-, wīt-

wiexð pres. 3 sg. of weaxan.

wīf n. *woman, female, lady*, BH,Bl,Cp,LG; Æ,AO,CP : *'wife,'* Bo,Mt; Æ,AO,CP.

+**wīf** I. n. *fate, fortune.* [wefan] II. n. *a disease of the eye,* Lcd3·292².

wīfcild n. *female child*, BH76⁹.

wīfcynn n. *womankind, female sex*, BH,Bl. [*'wifkin'*]

wīfcȳððu f. *company of a woman? intercourse with a woman?* Chr755A.

+**wīfe**=+wīf

wīfel I. m. *'weevil,' beetle*, Cp,Rd. II. (HGl; *'wifle'*)=wifer

wifer *missile, arrow, dart*, v. OEG1103.

wīfērend (KGl)=wegfērend

wīffæst *bound to a wife, married*, LL348,54.

wīffex n. *woman's hair*, WW. [feax]

wīffrēond m. *female friend*, LkLR15⁹.

wīfgāl *licentious, unchaste*, CP453³⁰.

wīfgemǣdla m. *woman's fury*, Lcd122b.

wīfgemāna m. *intercourse with a woman*, Lcd1·336.

wīfgeornes f. *adultery*, MtL15¹⁹.

wīfgifta fp. *dowry, outfit? marriage?* Jul38.

wīfhād m. *womanhood*, Æ : *female sex*, Æ.

wīfhand f. *female inheritor, female side*, Ct.

wīfhealf f. *woman's (i.e. mother's) side*, Chr p3'.

wīfhearpe f. *timbrel*, CPs150⁴.

wīfhīred n. *nunnery*, GD27⁸.

wīfhrægel n. *woman's clothing*, GD212¹⁰.

±**wīfian** *to take a wife, marry (of the man)*, Æ,Bo,LL. [*'wive'; 'i-wive'*]

wīflāc n. *cohabitation, fornication*, LL.

wīflēas *unmarried*, LL(190³). [*'wifeless'*]

wīflēast f. *lack of women*, ÆL10²¹⁶.

wīflic *womanly, feminine, female*, AO,BH, Gl. adv. -līce. [*'wifely'*]

wīflufu† f. *love for a woman.*

wīfmann (o²) m. *'woman,'* Æ,AO,BH,LG; CP : *female servant.*

wīfmyne m. *love for a woman*, Gen1861.

-wīfre v. gange-w.

+**wīfsǣlig** *fortunate*, WW496⁸.

wīfscrūd n. *woman's clothing*, ÆP142; TC530.

wīft=weft

wīfðegn m. *procurer*, WW.

wīfðing n. *marriage, cohabitation*, Lcd,LL. [*'wifthing'*]

±**wīfung** f. *marrying (of the man), wedlock*, Æ.

wīg (KGl)=weg

wīg I. n. *strife, contest, war, battle,* Æ,AO, CP : *valour* : *military force, army,* Æ. II. (wīh, wēoh)† n. *idol, image.*

wīga m. *fighter*, An,Men : *man.* [*'wye'*]

wīgan¹ *to fight, make war*, Æ,B.

wīgār m. *spear, lance*, WW143¹². [wīg, gār]

wīgbǣre *warlike*, WW193¹⁸.

wīgbealu n. *war-bale*, B2046.

wīgbed=wēofod

wīgbill n. *sword*, B1607.

wīgblāc *bravely caparisoned*, Ex204.

wīgblēd? m. *luck in war*, Rim26 (wilbec).

wīgbora m. *fighter*, ÆGr27¹⁶.

wīgbord† n. *shield*, B,Ex.

wīgcræft m. *war-power, art of war*, AO.

wīgcræftig *strong in battle*, B1811.

wīgcyng=wīcing

wīgcyrm m. *noise of battle*, Gen1990.

wīgelung=wīglung

wīgend† m. *warrior, fighter.*

wīgende *fighting*, Æ.

wīgfreca† m. *warrior.*

wīgfruma† m. *war-chief.*

wigg=(1) wīg I.; (2) wicg; **wīgga**=wicga
wīggebed=wēofod; **wīggend**=wīgend
wīggetāwe fp. *war-gear*, B368. [wīg, geatwe]
wīggild (wīh-) n. *idol*, DAN,NC.
wīggryre m. *war-terror*, B1284.
wīghaga† m. *war-hedge*, *phalanx*.
wīgheafola m. *helmet*, B2661.
wīghēap m. *troop of warriors*, B477.
wīgheard *brave in battle*, MA,OEG.
wīghete m. *hostility*, B2121.
wīghryre m. *slaughter, defeat*, B1619.
wīghūs n. *battlement, tower*, AO,CP : *turret (on an elephant's back)*, ÆL25⁵⁶⁰.
wīghyrst f. *war-gear, accoutrements*, RUIN 35.
wīgian *to fight*, LL132,6⁵.
wigle n. *divination*, A,OEG. ['*wiel*']
wīglēoð n. *war-cry, battle-signal*, Ex221.
wiglere m. *soothsayer, wizard*, Æ. ['*wiel-are*']
wiglian *to take auspices, divine*, Æ,LcD.
wīglic *warlike*, Ex;Gl. adv. -līce.
±**wīglung** f. *soothsaying, augury, witchcraft, sorcery*, Æ,WW (wīl-). [v. '*wiel*']
wīgmann m. *warrior*, LL,W.
wīgnoð m. *warfare, war*, WW442¹?
wigol *divining, foreboding*, WW133².
wīgplega† m. *war-play, battle*.
wīgrād (ō) f. *war-path*, GEN2084.
wīgrǣden f. *state of war, battle*, WALD1²².
wīgsigor† m. *victory in a battle*.
wīgslō m. *military expedition*, GEN2094.
wīgsmið I. m. *maker of idols*, PPs113¹². **II.†** m. *warrior*.
wīgspēd† f. *success in war*.
wīgspere n. *war-spear, dart*, WW143¹⁴.
wīgsteall n. *rampart, entrenchment*, LV,GL.
wīgstrang *mighty in war*, WW360³⁶.
wīgtrod n. *path of an army*, Ex491 (or ? wigrod *battle-pole*, Sedgefield).
wīgŏracu† f. *onslaught in battle, attack*.
wīgŏrīst *bold in battle*, JUL432.
wīgwægn m. *war chariot*, AO38.
wīgwǣpen n. *weapon of war*, W170⁸.
wīgweorðung† (ēoh¹) f. *idol-worship*.
wīh=wīg; **wīhaga**=wīghaga
wīhian=wōhhian
wihst pres. 2 sg. of weaxan.
wiht I. (u, y) fn. 'WIGHT,' *person, creature, being* : *whit, thing, something, anything*. II. adv. *at all*. ne w., nǣnig w. *not at all*. nān w. *no whit*. III. (+) f. *weighing, 'weight,'* Lcd,LL.
Wiht f. *Isle of Wight*, CHR. [L. Vectis]
wihte adv. (d. instr. of wiht) *at all*.
±**wihte** n. '*weight*,' Lcd.
wihtga=wītega
Wihtland n. *Isle of Wight*, BH,CHR.

wihtmearc f. *plumb-line*, OEG3005.
Wiht-sǣtan, -sǣte mp. *inhabitants of the Isle of Wight*, BH52⁴.
Wihtware mp. *inhabitants of the Isle of Wight*, CHR.
wīhūs=wīghūs; **wīl**=wiell
wīl n. '*wile*,' *trick*, CHR1128.
wil-=wiel-, wigl-, will-, wyll-
wīla (y) '*catenarum*,' v. OEG3560n and 7²⁵⁷.
wīlāwei=wā lā wā
wīlbec m. *stream of tears*, RIM26. [or? winbrec (*war's alarms*) ES65·189]
+**wilbod** n. *commandment*, WW191²².
wilboda m. *messenger of joy, angel*, GU1220.
+**wilcð** n. *rolling, tossing*, JPs88¹⁰. [weal-can]
wilcuma I. m. '*welcome*' *guest*, B,DHy,Sat. **II.**=wilcume
wilcume interj. '*welcome!*' GD,LG,WW.
±**wilcumian** *to 'welcome,' greet*, Æ,Mt.
wild? *wild*, OEG4706n.
wild-=wield-
wildæg m. *day of joy*, CR459.
wilddēor n. (occl. dp. wildrum) *wild beast*, Bo,Bl,VPs; AO : *deer, reindeer*. ['*wild-deer*']
wilddēorcyn n. *species of wild beasts*, RWH57¹⁵.
wilddēoren *like wild beasts, fierce*, Sc99⁷.
wilddēorlic *savage*, CP. adv. -līce.
wilde I. 'WILD,' *untamed, uncontrolled*, A, AO : *uncultivated, desert*, AO. **II.** adv.
+**wilde**=+wielde
wildēar (N), wil(de)dēor, wilder, wildor=wilddēor
wildefȳr n. *lightning*, CHR : *erysipelas*, WW.
wildeswīn m. *wild boar*, ANS129·44.
wildgōs f. *wild goose*, WW364!.
-wildian v. ā-w.
wildrum v. wilddēor.
wile pres. 3 sg. of willan.
+**wile**=+will
wileg(e)=wilige
wilewīse=wiligwīse
wilfægen *fain, glad*, Æ.
wilfullīce adv. *willingly*, Gl. ['*wilfully*']
wilgæst (e²) m. *welcome guest*, MOD7.
wilgedryht† f. *willing band*.
wilgehlēða m. *intimate companion*, RD15⁵. [hlōð]
wilgeofa=wilgiefa
wilgesīð† m. *willing companion*.
wilgest=wilgæst
wilgestealla=willgestealla
wilgiefa† (eo, i) m. *gracious giver, king*.
wilhrēmig *rejoicing in satisfied desire*, WW 376²⁶.
wilhrēðig *exultant*, EL1117.
wilia=wiliga; **wilian** (Æ)=wylwan

±**wilian** (y) *to connect, bind,* Sc 11⁸; W.

wilie=(1) wilige; (2) wielle

wiliga m., wilige (y) f. *basket, Æ,Mk,WW.* ['willy']

wiligwīse (wile-) *basket-wise,* Bl 125²¹.

wiliht (y) *full of willows,* Ct.

wilisc=wielisc

will (1) n.=willa m.; (2)=wiell

+**will** n. *will, wish, desire,* Bo; AO,CP. ['i-will']

will-=wiell-, wyll-

willa m. I.*mind,* 'WILL,' *determination, purpose, Æ,*CP. sylfes willum *of one's own accord* : *desire, wish, request* : *joy, delight, pleasure* : *desirable thing, valuable.* II. (æ, e, y) *fountain, spring.*

willan (y) anv. pres. 1, 3 sg. ind. and subj. wile, wille, wielle, pret. wolde *to* 'WILL*,' *be willing, wish, desire, Æ,AO,CP* : (denoting habit, repetition)· *to be used to, Æ* : *to be about to* : (sign of the future tense) *shall, will, Æ,CP.*

willcuma=wilcuma

willen I. *willing, desirous,* AS 63²⁴. II.= wyllen

-**willen** v. dol-w.

willendlic (BH)=hwilwendlic

willendīce adv. 'willingly,' *WW*; VH.

willes adv. *willingly, voluntarily, Æ.*

willfægen=wilfægen

willgebrōðor mp. *brothers,* Gen 971.

willgesīð=wilgesīð

willge-steald, -steall n. *riches, wealth,* Gen 2146? (or ? willgestealla m. *willing companion*).

willgesweostor fp. *sisters,* Gen 2607.

willgeðofta m. *pleasant companion,* Gen 2026.

±**willian** *to wish, desire,* Bo,Ps.

willic (y) *from a fountain,* WW. [wiell]

willīce (y) adv. *willingly, voluntarily, CM.* ['willy']

willnung=wilnung

willsele m. *pleasant dwelling,* Ph 213.

willsīð=wilsīð

willspell† n. *good tidings,* El.

willsum=wilsum

willung f. *desire,* BH. ['willing']

willwong m. *pleasant plain,* Ph 89.

willwyrdan *to be complaisant,* AB 34·10.

wilm=wielm

wiln (Æ)=wielen

+**wilnes** f. *desire, wish,* LPs 20³.

±**wilnian** (w. g. or a.) *to wish, long for, desire, will, An,B,Bo,Chr,CP,G*; AO : *beg for, supplicate, entreat, petition for* : *tend towards,* CP. ['wilne']

±**wilniendlic** *desirable* : *capable of desire,* ÆL 1⁹⁷ : (+) *unbridled,* ÆH 2·398'.

±**wilnung** f. *desire, longing (good or bad),* AO,CP. ['wilning']

wiloc=weoloc

Wil-sǣte, -sǣtan mp. *people o Wilts* : *Wiltshire,* Chr.

wilsc=wielisc

wilsīð m. *desired journey,* An,BH.

wilsum(lic) *desirable, delightful* : *ready, willing, voluntary, spontaneous* : *devoted.* adv. -līce.

±**wilsumnes** f. *willingness, devotion,* BH : *free-will offering,* LRPs : *vow.*

wilt I. pres. 2 sg. of willan. II. pres. 3 sg. of wealdan.

wiltīðe *having obtained one's wish, glad,* OEG 2219³⁵⁸⁹.

wilð pres. 3 sg. of weallan.

wilðegu f. *agreeable food,* An 153.

wiluc-=weoloc-

wiluncel (GPH 401)=wielincel

wilwendlic=hwilwendlic

wimman, wiman=wīfmann

wimpel (win-) m. 'wimple,' *covering for the neck, cloak,* Gl.

win-=winn

wīn n. 'wine,' B,Bl,OET,WW; CP. [L.]

wīnærn n. *tavern, cellar,* Gl : *drinking hall, wine hall,* B 655.

wīnbælg=winbelg

wīnbēam m. *vine,* WW.

wīnbeger n. *grape,* NG.

wīnbelg (æ) m. *(leather) bottle for wine,* Mt. [v. 'belly']

wīn-berge, -beri(g)e f. *whortle-berry,* OEG : *'wine-berry'* ('whimberry'), *grape, G,WW.*

wīnbōh m. *vine-shoot, vine, Æ.*

wīnbrytta m. *wine-seller, inn-keeper,* WW.

wīnburg† f. *festive city* : *walled vineyard, castle.*

wīnbyrele m. *inn-keeper,* WW 377⁴.

wincan=wincian

wince f. 'winch,' *pulley, WW* 416⁶.

wincel I. m. *corner,* Ct. [Ger. winkel] II.=wencel

wincettan *to wink,* PPs 34¹⁹.

wincian *to close one's eyes, blink, Æ,*CP. ['wink']

winclo=wenclu, nap. of wenceL

wīnclyster n. *cluster of grapes,* OEG 18B³.

wīncole *wine vat,* WW 439³⁰.

wīncynn n. *wine,* NC 333.

wind m. 'WIND,' *CP; Æ,*AO.

+**wind** n. *winding thing, winding path,* WW : *woven thing.*

windǣddre f. *windpipe,* WW.

±**windæg**† m. *day of strife or toil.*

±**windan**³ (tr.) *to* 'WIND,' *plait, curl, twist* : *unwind* : *whirl, brandish, swing* : (intr.) *turn, fly, leap, start, roll, slip, go, Æ,*CP;

AO : *busy oneself with,* Bo 18¹⁸ : *delay, hesitate,* Gu 265 : *roll up* : *repair,* AS (v. NED).

windbǣre (ē²) *windy,* OEG 43¹⁰.

windbland (o²) n. *blast of wind,* B 3146.

+winde *blowing,* BH 202⁷.

-winde v. ed-, næddre-, wudu-w.

windecræft=wyndecræft

windel m. *basket,* Æ,CP. ['*windle*']

windelocc m. *curly lock,* WW.

windelstān m. *tower with a winding stair-case,* (BT),WW 145¹⁷.

windelstrēaw n. '*windle-straw,*' Lcd,WW.

windeltrēow n. *oleaster, willow,* WW.

wind-fona, -gefonna m. *winnowing fan,* LkLR.

windfylled *blown down,* LL 452,19.

windgeard m. *home of the winds, sea,* B 1224?

windgereste f. *resting-place of the winds,* B 2456?

windhladen (æ²) *windy,* ANS 120·297.

windig '*windy,*' *breezy,* Æ,B,Lcd,Lk.

windiht (GPH)=wundiht; **windil**=windel

windiuscoful=windscofl

windles gs. of windel.

windong=windung

windrǣs m. *storm of wind,* MkL 4³⁷.

wīndrinc (e, y) m. *wine-drink, wine,* PPs; Æ. [v. '*wine*']

wīndruncen *elate, intoxicated with wine,* Da, RBL.

windscofl f. *fan,* WW 478²⁵.

windsele m.† (*windy hall*), *hell,* Sat.

windswingel f. (*wind-whip*), *fan,* WW 154¹⁰.

windumǣr (wudu-?) f. *echo,* WW 474⁸.

windung I. f. *winnowing, chaff, tares, straw,* NG. **II.** f. *something woven, hurdle,* WW. ['*winding*']

windwian wv. *to fan,* '*winnow,*' MH,VPs.

windwig=windig

windwigceaf n. *chaff,* OEG 2439.

windwigsyfe n. *winnowing-sieve, fan,* WW 141¹¹.

wine† m. [occl. gp. winig(e)a] *friend, protector, lord,* B : *retainer,* B,Chr. ['*wine*']

wīneard=wīngeard

wine-dryhten (i³)† m., gen. -dryhtnes *friendly lord, lord and friend.*

wīnegeard=wīngeard

winegēomor *mourning for friends,* B 2239.

winelēas† *friendless.*

winemǣg† m. *dear kinsman.*

wīnern=wīnærn

winescipe m. *friendship,* Gu,WW.

winestre=winstre

winetrēow f. *conjugal fidelity,* Hu 50.

wineðearfende† *friendless.*

winewincle f. *periwinkle* (*shell-fish*), Lcd, WW.

wīnfæt n. *wine-vessel, wine-vat,* WW.

+win-ful, -fullic *laborious, tedious, hard,* BH,GD. adv. -līce.

wīngāl† *flushed or intoxicated with wine.*

wīngeard m. *vineyard,* Bl,Bo,Chr : *vine?* WW. ['*winyard*']

wīngeardbōg m. *vine-tendril,* WW 118³.

wīngeardhōc m. *vine-tendril,* WW 201³¹.

wīngeardhring m. *cluster of fruit,* WW 213¹⁷.

wīngeardseax n. *vine pruning-knife,* WW 234⁴⁴.

wīngeardwealh (wīneard-) m. *worker in a vineyard,* Chrd 68².

wīngedrinc n.(†) *wine-drinking, drinking bout* : *wine,* WW.

wīngerd=wīngeard

wīngetredde=wīntredde

wīngyrd=wīngeard

wīnhāte f. *invitation to wine,* Jud 8.

wīn(h)rēafetian *to gather grapes,* LPs 79¹³.

wīnhūs n. *wine-house, tavern,* GL,LL.

winiga, winigea v. wine.

wining (eo, y) m. *leg-band, garter,* IM,WW.

wīnland n. *wine-growing country,* Chrd 15²¹. ['*wineland*']

wīnlēaf n. *vine-leaf,* OEG 18B⁷³.

wīnlic *vinous, like wine,* Æ.

wīnmere m. *wine-vat,* WW 439³⁰.

±winn n. *toil, labour, trouble, hardship,* BH, Lk : *profit, gain,* PPs : *conflict, strife, war,* Bo,Gen; AO. ['*win,*' '*i-win*']

±winna m. *enemy, adversary,* Æ,CP.

winnan³ (y) *to labour, toil, trouble oneself* : *resist, oppose, contradict,* Bo : *fight, strive, struggle, rage,* B,Bl. on w. *attack* : (+) *conquer, obtain, gain,* Chr,Met,Nar : *endure, bear, suffer* : *be ill.* ['*win*'; '*i-win*']

winnend m. *fighter* GL.

+winnesful=+winful

±winnstow f. *wrestling place,* WW.

winnung=windung; **winpel**=wimpel

wīnreced† n. *wine hall.*

wīnreopan⁵ (=e²) *to gather in the vintage,* VPs 79¹³.

wīnsæd *satiated with* '*wine,*' Jud 71.

wīnsæl n. *wine-hall,* WA 78.

wīnsele† n. *wine-hall.*

wīnsester m. *wine-vessel,* WW 122³¹. [L.]

winstōw=winnstōw

winstre I. adj. *left,* Æ,CP. **II.** f. *left hand.*

winsum=wynsum

wint pres. 3 sg. of windan.

wīntæppere m. *wine-tapster, tavern-keeper,* OEG 2652. [v. '*wine*']

winter mn. [ds. wintra; nap. wintru, winter] '*WINTER,*' Æ,AO,CP : pl. (in computing time) *years,* Æ,AO,CP.

winterbiter† *bitterly cold.*

winterburna m. *winter-torrent, BC,LG.* ['*winterbourne*']

wintercealdt† *wintry-cold.*

wintercearig *winter-sad, sad with years?* WA 24.

winterdæg m. '*winter day,*' *Bo.*

winterdūn f. *hill on which sheep were kept in winter?* LL453,1.

winterfeorm f. *Christmas feast,* LL452,21⁴.

Winterfylleð *October,* MEN,MH.

wintergegong m. *fate,* WW406⁶.

wintergerīm† n. *number of years.*

wintergetel n. *number of years,* CHR973A.

wintergewǣde n. *garment of winter, snow,* PH. [v. '*winter*']

wintergew(e)orp n. *snow-storm,* PH57.

winterhūs n. '*winter-house,*' ÆL36⁹⁸.

winterig=wintrig

winterlǣcan *to grow wintry,* CHR,LCD.

winterlic *wintry, winter,* Æ. ['*winterly*']

winterrǣdingbōc f. *lectionary for the winter,* TC430¹⁶.

winterrīm=wintergerīm

wintersǣt=wintersetl

winterscūr m. *winter-shower,* PH18. [v. '*winter*']

winterseld=wintersetl

wintersetl n. *winter-quarters,* AO; CHR. [v. '*winter*']

wintersteal m. *stallion a year old,* LL 378,7.

winterstund f. *winter-hour, short time, year?* GEN370.

wintersufel n. *food for winter,* LL450,9. [v. '*winter*']

wintertīd f. *winter-time,* Æ,BH. ['*wintertide*']

wintīber n. *wine-offering, libation,* WW 130¹³ (-tīfer).

+wintīd f. *time of affliction,* GD210¹⁵.

wintra v. winter.

-wintre v. ān-, twi-w., etc.

+wintred *grown up, adult, CP : aged, AO, LL.* ['*wintered*']

wintredde f. *winepress,* OEG2647.

wintreg=wintrig

wintrēow n. *vine, LG;* Æ. ['*winetree*']

wintrēowig adj. *of the vine,* GPH390.

wintrig '*wintry,*' *AO,Bo.*

wintrog m. *wine-vessel,* MtL21³³. [v. '*wine*']

wintunne f. *wine-cask* (or ? *wintūn wine-house*), ÆP19¹. [v. '*wine*']

wintwig n. *vine-twig,* WW.

winð pres. 3 sg. of winnan.

winðegu† f. *banquet of wine.*

winwircend m. *vine-dresser,* Mt pref. 19³.

+winworuld f. *world of care,* GU829.

winwringe f. *winepress,* Mt,GL.

wio-=weo-, wi-, wu-; **wiohbed**=wēofod

wīpian *to* '*wipe,*' *cleanse,* Æ,*Lcd,RB.*

wīr I.† m. '*wire,*' *metal thread, wire-ornament, B,Rd.* **II.** (ȳ) m. *myrtle,* GL; *Mdf.*

wir-=wear-, wier-, wyr-

wīrboga m. *twisted wire?* RD15³.

wirc-=weorc-, wyrc-

wird-=wierd-

+wīred *made of wire,* TC537'.

wirg- (Æ)=wierg-, wyr(i)g-

wīrgrǣfe? f. *myrtle-grove,* WW.

wirian=wiergan

wirig-=wierg-, wyr(i)g-

wirman (WW399¹⁶)=wyrman

wirpð pres. 3 sg. of weorpan.

wīrtrēow n. *myrtle,* LCD,WW.

wīrtrēowen (y¹, ȳ²) adj. *myrtle,* LCD 1·236¹.

wirtruma=wyrtruma

wirð I.=weorð I. **II.**=wierð pres. 3 sg. of weorðan.

wirðe=worð I.

wīs I. adj. '*WISE,*' *learned,* Æ,AO,CP : *sagacious, cunning : sane : prudent, discreet, experienced,* Æ,AO,CP. as sb. *wise man, CP.* **II.**=wīse I.

+wīs=+wiss

wīsa† m. *leader, director.*

wīsan=wesan; **wīsan** (DAN35)=wīsian

wīsbōc f. *instructive book?* PPs138¹⁴.

wīsc- (Æ)=wȳsc-

wīsce n. *meadow liable to floods, BC,KC;* PST95/98,542. ['*wish*']

wīschere m. *diviner?* ÆL21⁴⁶⁶.

wīsdōm m. '*wisdom,*' *knowledge, learning : experience, B,Bo,G,LL;* Æ,CP.

wīse I. f. '*WISE,*' *way, fashion, custom, habit, manner,* Æ,CP : *testamentary disposition : business, affair, thing, matter,* Æ,CP : *condition, state, circumstance,* AO,CP : *reason, cause,* Æ : *direction : melody,* MEN70 : *idiom.* **II.** adv. *wisely.* **III.** (ȳ) f. *sprout, stalk, Lcd,Rd,WW.* ['*wise*']

wīs-fæst, -fæstlic (PPs) *wise, sagacious, discreet, learned, intelligent.*

+wīsfullīce *knowingly,* GD95³¹.

wīshycgende *wise, sagacious,* B2716.

wīshȳdig† *wise, discreet, sagacious,* GEN.

±wīsian (w. d. or a.) *to direct, instruct, guide, lead, B;* Æ,CP : *point out, show,* GEN. ['*i-wisse*']

wīslic *certain, sure, true,* PPs. ['*wisly*'] adv. (±) -līce *certainly, truly, Lcd,Lk,PPs : moreover.* ['*iwisliche,*' '*wisely*']

wīslic *wise, sagacious, prudent, BH,W;* Æ, AO. adv. -līce *Bo,CP,Gen,LL,Met.* ['*wisely*']

wīsligan=hwistlian

wīsnes f. *teaching,* LCD3·82².

wisnian *to dry up, wither, waste away*, BL. [weornian]

+**wiss I.** n. *what is certain, certainty, surety*, Æ. **II.** adj. *certain, sure, trustworthy*, BH, Bo,Guth,Nic : *knowing.* tō (ge)wissan (Æ, OEG), gewissum; mid gewisse *especially, certainly*, RB,HL. ['*wis*,' '*i-wis*']

wiss-=wis-

wisse=wiste pret. 3 sg. of witan.

wissefa m. *wise-souled man*, SOL 438?

wissian (Æ,W; '*wis*')=wīsian

±**wissian** *to direct, instruct, guide*, Æ,Gen : *point out, show*, Æ. ['*i-wisse*']

wiss-iend, -igend m. *governor, director* : *driver (of chariot)*, Æ.

+**wisslīce**=+wislīce

wisste=wiste pret. 3 sg. of witan.

wissum (tō) adv. *altogether, completely*, OEG.

±**wissung** f. *showing, instruction, guidance*, Æ,LL : *certainty* : *rule, regulation, government*, Æ. ['*wissing*,' '*iwisse*']

wist f. *being, existence* : *well-being, abundance, plenty* : *provision, nourishment, subsistence, food, meal, feast, delicacy*, Æ,CP. [wesan]

wiste pret. 3 sg. of witan.

wistfæstlic=wīsfæstlic

wistful *productive*, CHR 1112.

±**wistfulgend** m. *banqueter*, EPs 41[5].

±**wistfullian** *to feast*, Æ.

wistfullīce adv. *luxuriously*, WW 513[6].

wistfulnes f. *good cheer*, BAS 50[25].

±**wistfullung** f. *feasting*, OEG.

wistfyllo f. *fill of food*, B 734.

wistgifende *fertile*, WW 457[25].

+**wistlan** *to feast*, G.

wistl-=hwistl-

+**wistlǣcan** *to feast, banquet*, G.

wist-mete m., nap. -mettas, *sustenance*, ÆL 23b[582].

wiston pret. pl. of witan.

wisōlung=hwistlung

wiswylle *wise in purpose*, PPs 118[40].

wīswyrdan *to be wise in speech*, A 13·38.

wīswyrde *prudent in speech*, W 72[18].

wit I. pron. 1 pers. (nom. dual), gs. uncer, d. unc, acc. unc(it) *we two*, B,Mt; CP. wit Æthered Æthered and I. ['*wit*'] **II.** (±)=witt

±**wita** (eo, ie, u) m. *sage, philosopher, wise man, adviser, councillor, elder, senator* (v. LL 2·737), Æ,BH,LG; AO : *witness, BH, LG*; Æ,CP : *accomplice.* ['*wite*'; witan]

±**witan** (eo, y) swv. pres. 1, 3 sg. wāt, 2 wāst, pl. witon, subj. pres. sg. wite, pl. wit-en, -on; pret. sg. wiste, pp. witen *to be aware of or conscious of, know, understand*, AO,CP : *observe, perceive* : (+)

ascertain, learn. andan w. *dislike.* incan w. (tō) *to have a grudge (against).* ege w. *to fear.* dōn tō witanne *to cause to know, inform.* ['WIT*'; '*i-wite*']

±**wītan**[1] **I.** *to guard, keep* : *look after*, Lcd, LL. ['*wite*[2]'] **II.** *to impute or ascribe to, accuse, reproach, blame*, AO,B,Bo. ['*wite*[1]'] **III.** *to depart, go, go out*, AO, Met : *leave off* : *pass away, die* (often forðgew.), Æ,CP. ['*wite*[3]']

wīte n. *punishment, torture, plague, injury*, Bo,Gen,VPs; CP : *penalty, fine*, LL : *contribution, in money or food, to sustenance of king or his officers*, LL 356,69[2] : *woe, misery, distress.* ['*wite*']

wītebend† mf. *bonds of torture or punishment*, AN.

wītebrōga m. *tormenting dread*, W.

wītedlīce=witodlīce

wītedōm (BH)=wītegdōm.

wītedōmlic *prophetic*, GUTH.

wītefæst *penally enslaved*, TC.

wīt-ega, -(i)ga m. *wise man* : *lawyer*, NG : *prophet, soothsayer*, CP,LG : *prophecy.* [witan; '*witie*']

wītegeard? m. *amphitheatre*, v. OEG 3333.

wītegdōm (i[2]) m. *prophecy, prediction* : *divination*, DA.

wītegestre f. *prophetess*, ÆT 715,Lk 2[36].

±**wītegian** *to prophesy, predict*, Æ,LG; AO. ['*witie*']

wītegung f. *prophecy, divination*, Æ,LG. ['*witieng*']

wītegungbōc f. *book of prophecy*, ÆL.

wītehrægl n. *penitential garb, sackcloth*, PPs 68[11].

wītehūs n. *torture-house, prison, hell* : *amphitheatre* (*as place of torture and martyrdom*), OEG.

wītel=hwītel

wītelāc† n. *punishment.*

wīteleas *without punishment or fine*, LL 360,73[4]. adv. -līce *with impunity*, TF 109[26].

wīteleast f. *freedom from punishment or fine*, Swt.

wītelic *toilsome, carking*, MFH 178 : *penal*, GD 330; 332.

witelīce (GD 102[24])=witodlīce

witenagemōt n. *meeting of the wise men, national council*, Æ,Chr. ['*witenagemot*'; wita]

+**wītende** *transitory*, MFH 165.

wītendlic=wītigendlic

+**wītendlic** *transitory, perishable*, Æ,CP.

wītendlīce=witodlīce

+**wit-endnes** (G), -ennes f. *departure, death*, BH,MH.

wīterǣden f. *punishment, fine*, BC,LL. ['*witereden*']

+witerian *to inform*, RWH 135[18]. [witter]
wītern n. *prison*, WW 199[31]. [ærn]
wītescræf n. *pit of torment, hell*, SAT 691.
wīt(e)steng m. *pole used for torture*, OEG.
wītestōw f. *place of torment or execution*, BH.
witeswinge f. *scourging, punishment*, GEN 1864.
wīteðēow adj. and sbm. *man reduced to slavery by the law*, Ct,LL.
witewyrðe *punishable*, GD 208[5].
+witfæst *of sound mind*, GUTH 66[17].
wītg-=witeg-
-wītian v. be-w., uð-w.
wītiendlīc=wītigendlic; wītig=wittig
wītīg-=witeg-
wītigende (BYH 102[26])=+wītende
wīt-igendlīc, -t(i)endlic *prophetic*, OEG.
wītiglīc *punitive, of punishment*, GD.
wītingstōw=wītnungstōw
±witlēas *foolish, mad*, Lcd,Met. ['*witless*']
witlēasnes f. *want of intelligence, folly*, OEG 47[3]. ['*witlessness*']
±witlēast f. *folly, madness*, Æ. [witt]
+witloca m. *mind*, MET,CP 469[2].
witmæreswyrt f. *spoonwort?* LCD 12a.
wītnere m. *tormentor, torturer*, Æ.
±witnes f. *knowledge, 'witness,' testimony*, Bl,Bo,DR,G : *a witness*, CP. nīwa gew. *the New Testament*. ['*i-witness*']
+witnian *to confess*, ÆH 2·124[22] (or ? +wītnian)
±wītnian *to punish, chastise, torture, afflict*, Æ,AO,CP.
wītnigend m. *punisher*, EPs 78[11].
wītnung f. *torment, torture, punishment, purgatory*, Æ.
wītnungstōw f. *place of punishment, purgatory*, ÆH.
witod=witodlīce
witodlīc *certain, sure*, LkR 20[6] (wutud-); adv. and conj. -līce *truly, for, verily, certainly, undoubtedly, indeed, thus, but, and, therefore, wherefore*, Æ,AO,CP. [witan]
-witol v. fore-w.
witolnes f. *wisdom*, GD 331[15]. [witan]
witon I. pres. pl. of witan. II.=wuton
wītrod=wīgtrod
+witscipe m. *evidence, knowledge*, BH. ['*witship*']
±witsēoc *possessed, insane*, Æ.
±witt n. *understanding, intellect, sense*, Æ, B,Bo,Lk,Met : *knowledge, consciousness* : *conscience*, CP. ['*wit*,' '*i-wit*']
+witt-=+wit-
witter *wise, prudent*, CHR 1067 D. [ON. vitr]
±wittig† *wise*, B,Cra,Ex,LL : *sagacious, reasonable : skilful*, Cra,OEG : *conscious, in one's right mind*, Æ. adv. -līce. ['*witty*']

wittignes f. *intelligence*, OEG 78 (wytti-).
wittol=witol
wītu nap. of wīte.
witud=witod
wituma (e, eo, y) m. *dowry* (v. LL 2·739).
witumbora m. *bridesman, paranymph*, OEG 1774.
wītungstōw=wītnungstōw
wītword n. *written evidence, will, covenant*, LL,TC. ['*witword*']
wið I. prep. (w. a.) WITH, *by, near, against, beside, at, through* : (w. d.) *from (separation), with (opposition), for, in return for, on condition of, beside, near, opposite* : (w. g.) *towards, to, at, against.* w. ēastan (1) adv. *to the east*; (2) prep. *east of.* w. ūp *upwards, above.* w. ðān ðe *because, in consideration of, provided that.* wið...weard prep. (w. a.) *towards.* II. conj. *until.*
wiðæftan I. adv. *from behind, behind, after*, AO. II. prep. *behind, at*, Æ.
wiðblāwan[7] *to blow away*, CP 439[24].
wið-bregdan[3], -brēdan[3] *to withhold, restrain, withstand, oppose*, Æ,CP : *take away*, GD 203[5].
wiðcēosan[2] *to reject*, Ps. pp. wiðcoren *rejected, reprobate, outcast*, BH,MH.
wiðcostian '*reprobare*,' EPs 32[10].
wiðcwædenes=wiðcwedennes
wiðcwedennes f. *contradiction*, CHR,Ps.
wiðcwedolnes=wiðercwedolnes
wiðcweðan[5] *to speak against, contradict, gainsay, oppose, resist*, Æ : *forbid, refuse, deny : reject, renounce*, CP.
wiðcweðenes=wiðcwedennes
wiðdrīfan[1] *to repel, drive off*, PPs.
wiðe-=wiðig-
wiðēadon (N)=wiðēodon pret. pl. of wiðgān.
wiðēastan *eastward, eastwards*, AO.
wiðeftan=wiðæftan
wiðer I. prep. and adv. *against.* II. adj. *hostile*, GPH 394. ['*wither*']
wiðerbersta m. *adversary*, SOL 86[5].
wiðerbreca (a[3], eo[3], o[3], u[3]) m. *adversary : the devil, Satan.*
wiðerbrocian *to oppose*, CVPs.
wiðerbrōga m. *adversary, the devil*, CR 564.
wiðerbruca=wiðerbreca
wiðercerran *to turn against, prance* (Swt). [cp. wiðercyr]
wiðercora m. *adversary, rebel, apostate, sinner*, Æ.
wiðercoren *rejected, reprobate, wicked*, Æ.
wiðercorennes f. *reprobation*, ÆH 2·290[19].
wiðercwednes (CP 143[20])=wiðercwidennes
wiðercwedol *opposing, contradicting*, Ps.
wiðercwedolnes f. *contradiction*, GL.

wiðercwedung f. *contradiction*, SPs51⁴.

wiðercweð-=wiðercwed-

wiðercweðan⁵ *to withstand*, LPs.

wiðercwida (y) m. *contradicter*, OEG 1893 : *opposer, rebel*, WW110²³.

wiðercwiddian (y³) *to murmur*, LPs40⁸.

wiðercwide m. *contradiction*, PPs : *opposition, resistance*, LL.

wiðercwidel-=wiðercwedol-

wiðercwidennes (e³, y³) *contradiction*, LPs.

wiðercwyd-=wiðer-cwed-, -cwid-

wiðercyr m. *rearing (of a horse)*, EL926.

wiðerdūne (ē³, y³) *narrow? uphill? steep?* (BTs), Mt7¹⁴.

-wiðere v. tō-w.

wiðerfeoht-=wiðfeoht-

wiðerflita m. *opponent, adversary*, AO,CP.

wiðerhabban *to resist*, PPs72²⁰.

wiðerhlinian *to lean against*, GL.

wiðer-hycgende, -hȳdig *refractory, perverse, antagonistic, hostile*. as sb. *rival, adversary*.

wiðerian *to resist, oppose, struggle against*, Æ : *irritate, provoke* : *be provoked*. ['*wither*']

wiðerlǣcan (y¹, ē³) *to deprive*, EPs83¹³.

wiðerlēan† n. *requital* : *compensation*.

wiðerling m. *opponent, adversary*, EHy4⁷. ['*witherling*']

wiðermāl n. *counter-plea, defence*, CHR1052.

wiðermēde *perverse, antagonistic*.

wiðermēdnes (oe) f. *perversity*, DR : *adversity*, DR.

wiðermēdo f. *antagonism*, GEN : *perversity*, PPs : *adversity*, DR.

wiðermetan⁵ *to compare*, WW.

wiðermōd *unwilling, contrary*, CP212⁷.

wiðermōdnes f. *adversity*, CP83¹⁹.

wiðermoednes (DR)=wiðermēdnes

wiðerrǣde *contrary, opposed, adverse, perverse, rebellious*, Æ : *disadvantageous* : *disagreeable, unpleasant*.

wiðerrǣdlic *contrary, adverse*, ÆGR264¹.

wiðerrǣdnes f. *opposition, discord, variance, disadvantage, adversity*, Æ.

wiðerræhtes (=rihtes) adv. *opposite*, B 3039.

wiðerriht n. *recompense*, WW118¹².

wiðersaca m. *adversary, enemy*, Mt,RB; Æ : *betrayer* : *apostate*, Æ. ['*withersake*']

wiðersacian *to renounce, become apostate*, OEG : *blaspheme*.

wiðersacung f. *apostasy*, GL : *blasphemy*, Sc.

wiðersæc I. n. *contradiction, hostility, opposition*, Æ : *apostasy*. [sacan] **II.** *unfavourable*, LCD97a.

wiðersprecend m. *a contradicter*, CHRD41²⁹.

wiðerstæger *steep*, WW.

wiðerstandan⁶ *to resist*, EPs16⁸.

wiðersteall (a³) m. *resistance, opposition*, Æ.

wiðersȳnes adv. *backwards*, BL93¹⁹.

wiðertalu f. *defence*, ÆH1·530⁶ (v. LL 3·226).

wiðertihtle f. *counter-charge*, LL.

wiðertrod† n. *return, retreat*.

wiðertȳme *troublesome, grievous*, LPs34¹³ : *contrary*, BF174¹.

wiðerweard *contrary, perverse, adverse*, Bo, G : *rebellious, hostile, Bl*; AO,CP : *inconsistent* : *unfavourable, noxious, bad*. ['*witherward*']

wiðerwearda m. *adversary*, BL,LPs17²⁷.

wiðerweardian (o³) *to oppose*, SPs.

wiðerweardlic *contrary, inimical, perverse*, Æ. adv. -līce.

wiðerweardnes f. *opposition, perversity, arrogance, enmity*, CP; Æ : *adversity, calamity, trouble*, CP. ['*witherwardness*']

wiðerwengel m. *adversary*, ARHy4⁷, RPs 73¹⁰.

wiðerwenning f. *controversy*, Sc146¹⁵. [winnan]

wiðer-werd-, -wi(e)rd-=wiðerweard-

wiðerwinn n. *contest*, OEG2³.

wiðerwinna m. *opponent, rival, adversary, enemy*, Æ,CP; AO. ['*witherwin*']

wiðerwinnan³ *to revolt*, GPH389.

+wiðerwordian=+wiðerweardian

wiðerwyrd=wiðerweard

wiðewinde=wiðowinde

wiðfaran⁶ *to come off, escape*, EX573.

wiðfeohtan³ *to fight against, rebel*, BH, WW.

wiðfeohtend m. *adversary*, BH,CP.

wiðfēolan³ *to apply oneself to*, BH.

wiðferian† *to rescue, redeem*, PPs.

wiðflita=wiðerflita

wiðfōn⁷ (w. d.) *to grasp at, clutch*, B760.

wiðforan I. prep. *before, in the presence of*. **II.** adv. *before, previously*.

wiðgān anv. -gangan⁷ *to go against, oppose* : *pass away, vanish, disappear*.

wiðgehæftan=wiðhæftan

wiðgemetnes f. *comparison*, BH430²⁰.

wiðgeondan prep. *beyond*, Mt3⁵.

wiðgrīpan† *to grapple with*, B2521.

wiðgȳnan *to reject*, ÆL23⁵⁴¹.

wiðhabban (æ²) (w. d.) *to oppose, resist, restrain, hold out*, AO.

wiðhæftan *to restrain*, A7·12.

wiðheardian *to harden*, ARSPs94⁸.

wiðhindan adv. *behind*, Æ.

wiðhogian (w. g.) *to disregard, reject*, GEN 2864.

wiðhycgan† *to reject, despise, scorn*.

wiði-=wiðig-

wiðig, wiði(g)e m. *withe, 'withy,' willow*, BC; Æ (Mdf) : *band, fetter, fillet, garland*.

wiðigrǣw f. *hedgerow*, KC. [v. '*rew*']

wĭðigrind f. *willow bark*, Lcd 37a.
wĭðing-=wĭðig-
wĭðinnan I. adv. '*within,*' *from within, Æ, Ps.* II. prep. (w. d. a.) *within.*
wĭð-inne, -innen, -innon=wiðinnan I.
wĭðir- (N)=wiðer-; wĭðl (GD)=wīdl
wĭðlǣdan *to lead away, remove, rescue,* Ps.
wĭðlǣdnes f. *abduction,* Ps (BT).
wĭðlan (N)=wīdlian
wĭðlicgan⁶ *to oppose, resist,* Chr, Chrd.
wĭðmetan⁵ *to compare with, liken to, Æ.*
wĭðmētednes f. *invention, device,* SPs.
wĭðmeten(d)lic *comparative (in grammar),* Ægr.
wĭðmetennes f. *comparison, Æ.*
wĭðmeting f. *comparison,* Sc.
wĭð-neoðan (Æ), -niðan, -nyðan adv. *below, underneath, beneath.*
wĭðobān (wido-) n. *collar-bone,* Lcd, LL.
wĭðobend (eo¹) *woodbine,* Lcd 113b. ['*withbind*']
wĭðone (Bl)=wið ðone
wĭðor-=wiðer-
wĭðowinde f. *convolvulus, woodbine,* Gl, Lcd. ['*withwind*']
wĭðrǣde=wiðerrǣde
wĭðret† n. *resistance, opposition,* B. ['*wither*']
wĭðrēotan² *to abhor? resist?* El 369 (GK).
wĭðrian=wiðerian
wĭðsacan² *to forsake, abandon, renounce, refuse, deny,* Bl, G; Æ, AO, CP : *oppose, strive against,* AO.
wĭðsacendlic *used in negations,* Ægr 226³.
wĭðsacung f. *denial, renunciation,* Sc 60¹⁴.
wĭðsceorian (o²) *to refuse,* CP 59¹².
wĭðscrĭðel=wĭdscrĭðol
wĭðscūfan² *to thrust back, refute, repel,* BH.
wĭðsecgan *to renounce,* DR. ['*withsay*']
wĭðsēon⁵ *to rebel, rise against,* AO.
wĭðsetnes f. *opposition,* Gl.
wĭðsettan *to withstand, resist,* HL, LPs : *condemn,* RWH 137²¹. ['*withset*']
wĭðslēan⁶ *to oppose, bring to naught, Æ,* CP.
wĭðsprecan⁵ *to contradict, gainsay* : *converse,* AS : *revile* : *speak with,* GD 345⁸.
wĭðspurnan³ *to hit against,* MtL 4⁶.
wĭðstæppan⁶ *to step or go out of,* Ps.
wĭðstandan⁶ (w. d.) *to '*withstand,*' resist, oppose,* Æ, Bl, Bo, Lcd, LG, Wa; AO, CP : *be lacking,* LL 102,31.
wĭðsteall=wiðersteall
wĭðsteppan=wiðstæppan
wĭðstond-=wiðstand-
wĭðstunian *to dash against,* Lcd 160b.
wĭðstyllan *to retreat,* WW 17²⁶.
wĭðstyltan *to hesitate, doubt,* MtL 21²¹.
wĭðtēon² *to take away* : *restrain,* CP.
wĭðtremman *to step back,* CP 441²⁷.

wĭððe f. *cord, band, thong, fetter, Æ, WW.* ['*withe*'; v. also wĭðig]
wĭðð er-=wiðer-
wĭððinglan *to be reconciled to,* MFH 178.
wĭððlr (DR 168²)=wiðer
wĭððyddan *to blunt,* v. OEG 4235.
wĭðufan I. prep. (w. d.) *above.* II. adv. *before, previously.*
wĭð-uppon, -uppan adv. *above.*
wĭðūtan I. prep. (w. d.) *outside of, AO, LL, Mt* : *except,* Lcd : '*without.*' II. adv. *from outside, outside,* HL.
wĭðweorpan³† *to reject, repudiate.*
wĭðwestan *to the west of,* AO 8¹².
wĭðwinde=wiðowinde
wĭðwinnan³ *to fight against, oppose,* AO, CP.
wĭðwĭðerian *to resist, withstand,* GD 117¹⁹.
wixlan (N)=wrixlan
wixð=wiexð pres. 3 sg. of weaxan.
±wlacian *to become lukewarm, be tepid, Æ,* CP.
wlaco, wlacu, wlæc *tepid, lukewarm, cool,* CP. ['*wlak*']
wlacunes=wlæcnes; wlæc v. wlaco.
wlæce n. *tepidity,* GPH 397.
wlæclic *lukewarm.* adv. -līce.
wlæclīce (PPs 148⁶)=wrǣclīce
wlæcnes f. *lukewarmness,* CP.
wlæffetere m. *stammerer,* GPH 403.
wlæffian (ea) *to stammer, speak indistinctly,* Chrd 74¹¹. ['*wlaffe*']
wlænc=wlanc, wlenc
wlænco=wlenco
wlǣta=wlætta
+wlǣtan *to defile, debase,* Bo 114²³.
wlǣtlīce=wlæclīce
wlǣtta m. *loathing, nausea, eructation, heartburn,* Lcd, RB; Æ : *an object of loathing* : *disfigurement,* OEG 4461. ['*wlat*']
wlǣtung (ā, ē) f. *nausea,* Cp, Lcd : *disfigurement,* OEG 4461. ['*wlating*']
wlanc (æ, o) *stately, splendid, lofty, magnificent, rich,* B, Ph : *boastful, arrogant, proud,* B. ['*wlonk*']
wlancian *to become proud or boastful, exult,* Gl.
wlanclic adj. *proud, arrogant.* adv. -līce, Gl.
wlāt pret. 3 sg. of wlītan.
wlātere m. *spectator,* Chrd 96²⁴.
-wlātful v. neb-w.
wlātian I.† *to gaze, look upon, behold.* [wlītan] II. (impers.) *to loathe, Æ, Lcd.* ['*wlate*']
wlātung I. f. *sight, spectacle,* Chrd 79⁴. II.=wlǣt(t)ung
wleaffian=wlæffian
±wleccan *to make tepid,* CP. [wlæc]

WLENC 417 WŌHHÆMERE

wlenc, wlenco (AO,CP), wlencu f. *pride, arrogance, haughtiness : glory, pomp, splendour,* AO,CP : (†) *bravado : prosperity, riches, wealth.* [wlanc]

+wlencan *to enrich, exalt,* EL,TC,VH.

wlēttung=wlǣtung

wlisp, wlips (Æ) *lisping.*

-wlispian v. ā-wl.

wlita m. *countenance,* GL.

wlītan[1]† *to gaze, look, observe.*

wlite m. *brightness : appearance, form, aspect, look, countenance,* LG : *beauty, splendour,* Bl,VPs; Æ : *adornment,* CP. ['wlite']

wlīteandet? n. *confession of splendour,* PPs 103².

wlitebeorht† *beauteous.*

wlitefull *beautiful,* Sc 21⁸.

wliteg-=wlitig-

wlitelēas *ugly,* AN 1171.

wlitelīce *handsomely,* BL 205⁶.

wlītescīne (ē³, ȳ³) †*lovely, beautiful,* LPs 80⁴.

wlitesēon f. *sight, spectacle,* B 1650.

wlitetorht† *brilliant, lovely.*

wlitewamm (o³) m. *disfigurement of the face.*

wliteweorð n. *legal value of a man's life, ransom,* GD 179²¹.

wlitig *radiant, beautiful, fair, comely,* Æ; CP. adv. -ige, -iglīce. ['wliti']

±wlitigian *to beautify, adorn : become beautiful,* SEAF 49 : *form, fashion,* Pss.

wlitignes f. *beauty, splendour,* BL.

wlitu=wlite; **wlō**=wlōh

wlōh f., dp. wlō(u)m *fringe, ornament, tuft : bit,* GU 1127.

+wlōh *adorned,* GEN 1789.

wlonc=wlanc

wlott *spot, blemish,* OEG 648?

wlōum v. wlōh.

wlyt-=wlit-; **wō**=wōh

wōc pret. of wacan (v. 'wake').

wōcer=wōcor

wōcie, wōcige *noose,* OEG 962; 3560.

wōclic=wōhlic

wōcor† f. (gs. wōcre) *increase, growth : offspring, progeny, posterity, race : usury*

wocorlīce=wacorlīce

wōcs=wōsc pret. 3 sg. of wascan.

wōd I. adj. *senseless, mad, raging,* AS,Chr, Cp,G,Lcd; AO : *blasphemous.* ['wood'] II. pret. 3 sg. of wadan.

wōda I. m. *madman,* Æ. II. m. *storm, flood? danger?* TC 341⁸.

wodawistle=wodewistle

woddor n. *throat, gullet?* SOL 95.

wōddrēam m. 'dæmonium,' RPs 95⁵ (v. ES 38²⁵).

wōdelic=wōdlic

Wōden m. *Woden : Mercury,* WW.

wōdendrēam m. *madness,* WW 245¹⁰. ['wid-dendream']

Wōdenesdæg=Wōdnesdæg

wōdewistle f. *hemlock,* GL.

wōd-frec, -fræc *madly ravenous,* LL,W.

wōdheortnes f. *madness,* MFH 178.

wōdian=wēdan

wōdlic *foolish, mad, furious,* Æ. adv. -līce *madly, furiously,* Æ,Bas,HL : *blasphemously.* ['woodly']

wōdnes f. *madness, frenzy, folly,* Æ.

Wōdnes gs. of Wōden.

Wōdnesdæg m. *Woden's day,* 'Wednesday,' G.

Wōdnesniht f. *Tuesday night,* LL,W. [v. 'Wednesday']

wōdōm=wōhdōm

wōdon pret. pl. of wadan.

wōdscinn n. *madness, folly,* W 80³.

wōdscipe m. *insanity,* WW 245¹².

wōdsēoc *mad,* GD 135¹.

wōdōrāg f. *paroxysm, madness, fury,* CP.

woecan (N)=wæccan

woerc- (N)=weorc-; **woerd-**=wird-

wofian *to shout, rave, blaspheme,* Æ.

wofung f. *madness, raving,* GD : *blasphemy,* Lk 24¹¹.

wōg=wōh

wōgere m. 'wooer,' *suitor, sweetheart,* Æ, Chrd.

wōgerlic *amorous,* CHRD 78³⁴.

wōgian *to 'woo,' court, marry,* Æ,Sc,TC.

wōgung f. 'wooing,' ÆL 7³⁰¹.

wōh I. n. *bending, crookedness : error, mistake,* Æ : *perversity, wrong, iniquity, depravity.* on w. *wrongly, wickedly.* ['wough'] II. adj. *bent, awry, twisted, crooked : uneven, rough : wrong, perverse, evil, depraved, bad, unjust,* CP : *false (weight),* W 70³. on wōn *wrongfully, in error.* ['wough']

wōhbogen† *bent, crooked.*

wōhcēapung f. *fine for illegal trafficking,* KC 5·143²².

wōhdǣd f. *wrong deed, crime,* BL,GD.

wōhdōm m. *unjust judgment,* BF 242⁶ (ōd).

wōhfōted *having deformed feet,* WW 161³⁰.

wōhfremmend m. *evildoer,* MET 9³⁶.

wōhful *wicked,* NG.

wōhfulnes f. *wickedness,* NG.

wōhgeorn *inclined to evil,* W 183⁸.

wōhgestrēon n. *ill-gotten property,* W.

wōhgod n. *false god, idol,* PPs 78⁵⁸.

wōhhǣmed n. *fornication, adultery,* CP.

wōhhǣmend m. *fornicator, adulterer,* CP.

wōhhǣmere m. *fornicator, adulterer,* CP 401³⁰.

wŏhhandede *maimed (of the hands)*, WW 161²⁹.

wŏhhian? *to speak wildly, rave?* GD 314⁷.

wŏhlic *perverse, wrong, unjust, evil.* adv. -lîce, Æ.

wŏhnes f. *crookedness, crooked place*, Æ : *wrong, error* : *wickedness*, Æ.

wŏhs, wŏhson=wŏsc, wŏscon pret. 3 sg. and pret. pl. of wascan.

wŏhsum *evil*, DR 27⁹ (wŏg-).

wŏl mfn. *pestilence, mortality, disease*, AO, CP.

wŏlbǣrnes f. *calamity, pest*, AO 62³⁴.

wŏlberende *pestilential, pernicious*, CP.

wŏlberendlic *pestilential*, CHR 1086.

wŏlbryne m. *pestilence*, AO 86²⁴.

wolc (WW 175²⁰)=wolcen

wolc-=walc-, wolcen-

wolcen nm. (nap. wolcnu) '*convolutio*,' *ball, lump*, PPs 147⁵ : *cloud*, B,Bl,Chr,CP,G, VPs : *sky, heavens*. ['welkin']

wolcenfaru† f. *scudding of clouds*.

wolcengehnäst n. *meeting of clouds (in a storm)*, RD 4⁶⁰.

wolcenrēad=weolocrēad

wolcenwyrcende? ptc. *cloud-making (Centaurs)*, WW 456²⁴.

wolcn=wolcen; **wolcrēad**=weolocrēad

wolcspinl=walcspinl

wol-cyrge, -cyrige=wælcyrige

wold=weald

wŏldæg m. *day of pestilence*, RUIN 26.

wŏldberendlic=wŏlberendlic

wol-de, -don pret. 3 sg. and pret. pl. of willan.

wŏlgewinn n. *calamitous war*, AO 64¹⁵.

wŏllic=wŏhlic

wollentēare *streaming with tears*, B 3032.

-wolma v. fŏt-w.; **wom**=wam(m)

wŏm I.=wŏgum dp. of wŏh, adj. **II.**=wŏma

wŏma m. *noise, howling, tumult* : *terror, alarm.* swefnes w. *dream-tumult, vision* : *eloquence?* OEG 8b¹⁰.

woman *to infringe*, EC 151¹⁶ : (+) w. d. pers. and g. thing *deprive of*, EC 151¹⁷. [wamm]

won I.=wan, wann. **II.** pret. 3 sg. of winnan.

wŏn I. wk. gdsn. and dpmn. of wŏh. **II.**=hwŏn

won-=wan-

wŏna gp. of wŏh II.

wondor=wundor

wŏnes=wŏhnes; **wong**=wang

wŏp I. m. *cry, shrieking, weeping, lamentation*, B,G; Æ,CP. ['wop'] **II.**=wēop pret. 3 sg. of wēpan.

wŏpdropa m. *tear*, SOL 283.

wŏpen pp. of wēpan.

wŏperian *to weep*, HL 18³².

wŏpig *sad, lamenting*, ÆL.

wŏplēoð n. *dirge, elegy*, OEG 3504.

wŏplic *tearful, sad*, Æ. adv. -lîce.

wŏpstōw f. *place of mourning*, Æ.

wŏr=wŏs, wāse

wŏra gp. of wŏh.

worc=weorc

word I. n. '*WORD*,' *speech, sentence, statement*, Æ : *command, order* : *subject of talk, story, news, report*, Æ,AO : *fame*, Æ : *promise* : *verb*, Æ : (*incarnate*) *Word*. **II.** *rod*, CPs : (*gooseberry*) *bush?* LkL 6⁴⁴ (v. ES 38·340; 40·152). **III.**=werod

word-bēot† n., -bēotung (Hu 14) f. *promise*.

wordcærse (WW 416⁸)=worðigcærse?

wordcennend m. *the begetter of the Word*, GPH 389.

wordcræft† m. *poetic art, eloquence*, El. [v. 'word']

word-cwide (e, y), -cwyðe m. *words, speech, language, utterance*.

worden pp. of weorðan.

wordes adv. *with words, verbally, orally*.

wordfæst *true to one's word, true*, OEH 301¹³.

wordful *talkative, verbose, fluent*, SC.

wordgebēot=wordbēot

word-gecwide (æ³) n., -gecweodu np. *verbal agreement*, LL,TC.

wordgemearc n. *definition or limitation by words*, GEN 2355.

wordgerȳne† n. *dark saying*.

wordglēaw *skilful in words*, DA 418.

wordgydd m. *lay, dirge*, B 3173.

wordhlēoðor† n. *voice, speech*.

wordhord† n. *treasury of words*.

wordig '*wordy*,' *verbose*, OEG 1416.

wordlāc n. *speech*, LPs 18⁴.

wordlār f. *teaching*, CHRD 53²².

wordlatu f. *delay in speech?* AN 1519.

wordlaðu† f. *conversation, speech*.

wordlēan n. *reward for song*, RD 78⁹.

wordlian (u¹) *to talk, commune*, BF : *conspire*, GD 106¹.

wordliend m. *speaker*, OEG 2321.

wordloc n. *art of logic*, WW 388¹¹.

wordloca m. (*word-hoard*), *speech*, AN 470.

wordloga m. *deceiver, liar*, W 40¹⁰.

wordlung n. *talk, discourse* : *empty talk*.

wordmittung f. '*collatio*,' WW 178³⁵.

wordpredicung f. *preaching*, CHRD 66²³.

wordrian=wordlian

wordriht n. *suitable word*, B 2631 : *spoken law*, Ex 3.

wordsāwere m. *rhetorician*, CP 97⁴.

wordsige m. *success in speech*, LCD 1·188'.

wordsnoter (o³) *eloquent, wise in words*.

wordsnoterlic *philosophical, learned,* OEG 2270.

wordsnoterung f. *sophism,* OEG 2268.

wordsomnere m. *enumeration, catalogue,* WW 212²⁷.

wordsomnung f. '*collatio,*' WW 178³⁵.

wordsprecende *able to speak,* VH 24.

wordwīsa m. *sophist,* WW 493³⁰.

wordwrītere=wyrdwrītere

wordwynsum *affable,* WW 191²¹.

wōre dsf. of wōh.

worf=weorf; **worfian**=woffian

wōrhana m. *moor-cock, cock-pheasant,* GL.

wōrhenn f. *hen pheasant,* WW.

wōrhona=wōrhana

worht pp. (*Bl;* '*ywrought*'), worhte pret. 3 sg. of wyrcan.

wōrht-=wrōht-

wōrigan *to roam, wander,* Æ : *move round, totter, crumble to pieces.* [wōr, wērig]

world=woruld; **worm**=wyrm

wormōd=wermōd

worms (u, rsm) nm. *matter, pus, virus, Ep, Lcd;* AO,CP. ['*worsum*']

worn (ea, eo) m. *large amount, number : troop, company, multitude, crowd : progeny.*

worngehāt n. *promise of numerous offspring,* GEN 2364?

wornlust=wamlust

worod=werod; **woroht**=wrōht

worold (AO,CP)=woruld

worpan=weorpan

worpen pp. of weorpan.

worpian *to cast, throw, pelt,* CP,EL.

worsm=worms; **wort**=wyrt

worð I. (eo, u) nm. *court, courtyard, curtilage, farm,* Mdf : *street.* II.=waroð

worð-=weorð-

worðig (eo, u, y) m. *enclosed homestead, curtilage, farm,* Æ,CP; Mdf : *street.*

worðigcærse f. *name of a plant,* LCD 3·303.

worðignetele f. *nettle,* LCD 44a.

worðscipe=weorðscipe; **worud**=werod I.

woruftord=weorftord

woruld (e¹, eo¹, ia¹; o²) f. '*WORLD,*' *age, AO, CP : men, humanity : way of life, life : long period of time, cycle, eternity.* tō worulde, ā on worulda world, in woruld worulde *world without end, for ever.*

woruldǣht f. *worldly possessions,* BH, LL.

woruldafol (-el) n. *secular or worldly power,* LL,W (ES 45·161).

woruldār f. *worldly honour,* CP : *secular property.*

woruldbearn n. *man,* RD 81²⁷.

woruldbebod n. *universal command, edict,* VH 24.

woruldbisgu f. *worldly occupation,* LL.

woruldbisgung (eo¹, y²) f. *worldly business : worldly misery, trouble.*

woruldbismer (o²) nm. *worldly reproach,* CP 61¹⁰.

woruldbliss f. *worldly bliss,* GU 135.

woruldbōt f. *compensation prescribed by the secular power,* LL 128,2.

woruld-broc n., -bryce (o²) m. *worldly trouble,* CP 259² : *use for secular purposes,* MH 136⁹.

woruldbūend† m. *world-dweller.*

woruldcamp m. *secular warfare,* ÆP 140⁴.

woruldcandel f. *sun,* B 1965.

woruldcearu (a³) f. *worldly care,* Æ.

woruldcempa m. *earthly soldier,* ÆL.

woruldcrǽft m. *secular art,* Æ. in pl. *world's hosts,* DA 362 (MP 26·434).

woruldcrǽftig *skilled in secular arts,* ÆP 128²⁵.

woruldcrǽft(ig)a m. *secular artificer,* ÆP 128¹⁰.

woruldcund *worldly, secular,* CP. adv. -līce, CP.

woruldcyning† m. *earthly king,* Æ.

woruldadǽd f. *worldly business,* LL (414').

woruldadēad *dead,* PPs 142⁴.

woruldadēma m. *secular judge,* LL.

woruldadōm m. *secular judgment,* Æ.

woruldadrēam† m. *earthly joy.*

woruldadrihten m. *world's lord, God,* MET 29¹.

woruldaduguð† f. *worldly riches,* GEN.

woruldearfoð† n. *earthly misery,* MET.

woruldege m. *earthly fear,* LL (310¹⁹).

woruldende m. *end of the world,* B 3083.

woruldfǽgernes f. *earthly beauty,* MH 34⁶.

woruldfeoh n. *earthly goods, wealth,* GEN 2142.

woruldfolgað m. *worldly occupation,* BL.

woruldfrætwung (world-) f. *worldly ornament,* BL 125³⁶.

woruldfrēond (ȳ³) m. *friend in this world,* W.

woruldfrið m. *worldly peace,* LL 220,1.

woruldfruma m. *primeval man, patriarch,* GUTH 12²⁸.

woruldgālnes f. *lust of pleasure,* W 219¹⁴.

woruldgebyrd n. *worldly origin,* BH.

woruldgedāl n. *death,* EL 581.

woruldgefeoht (o²) n. *earthly fight,* MH 36²⁶.

woruldgeflit n. *dispute, lawsuit?* LCD 3·174'.

woruldgerǣdnes (eo¹) f. *secular ordinance,* LL.

woruldgeriht n. *worldly justice, secular right or due,* LL 210,2¹.

woruldgerȳsnu np. *secular customs,* LL.

woruldgesǣlig *prosperous,* MA 219.

woruldgesǣlða (o²) fp. *worldly fortune,* AO.

woruldgesceaft† f. *creature of this world : world.*

woruldgestrēon† n. *worldly riches.*
woruldgeswinc (o²) n. *earthly toil, misery,* CP.
woruldgeðincð f. *worldly honour, dignity,* GD,W.
woruldgeðōht (world-) mn. *worldly thought,* Bl 15¹⁴.
woruldgewinn n. *earthly war,* ÆL 25⁸³².
woruldgewritu np. *secular writings,* BH.
woruldgewuna m. *customary law,* LL 206,1a.
woruldgielp (i³, y³) mn. *pride of this world, glory,* CP.
woruldgifu f. *worldly gift,* BH,CHR.
woruldgītsere m. *coveter of worldly things,* MET 14¹.
woruldgītsung f. *covetousness,* Bo,MET.
woruldglenge m. *worldly pomp,* BL,LL.
woruldgōd n. *worldly good,* Bo,BH.
woruldgylp (Æ)=woruldgielp
woruldgyrla (o²) m. *secular garment,* CHRD 96¹¹.
woruldhād m. *secular state,* BH,GD.
woruldhlāford m. *secular lord,* CP.
woruldhlīsa m. *worldly fame,* ÆH 2·566⁶.
woruldhremming (o²) f. *worldly hindrance,* CHRD 75³⁵,101⁴.
woruldhyht m. *earthly joy,* Az 136.
woruldlǣce m. *earthly physician,* ÆH 1·472¹³.
woruld-lagu f., -laga m. *civil law,* LL,W.
woruldlēan n. *earthly reward,* LL (422¹²).
woruldlic *earthly,* Æ,Bo : '*worldly*,' *secular,* MH ; Æ. adv. -līce *temporally.*
woruldlīf n. *life in this world : secular life,* BH.
woruldlufu f. *love of this world,* Æ.
woruldlust m. *worldly pleasure,* Bo.
woruldmǣg m. *earthly kinsman,* GEN 2178.
woruldman m. *human being, man of the world, layman,* Cr,Met; Æ,CP. ['*world-man*']
woruldmēd f. *earthly reward,* LL (422¹⁴).
woruldnēod f. *temporal need,* LL 267,32.
woruldnytt f. *worldly use or profit,* GEN, LCD.
woruldprȳdo f. *worldly pride,* Lcd 3·428', ByH 124³. [v. '*pride*']
woruldrǣden f. *way of the world,* B 1143 (v. MLN 25·113).
woruldrīca m. *great man,* Æ.
woruldrīce I. n. *earthly kingdom, CP : world-realm, world.* ['*worldriche*'] II. adj. *having worldly power or riches.*
woruldrīcetere (o²) n. *worldly power,* CHRD 68³⁴.
woruldriht (y³) n. *secular or civil law : God's law for the world.*
woruldsacu f. *worldly strife,* W 170⁹.
woruldsǣlða fp. *earthly blessings,* Bo.

woruldscamu (ea³) f. *public disgrace,* LL,W.
woruldsceaft† f. *earthly creature,* Az.
woruldscēat m. *part of the world, region.*
woruldscēawung f. *worldly sight,* CHRD 76³⁰.
woruldscipe m. *worldly matter, CP.* ['*worldship*']
woruldscīr (world-) f. *life in the world (i.e. not monastic), worldly affairs* GD 3⁷.
woruldscrift (eo¹, y³) m. *confessor,* ByH 132¹.
woruldsnotor *world-wise : scientific,* MH 44²⁵.
woruldsorg f. *earthly care,* CP,Bo.
woruldspēd f. *worldly wealth, success in the world,* CP.
woruldspēdig *rich in this world,* CP 333².
woruldsprǣc f. *worldly talk,* LL.
woruldstēor f. *secular penalty,* LL 258,51.
woruldstrang *having worldly power,* NC 334.
woruldstrengu f. *physical strength,* RD 27².
woruldstrūdere m. *spoliator, robber,* LL,W.
woruldstund *sojourn upon earth,* EL 363.
woruldðearf f. *this world's needs,* BH.
woruldðearfa m. *poor man,* PPs 69⁶.
woruldðearfende *poor in worldly goods,* CR 1351.
woruldðēaw m. *worldly affair,* Bo 7¹³.
woruld-ðegen, -ðegn, -ðēn m. *earthly or secular servant,* LL.
woruldðēnung (o²) f. *secular office,* NC 334.
woruldðēowdōm m. *secular service,* CHR 963.
woruldðing (o²) n. *worldly affair, thing, Æ,* AO,CP : *earthly riches.*
woruldðrymm m. *worldly glory,* ByH 124⁵ (world-).
woruldwǣpn (o²) n. *earthly weapon,* BL 213⁴.
woruldwæter n. *ocean, sea,* SOL 186'.
woruldwela m. *worldly wealth,* CP.
woruldwelig *rich in worldly goods,* NC 335.
woruldweorc n. *secular work,* LL : *mechanics.*
woruldweorðscipe m. *worldly honour,* LL.
woruldwīdl n. *world-filth,* CR 1007.
woruldwīg n. *worldly contest,* LL.
woruldwilla m. *earthly good,* Bo 24².
woruldwilnung f. *earthly desire,* CP.
woruldwīs (o²) *worldly-wise, CP : learned,* CP.
woruldwīsdōm m. *worldly wisdom, science,* Æ.
woruldwīse f. *custom of the world,* MH 68⁹B.
woruldwita m. *learned layman, sage,* LL.
woruldwīte n. *punishment, fine,* CR,LL.
woruldwlenco f. *magnificence, ostentation,* CP.
woruldwrenc (o²) m. *worldly cunning,* CP.
woruldwuldor n. *worldly glory,* CHRD 66²⁰.
woruldwunlende (o²) *dwelling,* MET 13¹⁷.
woruldyrmðu f. *earthly wretchedness,* AO.
wōrung f. *wandering, roving,* Æ,MFH 179.

wōs I. n. *sap, juice*, Lcd. [' *ooze*'] II. gs. of wōh.

+wosa m. *conversation, intercourse*, DR.

wōsan (NG)=wēsan

wōsc pret. 3 sg., wōscon pret. pl. of wascan.

wōse=wāse

wōsig *juicy, moist*, Lcd.

-wost v. fore-w.

wōð† f. *sound, noise : voice, song, poetry : eloquence*.

wōðbora† m. *orator, speaker, seer, prophet, poet, singer*.

wōðcræft† m. *art of speech or song*.

-woðe v. got-w.

wōðgiefu f. *gift of song*, Rd 32⁸.

wōðsong m. *song*, Cr 46.

wōum dp. of wōh, adj.

wōx I. pret. 3 sg. of weaxan. II.=wōsc

wracian I. *to be in exile, wander, travel*. II. *to carry on, prosecute*, AO 50²¹.

wraclīce=wræclīce

wracnian (æ) *to be a wanderer, traveller, pilgrim*, Æ.

wraco=wracu

wracu (e) f. (g. often wræce) *revenge, vengeance, persecution, enmity*, B,BH,G, LL,VPs,W; AO,CP : *punishment, penalty*, AO,CP : *cruelty, misery, distress, torture, pain, Ph*; AO. on ðā wrace *in retaliation*. [' *wrake*']

wræc I. (e) n(f?) *misery*, CP : *vengeance, persecution*, BH,Bl : *exile*. [' *wrack*'] II. *what is driven*, OET 37⁶². III. pret. 3 sg. of wrecan. IV.=wærc (A; v. Jaw 52)

wræca=wræcca; wrǣcan=wrecan

wræcca (e) m. ' *wretch*,' Jul; CP : *fugitive, outcast, exile*, B,Bo,Chr; AO : *adventurer, stranger : sojourner*.

wræccan=wrecan; wræce v. wracu.

wræcend=wrecend

wræcfæc n. *time of exile, banishment, misery*, Rim 64.

wræcful *wretched, miserable*, ÆH.

wræchwīl f. *time of exile or distress*, Ph 527.

wræclāst† (e) m. *path of exile*.

wræclāstian *to banish*, WW.

wræclic adj. *foreign : strange, unfamiliar, extraordinary : wretched, exiled*. adv. -līce.

wrǣclic=wrǣtlic

wræc-mæcg†, -mæcga (Jul 260) m. *exile, outcast, miserable man*.

wræcmon m. *fugitive*, Ex 137.

wræcnes=wrecnes

wræcnian=wracnian

wrǣcon pret. pl. of wrecan.

wræcscipe (e) m. *exile*, Bl,EPs 119⁵.

wræcsetl n. *place of exile*, Gu 267.

wræcsīð m. *journey of exile or peril, pilgrimage*, Æ : *exile, persecution*, Æ,AO : *misery*.

wræcsīðian *to wander, travel abroad, be in exile*, Æ.

wræcstōw f. *place of exile or punishment*, Bo, Gen.

wræcwīte n. *punishment*, Bl 5.

wræcworuld f. *miserable world*, W l²,VH.

wrǣd f. *band, bandage, wreath*, CP : *bundle : band, ftock*. [wrīðan]

wrǣdmǣlum adv. *in companies*, WW 411⁴².

wrǣg-=wrēg-

wrǣne (ē) *unbridled, loose, lustful*, AO.

wrænna (Æ)=wrenna

wrǣnnes f. *luxury, lust, wantonness*, AO, CP.

wrǣnsa m. *wantonness*, OEG 2347.

wrǣnscipe (ē) m. *wantonness*, OEG 5290.

wrǣnsian *to be wanton*, NC 335.

wrǣsnan *to alter, change, modulate*, Rd 25¹.

wrǣst (ā) *firm, able, strong, excellent : delicate*. adv. -e.

wrǣstan I. (±) *to* ' *wrest*,' *bend, twist, twang*, Sol,Wy. II. *to be or make elegant?* WW.

wrǣstlere m. ' *wrestler*,' WW 431²⁶.

wrǣstlic I. *pertaining to wrestling*, WW. II. (ā) *delicate, elegant*, WW.

wrǣstlend *wrestler*, WW 431²⁵. [wrǣstan]

wrǣstlung f. ' *wrestling*,' *struggling*, GD, OEG.

wræt=wrætt; wrǣt=wrǣtt

wrǣtbaso (e¹) *red*, Gl. [wrætte]

wræteread *red*, Lcd 111b.

wrætlic *artistic, ornamental : curious, wondrous, rare*. adv. -līce. [wrǣtt]

wrætt m., wrætte f. *rubea tinctoria? crosswort? hellebore?* Lcd,WW (A 30·248).

wrǣtt† f. *ornament, work of art, jewel*.

wrǣð I.=wrǣd. II.=wrǣððo

±wrǣðan (ē) *to anger*, ByH 112¹² : *get angry, be angry*, DR : *resist violently*, Lcd 3·212⁴.

wrǣðian=wreðian; wrǣððo=wrǣððo

wrǣð-studu, -stuðu (e) f. *column, pillar, support*, BH,W.

wrǣððo, wrǣð(ð)u (ā) f. ' *wrath*,' *anger, indignation*, DR,Leofric Missal,NG.

wrǣxlian=wraxlian

wrāh pret. 3 sg. of wrēon.

wrang (o) I. n. ' *wrong*,' *injustice*, LL,W. II. *rough, uneven*, KC. III. pret. 3 sg. of wringan.

wranga (pr-) *hold of a ship*, WW. [' *wrong*']

wrangwīs *rough, uneven*, OEG 1770.

wrāsen (ǣ) f. *band, tie, chain*, WW 34²⁴.

wrāst=wrǣst

wrāt pret. 3 sg. of wrītan.

wrāð I. adj. ' WROTH,' *furious, angry, hostile,
AO : terrible, horrible : grievous, harsh,
bitter, malignant, evil, cruel.* adv. -e, *Bo,
G,Gu,Ps.* ['wrothe'] II. f. *cruelty : hardship.* [wrīðan] III.=wrǣd. IV. pret. 3 sg.
of wrīðan.
+wrāðian (refl.) *to be angry, Chr* 1070,*RG.*
['wroth,' 'iwrathe']
wrāðlic† *grievous, severe, bitter.* adv. -līce,
B. ['wrothly']
wrāðmōd† *angry,* GEN.
wrāðscræf n. *pit of misery, hell.* RD 41⁴¹.
wrāððo=wrǣððo
wraðu† f. *prop, help, support, maintenance,*
BH.
+wraxl? *wrestling-place, gymnasium,* OEG
18b⁶⁸?
wraxlere m. *wrestler,* OEG.
wraxlian *to wrestle, Æ.* ['wraxle']
wraxliende *wrestling; contending, striving,*Æ.
wraxlung f. '*wrestling,' WW* 150⁸. ['wrax-
ling']
wrēah pret. 3 sg. of wrēon; wrec=wræc
wrecan⁵ (eo) *to drive, impel, push : press
forward, advance : fulfil, accomplish : utter,
deliver, pronounce : expel, banish, persecute,* CP : (±) 'WREAK,' *revenge, avenge,
punish, CP;* AO.
wreccan I. *to awake, arouse, Æ,CP.*
['wrecche'] II.=wrecan
-wrecel v. spor-w.
wrecend m. *avenger,* B,LL.
wrecnes (æ) f. *vengeance,* NG : *wickedness,*
BHCA 70¹².
wrecscip (æ?) '*actuaria'?* ES 43·336.
wrecu (VPs)=wracu
±wrēgan I.† *to excite, stir up.* II. *to accuse,
impeach, Æ,Chr,Cp,MH.* ['wray']
+wrēgednes f. *accusation,* ES 62·114².
wrēgend m. *accuser,* BH,GL.
±wrēgendlic *accusative,* ÆGR 22²⁰.
wrēgere m. *accuser, informer, Æ.* ['wrayer']
wrēgistre (ǣ) f. *female accuser,* ÆL 2²⁰⁸.
wrēgung f. *accusation,* ÆGr. ['wraying']
wrehte pret. 3 sg. of wrēgan.
wrehtend m. *instigator,* WW 420²⁹.
wrēhtend m. *accuser,* KGL 73²³.
wrēn-=wrǣn-
wrenc m. *wile, stratagem, trick, deceit, Bo,
Sc;* AO : (†) *modulation, melody, song.*
['wrench']
wrencan *to twist, IM : spin intrigues, devise
plots,* MOD 33. ['wrench']
wrenna (æ) m., wrenne f. '*wren,' Cp,WW.*
wreocan=wrecan
wreogan (M)=wrigon pret. pl. of wrēon.
±wrēon¹,² *to cover, clothe, envelop, conceal,
hide, Gen,Lcd,LG,LL : protect, defend, Gen,
Rd.* ['wry']

wrēotan=rēotan; wreotian=writian
wreotu nap. of writ.
wrēoð=(1) wrǣd; (2) wrǣððo
wreoðenhilt *with twisted hilt,* B 1699.
[=*wriðenhilt]
wreoðian=wreðian; wrēoðian=wrīdian
wretbasu=wrætbaso
±wreðian *to support, sustain, uphold, Bo,
GD;* CP. ['wrethe']
wreðstudu=wræðstudu
wrïanne (N)=wrēonne gerund of wrēon I
wricð, wriceð pres. 3 sg. of wrecan.
wrid m. *shoot, plant, bush, BC,Gl,Lcd;*
Mdf. ['wride']
+wrid I. n. *thicket?* GUTH. II. *husk,* WW
412³.
wrīdan¹ *to grow, thrive, flourish,* GEN,LCD.
wriden pp. of (1) wrīdan; (2) wrīðan.
wrīdian† *grow, flourish, spring up,* AA.
wriecð=wricð pres. 3 sg. of wrecan.
wriexl=wrixl
wrigelnes f. *covering,* JPs 60⁵.
wrigels mn. *covering, cloak, veil, HL,VPs.*
['wriels']
wrigen pp., wrigon pret. pl. of wrēon.
wrigennes (gn-) f. *a covering,* EPs 60⁵.
wrigian *to go, turn, twist, bend, Bo,Rd :
strive, struggle, press forward, endeavour,
venture, Bo.* ['wry']
wrīhst pres. 2 sg., wrīhð pres. 3 sg. of
wrēon.
+wrinclian *to wind about,* KC 4·34⁹. +wrin-
clod *serrated,* GPH 39⁸.
+wring n. *liquor, drink,* WW 128¹⁷.
wringan³ *to 'wring,' twist : (±) squeeze, press
out, Æ,Bo,GD,Lcd.*
wringe f. *(oil-)press, GD* 250¹⁵. ['wring']
wringhwǣg n? *strained whey,* LL 451,16.
+wrisc=+wrixl; wrislan=wrixlan
wrist f. '*wrist,' LL* 386,2.
±writ n. *letter, book, treatise, Ph : scripture,
writing, DR,LG : 'writ' ('i-writ'), charter,
document, deed, AO,Bl : 'stilus,'* GPH 402.
±wrītan¹ (ȳ) *to incise, engrave, 'WRITE,'
draw, Æ,Chr,CP;* AO : *bestow by writing.*
writbred n. *writing tablet,* MH,WW.
-wrīte v. wæter-w.; -writennes v. tō-w.
±wrītere m. '*writer,' scribe, author, por-
trayer, painter, Æ,Bf,Bo,CP,Mt : secretary,
CP,GD.*
writeȳren (MH 146¹²)=writīren
writian I. (eo) *to chirp, chatter,* v. OEG 37³.
II. *to cut? draw a figure?* ES 8·478.
writing f. *writing,* SPs 44².
wrītingfeðer f. *pen,* EPs 44².
wrītingīsen n. *style, pen,* MH 146¹²c.
writīren (ȳ²) n. *writing instrument, style,*
MH 146¹².
+writrǣden f. *written agreement,* WW 217⁷.

writseax n. *style, pen*, MtLp2[18].

writt-=writ-

+wriŏ n. *strap, thong*, WW143[13]? (v. A 8·451).

wriŏa m. *band, thong, bridle*, Æ,Sc : *collar, ring*, Æ,Rd. ['*wreath*']

±**wriŏan**[1] (ȳ) **I.** *to twist*, ÆGr : *wrap, bind up, bind, tie, fasten, fetter, check*, BC,LL : *vex, torture*, Æ. ['*writhe*'] **II.**=wridan

+wriŏelian *to bind?* OEG23[7]?

wriŏels m. *band, fillet, bandage*, WW411[17].

+wriŏennes f. *binding*, LCD.

wriŏian=wridian

+wriŏing f. *binding*, Sc202[13].

wrix(i)endlic *mutual*, GD2[7]. adv. -*lice turn about, one by one, by turns, in turn*, CP.

wrixl f., **wrixla** m. *change, exchange, barter*, CP.

+wrixl, +wrixle n. *turn, change* : *exchange, purchase, intercourse* : *requital* : *office*.

wrixlan (±) *to change, barter, exchange, reciprocate, lend*, AO. wordum w. *converse* : (+) *recompense, requite* : (+) *obtain*, CP.

+wrixle *alternate* : *vicarious*, GL.

wrixlian=wrixlan

+wrixlic *alternating*, OEG2[135].

±**wrixlung** f. *change*, BF120[20] : *loan*, WW 115,449.

wroegan=wrēgan

wrogen pp. of wrēon.

wroht=worht pp. of wyrcan.

wrōht I. f. *blame, reproach, accusation, slander* : *fault, crime, sin, injustice*, Æ : *strife, enmity, anger, contention, dispute*, AO,CP : *hurt, injury, calamity, misery*. [wrēgan] **II.** m. *tale-bearer*, ÆGR217[2].

wrōhtberend m. *accuser*, APs,WW.

wrōhtbora m. *accuser, monster*, WW : *the devil*, CR.

wrōhtdropa m. *criminal bloodshed*, GnE196.

wrōhtgeorn *contentious*, CP357.

wrōhtgetēme n. *series of crimes?* (BT),GEN 45.

wrōhtian *to do harm?* HL15[105].

wrōhtlāc n. *calumny*, W160[5]n.

wrōhtsāwere m. *sower of strife*, CP359.

wrōhtscipe m. *crime*, GEN1672.

wrōhtsmiŏ† m. *worker of evil, evildoer*.

wrōhtspitel *slanderous*, EGL. [spittan]

wrōhtstæf m. *accusation*, EL926 : *injury*, RD72[12,14].

wrong (WW201[35])=wrang II.

wrōt m. *snout, elephant's trunk*, Cp,WW. ['*wroot*']

wrōtan[7] *to root up*, Cp,Ps,Rd. ['*wroot*']

wrugon pret. pl. of wrēon.

wrungen pp. of wringan.

wrycŏ pres. 3 sg. of wrecan.

wryhta=wyrhta

wrȳhŏ=wrihŏ pret. 3 sg. of wrēon.

+wryndan (MtL7[25])=+gryndan

wrȳt-=writ-

wrȳte (CM56[83])=prȳte

wrȳŏan=wriŏan

wucaŏēn=wucŏegn

wuc-dæg, wuce-, wicu- m. '*week-day*,' BH Æ.

wuce=wucu

wucŏegn (i[1]) m. *monk or priest appointed for a week's duty, weekly servant*, CM,RB.

wucŏēnung f. *service for a week*, RB59,60.

wucu (i, ie, io) f. '*week*,' Bf,Lcd,RB; AO,CP.

wucubōt f. *penance lasting a week*, LL (278[12]).

wucweorc (i[1]) n. (*compulsory*) *work for a week, by a tenant*, KC,LL. ['*weekwork*']

wude=wudu

wudere m. *wood-man, wood-carrier*, WW 371[5]. ['*wooder*']

wudewe=wuduwe

wudian *to cut wood*, Æ,W.

wudig *wooded, having trees*, Az120.

wudigere, wudiere (WW; '*woodyer*')= wudere

wudiht *thick (with trees), forest-like*, GPH 402.

wudo-=wudu-

wudu (i, io) m., gs. wuda, wudes; nap. wudas, wuda '*wood*,' *forest, grove*, BC,CP, LL,VPs; Æ,AO; Mdf : *tree*, B,Cp,Ph : *the Cross, Rood* : *wood, timber*, Bo,CP,Gn : (†) *ship*, B : *spear-shaft*, B398.

wuduælfen (e[3]) f. *wood-elf, dryad*, WW.

wuduæppel f. *wild apple, crab*, LCD71a.

wudubēr f. *woodland pasture*, KC.

wudubǣre *wood-bearing*, OEG1806.

wudubǣrnett n. *burning of wood*, LL16,12; 24n[2].

wudubāt n. *wooden boat*, AN907.

wudubēam† m. *forest tree*.

wudubearo m. *forest, grove*, AA,W.

wudu-bend, -bind m.=wudubinde

wudubill n. *hatchet*, Cp; GD. ['*woodbill*']

wudubinde I. (-bindle) f. '*woodbine*,' *convolvulus*, Gl,Lcd,LG. **II.** f. *bundle of sticks*, OET35[18].

wudubior (=bora?) m. *wood-carrier*, HGL 427.

wudublǣd† (-blēd) f. *forest blossom*.

wudubucca m. *wild buck, wild goat*, LCD.

wudubyrōra m. *wood-carrier, camp-follower*, OEG869.

wuducerfille f. *wood-chervil, cow-parsley*, GL.

wuducocc m. '*woodcock*,' GL.

wuducroft m. *a croft with trees on it?* (BT) KC3·376[6].

wuduculfre m. *wood-pigeon*, WW.
wuducūnelle f. *wild thyme*, LCD.
wuducynn n. *an aromatic (?) wood*, JnL 12³.
wududocce f. *wild dock, sorrel*, LCD.
wuduelfen=wuduælfen
wudufæsten n. *place protected by woods, woodfastness : ship.*
wudufald *a fold in a wood*, KC.
wudufeld m. *wooded plain*, PPs 131⁶.
wudufeoh n. *forest-tax*, LCD.
wudufille=wuducerfille
wudufīn f. *pile of wood*, ÆGR.
wudufugol m. *forest bird, wild fowl*, BO, MET.
wudugāt f. *wild goat*, LCD.
wudugehæg n. *woodland pasture* (BTs), KC 3·176¹.
wuduhēawere m. *wood-cutter*, Æ. [v. '*wood*']
wuduherpaδ m. *public path through a wood*, KC 3·213².
wuduhīewet n. *illegal cutting of wood*, LL 567,37.
wuduholt n. *forest, wood, grove*, PH.
wuduhona m. *woodcock*, WW 38⁸.
wuduhrofe=wudurofe
wuduhunig n. *wild honey*, Mk; Æ. [v. '*wood*']
wudulād f. *carting wood*, LL 452,21⁴.
wudu-læs f., gs. -læswe *wood-pasture, run (for cattle) in a wood*, Ct.
wuduland n. '*woodland*,' BC.
wudu-leahtric, -lectric m. *wood-lettuce, wild sleepwort*, LCD.
wudulēswe=wudulæswe
wudulic adj. *woody, wooded, wild*, Æ,WW.
wudumǣr (ē³) f. *wood-nymph, echo*, GL.
wudumann m. *woodman*, KC 3·275⁹.
wudumerce m. *wild parsley, wood-mint*, LCD. [v. '*wood*']
wudung f. *getting of wood*, Æ : *right of estovers*, KC. ['*wooding*']
wudurǣden f. *wood-regulation, right of estovers*, LL.
wudurēc m. *smoke from a funeral pyre*, B 3144.
wudurima m. *border of a wood*, KC 3·34¹⁵.
wudurofe f. '*woodruff*,' Lcd,WW.
wudurose f. *wild rose*, LCD 34b?
wudusnīte f. *wood-snipe*, WW.
wudusūræppel f. *crab-apple?* LCD 160a.
wudutelga m. *branch of a tree*, SOL 421.
wudutrēow n. *forest tree*, LL,W.
wuduδistle m. *wood-thistle*, LCD.
wuduwa (wyde-) m. *widower*, LL. ['*widow*']
wuduwald m. *forest*, WW 426³⁵.
wuduwanhād m. *state of a woman who has not a husband, chastity*, 'widowhood,' CP, HL.

wuduwāsa m. *faun, satyr*, WW. ['*wood-wose*']
wuduwe (i, eo, y¹; e²) f. '*widow*,' Chr,G,Ps.
wuduweard m. *forester*, LL 452,19. ['*woodward*']
wudu-weax n., -weaxe f. *wood-waxen. genista tinctoria*, Lcd. ['*woodwax*']
wuduwēsten mn. *wild forest*, CHR p 5n.
wuduwinde f. *woodbine*, GL.
wuduwyrt f. *plant which grows in woods*, BL 59³.
wudwe=wuduwe
wuhhung f. *rage, fury, madness* : (pl.) *the Furies.*
wuht AO,CP=wiht; **wuhung**=wuhhung
wul=wull; **wulder**=wuldor
wuldor n. *glory, splendour, honour*, Bo, VPs; Æ,CP : *praise, thanks : heaven*, EL. ['*wulder*']
wuldor-bēag, -bēah m. *crown of glory*, Æ.
±**wuldorbēagian** *to crown*, ÆH.
wuldorblǣd m. *glorious success*, JUD 156.
wuldorcyning m.† *King of Glory, God.*
wuldordrēam m. *heavenly rapture*, MFH.
Wuldorfæder† m. *Glorious Father.*
wuldorfæst *glorious.* adv. -fæste, -fæstlīce.
wuldorfæstlicnes f. *glory*, Æ.
wuldorful *glorious*, Æ : *vainglorious*, SC.
±**wuldorfullian** *to glorify*, Æ.
wuldorfullīce adv. *gloriously*, ÆH.
wuldorgāst m. *angel*, GEN 2912.
wuldorgeflogena m. *one who has fled from glory, devil*, LCD 3·36¹⁵.
wuldorgesteald† np. *glorious possessions, realms of glory.*
wuldorgeweorc n. *wondrous work*, ES 43·167.
wuldorgifu† (eo) f. *glorious gift, grace.*
wuldorgim m. *glorious jewel, sun*, RD 81²⁰.
Wuldorgod m. *Glorious God*, BHB 344⁸.
wuldorhama† (o³) m. *garb of glory.*
wuldorhēap m? *glorious troop*, NC 335.
wuldorhelm m. *crown of glory*, BL.
wuldorlēan† n. *glorious reward.*
wuldorlic† *glorious*, BL,Ps. adv. -līce.
wuldormāga m. *heir of heaven*, GU 1067.
wuldormago m. *heir of heaven*, GU 1267.
wuldormicel *gloriously great*, †Hy 7⁹⁴.
wuldornytting f. *glorious service*, RD 81¹⁹.
wuldorsang m. *glorious song*, MFH 114¹⁰.
wuldorspēd f. *glorious wealth*, GEN 87.
wuldorspēdig *glorious*, AN 428.
wuldortān m. *plant with medicinal virtues?* (BT), LCD 3·34'.
wuldortorht† *gloriously bright, clear, brilliant, illustrious.*
wuldorδrymm m. *heavenly glory*, AN,BL.
wuldorweorud n. *heavenly host*, CR 285.
wuldorword n. *glorious word*, †Hy 7⁴⁶.

wuldrian (±) *to glorify, praise, extol,* Æ : *boast, brag,* Æ : *live in glory,* Æ.

wuldrig *glorious,* DR.

wuldrung f. *glorying, boasting,* Sc,DR.

wuldur=wuldor

wulf m. *(he-)'wolf,'* *Cp,LG,Wy*; Æ,AO, CP; Mdf : *wolfish person, devil,* Cr, MH.

wulfescamb m. *wild teasel,* Lcd,WW.

wulfeshēafod n. *head of a wolf,* Lcd : *outlaw,* LL (v. NED). *['wolfshead']*

wulfestæsel f. *(wolf's) teasel,* Lcd.

wulfhaga m. *shelter from wolves?* CC53.

wulfhēafodtrēo m. *cross, gallows?* RD56¹².

wulfheort† *wolf-hearted, cruel,* DA.

wulf-hlĭð n., nap. -hleoðu *hillside inhabited by wolves,* B1358.

wulfhol n. *wolf's hole,* WW.

wulflȳs n. *fleece of wool,* WW198²⁶.

wulfmod=wullmod

wulfpytt m. *wolf's hole?* BC,KC.

wulfsēað m. *wolf's hole,* KC3·264⁵.

wulfslæd n. *valley of wolves,* KC3·456⁶.

wull f. *'wool,'* *Gl,Lcd,VPs*; Æ.

wullcamb m. *comb for wool,* LL454,15¹. *['woolcomb']*

wullcnoppa (?hn-) m. *tuft of wool,* WW.

wulle=wull

wullen *(KC; 'woollen')*=wyllen

wullian *to wipe with wool,* Lcd1·356'.

wullmod m? *distaff,* Gl.

wulltewestre f. *wool-carder,* Lcd.

wulluc *cover, wrapper,* A31·65.

wullwēoga f. *scales for wool,* WW148²¹.

+**wun**=+wuna

±**wuna** I. m. (usu. +) *habit, custom, practice, rite,* Bo; Æ. on gew. habban *to be accustomed to,* CP. *['i-wune']* II. (+) *wonted, customary, usual,* Chr,LG. *['wone']*

wund I. f. *'wound,' sore, ulcer,* B,BH,Cr, Lcd,RB; CP : *wounding, injury,* Æ. II. adj. *wounded, sore,* AO.

wundel f. *wound,* LL,RB.

wundelīce=wundorlīce

wunden *(B; 'wounden')* pp. of windan.

wundenfeax *with twisted mane,* B1400.

wundenhals *with twisted prow,* B298.

wundenlocc† *with braided locks.*

wundenmǣl *etched, damascened (of a sword),* B1531.

wundenstefna m. *ship with curved or wreathed prow,* B220.

wunder=wundor

±**wundian** *to 'wound,'* Æ,CP,Chr,LL,Ps; AO.

wundiend *'vulnerator,'* ERHy6⁴².

wundiht, wundig *ulcerous, full of sores,* GPH.

wundle=wundel

wundlic *wounding, wound-inflicting,* GPH 402⁵¹.

wundon pret. pl. of windan.

wundor (often confused with wuldor) n. (gs. wundres) *'WONDER,' miracle, marvel, portent, horror,* Æ; AO,CP : *wondrous thing, monster.*

wundorāgræfen *wondrously graven,* AN712.

wundorbēacen n. *strange sign,* PPs73⁵.

wundorbebod n. *strange order,* B1747.

wundorblēo n. *wondrous hue,* CR1140.

wundorclam n. *strange bond,* CR310.

wundorcræft† m. *miraculous power.*

wundorcræftiglīce *with wondrous skill,* BH 324³o.

wundordǣd f. *wondrous·deed,* BL.

wundordēað m. *wondrous death,* B3037.

wundoreardung f. *wondrous dwelling.* VH24.

wundorfæt (e²) n. *wondrous vessel,* B1162.

wundorful (e²) *'wonderful,'* OEG; Æ. adv. -līce.

wundorgehwyrft (e⁴) *wondrous turn,* GPH 390.

wundorgeweorc=wundorweorc

wundorgiefu f. *wondrous endowment,* WY72.

wundorhǣlo (u²) f. *wondrous healing,* BH 446¹².

wundorhūs? n. *'solarium,' upper room,* GD 119²⁶.

+**wundorlǣcan** *to make wonderful, magnify,* SPs16⁸.

wundorlic *wonderful, remarkable, strange,* AO,Bl; Æ,CP. adv. -līce, Æ,CP,Lcd. *['wonderly']*

wundormāðm m. *wonderful treasure,* B2173

wundorsēon f. *wonderful sight,* B995.

wundorsmīð m. *skilled smith,* B1681.

wundortācen n. *miracle,* PPs104²³.

wundorweorc n. *'wonder-work,' miracle,* An,Bl.

wundorworuld f. *wonderful world,* RD40¹⁷.

wundorwyrd f. *wonderful event,* EL1071.

wundres v. wundor.

±**wundrian** (w. g.) *to 'wonder,' be astonished (at),* Bl,Bo,G,Ph; Æ,AO,CP : *admire : make wonderful, magnify.*

wundrigendlic *expressing wonder,* ÆGR 241¹⁶.

wundrum adv. (d. of wundor) *wonderfully, strangely, terribly.*

wundrung f. *wonder, astonishment, admiration,* Æ,Cr : *spectacle,* OEG4370. *['wondering']*

wundspring m. *ulcerous wound,* Lcd1·356'.

wundswaðu (e) f. *scar,* VPs37⁶.

wundur=wundor

wundwīte n. *compensation for wounding,* LL76H.

+**wunelic** *usual, customary,* Æ,CP : *accustomed (to), adapted (to).* adv. -līce, BH. ['*i-wuneliche*']

wunenes, wununes f. *dwelling, habitation :* *perseverance,* DR. [wunian]

wungynde=wuniende pres. ptc. of wunian.

wunian (±) *to inhabit, dwell, abide, exist, B, Bl,Cp,G;* AO,CP : (+) *remain, continue, stand, Æ,B,Bl;* AO,CP : (±) *be used to, be wont to, ÆGr :* (+) *habituate oneself to,* CP73[14]. ['*wone*']

wuniendlic *perpetually,* GD264[7].

wunigend m. *inhabitant,* RBL5[11].

+**wunlic**=+wunelic; **wunn**=wynn

wunnen pp., wunnon pret. pl. of winnan.

+**wunod** *domiciled,* GUTH9[23].

wunones=wunenes; **wunsum**=wynsum

wununes=wunenes

wunung f. *act of dwelling, living, Bl,RB :* *dwelling, habitation, Æ,HL.* ['*wonning*']

wunungstōw f. *abiding-place,* GD31[19].

wuraðo (N)=wræððo; **wurcan**=wyrcan

wurd=(1) wyrd; (2) word

wurdon pret. pl. of weorðan.

wurht, wurhton=worhte pret. sg., worhton pret. pl. of wyrcan.

wurm=wyrm

wurma m., wurme f. *murex, purple-fish :* *any dye, woad, purple : a plant used for dyeing.*

wur-mille, -mele (ea[1]) f. *wild marjoram,* GL.

wurms=worms; **wurnian**=weornian

wurpan=weorpan

wurpul *that which throws down,* GL.

wursm=worms; **wurst**=wierrest

wurt=wyrt; **wurð**=weorð

wurðe=weorð(e), wierðe; **wurðig**=worðig

wūscbearn n. *(dear) little child,* JnL13[33]. [wȳscan]

wūso (JnR13[33])=wūscbearn

wussung=wissung; **wuta**=wita

wutan=wuton

wutedlīce, wutodlīce (NG)=witodlīce

wuton 1 pers. pl. subj. of wītan *to go.* used to introduce an imperative or hortatory clause *let us...! come!* CP.

wutu (M), wutum, wutun (N)=wuton

wutudlīce=witodlīce

wūðwuta (DR)=ūðwita; **wȳc**=wīc

wyc-=wic-; **wȳd**=wīd; **wyd-**=wud-

wyder-=wiðer-; **wȳf-**=wīf-

wyglere=wiglere; **wyht**=wiht

wyl-=weal-, wel-, wi(e)l-; **wȳl-**=wīel-

wylcð pres. 3 sg. of wealcan.

wylf f. *she-wolf,* OET.

wylfen I. adj. *wolfish,* DEOR,OEG. **II.** f. *she-wolf, fury, Lcd ;* GL. ['*wolfen*']

wylian=wylwan

wȳliscmoru=wēalmoru

wyll I. f. *wool,* LL(166n[4]). **II.**=wiell

wyllan (æ, e;=ie) *to boil, Lcd.* ['*well*']

wylleburne †f. *spring.*

wyllecærse (i) *watercress, Lcd,WW.* ['*wellcress*']

wyllen (i) *made of wool, woollen.*

wyllestrēam m. *running water, Ph.* ['*wellstream*']

wyllewæter n. *spring water, Lcd.* ['*wellwater*']

wylleweg *road to a well or spring,* KC 5·150[12].

wyllflōd (i) *flood, deluge,* GEN1412.

wyllgespring n. *spring,* BH,PH.

wyllspring(e) (e[1], i[1]) m. *spring, Æ,CP, WW.* ['*wellspring*']

wyloc=weoloc; **wyn**=wynn

±**wyltan** (æ, e;=ie) *to roll.*

wylw-an, -ian (e, i;=ie) *to roll, roll together :* *compound, join.*

wyn-=win-, winn-; **wȳn-**=wīn-

wynbēam m. *tree of gladness, holy cross,* EL844.

wynburh f. *delightful town,* PPs127[2].

wyncondel f. *pleasant light, sun,* GU1186.

wyndæg† m. *day of gladness.*

+**wynde** n. *weaving,* GL.

wyndecræft m. *art of embroidery,* GL.

wyndle f. *wound,* LL381,23.

wyndrēam m. *jubilation, joyful sound,* Ps.

wyndrēamnes f. *jubilation,* LPs150[5].

wyndrian=wundrian; **wyne**=wine

wynele m. *gladdening oil,* PPs108[18].

wynfæst (e) *joyful,* PsC50[19].

wyngesīð m. *pleasant companion,* PPs100[3].

wyngrāf mn. *delightful grove,* PPs94[13].

wynigað=wunigað pres. pl. of wunian.

wynland† (o[2]) n. *land of delight.*

wynlēas† *joyless.*

wynlic *pleasant, beautiful, joyful, HL,Ph.* adv. -līce, *Ps.* ['*winly*']

wynlust m. *sensual pleasure,* Æ.

wynmæg f. *winsome maiden,* GU1319.

wynn f. (occl. late as. wyn) *joy, rapture, pleasure, delight, gladness, B ;* AO. ['*win*']

wynn- v. also wyn-, win(n)-.

wynnum† *joyfully, beautifully.* [wynn]

wynpsalterium n. *psalm of joy,* PPs56[10].

wynrōd f. *blessed cross,* SOL235.

wynsang m. *joyful song,* W265[31].

wynstaðol m. *joyous foundation,* RD92[3].

wynsum (e, i; once +wuns-) '*winsome,*' *pleasant, delightful, joyful, merry, B,MH, Ph ;* CP : *kindly, BH.*

+**wynsumian** *to rejoice, exult,* DR : *make glad, make pleasing.*

±**wynsumlic** adj. *pleasant, delightful* adv. -līce *pleasantly, happily* Æ

wynsumnes (i) f. *loveliness, pleasantness, rejoicing,* Æ.

wynwerod n. *'chorus,' joyous band,* GL.

wynwyrt f. *pleasant plant,* DD5.

wynyng=wining

wyorðmynd (BL)=weorðmynd

wȳr=wīr; **wyrc**=weorc

±**wyrcan** (e, eo, i) *to prepare, perform, do, make,* 'WORK*,' *construct, produce, effect,* Æ; AO,CP : *use (tools) : dispose, constitute : amount to :* (w. g.) *strive after : deserve, gain, win, acquire.* Eastron w. *to keep Easter, eat the passover.*

+**wyrce** n. *work : proceeds of work, perquisite,* LL449,7 (v. BTs).

wyrcend m. *worker, doer,* ÆH.

wyrcnes f. *work, operation,* BH.

wyrcta (Ep,MtL)=wyrhta

wyrcung f. *working, work,* DR.

±**wyrd** I. fn. *fate, chance, fortune, destiny,* B,Bo,Cp,Seaf; Æ,AO : *Fate, the Fates, Providence,* CP : *event, phenomenon, transaction, fact,* Bl,Cr : *deed :* (+) *condition : pleasure,* AO126³³. ['*weird*'; weorðan] II. f. *verbosity,* OEG1419.

wyrdan=wierdan

+**wyrde** I. n. *speech, conversation : ordinance.* II. *acknowledging, agreeing with,* CHR1055. III.=+wyrðe

+**wyrdelic** *historical, authentic,* Æ : *fortuitous,* OEG. adv. -lice *eloquently : accurately, verbatim : wisely,* OEG208.

+**wyrdelicnes** f. *eloquence,* A13·38³²¹.

wyrdgesceapum *by chance,* WW400²⁵.

+**wyrdignes** f. *eloquence,* OEG5488.

+**wyrdlian**=+wierdan

wyrdnes f. *condition, state,* Bo128n.

wyrdstæf m. *decree of fate,* Gu1325.

±**wyrdwrītere** m. *historian, chronicler,* Æ.

wyred=werod

wyregung=wyrgung

wyrest=wierrest; **wyrfan**=hwierfan

wyrg=wearg

wyrgan I. *to strangle,* Cp; Æ. ['*worry*'] II.=wiergan

wyrgcwedol (e;=ie) *ill-tongued, given to cursing.*

wyrgcwedolian (e) *to curse,* VPs.

wyrgcwedolnes (e¹, i²) f. *cursing,* Ps.

wyrged (æ) *the devil,* NG.

-**wyrgednes** v. ā-w.

wyrgels=wrigels; **wyrgelnes**=wyrgnes

wyrgend (e) m. *reviler, evildoer,* ÆL.

wyrgende *given to cursing,* W70¹⁸.

wyrgnes f. *abuse, cursing,* Æ,BH.

wyrgðu† (æ, e) f. *curse, condemnation, punishment : evil, wickedness.*

wyrgung (e) f. *curse, cursing, condemnation, banishment,* Æ.

+**wyrht** (eo) fn. *work, deed, service : desert, merit,* AO,CP : *transgression.* mid gewyrhtum *deservedly.*

wyrhta m. '*wright,' artist, labourer, worker, maker, creator,* Æ,Bl,Bo,G,LL; CP : (+) *fellow-worker :* (+) *accomplice.*

wyrī-=wearg-; **wyrian**=wiergan

wyricean=wyrcan; **wyrig**=werig

wyrig-=wearg-, wyrg-

wyrld=woruld

wyrm (eo, o, u) I. m. *reptile, serpent, snake, dragon,* Æ,AO : '*WORM,' insect, mite : poor creature,* VPs. [wurma] II.=wearm

wyrma=wurma; **wyrmæt**=wyrmæte (I.)

wyrmæte I. f. *attack of worms, worm-eaten state,* A,Lcd. II. adj. *worm-eaten,* Lcd. ['*wormete*']

±**wyrman** (æ, e, i;=ie) *to warm, make warm.*

wyrmbaso *red, scarlet,* OET113⁶⁷.

wyrmcynn n. *serpent-kind, sort of serpent,* AO,B,G. ['*wormkin*']

wyrmella=wurmille

wyrmfāh *adorned with figures of snakes, damascened?* B1698.

wyrmgal(d)ere (u) m. *snake-charmer,* Æ.

wyrmgealdor n. *charm against snakes,* Lcd 148a.

wyrmgeard m. *abode of serpents,* Sol469.

wyrmgeblǣd n. *swelling from snake-bite?* (*or insect-bite?*) Lcd162b.

wyrmhǣlsere m. *diviner by serpents,* WW 441³⁵.

wyrmhīw n. *likeness of a serpent,* ÆL10¹⁰⁴.

wyrmhord n. *dragon's hoard,* B2222.

wyrming (æ, e;=ie) f. *warming,* BHB196²⁷. [wearm]

wyrmlīc n. *form of a serpent,* WA.

wyrmmelu n. *worm-meal, 'pulvis e vermibus confectus,'* Lcd.

wyrmrēad (u¹) *purple, scarlet,* Æ.

wyrms nm. *virus, corrupt matter,* Æ.

±**wyrmsan** *to fester,* CP.

+**wyrms(ed)** *purulent,* Lcd,WW.

wyrmsele m. *hall of serpents, hell,* JUD119.

wyrmshrǣcing f. *spitting up of matter,* WW 113⁸?

±**wyrmsig** (u) *purulent,* WW.

wyrmslite m. *snake-bite,* W188¹.

wyrmsūtspiung f. *spitting up of matter,* WW 113⁸?

wyrmwyrt f. *worm-wort,* Lcd.

wyrn=wearn; **wyrnan**=wiernan

wyrp m. *a throw, cast,* Lk22⁴¹. ['*wurp*']

wyrpan=wierpan

wyrpe (e;=ie) f. *revolution, change, recovery, relief, improvement.* [weorpan]

+**wyrpe** n. *heap,* KC5·78'; Mdf.

wyrpel m. *jess (in falconry),* Wy87 (v. ES 37·195).

-wyrplic v. scort-w.

wyrpst, wyrpð pres. 2 and 3 sg. of weorpan and wyrpan.

wyrrest=wierrest; **wyrs**=wiers

wyrshræcung=wyrmshræcing

wyrslan (=ie) *to get 'worse,'* Æ,*VPs,W.*

wyrslic (=ie) *bad, vile, mean,* Rd,W.

wyrsm-=wyrms-

wyrst=(1) wrist; (2) wierrest

wyrt (e, i) f. **I.** *herb, vegetable, plant, spice,* *CP,Lcd,LG,VPs;* AO : *crop* : *root.* [*'wort'*] **II.** *'wort' (brewing),* Lcd.

wyrtbedd m. *bed of herbs,* Lcd.

+wyrtbox f. *fragrant herb or perfume box,* OEG 8²⁹⁹.

wyrtbræð m. *fragrance,* Æ.

wyrtcynn n. *species of plant,* JnL,WW.

wyrtcynren n. *the vegetable world,* LPs 146⁸.

wyrtdrenc m. *herbal drink, medicine, Cp.* [v. *'drench'*]

wyrteceddrenc m. *herbal acid drink,* Lcd 63b.

wyrtfæt n. *scent-bottle,* OEG.

wyrtforbor n. *restraint from action by the operation of herbs* (BT), Lcd 111b.

wyrtgælstre f. *witch who works with herbs,* Lcd 3·186¹¹.

wyrtgeard m. *(kitchen) garden,* CPs 143¹³.

wyrt-gemang (Æ) n., -gemangnes (e³) f. *mixture of herbs, spices, perfume.*

wyrtgyrd=wyrtgeard

±wyrtian *to season, spice, perfume,* Lcd, WW.

wyrtig *garden-like? full of herbs?* ÆL 30³¹².

wyrtmete m. *dish of herbs, pottage,* WW.

wyrt-rum, wyrt-(t)ruma m., -rume f. *root, root-stock,* CP : *origin, beginning, stock.* [v. CC68]

±wyr(t)trumian *to take root* : *establish* : *root out,* DR.

wyrttûn, ±wyrtûn (Æ) m. *garden.*

wyrttûnhege f. *garden enclosure,* GD 67¹⁸.

wyrtung f. *a preparation of herbs,* Lcd 1·342′.

wyrtwala (i, eo, u¹; æ, e²) m. *root, stock,* Lcd : *base, lower part,* KC.

wyrtwalian (æ²) *to set, plant, root* : *root up,* Ægr.

wyrtwalu f.=wyrtwala

wyrtweard m. *gardener,* GD 23; Jn 20¹⁵.

wyrtwela=wyrtwala

wyrð=weorð

wyrðan *to irrigate with manure,* A 36·77.

+wyrðan I. (=ie) *to value, appraise.* **II.**= +weorðan

wyrðe=weorð

+wyrðe (=ie) n. *bulk, contents, amount,* Lcd.

wyrðeland=yrðland

wyrðig I. *fitting, deserved,* AO 256¹¹. **II.**= worðig

wyrðing m. *fallow land? cultivated land?* WW 495²⁰.

wyruld-=woruld-; **wys-**=wis(s)-

±wŷscan (ī) (w. d. pers. and g. thing) *to 'wish,'* Æ,*CP;* AO : (+) *adopt,* ÆH.

+wŷscednes f. *adoption,* RBL 11¹⁴.

+wŷscendlic *desirable,* CM 109 : *optative (mood),* Ægr : *adoptive.* adv. -līce.

+wŷscing (ī) f. *adoption,* RB 10².

wŷsdōm (Æ)=wīsdōm; **wyt**=wit pron.

wyt-, wŷt-=wit-, wĭt-; **wytt**=wit pron.

wytuma m. *paranymph,* A 13·30⁸². [= witumbora? (BT)]

wyð-=wið-

wyxð pres. 3 sg. of weaxan.

Y

yb (AA)=ymb

ybilberende (OEG 53¹⁶)=yfelberende

ŷcan, ŷcean=īecan

yce (WW 468²²)=hice

ŷce (ī) fm. *toad, frog,* Lcd,WW.

ŷcte pret. 3 sg. of ŷcan.

ŷdæges=īdæges

ŷddisc n? *household stuff, furniture, possessions,* Æ. [ēad]

ŷde=ēode; **ŷdel**=īdel; **ydes**=ides

ŷdisc=ŷddisc; **ŷdl-**=īdl-; **yel-**=iel-

yfæsdrype=yfesdrype

yfel I. adj. gsm. yfel(e)s *bad, ill,* Bl,Lcd,Mt : *'evil,' wicked, wretched,* Bl,CP,Mt. comp. wiersa, wyrsa *worse.* superl. wierrest(a), wiersta, weorsta, wyr(re)sta *worst,* Æ,AO. **II.** n. *'evil,' ill, wickedness, misery,* B,Bl, CP,OET,RB,Ps.

yfelâdl f. *'cachexia,' consumption,* WW 113¹³.

yfelberende (ybil-) *bringer of evil tidings,* OEG 53¹⁶ (v. ANS 85·310).

yfelcund *evil, malignant,* LPs.

yfelcwedolian (ð) *to speak evil,* ERPs 36²².

yfel-cweðende, -cweðelgiende (EPs) *evil-speaking,* SPs 36²³.

yfeldǣd f. *ill deed, injury,* Æ.

yfeldǣda m. *evildoer,* ÆL.

yfeldǣde *evil-doing,* Æ,Lcd,Gl.

yfeldēma m. *wicked judge,* NC 335.

yfeldōnd m. *evildoer,* JnL 18³⁰.

yfeldōnde *evil-doing,* LL (424²⁰).

yfeldysig *'stultomalus,'* WW 165¹⁸.

yfole=yfle

yfelful *malicious, wicked,* A 11·116¹³.

yfelgiornes f. *malice, wickedness,* DR.

±yfelian *to inflict evil, hurt, wrong, injure,* Ps : *become bad, grow worse, suffer,* W. [*'evil'*]

yfelic, yfellic *evil, bad* : *poor, mean* : *foul, ugly.* adv. -lice.

yfellærrende *persuading to evil,* GPH 390.

yfellibbende *evil-living,* RBL 118¹⁰.

yfelnes f. *wickedness, depravity,* Æ; CP. ['*evilness*']

yfelsacend (eo¹, u²) m. *blasphemer,* GD 289²⁷.

±**yfelsacian** *to blaspheme,* BL 189; GD 289²⁷.

yfelsacung f. *calumny, blasphemy,* Æ,BL.

yfelsæc (eo¹, u²) n? *blasphemy,* EL 524.

±**yfelsian** (ebol-) *to blaspheme,* NG,WW.

yfel-spræce, -sprecende *evil-speaking,* Ps.

yfelsung (ebol-, eoful-) f. *blasphemy,* LL.

yfeltihtend m. *inciter to evil,* ÆH.

yfeltihtende *inciting to evil,* ÆH.

yfelwille *malevolent,* Sc 196¹⁸.

yfelwillende *vicious,* Æ,CP.

yfelwillendnes f. *malice,* LPs.

yfelwilnian *to desire evil,* LPs.

yfelwoerc n. *evil deed,* DR 103¹.

yfelwyrcende *evil-doing,* ÆL.

yfelwyrde *evil-speaking,* ES 39·354.

yfemest superl. adj. *highest, uppermost,* CP. [ufan]

ŷfer v. ŷfre.

yfera=yferra; **yferdrype**=yfesdrype +**yferian** *to exalt,* LPs.

yferra comp. adj. *after, subsequent* : *higher.* [ufan]

yfes f.=efes

yfesdrype (æ²) m. '*eaves-drop,*' EC 141¹⁶.

ŷfig=ĭfig

yfle adv. (comp. wirs) *evilly, badly, ill, wrongly, miserably, hurtfully,* Bl,G,Gen, Ps,Rd. ['*evil*']

±**yflian**=yfelian

yflung f. *injury,* GD 197¹².

yfmest=yfemest

ŷfre? ŷfer? *escarpment,* BC,KC (v. GBG).

ŷgett=iggað

ŷgland=iegland; **ŷgðelice**=ieðelice

ŷhte=ĭhte; **ŷl**=il; **ylca** (Æ)=ilca

ylcian=elcian; **yld**=ield; **yle**=ile

ylf, ylfe=ælf

ylfet, ylfetu, ylfette (Æ)=ilfetu

ylfig *raving, mad,* WW. [v. '*giddy*']

ylful (HGL 529)=ieldful

ylp m. *elephant,* WW; Æ. ['*elp*']

ylpen-=elpen(d)-; **ylpesbān**=elpendbān

yltsta=ieldesta wk. masc. superl. of eald.

yltwist f? *catching of birds,* WW 351⁶.

ym-=ymb(e)-; **ymb**=ymbe

ymb-=imb-

ymbærnan *to travel round,* BH 28⁸.

ymbbegang=ymbgang

ymbberan⁴ *to surround,* JUL,MkLR.

ymbbignes (bebīg-) f. *bending round, bend, circuit, sweep* (*of a river*), BH 424¹⁰. [bīegan]

ymbbindan³ *to bind round,* MkL 9⁴².

ymbcæflan *to embroider round, bedeck,* RPs 44¹⁵.

ymbceorfan³ *to circumcise,* NG.

ymbceorfnes f. *circumcision,* JnR 7²³ (-cernes).

ymbcerr (=ie) m. *turning about, going, migration,* NG : *tergiversation, trickery,* DR.

ymbcerran=ymbcyrran

ymbclyccan *to enclose,* RPs 16¹⁰ (ES 38·25).

ymbclyppan (i) *to embrace, clasp,* ÆGR.

ymbclypping f. *embracing,* OEG 4529 (emc-).

ymbcyme m. *assembly, convention,* LL 12 (ymc-).

ymbcyrran (e²; =ie) *to turn round, go round, make the circuit of* : *overturn, change,* NG.

ymbdringend=ymbhringend

ymbe (e¹, u¹) I. prep. w. a. d. and adv. (of place) *around, about, at, upon, near, along* : (of time) *about, at, after, before.* ymb utan *about, by, around* : (causal, etc.) *about, in regard to, concerning, on account of, owing to.* ðæs y. litel *soon after.* y. bĕon *to set about a thing.* ['EMBE,' 'UMBE'] II. (=i) n. *swarm of bees,* LCD 1·384'; Mdf.

ymbe-=ymb-

ymbeaht mp. '*collatio,*' WW; OEG 53²² (v. ES 11·492).

ymbeardian *to dwell round,* VPs 30¹⁴.

ymbebĕatan *to curb, restrain,* MET 24³⁷.

ymbebĕgnes=ymbbĭgnes

ymbeornan=ymbiernan

ymbesprĕc f. *talk, remark, criticism,* Æ.

ymbe-ðanc, -ðonc, -ðanca m. *thought, reflection,* CP.

ymbeðencan=ymbðencan

ymbeðridian *to think about,* NC 335.

ymb-fær (embef-) n., -færeld (Æ) nm. *journey round, circuit.*

ymbfæstnes f. *enclosure,* DR 174⁹.

ymbfæstnung f. *monument, tomb,* JnL 19⁴¹.

ymbfæðmian *to embrace,* SOL 150'.

ymbfaran⁶ *to surround,* AO 80²⁶ : *travel round,* GD 490³.

ymbfaru (emf-) n. *circuit,* HGL 422¹⁴.

ymbfeng I. m. *envelope, cover,* OEG 468. II. pres. 3 sg. of ymbfōn.

ymbfĕran *to go about, journey round,* AA 30¹⁰; GPH 396.

ymbfōn⁷ *to surround, encompass, embrace, grasp, seize,* AO.

ymbfrætewian *to decorate, deck round,* LPs, W.

ymb-gān anv., -gangan⁷ *to go round, surround.*

ymbgang (eo²) m. *going about, circuit, circumference, surrounding belt,* AO.

ymbgearwian *to clothe, dress*, NG.
ymbgedelf n. *digging round*, ÆH 2·408¹¹.
ymb-gefrætwian, -gefretwian (VPs)=ymbfrætewian
ymbgeong (N)=ymbgang
ymbgerēnian *to deck round*, BLPs 143¹⁵.
ymb-gesett, -geseten *neighbouring*, BH 2·362.
ymbgesettan=ymbsettan
ymbgirdan=ymbgyrdan
ymbgong=ymbgang
ymbgyrdan (i) *to gird about, encircle, surround*, Æ.
ymbhabban *to surround*, AO : *include, contain : detain*.
ymbhaga (=i¹) m. *enclosure for bees*, LCD 1·395⁴. [ymbe II.]
ymbhaldan=ymbhealdan
ymbhammen *surrounded, covered*, WW 340¹⁴.
ymbhangen pp. of ymbhōn.
ymbhealdan⁷ *to encompass*, SAT 7.
ymbhēapian *to crowd about*, WW.
ymbhēdig=ymbhȳdig
ymbhegian *to hedge round*, ÆGR.
ymbhēpan=ymbhȳpan
ymbhīwan (WW 381²)=ymbhȳpan
ymbhlennan (emb-) *to surround*, OEG 24.
ymbhoga m. *care, anxiety, solicitude, consideration*, Mt; CP. [v. '*embe*']
ymbhogian *to be anxious about*, LPs.
ymbhōn⁷ *to surround, deck, clothe*, HL,W.
ymb-hringan *to surround, fence round*, CP : *wind round*, WW.
ymbhringend m. *attendant member of a retinue*, GL.
ymbhūung=ymbhȳwung
ymbhwearft=ymbhwyrft
ymbhweorfan³ (e², u²) *to turn round, revolve : go round, encompass : tend, cultivate*, CP.
ymbhweorfnes f. *change, revolution*, DR 37¹⁸.
ymbhweorft (e²)=ymbhwyrft
ymbhwerf- (u², y²)=ymbhweorf-
ymbhwyrft (e, ea, eo, i) m. *rotation, revolution, turn : circle, extent, environment, circuit, orbit*, Æ,CP : *circle of the earth, orb, globe, world*, Æ,AO : *region, district : cultivation*, Æ.
ymb-hȳde, -hȳdi-=ymbhȳdig-
ymbhȳdig *anxious, solicitous, careful, suspicious : to be observed, needing attention*, Æ. adv. -līce.
ymbhȳdiglic *anxious, careful, solicitous*. adv. -līce.
ymbhȳdignes f. *anxiety, solicitude*, ÆH.
ymbhygd f. *anxiety*, BL,GD.
ymbhygdig=ymbhȳdig
ymbhȳpan *to press round, assail*, BH,WW.

ymbhȳwung (-hūung) f. *circumcision*, JnL 7²².
ymbiernan³ (io, y) *to run round : surround*, MH.
ymblǣdan *to lead round*, OET (VHy 7¹⁸).
ymblǣrgian (emb-) *to provide with a rim, surround*, OEG 8³⁷⁷. [lǣrig]
ymblicgan⁵ *to surround, enclose*, AO.
ymblīðan *to sail round*, BH 408²⁵.
ymblōcian *to look round*, NG.
ymblofian *to praise*, LPs 116¹.
ymblyt m. *circle, circuit, circumference*, SAT 7?
Ymbren n. '*Ember-'tide, Ember-day*, Lk,LL. [ymbryne]
Ymbrendæg m. *Ember-day*, BF,W.
ymbrene=ymbryne
Ymbrenfæsten n. *periodical fast (at Embertide)*, LL ; Æ. [v. '*ember*']
Ymbrenwuce (i³) f. *Ember-week*, LL 78,43. [v. '*ember*']
Ymbrigdæg=Ymbrendæg
ymbrine=ymbryne
ymbryne (e², i²) m. *revolution, circuit, course, anniversary*, Æ : *lapse of time*, Æ.
ymbscēawian *to look round*, NG.
ymbscēawiendlīce adv. *circumspectly*, BH 450²¹.
ymbscēawung f. *looking round*, DR.
ymbscīnan¹ *to shine round*, ÆH.
ymbscrīðan¹ *to revolve about*, MET 20²⁰⁸.
ymbscrȳdan *to clothe*, Æ. [scrūd]
ymbscūwan *to screen, defend* ('*obumbrare*'), EPs 139⁸.
ymbscīnan=ymbscīnan
ymbsēan (N)=ymbsēon II.
ymbsellan *to surround, enclose, beset*, Æ : *endue, clothe*, VH 24.
ymbsēon I. sv⁵ *to look round*. II. f. *beholding, regard*.
ymb-set, -setl n. *siege*, BH.
ymbsetennes f. *siege*, Ps.
ymbsetnung f. *sedition*, LkL : *siege*, GL.
ymbsett *neighbouring*, BH 362.
ymbsettan *to set round, surround, beset, encompass*, Æ : *plant*.
ymbsewen *circumspect*, GD 107¹¹.
ymb-sierwan, -sirwan pres. 3 sg. -sireð *to design, plot*, CP : *lay in wait for*.
ymbsittan⁵ *to set round, surround, invest, besiege*, Æ,AO,CP : *sit over, reflect upon*.
ymbsittend† m. *one living near, neighbour*.
ymbsmēagung (embe-) f. *consideration*, WW 165²⁸.
ymbsnāð, ymbsniden, pret. 3 sg. and pp. of ymbsnīðan.
ymbsnidennes f. *circumcision*, Æ.
ymbsnīðan¹ (em-) *to circumcise*, Lk ; Æ. [v. '*embe*']

ymbspænning f. *allurement*, CHRD 66³³.

ymbspannan⁷ *to span or clasp round, embrace*, BH 392⁶.

ymbspræc f. *conversation, comment, criticism*, Æ.

ymbspræce *spoken about, well known*, MET 10⁵⁹.

ymbsprecan³ *to speak about*, Lk 19⁷.

ymbstandan⁶ *to stand around, surround*, BO, BH.

ymbstandend m. *bystander*, Æ (emb-).

ymbstand(en)nes f. '*circumstantia*,' PSS.

ymbstocc (=i¹) m. *stump containing a swarm of bees*, KC 5·234.

ymbstrican *to smooth round*, LCD 36b.

ymbstyrian *to stir about, overturn*, LkL 15⁸.

ymbswæpe f. *digression*, WW 5²⁸.

ymbswāpan⁷ *to sweep round, environ : envelop, clothe.*

ymbswāpe=ymbswæpe

ymbswīfan¹ *to revolve round*, NC 352.

ymbsyllan=ymbsellan

ymbsyrwan=ymbsierwan

ymb-trymian, -trymman (Æ,CP) *to surround : fortify, protect.*

ymbtrymming m. *fortification*, Æ.

ymbtȳnan *to hedge round, surround*, MtR 21³³,W 146²⁷. [tūn]

ymbtyrnan *to turn round*, LCD : *surround*, WW.

ymbðeahtian *to consider, reflect*, CP.

ymbðencan *to think about, consider*, CP.

ymbðonc=ymbeðanc

ymbðreodian (embðryd-) *to deliberate*, GL.

ymbðreodung (i, y) f. *deliberation, consideration*, GL.

ymbðringan³ *to press round, throng about*, Ps,WW.

ymbðringend=ymbhringend

ymbðrydung=ymbðreodung

ymbūtan (e¹) prep. (w. a.) and adv. *around, about; outside, beyond*, Mk ; AO,CP. [v. '*embe*']

ymbwæfan *to clothe*, LPs 44¹⁵.

ymbwærlan *to turn (oneself) about, turn towards*, NG.

ymbweaxan⁶ *to grow round, surround*, AO.

ymbwendan *to turn round : turn away, avert.*

ymbwendung f. *reviving : behaviour*, DR.

ymbweorpan³ *to surround*, AN 1555.

ymbwīcigan *to surround, beleaguer*, Ex 65.

ymbwindan³ *to clasp round, hold : wind round.*

ymbwlātian *to contemplate*, Æ 145¹².

ymbwlātung f. *contemplation*, ÆGR.

ymbwrītan¹ *to score round*, LCD 124a.

ymbwyrcan *to hedge in*, CP : *weave*, MtL 27²⁹.

ymbyrnan=ymbiernan

ymcyme=ymbcyme

ymel (æ, e) m. *weevil, mite, beetle, caterpillar*, ÆGR; GD.

ymele, ymle f. *scroll*, ÆL,WW.

ymen m. '*hymn*,' *sacred song*, Bl,Ps. [L. hymnus]

ymenbōc f. '*hymn-book*,' BH 484²³.

ymener (BC 3·660')=ymnere

ymensang m. *hymn*, GD,AJPs.

ymesēne *blind*, ÆH 1·418'.

ymest=yfemest; **ymle** (Æ)=ymele

ymmon, ymn=ymen

ymnere m. *hymn-book*, BC,KC 4·275'. ['*hymner*'; L. hymnarium]

ymnyttan=emnettan; **ȳmon**=ȳmen

ymryne=ymbryne; **yn-**=in-

ynce m. '*inch*,' LL,Sol. [L. uncia]

yndse f. *ounce*, AO : *piece of money, shekel.* [L. uncia]

yngrian=hyngrian; **ynn-**=inn-

ynnelēac (ene-, yne-, ynni-) n. *onion*, GL.

ynse, yntse (Æ)=yndse

yplen (WW)=ypplen

±**yppan** *to bring out, open, manifest, disclose, display, reveal, betray*, BH,CP,WW : *come forth, be disclosed* : (+) *utter*. ['*uppe*']

yppe I. (u) f. *upper room : raised place, high seat, tribune : stage, platform*, WW 150⁹. II. *evident, known, open, manifest.*

ypping f. *manifestation : accumulation, extent, expanse?* Ex 498.

yppingiren (ip-) n. *crowbar?* LL 455,15 (or ? cippingiren ANS 115·164).

ypplen n. *top, height*, OEG 2862.

ypte pret. 3 sg. of yppan.

ȳr I.† m. *name of the rune for* y : *bow?* : *gold? horn?* RUN 27. II. n? *back of axe*, CHR,LCD.

yrcðu=iergðu; **yrd**=eard; **yrd-**=yrð-

ȳre I. m. *a coin of Danish origin*, BC 3·371². II.=ȳr

ȳren=īren

yreðweorh (JUL 90?)=ierreðweorh

yrf- v. also ierf-.

yrfan *to inherit : leave (by will) : honour with a funeral feast* (BTac), TC 611⁵.

yrfcwealm (a²) m. *murrain*, CHR 986 CE. [orf]

yrfebēc fp. *will, testament*, WW.

yrfecwealm=yrfcwealm

yrfeflit n. *dispute about an inheritance*, EC 145¹⁶.

yrfefyrst m. *legal formality or delay before entering on an inheritance*, LL 155³.

yrfegedāl n. *division of an inheritance*, Æ.

yrfegewrit (e¹) n. *will, testament, charter*, EC 145.

yrfehand (e¹) f. *natural successor*, EC 111¹⁴.

yrfelāf f. *bequest, inheritance : heir*, Ex 403.

yrfeland (ie) n. *inherited land*, CP.
yrfelēas (ie) *unprovided with cattle*, TC162'.
yrfe-numa, -nama (RWH53²⁰) mf. *heir, successor*, Æ.
yrfestōl† m. *hereditary seat, home*.
yrfeweard (ie) m. *heir, son*, AO,CP.
±**yrfeweardian** *to inherit*, CLSPs.
yrfeweardnes (ie) f. *heritage*, CP.
yrfeweardwrītere, yrfewrītend m. *will writer, testator*, Æ.
yrfweard-=yrfeweard-; +**yrgan**=eargian
yrgð, yrgðo, yrhðu=iergðu
yrm-=eorm-, ierm-; **yrnan**=iernan
yrre=ierre; **yrs-**=iers-
yrsebin f. *iron box*, LL455,17 (?=īsern, BT).
yrð (ea;=ie) f. *ploughing, tilling*, LL : *standing corn, crop, produce*, BH. ['*earth*']
yrðland (æ, ie) n. *arable land*, KC,WW; Æ. ['*earthland*']
yrðling (æ, e, eo, i) m. *husbandman, farmer, ploughman*, WW; Æ : *wagtail?* ANS 119·434. ['*earthling*']
yrðmearc f. *boundary of ploughed land*, KC.
yrðtilia=eorðtilia; **ys**=is, v. wesan.
ȳs=īs; **ysel**=esol; **ysele**=ysle
ȳsen, ȳsern=īsen, īsern
ysl, ysle f. *spark, ember*, Æ. ['*isel*']
yslende *glowing*, WW235²⁸.
ysope f., ysopo (indecl.) '*hyssop*,' Æ,Lcd, VPs.
ȳst f. *storm, tempest, hurricane*, AO,CP.
ȳstan *to storm, rage*, OEG.
ȳstas=ēstas np. of ēst.
ȳstig *stormy, of the storm*, LcD,PPs.
yt=itt pres. 3 sg. of etan.
ȳtan I. *to drive out, banish*, CHR1058D : *squander, dissipate*, RB55⁴. [ūt] **II.**=ūtan
Ytas=Iotas

ȳtemest superl. adj. *uttermost, extreme, last*, Bo,DR,LG,VPs; AO,CP. on ȳtemestum sīðe '*in extremis*.' ['*utmost*']
ȳtend m. *devastator*, WW232³⁷.
yteren *made of otter-skin*, AO18²¹. [otor]
ȳterra=ūterra
yteð=iteð pres. 3 sg. of etan.
ȳting f. *outing, journey*, Æ,RB.
ȳt-mest, -mæst=ȳtemest
ytst, ytt=itst pres. 2 sg., itt pres. 3 sg. of etan.
ȳttera, ȳttra=ūter(r)a
ȳð I. f. *wave, billow, flood*, An,B; Æ,CP : (†) *sea* : *liquid, water*. ['*ythe*'] **II.**=īeð
ȳð-=ēað-, ieð-
ȳðan=(1) īeðan; (2) ȳðgian
ȳðbord n. *ship? ship's side?* CRA57.
ȳðeg=ȳðig; **ȳðegan**=ȳðgian
ȳðfaru† f. *wave-course, flood*.
ȳðgebland† n. *wave-mixture, surge*, B.
ȳðgewinn† n. *wave-strife, life in the waves*, B.
ȳðgian *to fluctuate, flow, surge*, CP : *roar, rage*.
ȳðgung=ȳðung
ȳðhengest m. (*wave-horse*), *ship*, CHR1003E.
ȳðhof† n. *water-dwelling, ship*.
ȳðian (Æ)=ȳðgian
ȳðig *billowy, stormy*, ÆL16⁷⁰.
ȳðlād f. *sea-voyage*, B228.
ȳðlāf† f. *sand, shore, beach*.
ȳðlid† n. *ship, vessel*, AN.
ȳðlida m. *wave-traverser, ship*, B198.
ȳðmearh† m. *sea-horse, ship*.
ȳðmere m. *ocean of waves*, PH94.
ȳðung f. *agitation, commotion*, Æ : *inundation*, Æ.
ȳðwōrigende *wandering on the waves*, WW 243³.
ȳwan, ȳwian=īewan

SUPPLEMENT

ADDITIONAL SIGN AND ABBREVIATIONS

:   After an entry the colon indicates that the word is already in the main part of the dictionary and that a meaning given after the colon is believed to take precedence over the one given in the main part.

AHD   Die althochdeutschen Glossen, ed. E. Sievers and E. Steinmeyer, Bd. 1–4, Berlin, 1879–98.

AJP   American Journal of Philology.

ASPR   The Anglo-Saxon Poetic Records, 6 vols., ed. G. Krapp and E. Dobbie, New York, 1931–53.

BHW   The Homilies of Wulfstan, ed. D. Bethurum, Oxford, 1957.

BPG   The Old English Prudentius Glosses at Boulogne-sur-Mer, ed. H. Meritt, Stanford, 1959 (Stanford Studies in Language and Literature, 16).

CGL   Corpus Glossariorum Latinorum, 7 vols., ed. G. Goetz, Leipzig, 1888–1923.

CPC   The Peterborough Chronicle, ed. C. Clark, Oxford, 1958.

EGS   English and Germanic Studies.

EI   The Old English Exodus, ed. E. Irving, New Haven, 1953.

FF   Der Flussname Themse und seine Sippe, by Max Förster, Sitzungsberichte der Bayerischen Akademie der Wissenschaften, phil.-hist. Abt., Bd. 1, München, 1941.

FGR   Zur Geschichte des Reliquienkultus in Altengland, by Max Förster, Sitzungsberichte der Bayerischen Akademie der Wissenschaften, phil.-hist. Abt., Hft. 8, München, 1943.

FL   Fact and Lore about Old English Words, by H. Meritt, Stanford, 1954.

GAT   The Old English Apollonius of Tyre, ed. P. Goolden, Oxford, 1958.

GLL   Lehnbildungen und Lehnbedeutungen im Altenglischen, by H. Gneuss, Berlin, 1955.

HAW   Anglo-Saxon Writs, by F. Harmer, Manchester, 1952.

HBK   Kommentar zum Beowulf, by J. Hoops, Heidelberg, 1932.

HBS   Beowulfstudien, by J. Hoops, Anglistische Forschungen 74, Heidelberg, 1932.

HEW   Altenglisches Etymologisches Wörterbuch, by F. Holthausen, Heidelberg, 1934.

HSC   Studien zum altenglischen Computus, H. Henel, Beiträge zur Englischen Philologie 36, Leipzig, 1934.

JEGP-   Old English Glosses, Mostly Dry Point, by H. Meritt, to appear in JEGP.

JM   The Jespersen Miscellany, London, 1930.

JW   Wulfstanstudien, by K. Jost, Schweizer Anglistische Arbeiten, Bd. 23.

KCM   Catalogue of Manuscripts Containing Anglo-Saxon, by N. Ker, Oxford, 1957.

KF   One leaf of a Latin-Old English Glossary, now at the University of Kansas (see KCM 240).

KN   Untersuchungen einiger altenglischen Krankheitsnamen, by J. Geldner, Braunschweig, 1906.

KW   Die Wunder des Ostens, ed. F. Knappe, Berlin, 1906.

LCG   The Corpus Glossary, ed W. Lindsay, Cambridge, 1921.

MÆ   Medium Ævum.

MAG   The Battle of Maldon, ed. E. Gordon, London, 1937.

MNG   Notes on Some Old English Glosses in Aldhelm's De Laudibus Virginitatis, by T. Mustanoja. Bulletin de la Société Néophilologique de Helsinki, 51, 49–61 (1950).

SUPPLEMENTARY ABBREVIATIONS

MPS   The Poetical Dialogues of Solomon and Saturn, ed. R. Menner, New York, 1941 (MLA Monograph 13).

OEGC   Old English Glosses, A Collection, ed. H. Meritt, New York, 1945 (MLA General Series 16).

PM   Medicine in Anglo-Saxon Times, by J. Payne, Oxford, 1904.

RAC   Anglo-Saxon Charters, ed. A. Robertson, Cambridge, 1956.

RES   Review of English Studies.

SFF   Seasons for Fasting, ed. in ASPR 6, 98–104.

SHS   The Hymns in SPS.

SK   Lexicographical notes kindly sent to me by Sherman Kuhn.

SN   Studia Neophilologica.

SPS   The Salisbury Psalter, ed. C. and K. Sisam, EETS 242 (London, 1959).

TLG   The Later Genesis, ed. B. Timmer, Oxford, 1948.

VHF   Die Vercelli Homilien, 1 Hälfte, ed. Max Förster, Bibliothek d. ags. Prosa, Bd. 12 (Hamburg, 1932).

VLC   The Life of Saint Chad, ed. R. Vleeskruyer, Amsterdam, 1953.

VM   The Vercelli Manuscript (photostat reproduction), Rome, 1913.

WB   Beowulf, ed. C. Wrenn, revised ed. London, 1958.

YWES   The Year's Work in English Studies.

ADDITIONS TO DICTIONARY

abal *strength*, TLG 32, 499; v. afol
ābetēon *to accuse*, OEGC 4, 368
āblāwung: add *swelling*, LCD 18a
āblegned: add LCD 3, 42, 25
ācæglod: *locked with a key*, FL 2, A 1
accent m. *accent*, A 8, 333, 23
ācdrenc: lemma cirta = tiriaca, to which the part *ac* belongs?
āchangra m. *oak wood on a slope* (BTs)
ācholt m. *an oak wood* (BTs)
ācurslan *to malign*, SPS 36, 8
ādihtlan *to compose*, ASPR 6, 202, nn. 3–4
ādlberende *disease-bearing*, OEGC 8, 19
ādloma:=āðloga, FL 2, A 2
ādwollan *to degenerate*, OEGC 28, 234
æbbung: delete *gulf, bay*, FL 3, H 40
æcersplott m. *an acre* (BTs)
æcerweg m. *a field-road* (BTs)
āecgan? *to set on edge*, OEGC 30, 99, n.
æcin *a kind of law?*; lemma tabetum for tabletum? *a tablet of the law*, WW 279, 1 (printed wrongly cecin)
ǣfrelīce *in perpetuity*, ANS 111, 276
æfterfylgung: add *sect*, FL 2, B 20
æftergancnes,
   -gegencednes=æftergengnes, ÆL, 10, 219, v.l.
æfteronfōnd *one about to receive*, FL 3, A 1
ǣgmore:=angnere?
ǣgnian:=ængian, *to oppress?* (EI 265, n.)
± ǣlan: add [āl]

ælepe: delete, FL 2, B 2
ælere *fleabane?* FL 2, B 2
ælflsc? *elfish*, ES 38, 300; AHD 2, 162, 8
ælfsogoða: add *jaundice?*, KN 14
ælifn: *alum*, CGL 5, 343, 3 (Ep. Gl.); v. HEW s.v. ælefne
ǣmetla m. *one at leisure*, ASPR 3, 308, 183
ǣmynd: v. ANS 171, 22; HEW enters ǣmynde, *forgetfulness*
ǣmyrce: literally *not murky*, FL 3, D 1
ǣnetlīf n. *solitary life*, OEGC 9, 4; 10, 2
ǣrādl *early illness*, ASPR 3, 305, 31
ǣrǣt: *overeating*, HBS 20; for defence of *too early eating*, v. A 66, 17, n. 1
ǣreldo: delete, FL 3, A 2
ǣrglǣd: *very kind?*, HBS 23
ǣrgōd: *very good*, HBS 20
ǣrlsthyht *hope of resurrection*, BH 220, 28
ǣrlēof: delete, FL 2, B 3
ǣrlyft: delete, FL 2, B 4
ǣrnlgnweg=ærneweg, BHB 398, 30
ǣsmæl: *contraction of the pupil*, LCD 2, 338, 1
æstel: *bookmark*, FGR 11, n. 3
æthȳd: delete, FL 3, I 1
ætrihte II: add ætrihtes, VHF 2, n. 3 a
ætstandan: add *to blight (crops)*, CPC 1086, 20
āettan: delete, FL 2, B 59
ætwenian: add OEGC 28, 44 n.
ǣwiscberend: *middle finger* (lemma impudicus from Isid. *Etym.* 11, 1, 71)

æwul: delete, FL 2, A 11
æxfaru: = æscfaru, *military expedition*, FL 4, B 1
Africanisc *African*, WW 445, 39
āgan: add + (BTs)
āgānian *to gape*, GD 216, 17
agen *ear of grain*, ANS 117, 21
āgenland *land held in absolute possession?*, RAC p. 415
āgnian: delete *to enslave*; v. āegnian = ængian
āgniden: delete first entry; the word is a ptc.; v. LCG, D 78
āheordan? *to set free (from captivity)*, WB 2930 n.
āhlōend *a ravager*, WW 412, 19
āhwettan *to drive away with a curse*, TLG 31, 406
āhwilc: delete, FL 2, A 3
ahwlic *terrible*, FL 2, A 3
alb: read albe
aldgeddung *an old saying*, FL 4, B 2
alefne *alum*, WW 134, 38; 146, 21; ms. efne to which should be added the al of lemma alumen; v. ælifn
ālendan *to lease*, RAC 142, 24
Alexandrinesc *Alexandrian*, Mt p. 8, 13
allefne adj. or adv. *quite equal* or *universally*, RES 8, 162
Alleluia m. *the Alleluia*, HSC 40, n. 9
ālȳfednes? *granting*, FL 3, H 10
āmānsumung: add *Hermon*, KCM 319 a
amerian: delete, BPG 580 note
āmerian: add BPG 580
anbesettan *to inflict*, BPG 608
anbeweorpan *to cast into*, BPG 1000
anburge *sureties*, RAC p. 344
āncor: read ancor, HEW
andbicnian: add context of lemma concerns dogs harassing a cat
andēages: delete, HBK
andfenge: add *receptacle*, OEG 105
andfylstan *to aid*, SPS 43, 26
andlang: add B 2695, *by his side?* (ASPR 4, 255) *related?* (HBK)
andrecefæt: delete, FL 3, H 4
āndrencefæt *a cup emptied at one swallow*, FL 3, H 4
andwliteful: *with grim look*, BPG 382
ānhealfrūh *having one side rough*, FL 3, H 24
ānrǣde = ānrǣd, BTs
anspel: delete, FL 3, A 3
anstīg: v. FL 3, I 2
anstōr *incense*, GLL 68
āntīd: v. HBK
anung: = andung? (FL 2, A 4)
ānwald *monarchy*, WW 440, 25 (GLL 40)
ānwalda? *lone ruler*, VHF 112, n. 26
Arabisc *Arabian*, ÆGR 65, 12

āræfsan *to intercept*, KF
ārfæst(i)an *to show mercy*, SPS 102, 3
Arrianisc *Arian*, GD 240, 8
arscamu: delete, ASPR 5, 212
āscrīfan *to describe*, OEGC 4, 255
āscyled *made manifest*, OEGC 2, 212
āsēcendlic *to be sought*, LPs 110, 2
āslīding: *a slip of the tongue*, BPG 51
assedun *dun-coloured like an ass*, WW 163, 16
Assirisc *Assyrian*, OEG 26, 20
āstrīcan *to strike severely*, VHF 4, 38
āstrogdnis *sprinkling*, GLL 69; or āstregdnes, q.v.
āstrowenes: *spread?*, FL 3, A 4
āsyngian *to sin*, GLL 73
ātendnes *incentive*, A 65, 230
Athēnisc *Athenian* (BTs)
ātordrinca: delete; the part drincan is a verb at MH 94, 20
ātorgeblǣd: add *abscess*, BTs
ātwiccian *to excerpt*, OEGC 4, 222
āðȳtan: delete entry **II**; aðytið = aytið; v. OEG 4080
āwǣgnian *to fail to perform, annul*, HAW 458, 9
āwārnian: for ās-warnian read ā-swārnian
āwesnis *essence*, OEGC 72, 1
āwilnian *to wish for*, VM 67 a, 15
āyttan: delete (FL 2, B 59)

bædan: add a query; v. FL 5, A 1
+ bælcan: delete, FL 6, A 2
+ bǣran: for meaning exultare v. JEGP 49, 238
bǣrfōt: add W 181, 1
bancoða: read bāncoða, *bone disease*, LCD 2, 102, 16
bānloca: *muscle*, HBK p. 94
Barda m. *the Apennines*, AO 186, 33; v. FL 4, C 1
bēag: add *treasured things*, B 2635 (HBS p. 75); *a treasured thing (sword)*, B 2041 (WB)
bēaghyrne: delete, FL 3, H 5
bēagian: only +, not ±, GLL 222
bealuhycgende: v. OEGC 61, 52
bēansǣd: add RAC 252, 15
bebbisc = hehbiscop?, FL 2, A 6
bebyrwan: delete, FL 2, A 7
becierran: add *to change*, VHF 151, n. 11
bedbǣr: v. OEGC 51, 5 n.
+ bedgiht: *time for going to prayer*, FL 4, D 13
begēn *to affirm*, CR 1307 (ANS 166, 82)
begietend: add VHF 57, 47
begroren: = begnornende? (ASPR 1, 232)
behlēonian *to lean (something) against*, VHF 42, n. 197
bellringestre f. *bellringer*, A 76, 502

bemĭðan: add WW218, 21 (FL2, B6)
bēn: add *favour*, B428 (ASPR4, 138)
bēogang: *flight of bees*, FL2, A8
bēolǣs *pasture with flowers for bees?* (BTs s.v. lǣs)
bēotung: add+, WW408, 35
+**berbed:**= +byrded, *bordered*, FL2, A26
berigeblæ *an instrument for forking barley?*, WW411, 25
besceadwung f. *overshadowing*, *Selmo*, LPs67, 15
bescēawodnes: add, interprets *Sion*
bescirung glosses exordinatio, JEGP- v. unhādung
besparrian: add OEGC48, 1
beswicfalle: two words, not a cpd., JEGP46, 415
besylcan *to exhaust,* EL697
betellan: add *to prove one's claim to,* HAW481, 31
betweohceorfan glosses intercidere, GLL 209
beðrāwan: add (*in making candles*); v. BPG242
bīd: read bid and add on bid wrecen, *brought to bay,* B2962
biegan: add+, BTs
+**bignes:**= begegnes, FL2, A27
bigstandan *to stand by, help,* VHF35, n. 156
+**bind:** add *constipation,* WW232, 33
bisceopēðel *episcopal see,* BHB262, 11
bisceophādōēnung f. *episcopal service,* BHB232, 16
bisceophālgung f. *consecration of a bishop,* BHB72, 16
bisceopwyrtil: add *betony,* A41, 139
biscopstæf *bishop's staff,* FGR76, 162
biterlic *sad, bitter,* ÆL23, 250
bitrum adv. *bitterly,* EL1244 n. (ed. Gradon)
bizant m. *a coin,* BPG548
+**blǣcan:** add *to make pale,* FL6, A2
blǣce: add *psoriasis,* PM48, 134
blǣcern: *lantern*
bledu: v. heolorbledu
+**blīðlan:** add+, SPS91, 5 •
blōdiorn *bloody flux,* MkL p. 3, 7
blōdorc *sacrificial vessel,* BPG673
blōdspīwung *spitting of blood,* OEGC73b, 24
blōdwracu f. *revenge for bloodshed,* VHF28, n. 123
bōccynn n. *a kind of book,* SOLK192, 8
bōcholt *a beechwood* (BTs)
bogefōdder: *case for the bow,* FL3, H6
bōhtimber: v. HEW
bōl *necklace,* LCG, M302 (HEW)
bordstæð: *the rigging of a ship,* ASPR2, 110, 442
borgwedd: prob. not a cpd.

brādian: add *to become broad,* W262, 7d
brādsweord *broadsword,* Jud. 317 (ASPR4, 289)
brædrenc: add+, and read WW351, 28
brǣdīsen: delete, FL3, D2
brand: add brand Healfdenes, *Hrothgar,* B1020 (WB)
breahtmung: *flickering (of the eyelids),* FL3, A5
brēdīsern: delete
bredīsern *tablet knife, writing instrument,* FL3, D2
+**bregd:** add *fabric,* BPG852
+**bregdstafas:** *cunning skill in letters,* MPS
brēmelōȳfel m. *a bramble-thicket* (BTs)
brēmelwudu *a bramble-wood* (BTs)
breneð: 3 sg. of brȳnan, *to make brown?* (ASPR6, 157, 43)
brēosa: a ghostword that came to life; v. MLN51, 331
brēostgyrd: delete?; v. prēostgyrd
brīdelgym *a bridle ornament,* OEGC28, 456
brimsa?: v. MLN51, 331
broht:= broð, FL2, A10
broðhund:= roðhund, FL4, A2
brūmiddel *intercilium,* KF
brūneða: read bruneða, HEW
brȳdan = bregdan, ÆGR176, 3d
+**bryddan:** v. MPS16 n.
bryrdnes: add+, *compunction,* GLL50
brȳtofta: delete; fol. 18r of Additional MS. 32, 246 reads brytgifta
brȳðen: add WC p. 54, 10
bucheort *a tragelaph,* FL2, B29
buclic *like a goat* (gloss to tragicus) OEGC 28, 55
buf the interjection *buff,* FL4, E1 n.
būl: delete I after būla
būla: add DR4, 3; OEG8, 319
Bulgarisc *Bulgarian,* GD300, 21
burgende? *city boundary,* EL31 (ed. Gradon)
buterstoppa: add *churn?*
bȳl: delete the queries; add Mod. Eng. bile (HEW)
bylda: *builder* at CRA75
+**byrd:** to *fate* add MPS376 n.
byrdicge: prob. from same original gloss as byrding
byrdling: *offspring,* FL3, A7
byre: delete *storm,* BPG873
+**byrgen:** *grave,* WW277, 7 (FL2, A28)
byrst: add *a crash,* WW215, 27
byrstende: ptc. of berstan (BTs)
byrðincel n. *a little burden,* OEGC2, 193

cærswill m. *a spring where cress grows* (BTs)
caflwyrt: delete, FL2, A54

Caldisc *Chaldean,* OEGC 28, 118

camp *a fetter,* PPs 149, 8

căn: delete, ASPR 5, 216, 79

Cananisc *of Canaan,* MkR 3, 18

Cappadonisc *Cappadocian,* OEG 2302

Carles wǣn *Charles' Wain,* LCD 3, 270, 11

casebill: delete; v. cēasbill

cēacbora: *jugbearer?*; v. LCG A 659 n.

cēacfull *a jugful,* LCD 70 b

cealccrundel *a chalk ravine* (BTs)

cealfwyrt: delete, FL 2, A 54

cēaptoln f. *toll on buying and selling,* HAW p. 78

cēasbill *a club associated with philosophical dispute,* BPG 438 n.

ceasterwyrhta *city builder* (a mistaken glossing of polimitarium) WW 469, 21

cecil: = cēcel; v. LCG S 698 n.

cecin: delete; ms. æcin; v. æcin

cellod: cf. scutum cælatum?

cenep: add BPG 947 n.; and to meaning *bit* add (*bristling with points*)

cenningstān: delete, FL 4, A 3

ceorcing: delete, BPG 745 n.; v. ceorung

ceorung: add BPG 745

ceoselstān: add *stone (disease),* WW 113, 18; the lemma comes from Isid. *Etym.* 4, 7, 32

cicropisc: *Cecropean*; v. Isid. *Etym.* 9, 3, 16

+cīd: read ±cīd (v. gecīd in BTs)

cildild f. *childhood,* BF 12, 7

Cillinesc *Cyllenian,* WW 379, 4

cine I: read cīne (HEW)

cintōð: delete *front tooth* and add WW 85, 10

circwyrhta m. *church-builder,* HAW p. 510

cist: delete *horn,* FL 4, D 5

clangettung *clangour,* MLN 67, 554

clēot *a cleat,* LCG P 411 (v. HEW)

clericmann m. *a clerk* (BTs)

clifhlēp: delete the query, FL 4, A 5

±clifian: add BPG 982 n.

clifwyrt: *burdock?* (it is a glossary variant of clate)

clynian: delete entry I, BPG 982

cnēorift: delete *kneehose,* FL 4, D 2

cnēosār *pain in the knee,* OEGC 73 c, 12

cocer: delete *spear,* NP 1, 209

+cōcnian: add WW 372, 12 (misprinted gerecanade)

cocrōd f. *a clearing for netting woodcocks* (BTs)

Cōferflōd *the river Chebar,* MPS 20 n.

coitemære *boiled wine,* MNG 54

cōlcwyld: delete, FL 3, J 3

+collenferhtan: *to enhearten,* FL 6, A 3

corclō: delete; v. corncīð

+corded: delete the query, FL 3, H 18

corncīð *growth of grain,* FL 2, A 12; note also corwurm = cornwurm, OEG 1064

cornwurma: add OEGC 51, 7

corporale *a cloth for covering the Host,* FGR 90

corōr *a whisk?,* LCG V 93 (v. HEW)

costere: delete *spade, shovel,* FL 2, B 10; v. fostere

+cow: v. VHF 97, n. 148

cræftbōc f. *commentary,* OEGC 30, 88

crammingpohha: *a bag crammed with ill-gotten gains?,* FL 4, A 6

cranc *chronicle,* RAC 250, 16

credic?: = cremdisc?, *a cream dish,* FL 3, C 1

crinc: read cinc? *derision,* FL 4, D 3

crismclāð *chrism-cloth, headband,* FGR 90

crismsmyrels *anointment with holy oil,* FGR 90

crist: read crist, Förster, *Alteng. Lesebuch* 45

crompeht: add OEGC 19, 1

+crōwed = +crōged, OEGC 27, 21

cursian: delete *to plait,* FL 2, A 14; JEGP-

cūself: delete, BPG 280 n.

cūter *chewing gum,* FL 4, B 4

cwecesand: read cwece sund, *lively strait of water?,* FL 2, A 15

cwedelian = wyrgcwedolian, GLL 122

cwelderǣde: v. OEGC 36, 10 n.

Cwiccliende: for twincliende?, FL 4, D 4

Cwicelmingas *descendants of Cwicelm,* ÆGR 15, 3

cynehelm: on the meaning *royal power* v. HAW 477, n. to l. 24; add *garland,* GAT 26, 8 n.

cynesetl: add WW 71, 6

cynestrǣt: for 71, 6 read 467, 7

cynewāðen: delete, WC 14, 16 n.

cyninge f. *a queen,* BL 13, 1

cyningstān *an instrument used in casting dice,* WW 150, 24 (FL 4, A 3)

cyningwīc *stately dwelling,* GnE 107 (ASPR 3, 307, n. to 108)

cynling *clan,* ANS 111, 276

+cyrtan: *to lop off,* BPG 919

cyst: for meaning *picked host, company,* add EI 229 n.; v. ciest in HEW

cytwer: *a basket-weir;* v. cietwer in HEW

dæg: add ær dæge ond æfter dæge, *in perpetuity,* HAW 479, l. 10

dægmǣlspilu: delete; Additional MS. 32, 246, fol. 7r dægmeles-; add dægmæles pīl and dægmæles pinn, ÆGR 321, 6

dægword? *Chronicles,* Ex 519 (ASPR 1, 216, 519 n.)

dǣlnymendlic *participial,* ÆGR 134, 20

+ **dafenes** glosses oportuno at SPS 144, 15
+ **dăl**: add ± (BTs)
dalc: add Jos 7, 21
dalisc: lemma dedalei taken as de dalei, FL 3, K 1
dalmatice: omit the query
daroðæsc? *spear*, EL 140 (ASPR 2, 134, n. to 140)
dað: delete, FL 2, A 16
dĕagwyrmede: for assoc. with *gout* v. FL 4, D 6
dĕawdrīas: delete, ASPR 1, 224, 276
dĕawwyrm: add *itch-mite, foot-worm,* PM 44
delfīn: delete, FL 2, B 12
dengan: add CP 461, 16 (FL 3, F 2)
dennian: v. ASPR 6, 147, 12
dĕog: v. WB 850 n.
dĕopðancenlīce = dĕopðancollice, RWH 42, 3
+ **deorflĕas**: for GL read BPG 1017 n.
dĕð: delete entry II, FL 6, A 1
dīcsticce *stick supporting a dike,* FF 772, n. 1
dīerlingðegn *favourite follower,* A 73, 19
docga: add *(referring to cruel persons),* FL 3, J 4
dolhsmeltas: = dolhsweðlas?, FL 2, A 17
dōmesdæg = dōmdæg, VM 3 b 15; 114 a 18
doxian: v. VHF 100, n. 165
dracu f. *affliction,* W 91, 7 e
dragan: add *to suffer,* MLR 27, 452
droht: *a pull at the oars,* WW 486, 27; context of lemma remorum tractibus
dropa: delete the query (HEW)
+ **dropa**: for assoc. with drop v. FL 3, A 13
dryhtdōm: delete; part dryht repeated from preceding dryhten, SK
dryncelĕan: *entertainment given by the lord of the manor,* ANS 127, 196
dryslic: read ondryslic, FL 2, B 41
dūstswerm: add *atoms,* FL 4, A 7
+ **dwildæfterfolgung**: delete, FL 2, B 20
dwoligendlic *heretical,* GD 239, 21, o
+ **dyhtedum** adv. *splendidly,* OEGC 62, 17
dȳst, dȳð = dēst, dēð, ÆGR 3, 24 d; 210, 1 d; 212, 5 d

ĕabrycg f. *bridge over a river,* ÆL 27, 53
ĕad-: for eað- read ēað-
ĕaganbyrhtm m. *a flash of the eye, moment,* VHF 78, n. 41
ĕaghyll: *the hairless prominence between and above the inner corners of the eyes;* lemma glebenus from glaber
ĕaland: *maritime land* also at OEGC 4, 199
ĕalandcyning m. *island king,* BHB 308, 8
ealdgeðungen *old and distinguished,* W 99, 15

ealdhryðerflæsc *meat that has been stored away,* WW 127, 33; v. succidia at Isid. *Etym.* 20, 2, 24
ealdorlĕas: *lacking a leader,* B 15
ealdorlĕas: *lifeless,* B 1587
ealdwerig: read ealdorwērig? *fatally weary,* EI 50 n.
ĕallc *of a river,* OEGC 28, 216
ealleðern *wholly of leather,* Additional MS. 32,246, fol. 12r; scetra: ealleþern scyldas; v. Isid. *Etym.* 18, 12, 5
eallhālgung: *all worship,* FL 3, H 25
ealuscerwen: *serving of bitter ale,* EGS 4, 67 ff.; v. also WB
eardere *a dweller,* SHS 4, 15
eardlufu: delete the query (HBK)
eardrīce: delete; ms. eardwica
ĕarede: add *(of a pitcher having* duas ansas, Isid. *Etym.* 20, 5, 3); cf. ansa: auris, CGL 6, 73
earhwinnende *cowardly conquering (of a poisoned arrow),* VM 133 b, 23
earmheortnes *pity,* FL 2, A 38
earngĕap: add *falcon?* (HEW)
earningland: *land for which service was rendered?,* WC p. 178, 21
ĕarðyrel: in support of *ear-passage* v. FL 3, J 5
ĕastān *a river-stone?,* LCD 2, 218, 23
ĕaðbelg m. *irritability,* VHF 103, n. 176 a
Ebrēisclīce adv. *in Hebrew,* JnL 19, 13
eceddrinca: delete; v. VM 8 a, 9 where the part drincan is a verb
ecgclif n. *steep shore,* B 2893 (HBK)
edginnan *to begin again,* OEGC 27, 35
edspellung f. *recapitulation,* OEGC 20, 3
efengemetgian *to temper equally,* FL 5, A 5
efenhemman: delete, FL 5, A 5
Eficisc *of Ephesus,* FL 3, H 8
efne: delete *alum;* v. alefne
eftgān *to go,* GLL 215
eftgewæxen *grown again,* LCD 1, 378, 15
egnwirht: delete, FL 5, A 2
elðe = egðe; printed ciþe at WW 105, 2
eleberende *containing oil,* OEGC 8, 17
elegrēofa: *tinder from residue of pressed olives,* FL 3, A 9
elleahtor *misuse of the letter l,* FL 2, A 20
elleoht: delete; v. elleahtor
ellheort *disheartened;* v. hellheort
ellhygd = elhygd, GD 108, 4
emleahtor *misuse of the letter m,* FL 2, A 20
emleoht: delete; v. emleahtor
eoforhĕafodsegn: read eoforhĕafdod segn? *banner with a boar's head;* cf. geheafdod hring, *ring with a head,* WW 152, 45; mycelheafdod, 161, 19; and Latin aper, *military banner*
eolene: = eolha, *elk?* BPG 417 n.

eorle *the Eruli?*, WB6 n.
eorðgestrēon n. *earthly treasure*, W263, 24d
eorðryne *earthquake*, A73, 19 (ms. eorð-renas)
eotonweard: *watch against the monster*
ēowīgendlīc *demonstrative*, ÆGR231, 5, o
ern *grain, harvest*, ANS171, 19; v. rugern
esne: add *scholar*, FL3, H8
ēst: add *history? origin?*, B2157 (HBK)
ēstnes *bliss*, NP28, 49
ēt: for æt read ǣt

fācennes *deceitfulness*, JEGP-
fǣcnung *suspicion*, A65, 230
fædernama m. *surname*, RWH53, 21
fæderrīce n. *heaven*, VM70b, 22
fǣrblīfongen: add a query; not wholly legible
fǣrcumen *sudden*, OEGC9, 100
fǣrfrīge *with freedom to go*, JEGP33, 346
fǣrnes *suddenness*, JEGP-
fǣsting: for LL58, 7 read 58, 17
fæðel: delete, FL4, B5
fāg: add *tessellated*, WB725 n.
fāgwyrm: v. FL4, A8
faldwyrðe *entitled to have his own fold*, HAW p. 476
falðing: *something that falls*; glossaries assoc. lemma moles with ruina
farendlīc *pervious*, JEGP-
faul: *an expression used as a charm*
+feallan: add on lufe, *to fall in love*, GAT2, 10; 26, 22
fearhhama: *womb of a pig*, FL3, H12
fēawnes: add +, GLL188
feaxclāð: *band for the hair*
feaxēacan: delete, FL4, D7
feaxscēara: *hair shears*, FL3, H13
feht: add *shaggy pelt*, FL3, J6
felafrīcgende *well informed*, B2105 (HBS p. 119)
felarīce *very rich*, ÆH1, 582, 14
felasprecol = felaspecol, LCD3, 192, 22
felcyrf: add JEGP-
feltūngrēp: add *privy*, VHF146, n. 48
fenfugol: add (ms. fenfixas)
feohhord *treasury*, JEGP-
feohlufu f. *love of money*, BH(Sch)160, 13 (an elliptical compound)
fēolheard: *hard as a file*, MAG108 n.
fēondulf: on the authenticity of this word v. BPG617 n.
feorhcynn: *kinds of living creatures*, B2266 (ASPR4, 235)
feorhlegu *life* at B2800 (HBK)
feorhnest n. *provisions*, JEGP-
feorm: add *disposal*, WB451 n.
fēowergǣrede *four-pointed*, ÆGR288, 11
fēowerstrenge *four-stringed*, ÆGR288, 11 (bifidus taken as from fides)

fēowertȳnenihte *fourteen nights old*, BH206, 28
+fēra: for fera read fēra
ferhweard *guard of life*, B305 (EGS4, 67)
+fērlǣcan: add ±, ÆGR191, 17, j
ferð *crowd*, WA54 (EGS4, 84)
fetelhilt: v. NP28, 43
feðerberende adj. *feathered*, OEGC28, 481
flah = feoh, OET446, 9
fīfmægen: *quintuple powers*, MPS136 n.; delete fīfel
fingerdocca: *foxglove?* OEGC70, 22 n.
firenðēof: delete, FL2, B16
fiscfell: = fiscwell, FL2, A21
fiscflōdu: not a cpd.? (ASPR6, 204)
flǣre: *one of the spreading sides at the end of the nose*, FL3, H15
flǣsccostnung f. *carnal desire*, KCM p. 120, 3
flǣsclīce adv. *carnally*, CP207, 16
flǣsctāwere: *butcher*
flǣðecomb: two separate words? (FL2, A22)
+flenod: read +flerod, *flared?* (FL4, D14)
fleoðomum glosses flactris, WW239, 38; d. pl. of flēotham? *watery place*; note wætersteall to flactiris and cf. flōdham, wæterham
flīnd = flint, WW415, 10 (FL3, A11)
flocgian: v. BPG846 n.
flōdgrǣg *flood-grey*, GNC31 (ASPR6, 175)
flōdweard: *guardian of the flood?*, EI494 n.
flogoða: *venom*, BPG997
flustrian: *to flatter*, JEGP-
fnæs: delete ref. to WW425, 27, where fnasum is error for snasum; add LkL8, 44
fōdder: delete *hatchet*, FL5, B1
fōdderbill *an instrument for cutting fodder*, FL5, B1
fōgclāð *a patch*, FL2, A24
foldgrǣg: delete; v. flōdgrǣg
foldwylm *earth-stream*, PH64; usually, but unnecessarily, emended (SK)
fonfȳr *firefang*, JEGP-
foraldung *old age*, OEGC28, 312
forbēn: on this nonce word cf. FL2, A23
forbīgels: delete, FL2, B18
forboren *restrained from the effect of herb, bewitched?*, LCD2, 114, 9; v. 2, 306, 12; KN19
forcinnan? *to destroy*, MPS107 n.
forcompian? *to fight for*, BPG31 n.
ford: add *waterway*, B568 (HBS p. 99)
fordēad: *as if dead*, FL3, D3
fordēmednes: add GD345, 3
foreādihtian: delete; v. ādihtian
forebīcnung f. *prophecy*, ÆH1, 540, 26
foreblǣsting: delete, FL4, D8
forecennednes *progeny*, SHS8, 50

foredēman *to prejudge*, RBL 105, 6
forefæger: read forfæger
forefengnes *a protective skirting (of woods)*, OEGC4, 28
forefrēfrend *proconsul*, DR 190, 9b
foregesellan *to advance (money)*, BHB 330, 6
foregielpan: delete (BTs)
forehālig: delete; v. NP 28, 46
forelāttēow *leader*, LkL 22, 26
foresettendlic *prepositive*, ÆGR 267, 6
foretimbrigende *enclosing, impeding* BH (Sch) 552, 63
+**forewrit** *prologue*, KCM 280, 4
forgebind n. *stricture?*, LCD 1, 338, 3
forgiefednes *forgiveness*, GLL 39
forgīeman: insert ī before ȳ
forgifung: *the nuptial gift before the morning gift*, FL 3, H 16
forgrindet: 3rd sing. pr. of forgrindan (LCG C776)
forhrǣdlīce adv. *too soon*, CP 445, 1
forhtlēasnes f. *fearlessness*, VHF 4, n. 13a (context calls for un-)
forhto *fear*, SPS 88, 41
forlǣtu: v. VHF 138, n. 6
forlētere *a forsaker*, LkL p. 9, 17
formǣlan *to negotiate*, ANS 111, 280
forrǣpe *assart*, SN 16, 33
forrēcelēasian *to neglect*, BTs
forscēotan: add *to advance money*, NP 28, 45
forscired: based on same doc. as forscyrian
forsittan: add *to give out, fail*, B 1767 (v. FL 3, A 5 n. 2)
forsuncen *faded out (of the written page)*, KF
forsweflan: *to kill, perish*, FL 5, A 3
fortīn n. *a portent*, FL 4, B 6
fortog: read innanfortog, LCD 109b
fortogen: *griped*
forðāgān *to pass away*, Mt 14, 15
forðāloten *prone*, A 65, 230
forðātȳdred *propagated*, OEGC4, 91
forðegide *consumed*, SFF 214 (v. Sisam, *Studies*, p. 57)
forðgelǣdan *to bring forth, cause to grow*, GLL 232
forðhebban *to further*, GLL 220
forðmid *at the same time*, FGR 68
forðrǣsted *contrite*, GLL 52
forðringan: preferably *drive out* at B 1084 (HBK)
forðsecgan *to announce, proclaim*, GLL 90
forðsendan *to send forth*, ÆL 23b, 204
forðswebung *a killing?*, FL 5, A 3
forðtihtan *to persuade*, KCM p. 52, 8
forðtilian *to go on striving*, VM 72b, 11

forðwegan *to further*, GLL 220
forðyldegung *tolerance*, A 65, 230
forðysmed:=forðrysmed
foryldu: context calls for *weariness* at BPG 1030
fostere *a spade*, FL 2, B 10
fōtclāð: delete; v. fōgclāð
fōtgemet: delete *foot-fetter*, FL 5, A 5; add *a foot in measure*, HSC 60
fōtgeswell n. *swelling of the foot*, LCD 3, 70, 27
fōtlǣstlēas *soleless*, FL 3, H 32
fōtrāp: *rope by which the foot of a sail is tied*, JEGP 46, 416
fōðorn: delete; ms. slit mid ðe foðorne= mid ðefoðorne; v. ðefeðorn at LCD 3, 56, 27, and on the use of a thorn as a scalpel v. LCD 2, 106, 5
framādrȳfan: add VHF 69, 165
framāscūfan *to drive away*, VHF 69, 163
frēahbeorhtian: add+, GLL 103
frēawrāsn: *splendid band*, AJP 62, 338, n. 30
frēcenful *dangerous*, OEG 628
fregen II: add ANS 135, 399
fregensyllic: delete, ES 36, 325; ANS 135, 399
fregnðearle: delete; noun fregn and adverb ðearle; not a cpd.
frēols: add *charter of freedom*, HAW 447, n. 5
Fresiic: read Fresisc
Frīandæg *Friday*, RBL 43, 13
frigedōm m. *deliberation*, RBL 97, 8
frihtere: WE 61, 14 (ms. frif-)
frīs: *Frisian*, ASPR 3, 306, 95
frīðowang: *place of refuge* (WB)
fromācnȳslian *to degenerate*, OEGC30, 105
frumcenning m. *first-born*, SPS 77, 51
frummeoluc: *beestings*, JEGP 52, 372
frumtēam *first team (of animals harnessed in line)*, WW 427, 31
frysca: quite possibly a form of fersc, *fresh, youthful*; v. buteonem at CGL 6, 158 and butio glossed frysca, WW 10, 8
fugeldoppe: two words?, A 41, 111 n. 7
fulhealden: *sufficient, ample*; cf. German vollhaltig
fullhealden: delete; v. ful-
fullnes: read 111, 13 and v. SPS p. 37
fultumgestre f. *a helper*, A 65, 230
fyrclian: *to fork into many rays*, EGS 5, 84; CPC p. 81
fyrdhama: read fyrdhom (ASPR 4, 196)
fyrdtiber: delete the query (FL 3, H 14)
fȳrencylle f. *lamp*, BHB 476, 15
fyrgenhēafod? *mountain headland*, Charms 4, 27 (ASPR 6, 213)
fȳrrace: a dubious word, doc. as ferrece; note Latin ferrea in glosses to lemma vatilla at CGL 7, 395

fyrsrǣw f. *a row of furze* (BTs)

+fyxan *to trick*, FF 792, n. 8; v. also JEGP 33, 345, n. 25

gadinca: read gādinca, *maimed animal?*, FL 4, B 7

gæstlīðend *hospitable*, WE 66, 12

gafolgyld: delete the query, BPG 548 n.

galend *enchanter*, GLL 97

gangtūn m. *latrine*, ÆL 18, 379

gār: on the meaning at GEN 316 v. FL 4, B 8 and NP 39, 204

gāra: add *strip of cloth, saddle cloth*, WW 332, 10

gāstgifu: read WW 200, 18

gātaloc n. *goat-house*, WW 275, 31

gealga: delete entry II; galgan at WW 445, 35 and 499, 14 = geallan; v. OEG 2950

geallādl: add *jaundice*, KN 7

gealpettan: delete *to live gluttonously?*, VHF 76, n. 22

gēancyrrendlīc *relative*, ÆGR 231, 17 j

gēansprecan *to contradict*, GLL 124

gearofang *grappling hook?*, FL 4, D 12

Gēatisc? *of the Geats*, WB 3150 n.

gefestre f. *a giver*, A 76, 502

gēgan: v. FL 3, A 14

gēnde: delete = ; add = gīnde, gȳnde at ÆL 25, 636 c

gēoabbod m. *former abbot*, GDh 41, 27

gēomagister m. *former teacher*, BHc 410, 13

gēomēowle: only B 2931

gēotend: = gēotendæder, FL 2, B 51

gēotenlīc: for gegotenlic? BPG 437 n.

gētan: delete grētan; v. HBK

gielphlǣden: *laden with glorious words*, ASPR 4, 159

gilddagas: delete *guild-days*; lemma ceremonia from Isid. *Etym.* 6, 19, 36

gildet *gelded*, WW 120, 38; v. ðrysumer

gildfrēo *free of tax*, ANS 111, 276

gildlic: delete *of a guild*; v. FL 3, H 25 n.

gildsetl n. *meeting-place of a guild*, FF 792, n. 9

gilp: for doubt about meaning *dust, powder*, v. JEGP 46, 419; add = grip, *furrow?*

gilte: add *barren pig*, LCD 2, 88, 24

gimrodor: = gimhrōðor, *gem-splendour*, FL 3, A 17

ginfæsten: delete, EI 567 n.

+giscan: = giscian?, *to yex*, FL 3, A 15

+gite *conscious*, OEGC 28, 409

glæs: delete glæsas, BPG 678

glēd: add *an instrument of torture*, FL 4, D 22

glemm: read W 67, 18

glīwcynn: possibly for onclēow; v. JEGP 43, 438

glīwingman: *mocker*, FL 4, A 10

glōf: delete *pouch* (HBS p. 118)

gluto *glutton*, Ælfric's Colloquy, ed. Garmonsway, 297 n.

glyrende *looking askance*, FL 3, J 15; BPG 440

glȳs- = glēs-, ÆGR 293, 13 d

godcundlicnes = godcundnes, ÆL 23 b, 230 g

godē-: read gode-

godgesprǣcen = godsprǣce; v. godgesprǣce in BTs

godwebben: v. VHF 23, n. 103

goldhordhūs: *treasury*, not *privy*, FL 4, D 23; JEGP-

goldhwæt: v. WB 3074 n.

goldwreken *inlaid with gold*, WC p. 74, 7

gorettan: delete *pour forth, emit*, FL 3, J 16

gōseflǣsc n. *gooseflesh*, Klaeber, *Studies* (1929), p. 272

grammaticancræft = grammaticcræft, ÆL 35, 14

grēoðe: *a companion?*, FL 3, C 2

griffus *griffon*, MPS 256

grimena: ms. grimena ðus rendering bruchus cuius = grime maðu ðæs?; v. grame ceaferas at corres. passage in PPs 104, 30

grimhȳdig = gramhȳdig, VHF 77, n. 38

grimman: v. WB 306 n.

+grindswile *a swelling caused by friction, intertrigo*, KF

grinu: not necessarily a colour; v. FL 2, A 33

gristra: *miller*; glosses cerealis pistor, WW 141, 4; 202, 29

grōwan: delete *become*, FL 3, A 18

grundwiergen: *accursed monster of the deep*, HBK

grunian: *to desire*, not *chew the cud*, FL 3, E 1; v. gruncian, BPG 597

grytte: delete *spider*; = grytt, *dust*; aranea taken as arena (SK)

gullisc: *gilded*, MLN 59, 111

gūðfrēa: delete, FL 2, B 25

gūðgeorn *tempting, looking for a quarrel*, OEGC 60, 12

gūðmōd *of warlike mind* (Klb.); *warlike mind* (WB), B 306

gūðmōdig: v. gūðgeorn

Gūðmyrce: *warlike border-dwellers?* EI 59 n.

gydenlic: *of a goddess*; add (from the same context) OEG 3193; 7, 233; 8, 170

gyrdelbred: add (*carried in the purse?*) FL 2, A 34

gyrlgyden f. *goddess of dress*, BPG 670

hādswǣpa: = hādswǣpe, *bridesmaid*

hæcce: *frontal*, rather than *crozier*, EGS 5, 72, n. 22

hæcine: add, from Latin acinum, FL4, D24

hæfegītsung: delete, FL2,A35

hæferbīte: delete, FL4,D25

hæfergāt: delete; two words separated by point in Harley 3376

± hæftnīedan: only +

hǣlestre f. *saviour*, A65, 230

hǣmedrīm: *number of dallyings*, FL3,A20

+ hǣrede *hairy*, ANS117, 24

hǣðenfeoh: delete, FL2, B26

hǣðenwēoh *idol*, JUL53 (emended to -feoh in Woolf's ed.)

hǣwmænged *mixed purple*, OEGC4, 12

hafenian: *to lift up*, MAG42 n.; B1573

hālettend: *forefinger*, FL2,A36

hālewǣge *a holy cup*, ANS171, 29

hālgungbōc: *book containing coronation liturgy*, ASPR6, LXXXIX

hālswurðung: read halswurðung, *neck ornament*, EI549 n.

hamorian: delete, BPG580

hand: add ymb hand, *at once*, BPG52; bām handum twām, *zealously*, ANS162, 230

handæx: add *hatchet*

handwyrm: add *itch-mite*, PM44

harasteorra: read hāra-, FL4,A11

hāredagas *dog days*, OEGC63, 17

hāreminte *white mint?*, A41, 140 n.

hārewyrt: delete WW135, 5 and v. A41, 140 n.

hāsgrumel *sounding hoarsely*, OEGC15, 2

hātlīce: add *vehemently*, BHT352, 21

hattefagol: add a query; v. BTs under hæreanfagol

hāwung: *ability to see*, VHF99, n. 155

+ hēafdod: add (*referring to a ring*)

hēafodbeorg: *protection for the head* at B1030

hēafodbryce *breaking of the skull*, LCD1, 150, 22

hēafodclāð: add *the cloth used for covering the head of a dead person*, ÆL31, 1425 (v. B445)

hēafodsegn: read eoforhēafod segn?

hēafodslæge: *a head-stroke, beheading*, FL3,A21

hēafodsmæl: *part of a tunic* (BTs)

hēahdēma m. *high judge*, W254, 8d

hēahfexede a slavish gloss to alticomum (iubar), OEGC9, 35; v. hēahhelm in BTs and feaxede of a comet

hēahgræft: *prominent sculpture*, FL3,D6

+ healddagas: v. FL3,H20

healdend: add + at LCD3, 192, 23

healfes hēafdes ece *migraine*, LCD2, 20, 21

healfgewriten *half-written* LkL, 16, 6 (FL3, D16)

healfhrūh: v. ānhealfrūh

healfhundisc *semi-canine*, WNL191x

healfrūh: delete

healhālgung: delete, FL3,H25

hēalic = ēalic, FL2,A37

heallðegn: = healðegn

healðegn: *occupier of the hall* at B142 (WB)

hēanhād: delete; two words—context for the glosses is ardui formam propositi; v. BTsII, 2b under hēah

hēap: add forloren hēap, *ruined troop*, ÆH1, 342, 25

heardhīðende *ravaging*, RD33, 7 (ASPR3, 340)

hearma: add netila = nitella, *dormouse*

hearmdæg: delete; v. Klb., 2nd supplement, p. 470

hearmheortnes: delete, FL2,A38

hearplic *of a harp*, OEGC7, 21; 8, 15

hebbendlic: delete; ms. oferhebbendlic

hegessugge: read hegesugge

hellegāst: delete†; add GD189, 26

hellemūð *mouth of hell*, RWH118, 4

hellepīn *hell-torment*, RWH75, 28

hellerūne: delete B163; v. helrūna

hellfenlic *like a fen of hell*, FL2,B27

hellheort: prob. for ellheort, *disheartened*; cf. ellhygd

hellwendlic: delete, FL2,B27

helpendrāp: influenced by opiferra = opisphora

helrūna: add *one knowing the mysteries of hell*

helung *covering*, SPS35, 8

hemman: delete, FL2,B28

hēofon: read heofon, *heaven*, EI46n.

heofonarīce = heofonrīce, VHF46, 32

heofonhæbbend: read WW355, 21

heofonhlytta = efenhlytta, GLL60

heofonhūs *ceiling*, WW29, 22; v. hūshefen (FL4, A15)

heortbucc: delete, FL2,B29

heorða: delete the query, FL4,C3

heoruwearg: *accursed foe*, Klb.

herehorn m. *trumpet*, ÆGR40, 7 n.

herescipe *troop*, SFF18

hergere? *plunderer*, OEGC28, 341n.

herian: add *to help*, B1833 (HBS)

hīa = hīe, NG

hice(māse): read hīce(māse), HEW

hiellan: delete, FL5,A4

hierdung: delete *restoring*, FL3,H29

higesynnig? *sinful*, SFF168; or hige, synnig man (Sisam, *Studies*, p. 51)

hig, hig *o, o*, WW91, 7

hildefrōfor *battle-comfort*, WAL II, 12 (ASPR 6, 140)

hildelēoma: *battle-flame (sword)* B1143; *destructive flame (of the dragon)* B2583 (HBK)

hiltlēas: v. FL3, H26
hīredcniht: v. WC p. 127
hīredgerēfa: v. FL3, H27
hīwian: add hīwian on, to change to, VHF 101, n. 169
hīwiend one who forms, OEG 365 n.
hīwlic: of marriage, not matronly, JEGP 46, 420
hīwsprǣc artfully formed speech, SPS 39, 5 (ms. hwisprǣce); v. spǣcehēow
hlǣddisc: dish laden with varied viands, v. Isid. Etym. 20, 2, 8
hlǣfde: = lǣfðe
hlǣpewince: delete
hlāfhūs Bethlehem (domus panis), ÆH 1, 34, 15
hleg(i)ende: read hleg(l)ende
hlēohrǣscnes: v. hlēorhrǣscnes
hlēonian: delete, FL3, A22
hlēorhrǣscnes a striking in the face, FL6, A6
hlēoðrian: add to bark, WW 378, 3
hlēowfæst: add protected, VHF 143, 67
hlīdan: = liðian?, FL4, B12
hlīf m. moon-shaped ornament, OEGC 55, 5
hlīpcumb a valley with steep sides (BTs)
hlōse: add lewze, FL4, D37
hnoc: delete, FL4, D28
hnot: add hornless, WW 444, 19
hnȳlung: prob. = hlinung
hoferede: add strumous, ÆGR 322, 1
hofrede: = hoferede, hump-backed, FL2, A41
hōh: add headland, WB 3157 n.
hohfullīce carefully, RBL 89, 6
hōl: malice?, envy?, BHW 269, 57 n.
+ holen prince, protector, MÆ 12, 65
holstæf: delete, FL4, A12
hōn: delete tendrils of a vine, BTs
hōnende: read hōnede
+ hopp: delete small bag, FL3, D4
hoppetan: read hoppettan, LCD 2, 352, 1; GD 118, 25
hopscȳte: add WC p. 62, 22
hopsteort: read hōpsteort, FL4, D30
hordestre stewardess, A76, 502
horines filth, SHS 6, 5
hornādl a disease (connected with venery), LCD 60 b
hornungbrōðor bastard brother, OEGC 8, 13
hospan to reproach, SPS 41, 11; 118, 42
hracca: delete, JEGP 52, 373
+ hradod quick, A67, 126, n. 4
hræfnsweart black as a raven, VHF 101, n. 168
hrǣgltalu: supply of clothing, RAC 48, 26
hrǣglðēnestre f. keeper of the robes, A76, 502
hrandsparwa: delete?, FL2, A42

hrēodgyrd f. reed used as fishing rod, BPG 145
hrēðmann? glorious warrior, WB 445 n.
hrēðsecg? glorious warrior, WB 490 n.
hrician: add BPG 722
hrimpan: to wrinkle, contract, FL3, D5
+ hrin: delete, FL6, A4
hrinde frost-covered, B 1363 (HBK)
hring: on wopes hring cf. EGS 2, 68 ff.
hringgewindla: the coil of a serpent, FL3, A23
hrīstle: = hrīsel; v. LCG E 10
hrōflēas: add with no houses, RAC p. 460
hrohian to cough, MÆ 1, 208
hrohung spitting, MÆ 11, 90
hrycigan: = hrician, BPG 722
hrympel: delete the query; ms. hrympellum
hrȳmðe noise, A73, 23 n. 50
hūdenian: delete, FL3, F2
+ hūfud with pontifical headband, BPG 674
hund: delete sea-beast, FL4, A13
hundesberie nightshade?; glosses uua canina, OEGC 73 a, 8
hunigæppel: round cake made with honey, FL4, A14
hunigsmæc m. the taste of honey, ASPR 2, 60, 28
hunigtēaren: for GL read BPG 123
hūnsporu: part of the rigging of a ship?; gloss to dolon, q.v. at Isid. Etym. 19, 3, 3; v. hūnðyrlu
hunu?: v. FL2, B30
hwelpian to bring forth offspring, OEGC 61, 7
hwilpe: yarwhilp, YWES 14, 77
hwītian: add to make white, VHF 145, 86
hwītlēadtēafor salve of white lead, AB 34, 115
hwītstōw Lebanon (BT)
hwol: = wolma, FL5, D1
hwȳorf cattle, FL2, B31
+ hȳdan: delete to fasten with a rope?, JM 46
hȳdscip: a ship made with hides, FL3, H30
hȳge the top of the gullet, WW 264, 16; 405, 10 (HEW)
+ hyhtlīce suitably, VHF 62 n. 61
+ hylced: bent apart, BPG 764 n.
hylsung: = hwistlung, FL4, D32
hypsār sciatica, OEGC 73 c, 11
hȳreborg: prob. two words, each acc.
hyrsian: prob. = hȳrsumian, FL2, A43
hȳðscip: = hȳdscip

idelbliss f. vain joy, ANS 132, 330, 26
idellust vain desire, KCM p. 120, 3
idig: ms. idge = igde, ecgede, edged?, FL3, D7

īegclif: delete; v. ecgclif
ierfa: read 446, 4
+iht *yoked together*, ÆGR 289, 2
inbrecan *to break into*, BPG 330 n.
inbrēdan: delete; v. inbrecan
incūð: add *wicked*, SN 14, 216
indēpan: add +, BPG 162
in(for)lǣtan *to let in*, VHF 8 n. 26
ingebed: delete, FL 2, A 44
ingerǣcan *to give (something) in (to some-
body)*, BPG 235
inlād: for first entry subst. *toll on goods
carried into market*, HAW 477
inlendiscnes *habitation*, JEGP-
inmearg: delete, BPG 665
innanfortog *gripe*, LCD 2, 300, 27
innangund=innancund, LCD 1, 196, 17
innanonfeal *internal swelling*, LCD 2, 10, 11
innanwyrm *intestinal worm*, LCD 1, 82, 22
insǣte: *of ambush*, FL 3, H 31
insceaft f. *internal generation*, MPS 447 n.
inscūfan *to shove in*, VM 135 *b*, 18
± intimbrian *to edify*, VHF 67, n. 85
inðer: delete, FL 2, B 32
inðicce: delete; ms. inðicce but *in* dotted
for deletion
inwegan gloss to inlabi, GLL 230
inweorpan *to begin (the weft)*, OEGC 55, 9
inwrecg=inwærc, BPG 1077 n.
inylma pl. of innylfe, BPG 725
Iringes weg v. FL 4, C 4
Ispanisc *Spanish*, GD 237, 21
istoria *history*, MPS 4 n.

lāclic: delete, JW 130, n. 3
lācnystre f. *physician*, A 76, 502
lǣ *hair of the head*, WW 263, 21; 368, 14
(FL 3, H 55)
+lǣdendlic: add ±, SPS 97, 6
læfel: delete ref. to löffel
læfðe *a sprinkling*, FL 4, D 27
lǣlan?: add, v. ASPR 2, 120
lǣtcumen *late*, OEGC 27, 29
lahgewrit n. *rule*, KCM 414, 12
lāmen=lǣmen, RWH 76, 17
landefne: *the resources of the land*, CPC
1085, 12 n.
landgemirce: add *shore*, B 209
langlīfe: read langlif(e), ÆGR 320, 1
langmōdlīce *patiently*, GLL 113
lārfæsten: v. A 66, 29 n. 4
latimer m. *interpreter*, EHy 16, 5
lēad: add *an instrument of torture*, BPG 344
lēafsele: *place for shade*, FL 4, D 34
lēasbrēden f. *falsehood*, ÆL 17, 107 v.l.
lēasgespeca *a falsifier*, A 65, 230
lēasōlæccere *false flatterer*, ÆGR 303, 8
lēawfinger: v. FL 4, D 33
+led:=glēd

+legergield: v. FL 4, D 15
lengian: delete, MPS 262 n.
lengtogra: positive langtog at OEGC 27, 31
lent: delete?; v. BPG 152 n.
lēoht: add *world*, TLG 34, 310
leornestre f. *a student*, A 76, 502
lēoðucræft: read leoðu-
leoðuwācunga: read liðewācung, *mitigation*, FL 5, A 5
lēpene *a basket*, RAC 200, 9
lēwsa: add *misery*, WW 202, 31 (FL 4, D 35)
Libanisc *of Lebanon*, OEGC 28, 364
+līcbisen *an imitation*, DR 50, 4; *an
imitator*, 12, 11
līgfȳr: add VPs 28, 7 (SK)
līgrægel *a garment of varied hues*, WW 126,
1 (FL 4, D 36)
limgesihð: read limgesīð, FL 4, B 13
līnsētcorn *a grain of linseed*, ASPR 6, 128,
11
līð: add *point*, OEGC 4, 111 n.
liðelēaf *camomile*, OEGC 73 *c*, 9 (lemma
aviane=apiana)
liðerlic: v. FL 3, J 21
lodrung: read loðrung, *delusion*, A 36, 71
lōf: *band*, MLN 40, 411
lōhsceaft: v. HEW
lōse=hlōse, LCG F 342
lufe wk. f. *loved home*, B 1728 (WB)
lufen: *beloved home* (HBS 111)
Lundonisc *of London*, VLC 162, 11
lungencoðu f. *lung disease*, LCD 1, 388, 1
lyftedor: v. EI 251 n.
lyftwynn: *joyous air*, B 3043 (HBK)
lyge: delete section III (FL 2, A 45)
lȳpenwyrhta: *basket maker*, AB 29, 253
lȳtel: add lȳtlan ond lȳtlan, *little by little*,
OEGC 9, 69
lytwist? *deception*, FL 2, A 61

mādmōd: delete; v. vngemedemad
mǣdæcer m. *a meadow* (BTs)
mǣddīc f. *a dike in a meadow* (BTs)
mǣdmann *mower*, FGR 80, 4
mægdeneorðe f. *virgin soil*, NP 28, 49
mǣgmann m. *clansman*, BH(Sch) 115, 213
mægðblæd: read mægðblǣd, *glory of
virginity*, BPG 920 n.
mǣgðegesa? *viking*, GNE 106 (ASPR 3,
306)
mǣl: add 730 *meals* in a year, HSC 67
mænibrǣde: v. FL 3, H 33
mænihīwe *multiform*, AJP 59, 213
mǣrehwit *pure white*, ANS 132, 399
mǣr-hege: read mǣrhege
mǣrhlisa: delete? (FL 3, A 24)
mæssandæg=mæssedæg, ÆL 25, 203 *c*
mæssecapitel m. *chapter of the mass*, CM 536
māgatoga? *pedagogue*, OEGC 4, 117, n.

māhling *parent, kinsman*, ANS 117, 21
Mailrosisc *of Melrose*, OEGC 9, 22
+ **man** : delete WW 492, 20; add WE 57, 15
mānfolm: *hand* (FL 5, C 1)
market: add *market rights*, HAW 476, 16
masc *mash*, RAC 198, 31
mealmstān: *sandstone* (HEW)
meduscerwen: v. EGS 4, 74
meduwyrhta *brewer*, HAW 508, 12; or =
    mēdwyrhta?
Memfitisc *of Memphis*, OEGC 28, 415
menesoiling: add LCG L 277
mēoning: delete, FL 2, B 35
meoring: *hindrance?*, EI 63 n.
Merewīoing *the Merovingian*, B 2921
metenīōing *food-niggard*, ANS 117, 23
+ **metfæstlīce:** add + , ÆGR 294, 1, *j*
+ **methāt?** *temperate*, A 47, 51
mōōig: add SFF 228
micelnes: add + , GLL 45
middangeardtōdǽlend *cosmographer* (BTs)
middelfīēre: *the part of the nose between the
    flaring sides at the end*, FL 3, H 15
middelsǽ *middle sea*, RAC 160, 1
midfeorh adj. *middle-aged*, BH 440, 31
midgetellan *to count, include*, A 65, 230
midhlīte: two words? lemma *capulus* at
    Isid. *Etym*. 18, 6, 2 follows *ensis* glossed
    hiltlēas sweord
milescian *to become mellow*, WW 441, 28
min: add JEGP 43, 441 ff.
mindōm: *pusillanimity* (FL 4, D 38)
mīnlic adj. *in my manner*, GD 231, 17, 0
minnæn: delete, FL 6, A 7
misbēodan: add *to announce wrongly*,
    ANS 111, 280
misbregdan *to change*, JEGP-
misfēdan: v. GLL 208
mīōgihlytto *fellowship*, DR 93, 13
mōdhǽp: read mōdhēap, *bold host*, EI 242 n.
mōdsēocnes: *fright, sadness*; v. cardiacus at
    Isid. *Etym*. 4, 6, 4
mōdōrȳōo? *arrogance*, WB 1931 n.
moisn: add OEGC 28, 453
monigheōwlic *multifarious*, OEGC 4, 405
morgensēoc: for AN 241 read ASPR 3, 218,
    96
mōrhop: *a hollow in the moor*; v. fenhop
    and ASPR 4, 140, 450
morōcwalu = morōorcwalu, VHF 103, n. 179
muntgīu *the Alps*, W 152, 9
muscfīēote: read mustflēoge; lemma *bibi-
    ones* from Isid. *Etym*. 12, 8, 16 and
    among words glossed fleoge
mūsere m. *mouse-hawk*, OEGC 36, 14
mūsōēof *a thieving mouse*, WW 408, 4
    (FL 3, A 25)
mȳgō = mǽgō, KGL 876
mylenoxa *a mill-ox*, RAC 254, 7

mylma: delete, BPG 725
+ **myndblīōe:** delete, FL 2, A 30
mynetīsen: for 447 read 477
mynna m. *intention*, ANS 111, 276
mynsterōing n. *property of a monastery*,
    RB 56, 11 n.
myrōu: or myrōe?, *murderous*, WB
+ **mȳtan** = + mētan II, HGL 525, 3

nacudwrāxler *gymnosophist*, KCM 382; v.
    Isid. *Etym*. 8, 6, 17
nægl: delete *spear*, FL 3, A 26
nǽnigōinga *not at all*, VHF 148, 117
nǽrende: v. MPS 330 n.
nǽsc: WW 337, 3; LCD 2, 104, 13
nāhwanan *not at all*, VHF 11 n. 45
nāmrǽden: read namrǽden, *naming*, FL 3,
    A 27
Nazarenisc *Nazarene*, Mk 10, 47
nēahmynster = nēahnunmynster, BHB 254,
    10
nearoōanc: add *evil thought*, VHF 51, 99
nēobedd: *bed of spirits*, in GEN (TLG 36,
    343)
nēodlaōu: *urgent summons*, WB
nēodspearuwa: delete *restless*, FL 5, C 2
+ **neorō:** delete, FL 4, D 17
netwerōlicnes *utility*, OEGC 30, 20
Nicēnisc *Nicene* (BTs)
nīgecyrred: read OEG 3477
nīgende = hnīgende?, RD 8, 8 (ASPR 3, 326)
nihtbutorflēoge: v. FL 3, H 35
nihtēage: *a disease of the eye*, WW 114, 6;
    456, 34 (v. FL 3, H 36)
nihterne adj. *nightly*, ANS 132, 331
nip: delete, BPG 838
niōer(ā)settan *to set down*, GLL 238
niōerlǽtan *to lose heart*, ANS 117, 22
niōerlang *stretching downward* (BTs)
nīōing: v. metenīōing, unnīōing
norōgārsecg m. *northern ocean*, BHB 308,
    35
Norōmandisc *Norman* (BTs)
norōweall m. *north wall*, RAC 36, 8
nōō: read nōw?, *ship*, at WH 28 (FL 2, A 47)
nūhwænne *straightway*, VHF 14, n. 57
nūna: prob. scribal error for nū ōā occur-
    ring shortly before; infl. by following
    naviculam
nūten = nīeten, VLC 182, 218
nȳdgefēra *inevitable companion*, EL 1260 n.
    (ed. Gradon)
nȳdgylta *debtor*, GLL 145
nȳfellan = nīwfyllan, *to fill anew*, SOLK 85,
    12
nytōearfilc *useful*, HAW 340, 14; 358, 8
nȳōan = nēōan, GD 18, 10
nyōerāworpen *one who has been cast down*,
    KCM 169, 26

ōdencole: read ōdencolc, FL2, B63
oemseten: delete *shoot, slip*, FL4, D61
ofācennan *to generate*, KW63, 6
ofāstigan *to descend*, GLL211
ofdūneāstīgan *to descend*, GLL211
ofer: add *without*, B685
oferberan *to carry over*, VHF31 n. 130
oferblissian glosses supergaudeant, SPS34, 19; 24
oferbrū: add LCD3, 186, 25
oferbrūwa m. *eyebrow*, ÆGR298, 3; WW263, 25
oferbrycg(i)an: add MPS297 n.
oferclif: delete, FL3, D10
oferdæg m. *remaining day (in computation)*, HSC55
oferfæst *transfixed*, LkL p. 11, 13
oferfeallan: add *to fall upon*, A73, 26
oferflēdnes *fluctuation, vacillation*, GLL138
ofergemet: v. VHF66 n. 81
ofergeswincfull *excessively troublesome*, CHR1097 (p. 234, 2)
oferhīgian: *overpower* (HBK)
oferhrǣgan: delete, MPS297 n.
oferhrēosan *to fall*, SPS57, 9
oferhyrned: *having great horns?*, RUN 4 (ASPR6, 153, n. to 4)
ofermǣnan *to confute*, FL3, A28
ofermistian *to obscure*, OEGC4, 371
oferrǣdlīce *frequently*, RBL93, 4
ofersēam: *a special bag*, FL3, D11
ofersewenness *contempt* (BTs)
ofersiwenlic *contemptible*, CP208, 11 (v.l., p. 507, where read 208 for 206)
oferspyrian *to traverse*, OEGC28, 232
ofertǣlod p. ptc. of ofertalian, RWH70, 17
ofertredan: for GPH substitute ZDA20, 37
oferweorpan: delete the query after *stumble*
oferwēsnes *over-indulgence*, OEGC4, 259
oferwyrðe: delete, FL2, B37
oferȳð: *wavering, vacillation* (GLL138)
ofetrip: delete, NP5, 352
offrettan *to devour*, MkL12, 40
ofgeorn: delete, FL2, B38
ofheran: read ofhēran, =ofhīeran, *to hear, overhear*, RWH59, 16
ofnet: ms. ofnete=on fæte, *in a jug?*
ofsittan: add *to sit upon*, B1545
ofspræc: delete, FL2, B39
oftrahtung *a pulling out*, LkL, p. 8, 10
ofōȳstrian: add Pembroke College MS. 312 (binding fragment)
ofwyrtrumian *to eradicate*, LkL17, 6
ōgengel: =ongegnel?, *opposite*, FL4, D42
ohtrip: read ōhtrīp, *forced work at harvest*, NP5, 352
ōlōwong: part ol may be from note indicating corrigia=colligia
onācenned *inborn?*, OEGC9, 68

onǣht: *two words?*, v. II under ǣht in BTs
onǣlend: prob. for p.ptc. of onǣlan, BPG 801
onāgēotan *to infuse*, GLL228
onāhōn *to hang on*, VHF31, n. 130*a*
onālihtan *to illuminate*, GLL33
onāslīdan *to fall away, fail*, GLL230
onbebringan *to bring upon*, VM107*b*, 21
onbefeallan *to fall upon*, BPG18
onberan: delete *to be situated*, MLR42, 358
onbesendan *to send to*, FGR65, n. 2
onbesmītan *to defile*, A66, 27
onbrosnung: delete, FL2, B40
ondegslic *terrible*, FL2, B41
ondlēanian *to grant*, FL3, A22
ongeador *together*, B1595
ongēanclyppan *to call back*, A65, 230
ongēanryne *a course*, GLL216
ongēanstandan *to stand toward*, W252, 18
ongefealdan *to wrap*, OEGC61, 54
ongelīcnes: for 14, 20 read 17, 7; add *parable*, LkR4, 23
ongeniman *to take away*, WW397, 23
ongesendan *to send to*, FGR65, n. 2
onhiscend m. *a mocker*, OEGC2, 175
onīdlian *to empty*, SPS74, 9
onlūtung: *a lurking place*, BPG1011
onmeltan: delete, FL2, B42
onmētan: *to paint*, PPs88, 39
onnīed f. *oppression?*, EI139 n.
onopenian *to open*, SPS77, 23
onorðian *to inspire*, BPG200
onsǣlan: for B read B489?
onscǣgan *to deride*, MÆ1, 137
onsēcan: add B1942
onslīdan *to fall away, fail*, GLL230
onspǣtan *to spit on*, JEGP-; *to spew into*, WW526, 1 (onspec=onspet)
ontōblāwen *blown on*, BPG263
onweggewit: read onweggewite m. *departure* (SK)
orcðyrs: delete, HBS p. 19
orfgebitt: *food for cattle where there is no pasturage*, FL3, H30
orgel: for WW read W148, 32
orrest: *trial by battle*, EGS5, 85, n. 63; CPC p. 77
ōðer: delete *word, speech*, FL5, C3
oðhylde: delete, FL2, B43

pardus *a leopard*, AA123, 12
pēcung *deception*, OEGC24, 32
picgbrēad: v. FL4, A18
pīlstre: delete, FL2, B44
pīpe: add *tube for drinking sacramental wine from chalice*, RAC226, 25 n.
plegian: add p. mid hondum, *to clap hands*, EL805 n. (ed. Gradon)

plicettan: delete, BPG 682 n.
plicgan: = plyccan?, BPG 598 n.
plōgesland *ploughland*, RAC 164, 25
plyccan: add *to pluck with desire*, BPG 682
pocādl: add *smallpox*, PM 43, 130
prass: add *pomp*, W 148, 32; *proud array*, MA 68
preg m. *a pointed stick*; *pray*, OEGC 38, 3
prēostgyrd? *staff carried by member of clergy?*, FL 2, A 9
prodbor: = wrōhtbora?, FL 2, A 50
prologa *prologue*, MPS 89
pucian: delete, BPG 664 n.
pudd: *a sore, wound*, BPG 793 n.
puduc: *a little sore*, BPG 793 n.
purlamb: *a male lamb, a pur* (HEW)
pyflan *to blow*, BPG 664
pyrtan: = pȳtan?, BPG 934

+**rādod:** delete, A 67, 126 n. 4
+**rǣcan:** add *to wound*, FL 3, J 12
rǣdescamol: delete *couch* and add = rǣdingscamol, FL 3, D 12
rēada: delete *small intestines*; v. tolia at Isid. *Etym.* 11, 1, 57
+**rec:** delete entry **III?**; v. FL 2, A 31
+**recenes:** add *proof*, WW 381, 7 (context of lemma is testimoniorum congerie); add also BHB 436, 15 (lemma vocatio assoc. in glossaries with demonstrare)
recennes: delete; v. +recenes
recon: delete, FL 2, B 46
recondlic glosses numerosus, SPS 77 heading
redestān: read rēde-; delete the query and also read *sinopis*
regulares *regular days in computation*, HSC 53
reliquias: add r. rǣran, *to carry relics in procession*, FGR 7
+**rēne:** for *instrument, building* subst. *edification*, FL 6, A 4
rēnlend: delete; ms. wemend
rēnlic *rainy*, BPG 964
rēodmūða: *parrot*, FL 4, D 43
rēstan: delete, FL 4, D 44
rīcehéaldend *guardian of the kingdom*, A 67, 117 n. 12
+**rid** *food*, GD 323, 3; v. bedgerid
rīfnes *fierceness*, OEGC 4, 329
rihtgewittelic *rational*, SHS 15, 32; 37
+**rīm:** add *a calendar, numeral*, RAC 250, 13
rīpð *harvest*, OEGC 24, 23
risiendum: ptc. of hrisian, FL 4, B 14
rið: delete, FL 2, B 48
rōdetācen: add *crucifix*, VM 108 a, 11
rōmian: *to try to obtain*, TLG 28, 360
+**rōstian:** read +roscian, JEGP 52, 373

rudian *to be ruddy* ES 8, 478, 60
rūma: delete, FL 2, B 49
+**runnenes:** delete, BPG 721
ryplen: delete the query, BPG 843

sadolfæt *harness?*, WC 80, 22 n.
sadolgāra *saddle cloth*, WC p. 74, 11 (there taken as *harness*); v. gāra
sǣdsworn *a coalescing of seed*, FL 4, D 45
sǣebbung *ebbing of the sea*, FL 3, H 40
sǣhund: v. FL 4, A 13
sǣlwāg? *hall*, AN 1493 (ASPR 2, 121)
sǣmearh: for E 2 read EL 228
sǣsteorra: add *title of Virgin Mary* (BTs)
+**samhīwan:** add *members of a guild?*, FF 792, n. 4
samodherigendlic glosses conlaudabilis, GLL 57
samodwellung: add *(of substance in the birth of a bee)* FL 3, A 30
sārcrene: v. cren in HEW
scægan *to jeer*, MÆ 1, 137
scamlim: read WW 532, 31 and delete the query; ms. scamescan lim = scame, scamlim
sceadugeard: v. FL 4, A 19
scēatcod: read sceattcod, *bag for provisions*, FL 4, D 46
sceaðe: read sceaðu, VHF 143, n. 33
scēawungstōw: add *Sion* (BTs)
scenc: add *cupful*, GD 127, 11
scencen *pig's shank*, FL 4, A 20; also scencel
scencingcuppe: v. WC p. 112
scennum: v. EGS 2, 75
scer *clear, undisputed (in legal terminology)* HAW 62, 10 n.
scilfor: *glittering*, OEG 532 (v. FL 3, A 31)
scinncræftig *magical* (referring to Satan), A 65, 230
scinngedwola: delete, FL 3, A 32
scipberende *carrying ships*, OEGC 28, 321
scipgefeoht: v. BPG 89 n.
scipgefēre: read scipgefær (BTs)
scipwealh: *Welsh sailor*, RAC 204, 22 n.
scipwered: v. FL 4, B 15
scīrgesceat: delete; note the reading reported by Neil Ker at FF 784
scitte: add *diarrhoea* (BTs)
+**scola:** for *debtor* substitute *fellow-debtor*, MNG 55
+**scōla:** delete, MNG 56
scōm-: read scom; v. scamm in HEW
scoplic: for 119 read 199
scora: v. FL 4, D 47
scortwyrplic: *soon effecting an improvement?*, ES 60, 82
scræb: add OEGC 36, 17
scriccettan *to screech*, OEGC 15, 4

scrīftæcer *land whose yield served as payment for a priest?*, RAC 240, 4 n.

scrīpen: read scirpen?, *sharp*, FL 4, C 5

scufrægl *pullable curtains*, RAC 194, 20 n.

scūrheard: for relation to regnheard v. WB p. 81

scylfrung: *glittering*, FL 3, A 31

scypgescēot *ship-scot*, HAW 63, 2 n.

scȳr *a hut*, OEGC 55, 1

scyte: delete *stroke, blow?*, v. FL 3, A 33

Scyðōīsc Scythian, ÆL 7, 345

sealmbōc *psalter*, ÆH 1, 604, 24

sealmfæt: v. FL 5, C 4

sealtlēaf: read sealtlēap, *salt basket*, FL 4, A 23

sēamtoln *toll on the packhorse load*, HAW 117, 4

sēftēadīg: ms. eft eadig

selfǣte: *groundsel*; (senecio is glossed selbeza in OHG, gundswelga in OE)

± **sellan**: delete *lay by, hide*, FL 5, B 2

sendan: for *to feast* subst. *to put to death*, ASPR 4, 147

sendnes: *Mass*, WW 445, 34; 498, 39 (context missarum sacramentis)

seofonhīwe *septiform*, A 65, 230

sēoðan: add *to seethe (wrath)*, BPG 478 n.

sepulcer *grave*, FGR 70, n. 1

± **sēðedlīc** *probable*, OEGC 28, 20

sīa = sēo, OET 446; 447

sibgeleger = sibleger, W 164, 5 c

sicera m. *an intoxicating drink*, CHRD 74, 6

sīcing f. *sighing*, OEGC 30, 59

sīdung: *arrangement (of the dining table)?*, BPG 750 n.

sigehrēð: v. hrēðsecg

Sigelhearwa: = Sigelearpa, *sun-darkened?*, FL 2, A 40

siger: add *groundsel*, WW 301, 24 (syr = siger; v. WW 30, 39)

sigerīce: *realm of victory*, EI 27; 530

sinderhǣwe? *cinder-grey*, OEGC 51, 4 n.

sinewind: delete, FL 2, B 51

Sionbeorg *Sion*, SN 20, 202

sīoboren: the word misinterprets depost fetantes: v. GLL 200

± **sīoscipe**: add ±, BH 246, 18 n.

sinulīra *muscle*, FL 2, A 51

sixecge: add sixecgede, ÆGR 289, 5

slāpfulnes: delete; slapel at WW 541, 42 incomplete for slapfulnis at 162, 19; but fol. 4r of Antwerp MS. 47 reads slapulnis

slīdor: II, *slides for launching and pulling up ships*, WW 182, 18

slītol: delete, BPG 420 n.

slypton wk. pret. of slūpan?, VPs 75, 6 (SK)

smēa *titbit?*, RAC 74, 20 n.

smeringwyrt: = symeringwyrt, WW 135, 1

smyllan: *to smack*, BPG 4

snǣdan: add, a strongly urged (HBK) emendation for sendan at B 600

snāð: delete entry II, MNG 58

snyring: possibly for styrung, JEGP 46, 424

snyttruhūs: add *Silo*, FL 6, B 4

sōcnman *sokeman*, HAW 85, 13 n.

socða *broth, gruel*, FL 4, D 48

sol *dark, dirty*, FL 4, D 50

solcennes f. *laziness*, ANS 117, 22

sore: delete, FL 2, B 52

sorgbyrðen: read sorgbryðen, *brew of sorrow*, ES 67, 340

sōðlufu: two words? VHF 54 n. 1 a

sōðwundor n. *true wonder*, EI 24; EL 1121

spǣcehēow v. swæcehēow

spēd: delete *offspring*, FL 6, A 8

spircing: *sparkling*, BPG 755

stæf: add *Sunday letter (in computation)* HSC 47, n. 20

stæfplega: glosses ludus litterarius, LCG L 289; WW 433, 14 (context Ludi litterarii disciplina, Orosius 1, 18, 1)

stæfsweord: *swordstick*, FL 3, H 43

stæfwrītere: *grammarian*, WW 372, 34; 414, 11; 487, 14

stǣna *stone jug*, MtL 26, 7

± **stāl**: add ±, VHF 83, 113 n.

stānbryce *a piece of stone*, FL 2, A 53

stānbrycg: delete WW

stānfæt: add *jewelled sheath?* WAL II, 3 (ASPR 6, 139)

Stānhenge *Stonehenge*, FF 326, n. 2

stānwalu f. *a bank of stones* (BTs)

stānwyrht: delete WW 341, 10 and add WW 150, 32 (FL 4, D 51)

stānwyrhta: add WW 341, 10 (FL 4, D 51)

± **staðolfæstan** = ± staðolfæstnian ÆGR 192, 2

staðolnes *firmament*, GLL 174

stelscofl: = stēorsceofl, BPG 875 n.

stencan: delete *to afflict*, FL 3, D 14

stēordalc *steering pin, helm*, JEGP-

steornede: = steorrede

steorrede *starred (of a white mark on horse's forehead)* FL 4, D 52

stēða: delete; fol. 6r of Additional MS. 32246 reads steda

± **stīgan**: add hēanne bēam gestīgan, *to climb the high oak (to beat down acorns)* AJP 66, 1–12

stīgend: add *rider*, GLL 239

stincan: delete? *sniff*, B 2289 (HBK)

stincan *to move rapidly?*, B 2288 (HBK); RD 29, 12 (ASPR 4, 236, n. to B 2288)

stondnis *substance*, OEGC 72, 2

stōrsticca: *incense spoon*, RAC 226, 32 n.

strecednes: *spreading*, FL 4, B 16

+strēones: delete, BPG 93

± strīc: *plague* at BHW 269, 57 n.

strīcel, I: *teat*, FL 3, A 35; BPG 155 n.

strīpligan: = plyccan?, BPG 598 n.

strȳnd: delete *gain*; gestreonde at WW 488, 30 = gestreone; v. WW 190, 3

+strynge: = +styrung?, v. FL 3, A 16

stuntsprǣc: ms. stuntspæc

stȳcing f. *a clearing (of land)*, FF 771 n. 8

styntan: add +, *to repress*, BPG 278

+stynðo: v. VHF 97, n. 144

sum: add *an important one*, WB glossary

sunboga *arc of the sun*, JEGP-

sunderboren: *born of disparate parents*, FL 4, D 53

sūðēasthealf f. *the south-east*, OEGC 4, 384

sūðerne: add *of southern make*, MAG 134 n.

swǣcehēow: read spǣcehēow, *form of speech*, FL 6, A 9; note also hīwlice spǣce in BTs

swǣfan: read swǣlan?

swǣrbyrd?: for LCD 185a subst. LCD 3, 66, 22; ms. swærtbyrde

swǣsenddagas: v. FL 4, A 25

swǣslic: add + (BTs)

swǣðelyne: delete, FL 3, B 1

sweartbyrd: v. swǣrbyrd; for possible ref. to *blue baby* v. ANS 171, 33

swēgesweard: delete; ms. suge sweard (LCG U 222) *sow's hide*; v. vistilia at CGL 7, 423

sweglwered: *clothed with radiance* (HBK)

swelling: *swelling sail*, EL 245 n. (ed. Gradon); but a case can be made for ms. spellingum

swētwyrde: delete *stuttering*; add *lisping*, FL 4, A 26

swīnhege m. *a fence to keep swine from straying* (BTs)

swīnlic: delete the query; ms. swinlice

swiung: delete, JEGP-

swŏr: = swol?, EI 239 n.

swōrettan: add *to sigh (about something)*, VHF 85, n. 75

sworian? *to sigh*, VHF 101, n. 168

swūrplætt m. *a stroke on the neck*, FL 2, B 53

swȳrige? *troublesome*, JM 49

syllestre f. *a giver*, A 76, 495 n.

sylting *seasoning*, KCM 94, ix

symbelbrēad *bread for a feast (of water and a loaf in the desert)* SFF 122

symbelmōnaðlic: delete the query, FL 4, D 54

symeringwyrt: *mallow?*, A 41, 139

+taccian: delete, BPG 1022 n.

+tācnigendlīce *figuratively*, ÆH 2, 114, 25

tæg tæg *te-hee*, FL 4, E 1

± tæl: delete *competent*, WW 505, 3; add *having mastery of*, WW 502, 3 (lemma competem = compotem)

tæmespīle: *sieve-stake*, FF 463, n. 2

tala = talu, WW 204, 3 (FL 3, H 47)

tamcian: add +, BPG 1022 n.

tēafor: add *pigment, salve*, AB 34, 101

teltrē: = teldtrēow, *tent-peg*; v. claus · lignum tentorii, WW 205, 20

tēofrian: add: v. CP 153, 23

teolōyrl: *an opening in a beehive, service entrance*, FL 3, A 37

+tēwian *adorn*, W 262, 22 d

tīdfara: *one who goes at his allotted time?*, BPG 286 n.

tīmlic *suitable, of proper age*, BPG 922

Tīrisc *of Tyre*, OEGC 8, 14

tōǣtēacnes f. *increase*, BH 295, 12 (Sch)

tōǣtēacnian *to increase*, BH 295 n. (Sch)

tōātēon *to draw in*, GLL 243

tōāwrītan glosses conscribere, GLL 98

tōbesettan *to put to*, GLL 245

tōbringan *to bring to*, BPG 49

tōforlǣtan: add *to leave to*, VM 69 b, 7

tōgecīgan *to call to*, GLL 92

tōgegearwian *to prepare*, A 65, 230

tōgelǣdan glosses adducere, GLL 234

tōgelaðian *to invite along*, OEGC 60, 17

togetēohhian glosses apponere, GLL 245

tōgetēon *to draw in*, GLL 243

tōhāwiend *spectator*, JEGP 56, 65

tōhelpan *to help*, MkR 9, 24

tolcettende: *talking vainly?*, BPG 931 n.

tōlīhtan *to illuminate*, GLL 33

tōlūtan *to incline to*, VHF 24, n. 106

tōlynnan *to take away* (BTs)

top: on the meaning *plaything*, v. GAT p. 52

tōrǣcan: *proffer*, VHF 37, n. 171; *to apply (fire in torture)*, OEG 4489

toroc: the word is Celtic, like guohioc in same glossary

torr: with meaning *tower* this is a different word from torr, *rock*; v. HEW

tōsettan *to put to*, GLL 245; *to clamp*, BPG 302

tōspillan *to destroy*, SPS 82, 5

tōtrǣglian: v. BPG 602 n.

totrīda: delete the query, FL 4, E 2

trǣglian: *tear apart, destroy*, BPG 602 n.

trēowlēasnes: add + (BT)

+trēownes: add *faithfulness*, VHF 99, 309

treppan: delete *to trap*, FL 2, B 54

treumbicin? glosses (mel) silvestre Mt 3, 4 (KCM p. 476, 6)

+trīowed *shafted*, WW 143, 5 (FL 3, H 21)

trogscip: *boat made from a hollowed log*, FL 3, H 49

trym: add *ænge trym, step by step*, FL 4, D 1

tube: delete, BPG257 n.

tud: delete; v. tudenard

tudenard *a shield*, MNG59

tunge: add on halre tungan, *unequivocally?*, *viva voce?*, RAC p. 284, n. 11

tungele: delete; v. tunggelælle

tunggelælle adj. *verbose*, FL2,B55

tūnstede: add, based on loca inter agros, Isid. *Etym.* 15, 2, 14

turfgret *turfpit*, WC86, 19 n.

twelfmōnð *twelvemonth*, VM108a, 1

twentigesnihte *twenty nights old*, BHc206, 30

twifingre: add (*of fat on swine*)

twihǣmed *one who marries twice*, KCM p. 93c

twilafte: read twilāste (FL2,B56)

twiman renders homo dubius, WE55, 2

twing: delete, FL2,B57

twinwyrm: read twinwyrm, FL4,A27

twiseltōð: *with two protruding front teeth*, FL3, H50

twisnēse: v. BPG328 n.

tỹdrung *weakness, sterility*, OEG1031

tyncen: *little tub*, FL2,A55

tỹrlāca: delete WW

± **ðaccian:** delete *to tame*, BPG1022 n.

ðǣrgemang *thereamong*, BPG54

ðamettan: very likely scribal error for ðafettan

ðearfendlīce *poorly*, VHF128, n. 121

ðearflic: add *poor*, RBL100, 4

ðearmgyrd: read WW120, 1

ðeccbryce: delete?; v. OEG2256 n.

ðelneðung *some kind of plant*, OEGC73, 1

ðencan: add ± ðencan mid, *to remember someone with* (*a gift*), VHF99, 314

ðēodfēond: *archfiend*, BHW137, 52 n.

ðēodlāreow *great teacher*, SFF96

+ **ðicfyldan:** *to make dense* (*the material for a fire*), *to pile up*, BPG974

ðistra: delete the query, A76, 411–21

ðiustra: = ðēoster, FL4,D55

ðolle: *instrument on which a martyr was burned*, FL3,A38

ðornðỹfel m. *thorn bush*, FGR69, n. 3

+ **ðracen:** *stout of frame*, FL4,C2

+ **ðrǣsted** *contrite*, GLL53

ðrāg: add sume ðrāge, *at times*, OEGC4, 381

ðrāgmǣl n. *unhappy time*, JUL344 (ed. Woolf)

ðreclic *terrible*, SPS95, 4

ðrepel *a torture instrument of three stakes*, FL2,B60

ðrifingre: add (*referring to the fat of swine*)

ðrihǣmed *one who marries thrice*, KCM p. 93c

ðristlēasnes: delete, A66, 31 n.

ðrosm: add BPG760 n.

ðrōwungdæg m. *day of martyrdom*, Luick Festgabe (1925), p. 192

ðrūh: delete *chest*, BPG867 n.

ðrydægðyrn *period of three days*, OEGC7,13

ðrymdōm: *glorious judgement*

ðrỹpel: delete; v. ðrepel

ðrỹpelūf: delete, FL2,B60

ðrysumer? *three years old*, WW120, 38 (ms. triennis · þrywinter ł sumer gildeto(x))

ðunorbodu: v. FL3,H51

ðunorsliht m. *thunderstroke*, A73, 25

ðurh: add, with inst. case, VHF116, n. 43

ðurhlǣdan glosses perducere, SPS77, 52

ðurhlonge? adv. *continuously*, GEN307; v. TLG p. 38

ðurhrǣdan *to read through*, OEGC28, 23

ðurhūtlīce adv. *thoroughly*, NP28, 49

ðurhwunigendlic: add A65, 230

ðurhwunungnes *perseverance*, SPS p. 37

ðweorhtimber *resolutely made*, JUL550 n. (ed. Woolf)

ðwērian = ðwēorian, VHF148, 117

ðỹflen: delete, BPG843

ðỹflig *brambly*, OEGC30, 32

ðỹmele: add (*referring to the fat of swine*)

ðyrncin *kind of thorn*, FL4,A28

unǣtnes *affliction*, RAC p. 60, 8; **unætnessa** gebīdan, *to die*

unāhladen *unexhausted*, JEGP-

unāmyrred *uninjured*, ÆL35, 285

unbecweden: add *uncontested*, RAC p. 92,14

unbesprecen *uncontested*, RAC p. 60, 29

unbeðōht *unexpected*, JEGP-

unbỹergo: delete; ms. unbyengo, DR ed. Lindelöf, p. 206, n. 1

underbeðēodan *to subject*, JEGP-

underburhware: add SHS6, 32

undergrīpan *to seize*, RWH122, 23

underslīcende *slipping under*, JEGP56, 65

underðēodan: add *to instruct*, VLC172, 120 n.

+ **unfæstnian:** delete; see foll. word

± **unfæstnod** *not fixed in the mark* (*referring to an arrow*), VHF104, n. 182

unforhtlēasnes?: v. forhtlēasnes

unforðōht *unexpected*, JEGP-

unfrōforlīce: no *un* in ms.

unfūl: read unful, *empty*, FL4,D56

ungearwyrd: delete, JEGP52, 376

ungeblerde: add WW395, 16; OEG7, 247

ungedōn *not done*, OEGC28, 486

ungeearned *undeserved*, A65, 230

ungefynde: *undeveloped*, FL4,E3

ungemēde: substitute ungemedemad, *unmeasured*, ASPR3, 299, 25

ungemetlicnes *intemperance*, KF

ungenīwiendlic *unrenewable*, OEGC28, 188

ungeorwyrd *unsullied,* JEGP52, 377
ungescæōfulnes *innocence,* GLL134
ungeŏyre:=ungeŏwǣre; lemma *discensor*
=*dissensor,* a glossary equivalent of
discordator, q.v. at WW223, 10
ungewyldendlic *impatient,* OEGC30, 18
unglēaw: add *very sharp?,* WB2564 n.
unhālwendlic: add *not salutary,* ANS122,
257, 7
unhlitme: *without casting lots?* ASPR4,
177, 1128
unlǣdu *misery,* VHF29, n. 124
unlagu: delete *bad law,* BHW356, 16
unmiht: add *faintness?,* WW199, 36
unmihtiglic: add *faint?,* LCD2, 60, 8
unmihtiglīcnes *inability,* LCD1, 56, 15
unmōdnes *pride,* A66, 32, n. 4
unmyrge: delete the queries; v. colludium
at CGL6, 231, where dolus might be taken
to equal dolor
unnīŏing: add *liberal man,* ANS117, 23
unorne: *simple,* MAG256 n.
unrād f. *cruel raid,* CPC1111, 6 n.
unrēone? *very sad,* VHF92, n. 116a
unrihthād *improper manner,* VHF76, 44 n.
unrihthǣming f. *fornication,* ANS111, 280
unrihttīd: *time of evil,* VHF94, n. 128
unrihtwilla *bad intention,* A66, 28
unrīmgōd: *unnumbered good works,* ÆL33,
241
unsǣle: delete; ms. unfæle
unscæŏŏig *innocent,* ÆH1, 512, 12
unsceandlīce *shamelessly,* ÆL23b, 372
unsceŏŏiglīce *innocently,* FGR80, 3
unsēofene: read unseofiende
unslid:=unsilt, *unsalted;* v. LCG P400 and
LCD3, 18, 5
untamcul: *invincible,* BPG680 n.
untellendlic: add CPC1137, 20
untīdlic: add *timeless,* BPG452
untōdǣled: add *unshared,* VHF33, n. 146
untōslopen *undissolved,* JEGP-
untrum: add +, ÆL21, 187
unŏurhfǣre *impenetrable,* OEGC27, 25
ūpāhafen *exalted,* VHF75, 34
ūpālūcan *to eradicate,* GLL251
ūpfeax: *with bristling hair,* FL4, D57
ūpgelǣded *led up,* VM135a, 24
ūpgodu: delete *heathen gods,* FL3, A40
ūphebbe: delete, FL2, A57
ūprǣran *to raise up,* GLL249
ūpreccan *to erect,* GLL250
ūpscīnan *to rise shiningly,* OEGC62, 5
ūpsettan *to exalt,* SHS8, 52
ūpspringan *to rise up,* Lk1, 78
ūsspīung: delete; fol. 4v of Additional
MS. 32, 246 reads wyrmsspiung
ūtāblegned *ulcerated,* LCD2, 10, 5; 2, 98, 25

ūtālūcan *to pluck forth,* GLL251
ūtāslīdan: *to slip out,* BPG50 n.
ūtāwindan: *to slip out,* BPG50 n.
ūtāwyrtrumian *to root out,* VM75a, 5
ūtfaran *to go out,* SPS145, 4
ūtfēolan *to get out,* VHF95, 255, n. 130
ūtforlǣtan: add *to let out,* VHF133, 57
ūtlād: for *right of passage* substitute *toll on
goods carried out of market,* HAW477, 16
ūtofgān *to go out of,* VHF39, n. 182
ūtyrnan *to have diarrhoea,* LCD63b

wād: add cpds. with beorh, denu, lond
(BT)
wǣgbora: add *wave-bearer?* (HBK)
wægel: delete the query
wægngerefa:=wægngefēra,　　*wagon-com-
panion;* v. carpentarius, collegiatus at
CGL6, 230
wægnŏol: delete; v. wǣhŏoll
wǣhŏoll *battering ram,* FL3, A41
± **wǣlan**: add MPS143 n.
wælblēat: *deadly* (HBK)
wælgenga: read wǣlgenga and delete the
query, FL4, A29
wælkyrging renders gorgoneus, WE55, 6
wǣpenbǣre *weapon-bearing,* OEGC27, 11
wæterbucca: v. FL4, D58
wætergāt: v. FL4, D58
wæterlēod *fish,* OEGC28, 386
wætersol *pool,* Jn5, 2
wāgŏeorl: *a break in a wall;* v. ŏyrelung
ŏæs wages, CP153, 25
waled: *ridged,* FL3, D17
walu: *metal ridge on top of helmet, like that on
Sutton Hoo helmet* at B1031; v. WB, p. 319
wambecoŏu f. *stomach trouble,* LCD87b
wambegicŏa m. *itching of the stomach,*
LCD90a
wambewyrm *intestinal worm,* LCD90a
wambscyldig: read wamscyldig, *sinful,*
VHF93, n. 120
wancian *to waver,* RD87, 7 (ASPR3, 377)
wanfōta: v. Canopos at Isid. *Etym.* 12, 7, 26
wansēoc: *melancholic,* FL4, D59
wassen *vassal,* ANS111, 277 (Celtic); v.
HAW p. 532
wēagesīŏ: *companion in crime,* ASPR4,
282, 16
± **wealc**: add *military expedition,* ES72, 10
wealcol: *rolling in the waves,* BPG831
wealdweaxe *sinew,* OEGC52, 12 n.
wealhwyrt: *elecampane,* A41, 133 n. 6
weallstaŏol: delete the query, FF157, n. 1
weallwala: *wall panelling?,* AJP62, 336
wealte: add *a snare,* BPG138
wealword: v. A66, 34 n.
weardstōw *watchtower,* OEGC6, 1
wederāwendednes *variation of weather,* KF

wegend? *a bearer*, OEGC 28, 294
wegtwiflung: fol. 19 v of Additional MS. 32, 246 reads wegtwislung
wellere: WW 278, 19, prob. equivalent to wellyrgae, *walkyrie?*, LCG S 379 n.
wellwill *a spring*, KC 5, 344, 29
wenncïcen: v. ANS 171, 21
weolocbasu: add OEGC 51, 6
weoning: = wining, FL 2, B 35
weorcland *land subject to labour services*, RAC 166, 7 n.
+ **weorclïc:** delete, FL 2, A 32
weorf: = hwȳorf
weorŏŏearfa: delete, ES 62, 129
werbǣr f. *pasture land near a weir* (BTs)
werbēam: read wǣrbeam? *protecting pillar*, EI 486 n.
± **werian:** add *discharge obligations on (land)*, HAW p. 450, n. 3
werping *loss?* (gloss to iactura), ANS 117, 23
wēstenlïc *eremitic*, OEGC 4, 140
westrihte *westward*, OEGC 4, 112 n.
weŏel: delete, FL 2, B 62
wïcŏēnestre f. *weekly servant*, A 76, 502
wïcung *lodging*, WW 147, 26
wïdefeorlïc: delete wïder; fol. 5 v of Additional MS. 32, 246 reads widewïdl:** add JEGP 56, 66
wïdnes: add ÆH 2, 578, 10
wïdu f. *width*, KW 55, 13 (= WE 60, 18 c)
wïelïncel: delete, BPG 925
wïfcȳŏŏu: v. OEGC 4, 79 n.
wïfrian *to shake (a weapon)*, OEGC 25, 3
wïga *the Holy Spirit?*, EL 937 n. (ed. Gradon)
wïglian: add +, GLL 97
wïgnett? *gladiator's net*, FL 2, A 58
wïgnoŏ: delete the query, FL 4, C 8
willodlïce *willingly*, SPS 53, 8
willung: add +, GLL 109
wilnïncel *a little female servant*, BPG 925
wiluncel: delete; v. wilnïncel
wïlweg n. *desired way*, W 252, 17
winclian? *to wink*, FL 4, D 4
wïncole: read wïncolc, FL 2, B 63
windiht: delete
wïngeard: delete the query after *vine* and add WW 136, 36 (lemma brionia = vitem albam at Isid. *Etym.* 17, 9, 90)
wïngeardhring: *vine tendrils*, FL 3, H 56
wïnian *to pluck (grapes)*, LkL 6, 44
winnendlïc *fighting*, MNG 61
wiorŏegend *worshipper*, EPs 108, 11 (fenerator taken as venerator)
+ **wïred:** add *ornamented*, KCM p. 163 c; v. also WC 14, 12 n.
wïsbōc: *book of wisdom*, GLL 99
wïsnes: *wisdom*, VHF 59, n. 35; +, *understanding*, LCD 3, 82, 2

wïtecyll *sack in which parricides were put to death*, FL 4, D 31
witewyrŏe: read wïtewyrŏe
witnesman *witness*, ANS 111, 277
witod: = witodlïce, BHW 139, 87
witodlïce: add +, W 113, 13 n.; 119, 17 n.
wiŏerstede *substitution*, JEGP-
wiŏersȳnes: add *withershins*
wiŏerung *obstinacy*, KCM p. 319 a
wiŏgehæftan *to fight against*, BPG 822 n.
wïŏig: cpds. with bed, brōc, ford, grāf, lēah, mǣd, mere, mōr, pōl, pytt, slǣd, ŏȳfel (BT)
wiŏŏingian: *to talk against, contradict*, VM 65 b, 6
+ **wïxlan** *to change*, MLR 27, 453
wlæce: = wlæc?, BPG 652 n.
wlǣtlïc *foul*, OEGC 28, 431
+ **wlencan:** add ±, VHF 93, n. 118
wlïta: delete, FL 2, B 64
wlïteandet: delete the query, FL 5, C 4
wlïtescēawung *Sion*, BH 212, 11
wlïtiglïce: add VHF 39, 331 b
wōdscinn: *mad trickery?*, BHW 118, 34 n.
wordbebod *command*, VHF 113, 52
wordcennend: v. BPG 115 n.
wordclipinde *able to speak*, VHF 88, n. 93 a
wordriht: *statement of what is right according to law or custom*, WB 2631 n.
woruldbebod: *secular edict*, VHF 113, n. 30
woruldgeflit: delete the query (ANS 134, 288)
woruldgeŏingu *worldly things*, VM 69 b, 10
woruldhogu f. *worldly care*, BHW 204, 82
wrætbaso: add OEGC 51, 8
wraŏo = wraŏu?, FL 2, A 60
+ **wrinclod:** *wrinkled?*, BPG 750 n.
± **writ:** delete *stilus*, BPG 1018 n.
wrōhtbora: delete *monster*
wuduclāte *a plant*, aristolochia OEGC 73 b, 9
wuducynn: *a kind of tree*, FL 4, A 31
wuduhætt *leafy top*, OEGC 8, 16
wuldorbēacn *sign of glory*, A 73, 18, n. 12
wuldorbēag: add *iris of the eye*, FL 3, H 58
wulfsēaŏ: *pit in which wolves were trapped*, RAC 4, 12 n.
wyrmsūtspïung: delete; ms. wyrmsspiung
wyrpendlïc *suitable for throwing*, OEGC 9, 12

yfelmynan *to consider wickedly*, SPS 82, 4
yfelonbecweŏende *persuading to evil*, BPG 179
yltwist: v. lytwist
ymbeardung *dwelling around*, GLL 214
yrsebïn: read yrfebïn, *fodder basket for cattle*, FGR 55n.
ȳŏwōrigende: *wave-wandering (fish)*, FL 3, K 2